Readings in Ritual Studies

Readings in Ritual Studies

Edited by

RONALD L. GRIMES

Wilfrid Laurier University

PRENTICE HALL, Upper Saddle River, New Jersey 07458

Library of Congress Cataloging-in-Publication Data

Readings in ritual studies/edited by Ronald L. Grimes.
    p.   cm.
  Includes bibliographical references.
  ISBN 0-02-347253-7
  1. Ritual. I. Grimes, Ronald L.
BL600.R43 1996
 390—dc20   95-25288
                        CIP

Editorial/production supervision
   and interior design: Patricia V. Amoroso
Acquisitions editor: Ted Bolen
Editorial assistant: Meg McGuane
Manufacturing buyer: Lynn Pearlman
Cover design: Thomas Nery

 © 1996 by Prentice-Hall, Inc.
Simon & Schuster/A Viacom Company
Upper Saddle River, NJ 07458

Printed in the United States of America

10 9 8 7 6 5 4 3 2 1

0-02-347253-7

PRENTICE-HALL INTERNATIONAL (UK) LIMITED, *London*
PRENTICE-HALL OF AUSTRALIA PTY. LIMITED, *Sydney*
PRENTICE-HALL CANADA INC., *Toronto*
PRENTICE-HALL HISPANOAMERICANA, S.A., *Mexico*
PRENTICE-HALL OF INDIA PRIVATE LIMITED, *New Delhi*
PRENTICE-HALL OF JAPAN, INC., *Tokyo*
SIMON & SCHUSTER ASIA PTE. LTD., *Singapore*
EDITORA PRENTICE-HALL DO BRASIL, LTDA., *Rio de Janeiro*

Contents

Epigraphs

At about noon the first heavy drops of rain began to fall. The chimpanzees climbed out of the tree and one after the other plodded up the steep grassy slope toward the open ridge at the top. There were seven adult males in the group, including Goliath and David Graybeard, several females, and a few youngsters. As they reached the ridge the chimpanzees paused. At that moment the storm broke. The rain was torrential, and the sudden clap of thunder, right overhead, made me jump. As if this were a signal, one of the big males stood upright and as he swayed and swaggered rhythmically from foot to foot I could just hear the rising crescendo of his pant-hoots above the beating of the rain. Then he charged to, flat-out down the slope toward the trees he had just left. He ran some thirty yards, and then, swinging round the trunk of a small tree to break his headlong rush, leaped into the low branches and sat motionless.

Almost at once two other males charged after him. One broke off a low branch from a tree as he ran and brandished it in the air before hurling it ahead of him. The other, as he reached the end of his run, stood upright and rhythmically swayed the branches of a tree back and forth before seizing a huge branch and dragging it farther down the slope. A fourth male, as he too charged, leaped into a tree and, almost without breaking his speed, tore off a large branch, leaped with it to the ground, and continued down the slope. As the last two males called and charged down, so the one who had started the whole performance climbed from his tree and began plodding up the slope again. The others, who had also climbed into trees near the bottom of the slope, followed suit. When they reached the ridge, they started charging down all over again, one after the other, with equal vigor.

The females and youngsters had climbed into trees near the top of the rise as soon as the displays had begun, and there they remained watching throughout the whole performance. As the males charged down and plodded back up, so the rain fell harder, jagged forks or brilliant flares of lightning lit the leaden sky, and the crashing of the thunder seemed to shake the very mountains.

My enthusiasm was not merely scientific as I watched, enthralled, from my grandstand seat on the opposite side of the narrow ravine, sheltering under a plastic sheet. In fact it was

Jane van Lawick-Goodall, "The Rain Dance" from *Ritual, Play, and Performance,* edited by Richard Schechner and Mady Schuman (New York: Seabury, 1976), pp. 40–41. Reprinted with permission.

raining and blowing far too hard for me to get at my notebook or use my binoculars. I could only watch, and marvel at the magnificence of those splendid creatures. With a display of strength and vigor such as this, primitive man himself might have challenged the elements.

Twenty minutes from the start of the performance the last of the males plodded back up the slope for the last time. The females and youngsters climbed down from their trees and the whole group moved over the crest of the ridge. One male paused, and with his hand on a tree trunk, looked back—the actor taking his final curtain. Then he too vanished over the ridge.

I continued to sit there, staring almost in disbelief at the white scars on the tree trunks and the discarded branches on the grass—all that remained, in that rain-lashed landscape, to prove that the wild "rain dance" had taken place at all. I should have been even more amazed had I known then that I would only see such a display twice more in the next ten years. Often, it is true, male chimpanzees react to the start of heavy rain by performing a rain dance, but this is usually an individual affair.

—Jane van Lawick-Goodall

All rites begin in simplicity, are brought to fulfillment in elegant form, and end in joy. When rites are performed in the highest manner, then both the emotions and the forms embodying them are fully realized; in the next best manner, the emotional content and the forms prevail by turns; in the poorest manner, everything reverts to emotion and finds unity in that alone.

Through rites Heaven and earth join in harmony, the sun and moon shine, the four seasons proceed in order, the stars and constellations march, the rivers flow, and all things flourish; men's likes and dislikes are regulated and their joys and hates made appropriate. Those below are obedient, those above are enlightened; all things change but do not become disordered; only he who turns his back upon rites will be destroyed. Are they not wonderful indeed? When they are properly established and brought to the peak of perfection, no one in the world can add to or detract from them. Through them the root and the branch are put in proper order; beginning and end are justified; the most elegant forms embody all distinctions; the most penetrating insight explains all things. In the world those who obey the dictates of ritual will achieve order; those who turn against them will suffer disorder. Those who obey them will win safety; those who turn against them will court danger. Those who obey them will be preserved; those who turn against them will be lost. This is something that the petty man cannot comprehend.

The meaning of ritual is deep indeed. He who tries to enter it with the kind of perception that distinguishes hard and white, same and different, will drown there.[1] The meaning of ritual is great indeed. He who tries to enter it with the uncouth and inane theories of the system-makers will perish there. The meaning of ritual is lofty indeed. He who tries to enter with the violent and arrogant ways of those who despise common customs and consider themselves to be above other men will meet his downfall there.

If the plumb line is properly stretched, then there can be no doubt about crooked and straight; if the scales are properly hung, there can be no doubt about heavy and light; if the T

---

[1] A reference to the Logicians.

Hsün Tzu, from *Basic Writings of Mu Tzu, Hsun Tzu, and Han Fei Tzu,* translated by Burton Watson (New York: Columbia University Press, 1967), pp. 94–96, 100. Copyright © 1967 by Columbia University Press. Reprinted with the permission of the publishers.

square and compass are properly adjusted, there can be no doubt about square and round; and if the gentleman is well versed in ritual, then he cannot be fooled by deceit and artifice. The line is the acme of straightness, the scale is the acme of fairness, the T square and compass are the acme of squareness and roundness, and rites are the highest achievement of the Way of man. Therefore, those who do not follow and find satisfaction in rites may be called people without direction, but those who do follow and find satisfaction in them are called men of direction.

He who dwells in ritual and can ponder it well may be said to know how to think; he who dwells in ritual and does not change his ways may be said to be steadfast. He who knows how to think and to be steadfast, and in addition has a true love for ritual—he is a sage. Heaven is the acme of loftiness, earth the acme of depth, the boundless the acme of breadth, and the sage the acme of the Way. Therefore the scholar studies how to become a sage; he does not study merely to become one of the people without direction.

Ritual uses material goods for its performance, follows the distinctions of eminent and humble in creating its forms, varies its quantities in accordance with differences of station, and varies its degree of lavishness in accordance with what is appropriate. When form and meaning are emphasized and emotional content and practical use slighted, rites are in their most florid state. When form and meaning are slighted and emphasis placed upon emotion and practical use, rites are in their leanest state. When form and meaning, and emotion and practical use, are treated as the inside and outside or the front and back of a single reality and are both looked after, then rites have reached the middle state. Therefore the gentleman understands how to make rites florid and how to make them lean, but he chooses to abide in the middle state, and no matter whether he walks or runs, hurries or hastens, he never abandons it. It is his constant world and dwelling. He who abides in it is a gentleman and a man of breeding; he who abandons it is a commoner. He who dwells in it, who wanders widely and masters all its corners and gradations, is a sage. His bounty is the accumulation of ritual; his greatness is the breadth of ritual; his loftiness is the flourishing of ritual; his enlightenment is the mastery of ritual. This is what the *Odes* means when it says:

> Their rites and ceremonies are entirely according to rule,
> Their laughter and talk are entirely appropriate.[2]

. . . .

Rites trim what is too long and stretch out what is too short, eliminate surplus and repair deficiency, extend the forms of love and reverence, and step by step bring to fulfillment the beauties of proper conduct. Beauty and ugliness, music and weeping, joy and sorrow are opposites, and yet rites make use of them all, bringing forth and employing each in its turn. Beauty, music, and joy serve to induce an attitude of tranquillity and are employed on auspicious occasions. Ugliness, weeping, and sorrow induce an attitude of inquietude and are employed on inauspicious occasions. But though beauty is utilized, it should never reach the point of sensuousness or seductiveness, and though ugliness is utilized, it should never go as far as starvation or self-injury. Though music and joy are utilized, they should never become lascivious and abandoned, and though weeping and sorrow are utilized, they should never become frantic or injurious to health. If this is done, then rites have achieved the middle state.

—Hsün Tzu

---

[2] "Lesser Odes," *Ch'u-tz'u,* Mao text no. 209.

Introduction

Beginning in the mid-1960s, ritual's reputation changed dramatically. No longer the exemplar of dull routine, ritual was launched into prominence as a celebrated cause. No longer the glue of society and guardian of the status quo, it became subversive and creative. It has become the subject matter for thematic issues of mainline popular magazines such as *Life*. It is a recurrent topic in counterculture publications such *The Utne Reader* and *Shaman's Drum*. It is touted as a panacea for Western societies' cultural and psychological woes. Now ritual can provide women with solidarity, men with identity, adolescents with purpose, nations with a coherent ideology, and religious institutions with a reason for being.

Although both views—ritual as routine, ritual as panacea—can be instructive if understood in their social and historical contexts, neither attitude helps the student of ritual to understand it. The first view prevents notice of ritual's capacity for evoking creativity and challenging the status quo; it inhibits recognition of ritual's connection with play, drama, and other not-so-boring human activities. And the second threatens to set zealots loose plundering the symbolic goods of other cultures; it baits practitioners with the false hope that a little ritual spice exported from elsewhere can restore the savor to spirituality gone bland.

This change in reputation has provoked students into wanting to know what ritual is. Why does it evoke such indifference and such enthusiasm? Ritual is one of the oldest human activities—often considered as important as eating, sex, and shelter. Why has it persisted so long? Why does every attempt to suppress it result in creating it anew? What makes ritual seem at once so foundational that even the animals do it and so superfluous that Protestants once imagined that they could dispense with it altogether?

It is not easy to say what ritual is, although most of us can cite examples of it from our own experience: Sunday masses, Friday synagogue services, vigorous hymn singing, public prayers at graduations and inaugurations, temple chanting, the muezzin's call from a minaret, a masked dance by Hopis. If we reflect on it, most of us know firsthand ritual's capacity to weld a community, tranquilize inquiring minds, foment aggression, or inspire cooperation. Pressed, we might come up with other examples: the swearing in of a president, the archaic language and exaggerated decorum of the courtroom, high table at an exclusive girls' school.

But what about the ways doctors behave with nurses and patients? Is this ritual? And what about plays that take audience members on overnight treks through the woods? Or courtship behavior between adolescents? Or Olympic fanfare?

New, makeshift terminology in the field of ritual studies reflects considerable strain on the standard categories for classifying rites. Secular ritual, consumer ritual, ritualization, tacit ritual, interaction ritual, invisible religion, civil religion, and other such terms illustrate the extraordinary fuzziness of the notion of ritual. Much that would not have been regarded as ritual three decades ago now appears, either literally or metaphorically, to be ritual. Ritual can seem to exist in strictly circumscribed spaces (as if it were hiding in the corners of decrepit churches), and yet, almost magically, it can be everywhere, functioning as the very lifeblood of individuals and societies. Either the thing itself has changed or our eyes for seeing it have.

Several of the selections in this volume (most notably, those by Robbie Davis-Floyd, Richard Hardin, Roy Rappaport, Jonathan Z. Smith, and Stanley Tambiah) take up the issue of definition, and students of ritual will likely be driven to reflect on both the agreements and disagreements among these ways of conceiving ritual. Read by itself each selection can sound as if it were describing an obvious fact, but each is really a proposal, an attempt either to legislate or garner agreement in the scholarly community about the nature of ritual.

The study of ritual in the West has gone through at least three obvious stages. The first, research on ritual conducted by those who practice it, has a venerable history. The form of such study that is probably the most familiar to readers is Christian liturgical theology as written by Europeans and North Americans. The Christian tradition of theological reflection on ritual, though one of the most fully documented, is by no means the oldest. One of the delightful epigraphs for this book was written by Hsün Tzu in the third century B.C.E. There may be older documents reflecting on the meaning and function of ritual but none that are more articulate or thoughtful than this Chinese one. Undoubtedly, the oral exegesis of rites predates both Christian and Chinese documents.

In the second, quite late phase, the study of ritual was no longer in the sole possession of practitioners but also the purview of scholars from outside the ritual tradition which was the object of study. In the late nineteenth and early twentieth centuries ritual became a topic of special interest to the newly developing field of anthropology. Because one could observe and document ritual, and because it was sometimes especially visible and colorful, early anthropologists assigned it a privileged position in the study of societies. It was regarded by some as a window on culture, an opening into a culture's central values and persistent contradictions. In the social sciences ritual was studied formally in classrooms and at field sites rather than informally and by apprenticeship as is the case in most religious traditions. Those who studied it were observers rather than participants. In some instances observers became participant observers. They tried to understand ritual by momentary, short-term participation in it. The shift in attitude from participation to observation was enormous but not absolute. Scholarly observers who had no vested interest in sustaining the performance of the rites nevertheless maintained an investment in "performing" observed ritual in books, films, and lectures back home.

Although ritual as an intellectual category has existed at least since the inception of anthropology, ritual studies as a scholarly discipline is a recent invention. The mid-1970s witnessed the emergence of an interdisciplinary discussion of ritual that no longer confined it to either participating ritualists or observing anthropologists. *Readings in Ritual Studies* reflects this more recent turn in scholarship. Ritual studies has gained sufficient momentum as a field of study that an anthology has become necessary. An indication of the field's importance is the *Journal of Ritual Studies,* which is devoted exclusively to the topic of ritual. There are other indicators. For instance, there are a growing number of courses on ritual in secular universities as well as in religiously affiliated institutions such as seminaries. In addition to these courses there are now university graduate programs that specify ritual studies as one of their interests. Also, there have been discussions and proposals for Ph.D.'s in ritual studies. Whether or not there is ever a doctorate in ritual studies, the area is a regular part of the agenda of several professional associations, including the American Academy of Religion, American Anthropological Association, and North American Academy of Liturgy. Even in associations that have no subunit devoted to the study of ritual, for instance, the Modern Language Association, the topic appears with increasing frequency in published programs and proceedings. A striking feature of the conferences, proposals, and courses is their interdisciplinary composition.

Readings in Ritual Studies aims to illustrate and foster this interdisciplinary discussion. Its selections represent the most current scholarly thinking on the topic of ritual. Though it includes brief selections from those who fundamentally shaped the field in the first half of the twentieth century—Durkheim, Eliade, Freud, and van Gennep, for instance—it focuses on more recent writers from a variety of disciplines, including religious studies, anthropology, theology, history, psychology, law, media studies, ethology, performance studies, literature, and the arts.

The articles cover a range of topics, some theoretical (for instance, questions of definition, function, and interpretation), some on specific ritual types (for example, rites of passage, festival, and civil ceremony), and some on the rites of specific cultures and religious traditions. I have tried to provide cross-cultural breadth and to represent a wide variety of religious and nonreligious ritual traditions, though, as always, there are significant gaps in the presentation. The appendix lists the categories that the selections were chosen to represent.

Generally, I have favored selections that combine theoretical breadth with the concrete particulars that can be provided by ethnographic, textual, or historical research. The number of purely descriptive pieces is kept to a minimum, but *Readings* does include some purely theoretical pieces, because the goal is to provide a theoretical (rather than, say, an ethnographic or historical) basis for interdisciplinary teaching and research.

The table of contents is not organized topically but rather alphabetically by author. The reason for this choice is the glaring arbitrariness of any single set of subdivisions. To compensate, there is a subject bibliography in the appendix. Using this appendix, which lists the selections under major headings in ritual studies, is crucial for designing courses that make the best use of this text.

This collection is aimed at interdisciplinary audiences, especially those with interests in religious studies, anthropology, performance studies, and liturgiology but also in the other discipline-groups enumerated in section four of the appendix. *Readings* does not assume expertise in either ritual studies or in these disciplines. A few of the selections will seem easy to such readers; a few will seem difficult. Most, however, are in a middle range. With a good dictionary readers should be able to make sense of the arguments. Although I have tried to be aware of the technical vocabulary necessary for engaging in ritual studies, it was not possible to provide sufficient background and glossary to cover the complexity of the world's ritual traditions.

This is not a how-to-book. It includes neither primary ritual texts nor purely in-house apologies extolling the virtues of specific ritual practices and traditions. It does not pretend to make an adequate representation of any specific religious or secular ritual system. Rather, it aims to introduce students of ritual to the range of disciplinary and theoretical options in approaching the topic of ritual as it is framed in academic debate and discourse.

ACKNOWLEDGMENTS

I am grateful to the following colleagues and students for offering suggestions, critique, and comments on *Readings:* Bobby Alexander, Kathleen Ashley, Michael Aune, Ellen Badone,

Catherine Bell, Fred Clothey, Madeline Duntley, Armin Geertz, Ed Gilday, Bob Lester, Robert Petersen, Tony Swain, and Tod Swanson. I am indebted to Sam Gill, Mimi Ward, and Michael Zogry for their assistance, which was made possible by a University of Colorado Research Grant from the Graduate Committee on the Arts and Humanities. Laurie Goebel and Cathie Huggins helped me bring order to the final draft.

I would also like to thank the following reviewers: Mary McGee, Vassar College; Mary L. Collins, Catholic University of America; and Thomas V. Peterson, Alfred University.

Finally, I am most grateful to Pattie Amoroso, Prentice Hall's project manager, for her remarkable reliability in supervising the massive and complex editorial matters surrounding the production of this book.

Readings in Ritual Studies

*Arrange Me into Disorder: Fragments and Reflections on Ritual Clowning**

BARBARA A. BABCOCK

Facts of publication: *Babcock, Barbara A. 1984. "Arrange Me into Disorder: Fragments and Reflections on Ritual Clowning," from* Rite, Drama, Festival, Spectacle: Rehearsals Toward a Theory of Cultural Performance, *102–128. Edited by John J. MacAloon. Philadelphia: Institute for the Study of Human Issues, Inc. Reprinted with the permission of the publishers.*

Babcock's subject is the role of laughter and comedy in ritual and culture. She presents a provocative dialogue in the form of a pastiche of quotations that both describe and respond to ritual clowning. Her main examples are from Native American cultures of the Southwest (for instance, the Pueblos) and from cultures that employ humor in self-reflection and criticism. Drawing upon a surprising and delightful range of philosophers and critics, she metaphorically identifies academic concerns with ritual clowning. The essay is not only about play, it itself plays. It does so by engaging in back and forth movement between columns as well as between practitioners and commentators, readers and authors, quotations and endnotes. If we follow Hannah Arendt's notion that quotations are the modern equivalent of ritual invocation, we may see Babcock's work as a ritualizing of scholarship. Bruce Lincoln argues that footnoting is a form of ritual in "Two Notes on Modern Rituals" in the Journal of the American Academy of Religion *45.2 (1977): 147–60.*

About the author: Dates: *1943–, Danville, PA, U.S.A.* **Education:** *B.A., Northwestern University; M.A., University of Chicago; Ph.D., University of Chicago.* **Field(s):** *folklore; symbolic anthropology; Pueblo ethnography; feminist theory; cultural studies.* **Career:** *Regents Professor and Director, Comparative Cultural and Literary Studies, University of Arizona, Tucson.* **Publications:** *"The Novel and the Carnival World,"* Modern Language Notes *89.6 (1974): 911–937; editor,* The Reversible World *(Cornell University, 1978); "Too Many, Too Few: Ritual Modes of Signification,"* Semiotica *23.3–4 (1978): 291–302; "Ritual Undress and the Comedy of Self & Other: Bandelier's* The Delight Makers," *in* A Crack in the Mirror, *187–203, ed. Jay Ruby (University of Pennsylvania, 1981); "Reflexivity,"* The Encyclopedia of Religion, *1986: 234–238, ed. Mircea Eliade (Macmillan, 1986); "Mud, Mirrors, & Making Up: Liminality and Reflexivity in Between the Acts,"* in Victor Turner & the Construction of Cultural Criticism, *86–116, ed. Kathleen Ashley (Indiana University, 1990).* **Additional:** *President-elect, Society for Humanistic Anthropology, 1993; Regents Professor, University of Arizona, 1993; Distinguished Ford Foundation Visiting Professor, University of Chicago, 1993; Director, Pembroke Center for Teaching & Research on Women, Brown University, 1987–88. "For the last two decades my work has concentrated on interrelated aspects of cultural semiotics: ritual clowning and rites of reversal, reflexivity and metanarration, material culture, gender dynamics, and the politics of representation."**

The play of communicating and approaching
is the business and force of life;
absolute perfection exists only in death.[1]

One must still have chaos in oneself
to be able to give birth to a dancing star.[2]

*In addition to Carmen del Rio, to whom this assemblage is dedicated, my thanks to Barbara Myerhoff, Beverly Stoehje, Alfonso Ortiz, and Keith Basso. My title is drawn from A. R. Ammons's 1966 poem, "Muse." The English orthography of certain Pueblo words has been standardized.

Since 1872, when Darwin observed that "many curious discussions have been written on the causes of laughter with grown-up persons," many more curious and tedious discussions have been written on the same subject. While we acknowledge that all forms of creativity, especially clowning, involve a "disconfirmation of familiar forms," rarely are we willing to carry this disconfirmation into our scholarly practices. Unfortunately for those who make us laugh, "analysis has a way of failing to participate in the very spirit which it would analyse, and therefore not only involving itself in an ironic self-contradiction, but in a violation and negation of that to which it is attempting to do justice."[3] But can analysis participate in the comic spirit? Can one do what one describes?

After some years of writing conventional academic papers about assorted deconstructive phenomena, I can no longer deny the temptation to try. Moreover, my subject bespeaks fragments and motley and "artfully ordered confusion," and the philosophers and poets to whom I have turned to make a different sense of clowning embody their ironic aesthetic or metaphysic in unconventional, subversive, and self-mocking forms. Whether Kierkegaard or Nietzsche, Barthes or Derrida, Socrates or Zen masters, hierarchical and dialectical reasoning is displaced by playful, "horizontal," paralogical thought, and logical argument is eschewed in a paradoxical and paratactical discourse of fragments and aphorisms, dialogue and pastiche. "Kaleidoscope logic," "radical discontinuity," "inversive irregularity," "metaphysical free association," Zen "smashing" or "running sideways": these are all forms of meditation on play that remain in the realm of play, and I cannot separate this reading from my writing.

What is written here may or may not be "scientific" or "valid" ethnographic interpretation. It is a speculation, accomplished through rearranging a motley of written and unwritten cultural texts about clowning. Such a reading of readings may promise nothing more, and nothing less, than a few new tropes and concepts to enlarge the intelligibility of the text—ritual clowning—and to give its interpreters a little more room to play in, an open space of questioning, paracriticism as an attempt to recover the art of multivocation.[4]

What does philosophical pastiche have to do with Pueblo clowns, or Kierkegaard with *koyemci*? By the

philosopher's own definition, both may be described as "realities of decreation," as hypothetical and subjunctive modes of culture. Both are forms of play (as classically defined by Huizinga: occasions of questioning, speculation, self-commentary) and of what Nietzsche called "gay science" (wisdom + laughter). But too few have taken clowning seriously enough to realize that "the deepest source of knowledge involved in the perception of the ludicrous . . . is metaphysical, as having to do with the structure of truth and reality."[5] Unfortunately, with the growth of naturalism, the interpretation of the comic, particularly among "primitive" peoples, has increasingly lost its connection with rational thought. Yet all men "have an inclination, perhaps a need, to think beyond the limitations of knowledge, to do more with this ability than to use it as an instrument for knowing and doing."[6] In this sense, both clowning and philosophizing are liminal phenomena in their respective sociocultural contexts: "realms of pure possibility whence *novel* configurations of ideas and relations may arise," involving "the analysis of culture into factors and their free recombination in any and every possible pattern, however weird."[7] Both are marginal notes, parenthetical and paratactical to surrounding syntax and primary texts. Comedy, whether in written discourse or ritual drama, may be regarded as "an exercise in understanding, a planned confusion created in order to be clarified."[8] Comedy may be a spiritual shock therapy which breaks up the patterns of thought and rationality that hold us in bondage and in which the given and established order of things is deformed, reformed, and reformulated; a playful speculation on what was, is, or might be; a remark on the indignity of any closed system.

Since such planned and playful confusion involves donning masks and costumes of motley, it is not insignificant that it is in *Sartor Resartus* that Carlyle defines philosophy as "a continual battle against custom; an ever-renewed effort to transcend the sphere of blind custom."[9] Those who engage in thinking "are transported from the world of appearances to the invisible world of ideas where previous allegiances to established codes of conduct are gradually dissolved and everything stable is set in motion and rendered open to question. In short, thinking makes us aware of another order of reality than the one we had thoughtlessly taken over from sense experience and from our fellows. It undermines 'all established criteria, values, measurements for good and evil.' "[10] Like clowning, *theoria* is "an activity that defies all existing canons of the 'useful' or the 'realistic,' "[11] "perverting good sense and allowing thought to play outside the ordered categories of resemblance." (Foucault 1970:898). Despite the various uses to which interpreters put his activity, the clown like the thinker must hold out in the accursed bliss of his futility, for only

> by posing the unanswerable questions of meaning [do] men establish themselves as question-asking beings. Behind all the cognitive questions for which men find answers, there lurk the unanswerable ones which seem entirely idle and have always been denounced as such. It is more than likely that men, if they should ever lose this appetite for meaning which we call thinking and cease to ask unanswerable questions, will also lose not only the ability to produce those thought-things which we call works of art but also the faculty of asking all the answerable questions upon which every civilization is founded.[12]

The form that such "thought-things" often take brings me back to pastiche and parataxis and something of an explanation and justification of my own methods—a pretext for the texts I'm getting to. Whether by artist or theologian, clown or philosopher, seriously playful self-interpretation and commentary on the other do involve "the analysis of culture into factors and their free recombination" in weird assemblages of "orts, scraps, and fragments." The obvious example is the fool's costume of motley which "confuses and garbles the neat patterns of rationality and order and value that we use to organize experience"[13] and "characteristically contains chaotic and disproportionate elements . . . expressing both the emergence of form and meaning out of chaos and their reversion to it."[14] Such tattered garb implies an aesthetic and metaphysic of discontinuity, indeterminacy, and fragmentation common to various media and types of discourse. In theology, Clement of Alexandria's most mature work was a poetic and aphoristic *Rag Bag (Stromata)*. He insisted on the aphoristic, patchwork form of theology because "all things that shine through a veil show the truth grander and more imposing; as fruits through water and figures through veils, *which give*

added reflections to them."[15] Similarly in Zen religion, art, and literature there is "a preference for anecdotes and abbreviated discourse, if not simply shouts and exclamations . . . for an amorphousness and an ambiguity that represent an order of being and knowing that lies before and beyond all duality and hierarchy and intellection."[16] And in our own century and culture, David Miller has argued convincingly for a "theology of play" and Harvey Cox for a "theology of juxtaposition," of disrelation based on Surrealism's collage principle. And in philosophy from Heraclitus to Nietzsche and Wittgenstein to Derrida, the critique of metaphysical imperialism has involved the deconstruction of logical argument, and philosophical analysis regarded as most serious when most playful, embodying an attitude of contemplative celebration. One of the important moral philosophers of our time, Hannah Arendt, was heiress to an aphoristic technique. She collected quotations, stories, fragments of the broken tradition which she reworked, rewove into a collection of significant objects of reflection and understanding—a new, dynamic, illuminating collage or mobile. In visual art, ironic self-commentary takes many forms, most notably the collage or assemblage and the notion that the painting's surface should be an impartial collector of images—an aesthetic of process rather than product. Long before the German Romantics dignified an aesthetic of mixed genres, pastiche was an accepted mode in both literature and music. The notion that every creation is but a new arrangement of existing elements is a commonplace in literature. It is perhaps even more significant that the oldest forms of literary criticism were the dialogue and the *satura*. The Roman *satura* (a plate of mixed fruit) was the traditional vehicle for literary as well as social criticism and consisted of a mixture of genres, prose and verse, and inversive parodies. It is from this as well as the word *satyr* that *satire* derives.

As the preceding implies, the practice of criticism as pastiche and freeplay was not recently invented by Roland Barthes and Jacques Derrida, despite the remarks of some outraged commentators. They have, however, resumed the old game and said some very interesting things about what they're up to and why. Talking about himself (in both first and third persons) in his recent reflexive assemblage, Barthes has this to say about fragments:

To write by fragments: the fragments are then so many stones on the perimeter of a circle: I spread myself around: my whole little universe in crumbs: at the center, what?

His first, or nearly first text (1942) consists of fragments; choice is then justified in the Gidean manner "because incoherence is preferable to a distorting order." Since then, as a matter of fact, he has never stopped writing in brief bursts . . .

He already regarded the wrestling match as a series of fragments, a sum of spectacles, for "in the ring, it is each moment which is intelligible, not the duration" (*Mythologies*); with amazement and predilection he watched this sportive artifice, subject in its very structure to *asyndeton* and *anacoluthon*, figures of interruption and short-circuiting.

Not only is the fragment cut off from its neighbors, but even within each fragment parataxis reigns. This is clear if you make an index of these little pieces; for each of them the assemblage of referents is heteroclite; it is like a parlor game: "Take the words: *fragment, circle, Gide, wrestling match, asyndeton, painting, discourse, Zen, intermezzo*; make up a discourse which can link them together." And that would quite simply be this very fragment. The index of a text then is not only an instrument of reference; it is itself a text, a second text which is the *relief* (remainder and asperity) of the first: what is wandering (interrupted) in the rationality of the sentences.

Liking to find, to write beginnings, he tends to multiply this pleasure: that is why he writes fragments: so many fragments, so many beginnings, so many pleasures (but he doesn't like the ends: the risk of rhetorical clausulae is too great: the fear of not being able to resist the *last word*).[17]

Many years ago Franz Boas said something similar about North American Indian mythology: "It would seem that mythological worlds have been built up, only to be shattered again, and that new worlds were built from the fragments."[18] More recently, Lévi-Strauss has described creation by fragments—*bricolage*—as characteristic of mythical thought and governed by a logic very different from, but every bit as rigorous as that of science. The logic of *bricolage* is that of the kaleidoscope in which structural patterns are realized by means of bits and pieces—patterns produced by the conjunction of contingency *and* constraint. Like the myth and the kaleidoscope, the performance and dress of the clown or the pastiches of the philosopher are constructed out of oddments of cultural debris and involve a mirror principle.

What all this implies and what this essay attempts to argue both formally and substantially is that metalanguage or reflexive statement can be other than a sustained and systematic discourse about another discourse. Motley, I and my authorities suggest, is a significant type of second-order discourse, a form of self-commentary characteristic of a great variety of cultural performances, both singular and plural. Such expressive assemblages involve an interrogation of, a dialogue with a culturally constrained set of materials and tools. The "freeplay" (infinite substitutions in the closure of a finite ensemble) and "decentering" of *bricolage* is, Derrida points out,[19] a discourse on method not only of mythologizing, but also of Lévi-Strauss's own intellectual activity and of signification in general. In the choices he makes among limited possibilities, the *bricoleur* both makes a formal and sociocultural critique as well as gives an account of his personality and life.[20] Using Lévi-Strauss's example, both Derrida and Genette argue that *bricolage* is essential criticism, especially literary criticism. In discussing the organization of his data in *Naven*, Bateson similarly argues that an arrangement *is* an interpretation. The noted critic Walter Benjamin would seem to concur, for he once suggested that the perfect critical essay would consist entirely of carefully selected and arranged quotations, "the craziest mosaic technique imaginable."[21] Yet people today, as Nietzsche remarked in his 1887 Preface to the *Genealogy of Morals*, have difficulty with the aphoristic form because they do not take it seriously enough.

The temptation to construct a critical argument entirely of footnotes is more than an urge to parody the repressive structures of academic discourse. Rather it suggests a desire to foreground the fact that thinking and writing always involve a dialogue with other texts, that "all knowledge is knowledge of a complex and interwoven textuality."[22] Quotations, Hannah Arendt once said, are the modern equivalent of ritual invocations, recalling or repre-

senting voices from the past. But more than invocations of authority, the quotation and the footnote
are the means of transforming a monological performance into a dialogue, of opening one's discourse to that of others. They are also the literate
way of interrupting and commenting on one's own
text, of acknowledging that reading and writing,
like any cultural performance, involve appropriating, absorbing, and transforming the texts of others. "Quotations in my work are like robbers by the
roadside who make an armed attack and relieve an
idler of his convictions."[23] Interestingly enough,
these notions of the literary and critical text as dialogue and as *satura* have been reformulated in Ju-
lia Kristeva's concepts of *dialogisme* and *intertextu-
alité*, developed in response to Bakhtin's masterful
study of Rabelais and medieval carnival. Clowning—on the ancient stage, under the big top, in the
Pueblo plaza—exemplifies these very principles and
creates a space where texts can talk to each other.[24]
The clown's performance is a *parabasis* and a
parataxis that disrupts and interrupts customary
frames and expected logic and syntax and creates a
reflexive and ironic dialogue, an open space of questioning. It is "as if a social function of circuses were
to clarify for patrons what the ordering and limits
of their basic frameworks are."[25]

All of this suggests two directions for consideration: that ritual clowning is much more than a functional steamvalve and should be considered in terms
of its aesthetics and metaphysics as well as its prag-
matics; and, conversely, that criticism, whatever the
discipline, should be considered as comedy, reminded of its playful origins, and reinvested with a
comic perspective. Both clowning and criticism are
"sanctioned disrespect," ways in which society paradoxically institutionalizes doubt and questioning.
Both, I suggest, are also forms of irony: "the great
comic means by which various factions within the
self and the community question one another, thus
uncovering the magic and mystery which lurks in
every social bond."[26] Unfortunately, our emphasis
on clowning as childlike and un-serious, and on the
primitive as simple has generally precluded our seeing ritual clowning as a sophisticated form of sociocultural self-commentary, as irony writ large. Further, it has blinded our own interpretive enterprise
to the fact that "the comic frame makes man the stu-

dent of himself" and therefore "provides maximum
opportunity for the resources of criticism."[27] Some
four decades ago in discussing the "planned incongruity" and "gargoyle thinking" of his own work,
Kenneth Burke declared that "whatever poetry may
be, criticism had best be comic."[28] More recently,
Harold Rosenberg has asserted that sociology needs
to bring comedy into the foreground, including "an
awareness of the comedy of sociology with *its* dis-
guises," and, like Burke and Duncan, he has argued
that comedy provides "the radical effect of self-
knowledge which the anthropological bias excludes."[29]

What follows are reflections and speculations—
my own and those of others—in both these directions *at the same time*. If a dialogue is "a chain or gar-
land of fragments,"[30] then this is a dialogue about
dialogues. And if Cox is right that "a festive occasion
has three essential ingredients: (1) conscious excess,
(2) celebrative affirmation, and (3) juxtaposition,"[31]
then this is also a festive occasion. It is also an attempt
to argue by arranging and to write criticism "that is
fragmentary both in form and content, simultaneously completely subjective and individual, and completely objective and like a necessary part in a system
of all the sciences."[32] Undoubtedly this is quixotic
and ironic. I hope so, for "cheerfulness—*gay
science*—is a reward: the reward of a long, brave, in-
dustrious and subterranean seriousness."[33] The double vision is deliberate, for irony is "not merely a matter of seeing a 'true' meaning beneath a 'false'; but of
seeing *a double exposure on one plate*."[34] The meaning is as transitional as it is transitory: in between, in
the interplay; in the interconnections, the disjunctions; at the intersections, the crossroads; in the journey, not the arrival. The danger as well as the significance of certain deviant acts is "that they undermine
the intelligibility of everything else we had thought
was going on around us, including all next acts, thus
generating diffuse disorder."[35] My only defenses
against such charges of diffuse order are that my subject demands it and that "self-consciousness about
modes of representation (not to speak of experiments
with them) has been very lacking in anthropology."[36]
One must remember that writing by fragments is "a
way of perceiving reality and of experiencing reality,
of being real, and not just *any* parlour witticism,
clownish caper or comedian's trick."[37]

I know of no other manner of dealing with great tasks than as *play*; this . . . is an essential pre-requisite.[38]

TEXTS	PARATEXTS

They chased after her, carried her back and threw her down in the center of the plaza, then while one was performing coitus from behind, another was doing it against her head. Of course, all was simulated, and not the real act, as the woman was dressed. The naked fellow performed masturbation in the center of the plaza or very near it, alternatively with a black rug and his hand. Everybody laughed.[39]

A disgusting rite . . . revolting . . . abominable dance . . . vile ceremonial.[40]

They were drinking urine out of bowls and jars used as privies on the house tops, eating excrement and dirt.[41]

Bourke [like Bandelier] solved the problem of what to do about a scatological rite he witnessed in Zuni in 1881 by relegating it to a place near the bottom end of a simple scale of man's cultural evolution.[42]

The appearance of the six men who have just tumbled into the arena is not merely strange, it is positively disgusting. They are covered with white paint, and with the exception of tattered breechclouts are absolutely naked. Their mouths and eyes are encircled with black rings; their hair is gathered in knots upon the tops of their heads, from which rise bunches of corn husks; fragments of fossil wood hang from their loins; and to the knees are fastened tortoise-shells. Nothing is worn with a view to ornament. These seeming monstrosities, frightful in their ugliness, move about quite nimbly, and are boldly impudent to a degree approaching sublimity. . . . If one of the spectators has the misfortune to display immoderate enthusiasm, forthwith he is made the target of merciless jeering. One of the merrymakers goes up to him and mimics his manners and actions in the crudest possible way. The people on the terraced roofs exhibit their joy by showering down corncakes from their perches, which the performers greedily devour. These things are delightful according to Indian notions, and are well fitted to show how much of a child he still is,—a child, however, it must be remembered, endowed with the physical strength, passions, and appetites of adult mankind. . . . The pranks of these fellows are simply silly and ugly; the folly borders on imbecility and the ugliness is disgusting, and yet nobody is shocked; everybody endures it and laughs. . . . To the *Koshare* nothing is sacred; all things are permitted so long as they contribute to the delight of the tribe.[43]

Funny as these are to the natives, however, they have elicited only emotions of repugnance and disgust from even the ethnologist.[44]

People think that the clown is just nothing, that he is just for fun. That is not so. When I make other masked dancers and they do not set things right or they can't find out something, I make that clown and he never fails. Many people who know about these things say that the clown is the most powerful.[45]

The purpose of our ceremonies is not entertainment but attainment; the attainment of the Good Life. Our dramas, dances, songs are not performed for fun; no, they are more than that: *they are the very essence of our lives*; they are sacred.[46]

I would only believe in a god who could dance.[47]

To us the clown is somebody sacred, funny, powerful, ridiculous, holy, shameful, visionary. He is all this and then some more. Fooling around, a clown is really performing a spiritual ceremony. He has a power. It comes from the thunder-beings, not the animals or the earth. In our Indian belief, a clown has more power than the atom bomb. This power could blow the dome off the Capitol. I have told you that I once worked as a rodeo clown. This was almost like doing spiritual work. Being a clown, for me, came close to being a medicine man. It was in the same nature.[48]

Two grotesques, swinging lariats and singing, came in on the west side of the court and, seeing the woman, drop on their hands and knees and crawl toward her, each loosening his breechclout and displaying a false penis made of a gourd neck. When she finishes washing an old fringe of rags, she washes her legs, displaying a great false vulva so that all the spectators can see it and laugh at her. The grotesques and the two clowns—all whitened with clay—finally converge on her, and as she sits on the sacred shrine they propose copulation with her. She points to the presence of her boy as an obstacle. The clowns send the boy to get a jar of water and then proceed upon the shrine either to copulate or to imitate copulation with the utmost grossness. The boy returning, rushes among them, thrashes his immoral mother, and a general brawl ensues amid loud plaudits.[49]

And what happens when an interpreter such as Levine does take clowning seriously, as in the preceding scene from Stephen's *Hopi Journal*?

> The release from ego control of archaic impulses in the service of the pleasure principle is achieved, in a contagion of hilarious mirth, by regression to infantile or progressively more primitive stages of abandon. . . . The function of humor in permitting the acting out of otherwise strictly prohibited regressive, infantile-sexual, and aggressive behavior is illustrated by such anthropological accounts of American Indian ceremonials. Its social value is . . . periodic catharsis and sublimation from a ritualistic return of the repressed without individual guilt and fear of retribution or disruption of communal life.[50]

The "phallacies" proliferate. Whether by missionary, psychologist, or anthropologist, most descriptions and interpretations of ritual clowning are denigratingly ethnocentric and refuse to understand clowning within its own cultural context. Clowns are rarely asked what they're up to, and seldom listened to when they're asked.

> Well, white man, you want to see what goes on, don't you? You have spoiled our prayers and it may not rain. You think this business is vulgar, but it means something sacred to us. This old *katcina* is impersonating the Corn Maiden; therefore we must have intercourse with her so that our corn will increase and our people will live in plenty. If this were evil we would not be doing it. You are supposed to be an educated man, but you had better go back to school and learn something more about Hopi life.[51]

Seemingly vulgar antics can be sacred. In many cases, such as the pantomine described above, they are associated with fertility and rain, with societal and cosmic regeneration and renewal. Clowns are sacred beings whose existence and behavior are sanctioned in their creation myths, who mediate between spirits and men, and who heal and enable as well as delight.

Longing for something to make her laugh, *Iyatiku* (Corn Maiden) rubs her skin and covers the ball of epidermis with a blanket. From underneath comes *Koshare* to make fun and make people forget their troubles. *Iyatiku* makes an arch [the rainbow] for him to climb up and down.[52]

Gods enjoy mockery: it seems they cannot suppress laughter even during holy rites.[53]

The humorist possesses the childlike quality but is not possessed by it, constantly prevents it from expressing itself directly, but lets it only shimmer through an absolute culture.[54]

For a long, long time they journeyed; but the land of sunshine was not reached. On, on they marched till their food supply became scanty and their blankets became worn out. Then one by one they died of cold and hunger. For a while those who survived kept up courage even under adverse conditions. . . . At last, their numbers being so depleted, they became despondent and wished all to die.

At this juncture the mother god, the Moon, prayed to her husband, the Sun, to save the remnant of men, their children. So the Sun took one of the survivors to our people, painted his body in transverse black and white bands, decorated his hair with corn husks, and suspended eagle feathers behind each ear.

As soon as he was painted and decorated, this man became a "funny man" and began to dance, cut capers, and make grimaces. So interested did the people become in his performing that they forgot their sorrows and became glad. Then they resumed their journey, which they continued till they reached the Rio Grande confluence. Here in this valley they ceased their wanderings and took up their abode.[55]

Yet even the best ethnographers have little to say about the clowns and are given to simplistic explanations. Literary critics do little better, despite their lack of concern with social function. The criticism of comedy lags far behind that of tragedy, for the cultural biases are too strong.

. . . that divine malice without which I cannot imagine perfection: I estimate the value of human beings, of races, according to the necessity with which they cannot understand the god apart from the satyr.[56]

Judaeo-Christian religion is essentially tragic. Comedy is the business of devils, madmen, children. At least since Augustine, we have forgotten or denied that play is vital to the work of the gods; that there *are* divine forms of subversion. Rather we insist on a dichotomy between serious and ludic, good and evil, and value the former. Without a sense of irony and a perspective beyond good and evil, however, these sacred buffoons are incomprehensible and their comedy little more than a farce providing rebellious release. The absence of such a perspective is equally apparent in the targeting of Indian clowns by the Bureau of Indian Affairs "religious crimes code" in the 1920s, and in the sterile and reductive functionalist interpretations of clowning by intellectuals, even those who grant its religious significance.

> The highest earnestness of the religious life is recognizable by the jest.[57]

> What is here called "utility" is ultimately also a mere belief, something imaginary, and perhaps precisely that most calamitous stupidity of which we shall perish some day.[58]

Comedy is a complex, miscellaneous genre, embracing a plurality of impulses: farce, satire, irony, and so on. It is hazardous to declare that it has a single meaning or function, and yet its interpreters are prone to doing so. When, whatever the discipline, clowning is regarded as a means of catharsis and control, it is limited to simple farce or satire. Its complexities as a ludic genre of cultural performance are lost in its reduction to palliative remedies, substitute gratifications, or therapeutic reprieves from the oppressions of "reality." Whether in the terms of Arnold, Freud, or Gluckman, comedy seen simply as an escape from the pain and perplexity of life implies an identification of civilization with moral responsibility, spiritual seriousness, and social utility. The Indian, through his clown, is kept a child.

> Silly they were, yet wise as the gods and high priests; for as simpletons and the crazed speak from the things seen of the instant, uttering belike wise words and prophecy, so spake they, and became the attendants and fosterers, yet the sages and interpreters of the ancient dance dramas of the *ka'ka*. . . . And they are the oracles of all olden sayings of deep meanings; wherefore they are called the *kayemashi* (husbandmen of the *ka'ka*); and they are spoken of, even by the fathers of the people, as the *alshi tsewashi* (sages of the ancients). And most precious in the sight of beings and of men are they![59]

> [The cockfight] provides a metasocial commentary upon the whole matter of assorting human beings into fixed hierarchical ranks and then organizing the major part of collective experience around that assortment. Its function, if you want to call it that, is interpretive: it is a Balinese reading of Balinese experience; a story they tell themselves about themselves.[60]

Like Balinese cockfighting, Indian clown performances involve the paradoxical metacommentary that Bateson[61] and Geertz find characteristic of all forms of play. Pueblo ritual clowning has its own aesthetic, philosophy, and self-conscious awareness thereof.

Of burlesque and caricature generally, it can be said that they best permit insights into Pueblo modes of conception since they reveal what the Pueblos find serious or absurd, baffling or wrong, fearful or comical about life and about other people. When these center about the lives of other people, they can be particularly instructive. The wonder is that this has gone almost completely unrecognized by ethnographers.[62]

One of the best ways to understand a people is to know what makes them laugh. Laughter encompasses the limits of the soul. In humor life is redefined and accepted. Irony and satire provide much keener insights into a group's collective psyche and values than do years of research.[63]

The oldest form of social study is comedy. . . . If the comedian, from Aristophanes to Joyce, does not solve sociology's problem of "the participant observer," he does demonstrate his objectivity by capturing behavior in its most intimate aspects yet in its widest typicality. Comic irony sets whole cultures side by side in a multiple exposure, causing valuation to spring out of a recital of facts alone, in contrast to the hidden editorializing of tongue-in-cheek ideologists.[64]

We say that the disrelatedness of festive comedy leads to "clarification," to a "heightened awareness of all forms of relatedness."[65] We must not deny *Koyemci* or *Koshare* the perspective that we applaud in Shakespeare, Cervantes, or the *buffo* of commedia dell'arte. Any refusal of the possibility of detachment and double statement to "a people who can truly stand apart from themselves periodically, take an objective look and laugh"[66] is a bitter irony in itself. Pueblo ceremonialism is as complex, abstract, and powerful as any known, and its sacred clowning epitomizes the "transcendental buffoonery" and "beautiful self-mirroring" that Schlegel defined as irony.

Public rituals are the most important aesthetic expression of the Zuni people . . . a formal statement of Pueblo civilization.[67]

The comic frame should enable people to be *observers of themselves, while acting.* Its ultimate would not be *passiveness*, but *maximum consciousness*. One would "transcend" himself by noting his own foibles. The comic frame is one of acceptance but carries to completion the translative act. It considers human life as a project in "composition," where the poet works with the materials of social relationships. Composition, translation, also "revision," hence offering maximum opportunity for the resources of *criticism*.[68]

The Hopi newspaper *Quatöqti* carries two *koyala* clowns on the masthead and at the head of the editorial column. This may seem strange since clowns and everything they do and say are regarded as *ka-hopi*, that which is opposite of *hopi*, but things are in terms of what they are not. The social constructions of everyday life are perhaps most clearly seen when deconstructed. For literate Hopi, as well as for their ancestors, clowning is a most significant form of sociocultural commentary.

> Laughing at something is the first sign of a higher psychic life.[69]

> When we laugh we are free of all the oppression of our personality, or that of others, and even of God, who is indeed laughed away.[70]

> Whoever climbs the highest mountains laughs at all tragic plays and tragic seriousness.[71]

The Acoma say of the first clown, *Koshare*, that he is different from humans, never frightened, regarding nothing as sacred, able to go everywhere because "he knows something about himself."[72] Because he knows himself so completely, he can transcend himself: in his laughter is detachment, and in his detachment, freedom. Like all forms of reflexivity, clowning is paradoxical in that it involves a simultaneous subversion and transcendence of itself.

> Humour is not all innocence and play, however. At a more sophisticated and self-conscious level it stands more immediately within the sphere of duality, and in sensitivity to its conflicts and tensions, its alienations and anxieties. Here it is not a humour which leaves behind the world of dichotomy and rationality in a holiday of innocent abandon, but is a humour which moves within the terms and delineations of the objectified self in comic response to them. . . . On the one hand it becomes an act of *withdrawal* from that which is ordinarily taken as serious and sacred. And on the other hand it becomes an act of aggression against that which is ordinarily taken as sacred and serious.[73]

Mystics, radical philosophers, and theologians have long regarded laughter as a higher form of consciousness, a way of confronting the higher realities on which the whole of existence rests. The things that make life celebrative are the same which make life contemplative.[74] In Zen, for example, *satori* (awakening, enlightenment) is reached through both meditation and laughter. "Enlightenment is frequently accompanied by laughing of a transcendental kind, which may further be described as a laughter of surprised approval . . . at the moment of laughing something is understood; it needs no further proof of itself."[75]

> The question of the legitimacy of the comic, of its relationship to the religious, of whether it does not have a place in the religious address itself—this question is of essential significance for a religious existence in our times . . . It is certainly unjust to the comical to regard it as the enemy of the religious.[76]

Precisely because we are at bottom grave and serious human beings—really more weights than human beings—nothing does us as much good as the fool's cap: we need it in relation to ourselves—we need all exuberant, floating, dancing, mocking, childish, and blissful art lest we lose the *freedom above things* that our ideal demands of us. It would mean a relapse for us, with our irritable honesty, to get involved entirely in morality and, for the sake of the oversevere demands that we make on ourselves in these matters, to become virtuous monsters and scarecrows. We should be *able* also to stand *above* morality—and not only to *stand* with the anxious stiffness of a man who is afraid of slipping and falling at any moment, but also to *float* above it and *play*. How then could we possibly dispense with art—and with the fool?[77]

But we have forgotten religion as a festive art. We have made both our religious celebrations and our contemplative moments serious. In such contexts, laughter is regarded as inappropriate, subversive, and diabolical. This is not the case in other religions where a sanctioned, even prescribed relation is maintained between the serious and the ludic; where joking or clowning occurs in the most sacred moments of ritual. Pueblo ritual drama reveals this genius that can encompass impossible contradictions, illogicalities, and absurdities; can make them ring true in a synthesis *reflecting reality in a way that rational discourse does not know.*

By revealing the arbitrary, provisional nature of the very categories of thought, by lifting their pressure for a moment and suggesting other ways of structuring reality, the joke rite [or clown performance] in the middle of sacred moments of religion hints at unfathomable mysteries.[78]

We have in [Ndembu rites of] Chihamba the local expression of a universal human problem, that of expressing what cannot be *thought of,* in view of thought's subjugation to essences. It is a problem which has engaged the passionate attention of ritual man in all places and ages. It is a problem, furthermore, which has confronted artists, musicians, and poets whenever these have gone beyond the consideration of aesthetic form and social manners.[79]

It is likewise the project and problem of the clown. The sacred clown's part in expressing that which cannot be thought of suggests that he is in touch with higher mysteries, alternative realities. And indeed, he is so regarded by the Pueblos. The creation myths state this; his role and behavior in ritual drama enact it. He is the funniest *and* the most sacred of their priests, a delightmaker *and* a fearsome creature. *Koyemci* are the most frightening of all *katcinas.*

While thinking I am not where I actually am; I am not surrounded by sense-objects but by images which are invisible to everyone else. It is as though I had withdrawn into some never-never land, the land of the invisibles.[80]

In Tewa ritual dramas such as the Raingod ceremony, clowns are the "bringers of Katcinas," bringing them from the mythological lake of emergence in the north. *Kossa* can see what no one else can perceive, that is, the invisible; they "see" and announce the ap-

proach of the *katcinas*. Invisible themselves, they have the power of summoning the *katcinas* or sending them home. Further, they alone can understand the gestural language of the *katcinas* which they translate and interpret to the people during the dance.[81]

> The Hopi often regard clowns as personages who say and do things that are the *opposite* of normal expectancy; this inevitably links them with the realm of the dead, where conditions are frequently thought to be the opposite of those that prevail in the world of the living. . . . *Koyemci* often appear in stories pertaining to the home of the dead. . . . They are called "fathers" of *katcinas*. . . . They frequently appear with *katcinas*, who represent spirits of the dead; and, like those in the other world, they often behave in reverse fashion from the living.[82]

Any form of transgressive discourse, of anti-language, implies an alternative reality.[83]

The commonest form of reverse behavior is "talking backwards": saying the opposite of what one means. *Koyemci* are named "not with the names of men, but with the names of mismeaning."[84] From his birth the Acoma *Koshare* "talked nonsense,

talked backward."[85] The first Zuni *Newekwe* talked all the time, but "what he said was all the same to him; he did not care about the effect."[86] The clown through his language expresses a world behind and beyond words.

> The dance serves to reaffirm the basic tenets of the Hopi world view and fuses it with the Hopi ethos while the clowns remind the audience-participants that this, after all, is only life that we are living, and that like life everywhere it is fraught with all sorts of paradoxes, uncertainties, and outright contradictions. Between the *katcinas* and the clowns, we obtain a well-balanced portrayal of what the Hopi know about living; the *katcinas* remind men that if they but join their hearts periodically in these rites of mass supplication to the ancestral deities, life will continue as before in abundance and harmony; the clowns, by injecting a bit of the mundane and the commonplace, the ludicrous and the whimsical, into these most solemn of occasions, re-

mind the people that this other side of life, too, is their own and that it must not be forgotten in the commitment to an exacting calendar of religious observances. Perhaps one cannot go so far as to claim that the sacred clowns fuse the sacred and profane dimensions of existence, but they do at least serve to make the sacred relevant to the every-day.[87]

In Hopi theory, the regions of the living and of the dead make up a single universe, and the inhabitants of both realms must cooperate if a ceremony is to succeed.[88]

Translation between the realms of the living and the dead, between visible and invisible worlds, between the people and the *katcinas* is but one form of dialogue in which the clowns engage. Performing as they do between the seasons and between the acts and in the margins of Pueblo ritual drama, clowns are mediators par excellence between all types of cosmic, natural, and social dualities, between inside and outside, self and other, creation and destruction, order and chaos. The latter dialogues are exemplified in the very structure of ritual dramas in which the clowns interrupt and burlesque the solemn and orderly patterns of the masked and unmasked dancers, and in the juxtaposition of elegant and orderly dress with the clown's "holiday mongrel costume" of odds and ends. They are also expressed in the clown's double ceremonial role of maintaining order and disrupting it in the fashion of the Italian *buffo*. Like the *buffo*, the clowns "are in many ways responsible for creating and guiding an audience. They are constantly organizing; they create entrances which assemble and attract an audience, or they may physically gather an audience. Clowns constantly work to include, interest, and amuse the spectators, and their exits often provide theatrical and emotional finality and relief after a *Katcina* performance."[89]

If reality is the structure of facts consensually agreed upon in a given stage of knowledge, actuality is the leeway created by new forms of interplay. Without actuality, reality becomes a prison of stereotypy, while actuality always must retest reality to remain truly playful. To fully understand this we must study for each stage of life the interpenetration of the cognitive and the affective as well as the moral and the instinctual. We may then realize that in adulthood an individual gains leeway for himself, as he creates it for others; here is the soul of adult play.[90]

A man's maturity consists in having found once again the seriousness which one had as a child at play.[91]

The comical is present in every stage of life . . . for wherever there is life, there is contradiction, and wherever there is contradiction, the comical is present.[92]

It is contradiction that distinguishes men from angels, animals, and machines.[93]

Romantic irony, which takes many forms, is concerned essentially with the feeling that the human self *both is and is not* a part of the world in which it exists. Further, [it] is concerned with the feeling that art is designed both to absorb the observer or reader completely and at the same time to create in him a wariness or skepticism about the art object itself.[94]

Humor deals with being and nonbeing, and its true essence is reflection.[95]

Contrary to the denunciations of many critics, neither ritual clowning nor irony can be dismissed as nihilism or infinitely regressive negativity. Rather both are special forms of negation: what Burke calls "aesthetic negativity"; what Derrida defines as "deconstruction"; what Colie describes as "paradox"; what James labeled the "law of dissociation"; and what Arendt describes as "thinking." "All critical examinations must go through a stage of at least *hypothetically* negating accepted opinions and 'values' by searching out their implications and tacit assumptions, and in this sense nihilism may be seen as an ever-present danger of thinking."[96]

Gravity is the love of the object that falls for that which it falls toward.[97]

Irony is the handler of gravity.[98]

Science is irony. . . . At every point of its progress, science accepts implicitly, notes in its own margin, the possibility of contradiction, the progress to come.[99]

Irony is the contradiction of existing in terms of a contradiction, and this contradiction is precisely the awareness, on the one hand, of being a finite creature compelled by and subject to the demands of the world and, on the other hand, of being a free, responsible being who can never be compelled or subjected by any external force. The irony is that one *is* a contradiction, one exists dialectically [or better, dialogically].[100]

At base the clown, the ironist, is really an ethicist. Aesthetic negativity involves a double negation in which "any moralistic thou-shalt-not provides material for our entertainment" *and* our reflection as we applaud and consider the antics of "deviants who, in all sorts of ingenious ways, violate the very Don'ts of our/their society."[101]

Irony is a synthesis of ethical passion, which infinitely accentuates inwardly the person of the individual in relation to the ethical requirement, and of culture, which infinitely abstracts externally from the personal, as one finitude among all the other finitudes and particularities. . . . Irony is a specific culture of the spirit, and therefore follows next after immediacy; then comes the ethicist, then the humorist, and finally the religious individual.[102]

The clown, his job . . . is to make people think right . . . all night.[103]

As Klein has said, comparing Derrida's project to Nietzsche's, "It is [an] illusion to think that we can merely step outside the house of metaphysics and dance freely in the sunlight. . . . The only possible strategy is the much more patient and laborious one . . . by which the foundations of the structure may be carefully but decisively deconstructed, displaced, disorganized—giving rise, *not* to a new space *outside* the old enclosure, but to new angles, new possibilities of organization within it. The process requires that one use the elements of structure against the structure."[104] This is the way the clown uses his language or his ash house.

Redirecting thoughtful attention to the faulty or limited structures of thought, paradoxes play back and forth across terminal and categorical boundaries—that is, they play (*serio ludere*) with human understanding, that most serious of all human activities. . . . All paradoxes share with that mystifying dialogue (the *Parmenides*) respect and concern for the techniques they question or defy.[105]

Sacred clowning and other liminal aspects of ritual are deconstructive. As both Turner and Wallace argue, the factors of one's culture are learned by experiencing them confused, inverted, rearranged. But more than simply reinforcing traditional relations and structures, such displacements and contradictions prompt speculation about, reflection on, and reconsideration of the order of things. Both authors invoke William James's law of dissociation: what is associated now with one thing and now with another tends to become dissociated from either, and to grow into an object of abstract contemplation. Similarly, Piaget argues and Berlyne's experiments confirm that disequilibrium or discomfort arising from inconsistency and uncertainty motivates mature ways of organizing thoughts and perceptions.

Decomposing and superimposing . . . this double negation produces an affirmation which is never conclusive and which exists in perpetual equilibrium over the void . . . a work that turns in upon itself, that persists in destroying the very thing it creates. *The function of irony* now appears with greater clarity: its negative purpose is to be the critical substance that impregnates the work; its positive purpose, as criticism of criticism, is to deny it and so to tip the balance onto the side of myth. *Irony is the element which turns criticism into myth.*[106]

As both Socrates and the Zen masters demonstrate, there must be a frustration and confounding of the intellect for thinking to occur. And in both Zen and Pueblo clowning, humor is "fully developed and self-consciously employed as an integral part of both a pedagogical method and an enlightened outlook—both as one of the strategems for realizing enlightenment and as one of the consequences of enlightenment."[107]

Irony is permanent *parabasis*.[108]

Philosophy is the true home of irony, which might be defined as logical beauty: for wherever men are philosophizing in spoken or written dialogues, and provided they are not entirely systematical, irony ought to be produced and postulated; . . . compared to the lofty urbanity of the Socratic muse, rhetorical irony is like the splendor of the most brilliant oratory compared to ancient high tragedy. In this respect, poetry alone can rise to the height of philosophy . . . there are ancient and modern poems which breathe, in their entirety and in every detail, the divine breath of irony. In such poems there lives a real transcendental buffoonery. Their interior is permeated by the mood which surveys everything and rises infinitely above everything limited, even above the poet's own art, virtue, and genius, and their exterior form by the histrionic style of an ordinary good Italian *buffo*.[109]

Because they have not taken clowning seriously, Schlegel's interpreters have been greatly perturbed by his describing the Italian *buffo* as the ultimate expression of irony and by his comparing clowns' antics and Socratic irony. His parabases, like the *Koshare's* with their mocking and explicit burlesque of their role, the play and the audience, interrupt the illusion of fiction and upset theatrical convention. As such, they epitomize the very Socratic capacity of discourse to deconstruct and to comment upon itself. This is the capacity we call irony.

The trope of irony is a linguistic paradigm of a mode of thought which is radically self-critical with respect not only to a given characterization of the world of experience but also to the very effort to capture adequately the truth of things in language. . . . In irony, the figurative language folds back upon itself and brings its own potentialities for distorting perception under question. [Hence it is] metatropological, "the trope of tropes."[110]

The ironist is like the circus clown on the tightrope. First the ordinary tightrope walker [or *katcina*] performs his feats seriously. Then the clown, sent aloft by the ring-master, pretends to be afraid of heights, pretends to fall, perhaps falls, but the wire catches him by one of his enormous buttons, recovers himself and runs the rest of the way quickly; but all the time he is much more skillful than his fellow acrobat. He has raised tightrope walking to a higher power, in that he is performing at two levels simultaneously—as a clown and as a tightrope walker, and demonstrating at the same time both the possibility of tightrope walking and its sheer impossibility.[111]

Freedom is not knowledge but what one has become after knowledge. It is a state of mind which not only admits contradiction but which seeks it out for its nourishment and as a foundation. The saints do not laugh nor do they make us laugh but the truly wise men have no other mission than to make us laugh with their thoughts and make us think with their buffoonery.[112]

When a people can laugh at themselves and laugh at others and hold all aspects of life together without letting anybody drive them to extremes, then it seems to me that people can survive.[113]

With irony the subject is negatively free . . . and as such hovering, because there nothing is which binds him. It is this very freedom, this hovering, which gives the ironist a certain enthusiasm, for he becomes intoxicated as it were by the infinity of possibles; and should he require consolation for all that has passed away, then let him take refuge in the enormous reserves of the possible.[114]

Objections, digressions, gay mistrust, the delight in mockery are signs of health: everything unconditional belongs in pathology.[115]

For people who are as poor as us, who have lost everything, who had to endure so much death and sadness, laughter is a precious gift. When we were dying like flies from the white man's diseases, when we were driven into the reservations, when the Government rations did not arrive and we were starving, at such times watching the pranks of a *heyoka* (Sioux ritual clown) must have been a blessing.[116]

NOTES

1. Friedrich Schlegel, *Dialogue on Poetry and Literary Aphorisms* (University Park, Pa., 1968), p. 54.
2. Friedrich Nietzsche, *The Portable Nietzsche* (New York, 1954), p. 129.
3. Conrad Hyers, *Zen and the Comic Spirit* (Philadelphia, 1973), p. 18.
4. Ihab Hassan, *Paracriticisms: Seven Speculations of the Times* (Urbana, 1975), p. 25.
5. Marie C. Swabey, *Comic Laughter: A Philosophical Essay* (New Haven, 1961), p. 11.
6. Hannah Arendt, *Thinking* (New York, 1978), pp. 11–12.
7. Victor W. Turner, *The Forest of Symbols: Aspects of Ndembu Ritual* (Ithaca, 1967), p. 97; *Dramas, Fields, and Metaphors* (Ithaca, 1974), p. 255.
8. Harry Levin, *Refractions: Essays in Comparative Literature* (New York, 1966), p. 128.
9. Thomas Carlyle, *Sartor Resartus* (New York, 1970), p. 237.
10. Arendt, p. 175; Arien Mack, ed., "Hannah Arendt," *Social Research* 44(1):47, 1977.
11. Harvey Cox, *The Feast of Fools* (New York, 1969), p. 70.
12. Arendt, p. 62.
13. Hyers, p. 55.
14. W. Willeford, *The Fool and His Scepter* (Evanston, 1969), pp. 18–19.
15. Clement of Alexandra, *Selections from the Protreptikos* (New York, 1962), V. 9.
16. Hyers, p. 71.
17. Roland Barthes, *Roland Barthes* (New York, 1977), pp. 92–94.
18. Franz Boas, "Introduction," in James Teit, "Traditions of the Thompson River Indians, British Columbia," *Memoirs of the American Folklore Society* 7:18, 1898.

19. Jacques Derrida, "Structure, Sign, and Play in the Discourse of the Human Sciences," in R. Macksey and E. Donato, eds., *The Languages of Criticism and the Sciences of Man* (Baltimore, 1970), p. 254ff.

20. Claude Lévi-Strauss, *The Savage Mind* (Chicago, 1966), p. 21.

21. Walter Benjamin, *Illuminations* (New York, 1969), p. 8.

22. Geoffrey H. Hartman, "Crossing Over: Literary Commentary as Literature," *Comparative Literature* 28(3):266, 1976.

23. Benjamin, p. 38.

24. See Paul Bouissac, *Circus and Culture: A Semiotic Approach* (Bloomington, 1976).

25. Erving Goffman, *Frame Analysis: An Essay on the Organization of Experience* (New York, 1974), p. 31.

26. Hugh D. Duncan, *Communication and the Social Order* (New York, 1962), p. 386.

27. Kenneth Burke, *Attitudes toward History* (Boston, 1961), pp. 171, 173.

28. Burke, p. 140.

29. Harold Rosenberg, "Community, Values, Comedy," in *Discovering the Present: Three Decades in Art, Culture and Politics* (Chicago, 1973), p. 151.

30. Friedrich Schlegel, *Lucinda and the Fragments* (Minneapolis, 1971), p. 170.

31. Cox, p. 22.

32. Schlegel, *Lucinda*, p. 170.

33. Friedrich Nietzsche, *On the Genealogy of Morals and Ecce Homo* (New York, 1969), p. 21.

34. Allan Rodway, "Terms for Comedy," *Renaissance and Modern Studies* 6:113, 1963.

35. Goffman, p. 5.

36. Clifford Geertz, *The Interpretation of Cultures* (New York, 1973), p. 19.

37. Hyers, p. 20.

38. Nietzsche, *Genealogy of Morals*, p. 65.

39. Adolf Bandelier, in Charles Lange, *Cochiti* (Carbondale, Ill., 1968), p. 303.

40. John G. Bourke, *The Urine Dance of the Zuni Indians of New Mexico* (privately published, 1920), pp. 5–6.

41. Lange, p. 304.

42. Alfonso Ortiz, *New Perspectives on the Pueblo* (Albuquerque, 1972), p. 139.

43. Adolf Bandelier, *The Delight Makers* (New York, 1971), pp. 134–140.

44. Julian H. Steward, "The Ceremonial Buffoon of the American Indian," *Papers of the Michigan Academy of Science, Arts, and Letters* 14:199, 1931.

45. Apache Medicine Man, quoted in Morris E. Opler, *An Apache Life-way: The Economic, Social and Religious Institutions of the Chiricahua Indians* (New York, 1965), p. 276.

46. Pueblo medicine man, quoted in Vera Laski, *Seeking Life* (Philadelphia, 1958), p. 2.

47. Nietzsche, *The Portable Nietzsche*, p. 153.

48. Richard Erdoes and John Fire, *Lame Deer: Seeker of Visions* (New York, 1971), p. 236.

49. Alexander M. Stephen, *Hopi Journal of Alexander M. Stephen* (New York, 1936), p. 331.

50. Jacob Levine, "Regression in Primitive Clowning," *The Psychoanalytic Quarterly* 30(1):75, 81, 1961.

51. Don C. Talayesva, quoted in Leo W. Simmons, ed., *Sun Chief: The Autobiography of a Hopi Indian* (New Haven, 1942), p. 190.

52. Laguna creation myth, cited in Elsie Clews Parsons, *Pueblo Indian Religion* (Chicago, 1939), p. 246.

53. Friedrich Nietzsche, *Beyond Good and Evil: Prelude to a Philosophy of the Future* (New York, 1966), p. 233.

54. Soren Kierkegaard, *Concluding Unscientific Postscript* (Princeton, 1941), p. 490.

55. Jemez creation myth, cited in Albert B. Reagan, "Notes on Jemez Ethnography," *American Anthropologist* 29(4):723, 1927.

56. Nietzsche, *Genealogy of Morals*, p. 244.

57. Kierkegaard, p. 235.

58. Nietzsche, *The Gay Science* (New York, 1974), p. 300.

59. Frank H. Cushing, "Outlines of Zuni Creation Myths," *Thirteenth Annual Report of the Bureau of American Ethnology* (Washington, D.C., 1896), p. 402.

60. Clifford Geertz, "Deep Play: Notes on the Balinese Cockfight," *Daedalus* 101:26, 1972.

61. Gregory Bateson, "The Position of Humor in Human Communication," in J. Levine, ed., *Motivation in Humor* (New York, 1969), "A Theory of Play and Fantasy," in *Steps to an Ecology of Mind* (New York, 1972).

62. Ortiz, p. 147.

63. Vine Deloria, Jr., *Custer Died for Your Sins* (New York, 1969), p. 148.

64. Rosenberg, pp. 149–150.

65. C. L. Barber, *Shakespeare's Festive Comedy: A Study of Dramatic Forms and Its Relation to Social Custom* (Princeton, 1959), p. 3.

66. Ortiz, p. 159.

67. Ruth Bunzel, *Introduction to Zuni Ceremonialism* (Washington, D.C., 1932), p. 509.

68. Burke, pp. 171, 173.

69. Nietzsche, *Beyond Good and Evil*, p. 232.

70. Zen student, quoted in Nancy Wilson Ross, *The World of Zen* (New York, 1960), pp. 184–185.

71. Nietzsche, *The Portable Nietzsche*, p. 153.

72. M. Stirling, *Origin Myth of Acoma* (Washington, D.C., 1942), p. 45.

73. Hyers, pp. 170–171.

74. Cox, p. 104.

75. Hyers, pp. 163–164.

76. Kierkegaard, pp. 459, 465.

77. Nietzsche, *The Gay Science*, p. 164.

78. Mary Douglas, "The Social Control of Cognition: Some Factors in Joke Perception," *Man* 3(2):374, 1968.

79. Victor W. Turner, *Chihamba, the White Spirit* (Manchester, 1962), p. 87.

80. Arendt, p. 85.

81. Laski, pp. 3, 13ff.

82. Mischa Titiev, "Some Aspects of Clowning Among the Hopi Indians," in M. Zamora et al., eds., *Themes in Culture* (Quezon City, 1971), pp. 327–334; *The Hopi Indians of Old Oraibi; Continuity and Change* (Ann Arbor, 1972), p. 229.

83. M. A. K. Halliday, "Anti-Languages," *American Anthropologist* 78(3):572, 1976.

84. Cushing, p. 401.

85. Stirling, p. 33.
86. Elsie Clews Parsons, "Notes on Zuni," *Memoirs of The American Anthropological Association* 4:229–230, 1917.
87. Ortiz, p. 160.
88. Titiev, "Some Aspects of Clowning," p. 334.
89. Seymour Koenig, ed., *Hopi Clay, Hopi Ceremony: An Exhibition of Hopi Art* (Katonah, N.Y., 1976), p. 45.
90. Erik H. Erikson, "Play and Actuality," in Maria W. Piers, ed., *Play and Development* (New York, 1972), p. 165.
91. Nietzsche, *Beyond Good and Evil*, p. 83.
92. Kierkegaard, p. 459.
93. Octavio Paz, *Marcel Duchamp, or the Castle of Purity* (London, 1970), p. 41.
94. Gordon Mills, *Hamlet's Castle: The Study of Literature as a Social Experience* (Austin, 1976), p. 171.
95. Schlegel, *Lucinda*, p. 206.
96. Arendt, p. 182.
97. O. K. Bouwsma, *Philosophical Essays* (Lincoln, Neb., 1965), p. 22.
98. Paz, p. 32.
99. D. C. Muecke, *The Compass of Irony* (London, 1969), p. 129.
100. Thomas Hanna, *The Lyrical Existentialists* (New York, 1962), pp. 281–282.
101. Kenneth Burke, *Language as Symbolic Action: Essays on Life, Literature, and Method* (Berkeley, 1966), p. 13.
102. Kierkegaard, pp. 448–450.
103. Roy Quay, Cibecue Apache, quoted February 10, 1978.
104. Richard Klein, "Prolegomenon to Derrida," *Diacritics* 2(4):31–32, 1972.
105. Rosalie Colie, *Paradoxia Epidemica: The Renaissance Tradition of Paradox* (Princeton, 1966), pp. 7–8.
106. Paz, p. 32.
107. Hyers, p. 33.
108. Paul de Man, "Lecture on Irony," University of Texas, March 25, 1977.
109. Schlegel, *Dialogue on Poetry and Literary Aphorisms*, p. 126.
110. Hayden White, *Metahistory: The Historical Imagination in Nineteenth-Century Europe* (Baltimore, 1973), p. 37.
111. Muecke, pp. 198–199.
112. Paz, pp. 41–42.
113. Deloria, p. 168.
114. Soren Kierkegaard, *The Concept of Irony* (Bloomington, 1968), p. 279.
115. Nietzsche, *Beyond Good and Evil*, p. 91.
116. Erdoes and Fire, p. 237.

Constructing Ritual

CATHERINE BELL

Facts of publication: *Bell, Catherine. 1992. "Constructing Ritual," from* Ritual Theory, Ritual Practice, *19–37, 57–61. New York: Oxford University Press. © 1992 by Catherine Bell. Reprinted with the permission of Oxford University Press, Inc.*

This selection is less about ritual and more about theories of ritual, especially the way they function in academic discourse. Catherine Bell argues that scholars employing theories invent *the very phenomenon they claim to discover. She believes that at the root of the idea of ritual is a longstanding Western philosophical split between thought and action in which ritual is associated with action rather than thought. However, she says, ritual is also construed by theorists to be the means by which this rift is bridged. Can we have it both ways? she asks. She explores the question in the context of several theories, especially that of Clifford Geertz.*

Subsequent to the section reproduced here Bell's book maintains that ritualization is always strategic. Its interests are always vested, functioning to dominate, therefore it is inherently political. In her view the real, but typically unacknowledged, or "misrecognized," goal of ritualization is that of producing a body infused with the values of such strategizing. When successful, this process makes ritual activity seem natural, but in so doing it also creates a certain blindness among those engaged in its practice.

For an even stronger critique of the notion of ritual see Jack Goody, "Against 'Ritual'" in Sally F. Moore and Barbara G. Myerhoff, ed., Secular Ritual, *25–35. Assen, The Netherlands: Van Gorcum, 1977. For further reading on ritual and the body see Jean Comaroff,* Body of Power, Spirit of Resistance *(Chicago: University of Chicago Press, 1985).*

About the author: Dates: *1953–, New York, NY, U.S.A.* Education: *B.A., Manhattanville College; M.A., University of Chicago; Ph.D., University of Chicago.* Field(s): *Chinese religion; history of religions methodology; ritual studies.* Career: *Associate Professor, Department of Religious Studies, Santa Clara University.* Publications: The Ritual Dimensions of Religion *(Routledge, forthcoming);* Ritual Theory, Ritual Practice *(Oxford University, 1992).* Additional: *The author's main focus of research and publishing is Chinese religion.*

Theoretical descriptions of ritual generally regard it as action and thus automatically distinguish it from the conceptual aspects of religion, such as beliefs, symbols, and myths. In some cases added qualifications may soften the distinction, but rarely do such descriptions question this immediate differentiation or the usefulness of distinguishing what is thought from what is done. Likewise, beliefs, creeds, symbols, and myths emerge as forms of mental content or conceptual blueprints: they direct, inspire, or promote activity, but they themselves are not activities.[1] Ritual, like action, will act out, express, or perform these conceptual orientations. Sometimes the push for typological clarity will drive such differentiations to the extreme. Ritual is then described as particularly *thoughtless* action—routinized, habitual, obsessive, or mimetic—and therefore the purely formal, secondary, and mere physical expression of logically prior ideas. Just as the differentiation of ritual and belief in terms of thought and action is usually taken for granted, so too is the priority this differentiation accords to thought. For example, Edward Shils argues that ritual and belief are intertwined and yet separable, since it is conceivable that one might accept beliefs but not the ritual activities associated with them. He concludes that logically, therefore, "beliefs could exist without rituals; rituals, however, could not exist without beliefs."[2] Claude Lévi-Strauss takes this logic much further when an initial distinction between ritual and myth eventuates in a distinction between living and thinking.[3]

Aside from this basic structural pattern in which ritual is differentiated from mental categories as readily as action is differentiated from thought, there is a second structural pattern in theoretical discussions of ritual. This second pattern describes ritual as a type of functional or structural mechanism to reintegrate the thought–action dichotomy, which may appear in the guise of a distinction between belief and behavior or any number of other

homologous pairs. Both of these structural patterns—the differentiation of ritual as action from thought and the portrayal of ritual as a mechanism for integrating thought and action—can be demonstrated in several representative approaches to ritual.

Durkheim argued that religion is composed of beliefs and rites: beliefs consist of representations of the sacred; rites are determined modes of action that can be characterized only in terms of the representations of the sacred that are their object. "Between these two classes of facts," he wrote, "there is all the difference which separates thought from action."[4] Yet despite the secondary nature of ritual given in these initial definitions, Durkheim's important discussion of cult at the end of *The Elementary Forms* reintroduces ritual as the means by which collective beliefs and ideals are simultaneously generated, experienced, and affirmed as real by the community. Hence, ritual is the means by which individual perception and behavior are socially appropriated or conditioned.[5] In Durkheim's model the ritual activity of cult constitutes the necessary interaction between the collective representations of social life (as a type of mental or metamental category) and individual experience and behavior (as a category of activity).[6]

These two patterns turn up also in another, loosely structural, model employed with great sophistication by Stanley Tambiah but more simplistically by many others. There ritual is provisionally distinguished as the synchronic, continuous, traditional, or ontological in opposition to the diachronic, changing, historical, or social. However, ritual is also subsequently portrayed as the arena in which such pairs of forces interact. It is the mediating process by which the synchronic comes to be reexpressed in terms of the diachronic and vice versa.[7]

A third model, presented most fully in the early work of V. Turner, also portrays these two patterns. Turner initially described ritual as the affirmation of communal unity in contrast to the frictions, constraints, and competitiveness of social life and organization.[8] Rite affords a creative 'antistructure' that is distinguished from the rigid maintenance of social orders, hierarchies, and traditional forms. However, when subsequently portrayed as embodying aspects of both structure and antistructure, he describes rituals as those special, paradigmatic activities that mediate or orchestrate the necessary and opposing demands of both *communitas* and the formalized social order.

Each of these examples employs the two structural patterns described previously: ritual is first differentiated as a discrete object of analysis by means of various dichotomies that are loosely analogous to thought and action; then ritual is subsequently elaborated as the very means by which these dichotomous categories, neither of which could exist without the other, are reintegrated. These two structural patterns are rarely explicit and the first, in particular, in which ritual is differentiated from conceptual categories, is routinely taken for granted. However, the relationship that develops *between* these two patterns when they are simultaneously operative in a theoretical description of ritual is even less acknowledged and much more powerful. In effect, the dichotomy that isolates ritual on the one hand and the dichotomy that is mediated by ritual on the other become loosely homologized with each other. Essentially, as I will demonstrate, the underlying dichotomy between thought and action continues to push for a loose systemization of several levels of homologized dichotomies, including the relations between the ritual observer and the ritual actor. It is this invisible process of 'homologization', driven by the implicit presence of an opposition between conceptual and behavioral categories, that begins to construct a persuasive and apparently logical body of discourse.

DICHOTOMIES AND DIALECTICS

Jameson analyzes a type of logical structure within linguistical theory that is similar to the two patterns sketched out earlier for ritual theory.[9] The structured argument that he isolates provides a useful contrast to the one I am recovering here. Jameson points to a logical structure in which an initial differentiation, originally proposed to enable the theorist to concentrate on just one of the differentiated terms, surfaces again and again within subsequent analysis of that term. Specifically addressing Ferdinand Saussure's system of linguistics, Jameson shows that an initial distinction between structure and history (synchrony and diachrony) enables Saussure to focus upon and systematically elucidate one aspect of language, the synchronic or structural aspect. However, Saussure never resolved or transcended the dichotomy between synchrony and diachrony but reproduced it even in the final terms of his system.[10] How did such a replication occur?

In reaction against historicism in linguistics, Jameson explains, Saussure attempted to talk about the nonhistorical aspects of language. On a primary level, he distinguished between diachrony and synchrony, thereby providing himself a clear focus on the synchronic side of linguistics as opposed to the other side, where, he argued, everyone else was working. On a second level, and therefore within the synchronic system itself, Saussure also distinguished between *langue* and *parole* in order to further differentiate synchronic language from speech. He therein had his first internal replication of the original opposition. On yet a third level, Saussure took *langue* as a system and within it distinguished two ways in which signs are related, the syntagmatic and the associative (or paradigmatic), replicating his original dichotomy for a second time within the system as a whole.[11] The original differentiation between diachrony and synchrony was applied, through various pairs of categories, to three levels of analysis. In other words, the continual application of the dichotomy between synchrony and diachrony systematically generated successive and homologous levels of analysis.

At this point, Jameson suggests that it becomes quite "problematical to what degree the object of study is the thought pattern of the linguist himself, rather than that of the language." Moreover, this is also the point at which the originality of Saussure's initial distinction becomes a constraint on the whole system he has generated from it. Saussure's "initial repudiation of history," remarks Jameson, "which at the very outset resulted in an inability to absorb change into the system as anything but a meaningless and contingent datum, is now reproduced, at the very heart of the system itself, as an inability to deal with syntax as such."[12]

Theoretical discourse on ritual displays a similar logical structure: a distinction between belief and rite, made as readily as the heuristic distinction between thought and action, clears the way to focus on ritual alone. This is the first structural pattern noted previously. Ritual, however, becomes in turn a new starting point at which to differentiate once again between conceptual and behavioral components. This is the second structural pattern described earlier. However, ritual theory goes on to do something that Saussure, in the rigor of his focus and logic, according to Jameson, failed to do, namely, provide a stage of synthetic integration. Differentiated from belief in the first structural pattern, ritual becomes a second point at which to distinguish thought and action. Yet at this second stage ritual is seen as synthetic, as the very mechanism or medium through which thought and action are integrated. The elaboration of ritual as a mechanism for the fusion of opposing categories simultaneously serves both to differentiate and unite a set of terms. That is, the second structural pattern in ritual theory, in which ritual mediates thought and action, posits a dialectical relation between the differentiated entities instead of replicating an unmediated dichotomy. Ritual emerges as the means for a provisional synthesis of some form of the original opposition.

Saussure generated his linguistic system by positing an initial distinction, the successive and systematic replication of which rendered the distinction an ahistorical, nondialectical, or pure opposition.[13] Most ritual theory avoids this by incorporating the notion of dialectic or synthesis: ritual is a dialectical means for the provisional convergence of those opposed forces whose interaction is seen to constitute culture in some form.

The three representative theories of ritual briefly described clearly present ritual as just such a medium of integration or synthesis for opposing sociocultural forces. These are not isolated examples. There is a strong impetus within theoretical studies of religion and culture for this type of dialectic. This impetus can be seen, for example, in contemporary evaluations of Durkheim's theory of ritual. Some argue that his notion of ritual contains a dialectical mediation of the social and the individual; others argue that its fundamental weakness is precisely that his notion of ritual lacks such a dialectic. E. E. Evans-Pritchard has pinpointed Durkheim's theory of ritual as the central but "most obscure" and "unconvincing" part of his notion of society and religion.[14] Nancy Munn, on the other hand, has found it to be of "signal importance" for ritual studies today.[15] She argues that Durkheim developed a model of "social (ritual) symbolism as the switch point between the external moral constraints and groupings of the socio-political order, and the internal feelings and imaginative concepts of the individual actor."[16] Although it is precisely the nature of this switch point that Evans-Pritchard finds obscure, Munn is clearly attempting to find rooted in Durkheim a dialectical relationship between two irreducible entities, the individual's subjective state and the communal order, a dialectic mediated therefore by the collective representations generated and appropriated in the cult.

Sahlins has also looked for a synthetic reintegration of thought and action, self and society within Durkheim's theory and not found it. He argues that Durkheim's collective representations fail to mediate at all. Rather, as idealized representations of social values and structures, they merely act upon subjective states to mold them. For Sahlins, Durkheim's collective representations are unable to mediate or rearticulate individual experience within social categories; all they can do is simply appropriate and organize it into a "metalanguage."[17] In a somewhat similar argument, Lévi-Strauss suggested that Durkheim lacked an "adequate" notion of a symbol and symbolic action.[18] That is, in contrast to how symbols function, Durkheim's collective representations are mere signs, idealizations of the forms of social morphology that have become independent of these forms, and thus act solely to subordinate and structure individual perception and experience.[19]

Ultimately, Sahlins and Lévi-Strauss find Durkheim's theory of cult and ritual action less than complete for two reasons: first, it does not generate a level of cultural analysis as such; and second, it does not overcome the fundamental duality that resurfaced for Durkheim even in his portrayal of human nature itself. "This is the objective foundation of the idea of the soul: Those representations whose flow constitutes our interior life are of two different species which are irreducible one into another. Some concern themselves with the external and material world; others, with an ideal world to which we attribute a moral superiority over the first." For Durkheim, therefore, "we are really made up of two beings facing in different and almost contrary directions, one of whom exercises a real pre-eminence over the other. Such is the profound meaning of the antithesis which all men have more or less clearly conceived between the body and the soul, the material and the spiritual beings who coexist within us."[20]

Whether Durkheim provides a complete notion of ritual or not, we can see in his work and in the arguments of those reading him a tendency to isolate two types of sociocultural processes or entities and then to seek in ritual theory a model of their necessary reintegration. Indeed, given any initial avowal or assumption of such differentiated processes, a theoretician would have to come up with some phenomenon structured to mediate them if it did not already exist. Hence, I am suggesting that descriptions of how rituals work have been constructed according to a logic rooted in the dynamics of theoretical speculation and the unconscious manipulation of the thought–action dichotomy is intrinsic to this construction.

Saussure could not see how his initial distinctions radically limited the descriptive power of his system. Likewise, we do not see how such dichotomies as continuity and change, individual experience and social forms, and beliefs and behavior invoke an assumption about thought and action that runs particularly deep in the intellectual traditions of Western culture. We do not see that we are wielding a particularly powerful analytical tool, nor do we see how our unconscious manipulation of it is driven not only by the need to resolve the dichotomy it establishes, but also simultaneously to affirm *and* resolve the more fundamental opposition it poses—the opposition between the theoretician and the object of theoretical discourse. In other words, we do not see how such dichotomies contribute to the relational definition of a knower, a known, and a particular type of knowledge.

GEERTZ AND THE WINDOW OF RITUAL

To clarify the relationship between dichotomies and dialectics within the structure of ritual theory, a fuller example is needed to demonstrate how a coherent discourse on ritual is generated. The work of Geertz provides an excellent extended illustration for this purpose. Geertz has been a major influence in the study of religion and ritual, as well as a navigator for many through the shoals and reefs of various methodological issues. This is due in part to the symmetry of his terminology, its appeal to common sense, and his richly anecdotal ethnographies in which texture and nuance appear to defy ethnographic reductionism.

Geertz maintains that the thrust of his theoretical approach is the explanation of "meaning" in cultural phenomena.[21] With this focus he wishes to go beyond the functional or mechanistic analyses of human activity that he correlates with the reductionism of subordinating either the social to the cultural or vice versa.[22] Basic to this project is a distinction between "ethos" and "worldview." Ethos designates the moral and aesthetic aspects of a culture—a people's "underlying attitude toward themselves and their world."[23] Elsewhere Geertz describes ethos in terms of "dispositions," defined not as activity but as the likelihood of activity taking place under certain circumstances. Such dispositions are, in turn, further differentiated into two kinds: moods and motivations.[24] Worldview, on the other hand, indicates for Geertz the "cognitive, existential aspects" of a culture, a people's sense of the really real, their most comprehensive idea of a general order of existence.[25] Understood in this way, these two terms clearly lend themselves to a polarization in which ethos is to worldview as action is to thought.

At times Geertz explicitly correlates religious ritual with ethos and religious belief with worldview, thus invoking the first structural pattern in which ritual is taken for activity in contrast to belief as thought.[26] At other times he presents ethos and worldview as synthesized, fused, or stored in symbols that are arranged in various systems, patterns, or control mechanisms such as ritual, art, religion, language, and myth.[27] However, these systems do not only store a synthesis of ethos and worldview; they are also seen to effect it. Geertz argues with regard to ritual that "any religious ritual no matter how apparently automatic or conventional . . . involves this symbolic fusion of ethos and world view."[28] Here the second structural pattern appears in which ritual involves the integration of thought and action categories.

The dialectical nature of this fusion of ethos and worldview is made clear in Geertz's related discussion of symbolic systems, such as religion, which involve both "models for" and "models of" reality. These systems are "culture patterns." That is, they "give meaning . . . [or] objective form, to social and psychological reality both by shaping themselves to it and by shaping it to themselves."[29] With regard to ritual per se, Geertz suggests that "it is in some sort of ceremonial form—even if that form be hardly more than the recitation of a myth, the consultation of an oracle, or the decoration of a grave—that the moods and motivations which sacred symbols induce in men and the general conceptions of the order of existence which they formulate for men meet and reinforce one another." He goes on: "In ritual, the world as lived and the world as imagined, fused under the agency of a single set of symbolic forms, turns out to be the same world."[30]

Here the simplest ritual activities are seen to "fuse" a people's conceptions of order and their dispositions (moods and motivations) for action. For Geertz, this opposition of conceptions and dispositions, or the world as imagined and the world as lived, constitutes cultural life per se. Moreover, our perception and analysis of their opposition and resolution constitute a theoretical explanation of 'meaning' in culture. Indeed, failure to grasp the interaction of these two fundamentally differentiated categories—conceptions and dispositions—is tantamount to the reductionism that Geertz specifically decries, the reductionism of the social to the cultural or the cultural to the social.[31] Thus, the dichotomous nature of conceptions of order (worldview) and dispositions for action (ethos) is fundamental to Geertz's approach, as is their resolution in such symbolic systems as ritual. The temporary resolution of a dichotomy is cast as the central dynamic of cultural life.

So far this analysis of Geertz has simply invoked the two structural patterns discussed earlier. However, Geertz also reveals a third pattern and the further implications of his model of ritual. He goes on to explain that cultural performances such as religious ritual are "not only the point at which the dispositional and conceptual aspects of religious life converge *for the believer*, but also the point at which the interaction between them can be most readily examined *by the detached observer*."[32]

What does he mean by this? Since ritual enacts, performs, or objectifies religious beliefs (action gives expression to thought) and in so doing actually fuses the conceptual and the dispositional aspects of religious symbols (ritual integrates thought and action), Geertz must be concluding that ritual offers a special vantage point for the theorist to observe these processes. Why and how, we might ask, does ritual work to facilitate the theorist's project? The answer is left implicitly in Geertz's text. To answer explicitly, we need to retrace the homologizations that silently push his argument forward.

Outsiders, states Geertz, will see in ritual only the mere presentation of a particular religious perspective which they may appreciate aesthetically or analyze scientifically.[33] Neither response, he implies, penetrates to the real meaning and dynamics of such a cultural phenomenon. For participants, on the other hand, rites are "enactments, materializations, realizations" of a particular religious perspective, "not only models of what they believe, but also models for the believing of it."[34] Thus, the outsider has only conceptual categories with which he or she approaches the ritual activity. Participants, in contrast, actually experience in the rite the integration of their own conceptual framework and dispositional imperatives. In this argument, Geertz is setting up a third structural pattern and a third permutation of the thought–action dichotomy. That is, ritual participants act, whereas those observing them think. In ritual activity, conceptions and dispositions are fused for the participants, which yields meaning. Meaning for the outside theorist comes differently: insofar as he or she can perceive in ritual the true basis of its meaningfulness for the ritual actors—that is, its fusion of conceptual and dispositional categories—then the theorist can go beyond mere thoughts about activity to grasp the meaningfulness of the ritual. By recognizing the ritual mechanism of meaningfulness for participants, the theorist in turn can grasp its meaningfulness as a cultural phenomenon. Ritual activity can then become meaningful *to the theorist.* Thus, a cultural focus on ritual activity renders the rite a veritable window on the most important processes of cultural life.[35]

Slipping in by virtue of its homologization with the other two structural patterns, the third one organizes the argument in such a way that the theoretical explanation of 'meaning' is itself a fusion of thought and action—the theorist's thought (conceptual categories) and the activity of the ritual participants (which is also a fusion of conceptions and dispositions in its own right). Herein lies the implicit structural homology: the fusion of thought and action described within ritual is homologized to a fusion of the theoretical project and its object, ritual activity. Both generate meaning—the first for the ritual actor and the second for the theorist.

Another example of an argument for a particular relationship between the project of the outside observer and the project of the ritual is laid out by Theodore Jennings.[36] Jennings describes ritual as, first of all, a display to an observer (god, theorist, etc.) or observers (the community itself) and, second, as an epistemological project. Both of these dimensions of ritual act as a "point of contact" between the rite and the attempt by outside observers to grasp a "theoretical-critical understanding of it."[37] We need not castigate our pursuit of the meaning of ritual as "voyeurism or whoring," Jennings asserts, since our cognitive concerns are simply an "extension" of those of the ritual we are "invited" to watch.[38]

All the delicate assumptions of Jennings's approach find their inevitable contrast in Stephen Greenblatt's account of the epistemological project of the amateur ethnographer Captain John G. Bourke. Bourke "witnessed among the Zuñi Indians extreme and simultaneous violations of the codes governing food and waste, and hence experienced extreme disgust." His reaction, Greenblatt speculates, was "not simply an occupational hazard; after all, it is the ethnographer's nausea that gives him his particular discursive field." The parameters of Bourke's lengthy 1891 opus, *Scatologic Rites of All Nations*, were defined, asserts Greenblatt, "precisely by the rising of his gorge." "It would be absurd," he

continues, "to conclude that a similar, if better disguised, revulsion lies at the constitutive moment of *all* ethnography, but one may easily find other and more respectable instances than the work of Captain Bourke, in which aversion serves to transform behavior and material substances into the objects of representation and interpretation."[39]

Greenblatt suggests that Bourke instinctively depended on his revulsion to define his epistemological project and the 'otherness' it both required and established. Geertz and Jennings, in contrast, would have us depend on the essential congruity or likeness of doing ritual and generating theoretical interpretations of ritual to establish both our difference from and access to the "other."

Constructing Meaning

The result, for Geertz, of the convergence of concepts and dispositions effected by ritual is the theorist's understanding of the cultural meaning of a ritual. What is this meaning exactly? What does it render meaningful and meaningless? Citing Milton Singer, Geertz suggests how the convergence effected in ritual enables one to understand the way in which people regard their religion as "encapsulated" in specific performances that can be performed for visitors and themselves.[40] He quotes with much approval a well-known passage by Singer: "Whenever Madrasi Brahmins (and non-Brahmins, too, for that matter) wished to exhibit to me some features of Hinduism, they always referred to, or invited me to see, a particular rite or ceremony in the life cycle, in a temple festival, or in the general sphere of religious and cultural performances. Reflecting on this in the course of my interviews and observations I found that the more abstract generalizations about Hinduism (my own as well as those I heard) could generally be checked, directly or indirectly, against these observable performances."[41]

Singer's comments are presented as the discovery of an insightful method. They are also, however, an excellent example of the naturalness of the thought–action dichotomy in ritual discourse. First, in regard to Hinduism, he says that the Hindus have rites which they can enact or exhibit, whereas the researcher has concepts which can be thought or talked about. As a consequence of this distinction, the particularity of any one local ritual is contrasted with the more embracing, abstract generalizations of the researcher. Second, such rites are seen not only as very particular enactments of that abstract totality, Hinduism, but they are also portrayed as enactments exhibited *to others* for evaluation or appropriation in terms of their more purely theoretical knowledge. Third, because enactment of the rite is already implicitly construed as effecting an integration for participants between a supposed conceptual totality (Hinduism) and the practical needs of a particular time and place (the dispositions within the ritual context), the researcher easily sees in the exhibition of these rites for theoretical interpretation an equally effective convergence of theory and practice on another level—our conceptual abstractions integrated with their specific practices.

Thus, a model of ritual based upon our two structural patterns—in which ritual is both activity and the fusion of thought and activity—ultimately involves a third pattern, one in which the dichotomy underlying a thinking theorist and an acting actor is simultaneously affirmed and resolved. It is this homologization that makes ritual appear to provide such a privileged vantage point on culture and the meaningfulness of cultural phenomena.

To question Geertz's or Singer's appreciation of the way that ritual obliges the detached observer is to discover that ritual does so by virtue of those very features with which it has been theoretically constituted in the first place. Again we are faced with the question raised by Jameson: To what extent is the object of study the thought pattern of the theorist rather than the supposed object, ritual?

We have seen in Geertz's work not only the two patterns of the thought–action dichotomy described here but a third one as well. First, ritual was said to dramatize, enact, materialize, or perform a system of symbols. This formulation invokes the notion that activity is a secondary, physical manifestation or expression of thought. Second, by enacting the symbolic system, ritual was said to integrate two irreducible aspects of symbols, the conceptual (worldview) and the dispositional (ethos). In this way a thought–action dichotomy is inscribed within the opposing sociocultural forces that Geertz isolates in order to be subsequently resolved in the performance of the rite. On a third level, or in a third structural pattern, ritual as performance likewise enables the integration of the theorist's abstract conceptual categories and the cultural particularity of the rite. With this third level or pattern, the thought–action dichotomy has differentiated native ritual as activity from the thought of the theorist, while casting the resolution of this thought–action opposition in a theoretical grasp of the meaning of the ritual acts. What constitutes meaning for the ritual actors is seen as the integration of their conceptual and dispositional orientations that takes place in ritual. What constitutes meaning for the theorist is the same model, the integration of his or her conceptual categories with the ritual dispositions of the native actors, an integration afforded by proper analysis of ritual.

To restate the structure of this argument more formally is to make ludicrously explicit a type of logic that is effective only when left unexamined. Most simply, we might say, ritual is to the symbols it dramatizes as action is to thought; on a second level, ritual integrates thought and action; and on a third level, a focus on ritual performances integrates *our* thought and *their* action. The opposition of the theorist and the ritual object becomes homologized with two other oppositions, namely, the opposition that differentiates ritual (beliefs versus activities) and the opposition of two fundamental sociocultural forces that is resolved by ritual (conceptual versus dispositional forces). This homology is achieved by a hidden appeal to a type of common denominator, the opposition of thought and action. In the end, a model of ritual that integrates opposing sociocultural forces becomes homologized to a mode of theoretical discourse that reintegrates the dichotomy underlying the identification of a thinking theorist and an acting object.

This type of expedient logic carries another inevitable corollary, however. That is, theories of ritual which attempt to integrate thought and action in any guise simultaneously function to maintain their differentiation. This type of discourse on ritual not only constructs a model that integrates a thinking observer and an acting object; it simultaneously functions to distinguish them clearly. The resolution of a dichotomy functions to affirm the polarity of the terms involved. The implications, therefore, of differentiating a subject and object on the basis of thought and action are rather striking. . . . At this point, a final example further illustrates the circular logic built up by these homologies and the theory of ritual that emerges.

WHEN RITUAL FAILS

In his study of a Javanese funeral ceremony, Geertz ventured to analyze "a ritual which failed to function properly."[42] The analysis is simple and compelling. He begins by discussing the inability of functionalism to deal with social change and transformational social processes.[43] The reason for this, he suggests, is the tendency of functional theory to identify social conflict as disintegration and to treat sociological and cultural processes unequally, reducing either one to the other.[44] Such reductionism makes it impossible to articulate social change, which arises in "the failure of cultural patterns to be perfectly congruent with the forms of social organizations."[45]

Thus, to develop theoretical tools capable of analyzing social change, Geertz wishes to distinguish clearly between culture and the social system. He defines culture "as an ordered system of meaning and of symbols, in terms of which social interaction takes place." The social system, on the other hand, is "the pattern of social interaction itself."[46] The conceptual-dispositional nature of this distinction is made apparent when he further describes them as a "framework of beliefs" in contrast to ongoing processes of "interactive behavior." Culture is the set of meaningful terms people use for interpretation and guidance; social system is the actual "form that action takes."[47]

With these categories and a great deal of contextual detail, Geertz analyzes the particular failure of funeral services held after the sudden death of a young boy. He considers the funeral rites to have failed for the following reasons: first, they heightened tension and distress in the community rather than producing the usual effects of *iklas*, a detached acceptance of death, and *rukun*, communal harmony; second, the usual Islamic procedures were not followed due to a local officiant's sense of conflict between these practices and the politics of a new group to which the household of the boy belonged; and third, the modifications desperately introduced in order to proceed with a funeral of some sort were ad hoc, unauthorized, and initiated by individual enterprise rather than by consensus.[48]

Geertz concludes that the conflict which surfaced at the funeral was the result of a growing discontinuity between the community's cultural framework of beliefs and the actual patterns of social interaction. That is, community members were urbanites who still thought like villagers, expecting village values to fit increasingly urban forms of organization behind which quite different values were actually operative.[49] Geertz argues that a conflict between the community's cultural categories (beliefs and values) and their customary social behavior (group affiliation) emerged in the funeral.

This example illustrates the expedient homologizing and collapsing of levels of analysis that can make an interpretation appear so effective.[50] Geertz's initial discussion contrasts the functionalism of sociological and social-psychological approaches with an approach that can articulate the dynamics of change in positive terms. Within the space of just a few paragraphs, however, these contrasting analytical perspectives have been rendered loosely equivalent to a distinction between sociological and cultural processes that Geertz argues should be considered independently and treated equally. These processes are then described as the forces that are mobilized and brought to confrontation in ritual. Since a ritual that does not work is identified as one in which cultural and sociological categories are experienced as discontinuous, we are led to assume that successful rituals are those in which these terms or forces are "perfectly congruent."

Geertz has done two things in this analysis. First, the two methodological perspectives (the sociological and the cultural) have been homologized with a pair of analytical categories (culture and the social system, as defined by Geertz), which were then found to be those very sundered forces underlying the dynamics of the unsuccessful ritual. This is a collapse of three levels and an implicit identification of three sets of oppositions. Ultimately, the discontinuity affirmed in the conclusion is a direct replication of the differentiation established in the beginning.

Second, there are some implications for ritual. Geertz's usual model of ritual is upheld in this analysis by the implication that a successful ritual is one in which the differentiated forces of culture and the social system can be effectively integrated. In addition, however, if an unsuccessful ritual effects change, then a successful one maintains stasis or no change. Thus, in Geertz's analysis, ritual as an integrative mechanism is also a synchronic force within the society, rendering it roughly equivalent to what he considers "culture." Although it is fairly clear that Geertz wants to conclude that ritual facilitates change, he is logically kept from such a conclusion by the description of this rite as a failure and by the pure oppositions that such an unsuccessful ritual leaves unresolved.

THE MYTH OF THE
FUNDAMENTAL CONTRADICTION

There are several other ways in which ritual has been cast as a mechanism for the resolution of basic oppositions or contradictions. The most common approach, I have argued, is exemplified in the work of Geertz. A slightly different form can be seen in the work of Max Gluckman and some of V. Turner's analyses. In this approach ritual is the arena in which purely social conflicts are worked out. In general, they describe how social conflict is recognized within the strategic limits of ritual where it can be systematically subsumed within a reaffirmation of unity.

Gregory Bateson and Lévi-Strauss both employ yet another permutation of the approach. For them, the conflict is not as general as that between ethos and worldview, nor is it as simple and concrete as a social conflict between two parties. The problem is identified as one embedded in the social structure, while the ritual solution is a more or less symbolic one that does not effect any real changes. For Bateson, an outstanding feature of the Iatmul *naven* ceremony was the cross-dressing of particular relatives and the specific sexual gesture of the mother's brother. Analyzing these acts and features led Bateson to conclude that the ritual strengthens the tense and ambiguous relationship between a child and his

or her mother's family.[51] For his part, Lévi-Strauss saw in the asymmetrical facial paintings of the Caduveo Indians the attempt to resolve a "lived" contradiction, namely, the dilemma of marriage in a rigidly hierarchical society lacking any institutional structure for unrestricted and egalitarian exchange.[52] He suggested that the facial paintings were the "symbolic" expression of an attempt at a compromise since the Caduveo were never really able to articulate and resolve effectively the contradiction in which they were caught.[53] Lévi-Strauss argued that ritual ultimately seeks the resolution of the inherent conflict of culture and nature.

As with Geertz's approach, these theories see ritual as designed to address fundamental conflicts and contradictions in the society, and there is similarly little evidence that the conflicts so addressed are not simply imposed through the categories of the observer. As we have seen, it is quite common for scholars to see ritual as resolving the conflict between thought and action, particularly in the guise of belief systems in conflict with the real world.

"Contradiction" is, of course, a standard Hegelian and Marxist term that figures prominently in analyses of social process.[54] For Marx, contradiction occurs when the forces of material production begin to outstrip the system of social relations to which they earlier gave rise.[55] Other Marxist analyses suggest that the perception of such contradictions can be repressed by the generation of ideological structures. Thus, cultural artifacts such as Caduveo face paintings or works of literature are seen as expressions of this repressed but lived contradiction, expressions that embody the contradiction while attempting to resolve some version of it. For Marxists and many cultural anthropologists, therefore, a basic contradiction at the root of social experience provides the impulse for the generation of a variety of integral social phenomena—historical change and revolution, or culture itself with its arts and institutions.[56] Whether the emphasis is on how such fundamental contradictions are repressed or expressed, displaced or resolved, they are usually linked to "fissures" of a type that provide the theorist with an interpretive *entré* into the ideological structures of a society, an activity, or a cultural artifact.

Lévi-Strauss and Bourdieu talk of "fundamental oppositions" that generate various oppositional series, which can all be reduced in turn to the most fundamental opposition. In some passages these fundamental oppositions do not seem to mean much in themselves but are effective for the internal organization of taxonomic schemes that generate the sense of a coherent cultural unity.[57] That is, such oppositions are not basic or fundamental in the sense of being underlying or absolute social, metaphysical, or logical values; rather, they are particularly useful tools for invoking and manipulating the taxonomic schemes of a culture. Bourdieu also describes ritual's role in effecting change in terms of how it breaks up the 'natural' taxonomic order so as to impose the reordering of 'culture.' Ritual, he states, always aims to facilitate and authorize passages or encounters between opposed orders, presumably the orders of nature and culture or, equally reified, the old order and the new order.[58]

In this general type of argument the notion of a fundamental social contradiction appears highly suspicious—at least by virtue of the way in which the imposition of a neat logical structure renders ritual action amenable to theoretical analysis. Certainly, the identification of a contradiction *out there* at the root of culture and society also works to construct an object and method of analysis by which theory can be seen to grasp and explain the puzzles that 'the other' simply lives. Roy Wagner states that "anthropology is theorized and taught so as to *rationalize* contradiction, paradox and dialectic."[59] Indeed, contradiction in some form is readily presumed in order to mandate the rational exercises, resolutions, and breakthroughs of theory. The notion that ritual resolves a fundamental social contradiction can be seen as a type of myth legitimating the whole apparatus of ritual studies.

Equally mythical, perhaps, is the notion that there is anything fundamental. As a counterpart in logic to the search for origins in historical studies, the notion of a fundamental force or conflict also functions suspiciously like some key to understanding. In an exasperated tone, Foucault has declared that "nothing is fundamental" and *that*, he continues, is what is really interesting about social phenomena: "There are only reciprocal relations, and the perpetual gaps between intentions in relation to one another."[60]

In the interests of identifying such seductive myths and exploring truly alternative conceptions of ritual activity, it is probably more useful to proceed with the notion that ritual is *not* some basic mechanism for resolving or disguising conflicts fundamental to sociocultural life.

NOTES

1. Gilbert Lewis discusses the general application of the notion of ritual to conduct or behavior rather than thought or feelings in *Day of Shining Red: An Essay on Understanding Ritual* (Cambridge: Cambridge University Press, 1980), pp. 10–11.
2. Edward Shils, "Ritual and Crisis," in *The Religious Situation: 1968*, ed. Donald R. Cutler (Boston: Beacon Press, 1968), p. 736. (This version of "Ritual and Crisis" differs substantially from a paper with the same name included in Sir Julian Huxley, ed., "A Discussion of Ritualization of Behavior in Animals and Man," *Philosophical Transactions of the Royal Society*, series B, 251 [1966]: 447–50.)
3. Claude Lévi-Strauss, *The Naked Man: Introduction to a Science of Mythology*, Vol. 4, translated by John Weightman and Doreen Weightman (New York: Harper and Row, 1981), pp. 669–75, 679–84.
4. Emile Durkheim, *The Elementary Forms of Religious Life*, translated by J. W. Swain (New York: Free Press, 1965), p. 51.
5. Durkheim, pp. 463ff.
6. James Peacock has noted how Weber's model, which he finds to be "the most systematic and comprehensive conceptualization of the relationship between belief and action," contrasts with the Durkheimian model. See Peacock, "Weberian, Southern Baptist, and Indonesian Muslim Conceptions of Belief and Action," in *Symbols and Society: Essays on Belief Systems in Action*, ed. Carole E. Hill (Athens: University of Georgia Press, 1975), p. 82. Action (*Handeln*) is the "fundamental unit" of Weber's sociology, a unit that represents the act *and* its subjective meaning to the actor, which cannot be separated from each other. Hence, for Weber action cannot be analyzed "independently of belief" (Peacock, p. 82). As such, Weberian analysis focuses on the relationship between the individual and his or her acts and involves the interpretation of the meanings of those acts to the actor. It does not focus on the relationship of beliefs to society as in the Durkheimian approach. This Weberian perspective was elaborated into a full theory of action by Talcott Parsons, of course, in *The Structure of Social Action* (New York: Free Press, 1937) and with Edward Shils in *Toward a General Theory of Action* (New York: Harper and Row, 1962).

   Yet the objection can be made that the results of both the Durkheimian and the Weberian approaches are rather similar. The Durkheimian is left with a vividly constructed social self (or spiritual being) oddly contrasted with that other vaguely noted being, the physical individual self. In his opposition of self and society, the self is left in somewhat mystical shadows. The Weberian on the other hand is left with a vivid construction of the subjective meanings attached to the objective acts of the individual in contrast to the social significance of these acts. Their social significance, or meaningfulness for others in the culture, cannot be depicted. Rather their transpersonal significance can be described only in terms of logical and idealized systems of socioeconomic behavior completely dissociated from real people and their activities. In both Durkheimian and Weberian conceptualizations, an underlying distinction between the individual and society, or belief and action, pushes the analysis to a dualism in which two entities or forces are simply juxtaposed and not really integrated.

Numerous Durkheimians and Weberians have attempted to complete the "integration" that their masters left incomplete. See Robert Wuthnow's discussion of such dualisms and their resolution in *Meaning and Moral Order* (Berkeley: University of California Press, 1987), pp. 23, 26–27, 37–41. For a critique of Parsons and his separate systems of culture and personality, see Marcus and Fisher (pp. 9–11) and Sherry B. Ortner, "Theory in Anthropology Since the Sixties," *Comparative Studies in Society and History* 26 (1984):150.

7. Stanley J. Tambiah, *Buddhism and the Spirit Cults in North-East Thailand* (Cambridge: Cambridge University Press, 1970).

8. Victor W. Turner, *The Ritual Process: Structure and Anti-Structure* (Chicago: Aldine, 1966).

9. Frederic Jameson, *The Prison-House of Language* (Princeton, N.J.: Princeton University Press, 1972), pp. 17–32.

10. Jameson, *The Prison-House of Language*, pp. 18–21.

11. Jameson, *The Prison-House of Language*, pp. 18–39 passim.

12. Jameson, *The Prison-House of Language*, p. 39

13. Jameson, *The Prison-House of Language*, p. 22.

14. E. E. Evans-Pritchard, *Theories of Primitive Religion* (Oxford: Clarendon Press, 1965), pp. 61–62.

15. Nancy D. Munn, "Symbolism in a Ritual Context," in *Handbook of Social and Cultural Anthropology*, ed. John J. Honigmann (Chicago: Rand McNally, 1973), p. 583.

16. Munn, p. 583. This is the basis for Munn's own view according to which "ritual can be seen as a symbolic intercom between the level of cultural thought and other complex meanings, on the one hand, and that of social action and immediate event, on the other" (p. 579).

17. Marshall Sahlins, *Culture and Practical Reason* (Chicago: University of Chicago Press, 1976), pp. 110–13, especially p. 111.

18. Claude Lévi-Strauss, "French Sociology," in *Twentieth Century Sociology*, ed. George Gurvitch and Wilbert E. Moore (New York: The Philosophical Library, 1945), p. 518.

19. In this context, Sahlins (*Culture and Practical Reason*, p. 111) draws attention to W. Doroszewki's theory of the influence of Durkheim's notion of a "sign" on Saussure, in Doroszewki's "Quelques rémarques sur les rapports de la sociologie et de la linguistique: Durkheim et F. de Saussure," *Journal de Psychologie* 30 (1993): 82–91.

20. Durkheim, p. 298.

21. Clifford Geertz, *The Interpretation of Cultures* (New York: Basic Books, 1973), p. 89. According to Sperber, Radcliffe-Brown regarded anthropology as a "natural science of society," while Evans-Pritchard put it among the humanities. Geertz, on the other hand, is a major representative of a third approach according to which "the only way to *describe* cultural phenomena is, precisely, to *interpret* them." Sperber goes on to criticize this approach and to "develop a fourth view of anthropological knowledge" (*On Anthropological Knowledge*, Cambridge: Cambridge University Press, 1985, pp. 9–10).

22. Geertz, *The Interpretation of Cultures*, pp. 143–44.

23. Geertz, *The Interpretation of Cultures*, pp. 89, 126–27.

24. Geertz, *The Interpretation of Cultures*, pp. 95–97.

25. Geertz, *The Interpretation of Cultures*, pp. 89, 98, 126–27.

26. Geertz, *The Interpretation of Cultures*, pp. 127 and 131.

27. Geertz, *The Interpretation of Cultures*, pp. 44–45, 48, 89, 113, 127, 137, etc.

28. Geertz, *The Interpretation of Cultures*, pp. 113 and 127. Also see Geertz's discussion of how symbols "synthesize" ethos and worldview (p. 89).

29. Geertz, *The Interpretation of Cultures*, pp. 92–93.

30. Geertz, *The Interpretation of Cultures*, pp. 112–13.

31. Geertz, *The Interpretation of Cultures*, pp. 143 and 163.

32. Geertz, *The Interpretation of Cultures*, p. 113. Emphasis added.

33. Geertz, *The Interpretation of Cultures*, p. 113.

34. Geertz, *The Interpretation of Cultures*, p. 114.

35. Frits Staal gives an interesting demonstration of the problems that arise when ritual is seen as "pure activity." By this characterization, made in the context of a clear and complete opposition between thought and action, Staal wishes to maintain the total resistance of pure activity to any theoretical appropriation whatsoever. Thus, Staal concludes that ritual cannot be understood, that it is "meaningless" ("The Meaninglessness of Ritual," *Numen* 26 (1975), pp. 2–22).

36. Theodore Jennings, "On Ritual Knowledge," *Journal of Religion* 62, no. 2 (1982): 111–27.

37. Jennings, pp. 113, 124.

38. Jennings, pp. 124–27.

39. Stephen Greenblatt, "Filthy Rites," *Daedalus* 111, no. 3 (1982): 3–4.

40. Geertz *The Interpretation of Cultures*, p. 113, quoting Milton Singer, *Traditional India: Structure and Change* (Philadelphia: American Folklore Society, 1959), pp. 140–82. Parentheses added by Geertz.

41. Geertz, *The Interpretation of Cultures*, p. 113, quoting Milton Singer, "The Cultural Pattern of Indian Civilization," *Far Eastern Quarterly* 15 (1955): 23–26.

42. Geertz, *The Interpretation of Cultures*, p. 146.

43. Geertz, *The Interpretation of Cultures*, p. 143.

44. Geertz, *The Interpretation of Cultures*, pp. 143 and 163.

45. Geertz, *The Interpretation of Cultures*, p. 144.

46. Geertz, *The Interpretation of Cultures*, p. 144.

47. Geertz, *The Interpretation of Cultures*, pp. 144–45.

48. Geertz, *The Interpretation of Cultures*, pp. 153–62.

49. Geertz, *The Interpretation of Cultures*, p. 164.

50. For an example of Geertz's approach taken on wholesale, see Carole E. Hill, ed., *Symbols and Society: Essays on Belief Systems in Action* (Athens, Ga.: Southern Anthropological Society, 1975), p. 4.

51. Gregory Bateson, *Naven*, 2nd ed. (Stanford: Stanford University Press, 1958), pp. 86–107.

52. Claude Lévi-Strauss, *Tristes Tropiques*, trans. John Weightmann and Doreen Weightmann (New York: Atheneum, 1975), pp. 178–97, especially pp. 196–97. Also see Fredric Jameson's discussion of this story in *The Political Unconscious* (Ithaca, N.Y.: Cornell University Press, 1981), pp. 77–80, as well as Dowling's comments on it (William C. Dowling, *Jameson, Althusser, Marx* [Ithaca, N.Y.: Cornell University Press, 1984], pp. 119–26).

53. This is Jameson's interpretation, which reads a bit more into Lévi-Strauss's account than the latter might have intended.

54. On the notion of contradiction, see Anthony Giddens, *Central Problems in Social Theory: Action, Structure and Contradiction* (Berkeley: University of California Press, 1979), especially pp. 132–45; and also a more recent work, *The Constitution of Society: Outline of a Theory of Structuration* (Berkeley: University of California Press, 1984), pp. 310–19.

55. In his analysis of the Javanese funeral, Geertz uses a very similar set of categories to generate his notion of social change as the result of a perceived discrepancy between the cultural ideals of a community and the real social relationships among them ("Ritual and Social Change: A Javanese Example," in *The Interpretation of Cultures*, pp. 144–46).

56. It could be argued that this formula is not unique to Marx but underlies much of the reorientation of late nineteenth- and early twentieth-century thought, including the theories of Sigmund Freud, Max Weber, and Emile Durkheim.

57. Pierre Bourdieu, *Outline of a Theory of Practice*, trans. Richard Nice (Cambridge: Cambridge University Press, 1977), pp. 114–24.

58. Bourdieu, *Outline of a Theory of Practice*, p. 120.

59. Roy Wagner, *The Invention of Culture*, rev. ed. (Chicago: University of Chicago Press, 1981), p. x.

60. "Space, Knowledge and Power," an interview with Michel Foucault, in *The Foucault Reader*, ed. Paul Rabinow (New York: Pantheon, 1984), p. 247.

Women's Business Is Hard Work: Central Australian Aboriginal Women's Love Rituals

DIANE BELL

Facts of publication: *Bell, Diane. 1981. "Women's Business Is Hard Work: Central Australian Aboriginal Women's Love Rituals,"* Signs: Journal of Women in Culture and Society *7(2): 314–337. Copyright 1981 by the University of Chicago. Reprinted with the permission of the author and The University of Chicago Press.*

Colonization of aboriginal land in Australia has changed aboriginal social structure. Whereas women's and men's work were once separate but more or less equal, now women's power has diminished because White male administrators have typically recognized male Aboriginals as figures of power. Against this background Diane Bell examines the ritual complex known as yilpinji *to show how women draw upon traditional processes to enhance their social power.* Yilpinji *deals with love relationships but, because of the nature of aboriginal cosmology and social structures, it necessarily deals with relationships to land as well. Drawing on teaching by aboriginal women, Bell presents reconstructions of women's myths that present the law and authority of dreamtime. She also shows how ritual innovations drawn from outside aboriginal culture are being integrated and traditionalized.*

About the author: Dates: *1943–, Melbourne, Australia.* **Education**: *T.P.T.C., Frankston Teachers' College (Victoria, Australia); B.A. (honours), Monash University (Victoria, Australia); Ph.D., Australian National University (Canberra, Australia).* **Field(s)**: *anthropology; religion; feminist theory and practice; Australian aboriginal history, art, religion, and gender relations.* **Career**: *Professor of Australian Studies and director of the Center for Australian Studies, 1986–1988, Deakin University; Henry R. Luce Professor of Religion, Economic Development, and Social Justice, 1989–present, Holy Cross College.* **Publications**: Daughters of the Dreaming, *2nd edition (University of Minnesota, 1993, [1983] Allen & Unwin); "In the Tracks of the Munga-Munga," in* Claiming Our Rites: Australian Feminist Essays in Religion, *213–246, ed. Penny Magee and Morny Joy (Allen & Unwin, 1994); "Aboriginal Women's Religion: A Shifting Law of the Land," in* Today's Woman in World Religions, *39–76, ed. Arvind Sharma (State University of New York Press,*

To appreciate the impact of the changes wrought by the colonization of aboriginal land in Australia, one must first appreciate the quality of gender segregation in the aboriginal society. While devastating for aboriginal men and women alike, segregation has affected the two sexes differently because of the sex-segregated nature of their society and the male-oriented nature of the colonial power.

The twin assumptions that gender values are ordered in an unchanging, rigid, hierarchical structure and that men are the most important social actors have led some anthropologists to conclude that aboriginal women are now and always have been a dominated sex. However, I suggest that while the division of labor by sex was fixed, gender values were (and still are to a limited extent) fluid. It is in the dynamic interweaving of sexual politics and social change that we find clues to the relationship between the sexual division of labor and women's marginal position today. In the ritual domain where women continue to engage in work that is distinctively theirs, the changing nature of women's work is starkly drawn. Thus, I look to the realm of religious ritual to probe the meaning of gender relations for the Kaititj women of Warrabri, a government settlement in the Central Australian region of the Northern Territory.

Underwritten by her critically important economic and ritual contribution to her society, aboriginal woman's independent manner, dignity, and autonomy of action once ensured that her voice would be heard and heeded. Although today women continue to assert their rights within their society and continue to celebrate these in their rituals, their position vis-à-vis men has been considerably weakened. For negotiations between the sexes are now conducted in an arena where white male

control is the norm, and the roles made available to women are restrictive and predicated on an image of women as sex object, wife, and mother. Where once there was interdependence, now there is dependence. The separation of the sexes that once provided a basis for woman's power now provides the means for her exclusion.

THE CHANGING FACE OF ABORIGINAL SOCIETY

For tens of thousands of years prior to the establishment by the British of a penal colony at Botany Bay in 1788, the Australian aborigines based their life and law on their complex relationship to land. They looked to the dreamtime, the creative era, when the mythical ancestors wandered across the land, named important sites and features, explained social institutions, and performed rituals. Today their living descendents must perform these rituals and celebrate the activities of the ancestral heroes in order to maintain and reaffirm the strength and relevance of the law as an ever-present and all-guiding force in people's lives. Under the law established in the dreamtime, men and women had distinctive roles to play, but each had recourse to certain checks and balances which ensured that neither sex could enjoy unrivaled supremacy over the other. Men and women alike were dedicated to observing the law that ordered their lives into complementary but distinct fields of action and thought: in separation lay the basis of a common association that underwrote domains of existence.

Today, plagued by ill health, chronic unemployment, a dependence on social security, and a general feeling of powerlessness, many of the 200,000 de-

The research for this paper was undertaken while I was a post-graduate scholar in the Department of Prehistory and Anthropology, School of General Studies, Australian National University. I gratefully acknowledge their assistance and that of the Australian Institute of Aboriginal Studies in funding my field work. For criticisms on the various drafts I am particularly indebted to Caroline Ifeka and my fellow participants in the Wenner-Gren Conference, August 1980. Finally I thank the women who sat with me in the field, taught me, and cared for me.

scendents of the original owners of Australia live as paupers, an enclave population within a rich and developing nation of 14 million. The loss of land over which to hunt has been more than an economic loss, for it was from the land that aboriginal people gained not only their livelihood but also their sense of being.

The spread of white settlement across the Australian continent has been uneven and often violent. In the Northern Territory some groups have lived in close contact with whites since the opening up of the north in the late nineteenth century; others have only recently come into sustained contact; still others have returned from centers of population density to their traditional homelands.

In Central Australia, where I have worked since 1976, the demands of the pastoral and mining industries have alienated the best lands and introduced ideas and goods not easily incorporated by the old law. Aborigines have found a precarious niche at the interface between the old law of the dreamtime and the new law of white frontier society. On the fringes of towns, in camps adjacent to homesteads, on cattle stations (ranches), herded together on missions and controlled settlements, many aborigines have lived in refuge-like communities poised on the edge of what was once their traditional land. However, with the passage of the Aboriginal Land Rights (Northern Territory) Act in 1976 some land has returned to the aboriginals, and they have the right to claim other parcels of land.[1] New and exciting life choices are now possible.

In the late 1970s Warrabri (then a government settlement, today aboriginal land) was home to four different groups: the Warlpiri (Walbiri) from an abandoned mission 210 kilometers to the north, the Kaititj and Alyawarra from neighboring cattle stations to the east, and the Warramunga from the mission and the town of Tennant Creek. The enforced coresidence of peoples with such different backgrounds, yet all with traditional ties to land, engendered many tensions and conflicts. Alcoholism and violence constantly disrupted family life. In 1976 this mixed aboriginal population of approximately 700 shared their lives with the 80–100 whites whose function it was to administer the affairs of the community and to deliver certain services, such as health, education, and law enforce-

ment. Since the proportion of whites is so high, any analysis of the lives of Warrabri aborigines must take account of their presence.

The dominant feature of the new law is that it is male oriented, controlled, and delivered. The idea that men have certain roles and that women occupy a particular place are today as clear cut as they were in the past. Women's work is still women's work; men's work is still men's work. However, the context within which this work is undertaken and the way in which the work is evaluated have altered radically. Today a woman has no security as an independent producer but is dependent on social security payments that entail relationships over which she has no control. She is a member of a household, one with a nominal male head and notional breadwinner; she is a dependent. In the past women lived with men in small mobile bands where female solidarity was possible. Today women live in settlements, missions, cattle stations, and towns where male solidarity is given new support and additional opportunities to be realized. While women are recognized as the "feeders and breeders," men are groomed as politicians by their fellow white male administrators and liaison officers. Further, because it is inappropriate for aboriginal men and women to sit together in large mixed gatherings, most consultations with settlement communities take place between aboriginal and white males.[2] Aboriginal women have been cut out of much of the political life of larger settlements and left in their camps to produce babies and small artifacts. Such, in European reasoning, is the wont of women.

Today the sexual politics of aboriginal society are no longer played out within the confines of that society. The ongoing dialogue between the sexes, the interplay, the exchange, the constant vying for power and status continues: male assertions of control and authority must still be balanced against female independence and solidarity. Women still actively participate in the construction of the cultural evaluations of their work, but they are constrained and defined by the male-dominated frontier society as the female sex, one necessarily dependent. In seeking to understand the changing role and status of aboriginal women and the sexual division of labor, we need to explore not only the basis of female autonomy and solidarity within aboriginal society but also to allow that claims to autonomy and expressions of solidarity now occur in a vastly changed and changing milieu.³

WOMEN'S WORK

In the aboriginal communities of Central Australia today, as in the past, the usual pattern is that during the day men socialize with men and women with women, each in an area taboo to the other. In most hunting parties there is also a division whereby women hunt the smaller game and search for grubs, berries, roots, and wild honey, while men seek out the larger game. In the past in the desert regions it was the women who provided the reliable portion of the diet (up to 80 percent) and the men who occasionally brought home a larger animal.⁴ The sharing that women enjoyed with each other during the day, the solidarity they enjoyed with their sister co-wives, and their contribution to the food quest could not easily be shrugged off by men.

Today, as in the past, at evening time when men and women come together in family camps, women do so with confidence and dignity. Matters of common concern are discussed between husband and wife, and the produce of the day is shared. In the ebb and flow of daily life the independence and interdependence of the sexes is clearly illustrated. However, this pattern varies, as does the weight women may bring to bear on the final decisions taken in contemporary communities. When aborigines live in small, relatively homogeneous family groups, as they do on some cattle stations and homeland centers, interaction between the sexes results in women's having a decisive role in family affairs—one, which, due to group composition, makes them participators in community decisions. Women have no such role on the larger, more heterogeneous settlements where family and community do not coincide.⁵

Crucial to women's status is their relation to aboriginal law. In seeking to make plain to whites the importance of their law, aborigines draw upon an extended work metaphor. The law is termed "business" and is made up of "women's business" and "men's business." No pejorative overtones adhere to the qualification of business as women's. Ritual activity is glossed as "work" and participants as "workers" and "owners." The storehouse for ritual objects is known as the "office." Ritual is indeed work for aborigines, for it is here that they locate the responsibility of maintaining their families and their land.

The separateness of the sexes, so evident in daily activities, reaches its zenith in ritual activity. Again men, this time anthropologists, have underestimated or underreported the religious life of women. Yet ritual is, I believe, an important barometer of male/female relations, providing, as it were, an arena in which the values of the society are writ large. There the sexual division of labor is manifested and explored by the participants, and men and women clearly state their own perceptions of their role, their relationship to the opposite sex, and their relationship to the dreamtime whence all legitimate authority and power once flowed. Both men and women have rituals that are closed to the other, both men and women allow the other limited attendance at certain of their rituals, and finally there are ceremonies in which both men and women exchange knowledge and together celebrate their membership in the one society and their duty to maintain the law of their ancestors.

THE RITUAL DOMAIN

The range of women's ritual activity in the desert is extensive. The most common is the *yawalyu* in which women celebrate the broad themes of attachment to country, maintain health and harmony within their community, and define their power to control and direct emotions. Rights to participate in these rituals are based on rights and responsibilities with respect to the land that a woman holds through the patrilines of both her mother and father. A woman has two "countries," but her rights and responsibilities in each are qualitatively different. She is *kirda* for the country of her father and is said to own that country. She is *kurdungurla* for the country of her mother, and she is said to manage that country. Country is jointly owned with members of one's patriline and managed through the children of the senior women of the patriline. The *kirda* to *kurdungurla* relationship entails a ritual reciprocity that binds together patriclans and is the basic structuring principle of the land-maintenance ceremonies that both men and women must perform.

Yawalyu are staged quite independently of men, although the particular natural phenomena or species of flora or fauna which is the focus of the ritual is shared with the men who are joint *kirda* and *kurdungurla* for that dreaming country. Men and women thus share a knowledge of country encoded in the designs and songs which they jointly own and manage, but these are elaborated by each sex in their own closed and secret rituals so as to enhance their status as men or women. For women I found it was not the role of child bearer per se that was being celebrated. Rather, women were casting themselves as the nurturers of emotions, of country, and of people. As women "grow up" children, so they "grow up" country and relationships. Women see themselves as responsible for the maintenance of social harmony; hence their concern with health and with potentially explosive emotions. Any imbalance in these domains is a threat to their community. In the strife-ridden context of settlement life in Central Australia this is a truly awesome responsibility.

Within their own ritual domain women exercise complete autonomy and totally exclude men. The entire area of women's camps, including the nearby ritual ground, is taboo to men. In the case of the Kaititj of Warrabri this area is located as far as possible from the central facilities of the settlement and from other aboriginal camps. The single women's camp, the *jilimi*, provides a home for widows, estranged wives, women visiting from other communities, unmarried girls, and in fact any women who have chosen to live beyond the control and purview of men. Between 1976 and 1978 approximately 25 percent of adult women at Warrabri were living in the various *jilimi* of the settlement. The *jilimi* is thus the home of a high proportion of important and influential women. Within those camps women are ritually independent and were once, and are still to a degree, economically independent of men.[6] Thus, the role of the *jilimi* as a power base and refuge for women is obvious. Yet, paradoxically, since most ritual activity is initiated from these camps, it is little wonder that men are vague about women's ritual activity. Moreover, aboriginal men will not and cannot discuss women's business: male anthropologists may not be made aware of the ac-

tivity, let alone be invited to attend. As a result the image of woman as lacking any important ritual responsibilities has been perpetuated by the male orientation of research.

An understanding of male/female power relations and the sexual division of labor in aboriginal society has often been sought by anthropologists within the context of arranged marriages, wherein old men are depicted as cheerfully allocating scarce resources and arrogating to themselves the right to bestow women's services in marriage.[7] It is thus possible to postulate an enduring and constant relationship between women's work and the cultural evaluations of her role, a relationship which makes both secondary. The institutions of polygyny and gerontocracy, sanctioned by the male control of the ritual domain, then become the means by which men control women. However, aboriginal women do not endorse this analysis, and my own observations offer support for their self-assessments.

For instance, women play a decisive role in maintaining the promise system of marriage through their politicking and ceremonial activity during male initiation.[8] . . . Seen from a woman's point of view, marriage is an evolving serial monogamy wherein women progressively contract marriages that are more and more to their perceived benefit.[9] In so doing they actively establish alliances and cement relationships that they deem desirable. Marriages resulting from such female-initiated action are correct within the kinship system. They are "arranged" marriages contracted between families of the couple, not "promised" marriages formally agreed upon at the time of male initiation. Women also organize male/female relations deemed legitimate by society through a particular form of women's ritual known as *yilpinji*.

During my period of field work, 80 percent of marriages were correct within the kinship system and 20 percent incorrect, but promised marriages accounted for only 5–10 percent of extant marriages. Formal business contracts entered into at initiation time did not organize the totality of marriage arrangements. In their own way, both men and women sought to regulate and thereby, so they hoped, to contain male/female relations and to gain control over the activities of the opposite sex. Women stated that they used love rituals, *yilpinji* business, to establish and to maintain marriages of their own preference. In these rituals women clearly perceived themselves as independent operators in a domain where they exercised power and autonomy based on their dreaming affiliations with certain tracts of land. These rights are recognized and respected by the whole society. Women are not, and never were, the pawns in male games, and they have always been actively engaged in establishing and maintaining male/female relationships of their own choosing, that is, they have engaged in women's work.

The focus on promised marriage has obscured and distorted the role women play in establishing and maintaining relationships deemed legitimate by the whole of aboriginal society. In part this has been because women's love rituals have been seen as "love magic," as a deviant and illegitimate activity pursued on the periphery of the real decision-making domain of men. According to Phyllis M. Kaberry, love magic was a safety valve and at times a form of vengeance.[10] To Geza Roheim it was the sort of activity in which women indulged.[11] It was magic; it could not be religion because women did not have access to the dreamtime power. Although Kaberry and Catherine H. Berndt have challenged this aspect of Roheim's characterization of women's lives,[12] the designation "magic," with all its pejorative overtones, has persisted. Love magic continues to be viewed as a haphazard activity, lacking any structure or purpose. It provides background noise, a low level of interference for descriptions of the activities of men. Women's ritual activity, their work, has been seen as of concern to women only, while that of the men is seen as of concern to the whole society. Men celebrate themes of a broad cohesive nature; women have narrow, personal, and particularistic themes and interests.[13] Such an interpretation of ritual misreads the way in which women state their role and the way in which that role is evaluated by aboriginal men and women.

It might be analytically convenient to set up an opposition whereby men controlled the formal arrangements (i.e., marriage) and women controlled the informal (i.e., love rituals), but the formal and informal are not so easily separated. Women take part in marriage arrangements and men perform love rituals, but each does so with a particular purpose in mind.[14] It is this which distinguishes men's work from women's work in the business of marriage.

Through an analysis of the themes, imagery, symbolism, and structure of women's love rituals, I demonstrate that *yilpinji* concerns the whole of aboriginal society, that it is underwritten by the dreamtime law, and that it concerns emotional management, not love magic. Women's business, like men's business, has to do with the maintenance of aboriginal society as a whole; both work to uphold the law.

YILPINJI AND COUNTRY

Women who worked magic were called witches by missionaries who banned such activities; unhappily, it is a label still in vogue at Warrabri today. Many Warrabri residents who lived at the Baptist mission at Phillip Creek during the 1940s before the establishment of Warrabri tell of the lengths to which women would go to perform *yilpinji* and of the trouble this caused because the missionaries and some aboriginal converts were deeply opposed to it. One reason for the opposition to *yilpinji* lay in the sexual nature of its subject matter; yet of the 300 Kaititj love songs that I have collected in the field and translated, only a few have to do with actual consummation of sexual relations. Major themes are longing for country and family, sorrow, anticipation, agitation, concern, shyness, and display. Country is both a basis of identity and an analogy for emotional states. Love is, in fact, a very poor translation of *yilpinji* but one that has found acceptance in the anthropological literature and has been fed back into the indigenous conceptualization, reinforcing the male notion of what women ought rightly to be about. For white itinerant road gangers and station hands with whom some aboriginal women have had sexual liaisons, love magic has been a smutty joke. It was something for which one could pay to enjoy. It clearly marked women as sex objects. Meanwhile, debasement of *yilpinji* as love magic allowed aboriginal men an avenue by which it could be defused. Thus, white men encouraged *yilpinji*, and aboriginal men could, with this newfound male support, construe *yilpinji* as magic. Aboriginal men were thereby able to score telling points in their ongoing tug of war with women.[15] In the process aboriginal women's religion was stripped of its actual complexities.

Kaititj women are not explicit in their sexual references but employ euphemisms like "going hunting together." They also use gesture: a graphic hand sign or one to indicate that a woman is being led away by the wrist. They may dance holding a rhythm stick or bunched up skirt before them as a mock penis, but consummation is always offstage or obliquely indicated. Had I asked for love songs and love myths, I am sure I would have collected fewer songs, but they would have been more explicitly sexual. The songs and myths glossed by the Kaititj as *yilpinji* have more to do with the elaboration of a common core of values underpinning and shaping male/female behavior than with the playing out of strictly sexual relationships.

Love and sex are aspects of *yilpinji*, which itself encompasses the sweep of tensions and emotions engendered by male/female relationships. Such relationships, however, must be seen in their cultural context, where country is a major symbol of attachment. Devil's Marbles and the surrounding area, known as *karlukarlu*, for instance, is a focus for rain dreaming. It is spectacular country, where enormous round rocks stand in the desert. During rains numerous small streamlets run from the rocks and ridges, wild figs grow from the crevices, and water collects in the rock holes and depressions high on the Marbles. The desert lives. The colors and contrasts are sudden and dramatic; red rocks and green water heavy with slime weed, tall ant hills and spinifex plains. The country is extremely rich in dreaming sites and ancestral activity, but when the road was built from Alice Springs to Darwin it was located through the very center of the Marbles so that important sites are no longer accessible to the Kaititj. Sorrowfully the women claim that they can still hear the old people crying from the caves. This loss has meant that certain important rituals can no longer be performed, but, since the area is within a day's travel of Warrabri, women may still hunt, camp, and dream there. Nonetheless, by losing access to important sites where they could express their attachment and whence they can draw power, women have been weakened. One ritual object associated with this area was so powerful that it was believed a man would meet a violent death if he came within close range of it. This terminal sanction is no longer available to women. Men have, however, retained their own violent sanctions and apply them during initiation time.

The ritual objects that act as title deeds for country are, for the men, mostly kept at the site to which they belong. Today many are kept in the ritual storehouse on settlements, for "the country" is often many inaccessible miles away from where people now live. Women, on the other hand, have always kept their ritual objects in their immediate care. On settlements fire risk is high, as is the danger of discovery, and so women are restricted in the range of objects they can safely maintain. Guided by male-oriented research, government officials have conceded that men need storehouses or "offices"; thus on all settlements there are brick, fireproof storehouses for men, but not for women. Only in 1977 was the first women's ritual storehouse opened at Yuendumu. This recognition of the value of men's ritual gear and disregard for women's ritual needs have placed restrictions on women while encouraging men in their ritual politics.

Settlement life also restricts women's access to country more than it limits men, since the latter may seek licenses and thus have access to vehicles, while women will not generally seek licenses from white police. Some do have licenses, however, and have managed to acquire vehicles. Once owned, a vehicle is kept as exclusively women's property, and this right is respected. On settlements such as Warrabri, where the village council is all male,[16] women have difficulty in obtaining permission to use community vehicles. Many visits to country are aborted because women can neither gain access to a vehicle nor provide a woman driver to take them on women's business.

In short, women have unequal access to the resources provided by the new law; moreover, they are denied a role as co-workers in the emerging social order of Northern Australia and are depicted as second-class citizens within their own society. Aboriginal men have successfully co-opted the white male representatives of the new law, who in their ignorance have provided new weapons for the male half of aboriginal society. The negotiating position of aboriginal women has been undermined, and their loss of land amounts to more than a loss of foraging grounds. To add insult to injury, their tie to land is deemed by many white observers never to have existed.

YILPINJI STRUCTURE AND RANGE

In discussing and analyzing any aspect of women's ritual domain, I am confronted with the problem of using material that is restricted as either secret/sacred or as exclusive to women. When this difficulty arises I have provided generalizations without giving details of song texts or describing the content of the rites. Besides, most women's rituals have a publicly known structure which can be briefly outlined. Owners and managers, *kirda* and *kurdungurla*, for a particular dreaming or country gather in the women's secluded ritual areas to prepare the ritual paraphernalia, paint their bodies, sing the country, do their secret business, and discuss the procedure and myth. They then proceed to a more public arena for the display of the painted boards and bodies that encode the myths, a singing of the country which sketches the travels and exploits of the ancestors, and an indication in sign and gesture of the broad categories into which the songs fall. Finally the boards are rubbed clean, the power absorbed, and the ritual objects returned to the women's ritual storehouse. The performance of such rituals consumes valuable resources: ochre, fat, psychic energy. It is, in short, hard work.

Yilpinji may be performed for a number of reasons other than that of attracting a lover. *Yilpinji* may force a wayward husband to return, remind a wife of her duty to family and country, or even repulse the unwanted advances of a spouse or lover. In Central Australia the focus of *yilpinji* is the community, not the individual for whom the ritual is performed. Both men and women respect its power. Great care is taken by women after a performance to nullify the power of *yilpinji* by throwing dirt and cleaning away all traces of the activity. It must bring about immediate consequences only for the subject of the ritual, not for the whole community. The latter will benefit rather from the restoration of harmony and maintenance of correct marriage alliances. Consultation before a performance is

undertaken to determine the rectitude of *yilpinji* in the particular case. I have never heard women admit that they sing for a "wrong way" partner, although such a union can result if the power is not properly controlled. Warlpiri women were forever accusing the Kaititj of making trouble with their *yilpinji* by the indiscriminate singing of songs. Although the Kaititj appear to exercise enormous care in *yilpinji*, these accusations have forced them to desist from using several powerful songs. Residence on the settlement in this way also has limited their range of expression and played a part in narrowing the recognition of women's religious activities.

Yilpinji is achieved through a creative integration of myth, song, gesture, and design, against a backdrop of country. The circle, the quintessential female symbol, finds expression in the body designs, gestures using rolling hands, and patterns traced out by the dancing feet. Certain *yilpinji* and health/curing designs are the same, because, as Kaititj women recognize, love, health, and sexual satisfaction are intertwined at the personal and community level. Exclusively *yilpinji* designs concern agitation, excitement, and longing. Such feelings are said to be located in the stomach that quivers and shakes like the dancing thighs of women or the shaking leaves of men's poles at initiation or the shimmering of a mirage or the iridescence of a rainbow.

YILPINJI AND MYTHS

The following discussion of myth develops the argument that women are claiming a right to express feelings that may superficially seem ambivalent. Ownership of myth and the rights to perform rituals provide the power base for women's claims, while the content of the myths explores women's autonomy and the nature of male/female encounters. Women in the myth encapsulate two warring principles that underpin women's identity. On one hand, there is autonomy; on the other, there is the desire for social intercourse which involves men. No invariable sequence is apparent in the mythic representation of encounters, although women's loss and pain are consistently present. Myth provides an explanation for male violence but not its justification. It serves rather as a warning of the treatment women may expect from men and of the danger they face when leaving their own country.

In extracting a story line from the ritual performances and presenting it in the form of a myth which has a beginning and end, I am doing violence to the ritual's cultural conception. My justification is that, short of a lifetime spent as a woman in women's camps, it is impossible to comprehend the kaleidoscopic range of nuances, ramifications, and elaborations of behavior by which the dreamtime ancestors act out *yilpinji* myths. By organizing the fragments I gleaned into such a form I was able, by way of clarification, to ask further questions of the women. On several occasions I have read back to the women my rendition of the myths; they have nodded assent but declared my version to be written text which constitutes another form, one peculiar to Europeans. Their telling of the myth in ritual emphasizes the richness of country, rather than the development of plot or character: two cultural views are thus encapsulated in "myth as action" compared with "myth as text." Country and the sites are part of a metaphysical knowledge system that is totally unlike the European system. The latter elaborates meanings and ideas about society and the significance of life through focusing on persons and their seemingly highly individual actions; Kaititj women's ritual myths look to country dreaming and other spiritually empowered events to discuss themselves and their relations to men.

I should also point out that by presenting the myths in this form I am providing an overview that no individual woman could recite. The different dreamings are the responsibility of different women, and although each is aware of the content of the dreamtime activity and characters of others, one may only rightly speak of one's own dreamings. Because I was able to record dreamings from all the women of the Kaititj group, my synthesis is not the product of one person's knowledge and would not occur in this form. Women would correct me if I misplaced the dreamings of others but would not comment on the content of the dreamings of others.

There are no occasions on which a woman would sit down and tell an *yilpinji* myth, although there is a corpus of songs which are glossed *yilpinji*. There are ritual practices, designs, gestures, and ritual paraphernalia which are used only in conjunction

with *yilpinji*, and certain conditions which are said to eventuate exclusively from *yilpinji*. I have put the myths together from actual performances I attended, subsequent discussions and translations of songs and symbols, women's explanations of ritual action and song furnished during performances or while listening to a replay of a tape. Once the women had decided I was a suitable candidate for investment into ritual knowledge, they were prepared to elaborate more than usual during actual performances. They were dedicated to my learning the business straight and to informing me of the background knowledge that a woman of my age and status should have.

As the mother of a son nearing the age of initiation and a daughter nearing the age of marriage, I was in a position to begin a course of important ritual instruction. I discovered quite late in my field work that I was deemed a suitable candidate because, as a divorced woman in receipt of a government pension, I approximated to the aboriginal model of women ritual leaders. Like women resident in the *jilimi*, my economic independence was marked with receipt of a pension. It is important that men are kept in ignorance of many of the women's activities, and this can be assured only if a woman lives basically with other women. Aboriginal women assume that white women tell their husbands of their daily activities and therefore that they cannot be entrusted with women's secrets (the "What did you do today dear?" syndrome). I was warned that I must not discuss certain ritual practices with men. During most of the first year of my stay I was on trial. Little wonder, then, that male field workers gain only a superficial understanding of women's rituals, that young single field workers are given information appropriate to their perceived age and status, and that married women are given the advantage of ritual participation without necessarily the accompanying ritual explanation.

The two interrelated myths that provide the scenario for most *yilpinji* songs, designs, and performances belong to the Kurinpi (old women) dreaming and the Ngapa (rain) dreaming. These dreamings belong to and are managed by the women of the Nampijinpa and Nangala subsections, all of whom trace descent from the founding drama of the Stirling Swamp and Devil's Marbles area. The behavior glossed as *yilpinji* (in myth) occurs only in the Devil's Marbles area, because, say the Kaititj women, Kaititj dreaming for that area also has rainbow, whereas Warlpiri rain dreaming (farther west) only has rain. This privilege prompts jealousy and suspicion on the part of Warlpiri and pride for Kaititj. On settlements it provides a further wedge for men to drive into women's solidarity.

Yilpinji and the Kurinpi Myth

Although I would like to provide a detailed analysis of the Kurinpi myth as it exemplifies the dilemma or warring principles facing women, in that they want the advantages of children and the company of a spouse but fear the unpredictability of men and men's challenge to their independence and autonomy, I shall discuss here only that portion of the Kurinpi myth which concerns *yilpinji*, women's claims to feelings as their right, and an exploration of the complexities of male/female interaction:

In the Kurinpi myth two elderly, knowledgeable, and respected women, known as the Kurinpi, wander about in the Stirling Swamp naming the country and performing such rituals as are their responsibility. Their life is one of ritual observance and celebration of the bounty of their country. Their power is manifest in their ability to turn red as they rub themselves with fat while traveling from their swamp home in search of company. On their journey they observe the ritual relationship of owner to worker, experience sorrow at death, and come into conflict with members of the younger generation and the opposite sex.

Once out of their swamp homeland they cease to name the country and travel more warily. They poke the ground with spearlike sticks. As they pass through another swamp area closer to Devil's Marbles, they enter a patch of tall spear trees. Fearing that perhaps someone might see them, they clutch their ritual packages to themselves and continue. Several young boys appear and dance flanking them, just as did the *kurdungurla* for the *kirda* in their previous encounter with this ritual relationship. The boys are carrying spears similar to the women's. The women teach the boys to throw spears in an overarm action. The women wonder why the boys, who are also carrying ritual packages, continue to travel with them. The young boys

have ritual packages such as are the right of older people. At the meeting and while traveling with the boys the women feel a mixture of shame and curiosity. Finally each reveals to the other the contents of their packages. The Kurinpi attempt to leave, but the boys beg them to stay so they can show them everything. "No," say the women, "you are too young and we are leaving." Suddenly the boys disappear and reappear as initiated men. The women look on in amazement, since these men are wearing their ritual headbands and armbands. Again the women hasten to leave and again the men beg them to stay. The women fear that these men might spear them, for they now have long strong spears such as men carry. The men follow the departing women who soon leave them far behind. "Never mind," say the men, "we shall sharpen our spears, harden them in the fire and spear the women when we catch them."

The women say to each other, "Come. Let them go their way. We have everything we need." As the men travel they say, "Let them go. We have all we need and can easily catch them later when we learn how to throw these spears." As the Kurinpi dance on, they see and join another group of women who are performing *yawalyu* rituals. The men with the spears are unsuccessful in catching the women because they are not prepared to violate the restrictions of the women's ritual area.

The meeting with the boys has many connotations, but here I shall comment only on the significance of the myth for women's perception of themselves in their social function and in relation to men. Before encountering the boys the women had never felt shame. They had confidently and authoritatively known their country and their relationship to it. The status of the boys, already ambiguous, becomes doubly so after their transformation, without ritual, into men. Each is prepared to respect the ritual packages of the other, but the men rather fancy the women and decide to pursue them. The women continue to display their power by their rubbing of fat into their bodies and by their color changes. The men decide to use force and a new technology to win the women but are thwarted when they discover that the women have sought sanctuary in the company of other women.

In another encounter of the Kurinpi with men,

they do not escape but are overpowered. These two encounters are not considered to exist in any temporal sequence but, like the women's ability to turn red and take on the colors of the desert, the stories are in constant flux, an ever-shifting and dynamically constituted power on which women may draw. The two accounts are not considered conflicting versions of the same myth but rather are taken to be an illustration of the vagaries and complexities of male/female relationships:

> The women were returning to the camp from a day of hunting when some men began throwing stones at them. "What is this?" asked the women. "We want to get food, not to run away." Unaware of the presence of the men, the women continued home and on the way dug for grubs. One man ran after one of the women and stood on her digging stick and asked the woman for food. The woman felt shamed because she had never met a man like that before. He told the woman to get up, promising that they would dig together. "Don't be shy," he said, "we shall go together." He gently took the woman by the arm and they all continued together. But as they traveled and the woman left her country behind, she held back and tried to go the other way. The man crippled the woman with a spear. As she lay naked and complaining of this cruelty, he began to beautify himself so that she would love him. He brought her animal skins to warm her body and sat with her. She tried to straighten herself, but it hurt too much. She looked back to her country but knew she must leave with her husband.

It is worth noting that hitherto in the myth the women were depicted as old. Here they appear to be younger, but this is of little consequence since in both myth and reality older women and men court each other but also younger partners. Women regard themselves as desirable regardless of age.

In women's perception, men are so insecure that violence is their sole means of expressing emotion. Roheim would interpret this myth as a description of the wild being tamed,[17] but if seen within the context of land and of male/female interaction as a power relationship, the myth argues the importance of women's power base and also shows that, through marriage, men can disrupt women's ties to land. The once kind suitor who took the woman by the

arm now spears her. Her tie to her country is also damaged. In being crippled by the spear wound the woman is also deprived of her land. In the loss of land she loses her autonomy and power base, but he gains a wife to whom he can now afford to show affection and from whom he now seeks love by beautifying himself. In her crippled state, she feels the pain, loss of autonomous movement, and loss of land. As they continue together she sees his country, like a mirage, before her, and he begins instructing her in the wonders of his country. Through men, women may thus gain knowledge of another country, but the price is high. It is worth noting that after marriage men in reality often do not succeed in carrying off young wives to another country. Frequently they take up residence in their wife's country.

Yilpinji and Ngapa Myth

In the section of the rain Ngapa myth which concerns *yilpinji*, a complex series of relationships is played out. The wise rain father, known as Jungkaji, attempts to restrain his overly pretentious sons, the rainbow men, who come into conflict with their older brother, Lightning, while pursuing young girls to whom they are incestuously related. Rain's wife, as mother of the boys, finally lures them from the dangers of their exploits by feigning illness. Their duty to their mother overwhelms them, and they return, only to die, at the insistence of their stern father. There are important themes involving the flouting of a father's authority over his sons and identification of devotion to the mother with the sons' destruction, but I shall concentrate on the aspects of male/female relationship that are explored in the myth. During the pursuit, both men and girls, in contemplating the possible outcome of their behavior, express fear, ambivalence, tenderness, aggression, and insecurities.

> The rainbow men, as older and younger brother, travel around in circles in the Devil's Marbles area from Dixon Creek to Greenwood Station. Their father warns them not to venture too far, but they ignore his warning. "Rainbows should stay close to rain," he says. "Let Rain rain himself," say the sons. "We shall travel further." They travel up so high that they can see

the sea. They sit on top of the clouds and display their brilliant colors. They swoop into the green water below. They hide from rain in hollow logs and from the girls in creek beds and behind ridges.

In most of the encounters the girls, who are classificatory sisters but not identified as younger and older, are unaware of the presence of the men who creep closer and closer to them. The younger brother warns the older not to go too close lest he frighten the girls. "Hold back," he warns. The older brother counters, "Don't be silly." To their delight the women are picking sweet fruits. "You'll frighten them if you go any closer," warns the younger brother. "Wait for rain before showing yourself." The men have rubbed themselves with red ant hill to dull their brightness and thus not frighten the girls. As they add marks to their bodies, they reflect on their own beauty and wonder if the girls will like them. "Why don't they love us? Have we shown ourselves for nothing?" they wonder. The younger brother questions the correctness of the pursuit of the girls. "They may be of the wrong subsection," he suggests. "We can take wrong skins," says the older brother, but the younger still holds back.

Finally the girls separate. One goes to dig yams, the other to swim. The older brother descends upon the girl who is digging, and such is his brightness that she closes her eyes. He woos her and finally convinces her that she should accompany him. As she leaves she looks back in sorrow for her country but also, like the Kurinpi, she knows she must leave with her husband. The younger brother goes to the water where the other girl is swimming, but she is too frightened to go with him and attempts to escape. He spears her in the leg, and while she lies naked before him, he beautifies himself with body scars, all the while gently wooing her with tender words.

In the exploits of the rainbow men their brightness and its malleability are the subject of constant reference. They can overpower women with it. They can thus tear women from their land. The Kurinpi women, on the other hand, change color in a way which demonstrates their power over their bodies and men. One of the stated reasons for the extreme power of Kaititj *yilpinji* is this access to color in the rainbow myth.

In yet another encounter, the young girls are camped with their mother who remains in camp while they go in search of spring water for her. They return very tired and do not realize that men have been working *yilpinji* for them. Like most dreamtime women (and women today) they have carried their ritual packages with them but because they are so tired, they have decided to leave them behind in the camp, high in a tree. The next day they return from hunting with two men they have met during the day, only to find their packages missing. The girls are reluctant to go with the men who then spear them and finally they travel, along with the mother, into the men's country.

In this myth women's power, in the form of their ritual packages—that is, their tie to the land—is stolen, thus rendering them comparatively helpless.

Yilpinji and Women in Myth

In many of the exploits of the rainbow men, the girls are actually working the *yilpinji* for the men who follow them through the scrub or who are far away. In a dream a man may see his beloved wearing her *yilpinji* design and hasten to join her. As he returns to her she makes a bed for him so that they may comfort each other when reunited. "Make my heart still," she pleads. "Lie with me." Or as he travels he may hear the sound of her voice like music from afar. He may fish by throwing grass into the water to attract the fish and see his loved one instead. Or she may have prepared a ball of the green slime weed that she threw out to him from a distance, and this has now reached him.

When they are finally reunited, he kneels before her, woos her, and gently encourages her to appreciate his charms; he may make a pillow of his woomera (spear thrower) or swish away the flies with it. Sometimes the girl is afraid, but he reassures her. In one song she lies in a tight ball, but he soothes her and covers her until she relaxes. He asks, "Do you love me? If not I shall go away forever. Please tell me." Such behavior is a far cry from the single-mindedness of the songs and myths discussed by Ronald M. Berndt and C. H. Berndt and Roheim where the end point is always copulation.[18] In the women's songs a man may even feign illness in order to gain his loved one's attention and hope that she will eventually come to love him.

Yilpinji: Themes and Symbols

A major symbol of *yilpinji* is color and its power to attract. The whiteness of the headband and feather twirled by the opening woman dancer is contrasted to the bursting color of the rainbow men which must be dulled with green slime weed so as not to dazzle women in the myth. Thus, paradoxically, in ritual practice women throw balls of green slime to attract a lover; in fact both men and women use green slime to attract. Like the men's colors the women's colors are not static. They shift and change hue. The Kurinpi turn red, the color of the country. The rainbow men burst dangerously with all colors but use red of the ant hill and green from the water to dull their brilliance. Women see their own and men's colors as dynamic, not fixed in a color spectrum but fluid, unpredictable, dramatic as the country itself, and ever changing.

The shining of watchbands and buckles, the sparkling of lightning, the lure of blond hair, the blackening of eyebrows, and the reddened legs of women dancers all induce a lover to notice and appreciate the charms of a possible partner. A major theme of ritual is display. Decoration and display have found expression in terms of both traditional and introduced items. The traditional male hair-string headband has been replaced in reality and in some songs by the scarf or band from a stockman's hat. The arm bracelets adorned with feathers which were celebrated in song may now appear as the shining watch that winks across the desert. The pubic cover which is pushed aside by the impatient lover becomes the shining belt buckle which is seductively left open but catches the sun and shines. A woman's digging stick may now be a shining crowbar; her wooden carrier, a metal billy can. Such items glisten as women travel and attract the attention of a lover. In the same way bald heads are said to shine in the sun and to attract lovers.

The intrusion of such themes and items, which are often associated with a particular person, has been construed by C. H. Berndt as evidence of the nonreligious nature of love magic.[19] I think it has more to do with the manner in which women dream and with the ever-present nature of the dreamtime. In ritual the dreamtime moves concurrently with the present so that the appearance of introduced goods and their evolving meanings is not a contradiction so much as proof of the relevancy of the dreamtime law. Many of the songs belong to, or depict, actual living people; in time these songs will become part of the repertoire and their characters will be given kin terms as are the characters of the songs already accepted by male anthropologists as bona fide dreaming songs. The mixture of songs suggests to me that these present-day themes are in the process of achieving the nonspecificity and vagueness that characterize the dreaming. The innovative themes have a relevancy for today's world. One Kaititj/Alyawarra woman commented to me as I watched in amazement while money, an alien concept, was added to a ritual exchange, "It does not matter what it is. It is what it stands for that is important!" However, the accommodation of such modern items within ritual lulls women into believing that they have retained control over the power to attract, a power demonstrated by successful liaisons with white men. For women this belief strengthens their self-image and demonstrates the power of *yilpinji*; for men it strengthens the destructive image of woman as a sex object.

EXEGESIS

In these myths various admired female stereotypes are presented. The Kurinpi are the ritually important women, while the young girls exude sweetness, youth, and the ability to hunt proficiently. In ritual the desirability of these qualities is celebrated by women for a number of reasons. In both the Kurinpi myth and the rainbow myth men are portrayed as cruel, unsure, vain. They continually ask each other, "Will she like me? Will we frighten them?" Insecure about their ability to woo and win, they win, then woo, beautifying themselves after wounding the women. Once they make contact there is no standard response. The stable, symbolically ordered positions on the axis become freed and negotiable. Like the shifts in color, like the unpredictability of the country from which women draw their power, men are inconsistent. One brother uses soft words and beauty. He has been the confident one all along. The other uses physical force but soft words.

In an Aranda men's song cycle recorded by Theodor G. H. Strehlow the sequence of attraction, violence, consummation, and travel to a new country is followed, but the male perception and articulation casts woman as the passionate partner, so passionate in fact that she leaves her own country to travel with him.[20] When sorrow fills her as she leaves, he empathizes and beautifies himself to console her. Thus, men also recognize that in marriage women may lose land but in the song explain it as women's passion and credit themselves with tenderness. In Nancy D. Munn's account of Warlpiri male *yangaridji* (closely related to *yilpinji*) the crippling motif is said to be used to ensure fidelity.[21] Uniting both the male and female versions of *yilpinji* myths is the depiction of love as crippling and the use of land—also an actual living resource—as a central symbol. By evoking their control of land women may attract men.

The display of color so powerful in the myths about the rainbow men and the Kurinpi women is given form in the body decorations and secret rituals of the women. In Kurinpi performances women redden themselves, and like the Kurinpi, have the power to attract and face possible violence or escape to the closed world of women. Women's ritual practices, unlike the action of men in myth, are deemed invariably successful. Such differentiation and separation of the qualities of powerful, cruel/gentle men in myth is dynamically opposed to powerful, irresistible women who give the myth form in the rites. Like the Kurinpi, women may remain apart or seek a spouse; like the girls in the rainbow myth they may lead a man to destruction or entrance him with their sweetness. It is their choice.

The conflicts and tensions that arise when men and women must enter into the direct negotiation of rights, privileges, and obligations with each other burst forth in violence such as that seen in the jealous fights common in many communities, but they also find expression in the ritual statements of women in *yilpinji*. In everyday life men fear that if they really hurt a woman she may take ritual action. If a woman turns away from a man she usually has good reason. Her response will certainly have been the subject of much public discussion. If she acts rashly, she will incur the censure of other women and have no security in their camps. Women are not considered to be fickle in the eyes of men or women, and if a woman uses *yilpinji* against a man he knows

he has deserved it. Fights begin with accusations of infidelity (a vastly expanded possibility in settlements), not fickleness. The heightened suspicion of women's infidelity, like the debasement of *yilpinji* to love magic, has been imposed on women; stereotyping of the women's highly predictable responses to maltreatment has been achieved without consideration of their perceived feelings or their attitudes toward the diminution of their enforceable rights.

In *yilpinji* women not only articulate their models of social reality but also attempt to shape their worlds. This latter aspect is, I believe, apparent in the way in which women comment on ritual as it proceeds. At one level they discuss the myth as I have delineated it, and at another they comment on the power and efficiency of the rituals. These two levels are interwoven in the seamless web of life that encompasses the now of today and the now of the dreaming. Particular songs or combinations of songs and actions are remembered as having been sung at a particular place for a particular person and with a particular result. Two older women married to much younger men did not see the action of a man taking an older wife as duty but saw it as a man desperately in love with an irresistible woman. Such is the women's perception of the affair. They do not see themselves as being shuffled around but as capable of deciding whether or not they will go to a younger man. Since women exercise wide choice in second and subsequent marriages it is hard to believe that they go to younger men merely to uphold the gerontocracy. They go if they wish. To ensure the success of the match they work *yilpinji*. The two older women mentioned above are celebrated cases of *yilpinji*, but all the women with whom I worked would admit to having used *yilpinji* to achieve results they desired and all attested to the success they had.

As songs are being sung, women comment on the possible outcome of the ritual and the action in the ritual. They assert their rights to feelings. "That is my feeling," I have heard women say in explanation on many occasions. "If you want to stay you may." If a woman wants to get out of a marriage which she finds distasteful because the man is playing around, taking a second wife, or acting violently, a wife may ask for her ritual group to perform *yilpinji* to make him turn away from her. These are powerful and allowed only after the women have weighed the case. However, if a woman says, "That is my feeling," her words are respected.

In the myths the lovers are often improperly related. Roheim cast *yilpinji* as a holiday from the rules,[22] but in my experience, love rituals are very carefully used and then only after extensive consultation and consideration of the merits of the request. *Yilpinji* only induces certain states; it does not have the power to condone "wrong way" unions which, in any case, are rare, notorious, and generally short-lived. *Yilpinji* is used to establish correct unions. It is therefore feared by men, because *yilpinji* impinges upon the set of relationships that men claim to control through marriage alliances. They know that they cannot negate women's *yilpinji* and often do not even know they are being performed. At any time a woman may thus overturn the plans of men. Men do not attempt to prevent women from staging *yilpinji* but rather turn to their own sphere of control of male/female relations and intensify demands in the domain of promised marriages. Women respect the marriage codes but not necessarily the plans of men. In using *yilpinji* for correct unions they are upholding the moral order but not endorsing men's rights to determine actual marriages. The charge made by the men and accepted at face value by some anthropologists that women use *yilpinji* for wrong way unions obscures women's endorsement of central values.

CONCLUSION

In exploring women's mythology I have argued that women represent their world as one which is self-contained, known, and secure. The authority to control this world and the power to exclude men from this domain are underwritten by the dreamtime—the all-encompassing law of the past and now. In acting out the responsibilities conferred upon them as women by this law, women engage in work which is distinctively theirs. In the past this ensured that they would be recognized as full members of their society. Today, although they continue to work in their domain, one which remains separate and distinct from that of the men, they no longer enjoy their former status. For Kaititj women

the sexual division of labor is, on the one hand, dynamic and changing, much affected by colonization and white patriarchial practices. On the other hand, these women remain firmly oriented toward the age-long values of renewal and bound to people, law, and the land. To the extent that women's rituals endure and encode crucial aspects of gender relations and therefore of aboriginal culture, women and their rituals contribute most significantly to the continuity of aboriginal structures in a colonial frontier society.

NOTES

1. Under this act aborigines in the Northern Territory may claim unalienated crown land and land in which all interests others than those held by the crown are held by or on behalf of aborigines.

2. Diane Bell and Pam Ditton, *Law: The Old and the New, Aboriginal Women in Central Australia Speak Out* (Canberra: Australian National University Press, 1980), for a detailed discussion of women's role in the decision-making process.

3. Diane Bell, *Daughters of the Dreaming* (Melbourne: McPhee & Gribble, 1982) presents an in-depth exploration of change, continuity, and dimensions of time.

4. Betty Hiatt Meehan, "Woman the Gatherer," in *Women's Role in Aboriginal Society*, ed. Fay Gale (Canberra: Australian Institute of Aboriginal Studies, 1970), pp. 2–7.

5. Bell and Ditton, p. 90.

6. Bell, *Daughters of the Dreaming*, pt. 4. "Woman's Domain."

7. Mervyn J. Meggitt, *Desert People* (Sydney: Angus & Robertson, 1962), pp. 264–70.

8. Bell, *Daughters of the Dreaming*, pt. 8. "Initiation."

9. Bell, "Desert Politics: Choices in the 'Marriage Market,'" in *Women and Colonization: Anthropological Perspectives*, eds. Mona Etienne and Eleanor Leacock (New York: Praeger Pubs., 1980), pp. 239–69.

10. Phyllis M. Kaberry, *Aboriginal Women, Sacred and Profane* (London: Routledge & Kegan Paul, 1939), pp. 265–67.

11. Geza Roheim, "Women and Their Life in Central Australia," *Journal of the Royal Anthropological Institute* 63 (July–December 1933): 208–9.

12. Kaberry, pp. 220–21, 276–78; and Catherine H. Berndt, "Women and the 'Secret Life,'" in *Aboriginal Man in Australia*, eds. Ronald M. Berndt and C. H. Berndt (Sydney: Angus & Robertson, 1965), pp. 238–82.

13. See Nancy D. Munn, *Walbiri Iconography* (London: Cornell University Press, 1973), p. 213.

14. See Theodor G. H. Strehlow, *Love Songs of Central Australia* (Sydney: Angus & Robertson, 1971), for a discussion of men's love rituals.

15. By locating *yilpinji* within the context of land and interpreting the myths in terms of power symbolisms, I have not dwelt upon the explicit themes of sex as have some previous

analyses of male/female relationships. See R. M. Berndt and C. H. Berndt, *Sexual Behaviour in Western Arnhem Land* (New York: Viking Fund, 1951).

16. Aboriginal councils established in the 1950s are now assuming greater powers in the running of settlements and are demanding legal recognition and status through incorporation. See Bell and Ditton, pp. 11–15.

17. Roheim, p. 237.
18. Ibid., passim; and Berndt and Berndt.
19. C. H. Berndt, "Women's Changing Ceremonies in Northern Australia," in *L'Homme* (Paris: Hermann, 1950), p. 43.
20. Strehlow, p. 4.
21. Munn, p. 47.
22. Roheim, pp. 209–10.

Political Witch-Hunt Rituals

ALBERT BERGESEN

Facts of publication: Bergesen, Albert. 1984. "A Theory of Political Deviance," from The Sacred and the Subversive: Political Witch-Hunts as National Rituals, 7–19, 22–24. Storrs, CT: Society for the Scientific Study of Religion. Copyright © 1984 by The Society for the Scientific Study of Religion. Reprinted with the permission of Edward C. Lehman, Jr., Executive Secretary, The Society for the Scientific Study of Religion.

Not all ritual processes are either intentional or explicitly recognized. Political witch-hunting, for instance, displays many of the qualities that scholars consider typical of ritual. Some sociologists and political scientists regard witch-hunting as ritual because of its scapegoating dynamics. "Witch-hunting" refers not only to literal trials of alleged witches in Salem, Massachusetts, or in medieval Europe, for instance, but to any social movement in which a particular group, imagined or real, is stigmatized as deviant and threatening to the state. In the theoretical tradition of Emile Durkheim and Kai Erikson, Albert Bergesen here argues that states do not merely tolerate deviance but actually need it and therefore generate it. In effect, states invent witches in order to dramatize their own enduring values. This process of imagining and then dramatizing a society as if it were divided into mutually opposed groups is, for Bergesen and some other sociologists, ritual. He proposes an explanatory model of the witch-hunting process that links its rate and dispersion with the degree to which the values of corporate organizations are immanent in the everyday life of a society.

For more on scapegoating see works by René Girard such as Violence and the Sacred *(Baltimore: Johns Hopkins University Press, 1977). See also David Cannadine and Simon Price,* Rituals of Royalty: Power and Ceremonial in Traditional Societies *(Cambridge: Cambridge University Press, 1987).*

About the author: Dates: 1942–, Rockville Centre, NY, U.S.A. **Education**: B.A., University of California, Santa Barbara; Ph.D., Stanford University. **Field(s)**: cultural studies; linguistic and interaction rituals; art, power, and political solidarity. **Career**: Professor of Sociology, 1973–present, University of Arizona. **Publications**: The Sacred and the Subversive: Political Witch-Hunts as National Rituals (Society for the Scientific Study of Religion Monograph Series, 1984); with R. Wuthnow, J. Hunter, E. Kurzweil, Cultural Analysis: The Work of Peter Berger, Mary Douglas, Michel Foucault, and Jurgen Habermas (Routledge, 1984); "The Rise of Semiotic Marxism," Sociological Perspectives 36 (1993): 1–22; "A Theory of Pictorial Discourse," in Vocabularies of Public Life, ed. Robert Wuthnow (Routledge, 1991). **Additional**: Distinguished Article Award given by the Pacific Sociological Association for the best article published in Sociological Perspectives (1992).

Theories of the origins and functions of political witch-hunts [are usually] inadequate in that they [can] not provide a generalized theoretical scheme capable (1) of explaining the appearance of witch-hunts across a sample of national societies, or (2) of generating a sociologically satisfying account as to why these events are accompanied by such extensive ritual; why trivial acts can become crimes against the nation; or why individuals with no seeming intention of taking political action against the state can come to be considered as subversive or treasonous. This [selection] puts forth a theoretical scheme to explain these properties of witch-hunts.

CRIMES AGAINST THE NATION: CORPORATE CRIME

Political crime can mean many things. It can refer to the study of collective violence and civil disorders, or it can refer to the social processes whereby individual acts of vandalism, assassination, terrorist bombing, or other "normal crimes," come to be defined by political authorities as constituting distinctly political acts.[1] In short, political crime could refer to any number of different processes. But, for this research the term will be used in a very specific manner.

Since the term *political crime* has numerous well understood meanings, the notion of *corporate crime* will be introduced. *Corporate crime refers to those activities which are defined by legitimate political authorities to be acts committed against the interests and purposes of the corporate nation-state.* For example, during the French Revolution there suddenly appeared counter-revolutionaries, loyalist agents, foreign spies, and clandestine clergy, who the Jacobins saw as a threat to all that the revolution had fought to achieve.[2] What all these groups shared in common was their purported intent to undermine the newly established revolutionary society. Similarly, during the Stalinist trials of the late 1930s, there appeared Wreckers, Trotskyites, and enemies of the Soviet people; during the McCarthy period there were Communists, Communist sympathizers, spies, and other seditious elements, and finally, during the Chinese Cultural Revolution of the late 1960s there were capitalist roaders, revisionists, rightists, and ul-

tra-leftists. In all these societies there appeared groups who possessed the common characteristic of being understood to be somehow acting against or undermining the very essence of the corporate nation itself.

EMILE DURKHEIM: CRIME AND MORAL SOLIDARITY

One of the most provocative sociological approaches to the study of crime has been that of Emile Durkheim.[3] One of Durkheim's primary concerns was over the question of what made some activities criminal and others not. It became obvious that the presence of community punishment was not a function of the danger that particular activities posed to the functioning of the community itself. Many white collar crimes which could clearly upset the economic functioning of the society were less severely punished than crimes of petty theft. The community reacts to certain actions not because they, in Durkheim's famous phrasing, are criminal, for they become "criminal" because the community reacts to them. Activities are criminal because they violate communities' mores or "shock the common conscience." No action is inherently criminal; all that is required is the violation of some community norm. Punishment, therefore, acts not to reform the offender but to bring the community together to ritually reaffirm that aspect of the normative order which was violated. As Durkheim noted:

> Crime brings together upright consciences and concentrates them. We have only to notice what happens, particularly in a small town, when some moral scandal has just been committed. They stop each other on the street, they visit each other, they seek to come together to talk of the event and to wax indignant in commons.[4]

Durkheim further reasoned that far from being disfunctional for a society, the presence of crime was, in fact, quite functional. The periodic punctuation of social life with normative violations functioned to bring the community together in common moral indignation and thereby ritually reaffirm the common moral order.

KAI T. ERIKSON: THE COMMUNITY CREATION OF DEVIANCE

Erikson (1966) took the basic Durkheimian assumption about the functional quality of crime and added another important assumption. Erikson reasoned that if the presence of deviance was functional, why should society wait for some periodic violation of community mores? The society, in effect, need not wait for individuals to stray across its moral boundaries to attain the consequent positive result of intensifying moral solidarity if it could create the deviance itself. This assumption has taken the original Durkheimian position as to the functions of and naturalness of deviance, and added another important assumption as to the origins of crime.

Deviance can, therefore, come about in two ways: (1) individuals can cross the moral boundaries, the original Durkheim position, or (2) the boundaries themselves can be shifted by the community and thereby reclassify groups and individuals as deviants, the Erikson assumption. For instance, consider a university professor who has been teaching courses on Russian social institutions for the past twenty or thirty years. During this time his activity did not violate normative boundaries and was not considered to be "un-American" or subversive in character. There then appears the McCarthy period and suddenly he finds his work being defined as disloyal and un-American. The contents of his classes have not changed. He has not, by his activity, crossed or violated some stationary moral boundary. What has changed is the definition of what constitutes subversive activity and this shifting boundary has now moved over to include his course on Russian institutions.

Every social community possesses a set of institutional arrangements allocated the responsibility of defining moral boundaries, and hence, deviance. The police, courts, jails, prisons, and mental hospitals are modern institutional arrangements which function to define deviant behavior and thereby to establish or reestablish the ever shifting symbolic boundary separating the deviant from the normal, thereby allowing the community to create and maintain a certain volume of deviance. The reaffirmation of moral solidarity need not wait for members of the society to commit "crimes themselves,"

that is, for the individuals to violate some rule. The community can, on its own, create deviance by processing groups and individuals through its institutions of social control, thereby publicly reaffirming the character and definition of its own moral order.

Erikson further reasoned that since deviance functions to maintain the moral boundaries of a community, when there appeared a dramatic increase in the volume of deviance it must be a consequence of some crisis in these moral boundaries. The community, through its institutions of social control, responds to this crisis by creating deviance. The definition of individuals as beyond the community's moral order functions to redraw or reestablish the threatened boundary. For instance, in his example of the Massachusetts Bay Colony, the withdrawal of the Colony's Charter by Charles II created a crisis in the meaning of collective existence for the Bay community, and the subsequent appearance of witches in Salem helped to reestablish the moral character of the Colony.

Erikson's boundary crisis theory, though, does not explain the particular features of political deviance that are of interest in this research.

CROSS-NATIONAL RATES OF WITCH-HUNTING

The boundary crisis hypothesis explains the appearance of deviance within only one society and has no theoretical implications for why some societies should experience more deviance than others. Erikson's concern was with differing rates within a society; that is, why the rate or volume of deviance should dramatically increase, creating what he termed a "crime wave." If we assume that the rates of political deviance vary across a sample of societies, and we are to use Erikson's boundary crisis hypothesis, must we also assume a similar variation in the rates of boundary crises? Or, are there different kinds of crises, such that some generate a larger volume of deviance than others? Or is there a range of boundary crises that a society can experience, such that those societies which have a larger volume of deviance are perhaps experiencing different kinds of crises than those societies which have a small volume of political deviance? Finally, are there characteristics of some societies which enable them to withstand a crisis and therefore not require the presence of deviance? All of these exist as theoretical possibilities within the present formulation of Erikson's theory, but there is no way of knowing which might be the case.

Further, when it appears that political crime is endemic in some societies, must we also assert constant boundary crises for these nations? China, for instance, has been constantly preoccupied with routing out counterrevolutionaries, reactionaries, capitalist roaders, rightists and ultra-leftists, but it seems highly implausible that for every new rectification campaign or other witch-hunting activity that there has to be a simultaneous crisis in moral boundaries. A boundary crisis seems a more plausible explanation for an occasional outbreak of deviance, such as the Salem witch trials, or the Cultural Revolution. The interest here, though, is with comparative rates of deviance. That is, with comparing whole national societies and being able to theoretically predict which ones should have the higher rates of political deviance. For the appearance of any particular witch-hunt, or any particular increase in the volume of deviance, the Erikson notion of a boundary crisis is a much more plausible theoretical position.

THE DISTRIBUTION OF DEVIANCE THROUGHOUT THE SOCIAL STRUCTURE

Erikson's formulation asserts that a large volume of deviance will appear; its distribution within a society's social structure is left unspecified. Political subversives are usually not discovered at large; they are embedded within certain institutional areas, like the government bureaucracy, educational institutions, or military facilities. Further, different nations seem to find different institutions infected with deviance. Some, such as the United States during the McCarthy period, discovered deviance primarily within political institutions such as the State Department. While others, like China during the Cultural Revolution, found "those taking the capitalist road" in virtually all aspects of social life. Whereas in the United States deviance was discovered principally within one institutional area, in China the discovery of subversive elements occurred in the army, the party bureaucracy, the government bureaucracy, on agricultural communes and within educational institutions.

A general formulation of political deviance should be capable of predicting the relative distribution of deviance throughout a nation's social structure. That is, in which societies should we expect deviance to be more extensively distributed throughout their institutional space, and in which societies should the discovery of deviance be limited to a few institutional areas? This is an important empirical aspect of political deviance for which there is no present explanation within the boundary crisis formulation.

Like Erikson, I assume that political deviance is not an inherent quality of either individuals or their actions, but a label conferred by the larger society. The authorized agents of the community, through the use of trials, accusations, investigations, purges and rectification campaigns, create subversive individuals by labeling them as such. I similarly assume along with Durkheim and Erikson that the function of creating political deviance is related to questions of social solidarity. But, I differ from Erikson by not attributing the appearance of witch-hunts to some kind of social crisis. *Instead of arguing that deviance acts to reestablish unstable moral bounds, I assert that political deviance dramatizes that which is permanent and enduring in group relations—the corporate nature of modern societies.*

The theory that will be developed here is based on two sets of ideas derived from Durkheim's *Elementary Forms of the Religious Life*: (a) that social rites performed to representations of the social collectivity act to periodically redefine the meaning of these symbolizations, and (b) that these representations can be infused into or immanent within the things and structure of everyday life.

THE RITUAL FUNCTION OF DEVIANCE IN CREATING AND MAINTAINING COLLECTIVE REPRESENTATIONS

Two lines of thinking have derived from Durkheim's analysis of religious ritual and religious myth and his analysis of the social functions of crime. Interestingly enough, although his work in religion and his work in crime both have a common concern with the function of ritual activity in creating and maintaining cultural material, whether collective representations as in the analysis of primitive religion or moral boundaries in the analysis of crime, there has been little contact between later students of Durkheim's sociology of religion and Durkheim's sociology of deviance.

Erikson's analysis of the community creation of crime clearly implies that the action taken by various institutions of social control, whether police, courts, the legal system, prisons, etc., is of a ritualistic character. That is, the concern is not with apprehending those individuals because of the danger they pose to the community, but rather, with apprehending them so that the particular moral boundary in question can be symbolically reaffirmed, making the action of social control institutions ritualistic in character.

What is interesting then, is to compare the analysis of ritual found in the *Elementary Forms* and the analysis of ritual that is found in the sociology of deviance as seen in Erikson's work. In the analysis of primitive religion, ritual was not a variable for Durkheim. All societies were thought to have some form of religious ritual and Durkheim did not propose that the amount of ritual would vary from society to society. In the analysis of deviance on the other hand, if we assume that the community creates deviance, and that the community creation of deviance is essentially a ritualistic activity, then the ritualistic activity of creating deviance becomes a variable. Erikson, for example, was concerned with those situations in which the community suddenly experienced a rapid increase in deviance. This was brought about by a rapid increase in the activity of social control institutions. Conceptualizing ritual as a variable, we now need to explain why some societies have more ritual than others. Erikson explained this variation in the amount of ritualistic activity as a response to some collective crisis in the community, some threat to the community's moral boundaries for which the apprehension of deviants acted to reestablish. My concern, though, is with rates of political deviance across societies, not with the sudden increase or decrease of a rate within any one society. The answer to explaining these differences among societies, therefore, does not lie in an-

alyzing the kinds of threat that could occur, but with the sociology of religion and particularly the analysis of the function religious ritual performs. It is there that ritual activity is a variable and it is there that the answer to the question of what role ritual plays in creating political deviance can be found.

SACRED-PROFANE AND DEVIANT-NORMAL: THE RITUAL SIGNIFICANCE OF CREATING POLITICAL DEVIANCE

As Durkheim noted in the *Elementary Forms*, there is a direct relationship between community rites and the collective representations to which they are performed. Rites, among other things, act to symbolically divide the world into that which is sacred and that which is profane. In doing this, community rituals periodically reaffirm the very sacredness of the symbolic objects in question. By defining that which is sacred or profane, its opposite is automatically defined. In Durkheim's classic analysis of religious rites, whether they be positive or negative rites, they organize the demeanor of individuals in the presence of sacred things. These rites act to create the sense of the sacred, for by defining that which is dirty or impure as opposed to that which is sacred, clean, or pure, this symbolic division acts to periodically reaffirm and redefine that which is sacred and that which is profane.

The community creation of political subversives, whether through trials, rectification campaigns, congressional investigations, or accusations by political authorities, is a ritual practice similar to traditional religious rites. The ritual function is the same. The community creation of political deviance performs the same symbolic classification that religious rites performed: *Instead of dividing things into sacred and profane, the community creation of deviance divides the world into that which is normal and that which is deviant.* The action of the community in creating political deviance performs the same function that religious rituals do in dividing the world into that which is sacred and that which is profane. The similarity between the symbolic classification of sacredness and profanity and that of deviance and normality is quite striking. For instance, just as the sacred is thought to originate from another world, so are deviants thought to exist outside the bounds of normal moral society. Similarly contact with sacred things is prohibited, and deviants, both through the label that is attached and more literally by placing them in prisons, jails, or hospitals, are kept from the more general society. The point is that these ritual separations, in creating sacredness or deviance, automatically create the other, profanity or normality. Political deviance may be considered in some sense either analogous to the profane or to the sacred. The distinction is irrelevant. What is important is that virtually all aspects of social life can be so categorized and ritually classified.

This ritual classification performs the same function in modern national societies that religious rites and their classifications perform for more traditional or primitive societies. Just as religious rites function to dramatize the presence of those collective representations of more traditional societies, so does the ritual creation of political deviance function to dramatize and create those collective representations of the modern nation state. *In effect, as the sacred requires profanity, so do ideas of what constitutes a country's national interest require the presence of elements that would oppose them.* Just as purity requires dirt for its very existence, so do political ideas of national interest require those that would undermine them to periodically dramatize their very meaning.[5]

THE MODERN NATION-STATE: ITS CORPORATE CAPACITY AND COLLECTIVE REPRESENTATIONS

Before continuing with our analysis of the creation of political deviance in the ritual reaffirmation of the central values or collective representations of the modern state, we need to make some assumptions about nation-states as corporate entities.

In line with Weber's (1946) notion of corporate groups, we will deal with the modern state in its distinctly corporate capacity. As political sociologists have noted (Bendix, 1968), the state is a unique institution of modern society, possessing its own set of interests and purposes independent of the interests of its constituent groups and individuals. The state, as Sutton (1959:1) observed, provides the "struc-

tures and symbols that permit the whole system to be represented over against its individual members and sub-groups, or outside groups and individuals." When we refer to the interest of the community or the creation of deviance by the community, we will be referring specifically to the apparatus of the state.

What we commonly refer to as government will be conceived of as representing the structural agency through which the corporate capacity of the state is realized. That is, government provides the apparatus for making collective decisions and taking collective action. This understanding of government as the agency for the modern political community is found in Swanson's (1971:611) discussion of the corporate capacity of all social collectivities where corporateness is contained "(a) in a legitimated procedure through which participants can undertake collective action, and (b) a legitimated sphere of action to which the procedures may apply—a sphere of jurisdiction."

Since Durkheim's seminal analysis in the *Elementary Forms* it has been understood in sociology that social collectivities present themselves to their members through a variety of symbolic material. As Durkheim noted, "the God of the clan, the totemic principle, can therefore be nothing else than the clan itself, personified and represented to the imagination under the visible form of the animal or vegetables which serves as totem."[6] It is interesting that although we have been aware of the notion of the great God: "the people," since the French Revolution, sociologists have not seriously approached the symbol, "the people," as a Durkheimian collective representation of the corporate nation-state. With the rise of the modern state there has simultaneously arisen the experience of "the people" or "the nation," "the masses" or "the Proletariat." All of these symbols are collective representations of the new form of ultimate social authority, the modern corporate state.

As with primitive beliefs, the spirit of "the people" is thought to intervene in the daily affairs of modern social life.[7] The spirit of "the people" watches over political institutions: "public opinion" causes political leaders to resign, as in the case of President Johnson; or "public opinion" is thought to force the Congress to pass civil rights legislation. In all these instances, whether it be bourgeois democratic, communist, or fascist states, there has arisen a sense of "the people" or "the public" which has been experienced as a great *force* in these societies. We traditionally have approached the notion of public opinion as members of modern nation-states, and hence have treated public opinion as a "real" force in our social environment and studied it through opinion polls. In modern national societies individuals describe a force, power, or mana, in their presence which they term public opinion. This is very similar to forces such as ancestor spirits which are experienced in more primitive societies. Just as ancestor spirits symbolize the corporate organization of a hunter-gatherer or traditional social systems, so does the power of public opinion symbolize the organization of the corporate nation-state.

The image of "the people" or of "public opinion" is not the only symbolization of the corporate nature of modern societies; flags, national anthems, and national holidays, also serve as collective representations. Similarly, ideas of national purposes or national security along with any one of a number of political ideologies can form part of the symbolic material through which the corporate state presents itself. As Durkheim noted, collective representation need not be found in material objects such as totems or even in the organic presence of "the people." Collective representations may also be embodied in systems of ideas, such as ideas of "American freedom," "Communism," or "socialist development." This is an important point for, as mentioned earlier, I want to view the community creation of deviance as a ritualistic mechanism for creating and maintaining that which is sacred in social life, and that which is sacred is also the collective representation of that society.

Hence, my theory is predicated upon the idea that the community creation of deviance is another way of creating and maintaining the unique set of collective representations which are a part of national societies.

SUBVERSIVE ELEMENTS AS RITUAL OPPOSITION

The key theoretical proposition of this study is that the modern nation-state manufactures subversives to create a ritual contrast with its set of collective representations. *The function of creating this symbolic contrast with images of collective political purposes is precisely to dramatize and reaffirm the very meaning of these images of the corporate political state.* Nation-states are no different from primitive societies in periodically renewing the central meaning of group life. Where community rites reaffirmed the meaning of the symbols of the tribe, they now reaffirm the symbolizations of the modern state.

What is central in this process is the creation of deviants who stand in opposition to the collective representations of the nation itself. As mentioned earlier, these collective representations can take different substantive forms. Subversives can be undermining the "people," the "nation," or a particular ideology. The creation of opposition to the nation and all that it stands for can be accomplished in a number of different ways.

Ideological Opposition. A nation can create ideological deviance by labeling individuals rightists, ultra-leftists, Trotskyites, Titoites, reactionaries or counterrevolutionaries as is done in Communist states. These deviants are, by definition, in opposition to the central ideology of their respective countries and this provides the necessary contrast with the nation's collective purposes. While most pronounced in socialist states, ideological opposition can be manufactured in other kinds of political systems.

Attacking or Undermining National Security. Deviance can also be defined in terms of individuals who are purportedly attacking or undermining the security of the nation. These include such political deviants as wreckers, saboteurs, traitors, or spies. By viewing ideas of what constitutes national security as a set of ideas which can function as a Durkheimian collective representation, the ritual creation of those who attack or subvert these interests provides a symbolic contrast with these images of the corporate state.

Loyalty to the Nation. Another way of creating the ritual opposition is the question of loyalty. Parsons (1955:218) in his analysis of McCarthyism observed that "readiness to make a commitment to a collective interest is a focus of what we ordinarily

mean by 'loyalty.' " The accusation of disloyalty by such agencies as the House on Un-American Activities dramatizes the very meaning of loyalty and hence the very meaning of the collective interest.

Personal Interests vs. Collective Interests. A final example involves the ritual distinction between personal or private interests and collective interests. This distinction, while similar to the question of loyalty, has been most dramatically found in China, particularly during the Cultural Revolution. The crimes of "economism" and the problem of being "red and expert" provide good examples.

Economism refers to the purported separation of economic issues from their larger political significance, and more specifically, giving primacy to the working of price mechanisms and material incentives. During a strike in Shanghai, for instance, workers who were seeking higher wages were told they had been "hoodwinked" into following the evil road of "economism" and were "pursuing only personal and short term interests" (Bridgham 1967:9). Accusations of economism by political authorities function to contrast the collective purposes of "building socialism" and "serving the people" with the personal interests of higher wages. The effect of this issue was to dramatize the meaning of such collective purposes as building socialism by the creation of its very opposite, "bourgeois-interest."

The problem of being Red and Expert provides another example of a ritual contrast which occurred during the Chinese Cultural Revolution. Such purposes as "national construction" require not merely the presence of technical skill, being an "expert," but also the proper ideological commitment, to hold the "ideology of collectivism" and to place one's skills "wholeheartedly at the service of the people." Those who are not "red" but merely "expert" do not offer themselves "to the people in socialist construction," but think instead in terms of "individual narrow interests" (Lee, 1966). Here the corporate purposes of "national construction" are ritually contrasted with their opposite—"individual narrow interests." These examples from China illustrate the myriad forms which this ritual classification can take. What they all share in common is the separation of collective purposes from anything which might oppose them. The most prominent mode of opposition has been the question of individual interests vs. the interests of the nation as a whole.

THE DISTRIBUTION OF POLITICAL DEVIANCE THROUGH THE SOCIAL STRUCTURE

The corporate state periodically renews itself by defining the presence of subversives who oppose its central values. These political deviants are not created at large within the society but are discovered within certain institutional areas. Not all nations find the same institutional areas infected, and the question remains why some societies find more institutional areas polluted with political subversives than others. We have argued that the creation of deviance is a ritual mechanism for renewing symbolizations of the corporate state. Now, if these symbolizations were infused into or immanent within certain institutional areas, we should expect the ritualistic discovery of deviance in just those areas. This process whereby images of collective purposes come to be distributed throughout everyday life is referred to in the sociology of religion as immanence.

POLITICAL IMMANENCE: THE INFUSION OF ULTIMATE PURPOSES INTO EVERYDAY LIFE

Swanson (1964; 1967) in his study of the religious belief of primitive societies and of the Protestant Reformation suggests that there is a direct relationship between the organization of a society as a corporate actor and the distribution of the symbols of that corporate capacity within the social structure of the community. What is referred to as immanence within the sociology of religion is the situation where the collective representations of the society come to be directly experienced as present within the things and structure of a society. As Swanson notes:

> The experience is that of the manner in which God— or other things people find of ultimate importance—

are believed to be present in the world of men, nature, and society. In some societies people discover that what they believe of highest value is itself incorporated, is immanent, in persons, organizations, or various objects in the natural world.[8]

For instance, in highly immanent societies, such as the Catholic countries studied by Swanson (1967), the church is considered the mystical body of Christ, and the eucharistic bread and wine, the body and blood of Christ. In Protestant countries, which have a low degree of immanence, ultimate values, such as notions of God, are not incorporated into the things and structure of everyday life. God exists in a transcendent fashion; his essence is not infused into either the organization of the Protestant church or into such material objects as the communion bread and wine.

Nation-states can also be categorized in terms of their degree of immanence. Collective representations, such as images of "the people" or "the masses" may exist in a transcendent fashion, much like the Protestant God, being all powerful and yet not incorporated into the world they supposedly created. The "American people" are understood to be the origins of our present institutions of government, continually guarding over them, and also the source of political virtue and justice. Although the "American people" remain a force of tremendous power they are not incorporated into those institutions of government they have created. The "people" or "public" as an organic entity is understood to exist independent of political institutions, and each is felt to possess its own set of purposes and goals. The public, or public opinion can, in effect, stand against agents of government; the public can oppose the President, the Congress or the Courts.

In socialist states the "people," "proletariat," or "masses" are similarly understood as the creators of political institutions and as the source of virtue and justice—in Mao's famous words, "The people, and the people alone, are the motive force in the making of world history." But the 'Proletarian will' is embodied within, or immanent within, the actions of the Communist party.[9] Here an organization can embody the collective purposes of the whole society. The actions of the party are also the actions of the "people," whereas in a less immanent society, such as the United States, a "public" and a government are each understood to be capable of independent action and each possesses separate purposes.

One of the more obvious indicators of immanence is the presence of charismatic leaders who embody the will of their people. Recent charismatic leaders, Castro, Nkrumah, Mao, Stalin, are all understood within their societies to, in some fashion, embody the collective purposes of their nation. This infusion of political purposes into political leaders has been commented on before, although not as an example of immanence. What is referred to as a politicized society in the literature of economic and political development is just such a situation. Collective purposes have been observed to be immanent within the political elite of modernizing nations, constituting a situation where "a leader's individual qualities become identified with the collective purposes of an entire nation" (Rustow, 1967). Similarly, Lipset's (1963) analysis of the United States as the "first new nation" referred to national leaders being considered in their society as the "symbol of the new nation, its hero who embodies in his person its values and aspirations." Apter (1963), in his discussion of political religion and new states, similarly speaks of how "many leaders are charismatic who represent the 'one.' They personify the monistic quality of the system." These societies where leaders are seen as embodying the larger collective purposes of their nation are usually described as being highly politicized. This, though, is but another way of saying they are highly immanent.

Because of the long association of the concept of charisma with Weber, it is not ordinarily seen as an instance of immanence. For Weber charisma was more a personal attribute of the leader that was derived from his performance of miraculous deeds: "above all, however, his divine mission must 'prove' itself . . . If he wants to be a prophet, he must perform miracles; if he wants to be a warlord, he must perform heroic deeds."[10] But a Durkheimian interpretation of charisma is also present in Weber's writings: "By its very nature, the existence of charismatic authority is specifically unstable. The holder may forgo his charisma; he may feel 'forsaken by his God,' as Jesus did on the cross; he may prove to his followers that 'virtue has gone out of him.' "[11] The notion of "virtue has gone out of him" is very

similar to ideas of immanence where larger purposes and meanings can reside in the things of this world, including individuals. Weber thought that charisma was essentially noninstitutional in character, as opposed to rational legal authority which derived from a set of bureaucratic rules, or patrimonial authority which derived from traditional customs.

We can, so to speak, turn Weber on his head by giving a Durkheimian interpretation to charisma. The specific quality of charismatic leaders, their larger than life image, is not derived from the kinds of acts they perform, or from the needs of their followers to create an imaginary supernatural hero. Rather, these properties are symbolizations of group structure and are, under certain conditions, found immanent within certain individuals, roles, or even organizations—as where the Communist Party is often felt to embody the purposes of the Soviet people. Charisma can derive from the character of society; it need not be solely an individual "personality" attribute as initially suggested by Weber. When the purposes and meanings of the larger social order become immanent we find charismatic leaders.

Other examples of immanence would include societies where moral incentives are understood to be replacing material ones, as in the "red and expert" issue within China. In this situation the performance of institutional roles is understood to be for the larger political purposes of "serving the nation" rather than the individual purposes of personal advancement or material incentives. Larger purposes can also infuse definitions of affect, a situation Inkeles (1968) refers to as the "nationalization of affect." Just as role performance is for a larger collective purpose of "building the nation," so can the meaning of love, hate, desire, or ambition be infused with political significance. Inkeles observes (1968:78):

> You don't have children for the pleasure they give you, but so that Hitler and Mussolini may have more workers and soldiers to effect the high purposes for which they were put on earth. Friendship is not for the gratification it gives, but because comrades may join in carrying out the greatest task of all.

Finally, and perhaps the most dramatic recent example of immanence, was the image of "the thought of Chairman Mao" which had become extensively infused into virtually all aspects of Chinese life (Bergesen, 1978). "Mao's thought" had provided new goals for universities, industrial organizations, and agricultural communes, and individuals possessed by "Mao's thought" had claimed super human efforts, whether learning to fly airplanes, performing medical operations, or playing Ping-Pong (Lifton 1968; Myrdal and Kessle, 1970; Urban, 1971).

THE REAFFIRMATION OF IMMANENT COLLECTIVE REPRESENTATIONS

It has been argued that for modern nation-states ideas of national purposes, national security, images of the people, the nation, or specific tenets of ideologies, such as "building socialism" or "building the nation," can be considered Durkheimian collective representations. These are the cultural objects whereby the presence of the larger social order is made known to individual members of modern states.

If these collective representations are immanent in or infused into the meaning of everyday life, then their periodic reaffirmation will entail the creation of their ritual opposition, subversive elements, in just the institutional areas in which they are embedded. This is the key theoretical assumption of this study. The creation of deviance is essentially a ritualistic activity and the function of that ritualistic activity is to reaffirm those symbols of corporate life, which in the case of nation-states are the variety of symbolic material ranging from images of people through specific tenets of political ideologies. When these symbols and images can be located within or infused into the structure of everyday life, as in pre-modern society Christ was immanent within the body of the church, then the Durkheimian reaffirmation of these symbolizations will involve the ritual discovery of deviance in different institutional areas. Since collective representations can be located within the structure of everyday life, their ritual reaffirmation will also surround the structures of everyday life. In more highly immanent societies there will be discovered a larger volume of deviance in more institutional sectors than in less immanent societies. This is the central empirical hypothesis of this study.

"Communists" are created within the state department to dramatize the political purposes contained within that structure; "enemies of the people" are discovered within industrial plants to dramatize that the purpose of productive activity is to "build socialism"; and "those taking the capitalist road" are found within the party, universities, military facilities, and on the smallest agricultural commune, to dramatize that the goal and purpose of these organizations is to "serve the people."

The question now is to explain the differential distribution of these collective purposes within different societies. The ritual creation of deviance is a means of reaffirmation of these symbolizations and if we can account for their differential distribution, we can thereby account for the differential distribution of deviance, allowing us to explain why societies like the United States discover political deviance within only a few institutions while other societies, such as China and the Soviet Union, discover deviance in many more institutional areas.

CORPORATE ORGANIZATION AND THE DISTRIBUTION OF POLITICAL DEVIANCE

Swanson (1971:621) has argued that the organization of a collectivity as a corporate actor is directly related to the extent to which collective purposes and symbols of that corporate reality will be immanent within the things and structure of that society. Specifically, he hypothesizes that:

> Corporate purposes and choices are more likely to be experienced as present and compelling in the acts of those societies in which the constitutional system— the collective apparatus for making authoritative choices—provided a legitimate role for corporate interests and traditions in the formulation of action, at the same time excluding the special interests and traditions of component groups and individuals in the society.

By considering government as the apparatus for making collective decisions for the corporate state, and categorizing nations in terms of their inclusion of the interests of the country as a whole into this apparatus, we can predict the extensiveness of immanence and hence the extensiveness of the ritually created deviance which functions to reaffirm these immanent collective purposes.

PARTY SYSTEMS: THE INCORPORATION OF GROUP INTERESTS INTO THE NATIONAL GOVERNMENT

Modern nation-states offer a particular advantage when it comes to classifying their constitutional systems, that is, their "collective apparatus for making authoritative choices." For in the very process of their development these societies had to face and resolve our central theoretical concern: to what extent should various constituent interests be given a formal role in the making of collective decisions. In effect, the very process termed "state formation and nation building" (Bendix, 1964; Rokkan, 1970) represents a movement toward constituting modern societies as corporate actors with the modern state representing the agency endowed with the authority to take legitimate collective action.

Most contemporary societies are constituted as nation-states, regardless of their level of social or economic development, and most nation-states organize their politics through some form of party system. Whether one thinks of the developing nations in Africa, Asia, or Latin America, the socialist states, Russia and China, the past fascist and Nazi polities, or the plural party systems of Anglo-America and Europe, the political party is, as LaPalombara and Weiner (1966) comment, "omnipresent." Students of political parties also seem to agree that one of the most important functions of parties is organizing the interests of the populace and representing them within governmental structures. The relationship between various constituent groups and political institutions is mediated by parties.[12]

In a sense, then, party systems are expressions of constitutional systems representing different ways of allowing constituent or corporate interests to penetrate the agency authorized for making collective decisions—the national government. . . .

RITUAL GOVERNMENT ACTIONS AND THE CREATION OF POLITICAL SUBVERSIVES

Political deviants are created by the social definitions and labels of deviancy the community can apply. Although it has traditionally been understood that deviant labels are applied by social-control institutions such as police, prisons, or hospitals, labels of deviance can also be generated and applied by institutions other than those formally chartered functions of social control. In line with Goffman's (1956) idea that the construction of social definitions can be accomplished by numerous ritual activities, we will include the actions of political authorities as the principal source of deviance labels.

As mentioned earlier, government authorities are formally constituted agents for the larger society, and in this capacity they act for that community in defining the meaning of political subversion. This social construction of deviance can be accomplished in at least three general fashions.

Ritual Accusations. The simplest mode of defining the presence of subversives, counterrevolutionaries, reactionaries, spies, or espionage rings is the mere statement that they exist. They would include Senator McCarthy's claim that there were "X" number of communists in the State Department, or the claim by Chinese political elites that "class enemies" have "sneaked into our ranks" and are "plotting capitalist restoration" and "infecting our minds with bourgeois ideas." In effect, any statement, speech, or press release offered by constituted political authorities to the effect that subversive elements exist, or that the nation is somehow endangered, constitutes a ritual mechanism for defining the presence of subversion.

Traditional Social Control Mechanisms. The definitional power of the community is greatly enhanced over mere accusations by the actions of formally constituted agencies of social control. Activities by police, courts, imprisonment, deportation, or the passage of new restrictions are all traditional control mechanisms that can be employed to define the presence of political subversives.

Community Ceremonies. Finally, the community can convene itself in the form of political trials and investigations, such as the Stalinist show trials and the McCarthy Army Hearings. These activities involve the most extensive use of ritual embellishment of all the mechanisms at the disposal of the state. Trials with their ritual confessions, self-criticisms, elaborate accusations, and extensive media coverage provide unsurpassed public drama. The employment of censorship campaigns or rectification campaigns, where the community makes extensive efforts to cleanse itself of subversive elements, is a further, large-scale, community effort which functions to ritually define the presence of deviants.

In short, the state possesses a great variety of ritual mechanisms for defining the presence of subversive activity and for labeling individuals as political deviants. All of these activities have, at one time or another, been employed to create the sense of internal danger or threats to national security.

A MODEL OF THE WITCH-HUNTING PROCESS

The theoretical argument that images of national purposes can be immanent within the things and structure of a community, and that political authorities create subversives in the very structures that are infused with political significance as a means of reaffirming these larger political purposes, can be represented in the causal model on pg. 60.

HYPOTHESES

From this model the following hypotheses can be derived:

(i) The greater the inclusion of corporate interests at the expense of constituent interests in the structure for making collective decisions (X_1), the greater the overall rate of witch-hunting (Y_1).

(ii) The greater the inclusion of corporate interests at the expense of constituent interests in the structure for making collective decisions (X_1), the greater the dispersion of witch-hunting (Y_2).

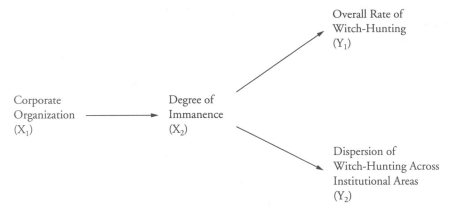

FIGURE 1

CONCLUSION

This formulation of political deviance suggests that the origins of deviance need not be considered solely as a response to some type of crisis. Political deviance has its origins in the very organization of collectivities as corporate actors. Similarly, deviance need no longer be viewed as functioning solely to repair problematical social boundaries. Deviance also serves to reaffirm that which is stable and enduring in social life—the corporate nature of all national societies. Finally, this theory allows for the comparative analysis of political witch-hunts, and as such provides an advancement over the previous piecemeal treatment they have been given. I have provided a general formulation that is not limited to the specific institutional properties of selected nations, but can be applied cross-nationally to a large sample of societies. This formulation also expands the understanding of witch-hunts from being previously considered as an institutional feature solely of totalitarian states to being a generalized social ritual employed by all societies to periodically reaffirm their corporate existence.

NOTES

1. See Turner (1969) or Silver (1969).
2. For a discussion of crimes during the Reign of Terror see Greer (1935) or Palmer (1941).
3. Particularly the chapter on Mechanical Solidarity (pp. 70–110) in Durkheim's *Division of Labor*.
4. Durkheim (1933:102)
5. See Douglas (1966) for a discussion of the ritual functions of pollution rules and ideas of dirt.
6. Durkheim (1965:236)
7. For a discussion of the spirits and gods of primitive societies see Guy E. Swanson, *The Birth of the Gods* (Ann Arbor: University of Michigan Press, 1964).
8. Swanson (1967:1)
9. For an interesting discussion of the infusion of ultimate political purposes into social structure see Benjamin Schwartz, "The Reign of Virtue: Some Broad Perspectives on Leader and Party in the Cultural Revolution." *The China Quarterly* 35(July–September 1968):1–17.
10. Weber (1946:249)
11. Weber (1946:249)
12. See Almond and Powell (1966). Kirkheimer (1966). Lipset (1960), Rokkan (1966).

BIBLIOGRAPHY

Almond, Gabriel and G. Bingham Powell. 1966. Comparative Politics: A Developmental Approach. Boston: Little, Brown.

Apter, David E. 1963. "Political Religion in the New Nations." In Clifford Geertz (ed.), Old Societies and New States. New York: The Free Press.

Bendix, Reinhard. 1964 Nation Building and Citizenship. New York: John Wiley.

———. 1968. State and Society: A Reader in Comparative Political Sociology. Boston: Little, Brown.

Bergesen, Albert. 1978. "A Durkheimian Theory of Political Witch-Hunts with the Chinese Cultural Revolution of 1966–1969 as an Example." Journal for the Scientific Study of Religion. 17 (March):19–29.

Bridgham, Philip. 1967. "Mao's 'Cultural Revolution': Origin and Development." The China Quarterly 29 (January–March):1–35.

Douglas, Mary. 1966. Purity and Danger. Harmondsworth: Penguin.

Durkheim, Emile. 1965. The Elementary Forms of the Religious Life. New York: The Free Press.

———. 1933. The Division of Labor in Society. G. Simpson, translator. New York: Macmillan.

Erikson, Kai T. 1966. Wayward Puritans: A Study in the Sociology of Deviance. New York: John Wiley.

Goffman, Erving. 1956. "The Nature of Deference and Demeanor." American Anthropologist 58 (June):473–502.

Greer, Donald. 1935. The Incidence of the Terror During the French Revolution. Cambridge: Harvard University Press.

Inkeles, Alex. 1968. Social Change in Soviet Russia. Cambridge: Harvard University Press.

Kirchheimer, Otto. 1966. "The Transformation of the Western European Party Systems." Pp. 177–200, in Joseph LaPalombara and Myron Weiner (eds.). Political Parties and Political Development. Princeton: Princeton University Press.

LaPalombara, Joseph and Myron Weiner (eds.). 1966. Political Parties and Political Development. Princeton: Princeton University Press.

Lee, Rensselaer W., III. 1966. "The Hsia Fang System: Marxism and Modernisation." The China Quarterly 26 (April–June):68–81.

Lifton, Robert Jay. 1968. Revolutionary Immortality. New York: Random House.

Lipset, S. M. 1960. "Party Systems and the Representation of Social Groups." European Journal of Sociology 1:50–85.

———. 1963. The First New Nation. New York: Basic Books.

Myrdal, Jan and Gun Kessle. 1970. China: The Revolution Continued. New York: Random House.

Palmer, Robert R. 1941. Twelve Who Ruled. Princeton: Princeton University Press.

Parsons, Talcott. 1955. "Social Strains in America." Pp. 209–238 in Daniel Bell (ed.), The Radical Right. Garden City: Anchor.

Rokkan, Stein. 1966. "Electoral Mobilization, Party Competition, and National Integration." Pp. 224–265 in LaPalombara and Weiner (eds.), Political Parties and Political Development. Princeton: Princeton University Press.

———. 1970. "Nation-Building, Cleavage Formation and the Structuring of Mass Politics," Pp. 72–144 in Stein Rokkan, Citizens, Elections and Parties. New York: David McKay.

Rustow, Dankwart, A. 1967. A World of Nations. Washington, D.C.: The Brooks Institution.

Schwartz, Benjamin. 1968. "The Reign of Virtue: Some Broad Perspectives on Leader and Party in the Cultural Revolution." The China Quarterly 35 (July–Sept.):1–17.

Silver, Alan. 1969. "Official Interpretations of Racial Riots" in Robert H. Connery (ed.), Urban Riots: Violence and Social Change. Proceedings of the Academy of Political Science 29 No. 1. New York.

Sutton, Francis X. 1959. "Representation and the Nature of Political Systems." Comparative Studies in Society and History 2:1–10.

Swanson, Guy E. 1964. The Birth of the Gods. Ann Arbor: University of Michigan Press.

———. 1967. Religion and Regime. Ann Arbor: University of Michigan Press.

———, 1971, "An Organizational Analysis of Collectivities." American Sociological Review 36 (August):607–623.

Turner, Ralph. 1969. "The Public Perception of Protest." American Sociological Review 34 (December):815–831.

Urban, George 1971. The Miracles of Chairman Mao. Los Angeles: Nash Publishing.

Weber, Max. 1946. The Theory of Economic and Social Organization. Glencoe: The Free Press.

The Function and Transformation
of Ritual Killing

WALTER BURKERT

Facts of publication: *Burkert, Walter. 1983. "The Function and Transformation of Ritual Killing," in* Homo Necans: The Anthropology of Ancient Greek Sacrificial Ritual and Myth, *35–48. Translated by Peter Bing. Berkeley: University of California Press. Copyright © 1983 by The Regents of the University of California. Reprinted with the permission of University of California Press.*

Walter Burkert believes that ritual sacrifice developed among ancient hunters. As males banded together for killing, sacrificial rituals performed in preparation for the hunt established primal social structures. Their collective aggression required social organization. In addition, humans experienced the sacredness of life in the act of killing. Killing nourished and gave power to those who caused death. Sacrifice is transformative, says Burkert. Through the experience of the sacrificial death men were made conscious of a new order, a new beginning. Thus, they reasoned, sacrifices appropriately accompany any creation, such as erecting a building. Taking an evolutionary perspective, Burkert considers the development of agriculture, asking what happened to the sacrificial killing of animals that was so common among earlier hunting societies. Though it underwent transformation, it survived in sacrificial acts performed during harvest celebrations. It also survived in secret societies in which initiates were ritually killed as sacrificial victims. Burkert finds in the rituals of ancient Greece all of the attributes of sacrificial ritual. He sees war and capital punishment in more contemporary societies as continuations of the sacrificial heritage.
Compare this view with the one articulated by Girard in this volume.

About the author: Dates: *1931– , Neuendettelsau, Bavaria, Germany*. **Education**: *Dr. Phil., University of Erlangen*. Habilitation, *University of Erlangen*. **Field(s)**: *classical philology; philosophy; anthropology of religion*. **Career**: *Professor of Classical Philology, 1966–1969, Technische Universität Berlin; 1969–present, University of Zürich; University of California, Berkeley, Sather Professor of Classical Literature, 1977*. **Publications**: Homo Necans: The Anthropology of Ancient Greek Sacrificial Ritual and Myth (*University of California, 1983 [German edition 1972]*); Greek Religion, Archaic and Classical (*Harvard University, 1985 [German edition 1977]*); Structure and History in Greek Mythology and Ritual (*University of California, 1979*); Ancient Mystery Cults (*Harvard University, 1987*); The Orientalizing Revolution: Near Eastern Influence on Greek Culture in the Early Archaic Age (*Harvard University, 1992*). **Additional**: *Foreign member, American Philosophical Society, American Academy of Arts and Sciences; member, Berlin-Brandenburgische Akademic der Wissenschaften; Balzan prize, 1990.*

Hunting behavior became established and, at the same time, transferable through ritualization. In this way it was preserved long after the time of the primitive hunter. This cannot be explained simply by the psychological mechanisms of imitation and imprinting; whereby customs are inherited. These rituals were indispensable because of the particular thing they accomplished. The only prehistoric and historic groups obviously able to assert themselves were those held together by the ritual power to kill. The earliest male societies banded together for collective killing in the hunt. Through solidarity and cooperative organization, and by establishing an inviolable order, the sacrificial ritual gave society its form.

As ethology has shown, a sense of community arises from collective aggression.[1] A smile can, of course, establish contact, and a crying child touches our hearts, but in all human societies "seriousness" takes precedence over friendliness and compassion. A community bound by oaths is united in the "sacred shiver" of awe and enthusiasm—the relic of an aggressive reflex that made the hairs bristle[2]—in a feeling of strength and readiness. This must then be released in an "act": the sacrificial ritual provides the occasion for killing and bloodshed. Whether in Israel, Greece, or Rome, no agreement, no contract, no alliance can be made without sacrifice. And, in the language of the oath, the object of aggression that is to be "struck" and "cut" becomes virtually identical with the covenant itself: *foedus ferire*, ὅρκια πιστὰ τέμνειν.[3] Families and guilds[4] organize themselves into sacrificial communities; so too cities at a festival, as well as gatherings of larger political groups. The inhabitants of the Peleponnesus, the "island of Pelops," meet at Pelops' grave for sacrifice at Olympia; the islanders celebrate in Delos; the Ionian cities slaughter a bull to Poseidon at Mykale.[5] In the time of Cicero, the cities of the Latin League still had the right "to demand their portion of meat"[6] from the sacrifice of a bull to Jupiter Latiaris. The Ionian League headed by Athens first met at Delos; later, Athens exacted a phallus for the procession at the Dionysia at Athens, and a cow for the Panathenaia.[7] It is in the sacrificial procession that the empire's power becomes manifest.

The closer the bond, the more gruesome the ritual. Those who swear an oath must touch the blood from the accompanying sacrifice and even step on the testicles of the castrated victim.[8] They must eat the meat of the victim as well, or at least the σπλάγχνα.[A,9] It was generally believed that conspiracies practiced human sacrifice and cannibalism.[10] And, in a secularized form among Athenian hetairiai, collective killing was an expression of loyalty.[11] Here, the *sacrilegium* normally contained in the *sacrum* no longer remains within the confines of ritual.

In a sacrifice the circle of participants is segregated from the outside world. Complicated social structures find expression in the diverse roles the participants assume in the course of the ritual, from the various "beginnings," through prayer, slaughter, skinning, and cutting up, to roasting and, above all, distributing the meat. There is a "lord of the sacrifice" who demonstrates his *vitae necisque potestas* (actually only a *necis potestas*, but it seems *e contrario* to include the power of life). And as for the rest, each participant has a set function and acts according to a precisely fixed order. The sacrificial community is thus a model of society as a whole, divided according to occupation and rank. Hence, the hierarchies manifested in the ceremony are given great social importance and are taken very seriously. An ancient epic, the *Thebaid*, relates that Oedipus cursed his sons because he was given the wrong piece of sacrificial meat.[12] Harmodios murdered Hipparchos, the Peisistratid, because his sister had been denied the honor of being a "basket carrier" in the Panathenaia.[13] And the Corinthians turned against the Corcyrans not least of all because "in their common festivals they would not allow them the customary privilege of founders and, at their sacrifices, they did not perform the rites of 'beginning' for a man of Corinth, as the other colonies did": this ultimately resulted in the Peloponnesian War.[14]

The sacrificial meal is particularly subject to sacred laws that regulate social interaction in distributing, giving, and taking. The very fact that eating became ceremonial clearly distinguishes human behavior from animal. Once the deadly knife has been used on the victim, intraspecific aggression must be set aside. This is accomplished through an eating inhibition evoked by rituals that excite anxiety and guilt. Since a hunting society must support women and children, abstinence becomes an excuse: we killed for the sake of others. Thus, there is often a rule that the killer, the sacrificer himself, must refrain from eating. And this is not so only in human-sacrifice;[15] Hermes, the cattle-killer, must also obey this rule, and similarly the Pinarii were excluded from the meal in the sacrifice at the Ara Maxima. Sometimes there is a rule that sacrificial meat must be sold at once;[16] in this way, the ritual inhibition becomes an economic factor. The tabu makes social interaction all the more intense.

The shock felt in the act of killing is answered later by consolidation; guilt is followed by reparation, destruction by reconstruction. Its simplest manifestation is in the custom of collecting bones,

A. σπλάγχνα: the collective term for the organs of the sacrificial animal. (Editor's note)

of raising the skull, the horns, or the antlers, thereby establishing an order whose power resides in its contrast to what went before. In the experience of killing one perceives the sacredness of life; it is nourished and perpetuated by death. This paradox is embodied, acted out, and generalized in the ritual. Whatever is to endure and be effective must pass through a sacrifice which opens and reseals the abyss of annihilation.

Building-sacrifices, for example, are for this reason widespread.[17] A house, a bridge or a dam will stay strong only if something lies slaughtered beneath it. One of the most detailed Latin descriptions of a sacrifice depicts the erection of a border-stone.[18] A sacrificial animal would be slaughtered in a pit and burned together with offerings of incense, fruits, honey, and wine. The stone was then placed on top of the remains while they were still hot. Thereafter, neighbors would return regularly on the anniversary of that sacrifice to repeat it. Similarly, altars and statues can be set up over a victim in the course of a ritual.[19] Any new creation, even the birth of music, requires ritual killing. Underlying the practical use of bone-flutes, turtle-shell lyres, and the tympanon covered with cowhide is the idea that the overwhelming power of music comes from a transformation and overcoming of death.[20] Thus, a slain man is easily made a hero or even a god, precisely because of his horrible end.[21] In any case, apotheosis is always preceded by death.

Sacrifice transforms us. By going through the irreversible "act" we reach a new plane. Whenever a new step is taken consciously and irrevocably, it is inevitably connected with sacrifice. Thus, when crossing frontiers or rivers, there are the διαβατήρια;[22] when opening an assembly, there are strange purifications;[23] when passing into a new age group or on entering an exclusive society, there will be sacrifice.[24] Before the sacrifice there is a period of abstinence, and if, after it, new barriers are erected as a sort of reparation, their limits can give new definition to life. If it is followed by a predetermined βίος, or lifestyle, the sacrifice becomes an initiation. Those who have undergone the unspeakable are both exonerated and consecrated, as expressed in the Greek word ὁσιωθίς.[25] Thus, the new lifestyle and the sacrifice at its inception are almost complementary: omophagy is followed by vegetarianism. Killing justifies and affirms life; it makes us conscious of the new order and brings it to power.

Following Rudolf Otto,[26] students of religion have used the following concepts to describe the experience of the Holy: terror, bliss, and recognition of an absolute authority, *mysterium tremendum, fascinans,* and *augustum.* The most thrilling and impressive combination of these elements occurs in sacrificial ritual: the shock of the deadly blow and flowing blood, the bodily and spiritual rapture of festive eating, the strict order surrounding the whole process—these are the *sacra* par excellence, τὰ ἱερά.[27] Above all, the young must confront the Holy again and again so that the ancestral tradition will become their own.

*   *   *

Although we can understand the persistence of sacrificial ritual through its social function, this by no means excludes change as an explanation. Ritual is a pattern of action redirected to serve for communication, and this means that the terms of expression are open to substitution, i.e., symbolization— this occurs even in the insect world, when a resourceful male offers his bride a white balloon or veil instead of an edible wedding gift.[28] Every communication is symbolic inasmuch as it does not use the real object it wants to communicate, but substitutes a sign that is familiar to and, hence, understood by the addressee. The object serving as sign is exchangeable. If the sender and the receiver are sufficiently familiar with one another, the complex of signs can be greatly reduced. On the other hand, when in competition with rival communications, the sign is exaggerated and heightened. Substitute signs thus used—whether consisting of natural or artificial objects, pictures, cries, or words—may be called *symbols* in a pregnant sense. They are not chosen arbitrarily, but are taken from a continuous tradition; they are neither independent nor self-evident, but bound to the system in which they function. Their richness of meaning coincides with the complex effects they produce in predetermined interactions.[29]

In ritual aggression, the ends and the means of aggression are exchangeable. Even mammals tear up tufts of grass or shred tree bark when performing the threatening rituals that both introduce and postpone a fight.[30] The triumphant cries of the greylag goose are directed toward a purely imaginary interloper. In human ritual, too, the aggressive gesture can become so important that its object is unessential. The wildest form of destruction, that of tearing an object to pieces ($\sigma\pi\alpha\rho\alpha\gamma\mu\acute{o}\varsigma$), can be carried out on an ivy plant,[31] and instead of a deadly club, a safe and flexible narthex stalk can be used.[32] Spiritual forces thus find release in a harmless game which heightens the sense of social ordering by means of dramatization.

Yet the theatrical character of the ritual may become so obvious here that it imperils its necessary function. In groups shaped by aggression, especially in the younger generation, forces that question the acceptance of tradition become active. Willfulness stands in the way of the impulse to imitate. Thus, along with its theatricality, human ritual must always have a strong underlying component of seriousness, and this means that time and again there is a regression from symbolism to reality. A non-instinctive ritual, transmitted by human beings, can fulfill its communicatory function only if it avails itself of a pragmatism that is unquestionably real.

In the hunting ritual, aggression between men was redirected toward an animal quarry which was thereby raised to the status of a personality, a blood-relation, even a father. It became the object of a "comedy of innocence," but because of the necessity of food, the hard underpinning of reality was never questioned. This all changed when mankind took its most important step, its mastery of the environment, in the Neolithic Revolution, the invention of agriculture, some 10,000 years ago.[33] Thereafter, hunting was basically dispensable. Characteristically, however, it was retained even in advanced cultures, as a ritual status symbol.[34] The pharaoh was celebrated as a hunter, as were his counterparts in Babylon and Nineveh; the Persian kings maintained animal parks for hunting, and Alexander followed in their footsteps. Of course, it was no longer a question of catching one's dinner, but purely a demonstration of the ruler's power to kill. Thus, the most prestigious quarry was the beast of prey. Through this emphasis the sport remained pragmatic and serious. Herakles, the bearer of the club, was more popular as a lion-killer than as the tamer of the bull.

We find a transitional phase documented at Çatal Hüyük.[35] The most important religious symbol in this farming town where goat and sheep had long been domesticated was a pair of horns from the wild bull, and wall paintings contain clear, thrilling depictions of the ritual hunt of a band of leopard men. We can even trace the gradual extinction of wild cattle in Çatal Hüyük, though not the critical step that followed: in place of the dwindling bands of wild animals, domestic ones were now used for sacrifice. The power of the traditional ritual to bind thus remained intact. The animal must, of course, now be removed from the everyday world; it must become sacred. Hence the adornment and the procession, and, sometimes, the animal being set free and recaptured. Hence, too, the many steps of "beginning," the incense and the music. In addition to the "action," which is no longer dangerous or even difficult, there are also words: prayers to the "stronger" powers and myths that tell of them. The reality of death and flowing blood is an unmitigated presence, perhaps all the more intense because the reaction is now inspired by a domestic animal, a familiar member of the household. The rapture attendant on eating game in the sacrificial meal is no less real now. Moreover, the domestic animal is a possession which must be given away;[36] thus, in addition to the old fundamental ambivalence of life and death in the sacrifice, there is now also renunciation and gratification. Even more than before, a sacred order is presumed and confirmed in this critical situation. In any case, with the integration of animal-sacrifice into agricultural society, a very stable socio-religious structure was established, which was to survive many thousands of years.

No less important was the expanded symbolism brought about by the newfound sources of food from farming—barley, wheat, the fruit of the vine—and added to the themes of ritual killing. The ritual pattern was so strong and inflexible that a festival meal without the preliminary horror of death would have been no festival at all. The farmer had to be just as reliable, enduring, and farsighted as the hunter. In particular, it was no mean task to overcome the inclination to eat the seed grain rather than throw it on the ground in the mere hope that something would grow. Here, too, the individual's desire for immediate profit could be controlled by the sacred tradition of the hunting ritual, which established the old order in a new context: renunciation and abstinence for the sake of long-range success, and with it a new order. Thus, the harvest is celebrated in a hunting festival and in sacrifice.[37] Gathering and storing at the sacred place now took on a new reality. Most importantly, the seed grain could not be touched as long as it was stored in sacred granaries, those mysterious, half-buried depositories of wealth.[38] At the same time, aggression had to look for new objects. Consequently, farming implements assumed the character of weapons. After all, a plow, a sickle, and a pestle were all used for chopping, cutting, and tearing apart. Cutting the wheat could thus become a symbolic substitute for castration; grinding the grain and pressing the wine could take the place of tearing up an animal in the hunt or sacrifice. Plowing and sowing could be seen as preliminary sacrificial renunciations.

We have already shown how, in hunting ritual, death gives way to a new order of life. In agriculture, the victory of life can be felt with even greater immediacy. The vine that has been pruned will bear all the more fruit; the grain that was buried in the earth sends up new shoots toward the light. The sacrificial ritual's power to bind is preserved on this level as well. Contracts are sealed with libations of wine (σπονδαί), and weddings are celebrated by cutting up cake or bread; cutting or breaking must still precede eating,[39] just as slaughtering precedes the eating of meat. The symbolism could easily become detached were it not for a counterforce guiding it back to the frightening reality. This occurs first of all in the myth, for the most gruesome tales of living creatures torn apart and of cannibalism are presented in conjunction with the achievements of civilized life. But the myth is not enough. Blood-sacrifice must be made at the harvest festival and at the preparations for it. Here the savagery beneath the seemingly civilized exterior is exorcised. In Greece, as far back as we can see, the victims were animal. But in the tropics, the very regions that had more favorable climates, the planters regressed to regular human sacrifice, to cultic cannibalism. Only in this way, it was said, could the seed grow and the fruit ripen.[40] Civilized life endures only by giving a ritual form to the brute force that still lurks in men.

Thus, aggression is once again directed toward human beings. Although the male societies that had been superimposed on the family structure lost their ostensible function when the hunt was abandoned, they were reestablished among planters as secret, or mask, societies.[41] At the center was a secret sacrifice, and if the aggression there did not suffice, it was worked out within the society itself. The contrast between the sexes was now played up—*Männerbund* versus female power—the more so because women now shouldered the main burden, supporting the family according to the new agricultural method. Likewise, the conflict between the generations became highly dramatized in the initiation rituals. Deprived of its hunting quarry, the secret society makes the initiand himself into a victim.[42] The group's aggression becomes focused on this man and he is forthwith killed—symbolically, of course; a sacrificial animal is substituted at the last minute. However, the bloodshed and the refined methods of torture are very real and guarantee the seriousness of the ritual. The gruesome "evil" at work in the ritual fulfills a function, i.e., to preserve a social structure over the course of generations. Once again, life rises up from the peril of death. Indeed, the individual experiences in himself how, after life had been endangered, there is a resurrection, a rebirth.

To some extent, this too was still a game, a show. With the progressive growth of consciousness, civilization came to demand absolute seriousness—one could no longer *pretend* to kill men. For this reason the death penalty became the strongest expression of governmental power,[43] and, as has often been shown, the criminal's execution at a public festival corresponded to a sacrificial ritual. In ancient times, the death penalty was not so much aimed at profane murderers as at those who entered an "untouchable" sacred precinct, went into a house of the mysteries unconsecrated, or laid a branch upon the wrong altar.[44] The tabu almost became an excuse to find a victim for releasing the sacred impulses of aggression.

There is another, far more serious, way to divert aggression toward the outside world: by integrating large groups of men in a common fighting spirit, i.e., war.[45] History, as far back as we can trace it, is the history of conquests and wars. Ever since Thucydides, historians have tried to understand the necessity of these events and, if possible, make them predictable. But it is precisely the irrational, compulsive character of this behavior mechanism that confronts us more clearly today than ever before.

War is ritual, a self-portrayal and self-affirmation of male society. Male society finds stability in confronting death, in defying it through a display of readiness to die, and in the ecstasy of survival. Such modes of behavior are so bound up with the governmental systems and values of our society that even today, when modern military technology has made war so distant that its absurdity is patent, when it is beginning to be the source of discord rather than of solidarity, still final emancipation from war lies far in the future.

For the ancient world, hunting, sacrifice, and war were symbolically interchangeable. The pharaoh and Herakles could be lord of the hunt, lord of the sacrifice, and warrior. On grave reliefs, Greek youths appear as hunters, warriors, or athletes. The emphasis may well have varied according to the social reality. A farmer, for instance, would put more weight on sacrificial ritual, whereas the nomadic animal breeder, wary of slaughtering his proud possessions, would become a conquering warrior.

Among the Greeks, a military expedition was prepared and ended by sacrificial ritual. There was sacrifice before setting off, then adornment and crowning with wreaths before battle—all as if it were a festival. A slaughtered victim introduced the subsequent deadly action which, in Homer, is simply called ἔργον. Afterward, a monument, a tropaion, was set up on the battlefield as a consecrated, enduring witness. This was followed by the solemn burial of the dead, a privilege the victor could not deny his defeated enemy. The burial, almost as important as the battle itself, was far more lasting in its consequences, for it left an enduring "monument." It almost seems as though the aim of war is to gather dead warriors, just as the Aztecs waged war in order to take prisoners to use as sacrificial victims.[46] The erected and consecrated monument is what endures, and it embodies the duty of the following generation. For war, necessary yet controlled because it is ritual, has this function above all: it must integrate the young into the patriotic community. The *senatus* resolves; the *inventus* must fight. As a rule, the Greeks' σπονδαί were for a period of thirty years at most. Each generation has the right and the obligation to have its war.

NOTES

1. Lorenz (1963) esp. 249–318 . . . Eibl-Eibesfeldt (1970) 145–48, 187–90 is somewhat reluctant; his example of the sudden effect of a smile in war (113–14) shows how shaky these other kinds of bonding are. A new theory of how human community is founded on aggression has been set out by Girard (1972); his model is not the hunting pack but the scapegoat complex (cf. Burkert [1979] 59–77) and Dionysiac σπαραγμός—a combination which is questionable. The practice of eating in sacrifice is not taken into account by him.
2. On the "sacred shiver" of awe see Lorenz (1963) 375–77.
3. As a formula, see *Il.* 3.73 and 19.191; *Od.* 24.483; R. Hirzel, *Der Eid* (1902); Stengel (1920) 136–38; Nilsson (1955) 139–42. On the Semitic "cutting" of a covenant see E. Bickermann, "Couper une alliance," *Archives d'Histoire du Droit Orientale* 5 (1950/51), 133–56. A special case of the encounter with death is passing through the severed halves of the sacrificial victim: see S. Eitrem, *Symb. Osl.* 25 (1947), 36–39; for the Hittites see O. Gurney, *RHR* 137 (1950), 5–25. On the sacrifice of the *fetiales* with the sacred *silex* see Latte (1960) 122–23; R. M. Ogilvie, *A Commentary on Livy* I (1965), 112; Burkert (1967) 287. Calling down a curse on oneself (Livy 1.24; Nilsson [1955] 139) does not explain the details of the ritual; the essential point is that the act, during which the one who swears raises himself above annihilation, is irrevocable. This can be shown, for instance, by sinking metal bars in the sea: Hdt. 1.165; Arist. *Ath. Pol.* 23.5. For this reason the σπονδή can take the place of blood sacrifice.
4. The phratries are constituted at the sacrifices of the μεῖον and κούρειον at the Apaturia: see Deubner (1932) 232–34. Amasis allowed the Greek merchants to construct "altars and sacred precincts for the gods" at Naukratis (Hdt., 1.178)—the permanent establishment of a trading company; cf. late Hellenistic Delos.
5. Hdt. 1.148; Strabo 8 p. 384; 14 p. 639; *Marm. Par., FGrHist* 239 A 27; G. Kleiner, P. Hommel, and W. Müller-Wiener, "Panionion und Melie," *Jdl Erg.-H.* 23 (1967); F. Sokolowski, *BCH* 94 (1970), 109–112.
6. Livy 32.1.9, 37.3.4; Cic. *Planc.* 23. Cf. Latte (1960) 144–46; A. Alföldi, *Early Rome and the Latins* (1965), 19–25.
7. Delos: Thuc. 1.96.2. For the phallus see *IG* II/III²673. βô[ν καί πανοπ]λ[ίαν ἀπάγεινὲς Παναϑ]ένια τὰ με[γάλα]ηαπάσας *IG* I²63 = R. Meiggs and D. Lewis, *A Selection of Greek Historical Inscriptions* (1969), #69, 55ff.; #46, 41; cf. IG I²10 = *SIG*³ 41; Schol. Aristoph. *Nub.* 386.
8. Stengel (1910) 78–85; *Hermes* 59 (1924), 311–21; στὰς ἐπὶ τῶν τομίων Demosth. 23.68, and cf. Dion. Hal. *Ant.* 7.50.1; Paus. 3.20.9, 4.15.8, 5.24.9. . . .
9. Thus Demaratos adjures his mother at the sacrifice: Hdt. 6.67, ἐσϑεὶς ἐς τὰς χεῖράς οἱ τῶν σπλάγχνων. Cf. Stengel (1920) 136, 14; Aristoph. *Lys.* 202 with Schol.; Antiphon 5.12; Aeschines 1.114; Isaeus 7.16; Lyk. *Leokr.* 20.
10. On the Catilinarians see Sall. *Cat.* 22; Plut. *Cic.* 10.4; Dio

Cass. 37.30.3. On the rebellious βουκόλοι in Egypt in A.D. 172 see Dio Cass. 71.4.1. The *Phoinikika*, a novel by Lollianos, contains a detailed description of such a gruesome sacrifice: A. Henrichs, *Die Phoinikika des Lollianos* (1972); cf. Henrichs, "Pagan Ritual and the Alleged Crimes of the Early Christians," in *Kyriakon, Festschr. J. Quasten* (1970), 18–35.

11. Thuc. 8. 73.3 'Υπέρβολον . . . ἀποκτείνουσιν, πίστιν διδόντες αὐτοῖς; cf. Plat. *Apol.* 32c on the request of the Thirty to Socrates, βουλόμενοι ὡς πλείστους ἀναπλῆσαι αἰτιῶν. The mutilation of the herms was a similar πίστις, Andoc. 1.67–and likewise a symbolic castration (Aristoph. *Lys.* 1094, Schol. Thuc. 6.27). Cf. also Diod. 1.21.2.

12. *Thebais* fr. 3 Kinkel/Allen—even the Grammarian who cited the passage (Schol. Soph. *OC* 1375) found this motivation utterly primitive, τελέως ἀγενῶς. Cf. the διμοιρία ἐν ταῖς θοίναις for the Spartan king, Xen. *Ages.* 5.1; the double portion for Hanna, Samuel's later mother, 1 Sam. 1:5.

13. Thuc. 6.56.

14. Thuc. 1.25.4 οὔτε Κορινθίῳ ἀνδρὶ προκαταρχόμενοι. The situation is explained by Andoc. 1.126: sacrificers bring the victim to the altar and ask the priest κατάρξασθαι.

15. For Mexico see E. Reuterskiöld, *Die Entstehung der Speisesakramente* (1912), 93; for cannibals see E. Volhard, *Der Kannibalismus* (1939), 443–44; for Persian youngsters, Strabo 15 p. 734, and cf. G. Devereux, *Mohave Ethnopsychiatry and Suicide* (1961), 42–43; J. P. Guépin, *The Tragic Paradox* (1968), 161–62. See *Hy. Merc.* 130–33; likewise at the Attic Buphonia, the βουτύπος, who flees and does not reappear, is excluded from the sacrificial meal. On the sacrifice at the Ara Maxima see Latte (1960) 213–21. On Pinarii see Cic. *Dom.* 134; Verg. *Aen.* 8.269–70 and Serv. on 269; Dion. Hal. *Ant.* 1.40; Diod. 4.21.2.; Macr. *Sat.* 3.6.14. On Egyptian customs see Hdt. 2.48.1.

16. *IG* I² 188 = *LS* 10 C 18, 21; *LSAM* 54, 1–3; Hdt. 2.39; Serv. *Aen.* 8.183 *de hoc bove immolato Herculi carnes carius vendebantur causa religionis, et inde alter redimebatur*—this is not just an expansion of Vergil's phrase *perpetui bovis* (Latte [1960] 217, 2) but, rather, evidence of a custom whose function it is simultaneously to insure exchange and continuity. The Manichaeans transfer the principle of exchange and assertions of innocence to all food, even vegetables: οὔτε σε ἐγὼ ἐθέρισα οὐδὲ ἥλεσα οὔτε ἔθλιψά σε οὔτε εἰς κλίβανον ἔβαλον, ἀλλὰ ἄλλος ἐποίησε ταῦτα καὶ ἤνεγκέ μοι. ἐγὼ ἀναιτίως ἔφαγον (Hegemon. *Acta Archel.* 10.6; cf. A. Henrichs and L. Koenen, *ZPE* 5 [1970], 146–54). E. Durkheim, *Les formes élémentaires de la vie religieuse* (1912), interpreted totemism as a system of reciprocal collaboration and supplementation.

17. Hock (1905) 75–83; Nilsson (1955) 404, 10; Müller-Karpe (1968) 336, 351, 361; K. Klusemann, *Das Bauopfer* (1919); cf. F. S. Krauss, *Volksglaube und religiöser Brauch der Südslaven* (1890), 158–64; B. Schmidt, *Das Volksleben der Neugriechen* (1871), 196–99. According to the *Enuma Eliš*, Ea kills his father Apsu and builds his temple upon him: *ANET* 61. However, animal sacrifice is rare, and human sacrifice unattested, for a building-sacrifice in the ancient Near East: see R. S. Ellis, *Foundation Deposits in Ancient Mesopotamia* (1968), 35–45.

18. Gromatici ed. Lachmann I 141: *lapides in solidam terram rectos conlocabant . . . unguento velaminibusque et coronis eos coronabant. in fossis . . . sacrificio facto hostiaque immolata atque incensa facibus ardentibus in fossa cooperta* (Lachmann; -i Cdd.) *sanguinem instillabant eoque tura et fruges iactabant, favos quoque et vinum . . . consumptisque igne omnibus dapibus super calentes reliquias lapides conlocabant.* On the festival see Ov. *Fast.* 2.639–78.

19. See the oracle ordering the construction of a statue of Apollo to ward off the plague: Kaibel, *Epigr.* 1034. K. Buresch, *Klaros* (1889), 81–86: a ram and a sheep are slaughtered in the sacrificial pit and burned; the fire is extinguished with wine and sea-water; the statue is then set up on the remains.

20. *Hy. Merc.* 38 ἥν δὲ θάνης τότε κεν μάλα καλόν ἀείδοις; Soph. *Ichn.* 281–93. On the νόμος πολυκέφαλος see Pind. *Pyth.* 12.4–24. The death of the lyre-player—not just Orpheus but Linos as well—was a favorite theme in Greek art (Brommer [1960], 84–85); cf. Aegisthus with the lyre on the Boston Oresteia-crater: E. Vermeule, *AJA* 70 (1966), 5, pl. 4.

21. Thus Agamemnon, when murdered, becomes an ἀνὴρ θεῖος: Aesch. *Ag.* 1547; and Rhesos becomes an ἀνθρωποδαίμων, Eur. *Rhes.* 962–73. Among the Hittites, "to become a god" is the normal expression for the death of the king: see Otten (1958) 119. The murder and deification of Caesar is historically the most significant example: see Burkert, *Historia* 11 (1962), 356–76; H. Gesche, *Die Vergottung Caesars* (1968), with A. Alföldi's review in *Phoenix* 24 (1970), 166–76.

22. *Il.* 11.726–30. For the special importance of these rituals for Spartans see Thuc. 5.54–55, 116; Pritchett (1979), 68–72. At the crossing of the Hellespont, Xerxes burned incense, poured libations, and sank valuable objects in the sea: Hdt. 7.54. Alexander made numerous sacrifices to the same end: Arr. *Anab.* 1.11.5–7.

23. Demosth. 54.39 τοὺς ὄρχεις τοὺς ἐκ τῶν χοιρίων, οἷς καθαίρουσι ὅταν εἰσιέναι μέλλωσιν. . . . Cf. Harp. καθάρσιον; Schol. Aeschines 1.23; Schol. Aristoph. *Eccl.* 128.

24. See n. 4, above.

25. Eur. fr. 472.12–15 τάς τ'ὠμοφάγους δαῖτας τελέσας μητρί τ'ὀρείῳ δᾷδας ἀνασχὼν καὶ κουρήτων βάκχος ἐκλήθην ὁσιωθείς; cf. Wilamowitz, *Berliner Klassikertexte* V/2 (1907), 77, 1 (reading μετὰ instead of καὶ). J. Bernays, *Theophrastos' Schrift über Frömmigkeit* (1866), 160, thought τελέσας corrupt. On ὅσιος see Harrison (1922) 504; M. van der Valk, *Mnemos.* III/10 (1942), 113–40; *REG* 64 (1951), 418; H. Jeanmaire, *REG* 58 (1945), 66–89. On the Delphic ὅσιοι who were consecrated through a sacrifice performed by a ὁσιωτήρ see II.5.n.47 below. There was presumably a similar contrast between the egg tabu (Plut. *Q. conv.* 635e) and ritual egg-swallowing among the Orphics (Mart. Cap. 2.140; P. Boyancé, *Mél. d'Arch.* 52 [1935], 112; Burkert [1968], 104n.25).

26. R. Otto, *Das Heilige* (1917; 1929¹⁷⁻²³); thereafter G. Mensching, *Wesen und Ursprung der Religion: Die grossen nichtchristlichen Religionen* (1954), 11–22.

27. See P. Weidkuhn, *Aggressivität Ritus Säkularisierung* (1965), 62: "Gipfelpunkt der Faszination . . . ist das Opfer seiner selbst. Gipfelpunkt des Tremendum . . . ist die Opferung des Nächsten."

28. Lorenz (1963) 99–101.

29. This is not far removed from the basic meaning of σύμβολον (on which see also W. Müri, "Symbolon," *Beil. z. Jahresbericht des Städt. Gymn. Bern* [1931]); the biological and traditional roots should not be lost sight of in the more sublimated use of the concept—see, for instance, P. Tillich, *Symbol und Wirklichkeit* (1962).

30. Morris (1967) 153–55.

31. Plut. *Q. Rom.* 291a αἱ γὰρ ἔνοχοι τοῖς βακχικοῖς πάθεσι γυναῖκες εὐθὺς ἐπὶ τὸνκιττὸν φέρονται καὶ σπαράττουσι δραττόμεναι ταῖς χερσίν.

32. On the mock combat of the ναρθηκοφόροι see Xen. *Cyrop.* 2.3.17; Ath. 631a. In myth, the thyrsos becomes a terrifying weapon: see Eur. *Bacch.* 762.

33. Earlier cultural historians thought that an era of nomadic shepherds formed an intermediate stage between hunters and farmers, but this has been made dubious by prehistoric finds, especially the discovery of Near Eastern Neolithic sites. Nomads seem, rather, to be offshoots of farming and city culture—see Müller-Karpe (1968) 20–21. Likewise, there is no archaeological support for the position—still held by some, and usually argued in connection with the theory of a matrilineal system (cf. P. W. Schmidt, *Das Mutterrecht* [1955])—that the cultivation of bulbous plants must have preceded grain-growing; cf. Müller-Karpe (1968) II.21–22, 249, and P. J. Ucko and G. W. Dimbleby, eds., *The Domestication and Exploitation of Plants and Animals* (1969). In this respect, the outlines of a universal history such as A. v. Rüstow's *Ortsbestimmung der Gegenwart* I (1951) and A. Weber's *Kulturgeschichte als Kultursoziologie* (1935; 1950²) have been rendered obsolete.

    G. Childe coined the term *Neolithic revolution* (*Man Makes Himself* [1936], ch. V), cf. S. Cole, *The Neolithic Revolution* (1959; 1963²). The term is, however, controversial: see R. Pittioni, *Propyläen-Weltgeschichte* I (1961), 229; Ucko and Dimbleby, *Domestication*.

34. For Egypt see E. Hornung, *Geschichte als Fest* (1960), 15–17; E. Otto, *JNES* 9 (1950), 164–77; *SB Heidelberg* (1958), 1, 20–21. For Assyria/Persia see B. Meissner, "Assyrische Jagden," *Der Alte Orient* 13 2 (1911). For the reliefs of Assurbanipal see *ANEP* 626; for the animal parks (παράδεισοι) see Xen. *Anab.* 1.2.7, *Hell.* 4.1.15; on the sarcophagus of Alexander, etc., see F. Orth, *RE* IX (1914) 558–604; J. Aymard, *Essai sur les chasses romaines* (1951); K. Schauenburg, *Jagddarstellungen in der griechischen Vasenmalerei* (1969); generally, cf. J. Ortega y Gasset, *Über die Jagd* (1956); W. Frevert, *Das jagdliche Brauchtum* (1969¹⁰).

35. Mellaart (1967) 268. On domestication see R. E. Zeuner in C. Singer, E. J. Holmyard, and A. R. Hall, *A History of Technology* I (1954), 327–52; F. E. Zeuner, *A History of Domesticated Animals* (1963), *Geschichte der Haustiere* (1967); Ucko and Dimbleby, *Domestication*. The oldest domestic animals are—apart from the special case of the dog—goats and sheep; shortly thereafter, the pig appears, followed in the seventh millennium by the cow. E. Hahn's thesis (*Die Haustiere* [1896], and cf. Ebert, *Reall. d. Vorgesch.* V 218) that the domestication of the cow occurred from the very start for sacral reasons, i.e., for sacrifice, has recently been resurrected: see E. Isaac, *Science* 137 (1962), 195–204; C. A. Reed in Ucko and Dimbleby, *Domestication*, 373. It remains an open question to what extent the ritual of human sacrifice had developed before animal-sacrifice. The evidence for ritual sacrifice of men in the Palaeolithic age is overwhelming.

36. In this way, ceremonies of bartering and buying developed. On Cos, the owner presents the sacrificial bull for Zeus Polieus "to the Coans," and Hestia, i.e., the coffers of the state, gets the proceeds of the sale; see *LGS* I 5 = *SIG*³ 1025 = *LS* 151 A 23–27. "Shepherds today in Crete will dedicate one of their animals to the village saint, selling it by auction on the Saint's Day to give the proceeds to the saint's church": S. G. Spanakis, *Crete, a Guide to Travel, History and Archeology*, Iraklion (n.d.) 291. Those who sacrifice a goat on the island of Leuke must deposit the buying price in the temple of Achilles: Arr. *Perip.* 22.

37. The researches of Wilhelm Mannhardt (*Roggenwolf und Roggenhund* [1865]; *Die Korndämonen* [1868]; *Wald- und Feldkulte* [1875/77]; thereafter *GB* VII/VIII), who developed the idea of the "Vegetationsdämon," are basic. The fact that it is precisely the "Vegetationsdämon" who is killed time and again in the ritual has been explained in various ways: the drowning is weather-magic for rain ([1875] 214, 417), the immolation is a purification (607–608), the burying is intended for sowing and germination (419–21), the whole process stimulates the annual cycle of the death and rebirth of vegetation. Indeed, in this case the rite cannot be derived from any attested or hypothetical mythology (1.3–4 above). The sacrificial rites are a given: no matter how great the hopes for increase and harvest are, the ritual can give form only to death and destruction.

38. For sacred circular structures functioning as granaries ever since Arpachija see Müller-Karpe (1968) 336. The myth of Trophonios and Agamedes (*Telegony*, p. 109 Allen; Charax, *FGrHist* 103 F 5; Egyptianized in the story of Rhampsinit's treasure house, Hdt. 2.121) deals with such a ϑησαυρός which can be opened only "secretly," accompanied by sacrifice. Cf. the underground ϑησαυρός at Messene: Plut. *Philop.* 19; Livy 39.50.3 (following Polybius).

39. Of course, apportioning presupposes a division, and it is precisely the latter act that is emphasized: taking/praying/breaking (I Cor. 11:24). Among the Hittites, breaking bread is one of the most common sacrificial ceremonies (*ANET* 345–51, 360–61); at an Attic wedding, the groom cuts (κόψαι) a sesame cake (Aristoph. *Pax* 869 with Schol. = Men. fr. 910) and divides it up (Men. *Sam.* 74, 125, 190; Phot. σήσαμον). . . .

40. Polynesian myths, especially the myth of Hainuwele from West-Ceram, about a being that was killed and out of which grew edible plants, "Dema," made a great impression: J. van Baal, *Dema: Description and Analysis of Marind Anim Culture* (1966); A. E. Jensen, *Hainuwele* (1939); *Das religiöse Weltbild einer frühen Kultur* (1948) = *Die getötete Gottheit. Weltbild einer frühen Kultur* (1966); C. G. Jung and K. Kerényi, *Einführung in das Wesen der Mythologie* (1941), 183–90. As applied to ancient myths and rituals, see A. Bre-

lich, "Quirinus," *SMSR* 31 (1960), 63–119, followed by I. Chirassi, *Elementi di culture precereali nei miti e riti Greci* (Rome, 1969). The notion that this represents a pre-agricultural stage has, however, been superseded through the excavations at Jericho and Jarmo. see n. 33 above.

41. H. Schurtz, *Altersklassen und Männerbunde* (1902); H. Webster, *Primitive Secret Societies* (1908); Höfler (1934); W. E. Peuckert, *Geheimkulte* (1961).

42. Aristoph. *Nub.* 257; Livy 10.38.9 *admovebatur altaribus magis ut victima quam ut sacri particeps* at the initiation into the *legio linteata* of the Samnites. On initiation rites generally see M. Eliade, *Birth and Rebirth* (1958).

43. On the ancient evidence see K. Latte, *RE* Suppl. VII 1599–1619; on its sacrificial character see Th. Mommsen, *Römisches Strafrecht* (1899), 900–904, 918; for an opposing view see Latte, *RE* Suppl. VII 1614–17; K. v. Amira, "Die germanischen Todesstrafen," *Abh. München* 31/3 (1922); L. Weiser-Aall, *ARW* 30 (1933), 209–27; Guépin (1968) 84. A traitor dies, according to the "law of Romulus," ὡς ϑῦμα τοῦ καταχϑονίον Διός, Dion. Hal. *Ant.* 2.10.3.

There are clear elements of a comedy of innocence in the "last meal" before an execution and in the expectation of goodwill; cf. also the executioner's mask. For the use of criminals in sacrificial ritual on Leukas, see Strabo 10 p. 452; on Rhodes (Kronia), Porph. *Abst.* 2.54; on Massalia, Petron. fr. 1 Buecheler; Schol. Stat. *Theb.* 10.793; on the Druids, Caes. *BGall.* 6.16.

44. . . . On Eleusis see Livy 31.14; . . . Kallias the Daduchos claimed that it was νόμος . . . πάτριος, ὅς ἄν ϑῇ ικετηρίαν μυστηρίοις, τεϑνάναι, Andoc, 1.110–16.

45. A "World History of War" such as L. Frobenius (1903) attempted could hardly be accomplished today. On the earliest evidence, that of Palaeolithic (?) drawings in Spain, see F. Cornelius, *Geistesgeschichte der Frühzeit* I (1960), 54, pl. 3. Today there are an enormous number of sociological and psychological studies on the problem of war: for instance, B. L. Richardson, *Arms and Insecurity: The Causes of War* (1960); G. Bouthoul, *Les guerres* (1951). K. R. Eissler, *Psyche* 22 (1968), 645, among others, stated that war is "the revenge of the elder generation on the younger." On Greece, see J. P. Vernant, ed., *Problèmes de la guerre en Grèce ancienne* (1968); on the distancing of modern historians from Thucydides see A. Momigliano, "Some Observations on the Causes of War in Ancient Historiography," in *Studies in Historiography* (1966), 112–26. On the cultic aspects see F. Schwenn, *ARW* 20 (1921), 299–322; 21 (1922), 58–71; 22 (1923/24) 224–44; and A. Brelich, *Guerre, agoni e culti nella Grecia arcaica* (1961). For the Hebrew term *to consecrate war* = to begin war, see W. R. Smith (1899) 122–23. On ceremonial war in Egypt and among the Aztecs see E. Hornung, *Geschichte als Fest* (1966).

46. On decoration see Hdt. 7.208–209; Plut. *Lac. inst.* 238 f.; on the σφάγια see Stengel (1910) 92–102, (1920) 132–33; Casabona (1966) 180–93; Pritchett (1979) 83–90; ἔργον

ll. 4.470, etc.; on burial see Thuc. 2.34. On human sacrifice among the Aztecs see Hornung, *Geschichte*, 43. For the metaphor of sacrifice applied to war see, for instance, Pind. fr. 78. On the Delphic oracle for king Philip see Parke and Wormell (1956) #266 = Diod. 16.91; Paus. 8.7.6.

ABBREVIATIONS

ANEP   *The Ancient Near East in Pictures Relating to the Old Testament,* ed. J. B. Pritchard. Princeton, 1954. Supplement 1968.

ANET   *Ancient Near Eastern Texts Relating to the Old Testament,* ed. J. B. Pritchard. Princeton, 1955.[2] Supplement (pp. 501–710), 1968.

ARW   *Archiv für Religionswissenschaft*

BCH   *Bulletin de Correspondance Hellénique*

FGrHist   F. Jacoby, *Die Fragmente der griechischen Historiker.* Berlin–Leiden, 1923–1958.

GB   J. G. Frazer, *The Golden Bough.* London, 1911–1936[3] (13 vols., cited by numerals as indicated in the Index, XII 147).

IG   *Inscriptiones Graecae*

JdI   *Jahrbuch der [kaiserlich] deutschen archäologischen Instituts*

JNES   *Journal of Near Eastern Studies*

LGS   I. v. Prott and L. Ziehen, *Leges Graecorum Sacrae e titulis collectae,* vols. I, II. Leipzig, 1896–1906.

LS   F. Sokolowski, *Lois sacrées des cités grecques.* Paris, 1969.

LSAM   F. Sokolowski, *Lois sacrées de l'Asie Mineure.* Paris, 1955.

RE   *Realencyclopädie der klassischen Altertumswissenschaft*

REG   *Revue des Etudes Grecques*

RHR   *Revue d'histoire des religions*

SIG[3]   *Sylloge Inscriptionum Graecarum,* ed. W. Dittenberger. Leipzig, 1915–1924.

SMSR   *Studi e materiali di storia delle religioni*

ZPE   *Zeitschrift für Papyrologie und Epigraphik*

BIBLIOGRAPHY

Brommer, F. (1956, 1960²) *Vasenlisten zur griechischen Heldensage*. Marburg.

Burkert, W. (1979) *Structure and History in Greek Mythology and Ritual*. Berkeley and Los Angeles.

Casabona, J. (1966) *Recherches sur le vocabulaire des sacrifices en Grec des origines à la fin de l'époque classique*. Aix-en-Provence.

Deubner, L. (1932) *Attische Feste*. Berlin.

Eibl-Eibesfeldt, I. (1970) *Liebe und Hass. Zur Naturgeschichte elementarer Verhaltensweisen*. München.

Girard, R. (1972) *La violence et le sacré*. Paris. (*Violence and the Sacred*, Baltimore, 1977).

Guépin, J. P. (1968) *The Tragic Paradox: Myth and Ritual in Greek Tragedy*. Amsterdam.

Harrison, J. E. (1922) *Prolegomena to the Study of Greek Religion*. Cambridge, (1903), 1922³ (reprint 1955).

Hock, G. (1905) *Griechische Weihegebräuche*. Diss. München.

Höfler, O. (1934) *Kultische Geheimbünde der Germanen*. I. Frankfurt.

Latte, K. (1960) *Römische Religionsgeschichte*. München. (Handbuch der Altertumswissenschaft).

Lorenz, K. (1963) *Das sogenannte Böse: Zur Naturgeschichte der Aggression*. Wien (1963), 1970.²⁵

Mannhardt, W. (1875) *Wald- und Feldkulte* I: *Der Baumkultus der Germanen und ihrer Nachbarstämme: Mythologische Untersuchungen*. Berlin, 1875 (1905² with minor amendments; reprint Darmstadt, 1963).

Mellaart, J. (1967) *Çatal Hüyük: Stadt aus der Steinzeit*. Bergisch Gladbach. (Çatal Hüyük: A Neolithic Town in Anatolia. London, 1967).

Morris, D. (1967) *The Naked Ape: A Zoologist's Study of the Human Animal*. New York.

Müller-Karpe, H. (1968) *Handbuch der Vorgeschichte*. II: *Jungsteinzeit*. München.

Nilsson, M. P. (1955) *Geschichte der griechischen Religion*. Vol. I. München, (1940), 1955² (-1967³ with supplements S. 848–70 and pl. 53) (Handbuch der Altertumswissenschaft).

Otten, H. (1958) *Hethitische Totenrituale*. Berlin, 1958.

Parke, H. W., and D. E. W. Wormell. (1956) *The Delphic Oracle*, vols. I, II. Oxford.

Pritchett, W. K. (1979) *The Greek State at War*. III: *Religion*. Berkeley and Los Angeles.

Stengel, P. (1910) *Opfergebräuche der Griechen*. Leipzig, 1910.

———. (1920) *Die griechischen Kultusaltertümer*. München, (1890), 1920³ (Handbuch der Klassischen Altertumswissenschaft).

Women's Stories, Women's Symbols: A Critique of Victor Turner's Theory of Liminality[1]

CAROLINE WALKER BYNUM

Facts of publication: *Bynum, Caroline Walker. 1984. "Women's Stories, Women's Symbols: A Critique of Victor Turner's Theory of Liminality," in* Anthropology and the Study of Religion, *105–125. Edited by Robert L. Moore and Frank E. Reynolds. Chicago: Center for the Scientific Study of Religion. Copyright © 1984 by Center for the Scientific Study of Religion. Reprinted with the permission of the publishers.*

No scholar has more fundamentally shaped contemporary ritual studies than Victor Turner. Many of the authors in this collection refer to him or are influenced by him. But, as is the case with all influential writers, Turner's views are not above question. Here Caroline Walker Bynum measures Turner's generalizations against the historical data of medieval European women's stories. She questions the adequacy of several of his most prominent ideas: dominant symbols, liminality, and social drama. These notions strongly inform his conception of ritual. Bynum argues that Turner's view assumes a position of looking at *women rather than* with *them. Consequently, she concludes that what Turner proffers as a social universal is really peculiar to men.*

For Bynum's critique of Clifford Geertz see her introduction to Gender and Religion: On the Complexity of Symbols, *8–11. Boston: Beacon, 1986.*

About the author: *Dates: 1941– , Atlanta, GA, U.S.A.* **Education**: *B.A., University of Michigan; M.A., Harvard University; Ph.D., Harvard University.* **Field(s)**: *medieval history; intellectual history; comparative religion; women's studies.* **Career**: *Assistant and Associate Professor, 1969–76, Harvard University; Associate and Full Professor, 1976–88, University of Washington; Professor, 1988–present, Columbia University; Morris and Alma Schapiro Professor of History, 1990–present; Associate Vice-President for Arts and Sciences, 1993–present.* **Publications**: *Docere Verbo et Exemplo: An Aspect of Twelfth-Century Spirituality (Scholars, 1979);* Jesus as Mother: Studies in the Spirituality of the High Middle Ages *(University of California, 1982); with Paula Richman and Stevan Harrell,* Gender and Religion: On the Complexity of Symbols *(Beacon, 1986);* Holy Feast and Holy Fast: The Religious Significance of Food to Medieval Women *(University of California, 1987);* Fragmentation and Redemption: Essays on Gender and the Human Body in Medieval Religion *(Zone Books, 1991);* The Resurrection of the Body in Western Christianity, 200–1336 *(Columbia University, 1994).* **Additional**: *MacArthur Fellow, 1986–91; Senior Scholar, Getty Center, 1987–88; Berkshire Prize winner for article "Women Mystics . . . ," 1985; Nelson Prize winner for article "The Body of Christ . . . ," 1987; Honorary Doctor of Humane Letters, University of Chicago, 1992; President of the American Catholic Historical Association, 1993; Elected Member, American Academy of Arts and Sciences, 1993. "During 1993–94, I gave my time to administration. In 1995, I spent time at the Wissenschaftskolleg in Berlin continuing my research on attitudes to the body in the Middle Ages. Having completed a study of the doctrine of the bodily resurrection, I shall explore the connections of this teaching with eucharistic doctrine, especially in the early Middle Ages."*

Having been asked to consider the usefulness of Victor Turner's "processual symbolic analysis" or "social drama approach" to my work as a historian of the religion of the western European Middle Ages, I should begin by saying what I do *not* intend to do.[2] First, I do not intend to address the general relationship of history and anthropology as academic disciplines or methods. Much has, of course, been written on this topic. Traditional historians are fond of the cliché that anthropology seeks to delineate general laws, history to describe particular events. But the more venturesome in both fields have sought a marriage of the two disciplines. The anthropologist Evans-Pritchard repeatedly argued that good history *is* good anthropology and vice versa, and dubbed eminent medieval historians such as Marc Bloch and F. W. Maitland the best of anthropologists.[3] The British historian Keith Thomas wrote recently that in the history departments of the 1980s the last vestiges of the innovations of the 60s may lie in the use of certain insights from cultural anthropology.[4] I cannot, on the basis of study of a single figure, launch a new theory of the relationship of the disciplines. But my sympathies have always lain with those in each camp who make use of the

other. And it seems clear to me that Victor Turner's own sense of what he is up to, taken very broadly, is appealing to any historian of religion. Turner's notion of the fundamental units of social reality as dramas builds temporality and change into all analysis;[5] Turner's sense of dominant symbols as multivocal requires that symbols and ritual be understood in their social context;[6] Turner's emphasis on the "orectic" (sensory) pole of meaning enables students of religion to talk of emotional, psychological and spiritual elements which psycho-history has tried, woefully unsuccessfully, I fear, to introduce into historical analysis.[7] Therefore, in concluding that certain of Turner's theories seriously misrepresent the complexity of religious experience, I shall *not* be suggesting that anthropology and history are incompatible. Rather I shall be arguing both that some of Turner's generalizations violate the subtlety of his own methodological commitments and that Turner's theory of religion is inadequate because it is based implicitly on the Christianity of a particular class, gender, and historical period.

Second, I do not intend to provide a critique of Turner's own application of his theory to the European Middle Ages, particularly in his well-known essays on Thomas Becket and Francis of Assisi.[8] It would be easy to show that, compared to the richness of Turner's analysis of Ndembu ritual, his sense of twelfth- and thirteenth-century symbols is thin. "Poverty" to Francis, the *imitatio Christi* or *via crucis* to Becket, become in Turner's own hands almost "signs" rather than "symbols"; they lose much of the multivocality they unquestionably have in their own historical context. For all Turner's effort to use a social drama analysis, his history of the Franciscan order sounds remarkably like the history of the institutionalization and, therefore, corruption of a dream which was the standard interpretation of Francis until recently;[9] his discussion of Becket does not advance much beyond the picture of radical conversion from one ideal to another which has always been seen as the crux of the matter—in legend and literature as well as in the work of historians.[10] It is not surprising that Turner uses Turner's model best when he knows the society under study most deeply. And indeed one is struck by the fact that even in his most recent writings, the Ndembu examples are the most powerful—the clearest, most precise, most analytical and cogent—whereas the modern examples are often tossed in without the care or the elaboration necessary to make the analysis convincing.[11] But for me to suggest simply that Turner could sometimes do a Turnerian analysis better than he does would contribute nothing to a study of Turner's model.

What I want to do, therefore, is to apply to my own research in the later Middle Ages Turner's notion of social drama as underlying both narrative and ritual. I want to focus especially on two aspects of Turner's notion of social drama, namely his understanding of "*dominant symbols*" (particularly as elaborated in *The Forest of Symbols* [1967]) and his notion of the central place in what he calls "liminality" of images of status reversal or status elevation (particularly as elaborated in *The Ritual Process* [1969] and in subsequent works).[12] I understand Turner to be arguing at his most general (and he is frequently quite general) that human experience, at least a great part of the time, occurs in units Turner calls "social dramas" (a subset of what he calls "processual units")—that is, that it takes a four-stage form: breach between social elements, crisis, adjustment or redress, and finally either reintegration of the group or person or "element" into the social structure or recognition of irreparable breach.[13] This social drama, to Turner, underlies both narrative—that is, the way we tell our important stories—and ritual—that is, the way we behave when we perform or enact certain formal, prescribed patterns that not only express but also move us into and elaborate our shared values. It is in the third stage that we find what Turner calls, borrowing the idea from van Gennep, "liminality"—a moment of suspension of normal rules and roles, a crossing of boundaries and violating of norms, which enables us to understand those norms, even (or perhaps especially) where they conflict, and move on either to incorporate or to reject them.[14] In the specific form of social drama called ritual, we find that rituals of life-crisis (i.e. change in life status, for example puberty or election as chief) often use images of inversion in the liminal stage (for example, the initiate becomes a "fool" or a "woman"); calendrical rituals (i.e. those that celebrate the recurring pattern of the year, for example harvest rituals) often use images of status elevation (for example, children wear masks of adults or of monsters at Halloween). Especially central in the liminal stage of ritual are what Turner calls "dominant symbols"—symbols which "condense" and "unify" into a moment disparate *significata* and bring together two poles of meaning: normative and emotional. A dominant symbol (for example, the Ndembu milk tree) can, therefore, only be understood in the context in which it is experienced. There it has meaning that includes as much the sensory, natural and physiological facts to which it refers (for example, milk, food, nurture, nursing, breasts, etc.) as the disparate social values for which it may stand (for example—in the case of the milk tree—both tribal custom and matriliny, on the one hand, and, on the other, conflict between mother and daughter, men and women).[15] From such fine and multitextured analysis of symbol and story, Turner sometimes moves on—quite a bit less successfully, I feel—to general cultural critique, calling for the liminoid (that is, the liminal-like) in modern life and cautiously praising *communitas*, his term for that feeling of union with one's fellow human beings which in pre-industrial societies was released in the liminal phase of ritual.[16]

There are some obvious problems with applying

Turner's writings to historical research, not least among them the fact that Turner does not have a complete and coherent theory to the extent that Geertz and Lévi-Strauss do. As I indicate above, all Turner's ideas involve in some way the insight that, in explaining human experience, one is explaining process or drama rather than structure, and that liminality or suspension of social and normative structures is a crucial moment in process. But the very fact that periods of liminality provide escape from roles and critiques of structures (in a functionalist sense of "structure") indicates that Turner has in certain ways never left the functionalist anthropology in which he was trained. And Turner himself, however quick he may have been to provide commentary on the modern world, has said repeatedly that for the industrialized world "liminality" is only a metaphor.[17] It is, therefore, not certain either how far Turner's insights fit together into a system or how many of Turner's own insights Turner himself thinks applicable to the European Middle Ages, a society between "primitive" and industrialized. I do not, however, want either to create a single "Turner theory" or to criticize such a theory by doing an exegesis of Turner. Others can do that better than I— among them Turner himself. Rather I want to apply what clearly *are* some of Turner's insights—his notion of narrative, his notion of dominant symbol, his notion of imagery of reversal and elevation—to my work on later medieval piety. Since Turner himself has extrapolated from analysis of ritual in "primitive" societies to more general theories about symbols and stories, I feel free to test his ideas against the religious texts which are the major source for historians of the Middle Ages. I want to show how certain of Turner's ideas, especially his sensitive and subtle notion of dominant symbols, enables me to describe aspects of European religiosity for which scholars have long needed terms. But I also want to argue that those places where Turner's notions fail to describe what I find in my research fit into a pattern and that that pattern suggests a fundamental limitation in the Turnerian idea of liminality, at least in the extended or metaphorical sense of the later Turner writings.

In evaluating Turner's social drama model and his theory of symbol, I want to concentrate on a major form of medieval narrative, the saint's life, and on a major Christian ritual or dominant symbol, the eucharist. I chose these initially because they seem to be the most obvious illustrations of Turner's ideas. Although many historians of religion and literature have pointed out that saints' lives as a genre are *not* chronologically or linearly arranged—the goal of the biographer being to depict the saint as static model—conversion *is* often the climax of the story which lies behind and generates the literary life.[18] And the eucharist is not only obviously a dominant symbol, condensing, unifying and polarizing meaning; it is also the central symbol in a clearly processual ritual, one which recapitulates what is certainly a social drama—the crucifixion—and one in which the moment of reception of sacred food was frequently accompanied by the extreme liminality of ecstasy or possession. Moreover, although the eucharist is not in any simple sense either a calendrical or a life-crisis ritual, the imagery of this liminal moment is obviously imagery of reversal: omnipotent God becomes dying man; the receiving Christian gains eternal life by eating and becoming the moment of death.[19] But when I have explored more closely the relationship of Turner's models to these medieval stories and symbols, a curious fact has emerged. (Turner's ideas describe the stories and symbols of men better than those of women.) Women's stories insofar as they can be discerned behind the tales told by male biographers are in fact less processual than men's; they don't have turning points. And when women recount their own lives, the themes are less climax, conversion, reintegration and triumph, the liminality of reversal or elevation, than continuity. Moreover, women's images and symbols—which, according to Turner's model, should reflect either inversion (for example, poverty) insofar as women are superior (for example, from the aristocracy) or elevation (for example, maleness, military prowess) insofar as women *qua* women are inferior—do not quite do either. They rather continue or enhance in image (for example, bride, sick person) what the woman's ordinary experience is, so that one either has to see the woman's religious stance as permanently liminal or as never quite becoming so.

These observations suggest to me that Turner's theory of religion may be based more than he is aware on the particular form of Christianity (with its strong emphasis on world denial and inversion of images) that has characterized elites in the western tradition—educated elites, aristocratic elites, and male elites. We will, however, understand this only if we use the category of gender very carefully. For my examination of Turner in no way implies that he fails to look at women either in his theory or in his fieldwork (where surely his analysis of women's rituals has been extensive and subtle).[20] In many places he suggests that women are liminal or that women, as marginals, generate *communitas*.[21] What I am suggesting is exactly that Turner looks *at* women; he stands with the dominant group (males) and sees women (both as symbol and as fact) as liminal to men. In this he is quite correct, of course, and the insight is a powerful one. But it is not the whole story. The historian or anthropologist needs to *stand with* women as well.[22] And when Turner attempts to stand with the inferior, he assumes symmetry—that is, he assumes that the inferior are exactly the reverse of the superior. If the superior in society generate images of lowliness in liminality, the inferior will generate images of power. To use Turner's own example, ghetto teen-agers in Chicago have first and second vice-presidents in their street gangs.[23] My research indicates that such things are very rare and that the images generated by the inferior are usually not reversals or elevations at all. Thus liminality itself—as fully elaborated by Turner—may be less a universal moment of meaning needed by human beings as they move through social dramas than an escape for those who bear the burdens and *reap* the benefits of a high place in the social structure. As recent liberation theologians have pointed out, it is the powerful who express imitation of Christ as (voluntary) poverty, (voluntary) nudity, and (voluntary) weakness. But the involuntary poor usually express their *imitatio Christi* not as wealth and exploitation but as struggle.[24]

Let me now turn to the later Middle Ages to illustrate the strengths and limitations of Turner's notion of liminality. First, then, the stories and symbols of men.

Male lives from the twelfth to the fifteenth centuries—both as lived and as told—may be nicely explicated as social dramas. As one would expect for religious *virtuosi*, charismatic figures, saints, the liminal phase usually issues in breach with previous role

and previous group—i.e., in conversion. Images of reversal and inversion are dominant in the converted life, particularly at moments of transition. If we take as an example one of the most famous of all medieval biographies, Bonaventure's life of Francis, we find that the story is not only told as a series of successful crises, breaches with former status and life, but that Francis, the wealthy merchant's son, adopts images not just of poverty but also of nudity, weakness and femaleness at key moments. At the two most decisive breaches of a life filled with crisis—i.e., when he renounces his earthly father and when he dies—Francis takes off all his clothes.[25] These two moments are each accompanied by adoption of disease and suffering (in the first case, dwelling among lepers; in the second, the union with the crucifix in stigmata).[26] And the moment of conversion is a moment of womanly fertility: Bonaventure tells us that Francis took off his clothes and his shoes, renounced his father, threw away his money, prayed to Mary, and like her gave birth to his first conceived child (his first disciple).[27] When the pope first rejects and later accepts Francis, Francis tells the story of a poor woman (by implication himself) who bears children of the Holy Spirit;[28] three women meet Francis and address him as "Lady Poverty";[29] Bonaventure suggests that ministers are fathers and preachers but Francis, who insisted on remaining layman rather than cleric, is a mother, laboring for her children by example—that is, by suffering birth pangs.[30] Francis is described as cradling all creation—from a rabbit to the baby Jesus—in his arms as a mother.[31] But Francis's renunciation of his earthly father is decisive; real change occurs. And, in Bonaventure's prose, the Francis who returns from being crucified in the stigmata is now a "knight," a captain of Christ's army, sealed (for all his lay status) by the seal of Christ the High Priest.[32] In death Francis is described as founder and leader, model and exemplar, and father of his friars.[33] The life is a drama. The story told of it is a drama. From the liminality of weakness, nudity and womanliness comes the leader and model who changes the religious life of the thirteenth century.

Not only are male lives social dramas; men themselves use images of reversal to express liminality. And chief among these images is woman—as fact and as symbol. As Simone Roisin has shown, recourse to and comfort by the Virgin is a more common theme in the visions of men than in those of women.[34] Men frequently describe not only themselves but even Christ and God as female and, as I have argued elsewhere, such descriptions are frequently part of their anxiety over administrative responsibilities. Abbots and novice masters in the throes of self-doubt about their leadership talk of themselves and their God as tender and maternal.[35] "Woman" was clearly outside medieval European notions of social structure, as Georges Duby repeatedly emphasizes in his study of the "three orders" of society;[36] and male writers clearly saw the image of the "female" (virgin, bride or mother) as an image for the male self when it escaped those three orders. In a very common metaphor, the monk Guerric of Igny wrote of the advancing soul as the "mother of Christ."[37] Bernard of Clairvaux not only elaborated the notion of the soul as bride and of the religious leader as mother but even suggested that monks, who fled the world, were women, whereas bishops, who led the world, were men.[38] To Bonaventure, not only the soul but also the illumined mind is bride, daughter, friend, sister and member of Christ.[39] Monks and friars, whose status as set-apart was what Turner calls institutionalized liminality, also spoke of themselves as "fools," "acrobats," and "children"—all images of reversal—and even in their clothing adopted the child's hood as a distinctive feature.[40] In a particularly vivid fourteenth-century example, Richard Rolle underlined his conversion and his rejection of family by fashioning hermit's clothing for himself out of two of his sister's dresses.[41]

To the well-known fact that men described themselves as women in moments or statuses of liminality, we can add the less commonly observed fact that men had recourse to actual women as liminal. Hildegard of Bingen, Birgitta of Sweden, Catherine of Siena and Joan of Arc are only the most obvious examples of women whose visions, attained while they were in a state of radical apartness (underlined by virginity or illness or low social status), were *for men* a means of escape from and reintegration into status and power.[42] Two important biographers of the early thirteenth century, Thomas of Cantimpré and Jacques de Vitry, created, through a number of lives, the image of the holy woman as critique of, re-

proach to, and solution for male pride, ambition and irreligiosity.[43] The biographers of two Franciscan tertiaries, Angela of Foligno and Margaret of Cortona, see these women as "mothers" who have only "sons"—i.e., the local friars for whom they provide healing, visions, advice, rebuke and comfort.[44] John Coakley in his study of fifteenth-century saints' lives points out that, in sharp contrast to male saints who often hold power and office in the world, all women saints from this period are known through the eyes of their male confessors and are depicted by these confessors as models of interiorized spirituality.[45] The woman is thus, to the man, a retreat from the world into inner, often mystical repose. What she says (and her rhetoric is sometimes strident) and what she is, is a criticism of male power and an alternative to it. Contact with her is, for the male, an escape from the world; after recourse to her he returns to that world girded with information and consolation.) The male biographers of Christina of Markyate in the twelfth century, Juliana of Cornillon in the thirteenth and Angela of Foligno in the fourteenth century stress explicitly that God chose to act through the weak vessel, the woman, as a condemnation of male religious failure, so that the last becomes first, the first last.[46] Victor Turner himself expresses this sense of woman as liminal for man in his recent work on pilgrimage when he refers repeatedly to the Virgin as expressing the affectional, emotional side of human character, holding up to society that escape from and evaluation of status and wealth which those who possess power apparently need in order to survive psychologically.[47]

Moreover, in the Middle Ages as today, men tended to assume that reversal was symmetrical. In other words, men writing about women assumed that women went through sharp crises and conversions and that their liminal moments were accompanied by gender reversal (in this case, of course, elevation). The twelfth-century biographer of Christina of Markyate tells a highly dramatic story of Christina escaping from marriage disguised as a man.[48] And from the patristic period (even more than from the later Middle Ages) there survive a host of stories of women disguising themselves as men in order to flee the world and join monasteries.[49] The lives of such early thirteenth-century saints as Margaret of Ypres or Mary of Oignies—although noticeably lacking in any images of gender reversal—are, as told by their male biographers, tales of high romance. Margaret avoided an earthly suitor by "marrying" Christ, and Mary, married young, more or less escaped marriage through extraordinary self-torture and starvation. It is only by reading between the lines that we realize that circumstances and social norms denied to Mary the mendicant poverty she really wanted as *imitatio Christi* or that Margaret sought in an unresolved pattern to become dependent on one male after another (uncle, lover, Dominican spiritual adviser, the other clergy of Ypres, finally Christ).[50] The stories are not exactly social dramas with crises, liminality, reintegration, although the male biographers shape them into the traditional medieval narrative form of situation, rupture, resolution.[51] Moreover, the male dress adopted in fact by such women as Joan of Arc, Margery Kempe, Dorothy of Montau and Christina of Markyate was less a religious symbol than a social mechanism. Joan of Arc wore it in order to be a warrior; Margery Kempe and Dorothy of Montau in order to go more safely on pilgrimage; Christina of Markyate in order to escape husband and family.[52] Although a powerful and sometimes threatening image to the *men* who encountered it, so much so that they perhaps saw female cross-dressing where none existed,[53] to women it was a means to change roles. In the later Middle Ages, it is male biographers who describe women as "virile" when they make religious progress. To men, women reverse images and "become men" in renouncing the world.[54] But medieval women do not describe themselves as men as a way of asserting either humility or spiritual prowess. Women either describe themselves as truly androgynous (that is, they use male and female images without a strong sense of a given set of personality characteristics going with the one or the other gender) or as female (bride, lover, mother). If we look at the relatively few women whose own writings survive, Gertrude of Helfta and the Flemish mystic Hadewijch are examples of the former; Mechtild of Magdeburg and Beatrice of Nazareth examples of the latter.[55]

The complex and powerful imagery in the writings by and about Catherine of Siena also illustrate this point. When Catherine's male biographer, Ray-mond of Capua, worried about the validity of her ecstatic experiences, he received from God a vision in which Catherine's face fused into or became a bearded male face, which Raymond understood to be Christ. Thus, the man needed the woman's visionary ability authenticated either by seeing her as male or by seeing a male Christ acting through her. But Raymond reported that God told Catherine herself that she need not adopt male disguise, as she had desired to do when she was a child; God, "who has created both sexes and all sorts of men," who can "create an angel as easily as an ant," would send her to preach and teach *as a woman* in order to shame immoral men. The woman in her own vision remains woman and the male dress once wished for (not, however, as image but as mechanism of actual role change) is not necessary.[56] In her *Dialogue*, Catherine's own images for herself are female; her Christ is androgynous—bridegroom but also mother.[57]

So, when we take our stand with male story tellers, whether their tales be of women or of men, we find social dramas everywhere, with liminal moments expressed in images of gender reversal. But when we stand with women and look at how their stories and their symbols really work, we find something different. The life of Beatrice of Ornacieux, for example, written by another Carthusian nun is an entirely static picture of extreme self-mortification and eucharistic frenzy.[58] There are dramatic elements certainly. At one moment Beatrice, locked in by her caretaker because she has made herself ill by extreme asceticism during Lent, passes through the locked door by putting a picture of the Virgin out through a little window.[59] But there is no conversion, no breach and reintegration. Beatrice's own self-image in her visions and her biographer's images for her are female. Like dozens of other thirteenth-century women, Beatrice repeatedly receives the Christ child at the eucharist and cradles him as a mother; her central images for her encounters with Christ in ecstasy are eating and illness or suffering.[60] To an astonishing extent, hers is a life in which "nothing happens," at least if we expect to find a social drama.

Moreover, if we turn to what is one of the most fascinating of all medieval texts, the autobiography of the English woman Margery Kempe, written in the early fifteenth century, we find constant change and excitement but no completed social drama. There are dozens of occasions on which, we might say, Margery strains desperately for liminality, strains for transition in status, for conversion, for escape from her normal role as "married woman" into the role, two hundred years old at least, of the *mulier sancta*. As the book opens, her depression about her failed business venture into brewing and her guilt about sex and food culminate in a vision in which Christ seems to substitute for her husband as her true lover, the eucharist to substitute for fleshly meat as her true food.[61] But the vision does not result in a conversion to chastity and abstinence. Margery must obey her husband, who, annoyed by her asceticism, says he will insist on the marriage debt unless she gives up her fasting. Margery then reports a conversation with Christ in which Christ says that she may give up the less important practice, fasting, in order to gain chastity. There is thus the amusing suggestion that Christ and Margery together have tricked the male, who has the power to grant to—and withhold from—the woman her own conversion.[62] Such manipulating and maneuvering then is the pattern of Margery's life. Wandering on pilgrimage, she must take her husband along or find another male protector; desiring weekly communion, she must get permission from her bishop and her confessor.[63] When Christ comes to tell her she is pregnant, he comforts her: "I love wives also, and especially those wives who would live chaste if they might."[64] And once her husband permits her to live in chastity (although for long years she cannot escape the responsibility of caring for him physically), Christ admonishes her: "Daughter, if thou knewest how many wives there are in this world that would love me and serve me right well and duly if they might be free from their husbands as thou art from thine, thou wouldst see that thou wert right much beholden unto me."[65] The message is almost: "be grateful for the little liminality permitted to you." In her own vivid prose, Margery sees herself as mother to the baby Jesus and bride to the human Christ, carrying such images to heights of literalism by actually feeling Jesus's toes in her hands in bed and weeping profusely at the sight of any male baby.[66] In her own eyes, Margery achieves spiritual growth not by reversing what she is but by being more fully

herself with Christ. It is not possible to see Margery's dominant symbols—virginity (which is also its opposite, sexuality) and eucharist (which is also its opposite, fasting)—as moving her through a crisis, redressing or consolidating a breach or a conflict of norms. This is because Margery, for all her fervor, her courage, her piety, her mystical gifts and her brilliant imagination, cannot write her own script.

Such constriction is what we find in women's stories generally, even when they are told by men. Juliana of Cornillon received a vision of the new liturgical feast of *Corpus Christi* and was ordered by Christ to have it established in the church. For twenty years she did nothing. She finally dared to approach a powerful male and, with his help, the observance made limited headway; but her further efforts to support monastic as well as liturgical reform led to her exile, and she wandered indecisively from religious house to religious house until her death. Dorothy of Montau, a fourteenth-century precurser of Margery Kempe, took her husband and her daughter along on pilgrimage. Although used by her confessor as propaganda for eucharistic devotion, she had to fight that same confessor in her lifetime for access to the eucharist and, when dying, was denied the final reception she craved. Even the life of Christina of Markyate, so skillfully organized by medieval narrative convention into a series of exciting crises, is, when one reads between the lines, a story of very *un*decisive change. Christina hangs from nails behind tapestries and leaps from windows to avoid her husband's advances; but it is years before she can legally escape the marriage and then only because her husband desires to marry someone else.[67] Umiltà of Faenza (or Florence) was able to adopt chastity only when doctors persuaded her husband that he must practice continence to preserve his health.[68] When Clare of Assisi's sister Agnes tried to flee her family, she was beaten half to death by her kinsmen; and the author of the nuns' book of Unterlinden tells a similar but even more gruesome story.[69] Although Clare herself did manage to renounce her noble family, shedding her jewels and her hair, she was never able to live the full mendicant life she so desired. Her story is a complex one, but it seems that, fleeing family and a possible husband only to accept the leadership of brother

Francis, she was led by Francis's rejection to accept enclosure, which she did not originally want. It was only two days before her death that her rule with its insistence on poverty was confirmed.[70] Indeed, in a recent quantitative study of saints' lives from 1000 to 1700, Weinstein and Bell have demonstrated that, in general, women's saintly vocations grew slowly through childhood and into adolescence; a disproportionate percentage of women saints were certain of their commitment to virginity before age seven. Despite the fact that both chastity and marital status were more central themes in women's lives than in men's, male saints were far more likely to undergo abrupt adolescent conversions, involving renunciation of wealth, power, marriage, and sexuality.[71]

The point I am making here is an obvious one. Women could not take off all their clothes and walk away from their fathers or husbands, as did Francis. Simple social facts meant that most women's dramas were incomplete. And there may be psychological reasons for women's images as well as social ones. Ramanujan, who has found a similar pattern in the lives of female Indian saints, has argued, using Nancy Chodorow's psychological research, that women are in general less likely to use images of gender reversal or to experience life-decisions as sharp ruptures because women, raised by women, mature into a continuous self whereas boys, also raised by women, *must* undergo one basic reversal (i.e., from wanting to "be" their mothers to acceptance of being fathers).[72]

If we turn from women's stories to women's symbols, we find that certain aspects of Turner's approach are extremely helpful. Although western Christianity had few women's rituals, certain key Christian rituals and symbols were especially important in women's spirituality in the later Middle Ages. One of these was the eucharist. And if one applies to late medieval eucharistic devotion Turner's notion of "dominant symbol," much that was before neglected or obscure becomes clear. Turner's idea of symbols as polysemic or multivocal, as including in some real sense the physiological and natural processes to which they refer as well as normative and social structural abstractions, provides a welcome escape from the way in which the eucharist and its related devotions have usually been treated by liturgists, historians of theology, and literary historians.

Such historians have frequently assumed that a devotion or an experience is "explained" once its literary ancestors or theological content are found: thus Dorothy of Montau's quite physical pregnancy (swelling) with Christ before receiving the eucharist is explained by the Biblical metaphor of the good soul as Christ's mother (Mark 3.35); Margery Kempe's cuddling with Christ in bed is simply a case of an uneducated woman's taking literally metaphors from the Song of Songs.[73] Turner's sense of ritual as process or drama moves us beyond this old-style history of theology or literature with its search for sources toward the new "history of spirituality"—where "spirituality" really means "lived religion"—which has been proposed recently by scholars like André Vauchez and Lester Little.[74]

When we turn to the eucharist in particular, Turner's notion of symbol as involving in some deep way a "likeness" between the orectic (the sensory) and the abstract or normative poles of meaning redirects our attention to the fact that the communion was *food*. People were eating God. The eucharist, albeit a recapitulation of Christ's execution, was not therefore a symbol of death but of life, birth, and nursing. As I have argued elsewhere, it stood for Christ's humanness and therefore for ours.[75] By eating it and, in that eating, fusing with Christ's hideous physical suffering, the Christian not so much *escaped* as *became* the human. By "saturating," as Turner puts it, the fact of eating, the eucharist itself summed up the asceticism (denial of the body, especially through fasting) and the antidualism (joy in creation and in physicality), which were part of medieval Catholicism. Not merely a mechanism of social control, a way of requiring yearly confession and therefore submission to the supervision of local clergy, the eucharist was itself both intensely feared and intensely desired. As symbol, it encapsulated two themes in late medieval devotion: an audacious sense of the closeness of the divine (Christians ate Jesus!) and a deep fear of the awfulness of God (if one ate without being worthy, one ate one's own destruction!). Moreover processual analysis helps us to see that the liturgy surrounding the eucharist was a drama. Thus we understand that when, in the thirteenth century, elevation of the host came to replace either conse-cration or reception of the elements as the climax of the ritual, the entire meaning was changed. God came to be taken in through the eyes rather than the mouth; he was thus taken in most fully where ec-static, out-of-the-body experiences added a deeper level of "seeing" to bodily seeing.[76]

But if Turner's notion of dominant symbol is useful in deepening any historian's understanding of this central Christian ritual, certain problems arise in seeing *women's* relationship to the eucharist in particular as processual. Turner's model would predict that, for women (excluded in theory from church office because of social and ontological in-feriority), the eucharist would express status eleva-tion.[77] To some extent, this is what we find. A not infrequent women's vision at the moment of re-ception of eucharist is the vision of self as priest.[78] Gertrude of Helfta, Angela of Foligno, and Lukardis of Oberweimar, among others, receive from Christ in the eucharist the power to preach, teach and criticize, to hear confessions and pro-nounce absolution, to administer the eucharist to others.[79] But the woman, released into another role in vision and image, never of course became a priest. And such visions, exactly as Turner's model would predict, serve as much to integrate the woman ec-static into basic Christian structures as to liberate her from them when they fail her. In some visions, recipient is elevated above celebrant, as when the host flies away from the corrupt priest into the mouth of the deserving nun or when Christ him-self brings the cup to a woman who has been for-bidden to receive it exactly because of her ecstatic possession.[80] But the very fact that the majority of visions which project women into power through reversed images in fact come in the context of the eucharist ultimately only integrates the woman more fully into clerically controlled structures. In order to have visions, she must attend the liturgy, controlled by exactly that clergy which her visions might seem to criticize.

There are thus elements of status elevation ritual in women's images. But the more thoroughly one explores women's experience the more unimportant images of reversal appear to be. Indeed, unlike teen-age gangs with second vice-presidents or Indian un-touchables who mimic high caste structures,[81] women's religious life in the later Middle Ages is strikingly without structure. The beguines, the only movement created by women for women before the modern period, were a puzzle to contemporary male chroniclers, who sought (as modern historians have continued to do) a specific founder for the move-ment and a specific legal status or rule or form of life characteristic of it.[82] But that which characterized the beguines (women who simply lived chastely and unostentatiously in their own houses or in groups, praying and working with their hands) was exactly *lack* of leaders, rules, detailed prescriptions for the routine of the day or for self-regulation, *lack* of any over-arching governmental structures. Moreover, many of the women saints of the later Middle Ages whose lives we know in detail cannot be located within any specific religious status. Although male orders fought to define themselves and each other in sometimes very uncharitable polemic,[83] women floated from institution to institution. Later claimed by the various orders as Premonstraten-sians, Cistercians, or Franciscans, a strikingly large number of the women saints of the thirteenth and fourteenth centuries cannot really be seen as affili-ated closely with any religious house or possessing any clear status. They were simply women in the world (in their fathers', uncles' or husbands' houses), being religious.[84] Historians have repeat-edly argued that women's failure to create or to join orders was owing to male oppression. In their dif-ferent ways, Grundmann, Greven, Southern, and Bolton all suggest that women were quasi-religious because male orders and supervisors would not take them on or because the church was not prepared to allow women to create their own structures.[85] It may be, however, that women's rather "structure-less" religion simply continued their ordinary lives (whose ultimate status they usually did not control), just as the economic activity of "holy women"— weaving, embroidery, care of the sick and small chil-dren—continued women's ordinary world. Recent research indicates that in some instances, women who could have chosen the more formal life of the convent chose the quasi-religious status instead. The loosely organized beguines were a desired alter-native.[86] In any case, if women's communities (convents or beguinages) were institutionalized liminality in Turner's sense, that liminality was imaged as continuity with, not as reversal of, the women's ordinary experience.

Of course, if one starts by assuming Turner's notion of "antistructure," one may describe this "structureless" aspect of woman's religious life by Turner's term *communitas*. But Turner's *communitas* is the antithesis to structure: the source for it, the release from it, the critique of it. What I am describing here is not something which "breaks into society through the interstices of structure" but something both simpler and more central: a normal aspect of women's lives.[87] If one looks *with* women rather than *at* women, women's lives are not liminal *to* women—but neither, except in a very partial way, are male roles or male experiences.[88]

Medieval women, like men, chose to speak of themselves as brides, mothers, and sisters of Christ. But to women this was an accepting and continuing of what they were; to men, it was reversal. Indeed all women's central images turn out to be continuities. Equally important, for women, in eucharist and in ecstasy, were images of eating and images of illness—and both eating and illness were fundamentally expressions of the woman's physicality. Told by the theological and exegetical tradition that they represented the material, the physical, the appetitive and lustful whereas men represented soul or mind, women elaborated images of self that underlined natural processes. And in these images, the woman's physical "humanness" was "saved," given meaning by joining with the human-divine Christ. Illness, self-induced or God-given, was identification with the crucifixion; eating was consuming and being consumed by the human body that was also God. We should not be misled by modern notions of illness or of brides as images of passivity. When the woman saw herself as bride or lover, the image was deeply active and fully sensual; when the woman sought illness as fact and as metaphor, it was a fully active fusing with the death agonies of Christ. Although each of these women's symbols is complex in ways I cannot elaborate here, none is in any obvious sense either elevation or reversal.[89]

Moreover, those women mystics like Margaret Porete (burned in 1310 for the "Free Spirit" heresy—i.e., antinomianism), who seem from the standpoint of the culture as a whole an extreme case of liminality or antistructure, are really not in their own context liminal at all.[90] It is true that Margaret (like Eckhart, whom Turner loves to cite) recommends by-passing all "works," all practices and disciplines, rules and formulae, to escape to an ultimate freedom, a sort of God beyond God.[91] But one questions whether, for women, such quietism and structurelessness (which in Margaret's case is intended to be permanent!) is a moment of oneness with humankind achieved as an escape from the weight of social structure and human responsibility. Is it not rather a reflection in image of the woman's own experience of the irrelevance of structure, of continuing striving without resolution, of going beyond only by becoming what one is most deeply?

My work on late medieval religiosity thus indicates that Turner's notion of liminality, in the expanded, "metaphorical" sense which he has used for nonprimitive societies, is applicable only to men. Only men's stories are full social dramas; only men's symbols are full reversals. Women are fully liminal only to men. I do not think the problem lies in the fact that later medieval Europe is a society which presented far greater variety of roles and possibility of choice than the society of the Ndembu, for which Turner first began to formulate his processual anthropology. If this were so, I would not find both his specific and his general insights so useful for understanding male stories. Bonaventure's view of Francis and Jacques de Vitry's view of Mary of Oignies seem well described and deeply penetrated when scrutinized through the lens of "liminality." The problem seems rather to be that the dichotomy of structure and chaos, from which liminality or *communitas* is a release, is a special issue for elites, for those who in a special sense *are* the structures. A model which focuses on this need for release as *the* ultimate sociopsychological need may best fit the experience of elites. Indeed in the western tradition, such a model may, however unwittingly, arise from a particular form of Christianity which has been that of the elites. The model of Jesus as poor, naked, defenseless, suffering, tender and womanly—which was particularly popular in the later Middle Ages—was an idea which especially appealed to the lower aristocracy and the new urban, merchant class.[92] As Herbert Grundmann pointed out many years ago, the Marxists were wrong to see medieval notions of the "poor of Christ" as the revolt of either the economically disadvantaged or of women; voluntary poverty *can* be a religious response *only* to those with some wealth to renounce.[93] But, as recent liberation theology reminds us, the "suffering servant" can be a more polysemic image than most Christians are aware. There are options beyond a claim to victory and kingship on the part of the oppressed, a release into poverty and suffering on the part of the advantaged.[94] To medieval women, at any rate, Christ on the cross was not victory or humility but "humanity." And in eating and loving that "humanness" one became more fully oneself. What women's images and stories expressed most fundamentally was neither reversal nor elevation but continuity.

I would object to any effort to make my description of women's images at a particular moment in the western tradition either universalist or prescriptive. A good deal of what seems to me irresponsible theologizing about women has been done recently, based on a superficial understanding of the history of Christianity; and certain claims about women's

need for female symbols or for affectivity or for the unstructured are among the most empty and ill-informed.[95] Indeed they may succumb to something of the same stereotype of "the female" that is built into Turner's notion of women as liminal *for men*. But my description of how actual women's stories and symbols function in the later Middle Ages does raise doubts about Turner's notion of liminality as universalist and prescriptive. Perhaps, after all, "social drama" and van Gennep's concept of liminality are less generalizable than Turner supposed and speak less fully to the complexity of human experience.

These doubts, however, throw us back exactly to the implications of the very best of the work of the early Victor Turner. Insofar as I am arguing that we must, at least some of the time, stand *with* those whom we study, Turner has already said it. If symbols are, in fact, multivocal, condensing and lived, we will understand them only when we look *with* as well as over and beyond the participants who use them, feeling as well as knowing their dramas in their own context. My critique of Turner's theory of liminality is thus one he might have given himself.

NOTES

1. Since I am writing here for an audience of non-medievalists, I have cited modern translations of medieval texts wherever possible. I have also tried to use examples that will be familiar, or at least accessible, to non-specialists through secondary literature. It is obviously not possible in an article of this sort to deal with the technical problems of recensions, authenticity, authorship, etc., associated with medieval texts. I would like to thank Peter Brown, Charles Keyes and Guenther Roth for arguing with me extensively about Victor Turner.

2. The term "processual symbolic analysis" was coined by Charles Keyes to describe the theory of symbol held by both Victor Turner and Clifford Geertz; see Keyes, "Notes on the Language of Processual Symbolic Analysis," unpublished paper, 1976. It has been adopted by Turner in *Process, Performance and Pilgrimage: A Study in Comparative Symbology*. New Delhi, 1979, pp. 143–154, which is reprinted in Victor and Edith Turner, *Image and Pilgrimage in Christian Culture: Anthropological Perspectives*, New York, 1978, pp. 243–255. A recent statement which scresses the centrality of social dramas in Turner's perspective is Victor Turner, "Social Dramas and Stories About Them," *On Narrative*, ed. W. J. T. Mitchell, Chicago, 1981, pp. 137–164.

3. E. E. Evans-Pritchard, *Essays in Social Anthropology*, London, 1962, pp. 13–65.

4. Keith Thomas, "The Ferment of Fashion," *Times Literary Supplement*, April 30, 1982, p. 479.

5. See, for example, *Dramas, Fields and Metaphors: Symbolic Action in Human Society*, Ithaca, 1974, pp. 33–34; *Image and Pilgrimage*, pp. 249–51; and "Social Dramas and Stories About Them."

6. See, for example, *The Forest of Symbols: Aspects of Ndembu Ritual*. Ithaca, 1967, chapters I and 2; *The Ritual Process: Structure and Anti-Structure*, Chicago, 1969, p. 41; and *Dramas, Fields*, pp. 50 and 55.

7. See *Forest*, chapters 1 and 2; and *Image and Pilgrimage*, pp. 245–49.

8. On Becket, see "Religious Paradigms and Political Action: Thomas Becket at the Council of Northampton," *Dramas, Fields*, pp. 60–97. On Francis, see "*Communitas*: Model and Process," *Ritual Process*, pp. 131–465 and passim.

9. New interpretations of Francis, not available to Turner, would make his ideal more complex than simply poverty. See, for example, E. Randolph Daniel, *The Franciscan Concept of Mission in the High Middle Ages*, Lexington, 1975; Barbara H. Rosenwein and Lester K. Little, "Social Meaning in the

Monastic and Mendicant Spiritualities," *Past and Present* 63 (1974), pp. 4–32; and Lester K. Little, *Religious Poverty and the Profit Economy in Medieval Europe*, Ithaca, 1978.

10. The novel aspect of Turner's analysis seems to me not his notion of the root paradigm of the cross or martyrdom or *imitatio Christi*, an understanding of which seems to have been implicit in all analyses of Becket, but the importance Turner places on Becket's incorporating the model into himself at the votive mass on October 13; see *Dramas, Fields*, pp. 84–85.

11. In "Social Dramas and Stories," Turner writes (p. 147): "I have found that among the Ndembu, for example, prolonged social dramas always revealed the related sets of oppositions that give Ndembu social structure its tensile character: matriliny versus virilocality; the ambitious individual versus the wider interlinking of matrilineal kin; the elementary family versus the uterine sibling group (children of one mother); the forwardness of youth versus the domineering elders; status-seeking versus responsibility; sorcerism (*wuloji*)—that is, hostile feelings, grudges, and intrigues—versus friendly respect and generosity toward others. In the Iranian crisis the divisions and coalitions of interests have become publicly visible, some of which are surprising and revelatory. Crisis constitutes many levels in all cultures." One is struck here by the lack of precision with which the modern analogy is used.

12. On dominant symbols, see also *Dramas, Fields* and *Image and Pilgrimage*, pp. 243–255. On status reversal or elevation, see especially "Humility and Hierarchy: the Liminality of Status Elevation and Reversal," *Ritual Process*, pp. 166–203.

13. For the four phases of social drama, see "Social Dramas and Stories," p. 145. The model of rites of passage from which Turner derives his notion of social drama has three phases: separation, margin or limen, and reaggregation (see *Image and Pilgrimage*, p. 249); and he frequently seems to assume three phases in social drama. See *Forest*, chapter 4.

14. See Arnold van Gennep, *The Rites of Passage*, 1908; reprint, London, 1960.

15. See *Forest*, chapters 2 and 3.

16. See especially *Process, Performance and Pilgrimage*.

17. For example, *Process, Performance, and Pilgrimage*, p. 23.

18. See Hippolyte Delehaye, *The Legends of the Saints: An Introduction to Hagiography*, tr. Crawford, London, 1907; Simone Roisin, *L'hagiographie cistercienne dans le diocese de Liege au XIIIe siècle*, Louvain, 1947; Charles Williams Jones, *Saints' Lives and Chronicles in Early England*, Ithaca, 1947; Baudoin de Gaiffler, "Hagiographie et historiographie: quelques aspects du problème," *La storiografia altomedievale*, Settimane di Studio del Centro italiano-de Studi sull'alto medioevo, 17, Spoleto, 1970, vol. 1, pp. 139–166.

19. On the eucharist generally, see Joseph A. Jungmann, *The Mass of the Roman Rite: Its Origins and Development*, tr. Brunner, 2 vols., New York, 1955: F. Baix and C. Lambot. *Le dévotion à L'eucharistie et le VIIe centenaire de la Féte-Dieu*, Namur, n.d.,; and n. 76 below.

20. See, for example, *Forest*, and *The Drums of Affliction: A Study of Religious Processes Among the Ndembu of Zambia*, Oxford, 1968.

21. For example, *Process, Performance and Pilgrimage*, pp. 104–105; *Ritual Process*, pp. 99–105.

22. I am aware that this is a very complicated issue, for it is difficult to sort out how a sub-group relates to the dominant culture; and we cannot *assume* that women will *not* agree with stereotypes of them generated by dominant males. The point is discussed well in Judith Shapiro, "Anthropology and the Study of Gender," *Soundings*, 64. 4 (1981), pp. 446–465. To "stand with" does not, of course, mean simply to take the view of informants. Turner himself discusses the problems with such an approach, which, he says, makes symbols merely "signs." See *Forest*, pp. 25–27, and "Symbolic Studies," *Annual Review of Anthropology* 4 (1975), pp. 145–161. What we see when we "stand with" a subculture will no more be simply what its members tell us than what we see when we stand with the dominant culture will be.

23. *Ritual Process*, pp. 192–193.

24. Gustave Gutiérrez, *A Theology of Liberation: History, Politics and Salvation*, tr. by Inda and Eagleson, Maryknoll, New York, 1973, especially chapter 3, pp. 287–306.

25. Bonaventure, The Life of St. Francis, in *Bonaventure: The Soul's Journey into God . . .*, tr. Cousins, New York, 1978, pp. 193–194 and 317. On Francis, see also n. 9 above. For many other examples of male lives characterized by crisis and abrupt conversion, see Donald Weinstein and Rudolph M. Bell, *Saints and Society: The Two Worlds of Western Christendom, 1000–1700*, Chicago, 1982, pp. 50–79 and 109–115.

26. Bonaventure, Life of Francis, pp. 195 and 303–307.

27. Ibid., pp. 199–200.

28. Ibid., pp. 204–206.

29. Ibid., p. 243.

30. Ibid., pp. 251–252.

31. Ibid., pp. 257 and 278.

32. Ibid., pp. 311–313.

33. Ibid., p. 321.

34. [Simone] Roisin, *L'hagiographie*, pp. 108, 111–113 and passim.

35. [Caroline Walker] Bynum, *Jesus as Mother: Studies in the Spirituality of the High Middle Ages*, Berkeley, 1982, pp. 110–169.

36. Georges Duby, *The Three Orders: Feudal Society Imagined*, tr. Goldhammer, Chicago, 1980, pp. 89, 95, 131–133, 145 and 209.

37. On Guerric, see *Jesus as Mother*, pp. 120–122 and passim.

38. Bernard of Clairvaux, sermon 12 on the Song of Songs, *The Works of Bernard of Clairvaux*, vol. 2: *On the Song of Songs*, vol. 1, tr. Walsh, Kalamazoo, 1976, pp. 77–85. And see *Jesus as Mother*, pp. 115–118 and 127–128.

39. Bonaventure, The Soul's Journey into God, in *Bonaventure . . .*, p. 93.

40. For Example, Bernard of Clairvaux, *The Letters of St. Bernard of Clairvaux*, tr. B. S. James, London, 1953, letter 90, p. 135. On clothing, see *RB: 1980: The Rule of St. Benedict*, ed. Timothy Fry, et al., Collegeville, Minnesota, 1981, pp. 261–263. In the modern world, of course, male religious clothing is a "reversed image" in another sense: monks and priests "wear skirts." On monasticism as institutionalized liminality, see *Ritual Process*, p. 107.

41. See the *Legenda* or Office of Rolle in Richard Rolle, *The Fire*

of Love or Melody of Love and The Mending of Life . . . translated by Richard Misyn, ed. and done into modern English by F. Cowper, London, 1914, p. xlvi.

42. For this argument see *Jesus as Mother,* pp. 257–262, and Bynum, "Women Mystics and Eucharistic Devotion in the Thirteenth Century," *Women's Studies,* 1984.

43. On Jacques and Thomas, see Ernest W. McDonnell, *The Beguines and Beghards in Medieval Culture with Special Emphasis on the Belgian Scene,* 1954, reprint, New York, 1969, pp. 20–40 and passim; and Brenda M. Bolton, "*Vitae Matrum*: A Further Aspect of the *Frauenfrage,*" in *Medieval Women,* ed. D. Baker, Studies in Church History: Subsidia I, Oxford, 1978, pp. 253–273.

44. *The Book of Divine Consolation of the Blessed Angela of Foligno,* tr. Steegmann, reprint, New York, 1966; the Life of Margaret of Cortona, *Acta sanctorum,* February, vol. 3, ed. Bollandus and Henschius, Paris and Rome, 1865, pp. 302–363.

45. "The Female Saint as Hagiographical Type in the Late Middle Ages," unpublished paper delivered at American Historical Association meeting, December, 1981. See also John Coakley, "The Representation of Sanctity in Late Medieval Hagiography: Evidence from *Lives* of Saints of the Dominican Order," Ph.D. dissertation, Harvard, 1980; and *Jesus as Mother,* chapter 5.

46. *The Life of Christina of Markyate,* tr. C. H. Talbot, Oxford, 1959; the Life of Juliana of Cornillon, *Acta sanctorum,* April, vol. 1, Paris and Rome, 1866, pp. 434–475; *The Book of Divine Consolation of Angela of Foligno.*

47. *Image and Pilgrimage,* pp. 161 and 236. See also *Process, Performance and Pilgrimage,* pp. 104–106; and *Ritual Process,* pp. 105, 183 and 200.

48. *The Life of Christina of Markyate.*

49. See John Anson, "The Female Transvestite in Early Monasticism," *Viator* 5 (1974), pp. 1–32. (See also Vern Bullough, "Transvestites in the Middle Ages," *American Journal of Sociology* 79 [1974], pp. 1381–1394.) Caesarius of Heisterbach tells a few such stories from the late twelfth century, but they are imitated from patristic examples: Caesarius of Heisterbach, *The Dialogue on Miracles,* tr. Scott and Bland, New York, 1929, vol. 1, pp. 51–59. One of the problems with the emphasis that Marina Warner places on Joan of Arc's transvestism in her recent book is her failure to give other late medieval examples of women cross-dressing: see Marina Warner, *Joan of Arc: The Image of Female Heroism,* New York, 1981. For two examples, see Michael Goodich, "Contours of Female Piety in Later Medieval Hagiography," *Church History* 50 (1981), p. 25. Delehaye, *The Legends of the Saints,* pp. 197–206, traces many of the later stories back to a single prototype.

50. The Life of Margaret of Ypres in appendix to G. Meersseman, "Les frères prêcheurs et le mouvement dévot en Flandre au XIIIe siècle," *Archivum Fratrum Praedicatorum* 18 (1948), pp. 106–130; the Life of Mary of Oignies by Jacques de Vitry, *Acta sanctorum,* June, vol. 5, Paris and Rome, 1867, pp. 547–572. On Mary's inability to adopt complete mendicant poverty, see Bolton, "*Vitae Matrum,*" pp. 257–59. For another parallel story, see Thomas of Cantimpré's Life of Lutgard of Aywières or of St. Trond, *Acta sanctorum,* June, vol. 4, Paris and Rome, 1867, pp. 189–210.

51. On medieval narrative technique see William J. Brandt, *The Shape of Medieval History: Studies in Modes of Perception,* New Haven, 1966.

52. On Joan, see Warner, *Joan of Arc.* On Dorothy of Montau (or of Prussia), see Stephen P. Bensch, "A Cult of the Maternal: Dorothea of Prussia (1347–94)," unpublished paper; Richard Kieckhefer, "Dorothy of Montau: Housewife and Mystic," unpublished paper; and Ute Stargardt, "The Influence of Dorothea von Montau on the Mysticism of Margery Kempe," Ph.D. dissertation, The University of Tennessee, 1981. Margery's life is available in a modern English translation: *The Book of Margery Kempe,* tr. W. Butler-Bowdon, New York, 1944. On Christina, see *The Life of Christina of Markyate,* and Christopher J. Holdsworth, "Christina of Markyate," *Medieval Women,* pp. 185–204.

53. Anson, "Female Transvestite," argues convincingly that these stories, like the later legend of Pope Joan, were the result of psychological projection. One of the major charges against Joan of Arc, who was accused of heresy (with overtones of witchcraft as well), was cross-dressing; see Warner, *Joan of Arc.*

54. See, for example, the biographies of Christina of Markyate and Juliana of Cornillon cited above.

55. Gertrude of Helfta, *Oeuvres spirituelles,* vols. 1–3, Sources chrétiennes, Série des textes monastiques d'Occident, Paris, 1967–68; *Hadewijch: The Complete Works,* tr. Hart, Paulist Press, New York, 1980; Mechtild of Magdeburg, *The Revelations . . . or the Flowing Light of the Godhead,* tr. Menzies, London, 1953; Beatrice of Nazareth (or Tienen), *Vita Beatricis: De Autobiografie van de Z. Beatrijs van Tienen O. Cist. 1200–1268,* Antwerp, 1964. On Gertrude and Mechtild of Magdeburg, see *Jesus as Mother,* chapter 5. Hadewijch, who uses intensely erotic language to describe her relationship to God, frequently casts herself in the role of a knight seeking his lady. On androgynous imagery in women's visions, see Elizabeth Petroff, *Consolation of the Blessed,* Alta Gaia Society, New York, 1979, pp. 66–78.

56. Raymond of Capua, Life of Catherine of Siena, *Acta sanctorum,* April, vol. 3, Paris and Rome, 1866, pp. 892 and 884. I have been unable to consult the English tr. by George Lamb, *The Life of St. Catherine of Siena,* London, 1960.

57. Catherine of Siena, *The Dialogue,* tr. Suzanne Noffke, Paulist Press, New York, 1980.

58. Marguerite of Oingt, Life of Beatrice of Ornacieux, *Les oeuvres de Marguerite d'Oingt,* ed. Duraffour, Gardette and Durdilly, Paris, 1965, pp. 104–137.

59. Ibid., pp. 136–137.

60. Ibid., p. 105 (she pierces her hands with nails to achieve stigmata); p. 117 (she sees Christ as a little child at every elevation of the host); p. 122 (the host swells in her mouth until she almost chokes, and after this she can eat no earthly food). For other lives of women by women, one can consult the several nuns' books from the early fourteenth century.

61. *The Book of Margery Kempe,* p. 10. It is interesting that the anchorite who advises her here describes Christ as mother and tells her to suck his breast; but Margery herself never uses reversed imagery. Her Christ is always male and she is always female; see, for example, pp. 22–23 and 76–77.

62. Ibid., p. 17.

63. On her need for male protection, see ibid., pp. 25, 28, 32, 98–100. Margery was quite bold about opposing authority figures. This may have been owing in part to her father's status (see Anthony Goodman, "The Piety of John Brunham's Daughter, of Lynn," *Medieval Women*, pp. 347–358), although to say this is not to detract from Margery's personal courage and insouciance.

64. Ibid., p. 39.

65. Ibid., p. 192.

66. Ibid., pp. 76 and 190; ibid., pp. 74–75 and 81.

67. For the texts discussed here see nn. 46 and 52 above, I should emphasize that later medieval women's lives include peasants as well as aristocrats, lay women as well as nuns and quasi-religious.

68. See Petroff, *Consolation of the Blessed*, p. 123; for other examples of circumstances constraining women's decisions, see ibid., p. 42. Weinstein and Bell, *Saints and Society*, pp. 88–97, give a number of examples of saintly women who are unable to determine their marital status and therefore the course of their lives.

69. *The Legend and Writings of Saint Clare of Assisi* (based on German work by E. Grau), St. Bonaventure, New York, 1953, pp. 35–37; Jeanne Ancelet-Hustache, ed., "Les *Vitae Sororum* d'Unterlinden: édition critique . . .," *Archives d'histoire doctrinale et littéraire du moyen âge* 5 (1930), pp. 374–375.

70. See *Legend of Saint Clare* and Rosalind B. Brooke and Christopher N. L. Brooke, "St. Clare," *Medieval Women*, pp. 275–287. For other women's lives in translation, see Petroff, *Consolation of the Blessed*.

71. Weinstein and Bell, *Saints and Society*, part I, especially pp. 34, 48, 71, 97, 108, 121 and 135.

72. A. K. Ramanujan, "On Women Saints," in *The Divine Consort: Rādhā and the Goddesses of India*, ed. Hawley and Wulff, Berkeley, 1982, pp. 316–324. Nancy Chodorow, *The Reproduction of Mothering: Psychoanalysis and the Sociology of Gender*, Berkeley, 1978. Ramanujan says about the Indian situation: "The males take on female personae . . . Before God all men are women. But no female saint, however she may defy male-oriented relational attitudes, takes on a male persona. It is as if, being already female, she has no need to change anything to turn toward God" (p. 324). See n. 89 below.

73. Examples of excellent scholarship in this vein, which nonetheless result in pejorative assessments of figures like Dorothy, Margery, Marguerite of Oingt, etc., are Edmund Colledge and James Walsh, eds., *A Book of Showings to the Anchoress Julian of Norwich*, 2 vols., Toronto, 1978, introduction; and Wolfgang Riehle, *The Middle English Mystics*, tr. Standring, London, 1981.

74. André Vauchez, *Le spiritualité du moyen âge occidental VIIIe–XIIe siècles*, Paris, 1975; Little, *Religious Poverty*.

75. On the eucharist, see Bynum, "Women Mystics and Eucharistic Devotion," *Women Studies*, 1984.

76. See Jungman, *Mass*, vol. 2. pp. 120–122 and 206ff.; Peter Browe, *Die Verehrung der Eucharistie im Mittelalter*, Munich, 1933; and Edouard Dumoutet, *Corpus Domini: Aux sources de la piété eucharistique médiévale*, Paris, 1942.

77. On women as inferior, according to scientific and theological theory, see Vern Bullough, "Medieval Medical and Scientific Views of Women," *Viator* 4 (1973), pp. 487–493; Eleanor McLaughlin, "Equality of Souls, Inequality of Sexes; Women in Medieval Theology," *Religion and Sexism*, ed. Ruether, New York, 1974, pp. 213–266; Marie-Thérèse d'Alverny, "Comment les théologiens et les philosophes voient la femme?" *La femme dans les civilisations des Xe–XIIIe siècles, Cahiers de civilisation médiévale* 20 (1977), pp. 105–129.

78. Mechtild of Hackeborn has a vision of herself distributing the chalice; see *Revelationes Gertrudianae ac Mechtildianae* 2: *Sanctae Mechtildis virginis ordinis sancti Benedicti Liber specialis gratiae*, ed. the monks of Solesmes, Paris, 1877, pp. 7–10. More common is the vision in which Christ is priest to the woman recipient; see Peter Browe, *Die Eucharistischen Wunder des Mittelalters*, Breslau, 1938, pp. 20–30. On Mechtild of Hackeborn and Gertrude (cited in n. 79 below), see *Jesus as Mother*, chapter 5.

79. Gertrude of Helfta, *Relevationes Gertrudianae ac Mechtildianae* 1: *Sanctae Gertrudis . . . Legatus divinae Pietatis . . .*, ed. the monks of Solesmes, Paris, 1875, pp. 392–395, and *Oeuvres spirituelles*, vol. 2, pp. 196–198; Angela of Foligno, *Book of Divine Consolation*, p. 223; the Life of Lukardis of Oberweimar, in *Analecta Bollandiana* 18 (Brussels, 1899), p. 337. See also the Life of Ida of Louvain, *Acta sanctorum*, April, vol. 2, Paris and Rome, 1865, p. 183.

80. For these examples, see the case of the Viennese beguine, Agnes Blannbekin, discussed by Browe, *Die Eucharistischen Wunder*, p. 34, and by McDonnell, *Beguines*, pp. 314–317; and the Life of Ida of Léau, *Acta sanctorum*, October, vol. 13, Paris, 1883, pp. 113–114.

81. See Michael Moffatt, *An Untouchable Community in South India: Structure and Consensus*, Princeton, 1979, for data which support Turner's idea of reversal.

82. On the beguines see the works cited in n. 85 below. In the south of Europe groups like the Humiliati and the mendicant tertiaries paralleled the beguines, who were a Low-Country and Rhineland movement.

83. See *Jesus as Mother*, introduction and chapter 3.

84. Brenda Bolton makes this point in "*Vitae Matrum*," p. 260. And note the number of female saints designated "lay" in Vauchez's list: André Vauchez, *La Sainteté en Occident aux derniers siècles du moyen âge d'après les procès de canonisation et les documents hagiographiques*. Bibliothèque des écoles françaises d'Athènes et de Rome, 241, Rome, 1981, pp. 656–676; see also pp. 315–18.

85. Joseph Greven, *Die Anfänge der Beginen: ein Beitrag zur Geschichte der Volksfrömmigkeit und des Ordenswesens im Hochmittelalter*, Münster in Westphalia, 1912; Herbert Grundmann, *Religiöse Bewegungen im Mittelalter*, 1935, reprint, Hildesheim, 1961; R. W. Southern, *Western Society and the Church in the Middle Ages*, Harmondsworth, England, 1970, pp. 318–331; Brenda Bolton, "*Mulieres Sanctae*," *Studies in Church History*, 10: *Sanctity and Secularity*, ed. D. Baker (1973), pp. 77–95, and "*Vitae Matrum*."

86. Frederick Stein, "The Religious Women of Cologne: 1120–1320," Ph.D. dissertation, Yale, 1977. The interpretation which blames male resistance to the religious needs of

women must also be modified in light of John B. Freed, "Urban Life and the 'Cura Monialium' in Thirteenth-Century Germany," *Viator* 3 (1972), pp. 311–327.

87. The quotation is from Turner, *Image and Pilgrimage*, p. 251.

88. The point I raise here parallels the criticism that has been made of certain interpretations of women's symbols that come out of the structuralist camp. For example, the much discussed essay by Sherry Ortner ("Is Female to Male as Nature is to Culture?" *Women, Culture and Society*, ed. Rosaldo and Lamphere, Stanford, 1974, pp. 67–87), which argues that women are universally imaged as "nature" to the image of man as "culture," has been criticized for, among other things, viewing culture monolithically as the dominant culture. See Eleanor Leacock and June Nash, "Ideologies of Sex: Archetypes and Stereotypes," *Issues in Cross-Cultural Research*, New York Academy of Sciences, vol. 285, New York, 1977, pp. 618–645; and C. P. MacCormack and M. Strathern, eds., *Nature, Culture and Gender*, Cambridge, England, 1980, especially p. 17.

89. For an example of fusion with Christ through eroticism, see Hadewijch, *Complete Works*; for fusion through eating, see the Life of Ida of Louvain, *Acta sanctorum*, April, vol. 2, Paris and Rome, 1865, pp. 156–189; for fusion through illness, see the life of Alice of Schaerbeek, *Acta sanctorum*, June, vol. 2, Paris and Rome, 1867, pp. 471–477, and Julian of Norwich, *Showings*, tr. Colledge and Walsh, Paulist Press, New York, 1978. See also Ernst Benz, *Die Vision: Erfahrungsformen und Bilderwelt*, Stuttgart, 1969, pp. 17–34. Ramanujan's formulation of differences in Indian lives of men and women (see n. 72 above) cannot be completely applied to the medieval tradition exactly because the passivity he implies in women's images does not accurately describe the intensely dynamic aspect of erotic and ascetic images in the west.

90. *The Mirror of Simple Souls*, long known to scholars but discovered only in this century to be Margaret's "heretical" treatise, has been printed in Romana Guarnieri, "Il movimento del Libero Spirito. II. Il 'Miroir des simples âmes' di Margherita Porete," *Archivio italiano per la storia della pietà*, vol. 4, Rome, 1965, pp. 513–635. On the work, see Robert E. Lerner, *The Heresy of the Free Spirit in the Later Middle Ages*, Berkeley, 1972, pp. 72–76 and 200–208.

91. Such mysticism is one of Turner's favorite examples of "metaphorical liminality." See *Process, Performance and Pilgrimage*, p. 125, where he claims that mysticism is interiorized ritual liminality, ritual liminality is exteriorized mysticism.

92. See Little, *Religious Poverty*, and Bynum, *Jesus as Mother*, p. 183. Turner is, of course, aware that reversal is more central in some religions than in others; see *Ritual Process*, p. 189. But his paradigm of Christianity seems late medieval, even Franciscan, rather than early modern or antique. In a rather obvious sense, the Reformation was a rejection of elaborate images of reversal—not just of carnival, monks and friars, but of the general notion of world denial as well.

93. Grundmann, *Religiöse Bewegungen*. On late medieval religiosity as upper class—and especially on conversion as an upper-class phenomenon—see Weinstein and Bell, *Saints and Society*, chapter 7, especially p. 216.

94. See above n. 24.

95. This writing has been surveyed recently by Rosemary Ruether, "The Feminist Critique in Religious Studies," *Soundings* 64.4 (1981), pp. 388–402; and Mark Silk, "Is God a Feminist?" *New York Times Book Review*, April 11, 1982.

Xunzi and Durkheim as Theorists of Ritual Practice

ROBERT F. CAMPANY

Facts of publication: *Campany, Robert F. 1992. "Xunzi and Durkheim as Theorists of Ritual Practice," from Discourse and Practice, 197–225, 227–231. Edited by Frank Reynolds and David Tracy. Albany: State University of New York Press. Copyright © 1992 by State University of New York. Reprinted with the permission of the State University of New York Press.*

Campany pioneers in studying premodern and non-Western ritual theory. He considers Xunzi, a Confucian who lived in the third century B.C.E. and wrote about the ritual practices of his community. By examining the strategies used in this discourse on local practice, Campany articulates Xunzi's general theory. The discourse includes a way of describing ritual, an account of its symbolism, and an explanation of its origins and functions.

Xunzi accounts for ritual practice as if he were an outsider, and Campany argues that assuming this point of view amounts to a theory of ritual. He finds surprising similarities, as well as differences, between Xunzi's theory and that developed by Emile Durkheim, who lived over two thousand years later. Campany uses the continuities between these theories to question the commonly assumed distinction between theorist and practitioner.

See also Herbert Fingarette, "Human Community as Holy Rite," which is chapter 1 of Confucius—the Secular as Sacred *(New York: Harper & Row, 1972); also Patricia Buckley Ebrey,* Confucianism and Family Rituals in Imperial China: A Social History of Writing about Rites *(Princeton: Princeton University Press, 1991).*

About the author: **Dates***: 1959– , Columbus MS, U.S.A.* **Education***: B.A., Davidson College; M.A., University of Chicago; Ph.D., University of Chicago.* **Field(s)***: religious studies; history of Chinese religions; methods for the cross-cultural study of religion and culture.* **Career***: Assistant and then Associate Professor of Religious Studies and East Asian Languages and Cultures, 1988–present, Indiana University.* **Publications***:* Strange Writing: Anomaly Accounts in Early Medieval China *(State University of New York, 1995).* **Additional***: "Supported by an NEH grant, I am currently on leave from teaching to prepare a motif-, theme-, and name-index, as well as a selective translation of the approximately 3,600 extant "anomaly accounts" (*zhiguai*) from early medieval China. I teach undergraduate and graduate courses on Taoism, East Asian Buddhism, death and the dead in comparative perspective, religion and food, and methods for the cross-cultural study of religion. I am also currently researching the history of local religious cults in early medieval China and am engaged in a detailed comparison of Taoist, Buddhist, and Confucian hagiographies from the same place and period."*

INTRODUCTION

It is no longer possible for Western academicians to presume that the other communities we study lack analogues to ourselves or to our ways of studying them. Until quite recently, our discourse on other cultures and religions was premised—almost totally unconsciously—on at least one fundamental difference between "us" and "them": we had the theory, while what they could provide amounted only to "raw" data; we theorized about their practices; we philosophized, they acted. A growing and increasingly sophisticated body of work has begun to deconstruct this notion as well as to imagine what our study of religions will look like in its absence. We are beginning both to recognize something analagous to our theories and philosophical discourses among the others we theorize about and to view our own theoretical and philosophical discourses as modes of cultural practice that might repay comparative study.

. . . I want to consider *theory about ritual practice*, or what might be called the philosophy of ritual, as itself a form of cultural practice; for this is an area in which the difference between "us" and "them" has been particularly clearly linked to the difference between "thought" and "practice."[1] To study ritual theory as a mode of practice is to "look [in some detail] at what we [and others] *do* when we theorize" about ritual. It is to become aware of the range of purposes served by ritual theory.[2] And, for the historian of religions, whose practice is always inherently comparative, it is to become aware of ritual theory as the locus of a *human* problem—not simply a modern Western problem—by searching for analogous practices across cultural, religious, and spatiotemporal boundaries.

The theorist of ritual to whom I will devote most of my attention here is the Chinese author Xun Kuang or Xunzi ("Master Xun"), whose name adorns the collectively authored text produced by a school of Ruist (or "Confucian") thinkers in the state of Qi sometime during the third century B.C.E.[3] Near the end, I will briefly sketch a few analogies with the work of Emile Durkheim (1858–1917), who, more than two millenia later and a world away, helped to lay the foundations for much of the subsequent comparative study of religions, and whose work continues to be an important part of its canon. In Xunzi and Durkheim we have two thinkers widely disparate in time, space, and culture who demarcated a certain realm of human practice as particularly important and problematic, who thought it possible and indeed necessary to "theorize" about that realm of practice, and who, as we will see, in some respects theorized about it in similar ways and for similar purposes. The point of this [study] is, first, to highlight certain features of Xunzi's ritual theory by comparison with a theory most readers . . . are probably more familiar with; second, to reinforce by means of the comparison the claim that Xunzi's theory of ritual is sophisticated and deserves to be taken as seriously as that of a figure such as Durkheim; and finally, perhaps to cast a ray of new light upon aspects of Durkheim's ritual theory that appear particularly salient when compared with Xunzi's theory.[4]

The questions that have shaped my reading of each of these figures are three: (1) What does each conceive a "theory" of ritual to be, and why does each think it necessary to construct a theory of ritual? (2) What specific shape does the theory take? In other words, what strategies does each writer use to describe, interpret, and explain ritual practice? (3) In the service of what larger social, moral, and religious aims does each construct a theory of ritual?

My answers to these questions have helped me to wrestle with a larger problem that arises from the linked dichotomies of us/them (or outsider/insider) and theory/practice. The problem is this: if we assume, as I think we must, that all practitioners of rituals have some self-understanding of why they do what they do and could offer some coherent account of what their practice "is" or "accomplishes" or "means," then how does a "theorist" of ritual differ from a "practitioner" of ritual—or is there a difference?[5] To put it another way: if we reject the notion, crudely put, that we as academic outsiders have a monopoly on thought about action, a monopoly we exercise as we think about others' action (where the "other" is virtually *defined* as one who acts, in contrast to the academic self, one who thinks), and if we replace it with the twin notions that all thought is already a species of action and that all actors already exercise thought about their action (or are "metapractitioners"), are there not still different—*practically* different—modes of thinking about action that might roughly be distinguished as "theoretical" versus "practical"? If so, what precisely is the difference?

Let us begin with Xunzi.

XUNZI'S RITUAL "THEORY": WHAT AND WHY?

In what sense does Xunzi offer a "theory" of ritual? Why does he consider it necessary to theorize about ritual at all?

I begin by noting some simple facts. From the total spectrum of human action, Xunzi isolates a particular sphere with its own distinctive form and coherence. In assigning that sphere a name—*li*, a term translatable both as a specific body of rites ("the" rites) familiar to Xunzi and his audience and as something like "ritual" in the generic sense—he already marks it off as somehow distinct from other sorts of activity. And in writing a treatise about it—*Li lun*, "A Discourse on Rites"—he already suggests that the rites are a sphere of activity that have become peculiarly problematic or opaque, requiring an effort of interpretation or explanation. These facts already point toward what constructing a "discourse" (*lun*) on ritual might have meant for Xunzi.

Consider further the following. Knowing that Xunzi belonged to the Ruist school, and that he looked upon the skillful performance of rites as an extremely valuable activity, we can assume that he, like most of his social class and orientation, participated in the rites he describes. Nevertheless, in writing a treatise on the rites—a treatise that, as we will see, goes far beyond merely describing performance, and that is in no sense a ritual manual or set of instructions for performance—Xunzi adopted a stance toward rites quite different from that of a participant in them. In fact, in doing so he engaged in a discourse that presumed a kind of cognitive distance from its object. By writing about ritual in the ways he did, he removed himself from the framework of ritual and placed its moments and gestures within an extra-ritual framework of his own devising. This remains true no matter how closely he thought his account of the rites matched their "real" meaning and purpose, and it remains true even if he valued ritual performance itself over mere writing (and reading) about ritual as a vehicle of culture. The point is that, in considering it possible and necessary to give a written account of ritual, he had already distanced himself from the arena of ritual no matter how sympathetic he was to its distinctive merits. He had become a spectator, which is exactly what a "theorist" is, etymologically speaking.[6]

Xunzi is no more explicit than some modern Western writers on what exactly he sees himself doing in his account of ritual, or why he is doing it. The best way to guess at his self-perception is to examine what he in fact does in his treatise, a task to which I will turn shortly. But embedded in his language we find a few subtle hints of Xunzi's stance toward his object and his task. At one point, writing of the need for personal examples when learning, he remarks that "rites and music provide models (*fa*) but no explanations (*shuo*)"; the implication seems to be that these performative genres—to each of which Xunzi devotes a chapter—are not immediately intelligible to the novice and require oral or written interpretation. We might speculate that Xunzi conceives of the *books* he goes on to cite as conversely providing "explanations" without "models," and thus find here a prototheory of the relation between written and performative genres; but Xunzi himself does not say this.[7] At another point he speaks in the first person of "being present as an observer at the community libation ceremony" and drawing conclusions from that experience about the way a true king should govern through ritual.[8]

In setting out to "explain" (*shuo*) or "discuss" (*lun*) ritual, as I said above, Xunzi suggests that the rites were the locus of a particular problem, that in his time they *needed* explanation or discussion, for as Charles Taylor has observed, "People reach for theories in order to make sense of a . . . universe which is full of conflict and rival interpretations, and which moreover everyone agrees is partly opaque."[9] Taylor's phrases aptly characterize the state of the "universe" of ritual in third century B.C.E. China. Consider for a moment the options on the table at that time.

Roughly three centuries before, Confucius had initiated a revolutionary understanding of the ancient rites of the Zhou dynasty as a medium for the cultivation of one's inner dispositions and for the perfect expression of one's humanity. He had declared that "one who knows the 'explanation' (*shuo*) of the [royal] sacrifice to the highest ancestor" would be able to govern the world "as easily as if holding it in his palm";[10] and he had set the "explanation" of rites on a new footing by removing it

from a "theological" ground, on which an account would be given of how the rites effected proper relations with ancestral spirits and with heaven and earth, to what I would call a "performative" ground: "Sacrifice to the spirits *as if* the spirits were present."[11] On this new demythologized ground, this ground of "as if" or "necessary fiction,"[12] "explanations" of rites now took the form of elucidations of the ways in which their performance expressed emotions or embodied moral principles.

Mencius had taken the new Ruist understanding of the rites one step further in this "performative" direction by grounding *li* as a disposition in the very nature of the self. For him, *li* was a realm of action generated by one of the four "germs" or "sources" (*duan*) of morality innate in human nature. Ritual—or more accurately, the attitudes of respect and modesty that find expression in ritual—well up spontaneously from the self unless obstructed.[13] Xunzi attacked this view—explicitly naming its proponent—in his famous chapter, "Human Nature is Evil," in part because it undercut what he saw as the compelling need for rites as the basis of human cultivation and social order.[14] One of Xunzi's opponents on the battlefield of rites, then, was the Ruist wing that portrayed rites as a natural, effortless flowing out from the self of certain of its innate dispositions.

Other schools had produced different sorts of challenges. Mozi and his followers decried many rites—especially the Ruist mourning ceremonies—as wasteful consumption of precious material resources; on the other hand, they advocated the old "theological" understanding of the rites, seeing them as expressions of gratitude and efforts to please the spirits, although belief in spirits was in turn advocated on purely pragmatic grounds.[15] The Taoists agreed with the position adopted by Xunzi (against Mencius) that the rites are a human artifice, the result of deliberate activity (*wei*), but they differed from him in seeing such artifice as an undesirable activity, a falsification of and disastrous departure from primordial simplicity and nondifferentiation.[16] The Legalists, who played the variant traditionalisms of the Confucians and the Mohists off against one another to good effect, proposed to replace the rites with a "behaviorist" system of rewards and punishments.[17] Finally, a crucial adversary for our purposes was a view that has been called "divinistic" or "shamanic naturalism";[18] it sought to explain the efficacy of rites by reference to either spiritual or cosmic "responses," not by reference to the human sphere. This view to some extent approximated that of the "commoners" on why rituals were performed and were efficacious. Its exponents rivaled the Ruists for imperial recognition and patronage.[19]

These competing understandings of the nature and significance of ritual are the background against which Xunzi's view of the need for and nature of a "theory" of ritual must be understood. From the above it can clearly be seen that in discussing ritual Xunzi is taking up a topic that has become a well-worn problem and a battleground on which various philosophical and religious issues were contested. To theorize about rites was therefore necessarily to take up this "transmit" of problems and to adopt a stand on some of the issues that had become attached to the interpretation of rites. We are not dealing with disinterested speculation about rites for its own sake; we are dealing with a world in which the understanding of rites has become a vehicle for debate among competing visions of how to organize a society and live one's life. It follows that the particular shape of Xunzi's theory of ritual must be understood, in part at least, as a response to the challenges posed by these other schools of interpretation. When set in its social context and viewed as a mode of practice, Xunzi's ritual theorizing, not surprisingly, comes to be seen as a vehicle of ideological contestation and moral-religious reform.

But we risk misunderstanding Xunzi if we forget that it is about *ritual* (among other things), after all, that he writes. His analysis of ritual performance cannot therefore be reduced to a mere pretext for ideological debate. The reason why the rites had become such fertile ground for disagreement, I suspect, is that their origin and purpose had to some extent been forgotten. They constituted so many "survivals" of an archaic, feudal world long since past. New life forms demanded reevaluation or an area or life now cut free from its old social and ideological moorings: should the rites be preserved, and if so, how could they now be understood?[20] Rites perhaps continued to provide pattern and order to the lives of at least some among the literate segments of Chinese society (although there is evidence that even here they were being departed from), but their rationale had become obscure. Since they could no longer be adequately understood from within the framework of the rites themselves, external (even if ritually derived) principles of explanation had to be brought to bear—a process initiated by Confucius and now to be continued (though in a new way) by Xunzi. The rites' opacity had made a *theory* about them both necessary and possible, and constructing a "theory" about them meant giving an account of them from some point of view other than themselves, a stance already adumbrated in the very act of *writing a treatise*. Ritual theory in China, in this sense, was born at the moment when the rites became a cognitive and religious *problem*—when they were something that demanded explanation instead of being the basis upon which other realms of activity were explained.

What shape, then, did Xunzi's theory of ritual take?

XUNZI'S STRATEGIES FOR THE DESCRIPTION, INTERPRETATION, AND EXPLANATION OF RITUAL

My goal here is not to summarize Xunzi's discourse on ritual but rather to characterize certain strategies used by Xunzi in his account, making explicit what are usually implicit moves made by him. For convenience I divide these strategies into descriptive, interpretive, and explanatory types, although I am aware that these categories often overlap, that (for instance) there is no "pure" description.

Description as Analysis

How does Xunzi describe ritual performance? He does so in a way that already presumes a spectator's distance in at least two senses: he never gives the sort of instructions that would be necessary to perform the ritual or participate in it, and with rare exceptions, he does not give a flowing narrative of the events of ritual performance from beginning to end, choosing intend to *analyze* the ritual process into discrete parts.

In his descriptive analysis of ritual, Xunzi uses an

array of what we might call "registers"—schematic devices in terms of which he breaks ritual performance down into parts and against which he plots those parts. He "describes" ritual, in other words, by providing a succession of lists of those of its aspects that fit under certain rubrics. His analysis is fairly clearly meant to give a rationale for particular aspects of the rites.

One of Xunzi's analytical registers for the organization of information about ritual performance is the set of human sensory faculties and body parts. Asserting that rites belong to that area of human activity concerned with "nourishing" or "bringing to maturity" (*yang*), he divides certain ritual acts and implements into categories according to the aspects of the body through which they nourish human nature. Thus, sacrificial foods nourish through the mouth; the odors of plants used during rites, through the nose; ornamentation of ritual objects, through the eye; musical instruments, through the ear; the spatial setting of ritual, through the body (13.1a–b; W89). At another point, he divides bodily modes for the expression of joy and sorrow: one's facial countenance and voice, what one eats and wears, where one dwells, are each described as markers of auspicious and inauspicious occasions (13.13a–14a; W102).

Time is another of Xunzi's analytic registers—or rather times, for Xunzi speaks of several kinds of duration. One kind is calendrical: he gives rationales for the number of days required for each of the stages of funeral ritual (13.11a; W99) as well as for the various lengths of mourning observed for those with whom one is related in different ways (13.18b–20b; W106–9).

Elsewhere, Xunzi seems more clearly to be dividing ritual duration into discrete segments and implying that each segment has (what we would call) a distinct "meaning." At one point, he tries to link different ritual acts according to the processual phase to which they belong: for instance, filling a goblet with water (an unfermented drink), laying out uncooked fish on the altar, and presenting unflavored soup, are all linked together as moments when raw food is offered;[21] other phases are those in which food or drink are not (or are only partially) consumed by the impersonator of the dead, those in which a particular ritual phase is about to begin, and

those in which rough or unfinished materials are used or music is performed in a deliberately imperfect way (13.5a–6b; W93–94). Elsewhere he charts the phasal structure of "all [the] rites" (*fan li*) as beginning in "simplicity" or a state of unadornment (*zho*, early glossed as *tuo*), coming to fulfillment in "form" or "pattern" (*wen*), and ending in "joy" or "pleasure" (*le*) (13.6b; W94). He also writes of how, "in all funerary rites" (*sangli zhi fan*), successive changes in the state of the dead are embodied in ritual display (*bian er shi*): the corpse is moved ever farther away from the living (*dong er yuan*) until a phase of rest or equilibrium is obtained (*jiu er ping*) (13.12.a; W99). In all of these passages Xunzi is charting the structure of ritual process: the discrete phases of one rite are classified with similar phases in other rites, a move that presumably aided understanding (although it is not clear just how), and individual ritual phases are linked with corresponding emotions or successive states of being.

Occasionally, Xunzi seems to want to correlate one analytical register with another, as if searching for ritual "principles." For example, he links the register of raw/cooked with that of temporal frequency: the greater the extent to which a food is cooked, the more frequently it is offered (13.4b–5a; W92–93). Elsewhere he links the nonconsumption of offerings by the impersonator of the dead (eating/not eating) with the completion phase of rites (incomplete/complete): when the impersonator no longer eats or drinks, invariably the rite is concluded (13.5b; W93).[22] These sorts of strategies lead us beyond Xunzi's descriptive analysis of ritual to his *interpretation* of it.

Interpretation: Decoding Ritual as Mimesis and as Expression

Symbolic Indirection. Xunzi is acutely mindful of what we might call "symbolic indirection" in ritual performance. In other words, he is concerned to show that certain ritual gestures and objects do not always "mean" what they seem to mean, that they are sometimes used in a nonapparent way to refer to something less than obvious. Ritual for Xunzi is a realm of "imitation" or "symbolization" (*xiang*). Further, while he thinks (as we will see below) that ritual performance has real, practical effects on human nature and social life, he wants to mark it off as a realm of practice distinct from other, "ordinary" forms of life by virtue, in part, of its "symbolic" or "indirect" nature.[23] His views on these topics can be seen most clearly in his analysis of funerary rites.

Xunzi gives the following principle for funerary and mourning rites: "One performs rites for the dead as though they were living, roughly imitating [or symbolically enacting, *xiang*] what one would do if they were alive while yet sending them to their final death."[24] Everything turns, then, on the tension between the ways in which one treats the living and the reality of the death of the person for whom the rites are performed. For Xunzi, funerary and mourning rites play across the contradiction and the gap between life and death: at times they seem to deny the contradiction and span the gap, while at other times they bespeak the contradiction and reveal the gap.

After this introductory passage he proceeds to analyze the symbolism of specific gestures and objects in the four basic ritual phases: preparation for burial, burial, mourning, and sacrificial offerings. Particularly in the case of the rites of preparation and burial, Xunzi's discourse takes the form of comparing the services rendered to the dead with those one would render to the living. This comparison allows him to isolate what we would call the "symbolic" quality of the ritual gestures. In preparing the corpse for burial, for instance, one washes, combs, and feeds it, here "imitating" (*xiang*) what one would for the living despite one's knowledge that the person in this case is dead. On the other hand, one seals off its orifices, thus "opposing" (*fan*) what one would do for a living person. In dressing the corpse and providing it with supplies, finally, one performs acts whose subtle ambiguity bodies forth the tension between our *connection with* and *separation from* the dead. One arranges the hair but adds no pin, provides jars but puts nothing in them, presents musical instruments but does not tune them, buries a carriage but takes the horses back home. Aspects of the burial—the "forms" (*mao*) of various constructed objects—likewise "imitate" or "symbolize" aspects of the world of the living from which the dead person is now separate: the form of the grave mound imitates (or symbolizes) that of a house, coffins imitate carriages, coffin covers imitate wall hangings in a room, and the wood lining of the grave pit imitates the railing and roof of a house (14b–18a; W103–5).[25]

Throughout this treatment, the key term is *xiang*, which I have translated as "imitate" or "symbolize." It is used repeatedly as (what we would term) a "verb" to specify how objects or gestures in the sphere of death ritual refer to, are modeled on, resemble, or reenact the forms appropriate to life. Xunzi's use of this word recalls the *Yi jing* (*Book of Changes*) account of how the ancient sages "were able to survey all phenomena under heaven and, considering their forms and appearances, 'symbolized' (*xiang*) things and their proper attributes. These were called 'symbols' (*xiang*)."[26] These mimetic signs reproduce in writing—a medium subject to human manipulation—the structure of nature and can thus be made to disclose the hidden patterns of cosmic change. Xunzi implies something similar of death ritual: that its elements, like graphic signs, imitate life forms while operating in a realm once removed from life, a realm of action and speech which is in fact (in this case) directed toward the opposite of life.[27] Ritual forms presume and play across a gap between ordinary life and the arena of ritual performance; they also, like the written signs of the *Yi jing*, allow a manipulation of ordinary life—or at least a real effect on it—by virtue of the mimetic correspondence between ritual gestures and life forms.

Conversely, it is this correspondence which allows Xunzi to "interpret" ritual, where "interpretation" entails linking ritual events with the external "meanings" to which they refer. This can be seen most clearly in a rare passage which seems to show Xunzi envisioning a "pure performance" that does not refer to anything outside itself and that is thus, strictly speaking, uninterpretable.

> How can one know the meaning (*yi*) of the dance? I say: the eyes cannot see it, the ears cannot hear it; and yet, when all the posturings and movements, all the steps and changes of pace are ordered and none are lacking in proper restraint, when all the power of muscle and bone are brought into play, when all is matched exactly to the rhythm of the drums and bells and there is not the slightest awkwardness or discord—*there*, in all these manifold actions of lively intensity, is the "meaning" of the dance![28]

We have here the exception that proves the rule: an

area of ritual practice whose "meaning" Xunzi is unable or unwilling to locate anywhere but within itself. The dance *is* its "meaning," that is, it is intrinsically meaningful; there exists no *other* register onto which one could map its gestures or in terms of which one could decode its symbols.[29] This passage is striking in its contrast to the many others in which Xunzi engages in "interpretation" and finds rites to have extrinsic meaning and function.

Expression. Xunzi also speaks of ritual as "expressing" through action states and dispositions internal to the self, although no single term in the text carries precisely the same range of connotations as our word "to express." One of the closest analogues is *jin*, "to exhaust," as in the phrase (said of the ways people should deal with their emotions through ritual) *lei zhi jin zhi* (13.14a), translated by Watson as "to express [them] completely and properly" (W102) and by Dubs as "made to fit the situation, completely expressed."[30] Other analogues include *fa*, "to issue from," "to burst out," and *xing*, "to be embodied," both of which appear in the following rationale for ritual music and dance: "Since people cannot help feeling joy, their joy must issue forth (*fa*) in the sound of the voice and be embodied (*xing*) in movement."[31]

Xunzi's notion of how ritual "expresses" inner states and dispositions is best seen in the dialectic he sets up between "emotion" or "sentiment" (*qing*) and "[ritual] form" (*wen*), each of which is ideally balanced against the other in ritual.[32] "When rites are performed at their best, emotion and form are both fully realized; next best is when emotion and form prevail by turns; last is when everything is based on emotion alone" (13.7a; W94). Elsewhere he imagines ritual "forms" to have been established as channels or outlets for human emotions that would otherwise lack proper media for expression (13.18a, W105; 13.21a, W109; 13.21b–22a, W110). In the lyrical conclusion to his chapter on rites, he even speaks of ritual as the literal *embodiment* of what would otherwise have no shape or image: "One serves the dead as though they were living, one serves the departed as though they were still present, thus giving body to that which has no shape or image. In this way are constituted the forms [of ritual]."[33]

But Xunzi's language of "embodiment" does not privilege inner emotions as the ultimate and unreachable source of ritual form. On the contrary, emotions—along with other aspects of human nature (*xing*)—are themselves subject to formation by ritual practice at the same time that they find expression in that practice. The rites constitute "models" or "molds" (*fa*) for a human nature that is pictured as naturally depraved but eminently malleable toward good.[34]

In Xunzi's chapter on "Self-Cultivation" we are told that "one who is without models (*wu fa*) is lost and without a guide"; that "ritual is the means whereby one can rectify oneself" (*zheng shen*), that "if you do unerringly as ritual prescribes, this means that your emotions have found rest in ritual (*qing an li*)"; and finally, that ritual (*li*) is itself the "model" (*fa*) one should adopt: "to reject ritual is to be without a model. . . . 'Learning' (*xue*) means learning to regard ritual as your model" (W30; 1.22a–b). So while, on one hand, ritual is pictured as channeling the expression of inner emotions into appropriate outward forms, on the other hand, it is also pictured as shaping emotions, informing by deliberate activity (*wei*) what is formless and entropic in human nature (*xing*).[35] In fact, Xunzi views human nature itself as split between innate dispositions (*xing*), on the one hand, and, on the other, dispositions instilled by conscious activity (*wei*) and directed by a mind capable either of directing desire or detaching itself from desire and becoming a "spectator." That is, the bipartite structure of the human self mirrors the bipartite distinction between inner, innate dispositions and the outer, learned "models" which are comprised in ritual. The structure of action is introjected into the self.[36]

We have now left Xunzi's methods of *interpreting* ritual, however, and have begun to approach his view of its *functions*, by means of which he seeks to *explain* its origin, its rationale, and its peculiar power.

Explanation: The Origins and Functions of Ritual

Origins. The strategy of searching for the *origins* of something as a way of explaining its existence and meaning is a familiar one. Xunzi's "Discourse on Ritual" opens with an account of the origins of ritual, an imaginative reconstruction of the conditions under which ritual first arose, not unlike the "state of nature" imagined by modern Western thinkers to explain the social contract.

> From whence did ritual arise? I reply: People are born with desires (*yu*). If they are unable to get what they desire, then they cannot help seeking it (*qiu*) all the more. If their seeking is not regulated and set within prescribed boundaries (*fen jie*), they will unavoidably contend with each other. Contending, they will grow disorderly; disorderly, they will wear themselves out. The ancient kings hated such disorder, so they established ritual principles (*li yi*) in order to contain (*fen*) it by training people's desires and providing that which they sought. By these means they ensured that desire did not exhaust the goods desired and that goods did not fall short of what was desired. By thus holding these two [goods and desires] in balance, each was allowed to flourish. This is how ritual arose (13.1a; cf. W89).

What is significant about this account is that, while it locates the origins of ritual in the distant past with the "ancient kings"—who were the subject of a fair amount of mythologizing on the part of other writers before and after Xunzi—it *explains* ritual's *rationale* by seeking to lay out general principles of human nature and behavior. It grounds ritual's origin, and hence its authority, not so much in the greatness and wisdom of its ancient inventors as in its efficacy for overcoming a fundamental obstacle to human flourishing anywhere and any time.[37] Ritual is that area of life that allows the expression of emotion (*qing*) and the fulfillment of human nature (*xing*) while at the same time enabling human community to exist by mitigating the innate, disorderly tendencies of human nature. Here, too, ritual involves a kind of indirection, only this time "functional" rather than "symbolic"; by obeying the dictates of ritual, which constrain one to act in a way one might not act by nature, one would appear to forfeit the objects of one's desires, because unlike ordinary life ritual is not about the direct pursuit of desires. But in fact it is only through the indirection of ritual that one's desires can be satisfied; if one attempts to satisfy them directly, one will fail (see 13.2b–3a; W90–91).

Xunzi gives another sort of explanation of the origins of ritual when he speaks of its "bases" (*ben*). At one point he says that "ritual has three bases: heaven and earth (*tiandi*), one's ancestors (*xianzu*), and one's lords and masters (*junshi*)" (13.3a–b; W91). This tripartite division sums up the categories of beings for whom one made offerings or performed rites in Xunzi's day. Xunzi seems to suggest that ritual performance is grounded in human relations with these types of beings; those relations are the context in which ritual becomes a meaningful activity.

In accounting for ritual's origins and rationale, then, Xunzi offers a view of what ritual *does*: in other words, he speaks of its functions.

Functions. Xunzi characterizes the functions of ritual with a rich array of metaphorical images. He first gives a "cosmic" characterization in which all natural processes, from the movements of heavenly bodies to the activities of human beings, are said to achieve their proper order through rites: "it is through ritual that the sun and moon shine, the four seasons proceed in order, the stars and constellations march, the rivers flow," and so on.[38] He next gives a "cultural" or "social" characterization in which it is through rites that human communal life reaches perfect form and apparent opposites (high and low, root and branch, beginning and end) are unified. Then comes a series of "directional" metaphors: ritual provides human life with requisite standards of measurement and degrees. To ignore these is to be "without direction" (*wufang*), while to abide by them is to "possess direction" or to be "oriented" (*youfang*); the sage is one who "possesses direction." Finally Xunzi describes the functions of ritual by resort to "habitative" metaphors: the rites are "the constant habitat and dwelling of the gentleman" because they allow a balance between "form and principle" (*wenli*), on the one hand, and "emotion and [practical] use" (*qingyong*), on the other. They constitute, in other words, the *world* of the gentleman, the environment in which he is comfortable, performs at his best, and achieves the full stature of humanity (13.8a–b; W94–96).[39]

These images do not exhaust Xunzi's views on the functions of ritual, however. We have already seen how, from the point of view of the individual participant, ritual functions as a vehicle not only for the expression but also for the transformation of emotions (which Xunzi conceives of as dispositions).[40] Concerning funeral rites, for instance, Xunzi says that they serve to channel disgust and loathing of the corpse—emotions that are natural but inappropriate—into a performance characterized by reverence (*jing*), which is what differentiates our approach to death from that of beasts (13.12a; W100).

Furthermore, from the point of view of the human community, ritual functions to reinforce social hierarchy and maintain social order. In the first place, the rites themselves encode distinctions (*bie* or *bian*) between hierarchical levels. For instance, the suburban sacrifice to heaven may be performed by the emperor (Son of Heaven) alone; altars of the soil (*she*) may not be established by anyone lower than a feudal lord (*zhuhou*). In this way "the rites distinguish [and make clear that] the exalted ritually serve the exalted and the humble serve the humble, that great corresponds to great and small to small" (13.4a; W91). Elsewhere we read that the three-year mourning period serves "to distinguish the ritual duties owed to near versus distant kin, to the eminent versus the humble" (13.18a; W105). The rites, then, are a domain given over to the marking of distinctions—not only, as we have seen, distinctions between different states and phases of the process of life (life/death, auspicious/inauspicious, joy/sorrow), but also distinctions between different social roles and hierarchical levels (ruler/noble/commoner, close/distant kin).

For Xunzi, ritual functions to preserve hierarchical social *distinctions* at the same time that it creates and maintains social *harmony*. A society must have status divisions in order to be unified and harmonious. The way in which Xunzi thinks ritual accomplishes this emerges quite clearly in his detailed analysis of the community libation ceremony (*xiang*).[41] As he moves through a rather lengthy narrative account of the gestures comprised in this ritual, he occasionally pauses to observe how they embody a particular principle of social distinction. For example:

> The host goes in person to fetch the guest of honor and his attendants, while the other guests [by contrast] come of their own accord. . . . This makes clear the principle of distinction between eminent and humble (14.5a; W118).

In his analysis of the *xiang* ceremony, then, Xunzi seeks to show how it functions to display the principles on which the community is built as well as to constitute the community as a cohesive group.[42]

Having discussed the ways in which Xunzi describes, interprets, and explains the origins and functions of ritual, we are now in a position to step back from these particular strategies and reflect on the larger aims of his theoretical project.

THE AIMS OF XUNZI'S RITUAL THEORY

As stated earlier, Xunzi's theory of ritual is not just a theory of ritual. To construct a theory of ritual in his day was to engage in a religious and ideological debate with others who had constructed other theories; it was to advance certain moral and religious aims. What Xunzi's own aims were can best be seen by considering the theories to which he fashioned an alternative, and how he responds to those theories in his text. Having briefly characterized above several of the competing academic theories of ritual current in his time, I will focus now on one particular competing view of ritual that apparently held sway among most of the common people as well as among a group of elite academicians who (to some extent at least) represented them.

I begin with the following passage, which comes near the end of Xunzi's "Discourse on Ritual."

> Only a sage can fully understand ritual. The sage has a clear understanding of it, the gentleman finds comfort in practicing it, the official takes it as something to be preserved, and the common people accept it as custom. To the gentleman it is the way of being human (*ren dao*); to the common people it is a matter of serving spirits (*gui shi*) (13.21b; W110).

This utterance is double-edged. On the one hand, it introduces a hierarchy of different ways of understanding and embracing the nature and significance of ritual performance. To one who understands its true nature it is seen for what it really is, "the way of being human." This is the view of ritual that Xunzi has been developing and would like his readers to accept. To see ritual as "the way of being human" is to see it as a symbolically and functionally "indirect" activity that is not, contrary to appearances, directed at the gods and ancestral spirits (save insofar as these are themselves symbolic entities) but at the human community and the human self. By contrast, to those who do not understand its true nature—the "hundred surnames," who are also lower on the status scale, whose entire social role is quite different— it is "a matter of serving spirits." This is one of the understandings of ritual Xunzi has been arguing against and to which he offers his own view as an alternative.[43]

Yet, on the other hand, each of these ways of participating in ritual—from understanding it to merely accepting it as custom, from seeing it as "the way of being human" to taking it as "a matter of serving spirits"—has a niche in what is an inclusive hierarchy of levels of participation. Ritual is a domain in which all participate (though in different ways corresponding to different social levels); it is a body of *practice* that members of all social levels share. It is only in their respective *understandings* of those practices that they differ. That difference is a crucial one for Xunzi, but at the same time, he seems to admit that his theory is not for everyone, that there will always be some who view ritual in ways he takes to be not so much false as limited, partial, or less than ultimate.

We have seen how Xunzi constructs a theory of ritual—involving a particular way of describing it, an account of its symbolism, and an explanation of it based on its origins and functions—in order to open up a ground from which ritual could be viewed as a "way of being human." In this respect his theory is aimed at countering the naive view of ritual as a matter of serving the gods and spirits. In a similar vein, he argues elsewhere that prayers for rain are best viewed in the way the gentleman views them, as "ritual forms" (*wen*), and not as the common people view them, as "[concerned with] spirits" (*shen*) (11.18b; W85); that visions of ghosts are due to overexcitement and not to real spectral appearances (W135), and so on.[44] Put simply, he is attempting to shift the meaning of ritual from the divine to the human sphere.

The difficulty facing him in this task is that, if taken "literally" or "at face value," rites seem to be

about nothing if not the service of gods and spirits. Victims are immolated; food is laid on altars; divine beings are invited to eat; ancestral spirits are impersonated by a ritual performer who eats, drinks, and converses with the living participants; grave goods are buried with corpses for their use in the other world; ancestors' names are inscribed on tablets. Then there is the fact, to which Xunzi himself attests, that most ordinary people in his day—most ritual participants—view the rites as a way of serving spirits. If the rites do not really serve spiritual beings, then whom or what *do* they serve? If these various gestures do not accomplish what they seem to, then what *do* they accomplish? And why, if the rites cannot be taken "literally," do they take the "divinistic" forms that they do, and why do so many participants view them literally?

We have already seen Xunzi's answers to the first two of these questions: ritual serves to train human desires, to express human emotions, to give structure and coherence to human society, to provide a total cultural habitat in which virtue and wisdom can flourish. But I do not think he provides answers to the last two questions. Xunzi does not tell us, that is, why rites that really serve humanity appear to serve spirits, nor does he explain why so many have misunderstood their real nature and function. He creates a notion of what I have called the "indirection" of ritual gestures and functions as a way of interpreting and explaining these, but he fails to explain why the indirection was necessary in the first place.

Now the most important difference between what we might call the "popular" or "received" account of ritual's nature and function, on the one hand, and Xunzi's account on the other, is this: Xunzi's account, seeks to shift the discourse on ritual from the ritual sphere to another sphere. Bypassing the apparent or surface-level referents of ritual acts, he seeks to put ritual on a different footing. Another way of saying this is that he gives an account of ritual from a point of view outside ritual.

In this respect, his discourse on ritual resembles that offered by other contemporary schools— Taoist, Mohist, Legalist, Mencian, Logicist, and others. Members of each of these other schools shared with Xunzi the quest to place ritual on some nonritual footing, to understand it not by reference to the world defined by its own internal logic but by reference to some other ground of knowledge or value they took as more fundamental. They differed over the ground on which ritual was to be set: was it to be natural processes, social utility, rewards and punishments, a self innately disposed toward good, linguistic analysis, or as Xunzi thought, a self innately disposed toward selfish action but capable through training of other-regarding action? For Xunzi, none of the other schools offered a satisfactory account of what ritual was, how it worked, what it accomplished, and most importantly, *why it was worth preserving.*[45]

Xunzi's key purpose in theorizing about ritual is to retrieve and preserve ritual as the center of human life, the locus of value and beauty. None of the other schools provided sufficient justification for the continued performance and preservation of ritual. The received or popular view of ritual, on the other hand, no longer sufficed to justify its practice, for it was being undermined by the various school theories each of which took ritual as secondary and other areas of life (or aspects of the self) as fundamental. Ritual had become opaque, the locus of a problem; it could no longer be defended from within, or justified internally in terms, as it were, of ritual itself. Paradoxically, then, in order to place ritual on a more secure footing, Xunzi had to resort to explaining it in nonritual terms; by adopting a stance outside of ritual he sought to justify ritual. He therefore adamantly maintains the *real function and effect* of ritual performance, but at the same time, he maintains that ritual performs functions and generates effects *indirectly*, not in the way that would be apparent from a point of view located inside the world of ritual. Ritual's demonstrated indirection saves it from agnostic or sceptical attack.

We are now in a position to return to one of the big questions mentioned at the outset as having generated this paper: given the breakdown of the old dichotomy between thought and action, is there any remaining way in which a theorist of ritual practice differs—in terms of practice—from a ritual participant? There is. Everyone involved in ritual performance, at least in principle (if often not in practice), has an account to offer of why they do what they do,

what it means, what their practice essentially is; so far, the practitioner and the theorist are indistinguishable. The real difference is not one between those who think and those who act. Nor is it one between a discrete group of participants and a discrete group of observers: Xunzi himself is probably an example of a person who was a "participant" and a "theorist" by turns. The essential difference is one between two *points of view* or roles, even if these are occupied at different moments by the same person. It is a difference between two ways of thinking about ritual practice (not one between thought and nonthought).

Quite simply, *theoretical* thinking about ritual practice is thinking from the point of view of a spectator, and this entails giving an account of ritual from a point of view outside ritual, using a language and a framework of understanding that are not derived from the ritual world but in terms of which that world is nevertheless described. "Theories" of ritual may take many forms, but they will all shift the discourse on ritual to some nonritual ground. Nontheoretical statements about ritual—statements made from within the realm of ritual—will take ritual itself as their point of departure; they will often use ritual itself as the reference point for explaining or describing other areas of life. For the theorist, ritual can no longer be the place from which to start, for *it* has become *the problem*; recourse must be had to some more secure foundation.

If ritual theory is an account of ritual from some point of view outside ritual, it is never a point of view outside *practice*. Theorizing about ritual is no less a mode of practice for being "theoretical": it is a project that takes on a particular shape, adopts a certain set of strategies, and perhaps most importantly, is undertaken for definite reasons. These reasons usually have to do with changing the way people live their lives—often even changing the way they participate in ritual. Ritual theory, in other words, often seeks to alter ritual practice as a social reality. This was certainly true of Xunzi and his contemporaries: those for whom they wrote about ritual were themselves participants in ritual. Paradoxically, Xunzi's aim in gaining an extra-ritual perspective on ritual was to enable his readers to perform and appreciate ritual in a new and better way.

DURKHEIM AS RITUAL THEORIST:
A BRIEF ANALOGICAL EXERCISE

If ritual is a ubiquitous human activity, ritual theory in the sense I have specified is hardly less so: wherever ritual has become a cognitive, moral, or religious problem, ritual theory will not have been far behind. We need more studies of premodern and non-Western ritual theory, and we need to know more about how modern Western theorists compare with their counterparts in other cultures and eras.[46] The following brief remarks are offered in that spirit, as a rough sketch for future work; space does not permit anything approaching a thorough comparison of Durkheim and Xunzi here.

In Durkheim we have a twentieth-century European who not only theorizes about ritual but does so in ways often strikingly analogous to those of Xunzi. In what follows I will highlight what are to me some of the most illuminating similarities and differences.

Like Xunzi, first of all, Durkheim views ritual gestures as subject to "symbolic indirection." Rites, like other religious practices and ideas, act as "symbolic expression[s]" or "allegories" or in the role of "mythological intermediary" for "forces" that are really moral, that is, social. They therefore need to be decoded; Durkheim seeks, as he says at one point, to "disengage [moral forces] from their symbols [and] present them in their rational nakedness."[47] Ritual objects and gestures are symbols of society created by society, which, however, has long forgotten that those symbols are its own.

> Between society as it is objectively and the sacred things which express it symbolically, the distance is considerable. It has been necessary that the impressions really felt by men, which served as the original matter of this construction, should be interpreted, elaborated and transformed until they became unrecognizable.[48]

We have seen that Xunzi, who came to something like the same conclusion, never explained why the "real" meaning and function of ritual gestures should be concealed by symbolic indirection. Durkheim has an explanation, arrived at with the aid of Kant and Hegel: humanity must undergo self-alienation in order to arrive at self-knowledge; to

know the self is perforce to come to terms with an "other." "Since collective sentiments can become conscious of themselves only by fixing themselves upon external objects, they have not been able to take form without adopting some of their characteristics from other things" (*EF* 466). This fixation of sentiments upon external objects takes place during periods of "collective effervescence," in which

> vital energies are over-excited. . . . A man does not recognize himself; he feels himself transformed and consequently he transforms the environment which surrounds him. In order to account for the very particular impressions which he receives, he attributes to the things with which he is in most direct contact properties which they have not, exceptional powers and virtues which the objects of everyday experience do not possess (*EF* 469).

It is society that creates the objects and categories of knowledge, that indeed creates the individual person as an entity. But here a particularly thorny problem confronts Durkheim, a problem from which Xunzi was relatively free: the dichotomy, inherited from his ancestors who discoursed on ritual, between thought and action, or belief and rite. Early on in this great decoding enterprise, he had maintained that "it is possible to define the rite only after we have defined the belief" (*EF* 51). But by the end, because of his stress on the collective as prior to the individual, he is forced to grant primacy to action— particularly ritual action—over belief or thought.[49] Rites, then, are metapractices that rejuvenate communal solidarity by recalling the primal acts and representations generated during "collective effervescence."[50] Again, although initially he says otherwise, rites for Durkheim do not simply reflect or "express" beliefs or sentiments: "The cult is not simply a system of signs by which the faith is outwardly translated; it is a collection of the means by which this is created and recreated periodically" (*EF* 464). One thinks of Xunzi's insistence that rites do not simply express inner dispositions but actively shape those dispositions.[51]

Durkheim, like Xunzi, seeks to "demythologize" ritual: by means of the notion of "symbol" and the dynamic of indirection, he criticizes the "theological" understanding of rites held by most of those who participate in them and substitutes another set of objects and forces to which ritual acts refer. And, as in Xunzi's case, those objects and forces are human, communal, and moral. It is society itself to which rites symbolically refer; it is the power of the collective upon which ritual power is based. Once again, as with Xunzi, Durkheim is concerned above all to maintain that the referents of ritual are *real* and that rites exert *real effects*. In decoding rites of sacrifice, for instance, Durkheim seeks to show that they are in fact an exchange between society and the individual, not between a god and an individual. Moreover, they effect "internal and moral regeneration": by the act of offering, persons periodically renew within themselves their social aspects, or their attachment to the collective (their "social sentiments"), which are otherwise in danger of decay (*EF* 384–90).

This leads us to another analogy: just as for Xunzi, for Durkheim the self is split into two parts, the religious symbols for which are body and soul: the one is "individual," is "rooted in our organism," and tends toward selfishness, while the other is not merely "social" in disposition but is an aspect of the self that is *created and implanted* by society.[52] The condition in which the self's individual aspect dominates and runs rampant, tearing the self loose from its social and moral moorings, is anomie, which often results in suicide.[53]

The key motivation for theorizing about ritual, then, for Durkheim as for Xunzi, is *education*. People must be taught the true and "rational" essence underlying the superficially absurd and outmoded forms of ritual and belief. Ritual must be set on a new foundation, that of human society and self cultivation; the alienation that characterizes unreformed religion must be abolished. Durkheim is more sensitive than Xunzi, however, to a problem inherent in this procedure: once society and its attendant moral code are stripped of the authority formerly lent them by religious symbols, and reduced to their "rational nakedness," whence comes their authority? It is an acute problem for Durkheim, who speaks of his desire to retain morality's old "sacred" character, to enable the schoolmaster to keep his sense of mission, so that he can feel himself to be "speaking in the name of a superior reality" as in the old days (*Moral Education*, 10). The only solution

he arrived at was the modern Western social theorist's old standby: the voluntary association as the new locus of social solidarity—for children, the school; for working adults, the occupational group, a form of association well suited to the modern division of labor.[54]

There are many other, perhaps less significant analogies between these two fertile thinkers: each holds out the possibility of what Durkheim calls "pure practice without theory" and what Xunzi sees exemplified in the dance, a realm of "pure" or "raw" practice that refers only to itself and cannot be decoded as ritual can;[55] each sees social solidarity as dependent on clear social divisions which are often embodied in ritual action; each stressed the different levels at which ritual may be understood, and each sought to raise the level of his audience's understanding to the point at which ritual's mask could be raised and ritual seen for what it "really is." Each, that is, engaged in ritual *theory* in the sense developed here: each described, interpreted, and explained ritual practice in nonritual terms, but for the eminently practical purpose of preserving its real and salutary social, moral, and psychological effects.

There are, however, at least two massive disanalogies. The first is that, unlike Xunzi, Durkheim felt it possible and helpful to reflect on the problem of ritual through the indirect vehicle of analyzing *other people's* rites—rites in which he never personally participated or even directly observed. His ritual theory gets refracted through what we noted at the outset to be a characteristically Western mode of encounter with "primitive" others. The second disanalogy is closely related: Xunzi wrote for a community of readers largely (if ideally) defined by its shared participation in a body of rites, whereas Durkheim wrote precisely because such a body of rites was lacking in his time and place. Too briefly put, Xunzi the premodern dealt with ritual in search of adequate theory, while Durkheim the modern dealt with theory in search of adequate ritual. Each of these disanalogies carries implications that cannot be explored here, perhaps the most salient is the extent to which a fully nuanced comparison of theorists (at which this essay only gestures) must take careful account of the total cultural and religious contexts in which their theories take on meaning as creative responses.

CONCLUSION

I would like to return to the point from which I departed: the question of the extent to which "we" (by which I mean late-twentieth-century Western-trained students of comparative culture and religion) are analogous to those we study, or the extent to which our "theories" are analogous to theirs. The notion that ours is to think, while theirs is to do, is happily departed from our midst. There is no more raw action or sheer actor. "They" turn out to be just like "us." But are they really? A book such as James A. Boon's *Other Tribes, Other Scribes* points up the problem sharply: when it is found that both the anthropological and the (say) Balinese communities are "dialectical" and "reflexive" and that both use signs in the Saussurian sense of engaging in an inherently contrastive enterprise, are we not still "dialectical" and "reflexive" and "Saussurian" in a way that they are not when we write a book about them—especially a book that compares ourselves to them—and gather around a table (in Chicago, say) to talk it all over? In the very stance of "studying" others are we not already placing ourselves on a level of practice definitionally distinct from theirs? In writing a [study], as I have here done, consisting of a theory of theories of ritual (which are already themselves "metapractices" and not merely "raw practice"), have I not thereby mock-triumphantly asserted my—and our—distance and difference from the makers of those theories, thus starting the problem all over again?

NOTES

1. On the pervasiveness of the distinction between thought and action in modern Western ritual theory (the very label for which already betrays the divide), including its relationship with the ways we differentiate ourselves from those we study, see Bell, "Discourse and Dichotomies." I have also learned much from Sullivan, *Icanchu's Drum*, chapter 1. I am grateful to Professors Frank Reynolds and David Tracy and Dean Franklin Gamwell for allowing me to serve as assistant to the Religions in Culture and History project while a graduate student at the University of Chicago. I would also like to thank the members of the sixth colloquium of the project, held in April 1989, for their thoughtful responses to an earlier draft of this [study], and in particular Dean Judith Berling, who gave a careful critique. My only regret is that space did not permit a more thorough incorporation of some of their suggestions in the revision.

2. I here follow Charles Taylor's mandate (see *Philosophy and the Human Sciences*, 116) to study social theory as a mode of practice. See also Bellah, "The Ethical Aims of Social Inquiry."

3. I am skirting here numerous problems of authorship and attribution that are more properly the work of the specialist. In what follows, I will often refer to the person named Xunzi as though I took him to be the sole author of the text called *Xunzi*, but this is of course a matter of convenience. As an excellent synposis of the evidence concerning the author, the text, and the Ruist school to which both belonged, I have relied on the important work of my colleague Robert Eno, *The Confucian Creation of Heaven*, especially chapter 6, which he kindly loaned me in its manuscript form. Other discussions of Xunzi in his historical and social context include Dubs, *Hsüntze, the Moulder of Ancient Confucianism*, and Fehl, *Rites and Propriety in Literature and Life*.

4. I realize that in many contexts it might be important to distinguish between a "theory" and a "philosophy" *of* something, including ritual, but for the purposes of this paper I make no such distinction. I henceforth use the term "theory"

when characterizing the discourses on ritual produced by Xunzi and by Durkheim, and what I mean by that term will become clear shortly.

5. This is, of course, not to deny what anyone knows who has questioned informants concerning their ritual practices: that not every individual is able (or willing) to articulate such a self-understanding when called upon to do so; as Taylor puts it, "the understanding is [often] implicit in our ability to apply the appropriate descriptions to particular situations and actions" (*Philosophical Papers*, 2:93).

6. Such was, apparently, the earliest English sense of the word: deriving from the Latin and Greek root *theoria*, the English *theorie* meant "a looking at, a viewing"; it also designated what offered to the viewer a particularly noteworthy "sight" or "spectacle" (this from *theoros*, a spectator). (I have consulted the *Oxford English Dictionary*, s.v. "theory." A 1605 sermon by Bishop Andrewes is cited to illustrate the sense of theory as a "spectacle": "Saint Luke . . . calleth the Passion *theorian* a Theory or Sight. . . . Of our Blessed Saviour's whole life or death, there is no part but is a Theorie of it selfe, well worthie our looking on.") In classical Greece, the same word in a more specialized sense also denoted a solemn legation of festal envoys sent by a state to observe religious sites in a neighboring state—a body of men who were apparently *sent to watch*. On this see Burkert, *Greek Religion*, 283. Compare Bourdieu, *Outline of a Theory of Practice*, 1, who, however, wants to return to the notion that there can be a "pure practice without theory."

7. For the context of this passage see Watson, *Hsün Tzu*, 20; I have consulted the annotated Chinese edition of Wang Xianqian, ed., *Xunzi jijie (Xunzi with Collected Commentaries)*, 1.9b (26). When citing Watson's translation I will henceforth abbreviate, for example, as W20. When citing the Chinese edition I will give the *juan* (chapter) number, followed by a period and the page number ("a" and "b" indicating recto and verso respectively). All translations from the Chinese are my own unless explicitly attributed to Watson, but

in all cases I give the location in Watson if one exists (his is only a partial translation). I have also occasionally consulted the older translation by Dubs, *The Works of Hsüntze*.

8. See 14.5a (539): *wu guan yu xiang er zhi wangdao zbi yi yi ye*; cf. W118.

9. Taylor, *Philosophical Papers*, 2:106, Cf. 2:93: "We could say that social theory arises when we try to formulate explicitly what we are doing, describe the activity which is central to a practice, and articulate the norms which are essential to it."

10. I refer to *Analects*, 3.11; cf. the translation in Lau, *Analects*, 69.

11. *Analects* 3.12: *ji shen ru shen zai*; cf. the translation in Lau, *Confucius: The Analects*, 69. Compare the things of which "the Master would not speak" mentioned in 9.1 and 7.21; most of them involve "spiritual" and "divine" matters.

12. I borrow this phrase from Yearley. "Hsün Tzu: Ritualization as Humanization," from which I have learned a great deal. I would like to thank Professor Yearley for kindly lending me his paper. I would also here like to thank Sally Gressums for lending me her unpublished paper (for which a title was lacking in my copy) on Xunzi, from which I also learned much.

13. See especially *Mencius* 2.A.6.

14. See W158ff. On Xunzi's response to Mencius, particularly as regards his alternative view of the mind and of human nature, see especially Yearley, "Hsün Tzu on the Mind," 465–68, and Lau, "Theories of Human Nature."

15. I do not pretend to have done justice to the fascinating subtleties of the Mohist position on rites and the spirits in such a short synopsis. For more thorough treatments, see Fehl, *Rites and Propriety*, 90–92; Schwartz, *The World of Thought*, 138–45 and 151–56; Mote, *Intellectual Foundations*, 87–89; and Graham, *Later Mohist Logic*, 270–72. Particularly relevant passages in the *Mozi* include sections 25, 31, and 32; see Watson, trans., *Mo Tzu*, 65ff. and 94ff.

16. See Schwartz, *The World of Thought*, 309–11. On certain of Xunzi's views on the mind and heaven as responses to Taoist "naturalism," see Yearley, "Hsün Tzu on the Mind," and Eno, chapter 6.

17. See Watson, trans., *Han Fei Tzu*, 118ff., and Schwartz, *The World of Thought*, chapter 8.

18. Eno, 142ff., gives an excellent discussion of this tendency of thought and how it differed from Xunzi's views on many points.

19. This is probably the view that later informs the specialists known as *fangshi*, on which see Ngo, *Divination*, and De-Woskin, *Doctors, Diviners, and Magicians*.

20. On the turbulent social changes that were culminating in Xunzi's day, see especially Hsu, *Ancient China in Transition*.

21. Watson's interpretation, though based on the Chinese commentarial tradition, that Xunzi thinks all of these acts "indicate respect for the basic materials of the meal" (W93), seems to me inadequate. All I am really sure of is that these gestures, in contrast to others used in the rites Xunzi describes, all involve *raw* foods; Xunzi's view of the significance of this fact remains unclear, though it is of course tempting to read him here as a proto–Lévi-Strauss.

22. "Completion" of ritual is a plausible but uncertain interpretation of what Xunzi is getting at in this passage.

23. I think Xunzi would agree, therefore, with the thesis advanced particularly clearly by Beattie, "On Understanding Ritual." I think he would disagree with the view advanced by Staal (in "The Meaninglessness of Ritual") concerning participants in ritual, that "there are no symbolic meanings going through their minds when they are engaged in performing ritual" (3), although he would agree with Staal and many other modern Western theorists that ritual is a "useless" activity in the sense that it is noninstrumental (or at least not *directly* instrumental) action (see 11–12). In any case, Xunzi clearly wants to affirm what Staal denies, that "ritual . . . consists in symbolic activities which refer to something else" (ibid.), and deny what Staal affirms, that "ritual . . . is meaningless, without function, aim or goal, or also that it constitutes its own aim or goal" (9). Indeed, Staal himself contradicts this, for he names a function performed by ritual, viz., the creation of a realm of perfect, risk-free activity, which has "a pleasant, soothing effect" (10). All of this is curious, since Staal cites Xunzi's opening passage on rites as a corroboration of his argument (14–15).

24. 13.14b: *sangli zhe yi shengzhe shi sizhe ye da xiang qi sheng yi song qi si ye*; cf. W103.

25. The term *mao*, which I have here rendered as "forms," connotes more specifically the *outward form taken by something that originates within*, and it usually refers to facial "expression." One of its classical lexical definitions is "whatever appears on the outside of something," the proof text being, significantly, another early text on ritual, the *Li ji* (*Ru xing* chapter): *Lijie zhe ren zhi mao ye*, "The rites and customs are the outward forms of benevolence [or humaneness—*ren*]" (cited in *Ci hai*, s.v. *mao*).

26. *Yi jing, Xi ci* section 1, 8.1; cf. the translations given in Wilhelm and Baynes, trans., *The I Ching or Book of Changes*, 304, and Legge, trans., *I Ching*, 360.

27. In his chapter on music—which immediately follows the chapter on rites in the received text of today—Xunzi also uses *xiang*, along with the semantically similar term *si*, when discussing the "symbolism" of musical instruments used in rites, what each "represents" and "resembles"; see W117–18, 14.4aff. For similar Ruist discourse on the symbolism of instruments, see Legge, trans., *The Li Ki*, chapter entitled *Li qi* (Ritual Implements), especially 1:398ff.

28. 14.4b–5a; cf. W118.

29. In other words, this is the one passage I have found in which Xunzi seems to be adopting something like Staal's position that ritual is, strictly speaking, "meaningless." Compare this statement by Staal: "To performing ritualists, rituals are to a large extent like dance, of which Isadora Duncan said: 'If I could tell you what it meant there would be no point in dancing, it'" ("The Meaninglessness of Ritual," 4).

30. See *The Works of Hsüntze*, 234.

31. 14.1a; cf. W112 and Dubs, *The Works of Hsüntze*, 247.

32. Peter Boodberg has argued, in fact, that the very term *it*, translated here as "rites" or "ritual," has the root etymological meaning of "form." See Boodberg, "The Semasiology of Some Primary Confucian Concepts," 34–35.

33. 13.22b: *shi si ru shi sheng shi wang ru shi cun zhuang yu wu xingying ran er cheng wen*; cf. W111.

34. I am here reminded of Geertz's well known observation that religion provides models *of* as well as *for* human life. See Geertz, *The Interpretation of Cultures*, 93–94.

35. Compare the passage in the "Discourse on Rites" 13.14a–b, translated at W102–3, which speaks of rites as "trimming or stretching, broadening or narrowing"—in short, forming and adjusting—the primal emotions of joy and sorrow, as a mode of "conscious activity" (*wei*) that works upon the "raw, material" (*caipu*) of human nature and its attendant spontaneous emotions.

36. The clearest treatment of this topic may be found in Yearley, "Hsün Tzu on the Mind," passim.

37. On the "universal" as distinct from merely "conventional" aspects of Xunzi's thought, see Yearley, "Hsün Tzu on the Mind," 476–79.

38. Yearley ("Hsün Tzu: Ritualization as Humanization," section 7) notes that this characterization of ritual is out of tune with most of his other statements in that it shifts discourse on ritual from the human to the natural sphere; he accounts for Xunzi's "cosmic" language, in a way reminiscent of Fingarette, by referring to "an experience many of us can have when humane order and power are at their most effective." But I think the passage is better seen as a cooptation of Taoist-style "naturalism": on the one hand, ritual belongs to the realm of *wei* or conscious activity and not that of *xing* or innate nature, but on the other hand, to the extent that ritual is patterned on the structure of, and can have real effects on, the course of nature itself, it takes on a "natural" dimension (no longer a mere human artifice) which lends it greater power in the eyes of Taoist opponents. I think Xunzi, in other words, is here trying to have his cake and eat it too, in direct response to the Taoist challenge—much as Eno convincingly shows Xunzi's theory of heaven to have been a response to Taoist naturalism. For examples of other, roughly contemporary "naturalistic" or "cosmic" characterizations of ritual emanating from the Ruist school, see Legge, trans., *The Li Ki*, 1:386–87 and 391.

39. I have omitted mention of a section of this passage (W94–95) in which Xunzi seems to be saying that one cannot measure ritual in certain other terms; I will consider it below, note 45.

40. On this see esp. Yearley, "Hsün Tzu on the Mind," 466.

41. On this ceremony see further Legge, trans., *The Li Ki*, 1:435–45; I have consulted the Chinese edition of Wang Meng'ou, 2:797–806.

42. Xunzi often speaks as if it is the particular function of music and dance to create social harmony, whereas ritual serves principally to reinforce social distinction. See, e.g., 14.3b; W117: "Music embodies an unchanging harmony, while rites represent unalterable reason. Music unites that which is the same; rites distinguish that which is different."

43. Note that the Taoist "naturalist" view—that people in their activities (though not in ritual activities as the Ruists understood these) should conform with natural patterns external to them and from which they have "fallen"—is structurally similar in locating the source of value outside the human realm. It comes under Xunzi's attack for just this reason, as in this passage: "Zhuangzi was obsessed by thoughts of heaven [that is, nature] and did not understand the importance of humanity. . . . He who thinks only of heaven will take the Way to be wholly a matter of harmonizing with natural forces" (W125–26). This passage comes in the context of a litany of the mistakes made by various academic schools, and in each case, their characteristic mistake could be applied to the realm of ritual, though space does not permit me to do so here.

44. On this line of argument in Xunzi, see esp. Machle, "Hsün Tzu as a Religious Philosopher," and Yearley, "Hsün Tzu: Ritualization as Humanization," who invokes the categories of "false consciousness" and "masochistic religion" to characterize Xunzi's objections to what I above called "divinistic naturalism" or a "theological" understanding of ritual practice and belief.

45. This explains the important passage, alluded to above, on 13.7b/W94–95, which seems to say that the "principles" (*li*) of ritual are incapable of being fathomed in terms of certain other standards. The first of these other standards is clearly that of the Logicians; the academic identity of the other two is unclear to me. But the essential point is that this passage does *not* say that ritual cannot be understood from any external point of view; it *does* say that ritual cannot be understood from three particular sorts of viewpoint, none of which, of course, Xunzi espouses.

46. A perusal of a recent work such as Grimes, *Research in Ritual Studies*, for instance, turns up nothing of this sort.

47. The quoted phrases are from Durkheim, *Moral Education*, 10–11.

48. Durkheim, *Elementary Forms*, 426. Hereafter abbreviated as *EF*.

49. "Society cannot make its influence felt unless it is in action, and it is not in action unless the individuals who compose it are assembled together and act in common. It is by common action that it takes consciousness of itself and realizes its position. . . . The collective ideas and sentiments are even possible only owing to these exterior movements which symbolize them" (*EF* 465–66).

50. On this point, see especially O'Keefe, *Stolen Lightning*, 189.

51. A key difference, however, is that Durkheim always speaks of this "shaping" in both *moral* and *cognitive* terms. In Durkheim and Mauss, *Primitive Classification*, for instance, social practice is pictured as the source of epistemological categories. Xunzi focuses much less on cognition and the source of epistemic categories, and more on the formation of dispositions to act appropriately.

52. The key locus for this idea is Durkheim's essay "The Dualism of Human Nature and Its Social Conditions," in Bellah, ed., *Emile Durkheim on Morality and Society*, 149–66. See also *EF* 298 and Bell, "Discourse and Dichotomies," 101.

53. I have relied especially on Giddens, *Capitalism and Modern Social Theory*, chapter 6.

54. See especially *Moral Education*, part 2, hints of which had already been given in Durkheim, *The Division of Labor*.

55. See especially Durkheim, *Education and Sociology*, 101.

REFERENCES

Beattie, J. H. M. 1970 "On Understanding Ritual." In *Rationality*, 240–68. Edited by Bryan R. Wilson. Oxford: Basil Blackwell.

Bell, Catherine. 1987 "Discourse and Dichotomies: The Structure of Ritual Theory." *Religion* 17:95–118.

Bellah, Robert N. 1973 *Emile Durkheim on Morality and Society*. Chicago: University of Chicago Press.

———. 1983 "The Ethical Aims of Social Inquiry." In *Social Science as Moral Inquiry*, 360–86. Edited by Norma Haan. New York: Columbia University Press.

Boodberg, Peter. 1979 "The Semasiology of Some Primary Confucian Concepts." *Philosophy East and West* 2 (1953):317–32; reprinted in Alvin P. Cohen (ed.): *Selected Works of Peter A. Boodberg*. Berkeley: University of California Press.

Boon, James A. 1982 *Other Tribes, Other Scribes: Symbolic Anthropology in the Comparative Study of Cultures, Histories, Religions, and Texts*. Cambridge: Cambridge University Press.

Bourdieu, Pierre. 1977 *Outline of a Theory of Practice*. Translated by Richard Nice. Cambridge: Cambridge University Press.

Burkert, Walter. 1985 *Greek Religion*. Translated by John Raffan. Cambridge: Harvard University Press.

DeWoskin, Kenneth J. 1983 *Doctors, Diviners, and Magicians of Ancient China: Biographies of "Fang-shih."* New York: Columbia University Press.

Dubs, Homer H. 1927 *Hsüntze, the Moulder of Ancient Confucianism*. London: Arthur Probsthain.

Dubs, Homer H., trans. 1928 *The Works of Hsuntze*. London: Arthur Probsthain.

Durkheim, Émile. 1933 *The Division of Labor in Society*. Translated George Simpson. New York: Macmillan.

———. 1956 *Education and Sociology*. Translated by Sherwood D. Fox. Glencoe, Ill.: Free Press.

———. 1961 *Moral Education*. Translated by E. K. Wilson and Herman Schnurer. New York: Free Press.

———. 1965 *The Elementary Forms of the Religious Life*. Translated by Joseph Ward Swain. New York: Macmillan, 1915; reprinted in Free Press Paperback Edition.

Durkheim, Émile, and Marcel Mauss. 1963 *Primitive Classification*. Translated by Rodney Needham. Chicago: University of Chicago Press.

Eno, Robert. 1990 *The Confucian Creation of Heaven: Philosophy and the Defense of Ritual Mastery*. Albany: State University of New York Press.

Fehl, Noah Edward. 1971 *Rites and Propriety in Literature and Life: A Perspective for a Cultural History of Ancient China*. Hong Kong: The Chinese University of Hong Kong Press.

Geertz, Clifford. 1973 *The Interpretation of Cultures*. New York: Basic Books.

Giddens, Anthony. 1971 *Capitalism and Modern Social Theory: An Analysis of the Writings of Marx, Durkheim and Max Weber*. Cambridge: Cambridge University Press.

Graham, A. C. 1978 *Later Mohist Logic, Ethics and Science*. Hong Kong: The Chinese University of Hong Kong Press.

Grimes, Ronald L. 1985 *Research in Ritual Studies: A Programmatic Essay and Bibliography*. Metuchen, N.J.: The American Theological Library Association.

Hsu Cho-yun. 1965 *Ancient China in Transition: An Analysis of Social Mobility, 722–222 B.C.* Stanford, Calif.: Stanford University Press.

Lau, D. C. 1953 "Theories of Human Nature in Mencius and Shyuntzyy." *Bulletin of the School of Oriental and African Studies* 15:541–56.

Lau, D. C. trans. 1979 *Confucius: The Analects*. Harmondsworth, England: Penguin.

Legge, James, trans. 1926 *The Sacred Books of China: The Texts of Confucianism*, Parts 3 and 4: *The Li Ki*, 2 volumes, 2nd ed. Sacred Books of the East volumes 527–28. Oxford: Oxford University Press.

———. 1973 *I Ching: Book of Changes*. New York: Causeway Books.

Machle, Edward. 1976 "Hsün Tzu as a Religious Philosopher." *Philosophy East and West* 26:443–61.

Mote, Frederick. 1971 *Intellectual Foundations of China*. New York: Knopf.

Ngo Van Xuyet. 1976 *Divination, magie et politique dans la Chine ancienne*. Paris: Presses Universitaires de France.

O'Keefe, Daniel Lawrence. 1982 *Stolen Lightning: The Social Theory of Magic*. New York: Vintage Books.

Schwartz, Benjamin I. 1985 *The World of Thought in Ancient China*. Cambridge: Harvard University Press.

Staal, Frits. 1975 "The Meaninglessness of Ritual." *Numen* 26:2–22.

Sullivan, Lawrence E. 1988 *Icanchu's Drum: An Orientation to Meaning in South American Religions*. New York: Macmillan.

Taylor, Charles. 1985 *Philosophical Papers*, volume 2: *Philosophy and the Human Sciences*. Cambridge: Cambridge University Press.

Wang Meng'ou, ed. 1980 *Li ji jinzhu jinyi*, 2 volumes. Taipei: Taiwan Commercial Press.

Wang Xianqian, ed. 1959 *Xunzi jijie (Xunzi with Collected Commentaries)*. Taipei: Yiwen Yinshu guan.

Watson, Burton, trans. 1963 *Hsün Tzu: Basic Writings*. New York: Columbia University Press.

———. 1963 *Mo Tzu: Basic Writings*. New York: Columbia University Press.

———. 1964 *Han Fei Tzu: Basic Writings*. New York: Columbia University Press.

Wilhelm, Richard, and Cary F. Baynes, trans. 1977 *The I Ching or Book of Changes*, 3rd ed. Princeton, N.J.: Princeton University Press.

Yearley, Lee H. 1980 "Hsün Tzu on the Mind: His Attempted Synthesis of Confucianism and Taoism." *Journal of Asian Studies* 29:465–80.

———. n.d. "Hsün Tzu: Ritualization as Humanization." Unpublished paper to appear in Wei-ming Tu, ed., *Confucian Spirituality*, volume 11 of *World Spirituality: An Encyclopedic History of the Religious Quest*. New York: Crossroads.

Etching Patriarchal Rule: Ritual Dye, Erotic Potency, and the Moroccan Monarchy

M. ELAINE COMBS-SCHILLING

Facts of publication: *Combs-Schilling, M. Elaine. 1991. "Etching Patriarchal Rule: Ritual Dye, Erotic Potency, and the Moroccan Monarchy." Journal of the History of Sexuality 1(4): 658–681. Copyright © 1991 by The University of Chicago. Reprinted with the permission of the author and publishers.*

In Moroccan Islam, rituals of first marriage constitute passage into adulthood for both males and females. Combs-Schilling shows that the marriage rite embeds the cultural particulars of Moroccan Islam in assumed universal truths about male-female relationships. By ceremonial and other means, boys, sometimes gentle, must learn to be assertive, and girls, sometimes forceful, must learn active submission. In the wedding ceremony a boy becomes a symbolic king. The girl who is to become a woman and his wife becomes his symbolic subject. Ritually, he must be made public and central, while she is made private and peripheral.

A central part of the ceremony is the use of hinna', a blood-red dye. The female's hands and feet are etched with it in a two- to six-hour rite. The male dips his hand in it and, upon striding into the nuptial chamber, presses his hand on the wall, leaving as many prints as the number of children he desires. He assumes patriarchal rule; she submits.

The symbolic act presages first intercourse, in which the emphasis is not on depositing sperm but on spilling the bride's blood. The act gives the new couple practice in the cultural roles they must assume. The bride's performance is supposed to be characterized by beauty, passivity, and sensuality; the groom's, by domination and power modeled on nothing less than the central ruler.

For further reading on the topic see M. Elaine Combs-Schilling, Sacred Performances: Islam, Sexuality, and Sacrifice. *New York: Columbia University Press, 1989.*

About the author: *Dates: 1949– , Knoxville, TN, U.S.A.* **Education**: *B.A., Stanford University; Ph.D., University of California.* **Field(s)**: *anthropology; rituals of dominance and resistance; gender and Islam.* **Career**: *Professor and Chair, 1983–present, Columbia University.* **Publications**: *Sacred Performances: Islam, Sexuality and Sacrifice (Columbia University, 1989); "Etching Patriarchal Rule: Ritual Dye, Erotic Potency, and the Moroccan Monarchy," Journal of the History of Sexuality 1 (1991): 658–681; Death and the Female Saint: Dominance in the Space of Opposition (Columbia University, forthcoming).* **Additional**: *"My research addresses the role of rituals in producing power as well as resisting it, especially in Morocco. I address the ways in which Morocco's millenium-old monarchy reconstitutes itself through the prison of ritual performances, as well as the role of the rituals surrounding a high mountain female saint in critiquing dominant forms. I also teach courses on ritual: ritual process, ritual and change, performance and power."*

Our bodies are our means of access to ourselves and to the world. They are also means of cultural communication and reproduction. Here, I focus upon the intersection between our bodies and the structures of political power. I argue that durable systems of domination are often ones in which the structures of power are so embedded within the body of self that the self cannot be easily abstracted from them.

Culture (that is, collective representations in thought and practice, abiding forms that are stored in the brain as abstractions) uses the body to elaborate its imagination.[1] It encodes its representations on body postures, patterns of eye contact, the structure of space, and the structure of physical movements. But culture also draws upon the body's inherent power in validating itself. It mobilizes the potency of crucial acts of humanity, notably sexual intercourse, birth, bloodspilling, and death, and shapes them to confirm its own designs, thereby embedding idiosyncratic cultural inventions within universal foundations with forceful consequence. By obscuring cultural particulars in the most potent of human actions—actions whose power almost all of humanity in some form knows—the cultural particulars lose the feel of particularity and come to appear as something intrinsic to existence, a natural part of the world, taken for granted. Culture does not have to whip up the potency of sexual intercourse; that potency exists beyond individual cultures, beyond the human species itself. Yet, its potency exists in rather fluid, nonspecific form and is thereby available for cultural channeling. We look at cultural manipulation of the panhuman potency of sexual intercourse in the construction and validation of one of the world's oldest still ruling monarchies, the Moroccan kingship.

MOROCCO'S MONARCHY

The Moroccan monarchy, like other largely legitimate, ruling monarchies, incorporates the population into it through a process of hierarchical solidarity, integration achieved through focus on the king. The king makes possible the community.[2] In the dominant forms of collective consciousness, political authority is conceived as passing from the king to prominent senior men, to other senior men, to junior men. Women are not represented as appropriate carriers of the public political domain.

The current king, Hassan II, is stunningly potent. He is the linchpin of Morocco's military, economic, and administrative structures. He decides all major issues of state, calls and dissolves parliament at will, and is the collective symbol of the Moroccan nation to itself. For the majority of Moroccans, the monarchy remains legitimate. Whatever individuals may think about any given occupant, the institution itself, like the U.S. presidency, remains an established reality through which large sectors of the population think about themselves, their collective history, and their distinctive political identity in the world.

The monarchy is not only powerful, it is remarkably old—one of the world's oldest, and probably *the* oldest still ruling monarchy.[3] Begun in A.D. 789, a hundred years before the British crown, the monarchy marked its twelve-hundredth anniversary in 1989. Six dynasties have occupied Morocco's central throne. The current dynasty, the 'Alawi, came to power in 1666.

The continuity in Morocco's political system makes it an important arena for examination. Much current political research addresses polities where the present-day forms of political authority are of recent origin, hotly contested, and where the boundaries of viable political units and the nature of political rule has been subject to frequent and radical changes over the last millennium. Not so in Morocco. There have been changes during the twelve centuries of rule, yet many of the essentials, mutatis mutandis, have endured, including the consistent focus on the monarch as the center of Islamic political identity.

There is no such thing as a static political system. If stability is a distinguishing feature, it has been actively achieved. Enduring political systems are dynamic, for they must address a population continually changing because of the basic parameters of birth, aging, and death. If a polity manages to endure, it has successfully regenerated mechanisms for incorporating new and old members into it, members born into constantly changing historical situations.

Much current gender research stresses the issue of contest to the dominant form of political authority. The research presented in this essay stresses active regeneration. Active contest and active regeneration are both parts of political systems. While it is true that systems of political domination are often contested, it is also true that some hierarchies of political domination (notably those embedded in gender and race) show remarkable resiliency even in the face of considerable assault and continue to persist long after repeated challenges have occurred. Contest is not so singular a political mode as current scholarship would make it. The interesting question in any particular situation is what is the mix of active contest and active regeneration and why. Morocco is an excellent case that illustrates the power of political regeneration; it illustrates how hierarchical political domination can be made a part of people's everyday lives—people on the top, people on the bottom—so that they actively help revitalize it because reality has been constructed in such a way that their own hopes, dreams, and accessible pathways of self-worth are tied to it. The clarity of the Moroccan case provides important insight that can be used to scrutinize acts of regeneration elsewhere, where the hierarchy of political domination is not so apparent, and yet its impact and durability continues to make itself felt. This essay is about regenerative political processes that exist in Morocco; it is also about regenerative political processes that exist elsewhere.[4]

The monarchy's potency during the first centuries of its rule (789–1350, especially the 1000s to the 1350s) is obvious and straightforward. That was Morocco's age of practical ascendancy.[5] Faith and legitimacy coincided with military might and economic power. Gold and silver flowed, Morocco's sugar industry flourished, its armies, navies, and administration thrived. Morocco was then a part of a great Islamic civilization, an Islamic expansionary core, if you will, for which Morocco was a western seat of power. At the height of its power, Morocco extended its dominion over much of the western Mediterranean; it ruled into Spain and Iberia in the north, Mauretania in the south, and the Libyan desert in the east.

The monarchy's potency during the past 650 years (the 1350s to the 1990s) is less straightforward and more intriguing.[6] During the years 1350 to 1415, the bubonic plague struck, the economy collapsed, the army and the administration fell apart, and Europe began to invade. It looked as if Morocco's polity and its distinctive Islamic monarchy were undone, but they were not. Despite the monarchy's loss of centralized institutions for controlling economic, military, and administrative might, the monarchy managed to survive by bolstering itself on cultural credit, which it then used as a means of gaining access to economic and military resources that existed, for the greater part of this post-1400s era, on the local level. Through culturally legitimated popular persuasion, the king could orient what he could not command and turn it to the monarchy's design. Ritual was a fundamental means of regenerating the foundation of credit.[7]

The monarchy's survival underlines Gramsci's and Foucault's notions on the peripheral and productive constitution of power, that is, that political power is not simply, and sometimes not even primarily, reproduced through state apparatus and coercive means, but also through a plethora of symbols, signs, and actions that are filled with compelling significance in people's daily lives. "What makes power hold good, what makes it accepted is simply the fact that it doesn't only weigh on us as a force that says no, but that it traverses and produces things, it induces pleasure, forms of knowledge, produces discourse. It needs to be considered as a productive network which runs through the whole social body, much more than a negative instance whose function is repression."[8]

In the long era of crisis (the 1350s to the 1900s), Morocco's monarchy was regenerated by diffuse, productive, and peripheral supports that continually renewed it in the hearts, minds, and deeds of the population. The supports were largely effective. Although Morocco was the first country attacked as Iberia came into its age of domination (1415), and although Morocco was repeatedly attacked in the centuries that followed, Morocco was nonetheless one of the last African countries to be formally colonized (1912) and one of the first freed from the colonial bond (1956). The specific details of that resistance and the role of rituals in it are told elsewhere.[9] Here I want simply to emphasize two of the embodied practices, two rituals, that helped renew Morocco's monarchy, and the implicit patriarchy upon which it rests, in the lives of individuals during the age of crisis and that help renew it still: the first marriage application of hinna' (henna) dye and the first marriage act of sexual intercourse.

First a few caveats: I am not suggesting that rituals were the monarchy's only means of survival or necessarily the most important means. Numerous factors enter into any history. But I am suggesting that, in post-1500s Morocco, rituals have been a crucial means of regenerating the dominant form of political authority and that this is because of what rituals are. Rituals, at their most effective, are real-life experiences; that is how the participants perceive them. Rituals are often heightened experiences, quintessential history, that can cast the rest of history into doubt, a fact too often forgotten by analysts who look at rituals as dubious occasions, doubting a priori their worth, and portraying them as comments on experience, reflections on experience, or elaborations of experience, rather than experience itself. But that approach is wrong. In

Morocco's resistance to western Europe (1400s–1900s), the local economy often faltered, battles frequently were lost, and the monarchy, in practical terms, was often frail, but in great ritual performances, participated in by nearly the whole of the population on numerous occasions every year, Moroccans experienced their ruler as powerful, their faith as unvanquished, and themselves as unified through focus on the reigning king. That experientially built reality was pivotal in maintaining the population's sense of self and purpose, their understanding of their monarchy, and their opposition to the west.

Ritual at its most persuasive is perceived by the participants as an on-the-ground experience that carries with it the substantive realism that the ground brings—colors, sights, sounds, smells, deep-seated longings. But ritual is orchestrated experience that has the ability to bring popular practice into line with the cultural imagination. In the rituals we examine, we see how the ritual process helps to solidify the bond between individuals and the accepted hierarchy of political authority. The rituals help to construct an experience in which the individual comes to see his or her self-definition as intertwined with the ruling power.

FIRST MARRIAGE

Popular rituals of first marriage take place throughout the Moroccan countryside. They are rites in which boys and girls are given passage into adulthood. The rites are explicitly local practices, embellished with local color and local meaning, but they also articulate and make convincing central cultural and political ideals. The rites embolden the characteristics of adult male and female, making them tangible for the participants, embedding them within their own bodies, at the same time that the rite revitalizes within the participants the monarchy as the proper form of political rule.

Marriages are still for the most part arranged, although the practices are undergoing alteration. Marriages link families, not simply individuals. Fathers typically have the final right of approval, while mothers are often the gatherers of information and the instigators of action.

The rite of marriage publicly inaugurates what the community marks as the legitimate unit of sexual intercourse and the legitimate unit of reproduction. Children born outside the bond of marriage (or outside the related bond of concubinage) are not legally recognized as existing. For children of casual sexual unions, it creates a momentous problem. Those individuals are not considered to be "illegitimate"; they simply are considered not to exist.[10]

First marriage ceremonies inculcate within the bodies of boys and girls the patterned actions, postures, and behavioral responses that they must exhibit if they are to be recognized as adults by others and by themselves. It is intensive training in a new stage of life. Within the Moroccan context, adulthood and marriage are considered for the most part coterminous. Later marriages do not call for the same intense preparation, since the transformation into adulthood has already been achieved.

We have descriptions of the ceremonies over the past three hundred years.[11] While there is local diversity in the practices, there is also much continuity in time and place. The following portrayal is drawn from my analysis of more than eighty ceremonies that took place in various parts of the countryside. I attended thirty-seven of them. The ceremonies included celebrations of urban as well as rural peoples, people from the mountains and from the plains, native Arabic speakers and native Berber speakers.[12] At first, my interests centered on the diversity of marriage ceremonies, but in analyzing the details of the eighty cases, what emerged as more striking was the commonality in basic substructure that characterizes them.

The transformation into adulthood is no easy task. Young men must be taken out of the house, put onto the streets, exercised in becoming central, public, and political, active participants in all that goes on, a communal link to transcendence, for that is how adult men in Morocco are culturally defined. Young women in contrast must be taken off the streets, exercised in becoming peripheral, private, and passive, responsive to needs of husband and mother-in-law. Upon marriage, the bride moves into her husband's household. In the early years typically that means moving into her husband's father's household, a patrilineally chartered household in which her mother-in-law is in charge of in-house affairs. The bride is an outsider, an interloper who is being judged by husband and mother-in-law. In order to earn the right to stay in the household, the bride is dependent upon their favor (divorce rates are high).[13] Active subservience is the likeliest means of gaining approval, especially during the early years of marriage. The birth of a male heir is the best way to secure that favor in the long term. (Until the turn of the century it was common in some regions for the bride not to be allowed to return to her natal household for a year, or until the birth of the first child.) Given this structure of reality, it is not surprising that women who are close to the bride try to give her active practice in submissive postures and attitudes during the wedding ceremonies.

For many young men and women, the traits the community demands in adulthood are not ones that they have been used to exhibiting. Boys can be tender and gentle; girls are often forceful and assertive.

Boys have been trained in subordinance. In many households the children kiss the father's hand on each occasion that they greet him. In some families, the weight of demonstrating patriarchal authority falls most heavily on sons, while daughters, who leave the household anyway, are given more room to maneuver. As junior members of their father's households, boys often carry out tasks that may be done by women or children but not by honored men, for example, serving their father's guests, with eyes downcast and body stances closed in. Boys have spent much of their time in the female quarters of their father's household, with mother or grandmother in charge. The rite of first marriage must move them unequivocally out of the female domain that they have inhabited as subordinates, so that they can reenter it as dominant males.

Young women must be exercised in the opposite qualities. Moroccan girls are often independent and forceful. In preadolescence, girls often carry out tasks that take them into the public sector, for instance, caring for animals, gathering firewood, fetching water from the wells. As married women, especially in the early years, they must greatly circumscribe their spatial movements. They must learn to operate and find meaning in enclosed household spaces, and if they should venture outside they must learn to enclose themselves there also.[14]

The important point here is that whatever the individual personalities and whatever traits they have exhibited in the past, males and females in adulthood must learn to channel systematically their own personalities into the traits collectively demanded of them in order to be recognized as adults by the community and honored in that state, a recognition for the most part necessary for viable adult existence. What men and women do in private is not so much the community's concern, so long as they continue to uphold collective expectations when they are with others. The reproduction of collective life depends on consistency in communal appearances. Days of preparation encode within the bodies of the bride and groom characteristics they must—in certain key situations—come to exhibit. I will focus upon two intense embodiments within the larger ritual: the ceremonies of the blood-red dye, hinna', and the ceremony of bloodspilling intercourse.

Groom's Transformation

The groom is taught how to be a man, how to become the head of household and enter the honored state of adult men, by having his identity merged into that of the quintessential man, the Moroccan king. The groom is transformed into the king at the beginning of the ceremonies and remains the king until they are complete.

At dawn on the day when the festivities begin, a group of young men (wazirs) come to the groom's father's household and call for the groom to come out—to come out of his state of dependence and enter the public world of real men. When the young man appears in the doorway, those who have called him out cover his entire body, including his face, with a large white blanket. He is now in-between. The identity he held as a child has been left behind. He is now in the process of becoming and is cocooned so that the metamorphosis successfully takes place. The groom is led to the public prayer grounds where the senior men of the community sacrifice a ram each year as a covenant with God on behalf of the community they represent.[15] At that sacred and public place, the young man is transformed into the king.

The transformation is often intense. For a time the groom appears to become the monarch. The young man is dressed in the monarch's clothing, surrounded by a court of advisors, and called by the monarch's favored titles "Mawlay al-Sharif" and "Mawlay Sultan," "My Lord the Descendant of the Prophet" and "My Lord the Powerful One." The bridegroom-king parades through the streets while his advisors wave flags, carry candles, and shout his praises, as is done for the real monarch. Sometimes they hold an imperial parasol over his head. The groom learns how to become a man by first "becoming" the nation's ruler, by inhabiting for the ritual time the body of the king. Personal metamorphosis is accomplished through political association, a profound political embodiment.

Groom's Hinna'

Culture often validates its creative illusions through the material, substantiating the cultural imagination within the physical world. The first marriage applications of hinna' are a case in point. Hinna' is a natural dye that leaves a blood-red stain. In Morocco, as in much of the Muslim world, it is a metaphorical signifier of blood, especially procreation's blood. The Qur'an is clear that human creation results from sperm drop and blood clot. Sperm is associated with men, and blood—in manifest practice—is associated with women (they shed menstrual blood; they spill the blood of childbirth). But first marriage ceremonies put the woman's dominion of procreative blood into question and in fact build an alternate reality in which it is shown that although women spontaneously spill blood, it is men who consciously guide the blood clot into life. First marriage is one of the few occasions in which Moroccan men are likely to use hinna'. This use makes great cultural sense because the ceremonies concern procreation.

As practiced in some parts of the countryside, the groom's final day of preparations includes a "Great Hinna'" ceremony.[16] After another public procession through the streets, during which drums beat, horns blare, and flags are waved to let the people know that the sacred and powerful one is there, the procession again comes to the public prayer grounds where the groom was first transformed into the "monarch." The groom formally sits on his "throne" and the festivities begin. First comes a ceremony of mockery leveled at the monarch-bridegroom, who must withstand the mockery with good-natured benevolence, as should the real monarch.[17] Then follows a ceremony of gift-giving. Finally the hinna' ceremony occurs. Several unmarried girls, sisters or cousins of the groom, mix the hinna' with raw eggs in a bowl to make a thick gooey paste which they then present to the monarch-bridegroom. This action is an embodiment—a palpable realization—of one of the ritual's main themes, that is, that although girls possess the blood clot, they must present it to the man, epitomized by the essential man, the monarch-bridegroom, in order for proper procreation to take place. This act heralds the intercourse that will occur that night.

The monarch-bridegroom puts his hand in the bowl of hinna'-blood and, leading his *wazirs*, strides to the still empty nuptial chamber where, that night, he will meet his bride. He opens the door, boldly enters, and with an authoritative brandish presses his right hand on the wall, leaving his imprint in the thick hinna' dye. The number of handprints is said to signify how many children he wants. Once the ritual is complete, those around the monarch-bridegroom recite in unison, "Now they are married. Now they are married."[18]

For the outsider, the words, "Now they are married," at first seem startling. After all, the female half of the bridal couple did not do anything, and, in fact, she was not even present. Yet those around the monarch-bride-groom are speaking of the marriage as having taken place. However, as it turns out, this is pretty much what happens on the marriage night anyway. The first marriage intercourse pivots on the bloodspilling of the man, and the hinna' ceremony is a rehearsal.

The hinna' ceremony gives the groom practice in what is expected of him. The metaphorical blood rehearsal verifies for him and those around him the cultural invention that he dominates earthly reproduction. Procreation is a power of God, but the hinna' ceremony helps to cultivate the perspective that it is the monarch-bridegroom who taps that creative power and brings it to earth. He takes the female's blood clot and guides it into life. Through metaphorical participation in the procreative act, the monarch-bridegroom is empowered, and he allows those gathered around him to partake in some of that power by dipping their little fingers into the hinna'-blood.

Female Places

The bride's preparations are in many ways the opposite of the groom's. As an embodied practice that gives the bride realistic preparation for the stances in which she will be rewarded this is culturally proper, for the role she occupies in adulthood is most often the opposite of the groom's. While he is made central, public, and sacred, she is rehearsed in becoming increasingly private, peripheral, and temporal. Most of the bride's preparations take place within enclosed household walls, many on the bed. Typically only women are present. While the groom is transformed into the king for his metamorphosis, the bride is transformed into no public figure. She does not become queen. In fact, there is no queen in Morocco. The women to whom the king is durably linked through contracts of marriage or concubinage are private individuals who do not appear (nor are they named) in public. The bride, like all women, including the king's women, remains herself, an inalienable member of her father's "bloodline" his patriline, who is being transferred to another patriline for purposes of reproduction. She will not become a member of that new patriline, and she does not pass on her blood heritage to her children. Children take their blood descent from their father. In the case of divorce and contest over children, the man has claim to them.[19] Songs sung to the bride often speak of her marriage as barter, and there is a dimension of barter about it: that is, the bartering of an inalienable part of the patriline, the bride, so that another patriline can birth its children, and in return the bride's own patriline can receive the women it needs to birth its children.

In terms of personality, the bride may well be forceful and decisive. Many Moroccan women, on their own or when alone with other women, are so. But collective consciousness does not valorize these traits for women. Lacking collective legitimacy, Moroccan women sometimes construct it—individually—for themselves. They engage, as Mernissi argues, in "auto-valorization," in self-legitimation, a very different kind of process than collective legitimation. On their own, some imagine worlds that offer them a noble place.[20] And in those worlds they are assertive and forceful, as many are when with women only. Given the traditional division of space, many Moroccan women spend most of their time separate from men. In the women's world, with no senior men present, women often negotiate a complex hierarchy of domination and submission. Yet, when a prominent man enters the room (for ex-

ample, husband or father), the female hierarchy for the most part collapses, and women as a category become subordinate to the man. The change in women's postures when a senior man enters is dramatic. In milliseconds, women can go from swaggering stances and boisterous laughter to submissive gestures, bodies turned inward, and eyes downcast. For most Moroccan women I know, passivity and silence are situational practices adopted when men of authority are present. That adoption reflects as well as reifies the accepted hierarchy of power.

Women as well as men tend to ascribe to the position that men have an intrinsic right to rule. If women wish to make their opinions felt, they must negotiate a space (their ability to construct that space is not institutionalized and inherited but must be continually rebuilt by individual women in their own lives). In terms of dominance hierarchy, men occupy first place.[21]

That women are resilient and take on power and exhibit authority in the domains allotted them does not mitigate the forcefulness of the ascribed hierarchy that puts the king on top, a hierarchy of elite senior men beneath him, a hierarchy of lower-ranking senior men beneath them, a hierarchy of junior men under them, and a hierarchy of women and children at the bottom. Although the majority of women take the hierarchy for granted, assuming that "this is the way it is," they often speak of it with pain, especially as it concerns the two most important dimensions of their lives—dimensions they do not control—that is, whether or not they will stay married, and whether or not they will be able to stay with their children (divorce and child custody are the rights of the husband). A man can divorce a woman simply by saying "I divorce thee," and many men, honorable men who have no intention of divorcing their wives, taunt wives with the threat as a form of "play," to the amusement of other males present and to the sorrow of women.

When it comes to culturally legitimated domination, the husband is in charge, and women as well as men tend to affirm the rightfulness of that division. Hence, if a bride is to have success in her new role as wife, she must learn to embody subordinance, and much of the marriage ceremony centers on women who are close to the bride (mother, aunts, and sisters) exercising the bride in postures and attitudes of subordinance and, furthermore, if she must come in conflict with her husband, teaching her how to express it in ways that do not openly conflict with the "appearances" of the dominance of men. The bride must learn to convey the image that her husband is in charge, that he is the unquestioned decision-maker in the household, whatever the private realities of in-house negotiations, for that is the appearance that will gain wife, husband, and children community-lauded honor.

The groom, in contrast, even if he should exhibit a tendency to be self-effacing and soft-spoken, must learn to appear in charge of the household—the decision-maker, the decisive actor, the mediating link between the household and the larger political and religious communities of which it is a part. Hence whatever the private variation, the adult male and the adult female must learn to express their personalities through acceptable channels if they are to receive communal affirmation. The hinna' ceremonies reflect and recreate proper channels of male and female expression.

Bridal Hinna'

The bridal hinna' is something done to the bride, not by the bride. What is demanded of her is that she actively bring her body into submission, which in fact demands considerable self-conscious control, but that control does not receive communal affirmation. Quite the contrary, the public perception is that the bride is "out of control," while the groom is "in control."[22] The bridal hinna' helps the bride to learn that she must force her body into submission so that others can take her blood and design it into things of beauty that will make her appealing to the man and by that process give her some security.

The bride typically sits or lies on a couch while a woman skilled in the art of hinna' application carefully etches her hands and feet with the dye. The ceremony can take from two to six hours. The hinna' applier dips a sharply pointed object into the bowl of thick hinna' paste, then lifts the sharp instrument so that a small thread-like cylinder of the paste dangles from its tip. The practitioner carefully lays the tiny cylinders one after the other on the bride's hands, wrists, ankles, and feet in delicate filigree patterns of abstract design and exquisite

beauty. The bride must remain perfectly still. Ideally she should not eat, drink, or move from the couch during this time. Carefully her hands are completed, and then her feet are etched by the same slow process.

After the hinna' application is complete, the bride must heat her hands and feet over hot coals; the heating is meant to set the dye. Next, those around the bride wrap her hands and feet with layers and layers of cotton or gauze. When they are finished the bride looks like a burn victim. The bindings remain in place for twelve to twenty-four hours. The bindings, like the heating, help set the dye. When bound, the bride is completely dependent on others. She cannot eat or drink or use the bathroom by herself. The ritual gives the bride embodied practice in the body stances, attitudes, and postures that are likely to gain her the most security and status during the early years of marital life. Through multiple senses, through multiple enactments, the bride is rehearsed in being the kind of individual that the society expects her to be and will reward her for being. Again, we must remind ourselves of the momentousness involved in the bride's change of households and her vulnerability as she enters a household in which she has no inalienable rights and never will (though she may achieve some earned rights that bring her a degree of security, especially if she bears many sons). Hinna' is a dramatic and realistic coding in the postures and attitudes of submission, one that embues the bride with the notion that she achieves a degree of empowerment from the submissive stance.

On the insistence of close friends, who presented me with what amounted to a fait accompli when I came into the female quarters one morning, I had the bridal hinna' done. It took six hours. My body was sore. My head ached. I did not eat, have anything to drink, or use the bathroom during the entire period. I had never in my whole life so actively had to constrain my body into stillness, actively force my body into passivity. I was exhausted from the effort, but it was also enjoyable being surrounded by women who cared about you, feeling enclosed, safe, and secure, the center of attention, having one's beauty constantly lauded. The designs are exquisite. There is much laughter, merrymaking, and ribald joking, especially about men's sexuality, about their need to assert their dominance, and about how women have to pretend to go along with it. Hinna' practitioners are perceived to be somewhat loose women and their presence brings a certain relaxation to the women's quarters. Some women whom I never saw smoking at any other time smoked while the hinna' practitioner was there. The sexual joking and relaxation give women lighthearted release and a degree of verbal control over the sexual dimension of their lives in which they lack practical control, while posing no threat to the accepted structure of male domination. In fact, one could argue, it helps accommodate women to it.

On the following day, the gauze is removed and the hinna' paste washed off. In the most elaborate ceremonies, the whole hinna' procedure is repeated again in order to reinforce the stain lines. The visual result of the dyeing is an etching of blood-red lace gloves and anklets, embedded in the skin itself, that can last for a month. But, more enduring, the hinna' application helps to strengthen the culture's inventions of what it means to be male and female. The ritual does not single-handedly build the cultural structure but, rather, draws certain dimensions together and presents them to the participants in crystalline form, emboldening them and embedding them in the participants during a time of high emotional pitch, when the learning facilities are on edge.

The hinna' is a compelling performance. Through icon, material substance, and action, the bride is rehearsed—in mind, body, and deed—in the understanding that she must submit to others while they guide her blood, so that it can be turned into things of creation that make her appealing to the man, sensual beauty on one level (communicated through the hinna' designs), the reproduction of children at a deeper level (communicated through the night's intercourse). These things are affirmed as making the wife valuable to the man. They are reliable pathways to viable existence, sensuality and beauty being more short-term, birth of male heirs being far more enduring. For women, the familiar modes of empowerment lie deeply embedded within the accepted structure of their own domination. The reality of this empowerment and domination is communicated by a group of caring women who read back to the bride the validity of what is done. Good times, laughter, caring for others, and collective worth are intimately intertwined

with the monarchical structure, making it durable and resilient.

Bloodspilling Intercourse

The hinna'-etched bride is carried to the nuptial chamber, her outer garments are removed, and she is placed on the nuptial bed, passive and white. If the bride does anything to affect her fate, she usually does so in private, after the preparers have left her and before the groom arrives. Sometimes, the bride waves her slipper seven times in front of the door and utters an incantation meant to bind the groom to her. In some local areas, she takes out a swab of cotton she has hidden in her garments. The cotton has been soaked in a bit of the blood of the ram that her father sacrificed for the wedding festivities and some drops of her own blood (obtained from a cut in her vulva).[23] The bride squeezes a bit of this mixed blood into a drink that she hopes the monarch-bridegroom will ingest. The culture allocates to women indirect and magical ways of influencing their fate (that is, by first influencing the men upon whom their fate depends), while it gives to men direct and political ways to affect their destiny. Both are means of empowerment, but they are different means and different kinds of power. The one is necessarily private and surreptitious, the other is direct and straightforward.

The bridegroom as monarch enters. Boldly opening the door, he steps into the room and greets the bride with a brandish of power. In some areas, he breaks her headdress. In others he tears her gown or places his sword on her shoulder. All are local variations on the common theme of male violence and domination. All are reminders of the rightful structure of authority in household and in nation-state.

Whatever his initial action, the most important exhibit of the monarch-bridegroom's power marks the act of intercourse, a biological act that is here culturally constructed to reinforce the culture's inventions. Ideally the bride arrives at the nuptial chamber with her hymen unbroken so that he—ruler and head of household—can break it. With dramatic thrust of finger or phallus, he pierces her, rupturing and causing to bleed the thin membrane that previously had lain across the birth canal. By the act, the monarch-bridegroom initiates the birth canal for children and lays claim to the offspring born from it, physically validating the rightfulness of the cultural principle of "blood inheritance" through the male line.

This is a sexual act, but it is a controlled act, a heightened sexual act different from other intercourses that will take place on two counts: (1) because the monarch is iconically present, and (2) because bloodspilling, not sperm-spilling, is the focus. (In fact, in some regions, as Daisy Dwyer notes, local custom prohibits the groom's spilling of sperm at the first marriage bloodspilling).[24] These two dimensions should alert us to the ritual's meaning. This inaugural intercourse is ritually constructed to bring the monarchy into every household, into every man and woman, through the most intimate act. And the ritual is constructed to undergird man and monarch's presumed dominance over procreation's blood.

As mentioned earlier, the Qur'an is clear that procreation emerges from sperm drop and blood clot. Sperm already belongs to the man; first marriage's intercourse gives to the male the dominance of procreation's blood also. The ritual affirms that although women unconsciously possess the blood clot, spontaneously spilling it each month, it is the man who consciously performs the definitive actions that guide that blood clot into life. This inaugural intercourse is ritually constructed to pivot on the man's domination of blood, an embodied action, a palpable expression, that confirms the rightfulness of patrilineality, patriarchy, and monarchy. Through dramatic physical act and enduring icon, blood descent and collective authority are verified as passing through, and belonging to, the male. In light of this ritually established cultural "truth," it is simply "natural" that the father gives the offspring his or her enduring name, his or her enduring sociobiological identity, for ritual shows the man to be the actor who initiates procreation itself. By the act, the monarch-bridegroom draws to himself the natural potency of sexual intercourse and bloodspilling and affirms the invented reality of his ascendancy as progenitor. Songs often sung to him as he walks through the streets confirm this role: "Glory to God, Glory to the Creator, Glory to the Eternal, the Creation has begun."[25]

The spilled blood is highly valued; it is caught on the bride's pantaloons or bedsheets and publicly exhibited. Elder women stand outside the door of the nuptial chamber waiting for the groom to hand them the mark of his accomplishment, the blood-soaked garment. The groom is typically credited with the successful completion of this act, while the bride is typically held to blame if the blood-soaked garment should not appear. Elder women ululate upon seeing the blood-stained cloth; unmarried girls dance with it through the streets for all to see; men sometimes use the blood-soaked garment for target practice. Sexual subtlety is not a characteristic of the rite.

In analyzing this ritual, I find striking the degree to which anthropologists have focused on women and virginity, when in fact the ritual, at least as practiced in Morocco, pivots on men and bloodspilling. The virginal womb, the unbroken hymen, is simply one way in which the culture "proves" that men dominate creation, one way that the culture physically verifies this illusion. The culture usurps the male-female act of first intercourse to affirm this invention of man's dominance, a dominance demonstrated—when the hymen is intact—by the physical response of the bride's body itself. If for any reason the bride's hymen should already be broken (the hymen can rupture through the girl's riding horseback or muleback), the proper order of things can still be established by the man's spilling of sacrificial blood. The groom sometimes brings a pigeon or a rooster into the nuptial chamber for this purpose, hiding it under his robes as he enters. There, following formal Muslim prescriptions, he sacrifices the bird: he takes a knife in his right hand, utters God's holy name, then, with swift motion, he pierces the thin membrane that covers the fowl's throat, allowing its sacrificial blood to flow on the bride's pantaloons or bedsheets, which are then handed outside to the women who begin the celebration.

Spilled blood physically confirms for the groom and for others the illusion that the groom dominates procreation. Hence, what matters is that the groom spill blood; it does not necessarily matter whether the blood comes from fowl or female.

Through the manipulation of physical substance and biological experience, the ritual makes men the cultural usurpers of the natural birth process. While biological foundations speak to the role of both women and men, and the physical foundations that most clearly manifest themselves in daily life speak to the importance of women (after all, the woman spills blood each month, conceives the child inside her, provides the womb in which it grows, and physically delivers the child into the world), the ceremony of hinna' and the rite of hymen, or hymen-substitute, bloodspilling are constructed to show man and monarch's true dominance, to give the cultural imagination priority over other forms of perception, and to confirm that domination through the physical processes themselves, through a male-initiated act of sexual bloodspilling.

Children are deeply valued in this culture. People want properly authorized reproduction to take place. The continuity of the man's name, his essence, and his patriline depends on it, as does a woman's status in this world. The most accessible means for a woman to achieve a position of worth is by becoming the mother of male offspring. As culturally constructed, the realization of these longings depends on the male's procreative dominance. What women typically want and work for, therefore, is man's exemplary performance.

The entire sequence of first marriage embodiments supports the cultural inventions of patrilineality, patriarchy, and monarchy, making them appear inevitable. If indeed men initiate and dominate the birth process, then it makes sense that men give children their enduring sociobiological identity. If indeed men successfully accomplish procreation through decisive actions made on behalf of the whole, then patriarchy also "naturally" follows. If indeed the king is the great progenitor par excellence, the template that other men use as stellar guide, then monarchy also follows.

Of all men, the ritual emboldens the king. The king enters the bedroom along with the groom and empowers him to carry out the momentous action. The king gives the young man his coming of age, while the groom gives the king entry into his intimate dimensions: his definition of self and his experience of the first act of marital intercourse. The identity of the head of household and the head of nation merge. Their power structures intermingle and each becomes dependent on the other. The mutual dependence of monarch and man makes it difficult for either to undo the other, for that would undo his own base of power and his own base of identity. The father of the nation and the father of the household become one, and the hopes of women are made to depend on them. Gender in this situation becomes precisely what Joan Wallach Scott suggests: "a primary means of signifying relationships of power."[26]

CULTURE'S SLEIGHT OF HAND

Culture has at its disposal a convincing mechanism for a great sleight of hand. Culture can make its elaborations appear true by embedding them within the body's most basic biological truths. The physical groundings —sexual intercourse, bloodspilling, and birth—independently and panhumanly exist, while the cultural elaborations do not (they are culture-specific). Once fused, they are hard to pull apart. The fusion of physical substratum with cultural elaboration is an enormously potent means of validating an invented structure of domination, for it encases cultural inventions within embodied truths, so that the biological truths themselves seem—naturally and implicitly—to support the structure of power.

Godelier remarks, "It is not sexuality that haunts society, but society which haunts the body's sexuality."[27] Sexual desires exist in potent but rather ill-defined form as seen in the varied patterns of sexual expression that exist the world over. Sexual intercourse exists as a basic potential, a basic human potency, to be tapped and shaped by society as it imposes external and rather rigid structures on internal and rather flexible human desires. The Moroccan ritual of first marriage is a profound occasion for monarchy's haunting of sexual intercourse. In it, the strivings of individual human agency and the strictures of political domination are made to converge. Strictures of polity become strictures of self; the erotic encodes the political.

When a literal "body politic" exists, it becomes difficult to bring the system of political domination to the level of self-conscious scrutiny without doing real damage to oneself, without bringing the system as a whole, internal and external, into question, for it is precisely the whole that is at stake. Embedding a system of domination within the male-female division of the world, and within the acts of human reproduction, is, to borrow from Bourdieu, "the best founded of collective illusions."[28]

First marriage rites are a generative mechanism through which the monarchy and the self are mutually constituted. In it, the Moroccan monarchy is written on and through people's own bodies at the same time that these people's selves are written on and through the monarchy. The durability of one of the world's oldest ruling monarchies in part results from the effectiveness with which the intimate link between ruler and constituent is made. The degree to which the definition of oneself lies in the central political institution makes the monarchy and its underlying patriarchy hard to undo.

Yet the structures of monarchy and patriarchy are invented and like all cultural inventions depend on their continual renewal in the lives of individuals in order to remain intact. Many dimensions of Moroccan life are changing.[29] The single most important source of change and potential conflict comes from public school education, with its stress on personal achievement as the legitimate mode of employment, on the power of the people as the legitimate foundation of political rule, and on the right of women to be educated and hold jobs in the public sector.

The access of females to education has the potential of being the most radical change, and its repercussions are beginning to be felt. Increasing numbers of women attend school, enter professions, marry later, and are beginning to demand, consciously and unconsciously, in thought and in body stances, alternative constructions.[30] The changes in practice are momentous, and yet one should not exaggerate their "inevitable" impact on the hierarchy of political authority. These changes, like all changes, are filtered through the dominant forms of collective consciousness and through the dominant institutions (economic, military, religious, political, and familial). The changes are substantial, yet they are not so cascading or cumulative as one might have thought in the abstract. As Mernissi and Naamane-Ghessous show, thus far the changes have not been dramatically incorporated into central cultural ideals, nor have they been integrated into the dominant forms of collective consciousness.[31] They are increasingly a part of everyday practice and as such are potentially significant, but only if they can be translated into basic definitional changes on the collective level. As of yet those changes have not occurred.

Basic cultural abstractions of male, female, and ruler have not kept pace with certain changes in lifestyle. This is often the case in times of dramatic social upheaval: innovative thoughts and experiences do not as easily become a part of the dominant forms of collective consciousness. Recent connectionist theories of cognition help us to understand why.[32] Its theorists, such as Quinn and Strauss, argue that memory is not stored in a central memory bank but rather in spiraling networks of neural connections, some of which are highly developed and elaborated (including those that result from consistencies in collective thought and practice), while others are underdeveloped or nonexistent. Innovative thoughts and practices are often harder to incorporate into the memory network precisely because they are novel; they do not have regular pathways of neural connections to carry and validate them, in sharp contrast to thoughts and practices that lie more in line with the dominant forms. Hence, in being novel, the new ideas and practices concerning women are not so easily synthesized.

However, their exclusion is not simply a case of the novel not being as easily integrated, for in fact there is much in daily life that revalidates the more enduring definitions (for example, patterns of the control and distribution of income, access to many jobs, and the organization of family life; familiar pathways of achieving happiness, satisfaction, and social status; the way in which individual Moroccans feel they participate in world affairs, that is, through a focus on their king). The rituals of first marriage are one mechanism of this renewal—not the only means, but an important one. First marriage rites are an emboldened and embodied mechanism through which the Moroccan monarchy and the implicit patriarchy upon which it rests continually become a part of the everyday lives of individuals throughout the land, attached to those things they hold most dear.[33] Through much of Morocco, first marriage ceremonies continue to be practiced in the basic form presented here and hence continue to infuse the monarchy into popular experience and consciousness by infusing it into the most basic understandings of male and female, writing definitions of political authority on definitions of gendered self, erotic longings, and hopes for progeny. I submit that the remarkable durability of the Moroccan monarchy lies in part in its success in fusing the structures of subordination with what the individual sees as the realistic means of empowerment, ennoblement, and hope. This fusion effects the most formidable kind of complicitous bonding that a power structure can create.

NOTES

1. For a thorough-going exploration of the role of the body in constituting human thought and human culture, see George Lakoff, *Women, Fire, and Dangerous Things: What Categories Reveal about the Mind* (Chicago, 1987); and Mark Johnson, *The Body in the Mind: The Bodily Basis of Reason and Imagination* (Chicago, 1987).

2. For a brilliant and amusing discussion of monarchy's hierarchical mode integration as opposed to more collective populist forms, see Marshall Sahlins, *Islands of History* (Chicago, 1985), pp. 32–72, especially pp. 36, 45–50.

3. Japan's emperorship is the contender. It is older than the Moroccan monarchy, but it does not hold the reigns of power in its hands. The Moroccan monarchy does.

4. Active contest of course exists in Morocco; I have written about it elsewhere (M. E. Combs-Schilling, "Capitulation and Resistance: The Life, Times, and Remembrances of a Female Saint of Morocco's High Atlas Mountains" [paper presented at the annual meeting of the American Anthropological Association, New Orleans, December 2, 1990]). Still I would argue that active contest is a less prominent mode of interaction between the ruling authority and the population in Morocco than is active regeneration. Active opposition, however, is expressed more in some regions than others, for example, in al-Rif. That opposition is also expressed more at some times than at others, for instance, in the early 1970s as opposed to the 1990s. Still, in Morocco, active regeneration remains the historically dominant mode. Even if the Moroccan monarchy were soon to fall, which I do not envision, a monarchy that has been actively renewed for twelve hundred years deserves scrutiny as to its mechanisms for bringing the population to the worldview of kings. The analysis of these processes can reveal important facets of popularly garnered legitimacy that are useful for the analysis of other polities where the modes of hierarchical reproduction are not quite so explicit but are nonetheless present.

5. For the history of this age, see Jamil Abun-Nasr, *A History of the Maghrib in the Islamic Period* (Cambridge, 1987); M. E. Combs-Schilling, *Sacred Performances; Islam, Sexuality, and Sacrifice* (New York, 1989), pp. 103–14; Abdallah Laroui, *The History of the Maghrib: An Interpretive Essay* (Princeton, NJ, 1977).

6. For the history of this age, see Abun-Nasr; Combs-Schilling, *Sacred Performances*, pp. 115–56; and Laroui. See also Muhammad al-Ifrani, *Nozhet-elhadi [Nushat al-hadi]: Historie de la dynastie Saadienne au Maroc (1511–1670)* (1700s), trans. and ed. O. Houdas (Paris, 1889).

7. See Combs-Schilling, *Sacred Performances*, pp. 115–309.

8. A. Gramsci, *Selections from Political Writings, 1910–1920*, ed. Q. Hoare (London, 1977); Michel Foucault, *Power/Knowledge: Selected Interviews and Other Writings, 1972–77*, ed. Colin Gordon (Brighton, 1980), p. 119. While the Moroccan case illustrates Foucault's point on the productive dimension of power, it calls into question Foucault's notions that Europe from the seventeenth century on has been the seat of a fundamentally different and much more efficient consolidation of productive power than had existed previously in the human community. Of the European center, Foucault states: "From the seventeenth and eighteenth centuries, there was a veritable technological take-off in the pro-ductivity of power. . . . There was . . . a new 'economy of power' . . . [which] was more efficient and less wasteful (less costly economically, less risky in their results, less open to loopholes and resistances) than the techniques previously employed" (p. 119). The analysis of Morocco's system of political domination and political regeneration (at least from the 1500s on) suggests that Foucault's assumptions, as is often the case in western scholarship, result from a Eurocentered bias, from a dominant form of western discourse that Foucault reproduces unawares.

9. Combs-Schilling, *Sacred Performances.*

10. A number of Moroccan lawyers currently are working on the lack of legal and cultural recognition of these children. The problem is exacerbated because adoption itself does not exist within Islamic legal parameters. Hence, not only are the children of casual sexual liaisons not recognized as existing, but there are no legal procedures within the traditional Islamic framework to give them a legal heritage. A number of orphanages have been established. They house mostly boys, because girls born into this state tend to be taken as servants (see n. 20 below). Since girls do not pass on blood heritage, their lack of it does not pose a serious problem. That is not the case for boys. Boys are the carriers of patrilineal identity. They do pass their blood heritage on to their children and thus, without knowledge of what that blood heritage is, they are truly ambiguous beings and tend not to even be taken as servants. The orphanages cater to adoption by foreigners who live in countries where legal adoption exists. Yet adding a further irony to this whole situation is the paradox that in order for these foreigners to take the children out of Morocco, they must, while in Morocco, legally declare themselves to be Muslim. Yet if they were really Muslims, given the Qur'anic text, they would not acquiesce to the practice of adoption.

11. Descriptions of Moroccan marriage ceremonies in more distant times can be found in Leo Africanus, *The History and Description of Africa and the Notable Things Therein Contained* (1526) (London, 1896); Lancelot Addison, *West Barbary; or, A Sort of Narrative of the Revolutions of the Kingdoms of the Fez and Morocco* (Oxford, 1671); M. Chenier, *The Present State of the Empire of Morocco*, 2 vols. (London, 1788); Germain Mouette, *The Travels of Sieur Mouette in the Kingdoms of Fez and Morocco* (London, 1710); John Windus, *A Journey to Mequinez* (London, 1725). The most important work on marriage is Edward Westermarck, *Marriage Ceremonies in Morocco* (London, 1914). Westermarck, a fluent Arabic speaker, made sixteen trips to Morocco to gather material for the book. In its 422 pages, it includes precise, detailed descriptions of ceremonies from all over Morocco.

12. The notes, interviews, and video recordings of the wedding ceremonies I attended were gathered during seven separate trips to Morocco that I made from 1976 to 1990. I lived for a total of four-and-a-half years in Morocco, spending twenty months in a small Berber-Arab town in the High Atlas mountains, eighteen months in Rabat, and six months in Casablanca (the majority of weddings were observed in these three locations). The rest of my time in Morocco was spent in shorter trips to the following places, where I also attended wedding ceremonies: Fez, Marrakesh, Midelt, Chefchaouen, Imichil, Lala Aziza, Boulawane, Oulad Teirna. In my analy-

sis, I drew upon the published research of others, including Susan Schaefer Davis, *Patience and Power: Women's Lives in a Moroccan Village* (Cambridge, MA, 1983); Daisy Dwyer, *Images and Self-Images: Male and Female in Morocco* (New York, 1978); Raymond Jamous, *Honneur et Baraka* (Paris, 1981); Roger Joseph and Terri Brint Joseph, *The Rose and the Thorn: Semiotic Structures in Morocco* (Tucson, AZ, 1987); Jane Kramer, *Honor to the Bride Like the Pigeon That Guards Its Grain under the Clove Trees* (New York, 1970). I first charted each of the eighty ceremonies in terms of their internal characteristics and then compared the characteristics and progressional flow of each ceremony to the others. From that I derived my assumptions about dominant forms. There is of course variation. The existence of variation does not necessarily conflict with the existence of dominant schemata; in fact one could argue that it is a necessary part of it. In trying to be a conscientious observer, one attempts not to exaggerate the structural coherency that exists in my given form, but one should not minimize it a priori either. Just as in the case of active contest versus active regeneration, so it is with the case of structural coherency versus individual variation, that is, no single one of these dimensions inevitably dominates the other. The degree of dominance of a given trait depends on time and place.

13. See Vanessa Maher, *Women and Property in Morocco* (Cambridge, 1974), which addresses the high divorce rate and the importance of women's networks of nurture and aid in helping women cope with the reality in which they live, where the structures of political authority and community decision making are not in their hands.

14. In some places this enclosure is accomplished through the wearing of layers of gowns and a veil across the face. In other places, the veil is not physically worn, but "veiling" is still accomplished through distinctive patterns of body closure and eye avoidance. By this summary of traits, I simply wish to illustrate some of the breadth that young men and young women exhibit in adolescence, and how this breadth is constrained in the postmarital life. I also do not mean to imply that young boys and girls have no training in the characteristics that will be demanded of them in adulthood. They have had considerable training. However, I wish to emphasize that first marriage ceremonies are a crystallization and an intensification of certain kinds of behaviors that must be effectively embodied if the groom and bride are to be successful adults.

15. The Great Sacrifice Feast is another ritual celebration that is canonical in Islam. Throughout the Muslim world the rite reinforces the legitimacy of patriarchy and patrilineality. In Morocco, it also reinforces monarchy, due to an innovation in the ritual performance accomplished in the late 1600s and continued to the present day (see Combs-Schilling, *Sacred Performances* [n. 5 above], pp. 221–71).

16. In some local areas, the groom dips only a single finger into the hinna' dye. In that case, there is close resemblance between the hinna'-dyed finger and the groom's blood-soaked phallus (or finger) of hymen-breaking intercourse.

17. Until the French banned them, ceremonies of ruler mockery were a part of Morocco's Great Sacrifice Feast. A scholar from one of the top Islamic universities would be selected as the "king" for a day and oversee ceremonies of raucous merrymaking in which the real king was the butt of the mock-

ery. The actual king often attended these ceremonies and laughed in good-natured amusement at himself. The ceremonies ended with affirmation of authority. The pretend king swore his allegiance to the real king, and the real king gave the imposter a valuable gift for his efforts.

18. Jamous, pp. 271–72.

19. If a divorced woman has children, they may be allowed to stay with her while they are young because many Moroccans believe that young children should be with their mothers. However, if the woman should remarry, she loses them. And in any event, by the time the children have reached the age of puberty, the father has taken them if he wants them (almost always the case with sons).

20. Fatima Mernissi, *Le Maroc raconte par ses femmes* (Rabat, 1986), p. 17. Mernissi notes that auto-legitimation sometimes takes the form of women imagining themselves as a race of giants daily battling the forces that would destroy them. Mernissi describes one case of "extreme" auto-valorization involving a nine-year-old girl, Aicha al-Hayyania, who had been taken out of her natal province to be engaged as a full-time domestic servant for a family in Fez. As a survival mechanism the girl often operated in a dream world of her rural infancy, in which she imagined herself in quasi-mythic terms as having nearly supernatural work capacities. She imagined that as a young child in the countryside she had been able to plant crops, press olive oil, gather firewood, carry water, fish, hunt, make bread, and take care of animals. It was with these thoughts that the young girl would sweep floors, sort grain, wash dishes, and care for children in the Fez household. The use of young girls, age five and up, as full-time domestic servants in Morocco is common. These girls, usually rural, are taken out of their natal families, often out of their natal locales, to live in households where they are servants, people on the bottom rung. The girl's family in the countryside, usually the girl's father, receives some small financial compensation for her work. As with other forms of servanthood, there is a great range of ways in which individuals are treated, but in structural terms, they rest unequivocally on the bottom. Child servants, almost all of whom are female, are an issue about which a number of Moroccans are fervently concerned and are working to change.

21. Women's postural code switching exists in numerous places in North Africa and the Middle East. It is described with poignancy and skill by Lila Abu-Lughod, *Veiled Sentiments* (Berkeley, 1986). Postural code switching also exists among men. While women as a category are dependent upon men as a category, each category has a dominance hierarchy within it (as well as a few crossovers between them, for instance, male servants and high-status, post-menopausal religious women). Lower-status individuals of the same sex must exhibit subordinate gestures when around higher-status individuals of that same sex.

22. Combs-Schilling, *Sacred Performances*, pp. 215–18.

23. Westermarck (n. 11 above), p. 147; Combs-Schilling interviews, 1977, 1985, 1988.

24. Dwyer (n. 12 above), pp. 64–65.

25. Jamous (n. 12 above), p. 271.

26. Joan Wallach Scott, *Gender and the Politics of History* (New York, 1988), p. 44.

27. Maurice Godelier, "The Origins of Male Domination," *New Left Review* 127 (1981): 17.

28. Pierre Bourdieu, *Le sens pratique* (Paris, 1980), p. 246. My colleague Robert E. Pollack, professor of biological sciences at Columbia University, reacted to the cultural construction in this way: "Biologically, it is completely unsound. In genetic terms neither the mother nor the father can pass on more than a random assortment of their mothers' and their fathers' alleles. It is disturbing that such strong and effective asymmetric cultural constructions, so damaging and unfair to women, can be built on a biological template which is genetically symmetric and physiologically tilted toward the centrality of women" (personal communication, May 1990).

29. Fatima Mernissi, *Beyond the Veil: Male-Female Dynamics in a Modern Muslim Society*, rev. ed. (Bloomington, IN, 1987); and Soumaya Naamane-Ghessous, *Au dela de toute pudeur: La sexualité féminine au Maroc* (Casablanca, 1987).

30. To illustrate the extent of the changes, I draw upon statistics derived from local documents in the small town in which I lived during 1977 and 1978 and to which I regularly return. The changes over the past decades have been momentous. In 1960–61, the first middle school was opened in Imi-n-Tanout (middle school follows elementary school and precedes high school). That first year 104 students attended; all were male. By 1963–64, middle school enrollment had grown to 326 students and, for the first time, included females. Six were enrolled. By 1976–77, the number of students in the middle school had grown to 598; sixty of them were female, 10 percent of the total (most of these girls were daughters of administrators and teachers from Morocco's urban centers who had come to town to work). By 1989–90, the number of students in the middle school has risen to 978; 277 students were female, 28 percent of the student body. The majority of these females came from local families. In 1984, a high school was opened in the town. As of the academic year 1989–90, the high school had 432 students, seventy-one of whom were female (16 percent). Most of these females also came from local families. School attendance has set in motion radical change in the gender organization of space. In 1976–77, females did not appear on the town's main streets; as of 1989–90, hundreds of these young women are seen on the streets each day with serious purpose as they go to and from school. Upon graduation from high school or college, some of these young women are entering jobs that take them into formerly uncontested male space (one of the town's doctors is a woman). The changes are dramatic, yet here, as in many other places, they have yet to be incorporated into and legitimated by the dominant forms of collective consciousness.

31. See Mernissi; and Naamane-Ghessous.

32. On connectionist theory, see especially Naomi Quinn and Claudia Strauss, "A Cognitive Cultural Anthropology" (paper presented at the annual meeting of the American Anthropological Association, Washington, DC, November 15–19, 1989); Naomi Quinn, "The Cultural Basis of Metaphor," in *Beyond Metaphor: The Theory of Tropes in Anthropology*, ed. James Fernandez (Stanford, CA, 1990); and Claudia Strauss, "Who Gets Ahead? Cognitive Responses to Heteroglossia in American Political Culture," *American Ethnologist* 17 (1990): 312–28.

33. The group that has most changed the ceremonies is the ruling elite of large urban centers, who frequently combine elements of wedding ceremonies in other countries with intrinsically Moroccan practices, including the bridal hinna'. But for them the change in ritual practice does not necessarily signal a change in gender and ruler definitions. Quite the contrary, this is the group whose economic fate and social standing is most directly linked with the king's, as Leveau clearly demonstrates (see Remy Leveau, *Le fellah marocain defenseur du trone*, 2d ed. [Paris, 1985]). This group has impelling socioeconomic reasons not to confront fundamentally definitions developed in the past even if their ritual foundations are more mixed.

Rite of Return: Circumcision in Morocco

VINCENT CRAPANZANO

Facts of publication: *Crapanzano, Vincent. 1980. "Rite of Return: Circumcision in Morocco" from* The Psychoanalytic Study of Society 9: *15–36. Edited by Werner Muensterberger and L. Bryce Boyer. New York: Psychohistory Press. Copyright © 1980 by The Psychohistory Press. Reprinted with the permission of the publishers.*

Using his own fieldwork observations among Muslims in Morocco, Vincent Crapanzano challenges the assumption that initiation rites such as circumcision necessarily transform boys into men. He doubts whether every rite labeled a rite of passage really effects passage from an old social status to a new one. He questions the universality of Arnold van Gennep's theory of transitional rites and calls attention to the dissonances between what people say a rite does and what that rite really effects.

For a general summary of Islamic ritual see Frederick M. Denny, "Islamic Ritual: Perspectives and Theories" in Approaches to Islam in Religious Studies, *edited by Richard C. Martin (Tucson: University of Arizona Press, 1985).*

About the author: Dates: *1939– , Glen Ridge, NJ, U.S.A.* **Education**: *B.A., Harvard College; Ph.D., Columbia University.* **Field(s)**: *epistemological foundations of interpretation; psychological and psychiatric anthropology; anthropology and literature.* **Career**: *Distinguished Professor of Comparative Literature and Anthropology, City University of New York Graduate Center.* **Publications**: The Hamadsha: A Study in Moroccan Ethnopsychiatry *(University of California, 1993);* Tuhami: A Portrait of a Moroccan *(University of Chicago, 1980, 1983);* Hermes' Dilemma and Hamlet's Desire *(Harvard University, 1993); with Vivian Corrison,* Case Studies in Spirit Possession *(Wiley, 1977).*

The primitive world, like the worlds of the child and the psychotic, offers a convenient space for projection. The line between folk anthropology and myth is hard to draw. The man-in-the-street with virtually no experience of the primitive will often discourse at great length about primitive customs. Even the serious ethnographies of the past, certainly past ethnological speculation, frequently impress later anthropologists rather more as myth than science; the vulgarized claims of such ethnographies and ethnologies are retained, symptomatically, in the popular imagination. They often appear as antithetical constructs, antiworlds really, which serve, as Lévi-Strauss (1963) maintains and Michel Foucault (1965) would maintain, a definitional function. This is of course most evident in nineteenth-century tracts on primitive sexual promiscuity (Bachofen 1967), marriage by abduction and female infanticide (McLennan 1865), incest (Morgan 1877; Tylor 1958), the priority of matriarchy (Bachofen 1967) or patriarchy (Maine 1861), and the absence even of religion among savages (Lubbock 1870). It is evident, too, in the writings of later anthropologists and will undoubtedly be observed by future scholars looking back at contemporary anthropology. If the fears and anxieties, the desires and longings, the needs for identity and definition of an age are not given direct expression in more scientific anthropological works, they do, nevertheless, influence the concerns, evaluations, and theoretical foci of such works. They determine, too, at least in part, the biases of these works.

In this paper[1] I suggest that the description of a certain class of rituals as rites of transition, *rites de passage*, may reflect less the reality of the ritual than the culture of the anthropologist. My point is that the emphasis on transition may be a (culturally if not psychologically induced) distortion of the ritual process: an oversimplification. I do not mean to deny the existence of the classical *rite de passage*; such rites undoubtedly exist. I mean simply to suggest that there may be rituals, traditionally described as rites of passage, that do not involve passage or give only the illusion of passage. These rites shall be called rites of return, *rites de retour*. In the second half of this paper I shall examine one such rite, the rite of circumcision of the Moroccan Arabs living in the countryside around the city of Meknes.

Arnold van Gennep (1960) first described the *rite de passage* in 1908. He noted that "the life of the individual in any society is a series of passages from one age to another and from one occupation to another." Progression from one occupational group to another is marked by special acts which, among the "semi-civilized," are enveloped in sacred ceremonies.

> Transitions from group to group and from one social situation to the next are looked on as implicit in the very fact of existence, so that a man's life comes to be made up of a succession of stages with similar ends and beginnings: birth, social puberty, marriage, fatherhood, advancement to a higher class, occupational specialization and death. *For every one of these events there are ceremonies whose essential purpose is to enable the individual to pass from one defined position to another which is equally well-defined.* (p. 3, italics mine)

All these ceremonies, van Gennep argues, exhibit a pattern (*schéma*) of three essential phases which vary in importance in different transitional contexts: separation (*séparation*), transition (*marge*), and incorporation (*agrégation*). The rite of circumcision is for van Gennep a rite of separation.

Despite van Gennep's assertion that the "essential purpose" of the rite of passage "is to enable the individual to pass from one defined position to another which is equally well-defined," he himself is not particularly clear about the nature of these "positions" (see Gluckman 1962). He refers to occupational groups, age grades, membership in societies, brotherhoods, religious, and tribal groups; he refers to such celestially determined units as months, seasons, and years. He lacks the conceptual apparatus of status and role that later scholars have (not without the danger of over-simplification) attached to his theories. Van Gennep's failure to define adequately "position" has, I believe, impeded an appreciation of the intricacy of the ritual process.[2] Moreover, his failure to consider ritual, however arbitrarily, from the experiential vantage point of any one of its participants has led him to simplify the ritual experience itself.[3] In this paper, I will look at the rite of circumcision from the point of view of a single participant, the boy who undergoes the operation. My decision is arbitrary but, hopefully, of heuristic value. In no way is it a denial of the significance of the rite for other participants.[4]

In their desire for analytic purity, if not in their fright, before the "subjective" vantage point of experience, many scholars have succumbed to what can be called the ritual illusion. Put, perhaps, too simply: the ritual illusion is the assumption that what the ritual is said to do is in fact what it does. That a boy is treated as a man, for example, that he is declared to be a man, *in a particular ritual context* does not necessarily indicate what his treatment and conceptualization will be in other contexts. He may well be treated as a man, or a boy, or an infant—or as in all three in different contexts. (These different contexts would include those of everyday life, those of other rituals, and those of such narratives as stories about the boy himself or myths and legends in which he is tacitly identified with one character or another.) What is important is to assume neither continuity nor discontinuity of both treatment and conceptualization between contexts. Ritual exegesis—and the exegetical method in ritual analysis—frequently (if not inevitably) promote the illusion of continuity and mask both discontinuities and dissonant experiences.

A striking example of how an analytic strategy can produce a scotoma, a blindness to possible discontinuities in the ritual process and dissonances in the ritual experience, is van Gennep's (1960) distinction between physiological and social puberty, a distinction which has provided the rationale for purely sociological analyses of ritual. Van Gennep notes quite simply that since the time of so-called puberty rites rarely coincides with the physical puberty of the initiate, "it is appropriate to distinguish between *physical puberty* and *social puberty*, just as we distinguish between *physical kinship* (consanguinity) and *social kinship*, between *physical maturity* and *social maturity* (majority)" (p. 68). With regard to circumcision, he notes:

> Variations in the age at which circumcision is practiced should themselves show that this is an act of social and not physiological significance. Among many peoples the operation is performed at fairly great intervals—for instance, every two, three, four or five years—so that children of different degrees of sexual development are circumcised at the same time. Moreover, within a single region inhabited by populations of the same somatic type (race), remarkable variations will be found. (p. 70)

As evidence, van Gennep quotes Doutté's findings on the age of circumcision in Morocco: from seven to eight days after birth to twelve or thirteen years among the Dukalla, from two to five years among the Rahuna, from two to ten in Fez, at eight in Tangiers, from five to ten among the Djabala, and from two to four around Mogador. Circumcision is, then, from van Gennep's point of view, a rite of social and not physiological significance. It is a rite of separation that removes the mutilated individual "from the common mass of humanity" and permanently incorporates him in a "defined group" "since the operation leaves ineradicable traces" (p. 72).

By isolating the physiological from the social, van Gennep precludes consideration of the significance of their frequent disjunction. He oversimplifies the ritual process and fails to appreciate the complexity of the ritual experience. It is important to note here too that *both* the physiological and the social are cultural categories.[5] Van Gennep frequently confuses an emic, or in-cultural, definition of group membership with an etic, or extracultural, definition of physiological puberty. From an experiential point of view, it is necessary to approach group membership, identity, role, and status as well as physical maturity emically.

Even among scholars who have accepted the experiential or phenomenological vantage point there is a marked tendency to succumb to the ritual illusion. Peter Berger and Thomas Luckmann note in *The Social Construction of Reality* (1967) that the socially constructed symbolic universe "makes possible the ordering of different phases of biography."

> In primitive societies the rites of passage represent this nomic function in pristine form. The periodization of biography is symbolized at each stage with the totality of human meanings. To be a child, to be an adolescent, to be an adult, and so forth—each of these biographical phases is legitimated as a mode of being in the symbolic universe (most often, as a particular mode of relating to the world of the gods.) *We need not belabor the obvious point that such symbolization is conducive to feelings of security and belonging.* (p. 99, italics mine)

Berger and Luckmann go on to suggest that a modern psychological theory of personality development can fulfil the same nomic function.

> In both cases, the individual passing from one biographical phase to another can view himself as repeating a sequence that is given in the "nature of things" or in his own "nature." *That is, he can reassure himself that he is living "correctly."* The "correctness" of his life program is thus legitimated on the highest level of generality. As the individual looks back upon his past, his biography is intelligible to him in these terms. As he projects himself into the future, he may conceive of his biography as unfolding within a universe whose ultimate coordinates are known. (pp. 99–100, italics mine)

Berger and Luckmann are correct in pointing to the nomic function that the rite of passage plays in the "periodization" of biography. But by failing to take into account a possible disjunction between the ritually periodized biography of the individual and his *everyday* experience of himself, and his personal history with all its contingencies, particularities, and deviations, Berger and Luckmann render personal history a stereotype, the individual a cypher, and time *angstlos*.

Indeed, one of the effects of the disjunction between these two orders, here ritualized biography and mundane personal history, is an anxiety which must

not be considered only in terms of pathology (Fromm-Reichmann 1955). Berger and Luckmann's "obvious point" that the ritual periodization of biography is "conducive to feelings of security and belonging" may not be so obvious after all. The ritual may give the individual no assurance whatsoever that he is living "correctly." As every therapist knows, it is the disjunction between a "normal" if not an *ideal* biography and one's own personal history that produces anxiety, guilt, and symptomatology. Civilization, as Freud (1930) has pointed out, imposes cruel sacrifice on man, on his sexuality and aggressivity. This sacrifice is dramatically portrayed in the Moroccan circumcision ritual that I will describe. We in the West may understand it in Oedipal terms as the birth of conscience, the repression of desire, and the creation of profound feelings of inadequacy, inferiority and worthlessness that demand constant compensation. To the Moroccan, the rite will be understood with little elaboration as a necessary prerequisite for both spiritual and sexual manhood.

The theories which have been put forth to explain the very widespread practice of circumcision (Jensen 1933) are, as Ashley-Montagu (1946) remarked, "as numerous as the leaves in the Vallombrosa." Bryk (1934) notes that the explanations for circumcision "furnish a splendid example of the versatility of human extravagant imagination, and are, at the same time, a document of the ambivalent validity of casuistic argumentation." Weston LaBarre (1970) remarks too on the ingenuity used to "explain" circumcision in conceptually comfortable terms. The Australian initiation rites which include circumcision and subincision have served as a prototype for much of the speculation on the "meaning" of circumcision (Bettelheim 1955; Radin 1957; Róheim 1942, 1945, 1972).

Early anthropological theories tended to be universal and rationalist. Briffault (1927) suggested that circumcision is an attempt on the part of the male to imitate female genital defloration; Westermarck (1926) saw it as a means of making the boy a man capable of procreation and marriage; Crawley (1927) regarded it as both a means of preventing the retention of magically dangerous secretions and as a sacrifice of a part that guaranteed thereby the well-being of the whole; Meiners, Boettiger, and Vatke among others (Bryk 1934) explained circumcision as a substitute for human sacrifice and castration. Frazer

(1922) understood it in terms of reincarnation. Circumcision has been explained too in terms of increased or decreased sensuality, the prevention of onanism and pederasty, ritual cleanliness, endurance tests and increased fertility (Bryk 1934, Gray 1911). Van Gennep (1960) as noted earlier, regarded it as a mark of group membership. This view had been carried to an absurd extreme in 1829 by van Autenreith (quoted in Bryk 1934) who derived circumcision from the barbarian warriors' custom of bringing back the genitals of fallen enemies. To avoid suspicion that these phallic trophies were plundered from their own dead, the warriors adopted the custom of circumcision. Numerous medical and hygenic reasons—the prevention of paraphimosis, phimosis, *calculi praeputiales*, cancer, gonorrhoea, and syphilis—have also been offered, usually without regard to native medical beliefs (Bryk 1934).

Aside from the more universalistic (statistical) explanations for circumcision such as Whiting's (1964) attempt to correlate it with rainy tropics, kwashkiokor, and patrilineal polygyny (!), most recent anthropological investigations have focused on the practice within a specific socio-cultural context. Circumcision is usually viewed as an important segment of an initiation ceremony. (As Radin [1957] pointed out, such initiations have the puberty rite as their prototype.) Raymond Firth (1963) writes, typically, with regard to the Tikopian practice of superincision (a longitudinal slitting of the upper surface of the anterior portion of the prepuce):

> The ceremonies of initiation cannot then be explained as the outcome of the particular operation of superincision; this must be explained in terms of the ritual as a whole from which it derives its justification. (p. 429)

Superincision for the Tikopian, Firth argues, "confers the appropriate material token of distinction upon the individual who has been the subject of the qualifying ritual." It characterizes the boy as sexually mature. (Here I should note that like circumcision in Morocco the operation is often precocious.) The initiation ritual itself shapes the boy's relation to other persons in the community and thus helps "to fit him for future life." Not only does Firth ignore the possible consequences of the disjunction between social and physical puberty but he tends to look at contradictory elements within the ritual context itself as ultimately integrative.

In his detailed analysis of *Mukanda*, the circumcision rite of the matrilineal Ndembu of Zambia, Victor Turner (1967; 1962) does recognize the complex, polysemic, sometimes contradictory, certainly bipolar referentiality of ritual symbols. Circumcision is the central episode in the Ndembu's seemingly classical rite of passage in which the boy is made a man. This rite, Turner stresses, not only changes the status of the initiate but serves to reconfirm or realign social relations. One of the most important of these is the parent-child relationship, which Turner (1967) understands in its broader socio-symbolic dimension.

> From being "unclean" children, partially effeminized by constant contact with their mothers and other women, boys are converted by the mystical efficacy of the ritual into purified members of a male moral community, able to begin to take part in the jural, political and ritual affairs of Ndembu society. (p. 265)

This change not only effects the relationship between sons and parents but also the "extrafamilial links of matrilineal descent and patrilateral affiliation."

> The separation of men and women in *Mukanda* is not only a ritualized expression, indeed an exaggeration, of the physical and psychological differences between men and women, but it also utilizes the idiom of sexuality to represent the difference between opposed modes of ordering social relations, which in Ndembu culture have become associated with descent through parents of opposite sex. The mother-son and father-son relationship have, in *Mukanda*, become symbols of wider more complex relationships. (p. 266)

Turner recognizes but does not explain the *force* of the sexual idiom. He notes that ritual symbols are a "compromise between the need for social control, and certain innate and universal human drives whose complete gratification would result in the breakdown of such control" (p. 37). Contrary goals are represented by the same form. Thus, *Mukanda* which explicitly seeks to bring life to boys as men implicitly (unconsciously) enables older men to "go as near as they dare to castrating or killing the boys." Turner does not, however, explore the effect of such disjunctions both within the ritual order and between the ritual order and everyday life. By seeking to distinguish all too completely between the socio-logical and the psychological, both Turner and Firth fail to recognize that the ritual disjunctions produce, *inter alia*, a unique frame for the (psychological) experience of time.

Psychoanalytic theories of circumcision have also ignored the role that the operation has on the individual's experience of time. They have tended to be speculative—and have ignored the effect of the operation on personality. Freud (1912, 1933, 1939; see also Kitahara 1976) regarded circumcision as a symbolic substitute for the actual castration practiced by the jealous father of the primal horde on his sons. Theodor Reik (1946) too considered circumcision as a castration equivalent that effectively supports the prohibition against incest. For the father, the puberty rite of which circumcision is an important component, "represents a number of hostile and homosexual acts, which in this form correspond to the paternal ambivalence toward the youth." They transform the youth's "unconscious impulses of hostility against his father into friendly ones."

> We recognize in all these rites the strong tendency to detach the youths from their mothers, to chain them more firmly to the community of men, and to seal more closely the union between father and son which has been loosened by the youth's unconscious strivings toward incest (p. 145).

Róheim (1942) argues, too, that puberty rites are based on the primal separation of the child from the mother. He follows Freud in viewing object loss as the contributing cause of all anxiety. Rites of transition are repetitions of the separation carried out on the body of the person who undergoes the rite. Separation from the mother is represented as separation of part of the body from the whole. Such separation is compensated for by a symbolic omnipotent penis (e.g., the bull roarer) and by a father-son unity.

Nunberg (1965; see also Orgel 1956) accepts the view that circumcision is a symbolic substitute for castration; he regards the foreskin as a symbolic residue of feminity—an identification that occurs in a number of mythologies including the Ndembu (Turner 1967) and the Dogon (Griaule 1970). Khan in his 1965 study of a foreskin-fetishist notes too that the uncircumcised penis is an "ideal bisexual object." Daly (1950; see also Schlossman, 1966)

suggests that the original function of circumcision and clitoridectomy was

> to modify the psycho-bisexuality which had resulted from the traumatic frustration of the hetero-sexual impulses in the original repression of incest. It represented a second wave of repression by means of which boys re-identified themselves with women. (220)

Bettelheim (1955) argues that an adequate explanation of initiation will have to take into account the consequences of pre-Oedipal emotional experiences, including those resulting from the infant's close attachment to the mother. He suggests that one sex envies the sexual organs and functions of the other. Male initiation rites may result then from "the desire to alleviate fear and envy of the mother and of women in general, and to reassert the relative power and importance of men as compared to women." (83) They may assert that men too can bear children. Genital mutilation, particularly subincision, may be an attempt to imitate female genital and sexual functioning.

Ozturk (1973) notes that the psychoanalytic studies of circumcision have been rather more concerned with the psychological origin of the practice than with its significance for the individual. He suggests that ultimately circumcision may have "acquired complete or relative autonomy from [its] original functions." The various forms, ages and social meanings of circumcision suggest that no one theory is applicable to all ritual circumcision. Ozturk's own research in Turkey, where the circumcision rite is not dissimilar to that in Morocco, reveals two conflicting effects of the operation. One is the fear of castration during and shortly after the operation; the other is "the provision of status, prestige, gifts, entertainment, and above all a sense of masculinity." Circumcision, Ozturk argues, "becomes an important ego need in the development of self-concept and identity." He notes that there is no passage from childhood to adulthood in the Turkish circumcision rite but probably passage from "an ambiguous sexual concept of self to a more clear-cut sexual concept of self." Ozturk's argument is well-taken as far as it goes, but it does not address itself to the question of why the excision of the foreskin should become an "important ego need," Cansever (1965), also in a study of circumcision in Turkey, notes that the operation is perceived by the child as an aggressive attack on his body; he feels inadequate, helpless, and functionally less efficient. His main reaction to the operation is one of defensive withdrawal accompanied by aggressive desires. In a rather noncommitted fashion, Cansever suggests

> that after the initial experience of defensive withdrawal disappears, during which time the ego will gain its strength over the instinctual drives and outside threats, it will integrate and synthesize the trauma and the resulting feelings from it into the structure of the personality. (329)

The question must still be asked: what are the effects of this painful operation on the structure of personality?

* * *

Although there is no specific Koranic authority, circumcision is obligatory and widespread for all Muslims.[6] It is of pre-Islamic origin (Patai 1969), and Mohammed seems to have accepted it without question. The several schools of Muslim jurisprudence differ as to its status. The Maliki, the dominant school in North Africa, regards it as commendable (*sunna*) but not indispensable (*wajub*). Muslim scholars justify its practice as being part of the religion of Muhammed or of the natural primitive religion (*fitra*), into which man is born (Levy 1962). In Morocco, among the illiterate Arabs with whom I worked, circumcision was considered an inviolable tradition based on (sic) Koranic authority. It was the mark not only of a Muslim but of a Maghrebi, for Jews too were circumcised.[7] Circumcision served to differentiate the Moroccan from the Nasrani, the Christian, the European.

Unlike female excision, which is usually veiled in secrecy and mystery, circumcision throughout the Middle East and North Africa is "always a public, joyous, and festive occasion" (Patai 1969). It is the first ceremony to follow the name-day celebration which occurs seven days after a child's birth and the celebration of the first haircut which takes place at an indeterminate age in the child's first year or two of life. Like the first haircut, circumcision is frequently performed in a saint's sanctuary and is accompanied by the sacrifice of a sheep or goat (von Gürnebaum 1951). The age at which the operation

is performed varies throughout the area. Although it is performed at fourteen, or later, on the island of Socotra and in some parts of Libya and Egypt, it usually takes place between the ages of three and seven (Patai 1969). There is, in fact, considerable variation even within a single family. Recently, with modernization, there has been a tendency to perform the operation within a few months of birth. In Meknes and its environs, I was told that it was better to circumcise a boy as early as possible, for then the operation would be less painful. Still, most of my informants were circumcised between the ages of three and six, one as late as twelve.[8] Often a family would wait until two or more brothers could be circumcised, or until the occasion of a marriage.

As Patai (1969) has noted, there is frequently a connection between circumcision and marriage. This is reflected in one of the words for circumcision, *khtana* in Moroccan Arabic, which is derived from the same Semitic root as the Hebrew for bridegroom, *hatan*, and for marriage, *hatanal* (Patai 1969). In some areas of Morocco the boy about to be circumcised is called a bridegroom and the circumcision itself the boy's first marriage (Westermarck 1926). (I have heard these terms used in Meknes in a joking fashion.) In some Arabian tribes a boy's circumcision is performed in the presence of his betrothed. Here the operation involves the removal of the skin of the entire penis and surrounding sections of the belly and inner thighs. The boy must stand upright, shout with joy, and brandish a dagger. His betrothed sits in front of him ululating and beating a drum. Should he utter a cry of pain, she has the right to refuse him (Henniger quoted in Patai 1969).[9] Among the 'Ababda of the Eastern Desert of Egypt, circumcision immediately precedes marriage; the hut in which the operation is performed is later used by the bride and groom as their residence. Both marriage and circumcision are called *'irs*, literally wedding (Murray quoted in Patai 1969). In Morocco the co-occurrence of a circumcision and marriage was not uncommon; it was never the groom, however, who was circumcised but a boy in his or his betrothed's family. (See also Lane 1963). The justification given was always economic. Most circumcisions and marriages took place after the summer harvest "when there was money."

Among the Moroccan Arabs with whom I worked, circumcision is an unquestioned given in the life of a man. It is said to make a boy a man and is justified on religious, hygienic, and sexual grounds. The sexual and, to a lesser extent, the hygienic are, in my observation, more important than the religious to the individual. With respect to religion, circumcision is considered a necessary prerequisite—a cleansing—for entering the mosque and for praying. In fact, one of the words for circumcision in Moroccan Arabic is *thara* which means, literally, a cleansing, an ablution. Both entering a mosque and reciting prayers, I should note, are male prerogatives.[10] Hygienically, an uncircumcised penis is said to be particularly vulnerable to infection from chafing, sweating and sexual intercourse. Men frequently remember getting sand painfully lodged in their foreskins before they were circumcised; they did not remember, however, that it was usually their mothers who cleaned it out. The uncircumcised are thought to be particularly vulnerable to *l-berd*, gonorrhea, and other venereal diseases. Indeed, women who have slept with uncircumcised men are said to spread *l-berd*. Sexually,[11] circumcision is thought to make the man more potent and sexual intercourse more pleasurable. One of my frankest informants wondered even whether the uncircumcised derived any pleasure whatsoever from sexual intercourse.

Although there is considerable variation in ritual detail, the circumcision rite is, nevertheless, surprisingly uniform throughout Morocco and bears a striking resemblance to the rite elsewhere in North Africa and the Middle East (see Westermarck 1926 for variations). I will restrict my discussion here to the rite as practiced by various Arab groups (Zerhana, Shrarda, etc.) who live in the countryside near Meknes (See Talha 1965).[12]

The circumcision rite is, as I have noted, conceived of as a festive occasion—an important and expensive ceremony to which considerable prestige is attached. It is in fact a very tense affair, marked, particularly within the boy's family, by a heavy sense of obligation. The rite *must* be carried out—and carried out correctly. It provides an arena (not as structured as that, for example, of the Ndembu) in which everyday social relations of envy and animosity as well as considerateness, friendship, and loyalty are sublated in ceremonial form and etiquette.

The tension between everyday and ritual relations can be near explosive. I remember attending a circumcision in a small hamlet on a large government farm where the men worked on a daily basis according to the whims of a rather corrupt farm manager. With more workers than jobs, there was, obviously, considerable strain among the men of the hamlet—strain that under normal circumstances was controlled by avoidance. During the circumcision ceremony avoidance was impossible; the entire hamlet was invited and with the exception of one man, a professed enemy of the sponsor, everybody came. At one point in the ceremony, well over twenty tense minutes were spent in deciding which guest would have the honor of preparing tea.[13] Exceptional attention was paid to the amount of tea each guest was served. Conversation was virtually precluded by the blasting of a transistor radio.

The ceremony places the sponsor,[14] usually the boy's family, under considerable financial strain. Poorer families will often wait several (anxious) years before they can afford to sponsor it correctly. I write "anxious" here because fathers "know" that the longer they wait the more painful the circumcision will be for their sons. It can be said that in certain cases the son is sacrificed for the prestige of his father. Of course, the son shares this prestige.

The circumcision ceremony begins the day before the actual performance. That evening, after a festive meal for which a sheep or goat has been slaughtered (*dbeh*) if the family can afford it, an older woman paints the boy's hands and feet with henna—like a girl's. The application of henna takes place in the woman's quarters in the exclusive presence of women who cluster tightly around the boy. Henna, which is deemed to have all sorts of curative and protective properties, is said to give the boy *baraka,* or blessing. The boy, who is considered unusually vulnerable to the evil eye and to demonic attack at this time is also given a protective amulet to wear. Most often this amulet consists of a string of beads, animal bones, and other miscellaneous objects, including a small pouch containing alum and harmal. (The latter are especially regarded for their apotropaic properties.) The amulet is worn on the boy's right ankle for seven days after the operation. The boy, or more accurately his mother, is given presents after the henna has been applied. There is dancing if the musicians arrive in the evening.

The following morning the boy is dressed in new clothes, usually a white chemise, occasionally a green one covered with a diaphanous white one, and a burnous. An embroidered bag which contains amulets is hung from his left shoulder. His head may be ritually shaved at this time in the presence of the male guests who give him gifts (*grama*). The donors are publicly praised by the village bard (*berrah*) who stands next to the boy. The head-shaving (*hsana*) is not obligatory.

The boy is then hoisted onto a horse or mule; his head is hidden in the hood of his burnous to protect him from the evil eye; and he is paraded through the village by his father to the local mosque or saint's sanctuary. *Ghiyyata*, or oboe-players, who in the smaller villages and hamlets are strangers, lead the parade, playing the whining circumcision music. Men, women and children follow behind the boy. After the mosque or sanctuary has been circumambulated three times, the boy's father carries him in to have a few prayers said for him. He is not allowed to touch the ground at this time. Unless the circumcision is to take place in the sanctuary—and I have not seen such a ceremony—the boy is led back to his house where the circumcision will take place. The boy's mother does not accompany her son on the parade. His father disappears as soon as the boy is home; for, as one Moroccan man put it, "what father can bear to see his son submitted to such pain."

I should add here, that in the poorer, more forlorn villages the parade is a rather shabby affair. The mosque may be circumambulated only once or the parade may be stopped altogether if "it is too hot." There is usually a clutch of people immediately behind the boy and then a chain of stragglers. A prostitute (*shikha*) who usually accompanies the musicians from one village circumcision to another is very much in evidence. Village boys are excited by the parade, but I have noticed that those who have been circumcised within a year or two withdraw when the parade returns to the boy's house. They look frightened or emotionally drained. Unmarried girls are unveiled and wear their hair down on this occasion.

The circumcision itself is performed by a barber shortly after the boy has returned from the mosque or sanctuary. In small villages the barber, like the musicians and prostitute, is a stranger, who in the month following the harvest rushes busily from village to village performing as many as a dozen circumcisions in a day. They seemed to me to be cold, efficient, and peremptory; they dictated the schedule of events, offered minimal advice, showed little or no sympathy to the boys they circumcised, and barely accepted the hospitality of their hosts. Although a boy is supposed to respect the barber who circumcised him, most younger circumcised boys disappeared when they saw him arrive.

The boy is carried by his mother to the room where the operation is to take place. A crowd of women, including the prostitute, and men, surrounding the women gather in front of the house. The mother—or some other female relative or a midwife—stands in front of the door. Her left foot is in a bowl of water which contains a piece of iron; in her left hand she holds a mirror into which she stares; in her right hand she holds a white flag. The iron is said to draw the pain from the scissors, ultimately from the wound, to the bowl where it is cooled down by the water. The mother stares into the mirror to prevent herself—and the boy—from crying; the flag represents the flag of Ali,[15] of Islam. Mother and son are for the moment symbolically equated.

The operation itself is a simple affair. The boy is held by an older man, preferably but not necessarily his paternal uncle, and is told to look up at a tiny bird.[16] The barber pulls the foreskin up, slips some sheep's dung in between the foreskin and the glans, and then with a single cut of a scissors, he snips off the foreskin. The dung is said to protect the glans from nicking. The penis is then plunged into a broken egg to which a little rabbit dung and henna have been added. This is said to cool the wound down and aid in healing.

As soon as the foreskin is clipped, a signal is given to the musicians who are waiting with the villagers in front of the house. They begin to play the circumcision music; women begin to dance. The boy is swaddled as an infant in a cloth (*izar*); heat is said to hasten healing. He is placed on his mother's naked back—or the back of another woman—in such a way that his bleeding penis presses against her.[17] His mother dances along with the other women until he stops crying. Then he is put to bed. In some ceremonies at this time women give him candies and other tidbits. He is fed a hard boiled egg and gravy when he wakes up—to give him strength. His mother cares for the wound until it has healed; she sprinkles it with powdered henna. His father returns after he falls asleep.

The dancing continues after the boy has been put to sleep. The prostitute who performs a belly dance is the center of attention. She is watched salaciously by the men and critically by the women. The circumcision rite affords one of the few occasions when both men and women can watch such dancing together. When the dance ends the prostitute eats with the men. (If the family is rich enough, a goat or sheep is slaughtered in the morning before the parade.) Conversation tends to be erotic.[18] When the meal is over, the prostitute makes love to any man in the village who can afford to pay her. She leaves with the musicians.

Many Moroccan men with whom I talked remember their circumcision vividly. It is often said that a circumcision should not be performed before a boy is old enough to remember it. It is in fact a subject of great anxiety. Moroccan men joke about it, especially in the baths. (Baths are considered to be a place of sexual temptation; they are said to be haunted by demons, or *jnun*.) They talk of the mutilated and those with jagged foreskins and those—they are actually very rare—who have lost their penis. They show, in my opinion, no particular pride in the operation. It is just carried out. An explanation is rarely offered to the boy either before or after the operation. He must simply submit without questioning, as he must submit to so much in a world that often seems needlessly arbitrary to the Westerner.

This attitude of unquestioned submission is aptly illustrated in the following retrospective account of the ceremony by a musician, a *ghita*-player (rather a Lothario) in his middle twenties who often played at circumcisions and marriages. He laughed nervously throughout this recitation. He did not remember exactly when the operation took place.

I was little. The barber came, and I came into the room. My paternal uncle was in the room. I did not know what was going to happen. I had been playing outside. First they circumcised my brother who left crying. I asked what had happened, but they said nothing had happened. Then they brought me into the room, telling me I was going to see some birds. I saw scissors next to me. My uncle held me. The barber touched my penis, and I was told to look up at the birds. Then I heard a drrrb. The moment he touched my penis, my tongue rolled to the back of my mouth.

And the blood that flowed tickled me. They put medicine on it, and I fell asleep. My friends watched me crying. I had a chemise on so that it would touch my penis. I did not wear pants. The worst was when I had to pee. It burned terribly. Slowly I began to go out, but I couldn't play with the other boys because I was afraid I would fall. I got better before my brother. Perhaps the barber nicked his glans. . . . My mother was not allowed to watch. She was at the door. Our custom is that when a boy is circumcised, his mother puts him on her back after she has removed the clothes from her back. The boy is against her naked back. The penis touches the mother's skin, and the blood flows down her back. The mother walks around and even dances a little. When the child is tired, she brings him to the room to sleep. . . . (How did you feel when your mother carried you?) I remember my penis touching my mother's skin. I wanted to jump in the air. It stung even more on my mother's flesh. I cried a lot. . . . (Where was your father?) No, I didn't see my father until I woke up. I was afraid of him. Even when my penis hurt, I didn't cry in front of him. My father told me not to cry, and he promised me all kinds of gifts. My mother put powder on my penis each day, and it stung for hours.

The operation is described matter-of-factly. The musician does not view the operation as a betrayal, as some of my informants did (Crapanzano 1977). It is described out of ritual context; his emphasis on the unexpected is not unusual. He is particularly conscious of how he appears in front of his father and friends; he compares his reaction to that of his brother. In Morocco there is considerable hostility between brothers and little overt hostility toward the father. Above all, the musician remembers the pain of his penis pressed against his mother's back.

The "movement" of the rite is circular. Symbolically—and in fact—the boy is led from the woman's world back to the woman's world. The circumcision rite itself is a period of liminality in which male and female elements are interrelated in a complex dialectic. The boy's (the bride's) hands and feet are hennaed like a woman's—by women in an intensely feminine atmosphere. His hair may be shaved. (I should note too that unmarried girls, presumably virgins, are permitted at this time to wear *their* hair down in public—a highly eroticized sign of immodesty permitted only at circumcisions and marriages. There is perhaps an element of role reversal here.) The boy is then declared a man—symbolized by the parade through town on horseback, his entrance into the mosque where women are not permitted, and the attention of his father and other men in village. In this "manly" condition he is, however, vulnerable to the evil eye and to demonic attack. He is protected by amulets; he hides his head in a hood; he must be carried. He is treated like a infant.

The boy is then returned from the public world of men back to the private world of female domesticity. He is led by his mother—his father disappears—into the room where he will be circumcised; that is, a woman who will symbolically bear his pain and give him strength, who is "one" with him, leads him into the room where he will be declared a man through an act that is unmanning. (I need not invoke Freud, Reik, or Bettelheim here; the anxiety aroused by circumcision is great. Several of my informants claimed that they thought their penises had been cut off and dared not look down for days.) The boy is then placed on his mother's back—the Oedipal implications are, to the Westerner, self-evident—in a manner that is at once intimate and painful. He is, of course, swaddled as a baby. He is in the presence, too, of a prostitute who dances erotically—a stranger whom he cannot know. He is carried to the woman's quarters and cared for by his mother. The men of the village, in a gesture that reaffirms *their* manhood—and differentiates them from the boy—have license to sleep with the prostitute. It is my impression that following the circumcision the boy is treated much as he was treated before the ritual interlude. He appears to suffer great anxiety when other circumcisions take place and when, in jest or as a disciplinary measure, he is threatened with a second circumcision, sometimes called a second marriage.

The circumcision rite is disjunctive. It declares passage where there is in both ritual and everyday life no passage whatsoever—only the *mark* of passage, the mutilation that is itself an absence, a negation. It is a precocious rite. The boy is declared a man before he is (emically as well as etically) physically a man—or is treated as a man. It removes him temporarily from the private world of women and children, from hearth and harem, to the public world of men, prowess and religion. It announces a transition yet to come—the passage into man-

hood—and provides him with an essential but insufficient prerequisite for that transition. It gives him, if I may speak figuratively, a preview of manhood—a preview that is, however, dramatically arrested. He is in his "manhood" deprived of his manhood. He is triumphantly carried back from the mosque to his mother who will not have him until he has been mutilated and then only as an infant. He is cruelly punished in the symbolic fulfillment of his *putative* desire: his penis, now mutilated, is pressed against his mother's sweating back. His separation—the root of all anxiety in the Freudian schema—is both declared and undeclared. He is ritually separated from his mother—only to be reunited with her in everyday life not as the man he has been ritually declared but as the infant he has been ritually undeclared. He suffers, one would surmise, an indelible sense of inadequacy and inferiority, particularly with respect to men, and an intense fear of women. These feelings of inadequacy, inferiority, and fear are reflected, presumably, in the Moroccan man's image of himself and of women and in the relations between the two sexes. It is perhaps no accident that the most virulent and capricious demons (*jnun*) in Morocco are female.

To look upon the Moroccan rite of circumcision as simply a ritualized punishment of incestuous desires, a disambiguation of the boy's primordial bisexuality, or a ritualized conversion of the infant's separation anxiety into castration anxiety, all determinant of Moroccan personality and culture is to lose sight of the complexity of the ritual process. The rite, as I have said, is essentially *disjunctive*: a series of contradictory messages that remain unresolved, at least in the ritual immediate. What resolution, if any, may come with time—the ritually unmarked time of physical maturation which culminates in an almost obsessive concern for frequency of sexual performance and in the ritually marked transition into marriage.[19] (The latter is reflected not only in the frequent symbolic and even temporal association of marriage and circumcision but in the Moroccan marriage ceremony itself, which is in many respects a symbolic undoing of circumcision [for details see Westermarck 1914].) It may come, too, with fatherhood and perhaps even with the son's circumcision. But here we must be careful. The father is not simply doing unto his son what was done unto him, as some theorists have rather too crudely suggested. The father is also vicariously reliving, anxiously remembering and repeating his own circumcision; he too is submitting now as he did then to the manifest message of the rite, to custom and tradition, ultimately to the will of God. Resolution may also come in the curing trance-dances of the Hamadsha, Jilala, and Isawa (Crapanzano 1973; Brunel 1926) which are so often accompanied by acts of self-mutilation. As I have suggested specifically regarding the Hamadsha, these rituals must not necessarily be conceived as affording resolution but similar to myth, the illusion of resolution.

The Moroccan circumcision rite renders the timeless repetition of (separation) anxiety into an event within time—to be remembered. It is the time of desire that has succumbed to symbolic substitutions, to culture and history. It is a time that rests cruelly upon mutilation and pain—the great sacrifice that to Freud necessitates civilization. It is a ritualized, discontinuous time. Rural Moroccans, Dale Eikelman (1977) has noted for the Bni Battu, "conceive events temporally in terms of sequences of irregular, island-like concrete experiences." These events serve as symbolic orientation points for the articulation of personal history, ultimately of self.

They rest—and this is the message that *I* see in the Moroccan circumcision ceremony—not on conjunction but on disjunction. It is for this reason perhaps that Moroccans say that circumcision should take place as early as possible to be as painless as possible, but not so early as to be forgotten. "Whenever man has thought it necessary to create a memory for himself," Nietzsche observed in *The Genealogy of Morals*, "his effort has been attended with torture, blood, sacrifice." It is this pain that grounds the individual in civilization and history. It may give him biographical and personal security, as Berger and Luckmann (1967) suggest, but only because the disjunction, ultimately the separation, are too painful to be acknowledged. What was desired can no longer be desired; what is desired must be seen as real—and not symbolic. The illusion of ritual must be denied; the ritual illusion must be taken as real—not only by the ritual participant but by the stranger to the ritual too, the anthropologist or the psychoanalyst, who understandably finds the impossibility of resolution intolerable. Transition, if only from a state of being uncircumcised to a state of being circumcised, must be witnessed—even where there is no transition, only repetition and return.

NOTES

1. The research for this paper was carried out under a grant from the National Institute of Mental Health (MH 13776-01) and a Quain Grant from the Institute of Intercultural Research. A preliminary version was delivered at the American Anthropological Association Meetings in San Francisco in 1975 and a more complete version at Harvard and Columbia in 1978 and at the University of Chicago in 1979.

2. A similar criticism may be advanced for Victor Turner's (1967) use of "state" in his discussion of rites of passage. Turner argues that such rites "indicate and constitute transitions between states." *State* he defines as "a relatively fixed or stable condition." He includes in its meaning "such social constancies as legal status, profession, office or calling, rank or degree"; he includes in it too the "culturally recognized degree of maturation" of an individual as well as his physical, mental or emotional condition. Such broad usage can only serve to mask ritual intricacy.

3. I do not use "experiential vantage point" here in a strictly phenomenological sense but rather in the sense of a "construct" as it is frequently used in psychoanalysis.

4. The rite of circumcision, like all rituals, is of significance to all ritual participants from their several vantage points. Frequently, the choice of a central figure—the boy or the father in the circumcision rite—masks the significance of the rite for other participants—the mother, brothers or sisters. The ritual must be understood not simply in terms of enactment or reenactment by any of its participants but also as a living or reliving—a remembering. See below.

5. Whatever validity Cohen's (1964) distinction between two stages of puberty may have would not effect my experiential argument here. Unless these two stages are culturally distinguished, they would not affect the perception of disjunction.

6. Female excision is less common and is not found in Morocco (Dostal n.d.). A spurious saying of the Prophet condones the practice: circumcision is a *sunna* (commendable act) for men and an honor for women (Margoliouth 1911).

7. Many of the women in the area in which I worked did not believe that Jews were circumcised. This is apparently true for some of the men as well (Rosen 1970).

8. Westermarck (1926) found that most circumcisions took place between two and seven.

9. Doughty (1964) heard tales of this practice for the Harb. When he came to them and asked about it, they answered: " 'Lord! That so strange things should be reported of us poor people! but, Khalil, these things are told of el-Kahtan'—that is of a further nation and always far off."

10. Frequently, circumcision is translated by North Africans into French as *baptème* (baptism) (Tillon 1966).

11. Here I encountered great resistance until I explained that I was circumcised—and then surprise and fraternal openness.

12. Berber tribes in the area such as the Majatte have essentially the same rite; the barbers who perform their circumcisions are usually the same as those who perform the rite for the Arabs. The Berbers consider the Arab circumcisions to be less joyous—couched more in secrecy. They criticize the Arabs for not explaining the operation to the boy ahead of time. I have no evidence to support this differentiation.

13. The serving of tea in Morocco provides an idiom for the articulation of social relations. The most honored guest is asked—encouraged, forced even—to prepare tea by the host and other guests who in round robin fashion politely refuse to prepare it. Special attention is paid to the level of tea in each glass. I have heard stories told of men being killed for having failed to serve equal amounts of tea. The preparer of tea always tastes the tea before serving it "to show that it is not poisoned."

14. The wealthy frequently sponsor circumcisions for the poor; the sponsor obtains great blessing (*baraka*) for such an act (Le Tourneau 1949). Westermarck (1926; Talha 1965) claims that some families are prevented by magical fright (*tera*) from sponsoring circumcisions for their sons. The sons must be carried off in secret by another family to be circumcised. In the cities there are yearly public circumcisions for the poor; these are usually held in a saint's sanctuary.

15. Ali is the Prophet's son-in-law. I have heard numerous tales of his bravery, his sexual prowess, and, of course, his spirituality. He is, in a sense, the ideal man.

16. Boys frequently catch a bird, tie a long string to one of its legs, and let it fly off, only to pull it back again. They repeat this letting go and pulling back until the bird dies.

17. Mothers frequently carry children on their backs.

18. The quality of such conversation is revealed in the following abbreviated excerpt from my field notes. The conversation occurred at breakfast before a circumcision. The prostitute and musicians had arrived the previous night. There had been dancing after the application of henna. The prostitute, who was about fifteen, had slept in bed with the men but had not made love to them.

There was joking about how the prostitute had sneaked off to bed before the men in order to have the most comfortable place. One man could not even find a place to sleep. She had taken up so much room! She flirted a lot with Driss (one of the musicians) and touched him and the other men a lot. She said, "Europeans eat only a little biscuit for breakfast. Moroccans will eat anything you put in front of them—a whole bowel of butter even. I have a girlfriend who lives with me. When we eat, I take all the meat and stick it in my mouth and then I take it out again. She can't eat any of the meat that way. Then my girlfriend sticks her hand in the food and messes it all up so that I can't eat it. Then we laugh and share it anyway. I wouldn't do this with anyone but her because she is my girlfriend." The prostitute thought all this very interesting; it was sexually loaded. Then men didn't pay much attention to details; they just enjoyed listening to her talk. The prostitute then began to flirt with Hasan (a shy villager). There was much joking about who would go into the backroom with her alone. Everyone said Hasan would not go with her because he was afraid he would be circumcised again. The prostitute gave Hasan a choice: he could go in with her alone or wait for the barber. Everyone laughed. Then several men suggested Hasan should hold the boy who was going to be circumcised. Hasan blanched. . . .

19. There are, to be sure, other unmarked transitions. Among these, I would include not only the boy's first heterosexual experience but also his homosexual adventures, especially his taking the dominant position. Younger boys play a passive part with older boys and then later, when they are older themslves, an active part in which they are dominant and enter the younger boy. I would also include a second, unmarked transition in which the son, especially the eldest, takes his father's "place" upon his father's death. Adult sons tend to avoid their fathers, do not smoke in front of them, do not talk about sex with them, or engage in flirtations in front of them. They do not show anger toward them (but often deflect anger to their brothers). The sons are generally submissive to their fathers and their fathers' authority.

BIBLIOGRAPHY

Ashley-Montagu, M. F. (1946). "Ritual Mutilation among Primitive Peoples." *Ciba Symposia* VIII; 421–436.

Bachofen, J. J. (1967). *Myth, Religion and Mother Right*. Princeton: Princeton University Press.

Berger, P. L. and T. Luckmann (1967). *The Social Construction of Reality: A Treatise in the Sociology of Knowledge*. New York: Doubleday.

Bettelheim, B. (1955). *Symbolic Wounds: Puberty Rites and the Envious Male*. London: Thames and Hudson.

Briffault, R. (1927). *The Mothers: A Study of the Origins of Sentiments and Institutions*. New York: Macmillan.

Brunel, R. (1926). *Essai sur la Confrérie religieuse des 'Aissaoua au Maroc*. Paris: Paul Geuthner.

Bryk, F. (1934). *Circumcision in Man and Woman: Its History, Psychology and Ethnology*. New York: American Ethnological Press.

Cansever, G. (1965). "Psychological Effects of Circumcision." *British Journal of Medical Psychology* XXXVIII: 321–331.

Cohen, Y. (1964). *The Transition from Childhood to Adolescence: Cross-Cultural Studies in Initiation Ceremonies, Legal Systems, and Incest Taboos*. Chicago: Aldine.

Crapanzano, V. (1973). *The Hamadsha: An Essay in Moroccan Ethnopsychiatry*. Berkeley: University of California.

———(1977). "Mohammed and Dawia: Possession in Morocco." In V. Crapanzano and V. Garrison (eds.) *Case Studies in Spirit Possession*. New York: John Wiley, pp. 141–176.

Crawley, E. (1927). *The Mystic Rose*. New York: Boni and Liveright.

Daly, C. D. (1950). "The Psycho-Biological Origins of Circumcision." *The International Journal of Psychoanalysis* XXXI:217–236.

Dostal, W. (n.d.) "Zum Problem der Madchenbeschneidung in Arabien." *Wiener volkerkundliche Mitteilungen* XI:83–89.

Doughty, C. M. (1964). *Travels in Arabia Deserta*. London: Jonathan Cape.

Eikelman, D. F. (1977). "Time in a Complex Society: A Moroccan Example." *Ethnology* XVI:39–55.

Firth, R. (1963). *We, The Tikopia: Kinship in Primitive Polynesia*. Boston: Beacon.

Foucault, M. (1965). *Madness and Civilization*. New York: Vintage.

Frazer, J. G. (1922). *Balder the Beautiful*. London: Macmillan.

Freud, S. (1912). "Totem and Taboo." Standard Edition 13:9. London: Hogarth Press, 1938.

———(1930) "Civilization and Its Discontents." Standard Edition 21:59. London: Hogarth Press, 1961.

———(1933) "New Introductory Lectures on Psychoanalysis." Standard Edition 22:3. London: Hogarth Press, 1957.

———(1939) "Moses and Monotheism." Standard Edition 23:3. London: Hogarth Press, 1967.

Fromm-Reichmann, F. (1955). *An Outline of Psychoanalysis*. New York: Random House.

Gluckman, M. (1962). "Les Rites de Passages." In *Essays on the Ritual of Social Relations*. Manchester: Manchester University Press, pp. 1–52.

Gray, L. H. (1911). "Circumcision." In J. Hastings (ed.) *Encyclopaedia of Religion and Ethics* III. New York: Scribners.

Griaule, M. (1970). *Conversations with Ogotemmeli*. New York: Oxford.

Gürnebaum, G. E. von (1951). *Muhammadan Festivals*. New York: Henry Schuman.

Jensen, A. E. (1933). *Beschneidung und Reifezeremonien bei Naturvolkern*. Stuttgart: Strecken and Schroder.

Khan, M. (1965). "Foreskin Fetishism and its Relation to Ego Pathology in a Male Homosexual." *International Journal of Psycho-Analysis*. 46:64–80.

Kitahara, M. (1976). "A Cross-cultural Test of the Freudian Theory of Circumcision." *International Journal of Psychoanalytic Psychotherapy* V:535–546.

LaBarre, W. (1970). *The Ghost Dance: The Origins of Religion*. New York: Doubleday.

Lane, E. (1963). *The Manners and Customs of Modern Egyptians*. London: Dent.

Le Tourneau, R. (1949). *Fez avant le protectorat: Etudes economique et sociale d'une ville de l'occident musulman*. Rabat: Publication de l'Institut des Hautes Etudes marocaines XLV.

Lévi-Strauss, C. (1963). *Totemism*. Boston: Beacon.

Levy, R. (1962). *The Social Structure of Islam*. Cambridge: Cambridge University Press.

Lubbock, J. (1870). *The Origin of Civilization and the Primitive Condition of Man*. London: Longmans, Green.

McLennan, J. F. (1865). *Primitive Marriage*. Edinburgh: Adam and Charles Black.

Maine, H. S. (1861). *Ancient Law*. London: Murray.

Margoliouth, D. S. (1911). "Circumcision (Mohammadan)." In

J. Hastings (ed.) *Encyclopaedia of Religion and Ethics* III. New York: Scribners.

Morgan, L. H. (1877). *Ancient Society*. New York: World Publishing.

Nietzsche, F. (1956). *The Genealogy of Morals*. New York: Anchor.

Nunberg, H. (1965). "Problems of Bisexuality as Reflected in Circumcision." In *Theory and Practice of Psychoanalysis* II. New York: International Universities Press, pp. 13–93.

Orgel, S. Z. (1956). "The Problem of Bisexuality as Reflected in Circumcision." *Journal of the Hillside Hospital* V:375–383.

Ozturk, O. M. (1973). "Ritual Circumcision and Castration Anxiety." *Psychiatry* XXXV: 49–60.

Patai, R. (1969). *Golden River to Golden Road: Society, Culture, and Change in the Middle East* (3rd ed.) Philadelphia: University of Pennsylvania Press.

Radin, P. (1957). *Primitive Religion: Its Nature and Origin*. New York: Dover.

Reik, T. (1946). *Ritual: Psychoanalytic Studies*. New York: International Universities Press.

Róheim, G. (1942). "Transition Rites." Psychoanalytic Quarterly XI: 336–374.

———(1945). *The Eternal Ones of the Dream: A Psychoanalytic Interpretation of Australian Myth and Ritual*. New York: International Universities Press.

———(1972). *Animism, Magic, and the Divine King*. New York: International Universities Press, (reprint).

Rosen, I. (1970). "A Moroccan Jewish Community during the Middle Eastern Crisis." In L. E. Sweet (ed.) *Peoples and Cultures of the Middle East*. II. New York: The Natural History Press.

Schlossman, H. H. (1966). "Circumcision as a Defense: A Study in Psychoanalysis and Religion." *Psychoanalytic Quarterly* 35:340–356.

Talha, A. (1965). *Moulay Idriss du Zerhoun: Quelques aspects de la vie sociale et familiale*. Rabat: Editions Techniques Nord-Africaines.

Tillon, G. (1966). "Le Harem et les cousins." Paris: Seuil.

Turner, V. (1962). "Three Symbols of *Passage* in Ndembu Circumcision Ritual: An Interpretation." In M. Gluckman (ed.) *Essays on the Ritual of Social Relations*. Manchester: Manchester University Press, pp. 124–173.

———(1967). *The Forest of Symbols: Aspects of Ndembu Ritual*. Ithaca, New York: Cornell University Press.

Tylor, E. B. (1958). *Primitive Culture* I & II. New York: Harper Torchbook.

van Gennep, A. (1960). *The Rites of Passage*. Chicago: University of Chicago Press.

Westermarck, E. (1914). *Marriage Ceremonies in Morocco*. London: Macmillan.

———(1926). *Ritual and Belief in Morocco* I & II. London: Macmillan.

Whiting, J. W. M. (1964). "Effects of Climate on Certain Cultural Practices." In N. Goodenough (ed.) *Explorations in Cultural Anthropology*. New York: McGraw Hill, pp. 511–544.

The Neurobiology of Myth and Ritual

EUGENE G. D'AQUILI
CHARLES D. LAUGHLIN JR.

Facts of publication: d'Aquili, Eugene G., Charles D. Laughlin Jr., and John McManus. 1979. "The Neurobiology of Myth and Ritual," from The Spectrum of Ritual: A Biogenetic Structural Analysis, 153–164, 168–182. New York: Columbia University Press. Copyright © 1979 by Columbia University Press. Reprinted with the permission of the publishers.

Eugene d'Aquili, a psychiatrist, and Charles Laughlin, an anthropologist, employ an interdisciplinary method called biogenetic structuralism in order to explain scientifically the connection between myth and ritual from a neurological and evolutionary point of view. Their explanation links, but does not identify, ritualization among animals with human religions ritual. Unlike Theodore Jennings, who argues that ritual behavior itself has a cognitive function, d'Aquili and Laughlin assign the cognitive dimensions of ritual to myth. They attempt to show that, given the structure of the brain, human beings inevitably construct myths to explain their world. Doing so is highly adaptive; it satisfies what the authors call the cognitive imperative, the drive to know. In their view myth constellates a conceptual and existential problem which ritual, then, attempts to solve by motor activity.
The fullest presentation of this view is found in Charles Laughlin and others, Brain: Symbol & Experience *(Boston: Shambala, 1990). The selection is well read alongside those by Jennings and Erikson in this volume.*

About the author: *Eugene G. d'Aquili.* **Dates**: *1940– , Trenton, NJ, U.S.A.* **Education**: *B.A., Villanova University; M.D., University of Pennsylvania; M.A. in anthropology, University of Pennsylvania.* **Field(s)**: *psychiatry, anthropology.* **Career**: *Assistant Professor of Psychiatry in the Department of Psychiatry of the Medical School, University of Pennsylvania, 1973. Medical practice, specializing in psychiatry, 1974–present.* **Publications**: *with Charles Laughlin and others,* Biogenetic Structuralism *(Columbia University, 1974); edited, with Charles Laughlin and John McManus,* The Spectrum of Ritual: A Biogenetic Structural Analysis *(Columbia University, 1979); with Charles Laughlin and John McManus,* Brain, Symbol & Experience: Toward a Neurophenomenology of Human Consciousness *(Shambala, 1990). Additional: Member: American Psychiatraic Association, American Anthropology Association, Institute of Religion in an Age of Science.*

About the author: *Charles D. Laughlin.* **Dates**: *1938– , Swampscott, MA, U.S.A.* **Education**: *B.A., San Francisco State College; M.A. University of Oregon; Ph.D., University of Oregon.* **Field(s)**: *neuroanthropology, transpersonal anthropology.* **Career**: *State University of New York, Oswego, 1970–1976; Carleton University (O Hawa, Canada) 1976–present.* **Publications**: *edited, with Eugene G. d'Aquili and John McManus,* The Spectrum of Ritual: A Biogenetic Structural Analysis *(Columbia University Press, 1979); with John McManus, R. A. Rubinstein, and J. Shearer, "The Ritual Transformation of Experience," in* Studies in Symbolic Interaction, *part A, 107–136, ed. N. K. Denzin (JAI, 1986); with John McManus and Eugene G. d'Aquili,* Brain, Symbol & Experience *(Columbia University Press, 1990); "Revealing the Hidden: The Epiphanic Dimension of Games and Sport."* Journal of Ritual Studies *7.1 (1993): 85–104.* **Additional**: *Member, International Consciousness Research Laboratory (ICRL); Former editor,* Anthropology of Consciousness *(journal of the Society for the Anthropology of Consciousness). "I have carried out ethnographic fieldwork among the So of Northeastern Uganda, Tibetan lamas in Nepal and India, and the Navajo of the American Southwest."*

[In this reading] we attempt to explain from a neuroevolutionary point of view why human ceremonial ritual is inevitably embedded within a mythic structure. It is indeed a fact that all human ceremonial rituals possess a cognitive rationale related to generation of the affective or dissociative states. . . . [Here] we attempt to . . . present a coherent neurobiological model for human ceremonial ritual. . . .

In many ways the most difficult task in doing a biogenetic structural analysis of human ceremonial ritual is to present a neural model for the development of myth in which human ritual is embedded. Yet . . . biogenetic structural methodology requires that all the major facets of a cultural institution be at least tentatively explained in terms of a neuroanatomical/neurophysiological model if sufficient data can be found to support the construction of such a model. Those who are well versed in the neural sciences may find fault with our choosing one set of data and interpretations rather than another in certain areas that are as yet controversial. The reader who may not be well versed in the neural sciences should be clearly aware that there are a number of such controversial areas in neurobiology. While biology may be a "hard" science compared to the social sciences, the "hardness" is only relative. At any rate, in areas where there is still legitimate controversy, we have chosen the data and interpretations that are most consonant with the evidence from ethology, psychology, and other sciences. Methodological purists from within the neural sciences may occasionally find this choice of data objectionable. But the entire thrust of biogenetic structuralism is an interdisciplinary approach to the social sciences, and, as such, an inter-disciplinary methodology must be followed. What such a methodology lacks in rigor it makes up for in scope, which is precisely the great need in the social sciences today. What follows, therefore, is not presented as scientific dogma, but rather as the most probable neural model, based on valid neurophysiological investigation and consonant with the evidence from other sciences, which can explain the generation of myth and its relationship to human ceremonial ritual.

. . . It is not sufficient for a biogenetic structural analysis of a human cultural institution merely to consider the evolution of the traits of man's behavior shared with lower animals. It is incumbent upon such an analysis to explain the differences as well. Furthermore those differences should be explained, if possible, in terms of evolution of the central nervous system (CNS), and in terms of the adaptive value that such accretions to the phylogenetically antecedent behavior have for *Homo sapiens.*

Since this attempt to provide a comprehensive neurobiological model for human ceremonial ritual involves the integration of data from various disciplines, and since the argument providing the basis for this model may appear at times somewhat difficult to follow, it is necessary to summarize. . . .

Let us begin our argument by considering the problem of those aspects of human ritual that man shares with other animals versus those aspects of human ritual, particularly its mythic basis, that appear to be unique to man. We would be the first to agree that cultic ritual as practiced by *Homo sapiens* has many unique characteristics. As we shall see, however, these unique characteristics, although an integral part of ritual as performed by man, can be viewed as being derived from other neurobiological systems that had selective advantages totally separate from those of ritual behavior. These unique elements of human ritual, particularly the myth structure or cognitive matrix in which ritual is embedded, appear to have been, as it were, grafted on the mainstream of the evolution of ritual behavior. While it is dangerous not to perceive the unique aspects of human ritual, particularly as exemplified in ceremonial ritual, it is even more dangerous to ignore those of its aspects that man has in common with other species. Tinbergen (1965) has strongly argued for the importance of homologous features in the study of origins of communicative behavior. To refuse to consider human ritual behavior within an evolutionary perspective is to commit the rankest of anthropocentrisms.

. . . A major problem for any organism whose adaptation depends on cooperation with one or more conspecifics is to decrease the distancing between itself and others so that some form of cooperation can be achieved. A number of ethologists such as Lorenz (1966), Tinbergen (1965), and Lehrman (1965) have observed that a certain amount of distance is normally maintained among vertebrates, probably to preserve the integrity of the individual's survival functions. Jay (1965), Chance (1965), and others have noted the importance of "social space" among nonhuman primates. Much has recently been written about personal space in man. There is increasing evidence that most vertebrates under normal conditions maintain a degree of distance or separateness. Most frequently this distancing is spatial, but it may also be relational in terms of hierarchy within a group.

If two or more animals must cooperate in a task, the most basic of which is the copulative function, their usually adaptive distancing becomes maladaptive. Some way must be found to circumvent the problem to permit greater spatial or relational proximity. One way in which proximity is achieved is by the performance of ritual behavior by one or more members of the group. Lorenz (1966), Lehrman (1965), Tinbergen (1965), and others have noted that such ritual courtship behavior prior to coition is common among many species and seems to aid the elimination of the distancing between the two individuals, allowing coition to take place. Ritual behavior before cooperative group action is also extremely common. Lorenz (1966) makes the important point that ritual behavior appears to be the trigger for much of the cooperative behavior within species for which cooperation is essential for survival. More importantly, Lorenz (1966) sees these same functions operative within culturally elaborated religious rituals in man. He notes:

> In cultural ritualization, the two steps of the development leading from communication to the control of aggression and, from this, to the formation of a bond, are strikingly analogous to those that take place in the evolution of instinctive rituals. . . . The triple function of suppressing fighting within the group, of holding the group together, and of setting it off, as an independent entity, against other, similar units, is performed by the developed ritual in so strictly analogous a manner as to merit deep consideration (1966:74).

At this point we must reiterate what is meant by ritual behavior. We [define] it as a sequence of behavior that (1) is sequentially structured (patterned); (2) is repetitive and rhythmic (to some degree at least)—that is, it tends to recur in the same or nearly the same form with some regularity; (3) acts to coordinate affective, perceptual (cognitive in man and other higher vertebrates), and motor processes within the CNS of individual participants; and, most particularly, (4) coordinates and synchronizes these processes among the various individual participants. Manley (1960) has considered this coordinating function of ritual among the black-headed gull in some detail. It appears, from the work of Schein and Hale (1965) with the domestic turkey, of Tinbergen (1951) with three-spined sticklebacks and queen butterflies, and of Rosenblatt (1965) with cats, that there is something about the repetitive or rhythmic emanation of signals from a conspecific that generates a high degree of limbic arousal. With respect to this rhythmicity of ritual Lorenz (1966) notes:

> The display of animals during threat and courtship furnishes an abundance of examples, and so does the culturally developed ceremonial of man. The deans of the university walked into the hall with a "measured step"; pitch, rhythm, and loudness of the Catholic priests chanting during mass are all strictly regulated by liturgic prescription. The unambiguity of the communication is also increased by its frequent repetition. Rhythmical repetition of the same movement is so characteristic of very many rituals, both instinctive and cultural, that it is hardly necessary to describe examples (1966:72).

Walter and Walter (1949), and Gellhorn and Kiely (1972; 1973) have shown that such repetitive auditory and visual stimuli can drive cortical rhythms and eventually produce an intensely pleasurable, ineffable experience in man (see also Abraham, 1976). Furthermore, Gellhorn and Kiely (1972; 1973) cite evidence that such repetitive stimuli can bring about simultaneous intense discharges from both the sympathetic and parasympathetic nervous systems in man. . . .

When one considers the evidence taken from the animal literature, together with the limited studies that have been done on man, one can infer that there is something about repetitive rhythmic stimuli that may, under proper conditions, bring about the unusual neural state of simultaneous high discharge of both autonomic subsystems. We would ask the reader to keep in mind the three stages of tuning of the sympathetic-parasympathetic subsystems (Gellhorn, 1967; Gellhorn and Kiely, 1973). In the first state, response in one system increases while, at the same time, reactivity in the other system decreases. If augmented reactivity of the sensitized system continues, the second stage of tuning is reached after stimuli exceed a certain threshold. At this point, not only is inhibition of the nonsensitized system complete, but also stimuli that usually elicit a response in the nonsensitized system evoke instead a response in the sensitized system. These behaviors comprise a "reversal phenomena." . . . If stimulation continues beyond this stage, increased sensitization can lead to a third stage characterized by simultaneous discharges in both systems. Normally, either the sympathetic or the parasympathetic system predominates, and the excitation of one subsystem inhibits the other. In the special case of prolonged rhythmic stimuli one can postulate that the simultaneous strong discharge of both autonomic systems creates a state of stimulation of the median forebrain bundle, generating not only a pleasurable sensation but, under proper conditions, a sense of union or oneness with conspecifics.

The simplest paradigm to explain the situation in man is the feeling of union that occurs during orgasm. During orgasm as during other states we shall consider later, there is intense simultaneous discharge from both of the autonomic subsystems. We are postulating that the various ecstasy states that can be produced in man after exposure to rhythmic auditory, visual, or tactile stimuli produce a feeling of union with other members participating in that ritual. In fact, social unity is a common theme running through the myth associated with most human rituals. Although it is very difficult to extrapolate from a human model to an animal model, it is clear that a homologous effective state is produced by rhythmic repeated ritual behavior in other species. This state may vary in intensity but always has the effect of unifying the social group.

Put simply, there is increasing evidence that rhythmic or repetitive behavior coordinates the limbic discharges (that is, affective states) of a group of conspecifics. It can generate a level of arousal that is both pleasurable and reasonably uniform among the individuals so that necessary group action is facilitated. We must note at this point that we have said nothing about the communicative aspect of this rhythmic signaling as separate from the affective responses. There is a body of evidence that many of these rhythmic stimuli serve as nonaffective communication as well. The position of most ethologists is that rhythmicity evolved in lower animal species is in the service of communication. However, many ethologists maintain that rhythmicity evolved an autonomous effect of its own separate from its signaling function. Thus Lorenz (1966) states:

> Both instinctive and cultural rituals become independent motivations of behavior by creating new ends or goals towards which the organisms strive for their own sake. It is in their character of independent motivating factors that rituals transcend their original function of communication and become able to perform their equally important secondary tasks of controlling aggression and of forming a bond between certain individuals (1966:72).

It is by no means certain that rhythmicity evolved first in the service of signaling and only secondarily developed its function of affective arousal. One may just as well maintain that the affective arousal is primary and that signaling became grafted onto the already present rhythmicity, using those very patterns of rhythmicity as signals. Whether signaling or affective arousal was first in the evolutionary sequence, however, is relatively unimportant. What is important is that we can distinguish two aspects of ritual behavior, one involving affective arousal as a result of rhythmic stimuli, and the other involving nonaffective communication using patterns of rhythmic stimuli, although both elements in fact seem inextricably woven together.

What we are suggesting, on the basis of the behavioral observations of ethologists, is that the rhythmic quality in and of itself produces positive limbic discharges resulting in decreased distancing and increased social cohesion. Even at the level of birds the communication quality of the signaling can be regarded as added to the effect of the rhythmicity on the nervous systems of the animals involved. Certainly in man the communicative quality of many aspects of ritual becomes very important and can enhance, or on occasion suppress, the immediate neural effect of the rhythmic or periodic stimuli. Similarly, in man, the cognitive, as opposed to the simply perceptual aspects of ritual behavior become extremely important. But the basic and relatively simple effect of ritual, that is, limbic coordination among conspecifics, is just as present in human ritual behavior as it is among other animals.

In higher organisms that require experiential input from their social environment for the adaptive potential of ritual behavior to reach fruition, ritual performed by adult members of the group has the secondary effect of socializing the young. A consideration of the adaptive significance of ritual becomes more complicated in this case, for the problem of obtaining social cohesion as an adaptive response arises anew with each generation. The process of socialization requires both passive and active participation by the young. The young may passively perceive innumerable occurrences of a repetitive ritual during which they learn to associate (1) the set of stimuli requiring or initiating the ritual, (2) the precise sequencing of behavioral events comprising the ritual, (3) affective states linked to the ritual behavior, (4) significant perceptual entities emphasized through the orientation of ritual participants, and (5) corporate group action concurrent with, or subsequent to, the ritual. In higher organisms, and especially among the primates, the young may enact the ritual during peer group play and thus further concretize the neural associations on which adequate functioning of the adult ritual depends.

We have presented the final common denominator of ritual behavior based on the exigencies of survival and crossing species lines. Let us now consider the problem of religious ritual in man. To do so we have to leave the theme that we have been considering up to this point to consider the aspects of ritual that appear to be unique to human religious action. We shall, however, return to the common biological theme toward the end of this [reading].

HUMAN RELIGIOUS RITUAL

The facet of religious ceremonial ritual that appears to be distinctly human is its seemingly inevitable association with myth. That is, religious ritual is always embedded in a cognitive matrix—a web of meaning, in Geertz's (1973) terms—that allows members of the society to interpret the conceptual significance of certain behavior. As numerous structural theorists have pointed out (Lévi-Strauss, 1963b; 1964; Maranda, 1973; Maranda and Maranda, 1971), mythic structure presents a problem that requires solution. In this regard it is the function of myth to supply a solution to the problem raised at the conceptual level and the function of concomitant ritual to supply a solution at the level of action. Man, who is at the mercy of certain forces of nature, must elaborate a cognitive structure that provides an explanation of those forces, the reasons why they affect him, and, most importantly, the means by which they may be controlled. An explanation generally takes the form of an elaborate story having the universal characteristics of employing powers, demons, personified forces, gods, or a supreme god as an integral element. The precise form the personalized power may take is limited only by the creative imagination of man. Elsewhere (d'Aquili, 1972; Laughlin and d'Aquili, 1974) we have suggested that man has a drive (termed the "cognitive imperative") to organize unexplained external stimuli into some coherent cognitive matrix. This matrix generally takes the form of a myth in nonindustrial societies and a blend of science and myth in Western industrial societies.

The solution at the level of action posed by a myth may (and usually does) require the ritual unification of the group, or a priestly representative of the group, with a personified being in such a fashion that the society gains some measure of control over the forces controlled by the being. All of this has been clearly delineated by Lévi-Strauss (1963a, b; 1964), among others. Thus, for example, the concepts of a Christ figure or a solar hero represent cognitive solutions to problems posed by the myths within which they are embedded as structural elements. Orthodox structuralists have, however, tended to deemphasize the role of ritual in organism-environment equilibration in favor of a stress on the analysis of the internal dialectics of mythic structure. There is, of course, much evidence supporting the contention that antinomies differentiated by myth are also in part resolved by myth. However, as Lévi-Strauss admits:

> And since the purpose of the myth is to provide a logical mode capable of overcoming a contradiction (an

impossible achievement if, as it happens, the contradiction is real), a theoretically infinite number of states will be generated, each one slightly different from the other. Thus, myth grows spiral-wise until the intellectual impulse which has produced it is exhausted. Its *growth* is a continuous process, whereas its *structure* remains discontinuous (1963a:226).

We can see that, considering the mythic process alone, complete psychological satisfaction of the inherent problem is never forthcoming. The process continues as long as the "intellectual impulse" remains unexhausted. Our contention is that total psychological resolution of the ambiguity contained in myth is never achieved within the confines of the structure of the myth per se, but rather by the articulation of the mythic structure with a mechanism specifically affecting limbic and autonomic functions. In other words the process of resolution requires some mechanism extraneous to the myth but intimately united with mythic expression through action. The mechanism must be capable of facilitating and sustaining a psychologically fulfilling resolution to problematic antinomies, thus providing active reinforcement of the mythic structure itself.

We contend that the only resolutions that are psychologically powerful to both individuals and groups are those that have an aspect of existential reality. We show in this [reading] that such a powerfully affective resolution arises primarily from ritual or meditation and rarely, if ever, from a cognitive unification of antinomies alone. The *ultimate* union of opposites that is the aim of all human religious ritual is the union of contingent and vulnerable man with a powerful, possibly omnipotent force. In other words we propose that man and a personified power or powers represent the ultimate poles of much mythic structure and that polarity is the basic problem that myth and ritual must solve. Side by side with this basic antinomy are usually other correlative antinomies that frequently must be resolved according to the specific myth before the basic god/man antinomy can be resolved. Such polar opposites include heaven/hell, sky/earth, good/bad, left/right, strong/weak, as well as an almost endless series of other polarities that recur in human myths.

Since we have stated a hypothesis that bases human religious ritual, in part, at least, on the evolution of the CNS, and since the structure of human religious ritual behavior arises directly out of its mythic structure, we must try to explain how man formulates myth.

The capacity to mythologize involves at least three critical higher cortical functions: conceptualization, abstract causal thinking, and antinomous thinking. First, all myths are couched in terms of named categories of objects that we call concepts or ideas. Second, all myths, like all other rational thoughts, involve causal sequences. Third, myths involve the orientation of the universe into multiple dyads of polar opposites. This latter characteristic is also present in everyday thought but is more markedly obvious in mythic structures. Indeed, it is this quality of human thought that has entranced psychologists and anthropologists from Jung to Lévi-Strauss to such a degree that other aspects of myth structuring have often been neglected.

At the risk of appearing overly simplistic, we note that all three of these higher cortical functions involve, in one way or another, a specific area of the brain. This area in man is composed of the supramarginal and angular gyri, as well as of certain adjacent areas. It can best be visualized as the area of overlap between the somaesthetic*, visual, and auditory association areas. It is, so to speak, an association area of association areas. It allows for direct transfer across sensory modalities without involvement of the limbic or affective system. It is as if three computer systems, one for each of the three major sensory modalities mentioned, were hooked into each other and the information from each became available to all. Such a system allows classes of objects to be set up that are vastly more inclusive than any classifying system possible within each individual sensory modality.

Ever since Goldstein's work in the 1940s it has been felt that the brain area we have described was intrinsically involved in conceptualization. After a period of research neglect, this position became powerfully supported by the evidence of Geschwind in his . . . classic monograph "Disconnection Syndromes in Animals and Man" (1965). Geschwind refers to this general area of the brain as the *inferior*

*somaesthetic: having to do with the body's sensing of itself (editor's note).

parietal lobule. Soviet researchers refer to roughly the same area as simply the parieto-occipital area, and Luria (1966) notes that it is intimately involved in the formulation of basic logical grammatical categories. Luria and others have shown that destruction of parts of this area of the brain inhibits the use of the comparative degree of adjectives. One object, for example, cannot be set off against another object in comparison. Such statements as "larger than," "smaller than," or "better than" become impossible for patients with lesions in portions of this area. Furthermore, such patients are not able to name the opposite of any word presented to them.

Although not conclusive, such evidence indicates that the inferior parietal lobule not only may underlie conceptualization but also may be responsible for man's proclivity for abstract antinomous thinking. Of course, a devastating lesion that destroys most or all of this area not only wipes out antinomous thinking but also drastically interferes with concept formation. The intellectual sequelae of such a lesion are profound. Furthermore, there is increasing evidence that the reciprocal connections between the anterior convexity of the frontal lobe on the dominant side and the inferior parietal lobule are intimately related to abstract causal thinking (Luria, 1966). Indeed Basso, De Renzi, Faglioni, Scotti, and Spinnler (1973) have presented impressive neurophysiological evidence for the existence of cerebral areas critical to the performance of "intelligence tasks." After reviewing the pertinent literature, as well as their findings, they conclude that:

> . . . there is one region of the brain, overlapping the language area, which plays a major role in several different intellectual tasks, independent of their specific features. This might mean that several intellectual abilities are focally organized in this area, or more likely, that the area subserves a superordinate ability entering into every intelligent performance and identifiable with the factor designated as "g" by psychologists.

We propose that this area comprises the inferior parietal lobule, the anterior convexity of the frontal lobes, and their reciprocal interconnections. It has long been known that the anterior portions of the frontal lobes, particularly on the dominant side, are involved in ordering not only sequential movement but also perceptual and cognitive elements in both space and time. . . .

. . . *Homo erectus* shows considerable elaboration of the inferior frontal convolution and middle temporal convolutions, as well as further development of the inferior parietal lobule. While we consider it improbable that *Australopithecus* was a complex mythmaker and religious ritual practitioner, we think it probable that *Homo erectus* was both. We do not wish at this time to be drawn into the controversy over the . . . Leakey finds from East Rudolf. If, indeed, the East Rudolf skull represents the genus *Homo,* then we simply push the cognitive, mythic, and ritual functions back from about 750,000 years ago to perhaps 2.5 million years ago or more. In any case we doubt that many physical anthropologists would disagree that, even if *Homo* were present on the earth 2 million years ago, he nevertheless had probably evolved from an australopithecine-like creature. The latter australopithecine types and *Homo* probably evolved from a common early australopithecine ancestor. Whenever it occurred, with the advent of the genus *Homo,* we get our first approximation of what we would probably recognize as human intellectual functioning, including both speech and . . . various abstract thinking faculties.

At this point we must return briefly to a topic we mentioned in passing earlier—that is, what we call the "cognitive imperative." The abstract problem solving that the evolution of these neural structures made possible aided man's adaptation to any environment. It permitted him to look for the causes of the phenomena that were occurring around him and to attempt to control them. Such problem-solving ability enhanced human adaptation from the arctic region to the tropical belt. It is not surprising, therefore, that, once these neural systems evolved, they rapidly spread over the globe. In this [reading] it is not possible to trace in detail the evolution of each of these neural mechanisms and the probable original selective pressures on them. Suffice it to say that in the aggregate these neural systems represent man's highest and most universal adaptive capability.

Their importance for survival is demonstrated by man's almost instinctive need to organize unknown or unexplained stimuli into some sort of cognitive framework. Work by Adler and Hammett (1973a, 1973b), Harvey, Hunt, and Schroder (1961), and others, as well as our own work involving people's responses to the Philadelphia earthquake . . . (accompanied by numerous other studies by cognitive psychologists), all support the hypothesis that man automatically, almost reflexly, confronts an unknown stimulus by the question "What is it?" Affective responses such as fear, happiness, or sadness and motor responses are clearly secondary to the immediate cognitive response. This appears to be true whether a person has normal intellectual functioning, is grossly psychotic, or has minimal to moderate brain damage. In all cases the immediate attempt of the human organism in the face of an unknown stimulus is the attempt to organize it within a known framework. It is this universal adaptive drive, related to abstract problem solving, that we have called the cognitive imperative. Such cognitive organization of external stimuli into a linear, causal, verbal mode of consciousness is an effect of the neural mechanisms whose evolution we have just described, all operating primarily within the dominant hemisphere of the brain. It is this linear analytic and verbal form of cognition that precisely constitutes man's most efficient form of adaptation to certain environments.

That there is a drive for organizing data in this distinctively human manner, together with an affective reward, is supported by the experiments of Terzian and Cecotto (1959; 1960), Rosadini and Rossi (1961), Alema and Rosadini (1964), and Hommes and Panhysen (1971). In summary these workers have demonstrated, among other things, that an intracarotid injection of sodium amytal on the dominant side of the brain, which interferes with the verbal and analytic functions that we have been discussing, and which prevents the organization of percepts into an analytical and verbal mode, results in a dramatic reaction that includes a sense of guilt and unworthiness, worries about the future, and a sense of loss of mastery over the environment. In a word such a chemical inhibition of the functions of the dominant hemisphere (analytic functioning) results in depression. On the other hand, injection of sodium amytal into the carotid artery on the nondominant side, in effect, releases the dominant analytic side from certain inhibiting influences and yields a state of very clear euphoria.

In the face of such evidence it is hard to deny the biological importance of ordering sensory data within an analytic framework. It is not hyperbole to speak of the need for order as a cognitive imperative. The point of all this is that man is driven to understand the world around him. He cannot do otherwise. He has no choice in the matter whatsoever. All the higher cognitive functions that we have described necessarily operate on incoming data—that is, percepts are categorized, organized, and modified into concepts, and concepts and percepts are both organized in causal chains and arranged in terms of antinomies or polar dyads. Strips of reality that can be understood within the bounds of given data are so understood and a model of reality is so constructed. If, however, the data available do not explain any unusual phenomenon, the machinery of the brain is not turned off. It still automatically constructs models of reality out of juxtaposed material drawn from the various sensory memory banks. It is here that Western science differs from myth formation. Ideally, Western science imposes a limitation on the functioning of the gnostic machinery of the brain and thus refuses to include in a model of reality elements that are not derived from observed data or that are not immediately inferable from such data.

At this point we should return to man's ability to think in terms of abstract causality. We have already discussed the relationship of the anterior convexity of the frontal lobe to the inferior parietal lobule in terms of the ability to juxtapose concepts in linear sequences. For convenience we refer to the anterior convexity of the frontal lobe, the inferior parietal lobule, and their reciprocal interconnections as the *causal operator*. The causal operator treats any given strip of reality in the same way that a mathematical operator functions. It organizes that strip of reality into what is subjectively perceived as causal sequences, back to the initial terminus of that strip or forward toward some desired final terminus. In view of the apparently universal human trait, under ordinary circumstances, of positing causes for any given strip of reality, we postulate that, if the initial terminus is not given by sense data, then the causal operator grinds out an initial terminus automatically.

Here again, we may note how Western science may differ from the more usual form of human cognizing. Science ideally refuses to postulate an initial terminus or first cause of any strip of reality unless it is observed or can be immediately inferred from observation. Under more usual conditions the causal operator grinds out the initial terminus or first cause of any strip of reality. This is a mental construct drawn from elements encoded in memory and characterized by the operator's nature itself. That is, the construct causes or in some sense has the power to generate the strip of reality. What we are implying is that gods, powers, spirits, personified forces, or any other causative ingredients are automatically generated by the causal operator. Note that in speaking of Western science *we have not been speaking of Western scientists.* The restrictions imposed on human thought are social and contractual in Western science. However, the brain of the scientist functions no differently from anyone else's brain. Although the scientist may reject the idea of gods, spirits, demons, or any other type of personified power, he nevertheless experiences them in his dreams and fantasy life. Any practicing psychiatrist or clinical psychologist can point to these phenomena in the fantasy life of the most rational man. The causal operator simply operates spontaneously on reality, positing an initial causal terminus when none is given. When the strip of reality to be analyzed is the totality of the universe, then the initial terminus or first cause that is automatically produced by the causal operator is Aristotle's First Mover Unmoved.

If the foregoing analysis is correct, then human beings have no choice but to construct myths to explain their world. The mythic materials may be social, or they may appear individually in dreams, daydreams, or fantasies. Nevertheless, so long as human beings ponder their existence in what often appears to be a capricious universe, then they must construct myths to orient themselves within that universe. This is inherent in the obligatory functioning of the neural structures considered earlier. Since it is highly unlikely that man will ever know the first cause of every strip of reality observed, it is highly probable that man will always create gods, powers, demons, or other entities as first causes to explain what he observes. Indeed, man cannot do otherwise. Myths are structured either socially or individually, according to the analytic and verbal mode of consciousness of the dominant hemisphere. Myths entail the codification of unexplained reality in terms of antinomies and of causal explanatory sequences.

The development of these higher cortical functions may be regarded as a major adaptive advance, insofar as they allow man abstract problem solving, an advantage in virtually any environment. They can, however, also be regarded as a curse. Because man can think abstractly and causally, he can transcend the world of his immediate perceptual field (see the "cognitive extension of prehension" in Laughlin and d'Aquili, 1974). From experience he can postulate probable events under given circumstances. Most of all, these functions make him acutely aware of his own mortality and of the contingency of his existence in an unpredictable world (Becker, 1973). This is the basis of the existential anxiety that all men bear. It is to relieve this "curse of cognition," this existential anxiety, that man first seeks mastery over his environment by attempting to understand it. He organizes reality into a cognitive framework. Often the organization is by means of a myth. But in and of itself, this organization of reality into mythic structures does not give man genuine control over the overwhelming forces of nature that confront him.

Satisfying the cognitive imperative, although necessary, is not sufficient. Since man ultimately attempts mastery of his environment by motor action, he tries to achieve mastery over disease, famine, and death by some form of motor activity as well. It is thus that religious ritual (i.e., mythically based, conceptualized ritual) necessarily arises out of the structuring of a myth. It can be argued that religious ritual is, in practice, no more effective in overcoming the grim forces of man's existential condition than cognitive organization is. To explain the persistence of religious ritual, Skinner and other behaviorists have proposed a model based on irregular scheduling of rewards. For example, if a ritual is performed often enough, a famine may be relieved in the natural course of events and the ritual is given the credit for it. It is certainly known from animal experimentation, as well as from observation of human behavior, that chance rewards may often sustain a behavior that is causally linked to the reward only in the cognized environment . . . of the subject. But religious ritual has persistence and intensity that seem to transcend the Skinnerian model. What really appears to maintain the force and persistence of religious ritual is the ineffable experience, the intense positive affect experienced by a participant, associated with the resolution of a crucial antinomy, usually the resolution of the god/man antinomy. How elements that are intrinsically opposite can at the same time be merged, and how this experience is joined with an ineffable affective experience, we now attempt to delineate.

RELIGIOUS RITUAL AND CEREBRAL ASYMMETRY

Over the [past few] years . . . the work of Sperry et al. (1969), Nebes and Sperry (1971), Gazzaniga (1970), Gazzaniga and Hillyard (1971), Bogen (1969), Levy-Agresti and Sperry (1968), and others has strongly pointed to what appears to be a rather startling situation in neuroanatomy and neurophysiology. Until these workers performed their experiments on split-brain animals and studied split-brain conditions in human beings, it had always been assumed that the higher cortical functions we have been considering, namely, language ability, conceptualization, abstract causal thinking, and certain basic logical processes such as abstract antinomous thinking, were pretty much all that was important in terms of higher cortical functioning. It had been known since the middle of the nineteenth century that, for the most part, these functions are lateralized to one hemisphere of the brain called the "dominant" hemisphere.

One can understand the prejudices regarding the prominence of these functions. Since they underlie abstract problem solving, and, to a great extent, most of human "culture," they were considered of paramount importance. The nondominant or "minor" hemisphere was usually ignored and even relegated to the status of a vestigial organ. By severing the connections between the two hemispheres in animals—that is, by severing the corpus callosum, the anterior commissure, and the optic chiasm—these workers were able to demonstrate that both sides of the brain could be taught different tasks and could respond differently to the same stimuli under appropriate conditions. To speak anthropomorphi-

cally, it was as if these animals possessed two minds or two spheres of consciousness.

The studies in relation to man were much more dramatic. In studying individuals with the corpus callosum severed to prevent the spread of epilepsy, it soon became clear that such individuals also acted as if they had two minds or spheres of consciousness, each independent of the other. This had not been noted before, because tests of the nondominant or minor hemisphere were usually given in terms of verbal questions requiring verbal answers. Since such verbal ability is almost completely lateralized to the dominant hemisphere, it is impossible to get accurate information concerning the minor or nondominant hemisphere, because both sides of the brain function essentially independently in these patients. By designing tests that did not require verbal responses it became possible to study functions of the minor hemisphere in split-brain patients.

At the risk of oversimplifying the situation it appears that the dominant hemisphere, as has been known for many years, is responsible for analytic, causal, verbal thought, and probably for discrete perception. In other words the neural mechanisms we have been discussing function primarily, although not solely, within the dominant or major cerebral hemisphere. What is new is the discovery that the so-called minor hemisphere has extremely important nonverbal, nonanalytic functions. First of all, it is related to the perception of visual-spatial relationships. Over and above this, there is good evidence that the minor hemisphere perceives the world, not in terms of discrete entities, but in terms of gestalts or nondiscrete holistic perceptions. The perception of wholeness or unity controlled by this hemisphere is extremely important to this discussion. Furthermore, there is evidence that the minor hemisphere may be chiefly responsible for creative or artistic ability.

Levy (personal communication) and Trevarthen (1969) are obtaining evidence that in the normally functioning individual both hemispheres may operate in solving problems via a mechanism of reciprocal inhibition controlled at the brain stem level. Put simply, the world is approached by a rapid functional alternation of each hemisphere. One is, as it were, flashed on, then turned off; the second flashed on, then turned off; the first flashed on, and so forth, in rapid alternation. The rhythm of this process, and the predominance of one side or the other, may account for various cognitive styles, from the extremely analytic and scientific to the extremely artistic and synthetic.

There is some evidence that this duality of cerebral functioning may parallel the duality of autonomic functioning we considered in the first part of this [reading]. Actually it is conceptually easier to integrate the two modes of consciousness into a more general duality of patterning within the CNS. [This has been done elsewhere] by using Hess's (1925) model of an energy-expending (or ergotropic) system and an energy-conserving (or trophotropic) system operating in a manner complementary to the human organism. In this model the ergotropic system consists not only of the sympathetic nervous system, which governs arousal states and fight or flight responses, but also of any energy-expending process within the nervous system. Conversely, the trophotropic system includes not only the parasympathetic nervous system, which governs basic vegetative and homeostatic functions, but also any CNS process that maintains the baseline stability of the organism. Thus the ergotropic/trophotropic model represents an extension to the CNS of the autonomic nervous system's functioning. We are now presenting an extended model according to which the minor or nondominant hemisphere is identified with the trophotropic or baseline energy state system, and the dominant or major hemisphere that governs analytical verbal and causal thinking is identified with the ergotropic or energy-expending system.

Alteration in the tuning of these systems has been offered as an explanation for various altered states of consciousness by varying investigators, including Gellhorn (1967), Gellhorn and Kiely (1972; 1973), and Ornstein (1972). These investigators present evidence that, at maximal stimulation of either the trophotropic or ergotropic system, there is, as it were, a spillover into the opposite complementary system. It has been postulated that the rhythmic activity of ritual behavior supersaturates the ergotropic or energy-expending system to the point that the trophotropic system not only is simultaneously excited by a kind of spillover but also on rare occasions may be maximally stimulated, so that,

briefly at least, both systems are intensely stimulated. The positive, ineffable affect that this state produces was alluded to in the first part of this [reading].

In man, we propose that, with the simultaneous stimulation of the lower aspects of both systems, their cerebral representations—that is, both hemispheres of the brain—may function simultaneously. This is manifested cognitively with the presentation of polar opposites by the analytic hemisphere (that is, the presentation of a problem to be solved in terms of the myth structure) and the *simultaneous* experience of their union via the excitation or stimulation of the minor hemisphere. This explains the often-reported experience of individuals solving paradoxical problems during certain states of meditation or during states induced by some ritual behavior. In one of the few experiments performed in any kind of a controlled manner on the experience of meditation, Deikman (1969) notes that one of the phenomena common to all subjects was what appeared to be simultaneity of conflicting perceptions during relatively advanced meditation states. He states:

> . . . the subjects' reports indicated that they experienced conflicting perception. For example, in the third session, subject B stated, about the vase, "it certainly filled my visual field" but a few minutes later stated "it didn't fill the field by any means." In the seventh session referring to the landscape he commented, ". . . a great deal of agitation . . . but it isn't agitating . . . it's . . . pleasurable." In general, subjects found it very difficult to describe their feelings and perceptions during the meditation periods—"it's very hard to put into words," was a frequent comment. This difficulty seems due in part to the difficulty in describing their experience without contradictions (1969:209).

It appears that, during certain meditation and ritual states, logical paradoxes or the awareness of polar opposites as presented in myth appear simultaneously, both as antinomies and as unified wholes. This experience is coupled with the intensely affective "oceanic" experience that has been described during various meditation states, as well as during certain stages of ritual. During intense meditative experiences such as yogic ecstasy and the *unio mys-*

tica of the Christian tradition, the experience of the union of opposites, or *conjunctio oppositorum,* is expanded to the experience of the total union of self and other or, as it is expressed in the Christian tradition, the union of the self with God.

We note what appears to be a different neurophysiological approach to essentially the same end state following meditation and ritual behavior. In both cases the end point appears to be the unusual physiological circumstance of simultaneous strong discharge of both the ergotropic and trophotropic systems, involving changes in the autonomic system and the onset of intense and unusual affective states, coupled with the sense of union of logical opposites, usually the self and a personified force or god. It appears that during meditation one begins by intensely stimulating the trophotropic system. There is a marked decrease of sensory input, the attempt to banish all thought and desire from the mind, and the attempt to maintain an almost total baseline homeostasis state with only enough intrusion of the ergotropic system to prevent sleep. The spillover in the case of meditation is from the trophotropic to the ergotropic side with the eventual result in strong discharges from both systems.

Ritual behavior apparently starts from the *opposite* system. Ritual is often performed to solve a problem that is presented via myth to the verbal analytic consciousness. The problem may be dichotomized as good and evil, life and death, or the disparity between god and man. The problem may be as simple as the disparity between man and a capricious rain god or as subtle as the disparity between man's existential contingent state and the state of an all-knowing, all-powerful, unchangeable "ground of being." In any case the problem is presented in the analytic mode, which involves ergotropic excitation. Like all other animals, man attempts to master the environmental situation by means of motor behavior. The motor behavior man chooses goes far back into his phylogenetic past. It usually takes the form of a repetitive motor, visual, or auditory driving stimulus, which strongly activates the ergotropic system. Even the cadence of words and chanting contributes to this repetitive quality. The slow rhythm of a religious procession or the fast beat of drums or rattles all serve to drive the ergotropic system. With prayers and chanting

this system is often driven in two ways. The myth may be presented within the ritual prayer and thus excite by its meaning the *cognitive* ergotropic functions of the dominant hemisphere. The rhythm of the prayer or chant, by its very rhythmicity, drives the ergotropic system independent of the meaning of words. If the ritual works, the ergotropic system becomes, as it were, supersaturated and spills over into excitation of the trophotropic system, resulting in the same end state as meditation but from the opposite neural starting point.

The difference between meditation and ritual is that those who are adept at meditation are often able to maintain an ecstatic state for prolonged periods of time. The ecstatic state and sense of union produced by ritual are usually very brief (often lasting only a few seconds) and may often be described as no more than a shiver running down the back at a certain point. This experience may, however, be repeated at numerous focal points during the ritual. Furthermore, the ecstatic states produced by ritual, although they are usually extremely brief, seem to be available to many or most participants. The ecstatic states attained through meditation, although they may last for hours or even days, require long practice and intense discipline.

In any case this unusual physiological state resulting from both approaches produces other cognitive effects besides a sense of union of opposites. Numerous reports from religious traditions point to the fact that such states yield not only a feeling of union with a greater force or power but also an intense awareness that death is not to be feared, accompanied by a sense of harmony of the individual with the universe. This sense of universal harmony may be the human cognitive extrapolation from the more primitive sense of union with other conspecifics that ritual behavior excites in animals. In point of fact the feeling of union with conspecifics carries through to human ritual as well. Even if the feeling is elaborated on a higher cognitive level to become a feeling of harmony with the universe (and a lack of fear of death), most human religious rituals also produce an intense feeling of union with the other participants. This oneness has contributed to the feeling of "a holy people," "a people of God," "a people set apart."

Thus, we see that the phylogenetic origins of ritual carry through in an unbroken line to the most complex human religious ritual. However, on these primitive functions are grafted other adaptive functions—namely, those of higher cognition. In point of fact, man is not simply the sum of neural mechanisms independently evolved under various selective pressures. Rather, man functions physiologically as an integrated whole. Although his higher cognition may have evolved as a very practical adaptive problem-solving process, this cognition carries with it, indeed, requires, the formation of myths that orient the person toward certain problems, problems rendered soluble through ritual. When ritual works (and it by no means works all the time), it powerfully relieves man's existential anxiety and, at its most powerful, relieves him of the fear of death and places him in harmony with the universe. It is no wonder that a behavioral phenomenon so powerful has persisted throughout the ages. Indeed, it is likely to persist for some time to come.

To summarize this rather complex argument, we are simply stating that, given an organism in which the neural mechanisms for abstract thought have evolved, which require causal and antinomous thinking as a highly adaptive trait, that organism must necessarily use these mechanisms in an attempt to explain his existential situation. Such explanation involves the obligatory structuring of myths, complete with the organization of the world into antinomies and with the positing of initial causal termini of strips of observed reality that man calls gods, spirits, demons, and the like. These mechanisms are not a matter of choice but are necessarily generated by the structure of the brain in response to the cognitive imperative. Once the problem is presented in myth form, man, in common with all animals, attempts to solve it (i.e., to master the environment) via motor action. In the presence of a problem presented in myth, and with the inherited ancient ritual mechanisms still intact, ritual becomes the motor vehicle by which the problem is solved. Indeed, ritual behavior is one of the few mechanisms at man's disposal that can possibly solve the ultimate problems and paradoxes of human existence. Thus, although ritual behavior does not always "work," it has such a powerful effect

when it does work that it is unlikely ever to pass out of existence within a social context, no matter what the degree of sophistication of society. Religious ritual behavior may take new forms within the context of highly developed Western technological societies. But whether in new form or in old, it is much too important to the psychological well-being of a society to lapse into oblivion.

This essentially ends what has necessarily been a rather sketchy outline of a theory of the evolution of religious ritual that takes into account the evolution of multiple, interrelated neural subsystems. We feel that we have presented a discussion that allows one to understand the evolution of the neural basis of human ceremonial ritual, as well as the *primary* pressures operating on the selection and maintenance of this behavior in human societies. It would be erroneous in the extreme to assume that this is the whole story or that the adaptive advantage of human ceremonial ritual presented in this [reading] exhausts its adaptive potential. On the contrary, ceremonial ritual (religious or otherwise) possesses a number of highly adaptive qualities, which, under specific circumstances, may respond to selective pressure from the environment even more strongly than the primary evolutionary components we have been considering. Specifically, we have not considered the relationship of ceremonial ritual either to the establishment of cognitive structures or to the institution and maintenance of social structures. Furthermore, we have not considered certain ancillary but very important aspects of human ritual in maintaining social well-being, such as the establishment and maintenance of ordered authority and the distribution of available resources in times of scarcity. We would urge the reader to bear in mind, however, that, no matter how complex the function of ceremonial ritual in any given society, under a specific set of environmental circumstances it cannot be adequately or fully understood apart from the evolution and function of those neural structures underlying ritual behavior, many of which arose far back in man's phylogenetic past, and some of which are responsible for his becoming *Homo sapiens*.

REFERENCES

Abraham, R. 1976. "Vibrations and the Realization of Form," in *Education and Consciousness: Human Systems in Transition* (E. Jantsch and C. H. Waddington, eds.). Reading: Addison-Wesley.

Adler, H. M. and V. B. O. Hammett. 1973a. "The Doctor Patient Relationship Revisited, and Analysis of the Placebo Effect," *Annals of Internal Medicine* 78:595.

———. 1973b. "Crisis Conversion and Cult Formation: An Examination of a Common Psychosocial Sequence," *American Journal of Psychiatry* 30:861.

Alema, G. and G. Rosadini. 1964. "Données cliniques et E.E.G. de l'introduction d-amytal sodium dans la circulation encéphalique, l'état de conscience." *Acat Neurochir* (Wien) 12:241–258.

d'Aquili, E. G. 1972. *The Biopsychological Determinants of Culture.* Reading, Pa.: Addison-Wesley Modular Publications.

Basso, A., P. De Renzi, L. Faglioni, G. Scotti, and H. Spinnler. 1973. "Neuropsychological Evidence for the Existence of Cerebral Area Critical to the Performance of Intelligence Tasks." *Brain* 96:715–728.

Becker, E. 1973. *The Denial of Death.* New York: Free Press.

Bogen, J. E. 1969. "The Other Side of the Brain, II: An Appositional Mind." *Bulletin of Los Angeles Neurological Society* 34:135–162.

Bourguignon, E. 1972. "Dreams and Altered States of Consciousness in Anthropological Research," in *Psychological Anthropology*, 2nd ed. F. L. K. Hsu, ed. Homewood, Ill.: Dorsey Press.

Chance, M. R. A. 1965. In *Primate Behavior* (E. DeVore, ed.). New York and London: Holt, Rinehart and Winston.

Clark, W. E. LeGros. 1963. *The Antecedents of Man.* New York: Harper and Row.

Deikman, A. J. 1969. "Experimental Meditation," in *Altered States of Consciousness* (C. T. Tart, ed.). Garden City, N. Y.: Doubleday.

Gazzaniga, M. S. 1970. *The Bisected Brain.* New York: Appleton-Century-Crofts.

Gazzaniga, M. S. and S. A. Hillyard. 1971. "Language and Speech Capacity of the Right Hemisphere." *Neuropsychologia* 9:273–280.

Geertz, C. 1973. *The Interpretation of Cultures.* New York: Basic Books.

Gellhorn, E. 1967. *Principles of Autonomic-Somatic Integration: Physiological Basis and Psychological and Clinical Implications.* Minneapolis: University of Minnesota Press.

Gellhorn, E. and W. F. Kiely, 1972. "Mystical States of Consciousness: Neurophysiological and Clinical Aspects." *Journal of Nervous and Mental Disease* 154:399–405.

———. 1973. "Autonomic Nervous System in Psychiatric Disorder," *Biological Psychiatry* (J. Mendels, ed.). New York: Wiley.

Geschwind, N. 1965. "Disconnection Syndromes in Animals and Man." *Brain* 88:237–294: 585–644.

Harvey, O. J., D. E. Hunt, and H. M. Schroder. 1961. *Conceptual Systems and Personality Organization.* New York: Wiley.

Hess, W. R. 1925. *On the Relationship Between Psychic and Vegetative Functions.* Zurich: Schwabe.

Hommes, O. R. and L. H. H. M. Panhuysen. 1971. "Depression and Cerebral Dominance." *Psychiatric Neurological Neurochir.* 74:259–270.

Jay, P. 1965. "The Common Langur of North India," in *Primate Behavior* (E. DeVore, ed.). New York and London: Holt, Rinehart and Winston.

Laughlin, C. and E. d'Aquili. 1974: *Biogenetic Structuralism.* New York: Columbia University Press.

Lehrman, D. S. 1965. "Interaction Between Internal and External Environments in the Regulation of the Reproductive Cycle of the Ring Dove," in *Sex and Behavior* (F. A. Beach, ed.). New York: Wiley.

Lévi-Strauss, C. 1963a. *Structural Anthropology.* New York: Anchor Books.

———. 1963b. *The Savage Mind.* Chicago: University of Chicago Press.

———. 1964. *Mythologiques: Le Crit et Le Cuit.* Paris: Plon.

Levy-Agresti, J. and R. W. Sperry. 1968. "Differential Perceptual Capacities in Major and Minor Hemispheres." *Proceedings of the National Academy of Science* 61:1151.

Livanov, M. N., N. A. Gavrilova, and A. S. Aslanov. 1973. "Correlations of Biopotentials in the Frontal Parts of the Human Brain," in *Psychophysiology of the Frontal Lobes* (K. H. Pribram and A. R. Luria, eds.). New York: Academic Press.

Lorenz, K. 1966. *On Aggression.* New York: Bantam Books.

Luria, A. R. 1966. *Higher Cortical Functions in Man.* New York: Basic Books.

———. 1973. "The Frontal Lobes and the Regulation of Behavior." in *Psychophysiology of the Frontal Lobes* (K. H. Pribram and A. R. Luria, eds.). New York: Academic Press.

Manley, G. H. 1960. Unpublished doctor's thesis on displays of the Blackheaded Gull. Oxford.

Maranda, P. 1973. *Mythology.* Baltimore: Penguin Books.

Maranda, P. and K. Maranda. 1971. *Structured Analysis of Oral Tradition.* Philadelphia: University of Pennsylvania Press.

Murdock, G. P. 1967. "Ethnographic Atlas: A Summary." *Ethnology* 6.

Nebes, R. D. and R. W. Sperry. 1971. "Hemispheric Deconnection Syndrome with Cerebral Birth Injury in the Dominant Arm Area." *Neuropsychologia* 9:247–259.

Ornstein, R. E. 1972. *The Psychology of Consciousness.* San Francisco: Freeman.

Pribram, K. H. 1973. "The Primate Frontal Cortex—Executive of the Brain," in *Psychophysiology of the Frontal Lobes* (K. H. Pribram and A. R. Luria, eds). New York: Academic Press.

Rosadini, G. and G. F. Rossi. 1961. "Richerche sugli effetti elettroencefalografici, neurologici e psychici della somministrazione intracarotidea di amytal sodico nell'uomo." *Acta Neurochir.* (Wien) 9:234.

146 ROBBIE E. DAVIS-FLOYD

Rosenblatt, J. S. 1965. "Effects of Experience on Sexual Behavior in Male Cats," in *Sex and Behavior.* (F. A. Beach, ed.). New York: Wiley.

Schein, M. W. and E. B. Hale. 1965. "Stimuli Eliciting Sexual Behavior," in *Sex and Behavior* (F. A. Beach, ed.). New York: Wiley.

Smith, W. J. n.d. Chapter II in *The Spectrum of Ritual: A Biogenetic Structural Analysis* (E. G. d'Aquili, C. Laughlin, J. McManus, G. R. Murphy, eds.).

Sperry, R. W., M. S. Gazzaniga, and J. E. Bogen. 1969. "Interhemispheric Relationships: the Neocortical Commissures; Syndromes of Hemisphere Disconnection," in *Handbook of Clinical Neurology* (P. J. Vinken and G. W. Bruyn, eds.). Vol. 4. Amsterdam: North Holland.

Terzian, H. and C. Cecotto. 1959. "Su un nuovo metodo per la determinazione e lo studio della dominanza emisferica." *G. Psichiat. Neuropat.* 87:889.

———. 1960. "Amytal intracarotideo per lo studio della dominanza emisferica." *Riv. Neurol.* 30:460.

Tinbergen, N. 1951. *The Study of Instinct.* London: Oxford University Press.

———. 1965. "Some Recent Studies of the Evolution of Sexual Behavior," in *Sex and Behavior* (F. A. Beach, ed.). New York: Wiley.

Trevarthen, C. 1969. "Brain Bisymmetry and the Role of the Corpus Callosum in Behavior and Conscious Experience." Presented at the International Colloquium on Interhemispheric Relations. Czechoslovakia, June 10–13.

Walter, V. J. and W. G. Walter. 1949. "The Central Effects of Rhythmic Sensory Stimulation." *Electroencephalography and Clinical Neurophysiology* 1:57–85.

Walter, W. G. 1973. "Human Frontal Lobe Functions in Sensory-Motor Association," in *Psychophysiology of the Frontal Lobes* (K. H. Pribram and A. R. Luria, eds.). New York: Academic Press.

Whitehead, A. N. 1927. *Symbolism: Its Meaning and Effects.* New York: Macmillan.

Ritual in the Hospital: Giving Birth the American Way

ROBBIE E. DAVIS-FLOYD

Facts of publication: *Davis-Floyd, Robbie E. 1994. "The Rituals of Hospital Birth in America," from* Conformity and Conflict: Readings in Cultural Anthropology, *8th ed., 323–340. Edited by James P. Spradle and David W. McCurdy. New York: HarperCollins. Copyright © 1993 by Robbie Davis-Floyd. Reprinted with the permission of the author.*

Birth is a neglected topic in the literature on rites of passage. Most of the theories about such rites are derived from initiation, not birth. Even when the notion of rebirth is evoked in initiation rites, it is often dissociated from physiological birth and the experience of women. Ritual or spiritual rebirth, often done at the hands of males, is sometimes treated as higher and more important than the birthing of women. Women, however, are now engaging in ethnographic fieldwork and paying sustained attention to actual births and their ritual circumstances. Some societies have specific rites surrounding birth. North American society imagines that in avoiding such rites it is not entangled with symbolism. However, Robbie Davis-Floyd shows how profoundly erroneous such a view is.

For a book-length treatment of the topic see Robbie E. Davis-Floyd, Birth as an American Rite of Passage *(Berkeley: University of California Press, 1992). For another treatment of tacitly ritualized behavior see Horace Miner, "Rituals of the Nacirema,"* American Anthropologist *58.3 (1956).*

About the Author: *Dates: 1951–   , Casper, WY, U.S.A.* **Education**: *B.A., University of Texas at Austin; M.A., University of Texas at Austin; Ph.D., University of Texas at Austin.* **Field(s)**: *medical and symbolic anthropology; gender studies; anthropology of reproduction; corporate futures planning.* **Career**: *Adjunct Assistant Professor, 1987–1989, Trinity University; Lecturer, 1990–1992, University of Texas at Austin; Visiting Lec-*

turer, 1993, Rice University; Research Associate, 1994–1995, Rice University; Research Fellow, 1994–1996, University of Texas at Austin. **Publications**: *"Obstetric Training as a Rite of Passage,"* Medical Anthropology Quarterly *1.3 (1987): 288–318; "Birth as an American Rite of Passage,"* in Childbirth in America: Anthropological Perspectives, *153–172, ed. Karen Michaelson (Bergin and Garvey, 1988); "The Role of Obstetrical Rituals in the Resolution of Cultural Anomaly,"* Social Science and Medicine *31.2 (1990): 175–189 (reprinted in* Pre- and Perinatal Psychology Journal *4.3: 162–175 and 5.1: 23–39);* Birth as an American Rite of Passage *(University of California Press, 1992); "The Technocratic Body: American Childbirth as Cultural Expression,"* Social Science and Medicine *38.8 (1994): 1125–1140; with Megan Biesele, "Dying as Medical Performance: The Oncologist as Charon,"* in The Performance of Healing, *ed. Carol Laderman and Marina Roseman (Routledge, 1995).* **Additional**: *"Since 1982 I have been conducting research, giving lectures, and writing about ritual and technology in American childbirth. I discovered that the obstetrical procedures through which birth is channeled in the U.S. are profoundly transformative rituals that enact the core values of American culture, making hospital birth into a technocratic rite of initation for mothers and babies. In both research and writing, I have applied this model as well to physicians, who must go through an eight-year-long initation into the core value system of the technocracy as it applies to the treatmant of the human body, so that they can most effectively represent society to the minds and bodies of its individual members. My interest in the rituals of hospital birth led me to study their cultural alternatives, the rituals of home birth, and by extension, the emergent rituals of midwives and holistic healers. Current research-in-progress includes postmodern midwifery, as well as the paradigm shifts made by increasing numbers of physicians as they move from technomedicine to holistic healing. In the past three years I have become concerned with the often naive and uncritical use of ritual by New Agers and others, who seem unaware of ritual's potential for ill (cult conversion, mind control) as well as good. So I give workshops around the country on 'The Power of Ritual' and am currently working on a book by that title."*

Why is childbirth, which should be such a unique and individual experience for the woman, treated in such a highly standardized way in the United States? To find out, between 1983 and 1991, I interviewed over 100 mothers, as well as many of the obstetricians, nurses, childbirth educators, and midwives who attended them during birth.[1] What I discovered was that childbirth in the United States is transformed into a cultural rite of passage designed to initiate the birthing woman into the core value and belief system of American society. The rituals to accomplish such initiation take the form of a set of standardized obstetrical procedures performed upon birthing women, regardless of the nature of their individual labors and desires.

Almost every woman in my study, no matter how long or short, how easy or hard her labor, had been hooked up to an electronic fetal monitor and an IV (intravenously administered fluids and/or medication), had been encouraged to use some form of pain-relieving drug, had an episiotomy (a surgical incision in her vagina to widen the birth outlet in order to prevent tearing) at the moment of birth,

and was separated from her baby shortly after birth. Most of them had also received doses of the synthetic hormone Pitocin to speed their labors, and had given birth flat on their backs; nearly one quarter of them, as of all American women today, gave birth by Caesarean section.

I knew from my study of anthropology that there were many other ways to give birth, and I wondered how such standardization of treatment was possible and what it meant. I was told by the obstetricians I interviewed that these procedures were medically and scientifically necessary, but the cross-cultural evidence I had did not confirm that they were. For example, the Mayan Indians of Highland Chiapas hold onto a rope while squatting for birth, a position that is far more physiologically efficacious than the flat-on-your-back-with-your-feet-in-stirrups (lithotomy) position required of most American women. Mothers in many low-technology cultures give birth sitting, squatting, or on their hands and knees, and are nurtured through the pain of labor by experienced midwives and supportive female relatives. Yet we seem to believe that the hospital management of birth represents its *de-ritualization*—the freeing of physiology from primitive custom and taboo.

Is this perception correct? Anthropologists have never found a society that does not ritualize important life transitions like birth, puberty, and death. Most societies, in fact, turn such events into cultural rites of passage, which serve to make it appear that society itself effects the biological transformation of the individual. Our culture is not so different from others as we sometimes assume, so I began to look beneath the veneer of "medical necessity" covering obstetrical procedures for the rituals that were, in some form or another, likely to be there.

It is hard to see the cognitive filter one is looking through! While poring over the transcriptions of my interviews, I began to understand that the forces shaping American hospital birth are invisible to us because they stem from the conceptual foundations of our society. I realized that American society's deepest beliefs center around science, technology, patriarchy, and the institutions that control and disseminate them, and that there could be no better transmitter of these core values and beliefs than the very obstetrical procedures whose raison d'être I had been questioning.

A *ritual* is a patterned, repetitive, and symbolic enactment of a cultural belief or value; its primary purpose is alignment of the belief system of the individual with that of society. *A rite of passage* may be simply defined as a series of rituals through which individuals are conveyed from one social state or status to another (for example, from boyhood to manhood, girlhood to womanhood, or from the womb to the world of culture), thereby transforming both society's perception of the individual and the individual's perceptions of herself or himself. Rites of passage generally consist of three stages, originally outlined by Arnold van Gennep: (1) *separation* of the individuals from their preceding social state; (2) a period of *transition* in which they are neither one thing nor the other; and (3) an *integration* phase, in which through various rites of incorporation they are absorbed into their new social state. In the year-long pregnancy/childbirth rite of passage in American society, the separation phase begins with the woman's first awareness of pregnancy; the transition stage lasts until several days after the birth; and the

integration phase ends gradually in the newborn's first few months of life, when the new mother begins to feel that, as one woman put it, she is "mainstreaming it again."

Victor Turner, an anthropologist famous for his writings on ritual, pointed out that the most important feature of all rites of passage is that they place their participants in a transitional realm which has few of the attributes of the past or coming state. Existing in such a non-ordinary realm facilitates the gradual psychological opening of the initiates to profound interior change. In many initiation rites involving major transitions into new social roles (such as military basic training), this openess is achieved through a ritualized combination of physical and mental hardships that serve to break down the initiates' *belief systems*—the internal mental structure of concepts and categories through which the initiates perceive and interpret the world and their relationship to it. The breakdown of their belief systems leaves the initiates profoundly open to new learning and the construction of new categories. The rite of passage then restructures the initiates' category systems in accordance with the dominant belief and value system of the society or group into which they are being initiated.

By making the naturally transformative process of birth into a cultural rite of passage, a society can ensure that its basic values will be transmitted to the three new members born out of the birth process: the new baby, the woman reborn into the new social role of mother, and the man reborn as father. Society must make especially certain that the new mother is very clear about these values and the belief system that underlies them, as she is generally the one primarily responsible for instilling this belief system in the minds of her children—society's new members and the guarantors of its future. This goal is accomplished through ritualizing the birth process.

CHARACTERISTICS OF RITUAL

Some primary characteristics of ritual are particularly relevant to understanding how this process of cognitive restructuring is accomplished in hospital birth. We will examine each of these characteristics in order to understand (1) how ritual works and (2) how the natural process of childbirth is transformed in the United States into a cultural rite of passage.

Symbolism

Ritual works by sending messages in the form of symbols to those who perform and those who receive or observe it. A *symbol*, most simply, is an object, idea, or action that is loaded with cultural meaning. The left hemisphere of the human brain decodes and analyzes straightforward verbal messages, enabling the recipient to either accept or reject their content. Symbols, on the other hand, are received by the right hemisphere of the brain, where they are interpreted holistically. Instead of being analyzed intellectually, a symbol's message will be *felt* in its totality through the body and the emotions. Thus, even though the recipient may be unaware of her incorporation of the symbol's message, its ultimate effect may be extremely powerful.

Routine obstetric procedures are highly symbolic. For example, to be seated in a wheelchair upon entering the hospital, as many laboring women are, is to receive through their bodies the symbolic message that they are disabled; to then be put to bed is to receive the symbolic message that they are sick. Although no one pronounces, "You are disabled; you are sick," such graphic demonstrations of disability and illness can be far more powerful than words. One woman told me:

> I can remember just almost being in tears by the way they would wheel you in. I would come into the hospital, on top of this, breathing, you know, all in control. And they slap you in a wheelchair! It made me suddenly feel like maybe I wasn't in control any more.

Another elaborated:

> It's funny—it seems so normal to lie down in labor— just to be in the hospital seems to mean to lie down. But as soon as I did, I felt that I had lost something. I felt defeated. And it seems to me now that my lying down tacitly permitted the Demerol, or maybe entailed it. And the Demerol entailed the Pitocin, and the Pitocin entailed the Caesarean. It was as if, in laying down my body as I was told to, I also laid down my autonomy and my right to self-direction.

The intravenous drips commonly attached to the hands or arms of birthing women make a very powerful statement: they are umbilical cords to the hospital. The long cord connecting her body to the fluid-filled bottle places the woman in the same relation to the hospital as the baby in her womb is to her. By making her dependent on the institution for her life, the IV conveys to her one of the most profound messages of her initiation experience: in American society, we are all dependent on institutions for our lives. The message is even more compelling in her case, for *she* is the real giver of life. Society and its institutions cannot exist unless women give birth, yet the birthing woman in the hospital is shown, not that *she* gives life, but rather that the *institution* does.

A Cognitive Matrix

A *matrix* (from the Latin *mater*-mother), like a womb, is something from within which something else comes. Rituals are not arbitrary; they come from within the belief system of a group. Their primary purpose is to enact, and thereby, to transmit that belief system into the emotions, minds, and bodies of their participants. Thus, analysis of a culture's rituals can lead to a profound understanding of its belief system. Analysis of the rituals of hospital birth reveals their cognitive matrix to be the *technocratic model* of reality which forms the philosophical basis of both Western biomedicine and American society.

All cultures develop technologies. But most do not supervalue their technologies in the particular way that we do. The U.S. entered the modern world as an industrial society. But in these postmodern times, as we have evolved from a production-based to an information-processing economy, we have turned into a *technocracy*—a hierarchical, bureaucratic society driven by an ideology of technological progress. In *Stealing Fire: The Mythology of the Technocracy*, Peter C. Reynolds discusses how we "improve upon" nature by controlling it through culture. The technocratic model is the paradigm that charters such behavior. Its early forms were originally developed in the 1600s by Descartes, Bacon, and Hobbes, among others. This model assumes that the universe is mechanistic, following predictable laws which those enlightened enough to free themselves from the limitations of medieval superstition could discover through science and manipulate through technology, in order to decrease their dependence on nature. The human body is viewed as a machine that can be taken apart and put back together to ensure proper functioning. In the 17th century, the practical utility of this metaphor of the body-as-machine lay in its separation of body, mind, and soul. The soul could be left to religion, the mind to the philosophers, while the body could be opened up to scientific investigation.

The dominant religious belief systems of Western Europe at that time held that women were inferior to men—closer to nature and feebler both in body and intellect. Consequently, the men who developed the idea of the body-as-machine also firmly established the male body as the prototype of this machine. Insofar as it deviated from the male standard, the female body was regarded as abnormal, inherently defective, and dangerously under the influence of nature. The metaphor of the body-as-machine and the related image of the female body as a defective machine eventually formed the philosophical foundations of modern obstetrics. Wide cultural acceptance of these metaphors accompanied the demise of the midwife and the rise of the male-attended, mechanically manipulated birth. Obstetrics was thus enjoined by its own conceptual origins to develop tools and technologies for the manipulation and improvement of the inherently defective, and therefore anomalous and dangerous, process of birth.

The rising science of obstetrics ultimately accomplished this goal by adopting the model of the assembly-line production of goods as its template for hospital birth. Accordingly, a woman's reproductive tract is treated like a birthing machine by skilled technicians working under semiflexible timetables to meet production and quality control demands. As one fourth-year resident observed:

> We shave 'em, we prep 'em, we hook 'em up to the IV and administer sedation. We deliver the baby, it goes to the nursery and the mother goes to her room. There's no room for niceties around here. We just move 'em right on through. It's hard not to see it like an assembly line.

The hospital itself is a highly sophisticated technocratic factory; the more technology the hospital has to offer, the better it is considered to be. As an institution, the hospital constitutes a more significant social unit than an individual or a family, so it can require that the birth process conform more to institutional than personal needs. As one resident explained, "There is a set, established routine for doing things, usually for the convenience of the doctors and the nurses, and the laboring woman is someone you work around, rather than with."

The most desirable end-product of the birth process is the new social member, the baby; the new mother is a secondary by-product. One obstetrician commented, "It was what we were all trained to always go after—the perfect baby. That's what we were trained to produce. The quality of the mother's experience—we rarely thought about that."

Repetition and Redundancy

For maximum effectiveness, a ritual concentrates on sending one basic set of messages which it will repeat over and over again in different forms. Hospital birth takes places in a series of ritual procedures, many of which convey the same message in different forms. The open and exposing hospital gown, the ID bracelet, the intravenous fluid, the bed in which she is placed—all these convey to the laboring woman that she is dependent on the institution.

She is also reminded in myriad ways of the potential defectiveness of her birthing machine. These include periodic and sometimes continuous electronic monitoring of that machine, frequent manual examinations of her cervix to make sure that it is dilating on schedule, and, if it is not, administration of the synthetic hormone Pitocin to speed up labor so that birth can take place within the required 26 hours. (In Holland, by way of contrast, where many births take place at home, midwives recognize that individual labors have individual rhythms; they can stop and start, can take a few hours or several days. If labor slows, the midwives encourage the woman to eat to keep up her strength, and then to sleep until contractions pick up again.) All three of these procedures convey the same messages over and over: *time is important, you must produce on time, and you cannot do that without technological assistance because your machine is defective.* Since hospital birth is the process that reproduces society, it is only fitting that these messages should be repeatedly conveyed during the birth of a new social member. Hospital birth reflects and reproduces this culture's standard for handling time.

Cognitive Simplification

In any culture, the intellectual abilities of ritual participants are likely to differ, often markedly. It is not practical for society to design different rituals for persons of different levels of intellectual ability, so ritual utilizes specific techniques such as rhythmic repitition to attempt to reduce all participants to the same simpler level of cognitive functioning. This low level of cognitive operation involves thinking in either/or patterns of little cognitive complexity that do not allow for consideration of options or alternative views. Such cognitive simplification must precede the conceptual reorganization accompanying true psychological transformation.

Three other techniques are often employed by ritual to accomplish this end. One of these is the *hazing* familiar to undergraduates in fraternity initiation rites. Another is *strange-making*—making the commonplace appear strange by juxtaposing it with the unfamiliar. A third is *symbolic inversion*—metaphorically turning things upside-down and inside-out to generate, in a phrase coined by Roger Abrahams, "the power attendant upon confusion."

For example, in the rite of passage of military basic training, the initiate's normal patterns of action and thought are turned topsy-turvy. He is made strange to himself, his head is shaved, so that he does not even recognize himself in the mirror. He must give up his clothes, those expressions of individual identity and personality, to put on a uniform identical to that of the other initiates. Constant and apparently meaningless hazing (e.g., orders to dig six ditches and then fill them up) breaks down his cognitive structure. Then through repetive and highly symbolic rituals (such as sleeping with his rifle), the basic values, beliefs, and practices of the Marines are literally incorporated into his body and his mind.

The transformative nature of ritual is a key to understanding the thorough internalization of the technocratic model by the medical students, residents, and physicians who are American society's representatives-in-charge of the rite of passage of birth. These medicine men must go through an extraordinarily intensive eight-year-long rite of passage (four years of medical school and four years of residency). As in any society, those responsible for the welfare of the human body (whether physician, shaman, priest—or all of these) are also responsible for conducting many of the rituals that will properly enculturate that body and the social member it carries; they must thoroughly internalize the values underlying these rituals.

In medical school and again in residency, the same ritual techniques that transform a youth into a Marine are employed to transform college students into physicians. Reduced from the high status of graduate to the lowly status of first-year medical student, initiates are subjected to hazing techniques of rote memorization of endless facts and formulas, absurdly long hours of work, and intellectual and sensory overload. As one physician explained:

> Medical school is not difficult in terms of what you have to learn—there's just so much of it. You go through, in a six-week course, a thousand-page book. The sheer bulk of information is phenomenal. You have pop quizzes in two or three courses every day the first year. We'd get up around 6, attend classes till 5, go home and eat, then head back to school and be in anatomy lab working with a cadaver, or something, until 1 or 2 in the morning, and then go home and get a couple of hours sleep and then go out again.

Subjected to such a process, medical students often gradually lose any idealistic goals of "helping humanity" they had upon entering medical school. A successful rite of passage produces new professional values structured in accordance with the technocratic and scientific values of the dominant medical system. The emotional impact of this cognitive narrowing is aptly summarized by a former resident:

> Most of us went into medical school with pretty humanitarian ideals. I know I did. But the whole process of medical education makes you inhuman. . . . I've seen people devastated when they didn't know *an* answer. . . . The whole thing can get you pretty warped. I think that's where the feelings begin that somebody owes you something, 'cause you really, you know, you've blocked out a good part of your life. People lost boyfriends and girlfriends, fiancees and marriages. There were a couple of attempted suicides. . . . So you forget about the rest of life. And so by the time you get

to residency, you end up not caring about anything beyond the latest techniques you can master and how sophisticated the tests are that you can perform.

Likewise, the birthing woman is socialized by ritual techniques. She is made strange to herself by being dressed in a hospital gown, tagged with an ID bracelet, and by the shaving or clipping of her pubic hair, which symbolically desexualizes the lower portion of her body, returning it to a conceptual state of childishness. (In many cultures, sexuality and hair are symbolically linked.) The physiological process of labor itself is painful, and is often rendered more so by the hazing technique of frequent and very painful insertion of someone's fingers into her vagina to see how far her cervix has dilated. This technique also functions as a strange-making device. Since almost any nurse or resident in need of practice may check her cervix, the birthing women's most private parts are symbolically inverted into institutional property. One respondent's obstetrician said to her, "It's a wonder you didn't get an infection, with so many people sticking their hands inside of you."

Cognitive Stabilization

When humans are subjected to extremes of stress and pain, they are likely, at least temporarily, to retrogress cognitively past the level of simplicity into a dysfunctional condition in which the individual becomes unreasonable and out of touch with reality. Whenever the danger of such retrogression is present, ritual plays a critical role, since it stabilizes individuals under stress by giving them a conceptual handle-hold to keep them from "falling apart" or "losing it." When the airplane starts to falter, even passengers who don't go to church are likely to pray! Ritual mediates between cognition and chaos by making reality appear to conform to accepted cognitive categories. To perform a ritual in the face of chaos is to restore order to the world. Ritual has high evolutionary value, for it must have been one of the adaptive techniques our hominid ancestors utilized to help them continue to function at a survival level whenever they faced conditions of extreme environmental stress.

The labor process itself subjects most women to

extreme of pain, which are often intensified by the hospital environment. Women who choose to birth at home generally experience more support from and control over their environments. These factors better enable the home birth mother to cope with the pain of labor without cognitively retrogressing to dysfunctional behavior. Most hospital birthers, on the other hand, no matter how supportive their husbands, must constantly cope with an unsupportive and alien environment over which they have no control. They look to hospital rituals to relieve the cognitive distress resulting from their pain and fear. Thus they utilize breathing rituals taught in hospital-sponsored childbirth education classes to prevent cognitive retrogression. They turn to drugs for pain relief, and to the reassuring presence of medical technology for relief from fear. One woman expressed it this way:

> I was terrified when my daughter was born. I just knew I was going to split open and bleed to death right there on the table, but she was coming so fast, they didn't have any time to do anything to me. . . . I like Caesarean sections, because you don't have to be afraid.

When you come from within a belief system, its rituals will comfort and calm you. Accordingly, those women in my study who were in basic agreement with the technocratic model of birth before going into the hospital (70%) expressed general satisfaction with their hospital births, even if they were distressed with some of the specific procedures used.

Order, Formality, and a Sense of Inevitability

Its exaggerated and precise order and formality set ritual apart from other modes of social interaction, enabling it to establish an atmosphere that feels both inevitable and inviolate. In hospital birth, this sense of inevitability is created by the order and formality of obstetric procedures such as electronic monitoring of the fetal heart tones, the administration of Pitocin, and the ever-present possibility of the performance of a Caesarean section. These procedures, while often bothersome and painful, work to give the laboring woman a sense that society is using the best it has to offer—the full force of its technology—to inevitably ensure that she will have a safe birth. When women who have placed their faith in the technocratic model are denied its rituals, they often react with fear and a feeling of being neglected:

> My husband and I got to the hospital, and we thought they would take care of everything. I kept sending my husband out to ask them to give me something for the pain, to check me, but they were short-staffed and they just ignored me until the shift changed in the morning.

To perform a series of rituals is to feel oneself locking onto a set of "cosmic gears" which will safely crank the individual right on through the danger to safety on the other side. The Trobriand sea fisherman who performs an elaborate series of rituals in precise order believes that, if he does his part with precision, so must the gods of the sea do their part to bring him safely home. Likewise, the obstetrician feels that if he performs all the ritual procedures correctly, they should result in a healthy baby. Without their rituals, neither obstetrician nor fisherman would have the courage daily to face the challenge and caprice of nature.

Once those gears have been set into motion, however, there is often no stopping them. Childbirth activists have noted that the very inevitability of hospital procedures makes them almost antithetical to the possiblity of normal, natural birth. Such activists observe that a "cascade of intervention" occurs when one obstetric procedure alters the natural birthing process, causing complications, and so inexorably "necessitates" the next procedure, and the next. Many of the women in my study experienced such a "cascade" when they received some form of pain relief, such as an epidural, which slowed their labor. Then Pitocin was administered through the IV to speed up the labor, but Pitocin very suddenly induced longer and stronger contractions. Unprepared for the additional pain, the women asked for more pain relief, which ultimately necessitated more Pitocin. Pitocin-induced contractions, together with the fact that the mother must lie flat on her back because of the electronic monitor belts strapped around her stomach, can cause the supply of blood and oxygen to the fetus to drop, affecting the fetal heart rate. In response to the "distress" registered on the fetal monitor, an emergency Caesarean is performed.

Acting, Stylization, Staging

Ritual's set-apartness is enhanced by the fact that it is usually highly stylized and self-consciously acted, like a part in a play. Those who perform the rituals of hospital birth are often aware of their dramatic elements. The physician becomes the protagonist in the play. The woman's body is the stage upon which he performs, often for an appreciative audience of medical students, residents, and nurses. Here is how one obstetrician played to his audience of students observing the delivery he was performing:

> In honest-to-God natural conditions babies were *sometimes* born without tearing the perineum and without an episiotomy, but without artificial things like anesthesia and episiotomy, the muscle is torn apart and if it is not cut, it is usually not repaired. Even today, if there is no episiotomy and repair, those women quite often develop a rectocele and a relaxed vaginal floor. This is what I call the saggy, baggy bottom. Laughter by the students. A student nurse asks if exercise doesn't help strengthen the perineum. . . . "No, exercises may be for the birds, but they're not for bottoms. . . . When the woman is bearing down, the levator muscles of the perineum contract too. This means the baby is caught between the diaphragm and the perineum. Consequently, anesthesia and episiotomy will reduce the pressure on the head and, hopefully, produce more Republicans." More laughter from the students.[2]

Cognitive Transformation

The goal of most initiatory rites of passage is cognitive transformation. It occurs when the symbolic messages of ritual fuse with individual emotion and belief, and the individual's entire cognitive structure reorganizes around the newly internalized symbolic complex. This transformation, or conceptual reorganization, must usually be preceded by the cognitive simplification described above.

The following quote from a practicing obstetrician presents the outcome for him of such transformative learning:

> I think my training was valuable. The people who trained us, and their philosophy, were unbeatable. Dr. Pritchard—he's *the* man in obstetrics today in this country. And his philosophy was one of teaching one way to do it, and that was *his* way. And it was basically the right way. . . . I like the set hard way. I like the riverbanks that confine you in a direction. Later on. . . . you can incorporate a little bit of this or that as things change, but you learn one thing real well, and that's *the* way.

For both nascent physicians and nascent mothers, cognitive transformation of the initiate occurs when reality as presented by the technocratic model and reality as the initiate perceives it become one and the same. This process is gradual. Routine obstetric procedures cumulatively map the technocratic model of birth onto the birthing woman's perceptions of her labor experience, thereby aligning her belief system with that of society. One woman described her experience of this process:

> As soon as I got hooked up to the monitor, all everyone did was stare at it. The nurses didn't even look at me anymore when they came into the room—they went straight to the monitor. I got the weirdest feeling that *it* was having the baby, not me.

The electronic fetal monitor—a machine that utilizes ultrasound to measure the rate of the baby's heartbeat through electrodes belted onto the mother's abdomen—has itself become *the* symbol of high technology hospital birth. Observers and participants alike report that the monitor, once attached, becomes the focal point of the labor, as nurses, physicians, husbands, and even the mother herself become visually and conceptually glued to the machine, which then shapes their perceptions and interpretations of the birth process. The above statement illustrates the successful progression of conceptual fusion between the woman's perceptions of her birth experience and the technocratic model. So thoroughly was this model mapped on to her birth experience that she began to *feel* that the machine itself was having the baby, that she was a mere onlooker. Soon after the monitor was in place, she requested a Caesarean section, declaring that there was "no more point in trying."

Consider the visual and kinesthetic images that the laboring woman experiences—herself in bed, in a hospital gown, staring up at an IV pole, bag, and cord on one side, and down at a steel bed and a huge belt encircling her waist. Her entire sensory field conveys one overwhelming message about our culture's deepest values and beliefs: technology is supreme, and the individual is utterly dependent upon it.

Internalizing the technocratic model, women come to accept the notion that the female body is inherently defective. This notion then shapes their perceptions of the labor experience, as exemplified by one woman's story:

> It seemed as though my uterus had suddenly tired! When the nurses in attendance noted a contraction building on the recorder, they instructed me to begin pushing, not waiting for the *urge* to push, so that by the time the urge pervaded, I invariably had no strength remaining but was left gasping, dizzy, and diaphoretic. The vertigo so alarmed me that I became reluctant to push firmly for any length of time, for fear that I would pass out. I felt suddenly depressed by the fact that labor, which had progressed so uneventfully up to this point, had now become unproductive.

Note that she does not say "The nurses had me pushing too soon," but "My uterus had tired," and labor had "become unproductive." These responses reflect her internalization of another basic tenet of the technocratic model of birth: when something goes wrong, it is the woman's fault. Michelle Harrison, a female physician, comments:

> Yesterday on rounds I saw a baby with a cut on its face and the mother said, "My uterus was so thinned that when they cut into it for the section, the baby's face got cut." The patient is always blamed in medicine. The doctors don't make mistakes. "Your uterus is too thin," not "We cut too deeply." "We had to take the baby," (meaning forceps or Cesarean), instead of "The medicine we gave you interfered with your ability to give birth."[3]

Affectivity and Intensification

The repetitious bombardment of the woman with symbolic messages will often, in ritual, intensify toward a climax, heightening the emotional effect of the event. Behavioral psychologists have long understood that people are far more likely to remember, and to absorb lessons from, those events that carry an emotional charge. The order and stylization of ritual, combined with its rhythmic repetitiveness and the intensification of its messages, methodically create just the sort of highly charged emotional atmosphere that works to ensure long-term learning.

As the moment of physical transformation approaches, the number of ritual procedures performed upon the woman will intensify toward the climax of birth. For example, once the woman's cervix reaches full dilation (10 cm), the nursing staff immediately begins to exhort the woman to push with each contraction, whether or not she actually feels the urge to push. When delivery is imminent, the woman must be transported, often with a great deal of drama and haste, down the hall to the delivery room. Lest the baby be born *en route*, the laboring woman is then exhorted, with equal vigor, *not* to push. Such commands constitute a complete denial of the natural rhythmic imperatives of the woman's body. They intensify the messages of the mechanicity of her labor and her subordination to the institution's expectations and schedule, as well as the atmosphere of drama that will pervade the rest of her birthing experience.

Preservation of the Status Quo

Through explicit enactment of a culture's belief system, ritual works both to preserve and to transmit that belief system, and so becomes an important force in the preservation of the status quo in any society. Whenever this stabilizing characteristic of ritual is paramount, one usually will find that those in positions of power will have unique control over its performance. They utilize the effectiveness of ritual to reinforce both their own importance and the importance of the belief and value system which legitimates their positions. It is no cultural accident that 99% of American women give birth in hospitals, where only physicians have final authority over the performance of the rituals through which births are culturally conducted.

In spite of tremendous advances in equality for women, the United States is still a patriarchy. Nowhere is this reality more visible than in the lithotomy position. Despite years of effort on the part of childbirth activists, including many obstetricians, the majority of American women still give birth lying flat on their backs. This position is physiologically dysfunctional. It compresses major blood vessels, lowering the mother's circulation and thus the baby's oxygen supply. It makes birth more difficult and increases the need for forceps because it both narrows the pelvic outlet and ensures that the baby, who must follow the curve of the birth canal, quite literally will be born heading upward, against gravity. We gain a clue to the peculiar tenacity of this position from an obstetric text:

> The lithotomy position is the best. Here the patient lies with her legs in stirrups and her buttocks close to the lower edge of the table. The patient is in the ideal position for the attendant to deal with any complications which may arise.

This lithotomy position completes the process of symbolic inversion that has been in motion ever since the woman was put into that "upside-down" hospital gown. Her normal bodily patterns are turned, quite literally, upside-down—her legs are in the air, her vagina totally exposed. As the ultimate symbolic inversion, it is ritually appropriate that this position be reserved for the peak transformational moments of the initiation experience—the birth itself. The official representative of society and its core values of science, technology, patriarchy, and institutions stands, in control, not at the mother's head nor at her side, but at her bottom, where the baby's head is beginning to emerge. (A completely different symbolic picture is presented in home birth—the father sometimes catches the baby, while the midwife sits at the mother's side. Or the mother sits, squats, or stands to deliver her child, with the midwife not towering above her, but waiting below.)

Structurally speaking, this puts the woman's vagina where her head should be. Such total inversion is perfectly appropriate from a social perspective, as the technocratic model promises us that eventually we will be able to have babies with our cultural heads instead of our natural bottoms. In our culture, "up" is good and "down" is bad, so the babies born of science and technology must be delivered "up" toward the positively valued cultural world, instead of down toward the negatively valued natural world. Interactionally, the obstetrician is "up" and the birthing woman is "down," an inversion that speaks eloquently to her of her powerlessness and of the power of society at the supreme moment of her own individual transformation.

The episiotomy performed by the obstetrician just before birth also powerfully enacts the status quo in American society. This procedure, performed on over 90% of first-time mothers as they give birth, expresses the value and importance of one of our technocratic society's most fundamental markers—the straight line. Through episiotomies, physicians can deconstruct the vagina (stretchy, flexible, part-circular and part-formless, feminine, creative, sexual—in short, non-linear), then reconstruct it in accordance with our cultural belief and value system. Doctors are taught (incorrectly) that straight cuts heal faster than the small jagged tears that sometimes occur during birth, and that straight cuts will prevent such tears (in fact, episiotomies often cause severe tearing that would not otherwise occur). These teachings mirror our Western belief in the superiority of culture over nature. Because it virtually does not exist in nature, the line is most useful in aiding us in our constant conceptual efforts to separate ourselves from nature.

Moreover, since surgery constitutes the ultimate form of manipulation of the human body-machine, it is the most highly valued form of medicine. Routinizing the episiotomy, and increasingly, the Caesarean section, has served both to legitimate and to raise the status of obstetrics as a profession, by ensuring that childbirth will be not a natural but a surgical procedure.

Effecting Social Change

Paradoxically, ritual, with all of its insistence on continuity and order, can be an important factor not only in individual transformation but also in social change. New belief and value systems are most effectively spread through new rituals designed to enact and transmit them; entrenched belief and value systems are most effectively altered through alterations in the rituals that enact them.

Nine percent of my interviewees entered the hospital determined to avoid technocratic rituals in order to have "completely natural childbirth," yet ended up with highly technocratic births. These nine women experienced extreme cognitive dissonance between their previously held self-images and those internalized in the hospital. Most of them suffered severe emotional wounding and short-term postpartum depression as a result. But fifteen percent did achieve their goal of natural childbirth, thereby avoiding conceptual fusion with the technocratic model. These women were personally empowered by their birth experiences. They tended to view technology as a resource that they could choose to utilize or ignore, and often consciously subverted their socialization process by replacing technocratic symbols with self-empowering alternatives. They wore their own clothes and ate their own food, rejecting the hospital gown and the IV. They walked the halls instead of going to bed. They chose perineal massage instead of episiotomy, and gave birth, like "primitives," sitting up, squatting, or on their hands and knees. One woman, confronted with the wheelchair, said "I don't need this," and used it for a luggage cart.

During the 1970s and early 1980s, the conceptual hegemony of the technocratic model in the hospital was severely challenged by the natural childbirth movement which these twenty-four women represent. Birth activists succeeded in getting hospitals to allow fathers into labor and delivery rooms, mothers to birth consciously (without being put to sleep), and mothers and babies to room together after birth. They fought for women to have the right to birth without drugs or interventions, to walk around or even be in water during labor—in some hospitals, Jacuzzis were installed. And for a while there, it looked as if American birthways would, by the 1990s, be radically transformed.

A common cultural response to the type of threat presented by the natural childbirth movement to the conceptual hegemony of the dominant technocratic model is to step up the performance of the rituals designed to preserve and transmit the reality model under attack. Even as the above changes in birth rituals were being achieved by those seeking greater choice and decision-making power for women, the use of high technology in hospital birth was intensifying. During the 1980s periodic electronic monitoring of nearly all women became standard procedure, the epidural rate shot up to 80%, and the Caesarean rate rose to nearly 25%. Concomitantly, malpractice suits against physicians have risen dramatically in recent years, forcing them to practice conservatively—that is, in strict accordance with technocratic standards. As one of them explained:

> Certainly I've changed the way I practice since malpractice became an issue. I do more C-sections, that's the major thing. And more and more tests to cover myself. More expensive stuff. We don't do risky things that women ask for—we're very conservative in our approach to everything. . . . In 1970 before all this came up, my C-section rate was around 4%. It has gradually climbed every year since then. In 1985 it was 16%, then in 1986 it was 23%.

The money goes where the values are. From this macro-cultural perspective, the increase in malpractice suits emerges as society's effort to make sure that its representatives, the obstetricians, perpetuate our technocratic core value system by continuing through birth rituals to transmit that system. Its perpetuation seems imperative, for in our technology we see the promise of our eventual transcendence of bodily and earthly limitations—already we replace body parts with computerized devices, grow babies in test tubes, build space stations, and continue to pollute the environment in the expectation that someone will develop the technologies to clean it up!

We are all complicit with our technocratic system, since we have so very much invested in it. Just as that system has given us increasing control over the natural environment, so it has also given not only doctors but also women increasing control over biology and birth. Contemporary middle-class women *do* have much greater say over what will be done to them during birth than [did] their mothers, most of whom gave birth during the 1950s and 1960s under general anesthesia. When what they demand is in accord with technocratic values, they have a much greater chance of getting it than their sisters who try for the natural way. Even as hospital birth still perpetuates patriarchy by treating women's bodies as defective machines, it now also reflects women's greater autonomy by allowing them conceptual separation from those defective machines.

Epidural anesthesia is administered in about 80% of American hospital births. So common is its use that many childbirth educators are calling the 1990s the age of the "epidural epidemic." As the epidural numbs the birthing woman, eliminating the pain of childbirth, it also graphically demonstrates to her through lived experience the truth of the Cartesian maxim that mind and body are separate, that the biological realm can be completely cut off from the realm of the intellect and the emotions. The epidural is thus the perfect technocratic tool, serving the interests of the technocratic model (by transmitting it) and of women choosing to give birth under that model, by enabling them to use it to divorce themselves from their biology:

> Ultimately the decision to have the epidural and the Caesarean while I was in labor was mine. I told my doctor I'd had enough of this labor business and I'd like to . . . get it over with. So he whisked me off to the delivery room and we did it. (Elaine)

For many women, the epidural provides a means by which they can actively witness birth while avoiding "dropping into biology." Explained Joanne, "I'm not real fond of things that remind me I'm a biological creature—I prefer to think and be an intellectual emotional person." These women tended to define their bodies as tools, vehicles for their minds. They did not enjoy "giving in to biology" to be pregnant and were happy to be liberated from biology during birth. And they welcomed advances in birth technologies as extensions of their own ability to control nature.

In dramatic contrast to such women, six of my interviewees (6%), insisting that "I am my body," rejected the technocratic model altogether. They chose to give birth at home under an alternative paradigm, the *holistic model*, which offers an integrated, connection-based approach to childbirth as well as to daily life. This model stresses the inherent trustworthiness of the female body, communication and oneness between mother and child, the integrity and self-sufficiency of the family, and self-responsibility. These homebirthers see the safety of the baby and the emotional needs of the mother as one. The safest birth for the baby will be the one that provides the most nurturing environment for the mother.[4] Said Ryla,

I got criticized for choosing a home birth, for not considering the safety of the baby. But that's exactly what I was considering! How could it possibly serve my baby for me to give birth in a place that causes my whole body to tense up in anxiety as soon as I walk in the door?

Although homebirthers constitute only about 1% of the American birthing population, their conceptual importance is tremendous, as through the alternative rituals of giving birth at home, they enact—and thus guarantee the existence of—a paradigm of pregnancy and birth based on the value of connection, just as the technocratic model is based on the principle of separation. The technocratic and holistic models represent opposite ends of a spectrum of beliefs about birth and about cultural life. Their differences are mirrored on a wider scale by the ideological conflicts between biomedicine and holistic healing, and between the representatives of industry and ecological activists. These groups are engaged in a core value struggle over the future—a struggle clearly visible in the profound differences in the rituals they daily enact.

SUMMARY: BIRTH RITUALS AND SOCIETY

Obstetrical procedures can be understood as ritual. They are patterned and repetitive; they are profoundly symbolic, communicating messages concerning our culture's deepest beliefs about the necessity for cultural control of natural processes. These procedures provide an ordered structure to the chaotic flow of the natural birth process. In so doing, they both enhance the natural affectivity of that process and create a sense of inevitability about their performance. Obstetric interventions are also transformative in intent. They attempt to contain and control the inherently transformative process of birth, and to transform the birthing woman into a mother in the full sense of the word—that is, into a woman who has internalized the core values of American society: one who believes in science, relies on technology, and recognizes her inferiority (either consciously or unconsciously) and so at some level accepts the principles of patriarchy. Such a woman will conform to society's dictates and meet the demands of its institutions, and will teach her children to do the same.

Every society in the world has felt the need to thoroughly socialize its citizens into conformity with its norms, and citizens derive many benefits from such socialization. If a culture had to rely on police [officers] to make sure that everyone would obey its laws, it would disintegrate into chaos, as there would not be enough police [officers] to go around. It is much more pratical for cultures to find ways to socialize their members from the *inside*, by making them *want* to conform to society's norms. Yet human beings are not automatons, and the extent to which this type of socialization succeeds depends to a great extent on the individual involved. One woman succinctly sums up:

It's almost like programming you. You get to the hospital. They put you in this wheelchair. They whisk you off from your husband, and I mean just start in on you. Then they put you in another wheelchair, and send you home. And then they say, well, we need to give you something for the depression. [Laughs] Get away from me! That will help my depression!

Through hospital ritual procedures, obstetrics deconstructs birth, then inverts and reconstructs it as a technocratic process. But unlike most transformations effected by ritual, birth does *not* depend upon the performance of ritual to make it happen. The physiological process of labor itself transports the birthing woman into a naturally transitional situation that carries its own affectivity. Hospital procedures take advantage of that affectivity to transmit the core values of American society to birthing women. From society's perspective, the birth process will not be successful unless the woman and child are properly socialized during the experience, transformed as much by the rituals as by the physiology of birth.

NOTES

1. The full results of this study appear in Robbie E. Davis-Floyd, *Birth as an American Rite of Passage*. Berkeley: University of California Press, 1992.
2. Nancy Stoller Shaw, *Forced Labor: Maternity Care in the United States*. New York: Pergamon Press, 1974, p. 90.
3. Michelle Harrison, *A Woman in Residence*. New York: Random House, 1982, p. 174.
4. For studies demonstrating the safety of planned, midwife-attended home birth, see *Birth as an American Rite of Passage*, Chapter 4, pp. 177–186.

Dirt: Purity and Danger

MARY DOUGLAS

Facts of publication: *Douglas, Mary. 1966. "The System Shattered and Renewed," from* Purity and Danger: An Analysis of Concepts of Pollution and Taboo, *188–210. London: Penguin. Reprinted with the permission of Routledge.*

Ritual sometimes incorporates forms of pollution such as blood, incest, or taboo. Surprisingly, pollutants are sometimes considered sacred. In her analysis of the symbolically dirty, Douglas shows that dirt as such does not exist. Rather, the dirty or polluting is matter out of place. Dirt is a product of the differentiating activity of the mind. As an apt symbol of creative formlessness, dirt has considerable potential for playing a powerful role in a variety of rites. Holding that the body provides the basic scheme for all symbolism, Douglas finds that most pollutants have some primary physiological reference.

Drawing heavily on William James's view that the most complete philosophies must find some way of affirming that which has been rejected, Douglas proposes a program for the comparative study of religions. Religions might be compared and classified, she suggests, on the basis of their tendencies to be dirt-affirming or dirt-rejecting. The powerful metaphor of composting shows clearly how pollutants, like weeds turned back into the soil as compost, have the power to enrich a dirt-affirming religion. While this is a promising idea, Douglas shows by extensive discussions of African ceremonies, particularly among the Lele, that some rites are dirt-rejecting; others, dirt-denying.

Douglas's discussion of Lele food laws is similar to her trenchant analysis of Jewish dietary laws in "The Abominations of Leviticus" in Purity and Danger: An Analysis of Concepts of Pollution and Taboo *(Harmondsworth, England: Penguin, 1966, pp. 54–72).*

About the author: Dates: *1921– , England.* **Education:** *B.Sc., St. Anne's College, Oxford; M.A., St. Anne's College, Oxford; D.Phil., St. Anne's College, Oxford.* **Field(s):** *anthropology.* **Career:** *Taught at University College London, 1951–1977, then at various institutions in the United States. Now retired in London.* **Publications:** *Purity and Danger (Penguin, 1966); Natural Symbols (Barrie and Rockcliffe, 1970); Essays in the Sociology of Perception (Routledge, 1982); with Aaron Wildaysky,* Risk and Culture *(California University, 1982); Risk Acceptability (Routledge, 1985); How Institutions Think (Syracuse University, 1986); Risk and Blame (Routledge, 1992); In the Wilderness: The Doctrine of Defilement in the Book of Numbers (Sheffield Academic, 1993).* **Additional:** *"I am an Africanist particularly interested in the following: methodology in the social sciences, how to avoid an ethnocentric basis for social thought, the politicization of nature; rival representations of danger, rival theories of psyche and justice. My current research is on pollution ideas in the Bible, with special reference to the priestly books of the Pentateuch."*

Can there be any people who confound sacredness with uncleanness? . . . The idea of contagion is at work in religion and society. . . . Powers are attributed to any structure of ideas, and . . . rules of avoidance make a visible public recognition of its boundaries. But this is not to say that the sacred is unclean. Each culture must have its own notions of dirt and defilement which are contrasted with its notions of the positive structure which must not be negated. To talk about a confused blending of the Sacred and the Unclean is outright nonsense. But it still remains true that religions often sacralize the very unclean things which have been rejected with abhorrence. We must, therefore, ask how dirt, which is normally destructive, sometimes becomes creative.

First, we note that not all unclean things are used constructively in ritual. It does not suffice for something to be unclean for it to be treated as potent for good. In Israel it was unthinkable that unclean things such as corpses and excreta could be incorporated into the Temple ritual, but only blood, and only blood shed in sacrifice. Among the Oyo Yoruba where the left hand is used for unclean work and it is deeply insulting to proffer the left hand, normal rituals sacralize the precedence of the right side, especially dancing to the right. But in the ritual of the great Ogboni cult initiates must knot their garments on the left side and dance only to the left (Morton-Williams, 1960, p. 369). Incest is a pollution among the Bushong, but an act of ritual incest is part of the sacralization of their king and he claims that he is the filth of the nation: '*Moi, ordure, nyec*' (Vansina 1964, p. 103). And so on. Though it is only specific individuals on specified occasions who can break the rules, it is still important to ask why these dangerous contacts are often required in rituals.

One answer lies in the nature of dirt itself. The other lies in the nature of metaphysical problems and of particular kinds of reflections which call for expression.

To deal with dirt first. In the course of any imposing of order, whether in the mind or in the external world, the attitude to rejected bits and pieces goes through two stages. First they are recognizably out of place, a threat to good order, and so are regarded as objectionable and vigorously brushed away. At this stage they have some identity: they can be seen to be unwanted bits of whatever it was they came from, hair or food or wrappings. This is the stage at which they are dangerous; their half-identity still clings to them and the clarity of the scene in which they obtrude is impaired by their presence. But a long process of pulverizing, dissolving and rotting awaits any physical things that have been recognized as dirt. In the end, all identity is gone. The origin of the various bits and pieces is lost and they have entered into the mass of common rubbish. It is unpleasant to poke about in the refuse to try to recover anything, for this revives identity. So long as identity is absent, rubbish is not dangerous. It does not even create ambiguous perceptions since it clearly belongs in a defined place, a rubbish heap of one kind or another. Even the bones of buried kings rouse little awe and the thought that the air is full of the dust of corpses of bygone races has no power to move. Where there is no differentiation there is no defilement.

> They outnumber the living, but where are all their
>   bones?
> For every man alive there are a million dead,
> Has their dust gone into earth that it is never seen?
> There should be no air to breathe, with it so thick,
> No space for wind to blow or rain to fall:
> Earth should be a cloud of dust, a soil of bones,
> With no room even for our skeletons.
> It is wasted time to think of it, to count its grains,
> When all are alike and there is no difference in them.
>
>   (S. Sitwell, *Agamemnon's Tomb*)

In this final stage of total disintegration, dirt is utterly undifferentiated. Thus a cycle has been completed. Dirt was created by the differentiating activity of mind, it was a by-product of the creation of order. So it started from a state of non-differentiation; all through the process of differentiating, its role was to threaten the distinctions made; finally it returns to its true indiscriminable character. Formlessness is therefore an apt symbol of beginning and of growth as it is of decay.

On this argument everything that is said to explain the revivifying role of water in religious symbolism can also apply to dirt:

> In water everything is 'dissolved', every 'form' is broken up, everything that has happened ceases to exist; nothing that was before remains after immersion in water, not an outline, not a 'sign', not an event. Immersion is the equivalent, at the human level, of death at the cosmic level, of the cataclysm (the Flood) which periodically dissolves the world into the primeval ocean. Breaking up all forms, doing away with the past, water possesses this power of purifying, of regenerating, of giving new birth. . . . Water purifies and regenerates because it nullifies the past, and restores— even if only for a moment—the integrity of the dawn of things. (Eliade, 1958, p. 194)

In the same book Eliade goes on to assimilate with water two other symbols of renewal which we can, without labouring the point, equally associate with dust and corruption. One is symbolism of darkness and the other orgiastic celebration of the New Year (pp. 398–9).

In its last phase then, dirt shows itself as an apt symbol of creative formlessness. But it is from its first phase that it derives its force. The danger which is risked by boundary transgression is power. Those vulnerable margins and those attacking forces which threaten to destroy good order represent the powers inhering in the cosmos. Ritual which can harness these for good is harnessing power indeed.

So much for the aptness of the symbol itself. Now for the living situations to which it applies, and which are irremediably subject to paradox. The quest for purity is pursued by rejection. It follows that when purity is not a symbol but something lived, it must be poor and barren. It is part of our condition that the purity for which we strive and sacrifice so much turns out to be hard and dead as a stone when we get it. It is all very well for the poet to praise winter as the

> Paragon of art,
> That kills all forms of life and feeling
> Save what is pure and will survive.
>
> (Roy Campbell)

It is another thing to try and make over our existence into an unchanging lapidary form. Purity is the enemy of change, of ambiguity and compromise. Most of us indeed would feel safer if our experience could be hard-set and fixed in form. As Sartre wrote so bitterly of the anti-semite:

> How can anyone choose to reason falsely? It is simply the old yearning for impermeability . . . there are people who are attracted by the permanence of stone. They would like to be solid and impenetrable, they do not want change: for who knows what change might bring? . . . It is as if their own existence were perpetually in suspense. But they want to exist in all ways at once, and all in one instant. They have no wish to acquire ideas, they want them to be innate . . . they want to adopt a mode of life in which reasoning and the quest for truth play only a subordinate part, in which nothing is sought except what has already been found, in which one never becomes anything else but what one already was. (1948)

This diatribe implies a division between ours and the rigid black and white thinking of the anti-semite. Whereas, of course, the yearning for rigidity is in us all. It is part of our human condition to long for hard lines and clear concepts. When we have them we have to either face the fact that some realities elude them, or else blind ourselves to the inadequacy of the concepts.

The final paradox of the search for purity is that it is an attempt to force experience into logical categories of non-contradiction. But experience is not amenable and those who make the attempt find themselves led into contradiction.

Where sexual purity is concerned it is obvious that if it is to imply no contact between the sexes it is not only a denial of sex, but must be literally barren. It also leads to contradiction. To wish all women to be chaste at all times goes contrary to other wishes and if followed consistently leads to inconveniences of the kind to which Mae Enga men submit. High-born girls of seventeenth-century Spain found themselves in a dilemma in which dishonour stood on either horn. St Theresa of Avila was brought up in a society in which the seduction of a girl had to be avenged by her brother or father. So if she received a lover she risked dishonour and the lives of men. But her personal honour required her to be generous and not to withhold herself from her lover, as it was unthinkable to shun lovers altogether. There are many other examples of how the quest for purity creates problems and some curious solutions.

One solution is to enjoy purity at second hand. Something of a vicarious satisfaction gave its aura, no doubt, to the respect for virginity in early Christendom, gives extra zest to the Nambudiri Brahmins when they enclose their sisters, and enhances the prestige of Brahmins among lower castes in general. In certain chiefdoms the Pende of the Kasai expect their chiefs to live in sexual continence. Thus one man conserves the wellbeing of the chiefdom on behalf of his polygamous subjects. To ensure no lapse on the part of the chief, who is admittedly past his prime when installed, his subjects fix a penis sheath on him for life (de Sousberghe [1954]).

Sometimes the claim to superior purity is based on deceit. The adult men of the Chagga tribe used to pretend that at initiation their anus was blocked for life. Initiated men were supposed never to need to defecate, unlike women and children who remained subject to the exigency of their bodies

(Raum [1940]). Imagine the complications into which this pretence led Chagga men. The moral of all this is that the facts of existence are a chaotic jumble. If we select from the body's image a few aspects which do not offend, we must be prepared to suffer for the distortion. The body is not a slightly porous jug. To switch the metaphor, a garden is not a tapestry; if all the weeds are removed, the soil is impoverished. Somehow the gardener must preserve fertility by returning what he has taken out. The special kind of treatment which some religions accord to anomalies and abominations to make them powerful for good is like turning weeds and lawn cuttings into compost.

This is the general outline for an answer to why pollutions are often used in renewal rites.

Whenever a strict pattern of purity is imposed on our lives it is either highly uncomfortable or it leads into contradiction if closely followed, or it leads to hypocrisy. That which is negated is not thereby removed. The rest of life, which does not tidily fit the accepted categories, is still there and demands attention. The body, as we have tried to show, provides a basic scheme for all symbolism. There is hardly any pollution which does not have some primary physiological reference. As life is in the body it cannot be rejected outright. And as life must be affirmed, the most complete philosophies, as William James put it, must find some ultimate way of affirming that which has been rejected.

> If we admit that evil is an essential part of our being and the key to the interpretation of our life, we load ourselves down with a difficulty that has always proved burdensome in philosophies of religion. Theism, wherever it has erected itself into a systematic philosophy of the universe, has shown a reluctance to let God be anything less than All-in-All . . . at variance with popular theism (is a philosophy) which is frankly pluralistic . . . the universe compounded of many original principles . . . God is not necessarily responsible for the existence of evil. The gospel of healthy-mindedness casts its vote distinctly for this pluralistic view. Whereas the monistic philosopher finds himself more or less bound to say, as Hegel said, that everything actual is rational, and that evil, as an element dialectically required must be pinned in, and kept and consecrated and have a function

awarded to it in the final system of truth, healthy-mindedness refuses to say anything of the sort. Evil, it says, is emphatically irrational, and *not* to be pinned in, or preserved, or consecrated in any final system of truth. It is a pure abomination to the Lord, an alien unreality, a waste element, to be sloughed off and negated . . . the ideal, so far from being coextensive with the actual, is a mere extract from the actual, marked by its deliverance from all contact with this diseased, inferior, excrementitious stuff.

> Here we have the interesting notion . . . of there being elements of the universe which may make no rational whole in conjunction with the other elements, and which, from the point of view of any system which those elements make up, can only be considered so much irrelevance and accident—so much 'dirt' as it were, and matter out of place. ([1901–1902] p. 129)

This splendid passage invites us to compare dirt-affirming with dirt-rejecting philosophies. If it were possible to make such a comparison between primitive cultures, what would we expect to find? Norman Brown (1959, chapter 8) has suggested that primitive magic is an escape from reality, on a par with infantile sexual fantasies. If this were right we should expect to find the majority of primitive cultures lined up with Christian Science, the only example of healthy-mindedness which William James described. But instead of consistent dirt-rejecting, we find . . . extraordinary examples of dirt-affirmation. . . . In a given culture it seems that some kinds of behaviour or natural phenomena are recognized as utterly wrong by all the principles which govern the universe. There are different kinds of impossibilities, anomalies, bad mixings and abominations. Most of the items receive varying degrees of condemnation and avoidance. Then suddenly we find that one of the most abominable or impossible is singled out and put into a very special kind of ritual frame that marks it off from other experience. The frame ensures that the categories which the normal avoidances sustain are not threatened or affected in any way. Within the ritual frame the abomination is then handled as a source of tremendous power. On William James's terms, such ritual mixing up and composting of polluting things would provide the basis of 'more complete religion'.

It may indeed be that no religious reconciliation with the absolute totality of things is possible. Some evils, indeed, are ministerial to higher forms of good, but it may be that there are forms of evil so extreme as to enter into no good system whatsoever, and that, in respect of such evil, dumb submission or neglect to notice is the only practical resource. . . . But . . . since the evil facts are as genuine parts of nature as the good ones, the philosophic presumption should be that they have some rational significance, and that systematic healthy-mindedness, failing as it does to accord to sorrow, pain and death any positive and active attention whatever, is formally less complete than systems that try at least to include these elements in their scope. The completest religions would therefore seem to be those in which the pessimistic elements are best developed . . . (p. 161)

Here we seem to have the outline of a programme for comparative religion. It would be to their own cost that anthropologists should neglect their duty of drawing up a taxonomy of tribal religions. But we find that it is not a simple matter to work out the best principles for distinguishing the 'incomplete and optimistic' religions from the 'more complete and pessimistic' ones. Problems of method loom large. Obviously one would have to be meticulously scrupulous in cataloguing all the ritual avoidances in any particular religion and in leaving nothing out. Beyond that, what other rules would objective scholarship need, to distinguish different kinds of religion according to these general criteria?

The answer is that the task is utterly beyond the scope of objective scholarship. This is not for the technical reason that the fieldwork is missing. Indeed, the scantier the field research the more practicable the comparative project appears. The reason lies in the nature of the material itself. All live religions are many things. The formal ritual of public occasions teaches one set of doctrine. There is no reason to suppose that its message is necessarily consistent with those taught in private rituals, or that all public rituals are consistent with one another, nor all private rituals. There is no guarantee that the ritual is homogeneous and, if it is not, only the subjective intuition of the observer can say whether the total effect is optimistic or pessimistic. He may follow some rules for arriving at his conclusion; he may

decide to add up each side of a balance sheet of evil-rejecting and evil-affirming rites, scoring each one equally. Or he may weight the score according to the importance of the rites. But whatever rule he follows he is bound to be arbitrary. And even then he has only come to the end of the formal ritual. There are other beliefs which may not be ritualized at all, and which may altogether obscure the message of the rites. People do not necessarily listen to their preachers. Their real guiding beliefs may be cheerfully optimistic and dirt-rejecting while they appear to subscribe to a nobly pessimistic religion.

If I were to decide where the Lele culture should be classed on William James's scheme, I would be in a quandary. These are a people who are very pollution-conscious in secular and ritual affairs. Their habitual separating and classifying comes out nowhere so clearly as in their approach to animal food. Most of their cosmology and much of their social order is reflected in their animal categories. Certain animals and parts of animals are appropriate for men to eat, others for women, others for children, others for pregnant women. Others are regarded as totally inedible. One way or another the animals which they reject as unsuitable for human or female consumption turn out to be ambiguous according to their scheme of classification. Their animal taxonomy separates night from day animals; animals of the above (birds, squirrels and monkeys) from animals of the below: water animals and land animals. Those whose behaviour is ambiguous are treated as anomalies of one kind or another and are struck off someone's diet sheet. For instance, flying squirrels are not unambiguously birds nor animals, and so they are avoided by discriminating adults. Children might eat them. No woman worthy of the name would eat them, and men only when driven by hunger. No penalties sanction this attitude.

One can schematize their main divisions as two concentric circles. The circle of human society encloses men as hunters and diviners, women and children and also, anomalously, animals which live in human society. These non-humans in the village are either domesticated animals, dogs and chickens, or unwanted parasites, rats and lizards. It is unthinkable to eat dogs, rats or lizards. Human's meat should be the game brought in from the wild by the hunters' arrows and traps. Chickens present something of a problem in casuistry which the Lele solve by regarding it unseemly for women to eat chicken, though the meat is possible and even good food for men. Goats, which were recently introduced, they rear for exchange with other tribes and do not eat.

All this squeamishness and discrimination would, if consistently carried through, make their culture look like a dirt-rejecting one. But it is what happens in the final count that matters. For the main part, their formal rituals are based on discrimination of categories, human, animal, male, female, young, old, etc. But they lead through a series of cults which allow their initiates to eat what is normally dangerous and forbidden, carnivorous animals, chest of game and young animals. In an inner cult a hybrid monster, which in secular life one would expect them to abhor, is reverently eaten by initiates and taken to be the most powerful source of fertility. At this point one sees that this is, after all, to continue the gardening metaphor, a composting religion. That which is rejected is ploughed back for a renewal of life.

The two worlds, human and animal, are not at all independent. Most of the animals exist, as the Lele think, to be the quarry of Lele hunters. Some animals, burrowing or nocturnal, or water-loving, are spirit animals who have a special connexion with the non-animal inhabitants of the animal world, the spirits. On these spirits humans depend for prosperity and fertility and healing. The normal movement is for humans to go out and get what they need from the animal sphere. Animals and spirits characteristically are shy of humans and do not come out spontaneously into the human world. Men, as hunters and diviners, exploit both aspects of this other world, for meat and medicines. Women, as weak and vulnerable, are those who specially need male action in the other world. Women avoid spirit animals and do not eat their meat. Women are never hunters and only become diviners if they are born as, or bear, twins. In the interaction of the two worlds their role is passive, and yet they particularly need the help of the spirits, since women are prone to barrenness, or, if they conceive, to miscarriage, and the spirits can provide remedies.

Apart from this normal relation of male attack and male ritual on behalf of women and children, there are two kinds of mediating bridges between the humans and the wild. One is for evil and the other for good. The dangerous bridge is made by a wicked transfer of allegiance by humans who become sorcerers. They turn their back on their own kind and run with the hunted, fight against the hunters, work against diviners to achieve death instead of healing. They have moved across to the animal sphere and they have caused some animals to move in from the animal to the human sphere. These latter are their carnivorous familiars, who snatch chickens from the human village and do the sorcerers' work there.

The other ambiguous mode of being is concerned with fertility. It is the nature of humans to reproduce with pain and danger and their normal births are single. By contrast, it is thought that animals are naturally fecund; they reproduce without pain or danger and their normal births occur in couples or in larger litters. When a human couple produce twins or triplets they have been able to break through the normal human limitations. In a way they are anomalous, but in the most auspicious possible way. They have a counterpart in the animal world and this is the benign monster to which Lele pay formal cult, the pangolin or scaly ant-eater. Its being contradicts all the most obvious animal categories. It is scaly like a fish, but it climbs trees. It is more like an egg-laying lizard than a mammal, yet it suckles its young. And most significant of all, unlike other small mammals its young are born singly. Instead of running away or attacking, it curls in a modest ball and waits for the hunter to pass. The human twin parents and the forest pangolin, both are ritualized as sources of fertility. Instead of being abhorred and utterly anomalous, the pangolin is eaten in solemn ceremony by its initiates who are thereby enabled to minister fertility to their kind.

This is a mystery of mediation from an animal sphere which parallels the many fascinating human mediators described by Eliade (1951) in his account of Shamanism. In their descriptions of the pangolin's behaviour and in their attitude to its cult, Lele say things which uncannily recall passages of the Old Testament, interpreted in the Christian tradition. Like Abraham's ram in the thicket and like Christ, the pangolin is spoken of as a voluntary victim. It is not caught, but rather it comes to the village. It is a kingly victim: the village treats its corpse as a living chief and requires the behaviour of respect for a chief on pain of future disaster. If its rituals are faithfully performed the women will conceive and animals will enter hunters' traps and fall to their arrows. The mysteries of the pangolin are sorrowful mysteries:

'Now I will enter the house of affliction,' they sing as initiates carry its corpse round the village. No more of its cult songs were told to me, except this tantalizing line. This cult has obviously very many different kinds of significance. Here I limit myself to commenting on two aspects: one is the way it achieves a union of opposites which is a source of power for good; the other is the seemingly voluntary submission of the animal to its own death.

For the purposes of studying pollution, I would need a broader approach to religion. Defining it as belief in spiritual beings is too narrow. Above all the subject of this [essay] is impossible to discuss except in the light of men's common urge to make a unity of all their experience and to overcome distinctions and separations in acts of atonement. The dramatic combination of opposites is a psychologically satisfying theme full of scope for interpretation at varying levels. But at the same time any ritual which expresses the happy union of opposites is also an apt vehicle for essentially religious themes. The Lele pangolin cult is only one example, of which many more could be cited, of cults which invite their initiates to turn round and confront the categories on which their whole surrounding culture has been built up and to recognize them for the fictive, man-made, arbitrary creations that they are. Throughout their daily, and especially their ritual life the Lele are preoccupied with form. Endlessly they enact the discriminations by which their society and its cultural environment exist, and methodically they punish or attribute misfortune to breaches of avoidance rules. The burden of the rules may not be oppressive. But by a conscious effort they respond through them to the idea that creatures of the sky are different in nature from creatures of the earth, so that it is held dangerous for a pregnant woman to eat the latter and nourishing for her to eat the former, and so on. As they prepare to eat they visibly enact the central discriminations of their cosmos no less than the ancient Israelites enacted a liturgy of holiness.

Then comes the inner cult of all their ritual life,

in which the initiates of the pangolin, immune to dangers that would kill uninitiated men, approach, hold, kill and eat the animal which in its own existence combines all the elements which Lele culture keeps apart. If they could choose among our philosophies the one most congenial to the moments of that rite, the pangolin initiates would be primitive existentialists. By the mystery of that rite they recognize something of the fortuitous and conventional nature of the categories in whose mould they have their experience. If they consistently shunned ambiguity they would commit themselves to division between ideal and reality. But they confront ambiguity in an extreme and concentrated form. They dare to grasp the pangolin and put it to ritual use, proclaiming that this has more power than any other rites. So the pangolin cult is capable of inspiring a profound meditation on the nature of purity and impurity and on the limitation on human contemplation of existence.

Not only does the pangolin overcome the distinctions in the universe. Its power for good is released by its dying and this it seems to take on itself deliberately. If their religion were all of a piece we might from the foregoing class the Lele as a dirt-affirming religion and expect them to face affliction with resignation, and to make death the occasion of comforting rituals of atonement and renewal. But the metaphysical notions which are all very well in the separate ritual frame of the pangolin cult are another matter when actual death has struck a member of the family. Then the Lele utterly reject the death that has occurred.

It is often said that in this African tribe or that, the people do not recognize the possibility of natural death. The Lele are not fools. They recognize that life must come to an end. But if matters were to take their natural course they would expect everyone to live out his natural span and to sink slowly from senility to the grave. When this happens they rejoice, for such an old man or woman has triumphed over all the pitfalls that lay in the way and achieved completion. But this rarely happens. Most people, according to Lele, are struck down by sorcery long before they reach their goal. And sorcery does not belong in the natural order of things as Lele see it. Sorcery was a late-coming afterthought, more an accident in creation. In this aspect of their culture they are a good example of the healthy-mindedness which William James described. For the Lele evil is not to be included in the total system of the world, but to be expunged without compromise. All evil is caused by sorcery. They can clearly visualize what reality would be like without sorcery and they continually strive to achieve it by eliminating sorcerers.

A strong millennial tendency is implicit in the way of thinking of any people whose metaphysics push evil out of the world of reality. Among the Lele the millennial tendency bursts into flame in their recurrent anti-sorcery cults. When a new cult arrives it burns up for the time being the whole apparatus of their traditional religion. The elaborate system of anomalies rejected and affirmed which their cults present is regularly superseded by the latest anti-sorcery cult which is nothing less than an attempt to introduce the millennium at once.

Thus we have to reckon with two tendencies in Lele religion: one ready to tear away even the veils imposed by the necessities of thought and to look at reality direct; the other a denial of necessity, a denial of the place of pain and even of death in reality. So William James's problem is turned into the question of which tendency is the stronger.

If the place of the pangolin cult in their world view is what I have described, one would expect it to be slightly orgiastic, a temporary destruction of apollonian form. Perhaps in its origin its feast of communion was a more dionysiac occasion. But there is nothing remotely uncontrolled about Lele rites. They make no use of drugs, dances, hypnosis or any of the arts by which the conscious control of the body is relaxed. Even the one type of diviner who is supposed to be in direct trance communion with the spirits of the forest, and who sings to them all night when they visit him, sings in a staid austere style. These people are much more concerned with what their religion can deliver in the way of fertility, cures and hunting success than in perfecting man and achieving religious union in the fullest sense. Most of their rites are truly magic rites, performed for the sake of a specific cure or on the eve of a particular hunt, and intended to yield an immediate tangible success. Most of the time the Lele diviners seem no better than a lot of Aladdins rubbing their magic lamps and expecting marvels to take shape. Only their initiation rites into this cult give a glimpse of another level of religious insight. But the teaching of these rites is overlain by the passionate absorption of the people in sorcery and anti-sorcery. Strong political and personal issues hang on the outcome of any sorcery accusation. The rites which detect sorcerers or acquit them, defend against them or restore what they have damaged, these are the rites which steal the public interest. Strong social pressures force people to blame each death on sorcery. Thus it is that whatever their formal religion may say about the nature of the universe and about the place of chaos, suffering and disintegration in reality, the Lele are socially committed to a different view. On this view evil belongs outside the normal scheme of things; it is not part of reality. So the Lele seem to wear the controlled smile of Christian Scientists. If they should be classified not according to their cultic practices, but according to the beliefs which periodically overthrow them, they appear to be frankly healthy-minded, dirt-rejecting, untouched by the lesson of the gentle pangolin.

It would be unfair to take the Lele as an example of a people who try to evade the whole subject of death. I cite their case mainly to show the difficulty of assessing a cultural attitude to such things. I learnt very little about their esoteric doctrines because they were carefully guarded secrets of male cult members. This esotericism in itself is relevant. Lele religious secretiveness is a clear contrast with the much more open rules of admission and publicity of the cultic ritual of the Ndembu, living to the south-east of them. If priests for various social reasons keep their doctrines secret, the anthropologist's misreporting is the least of the evils that can follow. Sorcery fears are less likely to overlay religious teaching, if the religious doctrine is more widely published.

To the Lele, then, it seems that the main reflections to which deaths give rise are thoughts of revenge. Any particular death is treated as unnecessary, due to a wicked crime on the part of a depraved anti-social human being. Just as the focus of all pollution symbolism is the body, the final problem to which the perspective of pollution leads is bodily disintegration. Death presents a challenge to any metaphysical system, but the challenge need not be squarely met. I am suggesting that in treating each death as the outcome of an individual act of treachery and human malice the Lele are evading its metaphysical implications. Their pangolin cult suggests a meditation on the inadequacy of the categories of human thought, but only a few are invited to make it and it is not related explicitly to their experience of death.

It may well seem that I have made too much of the Lele pangolin cult. There are no Lele books of theology or philosophy to state the meaning of the cult. The metaphysical implications have not been expressed to me in so many words by Lele, nor did I even eavesdrop on a conversation between diviners covering this ground. Indeed I have recorded (1957) that I started on the cosmic patterning approach to Lele animal symbolism because I was frustrated in my direct inquiries seeking reasons for their food avoidances. They would never say, 'We avoid anomalous animals because in defying the categories of our universe they arouse deep feelings of disquiet.' But on each avoided animal they would launch into disquisitions on its natural history. The full list of anomalies made clear the simple taxonomic principles being used. But the pangolin was always spoken of as the most incredible monster of all. On first hearing it sounded such a fantastic beast that I could not believe in its existence. On asking why it should be the focus of a fertility cult, I was again frustrated: this was a mystery of the ancestors, way back long ago.

What kind of evidence for the meaning of this cult, or of any cult, can be sensibly demanded? It can have many different levels and kinds of meaning. But the one on which I ground my argument is the meaning which emerges out of a pattern in which the parts can incontestably be shown to be regularly related. No one member of the society is necessarily aware of the whole pattern, any more than speakers are able to be explicit about the linguistic patterns they employ. Luc de Heusch [1964] has analysed my material and shown that the pangolin concentrates in its being more of the discriminations central to Lele culture than I myself had realized. I can perhaps justify my interpretation of why they ritually kill and eat it by showing that in other primitive religions similar metaphysical perspectives are recorded. Furthermore, systems of belief are not likely to survive unless they offer reflections on a more profound plane than used to be credited to primitive cultures.

Most religions promise by their rites to make some changes in external events. Whatever promises they make, death must somehow be recognized as inevitable. It is usual to expect that the greatest metaphysical development goes with the most pessimism and contempt of the good things of this life. If religions such as Buddhism teach that individual life is a little thing and that its pleasures are transient and unsatisfying, then they are in a strong philosophical position for contemplating death in the context of the cosmic purpose of an all-pervading Existence. By and large primitive religions and the ordinary layman's acceptance of more elaborate religious philosophies coincide: they are less concerned with philosophy and more interested in the material benefits which ritual and moral conformity can bring. But it follows that those religions which have most emphasized the instrumental effects of their ritual are most vulnerable to disbelief. If the faithful have come to think of rites as means to health and prosperity, like so many magic lamps to be worked by rubbing, there comes a day when the whole ritual apparatus must seem an empty mockery. Somewhere the beliefs must be safeguarded against disappointment or they may not hold assent.

One way of protecting ritual from scepticism is to suppose that an enemy, within or without the community, is continually undoing its good effect. On these lines responsibility may be given to amoral demons or to witches and sorcerers. But this is only a feeble protection for it affirms that the faithful are right in treating ritual as an instrument of their desires, but confesses the weakness of the ritual for achieving its purpose. Thus religions which explain evil by reference to demonology or sorcery are failing to offer a way of comprehending the whole of existence. They come close to an optimistic, healthy-minded, pluralistic view of the universe. And curiously enough, the prototype of healthy-minded philosophies as William James described them, Christian Science, was prone to supplement its inadequate approach to evil by a kind of demonology invented *ad hoc*. I am grateful to Rosemary Harris for giving me the reference to Mary Baker Eddy's belief in 'malicious animal magnetism' which she held accountable for evils she could not ignore (Wilson, 1961, pp. 126–7).

Another way of protecting the belief that religion can deliver prosperity here and now is to make ritual efficacy depend on difficult conditions. On the one hand the rite may be very complicated and difficult to perform: if the least detail gets into the wrong order, the whole thing is invalid. This is a narrowly instrumental approach, magical in the most pejorative sense. On the other hand the success of the rite may depend on the moral conditions being correct: the performer and audience should be in a proper state of mind, free of guilt, free of ill-will and so on. A moral requirement for the efficacy of ritual can bind the believers to the highest purposes of their religion. The prophets of Israel, crying 'Doom, Doom, Doom!' did much more than provide an explanation of why the rituals failed to give peace and prosperity. No one who heard them could take a narrowly magical view of ritual.

The third way is for the religious teaching to change its tack. In most everyday contexts it tells the faithful that their fields will prosper and their families flourish if they obey the moral code and perform the proper ritual services. Then, in another context, all this pious effort is disparaged, contempt is thrown on right behaviour, materialistic objectives are suddenly despised. We cannot say that they suddenly become religions of non-attachment, promising only disillusionment in this life. But they travel some way along this path. Thus, for instance, the Ndembu initiates of Chihamba are made to kill the white spirit that they have learnt is their grandfather, source of all fertility and health. Having killed him, they are told they are innocent and must rejoice (Turner, 1962). Ndembu daily ritual is very intensively performed as the instrument for gaining good health and good hunting. Chihamba, their most important cult, is their moment of disillusion. By it their other cults do not achieve immunity from discredit. But Turner insists that the object of the Chihamba rituals is to use paradox and contradiction to express truths which are inexpressible in any other terms. In Chihamba they confront a more profound reality and measure their objectives by a different standard.

I am tempted to suppose that very many primitive religions which offer material success with one hand, with the other protect themselves from crude experiment by extending their perspective in much the same way. For a narrow focus on material health and happiness makes a religion vulnerable to disbelief. And so we can suppose that the very logic of promises discreditably unfulfilled may lead cult of-

ficials to meditate on wider, profounder themes, such as the mystery of evil and of death. If this is true we would expect the most materialistic-seeming cults to stage at some central point in the ritual cycle a cult of the paradox of the ultimate unity of life and death. At such a point pollution of death, treated in a positive creative role, can help to close the metaphysical gap.

We can take for one illustration the death ritual of the Nyakyusa, who live north of Lake Nyasa. They explicitly associate dirt with madness; those who are mad eat filth. There are two kinds of madness, one is sent by God and the other comes from neglect of ritual. Thus they explicitly see ritual as the source of discrimination and of knowledge. Whatever the cause of madness, the symptoms are the same. The madman eats filth and throws off his clothes. Filth is listed as meaning excreta, mud, frogs: 'the eating of filth by madmen is like the filth of death, those faeces are the corpse' (Wilson, 1957, pp. 53, 80–81). So ritual conserves sanity and life: madness brings filth and is a kind of death. Ritual separates death from life: 'the dead, if not separated from the living bring madness on them.' This is a very perspicacious idea of how ritual functions. Now the Nyakyusa are not tolerant of filth but highly pollution-conscious. They observe elaborate restrictions to avoid contact with bodily rejects which they regard as very dangerous:

> Ubanyali, filth, is held to come from the sex fluids, menstruation and childbirth, as well as from a corpse, and the blood of a slain enemy. All are thought to be both disgusting and dangerous and the sex fluids are particularly dangerous for an infant. (p. 131)

Contact with menstrual blood is dangerous to a man, specially to a warrior, hence elaborate restrictions on cooking for a man during menstruation.

But in spite of this normal avoidance the central act in the ritual of mourning is actively to welcome filth. They sweep rubbish on to the mourners.

> The rubbish is the rubbish of death, it is dirt. 'Let it come now,' we say. 'Let it not come later, may we never run mad. . . . ' It means 'We have given you everything, we have eaten filth on the hearth.' For if one runs mad one eats filth, faeces . . . (p. 53)

We suspect that there is much more that could be said in the interpretation of this rite. But let us leave it at the point to which the brief remarks of the Nyakyusa have taken it: a voluntary embrace of the symbols of death is a kind of prophylactic against the effects of death; the ritual enactment of death is a protection, not against death but against madness (p. 89). On all other occasions they avoid faeces and filth and reckon it a sign of madness not to do so. But in the face of death itself they give up everything, they even claim to have eaten filth as madmen do, in order to keep their reason. Madness will come if they neglect the ritual of freely accepting the corruption of the body; sanity is assured if they perform the ritual.

Another example of death being softened by welcome, if we can put it that way, is the ritual murder by which the Dinka put to death their aged spearmasters. This is the central rite in Dinka religion. All their other rites and bloodily expressive sacrifices pale in significance besides this one which is not a sacrifice. The spearmasters are a hereditary clan of priests. Their divinity, Flesh, is a symbol of life, light and truth. Spearmasters may be possessed by the divinity; the sacrifices they perform and blessings they give are more efficacious than other men's. They mediate between their tribe and divinity. The doctrine underlying the ritual of their death is that the spearmaster's life should not be allowed to escape with his last breath from his dying body. By keeping his life in his body his life is preserved; and the spirit of the spearmaster is thus transmitted to his successor for the good of the community. The community can live on as a rational order because of the unafraid self-sacrifice of its priest.

By reputation among foreign travellers this rite was a brutal suffocation of a helpless old man. An intimate study of Dinka religious ideas reveals the central theme to be the old man's voluntary choosing of the time, manner and place of his death. The old man himself asks for the death to be prepared for him, he asks for it from his people and on their behalf. He is reverently carried to his grave, and lying in it says his last words to his grieving sons before his natural death is anticipated. By his free, deliberate decision he robs death of the uncertainty of its time and place of coming. His own willing death, ritually framed by the grave itself, is a communal victory for

all his people (Lienhardt [1961]). By confronting death and grasping it firmly he has said something to his people about the nature of life.

The common element in these two examples of death ritual is the exercise of free, rational choice in undergoing death. Something of the same idea is in the self-immolation of the Lele pangolin, and also in the Ndembu ritual killing of Kavula, since this white spirit is not angry but even pleased to be slain. This is yet another theme which death pollution can express if its sign be reversed from bad to good.

Animal and vegetable life cannot help but play their role in the order of the universe. They have little choice but to live as it is their nature to behave. Occasionally the odd species or individual gets out of line and humans react by avoidance of one kind or another. The very reaction to ambiguous behaviour expresses the expectation that all things shall normally conform to the principles which govern the world. But in their own experience as men, people know that their personal conformity is not so certain. Punishments, moral pressures, rules about not touching and not eating, a firm ritual framework, all these can do something to bring man into harmony with the rest of being. But so long as free consent is withheld, so long is the fulfilment imperfect. Here again we can discern primitive existentialists whose escape from the chain of necessity lies only in the exercise of choice. When someone embraces freely the symbols of death, or death itself, then it is consistent with everything that we have seen so far, that a great release of power for good should be expected to follow.

The old spearmaster giving the sign for his own slaying makes a stiffly ritual act. It has none of the exuberance of St Francis of Assisi rolling naked in the filth and welcoming his Sister Death. But his act touches the same mystery. If anyone held the idea that death and suffering are not an integral part of nature, the delusion is corrected. If there was a temptation to treat ritual as a magic lamp to be rubbed for gaining unlimited riches and power, ritual shows its other side. If the hierarchy of values was crudely material, it is dramatically undermined by paradox and contradiction. In painting such dark themes, pollution symbols are as necessary as the use of black in any depiction whatsoever. Therefore we find corruption enshrined in sacred places and times.

BIBLIOGRAPHY

Brown, N. O., 1959. *Life Against Death*, London.

de Heusch, L., 1964. 'Structure et Praxis Sociales chez les Lele', in *L'Homme*, 4, pp. 87–109.

de Sousberghe, L., 1954. 'Etuis Péniens ou Gaines de Chasteté chez les Ba-Pende', *Africa*, 24, pp. 214–19.

Douglas, M., 1957. 'Animals in Lele Religious Symbolism', *Africa*, 27, pp. 47–58.

Eliade, M., 1951. *Le Chamanisme*, Paris. (Translated into English 1964.)

———, 1958. *Patterns in Comparative Religion*, New York: Sheed & Ward.

James, W., 1901–2. *The Varieties of Religious Experience*, London.

Lienhardt, R. G., 1961. *Divinity and Experience: The Religion of the Dinka*, Oxford.

Morton-Williams, P., 1960. 'The Yoruba Ogboni Cult in Oyo', *Africa*, 30, pp. 363–74.

Raum, O., 1940. *Chagga Childhood*, London.

Sartre, J.-P., 1948. *Portrait of an Anti-Semite*, London.

Turner, V. W., 1962. 'Chihamba: The White Spirit', *Rhodes-Livingstone Paper* 33.

Vansina, J., 1964. 'Le Royaume Kuba', Musée Royale de l'Afrique Centrale, *Annales-Sciences Humaines*, 49.

Wilson, B. R., 1961. *Sects and Society*, London.

Wilson, M., 1957. *Rituals and Kinship among the Nyakyusa*, London.

Transformation: The Magic of Ritual

TOM F. DRIVER

Facts of publication: *Driver, Tom F. 1991. "Transformation," from* The Magic of Ritual: Our Need for Liberating Rites that Transform Our Lives and Our Communities, *166–191, 247–248. San Francisco: HarperSanFrancisco. Copyright © 1991 by Tom F. Driver. Reprinted with the permission of HarperCollins Publishers, Inc.*

Christian and Jewish theologians are increasingly entering into dialogue with social scientists and performance theorists. Theologian Tom Driver, in addition to writing Christian theology and theater criticism, has engaged in fieldwork in Japan, Haiti, and New Guinea. Here he argues for a theological reclamation of the notion of magic, by which he means ritual's transformative capabilities. The usual view of magic is that it amounts to bad science. Thus we typically regard magic as what "other" people do; it is not what "we" do. Driver argues against this prejudice and, by pointing to ritual's ability to evoke moral and social transformation, considers the ways that ritual both changes things and is subject to change.

Readers may find it provocative to compare Driver's ethical understanding of ritual transformation with the theatrical one proposed by Richard Schechner in this volume. For another theological treatment of ritual, this one by a Catholic rather than a Protestant theologian, see Mary Collins, Worship: Renewal to Practice *(Washington, D.C.: Pastoral, 1987). For other views of magic see the essays by Martin Hollis and J. H. M. Beattie in* Rationality. *Ed. Bryan R. Wilson. Oxford: Basil Blackwell, 1970.*

About the author: Dates*: 1925– , Johnson City, TN, U.S.A.* **Education:** *B.A., Duke University; M.Div., Union Theological Seminary; Ph.D., Columbia University.* **Field(s):** *theology and culture; ritual studies; religion and literature.* **Career:** *Faculty Member, 1956–1993, Union Theological Seminary; The Paul Tillich Professor of Theology and Culture, 1973–93, Union Theological Seminary; Emeritus, 1993–present, Union Theological Seminary; Visiting Professorships, Columbia University, Barnard College, Fordham University, University of Otago (New Zealand), Vassar College, Montclair State College (New Jersey), Doshisha Univer-*

sity *(Japan)*. **Publications:** The Sense of History in Greek and Shakespearean Drama *(Columbia University, 1960); editor with Robert Pack,* Poems of Doubt and Belief: An Anthology of Modern Religious Poetry *(Macmillan, 1964);* Jean Genet *(Columbia University, 1966);* Romantic Quest and Modern Query: A History of the Modern Theater *(Delacorte, 1970);* Christ in a Changing World: Toward an Ethical Christology *(Crossroad, 1981);* The Magic of Ritual: Our Need for Liberating Rites that Transform Our Lives and Our Communities *(HarperSanFrancisco, 1991).* **Additional:** *"In teaching and public speaking, my work on rituals is often documented with photographs and tape recordings that I have made in a number of countries. With Witness for Peace, I am presently engaged in human rights efforts on behalf of Haiti, where some years ago I learned much about ritualizing."*

Liminality is the mother of invention!

—Victor Turner[1]

From a purely theoretical point of view, if that were possible or desirable to achieve, it would be an open question whether rituals should be thought of first as instruments of order that happen to enhance communal bonds and to facilitate various kinds of transformation; or primarily as community-making events that incidentally generate order and transform it; or first of all as techniques of transformation that help to order life and to deepen communal relationships. Theory, however, is always affected by a thinker's social orientation and ideology. In my own case, although I belong to the privileged gender (male) and race (white) in the North American middle class, my theory is that ritual is best understood from a vantage point created by a "preferential option for the poor." That is to say, we cannot well appreciate the power of ritual unless we see its usefulness to those in need, especially those who, having little social power and, being the victims of injustice, have a need for the social structure to be transformed.

Here is the most difficult part of our entire discussion, for here ritual misapprehension is apt to be the greatest. Many persons in Western society are skeptical of any transformative powers that may be claimed for ritual, except perhaps the inducement of changes that can be taken as primarily subjective or psychological in nature. This skepticism, being partly a matter of ideology, is strongest in those sectors of society that would have the most to lose were any major social transformation to occur.

One way of guarding the status quo against change is to deny the rationality of any expectation that rituals can do much to alter it. The entire tradition of Enlightenment thought, with its strong antipathy to rituals, lends plausibility to such denial. This means that in order seriously to consider the idea that a ritual can serve as a technique of transformation, we must come straight out with the M-word and face the question of magic.

* * *

People educated in the Western style tend to assume that only cultures or subcultures less enlightened than our own have recourse to magic. Most Western intellectuals regard magic as superstition, and most theologians equate it with paganism as well. In these matters, it often seems that one person's "magic" is another person's "religion." Ronald Grimes's words are therefore refreshing: " 'Magic,' as I use it here, does not refer only to other people's rituals but to ours as well. It is not a pejorative term."[2]

... [A] Haitian woman, Mme. Victor, describ[ed] how to cure the *move san* (bad blood) that she and her culture understand to afflict women who have difficult pregnancies. [I am] interested ... in the precision of her instructions, their being rooted in a received sense of order in nature, implying a structured cosmos, and at the same time their *making* order, in the sense that her formulae are what she, the "doctor," orders. What she does as a practitioner of local herbal medicine, of course, is to *re*order: The medicine she prescribes, together with her instructions about how to prepare and administer it, are designed, as she says, to "make the milk return to its rightful place." At the same time, her metaphor of order and right place suggests also a transformation, since the aim of the cure is to transform the flow at the nursing mother's breast from a toxic to a nourishing substance. As outsiders we may suppose that Mme. Victor's intention is also to reorient the distraught mother to her child, her family, her friends, and herself, so that she will come to occupy her *own* rightful place.

Researcher Paul Farmer rightly noticed that Mme. Victor's magic is ritualized,[3] but to say so is to speak redundantly, since *all* magic is ritualized and, as we shall see, all ritual employs magic.

Techniques of transformation that are *not* magical, such as those based on scientific analyses or empirical observation without any transcendent reference—like building a car or boiling water—have a claim to being culture-invariant. They are understood to employ forces and "laws" that are the same in any cultural milieu. The techniques of ritual, however, appeal to forces, agents, and "laws" (understandings of how things work) that are culture-dependent. Magic operates within socio-cultural frameworks of reality.

Thorough analysis would show that "science" and "magic" overlap. On the one hand, while magic does not confine itself to empirically grounded methods, neither does it exclude them. For example, medical anthropologists often discover empirical bases for herbal cures that have been practiced and transmitted ritually. On the other hand, the procedures and understandings of science are by no means independent of local culture, even though science aims to achieve a body of knowledge that is universally valid.[4]

The bugaboo of regarding magic as nothing more than bad science is hard to shake off, but Suzanne Langer made a nice try when she wrote this:

> The apparently misguided efforts of savages to induce rain by dancing and drumming are not practical mistakes at all; they are rites in which the rain has a part. . . . A "magic" effect is one which *completes a rite.*[5]

In other words, the world seen by magic is the world as ritually ordered, a world in which society and nature usually are fused in a single vision. But it is not this vision alone to which I call attention. It is the vision as the enabler of transformative action.

We are on the best footing when we think of magic as what Grimes calls "ritual work." He says that if a ritual "not only has meaning but also 'works,' it is magical."[6]

This way of thinking about the subject is close to

that of Van Gennep, who had used "magic" to refer to the ceremonies, rites, and services that are the principal techniques of transformation employed by religion.[7] More than Van Gennep, however, Grimes directs attention to the presence of magic in "our own" culture:

> Magical acts seldom displace pragmatic or scientific ones [see Malinowski (1954), 85–87], and we have no reason to assume that magic is absent from technological societies, although it is probably adumbrated in them. I suspect magic is minimal in modern agriculture, but modern therapy and modern sexuality are as laden with magical thinking as healing and fertility rites ever were. In addition, advertising is full of it. People deny that they believe in magic, but ingest this pill and use that shampoo expecting "somehow" (the cue for magical transcendence) to become what they desire. A more responsible example of modern magic is Carl Simonton's [1975] use of imagery in therapy for cancer patients. A person treated in his clinic wills and imagines a cancer as soft or dissolvable and surrenders images of it as a rock, army, or steel armor. Considerable success is had in directly using symbols for such concrete ends.[8]

This is insightful, but it still holds magic at arm's length. More nearly on target is this:

> . . . a prayer, if one expects it to precipitate specifiable results such as healing or world peace, is magical. If the person praying is simply adjuring us to be peaceful, the prayer is hortatory and ceremonial. . . . Magic depends on the declarative to reach the imperative: "This is how things work; therefore, let this be the case."[9]

To reach from the declarative to the imperative requires a technique. The carpenter, aiming to let it be the case that the nail goes into the wood, uses a technique of hammering. For magic, the technique is ritual: What the act of hammering is to the carpenter, the performance of ritual is to the worker of magic.

Within the context of religion, as Van Gennep saw it, practice and theory are inseparable. If they do separate, religion dissolves, "the theory without the practice becoming metaphysics, and the practice on the basis of a different theory becoming science."[10]

Using the term *magico-religious*, Van Gennep expressed the conjunction of religious practice and theory. His point is excellent, for it reminds us that religion cannot be religion without performance, in all the senses of "performance" that we have earlier elaborated. The aim of religion is not simply intellectual understanding; it is also, and primarily, transformative action, for which the principal technique is "ceremonies, rites, and services." Ritual-making may not be a religion's first or last word but is surely its most essential. A religion is a *praxis*, a certain way of acting or attempting to act in the world, and this is established through a certain way of acting ritually.

Van Gennep's emphasis upon magic as the technique employed by religion should not blind us to the occurrence of magic outside religion also. Social life in general and political life in particular require ceremonies and rites, those quasi-dramatic enactments that express and define people's relationships and also make possible their transformation as part of the social dynamic. When the king is anointed, the President inaugurated, the scholar hooded, the couple wedded, or the dance floor rocked by the celebrators of Saturday night, we have instances of magical transformation. These events change things, and do so by the technique of ritual—that is, by magic.

While the literature on magic being published today offers no consistent point of view, there is considerable criticism of the idea, put forward most influentially in Frazer's *The Golden Bough*, that magic is primitive science, born of ignorance.[11] Here is Wittgenstein reflecting upon Frazer:

> When we watch the life and behaviour of [human beings] all over the earth we see that apart from what we might call animal activities, taking food &c., &c., [people] also carry out actions that bear a peculiar character and might be called ritualistic.
>
> But then it is nonsense if we go on to say that the characteristic feature of *these* actions is that they spring from wrong ideas about the physics of things. (This is what Frazer does when he says magic is really false physics, or as the case may be, false medicine, technology, &c.).[12]

Ridding himself of the notion that magic, the ac-

tion of ritual, is bad science, Wittgenstein helps us to glimpse the affinity between ancient or primitive ritualizing and modern instances:

> The religious actions or the religious life of the priest-king are not different in kind from any genuinely religious action today, say a confession of sins. This also can be "explained" (made clear) and cannot be explained.
>
> Burning in effigy. Kissing the picture of a loved one. This is obviously not based on a belief that it will have a definite effect on the object which the picture represents. It aims at some satisfaction and it achieves it. Or rather, it does not aim at anything; we act in this way and then feel satisfied.[13]

If I understand Wittgenstein's point, it is that magic should not be understood within the logic of cause and effect but rather in terms of symbolic and linguistic associations. This may be too little to claim for magic, but at least it avoids thinking of magic as false logic, and it does allow for a certain understanding of ritual as technique of transformation. Desire is transformed into satisfaction: "we act in this way and then feel satisfied." There is change, of however subjective a kind.

Some views of magic more recent than Frazer's challenge his idea of magic's being a "primitive" phenomenon but agree with him that it is unscientific and false. Instead of being false because primitive, magic is said to be false because decadent. "We are often told," says Suzanne Langer, "that savage religion begins in magic; but the chances are, I think, that magic begins in religion."[14] She assumes this to be a downhill course, as does Daniel O'Keefe, who expands the point with subtlety throughout his lengthy interpretation of magic as Promethean: *Stolen Lightening: The Social Theory of Magic.*[15]

Gregory Bateson's thoughts on the matter, lofty as they are, reveal a common misunderstanding of religion. For him science and religion are closely allied, and magic is "a degenerate 'applied' form of either":

> My view of magic is the converse of that which has been orthodox in anthropology since the days of Sir James Frazer. It is orthodox to believe that religion is

an evolutionary development of magic. Magic is regarded as more primitive and religion as its flowering. In contrast, I view sympathetic or contagious magic as a product of decadence from religion; I regard religion on the whole as the earlier condition.[16]

Bateson is right, of course, that magic is an application of knowledge, a technique, as Van Gennep called it. What is interesting, and erroneous, is the vaguely Neoplatonic point of view entertained by Bateson (and many others) that the application of knowledge for practical ends is a corruption. The following passage seems based upon an idealization of knowledge divorced from praxis:

> Consider such rituals as rain dances or the totemic rituals concerned with [the human's] relationship to animals. In these types of ritual the human being invokes or imitates or seeks to control the weather or the ecology of wild creatures. But I believe that in their primitive state these are true religious ceremonials. They are ritual statements of unity, involving all the participants in an integration with the meteorological cycle or with the ecology of totemic animals. This is religion. But the pathway of deterioration from religion to magic is always tempting. From a statement of integration in some often dimly recognized whole, the practitioner turns aside to an appetitive stance. He [sic] sees his own ritual as a piece of purposive magic to make the rain come or to promote the fertility of the totemic animal or to achieve some other goal.[17]

In other words, rituals are all right as long as they are not supposed to have any practical result. Then, in a second thought, Bateson allows that they may have results directed toward the celebrants, but not toward anything external to them:

> The criterion that distinguishes magic from religion is, in fact, *purpose* and especially some extrovert purpose. Introvert purpose, the desire to change the self, is a very different matter, *but intermediate cases occur.* If the hunter performs a ritual imitation of an animal to cause that animal to come into his net, that is surely magic; but if his purpose in imitating the animal is perhaps to improve his own empathy and understanding of the beast, his action is perhaps to be classed as religious. (Emphasis added)[18]

Rushing to repudiate magic, Bateson fails to notice that the "intermediate cases," in which introvert and extrovert purposes are mixed, are the most prevalent and the most interesting. They express, I would argue, the genius of religion, in which change in the self and change in the outer world are bound into an intimate connection.

It would be a poor anthropology, in the theological as well as the social-scientific sense, to categorize all desire as bad or corrupting. The better moral and theological question is not *whether* there is appetite or whether people perform rituals and other acts out of desire to change their situations, but *what* they desire, in what situations, and with what sense of responsibility for the common good. Bateson's assumption that an appetite for change in the external world makes religion degenerate flies in the face of the fervent desire present in many religions for transformation of the external world—that crops may grow, that disaster may be avoided, that illness be cured, or that justice roll down like a mighty stream. Religion is not about the elimination of desire but its *transformation* from lower to higher forms—the transformation of the suffering world into one more compassionate, loving, and just.

While Frazer, Bateson, and many other writers try to defend religion by denigrating magic, Van Gennep's position, holding magic and religion together, is better. We may say that some forms of magic and magical belief are less intelligent than others, remembering that the magico-religious, as Van Gennep called it, has crass as well as admirable examples; but without magic, religion is powerless. Since the rites of religion are techniques of transformation, Van Gennep realized, when people divorce religion from magic they end up with metaphysics on the one hand, empirical science on the other, and religion gone. This is the fate to which much liberal religion in Western society has very nearly come. Having mostly turned away from its own magic, it has little to offer, and its numbers are declining.

While some persons would like to preserve religion, if only it could be purified of all magic, some others hold that religion, no less than magic, is a system of illusion. The best argument against religion, however, is not that it is illusory but that because it is powerful it is dangerous. Since this argument could be used against *all* forms of power in the world, it proves not that religion should cease but that it should be subject to moral and intellectual critique. What is wanted is not the elimination of all power, without which life could not continue, but its transformation into beneficent forms. Religion should be judged by its contribution to that end.

The business of religions and their rituals, then, is to effect transformations, not only of persons' individual subjectivities but also transformations of society and the natural world. In a religious perspective, the personal, societal, and physical realms are not isolated from each other but participate together in a single field of divine power. The word "magic," which serves to remind us that ritual is a means of confronting power with power, is also a reminder that not all power is physical and material.

"From the viewpoint of the actor," Edmund Leach tells us,

> rites can alter the state of the world because they invoke power. If the power is treated as inherent in the rite itself, the analyst calls the action magic; if the power is believed to be external to the situation—a supernatural agency—the analyst says it is religious.

Leach is well aware of the tendency to analyze religion and magic into two different things, and the dichotomy bothers him. He continues:

> Current argument on this theme is highly contentious, and I must declare my own position: I hold that the rite is prior to the explanatory belief. This will be recognized as essentially the view of Robertson Smith.[19]

It was also the view of Wittgenstein, as we have seen, and the Cambridge anthropologists before him. Instead of holding the question of power at arm's length, Leach proceeds to discuss it. Of interest here is his conclusion that

> . . . every act by which one individual asserts his [sic] authority to curb or alter the behavior of another individual is an invocation of metaphysical force. The submissive response is an ideological reaction, and it is no more surprising that individuals should be influenced by magical performances or religious imprecations than that they should be influenced by the commands

of authority. The power of ritual is just as actual as the power of command.[20]

This is well said, reminding us that ritual and its magic cannot be understood except in relation to the socio-political world.

Perhaps we should add to Leach's comment the following: The power of ritual is not only just as actual as the power of command but also as actual as the power to *resist* command when the latter is unacceptable. Rituals of disobedience are perhaps less frequent but no less significant than those which induce conformity.

If the power of ritual to effect change is denied, causing religion to become, as Van Gennep said, metaphysics, then in that case the understanding of the world becomes the task of pure intellect, and its transformation the work of scientific technology. That is a dangerous situation because it masks two truths that are best known through the practice of ritual: first, that the agencies affecting human destiny, whether they be human or divine or aspects of nature or some combination of these, are of a personal character and should be addressed performatively; and second, that communal life without such performance becomes a mockery of itself, drained little by little of the experience of communitas and the recognition of the human as human.

Ritual, as I have indicated, refuses to recognize clear lines of demarcation between the psychological, the socio-political and the material worlds. It tends to personalize the latter and to objectify the former two, lessening the sharp distinction that scientific method likes to make between a material world of impersonal forces and a societal world of consciousness, custom, and choice. Ritual acts as if everything is alive and personal. We have already heard Wittgenstein on this:

> In magical healing one *indicates* to an illness that it should leave the patient.

> After the description of any such magical cure we'd like to add: If the illness doesn't understand *that*, then I don't know *how* one ought to say it.[21]

If one speaks *to* an illness and not just about it, if one *speaks* to an illness and does not just treat it as an impersonal condition, and if one expects that this speaking, done ritually, will affect the illness, is one's magic crass? I submit that a judgment about that should rest more upon ethical and practical considerations than upon metaphysical ones. It is necessary to judge the total situation of those performing the ritual. One needs to understand the situation personally, psychologically, socially, politically, culturally. What we can say in general, I think, is that there is something healthy about ritual's assumption that human reality is essentially dramatic, that at bottom life is not something to be *treated*, as scientifically based medicine *treats* a disease, but something to be *enacted*, as in the enactment of one's own being in the world or the enactment of a cure. Although this insight can perhaps be defended metaphysically, it is beyond my present purpose to do so. The clearer case is moral: when we understand ourselves as agents active in a world made up of other purposive beings, our sense of self and responsibility is heightened. The person who performs a rain dance or goes to church to pray for rain is at least *doing* something, and probably with more self-awareness than the person who watches the TV weather report and waits with passive impotence for the sky to change. Of course, there is nothing to prevent one's doing the ritual and also watching the TV weather, but in that case the passivity is gone.

* * *

Like any technique or value, magic is subject to distortion; and this happens especially when magic is viewed as a technique in direct competition with more empirical methods for transforming a situation. If we are to give up the Frazerian idea that magic is bad science, while retaining the knowledge that rituals do in fact bring about certain kinds of change, we must cease looking at magic and science as two means to the same end and realize instead that they are different means to different ends. At times the ends of magic and science may overlap, but they are not identical. Compared to science, magic is more holistic in its methods and aims.

Grimes helpfully points out that "the force of magic lies in its use of desire as a contributing factor in causing hoped-for results."[22] In other words, magic takes subjectivity seriously and includes it in its view of the overall situation that is to be trans-

formed. The inclusion of subjectivity, of "the human factor," as inherent in all aspects of any situation is part of what is meant by calling magic holistic; and it is this which most distinguishes it from scientific techniques. Science is primarily analytic and works by putting subjectivity in brackets and carefully delimiting the field of reference pertinent to any problem. By contrast magic is primarily synthetic; it works by emphasizing subjectivity and seeking to include as much as possible within the field of reference. When magic apes science by viewing its own techniques as valid without reference to subjectivity, and when it concentrates on narrow results narrowly achieved, then it is corrupted.

These considerations underscore two observations about ritual magic we have already made—its appeal to transcendent reference and its dramatizing character. Instead of narrowing its focus, as the pursuit of scientific techniques tends to do, magic broadens its view, always aware that the problem and situation of immediate concern is transcended by relevant factors that are likely to be hidden from view and probably lie on another plane of reality. In Haiti the *mambo* Melanie said to me, "If a disease has physical origins, then it can be cured by scientific methods; but if its causes are spiritual, then the *services vodou* are required." Such a view of the relation between science and magic, which one may encounter in many parts of the world, implies that the spiritual realm includes, yet surpasses, the physical. To put the point more clearly, the spiritual is the very act of transcending, while not excluding, the mundane.

Spirit is life. To call it transcendence is to speak abstractly. The same point is made more concretely by saying that spirit is personal. To view the world spiritually is to view it as full of personal agency, and this is precisely what ritual does: It takes reality as something to be enacted, a point we may also state the other way around by saying that ritual takes enactment as reality. The persons who perform a ritual are inserting their own present actions, their own subjectivity and interactions with others, into a holistic understanding of the world. They aim at a transformation of the world, or some part of it, through the *work* that they do; not as detached manipulators of objectified things that behave according to invariant rules, but as free agents actively impinging upon other free agents in a spirited world.

Ritual is the arena in which such action and interaction takes place. Hence in ritual, as in magic, the most distinctive feature is *not* the repetitive pattern but the performance of direct address to the powers being confronted or invoked.

Magical transformation, then, is not simply a transformation of subjectivity, leaving the external world unchanged except perhaps in appearance. Neither is it a transformation of the external world only, leaving subjectivity out of account and untransformed. Rather, it is transformation of a total situation by means of an enactment undertaken with strong subjective desire and producing an effect upon a number of subjects and objects together. It is, in short, a reordering of a totality. Let us take two examples: (1) a magical cure in Korea, and (2) exorcising apartheid in South Africa.

1. A Magical Cure

In Seoul, Korea, in 1983, I attended a *kut*, a ritual that employs song, dance, trance, and spirit possession. This one was led by a shamaness, known in Korea as a *mudang*, with several assistants. It took place in a medium-sized room in a large house where several similar services were going on simultaneously in other rooms. Attending were some fifteen or twenty persons, including the family who had requested the service. The father was going blind and needed a cure. He had received treatment in several hospitals and clinics, but his eyes continued to worsen, and so the *kut* had been arranged. At the request of my Korean host, David Suh, the *mudang* gave me permission to observe.

Except for a low altar at one end, laden mostly with food set out in colorful display, the room had no furniture. Three female drummers, one of them the *mudang* herself, sat on the floor along one wall near the altar. There was a male assistant who did little drumming, much more dancing and singing. The family sat along the wall opposite the drummers but not as near the altar. We observers, who included several apprentice *mudangs*, sat at the end of the room facing the altar. Not a lot of floor space was left over. Our arrangement resembled that of a quite intimate theater without chairs. Staring at me from among the food platters on the altar was a roasted pig's head.

I wondered how anything likely to go on in this room could cure blindness. Now that it's over, I am not sure that it did. At least no such cure was evident during the three hours I was present, and I did not learn what happened to the man's eyesight later. Nevertheless, the following things did happen.

The room became filled with a prodigious energy, emanating mostly from the *mudang*, her musicians, and their drums. There was, most of the time, a pounding, ebullient rhythm causing everyone's pulse to rise and leading to a keen level of anticipation. The *mudang* and her assistants danced vigorously. Some went into trance. At various times they became possessed by spirits, the two who impressed me most being the "petty official," with his felt hat, rapid-fire speech, and constant demands for money; and the "birth grandmother," with her huge fan, broad-brimmed straw hat, and flowing white robe.

The money that the "petty official" dunned out of the supplicating family and stuffed into his pockets, sleeves, collar, ears, and hat, as well as into the mouth of the pig's head, was, I learned, an amount that had been agreed upon ahead of time, a point which an uninformed observer would never have guessed, what with the "petty official" becoming ever more demanding in voice and gesture, the very picture of a small-time extortionist, and the family looking frantic and digging into pockets, purses, shopping bags, and bosoms in an apparently desperate effort to come up with ever more cash. The passing of money had been turned into a game. It is most likely that a bit more money was asked than had been agreed to, and equally likely that the family anticipated that. This serious play with money—serious because the money changed hands "for keeps," playful because of the conspiratorial and almost mocking style in which it was performed—increased the energy-pulse in the room.

Spirit possession, in my view, has also to be regarded as a kind of serious game. By that statement I definitely do not imply that there is nothing to it more than conscious role-playing. On the contrary, in many instances of spirit possession (some people would say in all) the possessed person loses consciousness throughout the trance and later has no recall of what occurred. I am as ready as any person to give this a theological, or if you please a mystical, interpretation. I take visiting spirits with much seriousness, whether they show up in a Korean *kut* or in a Christian service of worship. However, the seriousness and the truthfulness of spirit possession does not mean that it involves no role-playing, as is made obvious by the fact that costumes and props are made ready ahead of time, prepared for a panoply of spirits that is just as recognizable as the dramatis personae of any familiar script.

Is it sacrilege to use these theatrical terms? I think not, especially if we are willing to use them to speak respectfully of *our own* religion and its most hallowed traditions. Liturgical vestments are customes; and bread, wine, baptismal water, pulpit, and Bible are props for Christian worship, in just the same sense as props are used in the theater: They are the materials that need to be made ready for the anticipated action. In themselves they are not much. In the final analysis, it is the action, not the dress, that counts.

In spirit possession, "playing for keeps" is escalated to a very high level, as I could tell by watching not only the tone of the possessed performers at the *kut* but also the faces and demeanor of the family who needed help. They got it.

Thanks to David Suh's translation, I was able to follow what went on in the numerous exchanges between the visiting spirits and the family. Each member of the family was addressed, not just the father. They were told that hard times lay ahead. They were not to give up hope. Financial burdens would increase. The father would need much care. Everyone needed to see things they had not seen before, otherwise the family would find itself on the rocks. When the father regained his sight, everyone would have to readjust. And if he did not, who could tell what lay ahead? The family's roots were emphasized and interpreted as part of the historic roots of the nation. Each of the visiting spirits had died unjustly and carried, like the Korean nation itself, long victimized by its imperial neighbors, a spirit of *han*, a term that means both pride and resentment.

Courage and wisdom, I realized, were the ointment being applied to the father's eyes, and the "cure" was being given not to him only but to all his family network, and even to the rest of us present who cared about Korea.

The situation addressed was total. The father's particular affliction had been taken up into an entire cosmos of affliction. Everyone was being reoriented, renewed. Relationships were being transformed. You could see and feel it occur then and there, no matter how long or short it would subsequently endure.

Is this magic? I call it so, and think I do not misuse the word. If the transformation that occurred was not the one that had been anticipated by the family, it was nevertheless real and included a transformation of expectation. That there be a transformation is one half the definition of magic. The other half is that the technique for achieving it is ritual. I departed that room rather amazed, remembering the tag-lines with which Euripides often ended his plays:

> The gods bring many things
> to their accomplishment.
> And what was most expected
> has not been accomplished.
> But god has found a way
> for what no one expected.[23]

"But surely," someone will object, "this way of defining magic is equivocal." How shall we answer such a sober-minded critic? Magic's power rests upon the power of equivocation, through which not only blind eyes but also meanings and signifiers are transformed in a twinkling. If we cannot equivocate in speaking of magic, we cannot speak of it at all. It collapses into "bad science" or "falsehood" and is gone. Meanwhile, however, the ritualizing of the world and its sufferings continues, and because of it the world and its history come to be what they were not.

Consider a different example.

2. Exorcising Apartheid from South Africa

In 1987 two United States citizens, Walter Wink, the author of *Violence and Nonviolence in South Africa: Jesus' Third Way*,[24] and Richard Deats of the Fellowship of Reconciliation, were invited to South Africa to do workshops on nonviolent direct action. Because he had spoken against apartheid on a previous trip in 1986, Wink's visa application was denied outright. Deats's was granted after a long delay. The sponsors decided to hold a single large workshop in Lesotho, where Wink could legally go, inviting people from all over Southern Africa. This took place in May 1988. My account of the event is based on information given me directly by Walter Wink.

The workshop participants, thirty-eight in all, of whom about a third were black, were native to South Africa, Lesotho, Botswana, Swaziland, and Mozambique. They included a number of prominent religious leaders of South Africa, among them Sheena Duncan, president of Black Sash and vice president of the South Africa Council of Churches (SACC); Joe Seremane, acting justice and reconciliation secretary of the SACC; Sid Luckett, director of the justice division for the Cape Town diocese of the Anglican church; Emma Mashinini of SACC, subsequently elected to the steering committee of the Emergency Convocation of Churches; Richard Steele and Anita Kromberg, South African staff persons of the International Fellowship of Reconciliation, cosponsors of the event; the staff of the Transformation Resource Centre in Lesotho, cosponsors; Peter Kerchhoff, organizer of the Pietermaritzburg Agency for Christian Social Awareness; Rob Robertson, a leading spokesperson for nonviolence; three Quakers; four radicalized Afrikaners; and a contemplative Anglican nun. All the black participants had experience of detention and torture for their opposition to apartheid.

The workshop was held in a nondescript room about forty feet square in a Catholic seminary and retreat center in Roma. Chairs were set in a circle in one half of the room, which was furnished with a coal stove. The sponsors had covered the walls of the otherwise barren room with banners and political posters opposing apartheid. For the first worship service, someone had made a large wooden cross about eight feet high and four feet wide, and during the service participants were asked to affix their names to it. With this act, we may speak of ritual and the ambiguity of performance.

The reader may guess, as indeed the participants could only guess, at the symbolism of affixing one's name, along with others', to a large wooden cross during a Christian worship service improvised for a workshop concerning resistance to apartheid. I do not mean that the symbolism was secret, only that it

was richly polyvalent and was not verbalized at the time.

What the North American reader might not guess is that the act was risky. Although Lesotho is purportedly an independent country, in fact it is completely under the control of South Africa. As Wink reported to me, "We fully expected the security police at any time." The name-bearing cross would have provided the police with a ready-made roster of those apprehended in a raid. Hence the act of placing one's name upon a cross during a service of worship—in itself a performance in the *ritual mode*, combining doing and showing—took on in this context the additional implications of performance in the *confessional* and *ethical* modes.

The act signified: "I am a person who is willing to suffer in the struggle against apartheid." And this declaration entailed also a transformation, even in the case of those who had *already* endured such suffering, for it amounted to a rededication of the self, a renewal of commitment, a reenactment of devotion, and hence a *movement* (passage) of the self from an old stage to a new one. This is transformation effected in the confessional as well as the ritual mode.

The act further signified: "Not only am I willing in principle to suffer and risk for the sake of opposing apartheid, but I do put myself at risk here and now, by giving up the possibility of remaining anonymous on this occasion." Because the risk was actual (not only symbolic) and because it was undertaken for the sake of greater social justice, the act was transformational in the ethical mode of performance, too, in addition to the ritual and confessional modes. People often ask whether rituals "work." In cases like this one, we know that the ritual works from the simple fact that it has inescapable consequences. The risk that is here ritualized is real risk. In this sense, rites of passage always "work," since their enactment places their participants in a new social situation.

At the second worship service in the Lesotho workshop, the large cross was laid on the floor and the participants stood lighted candles upon it. Wink has not provided me with enough comment on this service to enable any analysis, but it is clear that the wooden cross was taking on additional layers of meaning through repeated usage. Meanwhile, the workshop sessions employed Bible study, some improvisational enactments of biblical stories, and reflections upon violence and nonviolence in South Africa today. The theme was the opposition that Christians faithful to God and Christ are required to make against the "principalities and powers" that are responsible for social injustice and oppression:

> For we are not contending against flesh and blood, but against the principalities, against the powers, against the world rulers of this present darkness, against the spiritual hosts of wickedness in the heavenly places. (Ephesians 6:12)
>
> . . . to make all [people] see what is the plan of the mystery hidden for ages in God who created all things; that through the church the manifold wisdom of God might now be made known to the principalities and powers in the heavenly places. (Ephesians 3:9–10)
>
> He disarmed the principalities and powers and made a public example of them . . . If with Christ you died to the elemental spirits of the universe, why do you live as if you still belonged to the world? Why do you submit to regulations . . . ? (Colossians 2:15, 20)

The workshop ended with a third service of worship. Wink asked each participant to write down on a piece of construction paper the name of the particular power that had him or her most in its thrall. Naming is always performative and is among the most obvious and consequential of the workings of ritual. Wink's aim was to provide occasion for persons to become conscious of the powers that prevent, or try to prevent, their being faithful to the Kingdom of God in their own Southern African context. As he expected, people wrote phrases like "Fear of Death," "Fear of Torture," "Separation from Family," and "Fear of Detention." Holding these insignia aloft, the people now formed a procession, at the head of which was the great cross with their names attached. The procession circled the room and sang:

> Thine be the glory,
> Risen, conquering Son!
> Endless is the victory
> Thou o'er death hast won.

The tune was from Handel's *Judas Maccabeus*, fa-miliar wherever this hymn is sung. When the procession and the hymn ended, the cross with its names attached was placed against a wall. Participants carried the signs bearing the names of the powers they feared to the coal stove. They burned them. Someone said a prayer, and the event was over.

If we speak of such a ritual as accomplishing transformation, we are not entitled to say that its direct result [was] the tumbling of the Jericho-walls of apartheid in South Africa. . . . What we can say is that certain transformations, as mentioned above, took place *during* the ritual, that these now become part of the history of the struggle for black liberation in Southern Africa, and that the rituals themselves are part of the movement for freedom that is now going on. We can say one thing more: If no people in South Africa were willing to undertake rituals of transformation in which they anticipate the liberation for which they long, then that freedom would never come. Ritual is, at the least, the preparation of groups of people for the spiritual work they must do; and the struggle for liberation is a spiritual work—that is, a work of moral courage—however physical and violent or nonviolent it may be.

Rob Robertson had persuaded Wink to try to enter South Africa illegally after the workshop ended. He thought it could be done at a certain border crossing and was worth the try. In a letter to friends written on June 16, 1988, Wink described how it happened:

> Sister Camilla, a contemplative nun in our group, arose at 2 A.M. to begin praying that we would get in. Others in the States were also focusing their prayers on that day. As we came in sight of the border we stopped and prayed that, as God had opened the prison doors and let Peter and Paul and Silas out, God would let us in! Then in a pouring rain, we drove up to the border post, jumped out, and ran under the shelter of the porch, where the senior soldier in charge was whistling—"Thine be the glory, risen, conquering Son . . ." The rain-darkened room was so dim that I virtually had to read my passport to the other soldier; he never even looked for a visa.
>
> Synchronicity, to be sure—only, it is rather awkward to give praise and thanksgiving to synchronicity.

In *Unmasking the Powers*, Wink has spoken of the

historic 1965 civil rights march from Selma, Alabama, to the state capital at Montgomery as an "exorcism." His words are pertinent:

> Waving holy water and a crucifix over Buchenwald would scarcely have stopped the Nazi genocide of Jews, but think about it—what if the church in Germany *had* staged ritual acts of protest outside those gates? What if, in churches all over the land, pastors had read from their pulpits prayers exorcising the spirit of Satan and Wotan from the national psyche? It could not have happened, of course, because the prior understanding of collective possession and the church's task in unmasking the Powers was not in place. . . .
>
> The march across the Selma bridge by black civil rights advocates was an act of exorcism. It exposed the demon of racism, stripping away the screen of legality and custom for the entire world to see. . . .
>
> Exorcism drives the devils first to reveal their names and then casts them out. Most do not come out without a struggle. When Phil and Dan Berrigan poured blood on the files of the Selective Service System, they were attempting to expose the demon of American messianic imperialism in Vietnam. They paid for it with stiff prison sentences.[25]

Actions such as these fit the definition of ritual that Bobby Alexander has proposed: "planned or improvised performance that effects a transition from everyday life to an alternative framework within which the everyday is transformed."[26] The everyday in Nazi Germany was the state's program of mass murder. In Alabama in 1965, the everyday was racial segregation. In South Africa in 1987, it was the apparently insuperable force of government by apartheid. The Selma march and the cross-bearing procession in Lesotho were the deliberate enactment of something different. They were magical acts. The word "magic" is not invoked here because of such things as the synchronicity that occurred for Walter Wink at the border crossing but rather because the Lesotho workshop and the Selma demonstration employed ritual as a technique in a holistic process of transformation. Without such ritualization, the Civil Rights Movement in the United

States could not have occurred, nor can any other liberation movement in the world. It was the genius of Martin Luther King, Jr., inspired by Mahatma Gandhi, Jesus, and others, to recognize this. At certain stages of their struggle, ritual magic is the principal technique available to oppressed peoples for the transformation of their historical situation. As one veteran of the Civil Rights Movement has said:

> . . . I came of age in the civil rights movement, in those demonstrations—in Mississippi, North Carolina, some parts of Alabama. We had white policemen coming at us and we had our spirituals, our songs. That's all we had.[27]

Rational political methods alone cannot bring about transformation of society from a less to a more just condition, because they cannot fuse the visionary with the actual (the absent with the present) as rituals do, thus profoundly affecting the moral life. Nor can ideas alone do this, for in order to bear fruit ideas require flesh-and-blood performance. Ritualization is required, as when the names are placed on the cross for the police to see if and when they come, or the marchers move across the Selma bridge, or (earlier) the freedom-loving people of Montgomery got off the segregated busses and walked in the open streets. They walked to get to their jobs, of course; but the magic is that they walked to get ever so much further than that. Dignity was their destination, and dignity is what they gave themselves by performing it, in public, in the dusty street, where the doing and the showing were one and the same.

* * *

The ability of rituals to assist in the transformation of society, which I have called part of their magic, is not magic in a fantastical sense. This is a point I want now to pursue by emphasizing that rituals not only can change, or help to change, a situation but that they themselves are subject to change in the course of time. In other words, rituals belong to human history. Ritual process belongs to historical process. It is not some kind of detached thing remote from the events that it influences. Agents of transformation, rituals are themselves transformed by the histories to which they belong.

This thought no doubt seems obvious to persons in the social sciences, but it can encounter resistance in some religious communities and some theologies. Even where it gains intellectual assent, there may be much resistance to change in a group's practice, especially if ritual is prized so highly for its ordering function that its ability to transform and to be transformed is feared.

Many people in fact think of a ritual as something that follows a set script and is always performed more or less the same way. However well sanctioned by usage such a meaning of ritual may be, it is very misleading, for it runs the risk of identifying ritual either with purely formal repetition or (what is similar) with a corrupted sense of magic.

I have argued that magic is corrupted by attempting to leave subjectivity out of account. By the same token, rituals are corrupted by trying to objectify them in such a way as to protect them from change. Instead of their being taken as part of the holistic situations they would transform, rituals are treated as impersonal objects. An effort is made to remove them from ongoing history, preserving as sacrosanct some form they have already assumed. The result is what theologians call *ritualism*. Its aim in some instances is to effect change in everything except the liturgical tradition, in others to ward off every kind of change whatever. In either case, such opposition to change amounts to corrupted magic, since it falls short of viewing transformation in a holistic way.

Rituals are in fact not changeless, and the attempt to make them so violates their nature. Instruments of transformation, they are themselves transformed by the processes of which they are a part: "To perform a ritual the same way twice is to kill it," said Stanley Walens, "for the ritual grows as we grow, its life recapitulates the course of ours."[28]

The changing of rituals under changed social conditions is so obvious that it would require no emphasis if it were not frequently denied. One example of such change was documented by Monica Wilson in "The Wedding Cakes: A Study of Ritual Change," which reports the influence of European wedding practices on nuptial ceremonies among the Nguni people in Pondoland and the Ciskei in Africa. Weddings, of course, are rites of passage in which the status of two persons, and the community's expectations concerning them, are transformed; but the rites themselves undergo change as they are employed in shifting circumstances. Wilson concentrated upon alterations in patterns of display in Nguni weddings that followed upon the arrival of missionaries and other Europeans prominent in the colonial system. Before long, she recounts, "the clothes worn and the parade of bride and groom [became] a copy so far as resources permitted of white patterns of display."[29] A European-style wedding cake was introduced, taking its place in the ceremony along with the type of cake that was already traditional. Changes like this did not amount simply to personal preferences:

> The style taken over by the converts tended to become the norm, and the black fringed shawl and kerchief survived a century longer among Nguni women than they did among the whites with whom they originated.[30]

Wilson generalizes that

> within a short space of time *new* forms are accepted as "traditional" in ritual. Some of the details of the contemporary marriage ritual . . . derive from traditional Nguni patterns, others from Europe, and others (such as *two* cakes) are brand new, but they are spoken of as *customary* among Christians, with an implication of antiquity.[31]

Wilson's is an example of ritual adaptation. In her description, it seems to include little or no critique of the social situation. There are times, however, when changes in familiar rituals are made deliberately to encourage social protest, and I choose an example from an unlikely source: the Anglican Book of Common Prayer. To find the example I have in mind, we must turn to the edition published in Philadelphia, the birthplace of American independence from Britain, by the Protestant Episcopal Church in 1789. The Preface to this edition declares:

> It is a most invaluable part of that blessed "liberty wherewith Christ has made us free," that in his worship different forms and usages may without offense be allowed, provided the substance of the Faith be

kept entire; and that, in every Church, what cannot be clearly determined to belong to Doctrine must be referred to Discipline; and therefore, by common consent and authority, may be altered, abridged, enlarged, amended, or otherwise disposed of, as may seem most convenient for the edification of the people, "according to the various exigency [sic] of times and occasions."

The authors of this passage were surely wrong to think that liturgy and doctrine can be so clearly separated one from the other, as if doctrine can remain immutable while forms of worship are altered; but they were right to recognize, as had their forerunners in the Church of England, that ritual does and must respond to "the various exigency of times and occasions." The preface continues with a quotation from the Prayer Book as published by the mother church:

> The particular Forms of Divine Worship, and the Rites and Ceremonies appointed to be used therein, being things in their own nature indifferent, and alterable, and so acknowledged; it is but reasonable that upon weighty and important considerations, according to the various exigency of times and occasions, such changes and alterations should be made therein, as to those that are in place of Authority should, from time to time, seem either necessary or expedient.

The American liturgical changes, like some that had preceded them in the Church of England, especially at the time of the English church's separation from Rome, were made in deliberate response to a changed political scene. Far from being simply adaptive, however, the American changes represented a conscious desire for the rituals to contribute to the new nation's experiment in democracy independent of the British crown.

In addition to their adaptation and responsiveness to particular occasions of social change, rituals are also transformed by processes less conscious and rational but no less consequential in the long run. This seems to be what Stanley Walens had in mind when he said that a "ritual grows as we grow." He might have added that *we* grow as our *rituals* grow. Thomas Peterson writes that the

meaning of ritual is never fixed and is always shifting because its meaning comes from its use. There can never be exactly the same meaning for any ritual act, because, while the form might be held constant, the context which is inseparable from the form will always vary.[32]

Theodore Jennings has pointed out that one reason rituals change is that they not only transmit ancient knowledge but also assist the discovery of new knowledge. He identifies three "moments" or types of knowledge provided by ritual, one of which, the most relevant here, is often overlooked. Calling this "the aspect of 'discovery' or 'inquiry' characteristic of ritual action," he writes:

> If we concentrate our attention upon ritual as an entirely fixed and unvarying sequence of actions, we are likely to overlook this aspect of ritual knowledge altogether. But such a "synchronic" approach to ritual is misleading when it is taken as the sole mode of gaining an understanding of ritual action. The problem might best be illustrated if we sought to compare the enactment of the Latin rite Mass in Western Africa, Central Mexico, a suburb of Chicago, and St. Peter's in Rome. Even if all are "performed" in Latin (the situation prior to Vatican II) the trained observer would notice significant variation which it would be at least premature to dismiss as incidental. Even if we attend to repeated performance of the same ritual in the same cultural setting over a period of time we would also notice differences in detail which eventually become very important. Even the liturgies of Eastern Orthodox churches with their strong emphasis on historical continuity and tradition have a history characterized both by development (amplification, elaboration) and by discarded alternatives. . . . A diachronic perspective on ritual, together with a cross-cultural comparison of putatively identical rituals, brings to light considerable variation which cannot be accounted for in the view of ritual as sheer repetition.[33]

Jennings argues that the changes rituals undergo are neither accidental nor incidental. As he says,

> variation in ritual performance is by no means the incidental and extraneous phenomenon it has often been thought to be by those who define ritual action in

terms of unvarying repetition. Instead, the variation in ritual performance may be understood as a decisive clue to the character of the ritual action as a relatively autonomous form of noetic exploration and discovery.[34]

We learn by doing. This includes the doing of ritual. What we learn by doing ritual is not only the ritual and how it has been performed before. We discover how to do it *next* time. We discover something of the world the ritual belongs to and aims to transform. "Ritual knowledge," Jennings holds, "is gained by and through the body . . . not by detached observation or contemplation but through action."[35]

One has to think here of the kinds of knowing that come to persons through physical activity rather than through the interpretation of words and icons. Jennings uses dancing as an example, and we might also think of athletics, carpentry, weaving, or lovemaking. On the radio, Davie Johnson, manager of the New York Mets, speaks of things that a pitcher can know only through "muscle memory," and Jennings speaks of learning how to use a chalice by handling it, just as the axe he himself had used elsewhere to chop firewood taught his hands, arms, and shoulders how it needed to be swung.

With such doing-knowledge in mind, Jennings goes on to observe that

> Ritual knowledge is gained through the alteration of that which is to be known. Even if we reduce the field of the object of ritual knowledge to the ritual itself— that is, claim that that which I seek to know is the ritual or the ritual action itself—even then we must say that the exploratory "doing" is a doing which alters the ritual complex or its constituent parts in some way. . . . Ritual knowledge is gained not through detachment but through engagement—an engagement which does not leave things as they are but which alters and transforms them. . . . ritual knowledge is not "descriptive" but is prescriptive and/or ascriptive in character. . . . Marx's formula that it is important not so much to understand the world as to change it is one which also neatly summarizes this aspect of ritual action.[36]

Jennings offers no specific evidence for his claim that ritual knowledge alters what it comes to know, but in my view the claim is defensible for the reason that Jennings assumes: Ritual is neither a detached contemplation of the world nor a passive symbolization of it but is the performance of an act in which people confront one kind of power with another, and rehearse their own future. At the least, as Jennings points out, this will result in the ritual itself being transformed over time; but the implication is that the world of which the ritual is a part will also be changed.

*   *   *

The transformative action of rituals is coming more and more to prominence in recent analyses, stimulated most perhaps by the thinking of Victor Turner and Richard Schechner, his sometime collaborator. The index of a recently published symposium edited by Schechner with Willa Appel lists thirty-one places in the volume where transformation is discussed. Colin Turnbull, for example, says that transition and transformation are "two basic elements of any ritual" and that "the latter is essential to our full understanding of liminality."[37] Schechner speaks of "the deconstruction/reconstruction process that performers use to effect transformations of self,"[38] and Turner, especially in his earlier writings, was interested in a dialectic between ritual and social structure which contributed to the dynamic of socio-historical change.

Although some of Turner's thoughts about this subject invite criticism . . ., Turner's contribution to the understanding of ritual process is immense. The concept of liminality, which he broadened and deepened beyond its origin in Van Gennep, . . . has become indispensable.

Turner showed that "ritual is not necessarily a bastion of social conservatism; its symbols do not merely condense cherished sociocultural values. Rather, through its liminal processes, it holds the generating source of culture and structure."[39] He argued cogently that "liminality is the mother of invention."[40]

The idea, however, is not simply that ritual is a cornucopia of inventiveness or a factory of fantasies. Rather, this inventiveness is related dialectically to the powers and structures of society as they exist at the time of the ritual performance. This means that ritual stands in contradiction to society, while at the same time being a part of it. We might say that ritual embodies the principle of growth or dynamic process through which a society transcends itself, praising, evaluating, rebuking, and remolding life as it is presently lived. As Turner puts it, "performance is often a critique, direct or veiled, of the social life it grows out of, an evaluation (with lively possibilities of rejection) of the way society handles history."[41] It follows that

> cultural performances are not simple reflectors or expressions of culture or even of changing culture but may themselves be active agencies of change, representing the eye by which culture sees itself and the drawing board on which creative actors sketch out what they believe to be more apt or interesting "designs for living."[42]

Turner is certainly not the only scholar to entertain a view of ritual as innovative and transformative. Here, for example, is Erik Erikson:

> . . . it should be noted that there can be no prescription for either ritualization or ritual, for, far from being merely repetitive or familiar in the sense of habituation, any true ritualization, while ontogenetically grounded, is yet pervaded with the spontaneity of surprise: it is an unexpected renewal of a recognizable order in potential chaos. Ritualization thus depends on that blending of surprise and recognition which is the soul of creative interplay, reborn out of instinctual chaos, confusion of identity, and social anomie.[43]

Roland Delattre has correctly insisted that ritual action, whatever else it may be, is always political action:

> For in ritual action we not only seek to articulate the state of affairs as we experience it, we also exercise in ritual action our creative capacities to re-order that state of affairs. Rituals may celebrate and confirm the rhythms and shape of an established version of humanity and reality, but they may also celebrate and render articulate the shape and rhythms of a new emergent version.[44]

The "social magic" of rituals, their character as "transformative performance" (Turner) or simply "transformance" (Schechner),[45] is only partly the result of their power to envision a reordering of the world. It comes also from their power to expose society's injustices and contradictions. Turner speaks of ritual as "a *transformative* performance revealing major classifications, categories, and contradictions of cultural processes."[46] He rightly assumes that such revelations are themselves transformative, and further supposes, again rightly, that revelation through *performance* is particularly potent. The liminality of ritual is the power of transcendence, of no-saying, of expressing what society and culture deny, of unmasking pretension, of elevating persons and things of "low degree," of "putting down the mighty from their seats" (Luke 1:52–53). It is the power Shakespeare called imaginative, to "give to aery nothing a local habitation and a name."[47]

While it is the business of literature to give names (the right descriptive words), that of ritual is to give "local habitation." Performance makes present. Because it is performance and not verbal description or exhortation, ritual brings the far-away, the long-ago, and the not-yet into the here-and-now. Because it is performance, ritual produces its effects not simply in the minds but also in the bodies of its performers. When it is imbued with the spirit of liberty, ritual becomes part of the work through which a body politic (a people) throws off its chains. But it is not always so imbued, and the transformations it brings about are not always liberating.

* * *

We have already noticed that ritual, employed as a means for the transformation of society is a kind of "social magic." It is important to remember that the morality of magic is determined by its practitioners. Nothing in the nature of ritual per se insures that the social transformations achieved by it will necessarily be good ones, for this depends upon the aim and will of the performers.

The insight of most religions is that the performers in sacred rite are not limited to the human ones. Rituals invoke the participation of spirits, animals, deceased ancestors, or gods, not simply as *objects* of ritual attention but as performers in their own right. For them also, the ritual is a technique of communication and transformation, and they seek to use it for purposes in line with their own natures.

The ritual world is a *personal* one, not the impersonal realm postulated by science. It is a world in which personal agents direct their interactive performances toward the reordering of social relationships. This is a moral project through and through, in the sense that it is never morally neutral but always aimed at something desired. Ritual is the work of beings who are characterized by their capacity to *perform* and hence to fabricate a social world that is not simply given to them but is compounded of desires and actions that are subject to moral evaluation.

Since the transformative potential of rituals is very high and not always directed toward ethically justifiable ends, it is fearsome. The totalitarian uses of ritual in our own time (and before) have shown that it holds the power to transform people not only into creatures of freedom but also into destructive armies and mass murderers. If the latter is not to be our own fate, we must learn to employ rituals as part of a more beneficent magic aimed at the transformation of society toward ever greater justice, peace, and freedom. We must see to the redemption of our rituals.

NOTES

1. Turner, "Symbols and social experience" (1974), 10.
2. Grimes, *Beginnings* (1982), 45.
3. Farmer, "Bad blood, spoiled milk" (1988), 89–90.
4. These points have been much discussed in recent times. See especially the articles collected in Wilson, *Rationality* (1970); Ulin, *Understanding cultures* (1984), xi–xiii, 10–11, 171–72; Taylor, *Beyond explanation* (1986), 79 ff.
5. Langer, *Philosophy in a new key* (1942, 1948), 139.
6. Grimes, *Beginnings* (1982), 45.
7. Van Gennep, *The rites of passage* (1908, 1960), 13.
8. Grimes, *Beginnings* (1982), 47.
9. Grimes, *Beginnings* (1982), 45.
10. Van Gennep, *The rites of passage* (1908, 1960), 13.
11. See Frazer, *The new Golden Bough* (1890, 1959).
12. Wittgenstein, *Remarks* (1979), 7e.
13. Wittgenstein, *Remarks* (1979), 4e.
14. Langer, *Philosophy in a new key* (1942, 1948), 135–36.
15. O'Keefe, *Stolen lightning* (1982).
16. Bateson and Bateson, *Angels fear* (1987), 56.
17. Bateson and Bateson, *Angels fear* (1987), 56.
18. Bateson and Bateson, *Angels fear* (1987), 56.
19. Leach, "Ritualization in man" (1966), 524.
20. Leach, "Ritualization in man" (1966), 525.
21. Wittgenstein, *Remarks* (1979), 6e–7e.
22. Grimes, *Beginnings* (1982), 46.
23. Adapted from William Arrowsmith's translation of *The Bacchae*, in *Euripides V* (Chicago: The University of Chicago Press, 1959), 220.
24. Wink, *Violence and nonviolence* (1987).
25. Wink, *Unmasking the powers* (1986), 64.
26. Alexander, *Pentecostal possession* (1985), 21.
27. Mud Flower Collective, *God's fierce whimsy* (1985), 121.
28. Walens, *Feasting with cannibals* (1981); quoted in Turner, *The anthropology of performance* (1986), 148.

29. Wilson, M., "The wedding cakes" (1972), 195.
30. Wilson, M., "The wedding cakes" (1972), 196.
31. Wilson, M., "The wedding cakes" (1972), 197.
32. Peterson, "Wittgenstein's theory" (1987), 7.
33. Jennings, "On ritual knowledge" (1982), 113.
34. Jennings, "On ritual knowledge" (1982), 114.
35. Jennings, "On ritual knowledge" (1982), 114–15.
36. Jennings, "On ritual knowledge" (1982), 116–17.
37. Turnbull, "Liminality" (1990), 55.
38. Schechner and Appel, *By means of performance* (1990), 41. This topic is discussed in detail in Schechner, *Between theater and anthropology* (1985). Schechner identifies performers' process of self-transformation with what Turner calls "ritual process," but I think they are not the same.
39. Turner, *The anthropology of performance* (1986), 158. The following comment by Bobby Alexander is apt: "The primary value of Turner's theory properly understood is the recognition that ritual is not an 'epiphenomenon' but has 'ontological status'. . . . In other words, ritual does not merely mirror nor rest on the surface of more fundamental social processes that underlie or precede it; it is not simply symptomatic of more primary social activity. Rather, ritual is part of the process of social change, given its capacity to generate new, communitarian social arrangements. . . . " Alexander, *Victor Turner revisited* (1991), 19.
40. Turner, "Symbols and social experience" (1974), 10.
41. Turner, *The anthropology of performance* (1986), 22.
42. Turner, *The anthropology of performance* (1986), 24.
43. Erikson, *Toys and reasons* (1977), 113.
44. Delattre, "Ritual resourcefulness" (1978), 288.
45. Schechner, *Essays on performance theory* (1977).
46. Turner, *The anthropology of performance* (1986), 157; Turner's emphasis.
47. *A Midsummer Night's Dream* (V.1.16–17).

REFERENCES

Alexander, Bobby C. 1985. *Pentecostal possession and Grotowski's ritual projects as social protest: A critical assessment of Victor Turner's theory of "ritual antistructure" as an interpretive tool.* Unpublished dissertation. Columbia University, NY.

———. 1991. *Victor Turner revisited: Ritual as social change.* Atlanta, GA: Scholars Press. Academy Series, American Academy of Religion, no. 74.

Bateson, Gregory, and Mary Catherine Bateson. 1987. *Angels fear: Towards an epistemology of the sacred.* NY: Macmillan Publishing Co.

Delattre, Roland. 1978. Ritual resourcefulness and cultural pluralism. *Soundings* 61(3): 281–301.

Erikson, Erik. 1977. *Toys and reasons: Stages in the ritualization of experience.* New York: W. W. Norton.

Farmer, Paul. 1988. Bad blood, spoiled milk: Bodily fluids as moral barometers in rural Haiti. *American Ethnologist* 15 (February): 80–101.

Frazer, James G. 1890, 1959. *The new Golden Bough: A new abridgment of the classic work* Ed. Theodore H. Gaster. New York: Criterion Books.

Grimes, Ronald L. 1982. *Beginnings in ritual studies.* Lanham, MD: University Press of America.

Jennings, Theodore W. 1982. On ritual knowledge. *The Journal of Religion* 62(2): 111–27.

Langer, Suzanne. 1942, 1948. *Philosophy in a new key: A study in the symbolism of reason, rite, and art.* New York: New American Library.

Leach, Edmund R. 1966. Ritualization in man in relation to conceptual and social development. *The Philosophical Transactions of the Royal Society of London*, 29th series, 251:403–8.

Malinowski, Bronislaw. 1954. *Magic, science and religion and other essays.* Garden City, NY: Doubleday.

Mud Flower Collective. 1985. *God's fierce whimsy: Christian feminism and theological education.* New York: The Pilgrim Press.

O'Keefe, Daniel L. 1982. *Stolen lightning: The social theory of magic.* New York: Continuum Books.

Peterson, Thomas V. 1987. Wittgenstein's theory of language and ritual change. Paper written for the Ritual Studies Group, American Academy of Religion Annual Meeting, Dec. 5–8, in Boston.

Schechner, Richard. 1977. *Essays on performance theory, 1970–1976.* New York: Drama Book Specialists.

———. 1985. *Between theater and anthropology.* Illustrated. Foreword Victor Turner. Philadelphia: The University of Pennsylvania Press.

Schechner, Richard, and Willa Appel, eds. 1990. *By means of performance: Intercultural studies of theatre and ritual.* New York: Cambridge University Press.

Simonton, Carl. 1975. Belief systems and management of the emotional aspects of malignancy. *The Journal of Transpersonal Psychology* 7(1): 29–47.

Turnbull, Colin. 1990. Liminality: A synthesis of subjective and objective experience. Chapter 3 in *By means of performance.* Ed. Richard Schechner and Willa Appel. New York: Cambridge University Press.

Turner, Victor. 1974. Symbols and social experience in religious ritual. *Studia Missionalia* 23: 1–21.

———. 1986. *The anthropology of performance.* New York: Performing Arts Journal Publications.

Tylor, Edward B. 1871, 1958. *Primitive culture: Researches into the development of mythology, philosophy, religion, art and custom.* 2 vols. Gloucester, MA: Smith.

Ulin, Robert C. 1984. *Understanding cultures: Perspectives in anthropology and social theory.* Austin: University of Texas Press.

Van Gennep, Arnold. 1908, 1960. *The rites of passage.* Trans. Monika B. Vizedom and Gabrielle L. Caffee. Chicago: University of Chicago Press.

Walens, Stanley. 1981. *Feasting with cannibals: An essay on Kwakiuti cosmology.* Princeton: Princeton University Press.

Wilson, Bryan R., ed. 1970. *Rationality.* New York: Harper & Row.

Wilson, Monica. 1972. The wedding cakes: A study of ritual change. In *The interpretation of ritual: Essays in honour of I. A. Richards.* Ed. J. S. La Fontaine, 187–201. London: Tavistock.

Wink, Walter. 1986. *Unmasking the powers: The invisible forces that determine human existence.* Philadelphia: Fortress Press.

———. 1987. *Violence and nonviolence in South Africa: Jesus' third way.* Philadelphia: New Society Publishers.

Wittgenstein, Ludwig. 1969. *On certainty.* Ed. G. E. M. Anscombe and G. H. von Wright. New York: Harper & Row.

———. 1979. *Remarks on Frazer's Golden Bough.* Atlantic Highlands, NJ: Humanities Press.

Ritual, Magic, and the Sacred

Emile Durkheim

Facts of publication: *Durkheim, Emile. 1915. "Definition of Religious Phenomena and of Religion" from* The Elementary Forms of the Religious Life: A Study in Religious Sociology, *36–45, 47. Translated by Joseph Ward Swain. London: Allen & Unwin. Reprinted with the permission of Routledge.*

Durkheim's conception of ritual construes it as half of a whole; the other half is belief. Together, rites and beliefs constitute religion. He also understands religion oppositionally. As the domain of the sacred, religion is antithetical to another domain, the profane (in this respect Eliade and van Gennep hold similar views). A third polarity is essential to Durkheim's conception: religion versus magic. Even though both religion and magic employ ritual means, religion, claims Durkheim, generates a "church," by which he means a collective, or social, expression that is not typical of magic.

Contemporary scholars often refuse to follow Durkheim's lead in defining ritual in a way that makes it essentially religious. See, for instance, Sally F. Moore and Barbara G. Myerhoff, ed., "Introduction." Secular Ritual. Assen, The Netherlands: Van Gorcum, 1977.

About the author: Dates: *1858–1917, Lorraine, France.* **Education:** *Ecole Normale Superieure.* **Field(s):** *sociology; philosophy.* **Career:** *University of Bordeaux, 1887–1902; Sorbonne, 1903–1917.* **Publications:** The Rules of Sociological Method *(1938 [1895]);* Suicide *(1952 [1897]);* Primitive Classification *(University of Chicago, 1963);* Durkheim on Religion: A Selection of Readings with Bibliographies and Introductory Remarks, *edited by W. S. F. Pickering (Routledge, 1975);* The Elementary Forms of the Religious Life: A Study in Religious Sociology *(1912 [1915 first English translation]; Free Press, 1965; second edition, 1976).*

Religious phenomena are naturally arranged in two fundamental categories: beliefs and rites. The first are states of opinion, and consist in representations; the second are determined modes of action. Between these two classes of facts there is all the difference which separates thought from action.

The rites can be defined and distinguished from other human practices, moral practices, for example, only by the special nature of their object. A moral rule prescribes certain manners of acting to us, just as a rite does, but which are addressed to a different class of objects. So it is the object of the rite which must be characterized, if we are to characterize the rite itself. Now it is in the beliefs that the special nature of this object is expressed. It is possible to define the rite only after we have defined the belief.

All known religious beliefs, whether simple or complex, present one common characteristic: they presuppose a classification of all the things, real and ideal, of which men think, into two classes or opposed groups, generally designated by two distinct terms which are translated well enough by the words *profane* and *sacred* (*profane, sacré*). This division of the world into two domains, the one containing all that is sacred, the other all that is profane, is the distinctive trait of religious thought; the beliefs, myths, dogmas and legends are either representations or systems of representations which express the nature of sacred things, the virtues and powers which are attributed to them, or their relations with each other and with profane things. But by sacred things one must not understand simply those personal beings which are called gods or spirits; a rock, a tree, a spring, a pebble, a piece of wood, a house, in a word, anything can be sacred. A rite can have this character; in fact, the rite does not exist which does not have it to a certain degree. There are words, expressions and formulæ which can be pronounced only by the mouths of consecrated persons; there are gestures and movements which everybody cannot perform. If the Vedic sacrifice has had such an efficacy that, according to mythology, it was the creator of the gods, and not merely a means of winning their favour, it is because it possessed a virtue comparable to that of the most sacred beings. The circle of sacred objects cannot be determined, then, once for all. Its extent varies infinitely, according to the different religions. That is how Buddhism is a religion: in default of gods, it admits the existence of sacred things, namely, the four noble truths and the practices derived from them.[1]

One might be tempted. . . to define [sacred things] by the place they are generally assigned in the hierarchy of things. They are naturally considered superior in dignity and power to profane things, and particularly to man, when he is only a man and has nothing sacred about him. One thinks of himself as occupying an inferior and dependent position in relation to them; and surely this conception is not without some truth. Only there is nothing in it which is really characteristic of the sacred. It is not enough that one thing be subordinated to another for the second to be sacred in regard to the first. Slaves are inferior to their masters, subjects to their king, soldiers to their leaders, the miser to his gold, the man ambitious for power to the hands which keep it from him; but if it is sometimes said of a man that he makes a religion of those beings or things whose eminent value and superiority to himself he thus recognizes, it is clear that in any case the word is taken in a metaphorical sense, and that there is nothing in these relations which is really religious.[2]

On the other hand, it must not be lost to view that there are sacred things of every degree, and that there are some in relation to which a man feels himself relatively at his ease. An amulet has a sacred character, yet the respect which it inspires is nothing exceptional. Even before his gods, a man is not always in such a marked state of inferiority; for it very frequently happens that he exercises a veritable physical constraint upon them to obtain what he desires. He beats the fetish with which he is not contented, but only to reconcile himself with it again, if in the end it shows itself more docile to the wishes of its adorer.[3] To have rain, he throws stones into the spring or sacred lake where the god of rain is thought to reside; he believes that by this means he forces him to come out and show himself.[4] Moreover, if it is true that man depends upon his gods, this dependence is reciprocal. The gods also have need of man; without offerings and sacrifices they

would die. We shall even have occasion to show that this dependence of the gods upon their worshippers is maintained even in the most idealistic religions.

But if a purely hierarchic distinction is a criterion at once too general and too imprecise, there is nothing left with which to characterize the sacred in its relation to the profane except their heterogeneity. However, this heterogeneity is sufficient to characterize this classification of things and to distinguish it from all others, because it is very particular: *it is absolute.* In all the history of human thought there exists no other example of two categories of things so profoundly differentiated or so radically opposed to one another. The traditional opposition of good and bad is nothing beside this; for the good and the bad are only two opposed species of the same class, namely, morals, just as sickness and health are two different aspects of the same order of facts, life, while the sacred and the profane have always and everywhere been conceived by the human mind as two distinct classes, as two worlds between which there is nothing in common. The forces which play in one are not simply those which are met with in the other, but a little stronger; they are of a different sort. In different religions, this opposition has been conceived in different ways. Here, to separate these two sorts of things, it has seemed sufficient to localize them in different parts of the physical universe; there, the first have been put into an ideal and transcendental world, while the material world is left in full possession of the others. But howsoever much the forms of the contrast may vary,[5] the fact of the contrast is universal.

This is not equivalent to saying that a being can never pass from one of these worlds into the other: but the manner in which this passage is effected, when it does take place, puts into relief the essential duality of the two kingdoms. In fact, it implies a veritable metamorphosis. This is notably demonstrated by the initiation rites, such as they are practised by a multitude of peoples. This initiation is a long series of ceremonies with the object of introducing the young man into the religious life: for the first time, he leaves the purely profane world where he passed his first infancy, and enters into the world of sacred things. Now this change of state is thought of, not as a simple and regular development of pre-existent germs, but as a transformation . . . of the whole being. It is said that at this moment the young man dies, that the person that he was ceases to exist, and that another is instantly substituted for it. He is reborn under a new form. Appropriate ceremonies are felt to bring about this death and re-birth, which are not understood in a merely symbolic sense, but are taken literally.[6] Does this not prove that between the profane being which he was and the religious being which he becomes, there is a break of continuity?

This heterogeneity is even so complete that it frequently degenerates into a veritable antagonism. The two worlds are not only conceived of as separate, but as even hostile and jealous rivals of each other. Since men cannot fully belong to one except on condition of leaving the other completely, they are exhorted to withdraw themselves completely from the profane world, in order to lead an exclusively religious life. Hence comes the monasticism which is artificially organized outside of and apart from the natural environment in which the ordinary man leads the life of this world, in a different one, closed to the first, and nearly its contrary. Hence comes the mystic asceticism whose object is to root out from man all the attachment for the profane world that remains in him. From that come all the forms of religious suicide, the logical working-out of this asceticism; for the only manner of fully escaping the profane life is, after all, to forsake all life.

The opposition of these two classes manifests itself outwardly with a visible sign by which we can easily recognize this very special classification, wherever it exists. Since the idea of the sacred is always and everywhere separated from the idea of the profane in the thought of men, and since we picture a sort of logical chasm between the two, the mind irresistibly refuses to allow the two corresponding things to be confounded, or even to be merely put in contact with each other; for such a promiscuity, or even too direct a contiguity, would contradict too violently the dissociation of these ideas in the mind. The sacred thing is *par excellence* that which the profane should not touch, and cannot touch with impunity. To be sure, this interdiction cannot go so far as to make all communication between the two worlds impossible; for if the profane could in no way enter into relations with the sacred, this latter could be good for nothing. But, in addition to the fact that this establishment of relations is always a

delicate operation in itself, demanding great precautions and a more or less complicated initiation,[7] it is quite impossible, unless the profane is to lose its specific characteristics and become sacred after a fashion and to a certain degree itself. The two classes cannot even approach each other and keep their own nature at the same time.

Thus we arrive at the first criterion of religious beliefs. Undoubtedly there are secondary species within these two fundamental classes which, in their turn, are more or less incompatible with each other.[8] But the real characteristic of religious phenomena is that they always suppose a bipartite division of the whole universe, known and knowable, into two classes which embrace all that exists, but which radically exclude each other. Sacred things are those which the interdictions protect and isolate; profane things, those to which these interdictions are applied and which must remain at a distance from the first. Religious beliefs are the representations which express the nature of sacred things and the relations which they sustain, either with each other or with profane things. Finally, rites are the rules of conduct which prescribe how a man should comport himself in the presence of these sacred objects.

When a certain number of sacred things sustain relations of co-ordination or subordination with each other in such a way as to form a system having a certain unity, but which is not comprised within any other system of the same sort, the totality of these beliefs and their corresponding rites constitutes a religion. From this definition it is seen that a religion is not necessarily contained within one sole and single idea, and does not proceed from one unique principle which, though varying according to the circumstances under which it is applied, is nevertheless at bottom always the same: it is rather a whole made up of distinct and relatively individualized parts. Each homogeneous group of sacred things, or even each sacred thing of some importance, constitutes a centre of organization about which gravitate a group of beliefs and rites, or a particular cult; there is no religion, howsoever unified it may be, which does not recognize a plurality of sacred things. Even Christianity, at least in its Catholic form, admits, in addition to the divine personality which, incidentally, is triple as well as one, the Virgin, angels, saints, souls of the dead, etc. Thus a religion cannot be reduced to one single cult generally, but rather consists in a system of cults, each endowed with a certain autonomy. Also, this autonomy is variable. Sometimes they are arranged in a hierarchy, and subordinated to some predominating cult, into which they are finally absorbed; but sometimes, also, they are merely rearranged and united. . . .

At the same time we find the explanation of how there can be groups of religious phenomena which do not belong to any special religion; it is because they have not been, or are no longer, a part of any religious system. If, for some special reason, one of the cults of which we just spoke happens to be maintained while the group of which it was a part disappears, it survives only in a disintegrated condition. That is what has happened to many agrarian cults which have survived themselves as folk-lore. In certain cases, it is not even a cult, but a simple ceremony or particular rite which persists in this way.[9]

Although this definition is only preliminary, it permits us to see in what terms the problem which necessarily dominates the science of religions should be stated. When we believed that sacred beings could be distinguished from others merely by the greater intensity of the powers attributed to them, the question of how men came to imagine them was sufficiently simple: it was enough to demand which forces had, because of their exceptional energy, been able to strike the human imagination forcefully enough to inspire religious sentiments. But if, as we have sought to establish, sacred things differ in nature from profane things, if they have a wholly different essence, then the problem is more complex. For we must first of all ask what has been able to lead men to see in the world two heterogeneous and incompatible worlds, though nothing in sensible experience seems able to suggest the idea of so radical a duality to them.

*   *   *

However, this definition is not yet complete, for it is equally applicable to two sorts of facts which, while being related to each other, must be distinguished nevertheless: these are magic and religion.

Magic, too, is made up of beliefs and rites. Like religion, it has its myths and its dogmas; only they are more elementary, undoubtedly because, seeking technical and utilitarian ends, it does not waste its time in pure speculation. It has its ceremonies, sacrifices, lustrations, prayers, chants and dances as well. The beings which the magician invokes and the forces which he throws in play are not merely of the same nature as the forces and beings to which religion addresses itself; very frequently, they are identically the same. Thus, even with the most inferior societies, the souls of the dead are essentially sacred things, and the object of religious rites. But at the same time, they play a considerable rôle in magic. In Australia [10] as well as in Melanesia,[11] in Greece as well as among the Christian peoples,[12] the souls of the dead, their bones and their hair, are among the intermediaries used the most frequently by the magician. Demons are also a common instrument for magic action. Now these demons are also beings surrounded with interdictions; they too are separated and live in a world apart, so that it is frequently difficult to distinguish them from the gods properly so-called.[13] Moreover, in Christianity itself, is not the devil a fallen god, or even leaving aside all question of his origin, does he not have a religious character from the mere fact that the hell of which he has charge is something indispensable to the Christian religion? There are even some regular and official deities who are invoked by the magician. Sometimes these are the gods of a foreign people; for example, Greek magicians called upon Egyptian, Assyrian or Jewish gods. Sometimes, they are even national gods: Hecate and Diana were the object of a magic cult; the Virgin, Christ and the saints have been utilized in the same way by Christian magicians.[14]

Then will it be necessary to say that magic is hardly distinguishable from religion; that magic is full of religion just as religion is full of magic, and consequently that it is impossible to separate them and to define the one without the other? It is difficult to sustain this thesis, because of the marked repugnance of religion for magic, and in return, the hostility of the second towards the first. Magic takes a sort of professional pleasure in profaning holy things;[15] in its rites, it performs the contrary of the religious ceremony.[16] On its side, religion, when it has not condemned and prohibited magic rites, has always looked upon them with disfavour. As Hubert and Mauss have remarked, there is something thoroughly anti-religious in the doings of the magician.[17] Whatever relations there may be between these two sorts of institutions, it is difficult to imagine their not being opposed somewhere; and it is still more necessary for us to find where they are differentiated, as we plan to limit our researches to religion, and to stop at the point where magic commences.

Here is how a line of demarcation can be traced between these two domains.

The really religious beliefs are always common to a determined group, which makes profession of adhering to them and of practising the rites connected with them. They are not merely received individually by all the members of this group; they are something belonging to the group, and they make its unity. The individuals which compose it feel themselves united to each other by the simple fact that they have a common faith. A society whose members are united by the fact that they think in the same way in regard to the sacred world and its relations with the profane world, and by the fact that they translate these common ideas into common practices, is what is called a Church. In all history, we do not find a single religion without a Church. Sometimes the Church is strictly national, sometimes it passes the frontiers; sometimes it embraces an entire people (Rome, Athens, the Hebrews), sometimes it embraces only a part of them (the Christian societies since the advent of Protestantism); sometimes it is directed by a corps of priests, sometimes it is almost completely devoid of any official directing body.[18] But wherever we observe the religious life, we find that it has a definite group as its foundation. Even the so-called private cults, such as the domestic cult or the cult of a corporation, satisfy this condition; for they are always celebrated by a group, the family or the corporation. Moreover, even these particular religions are ordinarily only special forms of a more general religion which embraces all;[19] these restricted Churches are in reality only chapels of a vaster Church which, by reason of this very extent, merits this name still more.[20]

It is quite another matter with magic. To be sure, the belief in magic is always more or less general; it is very frequently diffused in large masses of the population, and there are even peoples where it has as many adherents as the real religion. But it does not result in binding together those who adhere to it, nor in uniting them into a group leading a common life. *There is no Church of magic.* Between the magician and the individuals who consult him, as between these individuals themselves, there are no lasting bonds which make them members of the same moral community, comparable to that formed by the believers in the same god or the observers of the same cult. The magician has a clientele and not a Church, and it is very possible that his clients have no other relations between each other, or even do not know each other; even the relations which they have with him are generally accidental and transient; they are just like those of a sick man with his physician. The official and public character with which he is sometimes invested changes nothing in this situation; the fact that he works openly does not unite him more regularly or more durably to those who have recourse to his services.

It is true that in certain cases, magicians form societies among themselves: it happens that they assemble more or less periodically to celebrate certain rites in common; it is well known what a place these assemblies of witches hold in European folk-lore. But it is to be remarked that these associations are in no way indispensable to the working of the magic; they are even rare and rather exceptional. The magician has no need of uniting himself to his fellows to practise his art. More frequently, he is a recluse; in general, far from seeking society, he flees it. "Even in regard to his colleagues, he always keeps his personal independence."[21] Religion, on the other hand, is inseparable from the idea of a Church. From this point of view, there is an essential difference between magic and religion. But what is especially important is that when these societies of magic are formed, they do not include all the adherents to magic, but only the magicians; the laymen, if they may be so called, that is to say, those for whose profit the rites are celebrated, in fine, those who represent the worshippers in the regular cults, are excluded. Now the magician is for magic what the priest is for religion, but a college of priests is not a Church, any more than a religious congregation which should devote itself to some particular saint in the shadow of a cloister, would be a particular cult. A Church is not a fraternity of priests; it is a moral community formed by all the believers in a single faith, laymen as well as priests. But magic lacks any such community.[22] . . .

Thus we arrive at the following definition: *A religion is a unified system of beliefs and practices relative to sacred things, that is to say, things set apart and forbidden—beliefs and practices which unite into one single moral community called a Church, all those who adhere to them.* The second element which thus finds a place in our definition is no less essential than the first; for by showing that the idea of religion is inseparable from that of the Church, it makes it clear that religion should be an eminently collective thing.[23]

NOTES

1. Not to mention the sage and the saint who practise these truths and who for that reason are sacred.
2. This is not saying that these relations cannot take a religious character. But they do not do so necessarily.
3. Schultze, *Fetichismus*, p. 129.
4. Examples of these usages will be found in Frazer, *Golden Bough*, 2 edit., I, pp. 81 ff.
5. The conception according to which the profane is opposed to the sacred, just as the irrational is to the rational, or the intelligible is to the mysterious, is only one of the forms under which this opposition is expressed. Science being once constituted, it has taken a profane character, especially in the eyes of the Christian religions; from that it appears as though it could not be applied to sacred things.
6. See Frazer, *On Some Ceremonies of the Central Australian Tribes* in *Australian Association for the Advancement of Science*, 1901, pp. 313 ff. This conception is also of an extreme generality. In India, the simple participation in the sacrificial act has the same effects; the sacrificer, by the mere act of entering within the circle of sacred things, changes his personality. (See, Hubert and Mauss, *Essai sur le Sacrifice* in the *Année Sociologique*, II, p. 101.)
7. See what was said earlier of the initiation.
8. We shall point out below how, for example, certain species of sacred things exist, between which there is an incompatibility as all-exclusive as that between the sacred and the profane (Bk. III, ch. v, § 4).
9. This is the case with certain marriage and funeral rites, for example.
10. See Spencer and Gillen, *Native Tribes of Central Australia*, pp. 534 ff.: *Northern Tribes of Central Australia*, p. 463; Howitt, *Native Tribes of S.E. Australia*, pp. 359–361.
11. See Codrington, *The Melanesians*, ch. xii.
12. See Hubert, art. *Magia* in *Dictionnaire des Antiquités*.
13. For example, in Melanesia, the *tindalo* is a spirit, now religious, now magic (Codrington, pp. 125 ff., 194 ff.).
14. See Hubert and Mauss, *Théorie Générale de la Magie*, in *Année Sociologique*, vol. VII, pp. 83–84.
15. For example, the host is profaned in the black mass.
16. One turns his back to the altar, or goes around the altar commencing by the left instead of by the right.
17. *Loc. cit.*, p. 19.
18. Undoubtedly it is rare that a ceremony does not have some director at the moment when it is celebrated; even in the most crudely organized societies there are generally certain men whom the importance of their social position points out to exercise a directing influence over the religious life (for example, the chiefs of the local groups of certain Australian societies). But this attribution of functions is still very uncertain.
19. At Athens, the gods to whom the domestic cult was addressed were only specialized forms of the gods of the city (Ζεύς κτήσιος, Ζεύς ἑρκεῖ ος). In the same way, in the Middle Ages, the patrons of the guilds were saints of the calendar.
20. For the name Church is ordinarily applied only to a group whose common beliefs refer to a circle of more special affairs.
21. Hubert and Mauss, *loc. cit.*, p. 18.
22. Robertson Smith has already pointed out that magic is opposed to religion, as the individual to the social (*The Religion of the Semites*, 2 edit., pp. 264–265). Also, in thus distinguishing magic from religion, we do not mean to establish a break of continuity between them. The frontiers between the two domains are frequently uncertain.
23. It is by this that our present definition is connected to the one we have already proposed in the *Année Sociologique*. In this other work, we defined religious beliefs exclusively by their obligatory character; but this obligation evidently comes from the fact that these beliefs are the possession of a group which imposes them upon its members. The two definitions are thus in a large part the same. If we have thought it best to propose a new one, it is because the first was too formal, and neglected the contents of the religious representations too much.

Ritual and Myth

MIRCEA ELIADE

Facts of publication: *Eliade, Mircea. 1959 (1949). "Ritual and Myth" (originally titled "The Symbolism of the Center"), from* Cosmos and History: The Myth of the Eternal Return, *12–27. Translated by Willard R. Trask. New York: Harper and Row. Copyright 1953 and renewed © 1987 by Harper and Row, Publishers, Inc. Copyright 1954, © 1971, 1974, 1991 by Princeton University Press. Reprinted with the permission of Bollingen Foundation, Princeton University Press.*

This brief selection from Mircea Eliade's Cosmos and History: The Myth of the Eternal Return *is but one among his many presentations of what has become a classic theory of ritual. In this presentation Eliade focuses first on the symbolism of the center showing through numerous examples the sacredness of places designated as centers. The center is the world axis, the place at which earth contacts heaven and hell, the place at which the creation of the world began. Eliade presents examples of mountains, temples, palaces, and cities, showing how each is connected with creation, cosmic orientation, or the gods. The center is, in Eliade's terms, "the zone of the sacred, the zone of absolute reality."*

Eliade argues that creation, the gods, and absolute reality serve as models for human action. According to Eliade ritual amounts to a repetition of the acts of the gods. Eliade says that "every ritual has a divine model, an archetype." Thus every rite is a symbolic return to the time and place of the origin. Every rite takes place in the beginning. Through ritual, human beings realize what is real and meaningful. As narrative accounts of the acts of creation, myths often serve as models for ritual.

Eliade's theory of ritual has been among the most influential in the academic study of religion, yet it has its critics. See, for example, Jonathan Z. Smith's "The Wobbling Pivot," in his Map Is Not Territory: Studies in the History of Religions *(Leiden: E. J. Brill, 1978) and chapter one of his* To Take Place: Toward Theory in Ritual *(Chicago: University of Chicago Press, 1987).*

About the author: Dates: *1907–1986, Bucharest, Romania.* **Education:** *M.A., University of Bucharest; Ph.D., University of Bucharest.* **Field(s):** *history and phenomenology of religions.* **Career:** *Assistant Professor of Metaphysics, 1933–1939, University of Bucharest; Visiting Professor, 1946–1949, then Professor of the History of Religions, 1956–61, Ecole des Hautes Etudes, The Sorbonne; Distinguished Service Professor, History of Religions, 1962–86, University of Chicago.* **Publications:** Cosmos and History: The Myth of the Eternal Return *(Harper & Row, 1949 [1954, 1959]);* Patterns in Comparative Religion *(Sheed, 1958);* Myth and Reality *(Harper, 1963);* Shamanism *(Princeton University, 1964);* From Primitives to Zen *(Harper, 1967);* The Quest *(University of Chicago, 1969);* No Souvenirs *(Harper, 1977);* Histoire des Croyances et des Idées Religieuses *(Payot, 1979);* The Forbidden Forest *(University of Notre Dame, 1978);* Autobiography *(Harper, 1981).*

Paralleling the archaic belief in the celestial archetypes of cities and temples, and even more fully attested by documents, there is, we find, another series of beliefs, which refer to their being invested with the prestige of the Center. . . . The architectonic symbolism of the Center may be formulated as follows:

1. The Sacred Mountain—where heaven and earth meet—is situated at the center of the world.

2. Every temple or palace—and, by extension, every sacred city or royal residence—is a Sacred Mountain, thus becoming a Center.

3. Being an *axis mundi*, the sacred city or temple is re-

garded as the meeting point of heaven, earth, and hell.

A few examples will illustrate each of these symbols:

1. According to Indian beliefs, Mount Meru rises at the center of the world, and above it shines the polestar. The Ural-Altaic peoples also know of a central mountain, Sumeru, to whose summit the polestar is fixed. Iranian beliefs hold that the sacred mountain Haraberezaiti (Elburz) is situated at the center of the earth and is linked with heaven.[1] The Buddhist population of Laos, north of Siam, know of Mount Zinnalo, at the center of the world. In the *Edda*, Himinbjorg, as its name indicates, is a "celestial mountain"; it is here that the rainbow (Bifrost) reaches the dome of the sky. Similar beliefs are found among the Finns, the Japanese, and other peoples. We are reminded that for the Semangs of the Malay Peninsula an immense rock, Batu-Ribn, rises at the center of the world; above it is hell. In past times, a tree trunk on Batu-Ribn rose into the sky.[2] Hell, the center of the earth, and the "gate" of the sky are, then, situated on the same axis, and it is along this axis that passage from one cosmic region to another was effected. We should hesitate to credit the authenticity of this cosmological theory among the Semang pygmies if we did not have evidence that the same theory already existed in outline during the prehistoric period.[3] According to Mesopotamian beliefs, a central mountain joins heaven and earth; it is the Mount of the Lands,[4] the connection between territories. Properly speaking, the ziggurat was a cosmic mountain, i.e., a symbolic image of the cosmos, the seven stories representing the seven planetary heavens (as at Borsippa) or having the colors of the world (as at Ur).

Mount Tabor, in Palestine, could mean *tabbūr*, i.e., navel, *omphalos*. Mount Gerizim, in the center of Palestine, was undoubtedly invested with the prestige of the Center, for it is called "navel of the earth" (*tabbūr ereṣ*; cf. Judges 9: 37: ". . . See there come people down by the middle [Heb., navel] of the land. . . ."). A tradition preserved by Peter Comestor relates that at the summer solstice the sun casts no shadow on the "Fountain of Jacob" (near Gerizim). And indeed, Peter continues, "sunt qui dicunt locum illum esse umbilicum terrae nostrae habitabilis." Palestine, being the highest country—because it was near to the summit of the cosmic mountain—was not covered by the Deluge. A rabbinic text says: "The land of Israel was not submerged by the deluge."[5] For Christians, Golgotha was situated at the center of the world, since it was the summit of the cosmic mountain and at the same time the place where Adam had been created and buried. Thus the blood of the Saviour falls upon Adam's skull, buried precisely at the foot of the Cross, and redeems him. The belief that Golgotha is situated at the center of the world is preserved in the folklore of the Eastern Christians.[6]

2. The names of the Babylonian temples and sacred towers themselves testify to their assimilation to the cosmic mountain: "Mount of the House," "House of the Mount of All Lands," "Mount of Tempests," "Link Between Heaven and Earth."[7] A cylinder from the period of King Gudea says that "The bed-chamber [of the god] which he built was [like] the cosmic mountain. . . ."[8] Every Oriental city was situated at the center of the world. Babylon was a *Bāb-ilāni*, a "gate of the gods," for it was there that the gods descended to earth. In the capital of the Chinese sovereign, the gnomon must cast no shadow at noon on the day of the summer solstice. Such a capital is, in effect, at the center of the universe, close to the miraculous tree (*kien-mu*), at the meeting place of the three cosmic zones: heaven, earth, and hell.[9] The Javanese temple of Borobudur is itself an image of the cosmos, and is built like an artificial mountain (as were the ziggurats). Ascending it, the pilgrim approaches the center of the world, and, on the highest terrace, breaks from one plane to another, transcending profane, breaks from one plane to another, transcending profane, heterogeneous space and entering a "pure region." Cities and sacred places are assimilated to the summits of cosmic mountains. This is why Jerusalem and Zion were not submerged by the Deluge. According to Islamic tradition, the highest point on earth is the Kaaba, because "the polestar proves that . . . it lies over against the center of heaven."[10]

3. Finally, because of its situation at the center of the cosmos, the temple or the sacred city is always the meeting point of the three cosmic regions: heaven, earth, and hell. *Dur-an-ki*, "Bond of Heaven and Earth," was the name given to the sanctuaries of Nippur and Larsa, and doubtless to that of Sippara. Babylon had many names, among them

"House of the Base of Heaven and Earth," "Bond of Heaven and Earth." But it is always Babylon that is the scene of the connection between the earth and the lower regions, for the city had been built upon *bāb apsī*, the "Gate of the Apsu"[11]—*apsu* designating the waters of chaos before the Creation. We find the same tradition among the Hebrews. The rock of Jerusalem reached deep into the subterranean waters (*tehōm*). The Mishnah says that the Temple is situated exactly above the *tehōm* (Hebrew equivalent of *apsu*). And just as in Babylon there was the "gate of the *apsu*," the rock of the Temple in Jerusalem contained the "mouth of the *tehōm*."[12] We find similar conceptions in the Indo-European world. Among the Romans, for example, the *mundus*—that is, the trench dug around the place where a city was to be founded—constitutes the point where the lower regions and the terrestrial world meet. "When the *mundus* is open it is as if the gates of the gloomy infernal gods were open," says Varro (cited by Macrobius, *Saturnalia*, I, 16, 18). The Italic temple was the zone where the upper (divine), terrestrial, and subterranean worlds intersected.

The summit of the cosmic mountain is not only the highest point of the earth; it is also the earth's navel, the point at which the Creation began. There are even instances in which cosmological traditions explain the symbolism of the Center in terms which might well have been borrowed from embryology. "The Holy One created the world like an embryo. As the embryo proceeds from the navel onwards, so God began to create the world from its navel onwards and from there it was spread out in different directions." The *Yoma* affirms: "The world was created beginning from Zion."[13] In the *Ṛg-Veda* (for example X, 149), the universe is conceived as spreading from a central point.[14] The creation of man, which answers to the cosmogony, likewise took place at a central point, at the center of the world. According to Mesopotamian tradition, man was formed at the "navel of the earth" in *uzu* (flesh), *sar* (bond), *ki* (place, earth), where *Dur-an-ki*, the "Bond of Heaven and Earth," is also situated. Ormazd creates the primordial ox Evagdāth, and the primordial man, Gajōmard, at the center of the earth.[15] Paradise, where Adam was created from clay, is, of course, situated at the center of the cosmos. Paradise was the navel of the Earth and, according to a Syrian tradition, was established on a mountain higher than all others. According to the Syrian *Book of the Cave of Treasures*, Adam was created at the center of the earth, at the same spot where the Cross of Christ was later to be set up. The same traditions have been preserved by Judaism. The Jewish apocalypse and a midrash state that Adam was formed in Jerusalem.[16] Adam being buried at the very spot where he was created, i.e., at the center of the world, on Golgotha, the blood of the Saviour—as we have seen—will redeem him too.

The symbolism of the Center is considerably more complex, but the few aspects to which we have referred will suffice for our purpose. We may add that the same symbolism survived in the Western world down to the threshold of modern times. The very ancient conception of the temple as the *imago mundi*, the idea that the sanctuary reproduces the universe in its essence, passed into the religious architecture of Christian Europe: the basilica of the first centuries of our era, like the medieval cathedral,[17] symbolically reproduces the Celestial Jerusalem. As to the symbolism of the mountain, of the Ascension, and of the "Quest for the Center," they are clearly attested in medieval literature, and appear, though only by allusion, in certain literary works of recent centuries.[18]

The center, then, is pre-eminently the zone of the sacred, the zone of absolute reality. Similarly, all the other symbols of absolute reality (trees of life and immortality, Fountain of Youth, etc.) are also situated at a center. The road leading to the center is a "difficult road" (*dūrohaṇa*), and this is verified at every level of reality: difficult convolutions of a temple (as at Borobudur); pilgrimage to sacred places (Mecca, Hardwar, Jerusalem); danger-ridden voyages of the heroic expeditions in search of the Golden Fleece, the Golden Apples, the Herb of Life; wanderings in labyrinths; difficulties of the seeker for the road to the self, to the "center" of his being, and so on. The road is arduous, fraught with perils, because it is, in fact, a rite of the passage from the profane to the sacred, from the ephemeral and illusory to reality and eternity, from death to life, from man to the divinity. Attaining the center is equivalent to a consecration, an initiation; yesterday's profane and illusory existence gives place to a new, to a life that is real, enduring, and effective.

If the act of the Creation realizes the passage from

the nonmanifest to the manifest or, to speak cosmologically, from chaos to cosmos; if the Creation took place from a center; if, consequently, all the varieties of being, from the inanimate to the living, can attain existence only in an area dominantly sacred—all this beautifully illuminates for us the symbolism of sacred cities (centers of the world), the geomantic theories that govern the foundation of towns, the conceptions that justify the rites accompanying their building. We studied these construction rites, and the theories which they imply, in an earlier work,[19] and to this we refer the reader. Here we shall only emphasize two important propositions:

1. Every creation repeats the pre-eminent cosmogonic act, the Creation of the world.

2. Consequently, whatever is founded has its foundation at the center of the world (since, as we know, the Creation itself took place from a center).

Among the many examples at hand, we shall choose only one. . . . In India, before a single stone is laid, "The astrologer shows what spot in the foundation is exactly above the head of the snake that supports the world. The mason fashions a little wooden peg from the wood of the Khadira tree, and with a coconut drives the peg into the ground at this particular spot, in such a way as to peg the head of the snake securely down. . . . If this snake should ever shake its head really violently, it would shake the world to pieces."[20] A foundation stone is placed above the peg. The cornerstone is thus situated exactly at the "center of the world." But the act of foundation at the same time repeats the cosmogonic act, for to "secure" the snake's head, to drive the peg into it, is to imitate the primordial gesture of Soma (*Rg-Veda*, II, 12, 1) or of Indra when the latter "smote the Serpent in his lair" (VI, 17, 9), when his thunderbolt "cut off its head" (I, 52, 10). The serpent symbolizes chaos, the formless and nonmanifested. Indra comes upon Vrtra (IV, 19, 3) undivided (*aparvan*), unawakened (*abudhyam*), sleeping (*abudhyamānam*), sunk in deepest sleep (*suṣupaṇam*), outstretched (*aśayānam*). The hurling of the lightning and the decapitation are equivalent to the act of Creation, with passage from the nonmanifested to the manifested, from the formless to the formed. Vrtra had confiscated the waters and

was keeping them in the hollows of the mountains. This means either that Vrtra was the absolute master—in the same manner as Tiamat or any serpent divinity—of all chaos before the Creation; or that the great serpent, keeping the waters for himself alone, had left the whole world ravaged by drought. Whether this confiscation occurred before the act of Creation or is to be placed after the foundation of the world, the meaning remains the same: Vrtra "hinders"[21] the world from being made, or from enduring. Symbol of the nonmanifested, of the latent, or of the formless, Vrtra represents the chaos which existed before the Creation.

In our commentaries on the legend of Master Manole (cf. note 19, above) we attempted to explain construction rites through imitation of the cosmogonic gesture. The theory that these rites imply comes down to this: nothing can endure if it is not "animated," if it is not, through a sacrifice, endowed with a "soul"; the prototype of the construction rite is the sacrifice that took place at the time of the foundation of the world. In fact, in certain archaic cosmogonies, the world was given existence through the sacrifice of a primordial monster, symbolizing chaos (Tiamat), or through that of a cosmic giant (Ymir, Pan-Ku, Puruṣa). To assure the reality and the enduringness of a construction, there is a repetition of the divine act of perfect construction: the Creation of the worlds and of man. As the first step, the "reality" of the site is secured through consecration of the ground, i.e., through its transformation into a center; then the validity of the act of construction is confirmed by repetition of the divine sacrifice. Naturally, the consecration of the center occurs in a space qualitatively different from profane space. Through the paradox of rite, every consecrated space coincides with the center of the world, just as the time of any ritual coincides with the mythical time of the "beginning." Through repetition of the cosmogonic act, concrete time, in which the construction takes place, is projected into mythical time, *in illo tempore* when the foundation of the world occurred. Thus the reality and the enduringness of a construction are assured not only by the transformation of profane space into a transcendent space (the center) but also by the transformation of concrete time into mythical time. Any ritual whatever, as we shall see later, unfolds not only in a consecrated space (i.e., one different in essence from profane space) but also in a "sacred time," "once upon a time" (*in illo tempore, ab origine*), that is, when the ritual was performed for the first time by a god, an ancestor, or a hero.

Every ritual has a divine model, an *archetype*; this fact is well enough known for us to confine ourselves to recalling a few examples. "We must do what the gods did in the beginning" (*Satapatha Brāhmaṇa*, VII, 2, 1, 4). "Thus the gods did; thus men do" (*Taittirīya Brāhmaṇa*, 1, 5, 9, 4). This Indian adage summarizes all the theory underlying rituals in all countries. We find the theory among so-called primitive peoples no less than we do in developed cultures. The aborigines of southeastern Australia, for example, practice circumcision with a stone knife because it was thus that their ancestors taught them to do; the Amazulu Negroes do likewise because Unkulunkulu (civilizing hero) decreed *in illo tempore*: "Let men circumcise, that they may not be boys."[22] The hako ceremony of the Pawnee Indians was revealed to the priests by Tirawa, the supreme God, at the beginning of time. Among the Sakalavas of Madagascar, "all domestic, social, national, and religious customs and ceremonies must be observed in conformity with the *lilin-draza*, i.e., with the established customs and unwritten laws inherited from the ancestors. . . ."[23] It is useless to multiply examples; all religious acts are held to have been founded by gods, civilizing heroes, or mythical ancestors.[24] It may be mentioned in passing that, among primitives, not only do rituals have their mythical model but any human act whatever acquires effectiveness to the extent to which it exactly *repeats* an act performed at the beginning of time by a god, a hero, or an ancestor. . . .

Such a "theory" does not justify ritual only in primitive cultures. In the Egypt of the later centuries, for example, the power of rite and word possessed by the priests was due to imitation of the primordial gesture of the god Thoth, who had created the world by the force of his word. Iranian tradition knows that religious festivals were instituted by Ormazd to commemorate the stages of the cosmic Creation, which continued for a year. At the end of each period—representing, respectively, the creation of the sky, the waters, the earth, plants, animals, and man—Ormazd rested for five days, thus instituting the principal Mazdean festivals (cf. *Bundahišn*, I, A 18 ff.). Man only repeats the act of the Creation; his religious calendar commemorates, in the space of a year, all the cosmogonic phases which took place *ab origine*. In fact, the sacred year ceaselessly repeats the Creation; man is contemporary with the cosmogony and with the anthropogony because ritual projects him into the mythical epoch of the beginning. A bacchant, through his orgiastic rites, imitates the drama of the suffering Dionysos; an Orphic, through his initiation ceremonial, repeats the original gestures of Orpheus.

The Judaeo-Christian Sabbath is also an *imitatio dei*. The Sabbath rest reproduces the primordial gesture of the Lord, for it was on the seventh day of the Creation that God ". . . rested . . . from all his work which he had made" (Genesis 2:2). The message of the Saviour is first of all an example which demands imitation. After washing his disciples' feet, Jesus said to them: "For I have given you an example, that ye should do as I have done to you" (John 13:15). Humility is only a virtue; but humility practiced after the Saviour's example is a religious act and a means of salvation: ". . . as I have loved you, that ye also love one another" (John 13:34; 15:12). This Christian love is consecrated by the example of Jesus. Its actual practice annuls the sin of the human condition and makes man divine. He who believes in Jesus can do what He did; his limitations and impotence are abolished. "He that believeth on me, the works that I do shall he do also . . ." (John 14:12). The liturgy is precisely a commemoration of the life and Passion of the Saviour. We shall see later that this commemoration is in fact a reactualization of those days.

Marriage rites too have a divine model, and human marriage reproduces the hierogamy,[A] more especially the union of heaven and earth. "I am Heaven," says the husband, "thou art Earth" (*dyaur aham, pritivī tvam; Bṛhadāraṇyaka Upaniṣad*, VI, 4, 20). Even in Vedic times, husband and bride are assimilated to heaven and earth (*Atharva-Veda*, XIV, 2, 71), while in another hymn (*Atharva-Veda*, XIV, 1) each nuptial gesture is justified by a prototype in mythical times: "Wherewith Agni grasped the right hand of this earth, therefore grasp I thy hand. . . . Let god Savitar grasp thy hand. . . .

[A] hierogamy: sacred or holy marriage. (Editor's note)

Tvashtar disposed the garment for beauty, by direction of Bṛhaspati, of the poets; therewith let Savitar and Bhaga envelop this woman, like Sūrya, with progeny (48, 49, 52)."[25] In the procreation ritual transmitted by the *Bṛhadāraṇyaka Upaniṣad*, the generative act becomes a hierogamy of cosmic proportions, mobilizing a whole group of gods: "Let Viṣṇu make the womb prepared! Let Tvashṭṛi shape the various forms! Prajāpati—let him pour in! Let Dhātri place the germ for thee!" (VI, 4, 21).[26] Dido celebrates her marriage with Aeneas in the midst of a violent storm (Virgil, *Aeneid*, VI, 160); their union coincides with that of the elements; heaven embraces its bride, dispensing fertilizing rain. In Greece, marriage rites imitated the example of Zeus secretly uniting himself with Hera (Pausanias, II, 36, 2). Diodorus Siculus tells us that the Cretan hierogamy was imitated by the inhabitants of that island; in other words, the ceremonial union found its justification in a primordial event which occurred *in illo tempore.*

What must be emphasized is the cosmogonic structure of all these matrimonial rites: it is not merely a question of imitating an exemplary model, the hierogamy between heaven and earth; the principal consideration is the result of that hierogamy, i.e., the cosmic Creation. This is why, in Polynesia, when a sterile woman wants to be fecundated, she imitates the exemplary gesture of the Primordial Mother, who, *in illo tempore*, was laid on the ground by the great god, Io. And the cosmogonic myth is recited on the same occasion. In divorce proceedings, on the contrary, an incantation is chanted in which the "separation of heaven and earth" is invoked.[27] The ritual recitation of the cosmogonic myth on the occasion of marriages is current among numerous peoples; we shall return to it later. For the moment let us point out that the cosmic myth serves as the exemplary model not only in the case of marriages but also in the case of any other ceremony whose end is the restoration of integral wholeness; this is why the myth of the Creation of the World is recited in connection with cures, fecundity, childbirth, agricultural activities, and so on. The cosmogony first of all represents Creation.

Demeter lay with Iasion on the newly sown ground, at the beginning of spring (*Odyssey*, V, 125). The meaning of this union is clear: it contributes to promoting the fertility of the soil, the prodigious surge of the forces of telluric creation. This practice was comparatively frequent, down to the last century, in northern and central Europe— witness the various customs of symbolic union between couples in the fields.[28] In China, young couples went out in spring and united on the grass in order to stimulate "cosmic regeneration" and "universal germination." In fact, every human union has its model and its justification in the hierogamy, the cosmic union of the elements. Book IV of the *Li Chi*, the "Yüeh Ling" (book of monthly regulations), specifies that his wives must present themselves to the emperor to cohabit with him in the first month of spring, when thunder is heard. Thus the cosmic example is followed by the sovereign and the whole people. Marital union is a rite integrated with the cosmic rhythm and validated by that integration.

The entire Paleo-Oriental symbolism of marriage can be explained through celestial models. The Sumerians celebrated the union of the elements on the day of the New Year; throughout the ancient East, the same day receives its luster not only from the myth of the hierogamy but also from the rites of the king's union with the goddess.[29] It is on New Year's day that Ishtar lies with Tammuz, and the king reproduces this mythical hierogamy by consummating ritual union with the goddess (i.e., with the hierodule who represents her on earth) in a secret chamber of the temple, where the nuptial bed of the goddess stands. The divine union assures terrestrial fecundity; when Ninlil lies with Enlil, rain begins to fall.[30] The same fecundity is assured by the ceremonial union of the king, that of couples on earth, and so on. The world is regenerated each time the hierogamy is imitated, i.e., each time matrimonial union is accomplished. The German *Hochzeit* is derived from *Hochgezît*, New Year festival. Marriage regenerates the "year" and consequently confers fecundity, wealth, and happiness.

The assimilation of the sexual act to agricultural work is frequent in numerous cultures.[31] In the *Śatapatha Brāhmaṇa* (VII, 2, 2, 5) the earth is assimilated to the female organ of generation (*yoni*) and the seed to the *semen virile*. "Your women are your tilth, so come into your tillage how you choose" (*Qur'ân*, II, 223).[32] The majority of collective orgies find a ritual justification in fostering the forces of vegetation: they take place at certain critical periods of the year, e.g., when the seed sprouts or the harvests ripen, and always have a hierogamy as their mythical model. Such, for example, is the orgy practiced by the Ewe tribe (West Africa) at the time when the barley begins to sprout; the orgy is legitimized by a hierogamy (young girls are offered to the python god). We find this same legitimization among the Oraons; their orgy takes place in May, at the time of the union of the sun god with the earth goddess. All these orgiastic excesses find their justification, in one way or another, in a cosmic or biocosmic act: regeneration of the year, critical period of the harvest, and so forth. The boys who paraded naked through the streets of Rome at the Floralia (April 28) or who, at the Lupercalia, touched women to exorcise their sterility; the liberties permitted throughout India on the occasion of the Holi festival; the licentiousness which was the rule in central and northern Europe at the time of the harvest festival and against which the ecclesiastical authorities struggled so unavailingly[33]—all these manifes-

tations also had a superhuman prototype and tended to institute universal fertility and abundance.

For the purpose of this study, it is of no concern that we should know to what extent marriage rites and the orgy created the myths which justify them. What is important is that both the orgy and marriage constituted rituals imitating divine gestures or certain episodes of the sacred drama of the cosmos—the legitimization of human acts through an extrahuman model. If the myth sometimes followed the rite—for example, preconjugal ceremonial unions preceded the appearance of the myth of the preconjugal relations between Hera and Zeus, the myth which served to justify them—the fact in no wise lessens the sacred character of the ritual. The myth is "late" only as a formulation; but its content is archaic and refers to sacraments—that is, to acts which presuppose an absolute reality, a reality which is extrahuman.

NOTES

1. Willibald Kirfel, *Die Kosmographie der Inder* (Bonn, 1920), p. 15; Uno Harva, (formerly Holmberg), *Der Baum des Lebens* (Annales Accademiae Scientiarum Fennicae, Helsinki, 1923), p. 41; Arthur Christensen, *Les Types du premier homme et du premier roi dans l'histoire légendaire des Iraniens*, II (Stockholm, 1917), p. 42; our *Le Chamanisme et les techniques archaïques de l'extase* (Paris, 1951), pp. 242 ff.

2. Cf. Paul Schebesta, *Les Pygmées* (French trans., Paris, 1940), pp. 156 ff.; other examples in our *Le Chamanisme*, pp. 253 ff.

3. Cf., for example, W. Gaerte, "Kosmische Vorstellungen im Bilde prähistorischer Zeit: Erdberg, Himmelsberg, Erdnabel und Weltströme," *Anthropos* (Salzburg), IX (1914), pp. 956–79.

4. Alfred Jeremias, *Handbuch der altorientalischen Geisteskultur* (2nd edn., Berlin and Leipzig, 1929), p. 130.

5. Cf. E. Burrows, "Some Cosmological Patterns in Babylon Religion," in *The Labyrinth*, ed. S. H. Hooke (London, 1935), pp. 51, 54, 62, note 1; A. J. Wensinck, *The Ideas of the Western Semites Concerning the Navel of the Earth* (Amsterdam, 1916), p. 15; Raphael Patai, *Man and Temple* (London, 1947), p. 85. The same symbolism in Egypt: cf. Patai, p. 101, note 100.

6. E.g., among the Little Russians; Mansikka, cited by Harva, p. 72.

7. Theodor Dombart, *Der Sakralturm*, Part I: *Zikkurrat* (Munich, 1920), p. 34; cf. A. Parrot, *Ziggurats et Tour de Babel* (Paris, 1949). Indian temples are also assimilated to mountains: cf. Willy Foy, "Indische Kultbauten als Symbole des Götterbergs," in *Festschrift Ernst Windisch zum siebzigsten*

Geburtstag . . . Dargebracht (Leipzig, 1914), pp. 213–16. The same symbolism among the Aztecs: cf. Walter Krickeberg, "Bauform und Weltbild im alten Mexico," *Paideuma* (Bamberg), IV (1950), 295–333.

8. W. F. Albright, "The Mouth of the Rivers," *The American Journal of Semitic Languages and Literatures* (Chicago), XXXV (1919), p. 173.

9. Marcel Granet, *La Pensée chinoise* (Paris, 1934), p. 324; our *Le Chamanisme*, pp. 243 ff.

10. *Kisā'ī*, fol. 15; cited by Wensinck, p. 15.

11. Jeremias, p. 113; Burrows, pp. 46 ff., 50.

12. Texts in Burrows, p. 49; cf. also Patai, pp. 55 ff.

13. Texts cited by Wensinck, pp. 19, 16; cf. also W. H. Roscher, "Neue Omphalosstudien," *Abhandlungen der Königlich Sächsischen Gesellschaft der Wissenschaft* (Leipzig), *Phil.-hist. Klasse*, XXXI, 1 (1915), pp. 16 ff., 75 ff.; Burrows, p. 57; Patai, p. 85.

14. Cf. the commentary of Kirfel, p. 8.

15. Burrows, p. 49; Christensen, I, pp. 22 ff.

16. Wensinck, p. 14; Sir E. A. Wallis Budge, *The Book of the Cave of Treasures* (trans. from the Syriac, London, 1927), p. 53; Oskar Daehnhardt, *Natursagen*, I (Leipzig, 1909), p. 112; Burrows, p. 57.

17. On the cosmic symbolism of temples in the ancient East, cf. A. M. Hocart, *Kings and Councillors* (Cairo, 1936), pp. 220 ff.; Patai, pp. 106 ff. On the cosmic symbolism of basilicas and cathedrals, see Hans Sedlmayr, "Architectur als abbildende Kunst," *Österreichische Akademie der Wissenschaften, Sitzungsberichte* (Vienna), *Phil.-hist. Klasse*, 225/3 (1948), and *Die Kathedrale* (Zurich, 1950).

18. See our *Images et symboles*. (Paris, 1952).

19. *Comentarii la legenda Mesterului Manole* (Bucharest, 1943).

20. Mrs. (Margaret) Sinclair Stevenson, *The Rites of the Twice-Born* (London, 1920), p. 354 and note.

21. Mephistopheles too was *der Vater aller Hindernisse*, "the father of all hindrances" (*Faust*, v. 6209).

22. A. W. Howitt, *The Native Tribes of South-East Australia* (London, 1904), pp. 645 ff.; Henry Callaway, *The Religious System of the Amazulu* (London, 1869), p. 58.

23. Arnold van Gennep, *Tabou et totémisme à Madagascar* (Paris, 1904), p. 27 ff.

24. Cf. Gerardus van der Leeuw, *Phänomenologie der Religion* (Tübingen, 1933), pp. 349 ff., 360 ff.

25. W. D. Whitney and C. R. Lanman (trans.), *Atharva-Veda* (Harvard Oriental Series, VIII, Cambridge, Mass., 1905), pp. 750–51.

26. R. E. Hume (trans.), *The Thirteen Principal Upanishads* (Oxford, 1931).

27. Cf. E. S. C. Handy, *Polynesian Religion* (Honolulu, 1927), pp. 10 ff.; Raffaele Pettazzoni, "Io and Rangi," *Pro regno pro sanctuario* [in homage to G. van der Leeuw] (Nijkerk, 1950), pp. 359–60.

28. J. W. E. Mannhardt, *Wald- und Feldkulte*, I (2nd edn., Berlin, 1904–1905), pp. 169 ff., 180 ff.

29. Cf. S. H. Hooke, ed., *Myth and Ritual* (London, 1935), pp. 9, 19, 34 ff.

30. René Labat, *Le Caractère religieux de la royauté assyro-babylonienne* (Paris, 1939), pp. 247 ff.; cf. the traces of a similar mythico-ritual complex in Israel: Patai, pp. 90 ff.

31. See the chapter on agricultural mysticism in our *Traité d'histoire des religions*, p. 303 ff.

32. Trans. E. H. Palmer, *Sacred Books of the East*, VI, p. 33.

33. Cf., for example, the Council of Auxerre in 590.

The Development of Ritualization

ERIK H. ERIKSON

Facts of publication: *Erikson, Erik H. 1968. "The Development of Ritualization," from* The Religious Situation, *711–733. Edited by Donald R. Cutler. Boston: Beacon Press. Copyright © 1968, 1969 by David R. Cutler. Reprinted with the permission of Beacon Press.*

Sometimes we mistakenly talk as if ritual knowledge were only cultural and not also biological, and as if the capacity for ritual learning suddenly appears full-blown in adulthood. Erik Erikson, working on the basis of a modified Freudian theory of development, suggests that the psychosocial roots of ritual arise early, specifically in the interactions between parents and children. In Erikson's view ritualization, like any other sort of human competence, emerges in stages. He seems to imply that ritual skill cannot exceed the stage of human development on which it is based, and that neurotic development at any stage can result in flawed or destructive ritualization later in life. For example, it would seem to follow from Erikson's argument that flawed mutuality of recognition between mother and infant would distort one's sense for ritual numinosity. And flawed mastery of the rules of performance, usually learned during school age, would result in a diminished capacity for engaging in ritual formality.

This account of ritual's origins should be compared and contrasted with that of d'Aquili and Laughlin, as well as with that of Burkert (both in this volume).

About the author: Dates: *1902– , Frankfurt-am-Mein, Germany; moved to U.S.A., 1933.* **Education:** *Vienna Psychoanalytic Institute, 1933; M.A., Harvard University, 1960.* **Field(s):** *psychiatry; psychology.* **Career:** *Professor of Human Development and Lecturer on Psychiatry, 1960–1970, Harvard University; Research Associate in Child Development and Lecturer in Psychiatry, then Professor of Psychology, 1942–51, University of California, Berkeley.* **Publications:** Childhood and Society *(Norton, 1963 [1950]);* Young Man Luther: A Study in Psychoanalysis and History *(Norton, 1958);* Identity and the Lifecycle *(1980 [1959]);* Youth: Change and Challenge *(Basic, 1963);* Insight and Responsibility *(Norton, 1964);* Identity: Youth and Crisis *(Norton, 1968);* Ghandi's Truth *(Norton, 1969);* Life History and the Historical Moment *(Norton, 1975);* Studies of Play *(Arno, 1975);* Toys and Reasons: Stages in the Ritualization of Experience *(Norton, 1977); edited,* Adulthood *(Norton, 1978);* Dimensions of a New Identity *(Norton, 1979);* The Lifecycle Completed *(Norton, 1982); with Joan M. Erikson and Helen Kivnick,* Vital Involvement in Old Age *(Norton, 1987).* **Additional:** *Memberships: American Psychological Association American Psychoanalytic Association, American Academy of Arts and Science, National Academy of Education, Phi Beta Kappa. Pulitzer Prize and National Book Award, for* Ghandi's Truth, *1970.*

In this zoological setting, I may consider it a sign of hospitality that the ontogeny of ritualization in man is to be discussed before that in animals.[A] This permits me to give full consideration to man's complexity, and to dispense with the attempt to derive the human kind of ritualization from what has come to be called ritualization in animals. Rather, I will try to show what in human life may be the equivalent of the ethologist's ritualization, and to present a developmental schedule for its ontogeny. (For a conception of the human life cycle underlying this attempt, see [References] [1] and [3].) To do so, I must first set aside a number of now dominant connotations of the term. The oldest of these is the *anthropological* one which ties it to rites and rituals conducted by communities of adults (and sometimes witnessed by children or participated in by youths) for the purpose of marking such recurring events as the phases of the year or the stages of life. I will attempt to trace some of the ontogenetic roots of all ritual making but I will not deal explicitly with ritual as such.

A more recent connotation of "ritualization" is the *clinical* one. Here the term "private ritual" is used to conceptualize obsessional behavior consisting of repetitive solitary acts with highly idiosyncratic meanings. Such behavior is vaguely analogous to the aimless behavior of caged animals, and thus seems to provide a "natural" link with a possible phylogenetic origin of ritualization in its more stereotyped and driven forms. But it seems important to set aside this clinical connotation in order to take account of newer insights both in ethology and in psychoanalysis. There is now a trend in the etho-

logical literature (recently summarized in Konrad Lorenz's *Das Sogenannte Boese*) [8] which follows the original suggestion of Sir Julian Huxley to use the word ritualization (and this explicitly without quotation marks) for certain phylogenetically performed ceremonial acts in the so-called social animals. The study of these acts clearly points away from pathology, in that it reveals the bond created by a reciprocal message of supreme adaptive importance. We should, therefore, begin by postulating that behavior to be called ritualization in man must consist of an agreed-upon interplay between at least two persons who repeat it at meaningful intervals and in recurring contexts; and that this interplay should have adaptive value for both participants. And, I would submit, these conditions are already fully met by the way in which a human mother and her baby greet each other in the morning.

Beginnings, however, are apt to be both dim in contour and lasting in consequences. Ritualization in man seems to be grounded in the preverbal experience of infants while reaching its full elaboration in grand public ceremonies. No one field could encompass such a range of phenomena with solid observation. Rather, the theme of ritualization (as I have found in preparing this paper) can help us to see new connections between seemingly distant phenomena, such as human infancy and man's institutions, individual adaptation and the function of ritual. Here, I will not be able to avoid extensive speculation.

INFANCY AND THE NUMINOUS

Let me begin with the "greeting ceremonial" marking the beginning of an infant's day: for ritualization is to be treated here first as a special form of everyday behavior. In such matters it is best not to think at first of our own homes but of those of some

[A]The setting was a conference convened by ethologists, scientists who study animal behavior. *Ontogeny:* the origin and development of an individual animal or person; contrast *phylogeny,* the origin and development of a phylum or species. (Editor's note)

neighbors, or of a tribe studied or a faraway country visited, while comparing it all—how could some of us do otherwise—with analogous phenomena among our favorite birds.

The awakening infant conveys to his mother the fact that he is awake and (as if with the signal of an alarm clock) awakens in her a whole repertoire of emotive, verbal, and manipulative behavior. She approaches him with smiling or worried concern, brightly or anxiously rendering a name, and goes into action: looking, feeling, sniffing, she ascertains possible sources of discomfort and initiates services to be rendered by rearranging the infant's condition, by picking him up, etc. If observed for several days it becomes clear that this daily event is highly ritualized, in that the mother seems to feel obliged, and not a little pleased, to repeat a performance which arouses in the infant predictable responses, encouraging her, in turn, to proceed. Such ritualization, however, is hard to describe. It is at the same time highly *individual* ("typical for the mother" and also tuned to the particular infant) and yet also *stereotyped* along traditional lines. The whole procedure is superimposed on the periodicity of physical needs close to the requirements of survival; but it is an *emotional* as well as a *practical* necessity for both mother and infant. And, as we will see, this enhanced routine can be properly evaluated only as a small but tough link in the whole formidable sequence of generations.

Let us take the fact that the mother called the infant by a name. This may have been carefully selected and perhaps certified in some name-giving ritual, held to be indispensable by the parents and the community. Yet, whatever procedures have given meaning to the name, that meaning now exerts a certain effect on the way in which the name is repeated during the morning procedure—together with other emphases of caring attention which have a very special meaning for the mother and eventually for the child. Daily observations (confirmed by the special aura of Madonna-and-Child images) suggest that this mutual assignment of very special meaning is the ontogenetic source of one pervasive element in human ritualization, which is based on a *mutuality of recognition.*

There is much to suggest that man is born with the need for such regular and mutual affirmation

and certification: we know, at any rate, that its absence can harm an infant radically, by diminishing or extinguishing his search for impressions which will verify his senses. But, once aroused, this need will reassert itself in every stage of life as a hunger for ever new, ever more formalized and more widely shared ritualizations and rituals which repeat such face-to-face "recognition" of the hoped-for. Such ritualizations range from the regular exchange of greetings affirming a strong emotional bond, to singular encounters of mutual fusion in love or inspiration, or in a leader's "charisma." I would suggest, therefore, that this first and dimmest affirmation, this sense of a *hallowed presence*, contributes to man's ritual making a pervasive element which we will call the "Numinous." This designation betrays my intention to follow the earliest into the last: and, indeed, we vaguely recognize the numinous as an indispensable aspect of periodical religious observances, where the believer, by appropriate gestures, confesses his dependence and his childlike faith and seeks, by appropriate offerings, to secure a sense of being lifted up to the very bosom of the supernatural which in the visible form of an image may graciously respond, with the faint smile of an inclined face. The result is a sense of *separateness transcended*, and yet also of *distinctiveness confirmed.*

I have now offered two sets of phenomena, namely, ritualization in the nursery (as an enhancement by playful formalization of the routine procedures which assure mere survival) and religious rituals (which provide a periodical reaffirmation for a multitude of men) as the first examples of an affinity of themes, which seem to "belong" to entirely different "fields" but are necessarily brought together as subject matter for this Symposium. By suggesting such a far-reaching connection, however, I do not mean to reduce formalized ritual to infantile elements; rather, I intend to sketch, for a number of such elements of ritualization, an ontogenetic beginning and a reintegration on ever higher levels of development. In adult ritual, to be sure, these infantile elements are both emotively and symbolically reevoked; but both infantile ritualization and adult ritual are parts of a functional whole, namely, of a cultural version of human existence.

I will now try to list those elements of ritualization which we can already recognize in the first, the

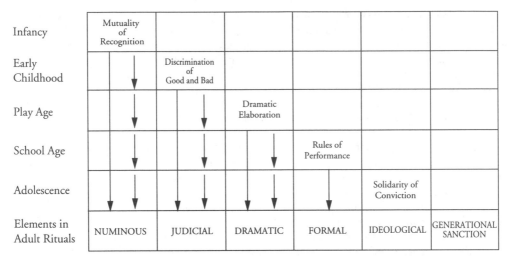

Infancy	Mutuality of Recognition					
Early Childhood		Discrimination of Good and Bad				
Play Age			Dramatic Elaboration			
School Age				Rules of Performance		
Adolescence					Solidarity of Conviction	
Elements in Adult Rituals	NUMINOUS	JUDICIAL	DRAMATIC	FORMAL	IDEOLOGICAL	GENERATIONAL SANCTION

FIGURE 1. **Ontogeny of Ritualization**

numinous instance—emphasizing throughout the opposites which appear to be reconciled. Its mutuality is based on the *reciprocal needs* of two quite *unequal* organisms and minds. We have spoken of the *periodicity of developing needs* to which ritualization gives a *symbolic actuality*. We have recognized it as a highly *personal* matter, and yet as *group-bound*, providing a sense both of *oneness* and of *distinctiveness*. It is *playful*, and yet *formalized*, and this in *details* as well as in the *whole* procedure. Becoming *familiar* through repetition, it yet brings the *surprise* of recognition. And while the ethologists will tell us that ritualizations in the animal world must, above all, be *unambiguous* as sets of signals, we suspect that in man the *overcoming of ambivalence* as well as of ambiguity is one of the prime functions of ritualization. For as we love our children, we also find them unbearably demanding, even as they will soon find us arbitrary and possessive. What we love or admire is also threatening, awe becomes awfulness, and benevolence seems in danger of being consumed by wrath. Therefore, ritualized affirmation, once instituted, becomes *indispensable* as a periodical experience and must find new forms in the context of new developmental actualities.

This is a large order with which to burden an infant's daily awakening, and, indeed, only the whole sequence of stages of ritualization can make this list of opposites plausible. Yet, even at the beginning,

psychopathology confirms this burdening. Of all psychological disturbances which we have learned to connect ontogenetically with the early stages of life, the deepest and most devastating are those in which the light of mutual recognition and of hope are forfeited in psychotic withdrawal and regression, and this, as Spitz and Bowlby have shown, can develop at the very beginning of life. For, the earliest affirmation is already reaffirmation in the face of the fact that the very experiences by which man derives a measure of security also expose him to a *series of estrangements* which we must try to specify as we deal with each developmental stage. In the first stage, I submit, it is a sense of *separation by abandonment* which must be prevented by the persistent, periodical reassurance of familiarity and mutuality. Such reassurance remains the function of the numinous and thus primarily of the religious ritual or of the numinous element in any ritual. Its perversion or absence, on the other hand, leaves a sense of dread, estrangement, or impoverishment.

In another context [3] I have suggested that the most basic quality of human life, *hope*, is the inner strength which emerges unbroken from early familiarity and mutuality and which provides for man a sense (or a promise) of a personal and universal continuum. It is grounded and fortified in the first stage of life, and subsequently nourished, as it were, by all those ritualizations and rituals which combat a sense of abandonment and hopelessness and promise instead a mutuality of recognition, face to face, all through life—until "we shall know even as also we are known."

THE PSEUDOSPECIES

In order to deal with the total setting which seems to give meaning to and to receive meaning from human ritualization, I must introduce three theoretical considerations of an incomplete and controversial nature.

Since ritualization in animals is for the most part an intraspecific phenomenon, it must be emphasized throughout that man has evolved (by whatever kind of evolution and for whatever adaptive reasons) in *pseudospecies*, i.e., tribes, clans, etc., which behave as if they were separate species created at the beginning of time by supernatural will, and each superimposing on the geographic and economic facts of its existence a cosmogeny, as well as a theocracy and an image of man, all its own. Thus each develops a distinct sense of identity, held to be *the* human identity and fortified against other pseudospecies by prejudices which mark them as extraspecific and, in fact, inimical to the only "genuine" human endeavor. Paradoxically, however, newly born man can fit into any number of such pseudospecies and must, therefore, become specialized during a prolonged childhood—certainly a basic fact in the ontogeny of familiarization by ritualization.

To speak of pseudospecies may be controversial enough. But I must now face a second conceptual dilemma in the form of Sigmund Freud's instinct theory. Whenever the noun "instinct" appears in psychoanalytic formulations it is helpful to ask whether the corresponding adjective would be "instinctive" or "instinctual," i.e., whether the emphasis is on an *instinctive pattern* of behavior, or an *instinctual drive or energy* more or less indifferent and divorced from prepared patterns of adaptiveness. As Freud put it in his *New Introductory Lectures*: "From the Pleasure Principle to the instinct of self-preservation is a long way; and the two tendencies are far from coinciding from the first." It will appear, then, that psychoanalysts usually mean instinctual drives, and this with the connotation of a quantitative ex-

cess devoid of instinctive quality in the sense of specific patterns of "fittedness" [6]. The evolutionary rationale for the free-floating quantity of instinctual energy lies, of course, in the very fact that man is, in Ernst Mayr's words, the "generalist animal," born to invest relatively nonspecific drives in such learning experiences and such social encounters as will assure, during a long childhood, a strengthening and widening of mutuality, competence, and identity—all, as I am endeavoring to show, supported most affirmatively by appropriate ritualizations.

I say "most affirmatively" because man's *moral prohibitions* and *inner inhibitions* are apt to be as excessive and maladaptive as the drives which they are meant to contain: in psychoanalysis we therefore speak of a "return of the repressed." Could it be, then, that true ritualization represents, in fact, a *creative formalization* which avoids both impulsive excess and overly compulsive self-restriction, both social anomie and moralistic coercion? If so, we could see at least three vital functions served by the simplest ritualization worthy of that designation:

(1) It binds instinctual energy into a pattern of mutuality, which bestows convincing simplicity on dangerously complex matters. As mother and infant meet in the first ritualization described so far, the infant brings to the constellation his vital needs, among them, oral, sensory, and tactile drives (subsumed as "orality" in Freud's libido theory), and the necessity to have disparate experiences made coherent by mothering. The mother in her postpartum state is also needful in a complex manner: for whatever instinctive mothering she may be endowed with, and whatever instinctual gratification she may seek in being a mother, she needs to be a *mother of a special kind* and *in a special way*. This she becomes by no means without an anxious avoidance (sometimes outright phobic, often deeply superstitious) of "other" kinds and ways typical for persons or groups whom she (sometimes unconsciously) dislikes, or despises, hates, or fears as godless or evil, unhygienic, or immoral.

(2) In permitting the mother to "be herself" and to be at the same time an obedient representative of a group ethos, ritualization protects her against the danger of instinctual excess and arbitrariness and

against the burden of having to systematize a thousand small decisions.

(3) In establishing mutuality in the immediacy of early needs, ritualization also does the groundwork for lasting mutual identifications between adult and child from generation to generation. For the mother is reaffirmed in her identification with those who mothered her well; while her own motherhood is reaffirmed as benevolent by the increasing responsiveness of the infant. The infant, in turn, develops a benevolent self-image (a certified narcissism, we may say) grounded in the recognition of an all-powerful and mostly benevolent (if sometimes strangely malevolent) "Other."

(4) Thus ritualization also provides the psychosocial foundation for that inner equilibrium which in psychoanalysis is attributed to a "strong ego"; and thus also a first step for the gradual development (to be sealed only in adolescence) of an independent identity [5] which—guided by various rituals of "confirmation" representing a "second birth"—will integrate all childhood identifications, while subordinating those wishes and images which have become undesirable and evil.

EARLY CHILDHOOD AND THE JUDICIOUS

Any ontological discourse suffers from the fact that it must begin to enumerate its guiding principles at the beginning, while only an account of their progression and differentiation as a whole can reveal their plausibility. The dimensions of ritualization suggested so far must now reappear on higher levels: mutuality between the child and that increasing number of adults with whom he is ready to interact, physically, mentally, and socially; the affirmation of such new mutuality by ritualization and this in the face of a new kind of estrangement; and the emergence of a new element of ritual.

A second basic element in human ritualization is one for which the best term would seem to be *judicial,* because it combines *jus* and *dicere,* "the law" and "the word." At any rate, the term should encompass methods by which the *discrimination* between right and wrong is ontologically established.

Eventually, this becomes an important aspect in all human ritual; for there is no ritual which does not imply a discrimination between the sanctioned and the out-of-bounds—up to the Last Judgment.

The ontological source of this second element is the second stage of life, that is, early childhood, which is characterized by a growing psychosocial autonomy and by rapid advances in development. As *locomotion* serves increased autonomy, it also leads to the boundaries of the permissible; as *discrimination* sharpens, it also serves the perception of conduct which "looks tight" or "does not look right" in the eye of others; while *language development* (obviously one of the strongest bonds of a pseudospecies) distinguishes with finite emphasis what is conceptually integrated in the verbalized world, and what remains outside, nameless; unmeaningful, strange, *wrong.* All of this is given strong connotations by what Freud called "anality." It brings with it a new sense of estrangement: standing upright, the child realizes that he can lose face and suffer shame; giving himself away by blushing, he feels furiously isolated, not knowing whether to *doubt himself* or *his judges.* His elders, in turn, feel compelled to utilize and thus to aggravate this trend; and yet, is it not again in the ritualization of approval and disapproval (in recurring situations of high symbolic meaning) that the adult speaks as a mouthpiece of a supraindividual righteousness, damning the deed but not necessarily the doer?

I will never forget an experience which I am sure I share with all anthropologists (professional and amateur): I mean the astonishment with which we "in the field" encounter for the first time old people who will describe what is appropriate in their culture with a sense of moral and aesthetic rightness unquestionably sanctioned by the universe. Here is an example of what I was told among the Yurok Indians in Northern California, who depended on the salmon and its elusive ways (long hidden to science) of propagating and migrating.

Once upon a time, a Yurok meal was a variable ceremony of self-restraint. A strict order of placement was maintained and the child was taught to eat in prescribed ways; for example, to put only a little food on the spoon, to take the spoon up to his mouth slowly, to put the spoon down while chewing the food—and above all, to think of becoming rich during the whole process. There was silence during meals, so that everybody could keep his thoughts concentrated on money and salmon. This ritualization served to lift to the level of a kind of hallucination nostalgic oral needs which may have been evoked by very early weaning from the breast (quite extraordinary amoung American Indians). Later, in the "sweat house" the boy would learn the dual feat of thinking of money and *not* thinking of women; and the adult Yurok could make himself see money hanging from trees and salmon swimming in the river during the off season in the belief that this self-induced "hallucinatory" thought would bring action from the Providers [2:177].

This ceremonial style which undoubtedly impressed the small child and had precursors in less formal daily occasions invested similar ritualizations along the whole course of life, for cultures (so we may remind ourselves in passing) attempt to give *coherence* and *continuity* to the whole schedule of minute ritualizations.

This second element of ritualization is differentiated from the first primarily by an emphasis on the *child's free will*. In the ritualizations of infancy avoidances were the mother's responsibility; now the child himself is trained to "watch himself." To this end parents and other elders compare him (to his face) with what he *might* become if he and they did not watch out. Here, then, is the ontogenetic source of the "negative identity" which is so essential for the maintenance of a pseudospecies for it embodies everything one is not supposed to be or show—and what one yet potentially is. The negative identity furnishes explicit images of pseudospecies which one must *not* resemble in order to have a chance of acceptance in one's own. Behind the dreaded traits are often images of what the parents themselves are trying not to be and therefore doubly fear the child might become, and are thus *potential* traits which he must learn to imagine in order to be able to avoid them. The self-doubt and the hidden shame attached to the necessity of "eliminating" part of himself as well as the suppression of urges create in man a certain *righteous rage* which can turn parent against parent, parent against child—and the child against himself. I paint this matter darkly because here we meet the ontological

origin of the divided species. Moral self-discrimination is sharpened by an indoctrination against evil others, on whom the small child can project what he must negate in himself, and against whom he can later turn that moralistic and sadistic prejudice which has become the greatest danger of the species man. His "prejudice against himself," on the other hand, is at the bottom of man's proclivity for compulsive, obsessive, and, depressive disorders; while irrational prejudice against others, if joined with mass prejudice and armed with modern weapons, may yet mark the premature end of a species just on the verge of becoming one [5]. All of this, however, also underlines the importance of true ritualization as a supraindividual formalization transmitting rules of conduct in words and sounds which the child can comprehend, and in situations which he can manage.

In its full elaboration in a *judiciary ritual,* however, this judicious element is reaffirmed on a grand scale, making all-visible on the public stage what occurs in each individual as an inner process: the Law is untiringly watchful as is, alas, our conscience. It locates a suitable culprit who, once in the dock, serves as "an example," on which a multitude can project their inner shame. The unceasing inner rumination with which we watch ourselves is matched by the conflicting evidence which parades past the parental judge, the fraternal jury, and the chorus of the public. Judgment, finally, is pronounced as based on sanctified agreement rather than on passing outrage or personal revenge; and where repentance does not accept punishment, the verdict will impose it.

Both the ritualized establishment of boundaries of good and bad in childhood and the judiciary ritual in the adult world fulfill the criteria for ritualized procedures as suggested earlier: meaningful regularity; ceremonial attention to detail and to the total procedure; a sense of symbolic actuality surpassing the reality of each participant and of the deed itself; a mutual activation of all concerned (including, or so it is hoped, the confessing culprit); and a sense of indispensability so absolute that the need for the ritualization in question seems to be "instinctive" with man. And, indeed, the judicial element has become an indispensable part of man's phylogenetic adaptation as well as his ontogenetic development.

In seeing the judicial element at work, however, in public and in private, we can also perceive where this form of ritualization fails in its adaptive function, and this means in the convincing transmission of boundaries from generation to generation. Failure is indicated where fearful compulsion to conform replaces free assent to what feels right; where thus the obsessively formalistic becomes dominant over the convincingly ceremonial or where considered judgment is swamped by instinctual excess and becomes moralistic sadism or sensational voyeurism. All of this increases the hopeless isolation of the culprit and aggravates an impotent rage which can only make him more "shameless." Thus, the decay or perversion of ritual does not create an indifferent emptiness, but a void with explosive possibilities—to which fact this Symposium should pay careful attention. For it explains why "nice" people who have lost the gift of imparting values by meaningful ritualization can have children who become (or behave like) juvenile delinquents; and why nice "churchgoing" nations can so act as to arouse the impression of harboring pervasive murderous intent.

Here, again, the psychopathology attending individual misfunctioning and the social pathology characterizing the breakdown of institutions are closely related. They meet in the alternation of impulsivity and compulsivity, excess and self-restriction, anarchy and autocracy.

CHILDHOOD: THE DRAMATIC AND THE FORMAL

I have now attempted to isolate two elements in human rituals which seem clearly grounded in ontogenetic stages of development. In view of the "originology" which is apt to replace defunct teleology, it seems important to reiterate that I am not suggesting a simple causal relationship between the infantile stage and the adult institution, in the sense that adult rituals above all serve persisting infantile needs in disguise. The image of the Ancestor or of the God sought on a more mature level is (as we shall see) by no means "only" a replica of the mother's inclined face, nor the idea of Justice "only" an externalization of a childish bad conscience. Rather, man's epigenetic development in separate and protracted childhood stages assures that each of the major elements

which constitute human institutions is rooted in a distinct childhood stage, but, once evolved, must be progressively reintegrated on each higher level. Thus the numinous element reappears in the judicial ritualizations as the aura adhering to all "authority" and later to a personified or highly abstract image of Justice, or to the concrete persons who as justices are invested with the symbolism and the power of that image. But this also means that neither the numinous nor the judicial elements, although they can dominate a particular stage or a particular institution, can "make up" a ritual all by themselves: other elements must join them. Of these, I will discuss in the following, the elements of *dramatic elaboration*, of *competence of performance*, and of *ideological commitment*.

First, then, the *dramatic* element. This I believe, is grounded in the maturational advances of the *play age* which permits the child to create with available objects (and then in games with cooperative adults and peers) a *coherent plot with dramatic turns* and some form of *climactic conclusion*.

While the second, the "judicial" stage was characterized by the internalization of the parental voice, this age offers the child a microreality in which he can escape adult ritualization and prepare his own, reliving, correcting, and recreating past experiences, and anticipating future roles and events with the spontaneity and repetitiveness which characterize all ritualization. His themes, however, are often dominated by usurpation and impersonation of adult roles; and I would nominate for the principal *inner estrangement* which finds expression, aggravation, or resolution in play, the *sense of guilt*. One might think that this sense should be subsumed under the judicial sphere; yet, guilt is an inescapable sense of self-condemnation which does not even wait for the fantasied deed to be actually committed, or, if committed to be known to others; or, if known to others, to be punished by them.

This theme dominates the great tragedies, for the *theater* is adult man's "play." The play on the toy stage and the plays acted out in official drama and magic ceremonial have certain themes in common which may, in fact, have helped to induce Freud to give to the dominant "complex" of this stage the name of a tragic hero: Oedipus. That common theme is the conflict between hubris and guilt, between the usurpation of father-likeness and punishment, between freedom and sin. The appropriate institution for the aweful expression of the dramatic is the stage, which, however, cannot do without the numinous and the judicial, even as they, in any given ritual, rite, or ceremony, cannot dispense with the dramatic.

What is the form of psychopathology characterizing the play age and the neurotic trends emanating from it? It is the weight of excessive guilt which leads to repression in thought and to inhibition in action. It is no coincidence that this pathology is most dramatically expressed in *Hamlet*, the tragedy of the *actor* in every sense of the word, who tries to solve his inhibitive scruples by the invention of a *play within a play* and prepares his perdition in and by it. And yet, this perdition almost seems a salvation from something worse: that pervasive boredom in the midst of affluence and power, that malaise and inability to gain pleasure "from either man or woman" which characterizes the absence of the dramatic and the denial of the tragic.

The *school age* adds another element to ritualization: that of the *perfection of performance*. The elements mentioned so far would be without a binding discipline which holds them to a minute sequence and arrangement of performance. The mental and emotional capacity for such accuracy arises only in the school age; or rather, because it *can* arise then, children are sent to "schools." There, with varying abruptness, play is transformed into work, game into cooperation, and the freedom of imagination into the duty to perform with full attention to all the the minute details which are necessary to complete a task and do it "right." Ritualization becomes truly cooperative in the whole arrangement called "school," that is, in the interplay between "teacher," "class," and individual child, and in the prescribed series of minute tasks which are structured according to the verbal, the mathematical, and the physical nature of the cultural universe. This, I submit, is the ontogenetic source of that *formal aspect* of rituals, provided by an order in space and time which is convincing to the sense as it becomes *order perceived* and yet also *participated in*. Adding this sense of detail, seriously attended to within a meaningful context, to the numinous, judicial, and dramatic elements, we feel closer to an understanding of the dimensions of any true ritual. But we also perceive the danger of overformalization, perfectionism, and

empty ceremonialism, not to speak of the neurotic "ritual" marked by total isolation (and all too often considered the model of ritualization by my psychiatric colleagues).

ADOLESCENCE AND BEYOND: THE IDEOLOGICAL AND THE GENERATIONAL

I have now concentrated on the ontogenetic and, as it were, unofficial sources of ritualizations in childhood. From here, one could continue in two directions: that is, one could discuss the always surprising and sometimes shocking spontaneous "rites" by which adolescents ritualize their relations to each other and demarcate their generation as (slightly or decidedly) different both from the adult haves and the infantile have-nots; or one could now turn to formal rites and rituals, for it is in the formal rites of confirmation, induction, etc., that adolescing man is enjoined for the first time to become a full member of his pseudospecies, and often of a special élite within it. For all the elements developed in the ontogenetic sequence already discussed now become part of formal rites which tie the infantile inventory into an ideological world image, provide a convincing coherence of ideas and ideals, and give youth the feeling of active participation in the preservation or renewal of society. Only now can man be said to be adult in the sense that he can devote himself to ritual purposes and can visualize a future in which he will become the everyday ritualizer in his children's lives.

Our ontogenetic sketch has to include this stage because the reciprocal mechanisms by which adult and young animals complete the interplay of their respective inborn patterns can be said to be paralleled in man by no less than the *whole period of childhood and youth*. To be fully grown in the human sense means the readiness to join not only the *technology* but also certain *irreversible commitments* to one's pseudospecies; which also means to *exclude* (by moral repudiation, fanatic rebellion, or warfare) inimical identities and outworn or foreign ideologies. Elsewhere [5] I have undertaken to delineate the identity crisis which precedes the emergence in youth of a sense of *psychosocial identity* and the readiness for the ideological style pervading the ritualizations of his culture. Only an integration of these two processes prepares youth for the alignment of its new strength with the technological and historical trends of the day. I have called the corresponding estrangement *identity confusion.* Clinically (i.e., in those so predisposed), this expresses itself in withdrawal or in lone-wolf delinquency; while it is often a matter of psychiatric, political, and legal definition whether and where borderline psychosis, criminality, dangerous delinquency, or unwholesome fanaticism may be said to exist. Much of youthful "demonstration" in private is just that: a dramatization (sometimes mocking, sometimes riotous) of the estrangement of youth from the impersonality of mass production, the vagueness of confessed values, and the intangibility of the prospects for either an individualized or truly communal existence; but, above all, by the necessity to find entirely new forms of ritualization in a technology changing so rapidly that change becomes one of its main attributes. There are historical identity vacua when the identity crisis is aggravated on a large scale and met only by an ideological renewal which "catches up" with economic and technological changes [1].

We have also witnessed in our time totalitarian attempts at involving new generations ideologically in staged mass rituals combining the numinous and the judicial, the dramatic and the precise in performance on the largest scale, which provide for masses of young individuals an ideological commitment encompassing perpetual change and, in fact, making all traditional (in the sense of prerevolutionary) values part of a decidedly negative identity.

I point to all this in the present context primarily because of problems concerning the ontogeny of ritualization. For what is in question is (1) the necessary coherence and continuity between early ritualization and overall technological and political trends, and (2) the role of youth in the rejuvenation of society and the integration of our humanist past with the technological age now emerging worldwide.

But before we come to the question of ritualization in the modern world we must mention a *dominant function of ritual in the life of the adult.* Parents are the earliest ritualizers in their children's lives; at the same time, they are participants of the instituted rituals in which the ritualizations of their child-

hoods find an echo and a reaffirmation. What, then, is the prime contribution of adult ritual to the ontogenesis of ritualization? I think ritual reaffirms the sanction needed by adults to be convincing ritualizers.

After the *rituals of graduation* from the apprenticeship of youth, *marriage ceremonies* provide for the young adult the "license" to enter those new associations which will transmit tradition to the coming generation. I am reminded here of a wedding ceremony which took place in a small town in the French Alps. The young Americans to be married faced the mayor; the tricolor was wound round his middle (which was soon to be regaled with ceremonial champagne). Above and behind him, *le Général* looked most distantly out of a framed picture into new greatness, and above him a bust of *l'Empéreur* stared white and vacant into the future, the brow wrapped in laurel; while even higher up, the afternoon sun streamed through a window, all the way down to the book out of which the mayor read phrases from a Code, to which a young bride from America could have agreed only with some reservations, had she fully understood them. Yet we few, in a foreign land, felt well taken care of, for the Western world shares many ceremonial values and procedures; and the couple accepted from the mayor a little booklet which provided for the entry of the names of the next generation.

Whether the ceremonies of the adult years call on personal ancestors in the beyond or on culture heroes, on spirits or gods, on kings or leaders, they sanction the adult; for his mature needs include the *need to be periodically reinforced in his role of ritualizer,* which means not more and not less than to be ready to become a numinous model in his children's minds, and to act as a judge and the transmitter of traditional ideals. This last element in the ontogenetic series I would call the *generational* which includes *parental* and *instructive, productive, creative,* and *curative* endeavors.

CONCLUSION

In the "freer" adult of the Western world we often observe an oppressive sense of responsibility in isolation, and this under the impact of two parallel developments, namely, the decrease of ritual reassurance from the ceremonial resources of a passing age, and the increase of a self-conscious awareness of the role of the individual, and especially of the parent and the teacher in the sequence of generations. Adults thus oppressed, however, are of little use to youth which prefers to gather around those who create new patterns of ritualization worthy (or seemingly worthy) of the energies of a new generation. The Symposium, having established the evolutionary significance of ritualization in man, may thus not be able to shirk the question whether fading rituals may or may not at this time be giving way to ritualizations of a new kind, dictated above all by new methods of communication and not always recognizable to the overtrained eye.

I hope, therefore, that this Symposium will come to discuss not only the question of the weakening of traditional ritual and of "our" traditional sense of ritualization, but also the agencies which provide a reinforcement of ritualization in line with a new world image. This new cosmos is held together by the scientific ethos, the methods of mass communication, and the replacement of "ordained" authorities by an indefinite sequence of experts correcting and complementing each other. Pediatric advice, for example, offers knowledge and prudence as guides to parental conduct; modern technology attaches new ritualizations to technical necessities and opportunities in homes and at work; and worldwide communication creates new and more universal parliaments. We must review the accreditation of those who rush in to occupy places left vacant by vanishing ritualization, and who offer new "rituals" of mechanistic or autocratic, self-conscious, totally thoughtless, or all too intellectual kinds.

However, new sources of numinous and judicial affirmation as well as of dramatic and aesthetic representation can obviously come only from a new spirit embodying an identification of the whole human species with itself. The transition will compound our estrangements; for could it not be that much of the ritualization discussed here owes its inescapability to a period in mankind's evolution when the pseudospecies was dominant? Will a more inclusive human identity do away with the necessity of reinforcing the identities and the prejudices of many pseudospecies—even as a new and more universal ethics may make old moralisms obsolete? If so, there seems to be a strong link between Huxley's Romanes lecture [7] and today's proceedings.

I am by no means certain that the elements of ritualization enumerated in this paper and charted with premature finality in Figure 1 represent a complete inventory. I have outlined what I was able to discern, and what I believe the principles of further inquiry to be. At any rate, there can be no prescription for ritualization, for, far from being merely repetitive or familiar in the sense of habituation, any true ritualization is ontogenetically grounded and yet pervaded with the spontaneity of surprise: it is an unexpected renewal of a recognizable order in potential chaos. Ritualization thus depends on that blending of surprise and recognition which is the soul of creativity, reborn out of the abyss of instinctual disorder, confusion of identity, and social anomie.

One major example of creative ritualization in the modern era, namely Gandhi's technique of nonviolent conflict (Satyagraha), has striking analogies to the pacific ritualization of animals as recently summarized by Lorenz [8]. For a preliminary report, see [4].

REFERENCES

1. Erikson, E H: *Young Man Luther* (W W Norton, New York, New York) 1958.
2. Erikson, E H: *Childhood and Society*, ed 2 (W W Norton, New York, New York) 1963.
3. Erikson, E H: *Insight and Responsibility* (W W Norton, New York, New York) 1964.
4. Erikson, E H: Psychoanalysis and Ongoing History, *American Journal of Psychiatry*, 1965, no 122, pp 241–250.
5. Erikson, E H: The Concept of Identity in Race Relations, in T Parsons and K B Clark, eds, *The Negro American* (Houghton Mifflin, Boston, Massachusetts) 1966.
6. Hartmann, H: *Ego Psychology and the Problem of Adaptation*, D Rapaport, translator (International Universities Press, New York, New York) 1958.
7. Huxley, J: *Evolutionary Ethics* (Oxford University Press, Oxford, England) 1943.
8. Lorenz, K: *Das Sogenannte Boese* (Borotha-Schoeler Verlag, Vienna, Austria) 1964.

Obsessive Actions and Religious Practices

SIGMUND FREUD

Facts of publication: *Freud, Sigmund. 1959 (1907). "Obsessive Actions and Religious Practices,"* The Standard Edition of the Complete Psychological Works of Sigmund Freud *9: 117–127. Reprinted in* Character and Culture, *17–26, translator unknown. Copyright © 1959 by The Institute of Psycho-Analysis. Reprinted with the permission of BasicBooks, Inc., a division of HarperCollins Publishers, Inc., Sigmund Freud Copyrights, The Institute of Psycho-Analysis, and The Hogarth Press, Ltd.*

Freud's work has been formative in cultivating scholars' willingness to (1) draw analogies between ritual and other kinds of behavior; (2) assume that dreams and rites share some of the same dynamics, for instance, displacement; and (3) posit meanings of which actors are unaware. Psychologists call these "unconscious meanings." Social scientists sometimes speak similarly of "operational" or "functional" meanings. These are similar to unconscious meanings insofar as ritualists are assumed to be unaware of them.

This article is one of the two or three most important of Freud's writings for understanding his view of religious ritual. In the popular mind Freud had little use for either ritual or religion. However, recent scholars have challenged both assumptions. This piece can be read as degrading religion to the status of an obsession. It can also be read as elevating obsessive neurosis to the status of ritual. Much hinges on how we regard Freud's claim that an obsessive person's actions are "perfectly significant in every detail."

Freud's interpretation of the ritualized dimensions of everyday behavior contrasts significantly with that of Goffman in this volume. See Volney Gay, Freud on Ritual *(Missoula, MT: Scholars Press, 1979).*

About the author: Dates: *1856–1939, Moravia, Czechoslovakia; moved to Vienna at age four.* **Education:** *M.D., Ll.D., University of Vienna.* **Field(s):** *psychology; psychoanalysis.* **Career:** *Lecturer in neuropathology, 1885, University of Vienna; Extra Professor, 1902; Professor, 1920.* **Publications:** The Interpretation of Dreams *(Basic, 1913 [1900]);* Totem and Taboo *(Routledge, 1950 [1913]);* The Future of an Illusion *(Norton, 1961 [1927]);* Moses and Monotheism *(Knopf, 1955 [1939]);* The Standard Edition of the Complete Psychological Works of Sigmund Freud *(Hogarth, 1959).* **Additional**: *Founder, Vienna Psychoanalytical Association. Editor of* Jarbuch der Psychoanalyse, Imago, International Journal of Psychoanalysis, Internationale Zeitschrift für ärztliche Psychoanalyse. *Goethe Prize, Frankfurt, Germany, 1930.*

I am certainly not the first person to have been struck by the resemblance between what are called obsessive actions in sufferers from nervous affections and the observances by means of which believers give expression to their piety. The term 'ceremonial', which has been applied to some of these obsessive actions, is evidence of this. The resemblance, however, seems to me to be more than a superficial one, so that an insight into the origin of neurotic ceremonial may embolden us to draw inferences by analogy about the psychological processes of religious life.

People who carry out obsessive actions or ceremonials belong to the same class as those who suffer from obsessive thinking, obsessive ideas, obsessive impulses and the like. Taken together, these form a particular clinical entity, to which the name of 'obsessional neurosis' is customarily applied. But one should not attempt to deduce the character of the illness from its name; for, strictly speaking, other kinds of morbid mental phenomena have an equal claim to possessing what are spoken of as 'obsessional' characteristics. In place of a definition we must for the time being be content with obtaining a detailed knowledge of these states, since we have not yet been able to arrive at a criterion of obsessional neuroses; it probably lies very deep, although we seem to sense its presence everywhere in the manifestations of the illness.

Neurotic ceremonials consist in making small adjustments to particular everyday actions, small additions or restrictions or arrangements, which have always to be carried out in the same, or in a methodically varied, manner. These activities give the impression of being mere formalities, and they seem quite meaningless to us. Nor do they appear otherwise to the patient himself; yet he is incapable of giving them up, for any deviation from the ceremonial is visited by intolerable anxiety, which obliges him at once to make his omission good. Just as trivial as the ceremonial actions themselves are the occasions and activities which are embellished, encumbered and in any case prolonged by the ceremonial—for instance, dressing and undressing, going to bed or satisfying bodily needs. The performance of a ceremonial can be described by replacing it, as it were, by a series of unwritten laws. For instance, to take the case of the bed ceremonial: the chair must stand in a particular place beside the bed; the clothes must lie upon it folded in a particular order; the blanket must be tucked in at the bottom and the sheet smoothed out; the pillows must be arranged in such and such a manner, and the subject's own body must lie in a precisely defined position. Only after all this may he go to sleep. Thus in slight cases the ceremonial seems to be no more than an exaggeration of an orderly procedure that is customary and justifiable; but the special conscientiousness with which it is carried out and the anxiety which follows upon its neglect stamp the ceremonial as a 'sacred act'. Any interruption of it is for the most part badly tolerated, and the presence of other people during its performance is almost always ruled out.

Any activities whatever may become obsessive actions in the wider sense of the term if they are elaborated by small additions or given a rhythmic character by means of pauses and repetitions. We shall not expect to find a sharp distinction between 'ceremonials' and 'obsessive actions'. As a rule obsessive actions have grown out of ceremonials. Besides these two, prohibitions and hindrances (abulias) make up the content of the disorder; these, in fact, only continue the work of the obsessive actions, inasmuch as some things are completely forbidden to the patient and others only allowed subject to his following a prescribed ceremonial.

It is remarkable that both compulsions and prohibitions (having to do something and having *not* to do something) apply in the first instance only to the subject's solitary activities and for a long time leave his social behaviour unaffected. Sufferers from this illness are consequently able to treat their affliction as a private matter and keep it concealed for many years. And, indeed, many more people suffer from these forms of obsessional neurosis than doctors hear of. For many sufferers, too, concealment is made easier from the fact that they are quite well able to fulfil their social duties during a part of the day, once they have devoted a number of hours to their secret doings, hidden from view like Mélusine.[1]

It is easy to see where the resemblances lie between neurotic ceremonials and the sacred acts of religious ritual: in the qualms of conscience brought on by their neglect, in their complete isolation from all other actions (shown in the prohibition against interruption) and in the conscientiousness with which they are carried out in every detail. But the differences are equally obvious, and a few of them are so glaring that they make the comparison a sacrilege: the greater individual variability of [neurotic] ceremonial actions in contrast to the stereotyped character of rituals (prayer, turning to the East, etc.), their private nature as opposed to the public and communal character of religious observances, above all, however, the fact that, while the minutiae of religious ceremonial are full of significance and have a symbolic meaning, those of neurotics seem foolish and senseless. In this respect an obsessional neurosis presents a travesty, half comic and half tragic, of a private religion. But it is precisely this sharpest difference between neurotic and religious ceremonial which disappears when, with the help of the psycho-analytic technique of investigation, one penetrates to the true meaning of obsessive actions.[2] In the course of such an investigation the appearance which obsessive actions afford of being foolish and senseless is completely effaced, and the reason for their having that appearance is explained. It is found that the obsessive actions are perfectly significant in every detail, that they serve important interests of the personality and that they give expression to experiences that are still operative and to thoughts that are cathected with affect. They do this in two ways, either by direct or by symbolic representation; and they are consequently to be interpreted either historically or symbolically.

I must give a few examples to illustrate my point. Those who are familiar with the findings of psychoanalytic investigation into the psychoneuroses will not be surprised to learn that what is being represented in obsessive actions or in ceremonials is derived from the most intimate, and for the most part from the sexual, experiences of the patient.

(*a*) A girl whom I was able to observe was under a compulsion to rinse round her wash-basin several times after washing. The significance of this ceremonial action lay in the proverbial saying: 'Don't throw away dirty water till you have clean.' Her action was intended to give a warning to her sister, of whom she was very fond, and to restrain her from getting divorced from her unsatisfactory husband until she had established a relationship with a better man.

(*b*) A woman who was living apart from her husband was subject to a compulsion, whenever she ate anything, to leave what was the best of it behind: for example, she would only take the outside of a piece of roast meat. This renunciation was explained by the date of its origin. It appeared on the day after she had refused marital relations with her husband—that is to say, after she had given up what was the best.

(*c*) The same patient could only sit on one particular chair and could only get up from it with difficulty. In regard to certain details of her married life, the chair symbolized her husband, to whom she remained faithful. She found an explanation of her compulsion in this sentence: 'It is so hard to part from anything (a husband, a chair) upon which one has once settled.'

(*d*) Over a period of time she used to repeat an especially noticeable and senseless obsessive action. She would run out of her room into another room in the middle of which there was a table. She would straighten the table-cloth on it in a particular manner and ring for the housemaid. The latter had to come up to the table, and the patient would then dismiss her on some indifferent errand. In the attempts to explain this compulsion, it occurred to her that at one place on the table-cloth there was a stain, and that she always arranged the cloth in such a way that the housemaid was bound to see the stain. The whole scene proved to be a reproduction of an experience in her married life which had later

on given her thoughts a problem to solve. On the wedding-night her husband had met with a not unusual mishap. He found himself impotent, and 'many times in the course of the night he came hurrying from his room into hers' to try once more whether he could succeed. In the morning he said he would feel ashamed in front of the hotel housemaid who made the beds, and he took a bottle of red ink and poured its contents over the sheet; but he did it so clumsily that the red stain came in a place that was very unsuitable for his purpose. With her obsessive action, therefore, she was representing the wedding-night. 'Bed and board'[3] between them make up marriage.

(*e*) Another compulsion which she started—of writing down the number of every bank-note before parting with it—had also to be interpreted historically. At a time when she was still intending to leave her husband if she could find another more trustworthy man, she allowed herself to receive advances from a man whom she met at a watering-place, but she was in doubt as to whether his intentions were serious. One day, being short of small change, she asked him to change a five-kronen[4] piece for her. He did so, pocketed the large coin and declared with a gallant air that he would never part with it, since it had passed through her hands. At their later meetings she was frequently tempted to challenge him to show her the five-kronen piece, as though she wanted to convince herself that she could believe in his intentions. But she refrained, for the good reason that it is impossible to distinguish between coins of the same value. Thus her doubt remained unresolved; and it left her with the compulsion to write down the number of each bank-note, by which it *can* be distinguished from all others of the same value.[5]

These few examples, selected from the great number I have met with, are merely intended to illustrate my assertion that in obsessive actions everything has its meaning and can be interpreted. The same is true of ceremonials in the strict sense, only that the evidence for this would require a more circumstantial presentation. I am quite aware of how far our explanations of obsessive actions are apparently taking us from the sphere of religious thought.

It is one of the conditions of the illness that the person who is obeying a compulsion carries it out without understanding its meaning—or at any rate its chief meaning. It is only thanks to the efforts of psycho-analytic treatment that he becomes conscious of the meaning of his obsessive action and, with it, of the motives that are impelling him to it. We express this important fact by saying that the obsessive action serves to express *unconscious* motives and ideas. In this, we seem to find a further departure from religious practices; but we must remember that as a rule the ordinary pious individual, too, performs a ceremonial without concerning himself with its significance, although priests and scientific investigators may be familiar with the—mostly symbolic—meaning of the ritual. In all believers, however, the motives which impel them to religious practices are unknown to them or are represented in consciousness by others which are advanced in their place.

Analysis of obsessive actions has already given us some sort of an insight into their causes and into the chain of motives which bring them into effect. We may say that the sufferer from compulsions and prohibitions behaves as if he were dominated by a sense of guilt, of which, however, he knows nothing, so that we must call it an unconscious sense of guilt, in spite of the apparent contradiction in terms.[6] This sense of guilt has its source in certain early mental events, but it is constantly being revived by renewed temptations which arise whenever there is a contemporary provocation. Moreover, it occasions a lurking sense of expectant anxiety, an expectation of misfortune, which is linked, through the idea of punishment, with the internal perception of the temptation. When the ceremonial is first being constructed, the patient is still conscious that he must do this or that lest some ill should befall, and as a rule the nature of the ill that is to be expected is still known to his consciousness. But what is already hidden from him is the connection—which is always demonstrable—between the occasion on which this expectant anxiety arises and the danger which it conjures up. Thus a ceremonial starts as an *action for defence* or *insurance*, a *protective measure*.

The sense of guilt of obsessional neurotics finds its counterpart in the protestations of pious people that they know that at heart they are miserable sinners; and the pious observances (such as prayers, invocations, etc.,) with which such people preface every daily act, and in especial every unusual undertaking, seem to have the value of defensive or protective measures.

A deeper insight into the mechanism of obsessional neurosis is gained if we take into account the primary fact which lies at the bottom of it. This is always *the repression of an instinctual impulse*[7] (a component of the sexual instinct) which was present in the subject's constitution and which was allowed to find expression for a while during his childhood but later succumbed to suppression. In the course of the repression of this instinct a special *conscientiousness* is created which is directed against the instinct's aims; but this psychical reaction-formation feels insecure and constantly threatened by the instinct which is lurking in the unconscious. The influence of the repressed instinct is felt as a temptation, and during the process of repression itself anxiety is generated, which gains control over the future in the form of *expectant* anxiety. The process of repression which leads to obsessional neurosis must be considered as one which is only partly successful and which increasingly threatens to fail. It may thus be compared to an unending conflict; fresh psychical efforts are continually required to counterbalance the forward pressure of the instinct.[8] Thus the ceremonial and obsessive actions arise partly as a defence against the temptation and partly as a protection against the ill which is expected. Against the temptation the protective measures seem soon to become inadequate; then the prohibitions come into play, with the purpose of keeping at a distance situations that give rise to temptation. Prohibitions take the place of obsessive actions, it will be seen, just as a phobia is designed to avert a hysterical attack. Again, a ceremonial represents the sum of the conditions subject to which something that is not yet absolutely forbidden is permitted, just as the Church's marriage ceremony signifies for the believer a sanctioning of sexual enjoyment which would otherwise be sinful. A further characteristic of obsessional neurosis, as of all similar affections, is that its manifestations (its symptoms, including the obsessive actions) fulfil the condition of being a compromise between the warring forces of the mind. They thus always reproduce something of the pleasure which they are designed to prevent; they serve the repressed instinct no less than the agencies which are repressing it. As the illness progresses, indeed, actions which were originally mostly concerned with maintaining the defence come to approximate more and more to the proscribed actions through which the instinct was able to find expression in childhood.

Some features of this state of affairs may be seen in the sphere of religious life as well. The formation of a religion, too, seems to be based on the suppression, the renunciation, of certain instinctual impulses. These impulses, however, are not, as in the neuroses, exclusively components of the sexual instinct; they are self-seeking, socially harmful instincts, though, even so, they are usually not without a sexual component. A sense of guilt following upon continual temptation and an expectant anxiety in the form of fear of divine punishment have, after all, been familiar to us in the field of religion longer than in that of neurosis. Perhaps because of the admixture of sexual components, perhaps because of some general characteristics of the instincts, the suppression of instinct proves to be an inadequate and interminable process in religious life also. Indeed, complete backslidings into sin are more common among pious people than among neurotics and these give rise to a new form of religious activity, namely acts of penance, which have their counterpart in obsessional neurosis.

We have noted as a curious and derogatory characteristic of obsessional neurosis that its ceremonials are concerned with the small actions of daily life and are expressed in foolish regulations and restrictions in connection with them. We cannot understand this remarkable feature of the clinical picture until we have realized that the mechanism of psychical *displacement*, which was first discovered by me in the construction of dreams,[9] dominates the mental processes of obsessional neurosis. It is already clear from the few examples of obsessive actions given above that their symbolism and the detail of their execution are brought about by a displacement from the actual, important thing on to a small one which takes its place—for instance, from a husband on to a chair.[10] It is this tendency to displacement which progressively changes the clinical picture and eventually succeeds in turning what is apparently the most trivial matter into something of the utmost importance and urgency. It cannot be denied that in the religious field as well there is a similar tendency

to a displacement of psychical values, and in the same direction, so that the petty ceremonials of religious practice gradually become the essential thing and push aside the underlying thoughts. That is why religions are subject to reforms which work retroactively and aim at a re-establishment of the original balance of values.

The character of compromise which obsessive actions possess in their capacity as neurotic symptoms is the character least easily detected in corresponding religious observances. Yet here, too, one is reminded of this feature of neuroses when one remembers how commonly all the acts which religion forbids—the expressions of the instincts it has suppressed—are committed precisely in the name of, and ostensibly for the sake of, religion.

In view of these similarities and analogies one might venture to regard obsessional neurosis as a pathological counterpart of the formation of a religion, and to describe that neurosis as an individual religiosity and religion as a universal obsessional neurosis. The most essential similarity would reside in the underlying renunciation of the activation of instincts that are constitutionally present; and the chief difference would lie in the nature of those instincts, which in the neurosis are exclusively sexual in their origin, while in religion they spring from egoistic sources.

A progressive renunciation of constitutional instincts, whose activation might afford the ego primary pleasure, appears to be one of the foundations of the development of human civilization.[11] Some part of this instinctual repression is effected by its religions, in that they require the individual to sacrifice his instinctual pleasure to the Deity: 'Vengeance is mine, saith the Lord.' In the development of the ancient religions one seems to discern that many things which mankind had renounced as 'iniquities' had been surrendered to the Deity and were still permitted in his name, so that the handing over to him of bad and socially harmful instincts was the means by which man freed himself from their domination. For this reason, it is surely no accident that all the attributes of man, along with the misdeeds that follow from them, were to an unlimited amount ascribed to the ancient gods. Nor is it a contradiction of this that nevertheless man was not permitted to justify his own iniquities by appealing to divine example.

NOTES

1. [A beautiful woman in mediaeval legend, who led a secret existence as a water-nymph.]
2. See the collection of my shorter papers on the theory of the neuroses published in 1906 [*Standard Ed.* 3].
3. [In German '*Tisch und Bett*' ('table and bed'). Cf. a paper on fairy tales in dreams (1913), *Standard Ed.*, 12, 282, footnote 3.]
4. [Equivalent at that time to four shillings or a dollar.]
5. [Freud discussed this case again at considerable length in Lecture XVII of his *Introductory Lectures* (1916–17).]
6. [The German word used here for 'sense of guilt' is '*Schuldbewusstsein*', literally 'consciousness of guilt'.—This seems to be the earliest explicit appearance of the 'unconscious sense of guilt' which was to play such an important part in Freud's later writings—e.g. at the beginning of the last chapter of *The Ego and the Id* (1923). The way had been prepared for the notion, however, very much earlier, in Section II of the first paper on 'The Neuro-Psychoses of Defence' (1894).]
7. ['*Triebregung.*' This appears to be Freud's first published use of what was to be one of his most used terms.]
8. [This passage foreshadows the concept of 'anticathexis', which is developed at length in Section IV of the paper on 'The Unconscious' (1915), *Standard Ed.*, 14, 180 ff.]
9. See *The Interpretation of Dreams* (1900), Chapter VI, Section B [*Standard Ed.*, 4, 305 ff.].
10. [Freud had already described this mechanism in his book on jokes (1905), near the end of Section 11 of Chapter II. He often recurred to the point—for instance, in the 'Rat Man' analysis (1909), *Standard Ed.*, 10, 241, and in the metapsychological paper on repression (1915), ibid., 14, 157.]
11. [This idea was expanded by Freud in the paper on sexual ethics written about a year later.]

Deep Play: Notes on the Balinese Cockfight

CLIFFORD GEERTZ

Facts of publication: *Geertz, Clifford. 1973. "Deep Play: Notes on the Balinese Cockfight," from* Myth Symbol and Culture. *Reprinted from* The Interpretation of Cultures: Selected Essays, *417–426, 432–433, 443–453. New York: Basic. Originally in* Daedalus *102 (Winter 1972):1–37. Copyright © 1971 by the American Academy of Arts and Sciences. Reprinted with the permission of the author and W. W. Norton & Company, Inc.*

Clifford Geertz views culture as an ensemble of texts. For him "texts" is a category that includes more than literary or verbal material. A text is any object of interpretation that says something about a culture. Though Geertz states that "to treat the cockfight as a text is to bring out a feature of it . . . that treating it as a rite or a pastime . . . would tend to obscure. . . ." cockfighting is nonetheless a ritual process. It is done as a sacrificial rite as part of every temple festival to appease the threatening demons.

Here Geertz comes, almost by coincidence, to consider cockfighting as text. Though cockfighting is a pastime, sport, occasion for gambling, display of violence, and work of art, it is also, according to Geertz's analysis, "a Balinese reading of Balinese experience, a story they tell themselves about themselves."

Through the careful description (only portions of which are selected for presentation here) and analysis of cockfights, Geertz shows a correlation between the spoken and unspoken rules of fighting and gambling and Balinese views on status. Surprisingly, though much money changes hands and winners and losers are determined, nothing in Balinese culture really changes. Geertz argues that what the fights depict is how the Balinese imagine the world to be rather than *how things are. The cockfight reveals the dark sides of Balinese hierarchy that are otherwise hidden: sentiments of jealousy, envy, and brutality.*

Others works by Geertz that are important for their contribution to ritual theory are "Religion as a Cultural System," "Ritual and Social Change," and "Ethos, World View, and the Analysis of Sacred Symbols." All are in The Interpretation of Cultures *(New York: Basic, 1973).*

About the author: Dates*: 1926–, San Francisco, CA, U.S.A.* **Education:** *B.A., Antioch College; Ph.D., Harvard University.* **Field(s):** *anthropology.* **Career***: Professor of Social Science, 1970–present, Institute for Advanced Study, Princeton, New Jersey. Also taught at University of California, Berkeley, 1958–60, and University of Chicago, 1960–1970.* **Publications:** The Religion of Java *(Free, 1960).* Islam Observed: Religious Development in Morocco and Indonesia *(Yale University, 1968).* The Interpretation of Cultures: Selected Essays *(Basic, 1973).* Negra: The Theatre State in Nineteenth Century Bali *(Princeton University, 1980).* Local Knowledge: Further Essays in Interpretive Anthropology *(Basic, 1983).* Works and Lives: The Anthropologist as Author *(Stanford University, 1988).* **Additional:** *Ten honorary doctorates, including Harvard University, University of Chicago, New School for Social Research, and Yale University. Talcott Parsons Prize, American Academy of Arts and Sciences, 1974; Sorokin Prize, American Sociological Association, 1974; Distinguished Lecturer, American Anthropological Association, 1983; National Book Critics Circle Prize in Criticism, 1988.* ˙

OF COCKS AND MEN

Bali, mainly because it is Bali, is a well-studied place. Its mythology, art, ritual, social organization, patterns of child rearing, forms of law, even styles of trance, have all been microscopically examined for traces of that elusive substance Jane Belo called "The Balinese Temper."[1] But, aside from a few passing remarks, the cockfight has barely been noticed, although as a popular obsession of consuming power it is at least as important a revelation of what being a Balinese "is really like" as these more celebrated phenomena.[2] As much of America surfaces in a ball park, on a golf links, at a race track, or around a poker table, much of Bali surfaces in a cock ring. For it is only apparently cocks that are fighting there. Actually, it is men.

To anyone who has been in Bali any length of time, the deep psychological identification of Balinese men with their cocks is unmistakable. The double entendre here is deliberate. It works in exactly the same way in Balinese as it does in English, even to producing the same tired jokes, strained puns, and uninventive obscenities. Bateson and Mead have even suggested that, in line with the Balinese conception of the body as a set of separately animated parts, cocks are viewed as detachable, self-operating penises, ambulant genitals with a life of their own.[3] And while I do not have the kind of unconscious material either to confirm or disconfirm this intriguing notion, the fact that they are masculine symbols par excellence is about as indubitable,

and to the Balinese about as evident, as the fact that water runs downhill.

The language of everyday moralism is shot through, on the male side of it, with roosterish imagery. *Sabung,* the word for cock (and one which appears in inscriptions as early as A.D. 922), is used metaphorically to mean "hero," "warrior," "champion," "man of parts," "political candidate," "bachelor," "dandy," "lady-killer," or "tough guy." A pompous man whose behavior presumes above his station is compared to a tailless cock who struts about as though he had a large, spectacular one. A desperate man who makes a last, irrational effort to extricate himself from an impossible situation is likened to a dying cock who makes one final lunge at his tormentor to drag him along to a common destruction. A stingy man, who promises much, gives little, and begrudges that, is compared to a cock which, held by the tail, leaps at another without in fact engaging him. A marriageable young man still shy with the opposite sex or someone in a new job anxious to make a good impression is called "a fighting cock caged for the first time."[4] Court trials, wars, political contests, inheritance disputes, and street arguments are all compared to cockfights.[5] Even the very island itself is perceived from its shape as a small, proud cock, poised, neck extended, back taut, tail raised, in eternal challenge to large, feckless, shapeless Java.[6]

But the intimacy of men with their cocks is more than metaphorical. Balinese men, or anyway a large majority of Balinese men, spend an enormous amount of time with their favorites, grooming them, feeding them, discussing them, trying them out against one another, or just gazing at them with a mixture of rapt admiration and dreamy self-absorption. Whenever you see a group of Balinese men squatting idly in the council shed or along the road in their hips down, shoulders forward, knees up fashion, half or more of them will have a rooster in his hands, holding it between his thighs, bouncing it gently up and down to strengthen its legs, ruffling its feathers with abstract sensuality, pushing it out against a neighbor's rooster to rouse its spirit, withdrawing it toward his loins to calm it again. Now and then, to get a feel for another bird, a man will fiddle this way with someone else's cock for a while, but usually by moving around to squat in place behind it, rather than just having it passed across to him as though it were merely an animal.

In the houseyard, the high-walled enclosures where the people live, fighting cocks are kept in wicker cages, moved frequently about so as to maintain the optimum balance of sun and shade. They are fed a special diet, which varies somewhat according to individual theories but which is mostly maize, sifted for impurities with far more care than it is when mere humans are going to eat it, and offered to the animal kernel by kernel. Red pepper is stuffed down their beaks and up their anuses to give them spirit. They are bathed in the same ceremonial preparation of tepid water, medicinal herbs, flowers, and onions in which infants are bathed, and for a prize cock just about as often. Their combs are cropped, their plumage dressed, their spurs trimmed, and their legs massaged, and they are inspected for flaws with the squinted concentration of a diamond merchant. A man who has a passion for cocks, an enthusiast in the literal sense of the term, can spend most of his life with them, and even those, the overwhelming majority, whose passion though intense has not entirely run away with them, can and do spend what seems not only to an outsider, but also to themselves, an inordinate amount of time with them. "I am cock crazy," my landlord, a quite ordinary *afficionado* by Balinese standards, used to moan as he went to move another cage, give another bath, or conduct another feeding. "We're all cock crazy."

The madness has some less visible dimensions,

however, because although it is true that cocks are symbolic expressions or magnifications of their owner's self, the narcissistic male ego writ out in Aesopian terms, they are also expressions—and rather more immediate ones—of what the Balinese regard as the direct inversion, aesthetically, morally, and metaphysically, of human status: animality.

The Balinese revulsion against any behavior regarded as animal-like can hardly be overstressed. Babies are not allowed to crawl for that reason. Incest, though hardly approved, is a much less horrifying crime than bestiality. (The appropriate punishment for the second is death by drowning, for the first being forced to live like an animal.)[7] Most demons are represented—in sculpture, dance, ritual, myth—in some real or fantastic animal form. The main puberty rite consists in filing the child's teeth so they will not look like animal fangs. Not only defecation but eating is regarded as a disgusting, almost obscene activity, to be conducted hurriedly and privately, because of its association with animality. Even falling down or any form of clumsiness is considered to be bad for these reasons. Aside from cocks and a few domestic animals—oxen, ducks—of no emotional significance, the Balinese are aversive to animals and treat their large number of dogs not merely callously but with a phobic cruelty. In identifying with his cock, the Balinese man is identifying not just with his ideal self, or even his penis, but also, and at the same time, with what he most fears, hates, and ambivalence being what it is, is fascinated by—"The Powers of Darkness."

The connection of cocks and cockfighting with such Powers, with the animalistic demons that threaten constantly to invade the small, cleared-off space in which the Balinese have so carefully built their lives and devour its inhabitants, is quite explicit. A cockfight, any cockfight, is in the first instance a blood sacrifice offered, with the appropriate chants and oblations, to the demons in order to pacify their ravenous, cannibal hunger. No temple festival should be conducted until one is made. (If it is omitted, someone will inevitably fall into a trance and command with the voice of an angered spirit that the oversight be immediately corrected.) Collective responses to natural evils—illness, crop failure, volcanic eruptions—almost always involve them. And that famous holiday in Bali, "The Day of

Silence" (*Njepi*), when everyone sits silent and immobile all day long in order to avoid contact with a sudden influx of demons chased momentarily out of hell, is preceded the previous day by large-scale cockfights (in this case legal) in almost every village on the island.

In the cockfight, man and beast, good and evil, ego and id, the creative power of aroused masculinity and the destructive power of loosened animality fuse in a bloody drama of hatred, cruelty, violence, and death. It is little wonder that when, as is the invariable rule, the owner of the winning cock takes the carcass of the loser—often torn limb from limb by its enraged owner—home to eat, he does so with a mixture of social embarrassment, moral satisfaction, aesthetic disgust, and cannibal joy. Or that a man who has lost an important fight is sometimes driven to wreck his family shrines and curse the gods, an act of metaphysical (and social) suicide. Or that in seeking earthly analogues for heaven and hell the Balinese compare the former to the mood of a man whose cock has just won, the latter to that of a man whose cock has just lost.

THE FIGHT

Cockfights (*tetadjen; sabungan*) are held in a ring about fifty feet square. Usually they begin toward late afternoon and run three or four hours until sunset. About nine or ten separate matches (*sehet*) comprise a program. Each match is precisely like the others in general pattern: there is no main match, no connection between individual matches, no variation in their format, and each is arranged on a completely ad hoc basis. After a fight has ended and the emotional debris is cleaned away—the bets have been paid, the curses cursed, the carcasses possessed—seven, eight, perhaps even a dozen men slip negligently into the ring with a cock and seek to find there a logical opponent for it. This process, which rarely takes less than ten minutes, and often a good deal longer, is conducted in a very subdued, oblique, even dissembling manner. Those not immediately involved give it at best but disguised, sidelong attention; those who, embarrassedly, are, attempt to pretend somehow that the whole thing is not really happening.

A match made, the other hopefuls retire with the same deliberate indifference, and the selected cocks have their spurs (*tadji*) affixed—razor-sharp, pointed steel swords, four or five inches long. This is a delicate job which only a small proportion of men, a half-dozen or so in most villages, know how to do properly. The man who attaches the spurs also provides them, and if the rooster he assists wins, its owner awards him the spur-leg of the victim. The spurs are affixed by winding a long length of string around the foot of the spur and the leg of the cock. For reasons I shall come to presently, it is done somewhat differently from case to case, and is an obsessively deliberate affair. The lore about spurs is extensive—they are sharpened only at eclipses and the dark of the moon, should be kept out of the sight of women, and so forth. And they are handled, both in use and out, with the same curious combination of fussiness and sensuality the Balinese direct toward ritual objects generally.

The spurs affixed, the two cocks are placed by their handlers (who may or may not be their owners) facing one another in the center of the ring.[8] A coconut pierced with a small hole is placed in a pail of water, in which it takes about twenty-one seconds to sink, a period known as a *tjeng* and marked at beginning and end by the beating of a slit gong. During these twenty-one seconds the handlers (*pengangkeb*) are not permitted to touch their roosters. If, as sometimes happens, the animals have not fought during this time, they are picked up, fluffed, pulled, prodded, and otherwise insulted, and put back in the center of the ring and the process begins again. Sometimes they refuse to fight at all, or one keeps running away, in which case they are imprisoned together under a wicker cage, which usually gets them engaged.

Most of the time, in any case, the cocks fly almost immediately at one another in a wing-beating, head-thrusting, leg-kicking explosion of animal fury so pure, so absolute, and in its own way so beautiful, as to be almost abstract, a Platonic concept of hate. Within moments one or the other drives home a solid blow with his spur. The handler whose cock has delivered the blow immediately picks it up so that it will not get a return blow, for if he does not the match is likely to end in a mutually mortal tie as the two birds wildly hack each other to pieces. This is particularly true if, as often happens, the spur sticks in its victim's body, for then the aggressor is at the mercy of his wounded foe.

With the birds again in the hands of their handlers, the coconut is now sunk three times after which the cock which has landed the blow must be set down to show that he is firm, a fact he demonstrates by wandering idly around the ring for a coconut sink. The coconut is then sunk twice more and the fight must recommence.

During this interval, slightly over two minutes, the handler of the wounded cock has been working frantically over it, like a trainer patching a mauled boxer between rounds, to get it in shape for a last, desperate try for victory. He blows in its mouth, putting the whole chicken head in his own mouth and sucking and blowing, fluffs it, stuffs its wounds with various sorts of medicines, and generally tries anything he can think of to arouse the last ounce of spirit which may be hidden somewhere within it. By the time he is forced to put it back down he is usually drenched in chicken blood, but, as in prize fighting, a good handler is worth his weight in gold. Some of them can virtually make the dead walk, at least long enough for the second and final round.

In the climactic battle (if there is one; sometimes the wounded cock simply expires in the handler's hands or immediately as it is placed down again), the cock who landed the first blow usually proceeds to finish off his weakened opponent. But this is far from an inevitable outcome, for if a cock can walk, he can fight, and if he can fight, he can kill, and what counts is which cock expires first. If the wounded one can get a stab in and stagger on until the other drops, he is the official winner, even if he himself topples over an instant later.

Surrounding all this melodrama—which the crowd packed tight around the ring follows in near silence, moving their bodies in kinesthetic sympathy with the movement of the animals, cheering their champions on with wordless hand motions, shiftings of the shoulders, turnings of the head, falling back en masse as the cock with the murderous spurs careens toward one side of the ring (it is said that spectators sometimes lose eyes and fingers from being too attentive), surging forward again as they glance off toward another—is a vast body of extraordinarily elaborate and precisely detailed rules.

These rules, together with the developed lore of cocks and cockfighting which accompanies them, are written down in palm-leaf manuscripts (*lontar; rontal*) passed on from generation to generation as part of the general legal and cultural tradition of the villages. At a fight, the umpire (*saja komong; djuru kembar*)—the man who manages the coconut—is in charge of their application and his authority is absolute. I have never seen an umpire's judgment questioned on any subject, even by the more despondent losers, nor have I ever heard, even in private, a charge of unfairness directed against one, or, for that matter, complaints about umpires in general. Only exceptionally well trusted, solid, and, given the complexity of the code, knowledgeable citizens perform this job, and in fact men will bring their cocks only to fights presided over by such men. It is also the umpire to whom accusations of cheating, which, though rare in the extreme, occasionally arise, are referred; and it is he who in the not infrequent cases where the cocks expire virtually together decides which (if either, for, though the Balinese do not care for such an outcome, there can be ties) went first. Likened to a judge, a king, a priest, and a policeman, he is all of these, and under his assured direction the animal passion of the fight proceeds within the civic certainty of the law. In the dozens of cockfights I saw in Bali, I never once saw an altercation about rules. Indeed, I never saw an open altercation, other than those between cocks, at all.

This crosswise doubleness of an event which, taken as a fact of nature, is rage untrammeled and, taken as a fact of culture, is form perfected, defines the cockfight as a sociological entity. A cockfight is what, searching for a name for something not vertebrate enough to be called a group and not structureless enough to be called a crowd, Erving Goffman has called a "focused gathering"—a set of persons engrossed in a common flow of activity and relating to one another in terms of that flow.[9] Such gatherings meet and disperse; the participants in them fluctuate; the activity that focuses them is discrete—a particulate process that reoccurs rather than a continuous one that endures. They take their form from the situation that evokes them, the floor on which they are placed, as Goffman puts it; but it is a form, and an articulate one, nonetheless. For the situation, the floor is itself created, in jury deliberations, surgical operations, block meetings, sit-ins, cockfights, by the cultural preoccupations—here, as we shall see, the celebration of status rivalry—which not only specify the focus but, assembling actors and arranging scenery, bring it actually into being.

In classical times (that is to say, prior to the Dutch invasion of 1908), when there were no bureaucrats around to improve popular morality, the staging of a cockfight was an explicitly societal matter. Bringing a cock to an important fight was, for an adult male, a compulsory duty of citizenship; taxation of fights, which were usually held on market day, was a major source of public revenue; patronage of the art was a stated responsibility of princes; and the cock ring, or *wantilan*, stood in the center of the village near those other monuments of Balinese civility—the council house, the origin temple, the marketplace, the signal tower, and the banyan tree. Today, a few special occasions aside, the newer rectitude makes so open a statement of the connection between the excitements of collective life and those of blood sport impossible, but, less directly expressed, the connection itself remains intimate and intact. To expose it, however, it is necessary to turn to the aspect of cockfighting around which all the others pivot, and through which they exercise their force, an aspect I have thus far studiously ignored. I mean, of course, the gambling.

ODDS AND EVEN MONEY

The Balinese never do anything in a simple way that they can contrive to do in a complicated one, and to this generalization cockfight wagering is no exception.

In the first place, there are two sorts of bets, or *toh*.[10] There is the single axial bet in the center between the principals (*toh ketengah*), and there is the cloud of peripheral ones around the ring between members of the audience (*toh kesasi*). The first is typically large; the second typically small. The first is collective, involving coalitions of bettors clustering around the owner; the second is individual, man to man. The first is a matter of deliberate, very quiet, almost furtive arrangement by the coalition members and the umpire huddled like conspirators in the center of the ring; the second is a matter of

impulsive shouting, public offers, and public acceptances by the excited throng around its edges. And most curiously, and as we shall see most revealingly, *where the first is always, without exception, even money, the second, equally without exception, is never such*. What is a fair coin in the center is a biased one on the side.

The center bet is the official one, hedged in again with a webwork of rules, and is made between the two cock owners, with the umpire as overseer and public witness.[11] This bet, which, as I say, is always relatively and sometimes very large, is never raised simply by the owner in whose name it is made, but by him together with four or five, sometimes seven or eight, allies—kin, village mates, neighbors, close friends. He may, if he is not especially well-to-do, not even be the major contributor; though, if only to show that he is not involved in any chicanery, he must be a significant one. . . .

Playing with Fire

Bentham's concept of "deep play" is found in his *The Theory of Legislation*.[12] By it he means play in which the stakes are so high that it is, from his utilitarian standpoint, irrational for men to engage in it at all. If a man whose fortune is a thousand pounds (or ringgits) wages five hundred of it on an even bet, the marginal utility of the pound he stands to win is clearly less than the marginal disutility of the one he stands to lose. In genuine deep play, this is the case for both parties. They are both in over their heads. Having come together in search of pleasure they have entered into a relationship which will bring the participants, considered collectively, net pain rather than net pleasure. Bentham's conclusion was, therefore, that deep play was immoral from first principles and, a typical step for him, should be prevented legally.

But more interesting than the ethical problem, at least for our concerns here, is that despite the logical force of Bentham's analysis men do engage in such play, both passionately and often, and even in the face of law's revenge. For Bentham and those who think as he does (nowadays mainly lawyers, economists, and a few psychiatrists), the explanation is, as I have said, that such men are irrational— addicts, fetishists, children, fools, savages, who need only to be protected against themselves. But for the Balinese, though naturally they do not formulate it in so many words, the explanation lies in the fact that in such play, money is less a measure of utility, had or expected, than it is a symbol of moral import, perceived or imposed.

It is, in fact, in shallow games, ones in which smaller amounts of money are involved, that increments and decrements of cash are more nearly synonyms for utility and disutility, in the ordinary, unexpanded sense—for pleasure and pain, happiness and unhappiness. In deep ones, where the amounts of money are great, much more is at stake than material gain: namely, esteem, honor, dignity, respect—in a word, though in Bali a profoundly freighted word, status.[13] It is at stake symbolically, for (a few cases of ruined addict gamblers aside) no one's status is actually altered by the outcome of a cockfight; it is only, and that momentarily, affirmed or insulted. But for the Balinese, for whom nothing is more pleasurable than an affront obliquely delivered or more painful than one obliquely received—particularly when mutual acquaintances, undeceived by surfaces, are watching—such appraisive drama is deep indeed. . . .

FEATHERS, BLOOD, CROWDS, AND MONEY

"Poetry makes nothing happen," Auden says in his elegy of Yeats, "it survives in the valley of its saying . . . a way of happening, a mouth." The cockfight too, in this colloquial sense, makes nothing happen. Men go on allegorically humiliating one another and being allegorically humiliated by one another, day after day, glorying quietly in the experience if they have triumphed, crushed only slightly more openly by it if they have not. *But no one's status really changes.* You cannot ascend the status ladder by winning cockfights; you cannot, as an individual, really ascend it at all. Nor can you descend it that way.[14] All you can do is enjoy and savor, or suffer and withstand, the concocted sensation of drastic and momentary movement along an aesthetic semblance of that ladder, a kind of behind-the-mirror status jump which has the look of mobility without its actuality.

Like any art form—for that, finally, is what we are dealing with—the cockfight renders ordinary, everyday experience comprehensible by presenting it in terms of acts and objects which have had their practical consequences removed and been reduced (or, if you prefer, raised) to the level of sheer appearances, where their meaning can be more powerfully articulated and more exactly perceived. The cockfight is "really real" only to the cocks—it does not kill anyone, castrate anyone, reduce anyone to animal status, alter the hierarchical relations among people, or refashion the hierarchy; it does not even redistribute income in any significant way. What it does is what, for other peoples with other temperaments and other conventions, *Lear* and *Crime and Punishment* do; it catches up these themes—death, masculinity, rage, pride, loss, beneficence, chance—and, ordering them into an encompassing structure, presents them in such a way as to throw into relief a particular view of their essential nature. It puts a construction on them, makes them, to those historically positioned to appreciate the construction, meaningful—visible, tangible, graspable—"real," in an ideational sense. An image, fiction, a model, a metaphor, the cockfight is a means of expression; its function is neither to assuage social passions nor to heighten them (though, in its playing-with-fire way it does a bit of both), but, in a medium of feathers, blood, crowds, and money, to display them.

The question of how it is that we perceive qualities in things—paintings, books, melodies, plays—that we do not feel we can assert literally to be there has come, in recent years, into the very center of aesthetic theory.[15] Neither the sentiments of the artist, which remain his, nor those of the audience, which remain theirs, can account for the agitation of one painting or the serenity of another. We attribute grandeur, wit, despair, exuberance to strings of sounds; lightness, energy, violence, fluidity to blocks of stone. Novels are said to have strength, buildings eloquence, plays momentum, ballets repose. In this realm of eccentric predicates, to say that the cockfight, in its perfected cases at least, is "disquietful" does not seem at all unnatural, merely, as I have just denied it practical consequence, somewhat puzzling.

The disquietfulness arises, "somehow," out of a conjunction of three attributes of the fight: its immediate dramatic shape; its metaphoric content; and its social context. A cultural figure against a social ground, the fight is at once a convulsive surge of animal hatred, a mock war of symbolical selves, and a formal simulation of status tensions, and its aesthetic power derives from its capacity to force together these diverse realities. The reason it is disquietful is not that it has material effects (it has some, but they are minor); the reason that it is disquietful is that, joining pride to selfhood, selfhood to cocks, and cocks to destruction, it brings to imaginative realization a dimension of Balinese experience normally well-obscured from view. The transfer of a sense of gravity into what is in itself a rather blank and unvarious spectacle, a commotion of beating wings and throbbing legs, is effected by interpreting it as expressive of something unsettling in the way its authors and audience live, or, even more ominously, what they are.

As a dramatic shape, the fight displays a characteristic that does not seem so remarkable until one realizes that it does not have to be there: a radically atomistical structure.[16] Each match is a world unto itself, a particulate burst of form. There is the matchmaking, there is the betting, there is the fight, there is the result—utter triumph and utter defeat—and there is the hurried, embarrassed passing of money. The loser is not consoled. People drift away from him, look around him, leave him to assimilate his momentary descent into nonbeing, reset his face, and return, scarless and intact, to the fray. Nor are winners congratulated, or events rehashed; once a match is ended the crowd's attention turns totally to the next, with no looking back. A shadow of the experience no doubt remains with the principals, perhaps even with some of the witnesses of a deep fight, as it remains with us when we leave the theater after seeing a powerful play well-performed; but it quite soon fades to become at most a schematic memory—a diffuse glow or an abstract shudder—and usually not even that. Any expressive form lives only in its own present—the one it itself creates. But, here, that present is severed into a string of flashes, some more bright than others, but all of them disconnected, aesthetic quanta. Whatever the cockfight says, it says in spurts.

. . . The Balinese live in spurts. Their life, as they arrange it and perceive it, is less a flow, a directional movement out of the past, through the present, toward the future than an on-off pulsation of meaning and vacuity, an arhythmic alternation of short periods when "something" (that is, something significant) is happening, and equally short ones where "nothing" (that is, nothing much) is—between what they themselves call "full" and "empty" times, or, in another idiom, "junctures" and "holes." In focusing activity down to a burning-glass dot, the cockfight is merely being Balinese in the same way in which everything from the monadic encounters of everyday life, through the clanging pointillism of *gamelan* music, to the visiting-day-of-the-gods temple celebrations are. It is not an imitation of the punctuateness of Balinese social life, nor a depiction of it, nor even an expression of it; it is an example of it, carefully prepared.[17]

If one dimension of the cockfight's structure, its lack of temporal directionality, makes it seem a typical segment of the general social life, however, the other, its flat-out, head-to-head (or spur-to-spur) aggressiveness, makes it seem a contradiction, a reversal, even a subversion of it. In the normal course of things, the Balinese are shy to the point of obsessiveness of open conflict. Oblique, cautious, subdued, controlled, masters of indirection and dissimulation—what they call *alus*, "polished," "smooth"—they rarely face what they can turn away from, rarely resist what they can evade. But here they portray themselves as wild and murderous, with manic explosions of instinctual cruelty. A powerful rendering of life as the Balinese most deeply do not want it (to adapt a phrase Frye has used of Gloucester's blinding) is set in the context of a sample of it as they do in fact have it.[18] And, because the context suggests that the rendering, if less than a straightforward description, is nonetheless more than an idle fancy; it is here that the disquietfulness—the disquietfulness of the *fight*, not (or, anyway, not necessarily) its patrons, who seem in fact rather thoroughly to enjoy it—emerges. The slaughter in the cock ring is not a depiction of how things literally are among men, but, what is almost worse, of how, from a particular angle, they imaginatively are.[19]

The angle, of course, is stratificatory. What, as we have already seen, the cockfight talks most forcibly about is status relationships, and what it says about them is that they are matters of life and death. That prestige is a profoundly serious business is apparent everywhere one looks in Bali—in the village, the family, the economy, the state. A peculiar fusion of Polynesian title ranks and Hindu castes, the hierarchy of pride is the moral backbone of the society. But only in the cockfight are the sentiments upon which that hierarchy rests revealed in their natural colors. Enveloped elsewhere in a haze of etiquette, a thick cloud of euphemism and ceremony, gesture and allusion, they are here expressed in only the thinnest disguise of an animal mask, a mask which in fact demonstrates them far more effectively than it conceals them. Jealousy is as much a part of Bali as poise, envy as grace, brutality as charm; but without the cockfight the Balinese would have a much less certain understanding of them, which is, presumably, why they value it so highly.

Any expressive form works (when it works) by disarranging semantic contexts in such a way that properties conventionally ascribed to certain things are unconventionally ascribed to others, which are then seen actually to possess them. To call the wind a cripple, as Stevens does, to fix tone and manipulate timbre, as Schoenberg does, or, closer to our case, to picture an art critic as a dissolute bear, as Hogarth does, is to cross conceptual wires; the established conjunctions between objects and their qualities are altered, and phenomena—fall weather, melodic shape, or cultural journalism—are clothed in signifiers which normally point to other referents.[20] Similarly, to connect—and connect, and connect—the collision of roosters with the divisiveness of status is to invite a transfer of perceptions from the former to the latter, a transfer which is at once a description and a judgment. (Logically, the transfer could, of course, as well go the other way; but, like most of the rest of us, the Balinese are a great deal more interested in understanding men than they are in understanding cocks.)

What sets the cockfight apart from the ordinary course of life, lifts it from the realm of everyday practical affairs, and surrounds it with an aura of enlarged importance is not, as functionalist sociology would have it, that it reinforces status discriminations (such reinforcement is hardly necessary in a society where every act proclaims them), but that it provides a metasocial commentary upon the whole matter of assorting human beings into fixed hierarchical ranks and then organizing the major part of collective existence around that assortment. Its function, if you want to call it that, is interpretive: it is a Balinese reading of Balinese experience, a story they tell themselves about themselves.

SAYING SOMETHING OF SOMETHING

To put the matter this way is to engage in a bit of metaphorical refocusing of one's own, for it shifts the analysis of cultural forms from an endeavor in general parallel to dissecting an organism, diagnosing a symptom, deciphering a code, or ordering a system—the dominant analogies in contemporary anthropology—to one in general parallel with penetrating a literary text. If one takes the cockfight, or any other collectively sustained symbolic structure, as a means of "saying something of something" (to invoke a famous Aristotelian tag), then one is faced with a problem not in social mechanics but social semantics.[21] For the anthropologist, whose concern is with formulating sociological principles, not with promoting or appreciating cockfights, the question is, what does one learn about such principles from examining culture as an assemblage of texts?

Such an extension of the notion of a text beyond written material, and even beyond verbal, is though metaphorical, not, of course, all that novel. The *interpretatio naturae* tradition of the middle ages, which, culminating in Spinoza, attempted to read nature as Scripture, the Nietzschean effort to treat value systems as glosses on the will to power (or the Marxian one to treat them as glosses on property relations), and the Freudian replacement of the enigmatic text of the manifest dream with the plain one of the latent, all offer precedents, if not equally recommendable ones.[22] But the idea remains theoretically undeveloped; and the more profound corollary, so far as anthropology is concerned, that cultural forms can be treated as texts, as imaginative works built out of social materials, has yet to be systematically exploited.[23]

In the case at hand, to treat the cockfight as a text is to bring out a feature of it (in my opinion, the central feature of it) that treating it as a rite or a pastime, the two most obvious alternatives, would tend to obscure: its use of emotion for cognitive ends. What the cockfight says it says in a vocabulary of sentiment—the thrill of risk, the despair of loss, the pleasure of triumph. Yet what it says is not merely that risk is exciting, loss depressing, or triumph gratifying, banal tautologies of affect, but that it is of these emotions, thus exampled, that society is built and individuals are put together. Attending cockfights and participating in them is, for the Balinese, a kind of sentimental education. What he learns there is what his culture's ethos and his private sensibility (or, anyway, certain aspects of them) look like when spelled out externally in a collective text; that the two are near enough alike to be articulated in the symbolics of a single such text; and—the disquieting part—that the text in which this revelation is accomplished consists of a chicken hacking another mindlessly to bits.

Every people, the proverb has it, loves its own form of violence. The cockfight is the Balinese reflection on theirs: on its look, its uses, its force, its fascination. Drawing on almost every level of Balinese experience, it brings together themes—animal savagery, male narcissism, opponent gambling, status rivalry, mass excitement, blood sacrifice—whose main connection is their involvement with rage and the fear of rage, and, binding them into a set of rules which at once contains them and allows them play, builds a symbolic structure in which, over and over again, the reality of their inner affiliation can be intelligibly felt. If, to quote Northrop Frye again, we go to see *Macbeth* to learn what a man feels like after he has gained a kingdom and lost his soul, Balinese go to cockfights to find out what a man, usually composed, aloof, almost obsessively self-absorbed, a kind of moral autocosm, feels like when, attacked, tormented, challenged, insulted, and driven in result to the extremes of fury, he has totally triumphed or been brought totally low. The whole passage, as it takes us back to Aristotle (though to the *Poetics* rather than the *Hermeneutics*), is worth quotation:

> But the poet [as opposed to the historian], Aristotle says, never makes any real statements at all, certainly no particular or specific ones. The poet's job is not to tell you what happened, but what happens: not what

did take place, but the kind of thing that always does take place. He gives you the typical, recurring, or what Aristotle calls universal event. You wouldn't go to *Macbeth* to learn about the history of Scotland—you go to it to learn what a man feels like after he's gained a kingdom and lost his soul. When you meet such a character as Micawber in Dickens, you don't feel that there must have been a man Dickens knew who was exactly like this: you feel that there's a bit of Micawber in almost everybody you know, including yourself. Our impressions of human life are picked up one by one, and remain for most of us loose and disorganized. But we constantly find things in literature that suddenly coordinate and bring into focus a great many such impressions, and this is part of what Aristotle means by the typical or universal human event.[24]

It is this kind of bringing of assorted experiences of everyday life to focus that the cockfight, set aside from that life as "only a game" and reconnected to it as "more than a game," accomplishes, and so creates what, better than typical or universal, could be called a paradigmatic human event—that is, one that tells us less what happens than the kind of thing that would happen if, as is not the case, life were art and could be as freely shaped by styles of feeling as *Macbeth* and *David Copperfield* are.

Enacted and re-enacted, so far without end, the cockfight enables the Balinese, as, read and reread, *Macbeth* enables us, to see a dimension of his own subjectivity. As he watches fight after fight, with the active watching of an owner and a bettor (for cockfighting has no more interest as a pure spectator sport than does croquet or dog racing), he grows familiar with it and what it has to say to him, much as the attentive listener to string quartets or the absorbed viewer of still life grows slowly more familiar with them in a way which opens his subjectivity to himself.[25]

Yet, because—in another of those paradoxes, along with painted feelings and unconsequenced acts, which haunt aesthetics—that subjectivity does not properly exist until it is thus organized, art forms generate and regenerate the very subjectivity they pretend only to display. Quartets, still lifes, and cockfights are not merely reflections of a pre-existing sensibility analogically represented; they are positive agents in the creation and maintenance of such a sensibility. If we see ourselves as a pack of Micaw-bers, it is from reading too much Dickens (if we see ourselves as unillusioned realists, it is from reading too little); and similarly for Balinese, cocks, and cockfights. It is in such a way, coloring experience with the light they cast it in, rather than through whatever material effects they may have, that the arts play their role, as arts, in social life.[26]

In the cockfight, then, the Balinese forms and discovers his temperament and his society's temper at the same time. Or, more exactly, he forms and discovers a particular facet of them. Not only are there a great many other cultural texts providing commentaries on status hierarchy and self-regard in Bali, but there are a great many other critical sectors of Balinese life besides the stratificatory and the ag-onistic that receive such commentary. The cere-mony consecrating a Brahmana priest, a matter of breath control, postural immobility, and vacant concentration upon the depths of being, displays a radically different, but to the Balinese equally real, property of social hierarchy—its reach toward the numinous transcendent. Set not in the matrix of the kinetic emotionality of animals, but in that of the static passionlessness of divine mentality, it ex-presses tranquillity not disquiet. The mass festivals at the village temples, which mobilize the whole lo-cal population in elaborate hostings of visiting gods—songs, dances, compliments, gifts—assert the spiritual unity of village mates against their sta-tus inequality and project a mood of amity and trust.[27] The cockfight is not the master key to Bali-nese life, any more than bullfighting is to Spanish.

What it says about that life is not unqualified nor even unchallenged by what other equally eloquent cultural statements say about it. But there is nothing more surprising in this than in the fact that Racine and Molière were contemporaries, or that the same people who arrange chrysanthemums cast swords.[28]

The culture of a people is an ensemble of texts, themselves ensembles, which the anthropologist strains to read over the shoulders of those to whom they properly belong. There are enormous difficul-ties in such an enterprise, methodological pitfalls to make a Freudian quake, and some moral perplexi-ties as well. Nor is it the only way that symbolic forms can be sociologically handled. Functionalism lives, and so does psychologism. But to regard such forms as "saying something of something," and say-ing it to somebody, is at least to open up the possi-bility of an analysis which attends to their substance rather than to reductive formulas professing to ac-count for them.

As in more familiar exercises in close reading, one can start anywhere in a culture's repertoire of forms and end up anywhere else. One can stay, as I have here, within a single, more or less bounded form, and circle steadily within it. One can move between forms in search of broader unities or informing con-trasts. One can even compare forms from different cultures to define their character in reciprocal relief. But whatever the level at which one operates, and however intricately, the guiding principle is the same: societies, like lives, contain their own inter-pretations. One has only to learn how to gain access to them.

NOTES

1. J. Belo, "The Balinese Temper," in *Traditional Balinese Cul-ture*, ed. J. Belo (New York, 1970) (originally published in 1935), pp. 85–110.
2. The best discussion of cockfighting is Bateson and Mead's *Balinese Character [A Photographic Analysis* (New York, 1942)], pp. 24–25, 140; but it, too, is general and abbrevi-ated.
3. Ibid., pp. 25–26. The cockfight is unusual within Balinese culture in being a single-sex public activity from which the other sex is totally and expressly excluded. Sexual differenti-ation is culturally extremely played down in Bali and most activities, formal and informal, involve the participation of men and women on equal ground, commonly as linked cou-ples. From religion, to politics, to economics, to kinship, to dress, Bali is a rather "unisex" society, a fact both its customs

and its symbolism clearly express. Even in contexts where women do not in fact play much of a role—music, painting, certain agricultural activities—their absence, which is only relative in any case, is more a mere matter of fact than so-cially enforced. To this general pattern, the cockfight, en-tirely by, of, and for men (women—at least *Balinese* women—do not even watch), is the most striking exception.
4. C. Hooykaas, *The Lay of the Jaya Prana* (London, 1958), p. 39. The lay has a stanza (no. 17) with the reluctant bridge-groom use. Jaya Prana, the subject of a Balinese Uriah myth, responds to the lord who has offered him the loveliest of six hundred servant girls: "Godly King, my Lord and Master/I beg you, give me leave to go/such things are not yet in my mind;/like a fighting cock encaged/indeed I am on my met-tle/I am alone/as yet the flame has not been fanned."

5. For these, see V. E. Korn, *Hei Adatrecht van Bali*, 2d ed. (The Hague, 1932), index under *toh*.

6. There is indeed a legend to the effect that the separation of Java and Bali is due to the action of a powerful Javanese religious figure who wished to protect himself against a Balinese culture hero (the ancestor of two Ksatria castes) who was a passionate cockfighting gambler. See C. Hooykaas, *Agama Tirtha* (Amsterdam, 1964), p. 184.

7. An incestuous couple is forced to wear pig yokes over their necks and crawl to a pig trough and eat with their mouths there. On this, see J. Belo, "Customs Pertaining to Twins in Bali," in *Traditional Balinese Culture*, ed. J. Belo, p. 49; on the abhorrence of animality generally, Bateson and Mead, *Balinese Character* [A Photographic Analysis (New York, 1942)], p. 22.

8. Except for unimportant, small-bet fights spur affixing is usually done by someone other than the owner. Whether the owner handles his own cock or not more or less depends on how skilled he is at it, a consideration whose importance is again relative to the importance of the fight. When spur affixers and cock handlers are someone other than the owner, they are almost always a quite close relative—a brother or cousin—or a very intimate friend of his. They are thus almost extensions of his personality, as the fact that all three will refer to the cock as "mine," say "I" fought So-and-So, and so on, demonstrates. Also, owner-handler-affixer triads tend to be fairly fixed, though individuals may participate in several and often exchange roles within a given one.

9. E. Goffman, *Encounters: Two Studies in the Sociology of Interaction* (Indianapolis, 1961), pp. 9–10.

10. This word, which literally means an indelible stain or mark, as in a birthmark or a vein in a stone, is used as well for a deposit in a court case, for a pawn, for security offered in a loan, for a stand-in for someone else in a legal or ceremonial context, for an earnest advanced in a business deal, for a sign placed in a field to indicate its ownership is in dispute, and for the status of an unfaithful wife from whose lover her husband must gain satisfaction or surrender her to him. See Korn, *Het Adatrecht van Bali*; Th. Pigeaud, *Javaans-Nederlands Handwoordenboek* (Groningen, 1938); H. H. Juynboll, *Oudjavaansche-Nederlandsche Woordenlijst* (Leiden, 1923).

11. The center bet must be advanced in cash by both parties prior to the actual fight. The umpire holds the stakes until the decision is rendered and then awards them to the winner, avoiding, among other things, the intense embarrassment both winner and loser would feel if the latter had to pay off personally following his defeat. About 10 percent of the winner's receipts are subtracted for the umpire's share and that of the fight sponsors.

12. The phrase is found in the Hildreth translation, International Library of Psychology (1931), note to p. 106; see L. L. Fuller, *The Morality of Law* (New Haven, 1964), p. 6 ff.

13. Of course, even in Bentham, utility is not normally confined as a concept to monetary losses and gains, and my argument here might be more carefully put in terms of a denial that for the Balinese, as for any people, utility (pleasure, happiness . . .) is merely identifiable with wealth. But such termi-

nological problems are in any case secondary to the essential point: the cockfight is not roulette.

14. Addict gamblers are really less declassed (for their status is, as everyone else's, inherited) than merely impoverished and personally disgraced. The most prominent addict gambler in my cockfight circuit was actually a very high caste *satria* who sold off most of his considerable lands to support his habit. Though everyone privately regarded him as a fool and worse (some, more charitable, regarded him as sick), he was publicly treated with the elaborate deference and politeness due his rank.

15. For four, somewhat variant, treatments, see S. Langer, *Feeling and Form* (New York, 1953); R. Wollheim, *Art and Its Objects* (New York, 1968); N. Goodman, *Languages of Art* (Indianapolis, 1968); M. Merleau-Ponty, "The Eye and the Mind," in his *The Primacy of Perception* (Evanston, Ill., 1964), pp. 159–190.

16. British cockfights (the sport was banned there in 1840) indeed seem to have lacked it, and to have generated, therefore, a quite different family of shapes. Most British fights were "mains," in which a preagreed number of cocks were aligned into two teams and fought serially. Score was kept and wagering took place both on the individual matches and on the main as a whole. There were also "battle Royales," both in England and on the Continent, in which a large number of cocks were let loose at once with the one left standing at the end the victor. And in Wales, the so-called Welsh main followed an elimination pattern, along the lines of a present-day tennis tournament, winners proceeding to the next round. As a genre, the cockfight has perhaps less compositional flexibility than, say, Latin comedy, but it is not entirely without any. On cockfighting more generally, see A. Ruport, *The Art of Cockfighting* (New York, 1949); G. R. Scott, *History of Cockfighting* (London, 1957); and L. Fitz-Barnard, *Fighting Sports* (London, 1921).

17. For the necessity of distinguishing among "description," "representation," "exemplification," and "expression" (and the irrelevance of "imitation" to all of them) as modes of symbolic reference, see Goodman, *Languages of Art*, pp. 61–110, 45–91, 225–241.

18. N. Frye, *The Educated Imagination* (Bloomington, Ind., 1964), p. 99.

19. There are two other Balinese values and disvalues which, connected with punctuate temporality on the one hand and unbridled aggressiveness on the other, reinforce the sense that the cockfight is at once continuous with ordinary social life and a direct negation of it: what the Balinese call *ramé*, and what they call *paling*. Ramé means crowded, noisy, and active, and is a highly sought-after social state: crowded markets, mass festivals, busy streets are all *ramé*, as, of course, is, in the extreme, a cockfight. *Ramé* is what happens in the "full" times (its opposite, *sepi*, "quiet," is what happens in the "empty" ones). *Paling* is social vertigo, the dizzy, disoriented, lost, turned-around feeling one gets when one's place in the coordinates of social space is not clear, and it is a tremendously disfavored, immensely anxiety-producing state. Balinese regard the exact maintenance of spatial orientation ("not to know where north is" is to be crazy), balance,

decorum, status relationships, and so forth, as fundamental to ordered life (*krama*) and *paling*, the sort of whirling confusion of position the scrambling cocks exemplify as its profoundest enemy and contradiction. On *ramé*, see Bateson and Mead, *Balinese Character*, pp. 3, 64; on *paling*, ibid., p. 11, and Belo, ed., *Traditional Balinese Culture*, p. 90 ff.

20. The Stevens reference is to his "The Motive for Metaphor" ("You like it under the trees in autumn,/Because everything is half dead./The wind moves like a cripple among the leaves/And repeats words without meaning") [Copyright 1947 by Wallace Stevens, reprinted from *The Collected Poems of Wallace Stevens* by permission of Alfred A. Knopf, Inc., and Faber and Faber Ltd.]; the Schoenberg reference is to the third of his *Five Orchestral Pieces* (Opus 16), and is borrowed from H. H. Drager, "The Concept of 'Tonal Body,' " in *Reflections on Art*, ed. S. Langer (New York, 1961), p. 174. On Hogarth, and on this whole problem—there called "multiple matrix matching"—see E. H. Gombrich, "The Use of Art for the Study of Symbols," in *Psychology and the Visual Arts*, ed. J. Hogg (Baltimore, 1969), pp. 149–170. The more usual term for this sort of semantic alchemy is "metaphorical transfer," and good technical discussions of it can be found in M. Black, *Models and Metaphors* (Ithaca, N.Y., 1962), p. 25 ff; Goodman, *Language as Art*, p. 44 ff; and W. Percy, "Metaphor as Mistake," *Sewanee Review* 66 (1958): 78–99.

21. The tag is from the second book of the *Organon, On Interpretation*. For a discussion of it, and for the whole argument for freeing "the notion of text . . . from the notion of scripture or writing" and constructing, thus, a general hermeneutics, see P. Ricoeur, *Freud and Philosophy* (New Haven, 1970), p. 20 ff.

22. Ibid.

23. Lévi-Strauss "structuralism" might seem an exception. But it is only an apparent one, for, rather than taking myths, totem rites, marriage rules, or whatever as texts to interpret, Lévi-Strauss takes them as ciphers to solve, which is very much not the same thing. He does not seek to understand symbolic forms in terms of how they function in concrete situations to organize perceptions (meanings, emotions, concepts, attitudes); he seeks to understand them entirely in terms of their internal structure, *independent de tout sujet, de tout objet, et de toute contexte*.

24. Frye, *The Educated Imagination*, pp. 63–64.

25. The use of the, to Europeans, "natural" visual idiom for perception—"see," "watches," and so forth—is more than usually misleading here, for the fact that, as mentioned earlier, Balinese follow the progress of the fight as much (perhaps, as fighting cocks are actually rather hard to see except as blurs of motion, more) with their bodies as with their eyes, moving their limbs, heads, and trunks in gestural mimicry of the cocks' maneuvers, means that much of the individual's experience of the fight is kinesthetic rather than visual. If ever there was an example of Kenneth Burke's definition of a symbolic act as "the dancing of an attitude" [*The Philosophy of Literary Form*, rev. ed. (New York, 1957), p. 9] the cockfight is it. On the enormous role of kinesthetic perception in Balinese life. Bateson and Mead, *Balinese Character*, pp. 84–88; on the active nature of aesthetic perception in general, Goodman, *Language of Art*, pp. 241–244.

26. All this coupling of the occidental great with the oriental lowly will doubtless disturb certain sorts of aestheticians as the earlier efforts of anthropologists to speak of Christianity and totemism in the same breath disturbed certain sorts of theologians. But as ontological questions are (or should be) bracketed in the sociology of religion, judgmental ones are (or should be) bracketed in the sociology of art. In any case, the attempt to deprovincialize the concept of art is but part of the general anthropological conspiracy to deprovincialize all important social concepts—marriage, religion, law, rationality—and though this is a threat to aesthetic theories which regard certain works of art as beyond the reach of sociological analysis, it is no threat to the conviction, for which Robert Graves claims to have been reprimanded at his Cambridge tripos, that some poems are better than others.

27. For the consecration ceremony, see V. E. Korn, "The Consecration of the Priest," in Swellengrebel, ed., *Bali: Studies*, pp. 131–154; for (somewhat exaggerated) village communion, R. Goris, "The Religious Character of the Balinese Village," ibid., pp. 79–100.

28. That what the cockfight has to say about Bali is not altogether without perception and the disquiet it expresses about the general pattern of Balinese life is not wholly without reason is attested by the fact that in two weeks of December 1965, during the upheavals following the unsuccessful coup in Djakarta, between forty and eighty thousand Balinese (in a population of about two million) were killed, largely by one another—the worst outburst in the country. [J. Hughes, *Indonesian Upheaval* (New York, 1967), pp. 173–183. Hughes' figures are, of course, rather casual estimates, but they are not the most extreme.] This is not to say, of course, that the killings were caused by the cockfight, could have been predicted on the basis of it, or were some sort of enlarged version of it with real people in the place of the cocks—all of which is nonsense. It is merely to say that if one looks at Bali not just through the medium of its dances, its shadow-plays, its sculpture, and its girls, but—as the Balinese themselves do—also through the medium of its cockfight, the fact that the massacre occurred seems, if no less appalling, less like a contradiction to the laws of nature. As more than one real Gloucester has discovered, sometimes people actually get life precisely as they most deeply do not want it.

Disenchantment: A Religious Abduction

SAM D. GILL

Facts of publication: *Gill, Sam D. 1987. "Disenchantment: A Religious Abduction," from* Native American Religious Action: A Performance Approach to Religion, *58–75. Columbia: University of South Carolina Press. Copyright © 1987 by University of South Carolina. Reprinted with the permission of University of South Carolina Press.*

The Hopi kachina initiation has long been characterized by the whipping of eight-to-ten-year-old initiates. The whipping has been associated with receiving the disenchanting knowledge that the kachina figures are not real gods, but mere impersonations. The record indicates that it is the shock of disenchantment more than the yucca switch that leaves a lasting impression on initiates, yet the religious significance of this response has not been taken seriously by observers of Hopi culture. Careful consideration of the initiation rites shows that disillusionment is treated by the Hopi as necessary to prepare the children for a meaningful religious life.

About the author: Dates: *1943– , Wichita, KA, U.S.A.* **Education:** *B.S., M.S., Wichita State University; M.A., University of Chicago; Ph.D., University of Chicago.* **Field(s):** *religious studies.* **Career:** *Associate Professor of Religion, 1975–1982, Arizona State University; Professor of Religious Studies, 1983–present, University of Colorado, Boulder.* **Publications:** Songs of Life: An Introduction to Navajo Religious Culture *(Brill, 1979);* Sacred Words: A Study of Navajo Religion and Prayer *(Greenwood, 1981);* Beyond "The Primitive": The Religions of Nonliterate Peoples *(Prentice Hall, 1982);* Native American Religions: An Introduction *(Wadsworth, 1982);* Native American Traditions: Sources and Interpretations *(Wadsworth, 1983);* Mother Earth: An American Story *(University of Chicago, 1987);* Native American Religious Action: A Performance Approach to Religion *(University of South Carolina, 1987).* **Additional:** *"My primary interests are in religion and dance and in religion and play, especially in the religious traditions of Australia, native North America, and southeast Asia."*

Some years ago I first observed portions of the ritual process by which Hopis initiate their children into their religious lives. I remember it clearly. It was early February, and the Hopi were celebrating the opening of their kivas and the return of the kachinas to the human world of the Hopi mesas. This occasion is Powamu, commonly known as the Bean Dance. Beans are planted and forced by the warmth maintained in the kivas to sprout early. The bean sprouting and the ceremonial events turn the attention of the Hopi toward the upcoming growing season.

The initiation of children accompanies Powamu. As I stood in the village of Mishong'novi, I observed groups of children, all decked out in new clothing and shoes, being instructed by their parents. These were the children being initiated into the kachina cult. Peering down one of the avenues between houses, I saw some of the children taken atop a kiva; one kachina held up a child's hands, while another whirled what appeared to be the cloth tassels of a sash gently against each child. The gentleness of this gesture belies the seriousness of the initiatory scenario of which it is a part. Were we to see the whole event, we would find that at least some Hopi children conclude their experience of initiation profoundly changed, bearing not the joys of conversion and revelation but rather feelings of betrayal and disenchantment. Hopi children are in a sense abducted from their childhood naïveté into maturity, and for us to consider more fully this initiatory process may open not only a deeper appreciation for Hopi religious practices, but also for widely used religious techniques.

The initiation into the kachina cult designates the formal beginning of participation in the myriad events of Hopi religious life. The rites of initiation are performed only once every several years during the annual celebration of Powamu, the first major winter ceremony in which the kachinas appear. Children around the age of ten enter the kachina cult by being inducted into either the Kachina Society or the Powamu Society. The rites of initiation into those societies vary somewhat, as do the privileges of the members, but both take place during Powamu, and until recently every child was initiated into one or the other. Most Hopi children still undergo this initiation.

Students of religion have recognized that initiation into the religious life occurs in a series of events that opens for our analysis the shape and meaning of a religion. The Hopi rites are commonly cited as a classic example. A careful scrutiny of the descriptive accounts of this particular Hopi initiation reveals that the interpretation usually given is limited and misleading. I will suggest an alternative interpretation based on the point of view that the ritual does what the Hopi say it does—that is, initiate the children into their religious lives by revealing to them the nature of the kachinas.

DESCRIPTION AND INTERPRETATIONS

The earliest description of the initiation version of Powamu I have found was written by Alexander M. Stephen at the Hopi village of Walpi, on First Mesa, in 1892.[1] The core of the ritual process, according to Stephen's description, takes place when the children are conducted into the kiva by their ceremonial fathers, whipped by Tungwup kachinas, and comforted by their mothers. Stephen advanced an explanation of this whipping rite that has been maintained by most other interpreters.

> The primary significance of the whipping (*wuvi'lauwû*) seems to be this: Until children have acquired some real intelligence or are, say eight or ten years old, they are made to believe that the kachina appearing at all celebrations are superhuman visitors, nor must such children even see an unmasked kachina. When they have grown old enough or are deemed to

have sufficient understanding, then they are instructed that the real kachinas have long since ceased their visits to mankind and are merely impersonated by men, but they must buy this knowledge at the expense of a sound flogging.[2]

Stephen revealed something in his interpretation that he did not mention in his description. He indicated that the initiation is for the purpose of teaching the children that the kachinas no longer come to the villages, but appear only through the efforts of impersonation which the children, as new members of the cult, may now begin to perform.

A problem for Stephen—indeed, the primary problem to which he spoke—was to explain what motivates the whipping of the initiates. He indicated that it is a kind of payment for the secret knowledge the initiates gain in the rites. Elsie C. Parsons, who undertook the task of editing Stephen's journal for publication, added a comment on the basis of her considerable experience, although it appears that she had not witnessed the initiation rites:

> The whipping of the children is interpreted by our Journalist [Stephen] as a kind of expiation in advance for learning about the kachina. It is no doubt a ritual of exorcism but possibly it is an exorcism for the children against the evils of life and to promote growth and well being.[3]

Parsons places both the Hopi and Stephen within Judeo-Christian categories of meaning. Stephen's journal actually says nothing of atonement. Parsons' introduction of exorcism, unfounded in the descriptive accounts she used, was perhaps based on her view that Powamu is generally a ceremonial focusing upon exorcism.[4]

Another description based on witness of the initiation rites prior to the turn of the century is that of Heinrick Voth, a Mennonite missionary at the Hopi village now known as Old Oraibi. Voth witnessed the initiatory form of Powamu in both 1894 and 1899. His account was published in 1901 and supplements the Stephen account. Voth described the whipping rite as separate from the initiates' education about the nature of the kachinas. He clarified the distinction between the Kachina and Powamu societies in terms of the rites of initiation and the privileges enjoyed by the initiated. He shed further light on the significance of the whipping rite with the following information:

> There is a tradition among the Hopi that this flogging ceremony was not always a part of the Powamu ceremony. It is stated that on one occasion a boy who had been initiated into the Powamu fraternity had revealed the secrets that he had seen and heard. A council of the leaders of the fraternity was at once called and the question discussed as to what to do about it. All urged that a severe punishment be inflicted upon the perpetrator. Only the *kalehtakmongwi* (Warrior chief), now represented by Koyongainiwa, remained silent. After having been asked four times by the others as to his opinion about the matter, he first also expressed his displeasure at the occurrence and then suggested that the boy be flogged before all the other novitiates by Kachinas as a punishment and as a warning to the rest. This was done, and the custom was continued.[5]

Voth recorded the whipping as occurring on the sixth day of the nine-day Powamu ceremonial and indicated that the children are protected against seeing unmasked kachinas even after their whipping. According to Voth, it was not until the ninth night that the children learned that the kachinas were masked impersonators.

> On this occasion the Kachinas appear unmasked, a very rare occurrence. The new Powamu and Kachina Wiwimkyamu (from Wimkya, member) that were initiated on the fifth and sixth days are to learn for the first time that Kachinas, whom they were taught to regard as supernatural beings, are only mortal Hopis.[6]

Stephen did not describe this event, but alluded to it two times by indicating that "the children are to be flogged this sunset in the court, after which they must not eat salt or flesh for four days, then they may look upon kachina and *wi'mi* in kivas."[7] *Wi'mi* are ceremonies.

Several witnessed accounts are available from the early decades of the twentieth century, but they add little to these earlier accounts.[8]

Descriptions and interpretations made through the 1930s placed major emphasis on the whipping rite.[9] The secondary literature has focused on this aspect of the initiation, maintaining with Stephen that the major information learned during the initiation is that the kachinas are masked impersonators rather than "real gods" as the children had been previously taught. Louis Gray, in the article on the Hopi in *The Encyclopedia of Religion and Ethics*, wrote, "Previous to this whipping the children have believed that the kachinas are real; after it they know that they are in reality only personifications." None of the secondary accounts raises the question of how this learning takes place, and not a single one gives any indication of how the Hopi children receive this knowledge.

It was not until 1942 that more was written about the effect the initiation has on the initiates. In that year the autobiography of the Old Oraibi Hopi Don Talayesva was first published. Talayesva had a vivid memory of his own initiation into the Kachina Society. He recalled,

> When the Kachinas entered the kiva without masks, I had a great surprise. They were not spirits, but human beings. I recognized nearly every one of them and felt very unhappy, because I had been told all my life that the Kachinas were gods. I was especially shocked and angry when I saw all my uncles, fathers, and clan brothers dancing as Kachinas. I felt the worst when I saw my own father—and whenever he glanced at me I turned my face away. When the dances were over the head man told us with a stern face that we knew who the Kachinas really were and that if we ever talked about this to uninitiated children we would get a thrashing even worse than the one we had received the night before.[10]

This Hopi account emphasizes the shock experienced upon learning that kachinas are masked Hopi. The whipping is described as a device to ensure secrecy, a role consistent with the story recorded by Voth.

For her study of Hopi personality development Dorothy Eggan interviewed a number of Hopis about their experience of the initiation into the kachina cult. Her evidence shows that Talayesva's response is typical. She wrote that

> at initiation the child learned that the Kachinas were not *real gods* but merely representatives of them, and

that they were an endless duty as well as a pleasure. The traumatic effect of this blow to a young Hopi's faith in his intimate world must be emphasized. All informants questioned by the writer have drawn the same picture of their reaction to initiation; their emphasis is rarely upon an anticipatory fear of it, nor upon the physical hardships endured during it. Rather they stress a previous struggle against disillusion in which the hints—not very specific because of the severe penalty for betrayal—of earlier initiates were dismissed; and finally the intense disappointment in and resentment toward their elders which survived in consciousness for a long time. . . . For Hopi children there was a double burden of disenchantment and modified behavior, for while an altered concept of the kachinas eventually became a vital part of their lives, excessive indulgence by their elders had disappeared never to return.

To exemplify this reaction Eggan quoted a Hopi woman as saying,

I cried and cried into my sheepskin that night, feeling I had been made a fool of. How could I ever watch the Kachinas dance again? I hated my parents and thought I would never believe the old folks again, wondering if Gods had ever danced for the Hopi as they said and if people really lived after death. I hated to see the other children fooled and felt mad when they said I was a big girl now and should act like one. But I was afraid to tell the others the truth for they might whip me to death. I know now it was best and the only way to teach the children, but it took me a long time to know that. I hope my children won't feel like that.[11]

On the basis of Hopi accounts it appears that the whipping is primarily an incentive for maintaining secrecy, but that the knowledge of the nature of the kachinas which is gained during the Bean Dance on the last evening of Powamu is experienced as a shocking disenchantment with the kachinas, Hopi ceremonials, and Hopi elders. This experience of disenchantment is vividly remembered throughout life.

Finally the most complete account based on an observed performance of the initiatory form of Powamu was written by Mischa Titiev. He and Fred Eggan were participants in the Powamu of 1934.

Titiev's account clearly indicates the distinction between the whipping part of the initiation rite and the moment when the initiates learn about the kachinas. He describes the initiatory element of the Bean Dance, which is performed in the kivas on the ninth night of Powamu:

Then the dancers enter the kiva while one of their number stands by the hatch and calls down all sorts of jests at the expense of each man as he comes down the ladder. Inasmuch as the performers announce on entering a kiva that they are the real Katcinas, and as they are unmasked, it does not take long for the recent initiates to discover that the Katcina impersonators are their relatives and fellow villagers. In such dramatic fashion is the most important of all Katcina secrets revealed to Hopi children.[12]

More details of this witnessed event are available in Titiev's 1972 publication of his Hopi field notes as well as the description of the rites which he observed in 1954, with comments on the observed changes during that period of time.[13]

Given the disenchanting nature of the secret learned by the kachina cult initiates, it is certainly not surprising that they respond with shock and displeasure. What is more shocking to me is that none of the observers has shown the least surprise at the anomaly presented by these Hopi rites. Not a single observer has responded to the revelation of the secret of the masked nature of the kachinas with more than passive acceptance. But in light of the fact that the Hopi have been commonly regarded as being almost excessively religious—as evidenced by their constant involvement in religious activities—I feel that it is startlingly incongruous that Hopis introduce their children into their religious lives with the revelation that the kachinas are not real gods, but men dressed as gods. Should this not raise the question of the motivation and meaning of all of Hopi religious practices that are associated with kachinas? Does it not seem utterly in opposition to the abundant references which attest to the Hopi belief that the donning of a kachina mask transforms a man into a god?[14] And finally, it is hard to overlook evidence that the initiated Hopis follow with the utmost care procedures of deception calculated to bring about an experience of disenchantment. The mere fact of the intentionality suggests that there is more to it than appears on the surface. Hints of this significance are suggested in Eggan's report by the Hopi who said, "I know now it was best and the only way to teach the children." Certainly a major element in the meaning of the mature Hopi religious life must stem from this shock of disenchantment. And I would suggest this may hold true for students of Hopi religion as well as for the Hopi children.

DISENCHANTMENT: DEATH TO NAÏVE REALISM

The esoteric aspects of the kachina cult initiation will probably never be known to non-Hopis, but the surface structure of the events of the ritual of initiation suggests much.[15] Prior to their initiation the children meet the kachinas in the villages in a wide array of associated experiences. Some kachinas present gifts to the children, while others frighten and discipline them. In all contacts the children are carefully guarded against either seeing an unmasked kachina or gaining knowledge that the kachinas are masked figures. In this way the children are nurtured in a perspective of naïve realism; that is, they are treated in such a way as to support the adequacy of their commonsense view of the world. The children are raised to accept the kachinas exactly as they appear to them in the village, as spirit beings who have come to the village to overlook and direct human and cosmic affairs. They identify the kachinas with their physical appearances and actions.

During the kachina cult initiation rites the final development of the perspective of naïve realism is made through a period of intense contact with the kachinas. Children are acutely aware of the kachinas' presence in the village; they watch them move about the village; they may be whipped by them; they are told special stories about them; and they are given special gifts, which they are told are brought from the kachinas' home in the San Francisco Peaks. While the children perceive the kachinas as beings of a wholly different category than themselves, they are not separated from these powerful beings. They observe the interaction of the Hopi people with the kachinas when they visit their villages on many ceremonial occasions. Further, the

children are taught that upon death a Hopi may become a kachina and return to work for the people.[16]

The nurturing of a perspective from which reality is viewed naïvely appears to lay the basis for the shock experienced at the conclusion of the initiation rite. This naïveté is shattered in the instant of realization that the kachinas are masked figures, impersonations perpetrated by members of their own village, even their own relatives. The loss of naïveté is always irreversible. The result, as is clearly indicated by Eggan's consultants, is that the reality of the kachinas, one's destiny, and the whole basis for reality are called into serious question. The interaction between the Hopi people and the kachinas, which the children had come to know as essential to the continuity of the Hopi way of life, appears now to be impossible. The kachinas are shown to be only disguised Hopi men, the relatives of the children, and not spirit beings at all. The disjunction between the kachinas and humankind, which had heretofore been rather easily bridgeable, has now become an abyss. And perhaps the most remarkable thing in light of the expected initiatory structure, the rites of initiation end on this note of discord.[17]

While the new initiates must enter their new lives suffering this disillusionment, the privileges enjoyed in their new status permit them to participate in the affairs they have found to be disappointing. They may now participate in kachina cult activities.[18] They may be present in the kivas during rehearsal and mask preparation activities. They are eligible to be initiated into secret societies, in which they may gradually come to know esoteric dimensions of the kachina cult. The initiation is constructed in such a way that a child's religious life begins in a state of seriousness and reflection, motivated by doubt and skepticism. The very nature of reality has become threatened. Each child must search out a new basis for perceiving a meaningful reality. There is tremendous incentive to listen more carefully to the stories of the old people. Don Talayesva describes his increased interest in these stories as stemming from his experience of initiation.[19] It is apparently through the stories and through participating in religious activities that new initiates find the meaningful equilibrium which gives them reprieve from the awful state of disenchantment. The kachina cult initiation is the formal introduction into the religious life of a

Hopi, not the culmination of this life. It turns an individual from the nonreligious life and provides the motivation for seeking religious awareness.

OTHER EXAMPLES

Disenchantment is not an uncommon technique used to bring about the fundamental changes so basic to rites of passage. Other examples may be briefly described to show the extent and variety of this abductive force.

Australia: The Broken Bullroarer. The process of disenchantment can be seen at work in the initiation rites of the Wiradthuri tribes of Australia. The occasion is the initiation of boys into manhood. The boys to be initiated are abducted from the village, taken from their homes and their mothers. The rites are loaded with chicanery. The boys are commanded to walk with their eyes fixed on their feet so that they may not observe the staging of the trickery. A principal focus of the several rites rests upon the revelation of the nature of the spirit Dhuramoolan. The boys are told frequently that Dhuramoolan is coming near, and they are advised to listen for his approaching voice. They hear a whirring noise that grows louder and louder, but they do not know that the sound is being made by men whirling bullroarers (thin pieces of wood whirled at the end of strings). At a critical juncture in the rites the boys are covered with blankets and told that Dhuramoolan is coming and that he may eat them. With bullroarers speaking close by, the elders reach under each blanket and with hammer and chisel they knock an incisor tooth from the mouth of each boy. The boys think the spirit is taking their teeth while sparing their lives.

In this initiation an illusion of the perceptual presence of a spirit is prepared, and it is fully accepted by the initiates. But, the initiation culminates in a disenchantment of this knowledge. On the last day the boys are covered with blankets and a crackling fire is built. The bullroarers are whirled nearby, and the boys are told that Dhuramoolan is going to burn them. When the boys become very frightened, the blankets are removed from their heads, and they are shown for the first time the men whirling the bullroarers. Thus they learn that this artificial noisemaking is what they have taken to be the voice of Dhuramoolan. Pointing to the men whirling the bullroarers, the head man shouts, "There he is! That is Dhuramoolan!" and he explains to the boys how the noise is made by whirling flat pieces of wood on strings. Then the boys are given the bullroarers to examine; they may even whirl them. They are forbidden to tell the uninitiated about them or ever to make a bullroarer except during the initiation rites. Then they destroy the bullroarers by splitting them into pieces and driving them into the ground, or sometimes by burning them.

There is little information about how the boys respond to this revelation, but clearly they can never again be terrified as they once were by the voice of the bullroarers. Nor can they retain the naïve knowledge of Dhuramoolan's nature engendered in them during the initiation rites. They have learned that the world is not always as it appears to be. They must now come to terms with the spiritual nature of the figure Dhuramoolan.[20]

Africa: the Killing of Kavula. A striking example of the defamation of sacred objects in the initiatory process occurs in the rites of initiation into one of the healing cults of the Ndembu of Africa. As we would expect, the revelation of the nature of Kavula, the spirit of the healing cult, is an essential part of the initiation. But the process by which the initiates learn of Kavula is startling. The adepts prepare a frame made of sticks covered with a white blanket to represent the divinity. It is called *isoli*. One of the initiated hides beneath the blanket to play the part of Kavula. The initiates are chased by the adepts, caught, interrogated with unanswerable questions, taunted for being unable to supply appropriate answers, and eventually led to the *isoli*. The initiates are instructed regarding the formal procedure of greeting Kavula. When they address the spirit in the *isoli*, its voice returns their greeting. The initiates approach the structure and, when instructed to kill Kavula, they beat the object with the butts of their rattles. With each blow "Kavula" shakes convulsively, as if dying. The initiates are then led back to the village. When they enter it, an adept takes a firebrand, strikes it violently on the ground, and cries out, "He is dead!" After a brief closing oration the initiation is concluded.

Victor Turner, who reported these events, elicited comment on the killing of Kavula from the Ndembu people. Muchona, a knowledgeable old man, said, "Kavula is killed to frighten the candidate. For he believes he is really killing Kavula. He has been instructed by the adepts that 'If you see the spirit of Kavula, you must consider this is a spirit which helps people.' . . . The adepts are just deceiving the candidates at *isoli*." One of the female initiates told Turner that it was "Kavula's back that we saw in *isoli*. When Kavula was killed the spirit flew away into the sky, not to Nzambi (the High God), but 'into the wind.' It could come again."

In this initiation rite the adepts use techniques of deception to build an illusion, a fictitious conception of reality, for the initiates. Bringing the initiates into Kavula's sacred presence, they confuse them with unanswerable questions, tell them to kill the very spirit that is to be revealed to them, and assure them at the conclusion of the rite that he is dead. Once the rites are over, the initiates are even shown the construction of the *isoli*. The illusion is disclosed; the enchantment with *isoli* is broken. Kavula, as presented to them, is shown to be nothing but a blanket-covered framework of sticks. Remarkably, however, the initiate domonstrated in her comments on the event that she discovered in it something of the mysterious nature of Kavula. She came to realize that Kavula is not limited to his appearance in the *isoli*, but is something more. Somehow in the process she gained the knowledge that Kavula is a spirit that flew "into the wind" and can come back; or perhaps, as Munchona told Turner, "Kavula takes all powers." It is through the creation of an illusion that is subsequently shattered by a dramatic and powerful act of disenchantment that the revelation of the spiritual dimension of reality is effected.[21]

DISENCHANTMENT: THE BIRTH OF THE RELIGIOUS PERSPECTIVE

In these examples from Australia, Africa, and North America the whole process of initiation builds to a climax in the shock of disenchantment. The ritual objects are destroyed or their ordinary character is revealed to the eyes of the initiates. Despite this, the initiations evidently succeed, although the revelation of the religious or the spiritual is as much a result of the initiatic process as a part of it.

When the dynamic of disenchantment is the driving power in an initiation rite, the first and essential ingredient is encouraging identification of the spiritual with some physical/sensual aspect of the world. The uninitiated must come to believe that the objects and entities observed are what they are presented as being. The white blanket in the framework of sticks *is* Kavula; the masked dancers *are* Hopi spirit beings; and the roar of the noisemakers *is* Dhuramoolan shouting. Ingenious techniques of secrecy and deception have been devised to nurture a perspective of naïve realism, and the effectiveness of the initiation depends on how firmly this viewpoint is established.

The whole initiatory process reinforces this sense that the fullness of the religious reality is invested in these figures and objects. Then in the concluding moments, upon the threshold of a new life, the illusion is dissolved, and the shock of disenchantment shatters all that went before. The experience makes a return to the previous state of life impossible. The naïve realism of the uninitiated perspective has been exploded. The rites have demonstrated irreversibly that things are not simply what they appear to be, that one-dimensional literalism is a childish faith that one has to grow beyond or else despair of a life rich in meaning and worth. Surely, being thus forced to abandon one's ingrained notion of reality is to experience a true death of the former self. And this loss of self constitutes the concrete transformation signified by the death experienced in the rites.

The purpose of initiation—to reveal the fullness of reality—is, of course, one with the nature of religion itself. For religion springs from the unique human capacity to grasp and to create dimensions of reality that are beyond the material, beyond the obvious, beyond even human existence, and to exercise this capacity by utilizing the material and obvious dimensions of ordinary human life.

Through initiation culminating in disenchantment, the novice is in a sense abducted into the religious life in a state of crisis, disappointment, or perplexity about the nature of reality. The only thing he knows is that he has been fooled and his sense of what is real and what is not is confounded. His options seem clear. He may see the world as meaningless, or he may undertake a quest for a fuller understanding of the world. This is scarcely a choice. The experience of disenchantment initiates the world-creating and world-discovering human and cultural processes we know as religion. It stimulates inquiry, thought, creativity, wonderment, and the eventual formation of the sense of the religious world. The newly initiated are invited and expected to participate in the religious activities of their communities. Through such participation they begin gradually to grasp the full scope of the reality that their initiatory experience has opened for them. With this expanding awareness, meaning may once again be conferred on the defamed objects, yet now in an enhanced and mature way.

The profound wisdom of the method of initiation by disenchantment lies in its capacity to bring the initiate through succeeding stages of perception to an encounter with a fuller reality. The rites necessarily must end on the threshold of revelation, for it is only through the living of the religious way that the nature of reality becomes fully known.

CONCLUSION

Following Victor Turner, who discussed the Gospel story of the empty tomb along with the killing of Kavula events, I too would like to briefly consider this biblical story, for I believe that this story of death and resurrection also involves the enchantment-disenchantment process at work in the initiation of the Christian tradition.

The Gospels recount the life and teachings of Jesus as the story of the incarnate revelation of God. The episode of the empty tomb concludes the books of Matthew, Mark, and Luke, and in John only one chapter follows it. It comes directly after the account of the crucifixion, and for those destined to be members of the first Christian community this death caused fear, despondency, and consternation. This is especially clear in the concluding words of the Gospel of Mark:

> And very early on the first day of the week they [the two Marys] went to the tomb when the sun had risen. And they were saying to one another, "Who will roll away the stone for us from the door of the tomb?" And looking up, they saw that the stone was rolled back—

it was very large. And entering the tomb, they saw a young man sitting on the right side, dressed in a white robe; and they were amazed. And he said to them, "Do not be amazed; you seek Jesus of Nazareth, who was crucified. He has risen, he is not here; see the place where they laid him. But go, tell his disciples and Peter that he is going before you to Galilee; there you will see him, as he told you." And they went out and fled from the tomb; for trembling and astonishment had come upon them; and they said nothing to any one, for they were afraid.

[Mark 16: 2–8]

If we consider this as the concluding event in the initiation of the first Christians, several elements are remarkably similar to the rites of initiation described above. As the Ndembu experienced the death of Kavula, the Hopi the unmasking of the kachina figures, the Wiradthuri the destruction of the bullroarers, so the followers of Jesus were forced to witness his death. They had come to know him well and had accepted him as their Lord. Yet they saw him captured, tortured, and crucified. They saw that he was a man who felt pain, suffered, and died. He, like any man, was placed in a tomb. The followers of Jesus had embraced a naïve view of his reality—that Jesus the man and Jesus the Christ were simply identical. But going to the tomb, they found that he was not there. The Ndembu who examined the *isoli* found only a framework of sticks—Kavula was not there. The Hopi found only their own relatives under the masks—the kachina spirit beings were not there. The Wirandthuri coming from under their blankets found only men whirling bullroarers—Dhuramoolan was not there.

The story of the empty tomb in Christianity follows a pattern akin to the abducting process of disenchantment. Christianity as a religion begins with the empty tomb which is received not with joy and comfort, but with trembling, astonishment, and fear. That which had appeared to be so real, the man Jesus, had ceased to be, and not even his body remained as an object to care for and reverence. It has been in the face of the fear and astonishment at the loss of Jesus, the man, that Christians throughout the Christian era have been led to grasp the reality of Jesus, the Christ, who was resurrected from the tomb, and hence the reality of God. It must follow that only with this relevation could it be clearly recognized that it is the life and teachings of Jesus that are the "living and the momentous revelation of the inexplorable" God.

In these few examples from a broad spectrum of religious contexts there appears the common structure of a technique of disenchantment used to initiate the process of developing the mature religious perspective and to promote authentic apprehension of the fuller nature of reality. The apparent effect of disenchantment is itself illusory. Acts which seem to spell the end of religion are the very techniques that thrust the initiate into the arena of adult religious life with incentive to plumb its full depths. They lay bare the limitations of naïve views of reality so that through deepened participation in a religious community and celebration of the day-to-day events of life in religious ritual, the individual may increasingly explore, create, and experience worlds of fuller meaning.

NOTES

1. It is not clear how much of the full initiation sequence Stephen observed. In [Elsie C.] Parsons' introduction to Julian H. Steward, "Notes on Hopi Ceremonies in Their Initiatory Form," *American Anthropologist* 33(1931): 56–79, she indicated that Stephen had not seen the whipping rites in 1892, yet the account in his journal (*Hopi Journal of Alexander M. Stephen*, ed. Elsie C. Parsons [New York: Columbia University Press, 1936], pp 198–202) certainly appears to be written on the basis of direct observation.
2. Stephen, *Journal,* p. 203.
3. Stephen, *Journal,* p. 156.
4. Parsons presents an extensive comparative discussion of the whipping practice in her *Pueblo Indian Religion* (Chicago: The University of Chicago Press, 1939), vol. 2, pp. 467–76, including various Pueblo peoples. Stephen's journal was not published until 1936, but an account based solely on his notes was published by J. Walter Fewkes, *Tusayan Kachinas*, Bureau of American Ethnography 15th Annual Report (Washington D.C., 1897). Since Fewkes had not witnessed the initiation form of Powamu, he added nothing to Stephen's notes.
5. H. R. Voth, *The Oraibi Powamu Ceremony* (Chicago: Field Columbian Museum Publication 61, Anthropological Series, vol. 3, no. 2, 1901), p. 105.
6. Voth, *Oraibi Ceremony*, p. 120.
7. Stephen, *Journal*, pp. 198, 202.
8. In Frank Waters, *The Book of the Hopi* (New York: Viking Press, 1963), pp. 176–79, an account of the kachina cult initiation is given as described by White Bear based on the 1914 initiation rites at Old Oraibi. The odd feature of this description is that it appears that the children see the dancers in an unmasked appearance before they undergo the whipping rite. When Waters describes the Bean Dance which concludes Powamu, he remarks, "All initiates know by now that the kachinas are mere men who impersonate them, and have full knowledge of Powamu" (p. 182). In Elsie C. Parsons, *A Pueblo Indian Journal* (Menasha, WI: American Anthropological Association, Memoirs no. 2, 1925), the account of the initiation into the kachina cult is described by the Hopi Crow-Wing, who mentions the whipping and the appearance of the Powamu kachinas as being without masks, but does not connect either very closely with the initiation.

Steward presents a witnessed account on First Mesa from his field notes in 1927, but it does not add to the earlier accounts and does not make clear when the children learn the nature of the kachinas. Steward indicates that the audience for the Bean Dance was "made up entirely of women who bring children, even small babies" ("Notes on Hopi Ceremonies," p. 71), but he does not make clear that only the initiated children and very small babies may be present.

9. For examples of this emphasis see Louis Gray, "Hopi," *Encyclopedia of Religion and Ethics*, ed. James Hastings (New York: Scribner's, 1920), 6: 783–89; Erna Fergusson, *Dancing Gods: Indian Ceremonials of New Mexico and Arizona* (Albuquerque: University of New Mexico Press, 1957), pp. 128–29; Walter C. O'Kane, *Sun in Sky* (Norman: University of Oklahoma Press, 1950); p. 185; and Alan W. Watts, *The Two Hands of God: The Myths of Polarity* (New York: Braziller, 1963), p. 206.
10. Don C. Talayesva, *Sun Chief: An Autobiography of a Hopi Indian*, ed. Leo W. Simmons (New Haven: Yale University Press, 1942), p. 84.
11. Dorothy Eggan, "The General Problem of Hopi Adjustment," *American Anthropologist* 45 (1943): 372.
12. Mischa Titiev, *Old Oraibi: A Study of the Hopi Indians of Third Mesa* (Cambridge: Paper of the Peabody Museum of American Archaeology and Ethnology, vol. 12, no. 1, 1944), p. 119.
13. Mischa Titiev, *The Hopi Indians of Old Oraibi: Change and Continuity* (Ann Arbor: University of Michigan Press, 1972), pp. 341–43.
14. See Titiev, *Old Oraibi*, p. 109.
15. For descriptions of these events see Titiev, *Old Oraibi*, p. 118; Stephen, *Journal*, pp. 224–27; Voth, *Oraibi Ceremony*, p. 118; E. Earle and E. A. Kennard, *Hopi Kachina* (New York: J. J. Augustin, 1938), Plates X, XI; J. Walter Fewkes, *Ancestor Worship of the Hopi Indians*, Smithsonian Annual Report for 1921 (Washington, 1923), Plates 2, 7, and "On Certain Personages Who Appear in a Tusayan Ceremonial," *American Anthropologist* 7 (1894): 32–53. Emory Sekaquaptewa; "Hopi Ceremonies," in *Seeing with a Native Eye*, ed. Walter H. Capps (New York: Harper & Row, 1976), pp. 35–43, has a particularly clear description of the view Hopi children develop toward kachinas.

16. This belief, which is alluded to by Eggan's consultant, is documented throughout Hopi literature.

17. The "betwixt and between" state of liminality as described by Arnold van Gennep, *Rites of Passage* (Chicago: The University of Chicago Press, 1901) and extensively explored by Victor Turner, *The Forest of Symbols: Aspects of Ndembu Ritual* (Ithaca: Cornell University Press, 1967), esp. chapter 4, may be applicable here. But instead of concluding the initiation by establishing a new equilibrium to resolve the state of liminality endured throughout the initiation process, it appears that it is the state of liminality that the children are being initiated into by these rites. A related discussion of liminality as associated with the Zuni ritual clown is presented by Louis Hieb, "Meaning and Mismeaning: Toward an Understanding of the Ritual Clown," in *New Prespectives on the Pueblos*, ed. Alfonso Ortiz (Albuquerque: University of New Mexico Press, 1972), pp. 163–95.

18. Titiev, *Old Oraibi*, p. 116, and others have indicated that children do not normally begin participating to any great extent for several years after their initiation.

19. Talayesva, *Sun Chief,* p. 85.

20. R. H. Matthews, "The Bŭrbŭng of the Wiradthuri Tribes," *Journal of the Anthropological Institute of Great Britain and Ireland* 25 (1896): 295–317. A. W. Howitt, *The Native Tribes of South-East Australia* (London: Macmillan, 1904), pp. 516–63.

21. Victor Turner, *Chihamba the White Spirit: A Ritual Drama of the Ndembu,* Rhodes-Livingstone Paper no. 33 (New York: Humanities Press, 1962).

Violence and the Sacred: Sacrifice

RENÉ GIRARD

Facts of publication: *Girard, René. 1977. "Sacrifice," from* Violence and the Sacred, *1–15, 17–33. Translated by Patrick Gregory. Baltimore: Johns Hopkins University Press. Reprinted with the permission of The Johns Hopkins University Press, Baltimore; London.*

Though "sacrifice" is in the title of this provocative essay, violence is its real subject. Girard thinks the human propensity toward violence is a persistent issue that must be faced by all cultures. According to Girard, humans are violent, and, if this violence is not deflected, properly channeled, or relieved, it will build to a climactic eruption resulting in endless chains of violence that threaten the destruction of society. Girard believes violence is at the core of human nature. Thus it is the "heart and secret soul of the sacred." Religion is a mechanism by which humans defend themselves against their own violent natures.

Cultures have developed several methods for dealing with violence. Girard understands these from an evolutionary perspective that assumes a development from primitive to modern societies, a premise severely questioned by many contemporary theorists. Girard defines primitive societies as those that lack a developed judicial system and that practice ritual sacrifice. In such societies retribution or revenge is the consequence of nonsacrificial acts of violence; each violent act evokes another. To prevent this sequence, a victim—often a slave, king, or animal—is chosen. On this victim violence may be practiced without fear of reprisal. Thus the "regular exercise of 'good' violence" is used to counter "bad" violence.

Modern societies, says Girard, developed judicial systems. Rather than attempting to prevent violent acts, they provide decisive retribution on the actual perpetrator, and they do so with such force and social authority that no further actions are possible.

On ritual and violence see also Robert D. Benford and Lester R. Kurtz, "Performing the Nuclear Ceremony: The Arms Race as a Ritual," in A Shuddering Dawn: Religious Studies and the Nuclear Age, *69–88. Ed. Ira Chernus and Edward Tabor Linenthal. Albany: State University of New York Press. 1989.*

About the author: Dates: *1923–, Avignon, France.* **Education:** *Baccalaureat Philosophie, Lycée d'Avignon; Archiviste-paleographe, École des Chartres, Paris; Ph.D., Indiana University.* **Field(s):** *religious studies; an-*

thropology; comparative literature, ritual studies, French literature and thought. **Career:** *Professor, Institut d'Études Françaises d'Avignon, 1962–present. Professor, 1981–present, Stanford University.* **Publications:** Deceit, Desire, and the Novel *(John Hopkins University, 1976 [1966]);* Violence and the Sacred *(John Hopkins University, 1991 [1977]);* with J. M. Oughourlian and Guy Lefort, Things Hidden Since the Foundation of the World *(Athlone, 1987; Stanford University, 1987, 1993);* "To Double Business Bound": Essays on Literature, Mimesis and Anthropology *(John Hopkins University, 1978; Athlone, 1988);* The Scapegoat *(John Hopkins University, 1989 [1986]);* Job, the Victim of His People *(Athlone, 1987; Stanford University, 1987);* A Theater of Envy: William Shakespeare *(Oxford University, 1991).* **Additional:** *Director, Program of Interdisciplinary Research, Stanford University, 1986–1991; Honorary Chair, Colloquium on Violence and Religion, 1991–present; Prize of the Académie Française for* La Violence et le sacré *(Violence and the Sacred), 1973; Chevalier de l'Ordre des Arts et des Lettres, December 1990; Médicis Prize for* Shakespeare, Les feux de l'envie *(A Theater of Envy: William Shakespeare), 1990; Principal organizer of several international symposia, including "Disorder and Order," 1981; "Understanding Origin," 1987; and "Vengeance," 1988.*

In many rituals the sacrificial act assumes two opposing aspects, appearing at times as a sacred obligation to be neglected at grave peril, at other times as a sort of criminal activity entailing perils of equal gravity.

To account for this dual aspect of ritual sacrifice—the legitimate and the illegitimate, the public and the all but covert—Henri Hubert and Marcel Mauss, in their "Essay on the Nature and Function of Sacrifice,"[1] adduce the sacred character of the victim. Because the victim is sacred, it is criminal to kill him—but the victim is sacred only because he is to be killed. Here is a circular line of reasoning that at a somewhat later date would be dignified by the sonorous term *ambivalence.* Persuasive and authoritative as that term still appears, it has been so extraordinarily abused in our century that perhaps we may now recognize how little light it sheds on the subject of sacrifice. Certainly it provides no real explanation. When we speak of ambivalence, we are only pointing out a problem that remains to be solved.

If sacrifice resembles criminal violence, we may say that there is, inversely, hardly any form of violence that cannot be described in terms of sacrifice—as Greek tragedy clearly reveals. It has often been observed that the tragic poets cast a glimmering veil of rhetoric over the sordid realities of life. True enough—but sacrifice and murder would not lend themselves to this game of reciprocal substitution if they were not in some way related. Although it is so obvious that it may hardly seem worth mentioning, where sacrifice is concerned first appearances count for little, are quickly brushed aside—and should therefore receive special attention. Once one has made up one's mind that sacrifice is an institution essentially if not entirely symbolic, one can say anything whatsoever about it. It is a subject that lends itself to insubstantial theorizing.

Sacrifice contains an element of mystery. And if the pieties of classical humanists lull our curiosity to sleep, the company of the ancient authors keeps it alert. The ancient mystery remains as impenetrable as ever. From the manner in which the moderns treat the subject of sacrifice, it would be hard to know whether distraction, detachment, or some sort of secret discretion shapes their thinking. There seems to be yet another mystery here. Why, for example, do we never explore the relationship between sacrifice and violence?

Recent studies suggest that the physiology of violence varies little from one individual to another, even from one culture to another. According to Anthony Storr, nothing resembles an angry cat or man so much as another angry cat or man.[2] If violence did indeed play a role in sacrifice, at least at one particular stage of the ritual, we would have a significant clue to the whole subject. Here would be a factor to some extent independent of those cultural variables that are often unknown to us, or only dimly known, or perhaps less familiar than we like to think.

Once aroused, the urge to violence triggers certain physical changes that prepare men's bodies for battle. This set toward violence lingers on; it should not be regarded as a simple reflex that ceases with the removal of the initial stimulus. Storr remarks that it is more difficult to quell an impulse toward violence than to rouse it, especially within the normal framework of social behavior.

Violence is frequently called irrational. It has its reasons, however, and can marshal some rather convincing ones when the need arises. Yet these reasons cannot be taken seriously, no matter how valid they may appear. Violence itself will discard them if the initial object remains persistently out of reach and continues to provoke hostility. When unappeased, violence seeks and always finds a surrogate victim. The creature that excited its fury is abruptly replaced by another, chosen only because it is vulnerable and close at hand.

There are many indications that this tendency to seek out surrogate objects is not limited to human violence. Konrad Lorenz makes reference to a species of fish that, if deprived of its natural enemies (the male rivals with whom it habitually disputes territorial rights), turns its aggression against the members of its own family and destroys them.[3] Joseph de Maistre discusses the choice of animal victims that display human characteristics—an attempt, as it were, to deceive the violent impulse: "The sacrificial animals were always those most prized for their usefulness: the gentlest, most innocent creatures, whose habits and instincts brought them most closely into harmony with man. . . . From the animal realm were chosen as victims those who were, if we might use the phrase, the most *human* in nature."[4]

* * *

Fieldwork and subsequent theoretical speculation lead us back to the hypothesis of substitution as the basis for the practice of sacrifice. This notion pervades ancient literature on the subject—which may be one reason, in fact, why many modern theorists reject the concept out of hand or give it only scant attention. Hubert and Mauss, for instance, view the idea with suspicion, undoubtedly because they feel that it introduces into the discussion religious and moral values that are incompatible with true scientific inquiry. And to be sure, Joseph de Maistre takes the view that the ritual victim is an "innocent" creature who pays a debt for the "guilty" party. I propose an hypothesis that does away with this moral distinction. As I see it, the relationship between the potential victim and the actual victim cannot be defined in terms of innocence or guilt. There is no question of "expiation." Rather, society is seeking to deflect upon a relatively indifferent victim, a "sacrificeable" victim, the violence that would otherwise be vented on its own members, the people it most desires to protect.

The qualities that lend violence its particular terror—its blind brutality, the fundamental absurdity of its manifestations—have a reverse side. With these qualities goes the strange propensity to seize upon surrogate victims, to actually conspire with the enemy and at the right moment toss him a morsel that will serve to satisfy his raging hunger. The fairy tales of childhood in which the wolf, ogre, or dragon gobbles up a large stone in place of a small child could well be said to have a sacrificial cast.

* * *

Violence is not to be denied, but it can be diverted to another object, something it can sink its teeth into. Such, perhaps, is one of the meanings of the story of Cain and Abel. The Bible offers us no background on the two brothers except the bare fact that Cain is a tiller of the soil who gives the fruits of his labor to God, whereas Abel is a shepherd who regularly sacrifices the first-born of his herds. One of the brothers kills the other, and the murderer is the one who does not have the violence-outlet of animal sacrifice at his disposal. This difference between sacrificial and nonsacrificial cults determines, in effect, God's judgement in favor of Abel. To say that God accedes to Abel's sacrificial offerings but rejects the offerings of Cain is simply another way of saying—from the viewpoint of the divinity—that Cain is a murderer, whereas his brother is not.

A frequent motif in the Old Testament, as well as in Greek myth, is that of brothers at odds with one another. Their fatal penchant for violence can only be diverted by the intervention of a third party, the sacrificial victim or victims. Cain's "jealousy" of his brother is only another term for his one characteristic trait: his lack of a sacrificial outlet.

According to Moslem tradition, God delivered to Abraham the ram previously sacrificed by Abel. This ram was to take the place of Abraham's son Isaac; having already saved one human life, the same animal would now save another. What we have here is no mystical hocus-pocus, but an intuitive insight into the essential function of sacrifice, gleaned exclusively from the scant references in the Bible.

Another familiar biblical scene takes on new meaning in the light of our theory of sacrificial substitution, and it can serve in turn to illuminate some aspects of the theory. The scene is that in which Jacob receives the blessing of his father Isaac.

Isaac is an old man. He senses the approach of death and summons his eldest son, Esau, on whom he intends to bestow his final blessing. First, however, he instructs Esau to bring back some venison from the hunt, so as to make a "savory meat." This request is overheard by the younger brother, Jacob, who hastens to report it to his mother, Rebekah. Rebekah takes two kids from the family flock, slaughters them, and prepares the savory meat dish, which Jacob, in the guise of his elder brother, then presents to his father.

Isaac is blind. Nevertheless Jacob fears he will be recognized, for he is a "smooth man," while his brother Esau is a "hairy man." "My father peradventure will feel me, and I shall seem to him as a deceiver; and I shall bring a curse upon me, not a blessing." Rebekah has the idea of covering Jacob's hands and the back of his neck with the skins of the slaughtered goats, and when the old man runs his hands over his younger son, he is completely taken in by the imposture. Jacob receives the blessing that Isaac had intended for Esau.

The kids serve in two different ways to dupe the father—or, in other terms, to divert from the son the violence directed toward him. In order to receive his father's blessing rather than his curse, Jacob must present to Isaac the freshly slaughtered kids made into a "savory meat." Then the son must seek refuge, literally, in the skins of the sacrificed animals. The animals thus interpose themselves between father and son. They serve as a sort of insulation, preventing the direct contact that could lead only to violence.

Two sorts of substitution are telescoped here: that of one brother for another, and that of an animal for a man. Only the first receives explicit recognition in the text; however, this first one serves as the screen upon which the shadow of the second is projected.

Once we have focused attention on the sacrificial victim, the object originally singled out for violence fades from view. Sacrificial substitution implies a degree of misunderstanding. Its vitality as an institution depends on its ability to conceal the displacement upon which the rite is based. It must never lose sight entirely, however, of the original object, or cease to be aware of the act of transference from that object to the surrogate victim; without that awareness no substitution can take place and the sacrifice loses all efficacy. The biblical passage discussed above meets both requirements. The narrative does not refer directly to the strange deception underlying the sacrificial substitution, nor does it allow this deception to pass entirely unnoticed. Rather, it mixes the act of substitution with another act of substitution, permitting us a fleeting, sidelong glimpse of the process. The narrative itself, then, might be said to partake of a sacrificial quality; it claims to reveal one act of substitution while employing this first substitution to half-conceal another. There is reason to believe that the narrative touches upon the mythic origins of the sacrificial system.

The figure of Jacob has long been linked with the devious character of sacrificial violence. In Greek culture Odysseus plays a similar role. The story of Jacob's benediction can be compared to the episode of the Cyclops in the *Odyssey*, where a splendidly executed ruse enables the hero to escape the clutches of a monster.

Odysseus and his shipmates are shut up in the Cyclops' cave. Every day the giant devours one of the crew; the survivors finally manage to blind their tormentor with a flaming stake. Mad with pain and anger, the Cyclops bars the entrance of the cave to prevent the men from escaping. However, he lets pass his flock of sheep, which go out daily to pasture. In a gesture reminiscent of the blind Isaac, the Cyclops runs his hands over the back of each sheep as it leaves the cave to make sure that it carries no passenger. Odysseus, however, has outwitted his captor, and he rides to freedom by clinging to the thick wool on the underside of one of the rams.

A comparison of the two scenes, one from Genesis and the other from the *Odyssey*, lends credence to the theory of their sacrificial origins. In each case an animal intervenes at the crucial moment to prevent violence from attaining its designated victim. The two texts are mutually revealing: the Cyclops of the *Odyssey* underlines the fearful menace that hangs over the hero (and that remains obscure in the Genesis story); and the slaughter of the kids in Genesis, along with the offering of the "savory meat," clearly implies the sacrificial character of the flock, an aspect that might go unnoticed in the *Odyssey*.

*   *   *

Sacrifice has often been described as an act of mediation between a sacrificer and a "deity." Because the very concept of a deity, much less a deity who receives blood sacrifices, has little reality in this day and age, the entire institution of sacrifice is relegated by most modern theorists to the realm of the imagination. The approach of Hubert and Mauss leads to the judgement of Claude Lévi-Strauss in *La Pensée sauvage*: because sacrificial rites have no basis in reality, we have every reason to label them meaningless.

The attempt to link sacrifice to a nonexistent deity brings to mind Paul Valéry's description of poetry as a purely solipsistic activity practiced by the more able solely out of love for art, while the less able persist in the belief that they are actually communicating with someone!

The two ancient narratives examined above make unmistakable reference to the act of sacrifice, but neither makes so much as a passing mention of a deity. If a god had intervened in either incident, its significance would have been diminished rather than increased, and the reader would have been led to conclude, in accordance with the beliefs common to late antiquity and to the modern world, that sacrifice has no real function in society. Divine intervention would have meant the elimination of the pervasive aura of dread, along with its firmly structured economy of violence. We would have then been thrown back upon a formalistic critical approach that would in no way further our understanding.

As we have seen, the sacrificial process requires a certain degree of *misunderstanding*. The celebrants do not and must not comprehend the true role of the sacrificial act. The theological basis of the sacrifice has a crucial role in fostering this misunderstanding. It is the god who supposedly demands the victims; he alone, in principle, who savors the smoke from the altars and requisitions the slaughtered flesh. It is to appease his anger that the killing goes on, that the victims multiply. Interpreters who think they question the primacy of the divine sufficiently by declaring the whole affair "imaginary" may well remain the prisoners of the theology they have not really analyzed. The problem then becomes, how can a real institution be constructed on a purely illusory basis? It is not to be wondered at if the outer shell finally gives way, bringing down with it even the most solid aspects of the institution.

Instead of rejecting the theological basis outright, qua abstraction (which is the same, in effect, as passively accepting it), let us expose its assumptions to a critical examination. Let us try to uncover the societal conflicts that the sacrificial act and its theological interpretations at once dissimulate and appease. We must break with the formalistic tradition of Hubert and Mauss.

The interpretation of sacrifice as an act of violence inflicted on a surrogate victim has recently been advanced once again. Godfrey Lienhardt (in *Divinity and Experience*) and Victor Turner (in a number of works, especially *The Drums of Affliction*), drawing from fieldwork, portray sacrifice as practiced among the Dinka and the Ndembu as a deliberate act of collective substitution performed at the expense of the victim and absorbing all the internal tensions, feuds, and rivalries pent up within the community.

Sacrifice plays a very real role in these societies, and the problem of substitution concerns the entire community. The victim is not a substitute for some particularly endangered individual, nor is it offered up to some individual of particularly bloodthirsty temperament. Rather, it is a substitute for all the members of the community, offered up by the members themselves. The sacrifice serves to protect the entire community from *its own* violence; it prompts the entire community to choose victims outside itself. The elements of dissension scattered throughout the community are drawn to the person of the sacrificial victim and eliminated, at least temporarily, by its sacrifice.

If we turn our attention from the theological superstructure of the act—that is, from an interpretive version of the event that is often accepted as the final statement on sacrifice—we quickly perceive yet another level of religious discourse, in theory subordinated to the theological dimension, but in reality quite independent of it. This has to do with the social function of the act, an aspect far more accessible to the modern mind.

It is easy to ridicule a religion by concentrating on its more eccentric rites, rites such as the sacrifices performed to induce rain or bring fine weather. There is in fact no object or endeavor in whose name a sacrifice cannot be made, especially when the social basis of the act has begun to blur. Nevertheless, there is a common denominator that determines the efficacy of all sacrifices and that becomes increasingly apparent as the institution grows in vigor. This common denominator is internal violence—all the dissensions, rivalries, jealousies, and quarrels within the community that the sacrifices are designed to suppress. The purpose of the sacrifice is to restore harmony to the community, to reinforce the social fabric. Everything else derives from that. If once we take this fundamental approach to sacrifice, choosing the road that violence opens before us, we can see that there is no aspect of human existence foreign to the subject, not even material prosperity. When men no longer live in harmony with one another, the sun still shines and the rain falls, to be sure, but the fields are less well tended, the harvests less abundant. . . .

In attempting to formulate the fundamental principles of sacrifice without reference to the ritualistic framework in which the sacrifice takes place, we run the risk of appearing simplistic. Such an effort smacks strongly of "psychologizing." Clearly, it would be inexact to compare the sacrificial act to the spontaneous gesture of the man who kicks his dog because he dares not kick his wife or boss. However, there are Greek myths that are hardly more than colossal variants of such gestures. Such a one is the story of Ajax. Furious at the leaders of the Greek army, who refused to award him Achilles' weapons, Ajax slaughters the herd of sheep intended as provisions for the army. In his mad rage he mistakes these gentle creatures for the warriors on whom he means to vent his rage. The slaughtered animals belong to a species traditionally utilized by the Greeks for sacrificial purposes; but because the massacre takes place outside the ritual framework, Ajax is taken for a madman. The myth is not, strictly speaking, about the sacrificial process; but it is certainly not irrelevant to it. The institution of sacrifice is based on effects analogous to those produced by Ajax's anger—but structured, channeled and held in check by fixed laws.

In the ritualistic societies most familiar to us—those of the Jews and of the Greeks of the classical age—the sacrificial victims are almost always animals. However, there are other societies in which human victims are substituted for the individuals who are threatened by violence.

Even in fifth century Greece—the Athens of the great tragedians—human sacrifice had not, it seems, completely disappeared. The practice was perpetuated in the form of the pharmakos,[A] maintained by the city at its own expense and slaughtered at the appointed festivals as well as at a moment of civic disaster. If examined closely for traces of human sacrifice, Greek tragedy offers some remarkable revelations. It is clear, for example, that the story of Medea parallels that of Ajax on the sacrificial level, although here we are dealing with human rather than with animal sacrifice. In Euripides' *Medea* the principle of human substitution of one victim for another appears in its most savage form. Frightened by the intensity of Medea's rage against her faithless husband, Jason, the nurse begs the children's tutor to keep his charges out of their mother's way:

> I am sure her anger will not subside until it has found a victim. Let us pray that the victim is at least one of our enemies![5]

Because the object of her hatred is out of reach, Medea substitutes her own children. It is difficult for us to see anything resembling a religious act in Medea's insane behavior. Nonetheless, infanticide has its place among ritualistic practices; the practice is too well documented in too many cultures (including the Jewish and the ancient Greek) for us to

---

[A] pharmakos: a person sacrificed in ancient Greece as a means of purification or atonement for a city or a community; often the person was one who had already been condemned to death. (editor's note)

exclude it from consideration here. Medea's crime is to ritual infanticide what the massacre of sheep in the *Ajax* is to animal sacrifice. Medea prepares for the death of her children like a priest preparing for a sacrifice. Before the fateful act, she issues the traditional ritual announcement: all those whose presence might in any way hinder the effectiveness of the ceremony are requested to remove themselves from the premises.

Medea, like Ajax, reminds us of a fundamental truth about violence; if left unappeased, violence will accumulate until it overflows its confines and floods the surrounding area. The role of sacrifice is to stem this rising tide of indiscriminate substitutions and redirect violence into "proper" channels.

Ajax has details that underline the close relationship between the sacrificial substitution of animals and of humans. Before he sets upon the flock of sheep, Ajax momentarily contemplates the sacrifice of his own son. The boy's mother does not take this threat lightly; she whisks the child away.

In a general study of sacrifice there is little reason to differentiate between human and animal victims. When the principle of the substitution is *physical resemblance* between the vicarious victim and its prototypes, the mere fact that both victims are human beings seems to suffice. Thus, it is hardly surprising that in some societies whole categories of human beings are systematically reserved for sacrificial purposes in order to protect other categories. . . .

This dividing of sacrifice into two categories, human and animal, has itself a sacrificial character, in a strictly ritualistic sense. The division is based in effect on a value judgement, on the preconception that one category of victim—the human being—is quite unsuitable for sacrificial purposes, while another category—the animal—is eminently sacrificeable. We encounter here a survival of the sacrificial mode of thinking that perpetuates a misunderstanding about the institution as a whole. It is not a question of rejecting the value judgment on which this misunderstanding is based, but of putting it, so to speak, in parentheses, of recognizing that as far as the institution is concerned, such judgments are purely arbitrary. All reduction into categories, whether implicit or explicit, must be avoided; all victims, animal or human, must be treated in the same fashion if we wish to apprehend the criteria by which victims are selected (if indeed such criteria exist) and discover (if

such a thing is possible) a universal principle for their selection.

We have remarked that all victims, even the animal ones, bear a certain *resemblance* to the object they replace; otherwise the violent impulse would remain unsatisfied. But this resemblance must not be carried to the extreme of complete assimilation, or it would lead to disastrous confusion. . . .

In order for a species or category of living creature, human or animal, to appear suitable for sacrifice, it must bear a sharp resemblance to the *human* categories excluded from the ranks of the "sacrificeable," while still maintaining a degree of difference that forbids all possible confusion. . . . No mistake is possible in the case of animal sacrifice. But it is quite another case with human victims. If we look at the extremely wide spectrum of human victims sacrificed by various societies, the list seems heterogeneous, to say the least. It includes prisoners of war, slaves, small children, unmarried adolescents, and the handicapped; it ranges from the very dregs of society, such as the Greek pharmakos, to the king himself.

Is it possible to detect a unifying factor in this disparate group? We notice at first glance beings who are either outside or on the fringes of society: prisoners of war, slaves, pharmakos. In many primitive societies children who have not yet undergone the rites of initiation have no proper place in the community; their rights and duties are almost nonexistent. What we are dealing with, therefore, are exterior or marginal individuals, incapable of establishing or sharing the social bonds that link the rest of the inhabitants. Their status as foreigners or enemies, their servile condition, or simply their age prevents these future victims from fully integrating themselves into the community.

But what about the king? Is he not at the very heart of the community? Undoubtedly—but it is precisely his position at the center that serves to isolate him from his fellow men, to render him casteless. He escapes from society, so to speak, via the roof, just as the pharmakos escapes through the cellar. The king has a sort of foil, however, in the person of his fool. The fool shares his master's status as an outsider—an isolation whose literal truth is often of greater significance than the easily reversible symbolic values often attributed to it. From every point of view the fool is eminently "sacrificeable," and the king can use him to vent his own anger. But it sometimes happens that the king himself is sacrificed, and that (among certain African societies) in a thoroughly regulated and highly ritualistic manner.

It is clearly legitimate to define the difference between sacrificeable and nonsacrificeable individuals in terms of their degree of integration, but such a definition is not yet sufficient. In many cultures women are not considered full-fledged members of their society; yet women are never, or rarely, selected as sacrificial victims. There may be a simple explanation for this fact. The married woman retains her ties with her parents' clan even after she has become in some respects the property of her husband and his family. To kill her would be to run the risk of one of the two groups' interpreting her sacrifice as an act of murder committing it to a reciprocal act of revenge. The notion of vengeance casts a new light on the matter. All our sacrificial victims, whether chosen from one of the human categories enumerated above or, *a fortiori*, from the animal realm, are invariably distinguishable from the nonsacrificeable beings by one essential characteristic: between these victims and the community a crucial social link is missing, so they can be exposed to violence without fear of reprisal. Their death does not automatically entail an act of vengeance.

The considerable importance this freedom from reprisal has for the sacrificial process makes us understand that sacrifice is primarily an act of violence without risk of vengeance. We also understand the paradox—not without its comic aspects on occasion—of the frequent references to vengeance in the course of sacrificial rites, the veritable obsession with vengeance when no chance of vengeance exists:

> For the act they were about to commit elaborate excuses were offered; they shuddered at the prospect of the sheep's death, they wept over it as though they were its parents. Before the blow was struck, they implored the beast's forgiveness. They then addressed themselves to the species to which the beast belonged, as if addressing a large family clan, beseeching it not to seek vengeance for the act that was about to be inflicted on one of its members. In the same vein the actual murderer was punished in some manner, either beaten or sent into exile.[6]

It is the entire species *considered as a large family clan* that the sacrificers beseech not to seek vengeance. By incorporating the element of reprisal into the ceremony, the participants are hinting broadly at the true function of the rite, the kind of action it was designed to circumvent and the criteria that determined the choice of victim. The desire to commit an act of violence on those near us cannot be suppressed without a conflict; we must divert that impulse, therefore, toward the sacrificial victim, the creature we can strike down without fear of reprisal, since he lacks a champion.

Like everything that touches on the essential nature of the sacrificial act, the true distinction between the sacrificeable and the nonsacrificeable is never clearly articulated. Oddities and inexplicable anomalies confuse the picture. For instance, some animal species will be formally excluded from sacrifice, but the exclusion of members of the community is never mentioned. In constantly drawing attention to the truly maniacal aspects of sacrifice, modern theorists only serve to perpetuate an old misunderstanding in new terms. Men can dispose of their violence more efficiently if they regard the process not as something emanating from within themselves, but as a necessity imposed from without, a divine decree whose least infraction calls down terrible punishment. When they banish sacrificial practices from the "real," everyday world, modern theorists continue to misrepresent the violence of sacrifice.

The function of sacrifice is to quell violence within the community and to prevent conflicts from erupting. Yet societies like our own, which do not, strictly speaking, practice sacrificial rites, seem to get along without them. Violence undoubtedly exists within our society, but not to such an extent that the society itself is threatened with extinction. The simple fact that sacrificial practices, and other rites as well, can disappear without catastrophic results should in part explain the failure of ethnology and theology to come to grips with these cultural phenomena, and explain as well our modern reluctance to attribute a real function to them. After all, it is hard to maintain that institutions for which, as it seems, we have no need are actually indispensable.

It may be that a basic difference exists between a society like ours and societies imbued with religion—a difference that is partially hidden from us by rites, particularly by rites of sacrifice, that play a compensatory role. This difference would help explain why the actual function of sacrifice still eludes us.

When internal strife, previously sublimated by means of sacrificial practices, rises to the surface, it manifests itself in interfamily vendettas or blood feuds. This kind of violence is virtually nonexistent in our own culture. And perhaps it is here that we should look for the fundamental difference between primitive societies and our own; we should examine the specific ailments to which we are immune and which sacrifice manages to control, if not to eliminate.

Why does the spirit of revenge, wherever it breaks out, constitute such an intolerable menace? Perhaps because the only satisfactory revenge for spilt blood is spilling the blood of the killer; and in the blood feud there is no clear distinction between the act for which the killer is being punished and the punishment itself. Vengeance professes to be an act of reprisal, and every reprisal calls for another reprisal. The crime to which the act of vengeance addresses itself is almost never an unprecedented offense; in almost every case it has been committed in revenge for some prior crime.

Vengeance, then, is an interminable, infinitely repetitive process. Every time it turns up in some part of the community, it threatens to involve the whole social body. There is the risk that the act of vengeance will initiate a chain reaction whose consequences will quickly prove fatal to any society of modest size. The multiplication of reprisals instantaneously puts the very existence of a society in jeopardy, and that is why it is universally proscribed. . . .

If primitive societies have no tried and true remedies for dealing with an outbreak of violence, no certain cure once the social equilibrium has been upset, we can assume that *preventive* measures will play an essential role. Here again I return to the concept of sacrifice as I earlier defined it: an instrument of prevention in the struggle against violence.

In a universe where the slightest dispute can lead to disaster—just as a slight cut can prove fatal to a hemophiliac—the rites of sacrifice serve to polarize the community's aggressive impulses and redirect them toward victims that may be actual or figurative, animate or inanimate, but that are always incapable of propagating further vengeance. The sacrificial process furnishes an outlet for those violent impulses that cannot be mastered by self-restraint; a partial outlet, to be sure, but always renewable, and one whose efficacy has been attested by an impressive number of reliable witnesses. The sacrificial process prevents the spread of violence by keeping vengeance in check.

In societies that practice sacrifice there is no critical situation to which the rites are not applicable, but there are certain crises that seem to be particularly amenable to sacrificial mediation. In these crises the social fabric of the community is threatened; dissension and discord are rife. The more critical the situation, the more "precious" the sacrificial victim must be.

It is significant that sacrifice has languished in societies with a firmly established judicial system—ancient Greece and Rome, for example. In such societies the essential purpose of sacrifice has disappeared. It may still be practiced for a while, but in diminished and debilitated form. And it is precisely under such circumstances that sacrifice usually comes to our notice, and our doubts as to the "real" function of religious institutions are only reinforced.

Our original proposition stands: ritual in general, and sacrificial rites in particular, assume essential roles in societies that lack a firm judicial system. It must not be assumed, however, that sacrifice simply "replaces" a judicial system. One can scarcely speak of replacing something that never existed to begin with. Then, too, a judicial system is ultimately irreplaceable, short of a unanimous and entirely voluntary renunciation of all violent actions.

When we minimize the dangers implicit in vengeance we risk losing sight of the true function of sacrifice. Because revenge is rarely encountered in our society, we seldom have occasion to consider how societies lacking a judicial system of punishment manage to hold it in check. Our ignorance engages us in a false line of thought that is seldom, if ever, challenged. Certainly we have no need of religion to help us solve a problem, runaway vengeance, whose very existence eludes us. And because we have no need for it, religion itself appears senseless. The efficiency of our judicial solution conceals the problem, and the elimination of the problem conceals from us the role played by religion.

The air of mystery that primitive societies acquire for us is undoubtedly due in large part to this misunderstanding. It is undoubtedly responsible for our extreme views of these societies, our insistence on portraying them alternately as vastly superior or flagrantly inferior to our own. One factor alone might well be responsible for our oscillation between extremes, our radical evaluations: the absence in such societies of a judicial system. No one can assess with certainty the amount of violence present in another individual, much less in another society. We can be sure, however, that in a society lacking a judicial system the violence will not appear in the same places or take the same forms as in our own. We generally limit our area of inquiry to the most conspicuous and accessible aspects of these societies. Thus, it is not unnatural that they should seem to us either horribly barbarous or blissfully utopian.

In primitive societies the risk of unleashed violence is so great and the cure so problematic that the emphasis naturally falls on prevention. The preventive measures naturally fall within the domain of religion, where they can on occasion assume a violent character. Violence and the sacred are inseparable. But the covert appropriation by sacrifice of certain properties of violence—particularly the ability of violence to move from one object to another—is hidden from sight by the awesome machinery of ritual.

Primitive societies are not given over to violence. Nor are they necessarily less violent or less "hypocritical" than our own society. Of course, to be truly comprehensive we ought to take into consideration *all* forms of violence, more or less ritualized, that divert a menace from nearby objects to more distant objects. We ought, for instance, to consider war. War is clearly not restricted to one particular type of society. Yet the multiplication of new weapons and techniques does not constitute a fundamental difference between primitive and modern warfare. On the other hand, if we compare societies that adhere to a judicial system with societies that practise sacrificial rites, the difference between the two is such that we can indeed consider the absence or presence of these institutions as a basis for distinguishing

primitive societies from "civilized" ones. These are the institutions we must scrutinize in order to arrive, not at some sort of value judgement, but at an objective knowledge of the respective societies to which they belong.

In primitive societies the exercise of preventive measures is not confined exclusively to the domain of religion. The way in which these measures are made manifest in normal social intercourse made a lasting impression on the minds and imaginations of the first European observers and established a prototype of "primitive" psychology and behavior which, if not universally applicable, is still not wholly illusory.

When the least false step can have dire consequences, human relationships may well be marked by a prudence that seems to us excessive and accompanied by precautions that appear incomprehensible. It is in this sense that we must understand the lengthy palavers that precede any undertaking not sanctified by custom, in this sense that we must understand primitive man's reluctance to engage in nonritualized games or contests. In a society where every action or gesture may have irreparable consequences it is not surprising that the members should display a "noble gravity" of bearing beside which our own demeanor appears ridiculous. The commercial, administrative, or ideological concerns that make such overwhelming demands on our time and attention seem utterly frivolous in comparison to primitive man's primary concerns.

Primitive societies do not have built into their structure an automatic brake against violence; but we do, in the form of powerful institutions whose grip grows progressively tighter as their role grows progressively less apparent. The constant presence of a restraining force allows modern man safely to transgress the limits imposed on primitive peoples without even being aware of the fact. In "policed" societies the relationships between individuals, including total strangers, is characterized by an extraordinary air of informality, flexibility, and even audacity.

Religion invariably strives to subdue violence, to keep it from running wild. Paradoxically, the religious and moral authorities in a community attempt to instill nonviolence, as an active force into daily life and as a mediating force into ritual life, through the application of violence. Sacrificial rites serve to connect the moral and religious aspects of daily life, but only by means of a lengthy and hazardous detour. Moreover, it must be kept in mind that the efficacy of the rites depends on their being performed in the spirit of *pietas*, which marks all aspects of religious life. We are beginning to understand why the sacrificial act appears as both sinful and saintly, an illegal as well as a legitimate exercise of violence. However, we are still far from a full understanding of the act itself.

Primitive religion tames, trains, arms, and directs violent impulses as a defensive force against those forms of violence that society regards as inadmissible. It postulates a strange mixture of violence and nonviolence. The same can perhaps be said of our own judicial system of control.

There may be a certain connection between all the various methods employed by man since the beginning of time to avoid being caught up in an interminable round of revenge. They can be grouped into three general categories: (1) preventive measures in which sacrificial rites divert the spirit of revenge into other channels; (2) the harnessing or hobbling of vengeance by means of compensatory measures, trials by combat, etc., whose curative effects remain precarious; (3) the establishment of a judicial system—the most efficient of all curative procedures.

We have listed the methods in ascending order of effectiveness. The evolution from preventive to curative procedures is reflected in the course of history or, at any rate, in the course of the history of the Western world. The initial curative procedures mark an intermediary stage between a purely religious orientation and the recognition of a judicial system's superior efficiency. These methods are inherently ritualistic in character, and are often associated with sacrificial practices.

The curative procedures employed by primitive societies appear rudimentary to us. We tend to regard them as fumbling efforts to improvise a judicial system. Certainly their pragmatic aspects are clearly visible, oriented as they are not toward the guilty parties, but toward the victims—since it is the latter who pose the most immediate threat. The injured parties must be accorded a careful measure of satisfaction, just enough to appease their own desire for

revenge but not so much as to awaken the desire elsewhere. It is not a question of codifying good and evil or of inspiring respect for some abstract concept of justice; rather, it is a question of securing the safety of the group by checking the impulse for revenge. The preferred method involves a reconciliation between parties based on some sort of mutual compensation. If reconciliation is impossible, however, an armed encounter can be arranged in such a manner that the violence is wholly self-contained. This encounter can take place within an enclosed space and can involve prescribed regulations and specifically designated combatants. Its purpose is to cut violence short.

To be sure, all these curative measures are steps in the direction of a legal system. But the evolution, if indeed evolution is the proper term, is not continuous. The break comes at the moment when the intervention of an independent legal authority becomes *constraining*. Only then are men freed from the terrible obligations of vengeance. Retribution in its judicial guise loses its terrible urgency. Its meaning remains the same, but this meaning becomes increasingly indistinct or even fades from view. In fact, the system functions best when everyone concerned is least aware that it involves retribution. The system can—and as soon as it can it will—reorganize itself around the accused and the concept of guilt. In fact, retribution still holds sway, but forged into a principle of abstract justice that all men are obliged to uphold and respect.

We have seen that the "curative" measures, ostensibly designed to temper the impulse toward vengeance, become increasingly mysterious in their workings as they progress in efficiency. As the focal point of the system shifts away from religion and the preventive approach is translated into judicial retribution, the aura of misunderstanding that has always formed a protective veil around the institution of sacrifice shifts as well, and becomes associated in turn with the machinery of the law.

As soon as the judicial system gains supremacy, its machinery disappears from sight. Like sacrifice, it conceals—even as it also reveals—its resemblance to vengeance, differing only in that it is not self-perpetuating and its decisions discourage reprisals. In the case of sacrifice, the designated victim does not become the object of vengeance because he is a replacement, is not the "right" victim. In the judicial system the violence does indeed fall on the "right" victim; but it falls with such force, such resounding authority, that no retort is possible.

It can be argued that the function of the judicial system is not really concealed; and we can hardly be unaware that the judicial process is more concerned with the general security of the community than with any abstract notion of justice. Nonetheless, we believe that the system is founded on a unique principle of justice unknown to primitive societies. The scholarly literature on the subject seems to bear out this belief. It has long been assumed that a decisive difference between primitive and civilized man is the former's general inability to identify the guilty party and to adhere to the principle of guilt. Such an assumption only confuses the issue. If primitive man insists on averting his attention from the wrongdoer, with an obstinacy that strikes us as either idiotic or perverse, it is because he wishes above all to avoid fueling the fires of vengeance.

If our own system seems more rational, it is because it conforms more strictly to the principle of vengeance. Its insistence on the punishment of the guilty party underlines this fact. Instead of following the example of religion and attempting to forestall acts of revenge, to mitigate or sabotage its effects or to redirect them to secondary objects, our judicial system *rationalizes* revenge and succeeds in limiting and isolating its effects in accordance with social demands. The system treats the disease without fear of contagion and provides a highly effective technique for the cure and, as a secondary effect, the prevention of violence.

This rationalistic approach to vengeance might seem to stem from a peculiarly intimate relationship between the community and the judicial system. In fact, it is the result not of any familiar interchange between the two, but of the recognition of the sovereignty and independence of the judiciary, whose decisions no group, not even the collectivity as a body, can challenge. (At least, that is the principle.) The judicial authority is beholden to no one. It is thus at the disposal of everyone, and it is universally respected. The judicial system never hesitates to confront violence head on, because it possesses a monopoly on the means of revenge. Thanks to this monopoly, the system generally succeeds in stifling the impulse to vengeance rather than spreading or aggravating it, as a similar intervention on the part of the aggrieved party would invariably do.

In the final analysis, then, the judicial system and the institution of sacrifice share the same function, but the judicial system is infinitely more effective. However, it can only exist in conjunction with a firmly established political power. And like all modern technological advances, it is a two-edged sword, which can be used to oppress as well as to liberate. Certainly that is the way it is seen by primitive cultures, whose view on the matter is indubitably more objective than our own.

If the function of the system has now become apparent, that is because it no longer enjoys the obscurity it needs to operate effectively. A clear view of the inner workings indicates a crisis in the system; it is a sign of disintegration. No matter how sturdy it may seem, the apparatus that serves to hide the true nature of legal and illegal violence from view eventually wears thin. The underlying truth breaks through, and we find ourselves face to face with the specter of reciprocal reprisal. This is not a purely theoretical concept belonging to the intellectual and scholarly realm, but a sinister reality; a vicious circle we thought we had escaped, but one we find has tightened itself, all unsuspected, around us.

The procedures that keep men's violence in bounds have one thing in common: they are no strangers to the ways of violence. There is reason to believe that they are all rooted in religion. As we have seen, the various forms of prevention go hand in hand with religious practices. The curative procedures are also imbued with religious concepts—both the rudimentary sacrificial rites and the more advanced judicial forms. *Religion* in its broadest sense, then, must be another term for that obscurity that surrounds man's efforts to defend himself by curative or preventative means against his own violence. It is that enigmatic quality that pervades the judicial system when that system replaces sacrifice. This obscurity coincides with the transcendental effectiveness of a violence that is holy, legal, and legitimate successfully opposed to a violence that is unjust, illegal, and illegitimate.

In the same way that sacrificial victims must in principle meet the approval of the divinity before being offered as a sacrifice, the judicial system appeals to a theology as a guarantee of justice. Even when this theology disappears, as has happened in our culture, the transcendental quality of the system remains intact. Centuries can pass before men realize that there is no real difference between their principle of justice and the concept of revenge.

Only the transcendental quality of the system, acknowledged by all, can assure the prevention or cure of violence. This is the case no matter what the consecrating institution may be. Only by opting for a sanctified, legitimate form of violence and preventing it from becoming an object of disputes and recriminations can the system save itself from the vicious circle of revenge.

A unique generative force exists that we can only qualify as religious in a sense deeper than the theological one. It remains concealed and draws its strength from this concealment, even as its self-created shelter begins to crumble. The acknowledgment of such a force allows us to assess our modern ignorance—ignorance in regard to violence as well as religion. Religion shelters us from violence just as violence seeks shelter in religion. If we fail to understand certain religious practices it is not because we are outside their sphere of influence but because we are still to a very real extent enclosed within them. The solemn debates on the death of God and of man are perhaps beside the point. They remain theological at bottom, and by extension sacrificial; that is, they draw a veil over the subject of vengeance, which threatens to become quite real once again, in the form not of a philosophical debate but of unlimited violence, in a world with no absolute values. As soon as the essential quality of transcendence—religious, humanistic, or whatever—is lost, there are no longer any terms by which to define the legitimate form of violence and to recognize it among the multitude of illicit forms. The definition of legitimate and illegitimate forms then becomes a matter of mere opinion, with each man free to reach his own decision. In other words, the question is thrown to the winds. Henceforth there are as many legitimate forms of violence as there are men to implement them; legitimacy as a principle no longer exists. Only the introduction of some transcendental quality that will persuade men of the fundamental difference between sacrifice and revenge, between a judicial system and vengeance, can succeed in by-passing violence.

All this explains why our penetration and demystification of the system necessarily coincides with the disintegration of that system. The act of demystification retains a sacrificial quality and remains essentially religious in character for at least as long as it fails to come to a conclusion—as long, that is, as the process purports to be nonviolent, or less violent than the system itself. In fact, demystification leads to constantly increasing violence, a violence perhaps less "hypocritical" than the violence it seeks to expose, but more energetic, more virulent, and the harbinger of something far worse—a violence that knows no bounds.

While acknowledging the differences, both functional and mythical, between vengeance, sacrifice, and legal punishment, it is important to recognize their fundamental identity. Precisely because these three institutions are essentially the same they tend to adopt the same types of violent response in times of crisis. Seen in the abstract, such an assertion may seem hyperbolic or simply unbelievable. It can only be appreciated by means of concrete examples. Only then will the utility of the comparison become apparent; customs and institutions that have remained incomprehensible, unclassifiable, and "aberrant" heretofore make sense when seen in the light of this identity.

Robert Lowie, discussing collective reactions to an act of violence, brings out a fact well worth noting here: "The Chukchi generally make peace after the first act of retribution. . . . While the Ifugao tend to protect a kinsman under almost all circumstances, the Chukchi often avert a feud by killing a member of the family."[7]

Whether it be through sacrificial killing or legal punishment, the problem is to forestall a series of reprisals. As the above quotation shows, Lowie is well aware of this aspect. In killing one of their own, the Chukchi abort the issue; by offering a victim to their potential enemies they enjoin them not to seek vengeance, not to commit an act that would constitute a fresh affront and oblige the other side to seek further retribution. This expiatory procedure brings to mind the sacrificial process; the fact that the victim is someone other than the guilty party drives the resemblance home.

The Chukchi practice cannot, however, be classified as sacrificial. A properly conducted ritual killing is never openly linked to another bloodletting of irregular character. It never allows itself to pass as a deliberate act of retribution. Because this link is consistently missing, the meaning of the sacrificial process has always eluded us, and the relationship between sacrifice and violence has remained obscure. Now the meaning is made clear, and in a manner too spectacular for the act to be mistaken for mere ritual.

Should one then classify this custom among legal punishments? Can one properly refer to it as an "execution of justice"? Probably not; after all, the victim of the second murder was in no way responsible for the first. To be sure, Lowie invokes the concept of "collective responsibility," but this is not a satisfactory explanation. Collective responsibility never specifically excludes the true culprit, and that is precisely what is being done here. Even if this exclusion is not clearly spelled out, there is sufficient evidence for us to assume that in many instances the true culprit is systematically spared. As a cultural attitude, this certainly demands attention.

To refer in this context to the so-called primitive mentality, to some "possible confusion between the individual and the group," is to hedge the issue. If the Chukchi choose to spare the culprit it is not because they cannot distinguish where the guilt lies. On the contrary, they perceive it with the utmost clarity. It is precisely because they see that the guilty party is guilty that they choose to spare him. The Chukchi believe that they have good reasons to act as they do, and it is these reasons we must now examine.

To make a victim out of the guilty party is to play vengeance's role, to submit to the demands of violence. By killing, not the murderer himself, but someone close to him, an act of perfect reciprocity is avoided and the necessity for revenge by-passed. If the counterviolence were inflicted on the aggressor himself, it would by this very act participate in, and become indistinguishable from, the original act of violence. In short, it would become an act of pure vengeance, requiring yet another act of vengeance and transforming itself into the very thing it was designed to prevent.

Only violence can put an end to violence, and that is why violence is self-propagating. Everyone wants to strike the last blow, and reprisal can thus follow reprisal without any true conclusion ever being reached.

In excluding the actual guilty party from reprisals the Chukchi hope to avoid the vicious cycle of revenge. They try to cover their tracks—but not entirely, for they do not want to deprive their act of its primordial meaning as a response to an initial killing, as the payment of a debt contracted by one of their number. To quell the passions aroused by this crime an act is required that bears some resemblance to the vengeance sought by the plaintiffs but that does not quite qualify as an act of revenge. The act resembles both a legal punishment and a sacrifice, and yet it cannot be assimilated to either. The act described here resembles a legal punishment in that it constitutes an act of reparation, a violent retribution; and the Chukchi show no hesitation in imposing on themselves the same loss they have inflicted on others. Their action resembles a sacrifice in that the victim of the second murder is not responsible for the first.

So flagrant a disregard of the principle of guilt strikes us as absurd. We hold that principle in such high esteem that any deviation from it appears to us an aberration of the intellect or malfunction of the senses. Yet our line of reasoning is rejected by the "primitives" because it involves too strict an application of the doctrine of vengeance and is thus fraught with peril.

When we require a direct link between guilt and punishment we believe that we adhere to a fundamental truth that has somehow eluded the primitive mind. In fact, we are ignoring a problem that poses a very real threat to all primitive societies: escalating revenge, unleashed violence—a problem the seeming extravagances of their customs and the violence of their religious practices are specifically designed to meet.

In Greek culture in particular, physical contact with the anathema is avoided. Behind this peculiar prohibition lurks a fear perhaps analogous to the one that inspires the Chukchi custom. To do violence to a violent person is to be contaminated by his violence. It is best, therefore, to arrange matters so that nobody, except perhaps the culprit himself, is directly responsible for his death, so that nobody is obliged to raise a finger against him. He may be abandoned without provisions in mid-ocean, or stranded on top of a mountain, or forced to hurl himself from a cliff. The custom of exposure, as a means of getting rid of malformed children, seems to find its origin in this same fear.

All such customs may appear to us unreasonable and absurd. In fact they adhere to a coherent logic. All of them concern themselves with formulating and practicing a form of violence incapable of serving as a connecting link between the violent act that preceded and the one that must follow. The aim is to achieve a radically new type of violence, truly decisive and self-contained, a form of violence that will put an end once and for all to violence itself.

Primitive peoples try to break the symmetry of reprisal by addressing themselves directly to the question of form. Unlike us, they perceive recurrent patterns, and they attempt to halt this recurrence by introducing something different into the picture. Modern man has long since lost his fear of reciprocal violence, which, after all, provides our judicial system with its structure. Because the overwhelming authority of the judiciary prevents its sentence from becoming the first step in an endless series of reprisals, we can no longer appreciate primitive man's deep-seated fear of pure, unadulterated vengeance. The Chukchi's behavior or the Greeks' cautious treatment of the anathema strike us as puzzling.

Of course, the Chukchi solution is not to be confused with retaliatory vengeance, ritual sacrifice, or legal punishment. And yet it is reminiscent of all these institutions. Their solution seems to occur at the point where all three intersect. Unless the modern mind can cope with the fact that the three are indeed capable of intersecting, it is not likely to shed much light on the questions that concern us here.

* * *

The Chukchi solution is fraught with psychological implications, all of rather limited interest. For example, it can be said that in choosing to kill someone close to the culprit rather than the culprit himself the Chukchi are trying to be conciliatory without risking a loss of face. That is indeed possible, but there are many other possibilities as well. It is easy to lose one's way in a maze of psychological speculation. The religious structure clearly transcends all "psychological" interpretations; it neither requires nor contradicts them.

The essential religious concern here is ritual impurity. And the cause of ritual impurity is violence. In many cases, this fact seems self-evident.

Two men come to blows; blood is spilt; both men are thus rendered impure. Their impurity is contagious, and anyone who remains in their presence risks becoming a party to their quarrel. The only sure way to avoid contagion is to flee the scene of violence. There is no question here of duty or morality. Contamination is a terrible thing, and only those who are already contaminated would wilfully expose themselves to it.

If even an accidental contact with a "contaminated" being can spread the impurity, it goes without saying that a violent and hostile encounter will guarantee infection. Therefore, the Chukchi reason, whenever violence is inevitable, it is best that the victim be *pure*, untainted by any involvement in the dispute. As we can see, these notions of impurity and contagion play an active role in social relations and are firmly rooted in reality. It is precisely this basis in reality that scholars have long denied. Modern observers—particularly Frazer's contemporaries and disciples—were totally blind to the reality that lay behind these ideas, because it was not *their* reality and because primitive religion succeeded in camouflaging its social function. Concepts such as impurity and contagion, because they translate human relations into material terms, provide a sort of camouflage. The peril that overshadows all human relations and that stems from these relations is presented either in a purely material or in a wholly otherworldly guise. The notion of ritual impurity can degenerate until it is nothing more than a terror-stricken belief in the malevolent results of physical contact. Violence has been transformed into a sort of seminal fluid that impregnates objects on contact and whose diffusion, like electricity or Balzacian "magnetism," is determined by physical laws. Far from dissipating the ignorance that surrounds these concepts, modern thinking only reinforces the confusion. By denying religion any basis in reality, by viewing it as a sort of bedtime story for children, we collaborate with violence in its game of deception.

In many religious communities—among the ancient Greeks, for instance—when a man has hanged himself, his body becomes impure. So too does the rope from which he dangles, the tree to which the rope is attached, and the field where the tree stands. The taint of impurity diminishes, however, as one draws away from the body. It is as if the scene of a violent act, and the objects with which the violence has been committed, send out emanations that penetrate everything in the immediate area, growing gradually weaker through time and space.

When a town has undergone a terrible bloodletting, and emissaries from that town are sent to another community, they are considered impure. Every effort is made to avoid touching them, talking to them, remaining in their presence any longer than necessary. After their departure rites of purification are undertaken: sacrifices offered, lustral water sprinkled about.

While Frazer and his disciples tend to view this fear of infection by the "impure" as a prime example of the "irrational" and "superstitious" element of religious thought, other observers regard it as an anticipation of sound scientific principles. They point out the striking resemblance between the precautions that modern medicine takes against bacterial infection and the ritualistic avoidance of pollution.

In some societies contagious diseases—smallpox, for instance—have their own particular gods. During his illness the patient is dedicated to the god; that is, he is isolated from the community and put under the supervision of an "initiate," or priest of the god, someone who has contracted the illness and survived it. This man now partakes of the god's power; he is immune to the effects of the divine violence.

It is easy to see why some observers have concluded that these impurity rituals reveal some sort of vague intuitive knowledge of microbiology; that the rituals, in short, are grounded in fact. Against this view it is argued that the procedures that are supposed to protect the believers from ritual impurity often disregard, or even flout, the principles of modern hygiene. This argument is not wholly satisfactory, however, for it fails to take into account the possible parallels between ritualistic precautions and the first tentative measures taken in the early days of public hygiene—in the nineteenth century, for example.

The theory that regards religious terrors or taboos as a sort of protoscience has hit on something of real interest, but too indefinite and limited to be of much use in our investigation. Such a theory can only arise in a culture that regards *sickness* as the sole fatal influence, the sole enemy man has to conquer. Clearly, medical considerations are not excluded from the primitive concept of contagion, and the prevention of epidemics plays a definite role in impurity rites. But these factors play only a minor role in primitive culture. They arouse our interest precisely because they offer the sole instance in which the modern scientific notion of contagion, which is exclusively pathological, coincides with the primitive concept, which is far broader in scope.

The aspects of religion in which contagion seems to have some reality for us are hard to distinguish from those in which it ceases to have any reality. That is not to say that primitive religion is afflicted with the sort of "confusion" that Frazer or Lévy-Bruhl attributed to it. The assimilation of contagious diseases and all forms of violence—the latter also regarded as contagious in nature—is based on a number of complementary inferences that combine to form a strikingly coherent picture.

A primitive society, a society that lacks a legal system, is exposed to the sudden escalation of violence. Such a society is compelled to adopt attitudes we may well find incomprehensible. Our incomprehension seems to stem from two main factors. In the first place, we know absolutely nothing about the contagion of violence, not even whether it actually exists. In the second place, the primitive people themselves recognize this violence only in an almost entirely dehumanized form; that is, under the deceptive guise of the *sacred*.

Considered all together, the ritual precautions against violence are firmly rooted in reality, absurd though some of them may appear to our own eyes. If the sacrificial catharsis actually succeeds in preventing the unlimited propagation of violence, a sort of *infection* is in fact being checked.

From the outset of this study, after all, I have regarded violence as something eminently communicable. The tendency of violence to hurl itself on a surrogate if deprived of its original object can surely be described as a contaminating process. Violence too long held in check will overflow its bounds—

and woe to those who happen to be nearby. Ritual precautions are intended both to prevent this flooding and to offer protection, insofar as it is possible, to those who find themselves in the path of ritual impurity—that is, caught in the floodtide of violence.

The slightest outbreak of violence can bring about a catastrophic escalation. Though we may tend to lose sight of this fact in our own daily lives, we are intellectually aware of its validity, and are often reminded that there is something infectious about the spectacle of violence. Indeed, at times it is impossible to stay immune from the infection. Where violence is concerned, intolerance can prove as fatal an attitude as tolerance, for when it breaks out it can happen that those who oppose its progress do more to assure its triumph than those who endorse it. There is no universal rule for quelling violence, no principle of guaranteed effectiveness. At times all the remedies, harsh as well as gentle, seem efficacious; at other times, every measure seems to heighten the fever it is striving to abate.

Inevitably the moment comes when violence can only be countered by more violence. Whether we fail or succeed in our effort to subdue it, the real victor is always violence itself. The *mimetic* attributes of violence are extraordinary—sometimes direct and positive, at other times indirect and negative. The more men strive to curb their violent impulses, the more these impulses seem to prosper. The very weapons used to combat violence are turned against their users. Violence is like a raging fire that feeds on the very objects intended to smother its flames.

The metaphor of fire could well give way to metaphors of tempest, flood, earthquake. Like the plague, the resemblance violence bears to these natural cataclysms is not limited to the realm of poetic imagery. In acknowledging that fact, however, we do not mean to endorse the theory that sees in the sacred a simple transfiguration of natural phenomena.

The sacred consists of all those forces whose dominance over man increases or seems to increase in proportion to man's effort to master them. Tempests, forest fires, and plagues, among other phenomena, may be classified as sacred. Far outranking these, however, though in a far less obvious manner, stands human violence—violence seen as something exterior to man and henceforth as a part of all the

other outside forces that threaten mankind. Violence is the heart and secret soul of the sacred.

We have yet to learn how man succeeds in positing his own violence as an independent being. Once he has accomplished this feat, however, the sacred presence invades his universe, mysteriously infects, without participating in it, and buffets him about rather in the manner of a plague or other natural disaster. Once all this has occurred, man is confronted with a group of phenomena that, despite their heterogeneous appearance, exhibit remarkable similarities.

As a general practice, it is wise to avoid contact with the sick if one wishes to stay healthy. Similarly, it is wise to steer clear of homicides if one is eager not to be killed.

As we see it, these are two distinct types of "contagion." Modern science concerns itself exclusively with one type, and has established its reality beyond all dispute. However, the other type could well be of greater importance to the members of a society that we have defined as primitive—that is, a society lacking legal sanctions.

Religious thought encompasses a large body of phenomena under the heading of ritual impurity—phenomena that seem disparate and absurd from the viewpoint of modern science but whose relationship and reality become perfectly clear when tested for the presence of basic violence, the prime ingredient and ultimate resource of the whole system.

There are undeniable similarities, for instance, between a bout of serious illness and an act of violence wilfully perpetrated by an enemy. The sufferings of the invalid are analogous to those of the wounded victim; and if the invalid runs the risk of dying, so too do all those who are involved in one fashion or another, either actively or passively, in a violent action. Death is nothing more than the worst form of violence that can befall a man. It is no less reasonable, therefore, to lump together all the possible causes of death, pathological and otherwise, than it is to create a separate category for only one of them: sickness.

To understand religious thought requires an empirical approach. The goal of religious thinking is exactly the same as that of technological research—namely, practical action. Whenever man is truly concerned with obtaining concrete results, whenever he is hard pressed by reality, he abandons abstract speculation and reverts to a mode of response that becomes increasingly cautious and conservative as the forces he hopes to subdue, or at least to outrun, draw ever nearer.

In its simplest, perhaps most elementary form, religion manifests little curiosity about the origins of those terrible forces that visit their fury on mankind but seems to concentrate its attention on determining a regular sequential pattern that will enable man to anticipate these onslaughts and take measures against them.

Religious empiricism invariably leads to one conclusion: it is essential to keep as far away as possible from sacred things, always to avoid direct contact with them. Naturally, such thinking occasionally coincides with medical empiricism or with scientific empiricism in general. This is why some observers insist on regarding religious empiricism as a preliminary stage of science.

This same empiricism, however, can sometimes reach conclusions so utterly foreign to our own way of thinking and can show itself so narrow, inflexible and myopic in its attitudes that we are tempted to attribute its functioning to some sort of psychological malaise. Such a reaction leads us to regard primitive society as an "ailing" society, beside which our "civilized" society presents a picture of radiant health.

The adherents of this theory show no hesitation in standing these categories on their heads, however, whenever the need arises. Thus, on occasion, it is "civilization" that is sick; and because civilized society is the antithesis of primitive society, it now appears that the primitive sphere must be the healthy one. Manipulate them as one will, it looks as if the concepts of sickness and health are not very useful in clarifying the relationship between primitive societies and our own.

Ritual precautions that appear lunatic or at least highly exaggerated in a modern context are in fact quite reasonable when viewed in their proper context—that is, in the context of religion's complete unawareness of the violence it makes sacred. When men believe that they can actually feel the breath of a Homeric Cyclops at their backs, they are apt to resort to all means at their disposal, to embrace all possible precautions. It seems safer to overreact than to underreact.

This religious attitude is not dissimilar to that of medicine when suddenly confronted with an unknown disease. An epidemic breaks out; the doctors and scientists are unable to isolate the pathogenic agent. Under the circumstances, what should they do? Clearly they must adopt, not *some* of the precautionary measures employed against familiar diseases, but *all* of them, without exception. Ideally, they would invent entirely new measures, since the enemy they are fighting is itself employing new weapons.

Once the microbe has been identified, it is seen that some of the measures employed were completely useless and should be abandoned in any future dealings with the disease. Yet it must be admitted that as long as the cause of the illness was unknown, their use was fully justified.

We must be careful not to push our metaphor too far. Neither primitive nor modern man has yet succeeded in identifying the microbe responsible for the dread disease of violence. Western civilization is hindered in its efforts to isolate and analyze the causes and to examine them in any but the most superficial manner because it has enjoyed until this day a mysterious immunity from the most virulent forms of violence—an immunity not, it seems, of our society's making, but one that has perhaps resulted in the making of our society.

NOTES

1. Henri Hubert and Marcel Mauss, *Sacrifice: Its Nature and Function* (Chicago, 1968).
2. Anthony Storr, *Human Aggression* (New York, 1968).
3. Konrad Lorenz, *On Aggression*, trans. Marjorie Kerr Wilson (New York, 1966).
4. Joseph de Maistre, "Eclaircissement sur les sacrifices," *Les Soirées de Saint-Pétersbourg* (Lyons, 1890), 2:341–42. Here,

and throughout the book, translations are by Patrick Gregory unless an English-language reference is cited.
5. Here, and throughout the book, quotations from the Greek plays have been translated by Patrick Gregory, from the original Greek.
6. Hubert and Mauss, *Sacrifice*, p. 33.
7. Lowie, *Primitive Society*, p. 400.

Ritual: Ceremony and Super-Sunday

GREGOR T. GOETHALS

Facts of publication: *Goethals, Gregor T. 1981. "Ritual: Ceremony and Super-Sunday," from* The TV Ritual: Worship at the Video Altar, *5–16, 18–31, 145–147. Boston: Beacon. Copyright © 1981 by Gregor T. Goethals. Reprinted with the permission of Beacon Press.*

Viewers do not ordinarily think of TV-watching as ritual. Gregor Goethals argues that it is and that it is not very different from traditional ritual. Both kinds of ritual share similar dynamics; their handling of space, time, imagery, and action are comparable. Televised papal blessings and presidential funerals are obvious examples of television's serving as a medium of ritual. Goethals, however, goes beyond this obvious claim to argue that even routine programs such as the evening news or occasional ones such as political conventions are no less ritualized.

For more on the topic of myth and ritual in the media see James W. Carey, ed., Media, Myths, and Narratives *(Newbury Park, CA: Sage, 1988).*

About the author: Dates: *1926– , Monroe, LA, U.S.A.* **Education:** *B.A., Louisiana State University; M.A., B.D., Yale University; Ph.D., Harvard University.* **Field(s):** *art history; religion and the arts.* **Career:** *Rhode Island School of Design, 1966–present.* **Publications:** The TV Ritual: Worship at the Video Altar *(Beacon, 1981);* The Electronic Golden Calf: Religion and the Making of Meaning *(Cowley, 1991).* **Additional:** *"Although my academic interests and research projects have focused on the ritual dimension of popular culture, I have worked as a practicing artist on mosaics for ritual settings in churches and synagogues. Currently, my interest in ritual and symbol has taken me into interactive media projects in which I work as a graphic artist and designer for multimedia experiments."*

From the rhythms of a Hopi rain dance to the liturgical motions of priest and communicants, ritual is a deeply rooted human activity. Studies by sociologists and anthropologists have shown how religious communities develop various forms of patterned action to put the group in touch with transcendent reality. Even those communities that disavow ritual objects and liturgy use repeated sequences of words, music, and action in their practice of worship. It is also true that the complexity of rituals does not depend upon the complexity of technological development; some of the most elaborate ritual patterns can be found in the simplest material cultures. The early Australian aborigines, with only a meager technological development, had a rich ritual life. Their rituals were, according to W. E. H. Stanner, evidence of the two abilities that have largely made human history what it is:

The first of these we might call "the metaphysical gift." I mean ability to transcend oneself, to make acts of imagination so that one can stand "outside" or "away from" oneself, and turn the universe, oneself, and one's fellows into objects of contemplation. The second ability is a "drive" to try to "make sense" out of human experience and to find some "principle" in the whole human situation.[1]

These human abilities Stanner understands as the basic source of both ritual and sacred images.

Ritual action, the dramatization of a significant event, is a major means of social integration. At its most fundamental level, ritual is the enactment of myth.[2] In the past, religious and political myths gave the members of a community a sense of their origins and destiny. In our present technological society, churches and synagogues often provide this kind of attunement to communal principles. For those who genuinely participate, the rituals offer occasions for identity and renewal. Through song, dance, and storytelling, people identify with their society. They gain a greater understanding of the whole of which each is a part. Although the mythic and aesthetic forms of ritual differ from culture to culture, its function remains the same—to provide an immediate, direct sense of involvement with the sacred, confirming the world view, indeed the very being, of the participant.

Throughout this [essay] two concepts of ritual will be used. The first presupposes that ritual is rooted in a propensity for order, rhythmic patterning, and play—a propensity not exclusively human but observable in other creatures as well. In *Homo Ludens*, Johan Huizinga has set forth the idea that the ritual act itself, or an important part of it, remains within the play category. And as he has observed, if one accepts the Platonic definition of play as a spiritual activity, there is nothing irreverent in applying it to the most solemn ritual occasions.[3] The theologian Hugo Rahner expressed a similar idea when he wrote of the "dance of the spirit" and of the "game of grace."[4] Thus ritual activity may range in scope from the religious rites in which people seek attunement with supernatural power to professional and amateur sports, which provide a communion of spectators and players.

The play and patterning motifs in ritual act as both stabilizing forces and means of introducing novelty and flexibility. On the one hand, ritual organizes, confirms, and conserves; it operates as a kind of adhesive, binding people to each other and to modes of living that have stood the test of time. On the other hand, the play of ritual opens up new ways of being and thinking. Ritual activity can incorporate revolutionary elements. Victor Turner has emphasized the antistructuralist elements that generate process and change in social groups.[5] Plays, songs, and ceremonies that were once in the secular area may in time be absorbed into sacred ritual. And the reverse is also true. Symbolic forms that were once a part of sacred ceremonies—drama in the medieval church, for example—spin off into secular culture and take on a life of their own.

The second concept of ritual presupposes a mystical or supernatural dimension. In the ritual play of traditional religion, persons seek communion with transcendent being; the myths that are enacted point to the beginning and the beyond. Through faith, the participants perceive dimensions of space, time, and destiny beyond finite experience—an "assurance of things hoped for and the conviction of things not seen."[6] Viewed in this way, ritual is concerned with the life of the soul, rather than with the play, knowledge, and kinship we experience in politics or sports. This view may, in fact, devalue those other rituals one participates in as citizen or fan. But it does not contradict the experience of ritual as the inexorable playing we share with other creatures. Instead, it extends ritual play to include a cosmic "game" whose measures and rhythms we perceive only dimly.

ELEMENTS OF TRADITIONAL RITUAL

The ritualistic power of television to bind people together can be illuminated by an analysis of some basic elements of ritual experience. Taken together, these fundamental elements form an interpretive structure that can be placed like a grid over particular kinds of television images. Using such an analysis we can identify analogous as well as contrasting elements in television communication.

The first element, and perhaps the most important for understanding ritual, is the active participation of individuals. If one is to experience its power as a form of social integration, one cannot be a detached observer. The participant must actually live the truth of the enacted myth. This action transcends time and space and has an aesthetic unity that one does not experience in ordinary everyday life. In other words, persons are actors in a ritual and their bodily gestures and motions affect others in the drama.

Another basic component of ritual experience is the space in which the action occurs. Ritual space is extraordinary, set apart from the ordinary spaces of daily life and specifically appropriate for particular events. Its sacredness does not depend upon architectural complexity. It may simply be ground that is designated as sacred, as, for example, in the rituals of the Australian aborigines. Or, it may be an intricately designed space like that of Chartres cathedral.

In some traditional religions, ritual space involves

special boundaries within which the presence of supernatural being is manifested. In that case it must be a fitting place for the holy and must allow for interaction between the divine and the human, between supernatural powers and finite creatures. Not all rituals, however, involve the presence of transcendent being. At its basic human level, ritual space must be related to the participation of the group and the action that occurs. Essentially it is space that is specially ordered for communion and interaction among persons with a common faith and loyalty.

A third element is the time in which ritual action takes place. Like ritual space, it is extraordinary in quality, not the ho-hum clock time of our workday. The time of ritual with its beginning, middle, and end is a carefully structured, cohesive unit. In time as we know it, we can point to a beginning, our birth, and we anticipate, ultimately, an ending in death. The middle, in-between, time stretches between these two poles. At no point in life are we able to perceive the whole of our existence, for ordinary time binds us to the middle. While we may conclude certain stages in our life cycle or accomplish certain projects, we can only experience the flow of the process. Ritual, on the other hand, deals with origin and destiny, the beginning and the end. Ritual casts us into measures that are outside ordinary time. The flow of everyday existence—open-ended and unresolved—is suspended and the believer leaps timelessly into creation and timelessly into eternity.

Extraordinary space and extraordinary time provide the context for the substantive core of ritual— the enactment of an event that is crucial for the life of the community and the individuals within it. The significant event that is enacted in ritual space and time is different for each religious tradition. The nature of the event depends upon the myths and history of the community. For some groups the events took place in the lives of historical figures such as Jesus of Nazareth or Buddha. Other ritual events involve "explanations" of what might be considered basically inexplicable phenomena, such as our fundamental origin and destiny. Australian aborigines, for example, had rituals that enacted the creation activity of Bolong the Rainbow Serpent. Whether the events are derived from historical persons and events, myths, or a combination of both, the constant element in all ritual action is the confirmation of the group and of the individual in the group. The

repeated enactment of such events assures the group's power to generate loyalty and faith. Ritual action offers full participation in a world view, not simply a set of concepts.

Just as the substance of ritual events differs with each tradition, so does the interpretation. For some groups, the enactment of these events may be a form for remembering. In other traditions, participation enables the believer to transcend the ordinary time boundaries and be a part of the original event. In Catholic ritual, "remembrance" has ontological overtones—to recall in order to live through the event. Communicants believe that through the grace of the sacrament they participate in the death, resurrection, and continuing being of Jesus. Ritual, in this sense, does more than "explain" the world. It creates the world, providing a sanctuary in which life is intensified. But, however widely the ontological interpretations of ritual action differ, the effect of participation in the drama is similar: believers experience a renewal of faith that sustains them as they return to ordinary time-space and its uncertainties.

The general pattern of ritual action, which involves withdrawal from the ordinary world into the extraordinary space, time, and action of ritual, transforms the person. Ritual participation can renew a person's faith in a center of values and meaning and can confirm one's place in a larger symbolic order. These experiences of renewal and confirmation occur, however, only to the degree that one is totally immersed in the ritual and its myth. For a disinterested observer a ritual might seem interesting or aesthetically pleasing but it would produce little effect. Tourists watching Hopi Indian dancers might be familiar with the myth involved, but they could not embrace it. The Indians do not dance to explain drought, to depict myth, or to illustrate tour books. For the Hopi who are still living in the myth, the rite and the myth are correlative. They dance in order to put themselves into a cosmic rhythm and to make it rain.[7]

Nor do rituals produce converts. Their power is manifested in the return of the believer from the sanctuary of metaphorical, ordered motions to the world of real life, better able to cope with its ordinariness and unpredictability. In addition to perpetuating the symbol systems of a tradition, repetition of ritual acknowledges the irresolution and disorder of common human experience. Even more, Eliade suggests, in repeating ritual one is

> tirelessly conquering the World, organizing it, transforming the landscape of nature into a cultural milieu. . . . Though the myths, by presenting themselves as sacrosanct models, would seem to paralyze human initiative, actually they stimulate [men and women] to create. . . .[8]

With its ordered cosmos of space and time, ritual, then, confirms and transforms the believing individual who, with renewed imagination, returns to see and shape the ordinary world in a new way.

TELECASTING TRADITIONAL RITUALS

At the conclusion of a very moving religious ritual, the inaugural mass of Pope John Paul II in October 1978, the pope pronounced blessings on all those present in St. Peter's Square. This was immediately followed by another blessing on all those present through the media of television and radio. Just how many millions of believers were thus blessed would be hard to determine, but the blessed were no longer confined to the time-space event in St. Peter's Square. Throughout the world believing Christians had tuned in and watched this solemn, ancient ritual performed by the new spiritual leader of the Roman Catholic world. In some sense, television viewers had been "present" and through that presence had received the pope's blessings.

In the [previous section], physical participation was discussed as one of the definitive elements of ritual. Today television takes countless viewers into important time-space events throughout the world. Although persons are not physically present, there is now an unprecedented opportunity for public participation in rituals that were once accessible to only a limited number of people. What is the nature of this transformation of ritual? What are some of its consequences? One new element is the electronic "ritual image." These electronic images contrast sharply with the ways images are employed in traditional ritual. For one who is physically present at a traditional ritual, the only visible images are those of liturgical objects or architectural surroundings, such

as mosaics, wall hangings, or sculpture. There are also those ineluctable images formed in the mind's eye as it registers the setting, gestures, and movements of persons taking part in the ritual. The extraordinary dimension television has introduced is the continous sequence of images that links the viewer to ritual action occurring in a different part of the world. The ordered time and space of traditional rituals can become "present" for persons wherever time zones and spaces are penetrated by the technology of television. Radio, of course, first broke down some of the time-space barriers and initiated wide participation in public events. But the visual image has had more dramatic and far-reaching consequences. Its impact has been great largely because there is so much to be seen—dance, gesture, color, and movement in space. The inaugural mass of Pope John Paul II included vestments, liturgical objects, and the gestures and motions of human figures.

The ritual image on television also communicates aspects of visual splendor that eludes those who are physically present. Those attending a ritual generally have a limited mobility and thus a limited view of the action. In contrast, the television participant is extravagantly mobile. Depending upon the importance of the event, numbers of cameras provide multiple perspectives—breathtaking shots of architectural spaces and environmental panoramas, close-ups of objects and celebrants, studies of an action from two or three different angles. Think of the view of the inaugural mass presented. Where in St. Peter's Square could one have seen the architectural intricacies of the cathedral dome and the detailed liturgical gestures and expressions of Pope John Paul II? If one participates in certain rituals only through the televised images, these unreal perspectives and details add to the sense of involvement. But there is, to be sure, a falsification of experience in the unreal images of television, and it could be argued that this lavish, imagistic emphasis calls attention to unimportant details. Television viewers, for example, saw the modern wristwatch of the pope and heard a newscaster comment on it. This observation broke into the spirit and rhythm of the ritual and reminded viewers of the two different environments—one in St. Peter's Square and another shaped by the TV image. Although gaining a proxy participation through technology, viewers lost the immediacy of the sights, smells, and perspectives of large crowds.

With the accessibility to ritual space through television, two levels of participation have merged. Those who are physically present at the sacred site are joined by the committed, faithful watchers of the TV image. The real division, then, comes between the believer and the nonbeliever. The believer is one who does not budge from the TV set during the high points of the time-space event. The nonbeliever, on the other hand, does not even bother to turn it on. Occasionally, when different rituals compete for the same time period, stations must choose between them. When one network started the telecast of a professional football game twenty minutes late in order to cover the funeral of Pope John Paul I, telephone lines were jammed by angry football fans, upset over the disruption of their sacred time.

The communicative possibilities of ritual images and their capacity to accommodate large public participation have also made television increasingly important in American political experience. One intense and powerful example of this was the funeral of John F. Kennedy. A shocked, grieving public was given the opportunity to take part in the process of mourning. The televised images had a sacramental and healing quality that helped absorb the loss. Like participants in a ritual, persons watching found comfort in the "presence" of others who shared their sorrow. A similar extension of ritual experience occurred in the telecast of funeral services for Hubert H. Humphrey. Although the tone of these services differed, the role played by the ritual images was similar: They provided the public with the opportunity to share with family, friends, and political figures the funeral rites and sacrament. Those in the larger American family who felt they had lost an honored, beloved friend and who wished to assemble in his memory could do so. Those who wanted to be a part of the liturgical events were able, through the ritual image, to enter many spaces: the spaces and ceremonies of the Rotunda at the Capitol, the liturgical space of the church in Minnesota, and finally, the grave site where only a small number of people could physically come together. Millions heard the bugle sound taps and the honor guard fire the final salute in the January twilight.

That ritual occasion was perhaps trivialized by the environments in which the telecast was received—a bar, the living room with the kids fighting, the kitchen where dinner was being prepared. Those who really cared about Senator Humphrey were there, and yet were not there. They saw the image, not the reality, of the ritual. But it was, nevertheless, a consolation.

The integrative and healing processes experienced by the American public when it mourns the deaths of its political leaders are instances of traditional rituals extended and transformed by television. Another example from political life is the inauguration of the president of the United States. This special event has generally been attended by a limited number of people. Now millions can take part through television. The telecast of Kennedy's inauguration taught us almost as much about the ritual power of television as did the images of his funeral. The inauguration, especially his speech, seemed to signal a new political awareness; citizens out there in electronic ritual space could join in this event. Political ritual has not been the same since.

Today, with the entrance of each new president, television coverage of the event and, even more important, the deliberate planning for such coverage, are increasingly elaborate. The inauguration is an institutionalized event which gives formal, symbolic authority to the most important leader in the American political system. Although it is a relatively short ceremony for such an authorization of power, an increasing amount of time has been given to programs and news relating to it. The telecasting of related events has created an elaborate pattern in which the inauguration itself is embedded. . . .

SECULAR RITUAL

In. . . Protestant tradition there is generally less expressed concern for liturgical rhythms and rituals than in a Catholic culture. If symbolizing is fundamental to human existence and if ritual is one way of accomplishing that, then, even in a Protestant environment, rituals arise outside of traditional institutions. Secular society, in fact, frequently develops its own sacramental forms.

One of the most obvious and popular examples of secular ritual is professional sports, especially football. A sports announcer once described the telecast event as a "tiny sanctuary in real life"—a description that could be a popular one-line definition of ritual. The Super Bowl represents the ultimate in ritualization. It has become a sacramental occasion more familiar, even to those who are not fans, than many events in the Christian liturgical year. Super-Sunday for most Americans refers not to Pentecost or the beginning of Advent but to Super Bowl Sunday. The big day is heralded in all the media and is generally featured on the cover of *TV Guide*. As with the inauguration of a president, there are pregame programs beginning the night before and others starting early Sunday morning. Some parts of the half-time entertainment specials are designed primarily for the television audience. In the shows that follow the game, superstars from the sports and entertainment world are featured.

Less obvious than the ritualization of sports is the ritualization of various political processes and of the nightly news programs. Like professional football and traditional rituals, political conventions, election coverage, and the nightly news are reshaped by television.

Looking first at political conventions, there is probably no way of knowing all that is going on at the different levels of human interaction—no way, really, to "cover" conventions like these. As television reporting has increased [since the 1960s], however, viewers have begun to have a sense of what is going on. The constant, complicated camera work brings viewers into the political realities. Live telecasts of the conventions, even to casual TV viewers, produce some degree of political awareness. Certainly, actions that are not accessible to the omnipresent camera continue to take place; the delegates are involved in unreported kinds of political activities. But TV coverage of the conventions has opened up new opportunities for public participation. Millions of viewers all over the nation become present through the electronic image.

The convention lends itself to ritualization because its very structure contains ritual elements. The event takes place in extraordinary space and has special time boundaries, running four days with formal opening and closing ceremonies. The space is perhaps more dramatically presented to the TV viewers than to those physically present. It is frequently de-

scribed by commentators as the cameras sweep over the interior. Viewers are moved from one place to another—the podium, the floor of the auditorium, the galleries. Most intriguing is the press box, where commentators sit like high priests. Some of the political personalities are interviewed in this special space.

The ritualization of the central event—the selection of the presidential and vice-presidential candidates—varies from convention to convention. Sometimes the event actually resembles the Super Bowl, where there are real struggles between competing quarterbacks, and fans are howling and blowing horns in the stands. At other times, especially when the primaries have more or less determined the outcome, the selection resembles a liturgical event. Although there may appear to be some kind of struggle between the god of light and the god of darkness, certain knowledge of the outcome gives more opportunity for luxurious ritual play.

In 1976, the Republican convention resembled the Super Bowl. The television commentators even called attention to the "battle of the wives," as Mrs. Ford cheered her team in one part of the "stadium" and Mrs. Reagan led cheers for the other team. Disruptions from the floor during the drama of the selection became a standard feature of this convention. Even on the last evening when Ford was chosen as the candidate, Reagan supporters continued their devotion to him. In the closing moments when all participants—those at the convention and those at home—expected a glowing reconciliation at the podium, the crowd still registered disharmony. Reagan supporters were not easy losers.

Perhaps because Carter—through his victories in the primaries—had virtually won the nomination before the 1976 convention, the Democrats, intentionally or unintentionally, exploited the ritualistic possibilities of the event. A rich variety of personages embellished the liturgical drama. Political heroes and heroines were highlighted in various parts of the program. It was Barbara Jordan, a black woman and a very powerful speaker, who sparked the first night. There was no way to measure the effect of her presence, but she was an inspiring figure for women all over the country. During the next four days of the convention there was a political model for everyone, liberal or conservative: Cesar

Chavez, Yvonne B. Burke, Jerry Brown, Hubert Humphrey, George Wallace. Even the draft resisters were represented. On one touching occasion when the paralyzed Vietnam veteran, Kovac, nominated one of the resisters for the vice-presidency, the two embraced at the podium. It was later reported that the event was staged, but as with Carter's walk down Pennsylvania Avenue, that simply reinforced the ritualistic intent.

Another unusual aspect of the convention was the simultaneous telecasting of images. As various speakers came and went, cameras on the floor picked up audience reactions as well as the image of the speaker. When the delegates were casting their votes, images from the convention floor were mixed with live shots from Carter's hotel room. Viewers saw Carter sitting with his mother, daughter, and grandson, watching the proceedings of the convention floor on their TV set. Then, at the very moment of victory, when there was a sufficient number of votes to assure him the candidacy, two live images were blended. Through the wizardry of technology, viewers saw the image of the victorious Carter in his hotel room simultaneously with the image of Mrs. Carter on the convention floor surrounded by reporters. What viewers saw was Carter watching himself watch himself. Carter must have had supreme confidence to permit this kind of symbolic telecast.

The final video spectacular of the 1976 Democratic convention came after the last speech. The Reverend Martin Luther King, Sr., gave the benediction. On their TV sets, viewers saw his expressive face and heard the Southern black preacher communicative with the Almighty, invoking blessings for the group. Viewers also saw, through a shift of cameras, Carter's face, hand on his chin, as he echoed a soft "Amen" to the prayer. Then came the parade of heroes and heroines, filing up to the podium in a great collection of video portraiture: Jerry Brown, Hubert Humphrey, Coretta King, George Wallace. Everyone moved about on the podium in a harmonious waltz. All joined in singing "We Shall Overcome."

Commercials, paid for by corporations, brought the convention rituals into the homes of the American public. While the conventions offered cross-sections of political opinions, the commercials indexed viewers' production and consumption: automo-

biles, dog food, underwear, soaps. Some commercials were the same for both conventions. On CBS, for example, Playtex and Volkswagen were among the sponsors for both the Democrats and the Republicans.

In November 1976, after a densely packed autumn of televised debates, political commercials, and opinion polls, election night came. Each of the three national networks prepared its own environment and format: charts, specially colored lights and maps, computers. Complex connections had been established in different sections of the country so that commentators could bring in live coverage from strategic places. The commercial advertisers were lined up and ready to hawk their wares. Cameras and newsmen took their positions at campaign headquarters and in spaces designated for victory celebrations. The viewer who cared about pictures and politics would soon be saturated with blinking lights; red, white, and blue maps of the United States; percentages and polls. Once a substantial number of precincts reported their results, the predictions, tabulations, and projections would begin flashing onto the viewers' screens.

While election night may not conform as closely to ritual structure as does the political convention, still it contains a number of ritualistic elements. The networks have appropriated and ritualized election night as a sports event. While it provides information and entertainment, it also draws millions of Americans together into an impassioned mass.

The candidates and their families are often well positioned on election night. As the computers projected Carter's victory in 1976, ABC immediately sent out images of Miss Lillian down in Georgia. At the moment of victory, Miss Lillian stood up, threw open her coat and revealed a JIMMY WON T-shirt. Behind her, in similar gestures a mini–chorus line of Carter supporters exposed their JIMMY WON T-shirts as well. Later on, viewers saw Jimmy and Rosalynn return to Plains to greet friends. One of the last images telecast in the early-morning hours was Carter carrying a sleeping Amy into their home.

The election night ritual is not over until the loser formally concedes the victory. The morning after the 1976 election Gerald Ford's statement was read with grace and dignity by Mrs. Ford on behalf of her husband, who was too hoarse to speak. Election night was over. There would be no such ritual for another four years. Yet those viewers who happened to see the reporting of the off-year elections in 1978 could see new ritual environments being tested. Innovative lights, new bright maps and charts, and computers were being put in readiness for Campaign 1980.

In 1980 TV viewers saw some unusual ritualistic elements at the Republican convention. The dramatic action centering around the choice of Ronald Reagan's vice-presidential running mate brought rumors and speculations, minute by minute, to those who tuned in. On the third evening of the convention, Walter Cronkite interviewed vice-presidential hopeful Gerald Ford and his wife, Betty. This interview allowed viewers to witness an unprecedented deliberation; apparently Ford was still weighing the pros and cons of joining the Reagan ticket as a "co-president." Some commentators later speculated that through the interview Ford was continuing his conversations with Reagan, as well as addressing the television public. Rumors about a Reagan-Ford ticket intensified during the evening, and there was widespread feeling that a deal had been struck between the two men. Meanwhile, George Bush, a discouraged aspirant, was reported to have conceded, "It looks like it's all set . . ." Evidently resigned to the alleged Reagan-Ford ticket, Bush cut his convention speech short by several minutes.

Excitement mounted during the roll call, and, as expected, Reagan was acclaimed the victorious candidate. Simultaneously, images were telecast live from the convention floor and from Reagan's hotel suite. The happy victor and his family saw their images and those from the convention blended on the TV screen. In the midst of the joyous demonstrations, however, all the networks busily forwarded hints to viewers that the deal between Ford and Reagan was off. They reported that George Bush had, in fact, received a call from Ronald Reagan inviting him to be his running mate. Even more excitement was generated when Reagan broke with tradition and came directly to the arena to address the delegates and announce his choice.

On the fourth and last evening of the convention, the Republicans' sense of togetherness resounded throughout all the activities. Prime time was saturated with happiness and harmony. When festivities

formally ended, loyal Republicans turned off their television sets, renewed and ready for battle.

The convention styles of 1976 were reversed for the two major parties in 1980. The Republican convention was a ritualistic confirmation of Reagan's candidacy similar to the one Jimmy Carter had received from his party four years earlier. Conversely, the Democratic convention had to cope with and conceal divided loyalties within the party, as the Republicans had in 1976. But, whatever the differences in convention styles, both Reagan and Carter had their campaigns ceremoniously launched in prime-time public view. John Anderson, the independent challenger, had no such symbolic time, space, or ritualistic form to dramatize and confirm his candidacy.

In the fall of 1980 TV viewers followed the major candidates through campaign speeches, polls and eventually two debates. The debates themselves spawned still more polls and debates about winners and losers. Finally came November 4. Voters made their choices during the day and in the evening tuned in to follow the dramatic interaction of computers, blinking lights, colored maps and commentators. *TV Guide* provided advice to viewers watching the events, indexing the times at which voting results might be expected. Before 10:00 P.M., commentators and President Carter alike agreed: Ronald Reagan had won the election. American voters had switched political channels and were prepared to tune in to the actor/politician who projected a soothing and trustworthy presence on television. Interested and enthusiastic Reagan supporters could look forward to the ritual of his inauguration and the preinaugural extravaganzas of January 1981.

The Super Bowl and World Series come only once a year and national conventions and election nights come once in four. But the public receives steady, if less spectacular, ritualistic nourishment through regularly broadcast professional sports such as football, baseball, basketball, and hockey. And every evening, without fail, there is the nightly news.

It will be remembered that ancient ritual provided its participants with an explanation of what the world was like; myths enacted in rituals explained the world to the believer. One difficulty in using myth to interpret newscasts is the common misunderstanding of the term. *Myth* is frequently interpreted as "falsehood" or "fantasy." Persons forget that myths enacted in ritual were ways of knowing and mediating truths about reality. It is this orienting and explanatory quality of myth that is found in the nightly news. The news presents public symbols through which contemporary persons understand reality.

The ritualistic power of the nightly news is due, in part, to its regularly scheduled time and uniform presentation. At a precise hour every evening viewers tune in their favorite national news program to find out what is going on. They read newspapers at random times and places, but the presentation of the nightly news is a shared perception of order and events. This collective viewing provides community solidarity since countless citizens are exposed to identical explanations of current realities.

Within the format of the nightly newscast there are patterns within patterns. Units within the half-hour segment are carefully organized in order of importance. Through words and pictures viewers get a sense of what is "true"—what is going on in the nation, Europe, Asia, even the cosmos. Outside of their immediate worlds of family and neighborhood, the nightly news tells viewers how it is, how things came to be, what might be expected.

Intermingled at regular intervals with information about national, international, and cosmic events are the sponsors' advertisements. Although detested by many, the commercials—in addition to making the program possible—play a comforting role. Many of the "truths" of the news deal with national and world events that are often dismal, tragic, without easy solution or resolution. The commercials break that mood of irresolution. One can, in fact, be comforted that there are some problems that are simple enough to be resolved through deodorants, laxatives, denture creams, cereals, antihistamines, or motor oil. The commercials set limits to the accounts of hard news and irreconcilable issues. They bring comfort where there might otherwise be none.

Taken together, the alternating news and commercials give us a tightly packaged symbolic record of reality. When Walter Cronkite said ". . . and that's the way it is . . .," many people had confidence in that knowledge. Viewers may know that the news gives incomplete, often misleading, information; still, to many, the camera does not lie. Ritualized by television, the symbols become the "reality."

According to sociologist Herbert J. Gans, journalists perform an important function when they report the actions and statements of national figures. In so doing, they help to form our concepts of the nation and of society. Moreover, through print and electronic media they are constantly reminding us of the reality and power of these human constructs—"nation" and "society." While journalists enhance the position of national leaders through their reporting, they also "inform an audience which lives in micro-societies that are often far removed from nation and society." Gans comments:

> Whether or not the audience actually needs information about them is a crucial question I cannot answer. Suffice it to say that news supplies that information. But when people say they keep up with the news, they may also be saying that they are maintaining contact with nation and society.[9]

One of the journalists' major functions is, in Gans's opinion, to manage, with others, the "symbolic arena" or public stage for communication. Because many people try to get their messages in and keep other messages out, the symbolic arena is a political battleground, and the management of it is a major political issue.

> In many countries, the issue is foreclosed because the government in power is its manager; in other countries, news organizations and journalists manage the arena, with the government retaining veto power. In America, the news firms are the nominal managers, but news organizations and journalists are the actual ones. In the process, they also regulate individuals and groups with messages; and, in so doing, they maintain order in the symbolic arena.[10]

ELECTRONIC POLITICS

Traditional rituals maintain social systems, but they can also change the systems. Roland A. Delattre, a scholar in American studies, writes of the creative role that ritual plays in our capacity to reorder as well as conserve: "Rituals may celebrate and confirm the rhythms and shape of an established version of reality, but they may also celebrate and render articulate the shape and rhythms of a new emergent version."[11]

Today the ritualistic patterning of television is changing the ways in which we think about and participate in our political processes. TV coverage of the 1976 and 1980 presidential campaigns emphasized activities which, before television, received little national attention. Extensive reporting of debates, caucuses, and primaries has increased the gamelike elements in politics. The events receive special attention and the rhythms of the primary campaigns have become a regular feature of the nightly news. Whereas the caucus was at one time a provincial affair in which decisions were made on the basis of direct contact between local politicians and workers, it is now a momentous media event that can enhance or detract from the aspiring candidates. Caucuses and primaries are like the Super Bowl playoffs. In fact, some of the terminology of professional sports has moved into the political sphere. Tuesday, June 3, 1980, became Super Tuesday because of the large number of primaries being held on that day and the unusually large number of delegates at stake in those contests.

Television news allows viewers to see and hear candidates in a unique kind of political portraiture. The candidates' images are like those of football heroes who are dramatically making end runs or successfully completing long passes. TV cameras, of course, also record the fumbles. The filmed replays of heroic actions or fumbles can circulate for days on local stations and national networks. John Anderson's statement favoring gun registration before a New Hampshire audience adamantly opposed to controls brought TV viewers the image of a candidate with guts.

Television news also packages dramatic action during political campaigns. Each evening viewers take their places at their sets and "live" in these dramatizations. As a result, this daily ritualization of the state primaries has shifted the process for selecting candidates from the national conventions to the earlier contests. On the basis of his commanding victories in the primaries, it was clear by early June

1980 that Ronald Reagan had enough delegates to win the candidacy of the Republican party. The convention was for him, as it was for Carter in 1976, a ritualistic celebration.

The changes in the quality and pace of political campaigning have been interpreted in various ways by participants and analysts. Jerry Brown, a presidential hopeful in 1980, said that the political process has been reduced to a chapter in *Wide World of Sports*. Political analyst Kevin Phillips, a participant on *The MacNeil/Lehrer Report*, following the Massachusetts and Vermont primaries, spoke of the "volatile" nature of the campaign:

> PHILLIPS: Well, maybe it's just a cliché . . . I suspect that the people are sufficiently disillusioned; they're not 100% sure what they are looking for; they're not sure what these politicians are; they go by on a screen. People don't know anything about a George Bush until all of a sudden, presto, George Bush wins. Then you start finding out what George Bush *is*, and maybe you don't like it. So you shift away from him, and then John Anderson flashes up there with his 31% and he's the hype. I think it's a very unfortunate thing. I think it's not the media's fault, it's the fault of a system, the interaction of the media, the fragmentation of the political process, the long drawn-out thing but—sure, it's volatile. It's also a mess.[12]

Yet Jim Lehrer, co-host of *The MacNeil/Lehrer Report*, pointed out that people were turning out in record numbers to vote. Another guest, Robert Shogan of the Los Angeles *Times*, responded:

> SHOGAN: Well, yeah, that's what *is* interesting. I don't know. Maybe it's a second stage. Not long ago, people were just staying home in record numbers and publishers were commissioning books about voter apathy, and now we've got this voter restiveness that the darned people won't stay home where they belong. They're turning out, the independents are voting, and it's upsetting everybody's prediction.[13]

Martin Linsky, media consultant to the Ford Foundation and the Institute of Politics at Harvard University, has voiced a positive attitude toward media-effected changes in the electoral process. In

"The System's Working Just Fine," an article in the Boston *Globe*, he said that we were engaged in a "great experiment." The emphasis of the media upon the primaries is "democratizing the process," taking the power to pick the presidential nominees away from party bosses and special interest groups and entrusting it to voters. "We are trusting their good judgment and the capacity of the nation's news media for keeping them informed." While there are "kinks" in the system, the surveys have shown a high degree of awareness of the candidates and their stands on issues. Rather than damage the system, the representation of events on television contributes positively to it; candidates themselves must respond to the changes.

> Television is the fastest, most intense, universal medium of communication devised so far. Every aspirant to national leadership in contemporary America must have among his or her skills the ability to communicate well on the tube and a finely tuned sense that the presence of television has shortened the time available for decision making.[14]

Politics and politicians are "caught up in a wider and genuine revolution, which is affecting almost every aspect of society," wrote Philip L. Geyelin, editor of the editorial page of the *Washington Post*. TV is part of a technological revolution in the field of communications and in computers as they relate to canvassing, polling, phone banks, and mail campaigns. He spoke of the changes in political events, such as a political rally, which is "staged almost entirely for the purpose of attracting television attention and getting the candidate on the evening news, where millions, as distinct from hundreds," can see and hear. He quoted the observations of Douglass Cater, analyst of politics and communications, who wrote in the London *Sunday Times*:

> After a quarter of a century's phenomenal growth, television has created a communication environment in no way comparable to the world of books, plays, cinema, newspapers and periodicals. Its ceaseless flow of electronic signals . . . affects fundamentally not merely our thoughts but the way we go about the business of thinking collectively. Society swims in this environment and is hardly conscious of its consequences.[15]

Geyelin concludes that this revolution is not all for the bad, but certainly not all for the good. It does threaten "a massive overloading of the thought processes which could blow out the political system unless we can adjust to it."

Whether viewed positively or negatively, the ritualized news patterns that flow across the screen each evening have contributed substantively to changing our political processes and to shaping our common electronic environment. Moreover, the format of the nightly news, along with other media, has nurtured persistent criticism of government action and of politicians in power.

NOTES

1. W. E. H. Stanner, "The Dreaming," *Reader in Comparative Religion, An Anthropological Approach*, eds. William A. Lessa and Evon Z. Vogt [Evanston, Ill. & Elmsford, N.Y.: Row, Peterson and Company, 1958], p. 518.

2. *Myth* and *ritual* are terms used and interpreted, sometimes very differently, by scholars in a variety of disciplines. Some scholars see myth and ritual as two different forms of ordering experience. Given the independence of symbolic expression, myth can be objectified in different kinds of literary and artistic works. Other scholars, by contrast, maintain that myth and ritual are essentially correlative. They emphasize that myth is most authentic and visual when enacted in ritual. Myth comes to life in ritual, and communicants live in the myth through ritual experience. Whether in literary form or actualized in ritual, myths express dimensions of human experience that do not lend themselves to scientific verification. They are the proper expression of what Eric Voegelin refers to as the "blind spot" in human experience, the mystery of the beginning and the beyond. (See Eric Voegelin, *Order and History*, vol. 1 [Baton Rouge: Louisiana State University Press, 1956], p. 2.)

3. Johan Huizinga, *Homo Ludens: A Study of the Play-Element in Culture* (Boston: Beacon Press, 1955), pp. 26–27.

4. Hugo Rahner, *Man at Play* (New York: Herder and Herder, 1972), pp. 8, 10.

5. Victor Turner, "Process, System and Symbol: A New Anthropological Approach," *Daedalus*, Summer 1977, p. 61. "My personal view is that anthropology is shifting from a stress on concepts such as structure, equilibrium, function, system to process, indeterminacy, reflexivity—from a 'being' to a 'becoming' vocabulary."

6. Heb. 11:1.

7. Discussions with Aidan Kavanagh, O.S.B., professor of liturgics, the Divinity School, Yale University, were especially helpful in making comparisons, and contrasts between traditional rituals and substitutes for them in contemporary life.

8. Mircea Eliade, *Myth and Reality* (New York: Harper and Row, 1963), pp. 140–141.

9. Herbert J. Gans, *Deciding What's News* (New York: Random House, 1979), p. 298.

10. Ibid., p. 299.

11. Roland A. Delattre, "The Rituals of Humanity and the Rhythm of Reality," *Prospects: An Annual of American Studies* 5 (1979).

12. WNET/Thirteen, Transcript from *The MacNeil/Lehrer Report*, "The Massachusetts and Vermont Primaries," air date: March 5, 1980, p. 7.

13. Ibid.

14. Martin Linsky, "The System's Working Just Fine," *Boston Globe*, March 12, 1980, p. 15.

15. Philip L. Geyelin, "New Technology and the Evolution of Politics," *Yale Alumni Magazine and Journal*, January 1979, p. 12.

Interaction Ritual: Deference and Demeanor

ERVING GOFFMAN

Facts of publication: *Goffman, Erving. 1967. "Interaction Ritual: Deference and Demeanor," from* Interaction Ritual: Essays on Face-to-Face Behavior, *53–67, 77–81, 85–91. Copyright © 1967 by Erving Goffman. Reprinted with the permission of the Estate of Erving Goffman.*

For readers who assume that all ritual is either religious or deliberately and highly formal, this selection will come as a jolt, since it argues that ceremony permeates everyday life. For Erving Goffman the self is "a ceremonial thing, a sacred object which must be treated with proper ritual care." He introduces a much-debated, but often-assumed distinction between substantive rules and ceremonial ones. Substantive ones bear on instrumental matters considered significant and efficacious in their on right, whereas ceremonial, or expressive, ones bear on the formalities with which things are done. In this view, even practical actions carry ceremonial meaning, since "ceremony" refers to the conventionalization of means of communication.

Readers may wish to compare this selection to two others. The selection by Robbie Davis-Floyd graphically illustrates that we ought not assume, after reading Goffman, that ceremonial acts—since they are not substantive—are, therefore, insubstantial. Another work by Goffman that is especially useful in understanding his view of ritualization is Presentation of Self in Everyday Life *(Garden City, NY: Doubleday, 1956).*

About the author: Dates: *1922–1982, born in Canada.* **Education:** *B.A., University of Toronto; M.A., University of Chicago; Ph.D., University of Chicago.* **Field(s):** *sociology; anthropology.* **Career:** *Assistant Professor, 1958–1959, University of California, Berkeley, then Associate Professor, 1959–1962, then Professor of Sociology, 1962–1968. Benjamin Franklin Professor of Anthropology and Sociology, 1968–1982, University of Pennsylvania, Philadelphia.* **Publications:** The Presentation of Self in Everyday Life *(Doubleday, 1956);* Asylums: Essays on the Social Situation of Mental Patients and Other Inmates *(Anchor, 1961);* Stigma: Notes on the Management of Spoiled Identity *(Prentice-Hall, 1963);* Behavior in Public Places: Notes on the Social Organization of Gatherings *(Free Press, 1963);* Interaction Ritual: Essays on Face-to-Face Behavior *(Doubleday, 1967);* Relations in Public: Micro-Studies of the Public Order *(Basic, 1971);* Frame Analysis: Essays on the Organization of Experience *(Harper, 1974);* Gender Advertisements *(Harper, 1979).* **Additional:** *LL.D., University of Manitoba; D.H.L., University of Chicago; Mead-Cooley Award in social psychology; Guggenheim Fellowship.*

Students of society have distinguished in several ways among types of rules, as for example, between formal and informal rules; for this paper, however, the important distinction is that between substance and ceremony.[1] A substantive rule is one which guides conduct in regard to matters felt to have significance in their own right, apart from what the infraction or maintenance of the rule expresses about the selves of the persons involved. Thus, when an individual refrains from stealing from others, he upholds a substantive rule which primarily serves to protect the property of these others and only incidentally functions to protect the image they have of themselves as persons with proprietary rights. The expressive implications of substantive rules are officially considered to be secondary; this appearance must be maintained, even though in some special situations everyone may sense that the participants were primarily concerned with expression.

A ceremonial rule is one which guides conduct in matters felt to have secondary or even no significance in their own right, having their primary importance—officially anyway—as a conventionalized means of communication by which the individual expresses his character or conveys his appreciation of the other participants in the situation.[2] This usage departs from the everyday one, where "ceremony" tends to imply a highly specified, extended sequence of symbolic action performed by august actors on solemn occasions when religious sentiments are likely to be invoked. In my attempt to stress what is common to such practices as tipping one's hat and coronations, I will perforce ignore the differences among them to an extent that many anthropologists might perhaps consider impracticable.

In all societies, rules of conduct tend to be organized into codes which guarantee that everyone acts appropriately and receives his due. In our society the code which governs substantive rules and substantive expressions comprises our law, morality, and ethics, while the code which governs ceremonial rules and ceremonial expressions is incorporated in what we call etiquette. All of our institutions have both kinds of codes, but in this paper attention will be restricted to the ceremonial one.

The acts or events, that is, the sign-vehicles or tokens which carry ceremonial messages, are remarkably various in character. They may be linguistic, as

when an individual makes a statement of praise or depreciation regarding self or other, and does so in a particular language and intonation;[3] gestural, as when the physical bearing of an individual conveys insolence or obsequiousness; spatial, as when an individual precedes another through the door, or sits on his right instead of his left; task-embedded, as when an individual accepts a task graciously and performs it in the presence of others with aplomb and dexterity; part of the communication structure, as when an individual speaks more frequently than the others, or receives more attentiveness than they do. The important point is that ceremonial activity, like substantive activity, is an analytical element referring to a component or function of action, not to concrete empirical action itself. While some activity that has a ceremonial component does not seem to have an appreciable substantive one, we find that all activity that is primarily substantive in significance will nevertheless carry some ceremonial meaning, provided that its performance is perceived in some way by others. The manner in which the activity is performed, or the momentary interruptions that are allowed so as to exchange minor niceties, will infuse the instrumentally-oriented situation with ceremonial significance.

All of the tokens employed by a given social group for ceremonial purposes may be referred to as its ceremonial idiom. We usually distinguish societies according to the amount of ceremonial that is injected into a given period and kind of interaction, or according to the expansiveness of the forms and the minuteness of their specification; it might be better to distinguish societies according to whether required ceremony is performed as an unpleasant duty or, spontaneously, as an unfelt or pleasant one.

Ceremonial activity seems to contain certain basic components. A main object of this paper will be to delineate two of these components, deference and demeanor, and to clarify the distinction between them.

DEFERENCE

By deference I shall refer to that component of activity which functions as a symbolic means by which appreciation is regularly conveyed *to* a recipient *of* this recipient, or of something of which this recipient is taken as a symbol, extension, or agent.[4] These marks of devotion represent ways in which an actor celebrates and confirms his relation to a recipient. In some cases, both actor and recipient may not really be individuals at all, as when two ships greet each other with four short whistle blasts when passing. In some cases, the actor is an individual but the recipient is some object or idol, as when a sailor salutes the quarterdeck upon boarding ship, or when a Catholic genuflects to the altar. I shall only be concerned, however, with the kind of deference that occurs when both actor and recipient are individuals, whether or not they are acting on behalf of something other than themselves. Such ceremonial activity is perhaps seen most clearly in the little salutations, compliments, and apologies which punctuate social intercourse, and may be referred to as "status rituals" or "interpersonal rituals."[5] I use the term "ritual" because this activity, however informal and secular, represents a way in which the individual must guard and design the symbolic implications of his acts while in the immediate presence of an object that has a special value for him.[6]

There appear to be two main directions in which the study of deference rituals may go. One is to settle on a given ritual and attempt to discover factors common to all of the social situations in which it is performed, for it is through such an analysis that we can get at the "meaning" of the ritual. The other is to collect all of the rituals that are performed to a given recipient, from whomever the ritual comes. Each of these rituals can then be interpreted for the symbolically expressed meaning that is embodied in it. By piecing together these meanings we can arrive at the conception of the recipient that others are obliged to maintain of him to him.

The individual may desire, earn, and deserve deference, but by and large he is not allowed to give it to himself, being forced to seek it from others. In seeking it from others, he finds he has added reason for seeking them out, and in turn society is given added assurance that its members will enter into interaction and relationships with one another. If the individual could give himself the deference he desired there might be a tendency for society to disintegrate into islands inhabited by solitary cultish men, each in continuous worship at his own shrine.

The appreciation carried by an act of deference implies that the actor possesses a sentiment of regard for the recipient, often involving a general evaluation of the recipient. Regard is something the individual constantly has for others, and knows enough about to feign on occasion; yet in having regard for someone, the individual is unable to specify in detail what in fact he has in mind.

Those who render deference to an individual may feel, of course, that they are doing this merely because he is an instance of a category, or a representative of something, and that they are giving him his due not because of what they think of him "personally" but in spite of it. Some organizations, such as the military, explicitly stress this sort of rationale for according deference, leading to an impersonal bestowal of something that is specifically directed toward the person. By easily showing a regard that he does not have, the actor can feel that he is preserving a kind of inner autonomy, holding off the ceremonial order by the very act of upholding it. And of course in scrupulously observing the proper forms he may find that he is free to insinuate all kinds of disregard by carefully modifying intonation, pronunciation, pacing, and so forth.

In thinking about deference it is common to use as a model the rituals of obeisance, submission, and propitiation that someone under authority gives to someone in authority. Deference comes to be conceived as something a subordinate owes to his superordinate. This is an extremely limiting view of deference on two grounds. First, there are a great many forms of symmetrical deference which social equals owe to one another; in some societies, Tibetan for example, salutations between high-placed equals can become prolonged displays of ritual conduct, exceeding in duration and expansiveness the kind of obeisance a subject may owe his ruler in less ritualized societies. Similarly, there are deference obligations that superordinates owe their subordinates; high priests all over the world seem obliged to respond to offerings with some equivalent of "Bless you, my son." Secondly, the regard in which the actor holds the recipient need not be one of respectful awe; there are other kinds of regard that are regularly expressed through interpersonal rituals also, such as trust, as when an individual welcomes sudden strangers into his house, or capacity-esteem, as when the individual defers to another's technical advice. A sentiment of regard that plays an important role in deference is that of affection and belongingness. We see this in the extreme in the obligation of a newly married man in our society to treat his bride with affectional deference whenever it is possible to twist ordinary behavior into a display of this kind. We find it more commonly, for example, as a component in many farewells where, as in our middle-class society, the actor will be obliged to infuse his voice with sadness and regret, paying deference in this way to the recipient's status as someone whom others can hold dearly. In "progressive" psychiatric establishments, a deferential show of acceptance, affection, and concern may form a constant and significant aspect of the stance taken by staff members when contacting patients. On Ward B,[7] in fact, the two youngest patients seemed to have become so experienced in receiving such offerings, and so doubtful of them, that they would sometimes reply in a mocking way, apparently in an effort to re-establish the interaction on what seemed to these patients to be a more sincere level.

It appears that deference behavior on the whole tends to be honorific and politely toned, conveying appreciation of the recipient that is in many ways more complimentary to the recipient than the actor's true sentiments might warrant. The actor typically gives the recipient the benefit of the doubt, and may even conceal low regard by extra punctiliousness. Thus acts of deference often attest to ideal guide lines to which the actual activity between actor and recipient can now and then be referred. As a last resort, the recipient has a right to make a direct appeal to these honorific definitions of the situation, to press his theoretic claims, but should he be rash enough to do so, it is likely that his relationship to the actor will be modified thereafter. People sense that the recipient ought not to take the actor literally or force his hand, and ought to rest content with the show of appreciation as opposed to a more substantive expression of it. Hence one finds that many automatic acts of deference contain a vestigial meaning, having to do with activity in which no one is any longer engaged and implying an appreciation long since not expected—and yet we know these antique tributes cannot be neglected with impunity.

In addition to a sentiment of regard, acts of deference typically contain a kind of promise, expressing in truncated form the actor's avowal and pledge to treat the recipient in a particular way in the oncoming activity. The pledge affirms that the expectations and obligations of the recipient, both substantive and ceremonial, will be allowed and supported by the actor. Actors thus promise to maintain the conception of self that the recipient has built up from the rules he is involved in. (Perhaps the prototype here is the public act of allegiance by which a subject officially acknowledges his subservience in certain matters to his lord.) Deferential pledges are frequently conveyed through spoken terms of address involving status-identifiers, as when a nurse responds to a rebuke in the operating room with the phrase, "yes, Doctor," signifying by term of address and tone of voice that the criticism has been understood and that, however unpalatable, it has not caused her to rebel. When a putative recipient fails to receive anticipated acts of deference, or when an actor makes clear that he is giving homage with bad grace, the recipient may feel that the state of affairs which he has been taking for granted has become unstable, and that an insubordinate effort may be made by the actor to reallocate tasks, relations, and power. To elicit an established act of deference, even if the actor must first be reminded of his obligations and warned about the consequence of discourtesy, is evidence that if rebellion comes it will come slyly; to be pointedly refused an expected act of deference is often a way of being told that open insurrection has begun.

A further complication must be mentioned. A particular act of deference is something an actor, acting in a given capacity, owes a recipient, acting in a given capacity. But these two individuals are likely to be related to one another through more than one pair of capacities, and these additional relationships are likely to receive ceremonial expression too. . . . Throughout this paper we must therefore keep in mind that a spate of deferential behavior is not a single note expressing a single relationship between two individuals active in a single pair of capacities, but rather a medley of voices answering to the fact that actor and recipient are in many different relations to one another, no one of which can usually be given exclusive and continuous determinacy of ceremonial conduct. An interesting example of this complexity in regard to master-servant relations may be cited from a nineteenth-century book of etiquette:

Issue your commands with gravity and gentleness, and in a reserved manner. Let your voice be composed, but avoid a tone of familiarity or sympathy with them. It is better in addressing them to use a higher key of voice, and not to suffer it to fall at the end of a sentence. The best-bred man whom we ever had the pleasure of meeting always employed, in addressing servants, such forms of speech as these—"I'll thank you for so and so,"—"Such a thing if you please"—with a gentle tone, but very elevated key. The perfection of manner, in this particular, is, to indicate by your language, that the performance is a favour, and by your tone that it is a matter of course."[8]

Deference can take many forms, . . . [one of which is avoidance rituals]. Avoidance rituals, as a term, may be employed to refer to those forms of deference which lead the actor to keep at a distance from the recipient and not violate what Simmel has called the "ideal sphere" that lies around the recipient:

Although differing in size in various directions and differing according to the person with whom one entertains relations, this sphere cannot be penetrated, unless the personality value of the individual is thereby destroyed. A sphere of this sort is placed around man by his honor. Language poignantly designates an insult to one's honor as "coming too close"; the radius of this sphere marks, as it were, the distance whose trespassing by another person insults one's honor.[9]

Any society could be profitably studied as a system of deferential stand-off arrangements, and most studies give us some evidence of this.[10] Avoidance of other's personal name is perhaps the most common example from anthropology, and should be as common in sociology.

Here, it should be said, is one of the important differences between social classes in our society: not only are some of the tokens different through which consideration for the privacy of others is expressed, but also, apparently, the higher the class the more extensive and elaborate are the taboos against contact. For example, in a study of a Shetlandic com-

munity the writer found that as one moves from middle-class urban centers in Britain to the rural lower-class islands, the distance between chairs at table decreases, so that in the outermost Shetland Islands actual bodily contact during meals and similar social occasions is not considered an invasion of separateness and no effort need be made to excuse it. And yet, whatever the rank of the participants in an action, the actor is likely to feel that the recipient has some warranted expectation of inviolability.

Where an actor need show no concern about penetrating the recipient's usual personal reserve, and need have no fear of contaminating him by any penetration into his privacy, we say that the actor is on terms of familiarity with the recipient. (The mother who feels at liberty to pick her child's nose is an extreme example.) Where the actor must show circumspection in his approach to the recipient, we speak of nonfamiliarity or respect. Rules governing conduct between two individuals may, but need not, be symmetrical in regard to either familiarity or respect.

There appear to be some typical relations between ceremonial distance and other kinds of sociological distance. Between status equals we may expect to find interaction guided by symmetrical familiarity. Between superordinate and subordinate we may expect to find asymmetrical relations, the superordinate having the right to exercise certain familiarities which the subordinate is not allowed to reciprocate. Thus, in the research hospital, doctors tended to call nurses by their first names, while nurses responded with "polite" or "formal" address. Similarly, in American business organizations the boss may thoughtfully ask the elevator man how his children are, but this entrance into another's life may be blocked to the elevator man, who can appreciate the concern but not return it. Perhaps the clearest form of this is found in the psychiatrist-patient relation, where the psychiatrist has a right to touch on aspects of the patient's life that the patient might not even allow himself to touch upon, while of course this privilege is not reciprocated. (There are some psychoanalysts who believe it desirable to "analyze the countertransference with the patient" but this or any other familiarity on the part of the patient is strongly condemned by official psychoanalytical bodies.) Patients, especially mental ones, may not even have the right to question their doctor about his opinion of their own case; for one thing, this would bring them into too intimate a contact with an area of knowledge in which doctors invest their special apartness from the lay public which they serve.

While these correlations between ceremonial distance and other kinds of distance are typical, we must be quite clear about the fact that other relationships are often found. Thus, status equals who are not well acquainted may be on terms of reciprocal respect, not familiarity. Further, there are many organizations in America where differences in rank are seen as so great a threat to the equilibrium of the system that the ceremonial aspect of behavior functions not as a way of iconically expressing these differences but as a way of carefully counterbalancing them. In the research hospital under study, psychiatrists, psychologists, and sociologists were part of a single ceremonial group as regards first-naming, and this symmetrical familiarity apparently served to allay some feeling on the part of psychologists and sociologists that they were not equal members of the team, as indeed they were not. Similarly, in a study of small business managers, the writer[11] found that filling-station attendants had the right to interrupt their boss, slap him on the back, rib him, use his phone, and take other liberties, and that this ritual license seemed to provide a way in which the manager could maintain morale and keep his employees honest. We must realize that organizations that are quite similar structurally may have quite different deference styles, and that deference patterns are partly a matter of changing fashion.

In our society, rules regarding the keeping of one's distance are multitudinous and strong. They tend to focus around certain matters, such as physical places and properties defined as the recipient's "own," the body's sexual equipment, etc. An important focus of deferential avoidance consists in the verbal care that actors are obliged to exercise so as not to bring into discussion matters that might be painful, embarrassing, or humiliating to the recipient. In Simmel's words:

> The same sort of circle which surrounds man—although it is value-accentuated in a very different sense—is filled out by his affairs and by his charac-

teristics. To penetrate this circle by taking notice, constitutes a violation of his personality. Just as material property is, so to speak, an extension of the ego, and any interference with our property is, for this reason, felt to be a violation of the person, there also is an intellectual private-property, whose violation effects a lesion of the ego in its very center. Discretion is nothing but the feeling that there exists a right in regard to the sphere of the immediate life contents. Discretion, of course, differs in its extension with different personalities just as the positions of honor and of property have different radii with respect to "close" individuals, and to strangers, and indifferent persons.[12]

Referential avoidance may be illustrated from Ward A, where rules in this regard were well institutionalized.[13] The fact that two of the female patients had had experience in a state-type mental hospital was not raised either in serious conversation or in jest, except when initiated by these women themselves; nor was a question of the age of these patients (who were in their middle thirties) raised. The fact that the two male patients were conscientious objectors was never raised, even by the CO's themselves. The fact that one of the patients was blind . . . was never raised by the others in [that patient's] presence. When a poor patient declined to participate in an outing on a claim of indifference, her rationalization for not going was accepted at face-value and her fiction respected, even though others knew that she wanted to go but was ashamed to because she did not have a suitable coat. Patients about to be given drugs experimentally, or who had just been given drugs, were not questioned about their feelings, unless they themselves raised the topic. Unmarried women, whether patients or nurses, were not directly questioned about boy friends. Information about religious affiliations was volunteered but rarely requested. . . .

DEMEANOR

It was suggested that the ceremonial component of concrete behavior has at least two basic elements, deference and demeanor. Deference, defined as the appreciation an individual shows of another to that other, . . . has been discussed and demeanor may now be considered.

By demeanor I shall refer to that element of the individual's ceremonial behavior typically conveyed through deportment, dress, and bearing, which serves to express to those in his immediate presence that he is a person of certain desirable or undesirable qualities. In our society, the "well" or "properly" demeaned individual displays such attributes as: discretion and sincerity; modesty in claims regarding self; sportsmanship; command of speech and physical movements; self-control over his emotions, his appetites, and his desires; poise under pressure; and so forth.

When we attempt to analyze the qualities conveyed through demeanor, certain themes become apparent. The well-demeaned individual possesses the attributes popularly associated with "character training" or "socialization," these being implanted when a neophyte of any kind is housebroken. Rightly or wrongly, others tend to use such qualities diagnostically, as evidence of what the actor is generally like at other times and as a performer of other activities. In addition, the properly demeaned individual is someone who has closed off many avenues of perception and penetration that others might take to him, and is therefore unlikely to be contaminated by them. Most importantly, perhaps, good demeanor is what is required of an actor if he is to be transformed into someone who can be relied upon to maintain himself as an interactant, poised for communication, and to act so that others do not endanger themselves by presenting themselves as interactants to him.

It should be noted once again that demeanor involves attributes derived from interpretations others make of the way in which the individual handles himself during social intercourse. The individual cannot establish these attributes for his own by verbally avowing that he possesses them, though sometimes he may rashly try to do this. (He can, however, contrive to conduct himself in such a way that others, through their interpretation of his conduct, will impute the kinds of attributes to him he would like others to see in him.) In general, then, through demeanor the individual creates an image of himself, but properly speaking this is not an image that is meant for his own eyes. Of course this should not prevent us from seeing that the individual who acts with good demeanor may do so because he places an appreciable value upon himself, and that he who fails to demean himself properly may be accused of having "no self-respect" or of holding himself too cheaply in his own eyes.

As in the case of deference, an object in the study of demeanor is to collect all the ceremonially relevant acts that a particular individual performs in the presence of each of the several persons with whom he comes in contact, to interpret these acts for the demeanor that is symbolically expressed through them, and then to piece these meanings together into an image of the individual, an image of him in others' eyes.

Rules of demeanor, like rules of deference, can be symmetrical or asymmetrical. Between social equals, symmetrical rules of demeanor seem often to be prescribed. Between unequals many variations can be found. For example, at staff meetings on the psychiatric units of the hospital, medical doctors had the privilege of swearing, changing the topic of conversation, and sitting in undignified positions; attendants, on the other hand, had the right to attend staff meetings and to ask questions during them (in line with the milieu-therapy orientation of these research units) but were implicitly expected to conduct themelves with greater circumspection than was required of doctors. (This was pointed out by a perceptive occupational therapist who claimed she was always reminded that a mild young female psychiatrist was really an M.D. by the fact that this psychiatrist exercised these prerogatives of informal demeanor.) The extreme here perhaps is the master-servant relation as seen in cases where valets and maids are required to perform in a dignified manner services of an undignified kind. Similarly, doctors had the right to saunter into the nurses' station, lounge on the station's dispensing counter, and engage in joking with the nurses; other ranks participated in this informal interaction with doctors, but only after doctors had initiated it.

On Ward A, standards of demeanor were maintained that seem to be typical in American middle-class society. The eating pace maintained at table suggested that no one present was so over-eager to eat, so little in control of impulses, so jealous of his rights, as to wolf down his food or take more than his share. At pinochle, the favorite card game, each player would coax spectators to take his hand and spectators would considerately decline the offer, expressing in this way that a passion for play had in no way overwhelmed them. Occasionally a patient appeared in the day-room or at meals with bathrobe (a practice permitted of patients throughout the hospital) but ordinarily neat street wear was maintained, illustrating that the individual was not making his appearance before others in a lax manner or presenting too much of himself too freely. Little profanity was employed and no open sexual remarks.

On Ward B, bad demeanor (by middle-class standards) was quite common. This may be illustrated from meal-time behavior. A patient would often lunge at an extra piece of food or at least eye an extra piece covetously. Even when each individual at table was allowed to receive an equal share, over-eagerness was shown by the practice of taking all of one's share at once instead of waiting until one serving had been eaten. Occasionally a patient would come to table half-dressed. One patient frequently belched loudly at meals and was occasionally flatulent. Messy manipulation of food sometimes occurred. Swearing and cursing were common. Patients would occasionally push their chairs back from the table precipitously and bolt for another room, coming back to the table in the same violent manner. Loud sounds were sometimes made by sucking on straws in empty pop bottles. Through these activities, patients expressed to the staff and to one another that their selves were not properly demeaned ones.

These forms of misconduct are worth study because they make us aware of some aspects of good demeanor we usually take for granted; for aspects even more usually taken for granted, we must study "back" wards in typical mental hospitals. There patients are denudative, incontinent, and they openly masturbate; they scratch themselves violently; drooling occurs and a nose may run unchecked; sudden hostilities may flare up and "paranoid" immodesties be projected; speech or motor activity may occur at a manic or depressed pace, either too fast or too slow for propriety; males and females may comport themselves as if they were of the other sex or hardly old enough to have any. Such wards are of course the classic settings of bad demeanor.

A final point about demeanor may be mentioned. Whatever his motives for making a well demeaned

appearance before others, it is assumed that the individual will exert his own will to do so, or that he will pliantly co-operate should it fall to someone else's lot to help him in this matter. In our society, a man combs his own hair until it gets too long, then he goes to a barber and follows instructions while it is being cut. This voluntary submission is crucial, for personal services of such a kind are done close to the very center of the individual's inviolability and can easily result in transgressions; server and served must co-operate closely if these are not to occur. If, however, an individual fails to maintain what others see as proper personal appearance, and if he refuses to co-operate with those who are charged with maintaining it for him, then the task of making him presentable against his will is likely to cost him at the moment a great deal of dignity and deference, and this in turn may create complex feelings in those who find they must cause him to pay this price. This is one of the occupational dilemmas of those employed to make children and mental patients presentable. It is easy to order attendants to "dress up" and shave male patients on visitors' day, and no doubt when this is done patients make a more favorable appearance, but while this appearance is in the process of being achieved—in the showers or the barbershop, for example—the patients may be subjected to extreme indignities. . . .

CEREMONIAL PROFANATIONS

There are many situations and many ways in which the justice of ceremony can fail to be maintained. There are occasions when the individual finds that he is accorded deference of a misidentifying kind, whether the misidentification places him in a higher or lower position than he thinks right. There are other occasions when he finds that he is being treated more impersonally and unceremoniously than he thinks proper and feels that his treatment ought to be more punctuated with acts of deference, even though these may draw attention to his subordinate status. A frequent occasion for ceremonial difficulty occurs at moments of intergroup contact, since different societies and subcultures have different ways of conveying deference and demeanor, different ceremonial meanings for the same act, and different amounts of concern over such things as poise and privacy. Travel books such as Mrs. Trollope's[14] are full of autobiographical material on these misunderstandings, and sometimes seem to have been written chiefly to publicize them.

Of the many kinds of ceremonial transgressions there is one which a preliminary paper on ceremony is obliged to consider: it is the kind that appears to have been perpetrated on purpose and to employ consciously the very language of ceremony to say what is forbidden. The idiom through which modes of proper ceremonial conduct are established necessarily creates ideally effective forms of desecration, for it is only in reference to specified proprieties that one can learn to appreciate what will be the worst possible form of behavior. Profanations are to be expected, for every religious ceremony creates the possibility of a black mass.[15]

When we study individuals who are on familiar terms with one another and need stand on little ceremony, we often find occasions when standard ceremonial forms that are inapplicable to the situation are employed in what is felt to be a facetious way, apparently as a means of poking fun at social circles where the ritual is seriously employed. When among themselves, nurses at the research hospital sometimes addressed one another humorously as Miss ———; doctors under similar conditions sometimes called one another "Doctor" with the same joking tone of voice. Similarly, elaborate offering of a chair or precedence through a door was sometimes made between an actor and recipient who were actually on terms of symmetrical familiarity. In Britain, where speech and social style are clearly stratified, a great amount of this unserious profanation of rituals can be found, with upper class people mocking lower class ceremonial gestures, and lower class people when among themselves fully returning the compliment. The practice perhaps reaches its highest expression in music hall revues, where lower class performers beautifully mimic upper class ceremonial conduct for an audience whose status falls somewhere in between.

Some playful profanation seems to be directed not so much at outsiders as at the recipient himself, by way of lightly teasing him or testing ritual limits in regard to him. It should be said that in our soci-

ety this kind of play is directed by adults to those of lesser ceremonial breed—to children, old people, servants, and so forth—as when an attendant affectionately ruffles a patient's hair or indulges in more drastic types of teasing.[16] Anthropologists have described this kind of license in an extreme form in the case of "siblings-in-law who are potential secondary spouses."[17] However apparent the aggressive overtones of this form of conduct may be, the recipient is given the opportunity of acting as if no serious affront to his honor has occurred, or at least an affront no more serious than that of being defined as someone with whom it is permissible to joke. On Ward B, when Mrs. Baum was given a sheet too small for her bed she used it to playfully bag one of the staff members. Her daughter occasionally jokingly employed the practice of bursting large bubblegum bubbles as close to the face of a staff person as possible without touching him, or stroking the arm and hand of a male staff member in parody of affectional gestures, gleefully proposing sexual intercourse with him.

A less playful kind of ritual profanation is found in the practice of defiling the recipient but in such a way and from such an angle that he retains the right to act as if he has not received the profaning message. On Ward B, where staff members had the occupational obligation of "relating to" the patients and responding to them with friendliness, nurses would sometimes mutter *sotto voce* vituperations when patients were trying and difficult. Patients, in turn, employed the same device. When a nurse's back was turned, patients would sometimes stick their tongues out, thumb their noses, or grimace at her. These are of course standard forms of ritual contempt in our Anglo-American society, constituting a kind of negative deference. Other instances may be cited. On one occasion Mrs. Baum, to the amusement of others present, turned her back on the station window, bent down, and flipped her skirt up, in an act of ritual contempt which was apparently once more prevalent as a standard insult than it is today. In all these cases we see that although ceremonial liberties are taken with the recipient, he is not held in sufficiently low regard to be insulted "to his face." This line between what can be conveyed about the recipient while in a state of talk with him, and what can only be conveyed about him when not in talk with him, is a basic ceremonial institution in our society, ensuring that face-to-face interaction is likely to be mutually approving. An appreciation of how deep this line is can be obtained on mental wards, where severely disturbed patients can be observed co-operating with staff members to maintain a thin fiction that the line is being kept.

But of course there are situations where an actor conveys ritual profanation of a recipient while officially engaged in talk with him or in such a way that the affront cannot easily be overlooked. Instead of recording and classifying these ritual affronts, students have tended to cover them all with a psychological tent, labelling them as "aggressions" or "hostile outbursts," while passing on to other matters of study.

In some psychiatric wards, face-to-face ritual profanation is a constant phenomenon. Patients may profane a staff member or a fellow-patient by spitting at him, slapping his face, throwing feces at him, tearing off his clothes, pushing him off the chair, taking food from his grasp, screaming into his face, sexually molesting him, etc. On Ward B, on occasion, Betty would slap and punch her mother's face and tramp on her mother's bare feet with heavy shoes; and abuse her, at table, with those four-letter words that middle-class children ordinarily avoid in reference to their parents, let alone their presence. It should be repeated that while from the point of view of the actor these profanations may be a product of blind impulse, or have a special symbolic meaning,[18] from the point of view of the society at large and its ceremonial idiom these are not random impulsive infractions. Rather, these acts are exactly those calculated to convey complete disrespect and contempt through symbolic means. Whatever is in the patient's mind, the throwing of feces at an attendant is a use of our ceremonial idiom that is as exquisite in its way as is a bow from the waist done with grace and a flourish. Whether he knows it or not, the patient speaks the same ritual language as his captors; he merely says what they do not wish to hear, for patient behavior which does not carry ritual meaning in terms of the daily ceremonial discourse of the staff will not be perceived by the staff at all.

In addition to profanation of others, individuals for varieties of reasons and in varieties of situations give the appearance of profaning themselves, acting in a way that seems purposely designed to destroy the image others have of them as persons worthy of deference. Ceremonial mortification of the flesh has been a theme in many social movements. What seems to be involved is not merely bad demeanor but rather the concerted efforts of an individual sensitive to high standards of demeanor to act against his own interests and exploit ceremonial arrangements by presenting himself in the worst possible light.

In many psychiatric wards, what appears to staff and other patients as self-profanation is a common occurrence. For example, female patients can be found who have systematically pulled out all the hair from their head, presenting themselves thereafter with a countenance that is guaranteed to be grotesque. Perhaps the extreme for our society is found in patients who smear themselves with and eat their own feces.[19]

Self-profanation also occurs of course at the verbal level. Thus, on Ward A, the high standards of demeanor were broken by the blind patient who at table would sometimes thrust a consideration of her infirmity upon the others present by talking in a self-pitying fashion about how little use she was to anybody and how no matter how you looked at it she was still blind. Similarly, on Ward B, Betty was wont to comment on how ugly she was, how fat, and how no one would want to have someone like her for a girl-friend. In both cases, these self-derogations, carried past the limits of polite self-depreciation, were considered a tax upon the others: they were willing to exert protective referential avoidance regarding the individual's shortcomings and felt it was unfair to be forced into contaminating intimacy with the individual's problems.

CONCLUSIONS

The rules of conduct which bind the actor and the recipient together are the bindings of society. But many of the acts which are guided by these rules occur infrequently or take a long time for their consummation. Opportunities to affirm the moral order and the society could therefore be rare. It is here that ceremonial rules play their social function, for many of the acts which are guided by these rules last but a brief moment, involve no substantive outlay, and can be performed in every social interaction. Whatever the activity and however profanely instrumental, it can afford many opportunities for minor ceremonies as long as other persons are present. Through these observances, guided by ceremonial obligations and expectations, a constant flow of indulgences is spread through society, with others who are present constantly reminding the individual that he must keep himself together as a well demeaned person and affirm the sacred quality of these others. The gestures which we sometimes call empty are perhaps in fact the fullest things of all.

It is therefore important to see that the self is in part a ceremonial thing, a sacred object which must be treated with proper ritual care and in turn must be presented in a proper light to others. As a means through which this self is established, the individual acts with proper demeanor while in contact with others and is treated by others with deference. It is just as important to see that if the individual is to play this kind of sacred game, then the field must be suited to it. The environment must ensure that the individual will not pay too high a price for acting with good demeanor and that deference will be accorded him. Deference and demeanor practices must be institutionalized so that the individual will be able to project a viable, sacred self and stay in the game on a proper ritual basis.

NOTES

1. I take this distinction from Durkheim (Emile Durkheim, "The Determination of Moral Facts," *Sociology and Philosophy*, tr. D. F. Pocock, Free Press, Glencoe, Ill., 1953, especially pp. 42–43); see also A. R. Radcliffe-Brown, "Taboo," *Structure and Function in Primitive Society* (Free Press, Glencoe, Ill., 1952, pp. 143–44), and Talcott Parsons, *The Structure of Social Action*. (McGraw-Hill, New York, 1937, pp. 430–33); sometimes the dichotomy is phrased in terms of "intrinsic" or "instrumental" versus "expressive" or "ritual."

2. While the substantive value of ceremonial acts is felt to be quite secondary it may yet be quite appreciable. Wedding gifts in American society provide an example. It is even possible to say in some cases that if a sentiment of a given kind is to be conveyed ceremonially it will be necessary to employ a sign-vehicle which has a given amount of substantive value. Thus in the American lower-middle class, it is understood that a small investment in an engagement ring, as such investments go, may mean that the man places a small value on his fiancee as these things go, even though no one may believe that women and rings are commensurate things. In those cases where it becomes too clear that the substantive value of a ceremonial act is the only concern of the participants, as when a girl or an official receives a substantial gift from someone not interested in proper relations, then the community may respond with a feeling that their symbol system has been abused.

An interesting limiting case of the ceremonial component of activity can be found in the phenomenon of "gallantry," as when a man calmly steps aside to let a strange lady precede him into a lifeboat, or when a swordsman, fighting a duel, courteously picks up his opponent's fallen weapon and proffers it to him. Here an act that is usually a ceremonial gesture of insignificant substantive value is performed under conditions where it is known to have unexpectedly great substantive value. Here, as it were, the forms of ceremony are maintained above and beyond the call of duty.

In general, then, we can say that all ceremonial gestures differ in the degree to which they have substantive value, and that this substantive value may be systematically used as part of the communication value of the act, but that still the ceremonial order is different from the substantive one and is so understood.

3. P. L. Garvin and S. H. Riesenberg, "Respect Behavior on Pronape: An Ethnolinguistic Study," *American Anthropologist*, 54 (1952), 201–20.

4. Some of the conceptual material on deference used in this paper derives from a study supported by a Ford Foundation grant for a propositional inventory of social stratification directed by Professor E. A. Shils of the University of Chicago. I am very grateful to Mr. Shils for orienting me to the study of deference behavior. He is not responsible for any misuse I may have made of his conception.

5. Techniques for handling these ceremonial obligations are considered in "On Face-Work," Erving Goffman, *Interaction Ritual: Essays on Face-to-Face Behavior* (Garden City, NY: Doubleday), pp. 5 ff.

6. This definition follows Radcliffe-Brown's (*op. cit.*, p. 123) except that I have widened his term "respect" to include other kinds of regard: "There exists a ritual relation whenever a society imposes on its members a certain attitude towards an object, which attitude involves some measure of respect expressed in a traditional mode of behavior with reference to that object."

7. Ward A was formally given over to pharmacological research and contained two normal controls, both nineteen-year-old Mennonite conscientious objectors, two hypertensive women in their fifties, and two women in their thirties diagnosed as schizophrenic and in fair degree of remission. For two months the writer participated in the social life of the ward in the official capacity of a normal control, eating and socializing with the patients during the day and sleeping overnight occasionally in a patient's room. Ward B was one given over to the study of schizophrenic girls and their so-called schizophrenogenic mothers: a seventeen-year-old girl,

Betty, and her mother, Mrs. Baum; Grace, fifteen years old, and Mary, thirty-one years old, whose mothers visited the ward most days of the week. The writer spent some of the weekday on Ward B in the capacity of staff sociologist. Within limits, it is possible to treat Ward A as an example of an orderly nonmental ward and Ward B as an example of a ward with somewhat disturbed mental patients. It should be made quite clear that only one aspect of the data will be considered, and that for every event cited additional interpretations would be in order, for instance, psychoanalytical ones.

I am grateful to the administrators of these wards, Dr. Seymour Perlin and Dr. Murray Bowen, and to their staffs, for co-operation and assistance, and to Dr. John A. Clausen and Charlotte Green Schwartz then of the National Institute of Mental Health for critical suggestions.

8. Anonymous, *The Laws of Etiquette* (Carey, Lee, and Blanchard, Philadelphia, 1836), p. 188.

9. Georg Simmel, *The Sociology of Georg Simmel*, tr., ed. by Kurt Wolff (Free Press, Glencoe, Ill., 1950), p. 321.

10. *E.g.* F. W. Hodge, *Etiquette: Handbook of American Indians* (Government Printing House, Washington, D.C., 1907), p. 442.

11. Unpublished paper prepared for Social Research, Inc., 1952.

12. Simmel, *op. cit.*, p. 322.

13. I am grateful to Dr. Seymour Perlin for bringing my attention to some of these avoidances and for pointing out the significance of them.

14. Mrs. Trollope, *Domestic Manners of the Americans* (Whittaker, Treacher; London, 1832).

15. A kind of ceremonial profanation also seems to exist with respect to substantive rules. In law what are sometimes called "spite actions" provide illustrations, as does the phenomenon of vandalism. But these represent ways in which the substantive order is abused for ceremonial purposes.

16. *Cf.* Harold Taxel, "Authority Structure in a Mental Hospital Ward," Unpublished Master's Thesis, Department of Sociology, University of Chicago, 1953, p. 68; and Robert H. Willoughby, "The Attendant in the State Mental Hospital," Unpublished Master's Thesis, Department of Sociology, University of Chicago, 1953, p. 90.

17. George P. Murdock, *Social Structure* (Macmillan, New York, 1949), p. 282.

18. Morris S. Schwartz and Alfred H. Stanton, "A Social Psychological Study of Incontinence," *Psychiatry*, 13 (1950), 319–416.

19. E. D. Wittkower and J. D. La Tendresse, "Rehabilitation of Chronic Schizophrenics by a New Method of Occupational Therapy," *British Journal of Medical Psychology*, 28 (1955), 42–47.

Ritual Criticism
*and Infelicitous Performances**

RONALD L. GRIMES

Facts of publication: *Grimes, Ronald L. 1990. "Ritual Criticism and Infelicitous Performances," from* Ritual Criticism: Case Studies in Its Practice, Essays on Its Theory, *210–216, 191–195, 199–209, 243–244. Columbia: University of South Carolina Press. Copyright © 1990 by University of South Carolina. Reprinted with the permission of University of South Carolina Press. Portions of this selection are from Ronald L. Grimes, "Infelicitous Performances and Ritual Criticism," Semeia 41:103–133. Reprinted with the permission of Scholars Press.*

The notion of ritual criticism is recent and probably unfamiliar to most readers of ritual theory. Commonly, it is assumed that ritual obviates or resists critique. In this widespread view ritualizing and thinking are construed as fundamentally opposed activities (for more on this opposition, see the selection by Catherine Bell in this volume). This selection argues that a rite, like any other cultural phenomenon, is likely to be less than perfect and therefore subject to criticism. Building on J. L. Austin's theory of performative utterances, it sketches a typology of "ritual infelicities" and offers brief biblical illustrations of each type. Other illustrations that might well evoke or benefit from ritual criticism are found in the hospital-based studies of both Goffman and Davis-Floyd.

For the basis of some of the ideas developed here see also Grimes, Beginnings in Ritual Studies, *rev. ed. (University of South Carolina Press, 1995).*

About the author: Dates: *1943–   , San Diego, CA, U.S.A.* Education: *B.A., Kentucky Wesleyan College; M.Div., Emory University; Ph.D., Columbia University and Union Theological Seminary.* Field(s): *religious studies; anthropology of religion; religion and the arts.* Career: *Assistant Professor of Religious Studies, 1970–1974, Lawrence University, Appleton, Wisconsin; Professor of Religious Studies, 1974–present, Wilfrid Laurier University, Waterloo, Ontario, Canada.* Publications: Symbol and Conquest: Public Ritual and Drama in Santa Fe, *(reissue, University of New Mexico, 1992 [1976]);* Beginnings in Ritual Studies, *(revised edition, University of South Carolina, 1995 [1982]);* Ritual Criticism *(University of South Carolina, 1990);* Reading, Writing, & Ritualizing *(Pastoral, 1993);* Marrying & Burying *(Westview Press, 1995).* Additional: *Director, Ritual Studies Laboratory, 1974–present; General Editor, then Founding Editor, Journal of Ritual Studies, 1987–present; Distinguished Visiting Professor, Department of Religious Studies, University of Colorado, 1993. Doctor of Humane Letters, Kentucky Wesleyan College, 1984. "Since 1982 most of my research and writing has concentrated on the study of ritual. I also teach courses on the topic—Rites of Passage, for instance, and Ritual and Illness. The geographical focus of my interests is the American Southwest. I regularly teach courses on religious conflict and convergence there. In addition, I teach and write about religious biography and autobiography."*

Ritual criticism is not a field, much less a discipline. There are no models for it, so one must begin forging them from bits and pieces found elsewhere. One must look for analogous practices. Obvious places to search are aesthetics generally (including literary criticism, theater criticism, and art criticism) and liturgiology (the theological criticism of the rites of one's own tradition).[1] Any serious attempt to formulate an ethic for engaging in ritual criticism must be interdisciplinary and take seriously the conflicts and convergences among the humanities, social sciences, and theology.

The phrase "ritual criticism" is not a familiar one. Many will hear it as analogous to "literary criticism."[2] Criticism is a notion nurtured specifically in

*[Introductory portions of this selection are] based on a paper, "On Ritual Criticism," presented in 1986 to the Ritual Studies Group of the American Academy of Religion and on an article, originally published as "Ritual Criticism and Reflexivity in Fieldwork," in the *Journal of Ritual Studies* 2(2):217–239. The latter is used with permission.

[The later] portions of this [selection], which are reprinted here with the permission of Scholars Press, were originally published in 1988 as "Infelicitous Performances and Ritual Criticism" in *Semeia* 41:103–122; the whole issue is on speech-act theory in religious and biblical studies. Both the chapter and the article grew out of a presentation in 1984 called "Infelicitous Performances, or, How Rituals Fail" to a joint meeting of the American Academy of Religion and the Society of Biblical Literature.

the humanities, but it has been appropriated in both the social sciences and theology. Ritual criticism is a practice thoroughly entangled with norms, judgments, and evaluation. But whether it is an artistic or a scientific practice is a matter of debate.

Literary scholars debate whether literary critics ought to exercise normative judgments, especially if they are made for the sake of a literature-consuming public, but, as far as I know, their differences do not lead them to reject the critical task altogether, as is sometimes the case in other fields. Criticism in literature has a longer history than in either religious studies or anthropology. A classic volume on literary criticism, with much to say about ritual, is Northrop Frye's *Anatomy of Criticism* (1968). In this book criticism assumes the form of an "anatomy," a laying out of parts in order to classify them and relate them to genres, literary slots, or categories. The book's usefulness to ritual criticism is limited, however, because ultimately it reduces ritual to repetitive patterns in literary works. Frye's theory does not enable one to take note of the ways literature implicates extra-literary moral and ritual behavior. However, Siebers' *The Ethics of Criticism* (1988) and Merod's *The Political Responsibility of the Critic* (1987) are clear evidence that more recent literary criticism is no longer necessarily confined to texts alone and that it is seriously interested in the relations among readers, texts, and the larger society. . . .

Another discipline in which important research

on criticism is going on is anthropology. It has the advantage of taking social and historical contexts seriously, whereas aesthetic criticism tends to ignore them. Also, the discipline of anthropology has been committed to overcoming the parochial biases one sometimes finds in theology. At an earlier time anthropology was considered only a scientific, and thus analytical or explanatory, discipline.[3] Recently, however, some anthropologists are speaking of anthropology as a critical discipline.

Though there is a large anthropological literature on ritual, there is no explicit, systematic research on the topic of ritual criticism. However, a great deal is either implied or said in an offhand way about it in anthropological writing. Among the most useful works on the critical dimensions of anthropology are Marcus and Fischer's *Anthropology as Cultural Critique* (1986), Clifford and Marcus's *Writing Culture* (1986), and Clifford Geertz's *Works and Lives: The Anthropologist as Author* (1988). These show increasing awareness of the literary dimensions of the ethnographic enterprise and also of the critical nature of writing about cultures other than one's own.

The so-called new, or meta-, ethnography is highly reflexive. By this I mean that it is self-conscious about its own processes, a theme that connects it with countercultural and postmodern concerns. The outcome in written ethnographies is the appearance (or reappearance) of the ethnographer as a character in his or her own account. No longer the omnipotent hand that paints the natives as if he or she were not present among them, the new ethnographer appears there in the photographs alongside the natives. No longer mere objects of an all-seeing camera's eye, these natives are less "informants" than consultants or collaborators.

To some this shift of attention seems narcissistic—the crass introduction of autobiography into ethnography. No doubt, in its worst examples this is the case. But in its best ones something else is going on. In these instances criticism is assuming the form of self-examination and self-criticism.[4] What becomes evident in reflexive ethnographies are the ways fieldworkers bear the values of dominating cultures, the ways author-ethnographers "construct" the very people they study. The ritual that gets criticized, then, is less that of indigenous people and more that of doing fieldwork. In new ethnographies

fieldwork functions as the initiation rite it tacitly is. The importance of anthropological study for ritual criticism lies in its historic commitment to understanding the politics of all intercultural activities, including research itself.

Theology is another field with strong commitments of the assessment of ritual. To their own detriment the humanities and social sciences studiously ignore theological disciplines, while the latter are busy reading, evaluating, and appropriating the former. Anthropological perspectives have deeply penetrated the heart of Christian theological reflection on ritual, otherwise known as liturgiology or liturgical theology.[5] The writings of Victor Turner, Clifford Geertz, and Mary Douglas are widely read by liturgical theologians.[6]

Unlike anthropologists, liturgiologists are not shy about making value judgments or covert in their assessments of rites. What they often lack, however, is cross-cultural perspective. What humanists and social scientists have to learn from them is how to sustain a long, literate tradition of ongoing criticism and consequent practice. The critical dimension of liturgics constellated in the late nineteenth century largely as a result of historical research on liturgical texts. Putting liturgical innovations in historical context began to relativize the liturgy itself.[7] Symbolic meanings no longer appeared timeless. Their meanings were seen as changing in relation to cultural and political contexts. Now it is not uncommon for liturgiologists to be articulate about the imperial politics of liturgical controversies and conciliar decisions and compromises.[8] Furthermore, liturgical theologians are beginning to engage in field study. Though insiders, they assume the postures of observers, pit texts against performances, and speculate about operational and unconscious meanings that differ from intended or explicitly stated meanings.[9] So the idea that a theological understanding of ritual is only in-house and thus incapable of examining its own presuppositions is clearly false.

Mary Collins wrote an essay, "Critical Ritual Studies: Examining an Intersection of Theology and Culture" (in her *Worship: Renewal to Practice*).[10] On the basis of field study she provides data illustrating how the rites for the profession of vows by women religious preceded, and thus implicitly criticized, systematic theological reinterpretation. Her field-work illustrates the fallacy of assuming that systematic theologians in seminaries are more critical than practitioners in the field. Her findings reverse the usual assumption that priests and women religious are mere technicians of the sacred, while the theologians are the critical minds. She concludes:

> To state the basic position of this paper succinctly, ritual studies are worth pursuing by researchers interested in the interplay between theology and culture precisely because ritual acts constitute a distinctive kind of religious and cultural expression, one which is corporate in its manifestations and bodily and nondiscursive in its presentation of content. These very characteristics make ritual inaccessible to ordinary theological methods, which work with texts [1987:97].

Just as utilization of historical methods in the late nineteenth and early twentieth centuries turned liturgiology into a critical discipline, so the contemporary shift of attention to nontextual, nonverbal aspects of ritual is an implicit critique of liturgy and liturgical theology. This shift has called attention to the local qualities of liturgy, which has the effect of tempering claims about its universality. It also has stirred a great deal of interest in enculturation, the process whereby rites are rendered indigenous and local.[11] No longer can liturgical theologians assume that symbols have meanings detached from relations of power and domination. Theologians have long understood that ritual is programmatic, or paradigmatic, and that critical judgment, therefore, must be exercised in the selection of rites and their constituent symbols. But now, as representatives of so-called world religions, they must face the fact that their own traditions are also "multinational religions." Like corporations, religious institutions ritualize local interests and bill them as if they were universal ones.

Religious studies is not identical with theology. Insofar as ritual studies is carried out within the field of religious studies, it often mediates between the analytical methods of anthropology and the prescriptive ones of theology. In practice, religiologists emphasize phenomenological, hermeneutical, and historical approaches to religious phenomena. The usual way of describing the differences between religious studies and theology is to say that religious studies is teaching *about* religion while theology is the teaching *of* religion. Fearing they might be accused of being covert theologians, religiologists have generally avoided evaluative methods. Typically, religious studies has left fieldwork to anthropologists and evaluation to theologians. As a result its study of ritual has been impoverished and in need of more sustained contact with critics in the humanities, theology, and the social sciences.

Religiologists have tried to avoid what one might call "religiocentrism," making judgments about one religious tradition from the point of view of a privileged other tradition. How is it possible, we have asked ourselves, to criticize ritual disinterestedly? Is not any act of assessing a rite necessarily centered in the religiosity (or lack of it) of one's own culture? Biblical criticism, which once seemed so scientific, now appears in historical retrospect to be rooted in the specificity of late nineteenth- and early twentieth-century Euroamerican societies. And if biblical criticism, having borrowed its objectivity from various kinds of literary and historical criticism, now has to admit to being an agent of enculturation rather than a universal science, how can we expect ritual criticism to fare any better? I do not argue that we can, because there is no such thing as disinterested criticism. For this reason we must systematically attend to the politics of critique. . . .

Infelicitous Performances

The practice of ritual criticism presupposes the possibility of ritual failure, which is seldom taken account of in theories of ritual. Engaging in ritual criticism presupposes that rites can exploit, denigrate, or simply not do what people claim they do. Consider these biblical passages:

> No enchantment against Jacob,
> No divination against Israel [Numbers 23:23].
>
> The magicians tried by their secret arts to bring forth gnats, but they could not [Exodus 8:18].
>
> But for Cain and his offering he [God] had no regard [Genesis 4:5].
>
> Now he [Jacob] has taken away my blessing [Genesis 27:36].

And [Nadab & Abihu] offered unholy fire before the Lord, such as he had not commanded them. And fire came forth from the presence of the Lord and devoured them [Leviticus 10:1–2].

I hate, I despise your feasts, and I take no delight in your solemn assemblies [Amos 5:21].

Do not lay your hand on the lad [Isaac] or do anything to him [Genesis 22:12].

Clearly, rites do not always go smoothly in the ancient Hebraic world any more than they do in modern synagogues, hospitals, or courtrooms. Often they seem to be more trouble than they are worth.

Amos's God has little use for solemn assemblies. Nadab and Abihu are killed for performing an unauthorized rite. Esau loses the benefits of the blessing rite to his brother Jacob. Cain's offering is disregarded for some unspecified reason. The Egyptian magicians' magic cannot match that of Moses and Aaron. Balak cannot get Balaam's oracle to tell him what he wants to hear. And if Abraham's ritual sacrifice of his son had been successful, it would have failed.

Curiously, little has been done in a theoretical way to take account of ritually related trouble, but speech-act theory has some promising features that might enable us to begin rectifying this gap in ritual studies. Speech-act theory, which developed out of philosophical linguistic analysis, is usually applied only to verbal phenomena. Here we shall extend its application to ritual, a performative phenomenon.

Specifically, I want to explore the applicability of J. L. Austin's typology of "infelicitous" (his term) performances to both biblical and nonbiblical examples of troublesome ritual. The reasons for putting speech-act theory to this use are simple: some of the examples used by Austin are ritualistic, and ritual contexts, more than any other, make use of what he calls "performative utterance," that is, speech insofar as it accomplishes tasks rather than merely describing them. Speech-act theory has proved generally useful in understanding the relations between "things said" and "things done," but I want to explore one specific dimension of the theory.

Austin's typology is applicable not only to things said in ritual contexts but also to things done in them, especially if the things done seem to go awry.

There is no necessary reason why one has to apply speech-act theory to failed rites as opposed to successful ones, but applying it to "happy" (Austin's term) instances has been done; applying it to unhappy ones has not.

Ritual is not a single kind of action. Rather, it is a convergence of several kinds we normally think of as distinct. It is an "impure" genre. Like opera, which includes other genres—for example, singing, drama, and sometimes even dancing—a ritual may include all these and more. Accordingly, applying speech-act theory to ritual is unlikely to explain every sort of action that can transpire in a rite. Initially, one might expect it to be of use only in understanding the verbal aspects of it, particularly those facets of ritual language that do rather than merely refer.

All speech acts are not ritual acts, and not all ritual acts include speech acts. Therefore we would suppose speech-act theory would be of little use in rites characterized mainly by silence or movement. Ritual is a more complex cultural form than speech, because it can include all the variants of speech, but speech cannot include all the varieties of ritual.

Just as what we label with the single term "ritual" is a complex phenomenon requiring multiple methods to understand it, so there are numerous ways a rite can succeed or fail. A fertility rite may not make crops grow. Nevertheless, it can succeed socially while it fails empirically. Worship can lapse into civil ceremony and thus serve a vested political interest, thereby failing ethically. Meanwhile, it can succeed in providing symbols that nourish or comfort individuals. A wedding may legally bind a couple but fail to generate a festive air. In short, different kinds of ritual fail in different ways. And a rite need not fail on every level or from every point of view for it to be worth our while to consider the question of ritual infelicity.

Since rites are often multiphased as well as multileveled, and since symbols have a fan of overlapping meanings as well as several kinds of meaning, one can seldom demonstrate that a rite has failed in all phases and on all levels. Of the many varieties of human behavior, ritual is probably the most difficult to evaluate. And when we do evaluate it, justifying our assessments is notoriously difficult. Consequently, quarrels over ritual are often settled by violence or counterritualization—not by discussion, argument, or vote-taking. Furthermore, criteria for considering a ritual as successful or failed may be inescapably religiocentric or ethnocentric.

Despite these difficulties and caveats, people still engage in ritual criticism. As religious traditions and cultures clash and converge, and individuals engage in overt and covert syncretism, criticism becomes increasingly necessary—if not for participants themselves, then for us who study ritual behavior.

Religious studies generally and ritual studies in particular typically ignore rites that do not do what they are purported to do. Although participants probably experience the failure of ritual as often as they do the success of it, people who study rites pay little attention to the dynamics of ritual infelicity. Questions such as the following remain not only unanswered but scarcely even considered: Does it make sense to consider rituals "happy," "true," or "successful," hence, "unhappy," "false," or "failed"? By what criteria do participants judge rites? Why is there such resistance to ritual criticism? Are there any cross-culturally valid ways to assess a rite? Are there specifically ritualistic, as opposed to moral, criteria? What do we mean when we say a ritual "works"? Is "working" a criterion equally applicable to every kind of ritual?

Understandably, anthropologists usually avoid making explicit, written judgments about the failure or success of the rites they observe and record. Liturgists are supposed to do so because of the normative, religious nature of their work, but they have difficulty in doing so. Liturgists do not typically pose their criticisms so as to make them open to cross-cultural assessment, nor are they always explicit about their grounds for engaging in ritual criticism in the first place. . . .

RITUAL INFELICITY IN SPEECH-ACT THEORY

Austin's *How to Do Things with Words* (1962) was originally delivered as the William James Lectures at Harvard in 1955. In it Austin introduces the idea of "performative utterance," which has become the foundation of . . . speech-act theory, whose leading contemporary proponent is John Searle. His *Speech Acts* (1969) and *Expression and Meaning* (1979) elaborate and refine Austin's original research.

Austin's stated intention is to describe the way words do things, as opposed merely to describing or expressing them. He employs a set of classifications that (1) enable us to distinguish words that say something ("constatives") from those that do something ("performatives"), and (2) help us judge when performatives are "happy," on the one hand, or "infelicitous," on the other.

Here we are concerned with types of "infelicitous performance" and the light they shed on ritual failure. I do not believe this approach stretches Austin's terminology. He recognized that it had implications for ritual (see, e.g., 1962:17, 20, 24, 36, 76, 84–85), but does not develop them. In the most explicit passage he says, ". . . Infelicity is an ill to which all acts are heir which have the general character of ritual or ceremonial, all conventional acts. . . ." (18–19).

Which infelicities are likely to occur in which types of ritual Austin never says. Nor does he consider any kind of act other than that of uttering words. So we are left to infer and imagine how to proceed from the kind he treats. He proposes two large categories of infelicity: "misfires" and "abuses." When a ritual misfires, its formula is not effective; the act is "purported but void." An example of a misfire would be a wedding performed by someone unauthorized to do it, say, the choirmaster rather than the priest. When a rite is abused, it is "professed but hollow." An abuse would be saying "I do" while secretly resolving not to do.

It is clear from Austin's analysis that recognizing ritual misfires requires attention to the total situation of the speech act, not just to the words alone. Assessment requires a consideration of the tradition and social context. I would add that recognizing ritual abuses requires that attention be paid to the psychology of the ritualist, especially insofar as one can infer such psychology from tones of voice, grammatical moods, and gestures.

Some performatives are easy to recognize, because they include explicit grammatical cues such as the first-person singular or certain adverbs: "I bid you welcome" or "I hereby name you the Queen Mary." But the line between explicit and implicit performatives is not always so clear. "I am sorry" can be the description of a feeling or the enactment of an apology, and pipe smoking can be either a habitual activity or a sacred gesture.

In John Searle's refinement of Austin's research, a great deal of effort is spent reformulating the taxonomy of illocutionary acts (see Searle 1979: chap. 1) and almost none on the infelicities. Searle (1969:chap. 5) argues that predication ("saying") is also an act, thus softening Austin's contrast between constatives and performatives. In addition, Searle (1969:136ff.) identifies the "speech act fallacy" that results from trying to overextend speech-act theory. But "defective" (see 1969:54) performatives receive little attention from him. So the main contribution of speech-act theory to a theory of ritual failure still consists of Austin's taxonomy, which he himself took to be provisional and incomplete. . . .

TYPES OF INFELICITOUS PERFORMANCE

Not all of Austin's examples depend solely on language-related features. His taxonomy turns out to be much broader than his declared intentions of developing a theory of utterance; it includes instances in which failure stems from some problem with attitude or action. In fact, examined carefully, only "breaches" necessarily involve words. In all the other categories failure could occur without the involvement of language at all, even though Austin often gives examples that are language-oriented. His categories are more general than one might initially suppose. Furthermore, we might surmise from the amount of space he devotes to infelicities that he expected them to occur as frequently as he did happy performatives.

Austin identifies two major types: (1) "misfires" and (2) "abuses." I shall describe the various subtypes and provide actual ritual examples to illustrate their usefulness beyond the arena of language.

(*1.11*)* "Nonplays" are procedures that do not exist, therefore the actions are disallowed. Strictly speaking, there would be no examples for this category (which may be one reason Austin never found a term for it that satisfied him). However, his inten-

---

*These numbers refer to the divisions outlined in illustration Fig. 1 p. 288.

tion seems to be that of defining a category of rites that someone, say, a ritual authority, believes to be nonexistent or illegitimate. I use the term to include invented or recently borrowed rites that are disconnected from the structures that might legitimate them. Austin says that nonplays lack "an accepted conventional procedure" (1962:14). Such a procedure does not fall within the boundaries of legitimacy or the domain of efficacy. For instance, recall that, when William O. Roberts, Jr. (1982:11), designed initiation rites for the youth of First Church of Christ in Middletown, Connecticut, a denominational executive responded, "In Christianity we confirm faith. We do not initiate people." In his view Christian initiation is a nonplay.

(*1.12*) If a rite fails by "misapplication," it is a legitimate rite but the persons and circumstances involved in it are inappropriate. An example is the funeral in 1954 of a ten-year-old Javanese boy named Paidjan. Clifford Geertz's (1973:153ff.) sensitive description and probing analysis show how the *slametan* (a communal feast) of the funeral became arrested because of social and political circumstances—because of what he deems "an incongruity due to the persistence in an urban environment of a religious symbol system adjusted to peasant social structure" (169). One might wish to add to this category procedures that fail because they are ill-timed, such as harvest celebrations (e.g., Thanksgiving) that occur two months later than the actual harvest or weddings that are undergone too soon or too late.

(*1.21*) "Flaws" are ritual procedures that employ incorrect, vague, or inexplicit formulas, including, I would add, nonverbal or gestural formulas. Indigenous attempts to account for the failure of magical rites often appeal to some such notion. If a ritual is considered merely flawed, participants may easily be convinced to repeat it. Obviously, ritualists themselves are not eager to keep records of their mistakes, so even though flawed enactments may be rife, recorded examples are rare. An interesting one is reported by Morris E. Opler (1969:92–93). Look-Around-Water, a Mescalero Apache, believed that a protective rite failed, allowing him to be struck by two bullets, because he had been singing a deer song instead of the one that properly belonged to him. As soon as he changed his song he was healed.

(*1.22*) "Hitches" are misexecutions in which the procedures are incomplete. One of Austin's (1962:37) fictional examples is the official who declared, "I hereby open this library," only to discover that the key had broken off in the lock. A more poignant instance is the case of Lulu (recounted in Leacock 1975:200ff.), a forty-year-old Afro-Brazilian woman who for twenty years was unable to have a trance experience even though she repeatedly showed the usual signs of incipient possession.

(*2.1*) "Insincerities" are a type of "abuse"—an act "professed but hollow." Ritual insincerity amounts to saying—I would add, doing—things without the requisite feelings, thoughts, or intentions. Lévi-Strauss (1967: 169ff.) retells the story (first told by Franz Boas) of Quesalid, a Canadian Kwakiutl who did not believe in shamanism. He learned it in order to expose it. Later, he continued to practice this "false supernatural" without believing in it, because people believed in him, and because he knew of techniques even more false than his own.

(*2.2*) "Breaches" are failures to follow through; they are abrogations of ceremonially made promises. Since "breaches" includes breaking promises and failure to abide by contracts, it is one of the more familiar types of infelicity. Sometimes rites fail to bind. One can avoid the conclusion that the fault is the rite's by claiming that persons, not ceremonies, fail—that rites are "victims," not agents. A widely publicized breach was former U.S. President Richard Nixon's violation of his oath of office by his involvement in Watergate. No longer "protecting and defending," he was guilty of undermining and attacking—at least this seemed to be the public verdict.

Here Austin's typology ends, yet there remain other examples that cannot be handled by his scheme, so further additions to the typology are necessary:

(*2.3*) "Glosses" are procedures that hide or ignore contradictions or major problems. Glossing over conflict is a function that rites proverbially (in anthropological theory) do well. In fact, some scholars argue that this is its primary function. However, rituals may also fail because a gloss is too thin and people see through it, or because it is too thick and

is recognizable only by its repercussions in the psyche or social structure. I once attended a wedding in which the bride was pregnant, followed a few months later by a child-blessing in which this same new wife participated with a black eye from her husband. Both ceremonies were "applied" in the same manner (and about as successfully) as her eye make-up. They "glossed" rather than "bridged" the chasms. It is not uncommon for participants to believe that one's wedding day should be perfect—ideal and unmarred by any recognition of difficulties.

(*2.4*) In a "flop" all the procedures may be done correctly but the rite fails to resonate. It does not generate the proper tone, ethos, or atmosphere. In some rites mood is less important than precise execution of procedures; this might be true of a healing rite or baptism. But in a fiesta or a birthday party, having a good time and being festive is a primary aim. At a retirement ceremony for a colleague things went without hitch or flaw (in Austin's sense of these terms), but the praise was so exaggerated and the jokes so strained that the farewell went flat; it flopped.

(*3*) Austin thinks of illocutionary acts almost solely in the context of interpersonal relations and legal procedures. Consequently, he omits consideration of the performative utterances that would be most obvious to scholars in religious studies and anthropology, namely, magic. Hence we need a new, major category, "ineffectuality."

Ineffectualities are procedures that fail to bring about intended observable changes. Ineffectualities are more serious than flaws, because the latter are partial. In the case of the former a rite may be properly performed, but it does not produce the goods. For instance, Maria Sabina (cited in Halifax 1979:213), a Mazatec shaman, was unable to heal seventeen-year-old Pefecto José García and concluded her chant, "Dangerous things are being done, tragedies are being worked out. We are left only perplexed, we mamas. Who can stand all these things? It's the same; it's the same here. Really this thing is big." The chant may have prepared those present for grief and loss; it was not a "flop." But it was, in her view, ineffectual inasmuch as the boy died.

(*4*) To label an act a ritual "violation" reflects a

moral judgment. Violations may be effective, but they are demeaning. From some points of view they are judged to be deficient. Rites such as initiations that deliberately maim or inadvertently degrade are difficult analytically as well as morally. Clitoridectomies are a case in point. Recently, some anthropologists, particularly women, have attacked them regardless of their indigenous support. Judging actions to be moral violations may be culturally relative, but this does not relieve us of moral responsibility. An example about which there seems to be obvious warrant for debate is the Aztec ceremony (see Vaillant 1962:205) in honor of Huehueteotl, the fire god. In it priests danced with prisoners bound to their backs and then, one by one, dumped them into the flames. Before death could relieve the pain, the priests dragged the captives out with hooks and cut out their still beating hearts. This example, along with burnings at the stake, head-hunting, and human sacrifices, challenges the easy cultural relativism of broad-minded academics.

(5) Ritual "contagion" occurs when a rite spills over its own boundaries. It may be effective, but it is uncontained. In *Violence and the Sacred* René Girard (1972:31ff.) has offered the most provocative analysis of this sort of infelicity. However, he typically emphasizes the way in which rituals contain the social contagion of violence rather than the way in which rituals themselves can contaminate. Maya Deren (1970:254ff.; 322n.8), a filmmaker, tells how the Voodoo rite she went to Haiti to study broke its bounds. It is rare for a non-Haitian to be possessed, but Deren was, producing considerable complications for her recording project. From one point of view this occurrence shows the power of the rite. From another, it is a problem, if not evidence of some sort of failure.

"Rituals of conflict" (Norbeck 1967:226) often spread as if they were a contagious disease. From the point of view of rebels and proponents of social change this is as it should be. From the point of view of the established elite, contamination is tantamount to failure.

(6) In instances of ritual "opacity" a ceremony or some element in it is experienced as meaningless; the act is unrecognizable or uninterpretable. Either it fails to communicate or it communicates such conflicting messages that someone—either participant or observer—fails to grasp its sense. There are short-lived varieties of opacity, but there are long-range ones too. Most rites probably contain some opaque symbols, and most religions, some opaque rites, but the situation becomes problematic if opacity is widespread. Opacity may incite one to curiosity, but when rife or sustained, it can damage a rite. Perhaps the most common example of opacity is the use of a sacred language (Latin, Hebrew, or Sanskrit, for instance) to such a degree that it ceases to create mystery and begins to obfuscate. How much opacity participants can tolerate seems to differ widely from culture to culture.

When tourists witness the Pueblo corn dance at Santo Domingo Pueblo, New Mexico, it is opaque to most of them; hence their concentration on the rhythm of the drums, the weather, or the color of costumes. The opacity may protect the rite from meddling, but it sometimes results in the spectators' inadvertently interrupting a sacred performance by an inappropriate response. In this case opacity is the result of being an outsider.

In the following case, recounted by Apuleius (1962:248–249) ritual opacity is deliberate, the result of priestly mystification:

> Thereupon the old man took me by the hand and led me towards the spacious temple. . . . He produced from the secret recesses of the shrine certain books written in unknown characters. The meaning of these characters was concealed, at times by the concentrated expression of hieroglypically painted animals, at times by wreathed and twisted letters with tails that twirled like wheels . . . so that it was altogether impossible for any peeping profane to comprehend.

(7) Ritual "defeat" is more common than might be supposed, because ritual competition and conquest are widespread. In a ritual defeat one ritual performance invalidates another. The eighteenth chapter of 1 Kings, for instance, tells of a contest between Elijah and Baal's prophets. The story is told from the point of view of the victors, so they are the ones who conclude that the opposing rite (and its attendant deity) are failures. Often a ritual defeat is

followed by ritual "theft," that is, the plundering of a conquered ritual system for its symbolic wealth.

That ritualists explicitly compete in magical battles is obvious enough. What scholars sometimes fail to notice is how rites may be thrown implicitly into competitive "market" situations. Fenn's (1982) analysis seems to imply that liturgy is sometimes defeated by courtroom ceremony. On occasion rites from the same system inadvertently become competitors, for example, a Sunday worship service and its televised counterpart.

(*8*) In cases of ritual "omission" the rite does not fail; rather, one fails to perform it. Ruth Finnegan (1969:545) says that if a Limba husband can complain against his wife, "You haven't greeted me," it is a serious breach of decorum. Like "flaws," omissions are a favorite way for participants to account for trouble. If one fails to make prayerful requests, offer the expected sacrifice, or give due thanks, then it is easy to claim that such omissions account for subsequent suffering or disaster. Omissions are the opposite of "nonplays." In the former there is no accepted procedure; in the latter there is a procedure but it is left undone.

(*9*) Outsiders are more likely than insiders to commit "misframes." When we misframe a rite, we misconstrue its genre. The result is akin to missing the point of a joke or taking irony literally. Perhaps we understand it on some level—it is not "opaque" to us—but on some other we miss the point. If one does not understand the shit devil rites described by Jeanne Cannizzo (1983:124–141), one might assume that boys who stumble, defecate, and wear ragged clothes were mentally ill instead of engaging in ritual caricature. It is not always easy to tell whether we are witnessing drama, symptoms, or ritual. It is a common error to misconstrue magic as drama or vice-versa. Since frames can shift or multiply in the course of a single cultural performance (e.g., a dramatic pageant within, or subsequent to, a civil ceremony), even participants can misframe the activities in which they participate. Sometimes this is an advantage, allowing ritualists to believe they share a common definition of the situation. In other instances, however, the misframing is disastrous or funny. Erving Goffman's *Frame Analysis* (1974: 324) is replete with examples, such as the story of a thousand enraged Mexican farmers who drive their priest out of town because he will not celebrate Mass

at a tree that, after lying five years dead on its side, is found upright after a thunderstorm. They frame the event as "miracle"; he does not.

To summarize, the complete typology, consisting of Austin's categories (without quotation marks) as well as my own (in quotation marks), is as follows:

FIGURE 1   Types of Infelicitous Performance

1. Misfire (act purported but void)

   1.1 Misinvocation (act disallowed)

      1.11 Nonplay (lack of accepted conventional procedure)

      1.12 Misapplication (inappropriate persons or circumstances)

   1.2 Misexecutions (act vitiated)

      1.21. Flaw (incorrect, vague, or inexplicit formula)

      1.22. Hitch (incomplete procedure)

2. Abuse (act professed but hollow)

   2.1. Insincerity (lack of requisite feelings, thoughts, or intentions)

   2.2. Breach (failure to follow through)

   2.3. "Gloss" (procedures used to cover up problems)

   2.4. "Flop" (failure to produce appropriate mood or atmosphere)

3. "Ineffectuality" (act fails to precipitate anticipated empirical change)

4. "Violation" (act effective but demeaning)

5. "Contagion" (act leaps beyond proper boundaries)

6. "Opacity" (act unrecognizable or unintelligible)

7. "Defeat" (act discredits or invalidates acts of others)

8. "Omission" (act not performed)

9. "Misframe" (genre of act misconstrued)

RITUAL INFELICITY IN THE HEBREW BIBLE

As anyone who has ever tried to apply and test some theory or scheme knows, all sorts of unanticipated problems appear as soon as one faces a specific tradition with that theory. When we engage in extended case studies rather than selecting examples, the lack of fit between theory and data begins to show. I am no biblical scholar and have neither the space nor the training to pursue a case study here, but it might be helpful at least to suggest lines along which a study of performative infelicity in the Hebrew Bible might proceed. Some of the more interesting examples are suggested by the [passage quoted earlier in this selection].

Beginning with biblical texts is basically, but not entirely, an inductive procedure. I have, after all, picked texts that appear to be relevant to the typology. For instance, the tale of the confrontation of Moses and Aaron with the Egyptian magicians seems to be, among others things, a story about magical combat. Comparative religion and symbolic anthropology are replete with similar stories about sorcerers and magicians who pit their rites against one another. This feature of the account appears to be a straightforward illustration of ritual "defeat" (#7).*

By itself this sort of labeling does not tell us very much; the work of interpretation has hardly begun when one categorizes the action. It begins to get interesting, however, when we inquire why these same magicians are said to have been successful in an earlier phase of competition. Like Moses and Aaron they too succeed in bringing frogs upon the land of Egypt by use of their secret arts (Exodus 8:7). It heightens suspense to have the magicians seem like real competition and then have them defeated. It may be that a symbolic, possibly ritualistic, issue is at stake when the magicians are successful in bringing frogs (amphibians associated with water) but fail with gnats (creatures of the air associated in the text with dust). Whether or not my speculations bear any fruit, the point is simply that categorizing the conflict as ritual defeat, a species of performative infelicity, precipitates an avenue of inquiry not entirely typical of biblical scholarship.

Consider a second biblical example, that of Cain's offering (Genesis 4). Popular interpretations of the story fill in the silence of the text by assuming that God rejects the offering because Cain hides some secret sin such as arrogance or that he is insin-

cere. Such an interpretation implies a classification of the problem as "insincerity" (#2.1), "lack of requisite feelings, thoughts, or intentions."

Modern scholarship, on the other hand, often reads the story as personifying a conflict between two ways of life: agricultural (symbolized by Cain and his vegetable/fruit offering) and nomadic (symbolized by Abel and his offering of livestock). Whereas the popular view treats Cain's failure as a form of "abuse" (#2), an act professed but hollow, the scholarly one treats it as a "misinvocation" (# 1.1) of some sort; "the act is disallowed." Following speech-act theory we would have to inquire whether it is disallowed because there is no accepted conventional procedure for such an offering or whether the persons or circumstances are inappropriate. If the latter, then we would have to ask, Inappropriate in what respects?

A third instance is Abraham's near sacrifice of Isaac, popularly regarded as a "test" but considered by some scholars as reflecting a cultural transition from child sacrifice to a more sublimated, more ethically sophisticated, rite in which an animal is substituted for a person. In the language of speech act theory we would say this is a "misapplication" (#1.12), because it involves an inappropriate object: a human rather than an animal.

But from the point of view of Isaac, we might imagine, it is better regarded as an instance of ritual "violation" (#4)—or near violation, since the act was not completed. From the point of view of a child-sacrificing culture (if there ever was one), Abraham's failure to follow through would have constituted a "breach" (#2.2). But modern Jews and Christians might well question whether any sort of infelicity or failure has occurred at all. The story, they might insist, is about a successful ritual revision or a successful attempt to resist a temptation to use ritual to satisfy an infanticidal obsession. What this third example illustrates is that the typology does not answer questions so much as precipitate them by providing a vocabulary.

A final example is the short folktale of Nadab and Abihu, the sons of Aaron (Leviticus 10). In one sense it parallels the Cain and Abel story: God is not happy with an offering. But instead of refusing it, he destroys the brothers with fire because they offered "unholy fire." The pun notwithstanding, the act is a "misfire" (#1), but of what sort? The only way to be

---

*Such references are to [the divisions in Fig. 1 in the previous section].

precise is to know more about what constituted un-holiness for the ancient Hebrews. Does the problem lie in intentions? In procedures? Or should we cir-cumvent these alternatives altogether and classify the action according to its results? If the latter, we need a new category, say, "backfires," which we could make an independent category or a subcategory of "contagion" (#5), which is what occurs when a per-formance leaps beyond proper boundaries.

FURTHER RESEARCH
ON RITUAL INFELICITY

I have raised far more questions than I have an-swered—deliberately so. The aim has not been to "apply" a theory of speech acts to biblical "data." Rather, it has been to experiment with the theory, both extending its scope and exposing its limits, as well as teasing a few texts with some new questions. The typology is incomplete, although I have shown how one might begin to expand beyond Austin's original aims and to build on his vocabulary. The categories need much more testing by application to specific rites. For the moment, the most one can ex-pect of them is that they call attention to what is of-ten ignored, namely, infelicitous performances, and that they provide a tentative glossary for beginning to assess them.

An obvious limitation of the typology is that it does not solve the problem of point of view. Who—participant or observer—is to decide whether proce-dures fail, and if they do, what sort of infelicity has been committed?

The typology does not fully explore how kinds of infelicity transpire in relation to one another. For instance, one may "gloss" a rite, deliberately making it "opaque," thereby laying the grounds for a ritual "defeat." Something like this happened when Span-ish conquistadors taught Native people of the new world to venerate crosses without fully conveying their meaning. Later, the conquerors used this de-votion as a means of discouraging rebellion among the conquered and of obtaining formal, ceremonial submission.

An unanswered question is this: What are the mo-tives and mechanisms for evading the judgment that a rite does not work? What is it about ritual itself that seems so regularly to discourage critical thinking?

One also might want to inquire whether the terms are ethnocentric. Austin's British, understated "infelicitous"/"happy" and my overstated, North American "failure"/"success" might suggest that rit-ual criticism is inextricably bound up with national or even temperamental sensibilities.

Another problem is that the typology does not systematically separate "failure in" and "failure of" rituals. In some types the problem lies with the rit-ualists, in others with the rite itself, and in still oth-ers with the relation between the rite and surround-ing religiocultural processes.

Finally, there are undoubtedly other types and examples. What shall we call the rite that is so rigid that it cannot change? How shall we name those ceremonies that are so weak dramatically, concep-tually, or socially that they simply have no effect? And what of annulments, for example, of weddings? As the types and examples proliferate, we must, of course, begin to examine the logic of sub- and su-per-ordination of the categories. Are there "levels" of failure?

Among these issues the point-of-view problem and the failure-in/failure-of distinction are in my es-timation the most important and troublesome, so a few additional comments may be necessary, if only to encourage further reflection and research.

Put simply, there is no resolving the point-of-view problem if one imagines there is some uni-versal, meta-ritualistic criterion which, like a meter stick, can be used to measure every rite cross-cul-turally. Even the exemplary meter stick lacks cur-rency not only in the New Guinea bush but in the United States. I have deliberately refrained from re-ferring to the categories as "criteria." They consti-tute a typology, an organized (perhaps in the fu-ture, systematized) phenomenology. Their worth consists of their ability to point to troublesome dy-namics and to provide a vocabulary for recogni-tions, debate, and discussion. They are useless as some kind of performative canon with which to prove failure or rebuke ritualists. Ritualists have so little difficulty evading ritual criticism that a set of a-cultural criteria would be of little practical use to anybody who is not already convinced that a prob-lem exists.

Since rites, especially religious ones, function as paradigms, they themselves are sometimes the ideal by which the ordinary is judged. Rites, like myths and dreams, resist criticism or, if you prefer, people resist having their rites, myths, and dreams subjected to criticism. The right to engage in it all is probably either bought with membership and participation or directly dependent upon the richness of one's observations and interpretations. Ritual criticism is but one phase—and not a privileged one either—of the hermeneutics of ritual. So if we are to speak of criteria at all, they are definitional not moral. Their weight comes from their ability to articulate, not their ability to prove or coerce. Consider, for instance "violations," those ritual acts that demean. Demeaning may be defined as in bounds for an initiation rite. If one chooses to resist this definition, he or she will probably have the most success by appealing to one part of the rite as a basis for criticizing some other part. In the Abraham-Isaac story ritual infanticide is prevented not by a bare moral interdiction but by a ritual substitute. The most effective ritual criticism is probably that which transpires on the basis of the ritual systems itself, not on some heteronomous rule.

This brings us to the failure-in/failure-of distinction. Infelicity is often taken by participants to be the result of a failure in some detail of performance. They will blame themselves before impugning the rite and will criticize some part of it before challenging the whole of it. It is a mistake always to blame persons rather than rituals—a tactic that prevents ritual criticism. Using a literary critical analogy, we might say that in such instances functional infelicity is translated into formal infelicity. Formally, a rite is a self-contained system; functionally, it achieves something in the environment or does something to or for participants.

However, I do not think a merely formal or morphological treatment of ritual failure will suffice, but neither will one that considers failure in purely functional, sociological terms. I doubt that one can ever judge a rite as failed or flawed in any absolute way. It is always flawed from person or group X's point of view or in relation to goal Y. If we learn to make such discriminations, we may become less susceptible to the wholesale waves of ritophobia and ritophilia that periodically sweep Western cultures. Analyzing ritual failure involves more than defining terms, supplying examples, or applying labels. But learning to do so is a first step toward a useful ritual criticism.

NOTES

1. One might want to examine other models and motives for evaluating cultural action. For example, Howard Richards in *The Evaluation of Cultural Action* (1985) attempts to reflect philosophically on the problem of evaluating programs in Latin America. Not only does he face the problem of how to integrate ethical concerns with those of productivity, he approaches the problem with considerable philosophical sophistication concerning the epistemology of cross-cultural evaluation.

2. Theologian and performance critic Tom Driver (1970) has said that theology is to religion what literary criticism is to literature. Literature, like religion, is a primary process upon which secondary, analytical processes depend.

3. For a good discussion of the tacit religious and ethical dimensions of anthropology, see Mark Kline Taylor's *Beyond Explanation: Religious Dimensions in Cultural Anthropology* (1986).

4. Some worry that self-criticism and self-consciousness would immobilize researchers.

5. Protestant theologians reflecting these social-scientific interests include Theodore W. Jennings, Jr., and Tom F. Driver. Driver has a forthcoming book on ritual and human transformation, which is deeply marked by ethnographic interests.

6. The works of James Fernandez (e.g., 1974, 1982, 1986) will soon have to be added to this list.

7. Many liturgical theologians learned their methods from biblical critics. Just as the Bible was made approachable by scholarly methods, so the liturgy is being relativized by historical and literary critical scholarship.

8. For a Protestant perception of the political ramifications of prayer and worship, see Theodore W. Jennings, Jr., *Life as Worship: Prayer and Praise in Jesus' Name* (1982: chap.3).

9. Theology and the social sciences both have their ways of putting judgments into force; each is normative in a different way. Social-scientific explanation exercises normative power by looking for latent social functions beneath the avowed intentions of those who enact the rites. As Talal Asad (1973:161) suggests, the attribution of implicit meanings to alien practices without the acknowledgment of the practitioners is a "theological" exercise.

10. Another volume relevant to the interface between theology and anthropology is John H. Morgan's *Understanding Religion and Culture: Anthropological and Theological Perspectives* (1979). See also Urban T. Holmes, "What Has Manchester to Do with Jerusalem?" (1977). Manchester is his symbol for the home of British social anthropology; Jerusalem, the home of three major religions.

11. For a fuller treatment of enculturation and liturgy see Chupungco (1982).

SOURCES CITED

Apuleius, Lucius. 1962. *The Golden Ass*. Translated by Jack Lindsay. Bloomington: Indiana University Press.

Austin, J. L. 1962. *How to Do Things with Words*. New York: Oxford University Press.

Cannizzo, Jeanne. 1983. The Shit Devil: Pretense and Politics among West African Urban Children. In *The Celebration of Society: Perspectives on Contemporary Cultural Performance*, edited by Frank E. Manning. London, Canada: Congress of Social & Humanistic Studies.

Chupungco, Anscar. 1982. *Cultural Adaptation of the Liturgy*. New York: Paulist.

Clifford, James, and George E. Marcus, eds. 1986. *Writing Culture: The Poetics and Politics of Ethnography*. A School of American Research Advanced Seminar. Berkeley: University of California Press.

Collins, Mary. 1987. *Worship: Renewal to Practice*. Washington, DC: Pastoral.

Deren, Maya. 1970. *Divine Horsemen: Voodoo Gods of Haiti*. New York: Chelsea House.

Driver, Tom F. 1970. The Study of Religion and Literature: Siblings in the Academic House. In *The Study of Religion in Colleges and Universities*, edited by Paul Ramsey and John F. Wilson. Princeton: Princeton University Press.

Fenn, Richard K. 1982. *Liturgies and Trials: The Secularization of Religious Language*. New York: Pilgrim.

Fernandez, James W. 1974. The Mission of Metaphor in Expressive Culture. *Current Anthropology* 15:119–145.

———. 1982. *Bwiti: An Ethnography of the Religious Imagination in Africa*. Princeton, NJ: Princeton University Press.

———. 1986. The Argument of Images and the Experience of Returning to the Whole. In *The Anthropology of Experience*, edited by Victor W. Turner and Edward M. Bruner. Urbana: University of Illinois Press.

Finnegan, Ruth. 1969. How to Do Things with Words: Performative Utterances among the Limba of Sierra Leone. *Man* (N.S.) 4:537–552.

Frye, Northrop. 1968. *Anatomy of Criticism*. New York: Atheneum.

Geertz, Clifford. 1973. *The Interpretation of Cultures*. New York: Basic Books.

———. 1988. *Works and Lives: The Anthropologist as Author*. Stanford, CA: Stanford University Press.

Girard, René. 1972. *Violence and the Sacred*. Translated by Patrick Gregory. Baltimore: Johns Hopkins University Press.

Goffman, Erving. 1974. *Frame Analysis: An Essay on the Organization of Experience*. New York: Harper & Row.

Halifax, Joan, ed. 1979. *Shamanic Voices: A Survey of Visionary Narratives*. New York: Dutton.

Holmes, Urban T. 1977. What Has Manchester to Do with Jerusalem? *Anglican Theological Review* 59(1):79–97.

Jennings, Theodore W., Jr. 1982. *Life as Worship: Prayer and Praise in Jesus' Name*. Grand Rapids, MI: Eerdmans.

Leacock, Seth and Ruth. 1975. *Spirits of the Deep: A Study of an Afro-Brazilian Cult*. Garden City, NY: Anchor.

Lévi-Strauss, Claude. 1967. *Structural Anthropology*. Translated by Claire Jacobson and Brooke G. Schoepf. Garden City, NY: Doubleday.

Marcus, George E., and Michael M. J. Fischer. 1986. *Anthropology as Cultural Critique: An Experimental Moment in the Human Sciences*. Chicago: University of Chicago Press.

Merod, Jim. 1987. *The Political Responsibility of the Critic*. Ithaca, NY: Cornell University Press.

Morgan, John H., ed. 1979. *Understanding Religion and Culture: Anthropological and Theological Perspectives*. Washington, DC: University Press of America.

Norbeck, Edward. 1967. African Rituals of Conflict. In *Gods and Rituals: Readings in Religious Beliefs and Practices*, edited by John Middleton. Garden City, NY: Natural History Press.

Opler, Morris E. 1969. *Apache Odyssey: A Journey between Two Worlds*. New York: Holt, Rinehart & Winston.

Richards, Howard. 1985. *The Evaluation of Cultural Action*. London: Macmillan.

Roberts, William O., Jr. 1982. *Initiation into Adulthood: An Ancient Rite of Passage in Contemporary Form*. New York: Pilgrim.

Royce, Anya Peterson. 1977. *The Anthropology of Dance*. Bloomington, IN: Indiana University Press.

Rubenstein, Richard. 1966. *After Auschwitz: Radical Theology and Contemporary Judaism*. Indianapolis: Bobbs-Merrill.

———. 1974. *Power Struggle: A Confessional Autobiography*. New York: Scribners.

Ruby, Jay, ed. 1982. *A Crack in the Mirror: Reflexive Perspectives in Anthropology*. Philadelphia: University of Pennsylvania Press.

Sacks, Oliver. 1984. The Lost Mariner. *New York Review of Books* 31(2):14–19.

Savage, Howard G. 1977. Meeting of Representatives of Indian Groups and Archaeologists of Ontario. *Arch Notes*, October-November, 34–36.

Scarf, Maggie. 1980. Images that Heal: A Doubtful Idea Whose Time Has Come. *Psychology Today* 14(4):32–46.

Schechner, Richard. 1977. *Essays on Performance Theory, 1970–1976*. New York: Drama Book Specialists.

———. 1980. The End of Humanism. *Performing Arts Journal* 4(1–2):9–22.

———. 1981a. Performers and Spectators Transported and Transformed. *The Kenyon Review*, N.S., 3(4):83–113.

———. 1981b. Restoration of Behavior. *Studies in Visual Communication* 7(3):1–45.

———. 1985. *Between Theater and Anthropology*. Philadelphia: University of Pennsylvania Press.

———. 1986. Magnitudes of Performance. In *The Anthropology of Experience*, edited by Victor W. Turner and Edward M. Bruner. Urbana: University of Illinois Press.

———, interviewer. 1989. Anna Halprin: A Life in Ritual. *The Drama Review* 33(2):67–73.

Searle, John. 1969. *Speech Acts: An Essay in the Philosophy of Language.* Cambridge, Eng.: Cambridge University Press.

———. 1979. *Expression and Meaning: Studies in the Theory of Speech-acts.* Cambridge: Cambridge University Press.

Siebers, Tobin. 1988. *The Ethics of Criticism.* Ithaca, NY: Cornell University Press.

Taylor, Mark Kline. 1986. *Beyond Explanation: Religious Dimensions in Cultural Anthropology.* Macon, GA: Mercer University Press.

Vaillant, George C. 1962. *Aztecs of Mexico.* Revised by Suzannah B. Vaillant. Baltimore: Penguin.

Holiday Celebrations in Israeli Kindergartens

DON HANDELMAN
LEA SHAMGAR-HANDELMAN

Facts of publication: *Handelman, Don, and Lea Shamgar-Handelman. 1990. "Holiday Celebrations in Israeli Kindergartens," from* Models and Mirrors: Towards an Anthropology of Public Events, *162–165, 168–179, 183–189, 288–290. New York: Cambridge University Press. Originally appeared as "Holiday Celebrations in Israeli Kindergartens: Relationships Between Representations of Collectivity and Family in the Nation-State" in* The Frailty of Authority *(Political Anthropology, Vol. 5), edited by Myron J. Aronoff (New Brunswick, NJ: Transaction, 1986), pp. 71–103. Copyright © 1986 by Transaction, Inc. Reprinted with the permission of Transaction Publishers.*

Ritual is not an adults-only exercise. Children both engage in it as they play and are put through it by adults. Not only does education employ ritual, some would say that it is *ritual, a protracted rite of passage in which children are transformed into socially acceptable adults. Don Handelman and Lea Shamgar-Handelman offer brief descriptions and discussions of three celebrations in Israeli kindergartens, showing how state and family vie to inscribe their values on these rites. The authors' contention is that in Israel "all children must learn that their parents are not the natural apex of hierarchy and authority; and that the rights of the collectivity can supersede those of familism." What seem* on the surface *to be innocent, mundane gestures aimed at having fun appear* upon analysis *to be symbols fraught with meaning—sometimes despite the denials of teachers that they intend such meanings. Handelman and Shamgar-Handelman attempt to articulate what some have called a school's "hidden curriculum" and to identify its operative hierarchy. Teachers are interpreted as embodiments of civil authority as it supersedes that of the family.*

About the author: *Don Handelman.* **Dates:** *1939–   , Montreal, Quebec, Canada.* **Education:** *B.A., McGill University; M.A., McGill University; Ph.D., University of Manchester.* **Field(s):** *symbol and ritual in state societies; play studies; bureaucratic organization; south Indian myth and ritual; Holocaust memorialism.* **Career:** *Lecturer to Professor, 1972–present, The Hebrew University of Jerusalem.* **Publications:** Models and Mirrors: Towards an Anthropology of Public Events *(Cambridge University, 1990); "Myths and Murugan: Asymmetry and Hierarchy in a South-Indian Puranic Cosmology,"* History of Religions *27 (1987): 133–170; "Symbolic Types, the Body, and Circus,"* Semiotica *85 (1991): 205–225; "Passages to Play: Paradox and Process,"* Play and Culture *5 (1993): 431–449.* **Additional:** *Mellon Fellow, University of Pittsburgh, 1977–1978; Distinguished Visiting Scholar, University of Adelaide, 1978; Fellow, Netherlands Institute for Advanced Study in the Humanities and Social Sciences, 1987–1988; member of the working group, Comparative Studies of Ritual; Academy of Finland Visiting Professor, University of Helsinki, 1991; Fellow, Swedish*

Collegium for Advanced Study in the Social Sciences, 1994. "My interest in ritual goes back to the 1960s, when I researched shamanism among the Washo of the Great Basin. My interest in play dates to the early 1970s, when I watched the nonverbal invention of a game in a sheltered workshop for the aged in Jerusalem. Currently, I do research on ritual, symbolism, and Holocaust memorialism in Israel, on Hindu myth, and on ritual in Andhra Pradesh. I regularly teach courses on anthropological theory, public events, and play."

About the author: *Lea Shamgar-Handelman.* **Birth place:** *Jerusalem, Israel.* **Education:** *B.A., The Hebrew University of Jerusalem; M.A., The Hebrew University of Jerusalem; Ph.D., The Hebrew University of Jerusalem.* **Field(s):** *family sociology; sociology of childhood; sociology of death; Holocaust memorialism in Israel.* **Career:** *Lecturer, then Associate Professor, 1979–present, Department of Sociology and Anthropology and the School of Education, The Hebrew University of Jerusalem.* **Publications:** Israeli War Widows: Beyond the Glory of Heroism *(Bergin & Garvey, 1986); "Childhood as a Social Phenomenon: Israel,"* Eurosocial Report *36.5 (1990); with Don Handelman, "Shaping Time: The Choice of the National Emblem of Israel," in Emiko Ohnuki-Tierney, ed.,* Culture Through Time: Anthropological Approaches, *193–226 (Stanford University, 1990); with Don Handelman, "Celebrations of Bureaucracy: Birthday Parties in Israeli Kindergartens,"* Ethnology *30 (1991):293–312; with Don Handelman, "The Presence of the Dead: Memorials of National Death in Israel,"* Journal of the Finnish Anthropological Society *16.4 (1991): 3–17.* **Additional:** *Senior Researcher, NCJW Research Institute for Innovation in Education, The Hebrew University, 1979–present; Fulbright Fellow, Family Studies Center, University of Minnesota, 1982–1983; Fellow, Netherlands Institute for Advanced Study in the Humanities and Social Sciences, 1987–1988; Fellow, Swedish Collegium for Advanced Study in the Social Sciences, 1994. "During the past few years my research and writing have concentrated on relationships between family and state, critical family theory, childhood as a social construction, responses in crisis of Israeli families to the 1991 Gulf War, and on Holocaust memorialism. The geographical focus of my interests is Israel. I regularly teach courses on family and state relationships, on the sociology of the family and childhood, and on the sociology of death."*

The object of education, contended Durkheim (1956: 71), 'is to arouse and to develop in a child a certain number of physical, intellectual, and moral states which are demanded of him by . . . the political society as a whole'. Processes of education, he added, are among the dominant means through which 'society perpetually recreates the conditions of its very existence' (1956: 123). Durkheim conjoined two themes that are salient for the modern nation-state. That the political economy of education, especially formal education, is a crucial expression of the ideology and authority of the state. And that the reproduction of social order depends in large measure on the exercise of the power of education through the requisite apparatus of the state.

In the case of Israel the tasks of formal education were less the replication of social order than the construction of an ideological blueprint that contributed to the very creation of the state. The fusion of political ideology and formal organization, in order to influence the maturation of youngsters who were the future generation of citizenry, began in the kindergarten.[1] For example, a veteran Jewish kindergarten teacher[2] reflected as follows on the intimate ties that developed between the Jewish community, the *yishuv*, in pre-state Palestine and the kindergarten. She declared that these were bonds between a form of early-age education and 'the ideas and aspirations that lifted the spirits of those parts of the nation that rebuilt the ruins of its homeland and rejuvenated this'. The Zionist vision of returning to work the land of Israel, she added, 'brought the garden into the kindergarten' (Fayence-Glick 1957: 141). As in numerous other aspects of the nation-building of Israel, that of the kindergarten was linked closely to the practice of proto-national ideology. In this the founders of the Jewish kindergarten in Palestine were influenced directly by the civil nationalism of the kindergarten movement in nineteenth century Germany (see Allen 1986).

Very young children experience and learn the lineaments of personhood and world through the family arrangements into which they are born. In these contexts they are enculturated into a sense of hierarchy and status, of division of labor, and of sentiment and loyalty, through notions of kinship and familism that come to be the natural ordering of things. Only later is the child made to realize that parental domination is itself subordinate to the idea of a wider moral order; and that on numerous occasions loyalty and obligation to the collectivity transcend that of familial ties. This transition, however obvious, is essential to the reproduction of the social orders of the state. It clearly is in the interests of representatives of the state to recruit the cooperation of the family in order to achieve societal goals; and so they phrase its relationships to the family in terms of cooperation and consensus. The rhetoric of politicians commonly likens the state and its citizenry to a great family; while the idioms of kinship and familism are used in cognate ways.

Yet this relationship between state and family is fraught with tension. This is evident in times of crisis, should officials intervene in the affairs of family; and especially when they insist that organs of the state are mandated for tasks of social control and affect that the family considers its own (Shamgar-Handelman 1981; Handelman 1978). With regard to children and their maturation, state and family do have overlapping and congruent interests; but their concerns also differ and are continually negotiated.

Bluntly put, all children must learn that their parents are not the natural apex of hierarchy and authority; and that the rights of the collectivity can supersede those of familism. This is integral to the process of maturation in the nation-state. In present-day Israel the young child's entry into the kindergarten is the onset of extended periods in educational settings that are regulated and supervised by organs of the state. The youngster is moved slowly during this lengthy transition from his embeddedness within home and family until, at age eighteen, he enters the army for compulsory service. At this time he is given over wholly by his parents to the authority and service of the state. The transition is one of offspring to citizen.

With regard to this transition, kindergartens in Israel are of especial interest, since their annual round is punctuated by numerous events that on a wider scale are of import to the civil and religious orders of state and nation. In kindergartens the celebration of such occasions is presentational and re-

presentational in form. The latter logic of organization is especially suitable to evoke in momentary but concentrated ways the kind of general transition to which we have referred above. Moreover, given the early ages of the youngsters, the experiencing of these celebrations often is designed in clearcut ways. Through such occasions children are involved outside their homes in focused representations that in general are thought to be of import to aspects of the nation-state. Many of these occasions explicitly celebrate versions of tradition and history of the Jewish people, of the renewal and coherence of the Jewish state, and of their integral and consensual synthesis. Scenarios emphasize the joint effort and viability of cooperation between kindergarten and parent, state and citizen, in order to inform the maturation of the child with experiences that begin to situate his personhood in relation to directives of the past and expectations of the future. On a more implicit level the 'hidden agendas' of these scenarios unearth the more problematic relationship between state and family.[3] Numerous celebrations can be understood as versions of the relationship between representations of collectivity and family, through which youngsters are shown and are encouraged to experience that the dominance of the former supplants that of the latter. This sort of exposure is especially important for children in urban locales where different spheres of living are quite compartmentalized, where settings of home and work are separated, and where the access of children to the world of adults is limited. The kindergarten is the first location where children learn of hierarchy and equality outside the home.

This [essay] discusses [three] cases of kindergarten celebrations in relation to the symbolic loads they convey and manipulate through re-presentation. The re-presentational aspects of their scenarios are not like the more cyclical sequence of inversion-reversion. Instead these are linear projections of irreversible maturation that the child is expected to undergo. It is surprising how little social analysis has been done on questions of whether and how kindergarten youngsters are exposed to the focused manipulations of symbols and symbolic formations of a suprafamilial character, whether in Israel or elsewhere. Studies of kindergartens emphasize the learning of competence in daily interaction (Jones 1969; Shure 1963; Shulz and Florio 1979). Our own argument is closer in spirit to that of Gracey (1975), who contends that the task of teachers in American kindergartens is to drill children in the role of student and, by extension, to prepare them for the rigid routines of bureaucratic, corporate society. Still, work on any kind of ceremonialism in kindergartens is minimal (Heffernan and Todd 1960; Moore 1959); while there are only bare traces of such discussion on higher grades (Bernstein, Elvin, and Peters 1966; Burnett 1969, Fuchs 1969; Judith Kapferer 1981; Waller 1932; Weiss and Weiss 1976).[4]

We will take up a small number of cases from our larger corpus of descriptions of such events, for the following reasons.[5] The integrity of the event as a viable performance is violated if it is not described in and of itself. The celebration, at least in part, should become the context for its own interpretation. Moreover, detailed description enables you to form interpretations alternative to those we argue for. We hardly would insist that there are singular constructions of significance in such celebrations. It also is advantageous to have concrete examples available, perhaps as parameters of discourse for future discussion.

Nonetheless we focus on aspects of these events that are related to our argument of explicit and implicit levels of communication in versions of the interplay of collectivity and family. In particular we attend to the sequencing of enactments. Sequencing may be of signal import in cultures that, according to Lee (1959), are made coherent to their members through lineal codifications of reality. Often in public events those acts placed, for example, 'before' and 'after' implicate the logic of design of the entire sequence of enactment. In occasions of presentation, sequencing is crucial to the emergence of coherent story-lines. In those of re-presentation, sequencing signals which version of reality will supplant another, to emerge climactic or dominant. We attend also to the prominence of symbolic formations in these enactments. These formations will be related to the three categories of person— teacher, child, and parent—whose positioning in relation to one another implicates the rudimentary praxis of collectivity and family that is enacted in the kindergarten. . . .

KINDERGARTEN CELEBRATIONS

The events to be discussed are representative of the range of holidays celebrated in Jewish Israeli kindergartens. Given the paucity of information available on such celebrations, we prefer to inform you with a sense of the variation among these occasions, rather than to limit our focus to one or two categories of holiday.[6] The first two of our cases, Ḥannuka and Purim, are traditional holidays, but not Days of Rest in the liturgical calendar. Both commemorate ancient victories: Ḥannuka of the Maccabees and of the rededication of the Temple in Jerusalem, and Purim the saving of the Jews of Shushan, in Persia, through the influence of Queen Esther. In varying degrees both are celebrated in home and synagogue, and Purim also in the street. Our analysis of a Ḥannuka celebration demonstrates the re-presentation of hierarchy, such that the family is shown to be enveloped by the collectivity. The case of Purim we discuss brings out an implicit premise that the maturation of children moves them from a condition closer to nature to one of civilization, and so towards their assumption of citizenship in the future. . . . The [third] case Jerusalem Day, is a secular state commemoration of the reunification of Jerusalem following the 1967 Six-Day War. Our analysis of this case points to the forging through symbolism of direct links between the collectivity and the child as citizen of the future, without the mediation of the family.

All of these cases offer implicit versions of hierarchical relationships between collectivity and family that should reverse the early-age experiences of the child. The re-presentations in these versions are hegemonic, sometimes approaching even that of encompassment. . . . We stress that youngsters experience dozens of such celebrations during their first few years of education. Explicit themes, contents, and forms vary within and among kinds of celebrations. But the kinds of implicit relationships between collectivity and family that emerge from our cases likely have a cachet of relevance that extends to numerous other kindergarten celebrations. It is the cumulative accretion of these experiences that has pervasive effects on the child.

All the celebrations described took place on the

kindergarten premises. The kindergarten is defined as 'the child's world', and the sole adult who has a legitimate place there is the teacher. Parents always are guests in the kindergarten. Nothing better exemplifies this attitude than the chairs in the kindergartens visited, where no more than one or two full-sized ones were found. As a rule the teacher sits on a full-sized chair, and at her feet as it were, the children on small chairs. When parents are invited, be it to a celebration, to a parent–teacher meeting or to their child's birthday party, they always are seated on the children's chairs. A parent in the kindergarten always occupies a child's place.

The children were given explanations in their respective kindergartens prior to a celebration with regard to the character of the holiday, its import for the people of Israel . . . , its dominant symbols, and some rudimentary historical background. More complicated enactments by the children were rehearsed beforehand. Unless otherwise specified, all the actions described were in accordance with the explicit instructions and orchestration of the teachers.

Ḥannuka: Hierarchy, Family, and Collectivity

Ḥannuka, the Festival of Lights, commemorates the victory of the Maccabees over the Seleucids, and their rededication of the Temple in 165 BCE. According to the *Talmud*, there was only enough undefiled oil for one day of lamp-lighting. Miraculously the oil multiplied into an amount sufficient for eight days. *Ḥannuka* is celebrated for eight consecutive days in the home, primarily by the lighting of an additional candle each day, in an eight-branched candelabrum, the *hannukia* (pl. *hannukiot*). An extra candle, the *shamash*, is used to kindle the others. *Ḥannuka* celebrates liberation from foreign domination: it is a triumph of faith, of the few over the many, the weak over the strong. In present-day Israel the martial spirit of this holiday casts reflections on the struggle of the Jewish people to create a unified national homeland.

Books of instruction for kindergarten teachers suggest that the major motif be heroism in Israel. The enactment should evoke the emotional experience of the occasion. The central signs of the celebration should be the *hannukia*, candles, tops,[7] and the national flag. The locale of the party should be filled with light, just as the shirts or blouses of the children should be white, to create an atmosphere of joyous luminosity. The best time is late afternoon or early evening: these hours evoke the uplifting illumination of the holiday from the midst of darkness and the depths of despair; and they connect the kindergarten to the home, where candles may be lit soon after. Scenarios suggest that a central *hannukia* be lit by an adult; that parents light small *hannukiot* made by their children; that the children form 'living *hannukiot*'; and that parents and children dance or play games together (Rabinowitz 1958). Certain of these motifs were incorporated into the example that follows.[8]

Description. The party began at 4.30 PM. Thirty-two children, aged four to five, and their mothers sat at tables placed along three walls of the room. Only a few fathers attended. A name-card marked the place of each child. White tablecloths covered the tables. At the centre of each were a vase of flowers, bags of candies, and candles equal to the number of children at that table. Before each child stood a little *hannukia* made by that youngster. On the walls and windows were hung painted paper *hannukiot*, oil pitchers, candles, and tops, all of which had been prepared in the kindergarten. Against the fourth wall stood a large *hannukia*, constructed of toy blocks covered with colored paper, that supported eight colored candles and the *shamash*.

An accordionist played melodies of the holiday. The teacher welcomed those present, and at a prearranged signal her helper extinguished the lights. Each mother lit a candle and aided her child to kindle his own little *hannukia*. The room lights were turned on. A father lit the large *hannukia* of toy blocks, and recited the requisite prayers. As he did so, the teacher instructed the children: 'Remember, when father says a blessing, you must sit quietly and listen to the blessing'. Holiday songs followed.

The teacher announced: 'Now we want to make a living *hannukia*. A living *hannukia* that walks and sings, a *hannukia* of parents and children'. She arranged the mothers and their children in a straight line, so that each child stood in front of his mother. An additional mother-child pair, the *shamash*, stood some feet to the side. Each mother held a candle, and each youngster a blue or white ribbon. Each child gave one end of his ribbon to the child-*shamash*. In this formation all children were attached to the *shamash* by their ribbons, and each mother to her own child. The mother of the *shamash* lit the candles held by the others. The lights were extinguished again, the room lit by the living *hannukia* in the gathering twilight. The accordionist played a melody of the holiday, 'We came to chase away the darkness', as each mother walked around her child. The lights were turned on. The mothers returned to their seats as a group, followed by their children.

The children and mothers of one table returned to the centre of the room and were told by the teacher: 'The children will be the spinning tops. Get down, children.' They fell to their knees, bent their heads, and curled their bodies forward. Each mother stood behind her child. The teacher narrated: 'The whole year the spinning tops were asleep in their box. From last year until this year, until now. And the children said to them, "Wake up, spinning tops. *Hannuka* has come. We want to play with you." ' To a background of holiday melodies the teacher moved from child to child, touching their hand. With each contact a child awakened, stood, raised his arms, and began to spin. Each mother spun her child, first clockwise, then counterclockwise. Next the mothers became the tops, spun by their children in one direction and then the other. The teacher instructed the second table: 'You'll also be the spinning tops. Each mother will spin her own child and when I give the signal, change roles. Alright? Let's start . . . The children are the spinning tops . . . the parents are the spinning tops'. Those at the third table followed.

Mothers and children held hands, formed an unbroken circle, and danced round and round the teacher. Only one father joined the circle. Singing and food followed. As 6 PM approached, the teacher gave the participants permission to leave, and the party broke up.

Discussion. This event is composed of three major segments, the overt symbolism of which is explicit. The first focuses on the serious traditionalism of the holiday, primarily through the *hannukia*.

This segment brings out the connectivity between past and present. The second works through the make-believe of the spinning top, and evokes the relationship between present and future.

The initial segment proceeds through a series of candle lightings: mother helps her child to kindle the small *hannukia*, father lights the large *hannukia*, and candles are lit on the living *hannukia*. These actions and others are embedded in the melodies and songs of the holiday that tell of heroism, victory, and the illumination of darkness. These themes weave together emotion and experience to carry the past into the present. The blue and white ribbons of the living *hannukia* are the official colors of the state, and of its flag and national emblem. In the living *hannukia* ancient triumph is fused with modern renaissance.

Here the idea of family is central. The enactment replicates symbolic acts—the kindling of candles and prayers—that should take place within the home, and that delineate familial roles and an elementary division of labor. Thus it is apt for mother to help her small child, in this instance to light the *hannukia*. Moreover it is appropriate for father, the male head of household, to recite the accompanying prayers on behalf of the family. Here one father does this on behalf of the assembly. The symbolism of this enactment then re-presents and transcends the level of the family. The 'living *hannukia*' envelops all the mothers and children, while respecting the singularity of individual families, shown here by the dyads of mother and child. Each mother stands behind her child, and walks around and envelops the latter, delineating the family unit. This living *hannukia* is a collective sign that also is emblematic of collectivity; while this collectivity itself is constituted of smaller family units.

The living *hannukia* projects into the present the presence of past heroism and dedication. This is done through the living bodies of mothers and children, who themselves compose the shape and substance of this central symbol. Thus the collectivity is re-presented as living through family units, just as the latter live within and through the former. Each is made to be seen as integral to the other. However the connotation is that the collectivity is of a higher order than the individual family, since here it subsumes the latter.

In contrast to the seriousness of the first segment,

the second is a playful re-presentation. Its motif is the top, a child's holiday toy that itself is inscribed with Hebrew letters that denote the miraculous. But in this segment commemoration and tradition are not marked. Instead the make-believe is evoked, slumber is shattered, and the participants act joyously in the holiday mood. Again the focus is that of the family unit, represented by dyads of mother and child. The hierarchy at the close of the first segment is kept. The teacher activates each child, and the latter performs under the direction of mother.

But in this make-believe segment, mother and child switch roles: the former becomes the sleeping top that is awakened and directed by her child. Unlike the inscription of tradition in the first segment, the playful is full of potential, as is the youngster who eventually will exchange the role of child for that of adult. As a mature adult the child will become a parent, bringing into being and controlling children of his own. This segment projects the child, as parent-to-be, towards a future in which he will replace his parents and will replicate their roles and tasks. Through the two segments past and future are joined together with a sense of the movement of generations. Whereas the first segment recreates family and collectivity in the images of tradition, the second segment shows the transitoriness of particular parents and the direction of succession. For the child the experience may evoke some feeling that his own parents are not timeless monoliths that will structure his world indefinitely.

The third segment opens with an unbroken circle dance of mothers and children who revolve around the axis of the teacher.[9] This formation is again a re-presentation of the relationship between family and collectivity. The circle dance blurs the distinctiveness of particular families and, within these, of parents and children, adults and youngsters. The delineation of family units has disappeared. Instead all are closer to being discrete and egalitarian individuals who themselves are part of a greater and embracing collectivity. This formation connotes the connectivity of present and future citizens, orientated towards an axial centre.

In this and other kindergarten celebrations the teacher is sole arbiter and ultimate authority. Children see her control parental figures before their very eyes. We argue that the teacher is a statist fig-ure, perhaps the earliest concretization of authority outside the home that very young children encounter. In these celebrations she is not an alternative source of authority to that of parents, as she may be perceived by children in the daily life of the kindergarten. Instead she is the pinnacle of hierarchy that supersedes and that subsumes the family. Thus the whole enactment is framed by the architectonics of hierarchy that are external to, but that act upon, the family unit. All actions of such celebrations, regardless of their explicit content, are imbued with this quality of hierarchy.

The implicit messages of this *Hannuka* celebration are of hierarchy from a more statist perspective. The first segment constructs a version of the superordination of roles within the family, and then embeds the latter within a version of collectivity. The second deconstructs the centrality of family status and alters hierarchical relationships among family members. The third emphasizes equality among citizens, all of whom are orientated towards the statist figure of the teacher. In other words, through these re-presentations the family is shown to be made over into a society of citizenry.

In the first segment the child is dependent upon and subordinate to his mother in order to light the little *hannukia*. In turn, both are dependent upon the figure of the father in order to light the large *hannukia* and to recite prayers on behalf of the whole family. This series is an accurate rendition of the comparative status of elementary roles within the family. Family units then are made to constitute a formation that is emblematic of the collectivity, the living *hannukia*. The collectivity is seen to exist as a coordinated assemblage of families. Here individual families are dependent upon and subordinate to the collectivity in order to relate to one another, and in order to create an alive and enduring vision of tradition and belief. The first segment builds up the sign of the *hannukia* in increasing degrees of envelopment and hierarchy. The apex is the living of this collective emblem. Integral to this are the ribbons, in the national colors, held by the children. Thus the *hannukia* itself is imbued with the symbolism of statehood; while implicit in this more traditional emblem is a modern version.

The second segment begins with a rendition of hierarchical family roles. The dyad of mother and child outlines the coherence of the family unit. The mother directs the movements of the spinning top, her child, in an accurate depiction of status and authority in relation to her offspring. But their switching of roles is at one and the same time a re-presentation of independence and equality. The autonomy of children, and their founding of families, is expected to be an outcome of maturation.[10] Through this process children partially are freed of their subordination to their family of procreation, and thereby are inculcated in their obligations of citizenship to the nation-state. As citizens, all Israelis are the theoretical equals of one another and are subordinate to the state without the intervening mediation of the family. In the third segment, the circle dance, there is no characterization of the family unit: the unbroken circle evokes egalitarianism and common effort, and all the dancers are orientated towards their common centre. There, orchestrating their actions, stands the teacher, just as the state is positioned in relation to its citizens.

Like the *ḥannukia* alive, the circle dance is a living, collective formation. But each is in structural opposition to the other. The *ḥannukia* depends on the family and on its internal hierarchy for its own existence. The circle dance eliminates the specificity of the family unit and simultaneously relates each participant in equality to all others and to a statist apex of hierarchy that is not representative of family. In the sequencing of this celebration the unbroken circle with its apical centre supplants the cellular *ḥannukia*; just as, for children, with time the state will supersede their parents as the pinnacle of authority.

Purim: The Evolution of Maturity

Purim commemorates the delivery of the Jews of Shushan from the evil designs of their enemies through the persuasions of Esther, the Jewish queen of the Persian monarch. This story is read in the synagogue; and the holiday is celebrated by a festive family meal, and by the exchange of gifts of food among relatives and friends. An especially joyous holiday, it is virtually the only time in the liturgical calendar when some license in dress and behavior is encouraged. Secular celebrations take the form of dressing up in costume and attending parties.

Instruction books designate the holiday as an entertainment, with children in costume and parents in attendance. Little mention is made of the traditional import of the holiday, and scenarios for its celebration rarely are given. The explicit enactment of the example we discuss was intended to entertain and to amuse the youngsters and their mothers. But within this is a degree of implicit patterning that connotes the role of the kindergarten in the maturation of children. Of this the teacher denied any conscious knowledge.

Description.   This celebration was held for three-year-olds. Some two weeks before, the teacher requested that the children be dressed in animal costumes. Her reason was that such figures were closest to the world of the child, and therefore more comprehensible to the youngsters. If this were not possible, then the child should be dressed as a clown. A few days prior to the party each mother informed the teacher of the costume her child would wear, to enable the teacher to prepare her program.

The party took place in the late afternoon, at the onset of the holiday. Mothers and children were arranged in a wide semi-circle, facing an open area in which the teacher stood. Mothers sat on the tiny kindergarten chairs, their offspring on the floor before them. Music of the holiday played in the background.

The celebration consisted of two segments, separated by an intermediate segment of an unbroken circle dance. In the first the children exhibited their costumes before the assembly in a set order of appearance. In the second, five mothers in clown costumes performed a rehearsed dance and song. The teacher, dressed as a clown, organized the showing of costumes through a simple narrative. Many years ago, she declaimed, there was a king, and she called out a boy dressed as a king. He was joined by a girl dressed as a queen. In their court, continued the teacher, there was a zoo full of animals. She called forth the inhabitants of the zoo. As each kind of character came forth a song that described its typical movements or activities was sung.

The following was the order of appearance. Five cats walked on all fours and meowed. Then three rabbits hopped out. A bear lumbered forth fiercely and was introduced as a 'teddy bear'. Three dainty dolls stepped out and were described as living in cardboard boxes. All of these dwelled in the royal zoo. The teacher told a soldier, a policeman, and a cowboy to come forward, introduced them as the 'royal guard', and marched with them around the semi-circle. This ended the narrative of the zoo within the royal court. The remaining children, all dressed as clowns, were called forth. After this, all the mothers and children formed an unbroken circle, with the teacher at its centre, and danced to the melody of a song about a little clown.

The teacher announced that the performance of the children had ended. She requested the performing mothers to sing. Each of their costumes was of a single color, and their song described the activities of clowns dressed in each of these colors. They sang in a line, with the teacher at their head. Food followed, and the party concluded.

Discussion. Unlike the *Ḥannuka* celebration, that of *Purim* was not thought to have any coherent scenario or explicit meaning. The declared intention was to have fun and to enable the youngsters to play make-believe characters. The teacher had hoped that all these characters would be animals. Faced with a mixed bag of costuming, she used a simple narrative to order their appearance. On a more implicit level this ordering is of direct relevance to our contention that kindergarten celebrations, in various ways, are engaged in the re-presentation of rudimentary socialization, in the direction of adulthood and citizenship.

The teacher recasts the kindergarten as the court of a king and queen. This role play is in keeping with the story of *Purim*, of Queen Esther and her Persian monarch. But there are no further connotations of the text of the holiday. Nonetheless, monarchy and court are emblematic of hierarchy, of moral order, and of social control. These are symbols of maturity and of statehood that exist above and beyond those of home and family. A zoo is situated within the court and is filled with characters. In Israel, zoos are institutions where wild animals, instinctive and unconstrained in their nature, are locked in cages, artifacts of civilization that place external restraints on these creatures. This is a popular view of the zoo. In the teacher's perception small children are close to the world of animals, driven by

their instincts and governed neither by obligations of maturity nor by norms of civilization. In the enactment children-as-animals are placed in a zoo, itself within a court. Through these metaphors the kindergarten is made over into a locale of moral order with connotations of ultimate authority and so of statehood, and into a place of confinement for those who have yet to learn internal restraint. Is it fortuitous in this instance that the kindergarten, called in Hebrew a 'garden of children' (*gan yeladim*), is turned into a zoo, called in Hebrew a 'garden of animals' (*gan ḥayot*)?

The order of appearance of the inhabitants of the zoo intimates strongly that the more 'natural' state of the youngsters is conditional. Their sequencing projects a developmental image of enculturation, of progressing towards maturity within metaphors of hierarchy and control. The first animal to appear is the cat. Although some cats in Israel are pets, its cities are pervaded by a profusion of undomesticated alley cats, fierce, and wary of humans. Even the pet cat is seen as a comparatively independent and autonomous creature. In her narrative the teacher describes the children-as-cats as 'looking for friends'. That is, these make-believe cats desire to establish relationships, connoting their potential domestication through sociability.

The next is the rabbit. In Israel this creature usually exists in the wild, and sometimes as a pet. In either instance it is thought of as timid, passive, and docile—a vegetarian in contrast to the predatory cat. Although wild, the rabbit is more easily caged and more controllable than the cat. The rabbit is followed by a child dressed as a bear. Although the child plays the gruff bear with gusto, the teacher turns this wild and fierce creature into a 'teddy bear'. Unlike cat and rabbit, the teddy-bear is a child's plaything. A toy, it is the human product of its natural counterpart—that is, a copy. Its animalism is man-made. A product of culture, it is a fully controlled and domesticated creation, in contrast to cat and rabbit. Still, the teddy-bear retains its animal form.

The doll appears next. Again this is a child's plaything and is man-made. Yet unlike the teddy-bear it is created in a human image, and its attributes of behavior are largely those of a person. According to the narrative the doll lives in a cardboard box, its own enclosure that is somewhat more akin to a home than is a cage. Where the teddy-bear is a play upon nature, the doll is a reflection of humanity and civilization. Of all these zoo creatures the doll is the most domesticated and restrained. These controls are inherent in and emerge from its human form and its attributes of culture. They are not a shell of strictures imposed from without, as in the case of cat and rabbit, nor an intermediate being, a domesticated animal, like the teddy-bear.

Left with a soldier, a policeman, and a cowboy, the teacher makes of them a 'royal guard'. These are not inhabitants of the zoo, but stand outside it. They close and complete the framework of social control introduced by the royal figures. Like the latter the royal guards are fully human figures whose roles embody a regimentation of maturity and order. They are guardians of moral codes against the predations of more impulsive, natural beings. These associations are reinforced as the teacher takes these guardians by the arm and they march together. As she had not done with those within the zoo, the teacher identifies herself with children who, by taking on roles of control and order, play themselves as they should become in the future—as mature adults.

Wittingly or not, the teacher has created a small drama about the evolution and the enculturation of humanity and hierarchy that leads to maturity and the assumption of responsibility beyond that of the familial. Framed at the outset and at the close by human figures with statist and hierarchical connotations, the characters of the zoo are transposed from the wild to the tame, from creatures of instinct to artifacts of culture. Just as their mothers watch this encoding from the periphery, so these youngsters see their mothers watching this happen to them.

The figure of the clown was intended by the teacher as a fallback costume for the children. Clowns were not included within court and zoo, but were shown afterward. These residual figures have no logical connection to prior actions in the sequence. The clowns are simply unabashed figures of fun, in keeping with the good humor of this holiday. But these figures also are depictions of immaturity, for their costumes lack the distinctiveness of gender differences. These child-clowns contrast with the adult clowns who perform a bit later on.

The appearance of the child-clowns is followed by a circle dance of all mothers and children. As noted, the connotations of this formation are of collectivity, egalitarianism, and joint effort. Here there is no delineation of the family unit, nor of the special bond between mother and child. The teacher reunites the children with persons who first and foremost are adults, rather than mothers, after these little people have been re-presented as trained and matured in an idiom of moral and social order. This process is validated in the second segment of the celebration. The teacher and clown-mothers perform. The figure of the clown appears here as the apex of authority and maturity, with the teacher at its pinnacle. In contrast to the clown-children, the clown-mothers and the teacher are big, adult clowns. They play consciously, with a freedom of action that accrues when self-discipline is more assured—when one is well-aware that one is not that which one plays at. But the similarity of costuming of the little clowns and the big ones puts them all on the same continuum of maturation. This then parallels and replicates, through another medium, the messages of maturation in the enactment of court and zoo. In the instance of the clowns the message is that maturation takes time but that the little ones are on the right track.

The entire enactment is an extended metaphor of a process of maturation that the child will undergo in order to turn into an adult member of a wider collectivity. The children are re-presented through court and zoo, in different stages of development. The egalitarian circle dance projects the enactment towards a future in which youngsters take their place of equality alongside their parents. Overlapping these activities, the clown-children blend easily into the figures of the clown-mothers and the clown-teacher, who here are at the apex of adulthood. . . .

Jerusalem Day: Statehood and Citizenship

Jerusalem Day was promulgated as a civil, state holiday to commemorate the reunification of the capital of Israel following the 1967 Six-Day War. It is celebrated primarily through official receptions and other functions, that presently include a festive, mass march around the perimeters of the city. The major thoroughfares are decorated with the national flag and with the banner of Jerusalem, a golden lion (the emblem of the ancient kingdom of Judea) rampant on a white field with blue borders. Jerusalem is the central place of the Jewish nation-state and, at present, of most varieties of Judaism, from those that are pillars of nationalism and its state religion to those who are ambivalent about, or who oppose, the existence of this state on religious grounds. From 1948 until 1967 the city was divided into western and eastern sectors, the former within Israel, the latter controlled by Jordan. Within the eastern sector is Mount Moriah, the Temple Mount, site of the first temple built by Solomon, and of the second, destroyed by the Romans in 70 C.E. This defeat is reckoned as the customary onset of the Diaspora, the widespread dispersion of the Jews into exile from ancient Israel. The only parts of this temple complex to survive are remnants of its outermost ramparts.

A short section of the western rampart is called the Wailing Wall, known in Israel as the Western Wall. Previously a place of popular worship, since 1967 the Wall also has been made the most dominant symbol of the state and of its organized religion. The Wall has become evocative of a nation whose florescence as a state awaited the return of its people, of a continuity that is perceived to have endured throughout the absence of Jewish sovereignty for close to 2,000 years. As does no other single physical presence in present-day Israel, it is perceived to condense the glory and then the desuetude of the past and the national redemption of the present. We raise these points because much of the symbolism of this kindergarten celebration is focused on this motif, in the context of Israeli state occasions.

Description. Three classes of three-, four-, and five-year-olds, totalling some sixty youngsters from the same kindergarten, participated on the morning of Jerusalem Day. Parents were not invited. The open courtyard of the kindergarten was decorated with national flags and with cutouts of the lion of Jerusalem. As requested, most of the youngsters were dressed in blue and white clothing. Each was given a lapel pin that depicted the lion. Each class was seated along one side of the courtyard, the teacher in the centre and an accordionist nearby.

The occasion opened with songs whose respective themes were: the ancient kingdom of Israel, rejoicing in Jerusalem, and the rebuilding of the temple. In a brief peroration the teacher declared that Jerusalem was the eternal capital of Israel; that this Day marked the liberation of East Jerusalem and the reunification of the city by the Israel Defence Forces; and that this Day was celebrated throughout the land.

Four five-year-olds recited a lengthy poem that told of two doves who dreamt of the arisal of the people of Israel. The doves flew to Jerusalem and alighted on the Wall. The closing lines stated: 'The children of Israel are singing a song; next year the city will be rebuilt.' The assembly then sang of the ancient longing of the Jewish people to return to Jerusalem. As this melody continued, six of the four-year-olds danced, each holding blue and white ribbons. During the dance each child gave the ends of his ribbon to two others. As their performance ended the children were joined by the ribbons in the form of a six-pointed Shield of David (the *magen david*, commonly translated as the Star of David), the central motif on the national flag.

The teacher told a story taken from a booklet of legends about Jerusalem. The narrative spoke of a lonely wall, dark with age, and laden with the memories of the great temple and of the free nation that dwelled here. Enemies burned the temple and drove out the Jews. Although they tried to destroy the wall, their tools broke. But the gentiles used the wall as a rubbish heap in order to obviate its presence. For centuries in their hatred of the Jews they dumped garbage about the wall, until it disappeared from sight.

One day a diaspora Jew came to see the wall at a time when gentiles ruled the land. All denied its existence. He found a great mound of rubbish and there learned of the custom of obliterating the Jewish wall. He swore to save it. A rumor spread that precious metals were buried there. The populace swarmed to sift through the garbage, found some coins of value, and uncovered the top stones. The next morning another rumor spread that treasure was buried at the base of the mound. People excavated the rubbish and gradually the whole of the wall was revealed. No treasure was found except for that of the Jew—the Wall itself. The Wall still was filthy, but clouds gathered and rains poured, cleansing and purifying the Wall. And the Jew gave thanks for this salvation.

Dancing and carrying toy blocks, the three-year-olds built a wall of roughly their own height. All the other youngsters formed a circle, held hands, and revolved singing and dancing around this edifice.

Discussion. Unlike the previous [two] celebrations, in this one no reference is made to the family. The relationship between nation-state and citizen is direct, immediate, and hierarchical. Here the family not only is superseded but is rendered irrelevant to the nation-state. The nation is depicted as the redeemer of the state, and the state as the protector of the nation. Both depend on the faith and loyalty of the citizenry.[11]

The courtyard is decorated in emblems of statehood, and acquires the semblance of an official locale. The dress of the youngsters is standardized through colors that shape these children into living emblems of the state. Their bodies are inscribed with signs of citizenship, of membership in the collectivity. Each child appears as a small part that embodies the greater whole, itself composed of many such parts. The ideal relationship between citizen and collectivity is one of synecdoche. This relationship is not manipulated during the occasion, but is re-presented in various ways.

The event consists of a preamble of song and speech, followed by formal enactments. The preamble enunciates themes and sentiments that are repeated and elaborated through performance. The opening songs connect past, present, and future. The words of each have references in common to verities that are held eternal. The first tells of King David, who made Jerusalem the capital of ancient Israel. The second rejoices in Jerusalem eternal. The third relates that the Temple, a metaphor of the nation in its reborn homeland, will be rebuilt. The words of the teacher situate these sentiments within constructions of reality in present-day Israel. The assembly celebrates the reunification of the eternal capital of this nation-state, accomplished by citizens in the people's army, in which these youngsters will serve on their completion of high school. Collectivity and citizenship are made interdependent.

The enactments begin with a poem that evokes prophecy. The doves dream that the renewed people of Israel will rebuild the city around the central focus of the eternal Wall. In Israel the dove is an emblem of peace that harks back to the biblical story of Noah's Ark and the dove that returned with an olive branch, signing an end to God's wrath. The next song expresses the longing of the people to return and carry out this endeavor. The sense of prophecy is mated with feelings of deepest desire.

In turn, prophecy and desire are realized as six youngsters shape a living Shield of David. This is a complex, multivocalic motif used by the Zionist movement to encode rejuvenation and attachment to a national homeland (see Scholem 1971). We note again that it is a preeminent emblem of the State. Thus children who first sat in a loose assemblage create the precise, coordinated pattern of this emblem. As in other symbolic formations, just as they bring the emblem into being through their collective efforts, so its shape ties them to one another and incorporates them within a greater, enveloping design. The aesthetic and emotive effect is one of a symmetrical blending of part and whole, of the blue and white coloration of dress and of connecting ribbons. The implication is that the citizens of the future will continue together to carry through the design of this emblem, one that connotes the actualization of the collectivity.

The primary message of the narrative of the rediscovery of the Wall is that the Jews must defend their patrimony, otherwise they will lose this. The tale is an allegory: the world of Israel, of the Wall, must be demarcated clearly from that of non-Jews who threaten its integrity and viability. This also is the logic of the modern, precisely demarcated nation-state, one that resonates strongly with aspects of the historical Jewish experience. In terms of nationhood or peoplehood, one either is a Jew or one is not. In terms of statehood, one either is a citizen or one is not. In the ideology of the nation-state these axes of inclusion-exclusion become almost isomorphic. The outer boundaries of the permissible are set by the collectivity, to which the desires of the citizen are subordinate. This is perhaps the highest level of contrast between 'inside' and 'outside' that is set for the Jewish citizen of modern Israel. Moreover it is a lesson that youngsters will have reason to learn in numerous contexts beyond that of the family in years to come. At this level of contrast the hierarchy, values, and relationships of the family always are of lesser relevance.

The tale posits a series of contrasts between Jew and gentile that derive from a simple postulate: that the Wall, and by analogy the nation and state, are indestructible despite all the depredations of enemies. This is its internal and eternal truth. By comparison all else is transitory. The Jew who returns to his source, across the gap of generations, is motivated by ideology. His is the wisdom of spirituality. The gentiles who try to destroy his roots are driven by materialism. He uses their cupidity to reveal his truth. In the context of the celebration the qualities of Wall and Jew are those of the nation-state and its citizenry. The attributes of the gentiles are associated with all those who would deny to the Jews their homeland. The tale is at once a metaphor of renewal and a parable on boundaries of national salvation that in the present-day world the state views itself as best able to uphold.

The closing enactment brings the message of the story into 'existence through the cooperative efforts of the children, just as the living Shield realized the prophecy of the doves. The youngsters build the Wall from the ground up, just as modern Israel is redeemed through the joint efforts of its citizenry. The simulated labors of the children show that which will be expected of them upon adulthood. The children dance in an unbroken circle around the completed Wall. Again their formation evokes egalitarianism, connectivity, synchronization, and perhaps the outer boundary of statehood that must be protected by its citizenry. Once more the centre of the circle is filled, here by the edifice of the Wall—an emblem that is hierarchical, authoritative, and nationalistic.

CONCLUSIONS

In the world of the little child the kindergarten celebration is among the few categories of occasion when the order of things that structures the wider social world directly intersects with and dominates that of the home. This is evident through explicit symbolism. But more profound in their impact are the architectonics of enactment. Their influence derives from the very ways in which persons in unison are mobilized and synchronized in social formations in order to do the more explicit scenarios of celebration. The lineal progressions of such formations constitute their own implicit sets of messages, and it is these that we have addressed.

These celebrations, and numerous others like them, make extensive and intensive use of living formations. Some of these forms are shaped explicitly, like the *ḥannukia* and the Shield of David. Others, like the unbroken circle and the dyad, stay more implicit. In either instance these are powerful media. Through them the meaning of things is turned into the shape of things. The shape of things is graspable through the senses, as is the case of icon and emblem. Yet in the latter instances these shapes still are largely external to the human body, to the source of emotions and feelings. But the shape of things in living formations is grasped by living through them. This is a more sensual experience, one that engages the senses more fully to create a holistic experiential environment. Architects and others sometimes refer to haptic space, of coming to know the shape of space and the feelings this engenders through the sense of touch. Through living formations the visual, the auditory, the tactile, and perhaps the olfactory senses are all 'touched' by the shape of things. The meaning of form and the form of meaning become inextricable.

Re-presentation through the sequencing of formations, in keeping with premises of linearity, are at the experiential heart of the kinds of enactments we have addressed. As noted, they are intended to touch the heart of the little child, and so to impress upon his being lessons that otherwise may remain more exterior to his sense of self. In particular we have stressed themes that will be adumbrated for the child in numerous ways and contexts in the years to come: for example, the relationship between hierarchy and equality. The interior hierarchy of the family is supplanted by and is subsumed within the collectivity. The collectivity, the nation-state, is superior to each of its citizens; yet they compose it, and it exists only through their cooperative efforts. As citizens they in principle are the equals of one another. So too as children grow, they will succeed and replace their parents, as heads of family and as citizens. These processes depend on the proper outcome of that of maturation. Here the kindergarten sees its role to infuse the child with internal restraint and with feelings of responsibility towards the collectivity and its parts. In turn, all of the above seems to evoke elementary patterns of social boundedness, and of the categories and entities that these demarcate and define. Thus boundaries between people, as members of categories and as persons, between family and collectivity, and between the nation-state and whatever lies without, are re-presented and constructed anew.

This kind of re-presentation is a way of projecting desired and expected futures of linear, irreversible development. In this it has some superficial similarity to modelling. But obviously these futures are not actualized in the course of kindergarten celebrations. The logic of these occasions is otherwise; and so they contain no rules of, nor procedures for, transformation. But in additive fashion these occasions do help to remake the biographies (and retrospectively, perhaps the autobiographies) of little children, during a time when these personalized narratives of self are embryonic. And this from another perspective of power—that of the nation-state.

The messages outlined above are essential to the production of moral order, and to the reproduction of social order in terms of this. In kindergarten celebrations they are communicated in ways easy to grasp for the little child. Youngsters are full of feeling, but they have yet to develop the critical attitudes that buffer personal choice against the demands of group pressure and the inducements of collective sentiments. Enculturation through celebration, as instruction books for kindergartens note, is first and foremost an appeal to the emotions of little children. Moods and feelings about centricity, control, collectivity, and cooperation are communicated early on to these Israeli youngsters. These sentiments were crucial to the periods of the *yishuv* and the early state, years of self-defense for survival and growth. Still we should inquire whether the emphasis today on these and related values survives primarily as an ideological tool, and through the inability of the apparatus of education and polity to check the viability of its own involution. The quality of life of this nation-state may depend as much on the teaching of critical perspectives and personal choice as it does on values that continue to close the collective circle.

NOTES

1. In both the pre-state and state periods there is no especial distinction between nursery school and kindergarten. Youngsters may be in kindergarten by age two, and at age six continue on to elementary school.

2. The Hebrew word for kindergarten teacher, in the feminine gender, is *gannenet*. Its meaning is literally that of 'gardener'. As in English, the connotations of the terms are those of one who is an active agent in the processes of growing, of cultivating, and of taming. The word likely is a translation of the German, *kindergärtnerin*, a gardener of children, and is distinguished clearly in Hebrew from 'educator' (fem. *m' hane het*) and 'teacher' (fem. *mora*). The Hebrew term for kindergarten, *gan yeladim*, again is a translation from the German.

3. Our usage is analogous to that of 'hidden curriculum' (Gearing and Tindall 1973: 103), although we stress more the contested relationship between parents and state that is implicit in the maturation of youngsters, from offspring to citizens. In a similar vein, the at times conflicted relationships between 'nation' and 'state' in the hyphenated nation-state (Handelman 1986) are not made explicit in such scenarios.

4. These comments hold as well for social science in Israel. The major exceptions are the studies of kindergarten birthday parties by Doleve-Gandelman (1987) and by Shalva Weil (1986). These events emphasize more the development of the child as a certain kind of social person. The cases in this [essay] relate more to the implicit figuration of a statist view of moral and social order. Therefore birthday parties are excluded from our discussion.

5. Descriptions of daily life and of celebrations in kindergartens were collected during the course of a seminar conducted by Lea Shamgar-Handelman at The Hebrew University. The ethnographers were supervisors employed by the Ministry of Education. They observed kindergartens that they themselves supervised, and so with which they were conversant. Their observations and responses, and those of the teachers they reported on, convinced us that the distinction between explicit and implicit agendas of celebrations was a valid one. These educators consistently understood such events in terms of the obvious occasions that were celebrated; and in terms of that which they perceived as the cooperation between teacher and parent in the establishment of a consensus on the education of the child. They did not acknowledge that the form and substance of celebratory enactments in the kindergarten implicitly conveyed a statist perspective. However they did agree that the task of the teacher was to educate not only the child but also the parents.

   All the kindergartens observed belonged to the secular stream of state education in Israel. All their classes consisted of both boys and girls; although for the sake of convenience we use the masculine gender to refer to the child in categorical terms. These kindergartens operated six days a week, four to five hours a day.

6. We do not discuss an example of holy days, the Days of Rest, like Passover and the weekly Welcome of the Sabbath (*kabbalat shabbat*). These occasions are celebrated primarily within the family. In the kindergarten they are done as rehearsals for family celebrations rather than as enactments in their own right. Their performance in earnest is permitted

only in accordance with the liturgical calendar, and associated texts of sacred standing.

7. On each of the four sides of the *Ḥannuka* top is inscribed the first letter of each of the Hebrew words, '*Ness Gadol Haya Po*' (There was a great miracle here). Spinning the top is a popular children's game. Regardless of which side remains uppermost when the top topples, its letter signifies the integrity and unity of the whole message, as does the top in its circular spinning.

8. The *hannukia* is distinguished from the *menora* (the seven-branched candelabrum) that appears as the official emblem of the State of Israel, that once stood in the Temple, and that was relit for eight days following the victory of the Maccabees. Hence the eight branches of the *hannukia*.

9. The circle dance became popular during the period of the *yishuv*, as a form through which to show the egalitarianism and dynamism of enduring bonds between persons who,

through their collective efforts, forged the embracing collectivity of which they were a part.

10. This switching is a variety of inversion, but one that differs in a major respect from those [in which the] intentionality is synchronic. Ideologically [the] reversion [of the latter] is final, and therefore timeless. There ideology and devices of enactment are homologous. However the inversion of this example, although clearly followed by reversion, projects a future condition that will come to fruition in all legitimacy. Therefore the intentionality of this kind of inversion is diachronic. Paralleling this, there is some contradiction between ideology and this device of enactment.

11. Other such celebrations involved the family in the scenario. Fathers reminisced about their experiences as soldiers fighting for Jerusalem; or parents told of life in Jerusalem under siege during the War of Independence. In these instances the stress was on the obligation, transferred from parents to children, to serve the country under any circumstances.

BIBLIOGRAPHY

Allen, Ann Taylor. 1986. Gardens of Children, gardens of God: kindergartens and day-care centers in nineteenth-century Germany. *Journal of Social History*, 19:433–50.

Bernstein, Basil, H. L. Elvin and R. S. Peters. 1966. *Ritual in education*. Philosophical Transactions of the Royal Society of London, Series B, no. 772, 251:429–36.

Burnett, J. H. 1969. Ceremony, rites and economy in the student system of an American high school. *Human Organization*, 28:1–10.

Doleve-Gandelman, Tsili. 1987. The symbolic inscription of Zionist ideology in the space of Eretz Yisrael: why the native Israeli is called tsabar. In *Judaism Viewed From Within and From Without: Anthropological Studies*, ed. H. E. Goldberg, pp. 257–84. Albany, SUNY Press.

Durkheim, Emile. 1956. *Sociology and Education*. Glencoe, The Free Press.

Fayence-Glick, S. 1948. Ḥannuka in the kindergarten. *Oshiot*, 2:28–39 (in Hebrew).

———1957. Kindergartens in Eretz Yisrael. In *The Book of the Fiftieth Anniversary of the Teachers' Union*, pp. 132–44. Tel-Aviv, Histadrut Hamorim b'Eretz Yisrael (in Hebrew).

Fuchs, E. 1969. *Teachers Talk*. New York, Doubleday.

Gearing, F. O. and B. A. Tindall. 1973. Anthropological studies of the educational process. *Annual Review of Anthropology*, 2:95–105.

Gracey, Harry L. 1975. Learning the student role: kindergarten as academic boot camp. In *Lifestyles* (2nd ed.), ed. S. D. Feldman and G. W. Thielbor, pp. 437–42. Boston, Little, Brown.

Handelman, Don. 1978. Bureaucratic interpretation: the perception of child abuse in urban Newfoundland. In *Bureaucracy and World View: Studies in the Logic of Official Interpretation*, by D. Handelman and E. Leyton, pp. 15–69. St. John's, Institute of Social and Economic Research, Memorial University of Newfoundland.

——— 1986. Comments on state and religion in Israel. Annual

Meeting of the American Anthropological Association, Philadelphia, December 3–7.

Heffernan, Helen and Vivian E. Todd. 1960. *The Kindergarten Teacher*. Boston, D. C. Heath.

Jones, N. Blurton. 1969. An ethological study of some aspects of social behavior of children in nursery school. In *Primate Ethology*, ed. D. Morris, pp. 437–63. New York, Doubleday.

Kapferer, Judith L. 1981. Socialization and the symbolic order of the school. *Anthropology and Education Quarterly*, 12:258–74.

Lee, Dorothy. 1959. *Freedom and Culture*. Englewood Cliffs, N.J., Prentice-Hall.

Moore, Elenora Haegele. 1959. *Fives at School*. New York, Putnam's.

Rabinowitz, Esther, ed. 1958. *Holidays and Times in Education*. Tel-Aviv, Urim (in Hebrew).

Scholem, Gershom. 1971. The Star of David: history of a symbol. In *The Messianic Idea in Judaism*, pp. 257–81. New York, Schocken.

Shamgar-Handelman, Lea. 1981. Administering to war widows in Israel: the birth of a social category. *Social Analysis*, 9:24–47.

Shulz, Jeffrey and Susan Florio. 1979. Stop and freeze: social and physical space in a kindergarten/first grade classroom. *Anthropology and Education Quarterly*, 10:166–81.

Shure, M. 1963. Psychological ecology of a nursery school. *Child Development*, 34:979–92.

Waller, Willard. 1932. *The Sociology of Teaching*. New York, Wiley.

Weil, Shalva. 1986. The language and ritual of socialisation: birthday parties in a kindergarten context. *Man* (N.S.), 21:329–41.

Weiss, M. S. and P. H. Weiss. 1976. A public school ritual ceremony. *Journal of Research and Development in Education*, 9:22–28.

"Ritual" in Recent Literary Criticism:
The Elusive Sense of Community

RICHARD F. HARDIN

Facts of publication: *Hardin, Richard F. 1983. " 'Ritual' in Recent Criticism: The Elusive Sense of Community," from* Publications of the Modern Language Association *98(5):846–862. Copyright © 1983 by the Modern Language Association of America. Reprinted with the permission of the Modern Language Association.*

Richard Hardin weighs the pros and cons of the notion of "ritual" in literary criticism. He implies some important questions: Is it helpful to consider every narrative with a death-and-resurrection motif a ritual? Does it make a difference if we regard a poem "as" as ritual rather than saying that it is a ritual? If a play is like an ancient rite, does that mean that it is derived from, or is a remnant of, that rite? Hardin summarizes the work of the Cambridge myth-and-ritual school, which was popular in the early part of this century, considers criticisms of this viewpoint, and then examines more recent attempts, particularly those inspired by Victor Turner and René Girard, to utilize the idea of ritual in interpreting literary works.

Readers wanting to consider some specific literary examples should consult the journal Religion and Literature, *currently published at the University of Notre Dame.*

About the author: Dates: *1937– , Los Angeles, CA, U.S.A.* **Education:** *B.A., St. Mary's University (Texas); M.A., University of Texas; Ph.D., University of Texas.* **Field(s):** *English; comparative literature.* **Career:** *Professor of English, 1976–present, University of Kansas.* **Publications:** *"Chapman and Webster on Matrimony: The Poets and the Reformation of Ritual."* Renaissance and Reformation *17 (1980): 65–73; with Bernard Accardi, and others,* Recent Studies in Myths and Literature, 1970–1990: An Annotated Bibliography *(Greenwood, 1991);* Civil Idolatry: Desacralizing and Monarchy in Spenser, Shakespeare, and Milton *(University of Delaware, 1992).* **Additional:** *Chair, University of Kansas Humanities Program, 1979–1982. "Although my focus is English Renaissance literature, I often teach courses relating myths to literature across periods. I am writing a book on the vogue of Daphnis and Chloe in literature."*

A reader of modern criticism learns to live with uncertainty when encountering some of the most ordinary terms. Words like "symbol," "rhythm," or "irony" require our patience, our openness to an unpredictable set of theoretical assumptions. Not many readers are so fastidious as to demand a new word for every shade of difference from an "accepted" meaning, and this is probably a healthy condition. "The abuse of an old word, if explained, may give less trouble than the invention of a new," writes C. S. Lewis (550). The mania for new phraseology has not always helped the social sciences, and there is no reason to think it would advance the understanding of literature. Still, explanations should be forthcoming when words undergo their necessary abuse. What, for example, does it mean to call a literary work a ritual? Some of the most reputable critics over the past decade have said that Milton's *Lycidas* is "a mourning ritual" (Wittreich 98), that Goethe's *Faust* "is an exceptionally clear instance of the work of art conceived as a socializing *rite de passage*" (Hartman, *Fate* 110), that Eliot's "Love Song of J. Alfred Prufrock" ends "with a ritual drama of rolling the universe toward an overwhelming question" (Feder 221), that a minor Jacobean play exemplifies the principle that "poetry is a ritual of resurrection and rebirth" (Cope 174). For the most part these statements are illuminating when read in the context of their arguments, so it would be churlish to accuse the authors of irresponsibility. "Ritual," however, has become a wonderfully unstable and intriguing word, owing, as I hope to show, to developments in our understanding of both ritual and literature. . . .

The use of "ritual" has quite properly been associated with myth criticism, but if we examine John B. Vickery's classic collection of essays in this field, *Myth and Literature*, we may find that as late as the 1960s myth critics held certain notions about ritual that are no longer tenable. Stanley Edgar Hyman's 1958 essay in that collection stands as the most confident assertion of these beliefs. A great student of Darwin's prose, Hyman seems to view literary theory as undergoing its own modest evolution within the larger progress of the human sciences, from E. B. Tylor's *Primitive Culture* to James G. Frazer's *Golden Bough* and the applications of Frazer by the so-called Cambridge school of criticism (Jane Harrison, Gilbert Murray, A. B. Cook, and F. M. Cornford). Since the 1960s virtually every "discovery" that Hyman attributes to this movement has been seriously challenged. Few people believe that all myth, including the bulk of Homer and "the whole body of Near East sacred literature" (51), originates in ritual. Few classical scholars would now say that "the ritual view has illuminated almost the whole of Greek culture" (56) or even that "the forms of Attic tragedy arise out of sacrificial rites of tauriform or aegiform Dionysos" (57). Although the ritual origins of drama in general are not so readily assumed as they were in Hyman's day, it remains true that, as Heinrich Dörrie observes, the specialist criticism of classicists "has not sufficiently prevailed in those areas in which more than one area of scholarship connect (ethnology, religious studies, psychology). In these fields it is still true that whatever pleases is allowed" (129, n. 13). The most influential developments of Frazer and the Cambridge school came, of course, not from Hyman but from Northrop Frye, whose elegant theories of myth, genre, mode, and archetype promoted a rich harvest of myth criticism in the 1960s. Still, Frye's assumptions are not all that different from Hyman's. At least one advance in myth criticism, and in our perceptions of "ritual" in literature, has come since Frye, in the theories of René Girard, whose ideas often resemble Frye's in their comprehensiveness, though they usually lead to conclusions diametrically opposed to his.

In this essay I propose that many critics . . . have still not come to terms with the meaning of "ritual," often because they base their assumptions on outdated notions about the origins of myth in ritual, about the connections between Greek or medieval drama and ritual, or about narrative as displaced ritual. It needs to be more generally known that these subjects have undergone serious reexamination . . . and that the very concept of ritual (or ceremony—I use the terms interchangeably, as indeed most scholars do) has received much scrutiny in the social sciences. . . . One particular theory, that of Victor Turner, has received wide acceptance, and I propose it as the most adequate for criticism today. Besides its clarity and precision, the theory has the advantage of recognizing the social foundations of ritual, a characteristic that critics have often overlooked. Rites cannot exist in an aesthetic or formalist vacuum; they require the context of community. We do not invent the great ceremonies of our culture but, rather, come to them as parts of a whole. Although rites may share their symbolic nature with art, they convey the sense of satisfaction peculiar to them alone in the intense experience of community that is their chief reason for being. The first two sections of the essay summarize some important new insights into relations between literature and ritual since mid-century and some of the ideas recently brought to bear on the subject by the social sciences. The third section surveys criticism, chiefly of the 1970s, that employs ritual as a central concept. I make no pretensions to have covered all literary studies, however, and in fact have had to leave out some items that, worthwhile in themselves, are not sufficiently relevant to my essay. There are critics, I believe, who have dealt quite aptly with this subject, though they may show no signs of having read anthropology; it is from them, perhaps, that we have the most to learn.

I

We can attribute many assumptions regarding a ritual element in literature to the influence of handbooks, anthology introductions, and such widely read critical works as Francis Fergusson's *Idea of a Theater* and those of Frye. These perpetuate the view that Greek tragedy originated in primitive Greek ritual, with the corollary that other forms of drama, perhaps all drama, had such roots. Jane Harrison believed that *drama* was related to *dromenon*, "the thing done" in a rite, which had a corresponding myth or *legomenon*, "thing spoken" (Hyman, "Ritual" 48–49). Thus the ritual theory of myth arises simultaneously with the ritual theory of drama, so that discussion of one inevitably leads to the other.

Of the many classical scholars who now dispute the ritual origins of tragedy none is more convincing or more aware of the implications of the theory for criticism at large than Gerald F. Else, whose *Origins and Early Form of Greek Tragedy* takes up the cudgels where Sir Arthur Pickard-Cambridge left off.[1] From the beginning, Else is alarmed that so influential a book as *The Idea of a Theater* would depend so fully on the exploded ideas of the Cambridge school, whose theory of tragedy "is not now held, at least in its strictest form, by any leading scholar." The disrepute of this theory "appears to have been unknown to Fergusson, and it is certainly unknown to many others" (3). Else's book questions, if it does not exactly overturn, many handbook truisms about tragedy. On the "Dionysiac" element, Else claims that nothing known about the history of early tragedy implies a Dionysiac content (31); he reminds us that Aristotle's *Poetics* never mentions the god or the spirit Dionysus is supposed to represent (14). As for the later plays,

> The content of the overwhelming majority of known tragedies (and we know the title and/or content of many more than are now extant) is *heroic* myth and legend, from Homer and the epic cycle. Affiliations with cult-myths and cult-rituals, especially those of Dionysos, are secondary both in extent and importance. In other words the regular source of tragic material is heroic epic, not religious cult. (63)

The self-awareness of the Greek tragic hero as we know him "is at the opposite pole from the Dionysiac frenzy of self-abandonment" (69). Skeptical of the belief that literary forms like tragedy must "evolve," Else poses the equally credible hypothesis that tragedy was invented in two successive acts of genius: first by Thespis, who created *tragoidia* (not, in the received sense, derived from "goat-song" [25, 70]). This was a "self-presentation" by a single epic hero in his moment of pathos. After Thespis invented this recitative event, Aeschy-

lus, adding the second character, gave us tragic drama (65, 78).

Else mentions a number of European scholars who have rejected the ritual theory, including Albin Lesky, C. del Grande, and Harold Patzer; in this country he might have added Bernard Knox (6, 71), William Arrowsmith, and Oliver Taplin, among others. Taplin is one of many classicists who have reminded us that the requirement for sameness marks ritual as distinct from dramatic art; Greek tragedies are not the same, as anyone knows who has tried to apply the Aristotelean model to, say, Sophocles' *Philoctetes*. Indeed, "The break with the repetitiousness of ritual may well have been one of the great achievements of tragedy's creators" (*Greek Tragedy* 161). Else wrote at a time when the old order was passing—Jessie Weston, William Troy, Fergusson, Theodor Gaster, Richard Chase, Hyman, and Lord Raglan—and if we are to accept his arguments we may find that to learn anything about tragedy from the examination of ritual we must, as Michael Hinden says, study the two forms as analogous, not interdependent.[2]

A notion that Else finds especially scandalous is the modern belief that Greek audiences approached tragedy in a spirit of "ritual expectancy," a critical assumption that "does serious damage to our interpretation of the plays and through them to our conception of tragedy as a whole" (4). This view, however, has influenced theatrical productions and criticism alike, as anyone knows who has seen Tyrone Guthrie's celebrated film of *Oedipus*. Bernard Knox finds fault with that production, and Oliver Taplin, in a recent survey of Greek tragedies on film, suggests that those who liked the Guthrie version "were impressed in the way that one might be by witnessing the dances and rituals of some primitive tribe, though with no notion of their significance" ("Delphic Idea" 811). The strangeness of the film creates a response in the audience, but—and the issue will recur in this discussion —it remains to be seen whether the sense of awe or transcendence is equivalent to a response to the work as drama. On the whole, Else gives us cause to rethink, if not to reject outright, the notion of "ritual expectancy" in drama. Anthony Graham-White proposes that it is just in the matter of expectations that ritual differs from drama. Rituals are believed to be efficacious;

they never exist for their own sake. It will not do, Graham-White maintains, to equate audience participation with ritual. Rites in traditional societies "usually are carried out by a clearly defined group," with the general public carefully excluded (323).[3]

On the whole it seems that the ritual hypothesis does more violence to the evidence than do some of the less exciting proposals of later classical scholarship. Furthermore, there is much to be said for the idea that the form and purpose of rites differ from those of drama, especially tragedy. A rite can be carried on by a single "actor"; the audience seldom identifies itself with a ritual celebrant in a spirit of pathos as it does when watching an actor; even when the audience knows the "fable" behind a play, it does not know how the expected end will be reached, though such familiarity is often required in ritual, and innovation is sure to arouse controversy. Victor Turner, Margaret Mead, and other anthropologists have declared the smallest unit of ritual to be the symbol.[4] If so, then perhaps in those dramas that are most frequently seen as ritualistic we focus on the symbols rather than on the hero's pathos or the development of plot (Fichte 15; quoted in Flanigan's second article, 115).[5] Although *Oedipus* is a well-plotted mimetic drama, the richness of the symbolism almost justifies Guthrie's treatment: one thinks of plague, blindness, the crossroads, the shepherd-king, the lame savior, incest, and countless other images in the language and action of the play hinting at a latent meaning of far greater consequence than the experienced events. Ritual drama is thinly plotted, but like much Greek tragedy it creates deep emotion through the use of symbols. Yeats, who called his own plays "not drama but the ritual of a lost faith," wrote with great success in this way, using incantatory language, masks, and archetypal characters "to draw the audience away from daily life and into the deeper levels of contemplation and response" (Gorsky 176). Yet because no theory of tragedy has ever elevated the symbol to so crucial a place in the genre, we may question whether the ritual hypothesis serves as useful a purpose in criticism of drama, particularly tragedy, as scholars once thought.

Although the ritual theory of myth, like that of tragedy, was already in the air during the later nineteenth century, we may trace its debut in English literary studies to the year 1890, when William Robertson Smith's *Religion of the Semites*, Jane Harrison's *Mythology and Monuments of Ancient Athens*, and Frazer's *Golden Bough* all first saw publication. To an outsider the theory that all myths derive from rituals may seem needlessly reductive, so that Clyde Kluckhohn's well-known critique of the theory in 1942 would appear to right the balance on behalf of common sense. Other serious flaws in the theory came to light during the next two decades, as in Joseph Fontenrose's book on the Delphic myth, which shows that the Babylonian myth of beginnings as told in the *Enuma elish* was recited in the Akitu festival but not enacted or symbolized in the rites of the occasion (ch. 15).[6] Such research has led us to see that although some myths are indeed "the spoken correlative of things done," as Harrison insisted, there are fundamental differences between myth and rite that obviate the ritual theory. "The truth is," G. S. Kirk has recently observed, "that myths seem to possess essential properties—like their fantasy, their freedom to develop, and their complex structure—that are not reproduced in ritual and suggest that their motive and origin are in important respects distinct" (25). Frazer himself, despite a certain positivist disdain for religion that led him to repudiate both Robertson Smith and the Cambridge group (Ackerman), is viewed by many folklorists as responsible for the confusion introduced by the ritual theory: "The fact is that he was not clear on the difference between fable and cult when he began to write *The Golden Bough*. . . . he gave cult an absolute priority over narrative, and viewed all cult from the peculiar vantage of a classicist, which does not in any case give a very full or unobstructed prospect of either cult or fable." (Bynum 158, 160; on the "ritual fallacy," see 149–254. An earlier folklorist critique is Bascom's "Myth-Ritual Theory.")

The work of Harrison and her adherents is well known for its concept of the original myth, the mono-myth from which all other myths descend and diverge: the divine king who must be sacrificed so that his society may prosper. A decisive, perhaps fatal blow to this theory came from Joseph Fontenrose in his 1966 critique of the Cambridge group and its later adherents. In its own sphere this book does what Else's nearly contemporaneous series of lectures does in the study of tragedy. Fontenrose reviews the case made by Andrew Lang in *Magic and Religion* (1901) that Frazer's theory was wholly based on misrepresentation or exaggeration of the evidence. We thus encounter a parallel between the ritual theories of myth and tragedy, in that although specialists had long ago repudiated the principal facts and assumptions supporting the theory, it nonetheless continued to be nourished by literary critics (Fontenrose singles out Lord Raglan and Stanley Edgar Hyman as principal offenders). "In all the ancient world [Greece included] we find no record, clear or obscure, of an annual or periodic sacrifice of divine kings" (8). The anecdote of the "king of the woods" in the grove at Nemi, Frazer's one clear instance of a king put to death when his strength fails, proves to have been an Italian folk custom that cannot be documented as involving the murder of a king (36–49). There is no ethnographic evidence, moreover, of any society anywhere in the world practicing the periodic sacrifice of a king. Well-known instances of a tribe's killing its kings in Africa cannot be used to support the mono-myth: these executions are not conducted periodically—they usually occur when the king is too old to govern—and they are not enacted ritually (9–13). Thus, what Frazer's early readers believed to be a truth grounded on historical and anthropological facts ought rightly to be recognized as a fiction about primitive life. Although Joyce, Eliot, and D. H. Lawrence appear to have credited Frazer's theory with as much historicity as did Harrison, Murray, and Cornford (see Vickery, *Literary Impact*), any myth critic has to admit that the assumptions behind, say, the notes to Eliot's *Waste Land* have lost much of the authority that they had a half century ago. Northrop Frye's recent apologia on the subject employs a rather qualified language compared to some of his earlier statements on the subject:

> Frazer demonstrated the existence *in the human mind* of a symbolism *often latent in the unconscious, perhaps never emerging in any complete form*, but revealed through many ritual acts and customs, of a divine man killed at the height of his powers whose flesh and blood are ceremonially eaten and drunk. This symbolism expresses the social anxiety for a continuity of vigorous leadership and sexual vitality, and for a constant

renewal of the food supply, as the bread and wine of the vegetable crops and the bodies of eaten animals are symbolically identified with the divine-human victim.

("Expanding Eyes" 111–12; italics mine)

Divine king has become a "divine man," but the critic at least saves the appearances of consistency with his earlier opinion of Frazer and his view of *The Golden Bough* as key to the origins of drama: "it reconstructs an archetypal ritual from which the structural and generic principles of drama may be logically, not chronologically, derived. It does not matter two pins to the literary critic whether such a ritual had any historical existence or not" (*Anatomy* 109).

This tendency to dismiss the question of Frazer's historicity (certainly Frazer, Harrison, and even Murray believed that they were recovering evidence of things that had really happened) is a disturbing feature of much myth-and-ritual theory. Those who apply the theory seldom admit that it has no basis in fact. Anne Righter, in her justly acclaimed *Shakespeare and the Idea of the Play*, speaks in factual terms about the resemblance of the murdered York in *Henry VI* to Frazer's ill-fated king:

> The story has reverberations that are even older than the mocking of Christ, echoes that call up the Golden Grove at Nemi and the whole problem of the temporary king. Many primitive societies, reluctant at last to slay the true king, as custom demanded, habitually elected a substitute ruler who took the ritual death upon himself in return for a brief reign. (106)

Yet Fontenrose has shown the wholly fictitious nature of Frazer's King of the Woods and the thin ethnographic evidence for the periodic sacrifice of a king (*Ritual* 36, 8–14). If this kind of thing never really happened, where does such a theory come from? If Frye's theory of drama and myth "may be" logically derived from a never-observed archetypal ritual, may it also *not* be derived? The strange, terrible specificity of the young man killed and eaten contrast sharply with the obscurity of a symbolism that according to Frye not only remains "latent in the unconscious" but has perhaps never come out of the incubator.

II

The potential fallacy of ritual origins is seriously compounded by the likelihood that "ritual" will be applied with no serious reflections on the exact meaning of the word. Critics using "mythic" to bestow value on a literary text (a practice noted well before Frye's *Anatomy*; see Wallace Douglas 127) have often done the same with "ritual." Yet the nature of ritual has evaded even social scientists and theologians during the past decade.[7] Scholars still debate, for example, whether rituals are independent of the social structure or whether they make statements about the relative status of persons in society (Crocker 48). Edmund Leach prefers to think of ritual as, narrowly, "a body of custom specifically associated with religious performance" but, more generally, "any noninstinctive predictable action or series of actions that cannot be justified by a 'rational' means-to-end type of explanation" (520–21). The latter definition has the advantage of incorporating the psychiatrist's sense of personal or private ritual, but some have doubted the appropriateness of this word to describe individual compulsive or idiosyncratic behavior, since "ritual" has traditionally referred to a social and communicative activity (Burkert 49; see also Thomas J. Scheff's critics, who are quoted on pp. 490–500 of his article). Viewed as implying compulsive behavior, the word still has connections with the rough-and-ready formulas of early twentieth-century psychiatric thought. If the study of myth and folklore has led us to understand that an apparently similar myth should not be interpreted identically for all cultures (Ferris 265), the same must be true of ritual, in which the symbols and structures are at least as arbitrary. For this reason, to associate "compulsive" or highly systematic literary structures with ritual, as Fletcher does in linking allegory and ritual, represents a straining of the word, if not a complete misapplication.[8]

Scheff has used another psychological definition of ritual—"the distanced reenactment of situations which evoke collectively held emotional distress"—to establish a theory of catharsis in drama by working from the assumption (debatable, as we have seen) that drama is in its origins ritualistic ("Distancing" 489; the theory forms the basis of Scheff's *Catharsis*). Critics of this theory have rightly noted

that the definition neglects the positive, celebrative role of ritual; the theory also requires that social institutions be interpreted in terms of individual behavior, despite massive evidence that the influence is in the opposite direction. Whatever contributions psychology has made to criticism have not been made in association with ritual. It might even be said that an unexpected consequence of the whole literature-as-ritual approach has been to move literature from the province of the self, making us more aware of the "world" of the play or poem, outside the confines of the author's or reader's psyche. If only psychoanalytic critics would admit the deficiencies in their concept, much confusion on the topic would disappear.

The most widely discussed work on ritual during the last two decades approaches the subject as a purely communal act. Victor Turner has described ritual as "prescribed formal behavior for occasions, not given over to technological routine, having reference to beliefs in mystical beings or powers" (*Forest* 19; cf. Goody). This definition lies behind Geoffrey Hartman's usage quoted in the beginning of this article, and it has won many adherents. The inclusion of "beliefs" in Turner's account would seem to limit the term, more than Leach's definition does, by excluding such formal gestures as handshaking, not to mention animal and insect "rituals" (on such rituals see LaFontaine and *Discussion of Ritualization*). In this view, however, it is the *belief* that effects the communal bonding that ritual achieves. Turner, in his study of the Ndembu people in Africa, observes that rites oblige the participants to undergo a change in social status, in which they momentarily exchange their established place in the social structure for a condition of "communitas." During this state the bonds are "anti-structural in that they are undifferentiated, equalitarian, direct . . ." (*Dramas* 46–47). Structure, rank, and social and economic status are what hold people apart; "communitas" unites people across the barriers. Following Arnold Van Gennep's classic *Rites of Passage*, Turner calls this state of being outside the categories of ordinary social life "liminality"—literally "thresholdness"—explaining that it can occur both in the state of communitas and in a condition of solitude away from society (*Dramas* 52–53). Acknowledging these two kinds of liminality may explain why "ritual" feelings or expectations are attributed to some literary works—feelings that can be identified with the timeless, dislocating effect that is perhaps essential, but is not peculiar, to ritual. Margaret Mead thus defines ritual as "the repetition of those symbols which evoke the feeling of that primordial event which initially called the community into being with such power that it effects our presence at that event—in other words, represents the primordial event" (127). This feeling can, however, be evoked by other than ritual means. Neither Mead nor Turner, I should note, equates ritual with the festive spirit, as scholars do in studies that follow the lead of C. L. Barber's *Shakespeare's Festive Comedy*, where "puritan" antiritualism is opposed to the natural impulse toward the celebrative and saturnalian. In the wake of the nostalgia for our primitive past developed by Mircea Eliade, Roger Callois and others, we should keep in mind that not all primitive people indulge in saturnalian release during festivals; some behave quite otherwise, in fact (Isambert).

At the same time that rituals help us rise above personal and social limitations, even above time and space, they also work, as Mary Douglas argues, to strengthen social status and respect for authority. This function is attested in rites of passage for adolescents throughout the world. According to Turner, this paradoxical effect results from the continuing cycle of "social dramas" in which the tension between elements of the "structure" leads to redress in order to reintegrate the disturbed social group—in effect a movement from structure to communitas to (if the rite is successful) renewed structure. The superbly literate and civilized Turner himself occasionally mentions possible applications of his "ritual process" to literature (e.g., *Dramas* 265). . . . He has suggested that we might profitably think of modern activities that seem ritualistic, like sports and the theater, as "liminoid" rather than liminal. "Many of the symbolic and ludic capacities of tribal religion have, with the advancing division of labor, with massive increase in the scale and complexity of political and economic units, migrated into nonreligious genres." Liminoid events are not necessarily collective; they are usually produced by known, named individuals. Although separated from the work place, they are unrelated to "calen-

drical or social-structural cycles or crises in social processes." Turner leads us to consider the presence of liminal experiences in literature rather than the structure of literature as ritual:

> If we focus, for example, on the liminoid genres of literature, on scenes and moments famous for the quality of their communitas and flow, such as Achilles's encounter with Priam in the *Iliad*, the episode of Raskolnikov's and Sonya's long, painful discovery of one another in *Crime and Punishment*, so well discussed by Paul Friedrich, the communitas of the liminary outcasts, Lear, Tom O'Bedlam, Kent, and the Fool in the scene on the heath in *King Lear*, in the serious vein; and the woman's communitas in Aristophanes' *Lysistrata*, and many episodes in *Tom Jones*, *Don Quixote*, and other "carnivalized novels," in the ludic, my hunch is that there will be key symbols which "open" up the relationship to communitas. ("Variations" 52)[9]

Florence Falk has recently applied the theory to *A Midsummer Night's Dream*, showing how the Athens-woods-Athens sequence resembles that of structure-communitas-structure. (For other uses of Turner and Van Gennep, see Boose.) Yet in this, as in so much similar criticism, we may be left feeling that we have been told what we already knew—though no doubt our knowledge can be sharpened and clarified. Shakespeare very likely has more to teach the anthropologists about ritual than he or even his audiences could learn from them.

III

Reviewing some of the criticism that has used the concept of ritual during the past decade, we may appreciate the advantage of a precise and informed notion of the subject. Studies of drama especially can benefit from a socially grounded theory like Turner's. Often those who speak of drama as rite neglect these social implications, emphasizing instead the mere feeling of transcendence or the "flow" of liminal and liminoid activities alike. Jackson Cope writes of the timeless quality inherent in both ritual and drama:

'Ritual,' I take it, is a ceremonial order of acts which at first level imitates; that is, it re-enacts an established pattern. But at its second level of definition, ritual demands that this conservative reenactment be really efficacious, effective in its repetitions as it was in its origins. Thus ritual is a present act which historically recalls the past for the purpose of reordering—even predetermining—the future. But that present moment of re-enactment merges into the future, and so makes the efficacy of predictive action inevitable as its pattern evolves from contingency into control. In short, ritual is a prediction which, completed, fulfills itself. (171)

This definition appears carefully designed to bring ritual into perfect accord with the aims and province of art. A tragedy of kingship, for example, will repeat the original king's moment of pathos with a view to evoking in the audience those feelings that once were or should have been. Thereafter no one will regard the king apart from the original pathos of the dream time. "Know ye not, I am Richard the Second?" Shakespeare's queen is reported to have said. Such a conception, encompassing as it does the long-acknowledged capacity of art to mediate between the historical and the ideal, is too broad to be serviceable. To further delineate the boundaries of rite and art, I have already mentioned the possibility of ritual drama, a special form that appeals to the audience chiefly in its use of symbols rather than in imitated actions. It is these symbols that evoke the necessary community of belief.

Much comment on the union of rite and drama has occurred in the field of medieval theater, especially since the influential findings of Hardison and Wickham on the subject. Confuting the idea that English religious and secular drama evolved out of Christian worship—a theory quite compatible with Frazer and the Cambridge school, as the writings of E. K. Chambers show—these two scholars have proved the existence of two distinct, largely independent dramatic traditions in the Middle Ages: "the drama of the Real Presence within the liturgy" and "the imitative drama of Christ's humanity," in Wickham's terms (314).[10] During the 1960s, however, one still encountered the view that the mystery play is based on rite, so that the audience and the actors "shared the same ritual world" during performance, "a world more real than the one which existed outside its frame" (Righter 21). We now see that although there was a shared belief in the transcendent meaning of the events enacted, the principal effect of, say, the grisly realism of the York *Crucifixion* is to draw the audience closer to the event not through symbols but through representation of recognizable human experiences, familiar human types. In an important article Martin Stevens aids our perspective on the separation of rite from drama and even raises doubts whether the Mass ought properly to be considered dramatic.[11] Following Brecht, Stevens proposes that drama, unlike rite, consists of enacted illusion; even "ritual drama" if performed in the church would lose ritual aspects entirely. Thus the sense of shared belief, the possibility for communitas, would be emptied from such "liturgical drama" as the Easter visitation at the tomb, which was performed as part of the Easter rite at a stylized sepulcher within the church. If a "play" cannot be staged without becoming representational drama, then ritual plays of the Yeatsian type would seem impossible. Although the persistence (documented by Hardison) of liturgical drama centuries after the establishment of "competing" mystery plays indicates that two entirely different sets of needs were being met (and the persistence of rites would of course add a third), many scholars still maintain, like Stevens, that rite and drama are mutually exclusive. "It is quite evident," writes Gauvin, using a concept resembling Mead's and Turner's,

> that a rite is composed of both the prescribed gesture and of its theological significance, which goes far beyond that. In Catholic liturgy the gesture has a deep symbolic and mystic value: it actualizes, in the present time of the ceremony, a past or future event that is thus mysteriously recreated or anticipated. The Catholic rite par excellence is the Mass, which can be said to reconstitute systematically the mystery of the Redemption by the death and Resurrection of Christ. (131; my trans.)[12]

To equate theater with ritual is therefore to say that theater recreates in the present that which it represents. This position, Gauvin believes, entails two untenable consequences for the English mystery plays: first, that these dramas-ceremonies are truly religious, though conducted by laymen; second, that the persons represented, including the Father and the incarnate Son, are not disguised actors but themselves. Perhaps, he concludes, the cycle plays and other religious representational drama (presumably including liturgical drama, if no play can be a rite) are best classified with devotional images. They do not stand in place of the Mass or any other rite, but they do arouse devout feelings in the viewer, just as a statue or a painting does (138–39; Hanning also argues the theological impossibility of ritual drama). The dramatic element of playing or pretending, however, is quite at odds with the nature of ritual, in which participants act for a purpose (to become adults, to join in marriage, to receive the eucharistic elements).

[In 1961] a critic struggling with the supposed ritual element in Shakespeare's plays could say, "I shall not be arguing that imaginative works *are* rituals in disguise, nor (save of course for the cases like Greek tragedy or medieval miracle plays, where it is already common knowledge) that they derive from rituals or explain or justify them. Such extravagances would be absurd" (Holloway 176). Yet at the outset we saw that some respectable scholars do speak of some literary works as rituals; we have also seen that the ritual origins of Greek and medieval theater are no longer accepted as "common knowledge," at least not among specialists in these fields. Hallett Smith's criticism of ritualist approaches to Shakespeare's late plays proceeds from a view similar to Gauvin's: that the plays inhibit the participation essential to true ritual because their theatricality distances the audience (197–202). As with studies of other literature, so with Shakespeare, the decline of myth criticism seems to have brought a waning of enthusiasm for the ceremonial element in the plays, at least as they are construed through the dubious methods of the Cambridge school.[13] The influence of the Christian liturgy is another matter, and it is the focus of Coursen's lengthy study of the tragedies (Hassel also examines drama and liturgy of the period). Coursen believes that Shakespeare conceived both comedy and tragedy in terms of the communion service, comedy working toward communion while "The tragic world divorces itself from the unifying powers expressed in communion" (34). The tragedies thus present an array of counterrituals

like the murder of Caesar or Richard II's parting from his queen, which Coursen views as an "anti-marriage" (77). Since the audience is not participating in these actions, they can of course be considered rites only from the characters' standpoint. And if we reflect on Victor Turner's definition, we have to add that these moments of disunion are not prescribed or occasioned. We may compare the . . . claim that the nunnery scene in *Hamlet* is an "inverted marriage ceremony," in which Ophelia "violates the ritual" by siding with her father rather than with her potential husband (Boose 329).[14] From the audience's perspective such scenes may be symbolic, but (again) the audience does not participate in them; to the characters they are not rites but quite real sets of actions. It is true that Brutus wants to make Caesar's murder an act of sacrifice, but that effort would seem the result of Brutus' special derangement.[15] An approach tying the plays to the Book of Common Prayer invites a return to earlier theories of drama and ritual as performative equivalents, a path fraught with difficulties. The tradition of the masque, however, should be sufficient to silence those who uncompromisingly separate rite from drama in this period. Jonson's masques especially disclose a sense of drama in the antimasque (when the characters show no awareness of the audience); yet they also contain a ceremonial sense in the mythological-symbolic trappings of the major figures, who mingle with the spectators in dance (see Orgel).

Criticism of narrative during the past decade has been influenced by ritual theories, though not quite as strongly as drama has been. Frazer's ideas inspired a number of modern authors to weave into their stories rites of rebirth, baptism, initiation, and so forth. Among novelists, D. H. Lawrence is especially fascinated with the idea that, as one critic puts it, "ritual as an organizing principle in the novel could link the pattern of an individual's life with that of society at large, and, beyond that, with Nature" (Ross 6). Lawrence's reading of Jane Harrison's *Ancient Art and Ritual*, Eliot's acquaintance with Jessie Weston, and of course the widespread interest in Frazer led to that deliberate infusion of ritual into fiction which John B. Vickery explores amply in *The Literary Impact of* The Golden Bough. Critics of such myth-dominated fiction would probably gain from careful thought about its ritual content. It is well to see John Updike's *The Centaur* as a series of mythic and timeless moments experienced by a father and relived by his son; but is it true that "By its transformation of a particular situation into a paradigm, myth makes rite dynamic and meaningful" (Vargo 459)? This statement implies that rites consist of details that cannot be "meaningful" without a mythic content. Yet we have seen that rites often exist without myths and that rites, being constituted of symbols, still convey meaning. We shall return later to this widely held assumption that ritual is inferior to myth, often because it is supposed prior to myth. In one of Faulkner's stories, the fact that a cardplayer throws the game supposedly signifies the victory of ritual as "a formal agent of hidden necessity" over game, the "formal agent of apparent freedom" (Zender 59; in fact, game is often defined in terms of social necessity [see n. 2, below]). Faulkner, the critic says, "is concerned with the tension between the predetermined movement of characters through a pattern analogous to a traditional myth or ritual, and their free movement in an invented dramatic action" (53). Zender seems to mean that the freedom we exercise contrasts with the predetermined part of our lives, which is a ritual. But the card game is "analogous" to ritual at best, for the program of fated action is like a rite only in that it is prescribed. There is no sense that the one who throws the game does so for communal purposes—to guarantee the harvest or restore the vitality of his community. In all likelihood the claimed association or ritual with "hidden necessity" was suggested by the role of the Fates in a ritualist theory of Greek tragedy. Even in the most familiar kind of fiction involving rites—stories of initiation like Faulkner's *The Bear* or Dickey's *Deliverance*—we should ask whether the stories *are* "rites of passage" when in fact they are *about* human lives in which initiation occurs.[16] By contrast, in many real initiation rites there is no myth or story involved, only a series of arbitrarily chosen and ordered symbols for the initiate.

In summary, despite the careful work of anthropologists, classical scholars, and others who aim to disentangle the term from irrelevant and dubious associations, much criticism has continued to tie literature with an imprecise concept of ritual. The major problems seem to be the tendencies to equate rite

with literature because of literature's emotional effects, its use of the symbol, its performative features, and its creation of a sense of kinship with fictional characters and hence with humanity at large. An uninformed, Cambridge-style ritualism also continues despite the efforts of Fontenrose, Else, and others. A 1981 study of the Soviet novel assumes a ritual theory of myth to show that the triteness and predictability of these novels shape them into "a sort of parable for the working-out of Marxism-Leninism in history" (Clark 9).[17] Especially in view of the communal roots of ritual, one may ask whether it makes sense to think of the lonely novel reader entering into a ritual of anything.

We should not deny the usefulness of some recent criticism aimed at the discovery of ritual content. I have already noted the rites embedded in Lawrence's stories. One recent study proposes that the setting of Joyce's "The Dead" is not a New Year's party but a funeral celebration featuring the "dance of the dead," a rite noted by Van Gennep and mentioned in one of Joyce's poems (J. W. Foster). John Vickery analyzes the pattern of the scapegoat ritual in the work of several authors whom we have every reason to believe were fully aware of this material ("Scapegoat"). (In the same collection, however, a recanting ritualist offers a caveat on interpreting quest narratives like *Gawain and the Green Knight* as rites of passage [Moorman, "Comparative"].)[18] The demonstrable influence of Nietzsche moved André Gide to construct *L'Immoraliste* around "symbolic rituals of death and revival" and to have his hero pass through rebirth and "a pagan-like cleansing ceremony in which sun, water, and a variation of tonsuring are used" (O'Reilly). Frazer's influence may also have indirectly moved Christian authors to incorporate their ceremonies into their works. In one of Charles Williams' "liturgical novels," *The Greater Trumps*, a character discovers that the Christian service in her village is part of a hidden cosmic dance, a means to participate in the universal delight that leads to mystic ecstasy (Manlove 169).[19] Such narratives not only contain rituals, they are about them, about the feelings they generate and the needs they serve, so that we may justly speak of a ritual ambience in these works, if not quite a ritual form.

It need hardly be said that this projection into

narrative and drama of details suggesting religious worship owes much to the nineteenth-century dream of a cult of art that would supplant traditional religion. This familiar theme takes various forms in Arnold, Nietzsche, and Joyce, who has Stephen Dedalus expound such a theory near the end of *Portrait of the Artist.* Renouncing Catholicism, Mallarmé nevertheless tries as Joyce does to retain a sense of the sacred through invented rites in his work (see, e.g., Danahy). Karl Beckson traces the course of British religious aestheticism in Yeats's "infallible church of poetic tradition," in the poets Lionel Johnson (who believed that "Life should be a ritual") and Ernest Dowson, and in the novels of Walter Pater (*Marius the Epicurean*) and Frederick Rolfe (*Hadrian the Seventh*). So many scholars still believe that "literature in man's historical evolution was once religious liturgy and dance, charms and oracles" (Ruland 119), that the "mythology of aestheticism" is often taken for granted by both the religious and the nonreligious.[20] Such assumptions are evident in the typical late twentieth-century observation that *A Midsummer Night's Dream*, although a secular play, embodies "more successfully than the religious and folk traditions, an extra-temporal moment of achieved harmony in human life, a triumph formerly shared with ritual, now in the sole possession of the work of art" (Vlasopolos 29).

A major voice of the past decade, questioning older theories regarding literature, especially drama, and the ritual process, has been René Girard. Following Freud in *Totem and Taboo*, Girard proposes that a primal killing threatened to destroy human community through successive retributions. This violence could be avoided only by the appointment of a scapegoat who would receive the full force of the community's wrath. The sacrificial victim becomes a characteristic human expedient and "constitutes a major means, perhaps the sole means, by which men expel from their consciousness the truth about their violent nature—that knowledge of past violence which, if not shifted to a single 'guilty' figure, would poison both the present and the future" (*Violence* 83). In all human relations, Girard sees three figures locked in a circle of "mimetic desire": the subject, the rival, and the object. "The subject desires the object because the rival desires it" (146). A telling instance is Shakespeare's *Troilus and Cres-*

sida, in which the Greeks want Helen back because the Trojans have taken her away and the Trojans want to keep her because the Greeks want her back ("Shakespeare's Theory" 113). Mimetic desire is "the immediate interplay of imitating and imitated desire. Mimesis generates rivalry, which in turn reinforces mimesis" (*Double Business* 53).

The scapegoat process gives birth to a vast array of myths and rituals, all of which serve merely to conceal the ugly facts of the surrogate victim sacrificed to this mimetic, desire-caused violence. Since myths exist to rationalize the scapegoat mechanism, mythology is little more than "a text of persecution" that rituals exist to enact ("Interview" 40): "Ritual is nothing more than the regular exercise of 'good' violence" (*Violence* 37), that is, violence that will prevent the spread of retribution or revenge and similar kinds of hostility throughout the community. Like almost all culture, drama originates in violence: "All religious rituals spring from the surrogate victim, and all the great institutions of mankind, both secular and religious, spring from ritual. Such is the case . . . with political power, legal institutions, medicine, the theater, philosophy and anthropology itself" (*Violence* 306). By "religion" Girard here means primitive religion as opposed to the beliefs of the Hebrew prophetic books and the Gospels (a point he makes clear in *Des choses* 178).

Although to skeptics his theory must seem a quaint throwback to mono-myth, Girard, like Frye, has built his hypothesis on an intricate theoretical structure. A fundamental principle is social differentiation: "Order, peace, and fecundity depend on cultural distinctions," the loss of which gives birth to rivalries and violence (*Violence* 49). Thus in *Troilus*, "degree" is what "permits individuals to find a place for themselves in society" (50). The final annihilation of differences can only lead to the triumph of the strong over the weak in a Hobbesian state of nature (51). This view accounts for the frequent concern in Girard's work with myths of twins or doubles (Cain and Abel, Romulus and Remus, Eteocles and Polyneices). Our modern loss of differences is attested by the change from these ancient myths of warring twins to the modern concept of affectionate family relations (61). Girard attacks the structuralist notion, shared by Lévi-Strauss and Frye, that literature and myth deal with differentiation, while ritual searches for an "undifferentiated immediacy." In fact both ritual and myth tend to destroy difference ("Shakespeare's Theory" 109, "Lévi-Strauss"). "The sacred concerns itself above all with the destruction of differences, and this nondifference cannot appear as such in structure" (*Violence* 241). Thus what Nietzsche called the "Dionysiac" state must aim to "erase all manner of differences: familial, cultural, biological, and natural" (160).

When the sacrificial rites disappear, at a time coinciding with the loss of the difference between "good" and "bad" violence, difference cannot be reasserted as it was each time on completion of the old rites. We then have a "sacrificial crisis," a time of deterioration for the system by which reciprocal violence is channeled off. When we "demystify" religion, our doing so "necessarily coincides with the disintegration of that system. . . . In fact, demystification leads to constantly increasing violence, a violence less 'hypocritical' than the violence it seeks to expose, but more energetic . . . a violence that knows no bounds" (24–25). Euripides' *Bacchae* concerns just such a crisis (126–42). Thus, while for Turner rites exist to instill a sense of *communitas*, of values shared across social boundaries (especially when violence threatens), Girard believes that rites are used to redirect violence. Violence, however, is the inescapable condition of society.

These ideas have particular relevance to drama, since drama, especially the great tragedies of the Greeks, "is by its very nature a partial deciphering of mythological motifs" (64). In Sophocles and Euripides (as later in Shakespeare), the poet at certain moments "lifts the veil long enough for you to glimpse the long hidden historical truth that lies at the origin" ("Interview" 35; this is the interviewer's paraphrase). Even though tragedy originated in ritual, the inspiration of a play like *Oedipus Rex* is "essentially antimythical and antiritualistic" (*Violence* 95). In "Myth and Ritual in Shakespeare's *A Midsummer Night's Dream*," Girard warns Shakespearean critics of the myth-ritual school to reconsider their assumptions: "Instead of viewing myth as a humanization of nature, as we always tend to do, Shakespeare views it as the naturalization as well as the supernaturalization of a very human violence. Specialists on the subject might be well advised to take a close look at this Shakespearean view; what if

it turned out to be less mythical than their own!" (200–01; the word "ritual," although it appears in the title, scarcely appears in the essay itself). In the same essay, Girard proposes that *A Midsummer Night's Dream* is a drama of mimetic desire in which the self idolizes the "other" for the sake of the self—in effect, the self mythologizes the other. This play shows that the myth always captivates sooner than the truly human does; thus, in *The Merchant of Venice*, where the same rules operate, Bassanio falls in love with Portia's picture, not with Portia.

It is in [an] essay on this play, in fact, that Girard offers by implication a way of resolving some of the confusion inherited from the past about ritual and literature. Ritual may inhere thematically, structurally, or, in certain special cases, affectively, by a deliberate appeal to audience participation. Girard sees *The Merchant of Venice* as a play about revenge and retribution, with Shylock as the "grotesque double" ("To Entrap" 105) of Antonio. He points out the telling evidence of Portia's question when she enters the courtroom, "Which is the merchant and which is the Jew?" The classic Jew of European anti-Semitism, Shylock, is widely recognized as a scapegoat, hence his doubling in the play. Yet, Girard asks, should we see scapegoat as theme or structure here? If scapegoat is theme, the author will actually realize the evil of the scapegoat mechanism, as did the Greek tragic dramatists; if structure, though, the scapegoat ritual will be "a passively accepted delusion" of the author (109). In Girard's view Shakespeare, like the Greeks, fully intends his meaning—scapegoat is theme; but for those unable to be reached by Shakespeare's meaning, there is also a scapegoat structure. Finally a special quality of *The Merchant of Venice* that evokes the audience's wishful participation gives the play what Turner would call its "liminoid" characteristics. "The crowd in the theater becomes one with the crowd on the stage. The contagious effect of scapegoating extends to the audience" during the trial scene, when "the presence of the silent Magnificoes, the elite of the community, turns the trial into a rite of social unanimity" (111). The crowd involvement in *Julius Caesar* is similar; in all such examples drama merges almost totally with ritual.

In Girard's view, the great tragedies signal a reaction against the excess of communality in ritual by asserting the claims of the suffering individual compelled by a socially determined necessity. Girard is always careful to admit that his hypothesis about human desire and the scapegoat mechanism is just that, and he denies that he is working toward a universally applicable "theory of literature." Although I cannot offer here a critique of his hypothesis, I might suggest that the equation of ritual with sacrifice (and therefore with the scapegoat process) narrows the concept excessively. Nevertheless, Girard's position does furnish a serviceable alternative to the familiar view that all literature gains profundity or beauty from a touch of the ritualistic.

IV

If there have been great authors who found the ritual sense dangerous or irrelevant (in *Madame Bovary* it is even a refuge for banality and superstition) there have always been those who have sought to recover that sense. Charting this recovery in the novels of George Eliot, Barbara Hardy calls to our attention a passage from *Daniel Deronda*:

> The most powerful movement of feeling within a liturgy is the prayer which seeks for nothing special, but is the yearning to escape from the limitations of our own weakness and an invocation of all Good to enter and abide with us; or else a self-oblivious lifting-up of gladness, a *Gloria in Excelsis* that such Good exists; both the yearning and the exultation gathering their utmost force from the sense of communion in a form which has expressed them both, for long generations of struggling fellowmen.(5)

What George Eliot conveys here is an appreciation of the flow and communitas that Turner finds in ritual, for the worshiper joins both other human beings and his or her ancestors in a momentary "time out of time." "Human feeling," Barbara Hardy observes, "is given clarity and definition by ritual, and shown at crucial moments to feel itself a part of a larger tradition" (14). Instead of attempting to bring ritual and literature together, she suggests reasons for appreciating their difference. Ritual is really "the ground, the bass," in much fiction, while "counterpointed against it is the change in feeling and circumstance" necessary in a novel or play (9).

Geoffrey Hartman's description of *Faust* as a ritual may be ascribable to the "liminoid" relation between the sacred and secular that Turner discusses. Art "seems generically and ambiguously involved with the sacred and profane . . ."; "it is always inauthentic vis-à-vis a thoroughgoing realism" (*Beyond Formalism* 21–22). Elsewhere in the same book, thinking of the romantic period, Hartman says, "There clearly comes a time when art frees itself from subordination to religion or religiously inspired myth and continues or even replaces them." He sees *Faust*, in fact, as attempting to "bridge the gap between the myth-centered age of romance and the modern spirit" (305, 310). Hartman proposes the evolutionary continuum in a critique of the "structuralist adventure," the program that in many respects includes Frye and that would reject Hartman's distinction between ancient and modern art, primitive and civilized mind. Understanding the testament of ancient art has been a task of modern civilization since the inception of the "modern," and a share of the task has been to discover the place of ritual in art. In literary thought, this enterprise begins not with Frazer's admirers but with the young Nietzsche's *Birth of Tragedy*. Nietzsche's book met with outrage from his fellow classical scholars, especially from the future prince of *Altertumswissenschaft*, Ulrich von Wilamowitz-Moellendorff. Twenty-five years later Nietzsche would agree with Wilamowitz in many respects: his first book was "badly written, ponderous, embarrassing, image-mad and image-confused, sentimental, . . . an arrogant and rhapsodic book." He particularly regretted that "the Dionysiac" remained as obscure and elusive a concept as ever. (Silk and Stern 95, 119–20. See also J. B. Foster on Gide, Lawrence, Malraux, and Mann.) The Dionysiac-Apolline polarity, so persistent in ritual conceptions of drama during our century, retains a certain hold on contemporary theater, but in criticism it has been reduced to an instance of the "radical indeterminacy" supposedly at the heart of literary discourse (de Man). The prospects for a fuller understanding of ritual in relation to literature might be improved if we could agree that both these features of cultural life exist in an ecology not unlike what George Eliot proposed, in which subject and object, worshiper and cult, reader (writer) and text acquire meaning only in the context of a community.[21]

NOTES

1. The posthumous 1962 edition of Pickard-Cambridge's book omits much of the rebuttal of the Cambridge school.

2. Using terminology borrowed from Richard Schechner, Hinden proposes that classical tragedy moves toward community—from the arena of play and the self-assertive "I" to that of game (the social "we") to the self-transcendent "other" of ritual.

3. Graham-White cites a number of theater critics who use "ritual" imprecisely. Yet one of these, Richard Schechner, has since developed his ideas impressively in a study of the common features of ritual and theater as recreations of past events or "restored behavior." Jerzy Grotowski is among the more recent experimenters in the ritualizing of theater (see Findlay).

4. Yet Herbert Weisinger restricts symbol to art alone: "To speak of symbolic meaning is already to have made the leap from myth to art" (152). I agree with Ernst Cassirer that symbolism is an inevitable human response, whether in art, religion, or politics (41–62).

5. See C. Clifford Flanigan's comprehensive discussions of Christian liturgical drama, which have considerable relevance to my subject.

6. Reviewing this book, Hyman says Fontenrose is "proudly enrolled under Henri Frankfort's obscurantist banner, in a crusade to undo the last seventy years of generalization in comparative mythology by the denial of the ancient Near East as a unified culture area" (127).

7. See Robert Goodin's strictures on this point (281). Various definitions are proposed in Moore and Meyerhoff, and Roy A. Rappaport's "Obvious Aspects of Ritual" is of great importance.

8. Also questionable is Fletcher's association of "contagious magic" with ritual form (195–99). For the distinction between religion and magic in ritual, see Goody. Wittgenstein remarks that such an act as burning in effigy "is obviously *not* based on a belief that it will have a definite effect on the object which the picture represents. It aims at some satisfaction and it achieves it. Or rather, it does not *aim* at anything; we act in that way and then feel satisfied" (4e).

9. "Flow" is a term borrowed from the social psychologist Mihali Csikszentmihalyi, meaning the "holistic sensations present when we act with total involvement," as in religious or creative experience or in sports ("Variations" 48).

10. Francis Edwards' guide for students still speaks of drama as moving "from the confines of the church to the open air" (64).

11. Blandine-Dominique Berger argues against Hardison's view that the Mass is drama. She sees liturgical drama "at the heart of a new type of liturgy" in the Middle Ages (132) but believes that liturgy was not the simple source for Western drama.

12. Mary and Max Gluckman, two social scientists, make a similar point: "When an ancient myth is reenacted in a drama, there is no idea that the events are in any way occurring then and there, with the actors becoming the heroes and heroines of that distant event, and the audience participating in the event itself. The drama is presentation, not a representation as ritual is" (235).

13. Cambridge-style criticism has persisted, however. See Isaacs and Reese and Bryant. The opening section of Robert Weimann's *Shakespeare and the Popular Tradition* (1–6) does not inspire confidence when it cites Frazer, E. K. Chambers, and Christopher Caudwell as its principal authorities on the alliance of ritual and theater. Weimann concurs with Hardison's doubts about the evolutionary view but claims that Hardison underestimates "the historical element of change" that links liturgy to Shakespearean drama (271, n. 23). Yet Weimann's opening section, entitled "Ritual and Mimesis," seems to treat "the gradual movement from myth to realism" (3) in evolutionary terms.

14. Boose discusses several such "rituals." Although she cites anthropological studies, she is much influenced by psychological conceptions of ritual, as when she asserts that "What the church service is actually all about is the separation of the daughter from the interdicting father" (326).

15. Ritualist readings of Caesar's murder have continued since Brents Stirling and Ernest Schanzer; see, e.g., de Gerenday's study, which shows the influence of Freud and Erik Erikson.

16. William Stephenson argues the primacy of the inner rite of Drew the artist over the initiation of the "antinomian" rugged hero Lewis. Cf. Lindberg.

17. Clark also observes that "The majority of initiating ordeals more or less clearly imply a ritual death—or at least some token mutilation—followed by a resurrection or new birth. In the Stalinist novel, death and token mutilation have a predominantly mythic function" (178).

18. Moorman reconsiders his earlier "Myth and Medieval Literature."

19. The entire issue of *Mosaic* in which Manlove's article appears (Winter 1979) is devoted to liturgy and literature.

20. Ruland's bibliographical survey is well informed from the standpoint of both religious and literary studies.

21. This study was supported by a grant from the General Research Fund of the University of Kansas.

WORKS CITED

Ackerman, Robert. "Frazer on Myth and Ritual." *Journal of the History of Ideas* 36(1975):115–34.

Arrowsmith, William. Introd. *The Bacchae.* In *Euripides V.* Ed. David Grene and Richmond Lattimore. Chicago: Univ. of Chicago Press, 1959, 142–53.

Bascom, William. "The Myth-Ritual Theory." *Journal of American Folklore* 70(1957):103–14.

Beckson, Karl. "A Mythology of Aestheticism." *English Literature in Transition* 17(1974):233–49.

Berger, Blandine-Dominique. *Le Drame liturgique de Pâques.* Paris: Editions Beauchesne, 1976.

Boose, Lynda E. "The Father and the Bride in Shakespeare." *PMLA* 97(1982):325–47.

Bryant, J. A., Jr. "Falstaff and the Renewal of Windsor." *PMLA* 89(1974):296–301.

Burkert, Walter. *Structure and History in Greek Mythology and Ritual.* Berkeley: Univ. of California Press, 1979.

Bynum, David E. *The Daemon in the Wood: A Study of Oral Narrative Patterns.* Cambridge, Mass.: Center for the Study of Oral Literature, 1978.

Cassirer, Ernst. *An Essay on Man.* 1944; rpt. New York: Doubleday, 1954.

Clark, Katerina. *The Soviet Novel: History as Ritual.* Chicago: Univ. of Chicago Press, 1981.

Cope, Jackson I. *The Theater and the Dream: From Metaphor to Form in Renaissance Drama.* Baltimore: Johns Hopkins Univ. Press, 1973.

Coursen, Herbert N., Jr. *Christian Ritual and the World of Shakespeare's Tragedies.* Lewisburg, Pa.: Bucknell Univ. Press, 1976.

Crocker, Christopher. "Ritual and the Development of Social Structure: Liminality and Inversion." In *The Roots of Ritual.* Ed. James D. Shaughnessy. Grand Rapids, Mich.: Eerdmans, 1973, 47–86.

Danahy, Michael. "The Drama of Herodiade: Liturgy and Irony." *Modern Language Quarterly* 34(1973):292–311.

de Gerenday, Lynn. "Play, Ritualization, and Ambivalence in *Julius Caesar.*" *Literature and Psychology* 24(1976):24–33.

de Man, Paul. "Genesis and Genealogy in Nietzsche's *The Birth of Tragedy.*" *Diacritics* 2.4(1972):44–53.

A Discussion of Ritualization of Behaviour in Animals and Man. Philosophical Transactions of the Royal Society of London. Series B. Biological Series 251. London: Royal Society of London, 1966.

Dörrie, Heinrich. "The Meaning and Function of Myth in Greek and Roman Literature." *Yearbook of Comparative Criticism* 9(1980):109–31.

Douglas, Mary. *Natural Symbols: Explorations in Cosmology.* New York: Random, 1973.

Douglas, Wallace. "The Meanings of Myth" (1953). In *Myth and Literature: Contemporary Theory and Practice.* Ed. John B. Vickery. Lincoln: Univ. of Nebraska Press, 1966, 119–28.

Edwards, Francis. *Ritual and Drama: The Medieval Theatre.* London: Lutterworth, 1976.

Else, Gerald F. *Origins and Early Form of Greek Tragedy.* Martin Classical Lectures, vol. 20. Cambridge: Harvard Univ. Press, 1967.

Falk, Florence. "Drama and Ritual Process in *A Midsummer Night's Dream.*" *Comparative Drama* 14(1980):263–79.

Feder, Lillian. *Ancient Myth in Modern Poetry.* Princeton: Princeton Univ. Press, 1971.

Ferris, William R., Jr. "Myth and the Psychological School: Fact or Fantasy." *New York Folklore Quarterly* 30(1974):254–66.

Fichte, Jörg O. *Expository Voices in Medieval Drama.* Nürnberg: Hans Karl, 1975.

Findlay, Robert. "Grotowski's 'Cultural Explorations Bordering on Art, Especially Theatre.'" *Theatre Journal* 32(1980):349–56.

———. "Grotowski's Laboratorium after Twenty Years: Theory and Operation." *Kansas Quarterly* 12(Fall 1980):133–39.

Flanigan, C. Clifford. "The Liturgical Drama and Its Tradition: A Review of Scholarship 1965–1975." *Research Opportunities in Renaissance Drama.* 18(1975):81–102.

———. "The Liturgical Drama and Its Tradition: A Review of Scholarship (Part II)." *Research Opportunities in Renaissance Drama* 19(1976):109–36.

Fletcher, Angus. *Allegory: The Theory of a Symbolic Mode.* Ithaca, N.Y.: Cornell Univ. Press, 1964.

Fontenrose, Joseph. *Python: A Study of Delphic Myth and Its Origins.* Berkeley: Univ. of California Press, 1959.

———. *The Ritual Theory of Myth.* Folklore Studies, no. 18. Berkeley: Univ. of California Press, 1966.

Foster, John Burton, Jr. *Heirs to Dionysos: A Nietzschean Current in Literary Modernism.* Princeton: Princeton Univ. Press, 1981.

Foster, John Wilson. "Passage through 'The Dead,'" *Criticism* 15(1973):91–108.

Frye, Northrop. *Anatomy of Criticism: Four Essays.* 1957; rpt. New York: Atheneum, 1967.

———. "Expanding Eyes." In his *Spiritus Mundi: Essays on Literature, Myth, and Society.* Bloomington: Indiana Univ. Press, 1976, 99–122.

Gauvin, C. "Rite et jeu dans le théâtre anglais du Moyen Age." *Revue d'Histoire du Théâtre* 29(1977):128–40.

Girard, René. *Des choses cachées depuis la fondation du monde.* Paris: Bernard Grasset, 1978.

———. "Interview." *Diacritics* 8.1(1978):31–54.

———. "Lévi-Strauss, Frye, Derrida, and Shakespearean Criticism." *Diacritics* 3.3(1973):34–38.

———. "Myth and Ritual in Shakespeare's *A Midsummer Night's Dream.*" In *Textual Strategies: Perspectives in Post-Structuralist Criticism.* Ed. Josué Harari. Ithaca, N.Y.: Cornell Univ. Press, 1979, 189–212.

———. "Shakespeare's Theory of Mythology." *Proceedings of the Comparative Literature Symposium* 11(1980):107–24.

———. *To Double Business Bound: Essays on Literature, Mimesis, and Anthropology.* Baltimore: Johns Hopkins Univ. Press, 1978.

———. "'To Entrap the Wisest': A Reading of *The Merchant of Venice.*" In *Literature and Society: Selected Papers of the English Institute.* Ed. Edward W. Said. Baltimore: Johns Hopkins Univ. Press, 1978, 100–19.

———. *Violence and the Sacred.* Trans. Patrick Gregory. Baltimore: Johns Hopkins Univ. Press, 1977.

Gluckman, Mary, and Max Gluckman. "On Drama, and Games and Athletic Contests." In *Secular Ritual.* Ed. Sally Moore and Barbara C. Meyerhoff. Assen, Neth.: Van Gorcum, 1977, 227–43.

Goodin, Robert. "Rites of Rulers." *British Journal of Sociology* 29(1978):281–99.

Goody, Jack R. "Religion and Ritual: The Definitional Problem." *British Journal of Sociology* 12(1961):142–64.

Gorsky, Susan R. "A Ritual Drama: Yeats's Plays for Dancers." *Modern Drama* 17(1974):165–78.

Graham-White, Anthony. " 'Ritual' in Contemporary Theatre Criticism." *Educational Theater Journal* 28(1976):318–24.

Hanning, R. W. " 'You Have Begun a Parlous Playe': The Nature and Limits of Dramatic Mimesis as a Theme in Four Middle English 'Fall of Lucifer' Cycle Plays." *Comparative Drama* 7(1973):22–50.

Hardison, O. B. *Christian Rite and Christian Drama in the Middle Ages.* Baltimore: Johns Hopkins Univ. Press, 1965.

Hardy, Barbara. *Rituals and Feeling in the Novels of George Eliot.* W. D. Thomas Memorial Lecture. Swansea, Wales: University College of Swansea, 1973.

Hartman, Geoffrey H. *Beyond Formalism.* New Haven: Yale Univ. Press, 1970.

———. *The Fate of Reading and Other Essays.* Chicago: Univ. of Chicago Press, 1975.

Hassel, R. Chris. *Renaissance Drama and the English Church Year.* Lincoln: Univ. of Nebraska Press, 1979.

Hinden, Michael. "Ritual and Tragic Action: A Synthesis of Current Theory." *Journal of Aesthetics and Art Criticism* 32(1974):357–73.

Holloway, John. *The Story of the Night: Studies in Shakespeare's Major Tragedies.* Lincoln: Univ. of Nebraska Press, 1961.

Hyman, Stanley Edgar. "The Ritual View of Myth and the Mythic" (1958). In *Myth and Literature: Contemporary Theory and Practice.* Ed. John B. Vickery. Lincoln: Univ. of Nebraska Press, 1966, 47–58.

———. Rev. of Joseph Fontenrose's *Python. Carleton Miscellany* 1(1960):124–27.

Isaacs, Neil D., and Jack E. Reese. "Dithyramb and Paean in *A Midsummer Night's Dream.*" *English Studies* 55(1974): 351–57.

Isambert, F. A. "Feasts and Celebrations: Some Critical Reflections on the Idea of Celebration." Trans. Bernd Jager. *Humanitas* 5(1969):29–42.

Kirk, G. S. *Myth: Its Meaning and Function in Ancient Greece and Other Cultures.* Cambridge: Cambridge Univ. Press, 1970.

Kluckhohn, Clyde. "Myth and Ritual: A General Theory." *Harvard Theological Review* 35(1942):45–79.

Knox, Bernard. *Word and Action: Essays on the Ancient Theater.* Baltimore: Johns Hopkins Univ. Press, 1979.

LaFontaine, J. S., ed. *The Interpretation of Ritual.* London: Tavistock, 1972.

Leach, Edmund. "Ritual." *International Encyclopedia of the Social Sciences.* New York: Macmillan, 1968, 13:520–26.

Lewis, C. S. *English Literature in the Sixteenth Century excluding Drama.* New York: Oxford Univ. Press, 1954.

Lindberg, Henry J. "James Dickey's *Deliverance:* The Ritual of Art." *Southern Literary Journal* 6(1974):83–90.

Manlove, C. N. "The Liturgical Novels of Charles Williams." *Mosaic* 12(Winter 1979):161–81.

Mead, Margaret. *Twentieth Century Faith: Hope and Survival.* New York: Harper, 1972.

Moore, Sally, and Barbara G. Meyerhoff, eds. *Secular Ritual.* Assen, Neth.: Van Gorcum, 1977.

Moorman, Charles. "Comparative Mythography: A Fungo to the Outfield." In *The Binding of Proteus: Perspectives on Myth and the Literary Process.* Ed. Marjorie W. McCune et al. Lewisburg, Pa.: Bucknell Univ. Press, 1980, 63–77.

———. "Myth and Medieval Literature: *Sir Gawain and the Green Knight.*" In *Myth and Literature: Contemporary Theory and Practice.* Ed. John B. Vickery. Lincoln: Univ. of Nebraska Press, 1966, 171–86.

O'Reilly, Robert F. "Ritual, Myth and Symbol in Gide's *L'Immoraliste.*" *Symposium* 28(1974):346–55.

Orgel, Stephen. *The Jonsonian Masque.* Cambridge: Harvard Univ. Press, 1967.

Pickard-Cambridge, Arthur. *Dithyramb, Tragedy and Comedy.* Oxford: Clarendon, 1927.

Rappaport, Roy A. "The Obvious Aspects of Ritual." In his *Ecology, Meaning, and Religion.* Richmond, Calif.: North Atlantic, 1979, 173–221.

Righter, Anne. *Shakespeare and the Idea of the Play.* 1962; rpt. Harmondsworth, Eng.: Penguin, 1967.

Ross, Charles L. "D. H. Lawrence's Use of Greek Tragedy: Euripides and Ritual." *D. H. Lawrence Review* 10(1977):1–19.

Ruland, Vernon. *Horizons of Criticism: An Assessment of Religious-Literary Options.* Chicago: American Library Assn., 1975.

Schechner, Richard. "Collective Reflexivity: Restoration of Behavior." In *A Crack in the Mirror: Reflexive Perspectives in Anthropology.* Ed. Jay Ruby. Philadelphia: Univ. of Pennsylvania Press, 1982, 39–81.

Scheff, Thomas J. *Catharsis in Healing, Ritual, and Drama.* Berkeley: Univ. of California Press, 1979.

———. "The Distancing of Emotion in Ritual." *Current Anthropology* 18(1977):483–505.

Silk, M. S., and J. P. Stern. *Nietzsche on Tragedy.* Cambridge: Cambridge Univ. Press, 1981.

Smith, Hallett. *Shakespeare's Romances: A Study of Some Ways of the Imagination.* San Marino, Calif.: Huntington Library, 1972.

Stephenson, William. "*Deliverance* from What?" *Georgia Review* 28(1974):114–20.

Stevens, Martin. "Illusion and Reality in the Medieval Drama." *College English* 32(1971):448–64.

Taplin, Oliver. "The Delphic Idea and After: Greek Tragedy on Film." *TLS,* 17 July 1981, 811–12.

———. *Greek Tragedy in Action.* Berkeley: Univ. of California Press, 1978.

Turner, Victor. *Dramas, Fields, and Metaphors: Symbolic Action in Human Society.* Ithaca, N.Y.: Cornell Univ. Press, 1974.

————. *The Forest of Symbols: Aspects of Ndembu Ritual.* Ithaca, N.Y.: Cornell Univ. Press, 1967.

————. "Variations on a Theme of Liminality." In *Secular Ritual.* Ed. Sally Moore and Barbara G. Meyerhoff. Assen, Neth.: Van Gorcum, 1977, 36–52.

Vargo, Edward P. "The Necessity of Myth in Updike's *The Centaur.*" *PMLA* 88(1973):452–60.

Vickery, John B. *The Literary Impact of* The Golden Bough. Princeton: Princeton Univ. Press, 1973.

————. "The Scapegoat in Literature: Some Kinds and Uses." In *The Binding of Proteus: Perspectives on Myth and the Literary Process.* Ed. Marjorie W. McCune et al. Lewisburg, Pa.: Bucknell Univ. Press, 1980, 264–78.

————. ed. *Myth and Literature: Contemporary Theory and Practice.* Lincoln: Univ. of Nebraska Press, 1966.

Vlasopolos, Anca. "The Ritual of Midsummer: A Pattern for *A Midsummer Night's Dream.*" *Renaissance Quarterly* 31(1979): 21–29.

Weimann, Robert. *Shakespeare and the Popular Tradition.* Baltimore: Johns Hopkins Univ. Press, 1978.

Weisinger, Herbert. "The Myth and Ritual Approach to Shakespeare." In *Myth and Literature: Contemporary Theory and Practice.* Ed. John B. Vickery. Lincoln: Univ. of Nebraska Press, 1966, 149–60.

Wickham, Glynne. *Early English Stages.* London: Routledge, 1959.

Wittgenstein, Ludwig. *Remarks on Frazer's* Golden Bough. Ed. and trans. R. Rhees and A. C. Miles. Retford, Eng.: Brynmill, 1979.

Wittreich, Joseph A., Jr. *Visionary Poetics: Milton's Tradition and His Legacy.* San Marino, Calif.: Huntington Library, 1979.

Zender, Karl F. "A Hand of Poker: Game and Ritual in Faulkner's 'Was.' " *Studies in Short Fiction* 11(1974):53–60.

On Ritual Knowledge

THEODORE W. JENNINGS JR.

Facts of publication: *Jennings, Theodore W., Jr. 1982. "On Ritual Knowledge," from* Journal of Religion *62(2):111–127. Copyright © 1982 by The University of Chicago. Reprinted with the permission of The University of Chicago Press.*

It is often popularly assumed that knowledge resides in the brain and that ritual is a way of tranquilizing or avoiding rational thought. If this were the case, ritual and knowledge would be antithetical. Against such assumptions Theodore Jennings, a Christian theologian, argues for a ritually based epistemology, or theory of knowledge. This article, widely cited among educators as well as liturgical theologians, argues that the body is not stupid. Rather it has its own ways of knowing, and these are especially evident in ritual action. Jennings is especially concerned not to treat ritual as secondary or subordinate to verbal expressions of religion such as theology. Instead, he considers ritual as a primary, engaged, bodily way of knowing.

For an application and discussion of this selection see Ron G. Williams and James W. Boyd, "Two Stances toward Ritual Repetition," in their Ritual Art and Knowledge: Aesthetic Theory and Zoroastrian Ritual, *61–82 (Columbia: University of South Carolina Press, 1993).*

About the author: Dates: *1942–   , Gainesville, FL, U.S.A.* **Education:** *B.A., Duke University; B.D., Candler School of Theology, Emory University; Ph.D., Emory University.* **Field(s):** *systematic theology, philosophy of religion.* **Career:** *Assistant Professor, then Professor of Constructive Theology, Chicago Theological Seminary, 1972–1978, 1991–present; Professor of Theology, Seminario Metodista de Mexico, 1983–1986; Associate Research Professor of Theology, 1975–1984, Candler School of Theology, Emory University.* **Publications:** Introduction to Theology *(Fortress, 1976);* Life as Worship *(Eerdmans, 1982);* Beyond Theism *(Oxford University, 1985);* Liturgy of Liberation *(Abingdon, 1988),* Loyalty to God *(Abingdon, 1992);* "Liturgy" *and* "Sacraments" in Encyclopedia of Religion, *ed. Mircea Eliade (Macmillan, 1987).* **Additional:** *Editorial board,* Journal of the American Academy of Religion. *"I am currently working on a series of books that engage in theological reflection of elements of Christian liturgy."*

The study of ritual forms of religious expression is, in many respects, still in its infancy. This is largely due to the greater attention given by religionists to the narrative and mythic forms of religious expression. Despite the pioneering work of Victor Turner and others much remains to be done in identifying the character and structure of ritual action. To this task many disciplines may contribute their own perspectives and lines of inquiry. My own field is that of Systematic Theology and it is precisely by way of this engagement and commitment that I have become interested in the study of ritual. In order to give an account of the nature and method of theological reflection, I found it necessary to give some account of the field of imaginative forms within which the data of theology (scripture, tradition, etc.) are to be located. While in my *Introduction to Theology* I concentrated most upon narrative forms of the religious imagination, it was clear then, and has become even more clear since, that ritual forms are also basic to theological reflection. This is especially the case if one acknowledges the unity of theology and ethics (as in the theology of Karl Barth) or of theory and praxis (as in liberation theology). Ritual is above all a pattern of action, and the more theology concerns itself with action (praxis, ethics) the more carefully it will have to attend to the patterns of action displayed in ritual.

The danger in this move to a consideration of ritual forms is that these will be simply subsumed under the better known mythic or narrative forms so familiar to us through the study of literature, anthropology of religion, or biblical criticism. When this happens, ritual becomes simply an illustration of that which is known or manifested through myth. Such a move is formally analogous to the Reformation insistence on the priority of Word to Sacrament—a priority which may or may not be dogmatically appropriate but which ought not to be made the a priori basis for an understanding of ritual generally.

Accordingly, it seems best to take the supposition that ritual is a symbolic structure which is *sui generis* as the starting point for any inquiry into the nature and character of ritual action. In this way, we will be able to take into account the complex interplay between symbolic structures as diverse as myth and ritual without prematurely granting precedence to one or the other.

A second thesis which will enable us to gain a better understanding of ritual is that ritual may be understood as performing noetic functions in ways peculiar to itself. Ritual is not a senseless activity but is rather one of many ways in which human beings construe and construct their world. Focusing on the noetic functions of ritual will enable us to develop the basis for a theoretical/critical reflection on ritual. That, in brief, is the thesis which this essay will elaborate and seek to make persuasive.

An inquiry into the noetic functions of ritual does not entail the view that such an approach will prove exhaustive of the "meaning" of ritual. It is not necessary at this point to debate the relative importance of playful, habitual, diversionary, or other possible aspects of ritual activity. It is enough for my thesis to claim that noetic functions do characterize rituals to some degree, allowing that other functions may even predominate in some examples of ritual action.

From whatever other points of view we may elect to study rituals, the perspective afforded by our investigation of the noetic dimensions of ritual will have great importance for any attempt to understand ritual. Precisely to the degree that rituals serve noetic functions, to that degree we may gain epistemological access to them, without violating their basic character. This problem of the investigation of ritual as violation, or alternatively as an extension of the ritual process, is one which has been the focus of attention in the Ritual Studies Consultation of the American Academy of Religion and will be the theme of the last section of this essay.

I wish to distinguish three "moments" in the noetic function of ritual. First, ritual action is a way of gaining knowledge. Ritual activity may serve as a mode of inquiry and discovery. This is perhaps the most controversial but, at the same time, most critical aspect of my thesis concerning the noetic function of ritual. It is critical because the relative autonomy of ritual as a symbolic structure hinges on it.

Second, ritual serves to transmit knowledge. This may be termed the pedagogical mode of ritual knowledge. Here the decisive importance of ritual in forming a way of being and acting in the world comes especially into focus. The elaboration of this and of the first subthesis will entail making good the claim that ritual is not primarily the illustration of theoretical knowledge nor the dramatization of mythic knowledge (though of course it may also do these things). Instead ritual action transmits the "knowing" gained through ritual action itself.

Third, ritual performance is a display of the ritual and of the participants in the ritual to an observer who is invited to see, approve, understand, or recognize the ritual action. This aspect of ritual knowledge serves as the point of contact between the ritual action and the attempt to gain a theoretical-critical understanding of ritual. Taken together, then, these aspects or moments of ritual knowledge will invite and guide the knowledge of ritual which is our task.

RITUAL AS COMING TO KNOW

Ritual action is a means by which its participants discover who they are in the world and "how it is" with the world. If we concentrate attention on ritual as an entirely fixed and unvarying sequence of actions, we are likely to overlook this aspect of ritual knowledge altogether. But such a "synchronic" and ahistorical approach to the study of ritual is misleading when it is taken as the sole mode of gaining an understanding of ritual action. The problem might best be illustrated if we sought to compare the enactment of the Latin rite Mass in Western Africa, Central Mexico, a suburb of Chicago, and Saint Peter's in Rome. Even if all are "performed" in Latin (the situation prior to Vatican II) the trained observer would notice significant variation which it would be at least premature to dismiss as incidental. Even if we attend to repeated performances of the same ritual in the same cultural setting over a period of time we would notice differences in detail which may cumulatively become quite important. Even the liturgies of Eastern Orthodox churches with their strong emphasis on historical continuity and tradition have a history characterized both by development (amplification, elaboration) and by discarded alternatives. A historical approach to liturgies may have much to contribute to the religionist's quest for an understanding of ritual by enabling him or her to overcome the bias toward understanding ritual as unvarying repetition. A diachronic perspective on ritual, together with a cross-cultural comparison of putatively identical rituals, brings to light considerable variation which cannot be accounted for by the view of ritual action as sheer repetition.

Now it is precisely this variation which makes possible (though it does not yet require) the view that ritual may be understood as a search for an understanding of the world, as a mode of inquiry and of discovery. If there were no variation in the ritual performance, we would have to conclude that there is here neither search nor discovery but only transmission and illustration of knowledge gained elsewhere and otherwise. This would then compel us to suppose that ritual is, in fact, not an autonomous, but a derivative, mode of the religious imagination.

The case for the autonomy of ritual forms and for the exploratory character of ritual action is strengthened by two additional considerations. The first additional clue is provided by the observations of Ronald Grimes in his participant-observer studies of the Actor's Lab of Hamilton, Ontario.[1] Grimes describes the emergence or "creation" of ritual forms in the work of this experimental theater company. This study suggests that the ritual action is not only the product but is also the means of a noetic quest, an exploration which seeks to discover the right action or sequence of actions. If, as these observations suggest, ritual action is not only the dramatic representation of the already known but is also a mode of exploration, discovery, and "coming to know," then the relative autonomy of the ritual form is further buttressed.

It would still be possible to argue that the transition from not-knowing to knowing is extrinsic to the ritual itself were it not for the groundbreaking work of Victor Turner who has located the transitional or liminal state within the ritual itself.[2] This liminality, Turner has shown, is not accidental to, but is constitutive of, the ritual process. The generative mode of ritual knowledge is inscribed in the ritual process through this liminal and transitional moment.

These reflections suggest that variation in ritual performance is by no means the incidental and extraneous phenomenon it has often been thought to be by those who define ritual action in terms of unvarying repetition. Instead, the variation in ritual performance may be understood as a decisive clue the character of the ritual action as a relatively autonomous form of noetic exploration and discovery. To be sure, this exploration and discovery take place within the already known repertoire of ritual action. This relatively stable repertoire provides the necessary framework for exploration in much the same way that a mastery of relevant data and theoretical construction is indispensable for "scientific" exploration and discovery. Without seeking to push the tenuous analogy between ritual and other noetic processes too far, we may nevertheless maintain that it is the openness to novelty inscribed in ritual liminality and the exploratory quest for the appropriate action which constitute the possibility of a history of ritual action even within a relatively stable ritual tradition. The pertinence of these reflections for the uncovering of the noetic dimension of ritual action is clarified by Gerardus van der Leeuw's reflections upon the ritual dance: "In the dance man discovers the rhythm that surrounds him. . . . He discovers the rhythm and invents a response. . . . He places his own movements and those of the creatures which surround him in an ordered whole."[3]

More light may be shed on this exploratory and generative aspect of ritual knowledge if we attend to the "how" of this exploration. This may also help us to identify more precisely the specific character of ritual itself. Ritual knowledge is gained through a bodily action which alters the world or the place of the ritual participant in the world. This summary statement proposes three interrelated aspects to the way of gaining knowledge in ritual: It is primarily corporeal rather than cerebral, primarily active rather than contemplative, primarily trans-formative rather than speculative. Let us see in more detail the meaning of these aspects of ritual knowledge.

1. Ritual knowledge is gained by and through the body. We might speak here of the "incarnate" character of ritual knowledge or say that it is gained through "embodiment." This would be somewhat misleading, however. It is not so much that the mind "embodies" itself in ritual action, but rather that the body "minds" itself or attends through itself in ritual action. When engaged in ritual action (let us take the performance of the Eucharist and the ritual-like activity of disco dancing as disparate exam-

ples), I do not first think through the appropriate action and then "perform" it. Rather it is more like this: My hand "discovers" the fitting gesture (or my feet the fitting step) which I may then "cerebrally" *re*-cognize as appropriate or right. I may then attempt to give an account of this appropriateness. These are different epistemological steps of which only the first (attending and discovering through the body) is constitutive of ritual knowledge.

2. Ritual knowledge is gained not by detached observation or contemplation but through action. It is in and through the action (gesture, step, etc.) that ritual knowledge is gained, not in advance of it, nor after it. If ritual knowledge were prior to the action, then we would be reduced once again to understanding the ritual as an illustration or demonstration of what is already known in some other way. If ritual knowledge were gained primarily after the action, then an unwarranted priority would be given to the re-cognitive as opposed to the cognitive, to the reflective-critical rather than to the active. That is, priority would be given to something other than ritual action itself. To say that there is such a thing as ritual knowledge is to say that it is knowledge which is identical with doing or acting, with a bodily doing or acting.

3. Ritual knowledge is gained through the alteration of that which is to be known. Even if we reduce the field of the object of ritual knowledge to the ritual itself—that is, claim that that which I seek to know is the ritual or the ritual action itself—even then we must say that the exploratory "doing" is a doing which alters the ritual complex or its constituent parts in some way. I do not discover what to do with the chalice by observing it but by "handling" it. (Just as I do not discover how to use an axe to chop firewood unless I actually chop firewood—unless, to speak metaphorically, the axe "teaches me" through my hands, arms, and shoulders how it is to be used.) Ritual knowledge is gained not through detachment but through engagement—an engagement which does not leave things as they are but which alters and transforms them.

To the extent to which we may be prepared to say that ritual knowledge is a knowledge of the world or of the world as encountered by the Sacred, then to that extent we shall also be led to say that the world is known by being changed or transformed. This occurs in and through the handling of those objects (masks, scepters, chalice, etc.) in which the cosmos is concentrated and represented in the ritual action. Ritual knowledge, then, is not so much descriptive as it is prescriptive and ascriptive in character. It prescribes and ascribes action. Victor Turner notes that "all rituals have this exemplary model: displaying character; in a sense they may be said to 'create' society in much the same way as Oscar Wilde held life to be an imitation of art."[4] More radically, we could say that ritual does not depict the world so much as it founds or creates the world.

Marx's formula that it is important not so much to understand the world as to change it is one which also neatly summarizes this aspect of ritual action. In the sphere of the Christian theological tradition, we may also be reminded here of the doctrines of transubstantiation and of consubstantiation. These doctrines may be understood as attempts to articulate in a reflective-critical mode the way in which ritual action entails the transformation of its primary "elements." By the same token, the tendency of left-wing reformers to speak of representation rather than transformation at this point is a clear sign of the rise of the intellectualistic bias of modernity. It is this bias which has rendered the phenomenon of ritual so opaque and has deflected the attention of the students of religion away from its ritual forms and to its narrative and mythic expressions.

THE PEDAGOGICAL CHARACTER OF RITUAL KNOWLEDGE

I have been describing ritual as a way of coming to know, that is, as a way of searching for and discovering knowledge. In doing so I have focused attention on the variation of ritual performance rather than on the repetition of action which is so noticeable in the observation of ritual. It is to this "repetition" that I now wish to turn in describing the way in which ritual transmits or "teaches" knowledge.

Ritual action does not primarily teach us to see differently but to act differently. It does not provide a point of view so much as a pattern of doing. The following reflections are an expansion on this theme, with particular attention to how this is done in ritual.

Our starting point here is the observation that a ritual is an action, a doing, a praxis, and above all a bodily doing, acting, performing. It is precisely this doing which is "communicated" or "transmitted" or taught by ritual action. On one level we can say that the doing of the ritual teaches us to do the ritual. The doing of the Eucharist, for example, teaches us to do the Eucharist. Ritual action incites or provokes the imitation of itself. The most direct such imitation is the repetition of the ritual itself.

We may extend this somewhat by saying that ritual action incites or provokes not only an imitation but also a response. This response, while being both provoked and patterned by the ritual action, is not itself necessarily "controlled" or "dictated" by that action. Again Grimes's reflections on the Actor's Lab experience are useful here in describing the way in which action invites action, which "carries forward" the "work" without dictating that action. This can also be recognized in that "profane" ritual of disco dancing where the actions of one partner invite, without foreclosing, the action of the other. Similarly Eucharistic action (consecration and elevation) invites but does not coerce a responding action—eating and drinking.

Ritual action, then, proposes a pattern of action, through provoking either an imitation or a response. Both imitation and response are themselves ritual actions, repeating or completing the ritual.

I think it is possible and necessary to go further here in order to say that ritual action patterns all action "governed" or "epitomized" by the ritual itself. This point may be illustrated by looking at the function of "the Lord's Prayer" when it is used in Christian worship. Its ritual use provokes imitation—that is, it teaches a congregant to "say" this prayer and to do so in a way which is repeatable both within and outside the ritual context. Beyond this, however, this prayer may serve as a model for acts of prayer which are not repetitions of this prayer. This has long been maintained in the Christian tradition, though the formulation of Johannes Wollebius is especially clear: "The form or true and religious pattern of prayer is the Lord's prayer."[5] The field of action governed or epitomized by this prayer, then, would be all praying activity, which includes that praying activity, presumably the greatest proportion, which occurs outside the ritual or liturgical context.

The field of action governed or patterned by the ritual action extends even further, however. As early as the third century Cyprian remarked, "If we call God Father we should behave as his children."[6] What Cyprian is proposing is that this ritual act may be understood as the epitome of all specifically Christian action—that is, as the précis of Christian ethics. This proposal is taken up by Karl Barth in a programmatic fashion through his announced intention to develop a specifically Christian ethic on the pattern of a commentary on baptism, the Lord's Prayer, and the Eucharist.[7] This proposal may be reformulated by the thesis that Christian ritual patterns all doing which is a doing *coram deo.* Ritual serves as a paradigm for all significant action. While the ritual itself may be specifically "religious," it serves as a paradigm for all important action whether or not that action is, in some restricted sense, religious.

The performance of ritual, then, teaches one not only how to conduct the ritual itself, but how to conduct oneself outside the ritual space—in the world epitomized by or founded or renewed in and through the ritual itself. Ernst Käsemann's reflection on Rom. 12:1 is quite pertinent here when he observes that worship and ethics converge.[8] The ritual serves to focus paradigmatic gestures which pattern world-engaging activity generally.

We can now state more precisely the relationship between the generative mode of ritual knowledge (exploration and discovery) and the pedagogical mode of ritual knowledge (transmission and formation). Ritual knowledge is, in both cases, the knowledge gained in bodily action, a knowledge which is a knowledge of bodily action. The known action (the traditional and transmitted action) serves as the field within which the quest for the action not yet known may be carried forward. The quest for the new action is dependent on the repertoire of received action. But if this repertoire is to fulfill its function (namely, to pattern all significant action), then it must remain open to the quest for this newly appropriate action, that is, for the action which is "fit" to be a paradigm for the world of action generally.

These remarks carry us over the threshold of a consideration of the truth or falsity of a ritual action and so of ritual knowledge. After all, if we are to speak of "knowledge" here, must we not also be prepared to speak of criteria in terms of which the truth or falsity, adequacy or appropriateness of such cognitive acts may be assessed? We may, in fact, discern in ritual the presence of something like coherence and correspondence tests of adequacy. I have indicated that, at the very least, what is sought in the exploratory moment of ritual knowledge is the fitting or appropriate act. "Fittingness" is a relational notion which suggests something very like coherence tests of adequacy. Here we could say that it is a question of ritual consistency—does this act fit with other acts or gestures? We might be tempted to call such a criterion "aesthetic," but this would not be to undermine the claim to knowledge. We have long since learned the role of aesthetic criteria of adequacy, even in development of scientific theory, through the work of Michael Polanyi and Thomas Kuhn.[9]

With respect to correspondence tests of adequacy, the situation may be somewhat more complex. In rough terms, however, we may say that a ritual is "falsified" to the extent to which it cannot serve as a paradigm for significant action outside the ritual itself and is validated to the extent to which it does function in this way. Ritual action which does not "correspond" in this way to the world of significant action generally becomes autistic and solipsistic and thus becomes, in the misinformed (but still informative) phrase, "mere ritual." Interestingly, it is precisely this autistic or solipsistic action which is the subject of psychoanalytically oriented reflections on "ritual behavior." The assertion that not all ritual action is pathological in character depends, then, on the development of ways to display the correspondence of this action to diverse ways of being and acting in the world. This criterion is more complex than it seems at first sight, however. That to which the ritual action corresponds is not some discrete and immutable state of affairs but "world in act." The ritual does not simply "mirror" but intends to transform this world in act. This suggests, then, that coherence and correspondence tests of adequacy require supplementation by something like a pragmatic test. Further development of an inquiry into ritual knowledge will have to be careful, however, not to make use of such a "pragmatic" theory of ritual in ways which efface the distinctions between ritual and magic or prototechnology.

THE OBJECT OF RITUAL KNOWLEDGE

These reflections press on us the need to give some provisional account of the object of ritual knowledge.

So far the object of ritual knowledge has been tentatively identified as "knowing how to act," or a knowledge of "the fitting action," or, more grandiosely, as "ontological praxis." Our problem is to give some answer to the question, What do I gain knowledge of when I acquire "ritual knowledge"? It is crucial that our answer to this question prescind from those instances where the ritual is serving the purpose of illustrating knowledge which is gained in some way other than the ritual itself. Thus, there may be cases where a ritual is understandable as the dramatization of myth (in which case we have primarily to do with mytho-poetic knowledge rather than ritual knowledge). There may also be cases where the ritual may be understood as "ceremonializing" knowledge whose character is technological—as in the case of a ceremonial "enactment" of planting, harvesting, canoe making, and so on. In this case, the ritual would be functioning as a pedagogical technique for the transmission of some store of knowledge which is only accidentally, rather than essentially, associated with the ritual performance itself. Many theories of ritual tacitly assume or explicitly maintain that all ritual is reducible to such a pedagogical, illustrative, or ceremonial activity and is, thus, devoid of any noetic function specific to itself. If this widespread view is to be countered, we must at least be able to give a provisional description of the object of ritual knowledge as such.

The formula which shall guide our reflections is this: Ritual knowledge is knowledge gained in action of action. The means of acquiring ritual knowledge correspond to its aim or object.

At its most circumscribed, this will mean that participation in the ritual action is generative of knowledge of the ritual action itself. The "fitting act" of the ritual performance is discovered and transmitted through the ritual performance. In this way ritual knowledge is reflexive.

But to leave the matter here is to render the ritual solipsistic. To the extent to which ritual action is "paradigmatic" it conveys the knowledge of the acts governed by the paradigm. Thus, in terms of our earlier illustration, the ritual performance of the Lord's Prayer models the praying activity of the community of its participants generally; or a burial ritual may model a way of handling grief, as when a child buries a canary or a lover mourns the temporary absence of the beloved. The knowing of the ritual action provides a model for fitting action in contexts or situations not themselves ritualized.

So far we have seen that the object of ritual knowledge is itself an action or set of actions. On the reflexive level, this is the ritual action itself. More generally, this will also include the knowledge of that set of actions for which the ritual action serves as a paradigm. But the object of ritual knowledge may be understood both more radically and more comprehensively.

The ultimate object of ritual action we will term an ontological or cosmogonic praxis. To participate in a ritual is to know how the world acts, how it "comes to be." Gerardus van der Leeuw quotes Lucian as follows: "He who does not dance does not know what will happen."[10] Participation in the ritual performance permits access to the world or community as a "happening" and a "doing." Perhaps the most familiar way in which this is formulated is to say that the most important rituals "repeat" the act which founds the world. Thus, the spring rituals of some agrarian societies "enact" the coming into being of the earth, its fertility, or the means of agriculture. The original and originative act which the ritual enacts may be comprehensive in scope (the origin of the world) or more restricted (the origin of the community, the origin of some crucially important feature of the life of the community). The more comprehensive in scope and radical in character the act, the more it warrants the term "cosmogonic praxis." In some cases of ritual, we may not have reference to an original act but to "the way things happen." In these cases it might be better to use the term ontological praxis so as not to bias interpretation in the direction of origins or a "time of origin." In any case, the ritual action seems to have this ontological dimension of exhibiting the action or rhythm of reality.

To the extent to which the originative act or ontological rhythm which is known by the ritual performance is comprehensive in character, it may be taken to be paradigmatic for a correspondingly wide variety of behavior by its participants. If this is true we would expect to find a correlation between the ontological radicality of a ritual and its importance as a model of, or paradigm for, other actions. The expectation of such a correlation would serve as an important heuristic tool in the investigation of ritual.

We may further anticipate that the more a ritual performance exhibits these features, the more central it will be to the "religion" of the community. This would enable us to distinguish between rituals and ceremonies where the former have both a greater radicality (ontological "depth") and are more comprehensively paradigmatic than the latter.

In summary, then, the object of ritual knowledge may be abstractly identified as the coordination of three kinds of action: (*a*) the ritual action, (*b*) the constituting action, (*c*) the extraritual behavior modeled by ritual action. In each case, the object of knowledge is an action or set of actions (or rhythm of actions) rather than a state or condition. Further, we may expect some correlation between the religious importance ascribed to the ritual performance and the radicality of the act (or "ontological depth" of the rhythm) which it enacts, as well as a correlation between its religious importance and the breadth of the field of behavior for which that performance serves as a paradigm.

Already, in inquiring into the object of ritual knowledge, we have had to refer to the questions of the investigation of ritual. It is to that issue that we now turn.

THE RITUAL AS OBJECT OF KNOWLEDGE

The ritual is performed. It is characteristic of any ritual that it entails an "audience," a "spectator." To vastly oversimplify a complex matter, we may say that the auditor or spectator is often "the god." Through the ritual the community identifies itself, that is, depicts itself to this auditor or spectator. Whether from the standpoint of an outside observer this self-identification is an actual or a disguised (masked) one is not important. What is important is that a certain display is inherent in the ritual action and that this display is directed exteriorly. This is, perhaps, most obvious in "sacrifice" rituals, which putatively at least allay the disfavor or seduce the favor of sacral forces. In Grimes's description of the Actor's Lab, this function of "critical" observer is played primarily by the "director," who awaits the proper or fitting ritual action and pronounces it "complete." To the extent to which drama and dance are derivative from ritual, we could say that the place of this "ideal observer" is taken by the audience or the critic who play their own parts in the "success" of the performance.

What is of great importance here is that ritual involves the movement whereby the ritual agent (the community, its priestly representatives, etc.) makes itself known in a particular way to another. This other is invited to participate responsively in the ritual action itself, to complete it, or continue it, or perfect it. I say "invited" since an essential difference between ritual and technology (or the pretechnology of some forms of magic) is that ritual does not coerce but invites response—it seduces rather than manipulates, just as the formulation of a question anticipates but does not foreclose the response.

To return directly to our theme of ritual knowledge, then, the ritual communicates two kinds of knowledge to an ideal observer, namely, the knowledge of the agent of the action (we are as we act) and the knowledge of the action anticipated from the observer/other. These two kinds of knowledge are, indeed, inseparable. The ideal observer of ritual action is not the removed or detached observer. Instead, this observer is one who is not only one who sees, but one who does—whose action will in some way extend or continue the ritual action itself and thereby "validate" it. Once again, the knowledge which is ritual knowledge is knowledge in act—it is praxological. It is knowledge gained, transmitted, and received in action.

These last reflections on the intention of ritual to be "seen" in a particular way open up to view the complex question of the "viewing" of ritual on the part of those of us who are engaged in the study of ritual. It is to that question I want to turn now.

Our task is to find ways to gain an understanding of ritual, a knowledge of ritual. Our problem is to discover whether there are ways of gaining such knowledge without distorting fundamentally the ritual process, on the one hand, or distorting the character of knowledge—more precisely, critical discursive knowledge—on the other.

Within the context of this "problematic," the question of whether ritual itself is involved in the quest for, and transmission of, knowledge assumes some importance for us. I have maintained that ritual does have such a noetic function and have suggested some of the peculiar characteristics which ritual knowledge may have. I want now to propose that ritual knowledge is not only distinct from the reflective knowledge we seek but is also the "point of contact" for that knowledge. That ritual action and the "scientific" study of ritual action are both "epistemological" processes must be our starting point.

Throughout this paper I have presupposed that ritual activity is not a mindless repetition of action-in-sequence but is a "minded" action—one which is not unconscious, preconscious, but fully conscious; though in a way unique to itself. One way of describing this is to say that ritual action involves an embodied consciousness in a way that, for example, contemplation or mytho-poesis do not. Ritual action is intelligent action which is different in kind, though not in degree, from such other forms of intelligent action as toolmaking, theoretical formulation, or painting. This point requires some stress, since much conspires to make us forget it. Most important is our cultural valuing of relatively disembodied expressions of consciousness. This bias is inherent even in talk of "embodied" consciousness, since that language tacitly asserts that consciousness is first or primarily "separate" from bodiliness and then secondarily is "incarnated." It will not do to turn this hierarchy on its head in order to speak of an absolute primacy of body meaning, however. Rather, it is appropriate to accept a plurality of modes of consciousness, a plurality of modes of

knowing, and to inquire whether these are related to one another and how they are so related.

Even if we grant the relative autonomy of ritual knowledge and scientific or reflective-critical knowledge without making the one subservient to the other, we may still be perplexed about the possibility of relating them. I have maintained that ritual knowledge is a particular form of knowledge, utterly distinct from scientific knowledge—it is corporeal where our knowledge is cerebral, praxological rather than speculative, engaged rather than detached. It may seem, therefore, that ritual knowledge is at least impervious to, if not repulsive of, scientific inquiry. Does not its autonomy as a form of knowledge render our tasks of investigation impossible?

I believe, on the contrary, that the particular character of ritual knowledge invites our inquiry—that such an inquiry is or may be an extension of ritual knowledge itself.

An inquiry into the meaning of ritual action begins with the observation of ritual action. It is crucial to understand that the observation of ritual is not a violation of the ritual but is intrinsic to ritual action itself. The action intends itself to be witnessed. In the previous section I have maintained that a decisive moment of ritual knowledge is the way in which ritual action intends to make its agent known to an other/observer. This other is in some cases "the god"; in other cases, perhaps, this other is the community which performs the ritual in the stead of the god. However, this role of observer is actualized in the ritual—the role itself is already present in the ritual. We may object that the scientific observer of ritual is not the one intended by this role of observer. There is, no doubt, much truth in this reflection, but it is noteworthy that our knowledge of ritual is largely gained by the observations of "outsiders," whether missionaries or anthropologists. These observations are typically gained not by stealth or subterfuge but at the invitation of the ritual participants themselves.[11] In other cases where accounts are given by participants to outside observers (when the ritual excludes the latter), the one who gives the account assumes the role of observer in giving the account. All of this would be impossible if the ritual action precluded the role of observer. It is possible on the grounds I have suggested, namely, that the ritual action includes and intends this role.

Ritual action not only permits but invites, and even directs, attention to itself. It does this in order to evoke a response to itself on the part of the observer. This response may be variously construed as imitation, participation, approbation, and so on. In any case, some appropriate action is awaited from the observer, some active engagement is anticipated. How does this expectation comport with our own intentions as students of ritual? What are our intentions, after all? Most simply put, our intention is to understand the ritual. This will include careful attention to, and an accurate accounting of, the ritual action. Moreover, we will probably intend to discover something of the inner appropriateness of ritual action—its coherence with other actions which make up the ritual complex we are studying. Further, we will want to inquire how this ritual action relates to the life of the people who engage in it. What field of significant action does this ritual govern, to what, that is, does it correspond?

These cognitive issues are not imported into ritual from the outside. They are present in ritual itself, or so I have maintained in earlier sections of this paper. Our task is to know reflectively what is known ritually, to re-cognize ritual knowledge. This, of course, involves the transferral of ritual knowledge "outside" the ritual space and time. This may seem to be simply a restatement of our original problem. Is such a translation, in the nature of the case, not impossible? I think not. For ritual action intends and entails such a translation, if I am correct in maintaining that ritual governs and serves as a paradigm for action not enclosed but epitomized by the ritual action. It is this which distinguishes ritual from autistic routine.

There are a number of other considerations which may be brought to bear on this question: The coexistence and mutual interaction between ritual, mythic, magical, and technological modes of cognition in "primitive" cultures suggests that none of these are taken to be impermeable to the others. This suggests that processes of translation are not excluded but anticipated even in "prescientific" societies. The ritual-like activities of scholars of religion suggest that the transposition from practitioner of ritual to investigator of ritual is not altogether the quantum leap we might make it out to be. There is also the question of the extent to which the knowledge of ritual is "praxological" in the sense of intending the transformation of the world it seeks to understand. These are all subjects which may provoke further reflection. I want to conclude these reflections, however, by taking up a final problem in the relationship between ritual knowledge and the scientific knowledge of ritual.

The introduction of the outside observer has some impact on the ritual performance, since it alters the composition of the ritual world. This is true even though the ritual includes the role of "outside observer" (or, additionally, the role of the role-breaking/transcending fool). Those who take seriously this more-or-less subtle alteration of the ritual world may conclude that such alteration invalidates the observation of the ritual. If this were true, then no observation of ritual would be possible, and the project of understanding ritual would be abortive. There are, I believe, two reasons for rejecting this conclusion. The first has to do with the rejection of the supposition that it is essential to ritual that it be utterly unvarying in its performance. Only if this were true would the variation in ritual performance occasioned by the observer mean an abrogation of the ritual itself. But as I have insisted earlier, ritual is not unvarying by nature but adaptive and, thus, generative of knowledge. A full recognition of this point would, I think, enable students of ritual to discard some of those inhibitions which result from the overscrupulous "voyeuristic" model of attention and study, without thereby lurching into what Ron Grimes has called "whoring."[12]

Finally, ritual knowledge is knowledge which is gained through effecting an alteration of what it knows. The intention to leave the ritual unaffected by our observation is, thus, alien to the character of ritual itself. Properly understood, then, our attempt to gain a reflective-critical knowledge of ritual is complementary to the noetic dimension of ritual itself.[13] Thus, the ambiguity in the phrases "ritual knowledge" and the "knowledge of ritual" may serve as the appropriate designation of the hypothesis which I have sought to elaborate in these pages.

NOTES

1. Ronald L. Grimes, "Liminality and the Lab," an unpublished paper presented at the American Academy of Religion Annual Meeting held in San Francisco, 1977. Published materials on Actor's Lab have subsequently appeared: "The Rituals of Walking and Flying: Public Participatory Events," *Drama Review* 22(4):77–82; and "The Actor's Lab: The Ritual Roots of Human Action," *Canadian Theatre Review* 22:9–19. The present essay had its origin as a response to and reflection on Grimes's work in the field of ritual studies. Cf. Grimes, *Symbol and Conquest: Public Ritual and Drama in Santa Fe, New Mexico* (Ithaca, N.Y.: Cornell University Press, 1977).

2. Victor Turner, *The Ritual Process: Structure and Anti-Structure* (Ithaca, N.Y.: Cornell University Press, 1969), pp. 94 ff.

3. Gerardus van der Leeuw, *Sacred and Profane Beauty: The Holy in Art*, trans. David E. Green (Nashville, Tenn.: Abingdon Press, 1963), p. 14.

4. Turner, p. 117.

5. Johannes Wollebius, *Compendium Theologiae Christianae*, bk. 2 (5.2), in *Reformed Dogmatics*, trans. John W. Beardslee (London: Oxford University Press, 1965), p. 204.

6. Cyprian, *On the Lord's Prayer*, par. 11, in *St. Cyprian on the Lord's Prayer*, trans. J. Herbert Bindley (London: SPCK, 1914) 5:450. This thesis is developed further in my book, *In Jesus' Name: A Theology of Prayer and Praise* (Grand Rapids, Mich.: Wm. B. Eerdmans Publishing Co., 1982).

7. Karl Barth, *Church Dogmatics IV*, 4 (fragment), trans. G. W. Bromiley (Edinburgh: T. & T. Clark, 1969), p. ix. This proposal is carried a step further in Barth's *The Christian Life*, trans. G. W. Bromiley (Grand Rapids, Mich.: Wm. B. Eerdmans Publishing Co., 1981).

8. Ernst Kasemann, "Worship in Everyday Life: A Note on Romans 12," *New Testament Questions of Today* (New York: Harper & Row, 1969), p. 191.

9. Michael Polanyi, *Personal Knowledge* (Chicago: University of Chicago Press, 1959), pp. 3–15, 33–48, 132–202. Thomas Kuhn, *The Structure of Scientific Revolutions* (Chicago: University of Chicago Press, 1962).

10. Van der Leeuw, p. 29.

11. Victor Turner provides a typical illustration of this point when he remarks, "I soon discovered that the Ndembu were not at all resentful of a stranger's interest in their ritual system and were perfectly prepared to admit to its performance anyone who treated their beliefs with respect" (*The Ritual Process*, p. 9).

12. Ronald L. Grimes, "Methodological Problems in Ritual Studies; or Beyond Voyeurism and Whoring" (paper presented at the American Academy of Religion Meeting, held in San Francisco, 1977). This paper, together with the already cited "Liminality and the Lab," served as the starting point for the formation of the Ritual Studies Consultation of the AAR in 1978.

13. The transformation of this hypothesis to the level of philosophers and theological theory would require a number of additional steps beyond the elaboration of the hypothesis I have attempted in these pages. The working out of the implications for a general theory of actual meaning would, in my view, entail an appropriation of kinesthetic and structural-linguistic modes of understanding for the recording and analysis of ritual action. A phenomenology of action and the location or ritual action within this field, together with an understanding of "body" (in the double sense of corporate and corporeal), are necessary for an adequate comprehension of ritual action. The movement toward a theological theory of ritual action would entail a reflection on the intended and/or represented other of this action. From the standpoint of a specifically Christian theological investigation, we would have to undertake the substantiation of a number of theses, among which are: (1) that divine action provokes ritual action i.e., that ritual action is not (only) an imitation of divine action but (also) a response to the action of God in Christ; (2) that repudiation of cultic action and inauguration of liturgical action are homologous to the transition from law to grace (this entails a critique of the perpetuation of cultic action in the sphere of the church); (3) that Christian ethics are to be understood from the standpoint of an understanding of liturgical gesture (rather than causal efficiency); (4) that, to paraphrase Ricoeur, "the gesture gives rise to thought" entails an appropriation (and modification) of both Eastern Orthodox liturgical theology and Third World liberation theology in the generation of a theological method whereby praxis (as opposed to techne) gives rise to theory.

Ritual, Politics, and Power

David I. Kertzer

Facts of publication: *Kertzer, David I. 1988. "The Power of Rites," from* Ritual, Politics, and Power, *1–14; 92–101, and notes. New Haven: Yale University Press. Copyright © 1988 by Yale University. Reprinted with the permission of Yale University Press.*

Because ritual is commonly identified with religion it has been relatively ignored in the study of politics. Arguing that symbols give people a way to understand and transform the world through the use and production of new symbols, Kertzer establishes the inseparability of symbols and politics. Ritual, which for Kertzer is "action wrapped in a web of symbolism," is central in the construction of political reality. Kertzer illustrates his thesis by examining Ronald Reagan's cemetery rites at Bitburg, Germany, in 1985. The notion of cognitive dissonance is invoked as Kertzer considers the role that rites play in influencing political beliefs. He holds that ritual envelops political action and political power and does so for all cultures, far beyond the common view that political ritual merely serves to bolster the status quo in supposedly primitive cultures.

For further reading on political ritual see Eric Hobsbawn and Terence Ranger, eds., The Invention of Tradition *(Cambridge: Cambridge University Press, 1983); Christel Lane,* The Rites of Rulers *(Cambridge: Cambridge University Press, 1991).*

About the author: Dates: *1948–   , New York, NY, U.S.A.* **Education:** *B.A., Brown University; Ph.D., Brandeis University.* **Field(s):** *politics and symbolism; political ritual; social organization; anthropology and history; Italian society and politics.* **Career:** *William Kenan Professor of Anthropology, 1989–1992, Bowdoin College; Paul Dupee University Professor of Social Science, and Professor of Anthropology and History, 1992–present, Brown University.* **Publications:** Comrades and Christians: Religion and Political Struggle in Communist Italy *(Cambridge University, 1980; Waveland, 1990);* Ritual, Politics, and Power *(Yale University, 1988);* Sacrificed for Honor *(Beacon, 1993).* **Additional:** *President, Society for the Anthropology of Europe, 1994–96; Founding Editor,* Journal of Modern Italian History.

From national party convention to presidential inauguration, from congressional committee hearing to the roar of the football stadium crowd belting out the national anthem, ritual is a ubiquitous part of modern political life. Through ritual aspiring political leaders struggle to assert their right to rule, incumbent power holders seek to bolster their authority, and revolutionaries try to carve out a new basis of political allegiance. All of these political figures, from leaders of insurrections to champions of the status quo, use rites to create political reality for the people around them. Through participation in the rites, the citizen of the modern state identifies with larger political forces that can only be seen in symbolic form. And through political ritual, we are given a way to understand what is going on in the world, for we live in a world that must be drastically simplified if it is to be understood at all.

Yet few people recognize how important ritual is in modern politics. Because ritual is usually identified with religion and, since modern Western societies have presumably separated political affairs from religious life, there is an assumption that ritual remains politically significant only in less "advanced" societies.[1]

But is industrial society really any different in its sacralization of power? Are politics now the product of rational activities by bureaucrats, are political allegiances decided by cost-benefit analysis, and are leaders regarded by the public as essentially no different from themselves? In Polynesia, temporal rulers were viewed as descendants of the gods and, as such, they radiated *mana*, or supernatural power. Being so powerful, they were surrounded by a web of rituals that governed all interaction with their subjects.[2] Although no such supernatural rationalization of secular power prevails today in the United States or in other industrial states, the politically powerful nonetheless are still surrounded by rites that govern their interaction with the public and with each other when they are in the public eye. Political ritual, as Shils quips, has been given a "bad name" by Western intellectuals raised in utilitarian traditions.[3] Blinded by their rational model of the political universe, these intellectuals ignore the ritual that envelops political action and political power.[4]

In these pages I try to show why ritual is important in *all* political systems and to point out the many ways ritual is employed in politics. In doing this I argue against the common view that political ritual merely serves to bolster the status quo. Ritual is much more important to politics than this. True, kings use ritual to shore up their authority, but revolutionaries use ritual to overthrow monarchs. The political elite employ ritual to legitimate their authority, but rebels battle back with rites of delegitimation. Ritual may be vital to reaction, but it is also the life blood of revolution.

POLITICS, SYMBOLISM, AND RITUAL

Politics is expressed through symbolism. Rather little that is political involves the use of direct force, and, though material resources are crucial to the political process, even their distribution and use are largely shaped through symbolic means. To understand the political process, then, it is necessary to understand how the symbolic enters into politics, how political actors consciously and unconsciously manipulate symbols, and how this symbolic dimension relates to the material bases of political power.[5]

Symbolism is involved in politics in many ways. In these pages I focus on just one, ritual. Anthropologists have long been associated in the public view with the search for quaint rites and seemingly illogical behavior. My goal, however, is not to exhume the exotic but to challenge some comfortable assumptions about the bases of our own political

systems. Although many political observers in the United States and other industrial nations have noted the ritual behavior associated with politics, few have ever taken it seriously. They view ritual as mere embellishment for more important, "real" political activities. But, in fact, ritual is an integral part of politics in modern industrial societies; it is hard to imagine how any political system could do without it. . . .

THE POWER OF SYMBOLS

Since my argument rests on the importance of symbolism in politics, it makes sense to begin with some general observations about the role of symbolism in human societies and in people's lives. Thurman Arnold, a witty legal scholar of a half-century ago, observed that all human conduct and all institutional behavior are symbolic. Arnold attempted to puncture the common conceit that people in modern societies behave in pragmatic, goal-oriented ways. On the contrary, he declaimed, "Society is generally more interested in standing on the side lines and watching itself go by in a whole series of different uniforms than it is in practical objectives." Scholars, chided Arnold, cannot bear the idea that people are more influenced by symbolic forms than by utilitarian calculations. As a consequence, the "chief interest of the intellectual is to prove that such irrational conduct is inherently rational—or else the product of some form of group sinning."[6]

But let me back up a bit here and begin by considering the individual's relation to his or her culture. Human reality is not provided at birth by the physical universe, but rather must be fashioned by individuals out of the culture into which they are born and the experiences they have, experiences that bring them into contact with other people and with various parts of nature. The world out there confronts each individual with an infinite number of stimuli, yet no one can deal with all of them. We must be selective in our perceptions, and those aspects of the world that are selected must be further reduced and reordered in terms of some system of simplification (or categorization) that allows us to make sense of them. This order is largely provided by the symbol system we learn as members of our culture, a system that allows for both social creativity and individual idiosyncrasy.

Such symbol systems provide a "shield against terror."[7] They are a means, indeed the primary means, by which we give meaning to the world around us; they allow us to interpret what we see, and, indeed, what we are. Perhaps the most striking aspect of this symbolic process is its taken-for-granted quality.[8] People are not generally aware that they themselves endow the world with their own symbolically constructed version of reality. On the contrary, people believe the world simply presents itself in the form in which it is perceived. This may be naive, but it is nevertheless necessary. We could not get out of bed in the morning if we did not subscribe to this view, for if we fully recognized the extent to which our notions of reality are the product of an artificially constructed symbol system, it would be, as Kenneth Burke pointed out, "like peering over the edge of things into an ultimate abyss."[9]

Through symbols we confront the experiential chaos that envelops us and create order. By objectifying our symbolic categories, rather than recognizing them as products of human creation, we see them as somehow the products of nature, "things" that we simply perceive and recognize. Indeed, the very distinction we make between the objective world and the subjective world is itself a product of humanly created symbols that divide the world of fact from the world of opinion.[10]

That people perceive the world through symbolic lenses does not mean that people or cultures are free to create any symbolic system imaginable, or that all such constructs are equally tenable in the material world. There is a continuous interaction between the ways people have of dealing with the physical and social universe and the actual contours of that universe. When symbolic systems collide with refractory social or physical forces, the potential for change in the symbolic system is ever present. Moreover, symbols do not simply arise spontaneously, nor is the continuing process of redefinition of the symbolic universe a matter of chance. Both are heavily influenced by the distribution of resources found in the society and the relationships that exist with other societies. Though symbols give people a way of understanding the worlds, it is people who produce new symbols and transform the old.

SYMBOLISM IN POLITICS

In a playful passage, Thomas Carlyle asks us to envision a pompous ceremonial gathering in Britain, replete with dukes, colonels, generals, and others of lofty status. Imagine, he says, that with a wave of the wand their clothes were all to vanish and they were left entirely naked. What would happen to the dignity of the occasion? Pursuing the point, Carlyle asks, "Lives there a man that can figure a naked Duke of Windlestraw addressing a naked House of Lords? Imagination, choked as in mephitic air, recoils on itself, and will not forward with the picture." Carlyle's clothes are one example of how all objects function in human society, for they all act as symbols, endowed with special meaning. To say that a person is clothed with authority is something more than metaphorical.[11]

Through symbolism we recognize who are the powerful and who are the weak, and through the manipulation of symbols the powerful reinforce their authority. Yet, the weak, too, can try to put on new clothes and to strip the clothes from the mighty. In Kessler's words, "The symbolic is not a residual dimension of purportedly real politics; still less is it an insubstantial screen upon which real issues are cast in pale and passive form. The symbolic is real politics, articulated in a special and often most powerful way."[12] Political reality is in good part created through symbolic means, as many a candidate for political office has recognized. Creating a symbol or, more commonly, identifying oneself with a popular symbol can be a potent means of gaining and keeping power, for the hallmark of power is the construction of reality.[13]

Some political observers have gone so far as to say that people live in a "dream world," a world of "illusion." They contrast the "real" world with this phantom realm of the symbol. In a stirring passage written in the shadow of Hitler's preparations for war, Max Lerner, horrified by the adulatory allegiance evoked by the Fuehrer, warned that while the power of dictators derives from the "symbols that they manipulate, the symbols depend in turn upon the entire range of associations that they invoke." He concluded: "The power of these symbols is enormous. Men possess thoughts, but symbols possess men."[14] Yet, just as Hitler's skillful manipulation of symbols was inspiring the German people to war, so a different set of symbols was being powerfully framed by Churchill, Roosevelt, and others to mobilize the opposition.[15]

Modern wars depend on a sense of national allegiance, but the nation itself has no palpable existence outside the symbolism through which it is envisioned. As Walzer puts it, "The state is invisible; it must be personified before it can be seen, symbolized before it can be loved, imagined before it can be conceived."[16] People subscribe to the "master fiction" that the world is divided into a fixed number of mutually exclusive nations; they see these units as part of the nature of things, and assume an antiquity that the nations in fact lack. This symbolic conception of the universe leads people to believe that everyone "has" a nationality, in the same sense that everyone has a gender. It is in this light that Benedict Anderson defined a nation as "an imagined political community." Far from being window dressing on the reality that is the nation, symbolism is the stuff of which nations are made.[17]

Symbols instigate social action and define the individual's sense of self. They also furnish the means by which people make sense of the political process, which largely presents itself to people in symbolic form. When Americans form their opinions regarding the activities of the president or the Congress, they do so mainly on the basis of the manipulation of symbols by these officeholders, in conjunction with their own material experiences, which are themselves perceived in good part through a symbolic filter. For this reason one observer of the American presidency concluded that "Politics is primarily the art of understanding the symbols actually operative in society and learning how to make them issue forth in action. . . . It is the art of governing not rationalists, but people." In electing a president, we elect "the chief symbolmaker of the land. . . ."[18]

The strength of people's allegiance to political symbols was certainly evident in Ohio during the days of inflamed patriotic zeal accompanying the captivity of the American embassy personnel in Iran. When the workers at a construction site were ordered by their boss to remove the American flag decals they sported on their hard hats, they staunchly refused. As one worker explained, "The hat says who you are . . ."—and, of course, so did the miniaturized stars and stripes.[19]

As this example of national allegiance shows, modern politics depends on people's tendency to reify political institutions. Entities such as "government," "party," or the "state" are not viewed as symbolic constructions. Rather, they are thought of as objects that exist independently of people and their symbolic universe. Children find it easier to conceive of authority in terms of a person like the president (or a teacher) rather than a collectivity such as Congress. Similarly, adults use the metaphor of a "body" to conceive of Congress, which allows them to treat a variegated group of people as a single entity.

Perhaps this can be made clearer by recounting the story of the Indian who came to see the "government" in Ottawa. The Indian grew increasingly frustrated as he was led from one office to the next, meeting one man after another who claimed responsibility for government affairs, yet never confronting the "government" itself, who, he thought, did a good job of keeping himself hidden.[20]

Many of the most potent political symbols have a palpable quality to them, making it easier for people to treat concepts as things. This is evident in the metaphors that help define the political universe. For numerous Americans, an "iron curtain" [once lay] across Europe, separating those on the other side from the "free world." Similarly, a flag is not simply a decorated cloth, but the embodiment of a nation; indeed, the nation is defined as much by the flag as the flag is defined by the nation.

Studies of politics in modern states, with a few important exceptions, pay little attention to the role of the symbolic in the political process.[21] In many studies, politics is examined as a give-and-take in which people simply follow their material interests. These material interests are often taken to be self-evident. In other studies, people are viewed as consumers in a public relations market, or as empty slates socialized to reproduce the political views of their parents, peers, or neighbors.

The lack of systematic studies of the symbolic dimension of politics in contemporary Western societies is no doubt also due to the difficulty all people face in examining their own symbol systems. Since people perceive the world through symbolic lenses, it is difficult for them to be conscious of just what those symbols consist of and what influence they have.[22]

The underdevelopment of studies on the symbolic dimension of modern politics is also due to the kinds of empirical methods emphasized in modern social science. Symbols cannot be satisfactorily studied in quantitative terms, nor through surveys or electoral analyses. In emphasizing such methods, analysts have a tendency to assume that those aspects of politics that cannot be easily quantified must be unimportant. To complete the vicious circle, the resulting empirical studies then reinforce the view that modern politics is determined by rational action.[23] Clifford Geertz points out some of the flaws in such approaches:

> The main defects of the interest theory are that its psychology is too anemic and its sociology too muscular. Lacking a developed analysis of motivation, it has been constantly forced to oscillate between a narrow and superficial utilitarianism that sees men as impelled by rational calculation of their consciously recognized personal advantage and a broader, but no less superficial, historicism that speaks with a studied vagueness of men's ideas as somehow "reflecting," "expressing," "corresponding to," "emerging from," or "conditioned by" their social commitments.[24]

In short, people are not merely material creatures, but also symbol producers and symbol users. People have the unsettling habit of willingly, even gladly, dying for causes that oppose their material interests, while vociferously opposing groups that espouse them. It is through symbols that people give meaning to their lives; full understanding of political allegiances and political action hinges on this fact.[25]

To argue that symbolism and ritual play important roles in the political process in Western societies flies in the face of much received wisdom. Yet, far from arguing that politics becomes less encrusted in symbol and myth as a society grows more complex, I suggest that a case could be made that just the reverse is true. Living in a society that extends well beyond our direct observation, we can relate to the larger political entity only through abstract symbolic means. We are, indeed, ruled by power holders whom we never encounter except in highly sym-

bolic presentations. And what political environment could be more dependent on symbolism than one in which our decision whether to pat a person on the back or to shoot him in the back depends on the color of the uniform he wears? With the increase in the size of the state and the growth of bureaucracy, Michael Walzer observes, politics is transformed "from a concrete activity into what Marx once called the fantasy of everyday life."[26]

DEFINING RITUAL

Before examining the role of ritual in politics, I should clarify what "ritual" means. Here, I take a middle path between an overly restrictive definition, which would limit ritual to the religious sphere and identify it with the supernatural, and an overly broad definition, labeling as ritual any standardized human activity. In defining ritual, I am not, of course, trying to discover what ritual "really" is, for it is not an entity to be discovered. Rather, ritual is an analytical category that helps us deal with the chaos of human experience and put it into a coherent framework. There is thus no right or wrong definition of ritual, but only one that is more or less useful in helping us understand the world in which we live. My own use of the term reflects my goal of shedding light on how symbolic processes enter into politics and why these are important.

Until a generation ago, anthropologists typically defined ritual as culturally standardized, repetitive activity, primarily symbolic in character, aimed at influencing human affairs (or at least allowing humans to understand better their place in the universe), and involving the supernatural realm.[27] Durkheim offered the most influential early social scientific view of ritual, relating it to religious practices, which, he believed, divide the world into two classes: the sacred and the profane. Rites, he asserted, are the "rules of conduct which prescribe how a man should comport himself in the presence of these sacred objects."[28]

Although on the surface Durkheim's view seems to link ritual behavior to the supernatural realm, a closer look leads to a different conclusion. For Durkheim, worship of a god is the symbolic means by which people worship their own society, their own mutual dependency. Thus, the sacred ultimately refers not to a supernatural entity, but rather to people's emotionally charged interdependence, their societal arrangements. What is important about rituals, then, is not that they deal with supernatural beings, but rather that they provide a powerful way in which people's social dependence can be expressed.

I follow this perspective in defining ritual as symbolic behavior that is socially standardized and repetitive.[29] This is, in fact, the way in which many anthropologists now use the concept.[30] In doing so, some have been at pains to distinguish between religious and secular ritual.[31] I think, however, that such a distinction is more a hindrance than a help in understanding the importance of ritual in political life. I thus use the term *ritual* in the more general sense.[32]

CHARACTERISTICS OF RITUAL

Ritual action has a formal quality to it. It follows highly structured, standardized sequences and is often enacted at certain places and times that are themselves endowed with special symbolic meaning.[33] Ritual action is repetitive and, therefore, often redundant, but these very factors serve as important means of channeling emotion, guiding cognition, and organizing social groups.[34]

I have defined ritual as action wrapped in a web of symbolism. Standardized, repetitive action lacking such symbolization is an example of habit or custom and not ritual.[35] Symbolization gives the action much more important meaning. Through ritual, beliefs about the universe come to be acquired, reinforced, and eventually changed. As Cassirer puts it: "Nature yields nothing without ceremonies." Ritual action not only gives meaning to the universe, it becomes part of the universe.[36] As one observer noted, "Through ritualized action, the inner becomes outer, and the subjective world picture becomes a social reality."[37]

Ritual helps give meaning to our world in part by linking the past to the present and the present to the future. This helps us cope with two human problems: building confidence in our sense of self by providing us with a sense of continuity—I am the same person today as I was twenty years ago and as

I will be ten years from now—and giving us confidence that the world in which we live today is the same world we lived in before and the same world we will have to cope with in the future. "By stating enduring and underlying patterns," Myerhoff writes, "ritual connects past, present, and future, abrogating history and time."[38]

One of the perennial problems people face is coping with the frustrating indeterminacy of the world. People respond by doing what they can to fix a single, known reality so that they can know what behavior is appropriate and so that they can understand their place in the world.[39] The very fixity and timelessness of ritual are reassuring parts of this attempt to tame time and define reality.

But even though there are certain psychological and even physiological bases of ritual, understanding its political importance depends on recognizing the ways ritual serves to link the individual to society.[40] Through ritual the individual's subjective experience interacts with and is molded by social forces.[41] Most often, people participate in ritual forms that they had nothing to do with creating. Even where individuals invent new rituals, they create them largely out of a stockpile of preexisting symbols, and the rituals become established not because of the psychic processes of the inventor but because of the social circumstances of the people who participate in the new rite.[42]

The power of ritual, then, stems not just from its social matrix, but also from its psychological underpinnings. Indeed, these two dimensions are inextricably linked. Participation in ritual involves physiological stimuli, the arousal of emotions; ritual works through the senses to structure our sense of reality and our understanding of the world around us.[43]

These psychological attributes are evident in another characteristic of ritual: its frequently dramatic character. Indeed, Arnold argued that people relate to the world through a series of dramatic productions:

> Every individual, for reasons lying deep in the mystery of personality, constructs for himself a succession of little dramas in which he is the principal character. No one escapes the constant necessity of dressing himself in a series of different uniforms or silk hats, and watching himself go by.[44]

Perhaps it is in this light that the proposal made by a local socialist newspaper at the end of the nineteenth century should be seen. It called for construction of a little platform along the line of march at Vienna's May Day demonstration so that marchers could step up momentarily to see the huge crowd of demonstrators of which they were a part.[45]

Ritual provides one of the means by which people participate in such dramas and thus see themselves as playing certain roles. The dramatic quality of ritual does more than define roles, however, it also provokes an emotional response. Just as emotions are manipulated in the theater through the "varied stimuli of light, colour, gesture, movement, voice," so too these elements and others give rituals a means of generating powerful feelings.[46]

Ritual dramas are widely found in politics.[47] In the United States, as elsewhere, election campaigns involve the staging of such dramas by candidates as well as the attempts to get the mass media to broadcast these dramatic productions into people's homes. Indeed, candidates often try to limit all contact with the public and the mass media that does not take place through carefully arranged dramatic productions, heavily laden with well-choreographed symbols.[48]

Symbols provide the content of ritual; hence, the nature of these symbols and the ways they are used tell us much about the nature and influence of ritual. Three properties of symbols are especially important; condensation of meaning, multivocality, and ambiguity.

Condensation refers to the way in which individual symbols represent and unify a rich diversity of meanings. The symbol, whether verbal or iconic—that is, manifest in a physical form such as a bible or a flag—somehow embodies and brings together diverse ideas. At a subconscious, and hence more powerful, level, these various ideas are not just simultaneously elicited but also interact with one another so that they become associated together in the individual's mind.[49]

Closely tied to the condensation of meaning in ritual symbols is their *multivocality*, the variety of different meanings attached to the same symbol. Where condensation refers to the interaction of these different meanings and their synthesis into a new meaning for an individual, multivocality suggests another aspect, the fact that the same symbol may be understood by different people in different ways. This trait is especially important in the use of ritual to build political solidarity in the absence of consensus.[50]

Given the properties of condensation and multivocality, it should hardly be surprising that ritual symbolism is often *ambiguous*: the symbol has no single precise meaning. Put in more positive terms, this means that symbols are not arcane ways of saying something that could be more precisely expressed in simple declarative form. The complexity and uncertainty of meaning of symbols are sources of their strength.[51]

I have emphasized the fact that rituals have a standardized form and are presented to individuals by society rather than generated from individual psychological activity. But this does not mean that ritual is an inherently conservative force. Rituals do change in form, in symbolic meaning, and in social effects; new rituals arise and old rituals fade away. These changes come through individual creative activity. People, in short, are not just slaves of ritual, or slaves of symbols, they are also molders and creators of ritual. It is because people create and alter rituals that they are such powerful tools of political action.[52]

Yet even though ritual does have this creative potential, it also has a conservative bias. Ritual forms do tend to be slower to change than many other aspects of culture, as any student of Western religions knows. Indeed, their ability to give people a sense of continuity derives in good part from their constancy of form over time. The impact of a particular enactment of a ritual is a product of its past performances. Memories associated with those earlier ritual experiences color the experience of a new enactment of the rites.[53] Rites thus have both a conservative bias and innovatory potential. Paradoxically, it is the very conservatism of ritual forms that can make ritual a potent force in political change.

THE POLITICAL IMPORTANCE OF RITUAL

According to mainstream Western ideology, ritual occupies at best a peripheral, if not irrelevant, role in political life. Serious political analysts, we are led to believe, would hardly waste their time by distracting attention from the real nitty-gritty of politics—interest groups, economic forces, and power relations—in order to turn a critical eye to ritual.[54]

But this image of "political man" as a rational actor who carefully weighs his or her objective circumstances and decides on a course of action based on an instrumental calculation of self-interest leaves out culture and all that makes us human. Though we are rooted in the physical world and much affected by material forces, we perceive and evaluate them through our symbolic apparatus. We communicate through symbols, and one of the more important ways in which such symbolic understandings are communicated is through ritual. Mary Douglas puts this starkly: "Social rituals create a reality which would be nothing without them. For it is very possible to know something and then find words for it. But it is impossible to have social relations without symbolic acts."[55]

Each society has its own mythology detailing its origins and sanctifying its norms. Some of these revolve around great men (in Western society female cultural heroes are less common), while others revolve around notable events that, whether having a historical basis or not, are defined through a web of symbolically constructed meaning. In the United States, children grow up learning about the Puritans, the Indians, the slaves, life on the plantation, the melting pot, George Washington, Abraham Lincoln, Daniel Boone, John Kennedy, and Martin Luther King. Indeed, their conceptions of society are in good part based on understandings passed on through such symbols. They learn both what are the valued norms of conduct and what are the criteria of success. More to the point here, these symbols provide a way to understand such abstract political entities as the nation and a means (indeed the compulsion) of identifying with them. Lance Bennet, a political scientist, observes:

> Myths condition the public to the powerful symbols used by politicians. Myths underwrite the status quo in times of stability and they chart the course of change in times of stress. In the day-to-day business of politics myths set the terms for most public policy debate. When mythical themes and myth-related language are stripped away from policy discourse, very little of substance remains. Most political controversy centers around disagreement over which myth to apply to a particular problem.[56]

Ritual practices are a major means for propagating these political myths. The symbols at the heart of ritual observances are part of the tissue of myth that helps structure an understanding of the political world and the public's attitude to the various political actors that populate it.

Once constructed, such symbolic understandings of the political order are resistant (though not immune) to change. Here again, there is a conflict between the view of humans as rational actors and a view that stresses a more complex interaction of the symbolic with the material. In the former view, changing a person's political opinion is a matter of logical argumentation and the marshaling of facts. But the resistance of beliefs to change through such rational debate has long been recognized. In China many centuries ago, Chuang Tzu wrote: "Suppose I am arguing with you and you get the better of me. Does the fact that I am not a match for you mean that you are really right and I am really wrong? Or if I get the better of you, does the fact that you are not a match for me mean that I am really right and you are really wrong?"[57]

The Confucian philosophers understood the importance of ritual for efficient government. People's behavior, they realized, is not a simple product of consciously weighing options, but rather takes shape through the rituals in which they take part. Rulers should always avoid giving commands, opined one of these philosophers, for commands, being direct and verbal, always bring to the subject's mind the possibility of doing the opposite. He continued:

> But since rituals are non-verbal, they have no contraries. They can therefore be used to produce harmony of wills and actions without provoking recalcitrance; if a man finds himself playing his appointed part in *li* [ritual] and thus already—as it were *de facto*—in harmony with others, it no more occurs to him than it occurs to a dancer to move to a different rhythm than that being played by the orchestra.[58]

Not only does ritual have this cognitive effect on people's definition of political reality, it also has an important emotional impact. People derive a great deal of satisfaction from their participation in ritual. Rulers have for millennia (indeed, for as long as there have been rulers) attempted to design and employ rituals to arouse popular emotions in support of their legitimacy and to drum up popular enthusiasm for their policies. But, by the same token, rituals are also important for revolutionary groups who must elicit powerful emotions to mobilize the people for revolt. Trotsky recognized the need for such ritual forms in the early years of the Soviet state. He was especially disturbed by the church monopoly on everyday rites, arguing that "rationalistic" appeals to the masses were not sufficient. We must recognize, Trotsky insisted, "man's desire for the theatrical," his "strong and legitimate need for an outer manifestation of emotions."[59] . . .

THE RITES OF BITBURG

Symbols have a history of cognitive and emotional associations. Their power comes in part from this history: the childhood memories they arouse, feelings of past solidarity, the way they have been used to define one's own identity and one's understanding of the world. Meanings cannot be declared by fiat, although new shades of meaning are continually being created and old ones lost through the incessant attempts by political leaders to manipulate the symbols.

Ronald Reagan's phenomenal popularity in the United States was in no small part the result of his skills in reworking symbols and staging rites to guide perceptions of both the external world and of his own heroic role in it. It should not be surprising, then, that the most withering criticism he faced in his first five years in office regarded his planned participation in a ceremony, a rite to be held at Bitburg in the spring of 1985. He had overseen numerous controversial political and military actions, from the firing of thousands of striking air traffic controllers to the stationing of American troops in chaotic Lebanon, yet none of this produced the furor that met his planned cemetery rite.

The decision to stage this rite can be traced to two ceremonies observed in 1984. In the first, leaders of the World War II Allied powers celebrated the anniversary of the Normandy landing. German Chancellor Kohl expressed his consternation at being excluded and was, by way of consolation, invited by French President Mitterand to celebrate a memorial ceremony at a Verdun cemetery where victims of the First World War were buried. Kohl and Mitterand solemnly embraced amidst the sea of crosses.

But the Verdun ceremony was not what Kohl needed. In fact, no one was concerned about the memories of the First World War, and thus there was no need for ceremonial reconciliation. What the Germans were uneasy about was being identified with Nazism and all its evils. Mitterand had ritually absolved the Germans from the wrong war. What was needed was a rite of absolution for the Second World War, one that would take place on German soil and have powerful symbolic content. The place was the Bitburg German cemetery; the sacral aura would be furnished by Ronald Reagan.

The value to Kohl of the rites lay in dispelling the discomfiting hold the Nazi symbolic legacy had on his countrymen. In doing so it would bolster his own stature and that of his party. The very staging of the rites demonstrated Kohl's power, all the more so when Reagan, by coming, showed he valued his commitments to the German chancellor above the passionate pleas of American congressmen and the American people. Reagan, for his part, was repaying Kohl in this ritual currency for a variety of both symbolic and material expressions of support that Kohl's government had given Reagan in the past. The most notable of these involved stationing a new battery of nuclear missiles on German soil. More generally, such rites would help nourish a political alliance that kept large numbers of American troops in Germany.

If Mitterand had tried to substitute the symbolism of the First World War for that of the Second, Reagan's mission was to transform the symbolism of the Second into that of the First, to take a still festering historical sore and, in Habermas's words, "bestow on the present the aura of a past that had a settled look."[60] Reagan began these attempts to rewrite the past even before he left for Germany. Defending his planned visit to honor the German war dead, Reagan told an American audience that the dead

German soldiers were "victims of Nazism also, even though they were fighting in the German uniform, drafted into service to carry out the hateful wishes of the Nazis. They were victims, just as surely as the victims in the concentration camps."[61] The evils perpetrated by Nazi Germany, in other words, were the responsibility of a tiny group of leaders who forced the German population to do their wicked bidding. Although this was the message Reagan hoped his cemetery ceremonies would send, he ran afoul of the symbolic construction his listeners had already placed on the events of the past.

For many Germans, by contrast, the rites were a satisfying vindication of their view that Germans had been unfair victims of malicious propaganda, that the Second World War was but another in a long line of European conflicts for which no one people could be singled out for blame. And even in the United States, where a chorus of protest sang out, the rite had a significant cognitive effect on millions of people. The fact that their president could join the head of the German government in such a rite in a German war cemetery would bolster the intended view of German innocence, of Germans as victims, rather than perpetrators, of Nazism.

In the end, though, the symbolism of Nazism proved too powerful for Reagan. Years after they had killed their last Allied soldier, decades after they had herded their last victim into nearby concentration camps, these dead German soldiers continued to inflict pain. And just as Reagan struggled to redefine the symbolism associated with his ritual appearance, his antagonists sought to discredit the rite through their own manipulation of powerful symbols. This took various forms. Perhaps most notable was the "discovery" that among the thousands of graves were thirty-eight bearing the mark of the Nazi SS, the *Schutzstaffel*, Hitler's infamous secret police. So powerful was the stigma associated with the symbol of the SS that Reagan's own staff grew alarmed about his participation in the rites, while the presidential aides who had helped select the site were showered with scorn. The Nazi army was one thing—indeed, it was not a Nazi army but a *German* army—the SS quite another in the symbolic construction of the German past. Just what the one or the other had actually done many decades before, few but the historians knew, but the symbolic distinction remained potent.[62]

Reagan's ceremonial plans spawned special outrage in the wake of his earlier announcement that he would not visit a Nazi concentration camp memorial during the trip. Yet, when the president subsequently added a visit to the Bergen-Belsen concentration camp, many of these same critics protested. As a *Jerusalem Post* writer cried out, "Do not drag our dead into your reconciliation with Kohl's Germany. Do not mention our victims in the same breath with those who lie at Bitburg."[63] By holding the two ceremonies on the same day, the concentration camp victims and their killers would be placed on equal symbolic footing.

The ceremonies went ahead, but Reagan did what he could to douse the sacred flames he had helped kindle. From refusing to join hands with Kohl at the cemetery, to his last-minute pilgrimage to Bergen-Belsen, he was able to tailor the rites to reduce his political costs. Kohl, for his part, made sure that the lesson of the rites was not lost in the face of Reagan's backsliding. The "visit to the graves in Bitburg," he declared, is "a widely visible and widely felt gesture of reconciliation between our peoples, the people of the United States of America and us Germans, reconciliation which does not dismiss the past but enables us to overcome it by acting together."[64] The past exists through its symbolization in the present. Overcoming the past means changing the symbols of the present, and this is just what the rites at Bitburg were intended to do.

In its editorial the day before the cemetery visit, the *Chicago Tribune* lamented that we "live in a time when symbolism has replaced rational debate as the medium of political exchange."[65] The medium of political exchange has always been symbolism; it is an exchange that not only redistributes political rewards, but that also builds our political understandings. If symbols and rituals are used to build political reality, it is because, as humans, we can do it no other way.[66]

POLITICAL BELIEF

By repetitively employing a limited pool of powerful symbols, often associated with emotional fervor, rituals are an important molder of political beliefs.[67] Political reality is defined for us in the first place through ritual, and our beliefs are subsequently reaffirmed through regular collective expression.

But what does all this say about our rational faculties, our ability to think logically and independently, to examine a problem critically and come to a rational conclusion based on an examination of the evidence? Unfortunately, it suggests that this view of our essentially rational nature is hard to defend. As Edelman observed, our most cherished and deeply rooted political beliefs are rarely if ever subjected to debate or critical examination. It is just because they are so deeply held that any sincere debating of their validity is so threatening, for to do so is to recognize implicitly that they may be erroneous.[68]

Years ago, from his cell in a Fascist prison, Antonio Gramsci made a similar point in explaining why it is so difficult to change people's political beliefs. Among the masses, he argued, "philosophy can only be experienced as a faith."[69] People do not construct their basic political conceptions by critically analyzing competing political ideas. Rather, people acquire these ideas through the society they live in, and these ideas are largely determined by those who exercise control (*hegemony*) over the society. Indeed, Gramsci held that a world in which a person's political beliefs depend on rational argument is inconceivable, for in such a world individuals would have to change their beliefs whenever they encountered a better educated and more articulate antagonist.

Gramsci was certainly not claiming that it is impossible to change people's beliefs, only that it is naive to imagine that such change can be brought about simply through logical persuasion. For an individual to change his or her beliefs without subjecting them to rational debate, a conducive social context is needed. Ritual provides just such a context. For example, when political elites form new international alliances, there is commonly considerable ritualization—much public hand-shaking and mutual parading of symbols. The nation or group that had previously been mistrusted, or even loathed, is placed in a new symbolic nexus, viewed now as benevolent rather than threatening.[70] Reagan and Kohl were still engaged in this process decades after the end of the Second World War, while the periodic rites of Arab unity aim to shore up popular perception of alliances that have very little other basis.

Ritual can foster common action without necessitating common belief. People's behavior may in many circumstances be better explained as the reaction to situational pressures rather than as the manifestation of a deep-seated belief. Indeed, a number of psychologists have warned against assuming that people's attitudes determine their behavior, in spite of the fact that this notion seems intuitively correct.[71]

According to Snyder and Swann, people are especially likely to act on the basis of situational pressures rather than out of underlying beliefs in social settings that:

(a) are novel, unfamiliar, and contain sources of social comparison . . . (b) make individuals uncertain of or confused about their inner states . . . (c) suggest that one's attitudes are socially undesirable . . . or deviant . . . and (d) sensitize one to the perspective of others and motivate concern with social evaluation and conformity with reference-group norms. . . .[72]

But I would take this a step further by suggesting that the beliefs themselves are not so stable. In social settings of this sort, people may change their beliefs as well as their actions. Public political rituals meet many of these criteria. They are occasions on which people are brought closely together with others and in which failure to conform to the behavior of others can make one a pariah.

The powerful emotions that rituals can induce lend further force to this drive toward conformity. Bagehot, in 1912, observed the uncharacteristic servility of that imperious English statesman, Lord Chatham, when the peer went to consult the king. During these conferences with King George III, Lord Chatham remained kneeling at the king's bedside. "Now no man," Bagehot observed, "can argue on his knees. The same superstitious feeling which keeps him in that physical attitude will keep him in a corresponding mental attitude."[73]

The primacy of the ritual in determining behavior is expressed in a rather different way in the Islamic world. What is important to be a good Moslem, the Prophet Muhammad reportedly advised, is to pray five times each day; what goes on in the worshiper's mind, he said, is between him and Allah.[74] Participating in the common prayers with fellow worshipers is a firmer basis of religious allegiance than private belief. Yet, at the same time, people who participate in ritual tend to develop beliefs that rationalize their behavior and support their allegiance.

COGNITIVE DISSONANCE

In examining the role rituals play in influencing political beliefs, [we see that tension is] produced when people hold beliefs that are mutually inconsistent or when a person's beliefs differ from those of socially significant others. These are both situations in which an individual is especially likely to change beliefs. Such change, however, is not a foregone conclusion: people go through life holding logically inconsistent views, and they are also likely to hold some views that differ from those of their neighbors.

The now venerable theory of cognitive dissonance, first fully developed in the late 1950s by Leon Festinger, sheds some light on this problem. By dissonance, Festinger simply refers to inconsistency among cognitions; conversely, consonance refers to the mutual consistency of beliefs. The theory holds that when people find themselves holding dissonant beliefs, they experience psychological discomfort. This, in turn, motivates people to reduce the dissonance. Not only do people try to reduce dissonance when it appears, they also actively avoid situations and information that are likely to increase dissonance.[75]

One common kind of cognitive dissonance occurs when our perception of events in the world conflicts with our beliefs about those phenomena. In such cases, Festinger argued, "the reality which impinges on a person will exert pressures in the direction of bringing the appropriate cognitive elements into correspondence with that reality."[76] The greater the amount of dissonance an individual experiences, the stronger is the pressure to reduce it. Cognitive dissonance is especially powerful in situations where our beliefs conflict with those of socially important others, and where no simple empirical referent can be used to demonstrate the validity of one's own beliefs. Where strongly held views are shared with others, though those beliefs seem to conflict with what is observed in the outside world, little cognitive dissonance is experienced.

The Nazi salute offers a good case for applying this approach to political ritual. The salute symbolized allegiance to the Nazi regime in general and to Hitler in particular. One of its purposes was to provide a systematic means to spot disloyalty, while simultaneously serving to reinforce the allegiance of the masses. Bruno Bettelheim recognized the political and psychological potency of the rite:

> To Hitler's followers, giving the salute was an expression of self assertion, of power. Each time a loyal subject performed it, his sense of well-being shot up. For an opponent of the regime it worked exactly opposite. Every time he had to greet somebody in public he had an experience that shook and weakened his integration. More specifically, if the situation forced him to salute, he immediately felt a traitor to his deepest convictions. So he had to pretend to himself that it did not count. Or to put it another way: he could not change his action—he *had* to give the Hitler salute. Since one's integration rests on acting in accord with one's beliefs, the only easy way to retain his integration was to change his beliefs.[77]

The power the rulers exercised through this Nazi ritual, as Bettelheim pointed out, came not only from the fact that it reached "the minutest and most private life activities of the individual but more, that it [split] the inner person if he resist[ed]."[78]

EMOTION AND COGNITION

To celebrate the tenth anniversary of the death of Lassalle, the socialist workers in Breslau, then part of Germany, dedicated a new red flag. In addition to the inscription, "May 23 1863, Ferdinand Lassalle," the front of the flag bore the mottoes "Liberty, Equality, Fraternity," and "Unity is Strength." On the back was the legend: "The social-democratic workers in Breslau 1873." The power that this socialist icon held over those who identified with its symbolism is told by its checkered itinerary of the ensuing decades. When Bismarck's anti-socialist laws threatened the flag, it was smuggled into Switzerland. Later, during the Nazi regime, it was buried in a garden, then hidden in a plumber's cellar. When Red Army officers, moving into Breslau at the end of World War II, heard of its existence, they went to salute it, but its guardian refused to give it up to them. Later, when Breslau was annexed to Poland, the flag was smuggled out to West Germany, where it was given to the Social-Democratic Party, which was presumed to be the legitimate heir of all it represented. Over several decades, people had risked imprisonment and worse to guard the flag.[79]

If political rites encourage certain interpretations of the world, they do so in no small part because of the powerful emotions that they trigger. Our perceptions and interpretations are strongly influenced by our emotional states, but the process works very much in the reverse direction as well. Our fears are aroused, terror incited, joy created through rites that channel our political perceptions. Before concluding this look at how ritual affects people's political beliefs and perceptions, I should like, briefly, to consider the role played by emotion.

The "ultimate force of symbols," writes Ioan Lewis, "depends at least as much on their power to stir the emotions" as on their cognitive content.[80] But these psychological processes should not be split into two separate forces. Indeed, what makes the emotional side of ritual so interesting and so politically important is frequently its connection to particular cognitive messages. Rituals do not simply excite, they also instruct. But the potency of that instruction depends heavily on the power of ritual to place the individual in a receptive frame of mind. Sensory devices of all kinds are used to affect the person's emotional state, from rhythmic chanting to stylized dancing and marching, from powerful singing to the doleful tolling of bells. The most effective rituals have an emotionally compelling quality to them: they involve not just part of the personality but the whole personality.[81] In the intensity of ritual, people focus their attention on a limited range of symbols. The greater their emotional involvement the more the rest of the universe is obliterated, and the more the symbols embodied in the rites become authoritative.[82]

What is the source of the emotion found in ritual? A clue is provided by Durkheim, who attributes the emotional intensity of rites to the fact that they express the powerful dependence people feel toward their society. But in addition to regularly scheduled rites, rituals are also typically found when individuals confront transition points in their lives. The strong emotions associated with ritual here reflect the inner conflicts, uncertainties and fears that afflict people in such circumstances.

In funerary ritual, for example, the emotional state of the mourner is affected by confronting death and by the changes in his life implied by that death. People use ritual to cope with these strong emotions, a practice from which many political systems have profited by inserting their own symbolism. From burials at Arlington military cemetery in the United States, to party- or state-organized funerals in certain communist countries, there is a ceaseless quest to politicize these emotionally potent rites.

Political forces also create new rituals to produce emotional states that can be used to influence people's perceptions of the political world. This is found in all contemporary societies. In the Soviet Union, for example, earlier idealistic views of people as rational actors—and hence of ritual as a form of superstition to be jettisoned—gave way to intricate plans to use the emotional impact of ritual to structure political beliefs.[83]

Just how the emotions generated by ritual infuse and affect its cognitive message remains an intriguing question. Victor Turner provides one of the best-known anthropological answers to this question in discussing the two poles of ritual, the emotional and the cognitive. In the performance of ritual an exchange takes place between these poles, and the emotions aroused in ritual infuse the cognitive view fostered by the rite, rendering it compelling. Like Durkheim, Turner sees such beliefs largely in consensual terms. This exchange of meanings between the poles of ritual "makes desirable what is socially necessary by establishing a right relationship between involuntary sentiments and the requirements of social structure. People are induced to do what they must do."[84] But the value of his argument regarding the exchange of qualities between the poles of ritual goes beyond this static and homogeneous view of social life.

Observers of crowd behavior have often noted the contagiousness of emotion. This operates in collective rituals as well, where people's emotions are heavily influenced by the emotions displayed by others around them.[85] Collective rituals are seductive, and the emotions previously associated with such collective ritual celebrations continue to be felt when similar rites are performed later, alone, or in more limited company.

Ritual can be seen as a form of rhetoric, the propagation of a message through a complex symbolic performance. Rhetoric follows certain culturally prescribed forms whose built-in logic makes the course of the argument predictable at the same time that it lends credence to the thesis advanced. Kenneth Burke described this as the "attitude of collaborative expectancy" that the formal pattern of rhetoric elicits from its audience. The very form of the presentation leads us to believe in the message put forth. Of special relevance to an understanding of the political uses of ritual is the emotionally compelling structure of we/they imagery. As Burke writes:

> Imagine a passage built about a set of oppositions ("*we* do *this*, but *they* on the other hand do *that*; *we* stay

here, but *they* go *there*; *we* look *up*, but *they* look *down*," etc.). Once you grasp the trend of the form, it invites participation regardless of the subject matter. Formally, you will find yourself swinging along with the succession of antitheses, even though you may not agree with the proposition that is being presented in this form. Thus, you are drawn to the form, not in your capacity as a partisan, but because of some "universal" appeal in it. And this attitude of assent may then be transferred to the matter which happens to be associated with the form.[86]

Successful ritual has just this structure. It creates an emotional state that makes the message uncontestable because it is framed in such a way as to be seen as inherent in the way things are. It presents a picture of the world that is so emotionally compelling that it is beyond debate.

NOTES

1. Reynolds (1978:134).
2. Norbeck (1977); Sahlins (1981). On politics and sacrality, see also Bergesen (1977:221).
3. Shils (1966:447).
4. The foremost anthropological exponent of the importance of ritual in all political systems is Abner Cohen (1974, 1981). Mackenzie (1967:290), a political scientist, declared: "It seems an obvious idea that someone should tackle the subject of political rituals in the Western world, yet nothing (so far) has come of it." Although there have been a handful of attempts to examine modern political rites in the West since, to date not much progress has been made in putting this all in a larger framework.
5. Here I follow Clifford Geertz's (1966:5) broad use of the concept of the symbol. In this view, a symbol refers to "any object, act, event, quality, or relation which serves as a vehicle for a conception," and the conception constitutes the meaning of the symbol.
6. Arnold (1935:17).
7. Berger (1967:22).
8. Berger (1967:24).
9. Burke (1966:5).
10. Cassirer (1946); Bauman (1973).
11. Carlyle (1908:45–46, 54).
12. Kessler (1978:244–45).
13. Nieburg (1973:54).
14. Lerner (1941:235).
15. Duncan (1962:245–46).
16. Walzer (1967:194).
17. Anderson (1983:14–15). The idea that polities are governed by "master fictions" is Geertz's (1977). For a discussion of this usage, see Wilentz (1985).
18. Novak (1974:23), Turner (1974:55).
19. Singer (1982:76).
20. Sahlins (1981:70) recounts this story, citing an earlier version in Lévi-Strauss (1966:239*n*). Radcliffe-Brown (1940: xxiii) also sheds light on the problem of reification in politics, writing that "There is no such thing as the power of the State; there are only, in reality, powers of individuals— kings, prime ministers, magistrates, policemen, party bosses, and voters." On the development of children's political conceptions, see Niemi (1973:121–22).
21. The exceptions include Murray Edelman (1964) and some of those most influenced by his work, such as Bennett (1980). In addition, a few political scientists, such as Aronoff (1980) and Laitin (1986), have been directly influenced by symbolic study in anthropology. However, this line of work has remained outside the main stream in both political science and political sociology, as its practitioners recognize. In Laitin's (1986:171). words, "The systematic study of politics and culture is moribund."
22. Cohen (1974:8; 1979:87).
23. Cohen (1974:7) has also made this point. I do not want to leave the impression that quantitative studies have no place in political study, for such work is certainly of great value in dealing with certain problems.
24. Geertz (1964:53).
25. Turner (1974:140–41).
26. Walzer (1968:36). It may seem surprising to quote Marx in conjunction with an attack on materialist approaches to the study of politics, but there is no contradiction here. In some ways, as Cohen (1979:11) notes, the study of political symbolism is "essentially the child of Marxism, for it was Marx who initiated the systematic analysis of culture in relation to

the power structure." Gramsci's attempts to produce a more sophisticated Marxian analysis of the relationship between ideological and material bases of political power are also of interest here. See Gramsci (1971) and, for commentary on Gramsci's famous concept of hegemony, see Boggs (1976), Kertzer (1979), Fox (1985) and Laitin (1986).

27. See, for example, Firth (1951:222).

28. Durkheim (1915:37, 41).

29. Nadel (1954:99) should be mentioned as one of the earlier anthropologists to focus on the formalized, repetitive nature of ritual rather than limiting the term to action involving religious phenomena.

30. Ritual can also be seen as a quality of certain social behavior that is found where there is an important symbolic element present. In this perspective, actions are not categorized as either ritual or not, but rather both the ritual and nonritual aspects of particular human activities are examined (Leach 1954:12–13). See also Da Matta (1977:256–57).

31. Thus, Gluckman (1965:251) distinguished between "ritual" and "ceremonial"; for a similar distinction see Binns (1980:586). Referring to Gluckman's distinction, Aronoff (1979:277–78) clarifies his own use of ritual as a means of analyzing Israeli politics by specifying that "when I speak of ritual in the modern political context I am referring to secular, ritual-like activity in which mystical notions are absent."

32. Further discussion of some of these definitional issues are found in Mead (1973:87–88); Munn (1973:580); Lukes (1975:290); Goody (1977); Rappaport (1979:174–77); Lewis (1980); Lane (1981); and Silverman (1981:164).

33. On the political significance of spatial symbolism, see Kuper (1972:420–21). Trexler's (1973:126–27) analysis of the sacralization of city hall in Renaissance Florence provides valuable insight into this process.

34. Leach (1966:404); Rappaport (1979:175–76).

35. Myerhoff (1977:200) also makes this point. From a Freudian point of view, an individual may engage in ritual behavior even though his action is not intelligible to anyone else. In such cases, of course, the analyst attributes symbolic meaning to the standardized, repetitive action, even though it is idiosyncratic. However, I exclude such idiosyncratic forms of behavior from what I consider as ritual action in this book. For a discussion of such "neurotic ritual," see Freud (1907).

36. Cassirer (1955:38–39).

37. Nieburg (1973:30).

38. Myerhoff (1984:152).

39. Moore (1975:234).

40. On the physiological bases of the power of ritual, see d'Aquili and Laughlin (1979) and Lex (1979).

41. See Rappaport (1979:188).

42. Cohen (1974:4; 1979:102–03); Bennett (1979:109n). Ortner (1975:167) has made a related point that is worth noting here:

We cannot, if we understand the ritual fully, emerge with a clear-cut assertion of the primacy of the social or cultural or psychological dimension of its meaning. It is the ingenuity of ritual symbolism constantly to transpose these into one another, to solve problems in each mode by means of forms derived from other modes and thus to

show, ultimately, both their irreducible interdependence and the means of moving between them.

43. Along these lines, Lewis (1977:2) has written that "Symbols and sentiments feed upon each other and their fruitful interplay lies at the heart of social behaviour." Fernandez, in dealing with this question of the relationship between ritual and emotional arousal, views the metaphorical properties of ritual as enabling people to bring about changes they desire in "the way they feel about themselves and the world in which they live" (1971:56).

44. Arnold (1935:iii). This dramatistic perspective has been more fully developed in Goffman's (1959) works. The use of masks in so many rituals around the world may be seen as a manifestation of this dramatistic quality (Tonkin 1979).

45. Mosse (1975:168).

46. Lewis (1980:33).

47. I follow Cohen (1981:156) here in defining a drama as "a limited sequence of action, defined in space and time, which is set aside from the ordinary flow of purposeful social activity."

48. Bennett (1977:227).

49. Victor Turner (1967) has been the one to develop most fully the concept of condensation in this context.

50. Munn (1973: 580) discusses the multivocality of ritual symbolism. Turner (1967:50) uses the term multivocality to refer to the fact that "a single symbol may stand for many things."

51. Lewis (1980:9). On this point, too, see Sperber's (1975) attack on semiotic analysis of symbolism.

52. On the creative potential in ritual, see Munn (1973:592), Moore (1977:167), and Moore and Myerhoff (1977:5).

53. Mead (1973:90–91).

54. Skinner (1981:37) has made a similar point. See also Lane (1981:2) and Bennett (1980:170).

55. Douglas (1966:62).

56. Bennett (1980:168).

57. Quoted in Pocock (1964:14). More recently, Gramsci (1971:339) has made a similar argument:

The most important element is undoubtedly one whose character is determined not by reason but by faith. But faith in whom, or what? In particular in the social group to which he belongs, in so far as in a diffuse way it thinks as he does. The man of the people thinks that so many like-thinking people can't be wrong, not so radically, as the man he is arguing against would like him to believe; he thinks that, while he himself, admittedly, is not able to uphold and develop his arguments as well as the opponent, in his group there is someone who could do this and could certainly argue better than the particular man he has against him; and he remembers, indeed, hearing expounded, discursively, coherently, in a way that left him convinced, the reason behind his faith.

58. In Pocock (1964:6).

59. In Binns (1980:594).

60. Habermas (1986:44).

61. These remarks come from a presidential press conference, and are reproduced in "Responses of the President to queries

on the German visit," *New York Times* (19 April 1985), p. 13.

62. James M. Markham, "Kohl says he urged Reagan to visit a Nazi camp," *New York Times* (17 April 1985), p. 14.

63. Meir Merhav, "Honouring evil," *Jerusalem Post* (3 May 1985), reprinted in Hartman (1986).

64. Kohl's remarks were delivered at the U.S. air base at Bitburg following the cemetery ceremonies. The text is reproduced in "Transcript of speech by Kohl at U.S. air base," *New York Times* (6 May 1985), p. 8.

65. *Chicago Tribune* (4 May 1985).

66. In addition to the sources previously cited, this discussion of the Bitburg rites is based on the following accounts in the *New York Times:* Bernard Weinraub, "Aides review Reagan's plan to visit German war graves" (13 April 1985), pp. 1, 4; David Kaiser's op-ed piece, "No wreath for Hitler's army" (18 April 1985), p. 27; Anthony Lewis, "Appointment at Bitburg" (25 April 1985), p. 27; Flora Lewis, "History doesn't die" (26 April 1985), p. 31; and James M. Markham, "Bitburg visit: Is 'reconciliation' needed?" (2 May 1985), p. 16. Also of use were Eckardt (1986), Hilberg (1986), and Rosenfeld (1986).

67. McManus (1979:227).

68. Edelman (1971:45–46).
69. Gramsci (1971:339).
70. Edelman (1969:232).
71. Norman (1975:83).
72. Snyder and Swann (1976: 1041).
73. Bagehot (1914:147).
74. This is cited in a similar context by Cohen (1979:98).
75. Festinger (1957:2–3). On cognitive dissonance, see also Wicklund and Brehm (1976).
76. Festinger (1957:11).
77. Bettelheim (1960:290–91).
78. Bettelheim (1960:292).
79. Hobsbawm (1984:67).
80. Lewis (1977:2).
81. See Ortner (1978:5–6).
82. Of relevance here are the findings of some experimental psychologists that the more a person thinks about another person, an idea, or a thing, the more intensified that person's feelings become. See Tesser (1978:298–99).
83. Lane (1981:32).
84. Turner (1974:56).
85. Bandura (1977:65).
86. Burke (1950:58).

REFERENCES

Anderson, Benedict. 1983. *Imagined Communities: Reflections on the Origin and Spread of Nationalism.* London: Verso.

Arnold, Thurmon W. 1935. *The Symbols of Government.* New Haven: Yale University Press.

Aronoff, Myron J. 1979. Ritual and consensual power relations: The Israel Labor party. In S. Lee Seaton and Henri J. M. Claessen, eds., *Political Anthropology: The State of the Art,* pp. 275–310. The Hague: Mouton.

———. 1980. Ideology and interest: The dialectics of politics. In Myron J. Aronoff, ed., *Ideology and Politics, Political Anthropology,* volume 1, pp. 1–30. New Brunswick, New Jersey: Transaction.

Bagehot, Walter. 1914. *The English Constitution.* New York: Appleton.

Bandura, Albert. 1977. *Social Learning Theory.* Englewood Cliffs, New Jersey: Prentice-Hall.

Bauman, Zygmunt. 1973. *Culture as Praxis.* London: Routledge and Kegan Paul.

Bennett, W. Lance 1977. The ritualistic and pragmatic bases of political campaign discourse. *Quarterly Journal of Speech* 63:219–38.

———. 1979. Imitation, ambiguity, and drama in political life: Civil religion and the dilemmas of public morality. *Journal of Politics* 41:106–33.

———. 1980. Myth, ritual and political control. *Journal of Communication* 30:166–79.

Berger, Peter L. 1967. *The Sacred Canopy: Elements of a Sociological Theory of Religion.* New York: Doubleday.

Bergesen, Albert J. 1977. Political witch hunts: The sacred and the subversive in cross-national perspective. *American Sociological Review* 42:220–33.

Bettelheim, Bruno. 1960. *The Informed Heart.* Glencoe: Free Press.

Binns, Christopher A. 1980. The changing face of power: Revolution and accommodation in the development of the Soviet ceremonial system, part 1. *Man* 14:585–606.

Boggs, Carl. 1976. *Gramsci's Marxism.* London: Pluto Press.

Burke, Kenneth. 1950. *A Rhetoric of Motives.* New York: Prentice-Hall.

———1966. *Language as Symbolic Action.* Berkeley: University of California Press.

Carlyle, Thomas. 1908. *Sartor Resartus, On Heroes, Hero-worship and the Heroic in History.* London: J. M. Dent.

Cassirer, Ernst. 1946. *The Myth of the State.* New Haven: Yale University Press.

———. 1955. *The Philosophy of Symbolic Forms,* volume 2, *Mythical Thought.* Translated by Ralph Manheim. New Haven: Yale University Press.

Cohen, Abner. 1974. *Two-Dimensional Man.* Berkeley: University of California Press.

———. 1979. Political symbolism. *Annual Review of Anthropology* 8:87–113.

———. 1981. *The Politics of Elite Culture.* Berkeley: University of California Press.

Da Matta, Roberto. 1977. Constraint and license: A preliminary study of two Brazilian national rituals. In Sally F. Moore and

Barbara G. Myerhoff, eds., *Secular Ritual*, pp. 244–64. Amsterdam: Van Gorcum.

d'Aquili, Eugene G., and Charles D. Laughlin, Jr. 1979. The neurobiology of myth and ritual. In Eugene G. d'Aquili, Charles D. Laughlin, Jr., and John McManus, eds., *The Spectrum of Ritual: A Biogenetic Structural Analysis*, pp. 152–82. New York: Columbia University Press.

Douglas, Mary. 1966. *Purity and Danger*. New York: Praeger.

Duncan, Hugh D. 1962. *Communication and the Social Order*. New York: Bedminster Press.

Durkheim, Emile. 1915 (1974). *The Elementary Forms of the Religious Life*. Translated by Joseph Swain. Glencoe: Free Press.

Erkardt, A. Roy. 1986. The Christian world goes to Bitburg. In Geoffrey Hartman, ed., *Bitburg in Moral and Political Perspective*, pp. 80–89. Bloomington: Indiana University Press.

Edelman, Murray. 1964. *The Symbolic Uses of Politics*. Urbana: University of Illinois Press.

———. 1969. Escalation and ritualization of political conflict. *American Behavioral Scientist* 13:231–46.

———. 1971. *Politics as Symbolic Action*. Chicago: Markham.

Fernandez, James W. 1971. Persuasions and performances: On the beast in every body . . . and the metaphors of everyman. In Clifford Geertz, ed., *Myth, Symbol and Culture*, pp. 39–60. New York: Norton.

Festinger, Leon. 1957. *A Theory of Cognitive Dissonance*. Evanston, Illinois: Row, Peterson.

Firth, Raymond. 1951. *Elements of Social Organization*. London: Watts.

Fox, Richard G. 1985. *Lions of the Punjab: Culture in the Making*. Berkeley: University of California Press.

Freud, Sigmund. 1907. Obsessive actions and religious practices. In James Strachey, ed., *The Standard Edition of the Complete Psychological Works of Sigmund Freud*, volume 9, pp. 117–27. London: Hogarth Press.

Geertz, Clifford. 1964. Ideology as a cultural system. In David E. Apter, ed., *Ideology and Discontent*, pp. 47–76. New York: Free Press.

———. 1966. Religion as a cultural system. In Michael Banton, ed., *Anthropological Approaches to the Study of Religion*, pp. 1–46. London: Tavistock.

———. 1977. Centers, kings, and charisma: Reflections on the symbolics of power. In Joseph Ben-David and Terry N. Clark, eds., *Culture and its Creators*, pp. 150–71. Chicago: University of Chicago Press.

Gluckman, Max 1965. *Politics, Law and Ritual in Tribal Society*. Oxford: Blackwell.

Goffman, Erving. 1959. *Presentation of Self in Everyday Life*. Garden City, New York: Anchor.

Goody, Jack. 1977. Against 'ritual': Loosely structured thoughts on a loosely defined topic. In Sally F. Moore and Barbara G. Myerhoff, eds., *Secular Ritual*, pp. 25–35. Assen: Van Gorcum.

Gramsci, Antonio. 1971. *Selections from the Prison Notebooks*. Translated by Quintin Hoare and Geoffrey Smith. London: Lawrence and Wishart.

Habermas, Jürgen. 1986. Defusing the past: A politico-cultural tract. In Geoffrey Hartman, ed., *Bitburg in Moral and Political Perspective*, pp. 43–51. Bloomington: Indiana University Press.

Hartman, Geoffrey, ed. *Bitburg in Moral and Political Perspective* (Bloomington: Indiana University Press, 1986).

Hilberg, Raul. 1986. Bitburg as symbol. In Geoffrey Hartman, ed., *Bitburg in Moral and Political Perspective*, pp. 15–26. Bloomington: Indiana University Press.

Hobsbawm, E. J. 1984. *Worlds of Labour: Further Studies in the History of Labour*. London: Wiedenfeld and Nicolson.

Kertzer, David I. 1979. Gramsci's concept of hegemony: The Italian Church-Communist struggle. *Dialectical Anthropology* 4:321–28.

Kessler, Clive S. 1978. *Islam and Politics in a Malay State*. Ithaca: Cornell University Press.

Kuper, Hilda. 1972. The language of sites in the politics of space. *American Anthropologist* 74:411–25.

Laitin, David. 1986. *Hegemony and Culture*. Chicago: University of Chicago Press.

Lane, Christel. 1981. *The Rites of Rulers*. Cambridge: Cambridge University Press.

Leach, Edmund. 1954. *Political Systems of Highland Burma*. Boston: Beacon.

———. 1966. Ritualization in man in relation to conceptual and social development. *Philosophical Transactions of the Royal Society*, series B, 251:403–8.

Lerner, Max. 1941. *Ideas for the Ice Age*. New York: Viking.

Lévi-Strauss, Claude. 1966. *The Savage Mind*. Chicago: University of Chicago Press.

Lewis, Gilbert. 1980. *Day of Shining Red: An Essay on Understanding Ritual*. Cambridge: Cambridge University Press.

Lewis, Ioan M. 1977. Introduction. In Ioan M. Lewis, ed., *Symbols and Sentiments*, pp. 1–24. London: Academic.

Lex, Barbara W. The neurobiology of myth and ritual. In Eugene G. d'Aquili, Charles D. Laughlin, Jr., and John McManus, eds., *The Spectrum of Ritual: A Biogenetic Structural Analysis*, pp. 117–52. New York: Columbia University Press.

Lukes, Steven. 1975. Political ritual and social integration. *Sociology* 9:289–308.

Mackenzie, W. J. M. 1967. *Politics and Social Science*. Baltimore: Penguin.

McManus, John. 1979. Ritual and human social cognition. In Eugene G. d'Aquili, Charles D. Laughlin, Jr., and John McManus, eds., *The Spectrum of Ritual: A Biogenetic Structural Approach*, pp. 216–48. New York: Columbia University Press.

Mead, Margaret. 1973. Ritual and social crisis. In James D. Shaughnessy, ed., *The Roots of Ritual*, pp. 87–102. Grand Rapids, Michigan: Eerdmans.

Moore, Sally F. 1975. Epilogue: Uncertainties in situations, indeterminacies in culture. In Sally F. Moore and Barbara G. Myerhoff, eds., *Symbol and Politics in Communal Ideology*, pp. 210–39. Ithaca: Cornell University Press.

———. 1977. Political meetings and the simulation of unanimity: Kilimanjaro 1973. In Sally F. Moore and Barbara G. Myerhoff, eds., *Secular Ritual*, pp. 151–72. Assen: Van Gorcum.

———, and Barbara G. Myerhoff. 1977. Introduction: Secular ritual, forms and meanings. In Sally F. Moore and Barbara G. Myerhoff, eds., *Secular Ritual*, pp. 3–24. Assen: Van Gorcum.

Mosse, George L. 1975. *The Nationalization of the Masses.* New York: Fertig.

Munn, Nancy D. 1973. Symbolism in ritual context: Aspects of symbolic action. In John J. Honigmann, ed., *Handbook of Social and Cultural Anthropology*, pp. 579–612. Chicago: Rand McNally.

Myerhoff, Barbara. 1977. We don't wrap herring in a printed page: Fusion, fictions and continuity in secular ritual. In Sally F. Moore and Barbara G. Myerhoff, eds., *Secular Ritual*, pp. 199–226. Assen: Van Gorcum.

———. 1984. A death in due time: Construction of self and culture in ritual drama. In John J. MacAloon, ed., *Rite, Drama, Festival, Spectacle*, pp. 149–78. Philadelphia: ISHI.

Nadel, S. F. 1954. *Nupe Religion.* London: Routledge and Kegan Paul.

Nieburg, H. L. 1973. *Culture Storm: Politics and the Ritual Order.* New York: St. Martin's.

Niemi, Richard G. 1973. Political socialization. In Jeanne N. Knutson, ed., *Handbook of Political Psychology*, pp. 117–38. San Francisco: Jossey-Bass.

Norbeck, Edward. 1977. A sanction for authority: Etiquette. In Raymond D. Fogelson and Richard N. Adams, eds., *The Anthropology of Power*, pp. 67–76. New York: Academic.

Novak, Michael. 1974 *Choosing our King: Powerful Symbols in Presidential Politics.* New York: Macmillan.

Ortner, Sherry B. 1975. Gods' bodies, gods' food: A symbolic analysis of a Sherpa ritual. In Roy Willis, ed., *The Interpretation of Symbolism*, pp. 133–69. New York: Wiley.

———. 1978. *Sherpas through their Ritual.* Cambridge. Cambridge University Press.

Pocock, J. G. A. 1964. Ritual, language, power: An essay on the apparent meanings of ancient Chinese philosophy. *Political Science* 16:3–31.

Radcliffe-Brown, A. R. 1940. Preface. In Meyer Fortes and E. E. Evans-Pritchard, eds., *African Political Systems*, pp. x–xxiii. London: Oxford University Press.

Rappaport, Roy A. 1979. *Ecology, Meaning and Religion.* Richmond, California: North Atlantic Books.

Reynolds, Frank E. 1978. Legitimation and rebellion: Thailand's civic religion and the student uprising of October, 1973. In Bardwell L. Smith, ed., *Religion and Legitimation of Power in Thailand, Laos, and Burma*, pp. 134–46. Chambersburg, Penn.: ANIMA Books.

Rosenfeld, Alvin H. 1986. Another revisionism: Popular culture and the changing image of the Holocaust. In Geoffrey Hartman, ed., *Bitburg in Moral and Political Perspective*, pp. 90–102. Bloomington: Indiana University Press.

Sahlins, Marshall. 1981. *Historical Metaphors and Mythical Realities.* Ann Arbor: University of Michigan Press.

Shils, Edward. 1966. Ritual and crisis. *Philosophical Transactions of the Royal Society*, series B, 251:447–50.

Silverman, Sydel. 1981. Rites of inequality: Stratification and symbol in central Italy. In Gerald D. Berreman, ed., *Social Inequality: Comparative and Development Approaches*, pp. 163–80. New York: Academic.

Singer, Milton B. 1982. Emblems of identity: A semiotic exploration. In Jacques Maquet, ed., *On Symbols in Anthropology*, pp. 73–132. Malibu, California: Undena.

Skinner, Quentin. 1981. The world as a stage. *New York Review of Books* 26:6(16 April):35–37.

Snyder, Mark, and William B. Swann, Jr. 1976. When actions reflect attitudes. The politics of impression management. *Journal of Personality and Social Psychology* 34:1034–42.

Sperber, Daniel. 1975. *Rethinking Symbolism.* Cambridge: Cambridge University Press.

Tesser, Abraham. 1978. "Self-generated attitude changes." In Leonard Berkowitz, ed., *Advances in Experimental Psychology*, volume 11, pp. 290–338. New York: Academic.

Tonkin, Elizabeth. 1979. Masks and powers. *Man* 14:237–48.

Trexler, Richard. 1973. Ritual behavior in Renaissance Florence: The setting. *Medievalia et Humanistica* 4:125–44.

Turner, Victor. 1967. *The Forest of Symbols.* Ithaca: Cornell University Press.

———. 1974. *Dramas, Fields, and Metaphors.* Ithaca: Cornell University Press.

Walzer, Michael. 1967. On the role of symbolism in political thought. *Political Science Quarterly* 82:191–205.

———. 1968. Politics in the welfare state. *Dissent* 15:26–40.

Wicklund, Robert A., and Jack W. Brehm. 1976. *Perspectives on Cognitive Dissonance.* Hillsdale, New Jersey: Erlbaum.

Wilentz, Sean. 1985. Introduction. In Sean Wilentz, ed., *Rites of Power*, pp. 1–12. Philadelphia: University of Pennsylvania Press.

Women and Ritual in Family Therapy

JOAN LAIRD

Facts of publication: *Laird, Joan. 1988: "Women and Ritual in Family Therapy," from* Rituals in Families and Family Therapy, *331–351, 361–362. Edited by Evan Imber-Black, Janine Roberts, and Richard Whiting. New York: Norton. Copyright © 1988 by Evan Imber-Black, Janine Roberts, and Richard Whiting. Reprinted with the permission of W.W. Norton & Company, Inc.*

After illustrating how thoroughly rites throughout the world celebrate men's status and men's power, Joan Laird, a family therapist who characterizes her method as "the ethnographic stance in the therapeutic use of ritual," considers women's ritual in North American society. Her feminist critique of ritual's role in dominance and submission patterns draws on a growing body of evidence and theory that question the assumption that ritual is a mere neutral tool, equally available to both women and men. Not only does Laird consider the problems therapists have in interpreting family ritualization, but she provides brief, clinically derived examples of what one might call "constructive ritual intervention." In doing so, she reflects the influence of Mara Selvini Palazzoli and others who have pioneered in using ritual for family therapy.

For further reading on ritual in family relationships see Evan Imber-Black and Janine Roberts, Rituals for Our Times *(New York: HarperCollins, 1992). On women and ritual see Susan Starr Sered,* Women as Ritual Experts: The Religious Lives of Elderly Jewish Women in Jerusalem *(New York: Oxford University Press, 1992).*

About the author: Dates: *1934– , Rochester, NY, U.S.A.* **Education:** *B.A., Vassar College; M.S., Columbia University School of Social Work.* **Field(s):** *family theory and therapy; application of anthropological theory and method to social work and family therapy (ritual, story, narrative); gender; sexuality.* **Career:** *Professor, 1987–present, Smith College for Social Work; Associate Professor, 1974–1986, Eastern Michigan University; Co-founder, Ann Arbor Center for the Family.* **Publications:** Family-Centered Social Work Practice *(Free, 1983);* A Handbook of Child Welfare *(Free, 1985);* Revisioning Social Work Education: A Social Constructionist Approach *(Haworth, 1993).* **Additional:** *Editor,* Smith College Studies in Social Work; *Editorial boards and consulting for:* American Journal of Orthopsychiatry, Journal of Teaching in Social Work, Journal of Gay and Lesbian Social Services, *and* Reflections. *"A social work educator since 1974, my teaching, writing, and research interests are in the family, particularly in family culture. I worked as a family therapist for some twenty years and have taught courses in family theory and practice, as well as in sociocultural theory. My mission has been to bring cultural-anthropological thinking and practice into the fields of social work and family therapy, both in theory and in practice. My writing in the last several years has centered on the understanding and use of ritual, story, and narrative in work with women."*

Once upon a time, many ages ago, in the land of the Mundurucu, in Brazil, the sacred trumpets of the tribe were all owned by the women. These women kept the golden trumpets in the forest, where they convened secretly to play them. But, alas, the women devoted so much time to playing the trumpets that they eventually abandoned their husbands and their household duties. The women, as possessors of the trumpets, had thereby gained ascendancy over the men. The men had to carry firewood and fetch water, and they also had to make manioc bread. . . . But the men still hunted and this angered them for it was necessary to feed meat to the trumpets. . . . So one of the men suggested that they take the trumpets from the women. This they did, forcing the women to return to the dwelling houses and to remain subservient to the men. Subsequently the people were taught that the women should not be permitted to meddle in the affairs of men, or take part in the secret male rites when the sacred musical instruments were played. The woman who would violate this prohibition stands condemned to death, and any man who shows the instruments or reveals the secret laws to a woman will be obliged to kill himself or be killed by his fellow man.

(Myth constructed from text and quotations in Bamberger, 1974, p. 273)

The golden trumpets are, of course, symbols of sexual and political power. Speculation to the contrary, to date there exists little firm evidence that women, in any time or in any society, have actually owned the secret symbols of authority. Furthermore, the Mundurucu myth suggests that women do not know how to handle public power and responsibility. It warns us of the risks women take and the dangers they face if, indeed, they are allowed access to the idols of the tribe or to the central rites that express the society's cultural code. It tells us that, in Mundurucu society at least, it is gender that is central in the very definition of culture and of power. This is no less the case in our own world.

Sex, at birth a biological given, must be distinguished from gender, a social construction, defined and shaped over time in particular historical, political, and sociocultural contexts. In turn, social constructions of gender identity and role, as they are expressed and shaped in the family and in other social groups, are powerful determinants of individual identity and activity. In recent years, as the feminist critique has spread to family therapy, the field has, at times painfully, begun to examine the social constructions and normative gender prescriptions implicit in major family theories and models and their underlying assumptions about mental health.[1] At the same time, family therapists and other mental health professionals have been questioning the central organismic, mechanistic, and sociological metaphors that have dominated model-building, as well as the languages that not only express but also create and recreate our world views.[2]

In recent years some have moved toward the adoption of a sociocultural metaphor, emphasizing the social and individual construction of meaning. Such a stance calls for a different view of reality and of normative behavior and leads to the adoption of new metaphors for practice. Family therapists have redefined therapy as story (Hartman & Laird, 1987) or as conversation (Hoffman, 1985), implying a recursive, co-evolving process between therapist and client in which each is changed as a new "story" or construction of reality unfolds. If the sociocultural metaphor indicates a search for meaning, then it becomes clear that therapists must search for the important sources of meaning, for the ways that families build and make sense of their worlds and hand down their values and traditions. Thus, family therapists have become increasingly interested in many of the categories long familiar to anthropologists in the study of small societies, such as language and metaphor, world view, folklore and myth, belief and spirituality, religion and ritual.

In the last few years this last category, ritual, long ignored in the family therapy field, has attracted considerable attention from both researchers and clinicians. . . . What has not been addressed, however, is the very powerful relationship between gender and ritual. This [reading] offers a beginning look at that relationship, particularly as it pertains to women's lives and to women in therapy. The notion of gender as a cultural construction is introduced, followed by an overview of women's ritual lives, both in other societies and in our own. This material is followed by a discussion of women and ritual in family therapy. A . . . case example [is] presented, illustrating the use of ritual in family systems therapy with women, as individuals and in families.

A CULTURAL CONSTRUCTION OF GENDER

Ritual is probably the most potent socialization mechanism available to kin and other groupings for preparing individual members to understand the group's meanings, carry on its traditions, and perform those social roles considered essential to its continuation. Through ritual, as males and females, we learn who we are to be, what words we may speak to whom and on what occasions, what we can and will do and how we shall do it, with whom we are to be, to what we can aspire. Our identities are not only reflected in the rituals we perform, but also reinforced, changed in some way, and created anew in each action. Ritual *implies* action and performance.

Furthermore, no two such performances are ever identical, nor are the contexts in which they occur (Moore & Myerhoff, 1977). As Kenneth Burke once phrased it, "Ritual is dancing an attitude" (quoted in Myerhoff, 1983).

Anthropologists Gregory Bateson and Margaret Mead were among the first to attend to the cultural worlds of women and to suggest a cultural conceptualization of gender, a conceptualization that emerged largely from their studies of ritual in traditional societies. Bateson, in his effort to interpret the *Naven* ritual, demonstrated that the analysis of such a complex ceremonial required multidimensional perspectives on ritual, culture, and mind. To understand a single ritual, or a series of rituals, in even the least complex of societies requires not only an exploration of the ritual in terms of the society's ecology, its economy, its psychology and sociology, its sexual politics, its world view and symbolic system, but also a vision of "how such partial modes of understanding can be fitted together in a coherent process of explanation" (Keesing, 1982, p. 17). Keesing warns that "bridge building between partial explanations itself entails further dangers. We are likely to be left with nothing more than an ever more complex functionalist matrix of interconnection, ultimately static and circular: 'the system' endlessly reinforcing and perpetuating itself" (1982, p. 33). Careful attention to the societal construction of gender and the relationships between the sexes is an essential part of that vision.

It is clear that many rituals, particularly initiation rites and other rites of passage, are very directly concerned with definitions of power and status as well as definitions of gender identity and social role. In traditional anthropological analysis, from Durkheim (1915) to the present, rituals have been seen as taming chaos and imposing order, as reinforcing social integration and celebrating society itself. More recently, however, Keesing (1982), reviewing anthropological studies of the Eastern Highlands of New Guinea, observed that boys' initiation and other central social rituals celebrate the unity and power of *men*. As he points out:

> They celebrate and reinforce male dominance in the face of women's visible power to create and sustain life, and in the face of the bonds between boys and

their mothers which must be broken to sustain male solidarity and dominance. Women's physical control over reproductive processes and emotional control over their sons must be overcome by politics, secrecy, ideology, and dramatized male power. (p. 23)

Male initiation rites in the Highlands not only transform boys into men, but are transformations in which the senior men define themselves as special in relation to women and to uninitiated boys. Langness (1974) argues that "the social solidarity [expressed in ritual] rests upon a power structure entirely in the hands of males, a power structure supported where necessary by a variety of acts that are magical, pure and simple, and designed to keep power in the hands of males" (p. 19). Such power is obtained through maintaining a clear sexual polarization in the world of economic production and through controlling women's productive and reproductive powers, as men or male-dominated kinship groups exchange women and bridewealth. Since male power, status, and prestige are dependent in large part on women's labor, "it is ties with women that pose the greatest threat, from both within and without. The bond between mothers and sons could keep boys from becoming men: it must be broken dramatically and traumatically" (Keesing, 1982, p. 24). Men's shared secrets of ritual contribute to the maintenance of a supercommunity in which women are either excluded from the central society rituals or play roles complementary and subordinate to those of men, "as spectators and fringe participants in male-dominated ritual pageantry and politics" (Keesing, 1982, pp. 24–25).

While the Eastern Highlands of New Guinea may afford a dramatic illustration of these themes, in general male rituals throughout the world tend to be more public and more central to societal cosmology than female ones. Women's rituals are usually less dramatic or colorful, less important in terms of power definitions, and tend to define women's domain as domestic. What rituals exist tend to celebrate woman's role as nurturer or caretaker and her assignment to a particular lineage and a particular male. Rituals that portray and thus bestow great power and authority, as well as the respect that comes from the accumulation of such power, are not generally available to women. Whatever contributions women make to public life are rarely made explicit; their social personae are usually defined by virtue of their relationships to men.

While the above interpretations and generalizations emerge from the study of less complex and diverse societies than our own, societies in which ritual experiences rather than written words or abstract concepts are the primary sources of learning, nevertheless they draw attention to some of the issues of power and definitions of gender implicit in American ritual. A few observations about our own cultural rituals may be made and briefly illustrated.

1. Women's rituals in the United States are less central and less definitional in terms of national values than those of men.

2. National rituals tend to define and confirm the assignment of the public domain (and thus greater power and prestige) to men, the domestic domain to women.

3. Many rituals, both societal and familial, continue to define women's deference and subordination to men.

4. Women's power, in this society, continues to be feared by men; thus, as in many traditional societies, women are seen as dangerous and polluting and must undergo elaborate purification rituals.

Power and Authority

In this country, our most colorful national pageants, which send powerful messages concerning what is to be most celebrated and valued, are associated with the military and with male-dominated spectator sports, particularly football and baseball. In these public enactments, it is the corporate-military complex as well as characteristics associated with males, such as aggressiveness and physical prowess, that are celebrated. Women tend to play subordinate and supportive roles in these dramatic pageants, cheering on the real actors in the drama. There are no rituals equivalent in visibility or drama which celebrate female symbols, roles, or characteristics. The public domains (and thus the public rituals) that are associated with power in this society, those of politics, the military, banking, the corpora-

tion, and even academe, remain largely under the control of men. It is difficult for women to see themselves reflected in or to know how to participate in such rituals.

Question may be raised as to whether even those rituals in our society highly identified with women clearly celebrate women's lives and contributions or are under women's control. Reproduction provides one example. In pre-industrial societies, argue Paige and Paige (1981), the rituals of reproduction are essentially political, a means by which men control the reproductive powers of women in order to gain political and economic power. Rich (1986) vividly describes how birthing in our own society was stripped from the control of women, becoming an experience in which women were isolated from the support and comfort of other women. Women were encouraged to relinquish breast-feeding, which became an isolated, embarrassing, and somehow "primitive" practice. In spite of what appears to be a contemporary reclaiming of birthing on the part of women, Paige and Paige argue that the male-dominated medical profession still controls the processes of childbirth; the "natural childbirth" movement has offered only minor modification and, in fact, its major innovation is paternal participation in delivery, a practice they see as a new form of couvade. Furthermore, while some women may have assumed more control over their own rituals of birth, it is men who dominate the legislative and judicial bodies which will ultimately decide whether women can make decisions to terminate pregnancy, to whom and under what conditions birth control will be available, to whom custody will be granted, and so on.

In Lévi-Strauss's theory of kinship, marriage was seen as "the most basic form of gift exchange, in which it is women who are the most precious of gifts" (Rubin, 1975, p. 173). Rubin argues that "kinship and marriage are always parts of total social systems, and are always tied into economic and political arrangements" (p. 207), The marriage contract and kinship obligations serve as charters for bestowing or limiting rights in person and property. In Rubin's view, if in pre-capitalist society women were kept in their place by men's cults, secret initiations, and so on, "capitalism has taken over, and rewired, notions of male and female which predate it by centuries" (p. 163). The notion of the exchange of women is still enacted in the traditional American marriage ceremony, in which the daughter is "given" to the groom by her father and in the process exchanges the name of one male for another. It will be argued that in our society the powerful symbolism and language in this rite lack the literal meanings of ownership and connotations of women as property found in many traditional societies. Nevertheless, such words and symbols create recursive worlds of meaning which continue to tell women who they are and what they may become. Women must make conscious and unusual decisions to modify these symbols and rules of relationship and, in fact, in many marriages it is clear that what has been purchased is women's domestic labor.

The notions of exchange of and control over women by men through marriage and kinship alliances have other, very concrete applications in American marriage and family patterns. For example, men continue to earn far more money than their working or nonworking wives and, as sociologist Pepper Schwartz (1987) points out, in marriage as well as in the larger society, "money talks." Her research has demonstrated that money or earning power buys the right in marriage to make decisions—decisions concerning whether to stay or leave, what the family shall purchase, where they shall live, how the children shall be educated, whether therapy shall be paid for, whether father will attend, and so on. Furthermore, in many cases money buys the right of men to bind women to unhappy marriages and in some families to rituals of violence and humiliation, since many women lack the resources to live independently or the skills to compete in the public world.

Public : Male = Domestic : Female

Male rituals everywhere celebrate men's entry into and participation in public life. Female rituals everywhere celebrate and define women's entry into and participation in domestic life. Rosaldo (1974), whose own field work was done among the Ilongot in the Philippines, points out that in many societies there are radical divisions between the lives of men and the lives of the domestic group. Such arrangements leave men free to design rituals of authority that define themselves as superior, as special, and as separate. These rituals increase the distance between men and their families, creating barriers to the demands for intimacy which family life implies. She argues that "because men can be separate, they can be 'sacred'; and by avoiding certain sorts of intimacy and immediate involvement, they can develop an image and mantle of integrity and worth" (p. 27). An analogy may be made to American society, for it is clear that even in dual career families women continue to carry much greater responsibility for the care of the children and the maintenance of the home. It is much more difficult for women, even those who work outside of the home, to construct or control public images of authority, since they are weighted down with the demands of caretaking and the burdens of domestic life. In public life, men are the authors, women the helpers; in domestic life the reverse is the case. For Rosaldo, as for many feminist scholars, the distribution of work roles is key to issues of gender equality and distribution of power.

Women's Rites of Passage

In our own society, no clearly defined or universal initiation rites of passage exist, a phenomenon which contributes to the difficulties young men and women face in leaving home and defining adulthood. The period of adolescence is prolonged and poorly marked. For many the high school graduation serves as a diffuse transition rite, for others entry in the military, for still others marriage.

Those rituals that do exist for the young female in our society carry confusing and ambiguous messages that fail to ready her for public life, that continue to define her in relation to and contingent upon males. The imagery from the "sweet sixteen" party and the debutante's "coming out" party emphasize beauty, femininity, and grace—and the availability of young women for potential husbands. These messages are most powerfully portrayed and best exemplified in the national Miss America pageant, that male-directed annual rite of fall in which women parade their bodies in a ritual somewhat reminiscent of the slave or cattle auction.

There are few rites, at least rites for which cultural material is available to the individual family (with the exception of the wedding, the birthday, and her own funeral), that help women mark *any* of the major transitions in their lives. The married woman's life is most clearly marked by family rites that celebrate the movement through life of her children; the single woman lacks even these. While childbirth may bring special privileges and recognition for the new mother, it often lacks symbolically rich rites of passage which help women incorporate the new status of motherhood. It is her reproduction (product) that is celebrated. Similarly, the transition to post childrearing is inadequately honored as the loss of children is mourned. The fact that these transitions are so poorly marked through ritual may contribute to the common occurrence of depression during both of these life phases. Women never "retire" from their domestic jobs, while the family's movement in time is marked by the husband's career, the birth of grandchildren, and so on. There are no widely sanctioned rituals that celebrate or help her incorporate public roles, that move her into the company of senior women, that venerate her achievements and wisdom as she moves to old age. Since rites of passage are important facilitators in the definition of self in relation to society, there is clearly a need for women to reclaim, redesign, or create anew rituals that will facilitate life transitions and allow more meaningful and clear incorporation of both familial and public roles.

While women have made substantial inroads into many male-defined and male-dominated professions and occupations and thus into the public domain, the risks are often heavy and some gains are achieved with substantial costs in ritual degradation and humiliation. The contemporary heroine is often criticized and ridiculed by both men and women in a male-controlled myth-making process, which reminds us all continually that the public sphere belongs to men. For example, Eleanor Roosevelt was villified repeatedly, her appearance and her mothering held up for public approbation. More recently, the attack on Margaret Mead's work by Derek Freeman (1983) excited the media for many months, while the occasion of Mary Catherine Bateson's (1984) loving and eloquent memoir of her parents gave male reviewers license to disparage not only Mead's contributions to social science but her abilities as wife and mother. The caveat to all American women was clear: Women who try to gain the golden trumpets will fail in both the public and domestic domains. . . .

In the field of family therapy, perhaps Virginia Satir is the only genuine female folk heroine, although others are emerging. Satir's contributions to the field are increasingly unremarked as the history of the family therapy is constructed and reconstructed during the field's major rituals, that is, its conferences and organizational meetings, those places where its traditions are defined and transmitted. Women need to monitor the myth-making processes in the profession's central rituals, as women's ideas and contributions are frequently ridiculed, overlooked, or trivialized.

Dominance and Submission

Another theme repeatedly enacted in both domestic and public ritual is one of dominance and subordination, as women perform in ritual roles that define their supportive and ancillary positions in relation to men. In many societies, women's deference to men is demonstrated symbolically by, for example, walking several paces behind their husbands, covering their faces in the presence of men, keeping their eyes downcast, or sleeping at the feet of men (Bamberger, 1974). In our own society, the images are no less powerful nor the messages less clear. For example, in hospital rituals, (usually) female nurses hand over the tools of the trade to (usually) male surgeons. Nurses and female doctors are often called by their first names, while male doctors are addressed by their professional titles, actions that not only symbolize but also confer authority and prestige. In many American families, men sit at the head of the table, are waited on and often served first by their wives, and are usually offered the choicest part of the meal.

Purity and Danger

A final set of symbols common to many rituals throughout the world identifies women with notions of sexual pollution and danger. Women everywhere are, on the one hand, portrayed as virginal and pure and, on the other, as sexually dangerous and polluting. In this paradoxical position, women are identified with and seen as closer to "nature," men to "culture," a false but useful dichotomizing process in the world of sexual politics (Ortner, 1974). Women are the "other," a marked category in relation to the generic, unmarked category of "self," which is owned by the male.

In many societies, women undergo elaborate purification rites at particular times, such as after childbirth or menstruation. While such cleansing rites carry multiple layers of meaning, they can be used, according to anthropologist Mary Douglas (1966), to assert male superiority, to claim separate social spheres for men and women, or to blame male failure on women's transgressions. Purification rituals, argues Douglas, both mirror and reinforce existing cosmologies, social structures, and balances of power, binding men and women to their prescribed social roles. In her view, where social systems are stable and well-articulated, such purification rites may be largely unnecessary, but where the social structure is poorly articulated and gender roles and relationships are highly ambiguous or changing, those who would challenge the established hegemony represent danger and must be defined as polluting.

While few clearly defined purification rites exist in our society, we are subjected to a discourse and to a set of diffuse rituals that define women as unclean and as sexually dangerous. The onset of menstruation provides one example.

> The lord said to Moses and Aaron. . . . "When a woman has a discharge of blood which is her regular discharge from her body, she shall be in her impurity for seven days, and whoever touches her shall be unclean until the evening. And everything upon which she lies during her impurity shall be unclean; everything also upon which she sits shall be unclean. And whoever touches her bed shall wash his clothes, and bathe himself in water, and be unclean until the evening. . . ."
>
> (Leviticus 15:1, 19–22)

In some societies, for example among the Navajo, menarche is an occasion of joy and celebration. The Kinaalda ceremony "ushers the girl into society, invokes positive blessings on her, insures her health, prosperity, and well-being, and protects her from potential misfortune" (Weigle, 1982, p. 180). In most traditional societies, however, the onset of menstruation is an ambiguous occurrence, celebrated and feared. Says Washburn:

> This explains why the rituals appear to fall into two categories, a cause for dancing and a cause for seclusion of the girls. In either case, the ritual marks an understanding that the girl needs a symbolic, interpretive framework as she negotiates her first life crisis and redefines herself as a mature female. These rituals also express an understanding that discovering our identity as women is not to be a solitary struggle but is to be worked out within the context of the community. In each primitive ritual a form of self-transformation is expressed through trials, symbolic acts, and words which promote healing and integrate the forces at play. The girls and the community move into a new identity *through* the crisis.
>
> (Washburn, 1977, p. 9)

In our society, the onset of menstruation for the young girl has often been a solitary, secretive, and shameful experience, marked only by a furtive trip to the drugstore, and perhaps by her first pelvic examination, often a ritual of humiliation. The event is not, as Washburn says, *recognized* in a way that provides the young girl "with a symbolic framework within which to find resources for her questions of meaning" (1977, pp. 12–13). She does not usually, in our society, emerge from this crisis with an increased sense of pride in her own body or sense of worth and integrity as an individual. Furthermore, the well-documented tabooing of sexual relations during menstruation, pregnancy, and in the postpartum period, in spite of an absence of evidence of health hazard, "clearly suggests that the widespread notion of sexual pollution is shared by Americans" (Paige & Paige, 1981, p. 276).

If menstruation is associated with impurity and uncleanliness, it is also linked with notions of power. Weigle (1982) accumulates a rich cross-cultural sample of ritual, myth, and folklore demonstrating that the menstruating woman is seen as dangerous, as emitting a *mana* or supernatural power. Not only must men protect themselves from contamination, but in some societies male rites symbolize the taking over of the reproductive powers that menstruation implies, as in *couvade* rituals or in the ritual cutting of male genitals in circumcision or supercision. In fact, women's sexuality in general is seen as powerful and potentially dangerous, a vision handed down from ancient mythology and still expressed today in myth and ritual. If in traditional societies men must refrain from sex before a hunt or a raid, in our own society some athletes must observe similar sexual taboos. For example, "during summer training camp—a liminal period prior to the start of the football season—professional players are isolated from their wives or other women. Both college and professional players are also expected to abstain from sex on the night before a game" (Arens, 1976, quoted in Kottak, 1978, p. 513).

If in some societies the menstruating female is seen as powerful and dangerous to self and others and thus must be isolated, in our own society a form of isolation is accomplished through defining her as "sick" and in need of time-out or a rest. In both cases she removes herself from the public world and the company of men. Furthermore, it is ironic that, at a time when our society seems to be moving toward sexual liberation and equality for women, many young women are literally starving themselves and ritually gorging and emitting food. The latter theme, not unlike the theme of fasting or starving during menstruation seen in the mythologies of various traditional societies, may express the female's shame over her own body image and bodily processes, denying her sexuality and conforming to male-defined stereotypes of beauty.

WOMEN AND RITUAL IN FAMILY THERAPY

Ritual permeates family life and thus provides the therapist and family together with rich sources for understanding issues of gender as they affect women, as well as powerful sources for change. The family therapist should develop skill in understanding and interpreting the meanings and prescriptions embedded in existing family rituals, in assisting women and families in preserving rituals important to individual identity and family coherence, in reclaiming those that may have been passed over or now exist in truncated, outdated, or destructive

forms, and in sharing in the construction of new rituals. Ritual form and content can be drawn upon to help underritualized families to more meaningfully order their lives, to help newly joined couples to creatively forge new rituals, and to incorporate traditions from both heritages (tasks often made more complex because of remarriage or ethnic or religious difference), to help families master crises and expected life transitions, or to disrupt rigid, destructive, or humiliating rituals (Laird, 1984).

Interpreting Ritual

First of all, family therapists need to listen for the ways in which gender role and identity are being shaped in the central rituals of the client's life. Questions to be explored include:

1. How are women and women's roles portrayed and performed in major family celebrations and in everyday ritual interaction?

2. What messages do such rituals send concerning how women are defined and define themselves?

3. How are relationships between men and women portrayed and defined?

4. How and for what reasons are women's contributions valued and celebrated?

5. How are such definitions enforced? What rewards and punishments are sanctioned in ritual?

6. How are these meanings interpreted by women themselves and others in their interpersonal networks?

7. What impact do these messages have upon the family dance and upon women's lives and self-images?

The therapist needs to be sensitive to the family's rituals as they involve women and to the other rituals interwoven throughout the fabric of women's lives, in their relationships with work, recreation, religion and spirituality, in fact throughout their social and cultural networks. Much understanding of ritual occurs on an analogic level and is not consciously interpreted by the participant. Furthermore, participation in ritual often stimulates deeply felt emotions as it orders life in particular ways and is a powerful reinforcer of the behaviors enacted or performed. Thus, most of us are unaware of the ways in which our participation in ritual orders our social and emotional functioning and creates and recreates our self-images. Often women are aware of feeling sad, resentful, or discontented without connecting these feelings to the powerful rituals in which they participate. The therapist needs to be sensitive to the events and the discourse surrounding daily interaction rituals and to the ways women participate in periodic or intermittent rituals such as family vacations or situations of pain or illness. Further, the family therapist should be alert to the normative and idiosyncratic life transitions of individuals and the family as a whole, as well as to the religious and secular holiday patterns in families. All of these ritual events are in some way relevant to a woman's identity and to her well-being. Inasmuch as possible and, of course, determined by the purposes for which therapy is undertaken, these events need to be "unpacked," the family's symbolism and layers of meaning interpreted. The interpretation of ritual is risky business; each of us will see different meanings in family symbolism and action, influenced by our own gender, our ethnic heritages, our political ideologies, our family experiences, and many other factors. Thus, the therapist needs to be wary of "editing" any family ritual without understanding how such ritual fits into the family's larger cultural context and meaning system.

In the following example, a typical holiday festival is explored for its potential meanings in relation to women's lives. Each of us will see different arrangements of color and symbol in this kaleidoscope. The composite portrait is based on the stories of many women, colleagues, friends, students, and clients, here presented as the reminiscences of a daughter and focused primarily on her vision of her mother during this festival.

A CHRISTMAS CAROL

My mother began preparations for Christmas months in advance, shopping for and wrapping gifts, making new decorations for the house, and addressing cards. She began preparing and freezing some of our family's traditional dishes weeks ahead of time, plum pudding, the pumpkin and mince pies, her collection of cookies, the jams, sauces, and candies, the vegetable casseroles. Since she worked fulltime as an administrative assistant, as Christmas approached she often stayed up late at night wrapping gifts, getting my father to sign the tags for the gifts she had purchased for his parents, siblings and other family members. Mom still tries to make at least one gift for each person in the family, fussing when she can't get them all finished and sighing that she's glad Christmas comes but once a year. Every year she said, and still does, she will be relieved when it is over.

Christmas seems to have always been almost entirely her responsibility, even though all of us have helped in small ways. My sister and I used to help decorate the cookies when we were children, and now we help with last minute dinner preparations and with the cleanup. One of my father's jobs is to get the tree into the house and properly secured, but he refuses to become involved with the decorating. I remember he would sit reading his newspaper, occasionally criticizing the placement of an ornament or the way we were hanging the tinsel. My mother would struggle with the lights, always complaining that she got the worst job, while my sister and brother and I would unwrap each special ornament with great pleasure as we rediscovered old favorites. The lights would finally be lit, and after a moment for admiration, my mother would begin to try to tame the chaos in the living room.

While we sometimes had friends or relatives over for dinner or visiting on Christmas eve, Christmas morning was of course very special when we were children. I know now, as I prepare them for my own children, that the Christmas stockings, perhaps the most exciting tradition I remember, required a great deal of thought and work. My mother always cooked a special breakfast on Christmas morning, after which we were allowed to go into the living room. My father, of course, assumed the role of Santa and presided over the distribution of gifts until he grew bored, at which point we would all share that role. Mother would rush in and out of the living room, trying not to miss anything while cleaning up the breakfast dishes, stuffing the turkey, and getting the rest of the dinner ready in time for the arrival of other family members.

Although now that we children are married and spend Christmas morning in our own homes, the rest of the holiday hasn't changed very much over the years. We all gather at my parents' house about 1:00 P.M. After a half-hour or so of family greetings and conversation, the men usually retire to the family room to watch television, the children play, and the women help my mother get the feast to the table. When we are all seated, my mother, with considerable ceremony, places the bird at my father's place at the head of the table. After the suitable "ohs" and "ahs" he raises his polished and sharpened carving knife and with a dramatic flourish makes the first cut. My mother never sits for very long, running back and forth from dining room to kitchen for much of the meal, keeping the bowls filled and beginning the next course. We all complain about this, to no avail.

There are parts of the holiday I dread. For as long as I can remember, there has been some sort of painful argument at dinner, in the earlier years almost always a fight between my brother and me. Someone usually gets a migraine headache, and my mother ends up in tears at least once during the day, making all of us feel guilty and irritated, because she is overburdened and we know it. On the other hand, it seems a source of pride to her to "do it all" and she often refuses help.

After dinner the males retreat, some to play cards or watch more television and some to nap, while the women and older female children begin the long and tedious business of cleaning up, and my brother puts another log on the fire. This is the time I tend to experience the most resentment, for even though I enjoy this special time for talking and sharing with the women in the family, I would like nothing better than to sneak upstairs for a little nap, to play cards, to watch football, to call for a beer.

I try to carry on most of the same traditions, even though I have a very demanding job. It just doesn't seem like Christmas if anything is skipped. My husband, who helps some and who tells me he doesn't want a "traditional" wife nevertheless seems to, like me, want a "traditional" life! It is difficult to understand why this special day, looked forward to all year long, usually leaves me exhausted, depleted, experiencing a sense of relief, of loss, but already thinking about next year.

Caplow et al. (1982) have suggested that the symbolism and activities of American holiday festivals celebrate the role of woman as caretaker and nurturer, particularly in relation to her job of childrear-ing. In their view, the family is the institution most at risk in our society, at least in its traditional form, as well as an institution undergoing change, conflict, and contradiction. The secular part of the Christmas ritual "glorifies the hearth and home, and the housekeeper most of all" (p. 235). Wives and mothers are rewarded with gifts and praise, with respect and admiration from relatives, friends, and neighbors for a job well done, while father's role is recognized in the Santa Claus symbolism. Santa, like father, tends to drop off the toys (the paycheck), "bringing good things into the family from the harsh outside world" (p. 235), but thereafter plays only a minor role; it is mother who transforms the gifts/money into wonder and excitement, who affirms and symbolizes the family's complex social ties, each gift symbolizing and defining a particular social relationship. In their view, as more and more women have migrated to the marketplace, Christmas has played an increasingly important role in reminding the community of the dangers to the family. "By glorifying the raising of children and insisting on its importance, the symbols of the festival cycle quell any doubts that parents may have and shore up the emotional conviction that sacrifices for children are worthwhile" (p. 244).

If the above interpretation has merit, paradoxically (for rituals can mask the paradoxes in women's lives), it is women who must perform the difficult and exhausting tasks which are said to culminate in their own praise and reward. While some women who work outside of the home report that their husbands "help," the family Christmas ritual has not in general been modified to reflect the changes in many women's lives and can represent an enormous burden in time and anxiety. The ritual also reflects women's position as subordinate to that of men. One and all are reminded that women "serve" men, and it is the male who sits at the "head" of the table or in the comfortable armchair. Just as man the hunter is feted after bringing home the kill (the tree, the roast, the gifts), the American husband is celebrated through the carving rite and festival games. His mate has the tasks of cooking, serving, and cleaning up after him and their progeny, even though in our society it may have been she who brought home the bacon.

Many women in therapy report exhaustion and

resentment around such family celebrations. Often angry at their husbands, they remember feeling sorry for their mothers and resentful toward their brothers. Many women complain that they "give" a great deal at such times, while their husbands may fail even to remember their birthdays. Yet such rituals are very difficult to change because they have been performed in similar ways for many generations; each gender knows the proper steps to the dance. If men have been reluctant to serve, to toil on the domestic front, women are reluctant to give up their centrality in the family, the satisfaction and praise that accompany the success of the ritual, the gratification that comes from nurturing and giving, and the power that comes with orchestrating social relationships.

USING RITUAL FOR CHANGE

The therapist who would draw on the power of ritual for change has two choices. First, she may design and prescribe a ritual to be enacted by an individual or family members without necessarily calling upon their interpretations, meanings, or cognitive understandings of their own ritual life. Based on the therapist's understanding of a dysfunctional, symptom-maintaining pattern, the family may be directed to perform a new set of ritualistic behaviors with little understanding of why such a request is made. This kind of intervention, central in structural, strategic, and systemic therapies, is a hallmark of Mara Selvini Palazzoli's work. She and her colleagues maximize the ritual form of therapy itself with their skillful use of time, team, secrecy, and so on, and have pioneered the use of ritualized prescriptions as well as elaborate ritual enactments (1974). In recent years she has experimented with the "invariant prescription," actually a series of ritualized prescriptions designed to alter the family's interactional patterns and its system of meanings and beliefs (Pirrotta, 1984; Viaro & Leonardi, 1986).

In more cognitively oriented family therapies, particularly those devoted to growth and differentiation rather than symptom relief or structural change, or those that draw upon the "story" or "conversation" metaphor, the therapist may engage women and families in exploring and interpreting their own ritual lives, designing changes that reflect their desired meanings. The family therapist, for example, can help women and families consider, as they participate in such family celebrations, what meanings are being expressed, to claim and perhaps enhance or intensify those they wish to preserve, and to discard or transform those that no longer express their desired lives or identities. In this approach, the therapist takes the stance of the "stranger" or "ethnographer" who wishes as completely as possible to learn about the culture of the "other," to learn the native's point of view, her meanings, her interpretations. However, unlike the anthropologist, the therapist has the responsibility to provide a context in which change can occur. She may reflect back her own interpretations and ideas, some of which may fit with the family's system of meaning. Individual women or women in groups may be coached to develop strategies to negotiate such changes in their marriages or families. Couples and families may be invited to consider what meanings their central family rituals convey for males and females, and what they would like to preserve or change. In the examples below, it is the ethnographic stance in the therapeutic use of ritual that is illustrated.

Mastering Women's Transitions

It has been argued that few meaningful rituals exist in our society to mark or celebrate the young girl's movement through the life cycle, to help her shape her own identity as a female. Birth and death have become male-medical affairs, with women playing peripheral roles in these most universal of phenomena. Girls' puberty rites, for example, which may have very powerful meanings closely integrated with social and kinship structures and the cosmologies of more traditional societies, are in our society truncated. As alluded to earlier, in our society the onset of menarche often has been a joyless occasion, unmarked by celebration and accompanied by shame, secrecy, confusion, and a sense of uncleanliness. Menarche might be embraced as an event that defines new possibilities and welcomes the young girl into a new world of power and fulfillment, linking her to the larger context and to men and women in new ways. Rarely do families endow this event

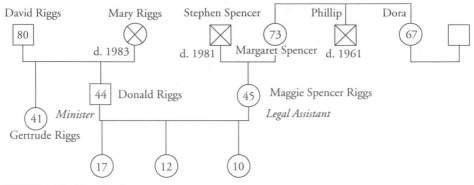

FIGURE 1 The Riggs Family

with the deeper and more lasting meanings that ritual potentiates. Family therapists can help families and their daughters incorporate this experience in new ways, helping them consider the implications of this transition for their individual and familial lives, as in the [above] illustration.

Brief Example: Becoming a Woman

The Riggs family includes Reverend Donald Riggs, a Congregational minister, his wife Maggie, a legal assistant, and their three daughters, Bonnie, 17, Trudie, 12, and Diane, 10 (see Fig. 1). The family had originally come for help in relation to Bonnie, a high school senior who seemed consistently depressed. A high achiever academically and a very serious and responsible eldest, Bonnie could not decide where to go to college, seemed to be increasingly anxious as high school graduation approached, and was experiencing long bouts of weeping. It was hypothesized that Bonnie, strongly identified with her mother, who had never dealt with her sorrows and disappointments in her own family of origin, was both weeping for her mother and reluctant to leave her with her sadness. Initially, the family therapist argued that young women matured at different rates, were not necessarily prepared to leave home at 17 or 18, and that Bonnie should get a job and remain at home for at least a year. This prescription was linked to a recommendation that Maggie, with

the help of the therapist, work on resolving some of the unfinished business with her own family. These interventions unleashed Bonnie's sense of humor and preparations for college, and Maggie's sharing with her daughters for the first time some of the "real" events in her own family, including a history of secret alcoholism on the part of her father. The therapist, however, was more concerned about the highly rebellious Trudie, the family joker, overly intense and thin, potentially anorexic, and full of scorn for both mother and older sister. Trudie envisioned moving to Australia and becoming a famous actress or writer, as soon as she was 18.

The onset of Trudie's menstruation, an event "spilled" in a session with mother and daughters by a giggling Diane, which occasioned much blushing and anger on Trudie's part, created an opportunity for the therapist to inquire about how the family had reacted to this event. She asked, for example, how Bonnie's menstruation had been handled and what meanings menstruation held for females in the family. Maggie, with some embarrassment, talked about how the subjects of sex and maturation had never been discussed in her family. Her mother had handed her a box of sanitary napkins and had said something about "the curse." She remembered feeling ashamed and humiliated, somehow tarnished, as well as feeling conspicuous; something about her was different—"everyone would know." Her menstrual periods were painful and embarrassing and it was several years before she was able to make a connection between menstruation and childbirth. While she had tried to be more open and positive with Bonnie, she had been very uncomfortable talking about menstruation, and Bonnie reported feeling confused and ignorant about the meanings of the event. Maggie reported that Trudie, earlier in the week, had said, "I know all about it, I don't need you to tell me," when she had tried to talk with her.

The therapist suggested that the family members talk about their ideas about menstruation and what meanings it had for each of them. This discussion revealed that even Maggie had little understanding of female biology or could allow herself to feel proud of her female reproductive abilities or sexuality. Bonnie, buried in her studies and sadness, had little pride in her femininity, while Trudie expressed disgust with the whole discussion, announcing she planned never to marry or have children anyway. Diane, the youngest, said that she had many questions but no one wanted to tell her anything. No one expressed joy or pleasure or pride. Donald seemed the least uncomfortable member of the family. For him it signaled the fact that his daughters were maturing and perhaps more "vulnerable." He indicated that he would not feel embarrassed to talk with his daughters about menstruation, but everyone in the family felt this was a female issue, an area in which they did not want father to assume family leadership. The therapist suggested that perhaps what was needed was instruction in and celebration of the ways of women by women, since in this family the girls' natural curiosity and opportunities for pride and self-valuing had been frustrated.

With father's consent, over the next several weeks, in a part of the therapy defined as "woman time," the family women and therapist worked together teaching and learning about becoming women and celebrating the beginning of Trudie's biological womanhood. Maggie, for the first time, was able to talk to her daughters about her own disappointments, her struggles to define herself as woman, wife, and mother, a contribution that seemed particularly meaningful and freeing for Bonnie. After a period of "education," during which time the girls were invited to ask questions and to contribute their ideas about what becoming a "woman" would mean and what they wanted it to

mean in their family, in school, in church, and in the community, a final celebration was planned, drawing upon ancient customs and the family's own symbols. This rite took place over a two-week period of time. The therapist had suggested that first Trudie needed to say goodbye to a phase of her childhood. She was to spend some time alone each day for a week, thinking very carefully about what she was giving up and leaving behind and what she thought ought to be changed in the family to recognize her maturing. At the end of the week, she and Diane were to have a special time alone. Trudie would pass on to Diane that childhood possession she thought Diane might most cherish. Trudie wrote and dedicated to Diane a very beautiful poem about a young girl's last joys of childhood, reading it to her aloud and giving her a locket Trudie said was a little young for her.

In a second assignment, Maggie was to preside over a family meeting, during which Trudie would describe for the family those changes she felt would appropriately define her new status. Trudie, for the first time without anger, was able to present her case for not attending church every Saturday and Sunday, taking further instruction, and so on. She agreed to attend once a month and to discontinue a series of antics in church which had been highly embarrassing for her parents. Her parents agreed to give her more autonomy in choosing her own clothes (her tastes were far more flamboyant and androgynous than the family norm), and to allow her to participate in school and community plays, an activity that had been discouraged.

The two weeks ended with a family celebration, to which Maggie's mother and aunt and Donald's father and sister were invited. These family members were told the nature of the occasion and asked to bring a gift for Trudie, while Donald and his father, both skilled cooks, were asked to ready a celebratory dinner. The gift that Trudie most valued came from her grandmother, a lovely gold ring that had belonged to her great-grandmother. Interestingly, the grandmother also presented Maggie and Bonnie with family heirlooms, a beautiful quilt made by her mother for Maggie and a carved crystal bowl for Bonnie, connecting these young women to the generations of women who had preceded them.

Donald composed a special blessing honoring his daughter's uniquely maturing self and her special gifts to the family of laughter and creativity, Diane read her poem, and the celebration ended with a toast to the family's newest young woman.

After a few more family sessions, during which time Bonnie, who had long since ceased her weeping, made the decision to attend a college in a nearby community and Maggie and Trudie greatly improved their relationship. Maggie contracted for ongoing individual family-of-origin work.

*   *   *

In this example, a normative life transition which happens to occur during the family's therapy is not ignored but becomes material for change and growth. Existing rituals and their definitions are examined, the family's meanings are explored, and the family is encouraged to ritualize the transition in a way that positively links the young girl to a wider world of pride and meaning. Other events may provide similar opportunities. For example, in our society women have "showers" when they are about to be married or to bear a child. No richly constructed rituals exist on the societal level to celebrate the movement to a new status of a young woman who is not marrying or bearing a child, aside from the high school or college graduation, and these rituals often celebrate a completion but leave indistinct, particularly for young women, what the implications are for a new status in family and community.

Family therapists may explore with families what the moving away from home means to both family and young person and what the terms of the new independence may be. Some families have created "independence" celebrations complete with party and gifts. In these situations, it is particularly important to help the family consider how the parents' roles will change, particularly the mother's role, to also define, mark, and celebrate her new status as her children leave. This latter point needs emphasis, since much of the field seems to have given more at-tention to extricating children from their "overin-volved" mothers than helping mothers define what these leavings mean for their self-definitions and their place in society. . . .

CONCLUSION

Family therapists have just begun to explore the richness and power of ritual life and its potential for therapeutic change, particularly in relation to issues of gender identity and relationships. In this [reading] an effort has been made to identify some of the common themes and issues that emerge when the relationships between ritual and women are explored. Certainly the focus on women's ritual lives and an accounting of some of the personal and social costs of women's rituals generates questions concerning the ritual lives of men. If male-controlled public rituals often are accomplished by power and prestige, men's work rituals can be accompanied by humiliation and drudgery. Furthermore, men may be excluded from meaningful participation in many of the important rituals of family life. Public and domestic rituals clearly carry both rewards and costs for both sexes.

We need not only to learn more about American national and family rituals and how to begin the difficult task of interpretation, but also to understand men's and women's ritual lives in the larger sociocultural and political contexts of gender relationships. It is our responsibility as family therapists to understand our role in contemporary ritual life and to consider how we may be participating in the social construction of gender definitions and relationships.

NOTES

1. See, for example, Goldner, 1985; Hare-Mustin, 1987.
2. See Fraser, 1984; Hoffman, 1985.

REFERENCES

Arens, W. (1976). Professional football: An American symbol and ritual. In W. Arens & S. P. Montague (Eds.). *The American dimension: Cultural myths and social realities* (3–14). Port Washington, NY: Alfred.

Bamberger, J. (1974). The myth of matriarchy: Why men rule in primitive society. In M. Rosaldo & L. Lamphere (Eds.). *Woman, culture, and society*. Stanford, CA: Stanford University Press.

Bateson, M. C. (1984). *With a daughter's eye: A memoir of Margaret Mead and Gregory Bateson*. New York: William Morrow.

Caplow, T., Bahr, H., Chadwick, B. A., Hill, R., & Holmes, M. (1982). Family symbolism in festivals. In *Middletown families: Fifty years of change and continuity*. Minneapolis: University of Minnesota Press.

Douglas, M. (1966). *Purity and danger: An analysis of concepts of pollution and taboo*. New York: Praeger.

Durkheim, E. (1915). *The elementary forms of religious life*. New York: Free Press (1965 reprint).

Fraser, J. (1984). Process level integration: Corrective vision for a binocular view. *The Journal of Strategic and Systemic Therapies*, 3(3), 43–57.

Freeman, Derek. (1983). *Margaret Mead and Samoa: The making and unmaking of an anthropological myth*. Cambridge, MA: Harvard University Press.

Goldner, V. (1985). Feminism and family therapy. *Family Process*, 24, 31–47.

Hare-Mustin, R. (1987). The problem of gender in family therapy theory. *Family Process*, 26, 15–27.

Hartman, A. & Laird, J. (1987, April). *Migration and family folklore*. Plenary paper, Ninth Annual Meeting, American Family Therapy Association, Chicago, IL.

Hoffman, L. (1985). Beyond power and control: Toward a "second order" family systems therapy. *Family Systems Medicine*, 3(4), 381–396.

Keesing, R. (1982). Introduction. In G. H. Herdt (Ed.). *Rituals of manhood: Male initiation in Papua New Guinea* (1–43). Berkeley, CA: University of California Press.

Kottak, C. (1978). *Anthropology: The exploration of human diversity*. New York: Random House.

Laird, J. (1984). Sorcerers, shamans, and social workers: The use of ritual in social work practice. *Social Work*, 29, 123–129.

Langness, L. L. (1974). Ritual power and male domination in the New Guinea highlands. *Ethos*, 2, 189–212.

Lévi-Strauss, C. (1969). *The elementary structures of kinship*. Boston: Beacon Press.

Moore, S. & Myerhoff, B. (1977). Introduction: Secular Ritual: Forms and Meanings. In S. Moore & B. Myerhoff (Eds.). *Secular ritual* (3–24). Amsterdam, The Netherlands: Van Gorcum.

Myerhoff, B. (1983, November). *Rites of passage*. Plenary speech, National Symposium, National Association of Social Workers, Washington, DC.

Ortner, S. (1974). Is female to male as nature is to culture? In M. Rosaldo & L. Lamphere (Eds.). *Woman, culture, and society* (67–87). Stanford, CA: Stanford University Press.

Pirrotta, S. (1984). Milan revisited: A comparison of the two Milan models. *Journal of Strategic and Systemic Therapies*, 3(4), 3–15.

Paige, K. & Paige, M. (1981). *The politics of reproductive ritual*. Berkeley: University of California Press.

Rich, A. (1986). *Of woman born: Motherhood as experience and institution*. (10th Anniversary Edition) New York: Norton.

Rosaldo, M. A. (1974). Woman, culture, and society: A theoretical overview. In M. A. Rosaldo and L. Lamphere (Eds.). *Woman, culture, and society* (17–42). Stanford, CA: Stanford University Press.

Rubin, G. (1975). The traffic in women: Notes on the "political economy." In R. Reiter (Ed.). *Toward an anthropology of women* (157–210). New York: Monthly Review Press.

Schwartz, P. (1987) *American couples: The intimate struggle for power*. Plenary paper, Ninth Annual Meeting, American Family Therapy Association, Chicago, IL.

Selvini Palazzoli, M., Boscolo, L., Cecchin, G., & Prata, G. (1974). The treatment of children through brief therapy of their parents. *Family Process*, 13(4), 429–442.

Viaro, M. & Leonardi, P. (1986). The evolution of the interview technique: A comparison between former and present strategy. *Journal of Strategic and Systemic Therapies*, 5, 1 and 2, 14–30.

Washburn, P. (1977). *Becoming woman: The quit for wholeness in female experience*. New York: Harper & Row.

Weigle, M. (1982). *Spiders & spinsters: Women and mythology*. Albuquerque, NM: University of New Mexico Press.

The Effectiveness of Symbols

CLAUDE LÉVI-STRAUSS

Facts of publication: *Lévi-Strauss, Claude. 1967 [1963]. "The Effectiveness of Symbols," from Structural Anthropology, 181–201. Translated by Claire Jacobson and Brooke Grundfest Schoepf. Garden City, NY: Anchor. Copyright © 1963, 1967 by Basic Books, Inc. Reprinted with the permission of BasicBooks, a division of HarperCollins Publishers, Inc.*

An extensive song text of the Cuna Indians of Panama incorporates a description of a shamanic cure performed to ease difficult childbirth. When a birthing mother loses the spiritual double on which her vital strength depends, a shaman leads a symbolic journey to recover and restore this spirit so the mother may successfully give birth. The remarkable emotional geography of this rescue traverses the vagina and uterus of the mother. Since the shaman treats the woman neither physically nor with any substance, Lévi-Strauss considers the cure psychological. Through a careful analysis of the text, he proposes a theory of disease and cure, suggesting that the shaman provides the sick woman with the language by which she can express previously unexpressed psychic states. To their mutual benefit Lévi-Strauss compares this shamanic cure with psychoanalysis.

On the role of symbols in healing see Arthur Kleinman, "How Do Psychiatrists Heal?" in his Rethinking Psychiatry, *108–141 (New York: Free Press, 1988).*

About the author: Dates: *1908–   , Brussels, Belgium.* **Education:** *Licentiate in philosophy and in law, University of Paris.* **Field(s):** *ethnology, anthropology, philosophy.* **Career:** *Lecturer in sociology, University of São Paulo, Brazil; New School for Social Research; Musée de l'Homme; École Pratique des Hautes Études; Collège de France (Chair, Social Anthropology).* **Publications:** Tristes Tropiques *(New York, 1961);* Totemism, *(Beacon, 1963);* The Savage Mind *(University of Chicago, 1966);* Structural Anthropology *(Basic, 1968; Anchor, 1967);* The Elementary Structures of Kinship *(Beacon, 1969).* **Additional:** *Huxley Memorial Medal, Royal Anthropological Institute, 1965; Viking Fund Prize, 1966; Gold Medal, Centre National de la Recherche Scientifique, 1967.*

The first important South American magico-religious text to be known, published by Wassén and Holmer,[1] throws new light on certain aspects of shamanistic curing and raises problems of theoretical interpretation by no means exhaustively treated in the editors' excellent commentary. We will re-examine this text for its more general implications, rather than from the linguistic or Americanist perspective primarily employed by the authors.

The text is a long incantation, covering eighteen pages in the native version, divided into 535 sections. It was obtained by the Cuna Indian Guillermo Haya from an elderly informant of his tribe. The Cuna, who live within the Panama Republic, received special attention from the late Erland Nordenskiöld, who even succeeded in training collaborators among the natives. After Nordenskiöld's death, Haya forwarded the text to Nordenskiöld's successor, Dr. Wassén. The text was taken down in the original language and accompanied by a Spanish translation, which Holmer revised with great care.

The purpose of the song is to facilitate difficult childbirth. Its use is somewhat exceptional, since native women of Central and South America have easier deliveries than women of Western societies. The intervention of the shaman is thus rare and occurs in case of failure, at the request of the midwife. The song begins with a picture of the midwife's confusion and describes her visit to the shaman, the latter's departure for the hut of the woman in labor, his arrival, and his preparations—consisting of fumigations of burnt cocoanibs, invocations, and the making of sacred figures, or *nuchu*. These images, carved from prescribed kinds of wood which lend them their effectiveness, represent tutelary spirits whom the shaman makes his assistants and whom he leads to the abode of Muu, the power responsible for the formation of the fetus. A difficult childbirth results when Muu has exceeded her functions and captured the *purba*, or "soul," of the mother-to-be. Thus the song expresses a quest: the quest for the lost *purba*, which will be restored after many vicissitudes, such as the overcoming of obstacles, a victory over wild beasts, and, finally, a great contest waged by the shaman and his tutelary spirits against Muu and her daughters, with the help of magical hats whose weight the latter are not able to bear. Muu, once she has been defeated, allows the *purba* of the ailing woman to be discovered and freed. The delivery takes place, and the song ends with a statement of the precautions taken so that Muu will not escape and pursue her visitors. The fight is not waged against Muu herself, who is indispensable to procreation, but only against her abuses of power. Once these have been corrected, relations become friendly, and Muu's parting words to the shaman almost correspond to an invitation: "Friend *nele*, when do you think to visit me again?" (413)[2]

Thus far we have rendered the term *nele* as shaman, which might seem incorrect, since the cure does not appear to require the officiant to experience ecstasy or a transition to another psychic state. Yet the smoke of the cocoa beans aims primarily at "strengthening his garments" and "strengthening" the *nele* himself, "making him brave in front of Muu" (65–66). And above all, the Cuna classification, which distinguishes between several types of medicine men, shows that the power of the *nele* has supernatural sources. The native medicine men are divided into *nele, inatuledi*, and *absogedi*. The functions of the *inatuledi* and *absogedi* are based on knowledge of songs and cures, acquired through study and validated by examinations, while the talent of the *nele*, considered innate, consists of supernatural sight, which instantly discovers the cause of the illness—that is, the whereabouts of the vital forces, whether particular or generalized, that have been carried off by evil spirits. For the *nele* can recruit these spirits, making them his protectors or assistants.[3] There is no doubt, therefore, that he is ac-

tually a shaman, even if his intervention in childbirth does not present all the traits which ordinarily accompany this function. And the *nuchu*, protective spirits who at the shaman's bidding become embodied in the figurines he has carved, receive from him—along with invisibility and clairvoyance—*niga*. *Niga* is "vitality" and "resistance,"[4] which make these spirits *nelegan* (plural of *nele*) "in the service of men" or in the "likeness of human beings" (235—237), although endowed with exceptional powers.

From our brief synopsis, the song appears to be rather commonplace. The sick woman suffers because she has lost her spiritual double or, more correctly, one of the specific doubles which together constitute her vital strength. (We shall return to this point.) The shaman, assisted by his tutelary spirits, undertakes a journey to the supernatural world in order to snatch the double from the malevolent spirit who has captured it; by restoring it to its owner, he achieves the cure. The exceptional interest of this text does not lie in this formal framework, but, rather, in the discovery—stemming no doubt from a reading of the text, but for which Holmer and Wassén deserve, nonetheless, full credit—that *Mu-Igala*, that is, "Muu's way," and the abode of Muu are not, to the native mind, simply a mythical itinerary and dwelling-place. They represent, literally, the vagina and uterus of the pregnant woman, which are explored by the shaman and *nuchu* and in whose depths they wage their victorious combat.

This interpretation is based first of all on an analysis of the concept of *purba*. The *purba* is a different spiritual principle from the *niga*, which we defined above. Unlike the *purba* the *niga* cannot be stolen from its possessor, and only human beings and animals own one. A plant or a stone has a *purba* but not a *niga*. The same is true of a corpse; and in a child, the *niga* only develops with age. It seems, therefore, that one could, without too much inaccuracy, interpret *niga* as "vital strength," and *purba* as "double" or "soul," with the understanding that these words do not imply a distinction between animate and inanimate (since everything is animate for the Cuna) but correspond rather to the Platonic notion of "idea" or "archetype" of which every being or object is the material expression.

The sick woman of the song has lost more than her *purba*: the native text attributes fever to her—

"the hot garments of the disease" (1 and *passim*)—and the loss or impairment of her sight—"straying . . . asleep on Muu Puklip's path" (97). Above all, as she declares to the shaman who questions her, "It is Muu Puklip who has come to me. She wants to take my *niga purbalele* for good" (98). Holmer proposes translating *niga* as physical strength and *purba* (*lele*) as *soul* or essence, whence "the soul of her life."[5] It would perhaps be bold to suggest that the *niga*, an attribute of the living being, results from the existence of not one but several *purba*, which are functionally interrelated. Yet each part of the body has its own *purba*, and the *niga* seems to constitute, on the spiritual level, the equivalent of the concept of organism. Just as life results from the cooperation of the organs, so "vital strength" would be none other than the harmonious concurrence of all the *purba*, each of which governs the functions of a specific organ.

As a matter of fact, not only does the shaman retrieve the *niga purbalele*; his discovery is followed immediately by the recapture of other *purba*, those of the heart, bones, teeth, hair, nails, and feet (401–408, 435–442). The omission here of the *purba* governing the most affected organs—the generative organs—might come as a surprise. As the editors of the text emphasize, this is because the *purba* of the uterus is not considered as a victim but as responsible for the pathological disorder. Muu and her daughters, the *muugan*, are, as Nordenskiöld pointed out, the forces that preside over the development of the fetus and that gives it its *kurgin*, or natural capacities.[6] The text does not refer to these positive attributes. In it Muu appears as an instigator of disorder, a special "soul" that has captured and paralyzed the other special "souls," thus destroying the cooperation which insures the integrity of the "chief body" (*cuerpo jefe* in Spanish, 430, 435) from which it draws its *niga*. But at the same time, Muu must stay put, for the expedition undertaken to liberate the *purba* might provoke Muu's escape by the road which temporarily remains open; hence the precautions whose details fill the last part of the song. The shaman mobilizes the Lords of the wild animals to guard the way, the road is entangled, golden and silver nets are fastened, and, for four days, the *nelegan* stand watch and beat their sticks

(505–535). Muu, therefore, is not a fundamentally evil force: she is a force gone awry. In a difficult delivery the "soul" of the uterus has led astray all the "souls" belonging to other parts of the body. Once these souls are liberated, the soul of the uterus can and must resume its cooperation. Let us emphasize right here the clarity with which the native ideology delineates the emotional content of the physiological disturbance, as it might appear, in an implicit way, to the mind of the sick woman.

To reach Muu, the shaman and his assistants must follow a road, "Muu's way," which may be identified from the many allusions in the text. When the shaman, crouching beneath the sick woman's hammock, has finished carving the *nuchu*, the latter rise up "at the extremity of the road" (72, 83) and the shaman exhorts them in these terms:

> The (sick) woman lies in the hammock in front of you.
> Her white tissue lies in her lap, her white tissues move softly.
> The (sick) woman's body lies weak.
> When they light up (along) Muu's way, it runs over with exudations and like blood.
> Her exudations drip down below the hammock all like blood, all red.
> The inner white tissue extends to the bosom of the earth.
> Into the middle of the woman's white tissue a human being descends. (84–90)

The translators are doubtful as to the meaning of the last two sentences, yet they refer to another native text, published by Nordenskiöld, which leaves no doubt as to the identification of the "white inner tissue" with the vulva:

sibugua	molul	arkaali		
blanca	tela	abriendo		
sibugua	molul	akinnali		
blanca	tela	extendiendo		

. . . .

sibugua	molul	abalase	tulapurua	ekuanali
blanca	tela	centro	feto	caer haciendo[7]

"Muu's way," darkened and completely covered with blood owing to the difficult labor, and which the *nuchu* have to find by the white sheen of their clothes and magical hats, is thus unquestionably the vagina of the sick woman. And "Muu's abode," the "dark whirlpool" where she dwells, corresponds to the uterus, since the native informant comments on the name of this abode, *Amukkapiryawila*, in terms of *omegan purba amurrequedi*, that is, "woman's turbid menstruation," also called "the dark deep whirlpool" (250–251) and "the dark inner place" (32).[8]

The original character of this text gives it a special place among the shamanistic cures ordinarily described. These cures are of three types, which are not, however, mutually exclusive. The sick organ or member may be physically involved, through a manipulation or suction which aims at extracting the cause of the illness—usually a thorn, crystal, or feather made to appear at the opportune moment, as in tropical America, Australia, and Alaska. Curing may also revolve, as among the Araucanians, around a sham battle, waged in the hut and then outdoors, against harmful spirits. Or, as among the Navajo, the officiant may recite incantations and prescribe actions (such as placing the sick person on different parts of a painting traced on the ground with colored sands and pollens) which bear no direct relationship to the specific disturbance to be cured. In all these cases, the therapeutic method (which as we know is often effective) is difficult to interpret. When it deals directly with the unhealthy organ, it is too grossly concrete (generally, pure deceit) to be granted intrinsic value. And when it consists in the repetition of often highly abstract ritual, it is difficult for us to understand its direct bearing on the illness. It would be convenient to dismiss these difficulties by declaring that we are dealing with psychological cures. But this term will remain meaningless unless we can explain how specific psychological representations are invoked to combat equally specific physiological disturbances. The text that we have analyzed offers a striking contribution to the solution of this problem. The song constitutes a purely psychological treatment, for the shaman does not touch the body of the sick woman and administers no remedy. Nevertheless it involves, directly and explicitly, the pathological condition and its locus. In our view, the song constitutes a *psychological manipulation* of the sick organ, and it is precisely from this manipulation that a cure is expected.

To begin, let us demonstrate the existence and the characteristics of this manipulation. Then we shall ask what its purpose and its effectiveness are. First, we are surprised to find that the song, whose subject is a dramatic struggle between helpful and malevolent spirits for the reconquest of a "soul," devotes very little attention to action proper. In eighteen pages of text the contest occupies less than one page and the meeting with Muu Puklip scarcely two pages. The preliminaries, on the other hand, are highly developed and the preparations, the outfitting of the *nuchu*, the itinerary, and the sites are described with a great wealth of detail. Such is the case, at the beginning, for the midwife's visit to the shaman. The conversation between the sick woman and the midwife, followed by that between the midwife and the shaman, recurs twice, for each speaker repeats exactly the utterance of the other before answering him:

> The (sick) woman speaks to the midwife: "I am indeed being dressed in the hot garment of the disease."
> The midwife answers her (sick woman): "You are indeed being dressed in the hot garment of the disease, I also hear you say." (1–2)

It might be argued[9] that this stylistic device is common among the Cuna and stems from the necessity, among peoples bound to oral tradition, of memorizing exactly what has been said. And yet here this device is applied not only to speech but to actions:

> The midwife turns about in the hut.
> The midwife looks for some beads.
> The midwife turns about (in order to leave).
> The midwife puts one foot in front of the other.
> The midwife touches the ground with her foot.
> The midwife puts her other foot forward.
> The midwife pushes open the door of her hut; the door of her hut creaks.
> The midwife goes out . . . (7–14).

This minute description of her departure is repeated when she arrives at the shaman's, when she returns to the sick woman, when the shaman departs, and when he arrives. Sometimes the same description is repeated twice in the same terms (37–39 and 45–47 reproduce 33–35). The cure thus begins with a historical account of the events that preceded it, and some elements which might appear secondary ("arrivals" and "departures") are treated with luxuriant detail as if they were, so to speak, filmed in slow-motion. We encounter this technique throughout the text, but it is nowhere applied as systematically as at the beginning and to describe incidents of retrospective interest.

Everything occurs as though the shaman were trying to induce the sick woman—whose contact with reality is no doubt impaired and whose sensitivity is exacerbated—to relive the initial situation through pain, in a very precise and intense way, and to become psychologically aware of its smallest details. Actually this situation sets off a series of events of which the body and internal organs of the sick woman will be the assumed setting. A transition will thus be made from the most prosaic reality to myth, from the physical universe to the physiological universe, from the external world to the internal body. And the myth being enacted in the internal body must retain throughout the vividness and the character of lived experience prescribed by the shaman in the light of the pathological state and through an appropriate obsessing technique.

The next ten pages offer, in breathless rhythm, a more and more rapid oscillation between mythical and physiological themes, as if to abolish in the mind of the sick woman the distinction which separates them, and to make it impossible to differentiate their respective attributes. First there is a description of the woman lying in her hammock or in the native obstetrical position, facing eastward, knees parted, groaning, losing her blood, the vulva dilated and moving (84–92, 123–124, 134–135, 152, 158, 173, 177–178, 202–204). Then the shaman calls by name the spirits of intoxicating drinks; of the winds, waters, and woods; and even— precious testimony to the plasticity of the myth— the spirit of the "silver steamer of the white man" (187). The themes converge: like the sick woman, the *nuchu* are dripping with blood; and the pains of the sick woman assume cosmic proportions: "The inner white tissue extends to the bosom of the earth. . . . Into the bosom of the earth her exudations gather into a pool, all like blood, all red" (84–92). At the same time, each spirit, when it appears, is carefully described, and the magical equipment which he receives from the shaman is enumerated at great length: black beads, flame-colored beads, dark beads, ring-shaped beads, tiger bones, rounded bones, throat bones, and many other bones, silver necklaces, armadillo bones, bones of the bird *kerkettoli*, woodpecker bones, bones for flutes, silver beads (104–118). Then general recruitment begins anew, as if these guarantees were still inadequate and all forces, known or unknown to the sick woman, were to be rallied for the invasion (119–229).

Yet we are released to such a small extent into the realm of myth that the penetration of the vagina, mythical though it be, is proposed to the sick woman in concrete and familiar terms. On two occasions, moreover, "muu" designates the uterus directly, and not the spiritual principle which governs its activity ("the sick woman's muu," 204, 453).[10] Here the *nelegan*, in order to enter Muu's way, take on the appearance and the motions of the erect penis:

> The *nelegan*'s hats are shining white, the *nelegan*'s hats are whitish.
> The *nelegan* are becoming flat and low (?), all like bits, all straight.
> The *nelegan* are beginning to become terrifying (?), the *nelegan* are becoming all terrifying (?), for the sake of the (sick) woman's *niga purbalele* (230–232).

And further, below:

> The *nelegan* go balancing up on top of the hammock, they go moving upward like *nusupane* (239).[11]

The technique of the narrative thus aims at recreating a real experience in which the myth merely shifts the protagonists. The *nelegan* enter the natural orifice, and we can imagine that after all this psychological preparation the sick woman actually feels them entering. Not only does she feel them, but they "light up" the route they are preparing to follow—for their own sake, no doubt, and to find the way, but also to make the center of inexpressible and painful sensations "clear" for her and accessible to her consciousness. "The *nelegan* put good sight into the sick woman, the *nelegan* light good eyes in the (sick) woman . . ." (238).

And this "illuminating sight," to paraphrase an expression in the text, enables them to relate in detail a complicated itinerary that is a true mythical anatomy, corresponding less to the real structure of the genital organs than to a kind of emotional geography, identifying each point of resistance and each thrust:

> The *nelegan* set out, the *nelegan* march in a single file along Muu's road, as far as the Low Mountain,
> The *nelegan* set out, etc., as far as the Short Mountain,
> The *nelegan*, etc., as far as the Long Mountain,
> The *nelegan*, etc., (to) Yala Pokuna Yala, (not translated)
> The *nelegan*, etc., (to) Yala Akkwatallekun Yala, (not translated)
> The *nelegan*, etc., (to) Yala Ilamalisuikun Yala, (not translated)
> The *nelegan*, etc., into the center of the Flat Mountain.
> The *nelegan* set out, the *nelegan* march in a single file along Muu's road (241–248).

The picture of the uterine world, peopled with fantastic monsters and dangerous animals, is amenable to the same interpretation—which is, moreover, confirmed by the native informant: "It is the animals," he says, "who increase the diseases of the laboring woman"; that is, the pains themselves are personified. And here again, the song seems to have as its principal aim the description of these pains to the sick woman and the naming of them, that is, their presentation to her in a form accessible to conscious or unconscious thought: Uncle Alligator, who moves about with his bulging eyes, his striped and variegated body, crouching and wriggling his tail; Uncle Alligator Tiikwalele, with glistening body, who moves his glistening flippers, whose flippers conquer the place, push everything aside, drag everything; Nele Ki(k)kirpanalele, the Octopus, whose sticky tentacles are alternately opening and closing; and many others besides: He-who-has-a-hat-that-is-soft, He-who-has-a-red-colored-hat, He-who-has-a-variegated-hat, etc.; and

the guardian animals: the black tiger, the red animal, the two-colored animal, the dust-colored animal; each is tied with an iron chain, the tongue hanging down, the tongue hanging out, saliva dripping, saliva foaming, with flourishing tail, the claws coming out and tearing things "all like blood, all red" (253–298).

To enter into this hell à la Hieronymus Bosch[A] and reach its owner, the *nelegan* have to overcome other obstacles, this time material: fibers, loose threads, fastened threads, successive curtains—rainbow-colored, golden, silvery, red, black, maroon, blue, white, wormlike, "like neckties," yellow, twisted, thick (305–330); and for this purpose, the shaman calls reinforcements: Lords of the wood-boring insects, who are to "cut, gather, wind and reduce" the threads, which Holmer and Wassén identify as the internal tissues of the uterus.[12]

The *nelegan*'s invasion follows the downfall of these last obstacles, and here the tournament of the hats takes place. A discussion of this would lead us too far from the immediate purpose of this study. After the liberation of the *niga purbalele* comes the descent, which is just as dangerous as the ascent, since the purpose of the whole undertaking is to induce childbirth—precisely, a difficult descent. The shaman counts his helpers and encourages his troops; still he must summon other reinforcements: the "clearers of the way," Lords-of-the-burrowing animals, such as the armadillo. The *niga* is exhorted to make its way toward the orifice:

> Your body lies in front of you in the hammock,
> (Her) white tissue lies in her lap,
> The white inner tissue moves softly,
> Your (sick) woman lies in your midst . . .
> . . . thinking she cannot see.
> Into her body they put again (her) *niga purbalele* . . . (430–435).

The episode that follows is obscure. It would seem that the sick woman is not yet cured. The shaman leaves for the mountains with people of the village to gather medicinal plants, and he returns to

---

[A] Heironymus Bosch (ca. 1450–1516), painter of the late Middle Ages. (Editor's note)

the attack in a different way. This time it is he who, by imitating the penis, penetrates the "opening of muu" and moves in it "like *nusupane* . . . completely drying the inner place" (453–454). Yet the use of astringents suggests that the delivery has taken place. Finally, before the account of the precautions taken to impede Muu's escape, which we have already described, we find the shaman calling for help from a people of Bowmen. Since their task consists in raising a cloud of dust "to obscure . . . Muu's way" (464), and to defend all of Muu's crossroads and byroads (468), their intervention probably also pertains to the conclusion.

The previous episode perhaps refers to a second curing technique, with organ manipulation and the administration of remedies. Or it may perhaps match, in equally metaphorical terms, the first journey, which is more highly elaborated in the text. Two lines of attack would thus have been developed for the assistance to the sick woman, one of which is supported by a psychophysiological mythology and the other by a psychosocial mythology—indicated by the shaman's call on the inhabitants of the village—which, however, remains undeveloped. At any rate, it should be observed that the song ends after the delivery, just as it had begun before the cure. Both antecedent and subsequent events are carefully related. But it is not only against Muu's elusive stray impulses that the cure must, through careful procedures, be effected; the efficacy of the cure would be jeopardized if, even before any results were to be expected, it failed to offer the sick woman a resolution, that is, a situation wherein all the protagonists have resumed their places and returned to an order which is no longer threatened.

The cure would consist, therefore, in making explicit a situation originally existing on the emotional level and in rendering acceptable to the mind pains which the body refuses to tolerate. That the mythology of the shaman does not correspond to an objective reality does not matter. The sick woman believes in the myth and belongs to a society which believes in it. The tutelary spirits and malevolent spirits, the supernatural monsters and magical animals, are all part of a coherent system on which the native conception of the universe is founded. The sick woman accepts these mythical beings or, more accurately, she has never questioned their existence. What she does not accept are the incoherent and arbitrary pains, which are an alien element in her system but which the shaman, calling upon the myth, will re-integrate within a whole where everything is meaningful.

Once the sick woman understands, however, she does more than resign herself; she gets well. But no such thing happens to our sick when the causes of their diseases have been explained to them in terms of secretions, germs, or viruses. We shall perhaps be accused of paradox if we answer that the reason lies in the fact that microbes exist and monsters do not. And yet, the relationship between germ and disease is external to the mind of the patient, for it is a cause-and-effect relationship; whereas the relationship between monster and disease is internal to his mind, whether conscious or unconscious: It is a relationship between symbol and thing symbolized, or, to use the terminology of linguists, between sign and meaning. The shaman provides the sick woman with a *language*, by means of which unexpressed, and otherwise inexpressible, psychic states can be immediately expressed. And it is the transition to this verbal expression—at the same time making it possible to undergo in an ordered and intelligible form a real experience that would otherwise be chaotic and inexpressible—which induces the release of the physiological process, that is, the reorganization, in a favorable direction, of the process to which the sick woman is subjected.

In this respect, the shamanistic cure lies on the borderline between our contemporary physical medicine and such psychological therapies as psychoanalysis. Its originality stems from the application to an organic condition of a method related to psychotherapy. How is this possible? A closer comparison between shamanism and psychoanalysis—which in our view implies no slight to psychoanalysis—will enable us to clarify this point.

In both cases the purpose is to bring to a conscious level conflicts and resistances which have remained unconscious, owing either to their repression by other psychological forces or—in the case of childbirth—to their own specific nature, which is not psychic but organic or even simply mechanical. In both cases also, the conflicts and resistances are resolved, not because of the knowledge, real or alleged, which the sick woman progressively acquires of them, but because this knowledge makes possible a specific experience, in the course of which conflicts materialize in an order and on a level permitting their free development and leading to their resolution. This vital experience is called *abreaction* in psychoanalysis. We know that its precondition is the unprovoked intervention of the analyst, who appears in the conflicts of the patient through a double transference mechanism, as a flesh-and-blood protagonist and in relation to whom the patient can restore and clarify an initial situation which has remained unexpressed or unformulated.

All these characteristics can be found in the shamanistic cure. Here, too, it is a matter of provoking an experience; as this experience becomes structured, regulatory mechanisms beyond the subject's control are spontaneously set in motion and lead to an orderly functioning. The shaman plays the same dual role as the psychoanalyst. A prerequisite role—that of listener for the psychoanalyst and of orator for the shaman—establishes a direct relationship with the patient's conscious and an indirect relationship with his unconscious. This is the function of the incantation proper. But the shaman does more than utter the incantation; he is its hero, for it is he who, at the head of a supernatural battalion of spirits, penetrates the endangered organs and frees the captive soul. In this way he, like the psychoanalyst, becomes the object of transference and, through the representations induced in the patient's mind, the real protagonist of the conflict which the latter experiences on the border between the physical world and the psychic world. The patient suffering from neurosis eliminates an individual myth by facing a "real" psychoanalyst; the native woman in childbed overcomes a true organic disorder by identifying with a "mythically transmuted" shaman.

This parallelism does not exclude certain differences, which are not surprising if we note the character—psychological in the one case and organic in the other—of the ailment to be cured. Actually the shamanistic cure seems to be the exact counterpart to the psychoanalytic cure, but with an inversion of all the elements. Both cures aim at inducing an experience, and both succeed by recreating a myth which the patient has to live or relive. But in one case, the patient constructs an individual myth with elements drawn from his past; in the other case, the patient receives from the outside a social myth which does not correspond to a former personal state. To prepare for the abreaction, which then becomes an "adreaction," the psychoanalyst listens, whereas the shaman speaks. Better still: When a transference is established, the patient puts words into the mouth of the psychoanalyst by attributing to him alleged feelings and intentions; in the incantation, on the contrary, the shaman speaks for his patient. He questions her and puts into her mouth answers that correspond to the interpretation of her condition, with which she must become imbued:

> My eyesight is straying, it is asleep on Muu Puklip's path.
> It is Muu Puklip who has come to me. She wants to take my *niga purbalele* for good.
> Muu Nauryaiti has come to me. She wants to possess my *niga purbalele* for good.
> etc. (97–101).

Furthermore, the resemblance becomes even more striking when we compare the shaman's method with certain recent therapeutic techniques of psychoanalysis. R. Desoille, in his research on daydreaming,[13] emphasized that psychopathological disturbances are accessible only through the language of symbols. Thus he speaks to his patients by means of symbols, which remain, nonetheless, verbal metaphors. In a more recent work, with which we were not acquainted when we began this study, M. A. Sechehaye goes much further.[14] It seems to us that the results which she obtained while treating a case of schizophrenia considered incurable fully confirm our preceding views on the similarities between psychoanalysis and shamanism. For Sechehaye became aware that speech, no matter how symbolic it might be, still could not penetrate beyond the conscious and that she could reach deeply buried complexes only through acts. Thus to resolve a weaning complex, the analyst must assume a maternal role, carried out not by a literal reproduction of the appropriate behavior but by means of actions which are, as it were, discontinuous, each symbolizing a fundamental element of the situation—for instance, putting the cheek of the patient in contact with the breast of the analyst. The symbolic load of such acts qualifies them as a language. Actually, the therapist holds a dialogue with the patient, not through the spoken word, but by concrete actions, that is, genuine rites which penetrate the screen of consciousness to carry their message directly to the unconscious.

Here we again encounter the concept of manipulation, which appeared so essential to an understanding of the shamanistic cure but whose traditional definition we must broaden considerably. For it may at one time involve a manipulation of ideas and, at another time, a manipulation of organs. But the basic condition remains that the manipulation must be carried out through symbols, that is, through meaningful equivalents of things meant which belong to another order of reality. The *gestures* of Sechehaye reverberate in the unconscious *mind* of the schizophrenic just as the *representations* evoked by the shaman bring about a modification in the organic *functions* of the woman in childbirth. Labor is impeded at the beginning of the song, the delivery takes place at the end, and the progress of childbirth is reflected in successive stages of the myth. The first penetration of the vagina by the *nelegan* is carried out in [single] file (241) and, since it is an ascent, with the help of magical hats which clear and light up the way. The return corresponds to the second phase of the myth, but to the first phase of the physiological process, since the child must be made to come down. Attention turns toward the *nelegan's* feet. We are told that they have shoes (494–496). When they invade Muu's abode, they no longer march in single file but in "rows of four" (388); and, to come out again in the open air, they go "in a row" (248). No doubt the purpose of such an alteration in the details of the myth is to elicit the corresponding organic reaction, but the sick woman could not integrate it as experience if it were not associated with a true increase in dilation. It is the effectiveness of symbols which guarantees the harmonious parallel development of myth and action. And myth and action form a pair always associated with the duality of patient and healer. In the schizophrenic cure the healer performs the actions and the patient produces his myth; in the shamanistic cure the healer supplies the myth and the patient performs the actions.

The analogy between these two methods would be even more complete if we could admit, as Freud seems to have suggested on two different occasions,[15] that the description in psychological terms of the structure of psychoses and neuroses must one day be replaced by physiological, or even biochemical, concepts. This possibility may be at hand, since . . . Swedish research[16] has demonstrated chemical differences resulting from the amounts of polynucleids in the nerve cells of the normal individual and those of the psychotic. Given this hypothesis or any other of the same type, the shamanistic cure and the psychoanalytic cure would become strictly parallel. It would be a matter, either way, of stimulating an organic transformation which would consist essentially in a structural reorganization, by inducing the patient intensively to live out a myth—either received or created by him—whose structure would be, at the unconscious level, analogous to the structure whose genesis is sought on the organic level. The effectiveness of symbols would consist precisely in this "inductive property," by which formally homologous structures, built out of different materials at different levels of life—organic processes, unconscious mind, rational thought—are related to one another. Poetic metaphor provides a familiar example of this inductive process, but as a rule it does not transcend the unconscious level. Thus we note the significance of Rimbaud's intuition that metaphor can change the world.

The comparison with psychoanalysis has allowed us to shed light on some aspects of shamanistic curing. Conversely, it is not improbable that the study of shamanism may one day serve to elucidate obscure points of Freudian theory. We are thinking specifically of the concepts of myth and the unconscious.

We saw that the only difference between the two methods that would outlive the discovery of a physiological substratum of neurosis concerns the origin of the myth, which in the one case is recovered as an individual possession and in the other case is received from collective tradition. Actually, many psychoanalysts would refuse to admit that the psychic constellations which reappear in the patient's conscious could constitute a myth. These represent, they say, real events which it is sometimes possible to date and whose authenticity can be verified by checking with relatives or servants.[17] We do not question these facts. But we should ask ourselves whether the therapeutic value of the cure depends on the actual character of remembered situations, or whether the traumatizing power of those situations stems from the fact that at the moment when they appear, the subject experiences them immediately as living myth. By this we mean that the traumatizing power of any situation cannot result from its intrinsic features but must, rather, result from the capacity of certain events, appearing within an appropriate psychological, historical, and social context, to induce an emotional crystallization which is molded by a pre-existing structure. In relation to the event or anecdote, these structures—or, more accurately, these structural laws—are truly atemporal. For the neurotic, all psychic life and all subsequent experiences are organized in terms of an exclusive or predominant structure, under the catalytic action of the initial myth. But this structure, as well as other structures which the neurotic relegates to a subordinate position, are to be found also in the normal human being, whether primitive or civilized. These structures as an aggregate form what we call the unconscious. The last difference between the theory of shamanism and psychoanalytic theory would, then, vanish. The unconscious ceases to be the ultimate haven of individual peculiarities—the repository of a unique history which makes each of us an irreplaceable being. It is reducible to a function—the symbolic function, which no doubt is specifically human, and which is carried out according to the same laws among all men, and actually corresponds to the aggregate of these laws.

If this view is correct, it will probably be necessary to re-establish a more marked distinction between the unconscious and the preconscious than has been customary in psychology. For the preconscious, as a reservoir of recollections and images amassed in the course of a lifetime,[18] is merely an aspect of memory. While perennial in character, the preconscious also has limitations, since the term refers to the fact that even though memories are preserved they are not always available to the individual. The unconscious, on the other hand, is always empty—or, more accurately, it is as alien to mental images as is the stomach to the foods which pass through it. As the organ of a specific function, the unconscious merely imposes structural laws upon inarticulated

elements which originate elsewhere—impulses, emotions, representations, and memories. We might say, therefore, that the preconscious is the individual lexicon where each of us accumulates the vocabulary of his personal history, but that this vocabulary becomes significant, for us and for others, only to the extent that the unconscious structures it according to its laws and thus transforms it into language. Since these laws are the same for all individuals and in all instances where the unconscious pursues its activity, the problem which arose in the preceding paragraph can easily be resolved. The vocabulary matters less than the structure. Whether the myth is re-created by the individual or borrowed from tradition, it derives from its sources—individual or collective (between which interpenetrations and exchanges constantly occur)—only the stock of representations with which it operates. But the structure remains the same, and through it the symbolic function is fulfilled.

If we add that these structures are not only the same for everyone and for all areas to which the function applies, but that they are few in number, we shall understand why the world of symbolism is infinitely varied in content, but always limited in its laws. There are many languages, but very few structural laws which are valid for all languages. A compilation of known tales and myths would fill an imposing number of volumes. But they can be reduced to a small number of simple types if we abstract, from among the diversity of characters, a few elementary functions. As for the complexes—those individual myths—they also correspond to a few simple types, which mold the fluid multiplicity of cases.

Since the shaman does not psychoanalyze his patient, we may conclude that remembrance of things past, considered by some the key to psychoanalytic therapy, is only one expression (whose value and results are hardly negligible) of a more fundamental method, which must be defined without considering the individual or collective genesis of the myth. For the myth *form* takes precedence over the *content* of the narrative. This is, at any rate, what the analysis of a native text seems to have taught us. But also, from another perspective, we know that any myth represents a quest for the remembrance of things past. The modern version of shamanistic technique called psychoanalysis thus derives its specific characteristics from the fact that in industrial civilization there is no longer any room for mythical time, except within man himself. From this observation, psychoanalysis can draw confirmation of its validity, as well as hope of strengthening its theoretical foundations and understanding better the reasons for its effectiveness, by comparing its methods and goals with those of its precursors, the shamans and sorcerers.

NOTES

1. Nils M. Holmer and Henry Wassén, *Mu-Igala or the Way of Muu, a Medicine Song from the Cunas of Panama* (Göteborg: 1947).
2. The numbers in parentheses refer to the numbered sections in the song.
3. E. Nordenskiöld, *An Historical and Ethnological Survey of the Cuna Indians*, ed. Henry Wassén, Vol. X of *Comparative Ethnographical Studies* (Göteborg: 1938), pp. 80 ff.
4. *Ibid.*, pp. 360 ff.; Holmer and Wassén, *op. cit.*, pp. 78–9.
5. Holmer and Wassén, *op. cit.*, p. 38, *n* 44.
6. Nordenskiöld, *op cit.*, p. 364 ff.
7. *Ibid.*, pp. 607–8; Holmer and Wassén, *op. cit.*, p. 38, *nn* 35–9.
8. The translation of *ti ipya* as "whirlpool" seems to be strained. For certain South American natives, as also in the languages of the Iberian peninsula (cf. the Portuguese *olho d'agua*), a "water eye" is a spring.
9. Holmer and Wassén, *op. cit.*, pp. 65–6.
10. *Ibid.*, p. 45, *n* 219; p. 57, *n* 539.
11. The question marks are Holmer and Wassén's; *nusupane* derives from *nusu*, "worm," and is commonly used for "penis"

(see Holmer and Wassén, p. 47, *n* 280; p. 57, *n* 540; and p. 82).
12. *Ibid.*, p. 85.
13. R. Desoille, *Le Rêve éveillé en psychothérapie* (Paris: 1945).
14. M. A. Sechehaye, *La Réalisation symbolique*, Supplement No. 12 to *Revue suisse de psychologie et de psychologie appliquée* (Bern: 1947).
15. In *Beyond the Pleasure Principle*, p. 79, and *New Conferences on Psychoanalysis*, p. 198, cited by E. Kris, "The Nature of Psychoanalytic Propositions and their Validation," in *Freedom and Experience, Essays presented to H. M. Kallen* (Ithaca, N.Y.: 1947), p. 244.
16. Caspersson and Hyden, at the Karolinska Institute in Stockholm.
17. Marie Bonaparte, "Notes on the Analytical Discovery of a Primal Scene," in *The Psychoanalytic Study of the Child*, Vol. I (New York: 1945).
18. This definition, which was subjected to considerable criticism, acquires a new meaning through the radical distinction between preconscious and unconscious.

---

*Olympic Games and the Theory of Spectacle in Modern Societies**

JOHN J. MACALOON

Facts of publication: *MacAloon, John J. 1984. "Olympic Games and the Theory of Spectacle in Modern Societies," from* Rite, Drama, Festival, Spectacle: Rehearsals Toward a Theory of Cultural Performance, *241–259, 275–278. Edited by John J. MacAloon. Philadelphia: Institute for the Study of Human Issues. Copyright © 1984 by ISHI, Institute for the Study of Human Issues, Inc. Reprinted with the permission of the publishers.*

John MacAloon considers ritual one of four nested and interrelated genres that comprise modern Olympic Games. The other three are spectacle, festival, and game. He is particularly interested in the interweaving of ritual and spectacle. The most obvious rites of the Games are the numerous and varied "ceremonies." The struc-

*I owe a special debt to each of my colleagues at Burg Wartenstein and to the Wenner-Gren Foundation for Anthropological Research. This essay was read by several additional persons whose encouragement, criticisms, and suggestions have benefited it. Among them are Don Handelman, Donald Levine, Michael Schudson, Carl Pletsch, Janet Harris, Thomas Buckley, Elihu Katz, Daniel Dayan, Jorunn Jacobsen, and Robert Stark. To Victor and Edith Turner, who nurtured my fascination with the Olympic Games, I owe particular gratitude.

ture of the Games, bounded by the opening and closing ceremonies, has the familiar form of a rite of passage (see van Gennep in this volume). MacAloon thinks the Olympic rites effect a global realization of a human kindness. He shows that Pierre de Coubertin, founder of the modern Olympic Games, understood modern athletics as a kind of religion aspiring to the ideals of world peace. MacAloon's analysis of the Games relies heavily on Victor Turner's studies of ritual (see his two selections in this volume), particularly his understanding of liminality.

In parts of the article not presented here, MacAloon uses a kind of frame analysis, based on Gregory Bateson's discussion of play and Erving Goffman's frame analysis. He shows how these genres interrelate and how these relations have changed as the Games have developed recently. He also outlines a sophisticated theory of spectacle capable of accounting for the history of the Games and their function in the contemporary world.

See the Journal of Ritual Studies, *vol. 7 no. 1, 1993; the entire issue is on ritual and sport.*

About the author: *Dates: 1947– , Detroit, MI, U.S.A.* **Education:** *B.A., Catholic University of America; M.A., University of Chicago; Ph.D., University of Chicago.* **Field(s):** *social and cultural theory; anthropology of performance; Olympic games; international organizations.* **Career:** *Professor of Social Sciences, 1974–present, University of Chicago.* **Publications:** This Great Symbol: Pierre de Coubertin and the Origin of the Modern Olympic Games *(University of Chicago, 1981); editor,* Rite, Drama, Festival Spectacle: Rehearsals Toward a Theory of Cultural Performance *(Institute for the Study of Human Issues, 1984); editor, with Kang Shin-pyo,* The Olympic Games and Intercultural Exchange in the World System *(Hanyang University, 1989);* Brides of Victory: Gender and Nationalism in Olympic Ritual *(Berg, 1995).* **Additional:** *"I have been chiefly engaged in the multinational, collaborative, and comparative study of the production, transmission, and reception of Olympic rituals. To that end, I ethnographically study and advise the International Olympic Committee, several National Olympic Committees, and the organizing committees of the Seoul, Barcelona, Lillehammer, and Atlanta Olympic Games, focusing on ritual and political communication."*

In merely eighty years, the Olympic Games have grown into a cultural performance of global proportion. Participants in the Games—athletes, officials, dignitaries, press, technicians, support personnel, as well as artists, performers, scientists, and world youth campers attending ancillary congresses and exhibitions—now number in the scores of thousands and are drawn from as many as 151 nations. Two or three million persons watch the events live, and the broadcast audience is staggering. According to reasonable estimates, 1.5 billion people—approximately one out of every three persons then alive on the earth—watched or listened to at least a part of the proceedings at Montreal through the broadcast media. Adding a "guesstimate" of the newspaper audience and of those interested in the Games but prevented by political censure or the lack of facilities from following them, the figure rises to something like half of the world's population. Had the 1980 Moscow Games not been truncated by boycotts, the television audience alone might have exceeded two billion.

The faces of entire cities have been permanently altered by the Games, and their impact on regional and national economies is considerable. Total expenditures in Montreal [1976] reached $1.5 billion and the ensuing debt, $990 million. The volume of symbolic exchange—interpersonal, national, and cross-cultural—defies quantitative description, but is even more prodigious and remarkable. Throughout their modern history, the Olympics have variously rejuvenated or destabilized political regimes. The first Games in Athens in 1896, helped topple two consecutive Greek governments.[1] More recently, an American president convinced much of his nation that, short of sending a bomb or an army, the most serious political step that could be taken against the Soviet Union was not sending an athletic team to "their" Games.

Not a few individuals have had their lives taken or saved, their pockets lined or emptied, their happiness ensured or stolen from them by the Olympics. For many, many more, the routines of daily life grind to a halt for two weeks every four years. Weddings are postponed, crops go untended, work is interrupted, and the Olympics crowd most other topics out of conversation. In short, the Games are an institution without parallel in nature and scope in the twentieth century. Insofar as there exists, in the Hegelian-Marxian phrase, a "world-historical process," the Olympics have emerged as its privileged expression and celebration.

THE GENRES OF OLYMPISM

As a self-consciously de novo enterprise born with few precedents into a world assumed by the Rénovateur Pierre de Coubertin (1863–1937) to be skeptical, if not hostile, Olympism's charter texts and official ideological statements are full of explicit consideration of various forms of symbolic action. Judgments on the qualities of performative genres are a central part of Olympic ideology itself. As Ernst Gombrich has argued for pictorial art, so is it also with the Olympic Games.[2] Form and purpose cannot be dissociated from one another if the Games are to be understood as dynamic sociocultural processes.[3]

Neither will it do to subsume the entire Olympic phenomenon under one traditional rubric—for example, "ritual." If it is true that genre theory is today moribund in literary studies, Raymond Williams is surely correct that this sort of "cramming" is in large measure to blame.[4] Such a tactic will also shatter the performative approach to cultural studies before it has the opportunity to consolidate. At the same time, unchecked multiplication of performance categories will sacrifice accumulated anthropological knowledge and will have a similarly crippling effect that Williams also notes in the history of literary criticism.

The genres discussed below—spectacle, festival, ritual, game—by no means exhaust the roster of performance types found in an Olympic Games. But they are semantically and functionally the most significant. The order in which they are discussed reflects a passage from the most diffuse and ideologically centrifugal genres to the most concentrated and ideologically centripetal. Spectacle and game appeared earliest, festival and ritual consolidated later, in Olympic history.[5]

Spectacle

Of all of the genres of cultural performance, the spectacle is the least well known by anthropologists. The ethnography of particular spectacles is in its infancy and comparative studies do not yet exist.

The following attempt to catalog the distinctive features of the spectacle is to my knowledge the first.

1. The English word "spectacle" derives from the Latin intensive *specere* "to look at," and ultimately from an Indo-European root *spek* "to observe." The dictionary definition echoes this etymology, defining "spectacle" first of all as "something exhibited . . . a remarkable or noteworthy sight." Spectacles give primacy to visual sensory and symbolic codes; they are things to be seen. Hence we refer to circuses as "spectacles," but not orchestral performances.

2. Not all sights, however, are spectacles, only those of a certain size and grandeur, or, as the dictionary puts it, "public displays appealing or intending to appeal to the eye by their mass, proportions, color, or other dramatic qualities." For example, only films employing a "cast of thousands," impressive scenery, and epic historical or religious themes are designated as spectacles.

3. Spectacles institutionalize the bicameral roles of actors and audience, performers and spectators. Both role sets are normative, organically linked, and necessary to the performance. If one or the other set is missing, there is no spectacle. Thus, in a strict sense, it is not the case that "most ceremonies and rituals are spectacles," as Max and Mary Gluckman have claimed.[6] Certain rituals require no audience, and though rituals involve grand interests and are often visually impressive, the congregation is rarely free simply to watch and to admire. If its attention to the altar, catafalque, or dance plaza is characterized by no more than "distanced observation," it is typically thought guilty of bad faith, sacrilege, or hypocrisy likely to threaten the efficacy of the performance. Nor does ritual usually permit the optionality generic to the spectacle. Ritual is a duty, spectacle a choice. Consequently, we speak of ritual "degenerating" ("de-genre-ating") into spectacle: Easter into the Easter Parade.

Of course, "exotic" rituals may be perceived as spectacles by outsiders who happen upon them—explorers, tourists, or anthropologists. But these outsiders commit a "genre error" analogous to what

Gilbert Ryle has called a "category error," and Clifford Geertz an error in "perspective." Since their roles as observers are not built into the structure of the performance itself, outsiders' typifications of ritual events as spectacles are at best metaphorical, or rhetorical, as with Freud adjuring his readers to call up before their eyes "the spectacle of a totem meal."[7]

Just as one culture's rituals may be erroneously taken for another's spectacles, so too unfamiliar styles of native ritual participation may seem like "simply watching" to an outside observer, as when Evans-Pritchard wrote of a Nuer exorcism:

> It was very noticeable during the ceremony how those present, as is often the case in Nuer ceremonies, chatted among themselves, asked for tobacco, and so on. They evidently, especially the children, enjoyed the *spectacle*. . . . [The possessed man] himself *showed little concern* for what was going on.[8] (emphasis added)

In his brilliant analysis of Sri Lankan exorcism, Bruce Kapferer shows how unwise it is to make such judgments without reference to the cultural determinants of audience style and the behavior of the afflicted. Other societies most certainly have their spectacles, and, as I shall show in this essay, rituals may be nested within true spectacles. But unless the genre is recognized as analytically and performatively discrete, and unless attention is paid to "emic" categories and norms, neither ethnographers nor culture theorists will find any coherent place for the spectacle within their accounts. Metaphor will overwhelm analytical precision in the theory of the spectacle in just the same way as it did Frobenius and Huizinga in their important early studies of play.[9]

This is not to say, however, that the metaphorical uses of the word "spectacle" are without interest in our own cultures. Our English trope "making a spectacle of oneself" (in French, *se donner en spectacle*) reflexively confirms the first three distinctive features of the genre by inverting them. What is private or hidden becomes publicly exhibited; what is small or confined becomes exaggerated, grand or grandiose when we make a spectacle of ourselves. And our comrades or strangers are forced into the role of spectators to our unusual behavior. In recent times, behavior so described is always untoward and embarrassing, and the trope is accusing and derogatory. But as recently as the turn of the century, "making a spectacle of oneself" could be a noble act. Here is William James's description of the death of a friend and colleague:

> Poor Frederick Myers died here a fortnight ago, in great suffering from his breathing, but a superb spectacle, awakening especially the admiration of his doctors, of the indifference to such temporal trifles which the firm conviction of continued life will give a man.[10]

The reasons for this shift in the history of speaking are as fascinating as they are unknown. Certainly, they must be discovered before a complete theory of the spectacle can be offered. . . .

4. Spectacle is a dynamic form, demanding movement, action, change, and exchange on the part of the human actors who are center stage, and the spectators must be excited in turn. Certain plastic artworks, like Christo's "Running Fence" or Smithson's "Spiral Jetty," are visually spectacular, but are not spectacles. And though "spectacle" is often confused in common speech with aesthetic categories like Kant's "sublime," the use of the former to describe natural phenomena is metaphorical, as the sixteenth-century Swiss humanist Konrad Gessner recognized when he wrote of the Alps: "It is such a pleasure for the mind to admire the immense masses of the mountains, *like* a spectacle, and to lift up the head almost into the clouds."[11]

The Olympic Games do not merely fulfill these criteria, they are spectacle par excellence, a type case against which all others may be compared. The Games are irreducibly visual. Quite literally, they must be seen, and seen in person, to be believed. Though it has played a capital role in the spectacular quality and growth of the Games, television, even of the highest technical standard, reduces the spectacle to constricted little rectangles of color and form, systematically impoverishing the spectacle's gifts to the human eye. The crowds streaming toward vast stadiums of concrete and glass, enclosing vibrant patches of brilliant green or burnished hardwood upon which athletes and officials in richly hued uniforms parade, process, and compete; the city transformed by banners and emblems, sidewalk art shows, impromptu dancers, singers, clowns, and street musicians; the hawkers of souvenirs and drinks, the scalpers of tickets, spilling over into the streets, calling their bids in a dozen languages; the hundreds of ushers, police, and civic authorities attempting to keep order among the thousands of tourists and fans milling about or congregating in bunches to exchange gossip, rumors, names, stories, and, lately, badges and emblems: the sheer scale and intensity of it all mock the puny efforts of the television camera to capture it in two-dimensional images. The Olympic Games have inspired a wealth of written and spoken commentary, and symphonic, balletic, and plastic artworks. Often these are rich and provocative, but they are commentaries on the spectacle, interpretive glosses that cannot capture the visual ecstasies and terrors of the original. Only film effectively translates the spectacle into another medium, and only two films of the scores that have been made—Leni Riefenstahl's *Olympia* of 1936 and Kon Ichikawa's film of the 1964 Tokyo Games—have really succeeded in capturing the epic visual quality in the Games.[12]

As for the spectators, their role is secure, and often predominant in organizational matters. Every effort is made to accommodate them in the choice of host cities, the design of stadiums, and the arrangement of the program. In the eleventh-hour controversy over whether to cancel the Montreal Games because of Canada's unprecedented refusal to admit the Taiwanese team into the country, even though it was recognized by the International Olympic Committee, the public statements of I.O.C. members expressed as much concern for the disappointment of the spectators as for that of the athletes. Fanciful proposals that the Games be conducted without spectators, proposals put forward occasionally in response to abuses, are taken by the I.O.C. to show fundamental ignorance of the aims of the Olympic movement, for, as Coubertin wrote in 1910, "the crowd has a part to play, a part of consecration."[13] Moreover, the movement is now utterly dependent upon television revenues, that is, upon the spectators, for fiscal viability.

Finally, it seems unnecessary to dwell on the dramatic character of the focal performances that bring spectators and participants alike to the Games. The athletic contests do not merely involve dramatic movement, they are pure movement dramatized.

Spectacle and Festival

Additional features of the spectacle can be highlighted by contrasting it with the related genre of festival. Again, etymology is enlightening. The English word "festival" derives from the Latin *festivus* "gay, merry, lighthearted" and from the noun *festum* "festival" or "festival time." The latter is used specifically for the great Roman feasts, such as the *Lupercalia, Lemuria, Saturnalia,* and *Vestalia.* Congruently, the dictionary defines "festival" as both a certain "joyous mood" and as "a time of celebration marked by special observances . . . a program of public festivity."

Spectacle, by contrast, denotes no specific style or mood aside from diffuse wonder or awe. Rather, a broad range of emotions may be intensified or generated in the spectacle. We speak of "fearful spectacles" as well as "joyous spectacles." Moreover, festivals are less bound externally to calendars and internally to fixed programs of "special observances." Spectacles tend to be irregular, occasional, open-ended, even spontaneous, and the ever aggrandizing ethos of the spectacle, with its generic maxim "more is better," tends to destroy the symmetries of balance, harmony, and duration that distinguish traditional festivals. Hence the genres of spectacle and festival are often differently valenced. While we happily anticipate festivals, we are suspicious of spectacles, associating them with potential tastelessness and moral cacophony. We tend, for example, to associate the Roman circus games rather than the medieval tournament with the term "spectacle." In festival, the roles of actors and spectators are less distinguishable than in spectacle, where the increased emphasis on sight, often at the expense of other modes of participation, seems to increase the threat of oversight. The following review, which appeared in a Chicago newspaper, makes the point with regard to cinematic spectacles, in this case *Alexander the Great* (1966). "Richard Burton (in blond hair) makes a good Alexander, but this attempt to film an intelligent spectacle mainly proves that an intelligent spectacle is a contradictory proposition."

Again we find that when individual experience is characterized through reference to the performative genre of spectacle, intellectual and moral ambiguity reappears. Christopher Isherwood's retrospective account of his Berlin days includes this passage:

Only a very young and very frivolous foreigner, I thought, could have lived in such a place and found it amusing. Hadn't there been something youthfully heartless in my enjoyment of the spectacle of Berlin in the early thirties with its poverty, its political hatred, and its despair?[14]

In Hermann Hesse's parable of 1919, "Zarathustra's Return: A Message to German Youth," the moral content of the trope is inverted. Yet this inversion too depends for its ethical surprise on the preexistent moral ambiguity and skepticism that surround the term "spectacle" for the reader. Zarathustra comes upon a demagogue haranguing the crowd from atop a vehicle. When the speech is finished, the young men rush up to Zarathustra to plead for leadership and salvation in their day of greatest affliction. Zarathustra remarks how pleased he is to see them "play-acting," for men are "never so honest as then."

The young men heard him and exchanged glances; they thought there was too much mockery, too much levity, too much unconcern in Zarathustra's words. How could he speak of play-acting when his people were in misery? How could he smile and be so cheerful when his country had been defeated and was facing ruin? How could all this, the people and the public speaker, the gravity of the hour, their own solemnity and veneration—how could all this be a mere spectacle to him, merely something to observe and smile at? Should he not, at such a time, shed bitter tears, lament and rent his garments?[15]

Again, it must be noted that such reflexive, intentionally negative, or unself-consciously skeptical literary uses of the term "spectacle" as we have seen in the quotations from Hesse, Isherwood, and Evans-Pritchard, respectively, were not at all typical of the middle and late nineteenth century. To the example of William James that of Ernest Renan may be added. Renan, we are told by a biographer, wished that his death and funeral would be "one of the finest moral spectacles of our age."[16] Are we to understand the literary image as a metaphorical reference to real cultural performances? Does the striking alteration over time of the meaning and moral

valence of the trope depend upon and give evidence for parallel changes in public spectacles themselves? What contemporary performances do these writers have in the backs of their minds as models? Or is the matter historically more complicated than this? Are the developments of the trope and of the performative genre both responses to a larger and more complicated skein of social and cultural changes in the modern world? Geertz has argued from the case of the Balinese cockfight that cultural performances may be understood as "stories a people tell about themselves."[17] Perhaps the growth of the spectacle genre in the modern world is to be understood as a public form of thinking out, of telling stories about certain growing ambiguities and ambivalences in our shared existence. In their performances, our poets reflect our spectacles back to us in single figures of speech.

For the moment, one thing is clear. Just as the word "festival" could not be substituted for "spectacle" in any of the texts cited, so too the performative genres of festival and spectacle are in frank opposition to one another. While the Olympic Games are our grandest spectacle, they are simultaneously a festival, and much of the character and history of modern Olympism is contained in the dialectic between these two genres of cultural performance. The same forces that have precipitated their spectacular quality are responsible for much of the global popularity of the Games. Yet the hierarchy of the Olympic movement has persistently declared itself against spectacle and for festival.

Coubertin called the Games "a festival of human unity" and, by 1935, he had grown worried that they might become "only theatrical displays, pointless spectacles."[18] Successive generations of Olympic officials have followed the founder's lead by banishing the word "spectacle" from the official lexicon in favor of "festival," which is endorsed and self-consciously pursued. For example, Monique Berlioux, former French swimming champion, press attachée to Georges Pompidou, and executive director of the I.O.C., created a storm in Montreal when she complained to the press that the Games there lacked "a sufficiently joyous and festive atmosphere." She cited the forbidding size of the facilities, the omnipresent security forces, and the paucity of colorful Olympic banners around the city. Candidate cities are conscious of the I.O.C.'s concerns and often include in their proposals promises to minimize the spectacular character of the Games. Munich, for example, pledged itself to an "intimate Olympics."

The official endorsement of the festival genre includes both mood and program. In 1918, Coubertin wrote, "If anyone were to ask me the formula for 'Olympizing' oneself, I should say to him, 'the first condition is to be joyful.' "[19] Yet as they have gained prestige and scope, the Games have become increasingly troubled by political, economic, and organizational struggles. The Moscow imbroglio, the huge Montreal debt, the Munich massacre, the South African and Rhodesian questions, the repression of the Mexican students, the ritual protests of black Americans, the cold war battles of Russia and the United States, and Hitler's attempt to co-opt the Games: these are the most recent, dramatic, and familiar examples. The joyfulness of the Games has become increasingly problematic. And on the microsocial level, for those spectators who take little interest in politics and for whom ever grander arrangements are made, the cautions of the ancient Stoic Epictetus are still salient today.

> But some unpleasant and hard things happen in life. And do they not happen at Olympia? Do you not swelter? Are you not cramped and crowded? Do you not bathe badly? Are you not drenched whenever it rains? Do you not have your fill of tumult and shouting and other annoyances? But I fancy that you bear and endure it all by balancing it off against the memorable quality of the spectacle.[20]

For most participants and spectators, at least enjoyment and probably joy have been the dominant moods during the Games. Personal discomforts and surrounding controversies retreat from the mind *in medias res*. "Let the Fun Begin" read a banner headline in a Montreal newspaper on opening day in 1976, expressing the anxious wishes of millions. But these days a strong foreboding remains about the fate of the Games in general and about the likelihood of joyfulness persisting from one day to the next within each Olympics. The immediate causes vary from one Games to the next, but the overall

shift is steady and unremitting. The emotional unpredictability of the spectacle has challenged, and perhaps now supersedes, the more reliable affective structure of the festival.

On the formal, programmatic level, the I.O.C. attempts to fix and to maintain the external and internal boundaries of space, time, and intention that distinguish the festival from the more centrifugal, diffusive, and permeable spectacle. The Games are bound to a calendar, occurring once, and only once, every four years. Indeed, the Olympic movement has its own calendar.[21] The I.O.C. has waged a persistent legal and rhetorical battle to protect its master symbols and emblems (the name "Olympic Games," the five-ringed flag, the motto *Citius, Altius, Fortius*, the Olympic medals, the sacred flame) from unauthorized use.[22] Self-consciously conservative with its symbolic resources, the hierarchy accedes to very few of the hundreds of requests it has received for patronage and support.[23] The I.O.C. has repeatedly rebuffed proposals that it decentralize and expand. Since 1915, when Coubertin chose Switzerland as the appropriately symbolic home for himself and for Olympism, the movement has been centered in Lausanne, where a paid staff of less than twenty labors in a municipally donated chateau. Though National Olympic Committees have bureaus in each member nation, the I.O.C. refuses to open any branch offices and has resisted other sorts of bureaucratic elaboration.

Olympic officials have sought not only to regulate the boundaries between the "outside world" and the festival but also to preserve balance and harmony within it. Long before the Games had attained their mass popularity and had begun their genre shift into spectacle, Coubertin worried incessantly about their "eurythmy." In 1906, he wrote:

> The crowd of today is inexperienced in linking together artistic pleasures of different orders. It is used to taking such pleasures piecemeal, one at a time, from special fields. The ugliness and vulgarity of settings do not offend it. Beautiful music thrills it, but the fact that it sounds amid noble architecture leaves it indifferent. And nothing in it seems to rise in revolt against these wretchedly banal decorations, these ridiculous processions, these detestable cacophonies and all this frippery which compose what nowadays is called a fes-

tival—a festival where one guest is always missing, taste.[24]

Coubertin saw the fragmentation of public celebrations not merely as a local problem for the Olympic Games to solve but as something diagnostic of modernity itself. In 1910, he asserted that:

> The men of old possessed the feeling for collective movement which we have lost. . . . They had acquired and developed their superiority through custom. . . . It must be admitted that the singularly human character of the then prevalent cults facilitated this acquisition and development. Nowadays scarcely any public cult is possible and its manifestations could in any case scarcely take a similar form. As for lay festivals, nobody has anywhere succeeded as yet in giving them an appearance of true nobility and eurythmy.[25]

The concern for order, nobility, and taste underlies most of the regulations issued by Coubertin and his successors. Among them are the statutory limitation of the festival to seventeen days or less, a maximum of three national entries (or one team) for each event, strict criteria for adding new sports to the program and concerted efforts to reduce the present number of competitions, representation by nation-states only, severe contractual restrictions on the powers of the host city and the organizing committee, minute supervision of rites and ceremonies, and a close watch on ancillary cultural programs. The more-is-better ethos of the spectacle, "gigantism" in Olympic vocabulary, is the sworn enemy in all this, even as the festival reaches out to encompass the whole world.

While spectacle and festival are in opposition to each other, at the same time they share a key feature. Both are, in fact, "megagenres" or "metagenres" of cultural performance. Neither specifies directly what sort of action the participants will engage in or see. Instead, each erects an additional frame around other, more discrete performative genres. There are religious festivals, drama festivals, commercial festivals, opera and film festivals, arts and crafts festivals, even culinary festivals, as well as combinations of these. So too with spectacles. These metagenres are distinguished by their capacity to link organically—or as Coubertin would have it, to reunite histori-

cally—differentiated forms of symbolic action into new wholes by means of a common spatiotemporal location, expressive theme, affective style, ideological intention, or social function. In each of these ways, Olympism attempts to marry the genres of ritual and game.

Ritual

From the earliest years of the movement, Coubertin emphasized the importance of Olympic ritual. In 1910, he wrote:

> It will be realized that the question of the "ceremonies" is one of the most important to settle. It is primarily through the ceremonies that the Olympiad must distinguish itself from a mere series of world championships. The Olympiad calls for a solemnity and a ceremonial which would be quite out of keeping were it not for the prestige which accrues to it from its titles of nobility.[26]

Ritual is usually distinguished from other forms of ceremonial behavior in two ways. Ritual invokes and involves religious or sacred forces or, in Paul Tillich's phrase, the locus of a people's "ultimate concern." And ritual action effects social transitions or spiritual transformations; it does not merely mark or accompany them. These two features are intimately related in the ritual process. As the works of Victor Turner have amply shown, the efficacy of ritual within the ongoing process of group life is dependent upon the ritual's capacity to place actors into direct, relatively unmediated contact with the very ground of structure itself. Or, as Terence Turner puts it, "the basic principle of the effectiveness of ritual action. . . . is its quality as a model or embodiment of the hierarchical relationship between a conflicted or ambiguous set of relations and some higher-level principle that serves, at least for ritual purposes, as its generative mechanism or transcendental ground."[27]

The "transcendental ground" of Olympic ritual is the idea of humankind-ness. In Olympic rituals, the symbols of generic individual and national identities are assembled and arrayed in such a way as to model, or to attempt to model, the shared humanity that is both the ground of the structural divisions the symbols condense and portray as well as the ultimate goal of Olympic ideology and practice. The experiential truth of the model, and, therefore, the efficacy of the rituals, is dependent upon experiences of what Victor Turner calls *communitas* within the ritual performances. In Olympic ritual, at least in official and many unofficial interpretations of it, the "higher-order principle" discussed by Terence Turner and the sought-for experience stressed by Victor Turner are one and the same thing.

Coubertin insisted repeatedly on the religious character of the Games. He wrote in 1929 that "the central idea" of the Olympic revival was that "modern athletics is a religion, a cult, an impassioned soaring."[28] But only Olympic athletics, by virtue of their "titles of nobility," could be fully connected with the worship of humanity. Coubertin belonged to the tradition of French social thought that D. G. Charlton has called the search for a "secular religion." Coubertin challenged the dualism of the conservative Catholicism in which he was raised and objected to the supernaturalism of the Church and its antagonistic attitudes toward the liberal political and social currents of the day. At the same time, he retained from Catholic practice the stress on ritual evocation of religious sentiments as against the elaboration of intellectual dogma. In 1897, he wrote:

> In reality, there is no such thing as a really rational religion. A really rational religion would exclude all idea of worship, and would consist only in a set of rules for upright living. . . . Reason, which the Frenchman so readily obeys, has finally established the necessity of the religious sentiment. Science has shown that it is powerless to take its place. If one glances about him, he perceives how profound is the religious sentiment of our epoch.[29]

It took Emile Durkheim rather longer to arrive at this conclusion. The Olympic Games can be seen as an answer in action to Durkheim's call for "new feasts and ceremonies" to guide mankind.[30]

Coubertin's class background, his personality, and his early identity struggles committed him throughout his life to the individual as the unit of human moral being, and he bequeathed this stance to Olympism. At the same time, as a French patriot and a political historian, he took the nation-state to be the most salient unit of modern social organization and solidarity. Olympic rituals incorporate the three structural identities of individual, nation, and humankind and, officially at least, recognize no other social units.[31]

Coubertin's vision of a world community was based upon a philosophical anthropology. Anticipating distinctions later made by Marcel Mauss,[32] Coubertin discriminated between "cosmopolitanism" and "true internationalism" in 1898.[33] The former view derides and devalues the significance of nationality and discrete cultural traditions and calls for a world citizenry in which all such differences are overcome and finally abandoned. The latter, "true internationalism," understands cultural differences as an enduring and marvelous feature of the human landscape and argues that world peace depends upon the celebration of human diversity and not the eradication of it. This was Coubertin's position. "Humankind" exists, he thought, not in spite of, but because of social and cultural diversity, and the task of revived Olympism was, in Ruth Benedict's phrase, to make the world "safe for differences." Generalizing from his own life, Coubertin insisted that internationalism is not incompatible with patriotism, at least with patriotism "rightly understood."

> Properly speaking, cosmopolitanism suits those people who have no country, while internationalism should be the state of mind of those who love their country above all, who seek to draw to it the friendship of foreigners by professing for the countries of those foreigners an intelligent and enlightened sympathy.[34]

In emotionally evocative ways, Olympic symbols condense and Olympic rituals model these broad and broadly modern social processes and psychological configurations.

In earlier studies I have subjected Olympic rituals to extensive processual symbolic analysis. Here I can only point out that Olympic rituals are organized around the classic schema of rites of passage first recognized by Arnold van Gennep. The opening ceremonies, including the lighting of the sacred flame at Archaia Olympia and its relay to the "New Olympia," are rites of separation from "ordinary life," initiating the period of public liminality. The opening ceremonies stress the juxtaposition of national symbols and the symbols of the transnational, Olympic, "human" community. The athletes and officials process into the stadium in national groups marked by the flags, anthems, emblems, and costumes of their motherlands. The procession and arrangement on the field expresses cooperative unity, though a unity of ordered segmentation. In the second stage of the rite, a liminal period reduplicating the overall liminality created by the opening ceremony as a whole, the Olympic flag is carried into the stadium and lifted above all the national flags, the Olympic anthem is played, and the sacred flame arrives to consecrate the festival. The president of the I.O.C. invites the chief of state of the host nation to pronounce the formula opening the Games. In each of these ways, the symbols of the Olympic community are positioned hierarchically over and above the symbols of the nation-states, but without contravening them. The third stage or phase of the opening ceremony has lately consisted of a highly choreographed and visually alluring pageant of dance and music that shifts the mood from the excited expectation and high solemnity of the first two phases to the joy that is prescribed as the dominant mood of the festival.

For the spectators, the games themselves and the victory ceremonies are rites of intensification, whereas, according to much official exegesis, they are rites of selection and initiation for the athletes. Here a third level of identity comes to the fore, that of the individual, represented by the individual athlete. In the victory ceremony, the individual's unique achievement, iconically symbolized by the athlete's body, is first honored with the symbolic rewards of the Olympic community—the medals and the olive fronds cut from the grove of Zeus in the sacred precinct of Archaia Olympia, handed over to or draped upon the victorious athletes by a presiding member of the I.O.C. Then the nations of the victors are honored by the raising of their flags and the playing of the champion's national anthem. Simultaneously, according to official exegesis, the nations, through their master symbols, are offered the opportunity of honoring the victors, presented now in their double identities as native sons and daughters and as initiated representatives of a wider human community, which, through them, these nations are

summoned to recognize. The sight of heretofore stoic and "Olympian" athletes weeping under the immense symbolic weight of the victory rite is surely one of the most powerful and evocative images generated by the modern world.

The closing ceremonies are rites of closure and reaggregation with the normative order. Here the role of the national symbols is altogether reduced. Only the anthems of Greece and of the present and of the subsequent host nations are heard. The flags and name placards of each country are separated from the athletes and carried into the stadium in alphabetical order by anonymous young women recruited from the citizenry of the host country. Since 1956, the athletes "march" in a band, not segmented by nationality, dress, event, or degree of Olympic success.[35] This is offered as a ritual expression of the bonds of friendship and respect transcending barriers of language, ethnicity, class, and ideology that the athletes are said to have achieved during the festival. At the same time, it is a symbolic expression of the humankindness necessary and available for all men and women, a final display and emotional "proof" that patriotism and individual achievement are not incompatible with true internationalism but are rather indispensable to it. After the Olympic flame is extinguished and the Olympic flag lowered and solemnly carried from the stadium, moments during which I observed widespread weeping in the stands at Montreal, the assembled thousands and the space that they occupied are released into an extraordinary expression of spontaneous *communitas*.[36]

Of course, there are other kinds of "typical" Olympic ritual experiences than those I have described, just as there are many unofficial exegeses of Olympic ritual symbols. Olympic rituals have been the staging place for international quarrels, chauvinistic episodes, intranational conflicts, and egotistical displays. Indeed, the Games have produced a debate over the social efficacy of public ritual that is in certain ways unique in the modern world, a debate that inevitably recalls for the anthropologist the famous controversy between Malinowski and Radcliffe-Brown over the anxiety-reducing and anxiety-producing character of traditional rites.

The fantastic release of human joy in the Olympic Games is intimately related to the festival frame that surrounds these solemn rites. But there is as well a terrifying fear, an omnipresent sense of tragic consciousness that haunts an Olympic Games. It has to do with the fate of ritual and festival experiences when they become embedded within a spectacle.

Games

Anthropologists have recently begun to appreciate the immense importance of games and sports in modern life.[37] In this they have lagged behind psychologists and behavioral scientists. Anthropology's traditional emphasis on "primitive" societies, where adult games tend to be irreducibly bound up with religious, mythic, or sociostructural processes, has impeded awareness of the discrete role games play in societies such as our own. *Mutatis mutandis*, games and sports have been taken for granted as features of the modern landscape when, in fact, organized sport as we now observe it is a remarkably recent innovation, barely a century old. When Coubertin called for the resurrection of the Olympic Games in 1892, he had simultaneously to win over a mass public to the concept of international sport itself.[38]

Even more than disciplinary priorities and historical myopia, the nature of the phenomenon itself has frustrated anthropological understanding. Games, and play-forms in general, are perhaps the most paradoxical of all cultural processes within societies with such value structures as our own.[39] In what follows, I present a condensed summary of the apparent paradoxes with which any study of Western play-forms must necessarily begin, aware of many phenomenological and conceptual complexities I ignore.

1. As *formal structures*, games always involve fixed and public rules, predetermined roles, defined goals, and built-in criteria for evaluating the quality of the performance. The rules are for the most part nonnegotiable and internally coercive. As long as they are respected, the game is a social system without deviance. And yet nowhere have adult games and sports made greater inroads than in cultures typified by individual autonomy, optional and diversified role choice, contempt for coercive norms or for the voluntary acceptance of such norms, cultural pluralism, and class and status stratification.

Moreover, game rules circumscribe an artificial and distinctively narrow subset of potential human actions. Nevertheless, games come to be "as large as life" ("Is chess like life? Chess is life!"—Bobby Fischer) typically in those societies that provide their members with unprecedented amounts and kinds of information about how varied human existence can be.

2. Certain *affective/experiential* qualities of games seem to conflict with the hidebound character of the rules, particularly in cultural milieus where "fun" is associated with deviance. Moreover, the affective spectrum of play is itself curiously polarized. Games are fun, "entertaining," "enjoyable," "lighthearted." And yet games regularly carry off the players into states of utter earnestness and commitment, at times becoming a rapture or a sickness unto death.

3. On the *motivational/functional* levels, games are the veritable type of free, voluntary activity. As Sartre has written: "As soon as a man apprehends himself as free and wishes to use his freedom, . . . then his activity is play."[40] Games are autotelic, intrinsically interesting, self-rewarding, self-actualizing. One plays for the experience of play. Games are, in and of themselves, "good for nothing" with respect to extrinsic rewards of self-esteem, money, status, and power. Yet games can and do have important psychological, economic, social, and political consequences of which the players and the larger audience are quite aware. Indeed, "playing games" has become a root metaphor and analogue for the generative process in science, art, warfare, commerce, and politics precisely in cultures that are at the same time derisive of "mere games" as standing apart from or in opposition to "the serious life."

4. As *semantic/symbolic/communicative* systems, games at one level seem absolutely simple. If one knows the rules, one can readily play across linguistic or even species lines. The meaning of games, however, is deeply paradoxical.

Gregory Bateson has drawn an elegant analogy between the semantic structure of games and Epimenides' classic logical paradox. The metacommunicative message "this is play," which composes the play frame, has the following logical structure:[41]

> All statements within this frame are untrue
>
> I love you
>
> I hate you

And on the communicative level of the actual contents of the frame, ludic symbols not only share multivocality and polysemy with other dominant cultural symbols but also tend to embody to an extreme degree what Victor Turner calls "polarization of meaning." Athletic body symbols, in particular, are at once highly iconic and have a rich variety of metonymic referents at the "sensory-orectic pole" and at the same time may take on an extraordinary perfusion of metaphorical referents at the "cognitive-ideological pole."[42] Athletic games, often on the evidence of the Olympics, have repeatedly been described as a universal language. The word "universal" clearly will not do.[43] But if one limits the claim to modern and "modernizing" societies, there is some irrefragable truth to it on what semiologists would call the level of the code. But on the level of the "dialect" it is something else again.[44] And on the level of the "message," there is often Babel in the absence of consecutive translation.[45]

There are as many routes through these dilemmas as there are theories, ideologies, and cultural contexts of play. Certainly, no full account of the Games can be made without considering the range of interpretations made of them. Here I can only sketch Coubertin's, which he bequeathed to generations of orthodox followers in the I.O.C.[46] Coubertin was profoundly discomfited by what he saw as the rigidification and spiritual desiccation of his contemporaries. His visions at Archaia Olympia and in the Chapel of Rugby School led him to the ancient Greek and British schoolboy athletes as contrasting models of human wholeness, of the integration of mind and body, effort and discipline, ambition and loyalty, self-sacrifice and joy. He asked:

> Is an individual a man in the full sense of the word if he is forever worried about husbanding his strength and limiting his initiatives, and takes no pleasure in expending himself beyond what is expected of him? But at the same time is an individual a man in the full sense of the word if he does not take pleasure in investing

the intensity of his effort with smiling calm and self-mastery, and in living within a framework of order, equilibrium, and harmony?[47]

Students of French thought and character will recognize in these lines the enduring tension between the values of *prouesse* and *ordre et mesure* in French social history.[48] *Prowess* is a value particularly associated with the French aristocracy. The marginality of the aristocracy in Third Republic France caused men like Coubertin to seek new realms in which to enact the traditional values in which they had been raised. Coubertin found a solution to his own marginal social identity in athletic games. So, too, he saw in them both an expression of the vibrant forces of the modern order and a therapeutic inversion of its deficiencies, an instrument of renewed hope and reform on a societal scale.

By contrast with the stultifying routines of modern life, game rules are freely and joyfully accepted. Because of, rather than in spite of, the rules, a "healthy drunkenness of the blood," an "impassioned soaring which is capable of going from play to heroism" is made possible. The game invites, indeed demands, what "ordinary life" inhibits—individual initiative beyond what is merely required—in contrast to both the sickly conformism and the antinomian excesses masquerading as "individualism" that Coubertin saw as characteristic of his contemporaries. In his study of Carnival, Roberto Da Matta has argued, following Dumont, that in hierarchical societies, to dramatize is to equalize; whereas, in ideologically egalitarian societies, to dramatize is to produce hierarchy. Athletic games do both at once, which is one reason why both hierarchical and egalitarian societies find Olympic contests dramatic and entrancing. As contests with winners and losers, games model hierarchical social arrangements. At the same time, and here Coubertin placed his stress, games model egalitarian social systems. Where the rules are known and accepted, they are equally binding on all, and a person's status or wealth has no direct bearing on the outcome of the game. In the Republic of Muscles, as Coubertin called it, the only inequalities recognized are those of achievement and not of ascription. Games are competitive, but they are also cooperative, voluntary competitions. Moreover, they produce events, not objects that can be bought and sold.

"In my opinion," Coubertin wrote in 1925, "the future of civilization rests at this moment neither on political nor on economic bases. It depends solely on the direction which will be given to education."[49] By "education" he meant both schooling in the narrow sense—the reform of pedagogy being his first concern—and, in a wider sense, the education of mankind's vision of itself. Coubertin passionately believed with his contemporary Durkheim that a society is "above all the idea it has of itself" and that the "revivification [of ideals] is the function of religious or secular feasts and ceremonies . . . moments [which] are, as it were, minor versions of the great creative moment."[50]

At the turn of the century, athletic games enjoyed a political and commercial irrelevance by comparison with what was to follow. Games struck Coubertin as peculiarly apt vehicles for delivering man from the constricting vision of *homo economicus*. The athlete devoted his extraordinary effort and discipline for no other reason than the love of the game itself, and only amateurs were to be admitted to Olympic competition. The Games would therefore provide, so Coubertin thought, dramatic evidence that men are not, and need not be, dominated by material interests in order to achieve moral status and collective approbation. So, too, I.O.C. members were to be sportsmen who donated their time and resources without material reward, and as unelected "trustees of the Olympic Idea," were to owe allegiance to no political unit but to the world community. Drawn from many nations, their corporate activity would model, as would that of the athletes, the belief that the capacity to recognize and to celebrate different ways of being human is a precondition for the notion of "human being" to have any meaning at all. Games provide, Coubertin thought, a universal dramatic form and a universal language through which otherwise distant and uncommunicative peoples might appear and speak to one another.

> To ask the peoples of the world to love one another is merely a form of childishness. To ask them to respect one another is not in the least utopian, but in order to respect one another it is first necessary to know one another. . . . Universal history is the only genuine foundation of a genuine peace. . . . To celebrate the Olympic Games is to appeal to history.[51]

Coubertin wrote volumes of "universal history" and meant the phrase in its French academic sense, but in the context of the Olympic games it takes on a new meaning, which he understood but could not quite formulate. The Olympic Games provide a kind of popular ethnography. Lured by the intrinsic appeal of games and the desire to back one's national champions, the spectators are additionally presented with a rich mosaic of cultural imagery in a festival designed to entertain and to delight, but also to educate and to inspire.

OLYMPIC GAMES: A RAMIFIED PERFORMANCE TYPE

The preceding sketch of the distinctive features of the four central performative genres of the Olympic Games ought to make clear why lumping the entire performance system under the single rubric of sports or creating some new bastard category like ludic secular ritual will not do. These genres are distinctive forms of symbolic action, distinguished from one another by athletes, spectators, and officials alike. While certain features are shared between genres, others are in tension or in opposition, both categorically and in context. On the level official ideology alone, we have seen that only three of the four genres are legitimated. The spectacle is regarded as intrusive. Moreover, we have noted in passing that official commitment to and confidence in the marriage of game, rite, and festival does not always work out so "happily" from the I.O.C.'s own perspective. This, we may be certain, has as much to do with the nature of the genres as it does with the potentially explosive themes and social arrangements performed differentially within them. At the same time, the Olympic Games form a single performance system. The genres are intimately and complexly interconnected on all levels: historically, ideologically, structurally, and performatively. Thus we are forced to recognize that the Olympic Games represent a special kind of cultural performance, a ramified performance type, and we are forced to seek for new models and methods of analysis that will allow us to understand the relationships between the various forms of symbolic action without losing sight of their distinctive properties.

NOTES

1. John J. MacAloon, *This Great Symbol: Pierre de Coubertin and the Origins of the Modern Olympic Games* (Chicago, 1981).
2. Ernst Gombrich, "Form and Purpose," Lecture given at the University of Chicago, May 1978; *The Sense of Order: A Study in the Psychology of Decorative Art* (Ithaca, 1979), pp. 145–148.
3. This is what makes the Olympic Games especially suited for the culture-as-performance approach. What distinguishes cultural performances from other kinds of cultural facts, and this approach from others, is the indivisibility of form and purpose.
4. Raymond Williams, *Marxism and Literature* (Oxford, 1977), pp. 180–182.
5. MacAloon, pp. 269–271.
6. Max and Mary Gluckman, "On Drama, Games, and Athletic Contests," in Sally F. Moore and Barbara G. Myerhoff, eds., *Secular Ritual* (Amsterdam, 1977), p. 227.
7. Sigmund Freud, *Totem and Taboo* (New York, 1950), p. 140.
8. E. E. Evans-Pritchard, *Nuer Religion* (Oxford, 1956), p. 37.
9. Leo Frobenius, *Kulturgeschichte Afrikas* (Zurich, 1932); Johan Huizinga, *Homo Ludens* (Boston, 1955).
10. Ralph Barton Perry, *The Thought and Character of William James*, vol. 1 (Boston, 1935), p. 439.
11. Quoted in E. Maeder, *The Lure of the Mountains* (New York, 1975), p. 8
12. Riefenstahl's *Olympia* is arguably the greatest documentary film ever made. The Games have played an important role in the creation of new artistic genres, such as Xalita Indian "tourist art" after Mexico City; in the revitalization of peripheral branches of artistic tradition, such as public sculpture and stadium architecture; and in the spread of electronic media, especially television. The first commercial transmission of any magnitude took place from the stadium in Berlin in 1936, and several other television firsts have been connected with the Olympics. Even now the sale of new TV sets rockets around the world every four years.
13. Pierre de Coubertin, *The Olympic Idea: Discourses and Essays* (Stuttgart, 1967), p. 32.
14. Christopher Isherwod, *The Berlin Stories* (New York, 1963), p. x.
15. Hermann Hesse, "Zarathustra's Return: A Message to German Youth," in *If the War Goes On: Reflections on War and Politics* (New York, 1971), pp. 88–89.
16. H. W. Wardman, *Ernest Renan: A Critical Biography* (New York, 1964), p. 206.
17. Clifford Geertz, *The Interpretation of Cultures* (New York, 1973), p. 448.
18. Coubertin, p. 131.
19. Coubertin, p. 57.
20. H. W. Pleket and M. I. Finley, *The Olympic Games: The First Thousand Years* (New York, 1976), p. 54. While the site of ancient Games was fixed in Elis, and while there are periodic calls within the movement for a stable venue, the modern Games remain a traveling show. Each host city is thought of as a "New Olympia," connected symbolically to the ancient tradition by the celebration of the festival. "People meet at Olympia," wrote Coubertin, "to make both a pilgrimage to the past and a gesture of faith in the future." The resemblances between religious pilgrimage and journey to the "New Olympia" are marked. As Victor and Edith Turner have noted, modern pilgrims and tourists (and Olympic "fans") are more closely related than we think.
21. Borrowed from the ancient Greeks, the Olympic calendar divides history into "Olympiads" and "Olympic Eras." An Olympiad is a four-year period opened and closed by the celebration of the Games. The succession of Olympiads from 1896 to the present compose the "Modern Olympia Era," whereas the period between 776 B.C. (traditionally the first Olympic Games) and A.D. 393 (the edict of Theodosius I banning pagan festivals, including the Olympic Games) composed the "Ancient Olympic Era." Coubertin quaintly referred to the intervening centuries as "The Dark Ages." If an Olympic Games cannot be held because of war (1916, 1940, 1944), the Olympic clock nonetheless keeps ticking. The period 1940–44, for example, is officially referred to as "an Olympiad during which no Games were held." The Olympic calendar is unlikely to surpass the Christian in salience, but it is more than a historical conceit. Several of my informants recall significant events in their lives by spontaneously placing them in reference to the Olympic Games. Moreover, the psychological and behavioral times of Olympic officials, top-class athletes, and devoted fans are very much organized into quadrennial rhythms by the Olympic calendar.
22. This effort has been surprisingly successful. Since international law is backward and offers little assistance in this matter, this success has to be attributed in no small part to the voluntary forbearance of would-be usurpers. The I.O.C. does permit the Games Organizing Committee of the host nation to sell the rights to its emblem to corporate sponsors, a controversial decision.
23. This reticence extends even to events conceived of as ancillary components of the festival, like the 1976 International Congress of Physical Activity Sciences in Quebec City. Even the International Olympic Academy, located at Archaia Olympia and dedicated to promulgating the orthodox Olympic gospel, required years to win I.O.C. patronage.
24. Coubertin, p. 17.
25. Coubertin, p. 34.
26. Coubertin, p. 34.
27. Terence Turner, "Transformation, Hierarchy, and Transcendence: A Reformulation of Van Gennep's Model of the Structure of Rites of Passage," in Sally F. Moore and Barbara G. Myerhoff, eds., *Secular Ritual* (Amsterdam, 1977).
28. Coubertin, p. 118; cf. John J. MacAloon, "Religious Themes and Structures in the Olympic Movement and the Olympic Games," in Fernand Landry and W. A. R. Orban, eds., *Philosophy, Theology and History of Sport and of Physical Activity* (Miami, 1978).
29. Pierre de Coubertin, *The Evolution of France under the Third Republic* (Boston, 1897), pp. 303–304.
30. Emile Durkheim, *The Elementary Forms of the Religious Life* (New York, 1965), p. 474ff.

31. It is not surprising that ritual protests at the Olympic Games are typically made in the name of ethnic, racial, or ideological groups, such as the protests of black Americans in 1968 and 1972. Gender distinctions are also formally represented, though they are understood by those concerned to be biological, not social categories.

32. Marcel Mauss, *Oeuvres*, vol 3 (Paris, 1969), pp. 573–639.

33. MacAloon, *This Great Symbol*, pp. 262–269.

34. Pierre de Coubertin, "Does Cosmopolitanism Lead to International Friendliness?" *American Monthly Review of Reviews* 17:429–434, 1898.

35. In Olympic folklore, this innovation is attributed to an anonymous Australian schoolboy of Chinese descent who wrote to I.O.C. president Avery Brundage, pointing out to him the symbolic appropriateness of the gesture. Until that time, Brundage is said to have feared the "disorder" such a change would introduce. The boy recognized the order in disorder that the old man could not see.

36. In Montreal, hours after the television cameras had been turned off and the officials had gone "home," indeed far into the night, thousands remained exulting together on the field and in the streets, hugging and kissing complete strangers no longer completely strange, holding impromptu races and long-jump contests in the suddenly liberated play spaces, cheered in a dozen languages by "common folk" now occupying the queen's box. Everywhere, persons exchanged flowers, seat cushions, pieces of clothing, photographs, currency, souvenir shards of pottery and splinters of wood broken from the equestrian apparatus left lying about. Athletes were seen to ask spectators for their autographs, and a harlequin in whiteface, who for two weeks had wandered through the festival wearing a sign reading The Olympic Clown, for the first time was seen to smile. Only at long last, and reluctantly, did this "holy riot of identities," this mass delight in "species-being," wind to an end as people drifted out to find their cars or a train back into the city.

37. For a useful historical review of this subject, see Helen Schwartzman, *Transformations: The Antropology of Children's Play* (New York, 1978). Much ink has been spilled on the definition of sport. I prefer the simple taxonomy of Guttmann (*From Ritual to Record: The Nature of Modern Sports*, 1978). The relationship between "play" and "game" is more complicated. Many take the position that the two categories are fundamentally disjunctive, arguing that play is spontaneous and free, while games are distinctively rule-bound. I believe this position is overstated and agree with Grathoff that play and game have a "common symbolic type." On the matter of rules, the difference is in their nature, not in their presence or absence. While game rules are explicit, conscious, corporate, and jural, play rules are often tacit, preconscious, individual, or natural. For example, the law of gravity is certainly a rule in the "free play" of kicking a ball around or gamboling in the park.

38. See Eugene Weber, "Pierre de Coubertin and the Introduction of Organized Sport in France," *Journal of Contemporary History* 5:3–26, 1970; and Jacques Ulmann, *De la gymnastique aux sports modernes* (Paris, 1971).

39. Richard H. Grathoff, *The Structure of Social Inconsistencies* (The Hague, 1970).

40. Jean-Paul Sartre, *Being and Nothingness* (New York, 1957), pp. 580–581.

41. Gregory Bateson, *Steps to an Ecology of Mind* (San Francisco, 1972), pp. 184 ff. This wonderful formulation itself invites playing around with. For example, change it to "all statements inside this frame are true; I love you; I hate you" and one has a blueprint for psychological ambivalence and an invitation to rethink and to revise Freud's theory of play as "repetition compulsion." Place the statement "all statements within this frame are untrue" *outside* the frame and one gets something else again, something also rather interesting.

42. See Victor Turner, *The Forest of Symbols* (Ithaca, 1967), pp. 59–91, and Mary Douglas, *Natural Symbols: Explorations in Cosmology* (New York, 1970), pp. 65–81, for contrasting accounts.

43. For example, the Tarahumara Indians of Chihuahua, Mexico, are widely known to be the finest long-distance runners in the world, judged according to empirical criteria of physiological performance. Repeated efforts made to enlist Tarahumara for the Olympic Games have failed. Away from their canyons, fed strange food, and enjoined to run around a flat ground of cinders, with no ball to kick and without the bracing ministrations of their sorcerers, all in service to a watch: this apparently made little sense to the Tarahumara. The world's finest distance runners could not "speak the language" of Graeco-European distance running.

44. Team handball "says" little to an American; baseball says little to a Bulgarian.

45. When Alberto Juantorena said that he won his Montreal victories "for the Cuban revolution," his American interlocutors understood what he meant. When he said that he won "because of the Cuban revolution," *that* did not compute. It is said that once a group of American sportswriters were granted an interview with Fidel Castro. Seizing their chance to "confront him," they asked, "Mr. Castro, isn't it true that in your country sport is entirely mixed up with politics?" "Mixed up with politics?" Castro responded. "No" (winks and conspiratorial elbowing all around), "sport *is* politics!" The reporters were dumbstruck; something in their cultural wires shorted out.

46. See MacAloon, *This Great Symbol*, for a full account.

47. Coubertin, *The Olympic Idea*, p. 55.

48. Jesse Pitts, "Continuity and Change in Bourgeois France," in Stanley Hoffman, ed., *In Search of France* (Cambridge, Mass., 1963).

49. Coubertin, *The Olympic Idea*, p. 99.

50. Durkheim, *Elementary Forms*, p. 470; *Sociology and Philosophy* (Glencoe, Ill., 1953), p. 92.

51. Coubertin, *The Olympic Idea*, p. 118.

Death in Due Time: Construction of Self
and Culture in Ritual Drama*

BARBARA G. MYERHOFF

Facts of publication: *Myerhoff, Barbara G. 1984. "A Death in Due Time: Construction of Self and Culture in Ritual Drama," from* Rite, Drama, Festival, Spectacle: Rehearsals Toward a Theory of Cultural Performance, *149–178. Edited by John J. MacAloon. Philadelphia: Institute for the Study of Human Issues. Copyright © 1984 by ISHI, Institute for the Study of Human Issues, Inc. Reprinted with the permission of the publishers.*

The birthday celebration of a ninety-five-year-old Jewish man in a senior citizens' center in California provides the case on which this study of ritual is based. The remarkable aspect of this seemingly ordinary ritual is that the honored guest dies at his own birthday party, transforming a secular event into a religious rite. The members of the surviving community reflect extensively on the significance of this dramatic death, discovering meaning in it for their own lives. Myerhoff's discussion of ritual and her analysis of these events illuminate a number of aspects of ritual: the distinction, yet interconnection, between secular and sacred ritual; the oscillation between planned aspects of ritual and improvised ones; the impact of ritual on time and continuity; the power of ritual to change experience and transform lives; and the capacity of ritual to demonstrate the continuity between one human being and all humanity. Myerhoff contrasts this birthday death with accounts of "tamed deaths." She shows how ritual can enable participants to return to earlier states of being or to retrieve fragments of the past

A comparative study of funeral rites is Richard Huntington and Peter Metcalf's Celebrations of Death: The Anthropology of Mortuary Ritual *(Cambridge: Cambridge University Press, 1979).*

About the author: Dates: *1936?–1985.* **Education:** *Ph.D., University of California, Los Angeles.* **Field(s):** *symbolic anthropology; film; life history.* **Career:** *Information not available.* **Publications:** *Peyote Hunt: The Sacred Journey of the Huichol Indians (Cornell University, 1974); edited, with Sally Falk Moore, Secular Ritual: Symbol and Politics in Communal Ideology (van Gorcum, 1977); edited, Life's Career (Sage, 1978); Number Our Days (Dutton, 1978); edited, with Elinor Lenz, The Feminization of America (Tarcher, 1985); with Deena Metzger and others, Remembered Lives: The Work of Ritual, Storytelling, and Growing Older (University of Michigan, 1992).* **Additional:** *The film version of Number Our Days (Direct Cinema, 1983, 29 minutes) won an Oscar from the Academy of Motion Picture Arts and Sciences in 1978 for best documentary.*

Humankind has ever chafed over its powerlessness when facing the end of life. Lacking assurance of immortality and insulted by the final triumph of nature over culture, humans develop religious concepts that explain that, if not they, someone or something has power and a plan. Thus death is not an obscene blow of blind chance. No religion fails to take up the problem, sometimes affirming human impotence thunderously. Nevertheless, people yearn for a good death, timely and appropriate, suggesting some measure of participation, if not consent. Occasionally, a subtle collusion seems to occur when human and natural plans coincide, revealing a mysterious agreement between mankind, nature, and the gods, and providing a sense of profound rightness and order that is the final objective of religion, indeed of all cultural designs. Belief and reality are merged at such times and death is more partner than foe. The questions of supremacy and power

*I am much indebted to many people who helped me in various ways, including Andrew Ehrlich, Laura Geller, Walter Levine, Riv-Ellen Prell-Foldes, Beryl Mintz, Morris Rosen, Chaim Seidler-Feller, and Dyanne Simon.

are rendered irrelevant, and an experience of unity and harmony prevails.

This essay describes such an event, tracing its origins and its consequences over a period of several months.[1] The entire sequence is treated as a single event, a drama of several acts. It is a social drama in Victor Turner's sense, but it is more strikingly a cultural drama, illustrating how a group draws upon its rituals and symbols to face a crisis and make an interpretation. It handles conflicts, not of opposing social relationships, but of opposition between uncertainty and predictability, powerlessness and choice. A final reconciliation is achieved when the community selects from and modifies its prevailing conceptualizations, using some traditional materials, improvising and developing others, until it has made a myth of a historical episode and found messages of continuity, human potency, and freedom amid threats of individual and social obliteration.

DEATH AS A CULTURAL DRAMA

Jacob Kovitz died in the middle of the public celebration of his ninety-fifth birthday, among friends and family gathered to honor him at the Aliyah Senior Citizens' Community Center, which had become the focus of life for a small, stable, socially and culturally homogeneous group of elderly Jews, immigrants to America from Eastern Europe. The case is remarkable for several reasons: it illustrates the use of ritual to present a collective interpretation of "reality," and it demonstrates the capacity of ritual to take account of unplanned developments and alter itself in midstream into a different event. Further, it illuminates how one man can make himself into a commentary upon his life, his history, and his community, mirroring his social world to itself and to himself at the same time. The case is an example of the transformation of a natural, biological event— death—into a cultural drama, shaped to human purpose until it becomes an affirmation rather than a negation of life.

Though quite rare in our times, such deaths are not unprecedented. The French social historian Philippe Ariès[2] refers to ritualized, ceremonial deaths as "tamed," and points out that in the Middle Ages, knights of the *chanson de geste* also tamed their deaths. Forewarned by spontaneous realization of imminent departure, the dying person prepared himself and his surroundings, often by organizing a ritual and presiding over it to the last. Death was a public presentation, often simple, including parents, children, friends, and neighbors. Tamed deaths were not necessarily emotional. Death was both familiar and near, evoking no great fear or awe. Solzhenitsyn, too, as Ariès notes, talks about such deaths among peasants. "They didn't puff themselves up or fight against it and brag that they weren't going to die—they took death calmly. . . . And they departed easily, as if they were just moving into a new house." Death was not romanticized or banished. It remained within the household and domestic circle, the dying person at the center of events, "determining the ritual as he saw fit."[3]

Later, as the concept of the individual emerges, distinct from the social and communal context, the moment of death came to be regarded as an opportunity in which one was most able to reach—and publicly present—a full awareness of self. Until the fifteenth century, the death ceremony was at least as important as the funeral in Western Europe.

In reading these historical accounts the anthropologist is reminded of similar practices in preliterate societies. Here is a description of a death ceremony among the Eskimos:[4]

> In some tribes an old man wants his oldest son or favorite daughter to be the one to put the string around his neck and hoist him to his death. This was always done at the height of a party where good things were being eaten, where everyone—including the one who was about to die—felt happy and gay, and which would end with the *angakok* [shaman] conjuring and dancing to chase out the evil spirits. At the end of his performance, he would give a special rope of seal and walrus skin to the "executioner," who then placed it over the beam on the roof of the house and fastened it around the neck of the old man. Then the two rubbed noses, and the young man pulled the rope. . . ."

All the elements of a tamed death are present also in the case of Jacob's birthday party: his foreknowledge of death, its occurrence in a public ceremony, which he directed, his attitude of calm acceptance, his use of the occasion to express the meaning of his life, and the presence and participation of those with whom he was intimate.

Unlike the Eskimo or the medieval knight, Jacob constructed his death alone, without support of established ritual and without expectation of cooperation from his community. This was his own invention, and his only partner was *Malakh-hamoves*, the Angel of Death, who cooperated with him to produce a triumphant celebration that defied time, change, mortality, and existential isolation. Through this ritual, Jacob asserted that his community would continue, that his way of life would be preserved, that he was a coherent, integrated person throughout his personal history, and that something of him would remain alive after his physical end.

It is not surprising that this accomplishment was achieved through ritual, which is unique in its capacity to convince us of the unbelievable and make traditional that which is unexpected and new.

THE WORK OF RITUAL

Ritual is prominent in all areas of uncertainty, anxiety, impotence, and disorder. By its repetitive character it provides a message of pattern and predictability. In requiring enactments involving symbols, it bids us to participate in its messages, even enacting meanings we cannot conceive or believe; our actions lull our critical faculties, persuading us with evidence from our own physiological experience until we are convinced. In ritual, doing is believing. Ritual dramas especially are elaborately staged and use presentational more than discursive symbols, so that our senses are aroused and flood us with phenomenological proof of the symbolic reality which the ritual is portraying. By dramatizing abstract, invisible conceptions, it makes vivid and palpable our ideas and wishes, and, as Geertz has observed, the lived-in order merges with the dreamed-of order.[5] Through its insistence on precise, authentic, and accurate forms, rituals suggest that their contents are beyond question authoritative and axiomatic. By high stylization and extraordinary uses—of objects, language, dress, gestures, and the like—ritual calls attention to itself, so that we cannot fail to see that its contents are set apart from ordinary affairs.

Ritual inevitably carries a basic message of order, continuity, and predictability. Even when dealing with change, new events are connected to preceding ones, incorporated into a stream of precedents so that they are recognized as growing out of tradition and experience. Ritual states enduring and underlying patterns, thus connecting past, present, and future, abrogating history and time. Ritual always links fellow participants but often goes beyond this to connect a group of celebrants to wider collectivities, even the ancestors and those unborn. Religious rituals go farther, connecting mankind to the forces of nature and purposes of the deities, reading the forms of macrocosm in the microcosm. And when rituals employ sacred symbols, these symbols may link the celebrants to their very selves through various stages of the life cycle, making individual history into a single phenomenological reality.

Ritual appears in dangerous circumstances and at the same time is itself a dangerous enterprise. It is a conspicuously artificial affair, by definition not of mundane life. Rituals always contain the possibility of failure. If they fail, we may glimpse their basic artifice, and from this apprehend the fiction and invention underlying all culture.

> Underlying all rituals is an ultimate danger, lurking beneath the smallest and largest of them, the more banal and the most ambitious—the possibility that we will encounter ourselves making up our conceptions of the world, society, our very selves. We may slip into that fatal perspective of recognizing culture as our construct, arbitrary, conventional, invented by mortals.[6]

Rituals then are seen as a reflection not of the underlying, unchanging nature of the world but of the products of our imagination. When we catch ourselves making up rituals, we may see all our most precious, basic understandings, the precepts we live by, as mere desperate wishes and dreams.

With ritual providing the safeguards of predictability, we dare ultimate enterprises. Because we know the outcome of a ritual beforehand, we find the courage within it to enact our symbols, which would otherwise be preposterous. In ritual, we incorporate the gods into our bodies, return to Paradise, and with high righteousness destroy our fellows.

What happens when a ritual is interrupted by an unplanned development, when it is not predictable, when accident rudely takes over and chaos menaces its orderly proceedings? What do we do if death appears out of order, in the middle of a ritual celebrating life? Such an occurrence may be read as the result of a mistake in ritual procedure, as a warning and message from the deities, or as a devastating sign of human impotence. But there is another possibility. The unexpected may be understood as a fulfillment of a different, loftier purpose, and a new, higher order may be found beneath the appearance or may take account of reality and thereby fulfill its purposes. Thus a new meaning and a new ritual emerge, made from older, extant symbols and rites.

ETHNOGRAPHIC SETTING

Before describing the birthday party, some social and historical background is necessary. At the time of this study, the relevant community consisted of about 4,000 people at the most. These individuals were spread over an area of about six miles around the Aliyah Center; the center membership included 300 people, about 200 of whom were present at the birthday party. The great majority of people belonging to the center were between 85 and 95 years old. Most had been residents in the neighborhood for 20 to 30 years.

Nearly all of them had lived as children in the little Jewish towns and settlements of Eastern Europe known as *shtetls*. Yiddish was their mother tongue and Yiddishkeit, the folk culture built around the language and customs of the *shtetl*, was a major emotional and historical force in their lives, though their participation in and identification with it varied in intensity throughout the life cycle. In great numbers, these people and others like them had fled their original homes, intent on escaping the extreme antisemitism, intractable poverty, and political oppression, which were becoming increasingly severe around the turn of the century.

As adolescents and young adults, they came to the New World and worked as small merchants, unskilled laborers, craftsmen, and artisans in the Eastern industrial cities of America. On reaching retirement age, with their children educated, married, and socially and geographically remote, they drifted into their present community, drawn to the mild climate, the ocean, and the intense Yiddishkeit of the area. Now they were isolated and old, but freed from external pressures to be "American." In this condition they turned more and more toward each

other, revived Yiddish as their preferred language, and elaborated an eclectic subculture, which combined elements from their childhood beliefs and customs with modern, urban American practices and attitudes, adapting the mixture to their present needs and circumstances.

These circumstances were harsh. Family members were distant or dead. Most of the group were poor, very old, and frail, suffering from social and communal neglect, extreme loneliness, and isolation. As a people, they were of little concern to the larger society around them. Their social, political, physical, and economic impotence was pronounced, and except on a very local level, they were nearly invisible.

Added to these afflictions was their realization that the culture of their childhood would die with them. The Holocaust wiped out the *shtetls* and nearly all their inhabitants. The center members clearly apprehended the impending complete extinction of themselves as persons and as carriers of a culture. The group was entirely homogeneous in age, and except for ceremonial occasions, no real intergenerational continuity existed. Their own membership were being depleted constantly, and there were no others to replace them. Death and impotence were as real as the weather, and as persistent.

Moreover, the social solidarity of the group was weakened by the members' ambivalence toward one another, due in part to enforced association and perhaps, too, to displaced anger. Their cultural traditions inclined them to a certain degree of distrust of nonkin, and despite the stability, homogeneity, and distinctiveness of past experiences, their circumstances, and extensive time spent together, they had less than entirely amiable feelings for each other. Factions, disagreements, and longstanding grudges marred their assemblies, most of which took place in secular and sacred rituals within the center building and on benches outside it.

But despite their ideological discord they were united by their common past. This was expressed as Yiddishkeit, in reference to the local customs, language, and beliefs that characterized these people's parental homes and early life in the *shtetl*. Very few were orthodox in religious practices. They had broken with strict religious Judaism before leaving the Old Country. A great many were agnostic, even atheistic and antireligious. But all were passionately Jewish, venerating the historical, ethnic, and cultural aspects of their heritage. Most had liberal and socialist political beliefs and had been active at one time or another in the Russian Revolution, various workers' movements, labor unions, or similar political activities. Since the Holocaust, all were Zionists, despite some ideological reservations concerning nationalism. For them Israel had become an extension of their family, and its perpetuation and welfare were identified as their own. This constellation of beliefs and experiences—the childhood history of the *shtetl*, Yiddish language and culture, secular and ethnic Judaism, and Zionism—were the sacred elements that united them.[7]

The subculture the group had developed comprised several distinct layers of historical experience: that of Eastern Europe, where they spent their childhood; of Eastern America from the turn of the century until the 1930s and 1940s, where they lived as adults; and of the California urban ghetto of elderly Jews, where they spent the latter part of their lives. Though there were many discontinuities and sharp disruptions during these 80 to 95 years, there were some notable cultural and social continuities, particularly between childhood and old age. These continuities seem to have helped them adapt to their contemporary circumstances. Not surprisingly, many of their rituals and symbols emphasized those situational continuities.

It is likely that the elders would not have elaborated this subculture had they remained embedded in a context of family and community. Their very isolation gave them much freedom for originality; they improvised and invented, unhampered by restraints of their original traditions and social disapproval of authorities. They had only themselves to please. For the first time since coming to America, now in old age they were able to indulge fully their old love of Yiddish and Yiddishkeit without fear of being ridiculed as greenhorns by their sophisticated, assimilated children. Now living again in a small, integrated community that emphasized learning, and where Yiddishkeit flourished and individual freedom and autonomy were exercised in isolation from mainstream society, they were able to revive their earlier responses to conditions they had known before. Their present poverty, impotence, physical in-

security, and social marginality repeated *shtetl* existence. Such continuity is adaptive despite its painful contents. People who have always known that life was hard and fate unreliable, if not downright treacherous, are not surprised to encounter these hazards again. They know how to cope with them and are not discouraged. They never expected life to be easy or happy. "Happiness," said Sarah, "happiness is not having a broken leg."

DRAMAS OF EXISTENCE, ARENAS FOR APPEARING

Ritual is a form by which culture presents itself to itself. In ritual, not only are particular messages delivered, but the ritual also creates a world in which culture can appear. Further, rituals create a setting in which persons can appear, by appearing in their culture, by devising a reality in which they may stand as part. In their rituals, we see persons dramatizing self and culture at once, each made by the other. There is a satisfying replication: Jacob made up himself and his interpretation of his life through his autobiographical writings. He performed the final chapter when he died. Center members make up a world, which they enact. They enact their own existence as individuals as they participate in that world. Jacob's death strengthened the center members' construction by making it more real, and by implying through his awesome performance that their constructed world was validated by divine or at least supernatural approval.

Center life, though vital and original, was conspicuously made-up. It was an assembly of odds and ends, adaptations and rationalizations built out of historical materials that were used to deny that their present life was an accommodation to desperate circumstances. It was further strained by the necessity of binding together people who had not chosen to be with each other, who were rejected by their kin, and who had lost most of those peers whom they regarded as truly like-minded. All culture is an invention, made-up in this sense, but greater depth of time and fewer contradictions often make its work easier than it was here. Only continual and protracted ceremonies could keep center members from appreciating their differences; only regular, elaborate rituals could convince them that their way of life was real—a given and not a construct.

The center provided a stage for the dramatization of their collective life, and also a place in which they could dramatize themselves as individuals. In it, they could appear, become visible, as continuing, living people. Without the center they were so cut off from human contact that it was possible to doubt their own existence. They needed each other as witnesses, particularly because in extreme old age the senses no longer give powerful messages of vitality. For many, sight, heating, taste have faded. Wakefulness has merged into dozing. Memory has overtaken the present and blended with dream. There is no one to touch them or whom they touch. They must reassure themselves of existence by receiving verification from outside their bodies. Their peers are only minimally useful in this: first, because they too are less acute and responsive; second, because they are in competition with each other for attention and often withhold or manipulate it to control one another.

The desire for attention is the dominant passion or dynamic force that gives the community its unique form. The attention of outsiders in general, and younger people in particular, is eagerly sought. The center people turn to them in an attempt to make a record of their existence and to leave behind with another a record that they have been here. Having a photograph taken, being interviewed and tape-recorded, even being listened to by someone who will return to the outside world and who will remember them after they are gone is urgent. By these activities the center people create arenas for appearing. Being overlooked is worse than being regarded as difficult, foolish, irrational, or selfish. Neglect is more unbearable. Naturally, if they can, they prefer to be seen as worthy and important, but in this they require certain uncommon attributes: a willing audience, a command of themselves, and demonstrable accomplishments.

Lacking assurance that their way of life will continue, finding no consolation that a God would remember their name, unable to draw on their own bodies for evidence of continuing vitality, they turn to each other as unwilling but essential witnesses to their dramas of existence. In their ceremonial life they created themselves, witnessed each other, proclaimed a reality of their own making.

Jacob was one of the most fortunate members of the community. He had the wherewithal to stage a drama not merely of existence but of honor. With his large, successful family, his accomplishments, and his command of himself, he was able to mount an exalted, ambitious proclamation on the meaning and value of his life.

For many years, birthdays had been celebrated by the members in their small, dilapidated center. These were collective occasions, grouping together all those born within the month—modest, simple affairs. Only Jacob Kovitz had regular birthday parties for him alone and these parties were great fetes. This reflected his unusual standing in the group. He was a kind of patriarch, a formal and informal leader of the group. He had served as its president for several years, and even after leaving the community to live in a rest home, he returned frequently and had been named president emeritus. He was the oldest person in the group and the most generally venerated. No one else had managed to provide leadership without becoming entangled in factional disputes. Jacob regarded himself, and was generally regarded by others, as an exemplar, for he had fulfilled the deepest wishes of most people and he embodied their loftiest ideals.

Jacob Kovitz enjoyed the devotion of his children, four successful, educated sons, who demonstrated their affection by frequently visiting the center and participating in many celebrations there. At these times they treated the members with respect and kindness, and they were always generous, providing meals, entertainment, buses for trips, and other unusual kindnesses. Moreover, when the sons came they brought their wives, children, and grandchildren, many of whom showed an interest in Judaism and Yiddishkeit. Family was one of the highest values among all the old people, and here was a family that all could wish for.

Jacob himself had been a worker. He had made and lost money, but never had he lost his ideals and concerns for charity and his fellows. Without a formal education he had become a poet and was considered a Yiddishist and a philosopher. He was not religious but he had religious knowledge and practiced the life of an ethical and traditional Jew. Jacob was a courageous and energetic man. After retirement he became active in organizing senior citizens' centers, and he drew the attention of the outside world for what his people regarded as the right reasons. All this he managed with an air of gentleness and dignity. Without dignity, no one was considered worthy of esteem by them. Without gentleness and generosity, he would have aroused sufficient envy to render him an ineffective leader. He was accepted by everyone in the group, a symbol and focus of its fragile solidarity.

Jacob also symbolized a good old age. He advised his followers on how to cope with their difficulties, and he demonstrated that old age was not necessarily a threat to decorum, pleasure, autonomy, and clarity of mind.

Following the program suggested by Moore and Myerhoff,[8] the ritual of Jacob's party–memorial is described in three stages: (1) its creation, (2) its performance, and (3) its outcome, sociologically and in terms of its efficacy.

CREATION OF THE CEREMONY

The explicit plan in the design of the ceremony specified a format with several ritual elements that had characterized Jacob's five preceding birthday parties. These were: (1) a *brocha*, here a traditional Hebrew blessing of the wine; (2) a welcome and introduction of important people, including the entire extended Kovitz family, present and absent; (3) a festive meal of kosher foods served on tables with tablecloths and flowers and wine, paid for mostly by the family but requiring some donation by members to avoid the impression of charity; (4) speeches by representatives from the center, sponsoring Jewish organizations under which the center operates, and local and city groups, and by each of the Kovitz sons; (5) entertainment, usually Yiddish folk songs played by a member of the family; (6) a speech by Jacob; (7) a donation of a substantial sum to the center for its programs and for Israel by the family; (8) an invitation to those present to make donations to Israel in honor of the occasion; and (9) a birthday cake, songs, and candles.

The format had a feature often found in secular ritual dramas. Within it fixed, sacred elements alternated with more open, secular aspects, as if to lend authenticity, certainty, and propriety to the open, more optional sections. In the open sections, modifications, particularizations, and innovations occur, tying the fixed sections more firmly to the situational details at hand, together providing a progression that seems both apt and traditional. In this case, for example, the *brocha*, songs, donations, and toasts are predictable; they are unvarying, ritual elements and symbolic acts. The personnel, as representatives, are also symbolic, signifying the boundaries of the relevant collectivities and the social matrix within which the event occurs, but the specific contents of their speeches are less predictable, although they inevitably repeat certain themes.

In this case the repeated themes of the speeches touched on the character, accomplishments, and personal history of Jacob; the honor he brought to his community and family; the honor the family brought to their father and their culture; the importance and worth of the attending center members; the beauty of Yiddish life; the commonality of all those individuals, organizations, and collectivities in attendance; and the perpetuity of the group and its way of life.

The style of the ceremony was another ritual element, familiar to all those who had attended previous parties, and familiar because it was drawn from a wider, general experience—that of many public festivities among strangers and mass media entertainment. It reached for a tone that was jovial, bland, mildly disrespectful, altogether familiar, and familial. It was set by a master-of-ceremonies (a son, Sam) who directed the incidents and the participants, cuing them as to the desired responses during the event, and telling them what was happening as the afternoon unfolded. Despite a seemingly innocuous and casual manner, the style was a precise one, reaching for a particular mood—enjoyment in moderation, and cooperation, unflagging within the regulated time frame. Things must always be kept moving, along in ritual; if a lapse occurs, self-consciousness may enter, and the mood may be lost. This is especially important in secular rituals, which are attended by strangers or people from different traditions, to whom the symbols used may not be comprehensible. Ritual is a collusive drama, and all present must be in on it.

In this case specific direction was unusually important. The old people are notoriously difficult to direct. They enter reluctantly into someone else's plans for them; for cultural and psychological reasons, they resist authority and reassert their autonomy. For biological reasons they find it hard to be attentive for extended periods of time and cannot long delay gratification. Programs must be short, emotionally certain and specific, skillfully interspersing food and symbols. The people can be engaged by the calling of their names, by praise, and by identifying them with the guest of honor. But their importance must not be inflated overmuch for they are quick to perceive this as deception and insult. Furthermore, the old people must not be too greatly aroused, for many have serious heart conditions. Perhaps it was the intense familiarity with their limits as an audience or perhaps it was the uncertainty that underlies all secular ceremonies that caused the designers to select as the master of ceremonies a directive leader, who frequently told the audience what was occurring, what would come next, and reminded them of what had occurred, reiterating the sequences, as if restatement in itself would augment the sense of tradition and timelessness that is sought in ritual.

The affair was called a birthday party, but in fact this was a metaphor. The son Sam said in his speech, "You know, Pa doesn't think a birthday is worth celebrating without raising money for a worthy Jewish cause." The event had a more ambitious purpose than merely celebrating a mark in an individual life. The birthday party metaphor was used because it symbolized the people's membership in a secular, modern society. But as only a birthday, it had little significance to them. None of them had ever celebrated their birthdays in this fashion. Indeed, it was the custom to remember the day of their birth by reckoning it on the closest Jewish holiday, submerging private within collective celebrations. More importantly, the event was a *simcha*, a *yontif*, a *mitzvah*—a blessing, a holiday, a good deed, an occasion for cultural celebration and an opportunity to perform good works in a form that expressed the members' identity with the widest reaches of community, Israel and needy Jews everywhere.

Its most important message was that of perpetuation of the group beyond the life of individual members. This was signified in two ways, both of which were innovations and departures from Kovitz's usual birthdays. First, temporal continuity was signified by the presence of a group of college students, brought into the center during the year by a young rabbi who sought to promote intergenerational ties. It was decided that the young people would serve the birthday meal to the elders as a gesture of re-

spect. That a rabbi was there with them was incidental and unplanned, but turned out to be important. Second was Jacob's announcement that he was donating funds for his birthday parties to be held at the center for the next five years, whether he was alive or not. Occasions were thus provided for people to assemble for what would probably be the rest of their lives, giving them some assurance that as individuals they would not outlive their culture and community.

Another of the repeated ritual elements was the personnel involved. Most of these have been identified, and reference here need be made only to two more. These were the director of the center and its president. The director, Abe, was a second-generation assimilated American of Russian-Jewish parentage. A social worker, he had been with this group a dozen years and knew the people intimately, usually functioning as their guardian, protector, interpreter, and mediator. He, along with Jacob and his sons, developed the format for the ceremony and helped conduct it. The president, Moshe, was a man of 82, with an Hasidic background.[9] He was a religious man with a considerable religious education, and a Yiddishist. It was to him that questions about Judaism and its customs were likely to be referred. After Jacob he was the most respected man in the group, and one of Jacob's closest friends.

Symbols carry implicit messages, distinguishable from the overt ingredients intended by the designers of a ritual; they are part of its creation but not clearly planned or controlled. When they are well chosen and understood, they do their work unnoticed. The following are the symbols within the planned ceremony. Others were spontaneously brought in when the ceremony was interrupted and they will be taken up later.

Many of the symbols employed have been mentioned. Every Yiddish word is a symbol, evoking a deep response. The man Jacob and his entire family were significant symbols, standing for success, fulfillment of Judaic ideals, and family devotion. The dignitaries and the publics they represented, too, were among the symbols used. The birthday metaphor with cake, candles, and gifts was a symbol complex along with "M.C.," "Guest of Honor," and the tone of the program, which incorporated American, contemporary secular life. Also present were symbols for the widest extension of Judaic culture and its adherents, in the form of references to Israel and *mitzvot* of charity and good works. The attendance of small children and young people symbolized the continuity and perpetuity of Judaism. The traditional foods symbolized and evoked the members' childhood experiences as Jews; they were the least ideological and possibly most powerfully emotional of all the symbolic elements that appeared in the ritual.

ANTECEDENT CONTEXT OF THE RITUAL

Everyone at the center knew that Jacob had been sick. For three months he had been hospitalized, in intensive care, and at his request had been removed by his son Sam to his home so that he could be "properly taken care of out of the unhealthy atmosphere of a hospital." Before Jacob had always resisted living with his children, and people interpreted this change in attitude as indicative of his determination to come to his birthday party. The old people were aware that Jacob had resolved to have the party take place whether he were able to attend or not. People were impressed, first, because Jacob had the autonomy and courage to assert his opinions over the recommendations of his doctors—evidently he was still in charge of himself and his destiny—and second, because Jacob's children were so devoted as to take him in and care for him. But most of all they were struck by his determination to celebrate his birthday among them. They were honored and awed by this and waited eagerly for the daily developments about the celebration: details concerning Jacob's health, the menu for the party, the entertainment—all were known and discussed at length beforehand.

As the day grew close, much talk concerned the significance of the specific date. It was noted that the celebration was being held on Jacob's actual birthday. The party was always held on a Sunday, and as the date and day coincided only every seven years, surely that they did so on this particular year was no accident. Again, they noticed that the month of March was intrinsically important in the Hebrew calendar, a month of three major holidays. And someone said that it was the month in which Moses was

born and died. He died on his birthday, they noted.

A week before the event, it was reported that Jacob had died. Many who were in touch with him denied it, but the rumor persisted. Two days before the party, a young woman social worker, a close friend of Jacob's, told the college group that she had dreamed Jacob died immediately after giving his speech. And she told the people that Jacob's sons were advising him against coming to the party but that he would not be dissuaded. Nothing would keep him away.

The atmosphere was charged and excited before the party had even begun. Abe, the director, was worried about the old peoples' health and the effects on them of too much excitement. There were those who insisted that on the birthday they would be told Jacob had died. Jacob's friend Manya said, "He'll come all right, but he is coming to his own funeral."

And what were Jacob's thoughts and designs at this point? It is possible to glimpse his intentions from his taped interviews with a son and a granddaughter. In these, common elements emerge: he is not afraid of death but he is tormented by confusion and disorientation when "things seem upside ways," and "not the way you think is real." Terrible thoughts and daydreams beset him, but he explains that he fights them off with his characteristic strength, remarking, "I have always been a fighter. That's how I lived, even as a youngster. I'd ask your opinion and yours, then go home and think things over and come to my own decisions." He describes his battles against senility and his determination to maintain coherence by writing, talking, and thinking. He concludes,

> I was very depressed in the hospital. Then I wrote a poem. Did you see it? A nice poem. So I'm still living and I have something to do. I got more clearheaded. I controlled myself.

Jacob had always controlled himself and shaped his life, and he was not about to give that up. Evidently he hoped he might die the same way. "I'll never change" were his last words on the tape.

It was difficult for Jacob to hold on until the party and to write his speech, which seemed to be the focus of his desire to attend. Its contents were noteworthy in two respects: first, his donation and provision for five more parties; and second, his statement that whereas on all his previous birthdays he had important messages to deliver, on this one he had nothing significant to say. Why, then, the desperate struggle to make this statement? The message, it seems, was that he could and would deliver it himself, that he was still designing his life and would do so to the end. The preparations for and the manner of the speech's delivery conveyed and paralleled its message.

THE PERFORMANCE OF THE RITUAL

The day of the party was fair and celebrants came streaming toward the center out of their rented rooms and boardinghouses down the small streets and alleys, several hours too early. That the day was special was clear from their appearance. The women came with white gloves, carrying perfectly preserved purses from other decades, and wearing jewelry, unmistakable gifts from their children—golden medallions bearing grandchildren's names, "Tree of Life" necklaces studded with real pearls; Stars of David; a gold pendant in the form of the letter *Chai*, Hebrew for life and luck. All were announcements of connections and remembrance. Glowing halos from umbrellas and bright hats colored the ladies' expectant faces. Men wore tidy suits polished with use over well-starched, frayed shirts.

The center halls, too, were festively decorated and people were formally seated. At the head table was the Kovitz family and around it the dignitaries. Jacob, it was learned, was behind the curtain of the little stage, receiving oxygen, and so the ceremony was delayed for about half an hour. At last he came out to applause and took his seat. Music called the assembly to order and people were greeted with *shalom*, Hebrew for peace. The guest of honor was presented, then introductions followed, with references to the Kovitz family as *mispoche* ("kin"), the term finally being used for the entire assembly. By implication, all present were an extended family. Each member of the Kovitz family was named, even those who were absent, including titles and degrees, generation by generation. The assembly was greeted on behalf of "Pa, his children, his children's children, and even from their children." The religious *brocha* in Hebrew was followed by the traditional

secular Jewish toast *l'chaim*. Sam set out the order of events in detail, including a specification of when Jacob's gift would be made, when dessert would be served (with speeches), when the cake would be eaten (after speeches), and so forth. The announcement of procedures was intended to achieve coordination and invite participation. The audience was appreciative and active. People applauded for the degrees and regrets from family members unable to attend, and recognized the implicit messages of continuity of tradition, respect from younger generations, and family devotion that had been conveyed in the first few moments.

The meal went smoothly and without any public events, though privately Jacob told the president, Moshe, that he wished people would hurry and eat because "*Malakh-hamoves* [the Angel of Death, God's messenger] is near and hasn't given me much time."

As dessert was about to be served, Sam, acting as master of ceremonies, took the microphone and began his speech, in which he recounted some biographical details of Jacob's life and certain cherished characteristics. He emphasized his father's idealism and social activism in the Old Country and in America, and spoke at some length about the courtship and marriage of his parents. Though his mother had died 24 years ago, she remained a strong influence in keeping the family together, he said.

During Sam's speech, Jacob was taken backstage to receive oxygen. People were restive and worried, but Sam assured them that Jacob would soon return and the program continue. Eventually Jacob took his seat, leaning over to tell one of the young people in English, and Moshe in Yiddish, that he had little time and wished they would hurry to his part of the program, for now, he said, "Ich reingle sich mutten *Malakh-hamoves*. "I am wrestling the Angel of Death."

The program was interrupted briefly when all those in charge recognized Jacob's difficulty in breathing and gave him oxygen at his seat. A pause of about ten minutes ensued. The thread of the ritual lapsed entirely while people watched Jacob being given oxygen. Moshe and Abe were worried about the impact of this sight on the old people. The previous year someone had died among them and they had been panic-stricken. But now all were rather quiet. They talked to each other softly in Yiddish. At last Sam took the microphone again and spoke extempore about his father's recent life, filling the time and maintaining the ritual mood until it became clear that Jacob was recovering. Sam told the group that maybe his wife's chicken soup—proper chicken soup prepared from scratch with the love of a Yiddishe mama—had helped sustain Jacob. This was received with enthusiastic applause. Most of those in the audience were women and their identity was much bound up with the role of the nurturant, uniquely devoted Jewish mother. In fact, the earlier mention of the importance and remembrance of the Kovitz mother had been received by many women as a personal tribute. They also appreciated the appropriateness of a daughter-in-law showing this care for a parent, something none of them had experienced. Sam went on to explain that since leaving the hospital Jacob had "embarked on a new career, despite his old age." He was teaching his son Yiddish and had agreed to stay around until Sam had mastered it completely. "Since I am a slow learner, I think he'll be with us for quite awhile." This too was full of symbolic significance. The suggestion of new projects being available to the old and of the passing on of the knowledge of Yiddish to children were important messages.

Sam went on, extending his time at the microphone as he waited for a sign that Jacob was able to give his speech. By now Sam was improvising on the original format for the ritual. He made his announcement of the gift of money, half to the center for cultural programs, half to Israel, reminding the audience that Jacob did not believe a birthday party was worth celebrating unless it involved raising funds for deserving Jewish causes.

Still Jacob was not ready, so the microphone was turned over to Abe, who improvised on some of the same themes, again and again, touching important symbolic chords. He, like Sam, referred to Jacob as a stubborn man and to Jews as a stiff-necked people, tenacious and determined. He reassured the assembly that they were important people and would be remembered, that outsiders came to their center to share their *simcha* and appreciate their unique way of life. They, he said, like Jacob, would be studied by scientists one day, for a better understanding of the indivisibility of mental and physical health, to see how people could live to be very old by using their traditions as a basis for a good and useful life.

He finished by emphasizing Jacob's most revered qualities: his devotion to his people, his learning and literacy, and his courage and dignity. He was an example to them all. "And," he went on, "you, too, you are all examples."

At last the sign was given that Jacob was ready. Abe announced the revised sequence of events: Jacob's speech in Yiddish, then in English, then the dignitaries' speeches, then the cake. Jacob remained seated but began his speech vigorously, in good, clear Yiddish.[10] After a few sentences he faltered, slowed, and finished word by word. Here are selections from his speech in translation:

> Dear friends: Every other year I have had something significant to say, some meaningful message when we came together for this *yontif.* But this year I don't have an important message. I don't have the strength. . . . It is very hard for me to accept the idea that I am played out. . . . Nature has a good way of expressing herself when bringing humanity to the end of its years, but when it touches you personally it is hard to comprehend. . . . I do have a wish for today. . . . It is that my last five years, until I am 100, my birthday will be celebrated here with you . . . whether I am here or not. It will be an opportunity for the members of my beloved center to be together for a *simcha* and at the same time raise money for our beleaguered Israel.

The message was powerful in its stated and unstated concepts, made even more so by the dramatic circumstances in which it was delivered. Jacob's passion to be heard and to complete his purpose was perhaps the strongest communication. He was demonstrating what he had said in the earlier interviews, namely, that he sustained himself as an autonomous, lucid person, using thinking, speaking, and writing as his shields against self-dissolution and senility.

Jacob finished and sat down amid great applause. His and the audience's relief were apparent. He sat quietly in his place at the table, folded his hands, and rested his chin on his chest. A moment after Sam began to read his father's speech in English, Jacob's head fell back, wordlessly, and his mouth fell open. Oxygen was administered within the surrounding circle of his sons as Abe took the microphone and asked for calm and quiet. After a few moments, his sons lifted Jacob, still seated in his chair, and carried him behind the curtain, accompanied by Moshe, Abe, and the rabbi.

Soon Abe returned and reassured the hushed assembly that a rescue unit had been called, that everything possible was being done, and that Jacob wanted people to finish their dessert.

> Be assured that he knew the peril of coming today. All we can do is pray. He's in the hands of God. His sons are with him. He most of all wanted to be here. Remember his dignity and yours and let him be an example. You must eat your dessert. You must, we must all, continue. We go on living. Now your dessert will be served.

People complied and continued eating. There were many who quietly spoke their certainty that Jacob was dead and had died in their midst. The conviction was strongest among those few who noticed that when the rabbi and Moshe left Jacob behind the curtain, they went to the bathroom before returning to their seats. Perhaps it was only hygiene, they said, but it was also known that religious Jews are enjoined to wash their hands after contact with the dead. Hence the gesture was read as portentous.

The room was alive with hushed remarks:

> He's gone. That was how he wanted it. He said what he had to say and finished.
>
> It was a beautiful life, a beautiful death.
>
> There's a saying, when the fig is plucked in due time it's good for the fig and good for the tree.
>
> Did you see how they carried him out? Like Elijah, he died in his chair. Like a bridegroom.
>
> He died like a *tzaddik*.[11]
>
> Moses also died on his birthday, in the month of Nisan.[12]

Order was restored as the dignitaries were introduced. Again the ritual themes reappeared in the speeches: Jacob's work among senior citizens, the honor of his family, his exemplary character, and so forth. A letter to Jacob from the mayor was read and a plaque honoring him proffered by a councilman. Then a plant was given to his family on behalf of an organization, and this seemed to be a signal that gifts were possible and appropriate. One of the as-

sembled elderly, an artist, took one of his pictures off the wall and presented it to the family. A woman gave the family a poem she had written honoring Jacob, and another brought up the flowers from her table. The momentum of the ritual lapsed completely in the face of these spontaneous gestures. People were repeatedly urged by Abe to take their seats. The artist, Heschel, asked what would be done about the birthday cake now that Jacob was gone, and was rebuked for being gluttonous. With great difficulty Abe regained control of the people, reminding them sternly that the ceremony had not been concluded. There remained one dignitary who had not yet spoken, Abe pointed out, and this was insulting to the group he represented.

Abe was improvising here, no longer able to utilize the guidelines of the birthday metaphor. The ceremony theatened to break apart. In actuality, Abe was worried about letting people go home without knowing Jacob's fate. It would be difficult for him to handle their anxieties in the next few days if they were left in suspense. No one wanted to leave. The circumstances clearly called for some closure, some provision of order. The last dignitary began to talk and Abe wondered what to do next. Then the phone rang and everyone was still. The speaker persisted, but no one listened. Abe came forward and announced what everyone already knew.

> God in His wisdom has taken Jacob away from us, in His mystery He has taken him. So you must understand that God permitted Jacob to live 95 years and to have one of his most beautiful moments here this afternoon. You heard his last words. We will charter a bus and go together to his funeral. He gave you his last breath. I will ask the rabbi to lead us in a prayer as we stand in solemn tribute to Jacob.

People stood. About a dozen men drew *yarmulkes* out of their pockets and covered their heads. The rabbi spoke:

> We have had the honor of watching a circle come to its fullness and close as we rejoiced together. We have shared Jacob's wisdom and warmth, and though the ways of God are mysterious, there is meaning in what happened today. I was with Jacob backstage and tried to administer external heart massage. In those few moments with him behind the curtain, I felt his strength.

There was an electricity about him but it was peaceful and I was filled with awe. When the firemen burst in, it felt wrong because they were big and forceful and Jacob was gentle and resolute. He was still directing his life, and he directed his death. He shared his wisdom, his life with us and now it is our privilege to pay him homage. Send your prayers with Jacob on his final journey. Send his sparks up and help open the gates for him with your thoughts. We will say Kaddish. "*Yitgadal veyitakadash shmeh rabba . . .* [Sanctified and magnificent be Thy Great Name]."[13]

The ritual was now unmistakably over but no one left the hall. People shuffled forward toward the stage, talking quietly in Yiddish. Many crossed the room to embrace friends, and strangers and enemies embraced as well. Among these old people physical contact is usually very restrained, yet now they eagerly sought each others' arms. Several wept softly. As is dictated by Jewish custom, no one approached the family, but only nodded to them as they left.

There were many such spontaneous expressions of traditional Jewish mourning customs, performed individually, with the collective effect of transforming the celebration into a commemoration. Batya reached down and pulled out the hem of her dress, honoring the custom of rending one's garments on news of a death. Someone had draped her scarf over the mirror in the ladies' room, as tradition requires. Heschel poured his glass of tea into a saucer. Then Abe took the birthday cake to the kitchen, and said, "We will freeze it. We will serve it at Jacob's memorial when we read from his book. He wouldn't want us to throw it away. He will be with us still. You see, people, Jacob holds us together even after his death."

Finally, the center had emptied. People clustered together on the benches outside to continue talking and reviewing the events of the afternoon. Before long, all were in agreement that Jacob had certainly died among them. The call to the rescue squad had been a formality, they agreed. Said Moshe,

You see, it is the Jewish way to die in your community. In the old days, it was an honor to wash the body of the dead. No one went away and died with strangers in a hospital. The finest people dressed the corpse and no one left him alone for a minute. So Jacob died like a good Yid. Not everybody is so lucky.

Over and over, people discussed the goodness of Jacob's death and its appropriateness. Many insisted that they had known beforehand he would die that day. "So why else do you think I had my *yarmulke* with me at a birthday party?" asked Beryl. Sam commented, "After a scholarly meeting it is customary to thank the man. Jacob was a scholar and we thanked him by accompanying him to Heaven. It's good to have many people around at such a time. It shows them on the other side that a man is respected where he came from." Bessie's words were "He left us a lot. Now the final chapter is written. No? What more is there to say. The book is closed. When a good man dies, his soul becomes a word in God's book." It was a good death, it was agreed. Jacob was a lucky man. "Zu mir gezugt," "It should happen to me" was heard from the lips of many as they left.

SOCIOLOGICAL CONSEQUENCES

Two formal rituals followed. The funeral was attended by most of the group (which, as promised, went in a chartered bus), and a *shloshim* or thirty-day memorial was held at the center, when the birthday cake was indeed served, but without candles.

At the funeral, the young rabbi reiterated his earlier statement concerning the electricity he had felt emitting from Jacob just before he died, described how Jacob used his remaining strength to make a final affirmation of all he stood for, and revealed that, at the last moment of his life, Jacob—surrounded by all the people he loved—believed in God.[14] In his eulogy, Jacob's son Sam said, "In our traditions there are three crowns—the crown of royalty, the crown of priesthood, and the crown of learning. But a fourth, the crown of a good name, exceeds them all." Spontaneously, at the graveside, without benefit of direction from funeral officials, many old men and women came forward to throw a shovel of earth on the grave, sometimes themselves tottering from the effort. Each one carefully laid down the shovel after finishing, according to the old custom. Then they backed away, forming two rows, to allow the Angel of Death to pass through. They knew from old usage what was appropriate, what movements and gestures suited the occasion, with a certainty that is rarely seen now in their lives. Moshe, one of the last to leave, pulled up some grass and tossed it over his shoulder. This is done he explained later, to show that we remember we are dust, but also that we may be reborn, for it is written: "May they blossom out of the city like the grass of the earth."

A month later, the *shloshim* was held. In it a final and official interpretation of Jacob's death was forged and shared. He was a saint by then. He must be honored, and several disputes were avoided that day by people reminding one another of Jacob's spirit of appreciation and acceptance of all of them and his wish for peace within the center. The cake was eaten with gusto as people told and retold the story of Jacob's death.

Funeral and *shloshim* were the formal and public dimension of the outcome of Jacob's death. Informal, private opinions and interpretations are also part of the outcome. These were revealed in subsequent individual discussions, informal interviews, casual group conversations, and a formalized group discussion on the subject. On these private, casual occasions people said things they had not, and probably would not, express in public, particularly about matters that they knew might be regarded as old-fashioned, un-American, or superstitious. In confidence, several people expressed wonder at and some satisfaction in what they regarded as the divine participation in the event. One lady said with a chuckle, "You know, if the Lord God, Himself, would bother about us and would come around to one of our affairs, well, it makes you feel maybe you are somebody after all." Said Bessie,

> You know, I wouldn't of believed if I didn't see with mine eyes. Myself, I don't really believe in God. I don't think Jacob did neither. If a man talks about the Angel of Death when he's dying that don't necessarily mean anything. Everybody talks about the Angel of Death. It's like a saying, you know what I mean? But you gotta admit that it was not a regular day. So about what really went on, I'm not saying it was God working there, but who can tell? You could never be sure.

Publicly the subject was discussed at great length. A debate is a cherished, traditional form of sociability among these people. And this was certainly a proper topic for a *pilpul*.[15] A kind of *pilpul* was held with a group in the center that had been participating in regular discussions. One theme considered by

them in detail was the young social worker's dream, in which she anticipated the time and manner of Jacob's death.[16] Dreams, they agreed, must be carefully evaluated, for they may be sent by God or the demons, and as such are not to be taken as prophecy on face value. After much discussion one of the learned men in the group said that perhaps the young woman should have fasted on the day after the dream. This assures that the previous night's dreams will not come true. Sam quoted Psalm 39, in which King David prayed to God to know the measure of his days. The request was denied because God decreed that no man shall know the hour of his death. Could it be that God granted Jacob what he had denied King David? Why had the girl had the dream? She knew nothing of these matters. Why had it not come to one of them, who understood the significance of dreams? After an hour or so of disagreement only two points were clear. First, that the news of the dream had received widespread circulation before the birthday party; and second, that it added to people's readiness to participate in a commemoration instead of a party. It made what happened more mysterious and more acceptable at the same time. Did it convince anyone that God had had a hand in things? Some said yes and some no. Perhaps the most general view was that expressed by Moshe, who on leaving said, "Well, I wouldn't say yes but on the other hand I wouldn't say no."

Another aspect of the ritual's outcome was the impact of the day on various outsiders. The attending dignitaries were included in the moment of *communitas* that followed Jacob's death, and were duly impressed. Before leaving, one of the Gentile politicians told the people around her, "I have always heard a lot about Jewish life and family closeness. What I have seen here today makes me understand why the Jews have survived as a people." This praise from an official, a stranger and a Christian, to a group that has always regarded Christians with distrust and often deep fear, was a source of great satisfaction, a small triumph over a historical enemy, and an unplanned but not unimportant consequence of the ritual.

The events of the day were reported widely, in local newspapers and soon in papers all over the country. Members of the audience were given opportunities to tell their version of what happened when children and friends called or wrote to ask them,

"Were you there that day . . . ?" The impact on the center members of the dispersion of the news to an outside world, ordinarily far beyond their reach, was to give them a temporary visibility and authority that increased their importance, expanded their social horizons, and accelerated their communication with the world around them. These, along with their heightened sense of significance, were the apparent sociological consequences of the ritual.

THE EFFICACY OF THE RITUAL

How shall the success of a ritual be estimated? How is one to decide if it has done its work? These are among the most complex and troublesome questions to be faced in dealing with this topic. It is not impossible to examine efficacy in terms of the explicit intentions of the performers. But it is necessary to go beyond this and inquire, too, about its unintended effects and the implicit, unconscious messages it carries. Then, one may ask, for whom did it work? For there may be many publics involved. In religious rituals even the deities and the unseen forces are addressed and, it is hoped, moved by the performance. The official plan for a ritual does not tell us about this. Many levels of response may be specified, for this is not given by the formal organization of a ritual. Sometimes audiences or witnesses are more engaged by watching a ritual than are its central subjects and participants. When we inquire about conviction, it is necessary to ask also about the degree and kind of conviction involved, since a range of belief is possible, from objection and anger if the ritual is incorrectly performed, through indifference and boredom, to approval and enjoyment, and finally total and ecstatic conviction. The long-range as well as immediate effects of the event must be taken into account, since rituals have consequences that reach past the moment when they occur; their outcome is usually to be known only in due time. It is impossible to take up all these questions. The fieldworker never has such complete information. And the symbols dealt with in ritual are by definition inexhaustible in their final range of referents. Subjects cannot verbalize the totality of their apprehensions in these areas because so much of their response is unconscious. Inevitably there are blanks in our inquiry,

and ultimately the fieldworker interested in such questions takes responsibility for inference in explanation, going beyond the observed behavior and "hard" data; to do otherwise would mean losing all hope of understanding the issues that make ritual interesting in the first place. In discussing ritual, an analysis of outcome is always an interpretation and an incomplete one.

All rituals are efficacious to some degree merely by their taking place. They are not purposive and instrumental, but expressive, communicative, and rhetorical acts. Their stated purpose must be regarded not as an illustration of a piece of life but as an analogy. No primitive society is so unempirical as to expect to cause rain by dancing a rain dance. Not even Suzanne Langer's cat is that naive. A rain dance is, in Burke's felicitous phrase, a dance with the rain, the dancing of an attitude. The attitude is the one described earlier—collectively attending, dramatizing, making palpable unseen forces, setting apart the flow of everyday life by framing a segment of it, stopping time and change by presenting a permanent truth or pattern. If the spirits hear and it rains, so much the better, but the success of the ritual does not depend on the rain. If a patient at a curing ceremony recovers, good, but he or she need not do so for the ritual to have successfully done its work. A ritual fails when it is seen through, not properly attended, or experienced as arbitrary invention. Then people may be indifferent enough not to hide their lack of conviction; their failure or refusal to appear to suspend disbelief is apparent and the ritual is not even efficacious as a communication.

In the case of Jacob's death, matters are complicated because two rituals must be considered: the intended birthday party, a designed, directed secular affair with nonreligious sacred nuances, transformed spontaneously by a collectivity into a nonplanned, fully sacred religious memorial.

The birthday party, as far as it went, was a success. It is hard to imagine how it could have failed to make its point and achieve its purposes, which were entirely social. It was convincing to all concerned and received by the audience with appreciation and cooperation. It demonstrated social connections and implied perpetuity of a collectivity beyond the limited life span of its central figure. It honored the man Jacob and his friends, values, and traditions. It reached beyond its immediate audience to include and allow for identification with a wider, invisible Jewish community. The goals of the birthday party were relatively modest and not unusual for secular ceremonies of this sort. The turning point occurred when Jacob died; the message and impact of the day's ceremonies took on a new dimension, and the sacred ritual replaced the social, more secular one.

In dying when he did, Jacob was giving his last breath to his group, and this was understood as a demonstration of his regard for them. His apparent ability to choose to do what is ordinarily beyond human control hinted at some divine collaboration. The collective and spontaneous reversion to traditional religious death rituals was hardly surprising. Death customs are always elaborate and usually constitute one of the most long-lasting and familiar areas of religious knowledge. According to some authorities, saying Kaddish makes one still a Jew no matter what else of the heritage one has relinquished.[17] The saying of Kaddish makes palpable the community of Jews. According to the rabbi at the party–memorial, the Kaddish always includes not only the particular death at hand but all a person's dead beloved and all the Jews who have ever lived and died.[18] Mourners coalesce into an *edah*, a community, connected beyond time and space to an invisible group, stretching to the outermost reaches of being a people, *Kol Israel*—the ancestors, those unborn—and most powerfully, one's own direct, personal experiences of loss and death.

For religious and nonreligious alike that day the Kaddish enlarged and generalized the significance of Jacob's death. At the same time, the Kaddish particularized his death by equating it with each person's historical, subjective private griefs, thus completing the exchange between the collective and the private poles of experience to which axiomatic symbols refer. When this exchange occurs, symbols are not mere pointers or referents to things beyond themselves. A transformation takes place: "symbols and object seem to fuse and are experienced as a perfectly undifferentiated whole."[19] Such transformations cannot be planned or achieved by will, because emotions and imagination, as D. G. James observes, operate more like fountains than machines.[20] Transformation carries participants beyond words and word-bound thought, calling into play imagination, emotion, and insight and, as Suzanne Langer says,

"altering our conceptions at a single stroke." Then participants conceive the invisible referents of their symbols and may glimpse the underlying, unchanging patterns of human and cosmic life, in a triumph of understanding and belief. Few rituals reach such heights of intensity and conviction. When this occurs, all those involved are momentarily drawn together in a basically religious, sometimes near ecstatic mood of gratitude and wonder. That Jacob's death was a genuine transformational moment was attested to by a profound sense of *communitas* and fulfillment that people appeared to have experienced with the recitation of the Kaddish.

We are interested in the unintended, implicit messages conveyed by ritual as well as the planned ones. Therefore, in this case it must be asked, What were the consequences of the set of items that suggested uncanny, inexplicable factors—Jacob's references to the presence of the Angel of Death, his seeming ability to choose the moment of his death, and the prophecy of his death in the form of a dream? The questions are particularly important because ritual is supposed to deliver a message about predictability and order, and here were intrusions beyond human control and therefore disorderly and unpredictable.

Paradoxically, these very elements of the uncanny, mysterious, and unpredictable made the ritual more persuasive and more convincing rather than less so. All these surprises were clothed in a traditional idiom, and while perplexing were not unfamiliar. There were well-used accounts for such matters; there were precedents for prophetic dreams, the presence of the Angel of Death, the deaths of the *tzaddikim*, and of Moses. Conceptions existed for handling them, and if most people involved did not deeply believe in the dogma, they were not unwilling to consider the possibility that explanations previously offered, though long unused, might have some validity after all.

Renewed belief in God at the end of life is hardly rare, and indeed it might even be that people were more reassured than frightened at the turn of events of the day. When a man dies, as Evans-Pritchard reminds us, a moral question is always posed: not merely, Why does man die? But why this man and why now? In our secular society, we are often left without an answer, and these celebrants, like most who have abandoned or drifted away from their religion, were ordinarily alone with these questions, dealing with ultimate concerns, feebly and individually. The result of Jacob's death, however, was the revival of the idea, or at least the hope and suspicion, that sometimes people die meaningfully; occasionally purpose and propriety are evident. Death in most cases may be the ultimate manifestation of disorder and accident but here it seemed apt and fulfilling. More often than not death flies in the face of human conception, reminding us of our helplessness and ignorance. It finds the wrong people at the wrong time. It mocks our sense of justice. But here it did the opposite and made such obvious sense that it came as a manifestation of order. It helped fulfill the purposes of ritual, establishing and stating form drawn forth from flux and confusion.

Remarkably enough, in this ritual the distinction between artifice and nature was also overcome. The ritual, though unplanned, was not susceptible to the danger of being recognized as human invention. Ironically, because no one was clearly entirely in control—neither Jacob nor the designers and directors—and because it unfolded naturally, the ritual was received as a revelation rather than as a construction. It did not suffer the usual risks of ritual, displaying the conventional and attributed rather than intrinsic nature of our conceptions. Had there been no intimations of the supernatural, the death would probably have been frightening, because it would have exaggerated mortal powers beyond the credibility of the people participating. The hints of mystery suggested powers beyond Jacob's control, making a religious experience of one that otherwise might have been simply bizarre. Despite the party and the resultant radical change of course, the celebration that occurred had that very sense of inevitability and predictability of outcome which is the goal of all human efforts in designing and staging a ritual.

RITUAL, TIME, AND CONTINUITY

Any discussion of ritual is also a discussion of time and continuity; when the ritual in question deals with death and birth, the themes of time and continuity are thrown into high relief. Ritual alters our ordinary sense of time, repudiating meaningless change and discontinuity by emphasizing regularity, precedent, and order. Paradoxically, it uses repetition to deny the empty repetitiveness of unremarked, unattended human and social experience. From repetition, it finds or makes patterns, and looks at these for hints of eternal designs and meanings. In ritual, change is interpreted by being linked with the past and incorporated into a larger framework, where its variations are equated with grander, tidier totalities. By inserting traditional elements into the present, the past is read as prefiguring what is happening in the here and now, and by implication the future is seen as foreshadowed in all that has gone before. Religious rituals are more sweeping than secular ones in this elongation of time and reiteration of continuity. The latter usually confine themselves to remembered human history, whereas the former transform history into myths, stories with no beginning and no end. Then time is obliterated and continuity is complete.

To do their work rituals must disrupt our ordinary sense of time and displace our awareness of events coming into being and disappearing in discrete, precise, discontinuous segments. This discontinuous experience is our everyday sense of time, used to coordinate collective activities; it is external in origins and referents, and does not take into account private responses, stimulation, states of mind, or motivation. Public chronological time is anathema to the mood of ritual, which has its own time. Rituals sweep us away from the everyday sense and from the objective, instrumental frame of mind that is associated with it. By merely absorbing us sufficiently, ritual, like art, lets us "lose ourselves" and step out of our usual conscious, critical mentality. When successful, ritual replaces chronological, collective time with the experience of flowing duration, paced according to personal significance; sometimes this is so powerful that we are altogether freed from a sense of time and of awareness of self. This is ritual time, and it must be present to some degree to mount the mood of conviction concerning the messages contained in a ritual.

But ritual is still a social event, and it is necessary that, within it, individuals' temporal experiences are coordinated somewhat. They must be delicately synchronized, without obliterating the individual's sense of an intense personal experience. Ordinary time is suspended and a new time instituted, geared to the event taking place, shared by those participating, integrating the private experience into a collective one. These moments of community built outside of ordinary time are rare and powerful, forging an intense communion that transcends awareness of individual separateness. Continuity among participants prevails briefly, in a sometimes euphoric condition, which Turner has described at length as a state of *communitas*,[21] and which Buber calls *Zwischenmenschlichkeit*.

Continuity of self may occur in rituals, especially rites of passage marking stages in the individual life cycle, and this produces yet another experience of time. Personal integration is achieved when the subject in a ritual retrieves his or her prior life experiences, not as past memories, but as events and feelings occurring in the present. Then the person is a child or youth once more, feeling one with earlier selves, who are recognized as familiar, still alive, coherent. Coherence of the "I," a sense of continuity with one's past selves, is not inevitable, as James Fernandez points out.[22] The choas of individual history, especially when that history has been great and often marked by numerous social and cultural separations, may be acute. The burden of memories weighs heavily on the elderly: the necessity for integration of a life is often a strong impulse. Reminiscence among the old is not merely escapism, nor the desire to live in the past.[23] It is often the reach for personal integration and the experience of continuity, and for the recognition of personal unity beneath the flow and flux of ordinary life.

Because ritual works through the senses, bypassing the critical, conscious mind, it allows one to return to earlier states of being. The past comes back, along with the ritual movements, practices, tastes, smells, and sounds, bringing along unaltered fragments from other times. Proust was fascinated with this process.[24] His work examines how the past may sometimes be recaptured with all its original force, unmodified by intervening events. This may occur when the conscious mind with its subsequent interpretations and associations is bypassed. Experiences of past time come back unaltered, often as spontaneous responses to sense stimuli; as Adam Mendilow describes this process, it occurs when the chemistry of thought is untouched by intervening

events and the passage of time.[25] These numinous moments carry with them their original, pristine associations and feelings. This is timelessness and the past is made into present. It is, says Mendilow, a kind of

> hermetical magic, sealed outside of time, suspending the sense of duration, allowing all of life to be experienced as a single moment. . . . These are pin-points of great intensity, concentrations of universal awareness, antithetical to the diffuseness of life (p. 137).

These pin-points of timelessness are beyond duration and change. In them one experiences the essence of life—or self—as eternally valid; simultaneity has replaced sequence, and continuity is complete.

Conceivably, any kind of ritual has the capacity to retrieve a fragment of past life. Rituals associated with and originating in childhood are more likely to do so, and these especially carry opportunities for finding personal-historical continuity. Two characteristics of these rituals are salient here: first, their intensely physiological associations; and second, their great power and immediacy, coming as they do from the individual's first emotional and social experiences. They are absolutely basic, arising in the context of nurturance and dependence, evoking the familiar, domestic domain, utterly fundamental, preceding language and conception. In our world of plural cultures, the first domestic nurturant experiences are often associated with ethnic origins, bound up with first foods, touch, language, song, folk ways, and the like, carried and connoted by rituals and symbols learned in that original context. Ethnic ritual and symbol are often redolent of the earliest, most profoundly emotional associations and it is often these that carry one back to earlier times and selves.

Consider the statement made by one of the old men present at Jacob's birth-death ritual.

> Whenever I say Kaddish, I chant and sway, and it all comes back to me. I remember how it was when my father, may he rest in peace, would wrap me around in his big prayer shawl. All that comes back to me, like I was back in that shawl, where nothing bad could ever happen.

The Kaddish prayer was probably the most important single ritual that occurred the day of Jacob's death. It was the most frequently and deeply experienced aspect of Jewish custom for the people there, the most ethnically rooted moment, sweeping together all the individuals present, connecting them with earlier parts of self, with Jacob the man, with each other, and with Jews who had lived and died before. The life of the mortal man Jacob was made into a mythic event, enlarging and illuminating the affairs of all those present. Here is ritual achieving its final purpose of transformation, altering our everyday understanding in a single stroke. Ultimately, we are interested in ritual because it tells us something about the human condition, the mythic condition, and our private lives all at once. It demonstrates the continuity between one human being and all humanity. It does more than tell us an eternal tale; it sheds light on our own condition. Jacob's death did this.

Jacob, when the celebration ended, had become a point from which radiated the enlarged meanings of his life and death, as well as the immediate ones, the grand and the minute, the remote and the particular, all implying each other, until continuity had become total unity.

Jacob's death could not change the harsh realities. But if people lived only by harsh realities there would be no need for rituals, for symbols, or for myths. The power of rituals, myths, and symbols is that they can change the experience we have of the world and its worth. Jacob's death rites may be considered an extraordinarily successful example of ritual providing social, cultural, biological, and spiritual continuity. More perpetuation, more connection, more interdependence, more unity existed when the day was over, making the oblivion of an individual and his way of life a little less certain than anyone had thought possible that morning.

NOTES

1. The methods used to gather information for this essay included participant observation, interviews, tape recording, group discussions, films, and still photography. I taped and photographed the event described and later had access to 8-mm film footage taken during the celebration by one of those attending. I interviewed Jacob Kovitz many times before he died, and interviewed members of his family before and after. The final interpretation I developed was discussed with the family, who had no objections to it, though it varied in some points with their own. All names used, including that of the center, have been changed.

2. See Philippe Ariès, *Western Attitudes toward Death from the Middle Ages to the Present* (Baltimore, 1974).

3. Alexander Solzhenitsyn, *Cancer Ward* (New York, 1968), pp. 96–97.

4. P. Freuchen, *Book of the Eskimos* (Cleveland, 1961), pp. 194–195.

5. Clifford Geertz, "Religion as a Cultural System," in M. Banton, ed., *Anthropological Approaches to the Study of Religion* (New York, 1966).

6. Sally F. Moore and Barbara G. Myerhoff, eds., *Secular Ritual* (Amsterdam, 1977), p. 22.

7. Here I am distinguishing between "religious" and "sacred" and treating them as categories that may exist independently or be joined. Where ideas, objects, or practices are considered axiomatic, unquestionable, literally sacrosanct, they are "sacred," with or without the inclusion of the concept of the supernatural. Their sacredness derives from a profound and affective consensus as to their rightness; their authority comes from their embeddedness in many realms of tradition. Over against the sacred is the mundane, which is malleable

and negotiable. When sacredness is attached to the supernatural, it is religious *and* sacred. When sacredness is detached from the religious, it refers to unquestionably good and right traditions, sanctified by usage and consensus.

8. Sally F. Moore and Barbara G. Myerhoff, *Symbol and Politics in Communal Ideology* (Ithaca, 1975).

9. Hasids (Hasidim) were, and are, a deeply religious, semi-mystical group practicing a vitalized, fervent form of folk Judaism originating in Eastern Europe during the mid-eighteenth century.

10. All these people are completely multilingual and use different languages for different purposes, with some consistency. For example, political and secular matters are often discussed in English; Hebrew is used to make poems, reminiscences, and arguments and bargaining. Yiddish, the *mamloschen*, punctuates all the areas, but appears most regularly in times of intense emotion. It is also used most in conversations about food, children, cursing, and gossiping. For some, Yiddish has connotations of inferiority since it was associated with female activities, domestic and familial matters (in the *shtetls*, few were educated in Hebrew and so Yiddish dominated the household). It was the language of exiles living in oppression and, later, of greenhorns. For others, the Yiddishists in particular, it is a bona fide language to be treated with respect and used publicly. Careful pronunciation, proper syntax, and avoidance of Anglicized words are considered signs of respect for Yiddishkeit. On the whole, Jacob was always careful in his Yiddish, and this was seen as an indication of his pride in his heritage.

11. A *tzaddik* in Hasidic tradition is a saintly man of great devotion, often possessing mystical powers. It is noted that

important Hasids sometimes died in their chairs, and it is said that they often anticipated the dates of their death. There is also a suggestive body of custom surrounding the symbolism of the chair, which figures importantly in at least two Jewish male rites of passage. In Hasidic weddings it is customary for the bridegroom to be carried aloft in his chair. And an empty chair is reserved for the prophet Elijah at circumcisions; this is to signify that any Jewish boy may turn out to be the Messiah, since Elijah must be present at the Messiah's birth.

12. In fact, Moses died on the seventh of Adar. He did, however, die on his birthday; he was allowed to "complete the years of the righteous exactly from day to day and month to month, as it is said, the number of thy days I will fulfill" (Talmud Bavli Kaddushin 38A). Hence the tradition in folklore that the righteous are born and die on the same day. Elijah did not die in his chair, however. He is believed to have "been taken up by a whirlwind into Heaven," passing out of this world without dying. His "passage" was not a normal death in any event, and this is probably why his death was brought up in this discussion. These points were clarified in personal communication by Rabbi Chaim Seidler-Feller of Los Angeles.

13. In Jewish mysticism, represented in the Kabbalah, a person's soul or spirit is transformed into sparks after death. "Kaddish" is a prayer sanctifying God's name, recited many times in Jewish liturgy; it is known also as the Mourner's Prayer and recited at the side of a grave.

14. Others disagreed with this and were certain that Jacob died an agnostic. They did not confront the rabbi on the matter, however; said Heschel, "If it makes the rabbi happy, let him believe it."

15. Literally, *pilpul* means "pepper" and refers to the custom of lively scholarly argument about religious texts.

16. Dreams were very significant among *shtetl* folk, being elaborately discussed and much used in pursuit of symbolic meanings and ritual usage. Indeed, four members of the group owned and used dream books, which they had brought with them from the Old Country.

17. Joseph Zoshin, "The Fraternity of Mourners," in J. Riemer, ed., *Jewish Reflections on Death* (New York, 1974).

18. The rabbi was in attendance fortuitously that day, in his capacity as leader of the young people. Without him the Kaddish would not have been said. His unplanned presence was subsequently interpreted by many as another sign that the memorial was meant to take place when it did.

19. Suzanne K. Langer, *Philosophy in the New Key* (New York, 1942).

20. D.G. James, *Scepticism and Poetry* (London, 1937).

21. Victor Turner, "An Anthropological Approach to the Icelandic Saga," in T. Beidelman, ed., *The Translation of Culture: Essays to E.E. Evans-Pritchard* (London, 1971).

22. James Fernandez, "The Mission of Metaphor in Expressive Culture," *Current Anthropology* 15(2):119–133.

23. See R.N. Butler, "The Life Review: An Interpretation of Reminiscence in the Aged," in B.L. Neugarten, ed., *Middle Age and Aging* (Chicago, 1968), for a discussion of the therapeutic functions of reminiscence in the elderly.

24. For further discussion of this process, see Barbara G. Myerhoff and Virginia Tufte, "Life History as Integration: Personal Myth and Aging," *Gerontologist* 15:541–543.

25. Adam A. Mendilow, *Time and the Novel* (London, 1952).

Ritual Structure in a Chicano Dance

MANUEL H. PEÑA

Facts of publication: Peña, Manuel H. 1980. "Ritual Structure in a Chicano Dance," Latin American Music Review *1(1) (Spring 1980): 47–73. Copyright © 1980 by The University of Texas Press. Reprinted with the permission of the publishers.*

For a ten-year period, Manuel Peña was a member of a band that played music for regular Saturday night dances among Chicanos in Fresno, California. Using Victor Turner's rites-of-passage model, Peña argues that these dance events have a ritual structure. He considers the dance a rite of intensification and uses, but does not develop, Gregory Bateson's theory of play in interpreting it. Seeing the dance event as a temporally and spatially structured whole, Peña shows that it is a form of ritualized play that reintegrates and reinvigorates dancers' social and cultural identity. This function is especially important, since the Chicanos who attended these dances did not enjoy full access to the traditions of the American culture to which they had otherwise accommodated themselves.

More on Hispanic ritual in North America can be found in Ronald L. Grimes, Symbol and Conquest: Public Ritual in Santa Fe *(Albuquerque: University of New Mexico Press, 1992).*

About the author: Dates: *1943–   , Weslaco, TX, U.S.A.* **Education:** *B.A., California State, Fresno; M.A. California State, Fresno; Ph.D., University of Texas, Austin.* **Field(s):** *Mexican and Mexican American music and folklore; ethnicity, class, gender.* **Career:** *Professor of Mexican American Studies and Anthropology, 1993–present, University of Texas, Austin.* **Publications:** The Texas-Mexican Conjunto *(University of Texas, 1985);* The Mexican American Orquesta *(University of Houston and University of Texas, 1994);* "Class, Gender, and Machismo," *Gender and Society 5.1 (1991): 30–46.* **Additional:** The Texas-Mexican Conjunto, *winner, third place, Chicago Folklore Prize.*

This paper presents ideas that I have elaborated as a result of ten years of experience (1967–1977) as a participant-observer in a series of regularly scheduled celebrations among a group of Chicanos[1] in Fresno, California. The paper attempts to formulate an analytical interpretation, by way of reconstructing the events, of the set of behavioral responses of the group as it participated in what were considered customary Saturday night dances. Most of the participants attended these dances more or less regularly for the greater part of the period. My own contribution to the musical occasions was as a member of *La Orquesta de Beto García y Sus G. G.'s*, a band that played in the style of music known as *orquesta tejana*. The style originated in Texas in the 1940s, but it has since gained currency in places far beyond, including the San Joaquin Valley of California.[2]

The basic thesis of the paper is that, as a specialized type of framed, festive play activity, the dances evinced a definite ritual structure, which in its totality of highly redundant, semantically, loaded elements defined an intensive adventure into a Chicano reality whose purpose was to revitalize a deeply felt (and threatened) ethnic boundary. The remarkable paradox surrounding these dances was accentuated by the essentially conservative public ideology of the participants; that is, these were not Chicanos caught up in the romantic nationalist *movimiento* of the 1960s and 1970s, which sought through political means to revitalize "Chicano" culture and improve the economic lot of the people. Rather, these were for the most part working-class people who outwardly maintained an unshaken loyalty to public American ideals. Yet, in the deep, liminal play that characterized these musical occasions, *every* symbolic effort was made to negate that very society which in everyday structured life these Mexican Americans endorsed. Thus, in its analysis the paper attempts to illuminate the complexities, that is, the conflict of values and ideologies, that mark the lives

of Mexicans in the United States. It does this by suggesting that in the ritualized structure of these musical occasions a microcosm of this conflict was symbolically played out and ultimately mediated.

In viewing the dances, first, as a form of framed play, I borrow from Bateson (1972); second, approaching them as ritual I borrow from Chapple and Coon (1942) and Leach (1972). Finally, as symbolic enactments the dances evinced elements of structure and *communitas* as these concepts have been elaborated by Van Gennep (1960) and Turner (1969). It is also important to note that although each of the dances that I observed over the period from 1967 to 1977 was essentially a re-creation of those before it, a gradual evolution did take place, the dances attaining maximum ritual effect over the last five years. This evolution undoubtedly went hand in hand with the band's growing popularity and its ever-increasing acceptance and identification with what the people saw as an established tradition. Nonetheless, the overall sequence of activities that structured each dance remained more or less constant throughout the period.

Thus, to encapsulate the argument, the Saturday night Chicano dances conformed to a type of framed play activity, but one with strong ritual features, inasmuch as the "redundancy factor [was] very high" (Leach, 1972:334). That is, as play activity the events were governed by a metacommunicative understanding among participants that the "set of all messages or meaningful actions, exchanged by them within a limited period of time," that is, within the dance, were delimited by this consciously recognized frame, which was at once physical and psychological (Bateson, 1972: 186–187). The people understood that the dance was a form of play in which the daily grind of life was suspended. Bateson's statement, "Attend what is within and do not attend what is outside" (1972: 187) was in operation here. In other words, the action within the dance was brought to the foreground to the exclusion of other orders of action. But at a tacit, extraconscious level the metacommunicative understanding elevated the dances to the status of, if not ritual, at least ritualized play. Characterized as they were by a repeated, drawn-out, redundant sequence, the actions within the dance communicated "loaded" information between members of the group, the historical and symbolic significance of which, in my estimation, served to reinforce the values, traditions, and attitudes that the group held as important. But this reinforcement can be understood only within the framework of the dynamics of intercultural contact and conflict (cf. Paredes, 1977, and Bateson, 1972) and ethnic boundary maintenance (see Barth, 1969), as these realities were negotiated generally in the daily lives of the people and specifically within the dance setting.

The full implications of intercultural contact cannot be developed here, but the nature of the participants' actions will be elaborated on in the course of the description of the dance. For the moment I merely wish to emphasize that it was both the "framing" and the more or less unconscious repetition of certain constituent parts, in being singled out for special treatment, that invested the dances with their peculiar ritual character.

Although the dances were used by the group primarily as a source of entertainment, on a functional and more deeply symbolic level the unique conduct of the events constituted a "special domain," to use Keil's terminology. In describing black entertainment Keil states that it is a domain "wherein black men have proved and preserved their identity. This domain or sphere of interest may be broadly defined as entertainment from the white or public point of view and as ritual, drama or dialectical catharsis from the Negro or theoretical standpoint" (1966: 15).

A similar assessment is possible with respect to the Chicano dances I am discussing here. That they were a form of entertainment is true, but they were clearly more than "mere decoration" or escape from reality in the lives of the people. They were, rather, "an adventure into reality," as Blacking has said of Venda music and dance (1973: 28). They symbolized the reality of men sharing a common and heightened cultural experience that made them "more aware of themselves and of their responsibilities towards one another" (ibid.). The dances were, in effect, something on the order of rites of intensification; to quote

Chapple and Coon: "In the technical (physiological) sense, the performance of these rites prevents the extinction of habits (orders of action) to which the individual has been trained" (1942: 508). In the context of the Chicano social group, the dances served to "prevent the extinction" of a way of life tied to the group's culture and ultimately to their ethnic identity. Thus, in actuality the performance of these rites (dances) was "technically" psychological and social, rather than physiological.

One final point needs to be stressed with respect to the analysis I propose. While it is generally acknowledged that dancing as an organized activity has universal symbolic significance, it is in culture-specific contexts that its ritual measure is determined. Dancing does not have the same ritual value everywhere. In our modern American society, for example, dancing, at least of the type I am discussing here, may be nothing more than an incidental (i.e., nonrepetitive) form of entertainment, or play. Such is the case in the generalized American society, where people dance in nightclubs, discotheques, ballrooms, and other places. This is not to say that such dancing is nonsymbolic; whatever the symbolic significance we can ascribe to such entertainment, it is still not comparable to the purposive, ritual behavior that marked the Chicano Saturday night dances in Fresno. This is an important distinction, because an otherwise desultory observation of the celebrations might have erroneously interpreted them as merely occasional manifestations of American pop culture, glossing over as nonsignificant the ritual, symbolic importance of such features as the *menudo* (a food with strong cultural overtones), the strategic placement of *gritos* (shouts) (another "loaded" message), the choice of powerfully evocative Mexican songs, and numerous other cues that clearly identified the events as ritualistic.

To give a brief history of the dance as an integrated feature in the cultural life of Chicanos I shall begin with the findings of Paredes and Limón. The former states: "The dance played but little part in Border folkways, though in the twentieth century the Mexicanized polka has become something very close to a native folk form. . . . There were community dances at public spots and some private dances in the homes, usually to celebrate weddings, but the dance on the Border was a modern importation, reflecting European vogues" (1958: 14).

I believe that Paredes is remarkably accurate in

this assessment considering the early date. Since the 1950s what we might call the "Chicanoized" polka[3] has, in fact, become a hallmark of both the musical and the dance styles in the Southwest, particularly in Texas, which has served as a sort of cradle of indigenous Chicano music and from which the forms have been exported to other parts of the country (e.g., California) where Chicanos have concentrated. Thus, as the twentieth century progressed, both public (in the form of profit-motivated dances) and private celebrations, such as weddings, *quinceañeras,* (fifteenth-birthday parties), anniversaries and other occasions, have shown a tremendous increase. Beginning especially in the 1940s, according to one of Limón's informants, public paid-admission dances have increased several times over previous years (1977), and my own observations as a dance-music performer certainly bear this out. We may accurately say, then, that public and private dancing has truly become an important element in the social lives of Chicanos. One has only to tune in to any Spanish-speaking commercial radio station in any part of the Southwest to learn how widespread dancing is among our people today.

Fresno is no exception. In the 1960s and 1970s there were a number of organizations in the city that sponsored regular Saturday night dances. Forming an interlocking social network among Chicanos from various working-class occupations, these included the Veterans of Foreign Wars, Post 8900, the *sociedades mutualistas,* El Comité Civico Mexicano, and a number of Catholic Church groups, such as Los Guadalupanos. These organizations were interrelated in the sense that an individual could and often did belong to more than one and in that all of the organizations evinced a working-class, Catholic *mejicano* outlook. A common sociocultural climate thus prevailed, with most members practicing a more or less selective acculturation, adapting in various ways to life in American society while at the same time retaining much of their Mexican identity. The *sociedades mutualistas,* particularly, tended to display a strong Mexican persuasion, bearing the names and emblems of such Mexican patriots as José María Morelos, Benito Juárez, and Justo Sierra, to name a few.

Yet, in spite of their Mexicanness, neither the *mutualistas* nor the other groups mentioned displayed any of the political fervor that at this precise period was sweeping *el movimiento* Chicano. Other political organizations existed, and a few individuals participated in them, but as a rule these organizations and their members eschewed the politics of the Chicano movement.[4] Some even expressed opposition to the tactics of the more militant Chicanos. Ironically, one goal of many an activist Chicano reformer, namely, the perpetuation of a distinct "Chicano" culture, was symbolically enacted by these "conservative" Mexican Americans at every Saturday night dance.

Aside from whatever peculiar goals these organizations might have (for instance, the *mutualistas* were primarily a funeral-fund brotherhood), fundraising was always important in obtaining money for scholarships, new churches or other buildings, and whatever other civic causes furthered a particular group's interests. And, invariably, the chief way to raise money was through public dances; this was the immediate rationale for the Saturday night dance. But obviously, as I have suggested, the dances had a significance far beyond the simple purpose of making money. They were, in fact, strongly supported by the people as a means of meeting friends and reestablishing social contacts. They were consequently well attended and marked by intense social interaction.

Here I should point out that the usual crowds which attended the Beto García dances had their counterparts in other similar places in Fresno and the surrounding area. There were actually at least a dozen or so groups which played within the same musical style as Beto, and each group tended to have its own following. Thus, on an given Saturday night there might be as many as a dozen dances, sponsored by the various organizations. Since each dance could be expected to draw anywhere from two hundred to four hundred celebrators, easily two thousand or more people shared in this activity on any given weekend. Add to these the number of dances in cantinas, weddings, and other social events, and one can accurately estimate five thousand people participating in this type of celebration.

La Orquesta de Beto García y Sus G. G.'s was essentially a family enterprise. It included Beto on trumpet (he also did most of the singing), his father Octavio on saxophone, his brother Alonso on electric piano, organ, and piano-accordion, and his sister (my wife) María on electric bass. I played trumpet and guitar, and at first Pete García (no relation) then later Reggie Peña, "El Güero" (no relation), pulled duty on the drums. Bill Giddings, an Anglo-American alto and tenor saxophonist who had played *orquesta* music for many years, joined the band in 1973. Originally, Octavio had started the band in Mercedes, Texas, but when the family migrated to California in 1960, Beto took over as leader. However, the old man, about sixty at that time, retained a special position of seniority and respect throughout the band's history in California.

Having originated in Texas, the band was steeped in the musical style popularized by Beto Villa *y Su Orquesta* and often referred to as *orquesta tejana* music, due greatly (though not exclusively) to the unique way of performing the polka (cf. Paredes, 1977). But, in addition to the polka, Mexican boleros and *cumbias* (the latter the latest variant in a long historical line of Afro-Hispanic popular genres) were very much a part of the band's musical repertory. Closer than the polka to the greater Mexican performance styles and clearly demonstrating the *orquesta*'s strong ties to popular greater Mexican musical culture, the *cumbia* and Mexican bolero nevertheless incorporated certain unique features common only to *tejano* musical groups. Incidentally, by this time, at least in Fresno, older forms, such as *redovas*, schottisches, and waltzes, had largely gone out of favor, although *redovas* were still occasionally requested (usually by older couples and late into the evening's celebration), and waltzes were still the standard, special dance for newlyweds at weddings.

Semiprofessional musicians (they all had other regular jobs), the Garcías were in many ways "folk" musicians in that they played a great deal of their music "by ear," simply picking up the melody of a popular tune and in impromptu sessions working out an "arrangement." Usually such arrangements, especially those of polkas, merely incorporated stock "licks," or formulas, that every other group used, and that in various combinations give form and identity to the *orquesta* style. In performing boleros, however, the group did not object to more sophisticated arranging, as long as it conformed to *el gusto de la gente* (the people's taste). In this respect the Garcías (Alonso excepted) were extremely conservative about "style" and had very definite ideas about *qué es lo que le gusta a la gente* (what people like).

Both Octavio and Beto were leery of some of the innovations within the *orquesta tejana* style that have been introduced by such groups as Little Joe y La Familia and Sunny Ozuna and the Sunliners. They were uncomfortable with these changes and considered them too "fancy" for the tastes of their particular dance patrons. I would, however, be remiss were I not to mention that, at the constant prodding of Alonso and this writer, more and more of those innovations were eventually accepted and incorporated into the group. In any case, as long-time performers in many different settings within Mexican American communities, both in Texas and in California, the Garcías had an instinctive understanding of who *la gente* were and what type of music they demanded. They were adept musicians, adaptable to many different crowds—even Anglo ones, when the occasion demanded it. But ultimately they were most at home among predictable audiences, with people who genuinely enjoyed dancing to their music, and who to them were synonymous with *la gente mexicana*, that is, the Saturday night Chicano dance crowd, who appreciated and shared fully in the Garcías' music, their class outlook, and their ethnic identity.

Octavio García, the oldest member in the group, had learned to play saxophone in the 1920s with a pair of blind musicians in Texas, *los hermanos* Verduzco. They had taught him a basic way of performing what was then called *orquesta tipica* music, which preceded the modern *orquesta* style, and he had merely modified that style slightly to accommodate the newer one. Having played for so long what to him was a valid mode of performance, he was vehemently averse to what he considered *mugrero* (i.e., "inferior" innovators). He was particularly critical of the modern jazz-influenced improvisations of such *orquestas* as Little Joe's, in which the melody is eschewed and, often, complexity of harmony preferred (e.g., altered chords like half-diminished sevenths, "flatted ninths," and so forth). I should add, however, that he was not critical of jazz itself for which he had a healthy respect and admiration, but only its introduction into Mexican music. His typical comments when this writer, or any other musician, tried such "modernistic" experiments were: "¡Pos si no tocas la melodía! Habiendo tan buen tono de do, ¿pa' qué quieren tanto periqueo? A la gente no le gusta ese mugrero"

("Why don't you play the melody? In a simple key like C, why all that fancy stuff? People don't like that junk!").

Although less opposed to such innovations, Beto still preferred straightforward tonic-dominant melodic interpretation with a minimum of "frills." When called upon to solo-improvise, particularly in *cumbias*, which in the *orquesta* style (as in others) call for some improvisation, Beto had a handy, well-rehearsed and oft-repeated solo that even Octavio poked fun at. He would burst into laughter when he compared Beto's "improvised" solo to a similar one he had kept handy many years before and had finally dropped in embarrassment when the Verduzcos, having memorized it too, had begun to follow his "ad lib"—in thirds! Then he would scratch his shaking head and, still laughing, say, "¡Ah, qué Chihuahua!" But Beto was undaunted, and, as leader of the group, he also acted as a sort of watchdog on individual performances. If Güero tried a particularly intricate new twist to the basic $\frac{4}{4}$ bolero rhythm, and especially if it altered the fixed three-four-one pulse normally sustained by the bass drum, Beto would stamp the beat on the floor with his foot while yelling to the drummer, "¡Dale derecho, dale derecho!" ("Keep it simple, man, keep it simple!"). Or, if the guitarist introduced too fancy a rhythmic pattern or harmonic progression, one Beto considered inappropriate, a reprimand could be expected. "Keep it simple, man, keep it simple," he would say. Always, to Beto *lo apropiado, al gusto de la gente* (the appropriate, geared to people's tastes) was the guiding principle for approval or disapproval.

Alonso García was recognized by the others as the most creative in the group. His was a quaint idiostyle, one fashioned after such Mexican orchestras as La Sonora Santanera (with shades of Luis Arcaraz) but strongly modulated by the *orquesta tejana* style. His piano solos, whether in polkas, boleros, or *cumbias*, were highly stylized—evincing a strong personal character, yet well within the amalgamation of traditional styles he had forged. Of course, when he played the piano-accordion, he flawlessly executed all the formulaic "licks" that have come to be associated with *conjunto* music, *orquesta's* sister style. (Alonso played the piano-accordion because he felt it was a more suitable link between the two styles, the button model

being too rigidly and harmonically *ranchera* to fit in with the more sophisticated style of the *orquesta*.)[5] In short, Alonso was an excellent example of a musician who is creative in a personal way yet firmly within the parameters of a collective musical style. He seemed to know, tacitly, what Beto, Octavio, and the audience would approve, and he seldom strayed beyond these constraints.

As a whole, then, the group of *Beto García y Sus G. G.'s* could be considered somewhat conservative and cautious in its approach to musical performance, carefully considering its preferences and those of its audience before accepting new stylistic features into its music. That is why Bill Giddings, an Anglo musician, fit in so well with the group: his addition did not significantly alter the band's style. On the contrary, through years of exposure he had mastered the nuances of *orquesta* music, his formal training on the saxophone merely adding polish to his execution.

I have not mentioned María, but she perhaps best exemplified the final consensus that usually emerged between the "innovators" and the "preservers" in the group. While she fully appreciated many distinct types of music, she also felt that the band was answerable to the dictates of the Saturday night crowd, as these dictates were translated into the band's popularity and appeal. As a member, and a very perceptive one, I believe, of the larger Chicano community, and one who had been exposed to many different styles of music, she was quite willing to incorporate new modes of performance, as long as they did not violate the established norms. Consequently, even in the most sophisticated arrangements her basic technique remained always the time-validated bass accompaniment patterns of *orquesta* music that had been set in the formative years of the 1940s and 1950s.

Significantly, the band was immensely popular with a large segment of the Mexican populace in Fresno and central California.

I have chosen to dwell at length on the musicians because I feel that they were an integral ingredient in the chemistry of the celebration itself and the social milieu within which the dance as ritualized play found expression. In their constant preoccupation with the social norms of performance, that is, in their attempts to create and protect a musical style shared by performer and audience alike, the Garcías demonstrated a focused attention on the need for a consensus between audience and performer, for a uniquely defined expression of group solidarity. This solidarity was displayed in the people's appreciation of Beto García's music; it was renegotiated and symbolically consummated at every Saturday night dance.

Typically, the people who attended these Beto García dances, aside from being exclusively Chicano and working-class, were for the most part middle-aged, from approximately thirty to sixty years of age. Usually married couples, they generally came to the dance in little parties. Two such couples will perhaps serve as examples.

Johnny and Rita Cuesta were typical of the "blue collar" participants. He was a truck driver for a meat-packing company and she worked at a raisin-packing plant. In their fifties, they came to the dances regularly, because, as Johnny said, "Pa' bailar no hay como la orquesta de Beto García" (for dancing there's no orchestra like Beto García's). Like many other patrons, Johnny and Rita were rather nondescript though reasonably well-adjusted members of the larger community. Like almost all of the other people, the Cuestas were bilingual, a consequence of their adaptation to American society. But, while they occupied a certain position in the American socioeconomic structure, their private lives, their primary contacts, were almost exclusively confined within a Chicano communicative network. Thus, to them the Saturday night dance with Beto García was an indispensable way of solidifying their place within that network, as well as a way to enjoy themselves in a stress-free situation among people like themselves. Consequently, Johnny and Rita celebrated often and hard, immersing themselves completely in the whirl of dance, laughter, and drink.

Frank and Cora Vera were considerably younger (in their late thirties) than the Cuestas, and, although working-class, their position, in the American sociological vernacular, would be considered higher in status because they were "white-collar" workers. He was a sales representative for a truck firm; she was a registered nurse. They were both active members in the veterans' organization, Post 8900, a primarily Mexican-American group that was a frequent dance sponsor. Like the Cuestas, the Veras were a nonpolitical couple, shunning the more political organizations like the Mexican Political Association (MAPA). Instead, they concentrated on civic-oriented, noncontroversial activities, such as the annual coronation of the *16 de septiembre* queen, sponsored by the Comité Cívico Mexicano, and, of course, those of the Veterans of Foreign Wars. The Veras were decidedly more anglicized than the Cuestas they spoke mainly English, for example—yet they, too, gravitated towards a Chicano social atmosphere. As active members in a Chicano community whose core was sharply distinguishable by its segregation from that of the Anglo, the Veras were clearly not ready to become integrated members of the latter community, if indeed that choice was open to them at all. Thus, like the Cuestas and all the other participants in the Saturday night celebration, the Veras' contact with the larger Anglo community was secondary, that is, confined to work and business, with perhaps an occasional party among co-workers. To Frank and Cora Vera, then, the Saturday night dance also served as an important reinforcement in their ties to the social network.

Finally, as members of an increasingly affluent working class within Chicano society, the Cuestas and the Veras represented a segment of that society that shared strongly in the musical outlook not only of the G. G.'s but also of the other musical groups in Fresno that played more or less within an *orquesta* tradition. And the dance was the focal point for intensifying the feelings of community, of being among one's own kind, participating in a shared esthetic experience. To be sure, there were other levels of Chicano society, namely, those occupied by farm workers, affluent professionals (doctors, lawyers), and businessmen, that were seldom represented at the dances. The reasons for this are complex, but they are based on such things as ascribed status and the differential identities (cf. Bauman, 1972) related to that status—in short, on the cultural diversity that existed among Chicanos in Fresno, as in any other community.

Since I am treating the dances as ritualized behavior, I want now to describe an event as it was typically enacted. The Fresno County fairgrounds cafeteria was a frequent site. A large, rectangular building with many windows, it offered a suitable atmosphere, with room for up to five hundred people. As a rule tables and chairs were set up in rows, with some kind of covering to adorn the bareness of the tables, mostly white papercloth with some additional decorative items, such as streamers or fresh flower arrangements. For each row, two or three tables were fitted end to end against the walls, so that a dozen people or so could sit on each side, with just enough walking space between rows. This deliberate crowding, I believe, enhanced the opportunity for close interaction, as well as maximizing the space available. The general arrangement left a large empty area in the middle of the hall that was the designated dance floor. The band was ordinarily set up on a portable platform, about two feet above the dance floor, at the far end of the hall.

The dance itself began at 9:00 P.M., a few couples arriving even before that time to get good seats and to socialize quietly before the noise and festivities set in. By 10:00 P.M. most of the celebrators had arrived. The procedure for entry was this: A small table with tickets and money change was set up at the door, one or two women from the sponsoring organization collecting. As the people arrived, some in groups of two, three, or more couples, they paid their admission fee and made their way to the tables. Often, since most people came at the same time, a line would form at the gate. By 9:30 the hall began to fill quickly, the cars parked around it forming a solid chain when all the dancers had arrived.

The nature of the celebration, by long-established custom, called for semiformal attire. Most of the men wore dress clothes—suits or sport coats and tie—although some, like Johnny Cuesta, dressed more casually, leaving out the tie. No one, however, would dress in blue-jean pants or jackets; this would have been considered in poor taste and inappropriate. The women often dressed rather lavishly in stylish gowns decked with ample jewelry, such as earrings, necklaces, bracelets, watches, and other common artifacts of adornment, including rouge, eye makeup, and so on. The Saturday night dance was, in effect, a distinct, clearly defined (or framed) play activity that required, among other things, "dressing up for the occasion." Members of the band marked the occasion by wearing identical uniforms. This was done consciously to distinguish the performers as a select group, whose purpose was to

add the "show-biz" touch to the event, but in a symbolic way the musicians' special garb invoked the power of their unique talent (often referred to, fittingly enough, as a *don de Dios* [gift from God]), which invested in them the responsibility for the bacchanalian deliverance of the festive throng. Their secular analogy to priests and shamans is, I believe, clear enough.

As well-paid and specially recognized participants, the *orquesta* musicians had of necessity to arrive early to set up the cumbersome electronic gear that is standard equipment for all modern dance bands. Again, without wishing to belabor the priestly analogy, I would add that the bandstand was, if not "sacred space," at least definitely *un lugar de respeto* (a respected place). Endowed with a special aura, it was off limits to everyone except by consent of the performers. The delicate nature of the equipment, whose massive array of microphones, speakers, and amplifiers certainly gave it an impressive appearance, provided the musicians with an excuse for discouraging audience encroachment. But such precaution was hardly necessary, since most people were duly respectful of the complicated machinery, only the most hardy (or intoxicated) ones venturing occasionally to disrupt the proceedings on stage.

Shortly before 9:00 P.M. Beto would mount the bandstand, and invariably, from force of habit, he would play a sort of D-minor arpeggio on his trumpet by way of warming up and as a signal to the other musicians that it was time to begin. Alonso would then hurry to the bar to buy his last beer before getting started, *para afinarse* (to tune himself up), as he said. El Güero would sit at his now-assembled drum set and play a few rolls as he tuned his snare and tom-toms; María started tuning her bass in the usual way: getting a G from the piano and tuning her strings successively down to the low E. And Bill, as was his wont, would liven things up with the latest joke he had heard, while he assembled his saxophones. Octavio, who did not believe in "warming up" (he warmed up with the first tune), was the last to climb on the bandstand. These preliminaries and warm-up habits were an economical way that each musician had devised for gearing up for the demands of the performance, and they were repeated more or less exactly every time. But in a sense most of these preliminaries were so stylized that I am tempted to include them as symbolic categories in the ritual scheme—a contribution on the part of the musicians to the order of things that characterized the first part of the dance.

This order was reflected in the first phase of the celebration. The dance began sedately enough. The participants were just settling in, they were generally sober, and the band played relatively softly. There was a sense of orderly decorum in the first hour of the dance: of subdued, restrained politeness, of freshly dressed men and women slightly unaccustomed to this moment of play. It was a structured quiet that preceded the full-blown hour of merriment. The band, in fact, always began with the same, strict order of music: the polka "Las alteñitas," the bolero "Sin ti," and the *cumbia* "El cable," the last a signal to the dancers that it was *taconazo* (dance) time. This initial order of songs was, as I indicated, unvarying, at least in the last five years; to the best of my recollection Beto only rarely changed this starting sequence. Moreover, it was significant in another way: it was a thematic exposition of the three main music genres that would, with minor variations, provide *el marco musical* (the musical frame), to borrow Beto's terminology, for the rest of the evening.

As the dance progressed, and by the first intermission at 10:40, the crisp order that had marked the initial phase of the celebration began to give way to a rising hum of musical and human sounds amid increasing movement. Couples who had earlier remained seated, enjoying polite conversation, now got up and began to dance. Some, who had at first danced in a constrained manner, mechanically or self-consciously, were by now quite loose and executing fancy turns. Faces began to glow with liquor and jollity, the mass of humanity going round and round in a counterclockwise circle, moving along in synchronous rhythm to the beat of Beto García's music. Mellowed by the beer, margaritas, screwdrivers, and other customary alcoholic drinks, the couples who had made such an orderly, even staid entrance could now be seen to interact freely and noisily across tables, on the dance floor, at the bar, and in the long, impatient lines in front the restrooms. Everywhere people socialized, the throng of voices rising in pitch, loudness, and incoherence until music and voices fused in a continuous din. The celebration was in full swing.

The musicians responded to this festive tumult by increasing the level of electronic amplification, even while the technical execution became less exact as the liquor became more available. At this time the crowd reacted to Beto's invitation for requests by increasing their trips to the bandstand and requesting more and more songs that evoked the past. Such selections as the ever-popular "Danzón Juárez," the *canción corrida*[6] "La del moño colorado," "La cumbiadel sol," and the only *corrido* popular with these crowds, "Gabino Barrera"[7] (featuring the exploits of a tough Mexican *campesino*), always remained in demand and part of Beto's repertory. The latter and other *ranchera* songs,[8] such as "Volver, volver" and "Me caí de la nube," inevitably called for a round of *gritos*, the song-and-*grito* pairing serving as a highly symbolic way of emphasizing *lo mexicano*. Associated with a simple rural life that has long been romanticized in Mexican movies (featuring charros and ranchero types) as the ideal Mexican existence (somewhat in the fashion of American westerns), the *rancheras* evoked feelings of nostalgia for an ungraspable "Mexican" reality. As is the case among Mexicans everywhere, *canciones rancheras* seemed to awaken the deepest national and cultural sentiments in many individuals in the crowd, sentiments that found expression in the lusty *gritos* that approached virtuosity in the throats of the best enthusiasts. By contrast, it is worth pointing out that boleros, because of their cosmopolitan, sophisticated nature (even if in most boleros the lyrical content, usually about love is identical to that in *rancheras*), never elicited such gusto. But, in the final analysis, these *gritos*, interspersed as they were in the appropriate places, formed yet another link in the symbolic categories of this Saturday night ritual.

The progression from sedate, orderly entrance to spontaneous, chaotic celebration reached its peak between the hours of midnight and 1:00 A.M. Under the influence of liquor, music, and the general gaiety, a strong esprit de corps marked this last hour of the dance. This was made possible because social and individual inhibitions were clearly broken down; at least some of the hierarchies that might exist in the outer world were here suspended. By mutual consensus the social norms of the world outside, or at least some of them, did not apply.

Let us take an example. Much has been made of the latent conflict in male-female relations in Mexican (and Chicano) society and its exacerbation by the male's exploitative, predatory nature (cf. Madsen, 1964, and Paz, 1961). Particularly sensitive is the husband-wife relation vis-à-vis other men. Some have seen such relations as guided by a pervasive mistrust (e.g., Madsen) that threatens continually to provoke violence. Without wishing to elaborate excessively on such misconceptions (cf. Paredes, 1977), I would add that, as is the case in many societies, there does exist a territorial barrier between a Chicano marital couple and individuals of the opposite sex outside—both men *and* women. Such sense of territoriality is reflected in the observance of *respeto* toward a man's wife *and* a woman's husband. As a result, a married individual's relations with members of the opposite sex (other than close relatives) tend to be formal, though not necessarily stiff. I emphasize the latter because subtle, witty joking, especially as it pits male against female, is quite acceptable and not uncommon. Thus, ordinarily for a man's wife to dance a slow, romantic bolero with someone else would be considered a breach of etiquette, a provocation if she danced too closely, and a breakdown of the formal relations. Nevertheless, in the atmosphere of the hour of *communitas* (the breakdown of structure, for Turner, 1969) partner swapping was common enough, although the proper decorum, that is, physical distance between the new partners, was always observed.

Other uncommon behavior, attributable to the antistructure (Turner, 1969) that marked this last hour, could be observed. Public intoxication, which is not condoned among these people, was quite common here, notably among the men, although the women, too, drank—and sometimes heavily. No one, however, drank so excessively as to "create scenes." Order was never dissolved sufficiently to lead to unruly behavior, even in the hour of spontaneous revelry. (*Communitas* is not, of course, synonymous with disorder.) Other behavior, not usual in the outside world, was evident: embracing, back slapping, boisterous laughter, exaggerated dancing (especially on the part of the men). At this time brisk and well-liked selections, such as the *cumbia* "El dale y dale," were greeted with enthusiasm and often roused the throng into particularly exuberant displays, the foot stomping, hand clapping, and cheers of elation continuing well after the final beat of the song. In sum, the scene at this time can best be described as festive and chaotic, the atmosphere charged with an air of intense "play," in which feelings of general camaraderie and mutual solidarity were given full expression.

The signal for the end of the dance was abrupt and usually unvarying. Beto would make his well-practiced farewell announcement over the microphone:

Damas y caballeros, con la siguiente selección se da por terminado el baile de esta noche. Se despide de Uds. la orquesta de un servidor, Beto García y Sus G. G.'s. Esperamos que nuestra de música haya sido de su completo agrado, y hasta la próxima. No se les olvide que todavía hay muy buen menudo; no se vayan con hambre. Hasta la próxima vez, que Dios los bendiga y manejen con cuidado. Good night everyone and we'll see you next time . . . [Singing] Échale un cinco al piano y que siga el vacilón . . .

(Ladies and gentlemen, the following song marks the end of tonight's dance. Always at your service, the band of Beto García bids you farewell. We hope you have enjoyed our music, and we will see you next time. Don't forget, there is still some good *menudo* left; don't leave hungry. Until next time, may God bless you, and drive carefully. Good night everyone, and we'll see you next time. [Singing] Échale un cinco al piano y que siga vacilón . . .)

With this introduction the band then struck up a *despedida* (farewell) medley of the *canción corrida* (polka) "Échale un cinco al piano" and the *cumbia* "La bala," two songs that Beto and the band had selected as appropriate to mark the end of the dance. The choice of these two songs merits some comment.

Like other aspects of the Saturday night dance, the musical selection was a dynamic process that evolved over the ten-year period. Thus, in the course of time some songs were discarded while new ones (or new arrangements of old ones) were added. As part of his efforts to find the most effective way to reach his audience, Beto had finally settled on this *despedida*, which in the last five years became, like the introductory set, a fixed part of the musical order. But it so happened that the celebration as has been described here reached its own maturity, or fell into place, so to speak, during the same period. We can suggest that this complementarity demonstrated how both performers and audience had been striving for a form that best captured the "quintessence," to borrow a term from Blacking, of the group's "socio-conceptual structure" (Blacking, 1974: 82). Furthermore, as Blacking again states, "Like ritual, music condenses a range of patterns of culture in a more concentrated fashion than daily social intercourse" (1974:75). In the immediate context, the final choice of farewell song that emerged out of the repertory (as well as other songs already mentioned) was a factor in the realization of the "perfect" ritual/music whole—one that captured in symbol, if not in word, the group's search for a satisfying collective expression.

Let me dwell further on this essential function of the *despedida* within the dance setting. We need to keep in mind that the hour of intense celebration extended to the very limits of the framed play period (see the schematic sequence on page 425). With only ten minutes or less to negotiate the change from chaos to order, a smooth transition was next to impossible. In "real" time this should have been simple to accomplish (the "goodnight" speech being enough), but in the symbolic time that operated here some sort of gearing-down mechanism seemed necessary. The polka/*cumbia* medley emerged as the ideal solution. But, in actuality, it was more of a mediator than a solution: in its combination of two disparate dance genres and in the awkwardness that necessarily marked the change from one rhythm to the other—the band literally had to stop for a fraction of a second—the music paralleled the emotional "hump" that was felt in such an abrupt switch from *communitas* to everyday structure. Thus, by experiencing the "braking" effects that the stop-and-go change from *cumbia* to polka produced, the dancers were literally jarred out of their festive flow and into the finale proper. None of this was ever consciously thought out, of course, but in due time the participants came to realize that this was an appropriate conclusion to the dance, and, as I will point out, it seemed to be an esthetically satisfying (if ritually protested) way to round out the celebration.

In addition to the polka/*cumbia* combination, the *despedida* medley, repeated as it was at every dance, consisted of a well-recognized gimmick that everyone had heard many times before but that never failed to elicit the same response. After polka and *cumbia* were played perhaps twice, the *cumbia* ("La bala") succeeded as the final selection. That

song was then repeatedly "ended," only to have Beto shout over the microphone, "¿Ya se cansaron?" (Are you tired yet?), whereupon the crowd, in unison, would respond with a loud "No!" After pausing a few seconds Beto would then begin the refrain again: ". . . A bailar la bala, . . ." This little sequence would be repeated perhaps two or three times, until Beto would once more cry out, "¿Ya se cansaron?" After another resounding "No!" he would answer in a resigned and falling voice, "Los músicos sí" (The musicians are). And after a loud collective groan the lights in the hall, which were always dimmed at the beginning, were turned back on again.

At this juncture the dance quickly came to its denouement, the final transition having been effected by the *despedida*. It was remarkable how the din that had just recently reached its peak was now replaced by a sobering quiet, as people prepared to "call it a night." Some couples would then start to file out, while saying their adieus. Others, who had not done so during the dance, stayed long enough to take in a quick serving of *menudo, para evitar la cruda* (to avoid a hangover), as was common knowledge. On the bandstand the tired musicians performed their last act: dismantling the electronic sound gear in preparation for loading. Within a half hour or so, the hall was almost empty. Only Beto and a handful of the organizers remained, *arreglando cuentas* (settling accounts) over a last drink, while the rest of the band members loaded and waited to be paid.

CONCLUDING REMARKS

In drawing analytic conclusions about the Chicano Saturday night dance, we must recognize the symbolic significance of several elements, particularly as these elements contributed to the overall meaning of the dance as a kind of rite of intensification. For it is in the combination of these elements that the dance emerged as a structured whole with its own functional significance. To illustrate what I mean, I would suggest, first, that some of these elements constituted a spatial paradigm with functions that gave definition to and imparted "loaded" information about the dance. Secondly, the temporal sequence of the dance constituted another paradigm in itself, evincing an import comparable to that of Ndembu ritual activity described by Turner (1969) in terms of structure and antistructure, albeit this was ritualized play, not ceremonial ritual. Thus, the progression of the dance, divided into definable phases (from an orderly, restrained entry to a chaotic, spontaneous celebration, and finally to a fixed, ordered conclusion) may be equated with structure, antistructure (*communitas*), and restructure, the sum of all elements, that is, the whole event, forming a rite of intensification.

It is clear that in coming together at a certain time and under specific conditions the group manifested a tacit need and desire to engage in a joint esthetic endeavor. Moreover, this endeavor, marked as it was by highly selective, expressive behavior, must clearly be seen as symbolically motivated. How else can we interpret the choice of Chicano music and dance, which by their uniqueness lend identity to the group? Or the choice of *menudo*, a native food with strong Mexican identification? And we must consider as well the choice of mutual co-participants, that is, fellow Chicanos. All of these cannot but be considered as highly purposeful. For what we witnessed here was a group of people, whose cultural heritage has often been disparaged,[9] coming together and through patterned, redundant, and meaningful communicative behavior bringing about the perpetuation of "orders of action to which the individual [had] been trained" (Chapple and Coon, 1942: 508). That is to say that through the enactment of this rite of intensification the group's threatened values and traditions were validated and their collective self-image reinforced.

Speaking of musical behavior among the Yoruba, Nketia says, "For the Yoruba in Accra, performances of Yoruba music . . . bring both the satisfaction of participating in something familiar and the assurance of belonging to a group sharing in similar values, similar ways of life, a group maintaining similar art forms. Music thus brings a renewal of tribal solidarity" (quoted in Merriam, 1964:226). Considering that Chicanos as a group have never enjoyed full access to American traditions, this kind of assessment is eminently applicable to the dance that I have been describing, particularly with respect to the renewal of group solidarity.

Let me elaborate on the concepts of structure and antistructure. The social group of Chicano dancers, belonging in ordinary life to a hierarchic social structure that has been shown to be hostile to Chicanos generally,[10] enacted this frequent (sometimes

weekly) rite in a manner that suggests a rite of passage, although, as I have indicated, rite of intensification seems a more appropriate description. In real and symbolic ways the frame of play activity marked by the gate itself, the admission fee (a symbolic token of initiation), the chain of cars parked around the building—all of these constituted a "threshold" through which the people were transported from the outer hierarchic, structured, and Anglo-dominated world into a "new reality," where, in the course of the dance, everyone shed his customary social status and entered into a shared state of *communitas*, born of a common sociocultural identity and a more or less shared (if not actually acknowledged) sense of alienation from the dominant American culture. In the predetermined breakdown of established structure that ensued within the dance setting, that is in the progression from orderly, restrained interaction to chaotic celebration, a spirit of *communitas* prevailed, in which all the people contributed to and partook of a strongly Chicano *ambiente*.

This is why the music of Beto García was so important, for in the mode of delivery that marked this uniquely Chicano musical style and its repertory of songs that evoked a concrete cultural history, the performers and audience created an ephemeral but binding Chicano reality, a strong bond based on commonality, "homogeneity and comradeship" (Turner, 1969: 96). This is also why *menudo* was prepared. It was symbolic of the group's social communion; no other food could have served as well. Lastly, this is why other dances in American society could not be ritual in the same way that these events were, for it was that very society that the assembled group was symbolically negating.

At these moments, then, within these dances we could witness what Turner has described as ". . . 'a moment in and out of time,' and in and out of secular social structure, which reveals, however fleetingly, some recognition (in symbol if not always in language) of a generalized social bond that has ceased to be and has simultaneously yet to be fragmented into a multiplicity of structural ties" (1969: 96). And the "emptiness at the center" that was created as people revolved in a counterclockwise direction while dancing the polka perhaps aptly symbolized the antistructure of this Saturday night Community that moved toward one goal, "a flowing from *I* to *Thou*"(Turner, 1969: 127).

Finally, it was in the combination of all the symbolic elements that constituted the dance and the transcendent spirit of shared exuberant celebration that the rite of intensification was enacted, ultimately accomplishing the reintegration and reinvigoration of the group's sociocultural identity. As Turner, again, puts it, "in rites de passage [in this case intensification] men are released from structure into communitas only to return to structure revitalized by their experience of communitas" (1969: 129). And so it was that the abrupt order reintroduced by the *despedida* at the end of the dance sent the revelers out into the night and to their respective statuses in structured Anglo society, their sense of identity reaffirmed by their renewed communion with fellow Chicanos. They would return to the dance again and again.

A STRUCTURAL REPRESENTATION

To round out the analysis I propose the following schematic representation [see p. 425] to categorize the various significant features of the dance. Somewhat in the structuralist fashion of Lévi-Strauss, I have set up paradigmatic (spatial) and syntagmatic (temporal) axes to designate significant constituent units, as these contributed to either the spatial or the temporal orders of the dance-as-ritual. Thus, aligned with the temporal axis are the sequential "phases" of the dance. The axis is, at the same time, a continuum, because, although junctures were temporally contiguous (music-intermission-music), the progression structure-*communitas*-structure was a continuous development. The elements on the spatial axis may be seen to mesh with the temporal, but their function was more readily metaphoric, that is, symbolic, than the temporal elements, which were more metonymic (cf. Leach, 1977: 12–13). But ultimately the division is a heuristic construct, not a hard and fast one; some elements evinced functions of both domains (e.g., intermissions did more than signify a break in the activity). Nonetheless, the schema will help to integrate (mainly) metaphoric and (mainly) metonymic elements as these combined to create a meaningful holistic structure.

NOTES

1. In this paper I use the terms *Chicano, Mexican American,* and *mexicano* interchangeably, although the first of these has achieved an increasing degree of political connotation and some controversy (cf. Limón, 1979).

2. A thorough musical analysis of Beto García and the *orquesta tejana* (also called "Tex-Mex") style is beyond the objectives of this paper (see Discography for selected samples). Made popular in the 1940s (but having a predecessor in the *orquesta típica*) by such commercial *orquestas* as that of Beto Villa, the style has become quite standardized in recent years, taking into consideration, of course, influences and changes that continue to occur. Originally showing affinities with such American bands as Tommy Dorsey, Glenn Miller, etc., *orquestas* have, for significant reasons that I believe are in reaction to the social, cultural, economic, and political domination of Chicanos, developed their own stylistic idiosyncracies (e.g., the "Chicanoization" of the polka) that are more attuned to the social realities and esthetic outlook of the people.

3. Insofar as this paper deals with the dance as a Chicano tradition (as distinguished from the greater Mexican tradition), the term "Chicanoized" seems more apt. The *orquesta* style of musical performance is virtually nonexistent south of the border, except for occasional and conspicuous borrowing by such Mexican groups as "Los Babys."

4. For a more comprehensive discussion of Chicano social and political organizations and their role in the integration of Chicanos, see Meier and Rivera (1972: chapter 14); for *el movimiento,* see F. Chris García (1974: chapter 1).

5. The relationship between *conjunto,* or *norteño,* music and *orquesta* has been an interesting one, reflecting class conflicts and accommodation among Chicanos, especially in Texas. The two styles have maintained a close, symbiotic relationship, tending strongly toward convergence in recent years. I am convinced that the same social forces that engendered the ritual character of the Saturday night dance are at work in the increasing convergence of these two musical styles indigenous to the Mexicans in the Southwest. In trying to mediate between the two, Alonso demonstrated his tacit awareness of that convergence.

6. A *canción corrida* (literally a "running song") is, in simple terms, a lyric composition (often a *ranchera*) sung to the $\frac{2}{4}$ beat of the *orquesta* polka. Not to be confused with a *corrido* (though Beto sang that in *tempo di polka* also), which is a ballad (see below), a *canción corrida,* or simply *corrida,* was referred to thusly by the people of Fresno because of the linguistic association that *correr* (to run) has with fast, i.e., polka music. Thus people would come up and ask for *una corridita,* snapping their fingers to indicate a polka beat.

7. See Mendoza (1964) for a formal analysis of the *corrido*. For the role of one hero *corrido* in the Chicano vs. Anglo conflict see Paredes (1958); for a broader treatment of the theme of intercultural conflict in *corridos* see Paredes (1976).

Phase I (9:00–10:40) : Structure
Entry and beginning of dance: first intermission

Phase II (11:00–11:50) : Transition
Third hour of dance: second intermission; decreasing order (structure)

Phase III (12:05–12:50) : *Communitas*
Total dissolution of structure

Phase IV (12:50–1:00) : Transition
"La despedida"

Phase V (1:00–1:30) : Re-Structure
End of dance; exit

TEMPORAL ELEMENTS

The hall—marked framed area of play (threshold)
Table arrangements—same as above
"Chain of cars"—same as hall and table arrangements
Dance floor—center of play activity
Mode of dress—formally defined event as "play"
Musicians' garb—defined them as celebrants, or secular "shamans"
Mode of entry—stressed structure
Admission fee—initiation token
Liquor—symbolic of social communion
Menudo—communal food; established cultural identity
Dimmed lights—intimate atmosphere; blurred perception (structure)
Choice of musicians—defined identity of the event (Chicano)
Musical selection—same as choice of musicians; evoked Chicano
    ambiente, cues to set sequential activities in motion
Gritos—a feature of *canciones rancheras*; expressed *lo mexicano*
Bandstand, electronic gear—analogous to religious altar,
    "lugar de respeto"

SPATIAL ELEMENTS

8. A *ranchera* song (from *rancho*: ranch) is a lyric composition that, by long association, evokes rural, pastoral settings. In contrast to urban, sophisticated music associated with large orchestras, including symphonic ones, people in Fresno and elsewhere link *rancheras* with the simple, unencumbered life of the common folk. *Rancheras* are consequently devoid of intricate harmonies, are generally played in a slow $\frac{6}{8}$ or $\frac{3}{4}$ time, and are commonly seen as most at home when played by *ranchero* groups—the mariachi in Mexico and the *conjunto de acordeón* in the United States. *Orquesta* groups play them too but often rework them into the ubiquitous polka tempo, thereby stripping them of their *ranchero* flavor.

9. For disparaging views of Mexicans in the nineteenth century see, for example, Robinson (1963); for a twentieth-century attitude see Webb (1935). See also the works of American social scientist Rubel (1966), Madsen (1964), Saunders (1954), and Heller (1968) and the scathing criticism of their work by Romano (1968). Biased, negative views are abundant in many areas of American popular culture, e.g., television's "Frito Bandito," which emphasizes lawlessness, and the roll-on deodorant ad, which emphasizes dirtiness. Accounts of racial/cultural prejudice and violence against Chicanos are legion, but see, for example, Valdez and Steiner (1972: 175–176), McWilliams (1968: chapters 12 and 13), . . .

10. Adequate discussion of the historical sources of this hostility which stems principally from the Mexican American War, is impractical here. Ample material already exists. For a sensitive (if dated) historical account of Chicanos' plight in the Southwest see McWilliams (1968); Acuña (1972) looks at the history of Anglo/Chicano relations from a colonizer/colonized perspective. See also Galarza (1964), and for a suggestive perspective and periodic bibliography with criticism see Gómez-Quiñones (1971).

DISCOGRAPHY

This list of commercial *orquesta* recordings is a sampling of selections from the most outstanding performers since Beto Villa. It is not an exhaustive one, by any means. For a comparison between these *orquestas* and their precursor, *la orquesta tipica*, see the readily available Arhoolie album listed first below.

PERFORMER	LABEL AND NUMBER	PERFORMER	LABEL AND NUMBER
Various: *Texas-Mexican Border Music: The String Bands*, v. 5 (Chris Strachwitz, ed.)	Arhoolie: 9007 (LP)	———— (y La Familia)	Buena Suerte Records: BSR-1038 (LP)
Beto Villa y su orquesta	Ideal: 475A&B (78) Ideal: ILP 104 (LP) Ideal: 777A&B (78)	Sunny Ozuna and the Sunliners	Leona Records: LRC 019 Teardrop: LPM 2003 (LP) Key-Loc: KL 3010 Key-Loc: 3028
Balde Gonzáles y su orquesta	RCA Victor: 235779 (78) Ideal: 695A&B (78) Melco: 3950-1A&B (78)	Augustine Ramírez y su orquesta	Freddie: LP 1095 (LP) Freddie: FR 1066 (LP)
Isidro López y su orquesta	Ideal: ILP 115 (LP) Ideal: 1582A&B (78) Torero: TO-116 (78)	Joe Bravo	Freddie: LP 1085 (LP)
Little Joe (and the Latinaires)	El Zarape: 1002 (LP)	Jimmy Edward	Texas Best Records: TXB–LP–1001 (LP)

BIBLIOGRAPHY

Acuña, Rodolfo. 1972. *Occupied America*. San Francisco: Canfield Press.

Barth, Fredrik. 1969. *Ethnic Groups and Boundaries*. Boston: Little Brown and Co.

Bateson, Gregory. 1972. *Steps to an Ecology of Mind*. San Francisco: Chandler Publishing Co.

Bauman, Richard. 1972. "Differential Identity and the Social Base of Folklore." In *Toward New Perspectives in Folklore*, edited by Américo Paredes and Richard Bauman. Austin: University of Texas Press.

Blacking, John. 1973. *How Musical Is Man?* Seattle: University of Washington Press.

————. 1974. "Ethnomusicology as a Key Subject in the Social Sciences." *In Memoriam, Antonio Jorge Dias*. Lisbon: Instituto de Alta Cultura.

Chapple, Eliot, and Carleton S. Coon. 1942. *Principles of Anthropology*. New York: Holt.

Galarza, Ernesto. 1964. *Merchants of Labor*. Santa Barbara, Calif: McNally and Loftin.

García, F. Chris. 1974. *La Causa Politica: A Chicano Politics Reader*, Notre Dame, Indiana: University of Notre Dame Press.

Gómez-Quiñones, Juan. 1971. "Toward a Perspective on Chicano History" *Aztlan* 2 (1971): 1–49.

Heller, Celia S. 1968. *Mexican-American Youth: Forgotten Youth at the Crossroads*. New York: Random House.

Keil, Charles. 1966. *Urban Blues*. Chicago: University of Chicago Press.

Leach, Edmund. 1972. "Ritualization in Man in Relation to Conception and Social Development." In *Reader in Comparative Religion*, edited by William A. Lessa and Evon Z. Vogt, pp. 333–337. New York: Harper and Row.

———. 1977. *Culture and Communication*. London: Cambridge University Press.

Limón, José. 1977. "Texas Mexican Popular Music and Dancing: Symbological Interpretation." Unpublished essay.

———. 1979. "The Folk Performance of *Chicano* and the Cultural Limits of Political Ideology." In press.

Madsen, William. 1964. *Mexican Americans of South Texas*. New York: Holt, Rinehart and Winston.

McWilliams, Carey. 1968. *North from Mexico*. New York: Greenwood Press.

Meier, Matt S., and Feliciano Rivera. 1972. *The Chicanos*. New York: Hill and Wang.

Mendoza, Vicente T. 1964. *Lirica narrativa de México: El corrido*. México, D. F.: Fondo de Cultura Económica.

Merriam, Alan. 1964. *The Anthropology of Music*. Evanston, Illinois: Northwestern University Press.

Paredes, Américo. 1958. *With His Pistol in His Hand*. Austin: University of Texas Press.

———. 1976. *A Texas-Mexican Cancionero*. Urbana: University of Illinois Press.

———. 1977. "On Ethnographic Work among Minority Groups: A Folklorist's Perspective." *New Scholar* 6: 1–32.

Paz, Octavio. 1961. *The Labyrinth of Solitude*. New York: Grove Press.

Robinson, Cecil. 1963. *With the Ears of Strangers: The Mexican in American Literature*. Tucson: University of Arizona Press.

Romano, Octavio. 1968. "The Anthropology and Sociology of Mexican Americans: The Distortion of Mexican-American History." *El Grito* 1: 13–26.

Rubel, Arthur J. 1966. *Across the Tracks: Mexican Americans in a Texas City*. Austin: University of Texas Press.

Saunders, Lyle. 1954. *Cultural Difference and Medical Care: The Case of Spanish-Speaking People of the Southwest*. New York: Russell Sage Foundation.

Turner, Victor. 1969. *The Ritual Process*. Chicago: University of Chicago Press.

Valdez, Luis, and Stan Steiner, eds. 1972. *Aztlan: An Anthology of Mexican American Literature*. New York: Vintage Books.

Van Gennep, Arnold. 1960. *The Rites of Passage*. Chicago: University of Chicago Press.

Webb, Walter Prescott. 1935. *The Texas Rangers*. Cambridge: Houghton Mifflin Co.

The Obvious Aspects of Ritual

ROY A. RAPPAPORT

Facts of publication: *Rappaport, Roy A. 1979, "The Obvious Aspects of Ritual," from* Ecology, Meaning, and Religion, *175–180, 188–195, 197–200, 208–214, 216–221. Berkeley, CA: North Atlantic. Copyright © 1979 by Roy A. Rappaport. Reprinted with the permission of North Atlantic Books.*

Known primarily as an ecological anthropologist, Roy Rappaport here proposes a largely formal theory of ritual. It defines liturgy in terms of its most conservative, or canonical, aspects. Consequently, liturgical theologians have become keenly interested in his theory. Although not a linguistic theory as such, much of Rappaport's view concentrates on the linguistic dimensions of ritual. For instance, for him sanctity is a quality of discourse, specifically the quality of unquestionability. Offering a very strict, succinct definition of liturgy, Rappaport argues the controversial thesis that sanctity itself is a product of ritual.

Regarding ecology and ritual see Rappaport's Pigs for the Ancestors: Ritual in the Ecology of a New Guinea People, *2nd edition (New Haven, CT: Yale University Press, 1984).*

About the author: Dates: *1926–　, NY, U.S.A.* **Education:** *B.S., Cornell University; Ph.D., Columbia*

University. **Field(s):** *religion; ritual; ecology; Melanesia.* **Career:** *University of Michigan, 1965–present (Chairperson, 1975–1980; Director, Program on Studies in Religion, 1991–present).* **Publications:** Ecology, Meaning, and Religion *(North Atlantic Books, 1979);* Pigs for the Ancestors *(Yale University, 1984); "Ritual, Time and Eternity,"* Zygon *27 (1992): 5–30; "Veracity, Verity and Verum in Liturgy,"* Studia Liturgica *23 (1993): 35–50; "Logos, Liturgy and the Evolution of Humanity," in Andrew Bartlet, and others, eds.,* Fortunate the Eyes That See: Essays in Honor of David Noel Freedman *(Eerdmans, 1994).* **Additional:** *President, American Anthropological Association, 1987–1989; Fellow, American Academy of Arts and Sciences, 1990; Appointed Mary and Charles Walgreen Jr. Professor for the Study of Human Understanding, 1991; Distinguished Lecturer, General Division American Anthropological Association, 1992.*

I take ritual to be a form or structure, defining it as the performance of more or less invariant sequences of formal acts and utterances not encoded by the performers. I shall be concerned to unpack the implications of this definition, noting first that no single feature of ritual is peculiar to it. It is in the conjunction of its features that it is unique. It is, nevertheless, convenient to consider its simple features at the beginning. The unique implications of their concatenation will emerge later.

First there is formality. Formality is an obvious aspect of all rituals: both observers and actors identify acts as ritual in part by their formality. Rituals tend to be stylized, repetitive, stereotyped, often but not always decorous, and they also tend to occur at special places and at times fixed by the clock, calendar, or specified circumstances.

There are problems in distinguishing some events from others by the criterion of formality because events are not easily discriminated into those that are formal and those that are not. There is, as Roger Abrahams (1973) has pointed out, a continuum of behavioral formality from (*a*) the formal words and gestures that intersperse ordinary conversation and acts, through (*b*) that of the "everyday ceremoniousness" of greeting behavior and formal expressions of deference and demeanor, through (*c*) the rather invariant procedures of, say, the courtroom within which the variant substance of litigation is contained, and through which it is presented in orderly fashion, through, next, (*d*) such events as coronations, in which the invariant aspects of the event begin to predominate over the variant, to, finally, (*e*) highly invariant events, like those of certain religious liturgies in which almost all of the performance is specified, and opportunities for variation are both few and narrowly defined.

Two points are to be noted. First, invariance emerges out of, or is an aspect of, increasing formality. Second, it may be useful to make a distinction between *ritual*, the formal, stereotyped *aspect* of all events, and *rituals*, relatively invariant *events* dominated by formality. Be this as it may, there is little value in separating rituals from other events by imposing an arbitrary discontinuity upon the continuum of formality at any particular point. I will simply note that the phenomena with which this essay is largely concerned lie toward the more formal, less variant end of the continuum. We shall be mainly concerned with rituals sufficiently elaborate to include what may be called "liturgical orders," more or less invariant sequences of formal acts and utterances repeated in specified contexts. The term "liturgical order" will, however, be extended here to include not only the fixed sequences of words and acts providing form to individual ritual events, but also, following Van Gennep (1909), to the fixed sequences of rituals that lead men around circles of seasons, along the straight paths that depart from birth and arrive at death, through the alterations of war and peace or along the dream tracks that cross Australian deserts.

While ritual is characterized by its formality, all that is formal, stereotyped, repetitive, or decorous is not ritual. Certain decorative art is similarly formal, and so are many buildings. It is of importance to recognize, although it seems banal, that performance as well as formality is necessary to ritual. Performance is the second *sine qua non* of ritual, for if there is no performance there is no ritual. This is not simply to say that a ritual is not a book or myth or television set, but to emphasize that performance is not merely a way to express something, but is itself an aspect of that which it is expressing.

Of course, not all formal performance is ritual. Ordinary usage would not so have it, and there is no analytic advantage here in violating ordinary usage. For instance, although they bear some resemblance to each other, ritual and drama, at least in their polar forms, are best distinguished. For one thing, dramas have audiences, rituals have congregations. An audience watches a drama, a congregation participates in a ritual. This participation often if not always requires more than the entertainment of a certain attitude. Participation is frequently active, and is likely to require of the members of a congregation that they sing, dance, stand, kneel, or respond in litanies at particular times. For another thing, those who act in drama are "only acting," which is precisely to say that they are not acting in earnest, and it is perhaps significant that drama's synonym in English is "play." Ritual in contrast, is in earnest, even when it is playful, entertaining, blasphemous, humorous, or ludicrous.

To say that ritual is in earnest is not to say that the formal action of ritual is instrumental in any ordinary physical sense. Indeed, another of ritual's criterial attributes—at least one proposed by many people—is that it is not. There seem to be two main lines of thought concerning this.

The first, clearly enunciated by Leach long ago (1954: 12ff.), implies the distinction already made between ritual and rituals. Ritual in this view is the non-instrumental aspect or component of events that may also include an instrumental component, "technique." Ritual is that frill or decoration that communicates something about the performance or the performer.

The other general view, which initially appears to be more different from the first than it actually is, would hold that ritual not only communicates something but is taken by those performing it to be "doing something" as well. There would seem to be support for this position from some of the words designating ritual in various languages. The Greek "dromenon" means "thing done," "liturgy" comes from the Greek for "public work," the English term "service" connotes more than talk; the Tewa Indians (Ortiz 1969: 98ff.), as well as the Tikopians (Firth 1940) refer to some rituals as "spirit work." However, that which is done by ritual is not done by operating with matter and energy on matter and

energy in accordance with the laws of physics, chemistry, or biology. The efficacy of ritual derives, to use a term that Fortes (1966) favors in a rather general way, from "the occult." The occult differs from "the patent" in that the patent can be known in the last resort by sensory experience, and it conforms to the regularities of material cause. The occult cannot be so known and does not so conform. Goody (1961) similarly characterizes ritual as "a category of standardized behaviour (custom) in which the relationship between means and ends is not intrinsic." . . .

* * *

There seem to be two broad classes of messages transmitted in ritual. First, whatever else may happen in some human rituals, in all rituals, both human and animal, the participants transmit information concerning their own current physical, psychic, or sometimes social states to themselves and to other participants. As Leach put it, ritual "serves to express the individual's status in the structural system in which he finds himself for the time being" (1954: 11). I shall, with some misgiving, follow Lyons (1970: 73) and refer to these transmissions as "indexical" transmissions, and to this information as "indexical."

In perhaps all animal rituals, and in some human rituals too, this is all there is. When one baboon presents his rump to another he is signaling submission; when the other mounts he signals dominance. The information content of the ritual is exhausted by the messages concerning their current states being transmitted by the participants. The ritual is only indexical.

But some human rituals are different, for in them the sum of the messages originating among and transmitted among the participants concerning their own contemporary states is not coextensive with the information content (using the term information in a broad sense) of the ritual. Additional messages, although transmitted by the participants, are not encoded by them. They are found by participants already encoded in the liturgy. Since these messages are more or less invariant obviously they cannot in themselves reflect the transmitter's contemporary state. For instance, the order of the Roman mass does not, in itself, express anything about the current states of those performing it. In recognition of the regularity, propriety, and apparent durability and immutability of these messages I shall refer to them as "canonical." Whereas that which is signified by the indexical is confined to the here and now, the referents of the canonical are not. They always make references to processes or entities, material or putative, outside the ritual, in words and acts that have, by definition, been spoken or performed before. Whereas the indexical is concerned with the immediate the canonical is concerned with the enduring. Indeed, its quality of perdurance is perhaps signified—its sense is surely conveyed—by the apparent invariance of the liturgy in which it is expressed.

. . . One of ritual's most salient characteristics is that it is not entirely symbolic. Since the term "symbol" is used in several ways in the literature it is important that I make clear that I am conforming to Peirce's (1960: 143ff.) tripartite classification of signs into *symbols, icons,* and *indices.* In this usage a symbol is merely "associated by law" or convention with that which it signifies. The word "dog" is a symbol designating a certain sort or class of creatures. Words are the fundamental, but not the only, symbols; for objects, marks, nonverbal sounds, gestures, movements may be assigned symbolic meaning by words. The virtues of symbolic communication are patent. With symbols discourse can escape from the here and now to dwell upon the past, future, distant, hypothetical, and imaginary, and with a complex symbolic system, such as a natural language, an unlimited variety of messages may be encoded through the orderly recombination of a small number of basic units. Although a few other species may make very limited use of symbols, symbolic communication is characteristic of the human species, and has made possible for men a way of life so different from that of other animals that some anthropologists would compare the emergence of the symbol in importance and novelty only to the emergence of life itself.

In contrast to symbols, *icons* by definition share sensible formal characteristics with that which they signify. A map is an icon of the area to which it corresponds, and many of what are called symbols in other usages are, in this terminology, iconic. A "phallic symbol," for instance, is an icon. In contrast to both symbols and icons, *indices* are, to use

Peirce's phrase, "really affected by" that which they signify. A rash is an index of measles, a dark cloud of rain. An index is caused by, or is part of, that which it indicates; in the extreme case it is identical with it.

Canonical messages, which are concerned with things not present and often not even material, are, and *can only be,* founded upon symbols, although they can employ, secondarily, icons and may even make limited use of indices. On the other hand, information concerning the current state of the transmitter may transcend mere symbolic designation and be signified indexically. It is for this reason that I refer to such information as "indexical." . . .

* * *

. . . It is from the canonical content of liturgy that are drawn the categories that give meaning to whatever indexical messages are transmitted. We come, this is to say, to the relationship of the indexical to the canonical. It is a complex relationship that I wish to address at first by [considering] an indexical message. . . .

By dancing at a *kaiko* a Maring man signals his pledge to help his hosts in warfare. Dancing signals a pledge because it is itself a pledging. As such . . . it indicates rather than merely symbolizes the pledge with which it is "identified," i.e., made identical. Now I wish to emphasize that "to pledge" is not merely to say something but to do something. A pledge is an act.

Ritual is full of conventional utterances which achieve conventional effects. "I name this ship the Queen Elizabeth." "We declare war." "I dub thee to knighthood." "I swear to tell the truth." "I promise to support you." "We find the defendant guilty." "I apologize." In all of these instances, we would agree, the speaker is not simply saying something but doing something, and what he is doing—achieving a conventional effect through some sort of conventional procedure—cannot be done by the application of matter and energy to some object in accordance with the laws of physics, chemistry, or biology.

The importance of such utterances in the conduct of human affairs is so patent as to obviate any need for comment, but philosophers have, in the last two decades especially, given considerable attention to their peculiar characteristics. J. L. Austin (1962) has called them "performative utterances" and "illocutionary acts"; J. R. Searle (1969) includes them among what he calls "speech acts"; F. O'Doherty (1973a) refers to an important subclass as "factitive" acts or utterances; J. Skorupski (1976) uses the term "operative acts" for a class resembling them closely.

It is important to note that the efficacy of what I shall, following Austin's earlier and simpler terminology, call "performatives" is not in the persuasive effect of these utterances upon others. If authorized persons declare peace in a proper manner peace is *declared*, whether or not the antagonists are persuaded to act accordingly. This is not to say that performative utterances may not be persuasive. They often have, to use Austin's terms, "perlocutionary" as well as "illocutionary" force. But an action of some sort (beyond the obvious act of producing sounds, or even meaningful sounds) is completed in the performative gesture or utterance itself. Performatives of course differ in the scope of the action they complete. Thus, if I am authorized to do so and name this ship the Queen Elizabeth, this ship is so named, and that is really all there is to it. You may call it "Hortense" if you like, but its name happens to be Queen Elizabeth (Austin 1962: 99 passim). On the other hand, if I have danced at your *kaiko*, thereby promising to help you in warfare, that is not all there is to it, for it remains for me to fulfill my promise, and I may fail to do so. Following O'Doherty, we may say that the naming, which not only constitutes an action but actually brings into being the state of affairs with which it is concerned, is not simply performative, but "factitive" as well. Whereas many actions completed in ritual—dubbings, declarations of peace, marriages, purification—are factitive, it is obvious that *all* are not. Some—among them are those Austin called "commissives" (1962: 150ff.)—do not bring into being the states of affairs with which they are concerned, but merely commit those performing them to do so sometime in the future.

While many liturgies are performative, while some sort of performative act is the main point of the performance, transforming war into peace, restoring purity to that which has been polluted, joining men and women in wedlock, performativeness is not confined to ritual. There is no advantage to be gained, for instance, in taking to be ritual the publican's utterance "The bar is closed." But when he says "the bar is closed" it is thereby closed, and we may as well go home. Performatives are not confined to ritual, but

it may be suggested that there is a special relationship between ritual and performativeness.

First, the formal characteristics of ritual enhance the chances of success of the performatives they include. Like any other acts performatives can fail. If, for instance, I were to dub one of my junior colleagues knight of the garter he would not thereby become a knight of the garter, even if the conduct of the ritual were letter-perfect. Conversely, if Queen Elizabeth dubbed Princess Anne's horse to knighthood it probably wouldn't make him a knight. And if a befuddled cleric recited the service for the dead rather than the marriage liturgy it is doubtful if the couple standing before him would thereby be married or become objects of mourning (Austin 1962: passim). All of these instances of faulty performatives are of ritual performatives, and ritual performatives can fail, but the ludicrous nature of these instances suggests that they are less likely to fail than other performatives. The formality of liturgical orders helps to ensure that whatever performatives they may incorporate are performed by authorized people with respect to eligible persons or entities under proper circumstances in accordance with proper procedures. Moreover, the formality of ritual makes very clear and explicit what it is that is being done. For instance, if one Maring casually said to another whom he happened to be visiting, "I'll help you when next you go to war," it would not be clear whether this was to be taken as a vague statement of intent, as a prediction of what he would be likely to do, or as a promise, nor would it necessarily be clear what might be meant by "help." To dance this message in a ritual, however, makes it clear to all concerned that a pledge to help is undertaken, and that that help entails fighting. Ritual, this is to say, not only ensures the correctness of the performative enactment; it also makes the performatives it carries explicit, and it generally makes them weighty as well. If a message is communicated by participation in ritual it is in its nature not vague. Moreover, there is no point in mobilizing the formality, decorum, and solemnity of ritual to communicate messages that are of no importance or gravity. Promises are often communicated in ritual, but vague statements of intent seldom if ever are.

I shall only mention two other closely related reasons for considering the performativeness of ritual here. First, the association of the sacred or occult (I do not take them to be synonymous) with performatives in magical and religious rituals may hide their conventional nature from the actors, and this obviously may enhance their chances of success. To take the state of affairs established by a king's enthronement to derive from the sacramental virtue of crown and chrism is perhaps more effective with respect to the maintenance of the order of which the king is a part than would be the recognition of enthronement as a naked performative. Second, as Ruth Finnigan (1969: 550) has suggested, albeit rather unspecifically, the "truth lying behind" assumptions concerning what is often called "the magical power of words" may be related to their illocutionary force or performativeness. It may be proposed, rather more specifically, that the magical power of some of the words and acts forming part of liturgies derives from the factitive relationship between them and the conventional states of affairs with which they are concerned. Magical power may be attributed to yet other words by extension of the principle of factitiveness beyond the domain of the conventional in which it is effective into the domain of the physical, in which it is not. But it behooves us to be wary about stipulating the limits of what may in fact be effected by ritual acts. The efficacy of factitiveness may, after all, be augmented by the perlocutionary force of the acts in which the factitiveness inheres, and no one yet knows how far into physical processes perlocutionary force may penetrate. It does seem safe to say, however, that the efficacy of ritual may extend beyond the purely conventional and into the organic, for people do occasionally die of witchcraft or ensorcellment, and they are sometimes healed by faith. The magical efficacy of words may rest upon their perlocutionary force or persuasiveness as well as upon their factitiveness.

*   *   *

Perhaps the most important reason for considering the performativeness of rituals is, paradoxically, that certain rituals are not themselves obviously performative but may make performatives possible.

There seems to be more to some or even all liturgies than the performatives they incorporate, and some liturgies may not seem to include performatives in any simple sense at all. Many religious rituals do not seem to be directed toward achieving simple conventional effects through conventional procedures. Although simple performativeness is not criterial of ritual, something like it, but of higher order, is. We approach here the conjunction of formality and performance. . . . We come, this is to say, to what is implicit in the act of performing a liturgical order.

The term "liturgical order," we may be reminded here, refers both to the more or less invariant sequences of formal acts and utterances that comprise single rituals, and to the sequences of rituals that make up ritual cycles and series. "Order" is an especially appropriate term because these series of events constitute orders in several senses beyond the obvious one of sequence. They are also orders in the sense of organization, form, or regularity (synonymous with the meaning of "order" in such phrases as "the social order"). As such they constitute order, or maintain orderliness, in contrast to disorder, entropy, or chaos. They are, further, orders in that they are in some sense imperatives or directives.

Liturgical orders . . . must be performed. Without performance there is no ritual, no liturgical order. There are still extant in books outlines of liturgies performed in Ur and Luxor, but they are dead, for they are no longer given voice by men's breaths nor energy by their bodies. A liturgical order is an ordering of *acts* or *utterances*, and as such it is enlivened, realized, or established *only when* those acts are performed and those utterances voiced. We shall return to this shortly. The point to be made here is that this relationship of the act of performance to that which is being performed—that it brings it into being—cannot help but specify as well the relationship of the performer to that which he is performing. He is not merely transmitting messages he finds encoded in the liturgy. He is participating in—becoming part of—the order to which his own body and breath give life.

Since to perform a liturgical order, which is by definition a relatively *invariant* sequence of acts and utterances *encoded by someone other* than the performer himself, is to *conform* to it, authority or directive is *intrinsic* to liturgical order. However, the account just offered suggests something more intimate, and perhaps even more binding than whatever is connoted by terms like "authority" and "conformity." The notion of communication implies, minimally, transmitters, receivers, messages, and channels through which messages are carried from transmitters to receivers. Sometimes, moreover, as in the case of canonical messages, the senders or encoders of messages are separate from the transmitters. . . . A peculiarity of ritual communication [is] that in ritual the transmitters and receivers are often one and the same. At least the transmitter is always among the receivers. . . . Another of ritual's peculiarities [is that] the transmitter-receiver becomes fused with the message he is transmitting and receiving. In conforming to that which his performance brings into being, and which comes alive in its performance, he becomes indistinguishable from it, a part of it, for the time being. Since this is the case, for a performer to reject the canonical message encoded in a liturgical order that is being realized by his performance as he is participating in it seems to me to be a contradiction in terms, and thus impossible. This is to say that *by performing a liturgical order the performer accepts, and indicates to himself and to others that he accepts, whatever is encoded in the canons of the liturgical order in which he is participating*. This message of acceptance is the indexical message that is intrinsic to all liturgical performances, the indexical message without which liturgical orders and the canonical messages they encode are nonexistent or vacuous. It is not a trivial message because men are not bound to acceptance by their genotypes. They are often free not to participate in rituals if they do not care to, and refusal to participate is always a possibility, at least logically, conceivable by potential actors. Participation always rests in some degree upon choice.

We see here, incidentally, how myth and ritual differ in an important way: ritual specifies the relationship of the performer to what he is performing while myth does not. A myth can be recounted as an entertainment by a bard, as an edifying lesson for his children by a father, or as a set of oppositions by a structuralist, although it may be recited as doctrine by a priest to a novice. To recite a myth is not necessarily to accept it, and a myth survives as well on the printed page as it does on the tongues of living men.

We are led here back to the matter of performatives and to the assertion that while all ritual may not be performative, rituals make performatives possible. Austin (1962: 26ff.) listed six conditions that must be fulfilled if performatives are to come

off. These include such obvious stipulations as that they be performed by proper persons under proper circumstances. Now his first and most basic condition is that for conventional states of affairs to be achieved there must *exist accepted* conventional procedures for achieving them. They cannot be achieved without such conventions. If young men are to be transformed into knights there must be a procedure for doing so, and this procedure must be acceptable to the relevant public. The acceptance of a procedure for dubbing knights also obviously presupposes the existence of an accepted convention of knighthood. This stipulation is not vacuous, for it can be violated. For instance, it is unlikely that in the contemporary United States a slap of the glove across the cheek would ever result in a duel. The conventions of honor, of which this ritual action was a part, are no longer accepted. They no longer exist except in memory or history.

Although Austin stipulated as requisite to the effectiveness of performatives that the relevant conventions exist and be accepted, he gave no attention to the matter of how this prerequisite is fulfilled. I am arguing here that it is fulfilled by ritual. The performance of ritual establishes the existence of conventions and accepts them simultaneously and inextricably. Ritual performance is not in itself merely, nor even necessarily, factitive. It is not always performative in a simple way, merely bringing into being conventional states of affairs through conventional actions. It is, rather, *meta*-performative and *meta*-factitive, for it *establishes*, that is, it stipulates and accepts, the conventions in respect to which conventional states of affairs are defined and realized. The canons accepted in their performance may, of course, represent conventional understandings concerning nature and the cosmos, or social and moral rules as well as simple performatives, but in any case the performance of a liturgical order realizes or establishes the conventions that the liturgical order embodies. It may be suggested that as the reality lying behind notions of the magical power of words is simple performativeness mystified, so may the reality lying behind the creative power of The Word—the Eternal Word—be meta-performativeness mystified—the establishment of conventions through participation in invariant liturgical orders.

* * *

The assertion that acceptance is intrinsic to performance is on the face of it either dubious or indubitable, and therefore requires some comment and clarification.

First, to say that the performer accepts the authority of a liturgical order in performing it is not to say that he is necessarily doing anything very grave. The gravity of the act of acceptance is contingent upon whatever the liturgical order represents. This, of course, varies.

Second, and more important, "acceptance" is not synonymous with belief. Belief I take to be some sort of inward state knowable subjectively if at all. Acceptance, in contrast, is not a private state but a *public act*, visible to both the witnesses and the performer himself. This is to [say] that participation in ritual marks a boundary, so to speak, between public and private processes. Liturgical orders are public, and participation in them constitutes a public acceptance of a public order, regardless of the private state of belief. Acceptance is, thus, a fundamental social act and it forms a basis for public orders, which unknowable and volatile belief or conviction cannot.

Acceptance not only is not belief. It does not even imply belief. The private processes of individuals may often be persuaded by their ritual participation to come into conformity with their public acts, but this is not always the case. This suggests that while participation in liturgical performance may be highly visible, it is not very profound, for it neither indicates nor does it necessarily produce an inward state conforming to it directly. But for this very reason it is in some sense very profound, for it makes it possible for the performer to transcend his own doubt by accepting in defiance of it. Acceptance in this sense has much in common with some theological notions of faith (O'Doherty 1973b: 8ff.; Tillich 1957: 16ff.). Nevertheless, it must be recognized that when the public and the private are so loosely related, a range of what Austin (1962: 95ff.) called "infelicities"—insincerities and the like—become possible, and they include possibilities for deceit. But the alternative to the possibility of deceit might well be the certainty of non-order or disorder if public order were required to depend upon the continuing acquiescence of the private processes of those subject to it—upon their belief, sincerity, good will, conviction, for these surely must fluctuate continu-

ously. While it is perhaps obvious it is worth reiterating that insincerity and the possibility of deceit are intrinsic to the very acts that make social life possible for organisms that relate to each other in acccordance with voluntarily accepted convention rather than in ways more narrowly defined by their genotypes. Our argument here suggests, however, that although liturgical performance does not eliminate infelicities, it does in some degree offset or ameliorate their effects by rendering them irrelevant. It is the visible, explicit, public act of acceptance, and not the invisible, ambiguous, private sentiment that is socially and morally binding.

To say, then, that a liturgical order is in its nature authoritative, or that the canons it encodes are accepted in its performance, is not to say that the performer will "believe" the cosmic order it may project or approve of the rules or norms it may incorporate. It is not even to claim that he will abide by these rules or norms. We all know that a man may participate in a liturgy in which commandments against adultery and thieving are pronounced, then pilfer from the poor box on his way out of church, or depart from communion to tryst with his neighbor's wife. But such behavior does not render his acceptance meaningless or empty. It is an entailment of liturgical performances to establish conventional understandings, rules, and norms in accordance with which everyday behavior is supposed to proceed, not to control that behavior directly. Participation in a ritual in which a prohibition against adultery is enunciated by, among others, himself may not prevent a man from committing adultery, but it does establish for him the prohibition of adultery as a rule that he himself has accepted as he enlivened it. Whether or not he abides by the rule he has obligated himself to do so. If he does not he has violated an obligation that *he himself* has avowed. . . .

In sum, ritual is unique in at once establishing conventions, that is to say enunciating and accepting them, and in insulating them from usage. In both enunciating conventions and accepting them, it contains within itself not simply a symbolic representation of social contract, but a consummation of social contract. As such, ritual, which also establishes a boundary between private and public processes, thereby insulating public orders from private vagaries (and vice versa)[1] is *the* basic social act.

* * *

To say that ritual is the basic social act must be to say that it is in some sense moral, for the social subsumes the moral. Not all rituals are explicitly moral, but it is worth making explicit that morality, like social contract, is implicit in ritual's very structure.

Moral dicta may, of course, form part of the canon that a liturgy carries, and we have already noted that it is also implied by obligation, which some philosophers, at least, would take to be entailed by the acceptance intrinsic to performance. Failure to abide by the terms of an obligation that one has accepted is generally, perhaps even universally, categorized as immoral, unethical, or wrong. It might even be argued that the violation of obligation is the fundamental immoral act. This is not our concern here, however, and morality is intrinsic to ritual's structure in a yet more subtle way. While not confined to them, the matter may be illustrated most clearly by reference to specifically factitive rituals like ordinations, dubbings, and peace declarations. It is of the essence to contrast such performative acts or utterances with ordinary descriptive statements. Austin initially tried to say that performatives are neither true nor false (1970: 233ff.) whereas statements are. Later he found this not always to be the case. However, they do differ from statements in a related way which he did not note but which does have to do with truth, and with the foundations of morality.

The adequacy of a descriptive statement is assessed by the degree to which it conforms to the state of affairs that it purports to describe. If it is in sufficient conformity we say that it is true, accurate, or correct. If it is not we say that it is false, erroneous, inaccurate, lying. The state of affairs is the criterion by which the statement is assessed. The relationship of performatives—particularly factitives and commissives—to the states of affairs with which they are concerned is *exactly* the inverse. If, for instance, a man is properly dubbed to knighthood and then proceeds to violate all of the canons of chivalry, or if peace is declared in a properly conducted ritual but soon after one of the parties to the declaration attacks the other, we would not say that the dubbing or the peace declaration were faulty, but that the states of affairs were faulty. *We judge the state of affairs by the degree to which it conforms to the stipulations of the performa-*

tive ritual. Thus, liturgical orders provide criteria in terms of which events—usage and history—may be judged. As such, liturgical orders are *intrinsically* correct or moral. Morality is inherent in the *structure* of liturgical performance *prior* to whatever its canons assert about morality itself or about whatever in particular is moral. This morality is not limited to the structure of simple factitive and commissive rituals, which seek to establish particular conventional states of affairs, but is intrinsic as well to rituals that seek to establish conventional orders. It is of interest here than ancient Persians and Indians referred to states of affairs that departed from the proper order, which was established liturgically, by a term, *anrta*, that also seems to have meant "lie" (Duchesne-Guillemin 1966: 26ff.; Brown 1972: 252ff.).

* * *

That virtually all rituals include acts as well as words, and often objects and substances as well, suggests that not all messages are communicated equally well by all media. . . . Formal postures and gestures may communicate something more, or communicate it better, than do the corresponding words. For instance, to kneel subordination, it is plausible to suggest, is not simply to state subordination, but to display it, and how may information concerning some state of a transmitter better be signaled than by displaying that state itself? . . . Although words may serve as indices and may even be necessary to stipulate the indexicality of physical acts (dancing would not be promising unless it were sometime so stipulated in words), physical acts carry indexical messages more convincingly than does language. "Actions," as the saying goes, "speak louder than words," even when the actions are ritual actions—or perhaps especially when they are ritual actions, for the acceptance of a particular order is intrinsic to a ritual act. Liturgy's acts may also speak more clearly than words. The very limitations of display may enhance its clarity. The subtlety of ordinary language is such that it can suggest, connote, hint at, or imply such delicately graded degrees of, say, subordination, respect, or contempt that it can shroud all social relations in ambiguity, vagueness, and uncertainty. But one kneels or one does not, and we may recall here the clarity that is intrinsic to binary signals.

It may be objected, however, that the language of

liturgy is not ordinary language, but stylized and invariant. As one kneels or one does not, so one does or does not recite a ritual formula, and so ritual words as well as acts can—and undoubtedly do—transmit indexical messages. Acts, however, have a related virtue not possessed by either words or the objects and substances that rituals may employ. Earlier I suggested that in ritual transmitter, receiver, and canonical message are fused in the participant, but nothing was said about what it is that constitutes the participant. Given the possibility or even probability of discontinuity or even conflict between public and private processes this is not a trivial question. Indeed, it is highly problematic.

I would now propose that the use of the body defines the self of the performer for himself and for others. In kneeling, for instance, he is not merely sending a message to the effect that he submits in ephemeral words that flutter away from his mouth. He identifies his inseparable, indispensable, and enduring body with his subordination. The subordinated self is neither a creature of insubstantial words from which he may separate himself without loss of blood, nor some insubstantial essence or soul that cannot be located in space or confined in time. It is his visible, present, living substance that he "puts on the line," that "stands up (or kneels down) to be counted." As "saying" may be "doing," "doing" may also be an especially powerful—or substantial—way of "saying."

As ritual acts and objects have special communication qualities so, of course, do words have others, as Tambiah (1968) has argued. Whereas acts and substances represent substantially that which is of the here and now, the words of liturgy can connect the here and now to the past, or even to the beginning of time, and to the future, or even to time's end. In their very invariance the words of liturgy implicitly assimilate the current event into an ancient or ageless category of events, something that speechless gesture, mortal substance, or expendable objects alone cannot. Because of their symbolic quality, this is to say, invariant words easily escape from the here and now and thus can represent felicitously the canonical, which is never confined to the here and now. Objects like the cross can have symbolic value, it is true, and thus make reference to that which is present in neither time nor space, but such objects must be assigned symbolic value by words, and words are ultimately necessary to representations of the canonical.

The informative virtues of the physical and verbal aspects of liturgy thus seem to complement or even complete each other. But terms like "complement" or even "complete" do not express adequately the intimacy of the relationship between liturgical words and acts. By drawing himself into a posture to which canonical words give symbolic value, the performer incarnates a symbol. He gives substance to the symbol as that symbol gives him form. The canonical and the indexical come together in the *substance* of the *formal* posture or gesture. . . .

* * *

Invariance . . . is characteristic of all rituals, both human and nonhuman, and it may be that both the sacred and the supernatural arose out of the union of words with the invariance of the speechless rituals of the beasts from whom we are descended. Be this as it may, both the sacred and the supernatural are, I believe, implied by liturgy's invariance. Before developing this point more must be said about the sacred.

Elsewhere (1971a, 1971b) I have argued that we take liturgies to be religious if they include postulates of a certain sort. The Shema, "Hear, O Israel, the Lord our God, the Lord is One," is an example. So is "Deceased Ancestors persist as sentient Beings," which is implicit in the rituals in which Maring men pledge their military support to their hosts. Such sentences have peculiar qualities. Having no material reference they are neither verifiable nor falsifiable, and yet they are regarded as unquestionable. I take *sanctity to be the quality of unquestionableness imputed by a congregation to postulates in their nature neither verifiable nor falsifiable.* This is to say that sanctity is ultimately a quality of discourse and not of the objects with which that discourse is concerned. It is of interest in this regard, however, that the objects with which sacred discourse is concerned are often themselves elements of discourse: instances of the Creative Word. The distinction between sacred discourse and the objects of sacred discourse may thus be masked or, to put it differently, sacred discourse and its objects may be conflated.

Let us turn now to the relationship of sanctity to

invariance. It was Anthony F. C. Wallace (1966: 234) who first pointed out that in terms of information theory ritual is a peculiar form of communication. Information is formally defined as that which reduces uncertainty, the minimal unit being the "bit," the amount of information required to eliminate the uncertainty between two equally likely alternatives. It is, roughly, the answer to a yes-no question. . . . Indexical messages, because they depend upon the possibility of variation, do contain information in the technical sense. But, Wallace observed, to the extent that a liturgy is invariant it contains no information because it eliminates no uncertainty. He further argued, however, that meaning and information are not the same thing, and that the meaning of this informationlessness is *certainty*. To put this a little differently, that which is stated in the invariant canon is thereby represented as certain because invariance implies certainty. Certainty and unquestionableness are closely related, and *one* of the grounds of the unquestionableness of these postulates, which we may call "ultimately sacred," is the certainty of their expression. It is not, however, the only ground.

Certainty is a property of information or messages. It is one thing to say that a message is certain and another to say that it goes unquestioned. Whether or not a statement will be challenged does not rest only or finally upon the properties of the statement itself, but upon the disposition toward it of the persons to whom it is presented. . . . To participate in a ritual is to accept that which it encodes. This acceptance is entailed by participation in an invariant order that the participants themselves did not encode. Liturgical invariance, at the same time that it invests what it encodes with certainty, secures the acceptance of its performers.

This account distinguishes the sacred from the divine or supernatural, but it may be that the invariance of sacred utterances may imply the objects of these utterances. Bloch's . . . (1973) arguments suggest that the notion of the supernatural as well as the idea of the sacred may emerge out of the invariance of liturgical performance. The words spoken by a performer are not his words. They are extraordinary and often immemorial words, and as such they imply extraordinary speakers who first uttered them in antiquity, or perhaps beyond antiquity, at the beginning of time. Gods and spirits as well as social contract and morality may be intrinsic to the structure of liturgical order.

While sanctity has its apparent source in ultimate sacred postulates which, being expressions concerning gods and the like, are typically without material significata, it flows to other sentences which do include material terms and which are directly concerned with the operation of society: "Henry is by Grace of God King." "It is more blessed to give than to receive." "Thou shalt not bear false witness." "I swear in the name of God to tell the truth." Thus it is that association with ultimate sacred propositions certifies the correctness and naturalness of conventions, the legitimacy of authorities, the truthfulness of testimony and the reliability of commissives. . . . That Maring men will honor the pledges to give military support that they undertake and display by dancing is certified by association with an ultimate sacred postulate.

It is important to observe here that the greater invariance of the sacred or spiritual than the social components of liturgical orders provides them with a certainty beyond the certainties of social orders currently existing. As the social content of canon is more or less enduring, providing an order within which the states represented in indexical messages may fluctuate, so the even less variable, more enduring references to gods and spirits provide an apparently eternal meta-order within which social orders themselves may be transformed. The adaptive implications of the greater invariance of the nonmaterial than the material are important, but are discussed elsewhere. Here I would like to suggest that although the concept of the sacred and the notion of the divine would be literally unthinkable without language it may also be that language and social orders founded upon language could not have emerged without the support of sanctity. . . . One of the problems inherent in language—its extraordinary talent for deceit [is]; . . . another—the innate ability of language users to comprehend the arbitrary nature of the conventions to which they are subordinated and their ability, also intrinsic to language, to conceive of alternatives. Lie and alternative, inherent in language, it is interesting to note, are taken by Buber (1952) to be the ground of all evil. At the very least they pose problems to any society whose structure is founded upon language, which is to say all human societies. I have therefore argued that if there are to be words at all it is necessary to establish *The Word*, and that The Word is established by the invariance of liturgy. It may be at least suggested, furthermore, that it emerged phylogenetically as some expressions drawn from the burgeoning language of earlier hominids were absorbed into, and subordinated to, the invariance of already existing nonverbal rituals which seem to be common in the animal world.

We may now note that liturgy ameliorates some of the problems intrinsic to symbolic communication, particularly lying, by moving in two opposite directions. On the one hand . . . it eschews symbolization in favor of indexicality in at least some of its representations of the here and now. On the other hand it sanctifies references to that which is not confined in the here and now. Like the lies to which they are a partial antidote, ultimate sacred postulates are made possible by denotative symbols, for denotative symbols free signs from that which they signify.

To summarize, truthfulness, reliability, correctness, naturalness, and legitimacy are vested in conventions and conventional acts by their association with ultimate sacred postulates. The notions of truthfulness, reliability, correctness, naturalness, and legitimacy are closely related to that of unquestionableness, which I have identified with the sacred. Unquestionableness in turn is closely related to certainty and acceptance, certainty and acceptance to invariance. The invariance of ritual, which antedates the development of language, is the foundation of convention, for through it conventions are not only enunciated, accepted, invested with morality, and naturalized, but also sanctified. Indeed, the concept of the sacred itself emerges out of liturgical invariance.

*   *   *

Yet, as important as liturgical invariance may be, surely language and the human way of life must be founded upon more than a trick in information theory. So far I have spoken only of the sacred, which is in language and which faces language and the public orders built upon language. But the sacred is only one component or aspect of a more inclusive phenomenon which I call the Holy. The other aspect of the Holy, which, following Rudolph Otto (1923), may be called the "numinous," is its nondiscursive,

ineffable, or emotional aspect—what is called "religious experience" (James 1903) in the broadest sense. We know that this, as well as the sacred, is invoked in at least some rituals. "Communitas" (Turner 1969) or "effervescence" (Durkheim 1961 [1915]) is one of its manifestations. Scholars differ with respect to the nature of religious experience. Some would apply the term to any emotional state taken by the individual to be a response to what is construed to be a divine object. Others, like Rudolph Otto (1923), would take it to be a general undifferentiated "ur-emotion" encompassing love, fear, dependence, fascination, unworthiness, majesty, connection. Witnesses agree that it is powerful, indescribable, and utterly convincing.

I do not mean to make too much of this, but Erikson (1966) suggests that the numinous emotion has its ontogenetic basis in the relationship of the preverbal infant to its mother. The child's experience of its mother has characteristics similar to those that Otto attributes to the worshiper's experience of . . . God: she is mysterious, tremendous, overpowering, loving, and frightening. It is learning to trust her upon whom he depends utterly that makes subsequent language learning and, for that matter, continuing socialization possible. This trust is learned in what Erikson calls "daily rituals of nurturance and greeting" (1966), stereotyped interactions between mother and child taking place dependably at regular intervals, or at times specified by the child's needs. Through the course of ontogeny the numinous emotions initially associated with mother are displaced to other objects. . . .

In sum, I earlier argued that liturgy's invariance gives rise to the sacred, meaning by the term "sacred" to designate only the discursive aspect of a more encompassing category which may be called the Holy. The sacred, the ultimate constituents of which are in language, is that aspect of the Holy which faces language, reason, the public order, and their problems. But the Holy also has a nondiscursive, affective and experiential aspect which we may, following Otto, call "the numinous." As the sacred may emerge out of the invariance of liturgical orders, so may the numinous be invoked by ritual's unison.

The canons of liturgy, in which are encoded both postulates concerning that which is ultimately sacred and sentences concerning temporal social orders may, then, receive in the rituals in which they are enunciated the support of numinous emotions. Numinous communitas, perhaps substantiated in acts of unison, may add a dimension—or a magnitude—to the orderliness of the sacred canonical. But unison is not all that is to be found at ritual's heart, nor is the relationship between canonical order and numinous emotion always complementary.

At the heart of some rituals there is not always heightened order but hilarity, confusion, aggression, and chaos, expressed in clowning, transvestism, attacks upon initiates, self-mortification, sexual license, blasphemy, and otherwise indecorous actions. Such behavior may challenge, tacitly or explicitly, the very canons that ordain it, and Abrahams (1973) suggests that the "vitality" of ritual springs from the confrontations of order and disorder for which it provides an arena. This is to say that liturgical orders may include not only canons of order but their antitheses as well. As Abrahams puts it "there is a simultaneous proclamation of the order of the world as seen by the group and its (almost) absolute denial" (1973: 15).

The orders of liturgy do generally manage to contain, and even to sublimate, the emotions that they themselves generate, and they surely may be vitalized or invigorated by confrontations with their anti-orders. But these confrontations may be more than invigorating. They may be limiting and corrective as well. The denials of order in ritual are seldom if ever absolute, and while they may be denials of this world's order, liturgical orders are usually concerned with more than the order of the world of here and now. They also proclaim an order that transcends time, an ultimate or absolute order of which the temporal order is merely a contingent part. It is the temporal, and not the ultimate, aspects of order that are most open to challenge, and that are most likely to be challenged by what appears to be anti-order. And it is the temporal and contingent nature of conventions that is exposed by ridiculing and violating them. In being exposed for what they are, they are prevented from themselves becoming ultimate. The king who is ordained by God is told—and so is everyone else—that he is no more than a man when he is demeaned in the name of God. Liturgy's challenges to the temporal are in the service of the ultimate, for they keep the conventions of time and place in their places by demonstrating that they are not ultimately sacred, but only

sanctified by the ultimately sacred. They are also thereby in the service of evolution, for they make it easier to discard temporal conventions when times and places change. . . .

* * *

Earlier I spoke of the acceptance of convention entailed by participation in liturgy. I insisted that ritual acceptance is a public act and that it is not necessarily associated with an inward state conforming to it. Acceptance does not entail belief but, I proposed, it is sufficient to establish the obligations upon which human societies stand. I would now suggest that formal acceptance in the absence of something more profound may be fragile and that the numinous, when it is experienced, supports acceptance with conviction or belief. Those who have reached those profound states called mystical report a loss of distinction, an experience of unification with what they take to be the divine object and perhaps the cosmos. The experience, they say, is ultimately meaningful, but being devoid of distinction is devoid of reference. It points to nothing but itself. Ultimate meaning is not referential but is, rather, a state of being or even of pure, seemingly unpredicated being. I cannot discuss the validity of the illuminations vouchsafed in those states in which meaning and being become one, but will only note that to say such meaning is convincing is inadequate, for, being directly experienced, it simply *is*. As such it is undeniable, and so, indeed, may be numinous experiences falling short of the mystical.

It is of interest that sacred propositions and numinous experiences are the inverse of each other. Ultimate sacred postulates are discursive but their significata are not material. Numinous experiences are immediately material (they are actual physical and psychic states) but they are not discursive. Ultimate sacred postulates are unfalsifiable; numinous experiences are undeniable. In ritual's union ultimate sacred propositions thus seem to partake of the immediately known and undeniable quality of the numinous. That this is logically unsound should not trouble us for, although it may make problems for logicians, it does not trouble the faithful. In the union of the sacred and the numinous the most abstract and distant of conceptions are bound to the most immediate and substantial of experiences. We are confronted, finally, with a remarkable spectacle. The unfalsifiable supported by the undeniable yields the un-questionable, which transforms the dubious, the ar-bitrary, and the conventional into the correct, the necessary, and the natural. This structure is, I would suggest, the foundation upon which the human way of life stands, and it is realized in ritual. At the heart of ritual—its "atom," so to speak—is the relationship of performers to their own performances of invariant sequences of acts and utterances which they did not encode. Virtually everything I have argued is implied or entailed by that form.

NOTE

1. Erving Goffman, in "The Nature of Deference and De-meanor" (1956) and later works, has argued that the rituals of deference and demeanor protect the psyche from lacerations that would inevitably result from naked encounters.

REFERENCES CITED

Abrahams, Roger. 1973. Ritual for fun and profit. Paper pre-pared for Burg-Wartenstein Conference-59 on Ritual and Reconciliation.

Austin, J. L. 1962. *How to do things with words.* Oxford Univer-sity Press.

———. 1970. Performative utterance. In *Philosophical papers,* 2d ed., ed. J. O. Urmson and G. J. Warneck. Oxford.

Bloch, Maurice. 1973. Symbols, song, and dance, and features of articulation. *European Journal of Sociology* 15:55–81.

Brown, W. Norman. 1972. Duty as truth in ancient India. *Pro-ceedings of the American Philosophical Society* 116:252–268.

Buber, Martin. 1952. *The eclipse of God.* New York: Harper & Bros.

Duchesne-Guillemin, Jacques. 1966. *Symbols and values in Zoroastrianism.* New York: Harper & Row.

Durkheim, Emile. 1961. *The elementary forms of the religious life.* Joseph Ward Swan, translator. New York: Collier.

Erikson, Eric. 1966. The ritualization of ontogeny. In *A discus-sion of ritualisation of behaviour in animals and man,* Julian Huxley, organizer. London: Philosophical Transactions of the Royal Society of London, Series B, Biological Sciences, vol. 251, no. 772.

Finnegan, Ruth. 1969. How to do things with words: performa-tive utterances among the Limba of Sierra Leone. *Man* 4:537–551.

Firth, Raymond. 1940. *The work of the gods in Tikopia.* London.

Fortes, Meyer. 1966. Religious premises and logical technique in divinatory ritual. In *A discussion of ritualisation of behaviour in animals and man,* Julian Huxley, organizer. London: Philosophical Transactions of the Royal Society of London, Series B, Biological Sciences, vol. 251, no. 772.

Goffman, Erving. 1956. The nature of deference and demeanor. *American Anthropologist* 58:473–503.

Goody, Jack. 1961. Religion and ritual: the definitional problem. *British Journal of Sociology* 12:142–164.

James, William. 1903. *The varieties of religious experience.* New York: Collier Books (1961).

Leach, E. R. 1954. *The political systems of Highland Burma.* Boston: Beacon Press.

Lyons, John. 1970. Human language. In *Non-verbal communica-tion,* ed. R. A. Hinde. Cambridge: Cambridge University Press.

O'Doherty, F. 1973a. Ritual as a second order language. Paper prepared for Burg-Wartenstein Conference-59 on Ritual and Reconciliation.

———. 1973b. Nature, grace, and faith. ms.

Ortiz, A. 1969. *The Tewa world.* Chicago: University of Chicago Press.

Otto, Rudolph. 1923. The idea of the holy. London: Oxford University Press. J. W. Harvey, translator.

Peirce, Charles. 1960. *Collected papers of Charles Sanders Peirce,* Vol. 2, *Elements of logic,* ed. Charles Hartshorne and Paul Weiss. Cambridge, Mass.: Harvard University Press.

Rappaport, Roy A. 1971a. Ritual, sanctity, and cybernetics. *American Anthropologist* 73:59–76.

———. 1971b. The sacred in human evolution. *Annual Review of Ecology and Systematics* 2:23–44.

Searle, J. R. 1969. *Speech acts.* Cambridge: Cambridge University Press.

Skorupski, J. 1976. *Symbol and theory: a philosophical study of the-ories of religion in social anthropology.* Cambridge: Cambridge University Press.

Tambiah, S. J. 1968. The magical power of words. *Man* 3:175–208.

Tillich, P. 1957. *The dynamics of faith.* New York: Harper.

Turner, Victor. 1969. *The ritual process.* Chicago: Aldine.

Van Gennep, A. 1909. *The rites of passage.* M. Vizedom and G. F. Caffee, translators, with introduction by Solon Kimball, Chicago: Phoenix Books, University of Chicago Press, 1960.

Wallace, Anthony F. C. 1966. *Religion: an anthropological view.* New York: Random House.

Restoration of Behavior

RICHARD SCHECHNER

Facts of publication: *Schechner, Richard. 1985. "Restoration of Behavior," from* Between Theater and Anthropology, *35–44, 55–65, 107–116. Philadelphia: University of Pennsylvania Press. Copyright © 1985 by The University of Pennsylvania Press. Reprinted with the permission of the publishers.*

Theater director and performance theorist Richard Schechner believes that "restored" behavior is at the root not only of theater and theme parks but also of ritual. Restored behavior consists of frames (compare the narrative sequence of frames in a comic strip) assembled into "strips" so as to create what appears to be a natural, coherent whole. Schechner throws into question any claim that a rite is truly original. Rather, all such performances are reinventions, and their actions are "re-behaved." They are, to use Victor Turner's apt phrase, in the "subjunctive mood"; even religious rites are "as if." In one example Schechner considers the Hindu agnicayana, a rite that was reenacted for a film by Robert Gardner and Frits Staal. Schechner claims that the film of the ritual, not the rite itself, was the generative, or originating, event. He raises questions concerning the effect of media on our sense of ritual authenticity not in order to argue for some impossible return to authenticity but to point to an emergent ritual sensibility far more rooted in dramatization and tourism than we sometimes imagine. If Schechner is correct, we must reconsider not only the relationship between original events and media events but the relationship of scholarship to both, since much scholarship is based on restored, rather than original, behavior.

Another of Schechner's books that makes significant contributions to the study of ritual is Essays in Performance Theory *(Drama Books, 1977; second edition in press with Methuen).*

About the author: *"Richard Schechner was born 23 August 1934 in Beth Israel Hospital, Newark, New Jersey, at 6:00 A.M., under the sign of the Lion. Eight days later he was circumcised as prescribed by rabbinic and Biblical law. He does not recall any trauma associated with the pinching of his foreskin. His birth was ordinary, vaginal, and medically uneventful. Both mother and son did well. (You may add any or all of this to my bio.)"* **Education:** *B.A., Cornell University; M.A., University of Iowa; Ph.D., Tulane University.* **Field(s):** *performance studies; anthropology and theater.* **Career:** *Assistant, then Associate Professor of Theater, 1962–1967, Tulane University; Professor of Performance Studies, 1967–1991, New York University; University Professor, 1991–present, New York University.* **Publications:** *edited with Mady Schuman,* Ritual, Play and Performance *(Seabury, 1976);* Essays on Performance Theory *(Drama Books Specialists, 1977);* Between Theater and Anthropology *(University of Pennsylvania, 1985);* The Future of Ritual *(Routledge, 1993); "Ritual, Violence and Creativity" in* Creativity/Anthropology, *296–320, ed. Smadar Lavie, Kirin Narayan, and Renato Rosaldo (Ithaca, NY: Cornell University, 1993); "Ritual and Performance," in* Companion Encyclopedia of Anthropology, *613–647, ed. Tim Ingold (London: Routledge, 1994);* Environmental Theater, *expanded edition (Applause, 1994).* **Additional:** *Editor,* The Drama Review, *1985–present. Sample of performances directed:* Faust/Gastronome, The Prometheus Project, Richard's Lear, The Balcony, Macbeth, Dionysus in 69.

Restored behavior is living behavior treated as a film director treats a strip of film. These strips of behavior[1] can be rearranged or reconstructed; they are independent of the causal systems (social, psychological, technological) that brought them into existence. They have a life of their own. The original "truth" or "source" of the behavior may be lost, ignored, or contradicted—even while this truth or source is apparently being honored and observed. How the strip of behavior was made, found, or developed may be unknown or concealed; elaborated; distorted by myth and tradition. Originating as a process, used in the process of rehearsal to make a new process, a performance, the strips of behavior are not themselves process but things, items, "material." Restored behavior can be of long duration as in some dramas and rituals or of short duration as in some gestures, dances, and mantras.

Restored behavior is used in all kinds of performances from shamanism and exorcism to trance, from ritual to aesthetic dance and theater, from initiation rites to social dramas, from psychoanalysis to psychodrama and transactional analysis. In fact, restored behavior is the main characteristic of performance. The practitioners of all these arts, rites, and healings assume that some behaviors—organized sequences of events, scripted actions, known texts, scored movements—exist separate from the performers who "do" these behaviors. Because the behavior is separate from those who are behaving, the behavior can be stored, transmitted, manipulated, transformed. The performers get in touch with, recover, remember, or even invent these strips of behavior and then rebehave according to these strips, either by being absorbed into them (playing the role, going into trance) or by existing side by side with them (Brecht's *Verfremdungseffekt*).[A] The work of restoration is carried on in rehearsals and/or in the transmission of behavior from master to novice. Understanding what happens during training, rehearsals, and workshops—investigating the subjunctive mood that is the medium of these operations—is the surest way to link aesthetic and ritual performance.

Restored behavior is "out there," distant from "me." It is separate and therefore can be "worked on," changed, even though it has "already happened." Restored behavior includes a vast range of actions. It can be "me" at another time/psychological state as in the psychoanalytic abreaction; or it can exist in a nonordinary sphere of sociocultural reality as does the Passion of Christ or the reenactment in Bali of the struggle between Rangda and Barong; or it can be marked off by aesthetic convention as in

drama and dance; or it can be the special kind of behavior "expected" of someone participating in a traditional ritual—the bravery, for example, of a Gahuku boy in Papua New Guinea during his initiation, shedding no tears when jagged leaves slice the inside of his nostrils; or the shyness of an American "blushing bride" at her wedding, even though she and her groom have lived together for two years.

Restored behavior is symbolic and reflexive: not empty but loaded behavior multivocally broadcasting significances. These difficult terms express a single principle: The self can act in/as another; the social or transindividual self is a role or set of roles. Symbolic and reflexive behavior is the hardening into theater of social, religious, aesthetic, medical, and educational process. Performance means: never for the first time. It means: for the second to the nth time. Performance is "twice-behaved behavior."

Neither painting, sculpting, nor writing shows actual behavior as it is being behaved. But thousands of years before movies rituals were made from strips of restored behavior: action and stasis coexisted in the same event. What comfort flowed from ritual performances. People, ancestors, and gods participated in simultaneously having been, being, and becoming. These strips of behavior were replayed many times. Mnemonic devices insured that the performances were "right"—transmitted across many generations with few accidental variations. Even now, the terror of the first night is not the presence of the public but knowing that mistakes are no longer forgiven.

This constancy of transmission is all the more astonishing because restored behavior involves choices. Animals repeat themselves, and so do the cycles of the moon. But an actor can say no to any action. This question of choice is not easy. Some ethologists and brain specialists argue that there is no significant difference—no difference of any kind—between animal and human behavior. But at least there is an "illusion of choice," a feeling that one has a choice. And this is enough. Even the shaman who is called, the trancer falling into trance, and the wholly trained performer whose performance text is second nature give over or resist, and there is suspicion of the ones who too easily say yes or prematurely say no. There is a continuum from the not-much-choice of ritual to the lots-of-choice of aesthetic theater. It is the function of rehearsals in

A. *Verfremdungseffekt*: "Alienation effect," that is, the effect of shattering the audience's illusion that what is being performed in front of them is real. This effect is usually produced by calling attention to the constructedness and artificiality of the play itself. (Editor's note)

aesthetic theater to narrow the choices or at least to make clear the rules of improvisation. Rehearsals function to build a score, and this score is a "ritual by contract": fixed behavior that everyone participating agrees to do.

Restored behavior can be put on the way a mask or costume is. Its shape can be seen from the outside, and changed. That's what theater directors, councils of bishops, master performers, and great shamans do: change performance scores. A score can change because it is not a "natural event" but a model of individual and collective human choice. A score exists, as Turner says (1982, 82–84), in the subjunctive mood, in what Stanislavski called the "as if." Existing as "second nature," restored behavior is always subject to revision. This "secondness" combines negativity and subjunctivity.

* * *

Put in personal terms, restored behavior is "me behaving as if I am someone else" or "as if I am 'beside myself,' or 'not myself,' " as when in trance. But this "someone else" may also be "me in another state of feeling/being," as if there were multiple "me's" in each person. The difference between performing myself—acting out a dream, reexperiencing a childhood trauma, showing you what I did yesterday—and more formal "presentations of self" (see Goffman 1959)—is a difference of degree, not kind. There is also a continuum linking the ways of presenting the self to the ways of presenting others: acting in dramas, dances, and rituals. The same can be said for "social actions" and "cultural performances": events whose origins can't be located in individuals, if they can be located at all. These events when acted out are linked in a feedback loop with the actions of individuals. Thus, what people in northern Hindi-speaking India see acted out in Ramlila tells them how to act in their daily lives; and how they act in their daily lives affects the staging of the Ramlila. Mythic enactments are often regarded as exemplary models. But the ordinary life of the people is expressed in the staging, gestures, details of costume, and scenic structures of Ramlila (and other folk performances). Sometimes collective events are attributed to "persons" whose existence is somewhere between history and fiction: the Books of Moses, the *Iliad* and *Odyssey* of Homer,

the *Mahabharata* of Vyas. Sometimes these actions and stories belong anonymously to folklore, legend, myth. And sometimes they are "original," or at least attributable to individuals: the *Hamlet* of Shakespeare, the *Ramcharitmanas* of Tulsidas, the *Oedipus* of Sophocles. But what these authors really authored was not the tale itself but a version of something. It's hard to say exactly what qualifies a work to belong to, and come from, a collective. Restored behavior offers to both individuals and groups the chance to rebecome what they once were—or even, and most often, to rebecome what they never were but wish to have been or wish to become.

Figures 1, 2, 3, and 4 are four versions of my fundamental thesis: Performance behavior is restored behavior. Figure 1 shows restored behavior as either a projection of "my particular self" (1 → 2), or a restoration of a historically verifiable past (1 → 3 → 4), or—most often—a restoration of a past that never was (1 → 5_a → 5_b). For example, interesting as the data may be, the "historical Richard III" is not as important to someone preparing a production of Shakespeare's play as the logic of Shakespeare's text: the Richard of Shakespeare's imagination. Figures 2, 3, and 4 elaborate the basic idea; I will discuss these elaborations later. A corollary to the basic thesis is that most performances—even those that apparently are simple 1 → 2 displacements or 1 → 3 → 4 re-creations—are, or swiftly become, 1 → 5_a → 5_b. For it is this "performative bundle"—where the project-to-be, 5_b governs what from the past is selected or invented (and projected backward into the past), 5_a—that is the most stable and prevalent performative circumstance. In a very real way the future—the project coming into existence through the process of rehearsal—determines the past: what will be kept from earlier rehearsals or from the "source materials." This situation is as true for ritual performances as for aesthetic theater. Even where there are no rehearsals in the Euro-American sense, analogous processes occur.

Figure 1 is drawn from the temporal perspective of rehearsal and from the psychological perspective of an individual performer. "Me" (1) is a person rehearsing for a performance to be: 2, 4, or 5_b. What precedes the performance—both temporally and conceptually—is either nothing that can be definitely identified, as when a person gets into a mood,

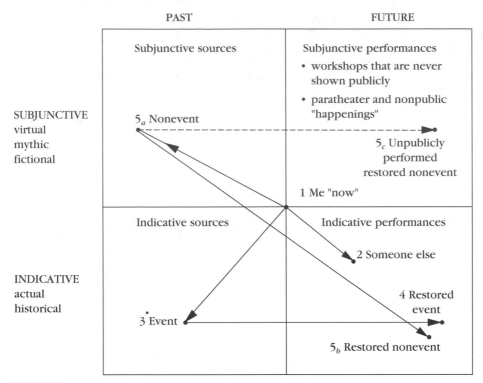

PAST   FUTURE

Subjunctive sources   Subjunctive performances
                                    • workshops that are never
                                      shown publicly
                                    • paratheater and nonpublic
                                      "happenings"

SUBJUNCTIVE 5_a Nonevent
virtual
mythic 5_c Unpublicly
fictional   performed
                                                    restored nonevent

                                    1 Me "now"

Indicative sources   Indicative performances

                                        2 Someone else

INDICATIVE   4 Restored
actual   event
historical
                 3 Event

                                        5_b Restored nonevent

FIGURE 1

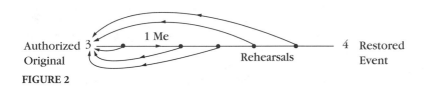

Authorized 3   1 Me   4   Restored
Original   Event
FIGURE 2   Rehearsals

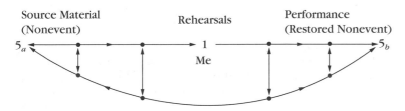

Source Material   Rehearsals   Performance
(Nonevent)   (Restored Nonevent)

5_a 1 5_b
                     Me

FIGURE 3

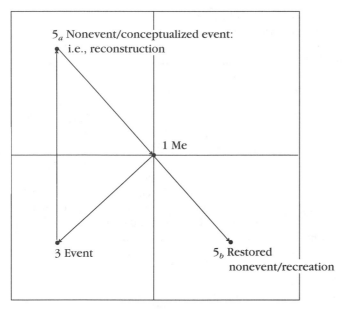

5_a Nonevent/conceptualized event:
i.e., reconstruction

1 Me

3 Event

5_b Restored
nonevent/recreation

FIGURE 4

or some definite antecedent event(s). This event will either be historically verifiable (3), or not (5_a). If it is not, it can be either a legendary event, a fiction (as in many plays), or—as will be explained—the projection backward in time of the proposed event-to-be. Or, to put it another way, rehearsals make it necessary to think of the future in such a way as to create a past. Figure 1 is divided into quadrants in order to indicate mood as well as temporality. The upper left quadrant contains mythic, legendary, or fictional events. The mood is subjunctive. In Turner's words:

> Here cognitive schemata that give sense and order to everyday life no longer apply, but are, as it were, suspended—in ritual symbolism perhaps even shown as destroyed or dissolved. . . . Clearly, the liminal space-time "pod" created by ritual action, or today by certain kinds of reflexively ritualized theatre, is potentially perilous. [1982, 84]

This past is one that is always in the process of transformation, just as a papal council can redefine Christ's actions or a great twentieth-century Noh performer can introduce new variations into a fifteenth-century mise-en-scène of Zeami's.

The lower left quadrant—that of the actual/indicative past—is history understood as an arrangement of facts. Of course, any arrangement is conventionalized and conditioned by particular world and/or political views. Events are always rising from the lower left to the upper left: today's indicative becomes tomorrow's subjunctive. That's one of the ways human experience is recycled.

The lower right quadrant—the future/indicative—is the actual performance-to-be-enacted. It is indicative because it actually happens. It is in the future because the figure is conceived from the temporal perspective of a sequence of rehearsals in progress: in figures 2 and 3, "me" is moving along with rehearsals from the left to the right.

There is nothing in the upper right quadrant—the future/subjunctive—because performances are always actually performed. But one might place some workshops and Grotowski's paratheater there, as a sequence $1 \rightarrow 5_a \rightarrow 5_c$. Paratheater and workshops are preparations and process implying performances that never-will-be. The paratheatrical work goes along "as if" there might be a performance, an end to the process; but the process doesn't end, it has no logical finality, it simply stops. There is no performance at point 5_c.

In 1 → 2 I become someone else, or myself in another state of being, or mood, so "unlike me" that I appear to be "beside myself" or "possessed by another." There is little rehearsal for this kind of performance, sometimes none. From birth, people are immersed in the kind of social performative actions that are sufficient preparations for entering trance. Watching children, infants even, at a black church or in Bali reveals a continuous training by osmosis. The displacement of 1 → 2 may be slight, as in some mood changes, or very strong, as in some trances. But in either case there is little appeal to either an actual or a subjunctive past. "Something happens" and the person (performer) is no longer himself. This kind of performance, because it is so close to "natural behavior" (maybe extraordinary from the outside but expected from within the culture)—either by surrender to strong outside forces, as in possession, or by giving in to moods within oneself—can be very powerful. It can happen to anyone, suddenly, and such instant performative behavior is regarded as evidence of the strength of the force possessing the subject. The performer does not seem to be "acting." A genuine if temporary transformation (a transportation) takes place. Most 1 → 2 performances are solos, even if these solos happen simultaneously in the same space. The astonishing thing about Balinese sanghyang trance dancing is that each dancer has by her/himself so incarnated the collective score that solo dances cohere into group performances. Upon recovering from the trance, dancers are often unaware that others were dancing; sometimes they don't remember their own dancing. I've seen similar meshing of solo performing into an ensemble several times at the Institutional Church in Brooklyn. As the gospel singing reached a climax more than a dozen women, men, and children "fell out" into the aisles. People watched them closely, grabbing them if they became too violent, preventing them from knocking against the chairs, calming them down when the singing subsided. The same kind of assistance is offered to trance dancers in Bali and elsewhere. The event in Brooklyn is very neatly organized. The singers whose gospel fired the trance dancing were definitely not in trance. They were the "transporters" propelling the dancers into trance. The dancers depended upon their friends to keep the dancing safe. The others in the church—potentially trance dancers but for the time being either more or less involved in the action—filled out a continuum from cool spectators to nearly wholly entranced clappers, foot stompers, and shouters. Each trance dancer was dancing in trance alone, but the whole group was dancing together, the whole church was rocking with collective performative energy. Peter Adair's film of a snake-handling, white, fundamentalist Christian sect in West Virginia, *The Holy Ghost People*, shows the same thing.

In 1 → 3 → 4 an event from some other place or past is restored—a "living newspaper" or a diorama at the American Museum of Natural History. Strictly speaking, dioramas are restored environments, not behaviors. But increasingly action is being added to the environments. [In] "restored villages" and "theme parks" . . . fact and fancy are freely mixed. Some zoos, however, try their best to make their displays genuine replicas of the wild. Reacting to the vanishing wilderness, zoo keepers are creating "breeding parks."

In the breeding park near Front Royal, Virginia, the attempt to keep an authentic and pristine environment is such that all visitors except breeders, veterinarians, and ethologists are excluded. At the San Diego Wild Animal Park in the lovely hills thirty miles northeast of the city, there is a combination of authenticity and local cultural values (shtick). Those riding the monorail around the 600-acre display are repeatedly reminded by the tour guide of the authenticity of the park. The brochure all visitors get begins:

> Join us here . . . to contemplate the wild animals of the world and nature's wilderness . . . to strengthen a commitment to wildlife conservation throughout the world . . . and to strive toward man's own survival through the preservation of nature.

Of course, there are adjacent to the monorail "wild preserve" a number of food stands, souvenir stores, and theaters offering animal shows (trained birds, a petting pen, etc.). Also, the park features nightly concerts of jazz, bluegrass, calypso, and "big band sounds." There is a McDonald's. This same brochure invites the more spendy visitors to "Join us for a tempting 10-ounce Delmonico steak dinner at Thorn Tree Terrace each evening, and take a new Caravan Tour into the preserve." Oh, well. But what interested me most was when I asked the monorail guide what the lions "roaming free" ate? Special food pellets packed with everything nutritious. Why not some of the wildebeests running across the fence from the lions? Well, I was told, although there is no shortage of wildebeests and lions do hunt them back in Africa, it would take too much space and, maybe, it wouldn't be so nice for the monorail visitors to witness such suppers. In this way, $1 \rightarrow 3 \rightarrow 4$ is transformed by specific cultural values into $1 \rightarrow 5_a \rightarrow 5_b$. The whole tone of the Wild Animal Park is of peaceful cohabitation. The hunting behavior of carnivores, though known, is not seen. The 5_a that the park restores is consistent with current California notions of how best "to contemplate . . . nature's wilderness."

Many traditional performances are $1 \rightarrow 3 \rightarrow 4$. So are performances that are kept in repertory according to a strict adherence to the original score. When the Moscow Art Theater visited New York in the mid-sixties, it claimed to present Chekhov according to Stanislavski's original mise-en-scènes. When I saw several plays of Brecht at the Berlin Ensemble in 1969 I was told that Brecht's Modelbuchs—his detailed photo accounts of his mise-en-scènes—were followed. Classical ballets have been passed on through generations of dancers. But even the strictest attempts at $1 \rightarrow 3 \rightarrow 4$ frequently are in fact examples of $1 \rightarrow 5_a \rightarrow 5_b$. $1 \rightarrow 3 \rightarrow 4$ is very unstable, simply because even if human memory can be improved upon by the use of film or exact notation a performance always happens within several contexts, and these are not easily controllable. The social circumstances change—as is obvious when you think of Stanislavski's productions at the turn of the century and the Moscow Art Theater today. Even the bodies of performers—what they are supposed to look like, how they are supposed to move, what they think and believe—change radically over relatively brief periods of time, not to mention the reactions, feelings, and moods of the audience. Performances that were once current, even avant-garde, soon become period pieces. These kinds of contextual changes are not measurable by Labanotation.[2] The difference between $1 \rightarrow 3 \rightarrow 4$ and $1 \rightarrow 5_a \rightarrow 5_b$ is shown in figure 2. In $1 \rightarrow 3 \rightarrow 4$ there is an event (3) that is always referred back to. This event serves as model and corrective. If during a rehearsal of one of Brecht's plays, according to his

authorized mise-en-scène, it is suspected that some gesture is not being performed as Brecht intended it, the gesture is checked back against the Modelbuch (and other documentary evidence). What the Modelbuch says goes. It is the authority. All details are checked against an "authorized original." Many rituals follow this pattern. This is not to say that rituals—and Brecht's mise-en-scènes—do not change. They change in two ways: first, by a slow slippage made inevitable by changing historical circumstances; second, through "official revisions" made by the owners-heirs of the "authorized original." In either case, it is my view that $1 \rightarrow 3 \rightarrow 4$ is very unstable: it is always becoming $1 \rightarrow 5_a \rightarrow 5_b$. . . .

* * *

A very clear example of a restoration of behavior of the $1 \rightarrow 5_a \rightarrow 5_b$ or $1 \rightarrow 3 \rightarrow 5_a \rightarrow 5_b$ type is the agnicayana that Frits Staal and Robert Gardner filmed in 1975 in Panjal, Kerala, India. Staal writes:

> The Agnicayana, a 3000-year-old Vedic ritual, was performed in 1975 in southwest India by Nambudiri Brahmans. This event, which lasted twelve days, was filmed, photographed, recorded and extensively documented. From twenty hours of rough footage, Robert Gardner and I produced a 45-minute film, *Altar of Fire*. Two records are planned with selections from the eighty hours of recorded recitation and chant. Photographs of the ceremonies were taken by Adelaide de Menil. In collaboration with the chief Nambudiri ritualists and other scholars, I am preparing a definite [*sic*] account of the ceremonies, which will appear in two illustrated volumes entitled: "Agni—The Vedic Ritual of the Fire Altar." . . . Vedic ritual is not only the oldest surviving ritual of mankind; it also provides the best source material for a theory of ritual. . . . Hubert and Mauss . . . used the Vedic animal sacrifice as source material for a construction of a ritual paradigm. However, they did not know that these rituals are still performed, so that many data were inaccessible to them. [1978, 1–2]

By now (1983) Staal's ambitious program has been achieved. Note that he uses the 1975 agnicayana as the basis for his construction of a ritual paradigm. I am not concerned with that theory because of an irony: were it not being filmed, photographed, and tape recorded, the 1975 Agnicayana would not have been performed. The impetus for the 1975 ag-nicayana was in America, not India: most of the money and much of the scholarly interest came from outside Kerala. Kerala was the 1975 ag-nicayana's location (as in ordinary films) but not its generative center. I doubt that American agencies would have responded with cash to an appeal from Nambudiri Brahmans to mount a ritual were it not to be filmed and studied. It was the threat of extinc-tion—the sense that "this is the last chance to record this event"—that created the 1975 agnicayana. Ac-tually, the 1975 agnicayana was either the one after the last of a series generated from within Kerala or the first of a new series generated by intercultural circumstances.

There are two related versions of the origins of the 1975 agnicayana. In the material accompanying the film, *Altar of Fire,* "a 16 mm color film on the world's oldest surviving ritual," a University of Cal-ifornia publicist writes:

> The background and problems of making *Altar of Fire* are perhaps as interesting as the ritual itself. The film's co-producer, Frits Staal, Professor of Philosophy and South Asian Languages at UC Berkeley, began study-ing Vedic recitation in southern India while a student in the 1950s. Later he discovered that the Nambudiri Brahmins not only transmitted the oral tradition through recitation but also continued to perform some of the larger Vedic rituals, the largest of which, the Ag-nicayana, had never been witnessed by outsiders.

> Western scholars had reconstructed this ritual from texts, but nobody had thought it possible that the cer-emony survived. Yet it has. There are only a few Nam-budiri families, however, whose members are entitled and able to carry out such a ceremony. It is expensive and requires years of training. Further, the tradition is rapidly dying because young people no longer believe in the efficacy of the ritual. As some Nambudiris be-came concerned about the disappearance of their tra-dition, Dr. Staal began to urge that the ceremony should be performed one last time so that it could be filmed and recorded.

> After years of intermittent discussion, the Nambudiris agreed. They asked only that in exchange for being given the privilege of attending, filming, and record-ing the performance, the scholars help defray the cost of the ritual. . . . Finally, by the end of 1974, almost $90,000 was raised from grants and donations by in-stitutions throughout the world. Robert Gardner, the noted ethnographic filmmaker (*Dead Birds, Rivers of Sand*) and professor at Harvard, was secured to direct the film. The Agnicayana was performed from April 12 to 24, 1975. [Extension Media Center, University of California]

The blurb goes on to describe the struggle involved in the filming itself. "There was a tendency to trans-form the sacrificial enclosure into a place of pil-grimage." Scuffles broke out between pilgrims and sightseers on the one hand and "scholars, Nam-budiri youths, and six policemen" on the other. But despite all efforts,

> At times, outsiders entered the sacrificial enclosure (a taboo place avoided scrupulously by the visiting schol-ars) and imperiled the filming—and indeed the ritual proceedings themselves. Some film footage was spoiled or its use made impossible by these fully dressed people who contrasted sadly with the Nam-budiris in their white loincloths, themselves disfigured only by an occasional wristwatch.

The University of California brochure describes a drama not shown in *Altar of Fire.* An endangered species—in this case, a rare, ancient ritual—is saved by the timely intervention of dedicated conserva-tionists from the outside who know both how to raise cash and how to behave on location. But the locals divide into two camps. The bad ones trans-form the event into something very postmodern: a combination media show and ad hoc pilgrimage center. These uncooperative locals dress according to their own mid-1970s codes—not as "natives"— and thereby "spoil" some footage. By contrast, and definitely in costume, the main actors—Nambudiri Brahmans—are "disfigured only by an occasional wristwatch." Scholarship plus media can turn the clock back three thousand years. Naturally enough, given the cinematic conventions of this kind of thing, the film itself shows very little of the struggle to make an "accurate" document of the agnicayana. The account of that struggle is reserved for the book, *Agni: The Vedic Ritual of the Fire Altar* (Staal 1983; two volumes, $250 for the set). Staal also gives the budgets for the project—a total of $127,207, of which $20,884 was spent in rupees on local expenses. That leaves more than $106,000 spent on the movie and all other non-Indian, non-local expenses. The agnicayana itself is probably out of financial reach for the Kerala Nambudiris. Certainly the filming is. The narrator of *Altar of Fire* makes no mention of the amount of money spent; credits at the film's end specify who, not how much. There is only the barest hint of the fierce local disagreements that surrounded the project. The UC press release makes a big thing out of these struggles because that underlines the heroic work of the film makers who were able to "overcome" all such difficulties.

But the UC brochure and the account in *Agni: The Vedic Ritual of the Fire Altar* are not the only "official" versions of what happened. Staal was attacked by Robert A. Paul (1978) for staging the agnicayana. In defending himself, Staal quotes the UC brochure. Then he adds:

> The Adhvaryu, the main priest, and several of the other priests who officiated in 1975 had earlier officiated in 1955 or 1956, or both [the most recent Kerala-generated performances of agnicayana]. All our films and recordings had to be made from the outside. Under such circumstances, without two decades of experience and several years of careful planning, it would not have been possible to film and record this event, which was quite possibly the last performance of the world's oldest surviving ritual. All those who were present realized that this was not a humdrum affair, but a historical event. [1979, 346–47]

But what kind of historical event? Is a ritual "surviving" if the filmed version of it is also a document of its "last [that is, final] performance"? Before 1975, the agnicayana was previously performed in the 1950s. In *Agni* Staal lists 103 performances including 22 that occurred in Kerala over the past one hundred years. In a letter to me (15 June 1983) disputing whether the agnicayana of the *Altar of Fire* is an event of the $1 \rightarrow 5_a \rightarrow 5_b$ type, Staal states that "such performances took place for almost three thousand years, and are well documented for many periods." He says that a reader can compare the 1975 performance step by step with "the ritual as it was before 600 B.C."

What I am saying is that no matter what textual documentation exists we do not know what agnicayana was. The transmission of the ritual is a very complicated interaction among elements of the oral tradition and written texts and formulas. The transmission of the ritual itself—as a performance text

(not a description, not a literary text, but as a thing done)—was largely oral, from man to boy, older Brahman priest to younger, employing a number of mnemonic devices used by Vedic reciters. Will *Altar of Fire*, *Agni*, and the eighty hours of sound tape, twenty hours of raw footage, and "thousands of color slides" now freeze the agnicayana texts? Freeze them in a way very different than the Sanskrit texts and memories of living persons charged with keeping and transmitting the oral tradition freeze things? In what way is the 1975 agnicayana a continuation of the oral tradition, and in what way is it a $1 \rightarrow 5_a \rightarrow 5_b$ or a $1 \rightarrow 3 \rightarrow 5_a \rightarrow 5_b$?

The agnicayana is very expensive by Kerala standards. That's why money had to be raised outside the community. Many priests are employed, a ritual enclosure built, an altar of firebrick constructed, food and shelter provided, and so on. The rite itself is archaic: long ago Vedic ritual gave way to later forms of Hinduism. Brahman priests reconstructed the 1975 agnicayana from a variety of sources: memory of previous performances, local opinion, Sanskrit texts. Also, and decisively for both the ritual itself and its filming, agnicayana requires animal sacrifice, a practice repugnant to many Kerala residents. Staal says, "Although discussion on the presence, dollars, and motives of foreign scholars and cameramen were relatively few, the outpouring of sentiment over the goats was practically unbounded" (1983, 2: 464). But it was the issue of the goats that was a magnet for discussions about dollars and foreign scholars. The controversy raged in the press, and because of Kerala's high literacy rate, 80 percent, almost everyone knew about the goats. In 1975 Kerala had a Marxist government, the Left is strong in the state, and animal sacrifice at the American-sponsored agnicayana became a prime political issue pitting old-fashioned entrenched interests, symbolized by the Nambudiri Brahman high-caste agnicayana, against more "proletarian" and "modern" interests. Finally, in Staal's words, "for the first time in the history of the Nambudiri tradition, the animals would be represented by rice flour folded in banana leaf" (1983, 2: 465). The heated politics of Kerala is absent from *Altar of Fire*.

The contextual situation of the 1975 agnicayana is extremely complex. The agnicayana is between an original event—the continuation of the oral tradition—and a social, political, and media event. In restoring agnicayana, considerations of how best to document the Vedic ritual—not the social or media event, certainly not the political controversy raging over the goats—were always first in the minds of Staal and Gardner. This intention to make a film of the agnicayana, as their texts and their Nambudiri Brahman priests said it was, rather than to make a film of what took place in 1975 is what makes *Altar of Fire* a $1 \rightarrow 5_a \rightarrow 5_b$. For *Altar of Fire* is what Staal and Gardner intended it to become—and to achieve their intention they had to shoot around the situation they found themselves in.

Their shooting script shows this—not that the passive recording of events is possible, even with the notebook and pencil. Like many rituals, agnicayana involves a great deal of simultaneous action over a wide range of spaces. But the camera and microphone are instruments of focus; and finished movies and sound casettes are the outcomes of rigorous selective editing. As performed in 1975, the agnicayana took 120 hours, plus many more hours of preparations—not to count the hours negotiating the fate of the goats. Staal and Gardner could shoot only twenty hours, and their script says that for "numerous episodes filming depends on remaining quantity of raw stock."[3] The twenty hours of raw footage were edited into a forty-five-minute film. The shooting script breaks the twelve-day ceremony into numerous episodes convenient to the camera. The script is very specific about who the main performers are and what is of interest:

> Adhvaryu I [chief priest]: as stage manager he performs most of the rites and commands the others. He is where the action is. . . .
>
> The final killing of the goat within the Camitra will not be filmed on this occasion [day 1] since this would upset many people; but hopefully on a later occasion. . . .
>
> [For day 2] No more than thirty minutes of filming for the entire day.

These procedures are only faintly reflected in *Altar of Fire*. On 11 April, the day before the agnicayana began, a statement was issued jointly in Malayalam and English by Muttathukkattil Mamunna Itti Ravi Nambudiri and Staal, explaining that a committee had been formed, government aid acquired, and a lot of money raised to "make it possible to film and record the [agnicayana] rituals so that a permanent

record would be available to scholars all over the world." The statement ends by declaring that "inanimate substances" would be used instead of goats. "The organizers hereby assure the public that no animal sacrifice will take place. We request the cooperation of the public for the successful conduct of the Yagna [agnicayana]" (Staal 1983, 2: 467–68). The shooting script had to be revised.

On camera, Edmund Carpenter, one of the visiting scholars invited to comment, says that there are three kinds of events going on simultaneously: the agnicayana, the social event surrounding the ritual, and the media event. He does not mention the political event. *Altar of Fire* focuses its attention on the agnicayana, all but forgetting social, media, and political events. But in India even noncontroversial ritual performances attract onlookers, merchants, beggars, entertainers, and crowds of curious. Media events are relatively rare, making the filming of the agnicayana a doubly powerful attraction for rural Panjal. On the last day, when the sacred enclosure was burned, a crowd of ten to fifteen thousand gathered. But *Altar of Fire* is carefully nonreflexive. The book, *Agni*, is more inclusive of these contextual events, but Staal still insists that the 1975 agnicayana is in no sense a reconstruction or restoration. The film he and Gardner made presents itself in such a way as to suggest that the film makers just happened to arrive and catch this ritual in time. But the film is actually at the convergence of two great streams of events: one to raise the money and gather the people necessary to perform and film agnicayana; the other the controversy, media, and social events that accumulated around the doing and filming of the ritual.

We need no new educating to the idea that the instruments and means of observing and recording things deeply affect what's being observed. The substantial financial-logistical energies that made *Altar of Fire* possible also made the 1975 agnicayana possible and also brought into existence much of the turmoil surrounding the project. These bundles of events have to be considered in relation to each other; and they need to be understood as parts of one complicated meta-event. We are also used to questioning the authenticity of performances like the 1975 agnicayana. But it is not authenticity that needs to be questioned. Rather, we want ways of understanding the whole bundle of relations that joins Sanskrit scholars, film makers, Nambudiri priests, the press, Marxists, curious and agitated crowds, and performance theorists. If the discussion stops shy of considering this whole bundle, we miss the chance to recognize in the Staal-Gardner project another harbinger of an important shift toward the theatricalization of anthropology—and maybe not just anthropology. By replacing the notebook with the tape recorder, the still camera with the movie camera, the monograph with the film, a shift occurs whereby we understand social life as narrative, image, crisis and crisis resolution, drama, person-to-person interaction, display behavior, and so on. Theatrical techniques blur temporal and causal systems, creating in their stead bundles of relations that attain only relative clarity and independence from each other—and those only within contexts or frames that themselves need definition. For example, in film an effect may precede its cause. Something that happened later—in the shooting of a film, in the rehearsal of a performance—may be used earlier in the finished product. Only $1 \rightarrow 5_a \rightarrow 5_b$ shows this kind of performative circumstance.

If I fault Staal and Gardner at all it is because they did not make a second film, "On Filming *Altar of Fire*," that dealt fully with all the contextual events—dramas, arrangements, rehearsals, struggles, negotiations—that truly characterize late-twentieth-century social life, a social life that delights in on-location intensity and focus—as at Panjal—but that also extends around the globe and involves hundreds of persons who collectively decide whether or not an agnicayana gets performed without necessarily knowing what agnicayana is.

People may believe the 1975 agnicayana to be a $1 \rightarrow 3 \rightarrow 4$. But actually it is a $1 \rightarrow 5_a \rightarrow 5_b$. It was restored in order to be filmed. Its "future as a film," 5_b, created its "past as a ritual," 5_a. When events like the fight over the goats erupted at time 1, threatening the agnicayana's future as a film, these events were thought also to threaten its past as a ritual. To keep the ritual "accurate" and "genuine" the fight had to be excluded from *Altar of Fire*. The camera and narrator had to glide lightly over those packets of rice wrapped in leaves. An event of the $1 \rightarrow 5_a \rightarrow 5_b$ type can get away with not sacrificing goats while

being proclaimed by Staal as an example of "animal sacrifice . . . still performed."

Altar of Fire ends with the narrator announcing that the viewer has seen what is probably the last performance of agnicayana. Not true. The viewer has seen the first of a new series of performances, a series where the event will never change because it is "on film." When people want to "see" the agnicayana they will not go to Kerala (where it may or may not be performed again), they will rent *Altar of Fire*. Funding agencies will not put up enough money to film agnicayana all over again; that would be redundant. Scholars using agnicayana will base their findings not on the series that ended in the 1950s—about which little is known—but on the material gathered by Staal and Gardner. And few, if any, scholars will examine all of the raw footage, listen to the full set of tapes, look at every one of the thousands of photographs. They will instead look at the movie, listen to the recordings, read the writings that came out of the Staal-Gardner project. Theories will be built on items extrapolated from strips of restored behavior.

Is this any different than building theories on writings? Writings are more easily recognized as interpretations than are restorations of behavior. Theories are presented in the same bundle as the data on which these theories rest. References are freely made to earlier interpretations and theories. Often writing is clearly reflexive. I don't prefer writings to restorations of behavior as a way of scholarship, but restorations are not yet understood as thoroughly as writing. Therefore, at present, restorations leave more mess than writing. People use restorations and consider them $1 \rightarrow 2$ or $1 \rightarrow 3 \rightarrow 4$ when actually they are $1 \rightarrow 5_a \rightarrow 5_b$ or $1 \rightarrow 3 \rightarrow 5_a \rightarrow 5_b$.

Figure 5 shows the full range of events flowing into and from the 1975 agnicayana. The movie becomes "now" for persons who in the future experience agnicayana through this medium. As Staal says, it is likely that most people will know agnicayana this way. Even if agnicayana is performed in Kerala again, it is possible that the Nambudiris will view the film and measure their ritual against it. The filming itself—as distinct from the finished film—is the core generative event. Before the filming comes planning, fund raising, consultations with ritual specialists, assembling people, material, and animals; and after the

	ORIGINAL EVENTS	MEDIA EVENTS	SCHOLARSHIP
Time "Then" 1	Agnicayana, 1950s and earlier: oral tradition		
"Now" 2	Agnicayana 1975		
2	Deciding how to do the ritual: consultations with priests, scholars, locals, film makers, etc.; remembering and rehearsing		
2	Making a shooting script		
2		Rough footage Still photos Recorded sound	
2	People who came to see the ritual		
2		People who came to see the filming	
2	Fight over sacrificing the goats		
"Later" 3		Finished film Finished writings Finished recordings	
4			Theory of ritual

FIGURE 5

filming comes the work of archiving and editing raw goods and, ultimately, items of Euro-American culture such as movies, cassettes, books. There are also items shared among Indians and Euro-Americans: theories of ritual, data on the agnicayana "then," "now," and "later." Most of the events shown in figure 5 are "betwixt and between." They happen between original events and media events and between media events and scholarship. The original series of agnicayanas was liminal, an old-fashioned ritual; but from 1975 on the agnicayana has become liminoid,

a voluntary performative event. Insofar as the agnicayana is liminoid it serves interests far beyond and different [from] those the old-fashioned agnicayana served when it belonged solely to Kerala. . . .

Why not think of Staal and Gardner as film directors? Their work in India is more easily understood when seen in performative terms. An earlier event is "researched" and/or "remembered"—actions equivalent to rehearsals. A performance is arranged that presumably duplicates this earlier event, or selects from a series of earlier events what is most "essential," "typical," or "authentic." An event created in the future (the film, *Altar of Fire*, 5ᵦ) is projected backward in time (the "original" agnicayana, 5ₐ) and restored "now" in order to be filmed (what happened in Kerala in 1975, 1). The items in this bundle cannot be separated; they must be considered as a unit. The so-called prior event (the "original" agnicayana is not strictly prior) certainly doesn't "cause" the 1975 performance. The 1975 performance is caused by the project of making a film. So in a sense the future is causing the present which, in turn, makes it necessary to research, remember—rehearse—restore the past. But this past—what is turned up by the rehearsal process—determines what is done in 1975, and those events are used to make the movie. The movie then replaces the "original" event. The movie is what we have of the past.

. . . .

Staal and Gardner are not alone in entering the field as theatrical producers-directors in the guise of anthropological fieldworkers. Not finding a ritual worthy of being filmed, they arranged for one to be performed. They made sure there was enough lead time to get money to make the movie and to import a planeload of important scholars. Their lie, if there is one, comes with the marketing of *Altar of Fire* as a document of a "living ritual" they just happened on in the nick of time. The film's audience may construe agnicayana as a "living ritual" when in fact it is a complicated kind of playacting. But I think I've shown how playacting is a kind of living ritual—though one made reflexive through the use of training, workshop, and/or rehearsal. *Altar of Fire* is more than a film of Vedic ritual. The filming itself ritualizes the action of restoring the agnicayana. But that work of ritualization took place in the out-of-sequence shooting, in the disputes surrounding the sacrifice (or nonsacrifice) of the goats, and in the editing room.

Maybe even today most anthropologists would agree with Turner, who in 1969 said of his stay with the Ndembu, "We never asked for a ritual to be performed solely for our own anthropological benefit; we held no brief for such artificial play-acting" (1969, 10). But the presence of the fieldworker is an invitation to playacting. And what should be done regarding traditions that are near extinction? Old-style patronage is finished. Yesterday patrons wanted performances either as entertainment, as celebration, or for ritual benefit. Today patrons want performances for the archives or as data from which to develop theories. Patrons such as the National Endowment for the Arts sponsor performances to "enrich cultural life"—which means a whole spectrum of things from paying off the upper middle class to keeping unruly youth in tow.

But what ought our response be to genres doomed by modernization and postmodernization? In Karnataka, South India, not too many miles from where Staal and Gardner filmed, Martha Ashton was "not only the first foreigner to study Yakshagana in detail, but . . . also the first and only female to perform it."[4] Ashton joined with her teacher Hiriyadka Gopala Rao in reconstructing old-style Yakshagana. They assembled a company, helped recollect old stories, steps, and songs. Not only did Ashton film the results of this reconstruction, she also wrote a book on Yakshagana (Ashton and Christie 1977) and organized a tour of the Rao-Ashton company to America in 1976—77. Was she wrong in doing all this? When I visited Kamataka in 1976 I saw three kinds of Yakshagana: the popular version; a style for modern audiences developed by K. S. Karanth, a well-known writer; and "classical Yakshagana" restored largely through the efforts of Rao and Ashton. Which style is most or least Indian?

The position of purists who refuse to stage the rituals or performances they are studying and recording (on film, on tape, and in books) is not pure but ambivalent. Their position is analogous to that of experimental theater auteur Richard Foreman who, in many of his productions, sat between his players and the audience, often running a tape recorder broadcasting his own voice interpreting and asking questions and giving instructions. To the society the fieldworker temporarily inhabits, he represents his home culture in one of its most inexplicable aspects: Why send somebody around the world to observe and record how another group lives? And to those of us who see or read the reports of the fieldworker, he is our main link with both fresh aspects of human behavior (fresh to us, that is) and our often asserted, sometimes tested, but never proven assertion that humans are one species culturally, "humanly," as well as biologically.

The situation precipitated by the fieldworker's

presence is a theatrical one: he is there to see, and he is seen. But what role does the fieldworker play? He is not a performer and not not a performer, not a spectator and not not a spectator. He is in between two roles just as he is in between two cultures. In the field he represents—whether he wants to or not—his culture of origin; and back home he represents the culture he has studied. The fieldworker is always in a "not . . . not not" situation. And like a performer going through workshops-rehearsals the fieldworker goes through the three-phase performance process isomorphic with the ritual process:

1. The stripping away of his own ethnocentrism. This is often a brutal separation, which in itself is the deepest struggle of fieldwork, and is never complete. What should he eat, how? And his toilet habits, his problems of hygiene. And the dozens of other things that remind the worker of the distance between his own culture and the one he wants to get inside of. But if his work is to succeed, he has to undergo some kind of transformation.

2. The revelation, often coming suddenly like inspiration, of what is "new" in the culture he temporarily inhabits. This discovery is his initiation, his transition, the taking on of a new role in his adoptive society, a role that often includes a new identity, position, or status. The worker "goes native," even inside himself.

3. The difficult task of using his field notes (or raw footage and sound tapes) to make an acceptable "product"—monograph, film, lectures, whatever: the way he edits and translates what he found into items understood by the world he returns to. In brief, he must make an acceptable performance out of all workshop-rehearsal material. His promotion to full professor ratifies his reintegration into his own society.

As fieldwork converges on theatrical directing, the third phase of the process includes making films—or, as Victor and Edith Turner did with their students, "performing ethnography" (see Turner and Turner 1982). It is this third phase of the process that is most problematical. Clearly, monographs are written in the style of the "home culture." Only recently, with an increase in "life histories," has there been some effort to make writing speak in the voice of the "away culture." But even life histories are translations. Films use images drawn directly from the away culture. These images make it seem as if the away culture were speaking for itself. But of course camera angles, methods of shooting, focus, and editing all reflect the world of the film maker. If the film maker is from the away culture, the point of view may be more from the inside—but maybe not: technology enforces its own logic. Or the resultant film may not be "ethnographic" in the classic sense. Ethnography demands a double vision, inside and outside simultaneously or alternately. If the fieldworker is able to show all this (maybe using local camerapersons and editors), the third phase of the fieldworker's progression folds back into phase 1. He tries to show his own people what the away culture is like in its own terms. It may be too much to ask—or the wrong thing.

In the past anthropologists have fancied themselves siblings of "hard scientists." But hard science works from models strictly fenced off from ordinary life; and it depends on predictive theory. The soft sciences are actually extensions of the arts and humanities. . . . Theory in the social sciences is little more than what Geertz calls "thick description" (1973, 3–32). Presently the theater director is leaving the shadowy, out-of-sight offstage and entering the stage not just as another performer but as a unique figure: the embodiment of the workshop-rehearsal process. Fieldworkers now not only watch but learn, participate, and initiate actions. Directors have been, and fieldworkers are becoming, specialists in restored behavior. In this epoch of information and reflexive hyperconsciousness we not only want to know, we also want to know how we know what we know.

* * *

D. W. Winnicott's ideas add an ontogenic level and a new set of categories to my description of what the performer does. Winnicott, a British psychoanalyst, studied the mother-baby relationship, especially how the baby learns to distinguish between "me" and "not me." Winnicott called certain objects "transitional"—in between the mother and the baby, belonging to neither the mother nor the baby (the mother's breasts, a security blanket, certain special toys). And the circumstances in which these transitional objects were used constituted "transitional phenomena."

I am here staking a claim for an intermediate state between a baby's inability and his growing ability to recognize and accept reality. I am therefore studying the substance of *illusion*, that which is allowed to the infant and which in adult life is inherent in art and religion. . . .

I think there is a use for a term for the root of symbolism in time, a term that describes the infant's journey from the purely subjective to objectivity; and it seems that the transitional object (piece of blanket, etc.) is what we see of this journey of progress toward experiencing. . . .

The transitional object and transitional phenomena start each individual off with what will always be important to them, i.e., a neutral sense of experience which will not be challenged. . . .

The important part of this concept is that whereas inner psychic reality has a kind of location in the mind or in the belly or in the head of somewhere within the bounds of the individual's personality and whereas what is called external reality is located outside these bounds, playing and cultural experience can be given a location if one uses the concepts of the potential space between the mother and the baby [1971, 3, 5, 12, 53]

This potential space is workshop-rehearsal, the liminal/liminoid space, the $1 \rightarrow 5_a \rightarrow 5_b$ bundle.

Winnicott's ideas mesh nicely with Van Gennep's, Turner's, and Bateson's, in whose "play frame" ([1955] 1972, 177–93) "transitional phenomena" take place. The most dynamic formulation of what Winnicott is describing is that the baby—and later the child at play and the adult at art (and religion)—recognizes some things and situations as "not me . . . not not me." During workshops-rehearsals performers play with words, things, and actions, some of which are "me" and some "not me." By the end of the process the "dance goes into the body." So Olivier is not Hamlet, but he is also not not Hamlet. The reverse is also true: in this production of the play, Hamlet is not Olivier, but he is also not not Olivier. Within this field or frame of double negativity choice and virtuality remain activated.

In children the movement from "not me" to "not not me" is seen in their relationship to security blankets, favorite toys that cannot be replaced no matter how old, dirty, or broken. Play itself deconstructs actuality in a "not me . . . not not me" way. The hierarchies that usually set off actuality as "real" and fantasy as "not real" are dissolved for the "time being," the play time. These same operations of dissolving ordinary hierarchies, of treasuring things beyond their ordinary worth, of setting aside certain times and places for the manipulation of special things in a world defined nonordinarily: this is also a definition of the workshop-rehearsal process, the ritual process, the performative process.

When such performance actualities are played out before audiences, the spectators have a role to play. Winnicott puts into his own terms an audience's "willing suspension of disbelief."

The essential feature in the concept of transitional objects and phenomena . . . is the paradox, and the acceptance of the paradox: the baby [performer] creates the object but the object was there waiting to be created [performance text]. . . . We will never challenge the baby [performer] to elicit an answer to the question: did you create that or did you find it? [1971, 89]

Olivier will not be interrupted in the middle of "To be or not to be" and asked. "Whose words are those?" And if he were interrupted, what could his reply be? The words belong, or don't belong equally to Shakespeare, Hamlet, Olivier. If such an interruption did take place the audience would assume Pirandello or Brecht was at work, building into the performance text its own reflexive double. But to whom would such an interruption belong? You see in the theater there is no place that is not make-believe. Even the shot that killed Lincoln, for a split second, must have seemed part of the show.

Restored behaviors of all kinds—rituals, theatrical performance, restored villages, agnicayana—are "transitional." Elements that are "not me" become "me" without losing their "not me-ness." This is the peculiar but necessary double negativity that characterizes symbolic actions. While performing, a performer experiences his own self not directly but through the medium of experiencing the others. While performing, he no longer has a "me" but has a "not not me," and this double negative relationship also shows how restored behavior is simultaneously private and social. A person performing recovers his own self only by going out of himself and meeting the others—by entering a social field. The way in which "me" and "not me," the performer and the thing to be performed, are transformed into "not me . . . not not me" is through the workshop-rehearsal/ritual process. This process takes place in a liminal time/space and in the subjunctive mood. The subjunctive character of the liminal time/space is reflected in the negative, antistructural frame around the whole process. This antistructure could be expressed algebraically: "not (me . . . not me)."

Figure 6 portrays this system. Figure 6 is a version of $1 \rightarrow 5_a \rightarrow 5_b$. Actions move in time, from the past thrown into the future, from "me" to "not me" and from "not me" to "me." As they travel they are absorbed into the liminal, subjunctive time/space of "not me . . . not not me." This time/space includes both workshops-rehearsals and performances. Things thrown into the future ("Keep that") are recalled and used later in rehearsals and performances. During performance, if everything goes right, the experience is of synchronicity as the flow of ordinary time and the flow of performance time meet and eclipse each other. This eclipse is the "present moment," the synchronic ecstasy, the autotelic flow, of liminal stasis. Those who are masters at attaining and prolonging this balance are artists, shamans, conmen, acrobats. No one can keep it long.

By integrating the thought of Winnicott, Turner, and Bateson with my own work as a theater director, I propose a theory that includes the ontogenesis of individuals, the social action of ritual, and the symbolic, even fictive, action of art. Clearly these overlap: their underlying process is identical. A performance "takes place" in the "not me . . . not not me" between performers; between performers and texts; between performers, texts, and environment; between performers, texts, environment, and audience. The larger the field of "between," the stronger the performance. The antistructure that is performance swells until it threatens to burst. The trick is to extend it to the bursting point but no further. It is the ambition of all performances to expand this field until it includes all beings, things, and relations. This can't happen. The field is precarious because it is subjunctive, liminal, transitional: it rests not on how things are but on how things are not; its existence depends on agreements kept among all participants, including the audience. The field is the embodiment of potential, of the virtual, the imaginative, the fictive, the negative, the not not. The larger it gets, the more it thrills, but the more doubt and anxiety it evokes, too. Catharsis comes when something happens to the performers and/or characters but not to the performance itself. But when doubt overcomes

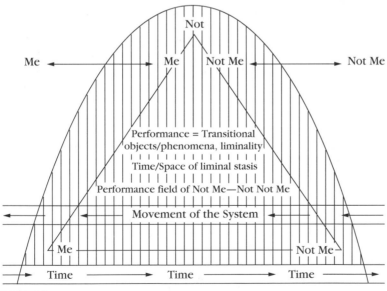

FIGURE 6

confidence, the field collapses like popped bubble gum. The result is a mess: stage fright, aloneness, emptiness, and a feeling of terrible inadequacy when facing the bottomless unappeasable appetite of the audience. When confidence—and the skills necessary to achieve what's promised—prevails, there is nothing performers can't do. A special empathy/sympathy vibrates between performers and spectators. The spectators do not "willingly suspend disbelief." They believe and disbelieve at the same time. This is theater's chief delight. The show is real and not real at the same time. This is true for performers as well as spectators and accounts for that special absorption the stage engenders in those who step onto it or gather around it. Sacred a stage may or may not be, special it always is.

*   *   *

The workshop-rehearsal process is the basic machine for the restoration of behavior. It is no accident that this process is the same in theater as it is in ritual. For the basic function of both theater and ritual is to restore behavior—to make performances of the $1 \rightarrow 5_a \rightarrow 5_b$ type. The meaning of individual rituals is secondary to this primary function, which is a kind of collective memory-in/of-action. The first phase breaks down the performer's resistance, makes him a tabula rasa. To do this most effectively the performer has to be removed from familiar surroundings. Thus the need for separation, for "sacred" or special space, and for a use of time different than that prevailing in the ordinary. The second phase is of initiation or transition: developing new or restoring old behavior. But so-called new behavior is really the rearrangement of old behavior or the enactment of old behavior in new settings. In the third phase, reintegration, the restored behavior is practiced until it is second nature. The final part of the third phase is public performance. Public performances in Euro-America are repeated until there are no more customers. In most cultures performances occur according to schedules that ration their availability. What we call new behavior, as I said, is only short strips of behavior rearticulated in novel patterns. Experimental performance thrives on these rearticulations masquerading as novelties. But the ethological repertory of behav-

iors, even human behaviors, is limited. In rituals, relatively long strips of behavior are restored, giving the impression of continuity, stasis: tradition. In creative arts, relatively short strips of behavior are rearranged and the whole thing looks new. Thus the sense of change we get from experimental arts may be real at the level of recombination but illusory at the basic structural/processual level. Real change is a very slow evolutionary process.

Many people these days fear a disruption of historical cultural variety brought about by world monoculture. Just as physical well-being depends on a varied gene pool, so social well-being depends on a varied "culture pool." Restored behavior is one way of preserving a varied culture pool. It is a strategy that fits into, and yet opposes, world monoculture. It is an artificial means of preserving the wild. Usually it is not local people who practice restored behavior in this conscious way. The devadasis were content to dance their sadir nac, even if it was doomed. The Mura and Dom danced and drummed their Chhau before Bhattacharyya arrived in 1961, even if it was "in decay." The agnicayana would or would not have been enacted again in Kerala without Staal and Gardner. As for Plimoth, the Pilgrims are long since gone. Modern sensibility wants to bring into the postmodern world "authentic cultural items." Maybe this is just a kind of postimperialist souvenir hunt. Or maybe it is something more and better. Within the frame of postmodern information theory all knowledge is reducible/transformable into bits of information. As such, these bits can be reconstructed in new ways to create new orders of facticity. An illusion of diversity is created backward in time to 5_a and forward to 5_b. This illusion is artful because it is art itself, pure theater. This illusion may have the status of "reality" as actual as any other order of reality. The underlying idea that information, not things, is the matrix of cultures, and maybe of "nature" itself, is at the root of such recent exploration as recombinant DNA, gene splicing, and cloning. What these experiments "create" is a liminal existence between nature and culture. The experiments suggest what the performing arts have long asserted, that "nature" and "culture" may be a false dichotomy, that actually these are not opposing realms but different treatments of identical information bits.

NOTES

1. In *Frame Analysis* Goffman used the term "strip of activity": The term 'strip' will be used to refer to any arbitrary slice or cut from the stream of ongoing activity, including here sequences of happenings, real or fictive, as seen from the perspective of those subjectively involved in sustaining an interest in them. A strip is not meant to reflect a natural division made by the subjects of inquiry or an analytical division made by students who inquire; it will be used only to refer to any raw batch of occurrences (of whatever status in reality) that one wants to draw attention to as a starting point for analysis" (1974, 10). My "strip of behavior" is related to Goffman's term, but it is also, as will be seen, significantly different.

2. Labanotation, roughly analogous to musical notation, was developed by Rudolf von Laban in 1928. According to an article in the *New York Times* (6 May 1979, "Arts and Leisure" section, p. 19) by Jack Anderson: "The system records dance movement by means of symbols on a page that is read from the bottom up. Three basic vertical lines represent the body's center, right, and left sides. Where the symbols are placed on the lines indicates what parts of the body are moving. The shape of the symbols indicates the direction of the movement, and their length indicates the movement's duration." This, plus other kinds of notation such as "effort-shape," makes it possible to more or less "keep" a dance or other bodily mise-en-scène long after it has stopped being performed. Such systems are now widely used in dance, less so in theater.

3. The *Altar of Fire* shooting script (Gardner[?] 1975) was given to me by someone who worked on the film—a local person. I obtained the script, in 1976. The script also gives detailed instructions to camerapeople, technicians, etc. It also provides drawings of the site, altars, etc. It includes lots of background material on agnicayana, as well as descriptions of what will happen.

4. From a publicity release announcing the Rao-Ashton company's tour to America.

REFERENCES

Ashton, Martha Bush, and Christie, Bruce. 1977 *Yakshagana.* New Delhi: Abhinav Publications.

Bateson, Gregory. 1972 *Steps to an Ecology of Mind.* New York: Ballantine Books.

Gardner, Robert. 1975 Presumed author of the shooting script used in the filming of the agnicayana of 1975. Script titled *Atiratra Agnicayana.* Undated photocopy of typescript.

Geertz, Clifford. 1973 *The Interpretation of Cultures.* New York: Basic Books.

Goffman, Erving. 1959. *The Presentation of Self in Everyday Life.* Garden City, N.Y.: Doubleday/Anchor.

———. 1974. *Frame Analysis.* New York: Harper Colophon Books.

Paul, Robert A. 1978 Review of *Altar of Fire. American Anthropologist* 80: 197–199.

Staal, Frits. 1978 "The Meaninglessness of Ritual." Manuscript.

———. 1979 "Comment: *Altar of Fire.*" a response to Robert A. Paul. *American Anthropologist* 81: 346–47.

———. 1983 *Agni: The Vedic Ritual of the Fire Altar.* Berkeley: Asian Humanities Press.

Turner, Victor. 1969 *The Ritual Process.* Chicago: Aldine.

———. 1982 *From Ritual to Theatre: The Human Seriousness of Play.* New York: Performing Arts Journal Press.

———, and Turner, Edith. 1982 "Performing Ethnography." *Drama Review* 26, 2: 33–50.

Van Gennep, Arnold. 1960 *The Rites of Passage* (originally published in 1908). Chicago: University of Chicago Press.

Winnicott, D. W. 1971 *Playing and Reality.* London: Tavistock.

Buddhism and Abortion in Contemporary Japan: Mizuko Kuyō *and the Confrontation with Death*

BARDWELL SMITH

Facts of publication: *Smith, Bardwell. 1992. "Buddhism and Abortion in Contemporary Japan:* Mizuko Kuyō *and the Confrontation with Death," from* Buddhism, Sexuality, and Gender, *65–89. Edited by José Ignacio Cabezón. Albany: State University of New York. Copyright © 1992 by State University of New York. Reprinted with the permission of the State University of New York Press. This article revised from an article published in* Japanese Journal of Religious Studies *15(1) (1988). Reprinted with the permission of* Japanese Journal of Religious Studies, *Nanzan Institute for Religion and Culture.*

Drawing on the research of a psychologist (Robert Jay Lifton) and anthropologist (Victor Turner), Bardwell Smith considers the psychosocial processes of grief, guilt, and healing after abortion in contemporary Japan. The mizuko kuyō, *a memorial service for unborn children, is one means of facilitating this process. Smith shows how it can function as a redressive rite in dealing with an experience that evokes considerable shame, isolation, and suffering among Japanese women.*

Compare this account with that of William R. LaFleur in Liquid Life: Abortion and Buddhism in Japan *(Princeton, NJ: Princeton University Press, 1992).*

About the author: Dates: *1925–   , Springfield, MA, U.S.A.* **Education:** *B.A., Yale University; M.A., Yale University; Ph.D., Yale University.* **Field(s):** *religious studies; anthropology of religion; Buddhism and society.* **Career:** *Professor of Religion and Asian Studies, 1960–present, Carleton College.* **Publications:** *with Frank E. Reynolds and Gananath Obeyesekere,* The Two Wheels of Dharma: Essays on Theravada Buddhism *(American Academy of Religion Monograph Series, 1972); editor, with John C. Perry,* Esssays on Tang Society *(Brill, 1976); editor,* Religion and the Legitimation of Power in Sri Lanka *(Anima, 1978); with George Elison,* Warlords, Artists and Commoners: Japan in the Sixteenth Century *(University of Hawaii, 1981); with Holly Reynolds,* The City as a Sacred Center: Essays on Six Asian Contexts *(Brill, 1987); editor,* Essays on Gupta Culture *(Motilal Banarsidass, 1993).* **Additional:** *American Council of Learned Studies research grant in Buddhist Studies, School of Oriental and African Studies, London University, 1972–1973; Fulbright research grant, Kyoto University, 1986–1987; National Endowment for the Humanities Collaborative Research Grant, 1991–1994; Memberships: American Society for the Study of Religion; American Academy of Religion; Association for Asian Studies. "Since 1986 I have been doing collaborative research with Elizabeth Harrison of the University of Arizona on the problem of child loss for Japanese women and Buddhist responses to abortion. We are hoping to complete a book on this subject. The topic involves much attention to ritual, though we seek to put the problem of ritualistic approaches to it in a larger social and religious context with Japan."*

The fact of death is the central human preoccupation. Other preoccupations are often skillful diversions from coping with one's mortality. In Reinhold Niebuhr's words, the human problem is not that we are finite but that we have trouble living with our finitude. To put the matter more directly, the central problem of life is not death but learning how to die. This chapter is about the confrontation with death set within the context of present-day Japan. It deals with the reality of death in the form of abortion, miscarriage, or stillbirth. It is not about abortion or infant death *in general*, but about the experience of mortality in personal terms. In particular, it is about the mother's experiencing of death, whether or not this death has been willed by her. And, it is also about factors within Japanese society that contribute to the dilemma surrounding abortion specifically.

Second, this chapter deals with various Japanese Buddhist reactions to the widespread modern phenomenon of abortion and raises questions about these responses. The primary response to this phenomenon is known as *mizuko kuyō: mizuko* mean-

ing water child or children, referring normally to an aborted fetus (induced or spontaneous) but also to stillborn infants and those who died soon after birth. *Kuyō* itself is a memorial service conducted in most cases by Buddhist priests for the spirits of *mizuko* and intended in part as consolation to the mother, as the one most directly affected, but often with other members of the family in mind as well. Understanding the many features of this widespread movement throughout Japan provides one example in the modern period of how diversely Buddhism and gender are found to be interrelated.

Although based on research that began intensively in 1986 and . . . extend[ed] through 1994, this [essay] is not primarily a report on that research but an initial attempt to view the contemporary phenomenon of *mizuko kuyō* against a wider socioreligious background in modern Japan. . . .[1]

The primary research is of several kinds. It includes extensive interviews with temple priests and women who have experienced the loss of a fetus or child. We have also distributed over 3000 questionnaires to worshippers who have participated in memorial services (*kuyō*) for aborted or stillborn children (*mizuko*). Beyond this, we have access to data being collected on *mizuko kuyō* by sociologists at two major Japanese universities and to more than 1500 questionnaires completed by women at an important temple in Kyoto. Finally, we have collected sizeable amounts of published materials in Japanese that deal with abortion and *mizuko kuyō* directly or seek to relate those to wider social and religious issues of both a contemporary and historical nature. These materials will be analyzed in the projected volume based upon this research.

THE GENERAL CONTEXT

In the *Japanese Journal of Religious Studies*, published by Nanzan University in Nagoya, two articles on *mizuko kuyō* have appeared in recent years, one by Anne Page Brooks (1981) and, in December 1987, a translation of an essay published two years before in Japanese by Hoshino Eiki and Takeda Dōshō.[2] Surprisingly, this is the extent of serious research on the subject yet to appear in English. The article by Anne Brooks is a good overview of the scene. The essay by Hoshino and Takeda is helpful in placing *mizuko kuyō* within the general conceptual framework of Japanese attitudes toward the spirits of the dead, in providing reasonably current statistics on abortions in Japan, and particularly in making careful distinctions between the meaning of abortion or infanticide (*mabiki*) within traditional life in Tokugawa Japan (1603–1867) and the meaning of *mizuko kuyō* today. This paper is addressed to the contemporary scene. Although the differences between traditional and contemporary Japanese social systems are complex, among the major assertions of the Hoshino article is the following: that with the gradual devolution of the traditional family system in modern urban areas the responsibility for abortion, which used to be shared by the local community in Tokugawa or Edo Japan, must now often "be borne in secret completely by the individual."[3]

It is precisely this "broken connection," as Robert Jay Lifton uses the term, that needs examining, not only with respect to earlier family systems and communal forms of support but also compared with former ways of relating death to life.[4] Arising out of his extensive interviews with survivors from several con-texts (including Hiroshima, the Chinese cultural revolution, and the Vietnam War), Lifton's studies have focused on the importance and difficulty of grieving, on the process by which one confronts death (or "death equivalents"), and on symbols relating death to the continuity of life.

> Images of death begin to form at birth and continue to exist throughout the life cycle. Much of that imagery consists of death equivalents—image-feelings of separation, disintegration, and stasis. These death equivalents evolve from the first moments of life, and serve as psychic precursors and models for later feelings about actual death. Images of separation, disintegration, and stasis both anticipate actual death imagery and continue to blend and interact with that imagery after its appearance.[5]

Lifton's research makes clear the importance of psychoanalytic studies that take seriously the human life process as well as an individual's feelings, such as anxiety, guilt, rage, and violence, which often accompany the confrontation with death or any of its equivalents. At the same time, his research indicates the equal importance of images of continuity, or life equivalents such as connection, integrity, and movement. Whereas modern existence is frequently the experience of broken connections of various sorts, Lifton believes that life-promoting connections are possible *provided* one confronts and learns to handle factors within human community that resist the facing of death, or death equivalents, such as injustice, collapse of communal order, profound disillusionment, and the like. Lifton's twofold approach (that is, of realism in the face of death equivalents and hope if these are seriously encountered), is central, implicitly, to the theme of this [essay] and the issue of Buddhism and gender.

Thus far, no attention has been paid to the implications of these sorts of findings on the widespread modern social and religious phenomenon known as *mizuko kuyō*. This seems ironic, because at the heart of this phenomenon lies both the experience of death and difficulties encountering this death. Lifton's research confirms my own suspicion that the problems experienced with abortion in Japan are not only more serious than often is acknowledged, but that complex factors exist within Japanese society related to abortion which are rarely discussed. It is part of this [essay]'s purpose to identify some of these.

As is commonly done by the media, one can easily dismiss the phenomenon of *mizuko kuyō* as another form of *shōbai* or business enterprise. Without question, there has been the tendency for it to become commercialized in many circles. Along with this there has been the inclination of some priest-practitioners to capitalize on feelings of guilt and fear that women frequently experience following abortion and to attribute many subsequent personal and family problems to the decision to abort. Our findings also reveal the problematic nature of economic support for many temples, thereby forcing some priests into activities even they may question. The present economic basis of temple support in Japan thus, in our estimation, is an important subject on which careful research needs to be done. As far as we are aware, no systematic studies exist.

But on whatever grounds one can legitimately question certain forms of *mizuko kuyō* practice, one quickly encounters the emotional problems that significant numbers of women attest to following abortions (in some cases years afterward). Our interviews reveal both the diversity of these experiences and the varied ways in which temple priests and sympathetic lay people have responded. The more deeply one looks, the more evident it becomes not only that widespread abortion creates genuine problems within Japanese society but that this society in fact has made it almost inevitable that these problems exist. Whereas problems connected with abortion are hardly unique to Japan, there are peculiar features here that one does not find elsewhere, or in earlier times within Japan. Hoshino and Takeda are right, for instance, in stressing that although early death was common in previous times there are new ingredients in the modern experience: for one thing, the very number of abortions today; for another, the more private nature of the experience and hence the greater emotional burden upon individuals. In Lifton's sense, the experiencing of this death becomes even more difficult within the framework of a vastly broken religious and cosmological world-view. The old connections are more problematic today. And this raises the interesting question as to whether the extraordinary public attention being paid to *mizuko* (whether aborted or stillborn) in Japanese society has arisen partly because the "image" of *mizuko* itself may have become yet another symbol of the broader social sense of disconnection.

The basic thrust of this [essay] therefore is to begin raising questions about what lies behind the complex phenomenon of *mizuko kuyō*. First, it will discuss the anomalous situation of birth control in Japan, in which abortion is the most effective of the widely used methods, with the result that the number of abortions is unusually high for a society like Japan. The very lack of significant procreative choices for most Japanese women contributes to the many problems not being adequately faced by the medical profession or other segments of Japanese society. Therefore, the [essay] also looks at the emotional needs women frequently have following abortion and asks what these represent. Third, as the *kuyō* or memorial service is the most common response offered by Buddhist temples, its general nature is examined briefly. Furthermore, because ritual and cosmology are necessarily related, the [essay] discusses certain forms of traditional Buddhist cosmology, especially the omnipresent Jizō figure and the concept of the six paths (*rokudō*) and asks about the appeal of these ancient ideas within a modern and "broken" era. Finally, the [essay] concludes by questioning whether the present Buddhist response addresses itself to certain deeper and often unstated grievances felt by Japanese women. In the context of this discussion other forms of ritual that seek to confront resentment and anger in particular will be mentioned. A concern of this kind is akin to Lifton's conviction that the life-cycle process and the rituals related to it help to create forms of renewal, with social as well as personal meaning, *only* when they address the pervasive experience of broken connections, in Japan or anywhere else.

THE PARADOX OF ABORTION: A WORLD OF NECESSITY AND SORROW

To enter the world of abortion is to observe a scene of resolution undermined by doubt, a scene of both conflict and relief. As one perceptive viewer of this world has put it: "This is the heart of the struggle. The quality of life pitted against life. Whichever we choose, we lose. And that, too, is part of being human. That too is the dilemma of abortions."[6] It is no longer surprising to hear American or European women, who have gone through an induced abortion and who affirm a woman's right to do so, express the emotional difficulty of such an experience, even to hear them reliving spiritual or psychic pain for years after the fact. It is clearly more anguishing still to absorb, through miscarriage or stillbirth, the death of a child one wished to have, let alone the death of an older child. Each instance is unique, though support from those who have encountered similar sorrow helps in offsetting isolation. The pain of grieving, inevitably personal, becomes more bearable when it can be shared, when it becomes less private.

In modern Japan the world of abortion is both similar to that of some other countries and very different. Although abortion has been legal in the United States only since 1973, Japan passed the Eugenic Protection Law in 1948 (with revisions in 1949 and 1952), making abortion legally possible for the first time. And yet, approaches to birth control exist here that are radically different than those found in most modern societies. As many studies reveal, there are but three primary methods of birth control practiced in Japan. *One* is the rhythm method, which lacks reliability. The *second* is the condom, which can be reliable if used properly, but this means of contraception frequently keeps the woman in a position of dependence on the male partner. The *third* method is by far the most effective, namely, abortion, thereby setting the stage for widespread emotional unrest—especially when adequate contraceptive alternatives are minimal. It therefore is accurate to say that the procreative choices available to Japanese women are remarkably slight.

Because of fears about side effects, oral contraceptives are not normally available; and because of their reluctance to be fitted by male gynecologists, Japanese women do not commonly use the diaphragm. It is possible that some form of abortificant (preventing the fertilized egg from becoming implanted in the uterus) may be available on the Japanese market in a few years if it proves free of serious side effects. The result would be a considerable lowering of the incidence of abortions and thus should be welcomed. The present conservative estimate of abortions per year is about 1 million, which is twice the officially reported number. More liberal estimates put the figure at close to 1.5 million. At any rate, obstetrician–gynecologists (Ob-Gyns) have a tremendous economic stake in abortions, deriving a large share of their income from this practice. The fewer reported, the less income declared. A clear conflict of interest exists: abortions pay off for the profession.

The most thorough analysis of birth control and abortion in Japan is by Samuel Coleman, *Family Planning in Japanese Society*, the data for which goes through 1976.[7] Although written in English, this study uses primarily Japanese sources along with the author's own research conducted over a period of twenty-eight months in Tokyo. This analysis spells out the inadequacies of family planning methods and sex education in Japan. The consequences of this situation appear not only in the general unavailability of modern contraceptive means but in the continued lack of reliable information provided to men and women regarding safe and effective methods of family planning. "Few private practice Ob-Gyns provide contraceptive counseling and methods for their patients. The most striking omission of this service appears among abortion cases, where contraceptive counseling should be a matter of routine."[8] The topic of sexual relations remains a taboo subject for discussion in most schools and in family circles (even between husband and wife, at least in early stages of marriage, let alone between parents and children). The result is naivete, embarrassment, misinformation, and an alarming rate of unwanted pregnancies within marriage and, increasingly in the past ten years, outside of marriage as well. It is common for women to have had at least two abortions by the time they are forty years old. Coleman speculates about what might alter this picture and believes that change will be prompted only from the bottom up, not from government or from the medical profession (primarily men in this case) with its vested interests.

Other, even more fundamental, differences in the Japanese social and cultural scene compound the problem of whether to keep or abort a pregnancy. It is perhaps true that the average relatively young, politically liberal Japanese professional woman, married or not, might have few qualms about an abortion if she wishes not to have the child. That category of person in Japan, however, is a tiny minority. As is well known, the vast majority of women are family bound, normally getting married in their middle to late twenties. For them, this path is deeply imbedded in their self-image and in social expectations. Within this customary pattern are two children, with a family beginning as soon as possible. For the married woman who does not wish to work full-time, therefore, the issue of abortion is not one she faces at the start. *Before* she is married, however, or *after* her complement of two children, the issue is real. At these times the lack of adequate family planning methods makes abortion a statistical probability if pregnancy occurs. The fact that women often have small procreative choice contributes not only to frustration but to considerable resentment, however diffused or obliquely expressed. Our findings reveal that women, trapped in this fashion, have strong feelings, even if these are seldom voiced in public. Indeed, frustrations mount precisely because so few contexts exist in which to discuss such matters.

At the most basic level, therefore, Japanese women possess insufficient procreative choice. Huge numbers become pregnant against their wishes or because of ignorance of adequate family planning methods. Husbands and wives rarely discuss matters of this kind in ways that help to open up communication on such issues, let alone correct the problem. As a result, women experience considerable frustration, and only after one or two abortions do they begin to assert their needs and rights in this arena. Japanese society does little to help in the areas of family planning and sex education. The medical profession would seem to be notably recreant in its responsibility to serve the needs of women who may neither want to get pregnant nor wish abortion to be their primary option. Often one hears the rationalization that more contraceptive means are not made available because this would simply encourage teenagers to become sexually promiscuous "like their Western counterparts." (Actually, women frequently express the same fear about their husbands: the safer sex becomes, the more he will play around.) As the statistics given in the Hoshino article make clear, the teenage years are one of two age brackets in which there have been sharp increases (almost double) in the number of abortions during the period 1974–1981, which simply means that more unmarried people are having sexual relations but without adequate birth control protection.

A SPECTRUM OF REACTIONS TO THE ABORTION EXPERIENCE

Even if a woman favors having an abortion, it does not mean she will go through this experience unscathed. Even with perfect assent she may later, much to her own surprise, encounter feelings of guilt, and if not that, then often a sense of sadness, brought about by something deeper than hormonal adjustments. Thoughts of "what might have been" surface in almost every person. The experience, in other words, is rarely simple relief, as though the object removed were an intruder, with no connection to the woman.

At a still-deeper level is the unexpected awareness that one's need to mourn this loss is very real and not unnatural. This is not simply because Buddhism teaches that human life begins at the instant of conception. Actually, it is more likely the reverse: Buddhism's teaching may be the endorsement of a profoundly human experience, namely, that nothing less than a human life is at issue. One question revolves around the symbolic nature of what are called *mizuko*, for in the case of *mizuko* there is obviously a fundamental inversion of the typical and expected sequence in the ancestor-descendent continuity. A child here dies before its parents. This naturally raises religious questions in Buddhism about what happens to the *mizuko*, as well as psychological questions as to how one experiences the loss, how one grieves. Even this prospective experiencing of family bond becomes an avenue for discovering hidden connections in life (in Lifton's sense) and a source of deep meaning. If so, whenever ambivalence exists in the decision to abort, mourning becomes the acknowledgement that something of consequence has occurred, that one is never quite the same again. It is therefore to acknowledge death, even a death which one has willed. Once more, therefore, in the words of Magda Denes, "That . . . is the dilemma of abortions."

At a still more painful psychic and spiritual level, there is the encountering of a reality so filled with sorrow that much deeper healing is required. One experiences a rupture or brokenness that tears at one's inner nature. Many Japanese words convey this quality of affliction: *nayami*, *kurushimi* and *modae*, each of which suggests anguish, ache, torment, agony. Perhaps the most appropriate term would be *kumon*, incorporating the Japanese *kanji* of *kurushimi* and *modae*, doubling their intensity. An apt Western equivalent might be Kierkegaard's "sickness unto death"; that is, a form of spiritual malaise for which there is no remedy without cost. There remains only the possibility of healing through deep suffering.

The earliest Buddhist example of this may be the story of Kisa Gotami who lost her only child, a young son. Her grief was such that she could not face the reality and refused to bury the child. Days ensued and the neighbors became alarmed, urging her to visit the Buddha. Although sympathetic, he advised her to make the rounds of each house in the village, requesting a grain of mustard seed from any family where death had not occurred. At the day's end she returned, with no mustard seeds. The universality of pain suddenly hit her. In Lifton's sense, she had in some authentic way confronted mortality itself. She could then bury her son and, although continuing to mourn his passing, became able to release her attachment to grief. As this happened, her own capacity for compassion emerged.

It is appropriate now to provide some sense of what the Buddhist memorial service called *mizuko kuyō* entails. To begin with, the term *kuyō* literally means "to offer and nourish." In this sense, it is the offering up of prayers for the nourishment of the spirit of the aborted or stillborn child. Also, as mentioned earlier, it is intended to console the parents, especially the mother, though not infrequently one finds fathers coming with the mother or even by themselves. This service may take place once, or once every month, or it may occur annually on the anniversary of death. Also, one may request a private service or include one's suffering with a service for many *mizuko*. This latter is more common. As one would expect, in Japanese Buddhism, because of the sectarian variety, there is no one pattern to this service. And, because the very existence of a memorial

service for an unborn child had no precedent until the past three decades in Japan, one finds considerable variation in content and emphasis. Although debate occurs in denominational circles among priests about all aspects of the *mizuko kuyō* phenomenon and about the service in particular, no official stated policy exists nor any recommended form of service.

On the other hand, the number of common elements are significant, as the general pattern that is followed bears some resemblance to what is used in regular services for the recent dead and even more to the memorial services for ancestors known as *senzo kuyō*. In general, priests conduct the service on behalf of those requesting it and face the altar during most of the service. At the beginning, the names of one or more forms of the Buddha and various bodhisattvas are invoked. Parts of several Mahāyāna *sūtras* are chanted, often including the *Heart Sūtra* (*Hannya-shin-gyō*) or the *Kannon Sūtra* (or *Kanzeon Bosatsu Fumon-bon* from the *Lotus Sūtra*), as well as selected *wasan* or songs of praise in behalf of figures such as Jizō Bosatsu. Frequently, the congregation joins in this chanting, but not always. Central to these services is the offering of light, food, flowers, and incense to the Buddha in behalf of the child and as tokens of the larger offering of one's life. In most cases, some sculpted representation of Jizō or of an infant symbolizing a *mizuko* is bought by the family and left in a specially designated place within the temple grounds. Quite frequently a *kaimyō*, or posthumous Buddhist name, is given the child; and this is inscribed on an *ihai* or mortuary tablet, which is left in a special chapel within the temple or taken home and placed in the family *butsudan*, or Buddhist shrine.

Clearly much more is involved in the memorial and grieving process than the externals of ritual. Often, for instance, a sermon is given, which tries to put the experience of those who attend into a wider human and Buddhist context. Furthermore, normally, a certain amount of counseling precedes and also may follow the service. In some cases there may be contact with other women who have already gone through a similar experience. On the other hand, for reasons of privacy, it is common for people to have these services performed at a temple where their identity is not known. Again, this supports the claim made by the Hoshino article that here we are dealing with a phenomenon in which there often is little, if any, communal support.

To provide another example both of the sorrow of losing one's child and of a *kuyō* in the child's behalf, a look at a well-known Noh play, *Sumidagawa*, is instructive. Written by Jūrō Motomasa (1395–1459), son of Zeami Motokiyo, this play is in the genre called *kyōjo-mono* or "mad woman" piece. The scene is set at the banks of the Sumida River in what is now Tokyo. A ferryman is about to take an unnamed traveler to the other shore when an obviously distraught woman appears, also seeking passage across. Unknown to the others, she is the widow of Lord Yoshida of Kita-Shirakawa in Kyoto and the mother of a twelve-year-old boy who was abducted the year before by a slave trader. Ever since, she has searched with "frenzied longing" for her lost son, Umewaka-maru. As the boat makes its way across, the woman divulges her mission, and the ferryman realizes that she is the mother of the boy whose death anniversary is just then being memorialized on the opposite shore by villagers who remember well his valor in the face of sudden illness and death.

One needs to see this play to appreciate the emotion portrayed by the mother as she takes part in the memorial service for her son.

> Before the mother's eyes the son appears
> And fades away
> As does the phantom broomtree.
> In this grief-laden world
> Such is the course of human life . . .
> Now eyes see how fleeting is this life.

On stage, the ghost of Umewaka-maru emerges from the burial mound, disappears, and reappears again. Each time the mother tries to touch him, but she cannot cross the boundary of life and death. The child speaks to her and echoes the villagers' chanting of the *nembutsu*. She reaches for his hand again.

> The vision fades and reappears
> And stronger grows her yearning.
> Day breaks in the eastern sky.
> The ghost has vanished;
> What seemed her boy is but a grassy mound

> Lost on the wide, desolate moor.
> Sadness and tender pity fill all hearts . . .

One is struck by how effectively the play creates in the viewer genuine feelings of loss and grief. The play not only incorporates a *kuyō* service but in a dramatic sense becomes one itself. By its very length on stage it draws out these feelings of grief in extended catharsis. The tragedy of the child's death remains, but of central importance is the way in which this has been faced in full, not glossed over or denied. A grief not encountered is a grief denied, and one thereby retains the "frenzied longing" in one guise or another. Only through realizing that the apparition is a ghost can she begin to accept his death and regain her sanity.

CONFRONTATION WITH DEATH AND DEATH EQUIVALENTS

Alongside the direct encounter with grief is the necessity of confronting feelings such as anger, guilt, or despair which frequently accompany the experience of another's death. For, as Lifton's research makes evident, these feelings may derive from significant exposure to what he calls *death equivalents*; that is, the sense of profound separation, fragmentation, and immobility or stasis. Sigmund Freud, in his rich essay "Mourning and Melancholia," makes a related point in distinguishing between two conditions whose symptoms often appear alike. "In mourning it is the world which has become poor and empty; in melancholia it is the ego itself. The patient represents his ego to us as worthless, incapable of any achievement and morally despicable."[9] As Freud knew, a gradation exists between these, not a sharp line. The clearest distinction is that the symptoms of mourning fade in time whereas the low esteem of melancholia persists. Freud also observed that in melancholia is a strong ambivalence toward the person who has died; an inner struggle occurs "in which love and hate contend with each other." Indeed, he correlates "obsessional self-reproach" with this ambivalence, regarding it as "the motive force of the conflict."

With Freud's thesis in mind it is reasonable to suggest that women who become pregnant against their wishes and who may also feel guilty over having to abort are prime candidates for a type of inner conflict that includes not only diffused resentment but self-reproach as well. This combination of repressed anger, guilt, and diminished self-esteem has many ramifications in the lives of women. This is not to imply that they are caused mainly by the problems over birth control and abortion. If anything, it is the reverse, namely, that problems arising there are attributable to less than satisfying relationships between men and women in so many areas of Japanese social life. The literature on women and the Japanese family is filled with portrayals of tensions within the home. The reality may be better or worse than the image, but it is certain that the widely read novels of Enchi Fumiko, Ariyoshi Sawako, and other women writers present a bleak picture.[10] In them one finds vivid portrayals of the kind of fragmentation and disconnectedness Lifton cites as death equivalents. Although the absence of realistic procreative choices discussed earlier, often leading to the necessity of abortion, is sufficient cause for frustration, the deeper causes are rooted within the whole social structure in which women have little opportunity to participate in the decision making that affects important areas of their lives. It must be acknowledged that Japan is hardly alone in this, as the women's movement, in its various forms throughout the world, makes clear.

A recent anthropological study by Takie Sugiyama Lebra, *Japanese Women: Constraint and Fulfillment*, provides a view different but not opposed to that of the Japanese women novelists just mentioned.[11] Her discussion of the well-known phenomenon of the close mother-child relationship is pertinent here. Referring to the mother's existence as filiocentric, in which she tends "to see a mirror image of herself in the child," Lebra calls the relationship one of "double identity" (herself and the child as one entity).[12] The most vivid expression of this relationship is suggested by the term *ikigai*, or that which is worth living for. In this case, the mother's worth is inherently related to her child. On one level this can mean genuine caring; on another level it suggests preoccupation, which is the usual connotation. What I am proposing here is that a correlation may exist between this heavy investment of self-esteem in her child and the ambivalence and dissatisfaction so many women feel (even if rarely expressed publicly) about their situation within Japanese society in general and their subjection to frequent abortion in particular. It would not be surprising if considerable melancholia (in Freud's sense) were present in the psyche of Japanese women, arising from a high level of ambivalence about their status in a male-governed society, a situation in which they develop various strategies to compensate for a sense of relative powerlessness. If so, Japanese women would not be alone, but they may have devised unique ways of approaching their dilemma. In another paper I have discussed this subject.[13]

At this point I turn to the concept of *redressive ritual*, as one means of confronting situations of frustration caused by broken connections of one sort or another. My thesis is that rituals of this kind can assist in providing imagery not only of death and death equivalents but also imagery of life's continuity, as Lifton uses these terms. In the process, people are assisted to confront threatening situations or broken connections both more deeply and more constructively.

In his last few years the anthropologist Victor Turner wrote at length on the topic of performative ritual and its relation to four phases of social drama (breach, crisis, redressive action, and outcome). His basic assumption is that society and social dramas are combative, filled with conflict, "agonistic," yet not yet settled, indeterminate.[14] Breach and crisis are chronic possibilities, not exceptional circumstances. The third phase, redress, implies the possibility of encountering conflict and moving through and beyond it, either to resolution or to recognition of stalemate. Although the latter may be unsatisfactory, it is at least honest. The phase of redress "reveals that 'determining' and 'fixing' are indeed processes, not permanent states or givens. . . . Indeterminacy should not be regarded as . . . negation, emptiness, privation. Rather it is potentiality, the possibility of becoming. From this point of view social being is finitude, limitation, constraint."[15] Turner sees ritual (and theater) as able "to mediate between the formed and the indeterminate" for these especially entertain the subjunctive mood, thus employing a serious engagement of new visions of reality.

There is a distinct similarity between the Turner thesis of ritual's potential within conflictive situations and Lifton's psychoanalytically based research into how one copes with life's broken connections. In both, there is the recognition of the commonness of conflict and of situations of fragmentation. In both, there is the stress on encountering these and learning how to experience them anew. In Lifton's words, there is a "three-stage process available to the survivor of actual or symbolic death encounter, consisting of confrontation, reordering, and renewal."[16] Within the second of these stages one discovers the possibility of "converting static to animating forms of guilt" or anger or despair. Using an anthropological approach, Victor Turner elaborates a theory of the therapeutic nature of "rituals of affliction" (as distinguished from the "prophylactic rituals" of life crises and seasonal festivals) and thereby takes his notion of redress a step further. Central to rituals of this kind is "divination into the hidden causes of misfortune, conflict, and illness (all of which in tribal societies are intimately interconnected and thought to be caused by the invisible actions of spirits, deities, witches, or sorcerers)," along with curative rituals that seek to move the afflicted person through and beyond the causes of this affliction.[17] As Turner well knew, these phenomena were not limited to tribal societies, and he had plans to study their presence in Japanese life before he died.

One could place *mizuko kuyō* precisely in the genre of rituals of affliction, for the sources of anguish are not only within each person's experience but within a larger cultural and social environment. Again and again, our research reveals how frequently women in Japan, in seeking explanations for repeated illness, financial troubles, or tensions within the family, begin to attribute these to an earlier experience of abortion. This search for causation is entirely understandable and analogous to Western explanation of evil from Job to Camus (questions of theodicy). One is struck, however, by how often abortion is cited as the cause for personal and social misfortune in Japan today. The simplest form of this is to view such misfortune as the punishment or evil spell (*tatari*) caused by the spirit of an aborted child. As the Hoshino and Takeda article states, "In traditional society the spirits of the children were not considered as possible purveyors of a curse, whereas in contemporary society the spirits of children are considered as the same as the spirit of an adult, and thus have the potential for casting a curse."[18] Although this is but *one* way of explaining the diverse phenomenon of *mizuko kuyō*, it is a common explanation offered by some proponents and cited by most critics.

It is our judgment, however, that behind the attribution of misfortune to abortion is a much larger issue, namely, the attempt to understand what underlies the confusions and fragmentation of a culture whose connections with its past are simultaneously broken and yet in many ways still alive. For this reason one needs to look at the forms of ritual and cosmology that are resorted to repeatedly in Buddhist temples and to ask whether these are potentially means of enabling men and women to confront the deeper and more systematic causes of what Lifton means by death equivalents. One problem, of course, is that in the modern period men and women live with several, often conflicting worldviews. On the other hand, world-views are always in process and traditional forms of cosmology and ritualistic expression respond in various ways to newly experienced human needs. This is again to put the anguish so often experienced after abortion into a larger cultural framework and to seek for more complex factors behind this widespread phenomenon.

PATHS TO HEALING THROUGH COSMOLOGY AND RITUALS OF AFFLICTION

In an essay on Thai Buddhist healing, Stanley Tambiah discusses the inevitable relationship between ritual and cosmology. "In the rituals we see cosmology in action. Ritual is symbolic action that has a telic or instrumental purpose—to effect a change of state. The cosmology and ritual are closely connected because the cosmological concepts and categories are translatable into an action medium that employs symbols of various kinds—verbal, visual, auditory, graphic, tactile, alimentary, and so on."[19]

To anyone familiar with Japanese Buddhist ritual that will be an apt description. Of particular importance here is ritual's instrumental purpose in effecting a change of state. In the case of some worshippers, the cosmological symbols as experienced in a ritual setting will be taken with a certain literalness. The ritual state is the real state. For most, the symbols will refer to something else, imperfectly understood but also real in some sense. For any one, their meaning in an age of broken connection becomes problematic. And yet, this happens frequently in history.

Within all forms of Buddhism, for instance, both Theravāda and Mahāyāna, there is reference to the six worlds or paths or destinies known as *rokudō* in Japan. These are paths within the realm of desire (the ego world), far removed spiritually from the realms of buddhas and bodhisattvas, and are composed of six graduated levels: the world of gods or heavenly beings, humans, *asuras* (warlike spirits who can also protect the Buddha Dharma), animals, hungry ghosts, and those who inhabit the many hells. Even if not taken literally as places, their meaning is metaphorically symbolic of real states of existence which all beings experience in one way or another. In the language of Japanese proverbs: "the Six Roads are right before your eyes"; "Hell and Heaven are in the hearts of man"; and "there is no fence to the Three Realms, no neighborhood to the Six Roads" (meaning "beyond there is only *nirvāna*; and short of that there is nowhere to escape"). In modern parlance, Sartre's play *No Exit* or Arthur Miller's *Death of a Salesman* might serve to convey analogous visions of entrapment, the central difference being that none of the six worlds or paths is a permanent place of residence. Each person is reborn or finds himself or herself in one or another because of previous karma, remaining a pilgrim in these realms until all sense of a separate independent self (what the French call *la moi*, the idea of "me") is extinguished. Because progress along these paths is slow and arduous, Buddhism provides symbols of hope and sources of grace. Foremost among the bodhisattvas who have vowed never to rest until all beings are rescued are Kannon and Jizō. Because Jizō is especially central to *mizuko kuyō* he will be singled out here.[20]

Jizō is omnipresent in Japan, from now-deserted but once-used mountain trails, to crossroads throughout the land, to tiny neighborhood shrines, to chapels and main altars in larger temples. He is the foremost protector of children, particularly those who have died early. As such, he is intimately identified with those who have been aborted, who never came into this realm of existence. Jizō Bosatsu is therefore the single most important figure in the drama of young children, infants, and unborn fetuses in Japanese Buddhist cosmology, and in ritual related to this. He is known as *migawari*, one who suffers in behalf of others, one who can transform his shape infinitely to rescue those in dire straits. He is the only bodhisattva who is associated with all six worlds, being present in each simultaneously, though he identifies especially with those in the three unhappy conditions (*san-akudō*): the realms for animals, hungry ghosts, and those in hell.

In other words, Jizō identifies with those in any kind of suffering. He is an apt paradigm for worlds where strife, discouragement, and passion reign. In such a world he represents the possibility of hope; he is the epitome of compassion in a realm where this is rare. In Turner's language he is the liminal figure par excellence; he is the androgyne who represents male and female equally. He is in the midst of life and death, present symbolically in the womb and tomb alike. Moreover, he is the alternative to chaos, but challenges all forms of order implicitly by his compassion, settling for nothing less than rescue from defeat and ultimate liberation. He thus is both antistructure *and* the hope for communitas (in Turner's words) beyond all present structures. In Lifton's sense, Jizō assists in the confrontation of death and death equivalents. Serene in appearance, he nonetheless confronts demonic and other forms of hellish experience.

He is thus potentially a symbol toward which all redressive action points. Within pan-Buddhist cosmology he is said to be the connecting link between Gotama (the last historical buddha) and Maitreya (*Miroku*), the buddha to be. This in-between age typically is depicted in Buddhism as one devoid of buddhas. It therefore epitomizes a time of broken connection; it is separation, disintegration, and stasis per se. It is the time once called *mappō*, the last days of the law, when conditions worsen, when hope seems impossible, and skillful means of rescue have powerful attraction. For these many reasons, Jizō's symbolic importance to the believer is clear. *Mizuko kuyō* needs to be viewed partially within this cosmological context, ancient but still alive. On the other hand, these are the words of conventional piety, and they may not reach those whose sense of broken connection is more than personal and who view the disorder of the modern world with greater seriousness.

As one seeks to understand a phenomenon as widespread and complex as this, is it possible that the Jizō and *mizuko* figures can be viewed as opposite yet virtually inseparable symbols at this point? And, in their dialectical relationship as life-death paradigms respectively? If Jizō is clearly the salvific boundary figure between all forms of life and death, one symbolic meaning of *mizuko* lies in its representation of radical isolation, a figure with no connection to anything living or dead, one whose "spirit" remains in limbo unless freed ritualistically to reenter, to be reborn within this world.

A traditional term in Japanese Buddhism for someone who has died without relatives is *muenbotoke,* one who has lived but who dies with no connections. This term was used for anyone who died without descendents to make offerings for his or her spirit. It was regarded as the ultimate desolation and also as a potentially dangerous circumstance because the person's spirit had not finally been put to rest. Its very restlessness was highly threatening, a concept that has been pervasive throughout East Asia, as well as elsewhere, since ancient days. As Emiko Ohnuki-Tierney has expressed it: "The freshly dead hover at the margin of culture and nature, the point at which the latter threatens the former . . . the world of the ancestors and the world of the living."[21] They therefore are in a condition of limbo, which always has been seen as both polluting and dangerous to the Japanese. Whereas it would be too simple to equate the *mizuko* with the *muenbotoke,* there is a sense in which they are genuinely homologous. Each represents a radical disconnection from its origins, and the departed spirit of each has not received proper treatment in the ancestral tradition. Indeed, in the case of the *mizuko* the point is precisely to put them *into* the ancestral lineage. It is also the function of ritual to assist in the process of transforming potentially malevolent or demonic forces

into ones capable of being protective and benevolent to the living. In the classical Buddhist sense, all mortuary ritual has this continuing transformation as central to its purpose.

It is but one step of the imagination to propose further that the condition of *muen,* or not-relatedness, is a pervasive experience in the modern world and certainly within Japan. In this vein, the symbolic power of the *mizuko* or the *muenbotoke* lies in the fact that they are not metaphors abstracted from living human existence, but indicators of what that existence commonly experiences. Perhaps only in this sense can one come to understand the rather extraordinary preoccupation with abortion manifested by so many Japanese women and with the various ways to encounter the meaning of this experience (as illustrated in *mizuko kuyō*). Further, this may also help one to understand the immense weight put upon the mother-child relationship, in which the average woman seeks to find her deepest identity. Without disparaging this bond, it is ironically a tie that tends to undermine the sense of wider, more corporate relationships with others within a pluralistic world. The price paid for forging a relationship so potentially narcissistic is not only that it may backfire (in cases of failure) but also that it fails to encourage broader, transpersonal bonds across lines of social difference. In other words, its very limited nature contributes paradoxically to the world of broken connection instead of helping to heal this condition in more basic ways. The current privatism of urban Japanese family life may be an attempt to construct connections of a closely personal sort, but most evidence suggests that this is rarely the outcome, either for parents or for children, and that it serves primarily to increase the sense of brokenness and isolation from a larger social fabric.

This, of course, is what Lifton is arguing on a more general level, and what he means by the term *broken connection.* His discussion of this condition is on many levels. Fundamentally, it deals with images of death and life and the symbolically broken connection between them. "Much more elusive is the psychological relationship between the phenomenon of death and the flow of life. Psychological theory has tended either to neglect death or to render it a kind of foreign body, to separate death from the general motivations of life. Or else a previous deathless cosmology is replaced by one so dominated by death as to be virtually lifeless."[22] It would be gratuitous to claim that a condition of nonrelatedness is the only experience men and women have in Japan or anywhere else. In fact, one might observe the very high premium put on relationships, especially close emotional relationships, in modern society. Again, there are innumerable forms of this within Japan. Yet it would be plausible to say that this emphasis exists, to a significant degree, precisely because so many of the old connections in traditional societies lack compelling power. This is not to romanticize these connections, but, in Lifton's words, "something has gone seriously wrong with everyone's images and models."[23]

In our research on *mizuko kuyō* we have come to realize that what is of central importance in any analysis of nonrelatedness or broken connection in Japan is the steady deterioration of traditional ancestral bonds. This cannot be overemphasized. Although these still exist in many forms and in certain circumstances they remain powerful, they are not strong enough to offset the more powerful experience of a people's increasing deracination from its past. Again, this phenomenon is worldwide. Half a century ago Walter Lippmann labeled this process as *the acids of modernity*. This is not to suggest that new forms of ancient traditions are not possible, only that the condition of disconnection is extreme. At the core of his research on survivors in many important contexts Lifton has observed a factor that has no precedent in history and that certainly affects the Japanese mind deeply, more so than that of any other people except perhaps the Jewish community (because of the Holocaust experience). The following words are telling:

> The broken connection exists in the tissues of our mental life. It has to do with a very new historical—one could also say evolutionary—relationship to death. We are haunted by the image of exterminating ourselves as a species by means of our technology. Contemplating that image as students of human nature, we become acutely aware that we have never come to terms with our "ordinary"—that is, prenuclear—relationship to death and life-continuity. We seem to require this ill-begotten imagery of extinction to prod us toward examining what we have steadfastly avoided.[24]

I wish to conclude this section by suggesting that many ingredients within the Japanese world-view are potential catalysts in this confrontation with both death and its equivalents and with the continuity of life and its equivalents. If the imagery of benevolent grace is powerfully expressed within Japanese religions, so too is the dark side of human existence with imagery of fury and malevolence. Although scarcely unique in this respect, the Japanese consciousness has managed to keep alive (whether in traditional or modern form) the awareness that these elements within the human and nonhuman scene (in worlds visible and invisible) are constants within psychic and spiritual existence. Japanese art and mythology are rich in depicting demons (*oni*), ghosts (*yurei*), raging deities (*araburu kami*), ferocious guardians at temple gates, and menacing divinities like Fudō-san who epitomizes sternness in the face of evil. In fact, Jizō and Fudō are often seen as complementary figures, two seemingly opposite forms of encountering tough reality. At least two features about these "dark" portrayals of the spirit world are central. First, they attest to the ambiguity of all existence, which clearly can be malevolent but is not *inherently* so. And second, intrinsic to all Buddhist mythology is a transformationist motif, meaning that (for those who seek wisdom and compassion) the most malign of forces can be transmuted into benevolent protective figures. Metaphorically, all of these forces suggest an august realism about the basic Japanese world-view; that is, an absence of sentimentality about the destructive potential within all existence, and at the same time, a basis for believing that even the most painful forms of nonrelatedness or separation are not the final or deepest expression of human experience. The key question here, of course, is how this might relate to the issue of abortion in modern Japanese society.

REDRESSIVE RITUAL AND SOCIAL DISORDER: A CONCLUDING PARADIGM

If the symbols of *mizuko* and *muenbotoke* have a homologous relationship, and if these represent human experience in some universal sense, then the question naturally arises of how ritual in particular can assist persons and communities to confront obstacles to the possibility of transformation and renewal. When one considers the full ritualistic process, as Arnold van Gennep did in his classic work *The Rites of Passage* (1909), one typically sees it as a movement from symbols of discontinuity to those of transition to those of continuity (or reincorporation).[25] In this final section my focus is on the first phase only, in part because I see it as crucial to the others and as frequently neglected in much modern expression of ritual. I have in mind *mizuko kuyō* in particular, for I also believe this same ritual has the potential to effectively help persons to face forms of *social* disconnection as well as the inner anguish they may feel personally after having lost a child or experienced deeply negative feelings following abortion.

For this purpose I return to Turner's idea of redressive ritual as one way to understand the deeper potential of a phenomenon such as *mizuko kuyō*. Central to any redressive ritual is its attempt to "include divination into the hidden causes of misfortune, conflict, and illness."[26] It is one thing to settle for the same explanation for all personal turmoil or family problems (attributing these to "vengeful spirits"), and it is another to allow for, even to smoke out, multiple interpretations. In the case of *mizuko kuyō* a major problem is to get society to conceive of a wider diagnosis. To pursue this wider diagnosis is to encounter the complexity of real existence. As Victor Turner writes, this openness to plural interpretation is evident "in ritual procedures, from divination to shamanistic or liturgical curative action, in which many invisible causes of visible afflictions are put forward by ritual specialists as they try obliquely to assess the main sources of discord in the communal context of each case of illness or misfortune."[27]

Such a diagnosis takes more time, though its value lies not only in inviting a richness of contending interpretations, but even more in its involvement of a wider community of people who then puzzle about their own implication in the misfortune at hand. As a way of gaining a certain perspective on the Japanese scene I wish to provide an example along similar lines from another culture with which I am familiar.

An eloquent discussion of this process is given by Bruce Kapferer in *A Celebration of Demons: Exorcism*

and the Aesthetics of Healing in Sri Lanka.[28] More often than not in cases of spirit possession it is unclear why someone has become possessed or who the possessing spirit is. In other words, the diagnosis is part of the cure, is even intrinsic to the cure. It becomes a means of widening the circle of involvement both sociologically and cosmologically. In Śrī Laṅkā, "demonic spirits" are not viewed as foreign to the natural or human realms but permanent ingredients within a more universal sphere. Demons, so-called, are allowed their place. Symbolically, they personify the possibility of disorder, confusion, and injustice, but they are seen within a deeper framework of social and cosmic order, not as independent of this order. The demonic element therefore is recognized as inherently present within a world of pain, not some intrusion into it.

This recognition is identical with Turner's view of existence as conflictive and agonistic. The demonic element may be found anywhere within the social and natural order, but its existence is not granted free play. It too is part of contingent reality. Demonic possession thus symbolizes the inversion of true order, somewhat like the death of a child represents a fundamental inversion of typical expectation. Also, this demonic possession manifests itself within normal human contexts of family and neighborhood. And, exorcism (which is one form of redressive ritual) is designed as the means of reestablishing harmonious order, but only *after* the roots of disharmony have been confronted and displaced. The relationship of order to disorder (the demonic) thus is ritualistically the same as that of life to death, for unless the threats of fundamental disorder and death are confronted (personally and communally) in symbolic, psychological, and liturgical ways one is avoiding the dark side of existence and hence the situation remains paralyzed by it.

In the process of encouraging over many days multiple diagnoses of the illness at hand, the Śrī Laṅkān exorcist invites those close to the victim (family, neighbors, friends) to assess *why* so-and-so has become afflicted. In the hands of a skillful practitioner, the speculations grow more and more complex and many plausible explanations are rehearsed. There are even acknowledgments by those who perceive how they may have contributed to a poisoned and disordered climate (not unlike what can happen in group counseling if candor emerges). At a certain point, the exorcist deems the time ripe for the ritual itself to begin; without that preparation, diagnosis would be premature. It would have settled on causes within the patient alone, raising no questions about the social environment in which he or she exists. All possibility of confronting the wider picture would have been neglected, and the ritual's impact would be severely limited. Whenever the social roots of the disease or of the broken connection are ignored, the communal involvement in healing is also diminished.

There are important implications in the preceding example for how one may approach the anguish of losing a child and the ritual of *mizuko kuyō* in Japan. Although afflictions take infinite shape there is a clue here in how one tries to assess what lies beneath the surface and who else may be involved in creating the situation at hand. On one level, through *mizuko kuyō* thousands of women are being helped to go through the mourning process after the turmoil of abortion, miscarriage, or stillbirth. That certainly has great value. On the other hand, there remains a need to address the specific factors that make abortion so frequently necessary. These are rarely being addressed, in part because doing so would reveal other sources of conflict and pain; but their very avoidance may also contribute to what Freud called *melancholia* and to diminished self-esteem. Although women can become skilled in coping with difficult aspects of a male-oriented society, the very strategies they employ successfully may serve to perpetuate the basic problems.

As mentioned earlier, this [essay] is not intended as a descriptive report on our research. Although admittedly speculative, it is one effort to see the *mizuko kuyō* phenomenon within a broader socioreligious background than is normally done. It is also an attempt to place it in the context of other research, notably that of Robert Jay Lifton and Victor Turner, as theirs has been concerned with issues very similar to what I find here. If one adopts the metaphor of social drama, as Turner and others do, then what one finds in relations between men and women in Japan is precisely what Michel Strickmann intriguingly calls a *theatre for the unspeakable* when discussing an ancient Taoist ritual in which resentment and anger against a dead parent are expressed, though obliquely through a priest. Thus the *form* of filial piety is maintained, but very unfilial emotions are given expression. The ritual is therapeutic, though not basically redressive.

It is a truism that whenever deep feelings cannot be expressed either with sufficient candor or in some effective ritualistic manner, then anger and frustration go underground. If indeed this is true, then the important phenomenon of *mizuko kuyō* must finally be seen within a larger context. When analyzed in this fashion, it illuminates more aspects of Japanese society and religion than one would initially suspect. The significance of any ritual and its healing powers usually will vary with the level of depth at which affliction is perceived and the extent to which the social fabric is seen as connected to the suffering of individuals, particularly when the extent of that suffering is so widespread. This [essay] represents the first stage of trying to outline certain connections between the momentum behind this movement and various features of the present Japanese social system and its economic values. It helps to illuminate also some of the very real tensions that Japanese Buddhism needs to address as it exists in an increasingly gender-conscious period of time.

NOTES

1. This research is being conducted collaboratively with Elizabeth Harrison who has a Ph.D. from the University of Chicago in Tokugawa intellectual history. For several years, while living in Kyoto, she was a research associate at Ryūkoku University. Currently, she is teaching in East Asian Studies at The University of Arizona. The project has been funded by grants from the Fulbright Commission and the Faculty Development Fund, Carleton College.

2. See Anne Page Brooks, "Mizuko Kuyō and Japanese Buddhism," *Japanese Journal of Religious Studies* 8, nos. 3–4 (1981); and Hoshino Eiki and Takeda Dōshō, "Indebtedness and Comfort: The Undercurrents of *Mizuko Kuyō*," *Japanese Journal of Religious Studies* 14, no. 4 (1987).

3. Hoshino and Takedo, ibid., p. 314.

4. Robert Jay Lifton, *The Broken Connection: On Death and the Continuity of Life* (New York: Basic Books, 1983).

5. Ibid., p. 53.

6. Magda Denes, *In Necessity and Sorrow: Life and Death in an Abortion Hospital* (New York: Penguin Books, 1976), p. 245.

7. Samuel Coleman, *Family Planning in Japanese Society: Traditional Birth Control in a Modern Urban Culture* (Princeton, N.J.: Princeton University Press, 1983), pp. 38–41.

8. Ibid., p. 40.

9. Sigmund Freud, "Mourning and Melancholia," *The Standard Edition of the Complete Psychological Works of Sigmund Freud*, trans. James Strachey in collaboration with Anna Freud (London: Hogarth Press, 1964), vol. 14, pp. 247–268. This quote is from p. 254.

10. See Fumiko Enchi, *Masks*, trans. Juliet Winters Carpenter (Tokyo: Charles E. Tuttle, 1984); and *The Waiting Years*, trans. John Bester (Tokyo, New York, and San Francisco: Kodansha International, 1980). Those by Sawako Ariyoshi are *The Doctor's Wife*, trans. Wakako Hironaka and Ann Silla Kostant (Tokyo, New York, and San Francisco: Kodansha International, 1981); *The River Ki*, trans. Mildred Tahara (Tokyo, New York, and San Francisco: Kodansha International, 1981); and *The Twilight Years*, trans. Mildred Tahara (Tokyo, New York, and San Francisco: Kodansha International, 1984).

11. Takie Sugiyama Lebra, *Japanese Women: Constraint and Fulfillment* (Honolulu: University of Hawaii Press, 1984).

12. Ibid., p. 165.

13. Bardwell Smith, "The Social Contexts of Healing: Research on Abortion and Grieving in Japan," . . . in Michael A. Williams, et. al., eds., *Innovation in Religious Traditions: Essays in The Interpretation of Religious Change* (New York and Berlin: Mouton de Gruyter, 1991).

14. Victor Turner, *Dramas, Fields, and Metaphors: Symbolic Action in Human Society* (Ithaca, N.Y., and London: Cornell University Press, 1974), pp. 38–44.

15. Victor Turner, *From Ritual to Theatre: The Human Seriousness of Play* (New York: Performing Arts Journal Publications, 1982), p. 77.

16. Lifton, *Broken Connection*, p. 177.

17. Victor Turner, "Dewey, Dilthey, and Drama: An Essay in Anthropology of Experience," in *The Anthropology of Experience* (Urbana and Chicago: University of Illinois Press, 1986), p. 41.

18. Hoshino and Takeda, "Indebtedness and Comfort," p. 316.

19. Stanley Jayaraja Tambiah, *Culture, Thought, and Social Action: An Anthropological Perspective* (Cambridge, Mass.: Harvard University Press, 1985), pp. 103–104.

20. Jizō is the Japanese name for this figure. In Chinese he is known as Ti-tsang; in Sanskrit, Kṣitigarbha.

21. Emiko Ohnuki-Tierney, *Illness and Culture in Contemporary Japan: An Anthropological View* (Cambridge: Cambridge University Press, 1984), p. 70.

22. Lifton, *Broken Connection*, p. 4.

23. Ibid., p. 3.

24. Ibid., p. 5.

25. Arnold van Gennep, *The Rites of Passage* (reprinted Chicago: University of Chicago Press, 1960).

26. Victor Turner, "Dewey, Dilthey, and Drama," p. 41.

27. Victor Turner, "Liminality and the Performative Genres," in *Rite, Drama, Festival, Spectacle*, ed. John J. MacAloon (Philadelphia: Philadelphia Institute for the Study of Human Issues, 1984), p. 25.

28. Bruce Kapferer, *A Celebration of Demons: Exorcism and the Aesthetics of Healing in Sri Lanka* (Bloomington: Indiana University Press, 1983).

The Bare Facts of Ritual

JONATHAN Z. (ZITTELL) SMITH

Facts of publication: *Smith, Jonathan Z. 1982. "The Bare Facts of Ritual," from* Imagining Religion: From Babylon to Jonestown, *53–65, 143–45. Chicago: University of Chicago Press. Copyright © 1982 by The University of Chicago. Reprinted with the permission of the author and the University of Chicago Press.*

Incongruity and incredulity are key factors that Jonathan Z. Smith considers in developing his understanding of ritual. He sees ritual as a "struggling with matters of incongruity." The world often does not comply with the way things ought to be; it cannot be fully controlled. Ritual is a way of performing things as they ought to be, a way of doing in which all things can be controlled. Smith argues that the difference, the incongruity, between the ritual and the nonritual world provides the occasion for people to think, rationalize, and accommodate the contradiction that is acknowledged by the very existence of ritual. Smith compares two accounts of seeming accidents in temples. Each reflects a differing ritual strategy. Temples are ritual places. Smith holds that a ritual place serves as a "focusing lens," a place where the ordinary becomes significant.

Smith's principal example is circumpolar bear hunting and its associated rites. In them hunting takes the form of ritualized etiquette towards prey. For example, hunters do not kill bears unless the bears are facing in the right direction, can be wounded in the correct spot, and are addressed properly or sung to before being killed. After Smith describes this etiquette, he inquires into the consistency of the hunters' statements. He concludes that not only are the ritual restrictions impractical and almost always impossible to comply with, they are not supported by the ethnographic literature. Smith points out the incongruity between what the hunters say and what they actually do, a gap that he fills with his own understanding of ritual.

Smith's theory is further developed in To Take Place: Essays toward Theory in Ritual *(Chicago: University of Chicago Press, 1987).*

About the author: Dates: *1938–   , New York, NY, U.S.A.* **Education:** *B.A., Haverford College; Ph.D., Yale University.* **Field(s):** *history of religion; Hellenistic religions; anthropology of religion; method and theory of religion.* **Career:** *Instructor of Religion, 1965–1966, Dartmouth College; Acting Assistant Professor, 1966–1968, University of California, Santa Barbara, then Assistant Professor, 1968–1973; William Benton Professor of Religion and Human Sciences, 1974–1982, then Robert O. Anderson Distinguished Service Professor of Humanities, 1982–present University of Chicago,* **Publications:** Map Is Not Territory: Studies in the History of Religion *(Brill, 1978);* Imagining Religion: From Babylon to Jonestown *(University of Chicago, 1982);* To Take Place: Essays Toward Theory in Ritual *(University of Chicago, 1987).* **Additional:** *Co-editor of* History of Religions, *1968–1981. Memberships: Society for Religion in Higher Education, Society of Biblical Literature, American Academy of Religion, Society for the Scientific Religion.*

There is one aspect of scholarship that has remained constant from the earliest Near Eastern scribes and omen interpreters to contemporary academicians: the thrill of encountering a coincidence. The discovery that two events, symbols, thoughts, or texts, while so utterly separated by time and space that they could not "really" be connected, seem, nevertheless, to be the same or to be speaking directly to one another raises the possibility of a secret interconnection of things that is the scholar's most cherished article of faith. The thought that the patterns and interrelationships that he has patiently and laboriously teased out of his data might, in fact, exist is the claim he makes when his work is completed as well as the claim that appears to be denied by the fact that he has had to labor so long. . . . And this is why coincidence is, at one and the same time, so exhilarating and so stunning. It is as if, unbidden and unearned by work and interpretation, a connection simply "chose" to make itself manifest, to display its presence on our conceptual wall with a clear round hand.

I should like to begin this essay with one such coincidence and juxtapose two texts separated in time by some eighteen centuries. The one is from Kafka, the other from Plutarch.

Leopards break into the temple and drink the sacrificial chalices dry; this occurs repeatedly, again and again: finally it can be reckoned on beforehand and becomes a part of the ceremony.[1]

At Athens, Lysimache, the priestess of Athene Polias, when asked for a drink by the mule drivers who had transported the sacred vessels, replied, "No, for I fear it will get into the ritual."[2]

These two texts illustrate the sovereign power of one of the basic building blocks of religion: ritual and its capacity for routinization.

Both fragmentary stories take their starting point in what we would most probably call an accident. Both give eloquent testimony, in quite different ways, to the imperialistic eagerness with which ritual takes advantage of an accident and, by projecting on it both significance and regularity, annihilates its original character as accident.[3] But our two texts, while remarkably similar in structure, differ quite sharply in how they see and evaluate this process. They seem to suggest, at least by implication, two differing theories about the origin of religion.

Both texts set the action they describe within a temple. In Kafka, the locale is apparently some jungle shrine; in Plutarch it is a sacred place within the heart of a cosmopolitan city—the dwelling place, north of the Parthenon, of the ancient wooden statue of Athene Polias, "the holiest thing" within all Athens.[4] This temple setting is more than mere scenery. It serves to frame all that follows.

When one enters a temple, one enters marked-off space in which, at least in principle, nothing is accidental; everything, at least potentially, is of significance. The temple serves as a *focusing lens*, marking and revealing significance. For example, in Jewish tradition gossip in the temple and in the Land of Israel (which they understood to be an extended temple) is Torah.[5] If an accident occurred within its precincts, either it must be understood as a miracle, a sign that must be routinized through repetition, or it will be interpreted as impurity, as blasphemy. Thus the lamp in the temple that unexpectedly burned for eight days according to a late rabbinic legend was retrojected as having given rise to the festival of Hannukah, the first feast to enter the Jewish liturgical calendar without scriptural warrant, claiming only human decree rather than divine command, and hence, itself, potentially blasphemy.[6] In the case of the oil lamp, the interpretation was one of miracle. On the other hand, when the high priest in Jerusalem spilled a basin of sacred water on his feet rather than on the altar the accident was understood as blasphemy and he was pelted by the crowd.[7]

A sacred place is a place of clarification (a focusing lens) where men and gods are held to be transparent to one another. It is a place where, as in all forms of communication, static and noise (i.e., the accidental) are decreased so that the exchange of information can be increased. In communication, the device by which this is accomplished is redundancy; in our examples, through ritual repetition and routinization. In Kafka's story, the leopards were received as a message (a miracle, a sign) and incorporated, through routinization and repetition, into the ritual. In Plutarch's story, this potential was refused by the priestess, who saw the possibility of blasphemy.

There is a vast difference between the actors in the two stories. But we are in danger of dwelling on this difference in such a way as to mislead ourselves badly. There appears to us to be something mysteri-

ous, awesome, and awful about the leopards, but there is nothing at all extraordinary about the mule drivers. Therefore the first may appear to us as being inherently religious, the latter, quite commonplace and secular. From the vantage of such an understanding, Kafka would appear to be drawing on romantic theories of religion as the epiphanic. That may well be what he had in mind, but I would opt for a different understanding. For leopards in a jungle seem as commonplace as mule drivers in an ancient city. The leopards in Kafka's story do nothing mysterious; in fact, they do what the mule drivers desire to do. They are thirsty, and they drink. That they drink from a "sacrificial chalice" is what the readers and celebrants know. The leopards presumably do not. They simply see a bowl of liquid, as the pigeons that sometimes make their way into Catholic churches do not know that the stand of holy water at the entrance was not put there for their relief as a bird bath.

Indeed this is necessarily so if we take seriously the notion of a temple, a sacred place, as a focusing lens. The ordinary (which remains, to the observer's eye, wholly ordinary) becomes significant, becomes sacred, simply by *being there*. It becomes sacred by having our attention directed to it in a special way. This is a most important point, one that is only recently gaining acceptance among historians of religion although it was already brilliantly described by A. van Gennep in *Les Rites de passage* (1909) as the "pivoting of the sacred."[8] That is, there is nothing that is inherently sacred or profane. These are not substantive categories, but rather situational or relational categories, mobile boundaries which shift according to the map being employed. There is nothing that is sacred in itself, only things sacred in relation.

To digress from Kafka and Plutarch to another set of ancient stories about ritual. In the extensive Egyptian *logos* in book 2 of his *Histories*, Herodotus tells that Amasis, "a mere private person" who was elevated to king but despised because of his "ordinary" origins, had a golden foot pan in which he and his guests used to wash their feet. This was melted down and remolded into the statue of a god which was reverenced by the people. Amasis called an assembly and drew the parallel as to "how the image had been made of the foot pan, in which they formerly had been used to washing their feet and to deposit all manner of dirt, yet now it was greatly reverenced. And truly it has gone with me as with the foot pan. If I were formerly a private citizen, I have now come to be your king, and therefore I bid you to do honor and reverence to me."9 This is a sophisticated story which foreshadows the kinds of subtle distinctions later political thought made between the king as divine with respect to office and human with respect to person. Divine and human, sacred and profane, are maps and labels not substances; they are distinctions, of "office." This is almost always misunderstood by later apologetic writers who used the Amasis story to ridicule idolatry.10 Likewise the analogous *topos* found independently in both Israelitic11 and Latin12 tradition of the carpenter who fashions a sacred object or image out of one part of a log and a common household utensil out of the other.13 Similar too is the opposite theme to the Amasis story, that a statue of a deity would be melted down and used to fashion a commonplace vessel: "Saturn into a cooking pot; Minerva into a washbasin."14 The *sacra* are sacred solely because they are used in a sacred place; there is no inherent difference between a sacred vessel and an ordinary one. By being used in a sacred place, they are held to be open to the possibility of significance, to be seen as agents of meaning as well as of utility.

To return to Kafka and Plutarch. Neither the leopards nor the mule drivers can be presumed to know what they do or ask. The determination of meaning, of the potentiality for sacrality in their actions, lies wholly with the cult. The cult in Kafka's story perceives significance in the leopards' intrusion and, therefore, converts it from an accident into a ritual. The leopards no longer appear whenever they "happen" to be thirsty: "It can be reckoned on beforehand and becomes a part of the ceremony." In the Plutarch story, the priestess rebuffs the potential for significance. Whether the mule drivers will ever thirst again, whether or not they wished to drink from the sacred vessels they had just transported or from some "ordinary" cup makes no difference. If done in the temple, with the authority of the priestess, their act is potentially a ritual.

Why does the priestess refuse? What should we understand her answer, "No, for I fear it will get into the ritual," to mean? There is a thin line, as

Freud most persuasively argued, between the neurotic act and religious ritual, for both are equally "obsessed" by the potentiality for significance in the commonplace.15 But this presents a dilemma for the ritualist. If everything signifies, the result will be either insanity or banality. Understood from such a perspective, *ritual is an exercise in the strategy of choice.* What to include? What to hear as a message? What to see as a sign? What to perceive as having double meaning? What to exclude? What to allow to remain as background noise? What to understand as simply "happening"? The priestess is exercising her sense of the *economy of signification.* To permit something as apparently trivial as a drink of water to occur in the temple runs the risk of blurring the focus, of extending the domain of meaning to an impossible degree. It is to run the risk of other ritual acts being perceived as banal, as signifying nothing. We do not know whether, in this particular instance, she was right. But we can affirm that, as priestess, she has acted responsibly.

*   *   *

. . . I shall take my cue for the latter part of this essay from [the] gifted Argentinian writer [Jorge Luis Borges]. In his short story, "Death and the Compass," Borges has his police commissioner, Lönnrot, declare to a colleague, "Reality may avoid the obligation to be interesting, but hypotheses may not. . . . In the hypothesis you have postulated [to solve the murder] chance intervenes largely. . . . I should prefer a purely rabbinical explanation."16 Let me raise a "rabbinical" question. What if the leopards do not return? What if the mule drivers had taken their drink without asking anyone and then were discovered? What then? Here we begin to sense the presence of one of the fundamental building blocks of religion: its capacity for rationalization, especially as it concerns that ideological issue of relating that which we do to that which we say or think we do.

This is not an unimportant matter in relationship to the notion of ritual as a difficult strategy of choice. It requires us to perceive ritual as a human labor, struggling with matters of incongruity. It requires us to question theories which emphasize the "fit" of ritual with some other human system.

For the remainder of this essay, I should like to

offer a concrete example which not only will illustrate the problematics and rationalizing capacities of religious ritual and discourse but also allows us to reflect on the dilemmas created for historians of religion by these capacities. I should like to direct attention to a set of bear-hunting rituals as reported, especially, from paleo-Siberian peoples. I have chosen this example because it is well documented in ethnography and has been of great importance in a number of theoretical discussions of ritual.

We need, at the outset, to fix on a traditional cultural dichotomy: agriculturalist and hunter. Within urban, agricultural societies, hunting is a special activity, remote from the ordinary rhythms of life, in which man steps outside of his cultural world and rediscovers the world of nature and the realm of the animal, frequently perceived as a threat. The hunter tests his courage in an extraordinary situation. It is this fortitude in confronting the dangerously "other" that has been celebrated in the novels of authors such as Hemingway, or in the compelling *Meditations on Hunting* by the Spanish philosopher Ortega y Gasset. Within agricultural, urban societies, the religious symbolism of hunting is that of overcoming the beast who frequently represents either chaos or death. The hunt is perceived, depending on the symbolic system, as a battle between creation and chaos, good and evil, life and death, man and nature, the civil and the uncivil. The paradigm of such a symbolic understanding is the royal hunt which persists from ancient Sumer and Egypt to the contemporary queen of England, mythologized in legends of heroic combats with dragons, and partially secularized in the relatively recent ceremony of the Spanish bullfight. The king, as representative of both the ruling god and the people, slays the beast.[17]

In contrast, among hunting societies, hunting is perceived as an everyday activity. It is not understood as an act of overcoming but as a participation in the normal course of things. The hunter and the hunted play out their roles according to a predetermined system of relationships. This system is mediated, according to the traditions of many hunting peoples, by a "Master of the Animals," a "Supernatural Owner of the Game," who controls the game or their spirits, in northern traditions most frequently by penning them. He releases a certain number to man each year as food. Only the allotted number

may be slain in a manner governed by strict rules. Each corpse must be treated with respect. The meat must be divided, distributed, and eaten according to strict rules of etiquette, and the soul of the animal must be returned to its "Supernatural Owner" by ritual means. If the system is violated, game will be withheld and complex ceremonies, frequently involving the mediation of a shaman, are required to remove the offense and placate the "Master."[18]

Beyond this mythology underlying the hunt, it has long been clear that the hunt itself can be described as a ritual having several more or less clearly demarcated parts. In what follows, I am largely dependent on the outlines provided by A. I. Hallowell's classic study, *Bear Ceremonialism in the Northern Hemisphere*, as well as Evelyn Lot-Falck's more recent monograph, *Les Rites de chasse chez les peuples sibériens*, supplementing them, where appropriate, with details from other ethnographies.[19]

The first group of rituals may be brought together under the heading "preparation for the hunt."[20] One set of rituals Lot-Falck interprets as ceremonies designed to "insure the success of the hunt" under which she includes various forms of "divination" (oracles from bones and flight of arrows predominate) and rites which she terms "magical ceremonies employing sympathetic magic"—a theme to which I shall return. These may be of several types: mimetic dances "prefiguring" the hunt, the stabbing of an "effigy" of the animal, and the like. There are also invocations to the "Master of the Animals" or to the individual hunter's "guardian spirit," or attempts, through ritual, to "capture the game animal's soul." The bulk of the rituals of preparation are concerned with the purification of the hunter, purification by smoke being the most widespread. A variety of avoidances are observed, particularly of women and sexual intercourse and of contact with the dead. Finally, almost universally, there is a ceremonial hunt language.[21] The animals are believed to understand human speech, and it would be a gross violation of etiquette to announce that one is coming to kill them. A variety of euphemisms and circumlocutions are employed.

The rituals surrounding the second important moment of the hunt, "leaving the camp," appear to express the hunter's consciousness of crossing a boundary from the human social world into a forest realm of animals and spirits.[22] Leaving in a rigidly prescribed order, as if to carry human social structures into another's domain, the chief rituals focus on gaining permission from the forest to enter, with the key image being that of guest. Thus the earliest extant Finnish bear rune addresses the forest as "lovely woman—hostess good and bountiful" and requests entrance.[23] I would argue that the complex of host/guest/visitor/gift comprises the articulated understanding of the hunt. The forest serves as a host to the hunter, who must comport himself as a proper guest. The hunter is a host inviting the animal to feast on the gift of its own meat. The animal is host to the hunters as they feed on its flesh. The animal is a gift from the "Master of the Animals," as well as being a visitor from the spirit world. The animal gives itself to the hunter. The hunter, by killing the animal, enables it to return to its "Supernatural Owner" and to its home, from which it has come to earth as a visitor.[24]

The third moment in the hunt seen as ritual is the "kill," which is likewise governed by strict rules of etiquette.[25] Most of the regulations seem designed to insure that the animal is killed in hand-to-hand, face-to-face combat. For example, in some groups, the animal may be killed only while running toward the hunter or (when a bear) only while standing on its hind legs facing the hunter. It may never be killed while sleeping in its den. In addition, it may only be wounded in certain spots (the most frequent interdiction is against wounding it in the eye) and the wound is to be bloodless. The controlling idea is that the animal is not killed by the hunter's initiative, rather the animal freely offers itself to the hunter's weapon. Therefore, the animal is talked to before the kill; it is requested to wake up and come out of its den or to turn around and be killed. To quote one example, from D. Zelenin:

> The Yakuts say that if one kills a bear in his hibernation den, without taking care to awake or warn him, other bears will attack the hunter while he sleeps. A Nanay hunter, upon encountering a bear in the open, does not kill him at once, but begins by addressing dithyrambic praise poems to him and then prays that the bear will not claw him. Finally he addresses the bear: "You have come to me, Lord Bear, you wish me

to kill you. . . . Come here, come. Your death is at hand, but I will not chase after you."[26]

Among almost all of these northern hunting groups, there is a disclaimer of responsibility recited over the animal's corpse immediately after it has been killed.[27] "Let us clasp paws in handshake. . . . It was not I that threw you down, nor my companion over there. You, yourself, slipped and burst your belly."[28] Even responsibility for the weapons will be disclaimed: "Not by me was the knife fashioned, nor by any of my countrymen. It was made in Estonia from iron bought in Stockholm."[29]

The conclusion of the hunt proper, the "return to camp," has been described by Lot-Falck as a "strategic retreat."[30] The hunters leave the world of the forest and return to that of the human, bearing the corpse of the slain animal. There is continued need for etiquette in the treatment of the corpse, in the reintegration of the hunters into human society, in the eating of the flesh, and in insuring that the animal's soul will return to its "Supernatural Owner." The corpse may be adorned and carried in solemn procession. The hunters continue to disclaim responsibility, reminding the animal that now its soul is free to return to its spiritual domicile and assuring it that its body will be treated with respect. "You died first, rather than us, greatest of all animals. We will respect you and treat you accordingly. No woman shall eat your flesh. No dog shall insult your corpse."[31] Ceremonies of purification are performed by and for the hunters on their arriving at camp; women play a prominent role in ritually greeting the men, reintegrating them into the domestic world.

The animal's corpse is butchered and divided according to strict rules of rank and prestige so that its body becomes a social map of the camp. Certain parts are set aside, in particular the head and bones. Among northern hunters, bones play an analogous role to that of seeds in agrarian societies. Bones endure; they are the source of rebirth after death. The bones are a reservoir of life; they require only to be refleshed.[32] The meal is governed by rules, as the animal is an invited guest at a banquet held in his honor and consisting of his meat. Each piece of meat, as it is consumed, is wedded, in some traditions, to the life of the one who eats. The animal's "generic" life endures in the bones; its "individuality" is preserved by its consumer.[33] The majority of these return elements are joined together in the series of ancient texts which were collected by Elias Lönnrot as the forty-sixth rune of the Finnish *Kalevala*.[34]

Having followed the standard reports and interpretations to this point, we must, at this time, ask some blunt questions. In particular, can we believe what I have summarized above on good authority? This is a question which cannot be avoided. The historian of religion cannot suspend his critical faculties, his capacity for disbelief, simply because the materials are "primitive" or religious.

First, some general questions. Can we believe that a group which depends on hunting for its food would kill an animal only if it is in a certain posture? Can we believe that any animal, once spotted, would stand still while the hunter recited "dithyrambs" and ceremonial addresses? Or, according to one report, sang it love songs![35] Can we believe that, even if they wanted to, they could kill an animal bloodlessly and would abandon a corpse if blood was shed or the eye damaged? Can we believe that any group could or would promise that neither dogs nor women would eat the meat, and mean it? Is it humanly plausible that a hunter who has killed by skill and stealth views his act solely as an unfortunate accident and will not boast of his prowess? These, and other such questions, can be answered from the "armchair." They do not depend on fieldwork but upon our sense of incredulity, our estimate of plausibility. Our answers will have serious consequences. For if we answer "yes" to these questions, if we accept all we have been told on good authority, we will have accepted a "cuckoo-land" where our ordinary, commonplace, common-sense understandings of reality no longer apply. We will have declared the hunter or the "primitive" to be some other sort of mind, some other sort of human being, with the necessary consequence that their interpretation becomes impossible. We will have aligned religion with some cultural "death wish," for surely no society that hunted in the manner described would long survive. And we will be required, if society is held to have any sanity at all, to explain it away.

If our sense of incredulity is aroused, we need, as historians of religion, to get up from the armchair and into the library long enough to check the sources. For example, despite the description of the hunt I have given, most of the groups from which this information was collected do not, in fact, hunt bears face-to-face but make extensive use of traps, pitfalls, self-triggering bows, and snares. In more recent times, the shotgun has been added to their arsenal.[36] This precludes most of the elements of ritual etiquette I have described: no hand-to-hand combat, no addressing of the bear, no control over where it is wounded. The Koryak and Chukchi are characteristic of those who actually encounter a bear. When attacking the bear in winter, while it is in its den, they block the entrance to the den with a log, "break in the roof and stab the beast to death or shoot it." When bears are encountered outside their den, in spring or autumn, they set packs of dogs on it to "worry the animal."[37] No sign of ritual etiquette here! Of even greater interest is the following. The Nivkhi *say* that "in order not to excite the bear's posthumous revenge, do not surprise him but rather have a fair stand-up fight," but the same report goes on to describe how they *actually* kill bears: "a spear, the head of which is covered with spikes, is laid on the ground, a cord is attached to it and, as the bear approaches [the ambush] the hunter [by pulling up on the cord] raises the weapon and the animal becomes impaled on it"[38] As this last suggests, not only ought we not to believe many of the elements in the description of the hunt as usually presented, but we ought not to believe that the hunters, from whom these descriptions were collected, believe it either.

There appears to be a gap, an incongruity between the hunters' ideological statements of how they *ought* to hunt and their actual behavior while hunting. For me, it is far more important and interesting that they say this is the way they hunt than that they actually do so. For now one is obligated to find out how *they* resolve this discrepancy rather than to repeat, uncritically, what one has read. It is here, as they face the gap, that any society's genius and creativity, as well as its ordinary and understandable humanity, is to be located. It is its skill at rationalization, accommodation, and adjustment.

I first became aware of this particular set of issues when reading the account of pygmy elephant-hunting in R. P. Trilles's massive study, *Les Pygmées de la forêt équatoriale*. Let there be no misunderstanding. A pygmy who kills an elephant by means other than a deadfall does so by an extraordinary combination of skill and nerve. After shooting it with poisoned arrows, an individual, possessing what Trilles terms an *audace singulière* runs under the elephant—what one of their songs describes as "this huge mass of meat, the meat that walks like a hill"—and stabs upward with a poisoned spear.[39] The corpse is then addressed in songs. Combining two of these, one hears an extraordinary set of rationalizations.

1. Our spear has gone astray, O Father Elephant.
   We did not wish to kill you.
   We did not wish to kill you, O Father Elephant.

2. It is not the warrior who has taken away your life—
   Your hour had come.
   Do not return to trample our huts, O Father Elephant.

3. Do not make us fear your visit,
   Henceforth, your life will be better,
   You go to the country of the spirits.
   ....
   We have taken you away. but we have given you back a different sort of life.
   Against your children, Father Elephant, do not be angry.
   You begin a better life.

This is immediately followed by the ecstatic cry:

O honor to you, my spear!
My spear of sharpened iron, O honor to you![40]

The progression is clear. (1) We did not mean to kill you; it was an accident. (2) We did not kill you; you died a natural death. (3) We killed you in your own best interests. You may now return to your ancestral world to begin a better life. The final ejaculation may be paraphrased: "Never mind all of that. Wow! I did it!"

Once we have heard this last prideful cry, and remember the details of the poisoned arrows and spears, we are in danger of dismissing the rest as

hypocrisy. The hunter does not hunt as he says he hunts; he does not think about his hunting as he says he thinks. But, unless we are to suppose that, as a "primitive," he is incapable of thought, we must presume that *he* is aware of this discrepancy, that he works with it, that he has some means of overcoming this contradiction between word and deed. This work, I believe, is one of the major functions of ritual.

I would suggest that, among other things, *ritual represents the creation of a controlled environment* where the variables (i.e., the accidents) of ordinary life may be displaced *precisely* because they are felt to be so overwhelmingly present and powerful. *Ritual is a means of performing the way things ought to be in conscious tension to the way things are in such a way that this ritualized perfection is recollected in the ordinary, uncontrolled, course of things.* Ritual relies for its power on the fact that it is concerned with quite ordinary activities, that what it describes and displays is, in principle, possible for every occurrence of these acts. But it relies, as well, for its power on the perceived fact that, in actuality, such possibilities cannot be realized.

There is a "gnostic" dimension to ritual. It provides the means for demonstrating that we know what ought to have been done, what ought to have taken place. But, by the fact that it is ritual action rather than everyday action, it demonstrates that we know "what is the case." Ritual provides an occasion for reflection and rationalization on the fact that what ought to have been done was not done, what ought to have taken place did not occur. From such a perspective, ritual is not best understood as congruent with something else—a magical imitation of desired ends, a translation of emotions, a symbolic acting out of ideas, a dramatization of a text, or the like. Ritual gains force where incongruency is perceived and thought about.

Two instances may be provided from the northern hunters by way of illustrating the implications of such an understanding of ritual.

As is well known, a number of these circumpolar peoples have a bear festival in which a bear is ritually slain.[41] To give a brief, highly generalized description. A young, wild bear cub is taken alive, brought to a village, and caged. It is treated as an honored guest, with high courtesy and displays of affection, at times being adopted by a human family. After two or three years, the festival is held. The bear is roped and taken on a farewell walk through the village. It is made to dance and play and to walk on its hind legs. Then it is carefully tied down in a given position and ceremonially addressed. It is slain, usually by being shot in the heart at close range; sometimes, afterward, it is strangled. The body is then divided and eaten with ceremonial etiquette (the same rules that pertain to the consumption of game). Its soul is enjoined to return to its "Owner" and report how well it has been treated.

Many valuable interpretations of these festivals have been proposed, each illuminating important elements of the ritual. I should like to suggest another aspect: that *the bear festival represents a perfect hunt.*[42] The etiquette of the hunt—the complex structures of host/guest/visitor/gift—presupposes a reciprocity that cannot be achieved in the actual hunt because, at the very least, one of the parties, the bear, will more than likely *not* play its appointed role. In the actual hunt, the hunter might attempt to play his part; the animal will not reciprocate, nor will it respond in the required manner. And the bear's failure to reciprocate will prevent the hunter from making his attempt if the hunt is to be successful qua hunt (i.e., the gaining of meat without injury or loss of life to the hunter). But in the bear festival all of the variables have been controlled. The animal has been compelled to play its part. The bear was treated correctly as a guest. It was constrained to rejoice in its fate, to walk to its death rather than run away, to assume the correct posture for its slaughter, to have the proper words addressed to it (regardless of length) before it is killed, to be slain face-to-face, and to be killed in the proper all-but-bloodless manner.[43] It is conceivable that the northern hunter, while hunting, might hold the image of this perfect hunt in his mind.[44] I would assume that, at some point, he reflects on the difference between his actual modes of killing and the perfection represented by the ceremonial killing.

I would advance a similar proposal for interpreta-

tion of what is usually termed "mimetic" or "sympathetic hunting magic."[45] The basic idea of such magic, according to most scholars, is that of "like producing like," with the notion that when the hunter has made a representation of the animal and then acted out killing it, there is an "expectation that the hunter will be able to inflict a corresponding injury to the real animal . . . [and] what was done to an accurate portrayal of the animal would, sooner or later, happen to the animal itself."[46] I would insist, on the contrary, that "sympathetic hunting magic" is not based on the principle that "like produces like," but rather on the principle that the *ritual is unlike the hunt.* Such "magic" is, once more, *a perfect hunt with all the variables controlled.* The figure, the representation of the animal, is immobile because it is inanimate. The proper words may be spoken, the animal may be placed in the proper position, it may be wounded in the proper place, and it surely will not bleed. Such a ceremony performed before undertaking an actual hunt demonstrates that the hunter knows full well what ought to transpire if he were in control; the fact that the ceremony is held is eloquent testimony that the hunter knows full well that it will not transpire, that he is not in control.

There is, I believe, an essential truth to the old interpretation of "sympathetic magic" as an "offensive against the objective world"[47] but that the wrong consequences were deduced. It is not that "magical" rituals compel the world through representation and manipulation; rather they express a realistic assessment of the fact that the world cannot be compelled. The ritual is incongruent with the way things are or are likely to be, for contingency, variability, and accidentality have been factored out. The ritual displays a dimension of the hunt that can be thought about and remembered in the course of things. It provides a focusing lens on the ordinary hunt which allows its full significance to be perceived, a significance which the rules express but are powerless to effectuate. It is in ritual space that the hunter can relate himself properly to animals which are both "good to eat" and "good to think."

NOTES

1. F. Kafka, "Reflections on Sin, Hope, and the True Way," in Kafka, *The Great Wall of China* (New York, 1970), p. 165.
2. Plutarch *De vitioso pudore* 534C.
3. For a familiar example, the Israelites at the time of their exodus from Egypt did not have time to leaven their bread. This domestic accident—assuming for the moment the historicity of the account in Exod. 12:39—was "discovered" to have significance (i.e., nothing of the old year carried over into the new) and was regularized as part of a spring New Year festival, later developed into Passover.
4. Pausanias I.26.6. See further, C. J. Herington, *Athena Parthenos and Athena Polias* (Manchester, 1955).
5. For example, Leviticus Rabbah, 34. See further, J. Z. Smith, *Map Is Not Territory* (Leiden, 1978), pp. 113–14 for other examples.
6. b. Shabbat 21b and scholion Megillat Ta'anit 25 Kislev. This story is not known to the authors of the books of the Maccabees. See 1 Macc. 4:36–59 and J. A. Goldstein, *I Maccabees* (Garden City, 1976), pp. 273–84.
7. The action appears to be attributed to Alexander Jannaeus in Josephus *Ant.* 13.372. It is attributed to an anonymous Sadducean priest in rabbinic texts, e.g., M. Sukka 4.8; Tosefta Sukka 3.16 [197]; b. Sukka 48b. For a comparison of these two interpretations, see J. Derenbourg, *Essai sur l'histoire et la géographie de la Palestine* (Paris, 1867), 1:96–101. For a sociological interpretation, see L. Finkelstein, *The Pharisees*, 3d ed. (Philadelphia, 1962), 2:700–708.
8. A. van Gennep, *Les Rites de passage* (Paris, 1909), p. 16.
9. Herodotus 2.172. I have adapted the standard translation by G. Rawlinson.
10. The story is explicitly cited by Minucius Felix *Octavius* 22.4; Theophilus *Ad Autolycum* 1.10 and elsewhere. It seems to lie behind texts such as Philo *Contemp.* 7; Justin *I Apologia* 9.3; Arnobius *Adversus Nationes* 6.12.
11. Isaiah 44:14–17.
12. Horace *Satires* 1.8.1–3.
13. E.g., Wisdom of Solomon 13:11–14:8; Tertullian *De idolatria* 8.
14. Tertullian *Apologia* 13.4.
15. S. Freud, "Obsessive Acts and Religious Practices," in J. Strachey, ed., *The Standard Edition of the Complete Psychological Works of Sigmund Freud* (London, 1959), 9:117–27. Compare L. Wittgenstein, "Remarks on Frazer's 'Golden Bough,'" *Human World* 3 (1971): 32, "The ceremonial (hot or cold) as opposed to the haphazard (lukewarm) is a characteristic of piety."
16. J. L. Borges; *Ficciones* (New York, 1962), p. 130.
17. For an archaic example, see T. Save-Söderberg. *On Egyptian Representations of Hippopotamus Hunting as a Religious Motif* (Lund, 1953).
18. For this complex within the circumpolar region, see I. Paulson, *Schutzgeister und Gottheiten des Wildes (der Jagdtiere und Fische) in Nordeurasien* (Stockholm, 1961).
19. A. I. Hallowell, "Bear Ceremonialism in the Northern Hemisphere," *American Anthropologist* 28 (1926): 1–175; E. Lot-Falck, *Les Rites de chasse sur les peuples sibériens* (Paris, 1953).

20. Lot-Falck, *Rites*, pp. 117–38; Hallowell, "Bear Ceremonialism," p. 32, n. 80.
21. Hallowell, "Bear Ceremonialism," pp. 43–53; Lot-Falck, *Rites*, pp. 103–6.
22. Hallowell, "Bear Ceremonialism," pp. 41–42; Lot-Falck, *Rites*, pp. 139–40, 143–51.
23. *Suomen Kansen Vahat Runot* (Helsinki, 1908–43), 9.4:1101, as translated by C. M. Edsman, "The Hunter, the Game, and the Unseen Powers: Lappish and Finnish Bear Rites," in H. Hvarfner, ed., *Hunting and Fishing* (Luleå, 1965), p. 176.
24. See, from quite different perspectives, K. Kindaichi, "The Concepts behind the Ainu Bear Festival," *Southwestern Journal of Anthropology* 5 (1949): 345–50; A. Slawik, "Zur Etymologie des japanischen Terminus marebito 'Sakraler Besucher,'" *Wiener Völkerkundliche Mitteilungen* 2 (1954): 44–58; J. M. Kitagawa, "Ainu Bear Festival (Iyomante)," *History of Religions* 1 (1961): 95–151, and I. Goldman, *The Mouth of Heaven: An Introduction to Kwakiutl Religious Thought* (New York, 1975), esp. chaps. 1, 7–8.
25. Hallowell, "Bear Ceremonialism," pp. 53–54; Lot-Falck, *Rites*, pp. 151–61.
26. D. Zelenin, *Kult ongonov v Sibiri* (Moscow and Leningrad, 1936), p. 209. I have followed the French translation by G. Welter, *Les Cultes des idoles en Sibérie* (Paris, 1952), p. 143. Cf. Lot-Falck, *Rites*, p. 153.
27. Hallowell, "Bear Ceremonialism," pp. 54–61; Lot-Falck, *Rites*, pp. 170–73.
28. *Suomen Kansen Vahat Runot*, 6.2:4883, in Edsman, "The Hunter," p. 186.
29. *Suomen Kansen Vahat Runot*, 1.4:1244, in Edsman, "The Hunter," p. 185.
30. Lot-Falck, *Rites*, pp. 173–85.
31. J. Teit, *The Lillooet Indians* (Leiden, 1906), p. 279, in the series American Museum of Natural History Memoirs, 4, Jessup North Pacific Expedition, 2.1.
32. See, M. Eliade, *Shamanism* (New York, 1964), pp. 158–64, and the literature he cites.
33. Hallowell, "Bear Ceremonialism," pp. 61–106; Lot-Falck, *Rites*, pp. 186–213.
34. In the translation by J. M. Crawford, *The Kalevala* (Cincinnati, 1898), 2:661–78.
35. Hallowell, "Bear Ceremonialism," p. 54, citing L. von Schrenck, *Reisen und Forschungen im Amurlande in den Jahren 1854–1856*, vol. 3.1, *Die Völker des Amurlandes* (St. Petersburg, 1891), p. 561.
36. Hallowell, "Bear Ceremonialism," pp. 33–42. Cf. M. G. Levin and L. P. Potapov, *The Peoples of Siberia* (Chicago, 1964), pp. 213, 254, 447, 520, 553, 590, 738, 770.
37. W. Jochelson, *The Koryak* (Leiden and New York, 1905–08), p. 142, in the series American Museum of Natural History Memoirs, 5, Jessup North Pacific Expedition, 7. Cf. Hallowell, "Bear Ceremonialism," p. 38.
38. Hallowell, "Bear Ceremonialism," p. 39, quoting E. G. Ravenstein, *The Russians on the Amur* (London, 1861), p. 379.
39. R. P. Trilles, *Les Pygmées de la forêt équatoriale* (Paris and Munster i. Wein, 1925), p. 325.

40. Ibid., pp. 460–61 and 358.

41. Hallowell, "Bear Ceremonialism," pp. 106–35. For a useful comparative treatment, see H. J. R. Paproth, "Das Bärenfest der Ketó in Nordsiberien in Zusammenhang gebraucht mit den Bärenzeremonien und Bärenfesten anderer Völker der nördlichen Hemisphäre," *Anthropos* 55 (1962): 55–88. It is to be regretted that, since the study by W. Koppers, "Der Bärenkult in ethnologischer und prähistorischer Beleuchtung," *Palaeobiologica*, 1933, pp. 47–64, the study of bear ceremonialism has been linked with the attempt to reconstruct paleolithic religion. See the careful review articles by K. J. Narr, "Interpretation alsteinzeitlicher Kunstwerke durch völkerkundliche Parallelen," *Anthropos* 50 (1955): 513–45, and especially, Narr, "Bärenzeremoniell und Schamanismus in der Alteren Steinzeit Europas," *Saeculum* 10 (1959): 233–72.

42. Cf. Hallowell, "Bear Ceremonialism," p. 132, who argues that the bear festival "is only an extension of the rite which is observed at the slaughter of every bear."

43. The desire for a bloodless killing seems to be behind the strangulation. Note that L. von Schrenck, *Die Völker des Amurlandes*, p. 711, records that the Gilyak (i.e., the Nivkhi) immediately cover with snow any blood that is spilled during the ritual kill. On this detail, see further Hallowell, "Bear Ceremonialism," p. 115, n. 484, and C. Coon, *The Hunting Peoples* (New York, 1976), pp. 380–81.

44. I can find no unambiguous evidence for this among northern hunters. See its appearance among Philippine Negritos as described in K. Stewart, *Pygmies and Dream Giants* (New York, 1954), p. 65.

45. Lot-Falck, *Rites*, p. 154 et passim.

46. I. Lissner, *Man, God, and Magic* (London, 1961), p. 246.

47. S. Reinach, "L'Art et la magie," *L'Anthropologie* 14 (1903): 257–66.

The Meaninglessness of Ritual

FRITS STAAL

Facts of publication: *Staal, Frits. 1979. "The Meaninglessness of Ritual," Numen 26(1): 2–22. Reprinted with the permission of Numen, E. J. Brill, Leiden, Netherlands.*

Staal asks sobering questions of several standard theories of ritual and shows their inadequacies. These theories hold in common an attempt to comprehend the meaning of ritual. In the face of the failure of these theories, Staal hypothesizes that ritual is pure activity without meaning, goal, or aim. The Vedic ritual of the fire altar (Agnicayana) provides the prime example by which Staal demonstrates his theory of the meaninglessness of ritual. From the perspective of his theory Staal is able to shed light on a number of problems and issues: why ritual scholars have ignored the rules that are essential to most rites; the likeness of ritual performances to neuroses (that is, the obsessiveness common to ritual performers); and the usefulness of the side-effects of ritual such as bonding participants and boosting morale. Staal speculates that the meaninglessness of ritual contributes to the evolution of language, religion, and humanity. He believes that ritual is the source of syntax and suggests it may also underlie the development of religious structures.

Hans Penner has written a stimulating response to this controversial theory in "Language, Ritual and Meaning," Numen 32. 1(1985): 1–16.

About the author: *Dates: 1930–   , Amsterdam, The Netherlands.* **Education:** *Kandidaats, Doctoraal, University of Amsterdam; Ph.D., University of Madras.* **Field(s):** *philosophy; Sanskrit; linguistics; anthropology.* **Career:** *Professor of Philosophy and of South and Southeast Asian Studies, 1968–1991, University of California at Berkeley; emeritus, 1991.* **Publications:** Nambudiri Veda Recitation *(Mouton, 1961);* The Science of Ritual *(Bhandarkar, 1982);* Agni: The Vedic Ritual of the Fire Altar I–II *(University of California, 1983);* Jouer avec le feu: Pratique et theorie du rituel védigue *(1990);* Rules without Meaning: Ritual, Mantras and the Human Sciences *(Peter Lang, 1989).*

The Agnicayana, a 3000-year-old Vedic ritual, was performed in 1975 in a village in southwest India by Nambudiri brahmins. This event, which lasted twelve days, was filmed, photographed, recorded and extensively documented. From twenty hours of rough footage, Robert Gardner and I produced a 45-minute film, "Altar of Fire." Two records are planned with selections from the eighty hours of recorded recitation and chant. Photographs of the ceremonies were taken by Adelaide de Menil. In collaboration with the chief Nambudiri ritualists and other scholars, I am preparing a definite account of the ceremonies, which will appear in two illustrated volumes entitled: "Agni—The Vedic Ritual of the Fire Altar."

I shall here be concerned not with empirical description, but with theoretical implications. Vedic ritual is not only the oldest surviving ritual of mankind; it also provides the best source material for a theory of ritual. This is not because it is close to any alleged "original" ritual. Vedic ritual is not primitive and not an *Ur*-ritual. It is sophisticated and already the product of a long development. But it is the largest, most elaborate and (on account of the Sanskrit manuals) best documented among the rituals of man. Hubert and Mauss, who noted these facts in 1909, used the Vedic animal sacrifice as source material for the construction of a ritual paradigm ("un schème abstrait du sacrifice").[1] However, they did not know that these rituals are still performed, so that many data were inaccessible to them. I shall use data from the 1975 performance and textual material from Sanskrit manuals, in particular the *śrauta sūtras*, a literature exclusively devoted to ritual which dates from the eighth through fourth centuries B.C.

* * *

A widespread but erroneous assumption about ritual is that it consists in symbolic activities which refer to something else. It is characteristic of a ritual performance, however, that it is self-contained and self-absorbed. The performers are totally immersed in the proper execution of their complex tasks. Isolated in their sacred enclosure, they concentrate on correctness of act, recitation and chant. Their primary concern, if not obsession, is with rules. There are no symbolic meanings going through their minds when they are engaged in performing ritual.

Such absorption, by itself, does not show that ritual cannot have a symbolic meaning. However, also when we ask a brahmin explicitly why the rituals are performed, we never receive an answer which refers to symbolic activity. There are numerous different answers, such as: we do it because our ancestors did it; because we are eligible to do it; because it is good for society; because it is good; because it is our duty; because it is said to lead to immortality; because it leads to immortality. A visitor will furthermore observe that a person who has performed a Vedic ritual acquires social and religious status, which involves other benefits, some of them economic. Beyond such generalities one gets involved in individual case histories. Some boys have never been given much of a choice, and have been taught recitations and rites as a matter of fact; by the time they have mastered these, there is little else they are competent or motivated to do. Others are inspired by a spirit of competition. The majority would not be able to come up with an adequate answer to the question why they engage in ritual. But neither would I, if someone were to ask me why I am writing about it.

Why ask such personal questions? It might be more proper and fruitful to ask specific questions about the meaning of particular rites. Some such questions do receive specific answers, on which participants and scholars generally agree. The Yajamāna, or Patron of the ritual, must keep his hands closed "like a child in the womb of its mother, ready to be reborn." The fire altar has the shape of a bird because fire, as well as Soma, were fetched from heaven by a bird. The priests do not go south if they can help it for the southern direction is inauspicious. Certain bricks of the altar are consecrated so that it may rain.

Such simple answers form a small minority. They are given rarely, and only in reply to similarly simple questions. Most questions concerning ritual detail involve numerous complex rules, and no participant could provide an answer or elucidation with which he would himself be satisfied. Outsiders and bystanders may volunteer their ideas about religion and philosophy generally—without reference to any specific question. In most cases such people are

Hindus who do not know anything about Vedic ritual. There is only one answer which the best and most reliable among the ritualists themselves give consistently and with more than average frequency: we act according to the rules because this is our tradition (*parampara*). The effective part of the answer seems to be: look and listen, these are our activities! To performing ritualists, rituals are to a large extent like dance, of which Isadora Duncan said: "If I could tell you what it meant there would be no point in dancing it."

Ritual, then, is primarily activity. It is an activity governed by explicit rules. The important thing is what you do, not what you think, believe or say. In India this has become a basic feature of all religion, so that we should refer, not to the faithful or orthodox, but to the orthoprax (from Greek *orthos*, "right" and *praxis*, "action"). It is precisely this feature which is least understood by English-writing Indian authors such as V. S. Naipaul and N. C. Chaudhuri, who have recently taken on the role of explaining India to Western intelligentsia.

* * *

If we wish to know the meaning or theory of ritual, we should not confine ourselves to practising ritualists; we have learned, after all, that it does not pay to ask elephants about zoology, or artists about the theory of art. Before asking anyone else, however, let us take a look at what the Indian tradition itself has to offer. Since in India ritual has always been a favorite topic for speculation, there is an abundance of material. Even prior to speculation we find suggestive ideas. In the earliest Vedic literature, rituals, along with metres and chants, are used by gods and demons to fight and conquer each other, and sometimes to create worlds. Even when the aims are not explicit, gods and demons are frequently depicted as engaged in ritual. Commentaries provide rituals with a great variety of interpretations, sometimes inconsistent with each other.

In due course specific rites came to be prescribed to fulfil specific desires: for health, power, offspring, victory, heaven, and the like. The list of wishes and desires is not so very different from that of modern man. It is certainly not exclusively spiritual, as some modern visionaries have claimed. But this trend re-

ceded again into the background. With increasing systematization of the ritual, we witness a codification of two kinds of rites: the *grhya* or domestic rites, which are "rites de passage," life-cycle rites or sacraments, accompanying such events as birth, initiation, marriage and death; and the *śrauta* rites, "rites solennels," or traditional rites. There are several general and formal differences between these two kinds of ritual. For example, the traditional rites require three fire altars and the services of several priests, whereas the domestic rites require only one fire (the domestic fire) and one priest (the domestic priest). While the function of the domestic rites appears to be fairly straightforward, the significance of the traditional rites is not obvious. The traditional ritual, with its myriad ramifications, exhibits the unhampered development of ritual construction and creativity. It is therefore more important for the understanding of ritual than the domestic rites. The latter, by themselves, might seem to be amenable to explanations along the lines of, e.g., van Gennep's *Rites de passage* (1909). But since such explanations are clearly inapplicable to the traditonal rites, and domestic and traditional rites are partly similar in structure, it follows that all such theories are inappropriate. There are, moreover, traditional rituals which last a thousand years, which shows that some of the rites were purely theoretical. Such theoretical constructs (which the grammarian Patañali compared to the infinite uses of language) should not be brushed aside, as was done by Hillebrandt, who referred in this connection, to "myth and fantasy" of the ritualists.[2] On the contrary, they are as important for the theory of ritual as are concrete ceremonies. Many rites have in fact an intermediate status. The Agnicayana, which was performed in 1975, is a traditional ritual which seems to have been always "real," though some of its extensions, which the texts describe, smack of theory.

The *śrauta sūtras* of the late Vedic period offer several definitions of ritual. One which is often quoted characterizes it as comprising three things: *dravya*, "the substance (which is used in oblations)"; *devatā*, "the deity (to which oblations are offered)"; and *tyāgā*, "renunciation (of the fruits of the ritual acts)." The *tyāgā* is a formula pronounced by the Patron at the culmination of each act of oblation. When the officiating priest, on behalf of the Patron, makes the oblation into the fire for one for one of the gods, for example Agni, the Patron says:

"this is for Agni, not for me" (*agnaye idaṃ na mama*).

At this point a contradiction begins to appear, which becomes increasingly explicit in the ritualistic philosophy of the Mīmāṃsā. The reason for performing a specific ritual is stated to be the desire for a particular fruit or effect. The stock example of the Mīmāṃsā is:

"he who desires heaven shall sacrifice with the Agniṣṭoma ritual" (*Agniṣṭomena svargakāmo yajeta*).

But this fruit is renounced whenever the Patron utters his *tyāga* formula of renunciation. The effect, therefore, is not obtained.

The resulting picture is further complicated by another apparent contradiction. The rites are subdivided into two classes: "obligatory," (*nitya*) and "optional" (*kāmya*). Unlike the Agnicayana, which is *kāmya*, the Agniṣṭoma is a *nitya* rite: every brahmin has the duty to perform it. So here is a ritual which appears to be optional, since it is confined to those who desire heaven (nobody's duty); but which is also not optional, because it is a prescribed duty; and which moreover in the final resort does not bear any fruit because its fruits are abandoned. The texts reflect such contradictions. The Mīmāṃsā Sūtra, basic manual of the Mīmāṃsā, lays down that the rites lead to happiness, but the subcommentary "Straight Spotless" (*Rjuvimalā*) observes that this does not apply to obligatory acts.

The Mīmāṃsā philosophers faced another difficulty. When a ritual performance is completed, no fruit is seen. The Yajamāna, on whose behalf the rites have been performed, does not raise up and go to heaven. Rather the opposite: he returns home and is, as the texts put it, the same as he was before. In particular, he must continue to perform the morning and evening fire rites (*agnihotra*) for the rest of his life. The Mīmāṃsā concluded, quite logically, that the fruit of ritual activity is—temporarily—unseen. It will become apparent only later, e.g., after death. An elaborate theory was devised to show that this is in accordance with the mechanism of *karman*, according to which every cause has an effect. A spe-

cial logical theorem, called *arthāpatti*, was invented in support of this theory. The followers of the Mīmāṃsā were criticized by others (e.g., the philosophers of the Advaita Vidānta) for postulating such unseen effects. For whatever our contemporary fads may suggest—in India, the unseen is resorted to only under duress. What the Mīmāṃsā in fact ended up teaching is that the rituals have to be performed for their own sake.

The notion of *tyāga*, "renunciation," has attained an important position in Hinduism through the teachings of the Bhagavad Gītā. Here Śrī Kṛṣṇa advocates as the highest goal of life a mode of activity, in which acts are performed as usual, but the fruit (*phala*) of action (*karman*) is always renounced (*karma-phala-tyāga*).

*   *   *

The Indian tradition offers suggestive speculations but it does not seem to come up with a single consistent theory of ritual. The most interesting Indian contribution is perhaps the term *karman* itself: originally and primarily used for ritual and similarity pure or ideal activity, it comes by extension to denote any kind of human activity. Now let us see what modern scholars have to offer. For a long time it has been fashionable to believe that rites re-enact myths. This idea was partly inspired by the Babylonian festival of the New Year, which involves a recital of the myth of creation. But this hypothesis is difficult to support and creates an unsolved problem: why should anybody wish to re-enact a myth? The same difficulty applies to several more recent theories, according to which ritual reflects social structure. It is true, again, that there are some remarkable parallels which require explanation. But the question remains: why should social structures be represented or enacted ritually, and in a very roundabout manner at that? Such unanswered questions, generated by the theory, suggest that theories of this type are best abandoned.

A related theory, current among anthropologists, is that rituals are used, in preliterate societies, to transmit "cultural and social values" to the younger generation. This would explain the informants' emphasis on tradition. But the assumption is, of course, unnecessary. Not only are rituals not confined to preliterate societies (it is anthropologists who tend to confine themselves to preliterate societies); but such values (e.g., gods, myths, kinship systems) are most readily transmitted by grandmothers and through language, and there is no need for them to be transmitted again by other means. The only cultural values rituals transmit are rituals.

Another widespread theory is that ritual effects a transition from the realm of the profane to that of the sacred. (Instead of "transition" we also meet with "communication": a weaker version of the theory.) This is very intriguing and unclear. Terms such as "transition" or "communication" do not pose too much of a problem; but "sacred" and "profane" certainly do. Either the theory expresses a tautology: the distinction between profane and sacred is the distinction between the status of a person or object before and after a relevant ritual is embarked upon; accordingly, if sacred and profane have been defined in terms of ritual, ritual cannot be defined in terms of sacred and profane. This is circular and uninformative.

On another interpretation, this theory would assume that the distinction between sacred and profane is already established and known from elsewhere. For example, in the realm of divinity, "sacred" might have been shown to be the domain of the gods, and "profane" that of men. But a satisfactory distinction of this kind is not easily found, especially outside the realm of ritual. Moreover, the terms do not introduce anything new. The theory would merely claim that ritual effects a transition from the realm of men to that of the gods (or a communication between the two). As a matter of fact, the Vedic ritual offers an immediate contradiction. During the Soma rituals, a transition is effected from the "Old Hall," (*prācīnavaṃśa*) to the "Great Altar" (*mahāvedi*). The former is said to be the abode of men, and the latter that of the gods. Thus a transition from the domain of men to that of the gods is effected *within* the ritual. The distinction therefore cannot serve as a concept in terms of which the ritual itself may be defined.

* * *

Why has it proved so difficult to define the meaning, goals and aims of ritual? Why are there so many different answers and theories, not only often contradictory between themselves, but of such disparate character that it is difficult to even compare them with each other? There is one simple hypothesis which would account for all these puzzling facts: the hypothesis that ritual has no meaning, goal or aim.

This is precisely what I suspect to be the case. Ritual is pure activity, without meaning or goal. Let me briefly digress for a point of terminology. Things are either for their own sake, or for the sake of something else. If I were defending the view that ritual is for something else, it would be necessary to distinguish between such other things as meaning, function, aim or goal. But since my view is that ritual is for its own sake, I shall not bother about these differences. To say that ritual is for its own sake is to say that it is meaningless, without function, aim or goal, or also that it constitutes its own aim or goal. It does not follow that it has no value: but whatever value it has is intrinsic value.

Ritual exhibits its character of pure activity most readily when it is contrasted with the applied activities of our ordinary, everyday life. In ritual activity, the rules count, but not the result. In ordinary activity it is the other way around. In Vedic ritual, for example, an important ceremony is *agnipranayana*, "transporting the fire (from the Old to the New Altar)." This is in fact a transition from the abode of men to that of the gods. But the priests do not first think of men and then meditate on the gods. They think of neither, at any time. What is essential in the ceremony is the precise and faultless execution, in accordance with rules, of numerous rites and recitations. The result is important, but it has only ritual use and can only be reached in the ritually prescribed manner. I could not come in and assist in the proceedings by picking up the fire from the Old Altar and depositing it on the New. In fact, if I did such a horrible thing, the entire ceremony would be desecrated, interrupted, and expiation rites would have to be performed. Similar disasters would result if anyone used the sacred fire for any but a ritual purpose, e.g., to heat water for tea.

Now contrast this with an ordinary activity. I am about to transport my suitcase from my house to the bus stop, which is about a mile away. There are no rules I have to follow, provided I obtain the desired effect. I may put my suitcase on a skate board. Or my brother may appear on a bicycle, and the two of us use this vehicle to transport my suitcase to its intended destination.

The two kinds of activity, ritual and ordinary, can be juxtaposed without conflict or contradiction. After making fire for the altar in the ritually prescribed manner by rubbing two pieces of wood together, a priest leaves the sacred enclosure and lights a cigarette with a match. Not so different, actually, from Arthur Rubinstein back home after a concert, putting on a gramophone record. But the two domains should not be mixed. If a priest would light a cigarette from the sacrificial fire, it would be bad. If he would light a cigarette from fire which he had produced by rubbing two pieces of wood together in the ritual manner, he would be considered mad or very eccentric. The ritual and ordinary ways of making fire are neatly demarcated.

A distinctive feature of ordinary activity is that it runs risks which ritual activity avoids. In ordinary activity, the entire performance may fail to have the desired effect. The bicycle together with its load may fall into a canal, or the suitcase may be seized by armed robbers. In ritual activity, the activity itself is all that counts. Not only have we established the rules ourselves, so that we are completely in control; we are also assured of success. If one rite goes wrong, another takes its place. This goes a long way to explain the curious fact that rituals, so apparently meaningless and useless, are at the same time readily engaged in. *Eo ipso* it explains that ritual activity has a pleasant, soothing effect. If you give up desire, you will be happy. This idea and the notion that ritual is performed for its own sake are closely connected and clearly foreshadowed by the Indian doctrine of *tyāga*, the teachings of the Bhagavad Gītā, and by similar notions in other traditions, e.g., *wu-wei*, "absence of (effective) action" in Taoism, or the categorical imperative in Kant. It also accounts for the similarity between rites and games, which are equally unproductive, as Huizinga and Caillois have pointed out. But ritual is one up on most games because you cannot even lose.

Several anthropologists have detected features of meaningless in ritual, without recognizing that these features express its essence. Lévi-Strauss says that ritual "consists of utterances, gestures and manipulations of objects which are independent of the inter-pretations which are proper to these modes of activity and which result not from the ritual itself but from implicit mythology" (*L'homme nu*, 1971, page 600). If we remove the word "implicit" from this sentence (which means forsaking the author's ideas about the complementarity of myth and ritual) we approximate what I believe to be the correct theory. Van Gennep came close to the idea that ritual is meaningless. After completing his *Rites de passage*, he noted that marriage ceremonies, in many societies, include an aspersion rite which he interpreted as a fecundity rite. But identical aspersion rites are employed, in the same and in different societies, when a slave is acquired, when a new ambassador arrives in town, to make rain or to expel someone. Like Indian commentators, van Gennep gave different interpretations to each of these rites. He concluded: "the aspersion rite does not have any personal or basic meaning in the state of isolation, but it is meaningful if seen as a component part of a particular ceremony. The meaning of the rite can, consequently, only be found by determining the relation it has with the other elements of the whole ceremony."[3]

Aspersion rites are not confined to humans. In his Sather lectures at Berkeley, Walter Burkert dealt with the ritual pouring of liquids for marking a territory and observed that this is quite common in mammals: "we all know the dog's behavior at the stone."—In the development of our concepts and theories of ritual it it only a small step from "changing meaning" to: "no intrinsic meaning" and "structural meaning," and from there to: "no meaning."

If ritual is useless this does not imply that it may not have useful side-effects. It is obvious, for example, that ritual creates a bond between the participants, reinforces solidarity, boosts morale and constitutes a link with the ancestors. So do many other institutions and customs. Such side-effects cannot be used to explain the origin of ritual, though they may help to explain its preservation. They explain why rituals are preserved though their meaninglessness is recognized, like the Jewish ritual of the Red Heifer which baffled even Solomon and which was considered the classic example of a divine command for which in a rational explanation can be adduced.

These side-effects fail to explain the most curious fact about ritual preservation: rituals are always guarded jealously and with extreme conservatism. This is directly explained by the theory that ritual has no meaning. A useful institution is open; it may undergo change, because efforts are made to render it more (or less) useful. A useless institution is closed; it is not understood and therefore can only be abandoned or preserved. There are parallels to this situation from outside the realm of ritual. In India, during the last 3000 years, the Vedic language gave way to classical Sanskrit which was in due course replaced by Middle and Modern Indo-Aryan languages. During all these changes the Vedic mantras were orally transmitted without any change. Why? Because they had become meaningless. Languages change because they express meaning, are functional and constantly used. Meaningless sounds do not change; they can only be remembered or forgotten.

Freud has drawn attention to similarities between ritual and neurosis. The obsessiveness which pervades ritual has led several anthropologists to emphasize the emotions and anxiety which sometimes accompany ritual, and which they claim underlie it. In *L'homme nu*, Lévi-Strauss has located such anxiety in the ritualists' fear that reality, which they have cut up ritually, cannot be put together again. But it is apparent that the obsessiveness of ritual is also an immediate consequence of its meaninglessness. Nothing is more conducive to uneasiness than to be entrapped in absurdity. If I detect a mistake in cooking or calculating, I perceive the result and understand the reason. But if I have made a ritual mistake, I don't notice any difference and don't see any reason. I am not even sure whether I made a mistake or not, and there is no way to determine it. It is like being in a foreign culture where strange things happen and it is not clear whether one has made a *faux pas*. The Agnicayana performance of 1975 was followed by a long series of expiation rites, for mistakes that might have been committed. Our anxiety is greatest when we don't know why we are anxious.

The meaninglessness of ritual explains the variety of meanings attached to it. It could not be otherwise. Ideal activity cannot fail to resemble actual activity. Therefore rituals resemble other things, including features of myth and social structure. However, though a ritual activity may resemble a meaningful non-ritual activity, this does not imply that it must itself be meaningful. This can be seen in the realm of animal ritualization, as well as in the human domain. Among animals, ritualization often implies that the goal of an activity has changed. Many ritual displays incorporate modes of action which originally had a different function, e.g., fighting. Such ritual displays may acquire a new function: they lead to copulation because they are sexually stimulating, for example. Some of the same ritual displays, however, are post-nuptial or post-reproductive, and therefore not clearly functional. Biologists find them puzzling (e.g., Huxley[4]).

Human ritualization often follows animal ritualization rather closely. Fighting, simulated or real, is still sexually stimulating among humans. But typical human forms of ritualization seem in general to dissolve meaning, not replace it. One of the earliest rituals originated in connection with the use of fire. During most of its existence, mankind did not know how to use it. Subsequently, more than 250,000 years ago, man learned the use of fire; but he could not make it. So fire was collected from natural conflagrations and was carefully kept and carried around. Elaborate techniques were devised for the preservation of fire. Finally, more than 50,000 years ago, man learned how to make fire. At this point ritualization and the cult of fire came into being. For instead of relying on his art of making fire, and producing it whenever he needed it (which is easy at least during a dry season or in a dry climate), man continued to carry fire around. A distinction was made between such "eternal" fire and the "new" fire which could now be made—a distinction we have since abandoned as irrational. To ancient man, and in several existing societies, fires have retained individuality. They should not be mixed. Fires have to be extinguished, or newly made, at set times by ritual experts. Alongside, the continued preservation of "eternal" fire reflects fossilized habits which had lasted some 200,000 years.

A more recent example comes from the Agnicayana.[5] During the ceremony of *agnipranayana*, when fire is transported from the Old to the New Altar, one of the priests engages in a long recitation. The recitation is of an ancient battle hymn, the Apratiratha or "Song to the Irresistible Warrior" (Taittirīya Saṃhitā 4.6.4, cf. Rgveda 10.103 and 6.75). Indra is invoked as a victorious warrior or hero, "fond of slaughter, disturber of peoples," who with the help of his arrows, chariots and troups, destroys the enemies. When the priest recites: "Comrades, follow in Indra's footsteps!" he sounds less like an officiating priest than like a gang leader or a commander-in-chief. And what is the origin of all of this? At an earlier period, the Vedic Aryans fought their way into the Indian subcontinent, moving from west to east and carrying fire. In the *agnipraṇayana* rite, fire is still carried from west to east. But the priests are not celebrating the ancient raids of their ancestors, of which they need not even be aware. The function of the hymn has not changed. It has become ritual, i.e., disappeared.

Can the hypothesis of the meaninglessness of ritual be formulated in terms of evolution or development? Necessarily so, but we have to speculate back to the origin of man. Philosophers, especially in Germany, have made much of self-consciousness as a characteristic of man, but we are rarely told what this means. I think that man became aware of himself primarily as an agent. Like many other animals, he was already aware of the outside world and could communicate to a limited extent with other members of the species (which does not imply that he possessed language). Abandoning a sense of being pushed around, man made the discovery that he affected the outside world by engaging in activity—a pursuit wrought with risk and danger. So he created a world of ritual or ideal activity, intrinsically successful and free from such contingencies. It expressed man's awareness of himself, and paved the way for theory construction and language, as we shall see. Much later, when ritual was contrasted with ordinary, everyday activity, its meaninglessness became patent and various rationalizations and explanations were constructed. Ritual became deeply involved with religion, which always stands in need of the mysterious and unexplained. Rites were attached to all important events. In the course of time rituals, instead of remaining useless and pure, became useful and meritorious.

Throughout the history of man's speculation on ritual we find inklings of its original function as perfect activity. Just as the Indians mused about *śrauta* rituals, the Chinese theorized about *li*, which means: rites, ceremonies, rules of good manners and proper conduct, etiquette. The Confucian philosopher Hsün Tzŭ (third century B.C.) explained the origin of the *li* as follows:

> Man at birth has desires. When these desires are not satisfied, he cannot remain without seeking their satisfaction. When this seeking for satisfaction is without measure or limit, there can only be contention. When there is contention, there will be disorder; when there is disorder, everything will be destroyed. The early kings hated this disorder, and so they established the *li* and standards of justice so as to set limits to this confusion, to satisfy men's desires, and give opportunity to this satisfaction, in order that desires should not be stretched to the breaking point by things, nor things be used up by desires; that both these two should mutually support one another and so continue to exist. This is how the *li* originated.[6]

Enough of generalities. If ritual consists in the precise execution of rules, it must be possible to know what its rules are. The rules of the *śrauta* ritual have been formulated with great care in the *śrauta sūtras*, and made accessible by Sanskrit scholars, foremost among them Willem Caland. Searching for the best literature outside the Vedic, one soon finds out that there is no literature at all. Lévi-Strauss, in *L'homme nu* (pages 601–603), distinguishes two basic ritual operations: "morcellement" (dismemberment, fragmentation) and repetition. But he offers no actual rules. Hubert and Mauss showed little more than that rites have a beginning, a middle and an end. Scholars and students of ritual seem to lag behind their colleagues who study the rules of measurement, counting or language, and who have for millenia been familiar with some of the rules which obtain in their respective domains. Among students of ritual—whether religiously, anthropologically or psychologically inspired—we mostly meet with generalities. The reason for this neglect is rooted in the nature of ritual itself: if a thing is useless, it is not taken seriously. Thus we do not possess much in the way of a science of ritual, even though the subject is certainly amenable to precise investigation, not unlike physics, mathematics or grammar.

Even at this early stage of pre-scientific groping, in which we find ourselves, it is not impossible to formulate ritual rules. I shall give a few examples from Vedic ritual. This will necessarily involve some detail (for more, see Staal[7]). We must start with the observation that the *śrauta* rituals constitute a hierarchy. Four of them, for example, which I shall refer to by capital letters, are listed in the following order:

D: "Full and New Moon ceremonies" (*darśapūrṇamāsa*)

P: "Animal Sacrifice" (*paśubandha*)

A. "Praise of Agni" (*agniṣṭoma*, paradigm of the Soma rituals)

C: "Piling of Agni" (*agnicayana*).

This sequence is not arbitrary. There is increasing complexity. A person is in general only eligible to perform a later ritual in the sequence, if he has already performed the earlier ones. Each later ritual presupposes the former and incorporates one or more occurrences of one or more of the former rituals. Sometimes these embedded rituals are abbreviated. In general, they undergo modifications. We find the following embeddings, among others:

In P, performances of D are embedded when a cake of eight potsherds is offered to Agni and when a cake of eleven potsherds is offered to Agni-Viṣṇu;

in A are embedded: two performances of P (for Agni-Soma and for Pressing Soma) and several performances of D (called Consecration, Going Forth, Final Bath, Conclusion and Departure, etc., not to mention performances of D embedded in P);

in C, a performance of A, fourteen performances of P and numerous performances of D, some already embedded in A and P, are embedded.

This enumeration is by no means complete, but it may serve to illustrate the "embedding" feature of the underlying structure.

Now for the modifications which rituals undergo when they are embedded, and, more generally, in different contexts. First of all, the deities to which rites on different occasions are dedicated are often different, which induces differences at least in the names which occur in many of the recitations. Even within D itself, one of the main oblations is for Agni-Soma at full moon, but for Indra-Agni at new moon. Sim-

ilarly, the different deities to which the different animals in performances of P are dedicated, induce differences in recitation. But apart from these substitutions there are numerous more complex modifications which are induced by embedding. I shall give one simple example. In the regular performance of D, there are *fifteen sāmidhenī* verses, recited when the twigs of firewood are put on the fire. But at the performance of D which is embedded in P when a cake of eleven potsherds is offered to Agni-Visnu, there are *seventeen sāmidhenī* verses. Such examples can be multiplied almost indefinitely.

Though all these rituals involve embeddings and modifications, it does not follow that there is a unique description in terms of these for each particular ritual. For example, C may be analysed differently as an Atirātra, viz., a modification of A, in which the construction of the New Altar is modified. Such an alternative analysis would necessitate a different structural analysis; what is important in the present context is only that it would involve embeddings and modifications.

In order to get an inkling of the syntax of these structures, we have had to enter into some complexity even though I have made several simplifications. In order to explicate the rules, I shall have to simplify differently and construct a model of a ritual—a more formal representation corresponding to what Hubert and Mauss called a "schème abstrait du sacrifice." In order to make this precise, a series of artificial assumptions will be made, defining D, P and A. The reason for these artificial assumptions and definitions is merely that they constitute a model which exhibits specific structures and rules of the ritual. This model is similar with respect to these structures to the really existing rituals, but is much less elaborate than the latter. What is important is that the existing rituals can be analysed in the same manner as the model with regard to the structures in which we are here interested.

Let us assume that a *ritual* consists of smaller units, which I shall call *rites*. The rites of ritual "D" will be written as "d," those of "P" as "p," etc. Now let us make more specific assumptions. Let D consist of three rites, d_1, d_2 and d_3. I shall write this as a rule:

$$D \rightarrow d_1\ d_2\ d_3. \tag{1}$$

This may be illustrated as:

Ritual P involves several performances of D. Let us assume:

$$P \rightarrow p_1 \; D \; p_2 \; D \; p_3 \; p_4. \tag{2}$$

Similarly, A involves performances of P, as well as of D directly, e.g.:

$$A \rightarrow D \; a_1 \; a_2 \; P \; D \; a_3 \; a_4. \tag{3}$$

A representation of the structure (3) is:

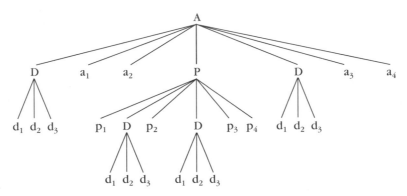

This picture does not correspond to any existing ritual. However, it expresses, precisely, one of the main features of ritual structure, which I have referred to as *embedding*.

We have already met with a second structure: rituals which are embedded undergo *modification*. We may introduce the example I gave into our model by assuming that in ritual D, the first rite, d_1, represents the recitation of fifteen *sāmidhenī* verses. Let us further assume that in the second occurrence of D in P, rite d_1 has to be replaced by a rite d_{*1}, in which seventeen *sāmidhenī* verses are recited. We cannot simply represent this transformation by

adding an expression:

$$d_1 \rightarrow d_1^* \tag{4}$$

for the effect of this would be that all occurrences of d_1 are replaced by occurrences of d_1^*. What we must do is, replace by d_1^* only the d_1 in the second occurrence of D in P. This can be done by introducing a different kind of rule which can be effected by means of an expression which uses a different symbol instead of the single arrow $\rightarrow$, for example a double arrow $\Rightarrow$. We have to represent the entire configuration in which d_1 occurs since it is not otherwise possible to single out the d_1 we wish to single out. This can be done as follows:

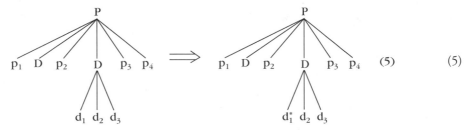

Again, this rule does not correspond to any actual rule, but it expresses, precisely, the feature of ritual structure which I have referred to as *modification*. In

the . . . article on "Ritual Syntax" I have shown that there are also other types of ritual rules than those which exhibit embedding and modification.

* * *

No linguist will have failed to observe the similarity of these ritual rules with the rules of syntax. The single arrow rules which pertain to ritual embedding correspond to the phrase structure rules of syntax; the double arrow rules which pertain to ritual modification correspond to its transformational rules. This correspondence is not due to the fact that I selected ritual rules which appear to resemble syntactic rules. The rules of embedding and modification are in fact very basic rules of ritual, or at least of Vedic ritual.

The partial similarity between ritual and syntax could mean that ritualists follow, albeit unconsciously, the rules of syntax which they had internalized when they learned their native language. I am inclined to the opposite view: syntax comes from ritual. A simple consideration in support of this idea is that animals have ritual, but not language. But there are weightier considerations. Syntax is the part of language which stands most in need of explanation. Language relates sounds to meanings, and so it must necessarily comprise a domain of sounds (studied in phonetics and phonology) and a domain of meanings (studied in semantics). If language were rational and adapted to its purpose, sounds and meanings would be related by means of a 1-1 correspondence. If this were true of natural languages, assuming semantics to be universal, different natural languages would also stand to each other in a 1-1 correspondence, and translation could be effected with the help of dictionaries only. There would be no need for artificial languages, and logicians would be out of business.

What we do find in language is something different. Meanings and sounds are related to each other through a vast and complicated domain of structured rules: syntax. The transition between sound and meaning is unnecessarily complex, roundabout and mathematically absurd. "Nobody in his right mind would attempt to build an artificial language based on phrase structure plus transformations" (J. A. Fodor[8]). How are we to explain such apparent redundancies? It is not enough to say, as communication theorists might, that redundancies are necessary for communication because they decrease mistakes in reception. That assumes that language is only for the sake of communication, which it is not. More importantly, such redundancies, to perform their al-

leged function, merely need be random: which cannot explain syntax, a structured domain of specific rules which in fact makes language unlogical and inefficient. These specific rules, which are without rhyme or reason, must come from elsewhere. They look like a rudiment of something quite diferent. The similarity between syntax and ritual suggests that the origin of syntax is ritual.

The ritual origin of syntax has implications not only in language but also in religion. I shall mention three. Ritual is replete with language, but it is very often meaningless language. When a small golden image of a man is buried under the fire altar of the Agnicayana, the Chief Priest of the Sāmaveda chants songs which contain such sounds as:

kā hvā hvā hvā hvā hvā
phal phal phal phal phal
hau hau hau hau hau
bham bham . . . (eighteen times).

Such structured sounds partake of the syntax of ritual, but do not relate to meaning. This applies to most mantras. Originally, language was born when such structured sounds were connected with meaning. The state immediately preceding language survives in religion as mantras and magical spells: *abracadabra*. Unlike language, these are universal and need no translation. The abundance of such formulas in Buddhism facilitated its introduction into China, where their way was paved by the sacred noises of popular Taoism.

A second feature is that mysticism is characterized by the absence of language. It points to a pre-linguistic state which can be induced by ritual, by recitation, by silent meditation on mantras, or by other means, as I have shown in *Exploring Mysticism*. All these methods help to eliminate meaning, sound and (ritual) structure.

Wittgenstein had an inkling of the place which language occupies in religion when he remarked:

> Is speech essential for religion? I can very well imagine a religion in which there are no doctrines, and hence nothing is said. Obviously the essence of religion can have nothing to do with the fact that speech occurs— or rather: if speech does occur, this itself is a component of religious behavior [the German original has: *Handlung*, "activity"] and not a theory. Therefore nothing turns on whether the words are true, false or nonsensical.[9]

The ritual origin of syntax is connected with another curious fact, which I mentioned in passing: the Vedic gods fought and created not only with ritual, but also with meters and chants. What an extraordinary thing to do! But no, it is not. Meters and chants are like ritual in that they fail to express meaning, but reflect syntactic structure in its pure form, hence pure activity.

*   *   *

We have not come to the end of our investigation. On the contrary, we have hardly begun. What I hope to have shown is that ritual, which has so far been impervious to our understanding, is meaningless and also a subject amenable to serious study. Once we abandon generalities and start working, a first adequate theory will undoubtedly emerge, sooner or later. Such a theory will not only elucidate ritual; it will throw light on the origins of language, religion, and perhaps man.

What will a theory of ritual be like?—Let us reflect once more on the Agnicayana. The main altar is constructed in the shape of a bird from 1005 kiln-fired bricks, 200 each in four layers, and 205 in the fifth layer which comes on top. The configuration of the first, third and fifth layer is the same; and so is that of the second and fourth. The surface of each layer is 7-1/2 times a square of the Yajamāna's length. The bricks are of ten different shapes. There are 136 squares, 48 oblongs of one size, and 302 of another. In addition there are 207 halves of squares, 202 halves of oblongs, and five more groups consisting of bricks arrived at by further subdivision of the former shapes. There are ten bricks which are half as thick as all the others. All the bricks constitute furthermore another set of groups, each with its

own name and consecrated by particular mantras. Most bricks have to be consecrated in a specific, very roundabout order; others may be consecrated in any order, provided one general direction is maintained and the location of the final brick is fixed. Some bricks have figures drawn on them. Others are lifted from their proper place, carried around the altar and put back before they can be fully consecrated. All of this, and much more, is in accordance with numerous precise rules, for which in almost all cases no explanation whatever is offered. Whether or not the rules are arbitrary, they are strictly adhered to. In case of controversy or differences of interpretation, various schools arise which establish different traditions. Unlike sects, ritual traditions co-exist peacefully, they are mutually exclusive and there is neither desire, nor mechanism for conversion. This feature, too, has become a mark of Indian religions.

And so we may return to the question what a theory of ritual would be like. It is unlikely that such a theory, if at all adequate, will be simple, viz., more simple than the ritual facts themselves. There will be complaints about its myriad rules, as there have been about Chomsky and Halle's *Sound Pattern of English*, Euclid's *Elements*, and the *śrauta sūtras*.

A final paragraph and consolation. There must be readers who are shocked, angry or depressed at the thought that ritual (not to mention religion and even language) is not only complex but also meaningless. I am not a bit sad about it. I prefer a thing, like a person, to be itself, and not refer to something or somebody else. For all we know life itself may be meaningless. Seen from without, the life of an ant seems to be just that, a thought that must have occurred to King Solomon (*Proverbs* 6:6). Neither ants, nor we are any the worse for it.

NOTES

1. H. Hubert and M. Mauss, "Essai sur la nature et la fonction du sacrifice." *Mélanges d'histoire et des religions*, 1909, page 22.
2. A. Hillebrandt, *Ritual-Literatur, Vedische Opfer und Zauber*, Strassburg 1897, page 158.
3. "De la méthode à suivre dans l'étude des rites et des mythes," *Revue de l'université de Bruxelles*, 1911, pages 505–23; English translation in J. Waardenburg (ed.), *Classical Approaches to the Study of Religion*. The Hague-Paris 1973, I, page 299.
4. J. Huxley (ed.), "A Discussion on Ritualization of Behavior in Animals and Man," *Philosophical Transactions of the Royal Society of London*, 1966, Series B, No. 772, Vol. 251, page 254.
5. Cf. J. C. Heesterman, "Vrātya and Sacrifice," *Indo-Iranian Journal* 6, 1962, pages 34–36.

6. Fung Yu-lan, *A History of Chinese Philosophy*, transl. Derk Bodde, Princeton 1952, I, page 297.
7. "Ritual Syntax," *Sanskrit and Indian Studies, Essays in Honor of Daniel H. H. Ingalls*; "Ritual Structure," *Agni. The Vedic Ritual of the Fire Altar*, volume II [Berkeley, Asian Humanities Press, 1983.]
8. In: F. Smith and G. A. Miller (eds), *The Genesis of Language: A Psycholinguistic Approach*, Cambridge, Mass. 1966, page 270.
9. F. Waismann, "Notes on Talks with Wittgenstein," *The Philosophical Review* 74, 1965, page 16.

A Performative Approach to Ritual*

STANLEY J. TAMBIAH

Facts of publication: *Tambiah, Stanley J. 1981. "A Performative Approach to Ritual," Proceedings of the British Academy, 1979 65: 116–142 (read 28 March 1979). Reprinted with the permission of The British Academy.*

Stanley Tambiah says that the distinction between ritual and nonritualistic action, like the distinction between religious and nonreligious ritual, is never absolute. Ritual shares qualities with other kinds of activity such as festivities, meetings, and conventions. He accounts for several of the prominent features of ritual such as its redundancy, formality, and stereotyped form, as well as the traditionalizing attitude of ritualists, by arguing that they are necessary if cosmological constructs enacted in ritual are to be taken by ritualists as immutable and unquestionable. From a theoretical position based in information theory, Tambiah offers a characterization of ritual that treats it as an indirect form of communication. In his view ritual does not directly express the feelings of individuals but employs conventionalized forms in order to distance participants from direct or spontaneous expression of emotion.

Tambiah's understanding of ritual resonates with the view of Rappaport (in this volume).

About the author: Dates: *1929–   , Sri Lanka.* **Education:** *B.A., University of Sri Lanka; Ph.D., Cornell University.* **Field(s):** *anthropology; Buddhist studies.* **Career:** *Professor of Anthropology, 1973–1976, University of Chicago. Professor of Anthropology and Curator of South Asian Ethnology at the Peabody Museum, 1976–present, Harvard University.* **Publications:** Buddhism and the Spirit Cults in Northeast Thailand *(Cambridge University, 1970); with Jack Goody,* Bridewealth and Dowry *(Cambridge University, 1973);* World Conqueror and World Renouncer: A Study of Buddhism and Polity in Thailand Against a Historical Background *(Cambridge University, 1976);* "A Performative Approach to Ritual*" (Proceedings of the British Academy, 1981);* Culture, Thought and Social Action: An Anthropological Perspective *(Harvard University, 1985);* Sri Lanka: Ethnic Fratricide and the Dismantling of Democracy *(University of Chicago, 1986).* **Additional:** *Curl Bequest prize, Royal Anthropological Institute, 1964; Rivers Memorial medal, Royal Anthropological Institute, 1973; D.Litt., Jaffna University, Sri Lanka, 1981; Guggenheim fellowship, 1982.*

Let me at the outset state firmly that we cannot in any *absolute* way separate ritual from non-ritual in the societies we study. But *relative* contrastive distinctions (rather than *absolute* distinctions) help us to distinguish between certain kinds of social activity. For example, although symbolic elements surround the activity of a scientist conducting an experiment in a laboratory—he may wear a white coat and observe a certain etiquette with his colleagues—yet there is a difference between the scientific experiment and a Roman Catholic mass with regard to the way words and acts are implicated and 'verification' procedures invoked, and results interpreted.

Although neither linguistically nor ostensively can we demarcate a bounded domain of ritual (separated off from other domains) in any society, yet every society has named and marked out enactments, performances, and festivities which we can identify as typical or focal examples of 'ritual' events. They constitute paradigmatic instances of the phenomenon I want to focus on.

In the Thai language the prefix *pithi*, usually translated as 'ceremony', demarcates certain events.

*I want to thank Dan Rosenberg for editorial help and critical comments while this essay was in first draft. Others who have kindly read and offered perceptive and constructive remarks are Shmuel Eisenstadt, Aram Yengoyan, Mariza Peirano, and Tullio Maranhao.

Pithi taengan means marriage ceremony, *pithi phaosob* means cremation rites, and *pithi wajkhru* means the ceremony of honouring one's teacher. Again the prefix *ngān* signifies some kind of festivity, and can label a temple fair (*ngān wat*) or a feast at home (*ngān liang*). While differentiating ceremonies or festivities from other events to which these labels are not attached, these examples do not however differentiate 'religious' events from 'non-religious', for in no Thai *pithi* or *ngān* is some feature of Buddhism or the supernatural not invoked.

Consider the following expressions in the English language: graduation ceremony, church service, prayer meeting, Republican Convention, communion rite, football match. The words 'ceremony', 'service', 'convention', 'meeting', 'match', and so on mark the events as being of a particular kind. Indeed, these events appear to share some features—an ordering or procedure that structures them, a sense of collective or communal enactment that is purposive (devoted to the achievement of a particular objective), and an awareness that they are different from 'ordinary' everyday events.

Some examples from India and Sri Lanka illustrate another feature associated with rituals, especially those of a festive kind: namely, the charged use of certain vehicles and devices of communication as a mode of experiencing and activating the extraordinary and extra-mundane. The *līlā* in North India means 'play' and as such labels games and dramas. But *līlā* is also used to describe one of the great cycles of religious festivals, the Rām Līlā, at which the epic Rāmāyaṇ is enacted. In this context, *līlā* means no 'ordinary' play, no 'ordinary' theatre, but communicates the fact of the gods and the divine becoming *activated and manifest in this world*, and thus stands for an intensified *experience* of the divine, characterized by a heightened use of many media of communication and a charged and expectant mass participation. The Tamil language equivalent for such a religious festival is *thiruvilaiyādal*, and in neighbouring Sri Lanka festive rites performed for gods are called *deiange sellama*, 'the play of the gods'. If you will permit me an unavoidable digression: it is perhaps not too far-fetched to say that the Tikopians express in a different idiom, immortalized for us by Raymond Firth—'the work of the gods'—a similar sense of prescribed communal activity and an

intensified experience during the ritual cycle when their gods initiate and regulate the cosmic round of activities.

We can of course find similar examples in the ancient Greek World where ritual, festival, and play belonged to a paradigmatic set (in the Saussurean sense). A brief reference to Johan Huizinga's *Homo Ludens* is apposite here. Asserting the refreshing proposition that the 'play activity is the basis of civilisation' (as a view of contest it is at least a nice antidote to Konrad Lorenz's attributing the same role to aggression), Huizinga enumerates many features characterizing 'play' in the Classical Greek period, of which the following are examples: play constitutes a stepping out of real life into a temporary sphere of activity with a disposition all of its own ('limitation of time'); it also takes place in a marked-off space, the playground and ritual stage sharing this 'limitation of space'; it assumes a fixed, culturally ordained form, constituted of 'elements of repetition and alternation (as in a refrain) [which] are like the warp and woof of a fabric'; it is a 'contest for something' as well as a 'representation' of something . . . it 'creates order, and is order', and in an imperfect world it brings temporary perfection. All these characteristics fit like a glove the examples of ritual we have earlier cited.

But Huizinga himself saw that there were elements of tension, uncertainty, and chanciness of outcome in play, a feature which Lévi-Strauss, continuing the challenging comparison between ritual and play,[1] singles out as the distinctive difference between them. In a famous passage in *Savage Mind* (1966) Lévi-Strauss remarked, 'All games are defined by a set of rules which in practice allow the playing of any number of matches', while ritual is played 'like a *favoured instance of a game*, remembered from among the possible ones because it is the only one which results in a particular type of equilibrium between the two sides' (p. 30). 'Games thus appear to have a disjunctive effect: they end in the establishment of a difference between individual players or teams where originally there was no indication of inequality. And at the end of the game they are distinguished into winners and losers. Ritual, on the other hand, is the exact inverse; it conjoins for it brings about a union . . . or in any case an organic relation between two initially separate groups, one ideally merging with the person of the officiant and the other with the collectivity of the faithful' (p. 32).

While no anthropologist will take Lévi-Strauss's formulation to be true of all rituals known, yet his comparison helps us to understand how the Trobrianders (in Jerry Leach's marvellous film 'Cricket in the Trobriands') have transformed the English competitive (and ritualized) game of cricket—a 'rubbish' game from the Trobriand point of view—into an elaborate formalized *kayasa* display, where not an outright win but a near equivalence of exchange (with the host team enjoying a slight edge) is the outcome.[2] The Trobriand transformation of a competitive game that evolved in an individualist Western society to a near-balanced reciprocity of formalized display and exchange does hint at a general, if not universal, feature of ritual: ritual usually specifies in advance not only the procedural rules but also the sequences of events, and in this sense stands in stark contrast to the unpredictable and unequal outcomes of sports (as they are understood in our time), with the jubilation of victory and the humiliation of defeat, all too well known in British football today.

Obviously such ritual enactments as various forms of divination, astrological consultations, mediumistic sessions do not predict their outcomes in advance, yet their ordering is so different from the uncertainties of a game. For they have as their aim the enabling of the client to effect a cure or a reconciliation, to make a decision, to avoid a danger, and in this sense the object of the exercise is to make a fruitful exchange between the occult and the human via the mediation of the officiant, a fruitful conjunction that will help to produce an orderly ongoing social existence.

We can now venture a working definition of ritual which highlights the features we have touched upon:

Ritual is a culturally constructed system of symbolic communication. It is constituted of patterned and ordered sequences of words and acts, often expressed in multiple media, whose content and arrangement are characterized in varying degree by formality (conventionality), stereotypy (rigidity), condensation (fusion), and redundancy (repetition). Ritual action in its constitutive features is performa-

tive in these three senses: in the Austinian sense of performative wherein saying something is also doing something as a conventional act; in the quite different sense of a staged performance that uses multiple media by which the participants experience the event intensively; and in the third sense of indexical values—I derive this concept from Peirce—being attached to and inferred by actors during the performance.

THE INTEGRATION OF CULTURAL ACCOUNT AND FORMAL ANALYSIS

Let us note at the outset that the definition insists on ritual's being a culturally constructed system of symbolic communication—that is to say, its cultural content is grounded in particular cosmological or ideological constructs. The definition also insists on ritual's portraying certain features of form and patterning, and using certain communicational and semiotic vehicles. Can a 'cultural account' and a 'formal analysis' be fused in one and the same analysis? Can the formal features of ritual in general be reconciled with the particular cultural contexts in which rituals are created and enacted? Are they not conflicting analytical frames? I hope to demonstrate that cultural considerations are integrally implicated in the form that ritual takes, and that a marriage of form and content is essential to ritual action's *performative* character and efficacy.[3]

At first sight this theoretical aim seems daunting, because it appears as if the battle lines have already been drawn between two schools of thought, the neo-Tylorians and the proponents of a semiotic theory of ritual. As we well know, the neo-Tylorians (e.g. Horton) conceive the critical feature of religion, and therefore of (religious) ritual, as being belief in, and communication with, the 'supernatural' world or a 'transtemporal' other world. In contrast, the semiotic school views the category ritual as spanning sacred—secular, natural—supernatural domains, and as having as its distinctive feature a tendency towards certain forms and structures of 'communication'.

My view is that we can liberate ourselves from the limitations of the neo-Tylorian natural—supernatural dichotomy by first recognizing that all societies have cosmologies which in their *several different classificatory ways* relate man to man, man with nature and animals, and man with the gods and demons, and other non-human agencies. The inevitability of the cosmological perspective was graphically stated by Wittgenstein in this aphorism: if the flea were to construct a rite it would be about the dog. We have also clearly to realize that cosmological conceptions are not merely—or even importantly—to be understood in terms of the subjects' stated 'beliefs' as the neo-Tylorians tend to do—but is most richly embedded in myths, rituals, legal codes, constitutional charters, and other collective representations. Moreover, when beliefs are taken to be prior to ritual action, the latter is considered as derivative and secondary, and is ignored or undervalued in its own right as a medium for transmitting meanings, for the construction of social reality or, for that matter, the creation and bringing to life of the cosmological scheme itself. In other words, ritual's performative and creative aspect as an enacted event tends to be lost sight of in neo-Tylorian discussions.

Thus, while we must grant the importance of cultural presuppositions, of cosmological constructs, as anterior and antecedent context to ritual, we must also hold that our understanding of the communicative aspects of ritual may not be furthered by imagining that such a belief context adequately explains the form of the ritual event *per se*. But the clue for synthesizing this seeming antinomy has already revealed itself to us, in the fact that cosmological constructs are embedded (of course not exclusively) in rites, and that rites in turn enact and incarnate cosmological conceptions. The integration of cultural account and formal analysis is revealed in this mutuality: if a society's major rituals are closely associated with its cosmology then we can legitimately ask *what* does a society seek to convey to its adherents in its main performances, which leads us to ask why certain communicational forms are chosen and used in preference to others as being more appropriate and adequate for this transmission.

By cosmology I mean the body of conceptions that enumerate and classify the phenomena that compose the universe as an ordered whole and the norms and processes that govern it. From my point of view, a society's principal cosmological notions are all those orientating principles and conceptions that are held

to be sacrosanct, are constantly used as yardsticks, and are considered worthy of perpetuating relatively unchanged. As such, depending on the conceptions of the society in question, its legal codes, its political conventions, and its social class relations may be as integral to its cosmology as its 'religious' beliefs concerning gods and supernaturals. In other words, in a discussion of enactments which are quintessentially rituals in a 'focal' sense, the traditional distinction between religious and secular is of little relevance, and the idea of sacred need not attach to religious things defined only in the Tylorian sense. Anything towards which an 'unquestioned' and 'traditionalizing' attitude is adopted can be viewed as sacred. Rituals built around the sacrosanct character of constitutions and legal charters, and wars of independence and liberation, and devoted to their preservation as enshrined truths, or to their invocation as great events, have (to borrow a phrase from Moore and Myerhoff) a 'traditionalizing role', and in this sense may share similar constitutive features with rituals devoted to gods or ancestors.[4] No wonder that an American sociologist—Bellah—has coined the label 'civil religion' to characterize some American national ceremonials.

Thus, supposing we say that the main and critical points of articulation in many (if not all) cosmologies[5] are (to give a few examples): the insistence on unquestioned acceptance of conceptions that cannot be subject to the criterion of independent validating experience, the promise held out that the committed members will experience a greater cosmic reality and truth if they will suspend doubt and simply follow the prescribed practices; the postulation of a relation between life and death, between a 'this world' and an 'other world', between the realms of gods, ancestors, humans, and creatures of nature; the predication of a morally evaluated hierarchy of all creatures that comprise the cosmos, and the transactions between them both desirable and undesirable, deserved and undeserved; the enshrinement of events of sacred beginnings and climactic events; supposing we say this, then certain corollaries necessarily follow which inflect and mould ritual action, which has for its objective the communication with and mediation between these culturally distinguished agents, levels, domains, and events which compose the cosmology.[6]

FORMALITY, CONVENTIONALITY, STEREOTYPY, AND RIGIDITY

This dynamic nexus between such cultural constructs and ritual as a mode of social action generates the set of features which in our definition we have referred to as formality, conventionality, stereotypy, and rigidity. If cosmological constructs are to be taken on faith and be considered as immutable, then it is a necessary corollary that the rites associated with them be couched in more or less fixed form, be transmitted relatively unchanged through time and be repeatedly enacted on ordained or crisis occasions. Moreover, especially in cosmic rites, but also in many rites of passage and in curing cults of mediumistic possession, the cosmogony is repeatedly enacted and the archetypes constantly reiterated in order to achieve the double feat of projecting concrete present time into mythical time (Eliade 1959, p. 20) and bringing the superior divine realm or moments of beginning into the present human world to achieve a cleansing and a charging with moral potency.

These objectives and constraints directly shape certain features of form in ritual as a medium, features which by a happy convergence of ideas more than one anthropologist has in recent times identified.[7] In some respects, of course, these recent discussions return to Malinowski's treatment of magical language as a distinct mode, separate from ordinary speech. For example, Rappaport (1971, 1974) enumerates a conjunction of features as distinctive of ritual such as formality (including stylization and repetition), invariance of liturgical form which generates sanctity (the quality of unquestionable truthfulness), and certainty of meaning. Bloch (1974) has . . . made a similar identification. Moore and Myerhoff in their . . . work (*Secular Ritual*, 1977) refer to ritual as a 'traditionalizing instrument' and single out repetition, stylization, ordering, evocative presentational style and staging, etc., as formal features which enable ritual to imitate the rhythmic imperatives and processes of the cosmos, and thereby attach permanence and legitimacy to what are actually social constructs. These last authors make the telling observation that even in the case of a newly invented ritual (or ritual performed only once), it is constructed in such a way that 'its

internal repetitions of form and content make it tradition-like' because 'it is supposed to carry the same unreflective conviction as any traditional repetitive ritual . . .' (pp. 8–9).

I want to begin my commentary by elaborating the point that the formalization of rituals is linked to ritual's being *conventionalized* action, and that this conventionality in turn psychically *distances* the participants from the ritual enactment. This very fact puts in jeopardy the usefulness of the intentionality theory of meaning for understanding ritual.[8] Let me explain.

Rituals as conventionalized behaviour are not designed or meant to express the intentions, emotions, and states of mind of individuals in a direct, spontaneous, and 'natural' way. Cultural elaboration of codes consists in the *distancing* from such spontaneous and intentional expressions because spontaneity and intentionality are, or can be, contingent, labile, circumstantial, even incoherent or disordered.

Now, if for the purposes of exposition we draw a crude distinction between 'ordinary' communicational behaviour and 'ritual' behaviour (accepting of course that both kinds are equally subject to cultural conventions), then we could say (forgetting the problem of insincerity and lying) that ordinary acts 'express' attitudes and feelings directly (e.g. crying denotes distress in our society) and 'communicate' that information to interacting persons (e.g. the person crying wishes to convey to another his feeling of distress). But ritualized, conventionalized, stereotyped behaviour is constructed in order to express and communicate, and is publicly construed as expressing and communicating, certain attitudes congenial to an ongoing institutionalized intercourse. Stereotyped conventions in this sense act at a second or further remove; they code not intentions but 'simulations' of intentions. People can act meaningfully in stereotyped ways because they have 'learned to learn' in Bateson's sense of deutero-learning, and because the enactment of ritual is the guarantee of social communication. Thus *distancing* is the other side of the coin of conventionality; distancing separates the private emotions of the actors from their commitment to a public morality. In a positive sense, it enables the cultural elaboration of the symbolic; but in a negative sense it also contributes to hypocrisy, and the subversion of transparent honesty.[9] The whole point about a vigorous culture as a social product is that it is capable of elaborating several orders of conventionality, superimposing and interweaving them, and juxtaposing several dimensions of meaning.

This of course means that any theory of ritual as directly modifying sentiments, as enabling persons to 'act out' their aggression or frustration and thereby reach a cow-like, placid state, is too simplistic and naïve. Radcliffe-Brown himself, at certain points in *The Andaman Islanders*, for example in his discussion of the peace-making ceremony (p. 238), viewed ritual as replacing aggressive feelings by those of 'friendship and solidarity'.[10] But he clearly saw that the objective was not achieved directly; for example, he commented that Andamanese ceremonies 'are not spontaneous expressions of feeling; they are all customary obligations to which the sentiment of obligation attaches' (p. 246).[11]

Susanne Langer (1951) saw very well how formalization in ritual involved the adoption of conventionalized gesture as opposed to improvised action, and how critical the phenomenon of psychic distancing of the participants was. She noted that ritual, usually bound to set occasions, is a 'presented idea'; ritual as symbolic activity involves 'conceptions' rather than an immediate relief of feelings which may or may not take place. Ritual, Langer continued, was a culturally constructed expressive act, 'expressive in the logical sense', that is, 'not as a sign of the emotion it conveys but a symbol of it; instead of completing the natural history of a meaning, it denotes the feeling, and may merely bring it to mind . . . when an actor acquires such a meaning it becomes a *gesture*' (pp. 123–4).

In other words, Langer's point was that ritual's distinctive characteristic is not the evoking of feelings in an immediate psychological sense, not to produce a catharsis in the Aristotelian sense, which it may or may not do, but the 'articulation of feelings' and 'the ultimate product of such an articulation is not a simple emotion, but a complex permanent attitude. This attitude, which is the worshippers' response to the insight given by the sacred symbols, is an emotional pattern, which governs all individual lives. It cannot be recognized through any clearer medium than that of formal-ized gesture'. Ritual is not a 'free expression of emotions', but a disciplined rehearsal of 'right attitudes'.[12]

All of a piece with the elaboration of the formalized gesture is the development together with ritual of what Hymes has called the 'polite style' as opposed to the normal unmarked colloquial and slang. The polite style, the style of rhetoric, the use of superior forms of address and pronouns, and of inflated vocabulary, comes to be preferred in important, serious ceremonies. 'The style becomes a formal marker of occasions of societal importance where the personal relationship is minimized' (Ervin-Tripp 1972, p. 235). We may add that where, as in many complex serious ceremonies, slang and low comedy—the indicators of 'vulgar' persons—are introduced at certain points, these 'crude' sequences make their import by unfavourable comparison with, and subordination to, the high style associated with the refined, the honoured, and the high-ranked *persona*.[13]

If we push this line of thought far enough a certain conclusion follows: when quintessential rituals are enacted, their meanings retreat further and further away from an 'intentional' theory of communication and meaning as developed by philosophers of language.[14] We can keep aside as more or less irrelevant the Gricean theory of intentional meaning, because in conventional ritual like marriage the immediate intentions of the officiating priest or of the bride and groom do not explain the meaning and efficacy of the rite iself (nor the unintended meanings). Whether one is marrying because one has made the girl pregnant, or whether the ceremony is being performed by a fallen, drunken priest (of the sort so powerfully depicted in Graham Greene's *The Power and the Glory*), is immaterial to the validity of the sacrament performed, provided certain conditions are satisfied (the priest has been ordained into his office, the couple are not marrying bigamously, etc.).[15] Thus, if we postulate a continuum of behaviour with intentional behaviour at one pole and conventional behaviour at the other, we shall have to locate formalized ritual nearer the latter pole. Although we leave intentionality as such behind us, we very much want to adopt and adapt the Austinian notion of performative acts and the Gricean notion of conventional (and non-conventional) implicature in our scheme for understanding the social meaning and efficacy of ritual.

At this point I can conveniently introduce the first of the three senses in which I consider ritual to be performative. This first sense obviously derives from Austin's well-known notion of the performative utterance in which the saying of the illocutionary speech act is 'the doing of an action'; this act, 'conforming to a convention' in 'appropriate circumstances', is subject to normative judgements of felicity or legitimacy and not to rational tests of truth and falsity.

Adapting Searle (1969)[16] for our purposes, we can say that rituals as performative acts may be subject to two different sorts of rules, *regulative* and *constitutive*. This distinction is not watertight, but it does afford us some analytic mileage. Regulative rules regulate (perhaps 'orientate' is a better word) a pre-existing activity, an activity whose existence is logically independent of the rules, as for instance when dinner-table manners regulate the eating of food. Constitutive rules constitute (and also regulate) an 'activity the existence of which is logically dependent on the rules' (pp. 34–5), as in the case of the rules of football or chess.

To Austin's classical examples of constitutive acts such as greeting, baptizing, naming a ship, and marriage vows—all of which are created and understood within the bounds of the conventions themselves—to these we can add several anthropological examples: the installation of a Tallensi chief, Ndembu circumcision rites, Lodagaa mortuary rites, a Japanese tea ceremony, a Catholic mass, and a multitude of cosmic rites and festivals which are self-constituting events and of which we have several classic descriptions.

Now, to these classic constitutive ritual acts, whose very performance achieves the realization of the *performative* effect, can be attached two kinds of *perlocutionary* (functional) consequences. There are certain constitutive rites in which certain *perlocutionary* effects are presupposed by the illocutionary force of the acts and actually take place: when a Tallensi chief is properly installed certain results must imperatively follow upon his exercise of the powers of office. The valid performance of Lodagaa mortuary rites must imperatively lead to the distribution of the rights and duties and property of the dead

man to his declared heirs (Goody 1962). But there are also constitutive acts which, although they realize their performative dimension, may yet be uncertain of realizing their expected perlocutionary effects. A classic example is curing rituals in cases of spirit possession, which, though performatively valid, may or may not induce a cure in the patient, traffic with the super natural being notoriously uncertain.

The way to account for people's continuation with so-called 'magical' rites that empirically may produce false results is a classic anthropological chestnut that has exercised, to give a few examples, the minds of Tylor, Frazer, Evans-Pritchard, and, more recently, Horton. Against this main-line tradition, I have earlier submitted that it might be misplaced to judge such rites solely against the perspective and truth canons of Western scientific rationality, for as constitutive and persuasive acts they cannot be 'falsified', though individual instances of them may be declared normatively infelicitous or illegitimate (Tambiah 1973). If anthropologists insist on seeing magical rites as acts launched by the actors to achieve practical results by suspending the laws of motion and force as we understand these laws in modern physics, then obviously such acts must be declared false. But in so far as anthropologists are open to the proposition that magical rites are conventional acts which should also be examined within a performative frame of social action, then a new horizon opens before us for viewing the logic of such purposive acts and the canons for their validity from the actors' point of view.

But let me add that this performative view also faces fuzzy instances which it has to situate within its framework. Where curing rites are intertwined with the use of herbal and other medicines and practical health care (as in many traditional societies), it may make sense to view the ritual component as having a strong 'regulative' character. In such cases, an improvement in medical techniques may render the older rites *obsolete* rather than proving them false or wrong. An example is the virtual disappearance of the rites addressed to the smallpox goddess in Sri Lanka in the face of dramatically successful Western medicine in eradicating smallpox. Another frequently observed fact can also be cited in this context. Curing rites, divinations, rain-making rites—

all promising an empirical result but not falsifiable on that account—are prone to proliferate, compete with rivals, and come into and go out of fashion quickly depending on their alleged results. But note that rival cults do not seek so much to 'disprove' as to outbid one another, and usually a great number of redundant cults coexist and are simultaneously resorted to by clients.

Certain special considerations apply to that second class of performative ritual acts which we have called *regulative*, in the sense that they orientate and regulate a practical or technical activity, and address themselves to the aesthetic style of that activity, or act as its diacritical features, without actually constituting it. The procedures for rice cultivation among the Kachin, which may entail ploughing in certain directions or allocate different roles to men and women, regulate or orient cultivation without constituting it. Again the Trobriand canoe-making ritual or agricultural rites, interwoven closely with practical technical acts of boat-building or gardening, do many things such as organizing labour, encoding aesthetic values and mythical associations, timing the work phases, and providing an anticipatory statement about the success to be achieved in Kula or yam harvests to be distributed as *urigubu*— yet these rites supplement and regulate the technical activity which is a separate strand in the coil.[17]

Thus regulative rituals have two characteristics. By themselves they can be seen to have a 'constitutive' element; but they are in fact interwoven with practical activity, and therefore the constitutive element does not exhaust the whole amalgam which is canoe-building or gardening in Trobriand terms. Secondly, the expected perlocutionary effect of the rites may happen uncertainly but this does not once again undermine their performative validity.[18]

THE APPLICATION OF INFORMATION THEORY TO RITUAL

We have so far explored some of the conditions that contribute to the formalization, conventionalization, and distancing of ritual as a medium of communication. One set of features that frequently accompanies the foregoing in most complex rituals is various kinds of abbreviations and elisions which are referred to in the literature as *condensation* and *fusion*. A second set consists of repetitive and recursive sequences which tend to be labelled as *redundancy*, a labelling that derives its reason by association with information theory. In actual fact condensation and redundancy are linked, dialectically related processes, that, as we shall see in due course, produce intensification of meaning as well as the decline of meaning.

Information theory has been promiscuously invoked by analysts of ritual, an invocation that is further compounded by different 'readings' of the theory that are then applied to the interpretation of ritual. It is necessary therefore to make a few preliminary clarifications even at the risk of sounding pedantic.

Information theory (Cherry 1961, Miller 1951) relates strictly to communication engineering, which is concerned with the technical problem of making the most economical use of the capacity of a transmission channel (or to put it in another way, of transmitting the maximum number of messages through the channel in the shortest possible time). In this technical science, the notion of 'information' has a precise statistical meaning. The amount of information carried by a unit in a code is a function of the probability of its occurrence; in fact, information content is inversely proportionate (and logarithmically related) to probability.[19]

The next set of concepts that are central in information theory are 'noise' and 'redundancy'. 'Noise' refers to any interference in a channel that affects the correct reception of signals. The use of 'superfluous' symbols to make sure that the message will be received correctly is known as redundancy. Redundancy is considered a necessary vice in information theory; some degree of it is thought to be desirable because of the interference upon the medium or channel of unpredictable physical or other disturbances, which would lead to a distortion or obliteration and loss of information.[20] 'Redundancy, like the unemployed worker, is unproductive, but only when the message is to be sent through a perfect noise-free channel to a perfect receiver' (Corcoran 1971, p. 33).

Messages can be repeated in many ways—they may be transmitted over several channels simultaneously, permitting the recipient to compare the several received messages and arrive at the correct message. More often it is necessary to use a single channel several times in a row, in which case either the entire message may be relayed and then repeated, or one section of the message may be repeated before proceeding to the next section.[21]

Now at first sight the fact that ritual has various features of redundancy and high probability of occurrence invites an application to it of information theory. But there are good reasons against a literal and limited application of that theory to ritual as communication.

The passage of new information as such from one person to another is only one aspect of social communication, and in ritual, which we have seen to be formalized and predictable, this aspect may be subordinate and of little relevance. But we should not commit the error that because most rituals are not concerned with transmitting new information they therefore lack any referential, propositional, and analogical meanings at all.[22] A further limitation is equating information as such (in the technical sense) with the concept of 'meaning'.[23] Indeed, the various ways meaning is conceived in our field are a deadly source of confusion.

Social communication, of which ritual is a special kind, portrays many features that have little to do with the transmission of new information and everything to do with interpersonal orchestration and with social integration and continuity. The orchestrational and integrational aspect of the communicative process (Birdwhistell 1970, pp. 86–7) includes many operations: the 'phatic' feature which keeps the communication system in operation, the certainty of message that eases an interpersonal anxiety or affective lesion, the battery of linguistic and other cues which act as triggering mechanisms and context markers, the regulative etiquette that orders what is considered as proper communication between persons in equal or asymmetrical statuses—these are a related set. Another set relates to features that cross-reference and link particular messages to enable their comprehensibility and reception as larger totalities, and features that relate the particular context of communication to the larger cultural context(s) of which it is a part. Here one can also appropriately invoke and apply to ritual Jakobson's

enumeration of functions of verbal communication—referential, poetic, phatic, emotive, conative, and metalingual, all of which in varying proportions are served by verbal communication. The coding of emotive elements in ritual speech through prosodic features of intonation and stress, emphatic vocal prolongations, etc., and the supplementary use of paralinguistic features such as kinetic movements and gestures, whether conventionally required or unconsciously manifested, are familiar indices that reveal the emotional attitudes of the officiants and participants. In Thailand one has only to compare the still, emotionless, detached postures of the Buddhist monk and the convulsive, overwhelmed movements of a spirit-possessed medium to realize instantly the different involvements being communicated. But rituals may also convey the metalanguage function of definitional, glossing learning, as for instance manifest in certain initiation and mystery cults whose initiates are 'taught' mysteries, identifies, and given new knowledge from which they were previously excluded.[24] Examples of such teaching of the cultural code in graduated terms are the Baktaman (Barth 1975), who progressively introduce initiates into the secret mysteries, and the Bemba, who in their Chisungu rite use mnemonic devices and songs for teaching young girls (Richards 1956).

Be these things as they may, I wish to elucidate and underscore one understanding of *meaning*, defined not in terms of 'information' but in terms of *pattern recognition* and *configurational awareness*. A hallmark of the arts and crafts—poetry, painting, dancing, music, pottery design and so on—is the reduction of the random by restraint (as Bateson put it),[25] indeed the creation of recognizable patterns and unanticipated tensions and outcomes, by means of redundancy and recursive loops. And of course a prime aesthetic censor which prevents the deterioration of art forms into degenerate banality is *controlled modulation*. One recognizes, in this characterization of meaning in terms of pattern recognition, a positive characterization of the role of redundancy in art forms. The antithetical image of this positive projection of meaning as pattern is the communication engineer's postulation of unpredictability and low probability of occurrence of an item as constituting its high information content.

We must now introduce a certain amount of rigour into the discussion of what we mean by 'redundancy' in ritual. Those of us who have done detailed studies of complex rites and ritual cycles are keenly aware of various kinds and patterns of repetitions that occur, sometimes boring us with their seemingly insistently unvarying recurrence, and sometimes subtly stimulating in us a sense of creative variation and attentive expectation. In this presentation I can only barely suggest the dimensions of our problem, locate some of the meaningful patterns, and urge the need for a closer analysis of them before indulging in gross generalities. There are, just to enumerate at random, repetitions of the same sequence, both within a long rite and between a series of related rites. But there are many rites in which redundancy, rather than being mere tedious repetitions of the same thing, can be demonstrated to be interesting and complex in the work it does.

A standard example is 'parallelism', the pairing of couplets, which Robert Lowth identified and made famous in the second half of the eighteenth century as being characteristic of Hebrew poetry, and which more recently Jakobson (1966) has brought to our notice in his analysis of Finnic and Russian oral traditions.

Parallelism in its more general sense refers to the poetic artifice of 'recurrent returns' at the semantic, syntactic, and phonemic levels of expression, and in its specific canonical sense refers to a compositional device wherein 'certain similarities between successive verbal sequences are compulsory or enjoy a high preference' (Jakobson 1966, p. 399). Parallelism expresses mainly a relation of symmetry, the two halves of the pair being slightly distinguished from each other by syntactic or semantic variations or slight differences in function or by other substitute devices.

In a . . . survey Fox (1977) enumerates the occurrence of canonical parallelism in its various forms and patterns, and reports its widespread occurrence in both literate and oral cultures distributed in time and space: in as diverse instances as Hebrew, Vedic, Chinese, Dravidian, and Mayan poetry, in the ritual language occurring in Vietnam, Mongolia, and Hawaii, and among the Todas, the Walbiri of Australia, the Navaho, the Kachin, the Thai, the Buang of Papua New Guinea, the Merina of Madagascar,

the Rotinese of the outer Indonesian Islands, and the Chamulas of the Chiapas Highlands of Mexico.

What is of particular interest to us is that parallelism is a pervasive device and idiom of formal speaking, chanting, singing, and of greetings, farewells, petitions, and courtship overtures. Especially throughout the world's oral traditions it is a 'speech form or language stratum reserved for special situations: for the preservation of past wisdom, for the utterance of sacred words, for determining ritual relations, for healing, and for communication with spirits . . .' (Fox 1975, pp. 127–8).

The question why such a language form should be considered appropriate for formal occasions, especially as a component of ritual language, could be approached from many angles.

Let me briefly allude here to the creative role of the 'formula', a term applied by Lord (1958), and Parry before him, to 'repeated word groups' that express an essential idea, in generating and producing an actual recitation as performance. The Slavonic singer of epic poetry has in his possession 'basic patterns of meter, word boundary, melody', and he is adept at using these compositional devices: 'the linking of phrases by parallelism, [the] balancing and opposition of word order', and the substitution of key words (Lord calls this paradigmatic operation a 'substitution system'). Lord has eloquently stated that 'for the oral poet the moment of composition is the performance'. He has demonstrated how the oral poet, whose basic capital is a stock of memorized formulas, varies and ornaments his songs, lengthens or shortens them, according to the demands and character of the audience and other situational circumstances, and how in fact he preserves the tradition by the constant recreation of it. Indeed, such a dynamic performative approach should save us from an overly simplistic view that, because oral specialists say and believe their sacred words are fixed and invariant, their actual renditions are reproductions of an invariant text. It surely cannot be the case that, while guided as well as constrained by sequencing rules and other prescriptions regarding language expression, the political orator—including the Merina and Balinese instances (Bloch 1975)—produces set congealed speeches.

In ritual too not only would the outputs of different specialists allegedly performing the same rite be different in certain respects but also the outputs of the same specialist—especially if he is not confined to the recitation of a written sacred text—would be variable at separate performances of the same rite. Indeed, complex rites, and long recitations, usually have some sequences more open than others, more open in terms of structure and more open to new contents. (Even in the Trobriand case Malinowski remarked that in the main body [*tapwana*] of the spell—which in content was constructed by combining and varying action words with metaphors and metonyms—there was more freedom as regards the order in which words were uttered, whereas words were not liable to 'even the smallest alteration' in the first part [*u'ula*] of the spell which was usually a recitation of ancestral names that established the magician's charter.) Thus, in summary, let us suppose that whatever the permissible features of creativity and variability in the 'production' of rites as performances, such features (*a*) function on a base or core of stereotyped or conventionalized formulas and 'substitution systems' and/or (*b*) are to some degree accountable for in terms of contextual demands and indexical factors.

Whatever the importance of these compositional considerations, we have yet to tackle here why *ritual language* resorts to, and how it exploits, redundant and patterned devices, of which parallelism is an example. An ethnographic illustration opens a window on to our problem by telling us why a certain people views a particular linguistic construction as an effective communication device with the divine. The Chamulas of highland Mexico consider formal ritual speech as 'heated' discourse (in comparison with the cool discourse of ordinary times). Heated discourse is an intensified medium which serves to establish contact with the higher holy entities which are themselves symbols of cyclical heat, a principle of great importance in Chamula thought. This ritual speech, rendered with voice modulations from higher to lower pitch with great regularity, is constructed in pairs, and multiples of pairs, which enter into numerous combinations in 'song', 'prayer', 'language for rendering holy', and sometimes in 'true ancient narrative', as these genres are distinguished by native speakers.

From the point of view of text or discourse con-struction, the 'stacking' (as Gossen calls it) of the parallel couplets one after the other enables the performers to extend texts, give them embellishments (within stylistic bounds), explore nuances of multivocal meanings; and from the point of view of performative efficacy the structure of the entire recursive recitation may be seen as an iconic analogue of the cycles of creations of the cosmic order in their temporal and spatial regularity and cumulative effect.

Let us next briefly recall the structural pattern of the Trobriand spells in order at least to confront, if not solve, the basis for the Trobriand view that their magical spells were 'verbal missiles' launched by man as 'magical power towards the entities or forces which they were meant to affect' (Malinowski 1935, vol. 2, pp. 248–9). At least part of the answer to the 'creative metaphor of magic' and its persuasive potency lay in the verbal construction of the spell, the mode of its recitation, and the physical manipulations which accompanied it. As Malinowski put it: in the main part of the spell (*tapwana*) 'several key words are repeated with inventory expressions' in such a way as to produce the effect of 'rubbing' the verbs of action into a succession of dazzling metaphors drawn from diverse sensory domains, or into the enumerated parts of the object—whether it be a tuber or a yam house—assembled as a whole through step by step metonymical recitation. The contours of this magical operation have been already described (Tambiah 1968; Nancy Munn, n.d.), but here I want to suggest the mechanisms by which this kind of redundant rhetoric 'generates' the magical missile. The formulaic pattern of the Trobriand spells insistently introduces a variety of metaphorical expressions or metonymical parts into a stereotyped stream of repeated words intoned with modulations of speed, loudness, and rhythm, thereby foregrounding them as well as telescoping or fusing them into an amalgam that is given motion and direction by compelling illocutionary words of command and persuasion or declaration. Malinowski's characterization of this process as a 'rubbing' effect is felicitous, for indeed in Trobriand magic the verbal creation of force is made more realistic and operational by using substances (which themselves have metaphorical associations named in the spell) metonymically, so that a transfer of effect is made through blowing, rubbing, smoking, and various tactile manipulations. The cross-linkages in this art are manifold, and combine to produce an arrow-like thrust.

The Trobriand formulaic structure and ritual operations are by no means idiosyncratic. The spell symbolism and structure of the Melpa-speaking people of Mount Hagen in New Guinea are remarkably similar as described by the Stratherns (1968). . . . Michelle Rosaldo (1975), with the Trobriand precedent in mind, suggested that the effectiveness of the magical spells of the Ilongot of Northern Luzon, Philippines (who are hunters, headhunters, and swidden agriculturists) 'depends on the fact that they invoke images from a number of diverse areas of experience and that these images, in turn, are regrouped and organized in terms of a small set of culturally significant and contextually desirable themes', and that this 'new organization', the creative product of the spell, itself depends on 'the repetitive and formulaic quality of magic' (p. 178).

One upshot of these analyses is that the ordering and the pattern of presentation of the ritual language, physical gestures, and manipulation of substances is the *form* of the ritual, that form is the arrangement of contents. Therefore I think Rappaport (1974) is mistaken—in the same way that McLuhan is mistaken—in thinking that the 'surfaces of ritual' whose features are stereotypy, liturgical invariance, and so on can be dealt with apart from the symbolism of ritual or, as he puts it, 'the relations among the symbols that may appear in rituals'. If then the neo-Tylorians err in accenting beliefs to the detriment of the ritual action, there is one extreme semiotic school that supposes that form can be tackled apart from the presentation of contents and the interpretation of symbolism.

Let us now review another order of redundancy which consists of recurrences which are not simply mechanical in their appearance but occur in *recursive* fashion to start new sequences or combine unit acts into different 'syntactic' sequences within the same rite.

There are in all complex rites discernible 'sequencing rules' and 'co-occurrence restrictions'. Socio-linguists in the United States have instructed us that almost all kinds of speech events constitute forms of discourse with their own sequencing rules: telephone conversations have their predictable sequencing, as revealed by Schegloff (1972);[26] therapeutic discourses have their coherent sequencing, as revealed by Labov and Fanshel (1977).[27] Since ritual discourse is in fact a more conventionalized event, we should not be surprised to find that it has even more conspicuous sequencing rules. And moreover, because the rituals we are focusing on are considered public, serious, and festive by the actors, we should expect various 'co-occurrence restrictions' and 'bound relations' in the proceedings, precisely because on the one hand the communication reflects and realizes cosmological and liturgical concepts and principles, and on the other hand that same communication is between persons in 'status marked situations' of authority and subordination, of competence and eligibility, of 'power and solidarity' (to repeat the famous phrase of Brown and Gilman [1960]), persons variously called priest, officiant, patient, communicant, addressor, and congregation. In other words, if ritual events are performative acts (in a much stronger sense than ordinary speech acts which also do something with words), then the connections between the unit acts and utterances of the ritual, the logic of the rules of obligatory sequences of the ritual acts *per se*, cannot be fully understood without realizing that they are the clothing for social actions; and these social actions cannot in turn be understood except in relation to the cosmological presuppositions and the social interactional norms of the actors. Once again, the form and content of ritual are necessarily fused, and our problem is to devise a conceptual system that sees the message 'as both itself internally patterned and itself a part of a larger patterned universe—the culture or some part of it' (Gregory Bateson 1972, p. 132).

There are two more general points to be made regarding the study of redundancy and patterning. The notions of sequencing rules and co-occurrence restrictions have to do with horizontal relations, the linear syntagmatic connections between actions and utterances as they unfold from beginning to end. The classical framework in the anthropological study of rites in this mode is of course the tripartite scheme of van Gennep—segregation, liminal period, and reaggregation—and Mauss's earlier scheme for sacrifice—entry, act, and exit. This scheme, if employed mechanically, can mask certain perceptions. For example, there are certain rituals of curing which are patterned into two halves, the second half being a repeated but stronger and more potent version of the first half. Or again there are both cosmic festivals and rites of affliction which have internal recursive loops, and shifts in the media emphasized, and a combined pattern of progressions and reiterations, whose subtleties are not revealed by a prior commitment to the tripartite straitjacket as the point of departure. A generative syntactic approach, or a pointillist dissection, or a configurational approach devoted to seeing how the whole is built up from, but is also greater than, the parts—all these perspectives will concentrate on how lower-level units build up into or fuse into higher-level units and processes, how different media are made to converge, and how total experiences are produced.

In other words, the horizontal relations and connections dynamically act upon one another to constitute the *vertical* dimension by which higher-level integration is achieved by 'the interplay of variation' (Terence Turner, n.d.), by the dialectic of paradigmatic 'oppositions' and syntagmatic 'contrasts' (Jakobson), and by the condensation of messages sent through 'the switching of metaphoric and metonymic modes' to produce a 'single experience' and a single 'message' (Leach 1966, 1976). Thus the second sense in which I see ritual as performative is as a dramatic actualization whose distinctive structure including its stereotypy and redundancy has something to do with the production of a sense of heightened and intensified and fused communication. The objectives of such intensification have been variously phrased: as the submission of persons to a compelling 'constraint' (as Radcliffe-Brown put it), or as their transportation into a supra-normal, transcendental 'antistructural', 'numinous', or 'altered' state of consciousness, or as a euphoric communion with one's fellow beings, or a subordination to a collective representation. If such is the case,

then we anthropologists have to delve deeper than we have done so far into the manner of interplay of the horizontal and vertical dimensions of the ritual, and the manner in which media such as chants, songs, dance, music, verbal formulae, material gifts are employed in the service of heightening communication. These media may, according to cultural definitions, be considered to be 'heated', 'compelling', 'forceful', and 'pleasing' to demons and deities; and at the same time they may be considered to make certain kinds of impacts on the officiants and participants as both senders and receivers of the message.

The media may, especially in their repetitive and/or punctuational use, serve to initiate and leave sacred time or to enter and leave supra-normal states. The employment of certain musical instruments for this purpose has been aptly noted by Needham (1967). Another classical example is the verbal formulae of Buddhist meditational exercise by which their mindful repetition is held to enable the achieving of the detached mental state of 'one pointedness of mind' (Maha Boowa 1976), or the *mantras* of Hinduism which 'are now mainly regarded as aids or means to meditation and concentration', or as 'instruments of therapy intended to bring about a change in mental state' (Staal 1975, pp. 27–8).[28] Whether literally meaningful or not,—some are and some are not—the prime value of these repeated sayings is their therapeutic value as 'focusing' mechanisms. But their efficacy is of an intriguing sort. I have previously referred to ritual's formalism as enabling the 'distancing' of actors, and participation in it as engaging not raw emotions but 'articulated' feelings and gestures. In a similar vein it makes sense to suggest that the repeated verbal formulae as 'supports of contemplation' or transporters into a trance state do so, not by a direct assault on the actor's senses and inflicting an immense psychic toll on him or her, but by a more indirect conventional illocutionary employment of them as instruments of passage and as triggering mechanisms.[29]

NOTES

1. Play, especially in its manifestation as contemporary competitive sports.

2. To give another example that fits the Lévi-Strauss scheme: the outcome of the *An Keliya* ritual performed as a contest in Sri Lanka is open in that either team may win, but the preferred and usual winner is the team representing the Pattini goddess. The final contest in a series is always won by her, and the ritual concludes as a conjunction between the two teams (see Nur Yalman, 1966).

3. McLuhan (1964), who has some relevance for our topic, has argued that the 'message' of any medium or technology is 'the change of scale or pace or pattern that it introduces into human affairs', and that it is mistaken to think that a medium's message lies in its contents. Rather the message is to be found in the character of the medium itself. This view errs on the side of formalism.

4. Thus, while I agree with Moore and Myerhoff (1977) that the term 'sacred' need not be conterminous with 'religious', I don't share with them the desire to carve out a category of 'secular ritual' when the analytic objective is to inquire into the features of ritual as a medium of communication.

5. These categories are of course not 'equivalent' or the same in different cosmologies. They are stated here for illustrative purposes.

6. To give concrete ethnographic examples. The rituals of the Walbiri of Australia (Munn 1973) cannot be understood outside of their cosmological ideas of how dream time and phenomenal time are related. Similarly, the Thai rites, whether Buddhist or pertaining to the spirits, derive their fullest meaning only when placed in relation to the cosmological scheme of three *lokas*, of a hierarchy of heavens, hells, and human habitat, and of the bodily, material, mental, and sensory values attached to the Buddha, to gods, to humans, and to demonic spirits (Tambiah 1970, 1977). A person alien to Christianity cannot feel moved or spiritually strengthened by the spectacle of wine and bread being transformed into the blood and flesh of Christ in the Roman Catholic mass. The special reverence in which Americans hold their constitution cannot be understood without a feel for their special historic experience which includes their War of Independence and the Civil War.

7. Leach's pioneering essay (1966) and Wallace (1966) (and of course Malinowski before them) should be considered our immediate predecessors who highlighted various implications of ritual's stereotyped form.

8. Let me make clear, so as to remove misunderstanding, that the 'conventional-intentional', and the 'ordinary' behaviour–'conventional' behaviour distinctions are *relative* ones. All social conduct is coloured by convention and subject to cultural understanding and codification. My distinction is between *degrees* of formalization and stereotyping in what I label conventional and ordinary behaviour, as modes of conduct that stand in a contrast of relative distinction.

9. And once again such elaborations into stereotyped forms may in certain extreme circumstances—as we shall see—reduce the ritual of social interaction to mere *phatic* communication, or to a mere buttressing of status differentials, allowing ritual to take on only pragmatic or indexical functions and to lose its referential and semantic meanings. . . .

10. Of the peace-making ceremony he wrote: the rite compels participants 'to act as though they felt certain emotions, and therefore does, to some extent, produce these emotions in them' (p. 241).

11. Skorupski (1976, ch. 6) is making the same point when he says that as 'interaction code behaviour' gets increasingly elaborated into 'convention-dependent communication', socially shared and socially on record, 'the allusion made to the original base of appropriate feeling may be increasingly indirect, increasingly mediated by a more direct allusion' (pp. 90–1). Thus as norms become ceremonialized 'what occupies the foreground is neither the feeling nor the expression of feeling, but the propriety of the expression of feeling' (p. 91).

12. Geertz in a well-known essay (1966) on religion as a cultural system also makes this Langerian point.

13. A good example is the *alus* (refined) etiquette as opposed to *kasar* (vulgar) manners as recognized in Javanese culture and explicitly coded in their popular theatre (*ludruk*). See, for example, Peacock's *Rites of Modernization* (1968) and Geertz's *The Religion of Java* (1960).

14. My reference here is to H. P. Grice, 'Meaning' in *Philosophical Review*, 1957 (and subsequent modifications by Searle, Strawson, and others). According to this formulation, communication is essentially the expression of an attitude, such as a belief (in the case of statements) or a desire (in the case of requests). To express an attitude one intends the recipient to regard what one is doing (e.g. saying something) as reason to believe one has that attitude. Communication succeeds only if the recipient recognizes this intention, and genuine communication can take place only between beings who not only have intentions and beliefs, but can have and recognize intentions of this complex sort. And this is possible only if each communicant is not only aware of the other's intentions but also aware that the other is aware of his own intentions, and so on.

15. If we still want to use the concept of 'intentionality' we can say that a large part of the intentions of the actors as regards the purpose and results of the ritual are already *culturally defined, presupposed, and conventionalized*. Of course, there may be other personal intentions and purposes shared by the participants which may additionally motivate them to engage in a ritual, but these motivations do not affect the validity and performative efficacy of the rite *per se*. For example, the intention to get married implies the cultural requirement, say, of undergoing the marriage rite. The fact that the bride and groom want to get married in order to attain respectability is immaterial to the rite's validity and efficacy.

16. Searle's revisions of Austin are noteworthy: he rejects Austin's distinction between locutionary and illocutionary acts (preferring to embed the propositional features within the illocutionary acts), but accepts the Austinian notion of perlocutionary effects or consequences as being separate from the conventional efficacy of the illocutionary or performative act *per se*.

17. It is interesting that Malinowski asserted that Trobrianders distinguished between 'the road of magic' (*megwa la keda*) and 'the road of garden work' (*bagula la keda*), while also maintaining that gardening rituals and cultivation made up one totality.

18. Of course drastic changes in technology introduced in traditional societies by modernization and development programmes may or may not affect the practice of the regulative rites. The evidence is uncertain and goes both ways; so is the evidence on adaptive changes in ritual. See Milton Singer (1972) for rituals addressed to modern machinery by Indian factory workers; they are transposed from a previous traditional milieu of crafts and handicrafts.

19. In more simple terms, this implies many things for the communication engineer. The more alternative units or signs there are in a code that may occur in a message, the less likely is each unit to occur, and therefore the more information it will carry when it occurs; conversely the fewer the alternative units that can occur in a message, the more probable is the occurrence of each unit, and the lower, therefore, is each unit's information content. In a message, the items that appear more frequently carry less information than those items that appear less frequently, and can also be more easily guessed at by the receiver if some of them are missed out or distorted. For these reasons, those items which occur frequently in a message can be transmitted in a shorter time by economical use of symbols or digits of a code.

20. Also, if the communication system is made entirely free of redundancy, the information lost could prove to be irrecoverable.

21. The latter procedure is usually preferred because by the time the entire message is relayed and then repeated, there is the risk of the recipient losing sight of the first message, and because it is easier for the recipient to catch mistakes caused by unexpected interruptions if sections of a message are repeated in turn.

22. Bloch (1974) commits this mistake of conflating stereotypy in ritual with lack of propositional force. See my analyses of Trobriand and Azande magic (1968, 1973) for examples of referential and analogical devices by which the performative transfer is made. An illuminating and useful . . . work on the various dimensions of metaphorical usage is Sapir and Crocker (1977). . . .

23. In this connection it is relevant to refer to an interpretation that is attributed to John Lyons (1963). Starting with the proposition, closely related to information theory, that 'meaning implies choice', Lyons asserted that any linguistic item whose occurrence in a given context is completely determined *has no meaning* in that context. Lyons proceeded to say 'that having meaning, as the notion is here defined, is a matter of *how much* meaning items have in context . . . not what meaning they have'. In so far as Lyons is equating 'meaning' with 'information' in the technical sense, we have to realize that it is a narrow or limited conception of meaning. Secondly, in so far as there are modes of meaning and functional uses of speech acts other than purely informational defined in terms of probability of occurrence, Lyons's

'how much' criterion becomes irrelevant as a criterion for judging the meaning of those modes and uses. As a matter of fact, Lyons in this work advances two notions of meaning—one in terms of information theory (probability of occurrence in context), and the other in the structuralist sense of paradigmatic relations between units (Saussure's *value*). In this latter sense—which is Lyons's more important conception—he discusses synonymy, antonymy, hyponymy, incompatibility, etc. It is clear that redundancy subject to the second kind of analysis will deliver meaning in terms of 'patterns' of various kinds, which is outside the view of meaning treated in the informational sense.

24. We should note here that what is stereotyped, predictable knowledge for the already initiated is *new information* for the initiates, for allegedly they hear it for the first time. In this context ritual speech is informational for the initiates.

25. Restraint in cybernetic terms, says Bateson, consists of 'factors which determine inequality of probability'. Elsewhere he writes: 'The essence and *raison d' être* of communication is the creation of redundancy, meaning, pattern, predictability, information, and/or the reduction of the random by restraint' (1972, pp. 131–2). As Aram Yengoyan has commented (personal communication), Bateson does not explore the different implications of externally imposed restraints, and internal restraints in which the cosmological axioms set a range in which meaning can operate.

26. Also see H. Sacks, E. Schegloff, and G. Jefferson, 'A simplest systematics for the organization of turn-taking for conversation' in *Language* 50 (4) (1974), 696–735.

27. The authors state at one point: 'The framework that we have provided so far indicates that conversations to be studied will form a complex matrix of utterances, propositions and actions. The matrix shows two kinds of relations: the vertical relations between surface utterances and deeper actions, which are united by rules of interpretation and production; the horizontal relations of sequencing between actions and utterances, which are united by sequencing rules.' See William Labov and David Fanshel, *Therapeutic Discourse* (1977), p. 37.

28. The 'great sentences' (makāvākya) of the Upaniṣads ('you are that' [brahman]) or the *koāns* of Zen Buddhism ('What is the sound of one hand clapping?') are held to be meaningful and capable of much interpretative commentary. On the other hand, many of the Tantric *mantras* are literally meaningless (though of course always open to symbolic interpretations)—and their main function is as aids in meditation (Staal 1975). On Zen formulae see Suzuki (1970).

29. In all the examples of mediumship and spirit possession I have seen, the entry into the trance or possession state is a 'conventional' act of passage marked by enacting a culturally defined ritual sequence; but of course once a supra-normal or dissociative state is reached the medium or the patient can manifest convulsive behaviour and talk in tongues. This behaviour, which is the opposite of 'normal' behaviour, is also inflected by cultural expectations of how the invasion of the other world manifests itself in the human vessel.

REFERENCES

Austin, John (1962). *How to Do Things with Words*, Oxford University Press.

Barth, Frederik (1975). *Ritual and Knowledge among the Baktaman of New Guinea*, Yale University Press, New Haven.

Bateson, Gregory (1972). *Steps to an Ecology of Mind*, Intertext Books, London.

Birdwhistell, Ray L. (1970). *Kinesics and Context; Essays on Body Motion and Communication*, Univ. of Pennsylvania Press.

Bloch, Maurice (1974). 'Symbols, Song, Dance and Features of Articulation' in *European Journal of Sociology* 15.

——— (ed.) (1975). *Political Language and Oratory in Traditional Society*, Academic Press.

Brown, Roger, and Gilman, Albert (1960). 'The Pronouns of Power and Solidarity' in *Style in Language*, ed. Thomas A. Sebeok, MIT Press, Cambridge, Mass., pp. 253–76.

Cherry, Colin (1961). *On Human Communication*, Science Editions, Inc., New York.

Corcoran, D. W. J. (1971). *Pattern Recognition*, Penguin Books.

Eliade, M. (1959). *Cosmos and History: The Myth of the Eternal Return*, Harper & Row, New York.

Ervin-Tripp, Susan (1972). 'On Sociolinguistic Rules: Alternation and Co-occurrence' in *Directions in Sociolinguistics, The Ethnography of Communication*, ed. John J. Gumperz and Dell Hymes, Holt, Rinehart & Winston, Inc.

Fox, James J. (1975). 'On Binary Categories and Primary Symbols' in Roy Willis (ed.), *The Interpretation of Symbolism*, John Wiley & Sons, New York.

——— (1977). 'Roman Jakobson and the Comparative Study of Parallelism' in *Roman Jakobson: Echoes of his Scholarship*, Lisse: The Peter de Redder Press.

Geertz, Clifford (1960). *The Religion of Java*, The Free Press of Glencoe.

——— (1966). 'Religion as a Cultural System' in *Anthropological Approaches to the Study of Religion*. ASA Monographs 3, ed. Michael Banton, Tavistock Publications.

Goody, Jack (1962). *Death, Property and the Ancestors, A Study of the Mortuary Customs of the Lodagaa of West Africa*, Tavistock Publications.

Gossen, Gary H. (1974). 'To Speak with a Heated Heart: Chamula Canons of Style and Good Performance' in *Explorations in the Ethnography of Speaking*, ed. R. Bauman and J. Sherzer, London and New York, Cambridge University Press, pp. 389–416.

——— (1978). 'Language as Ritual Substance' in *Language in Religious Practice*, ed. William J. Samarin, Newbury House Publishers, Inc.

Grice, H. P. (1957). 'Meaning' in *Philosophical Review*.

Jakobson, Roman (1966). 'Grammatical Parallelism and its Russian Facet' in *Language* 42, pp. 398–429.

Labov, William, and Fanshel, David (1977). *Therapeutic Discourse*, Academic Press.

Langer, Susanne K. (1951). *Philosophy in a New Key*, New York: New American Library.

Leach, Edmund (1966). 'Ritualization in Man' in *Philosophical Transactions of the Royal Society of London*, Series B, vol. 251, no. 722, pp. 403–8.

——— (1976). *Culture and Communication*, Cambridge University Press.

Lévi-Strauss, Claude (1966). *The Savage Mind*, Weidenfeld & Nicolson, London.

Lord, Albert (1958). *The Singer of Tales*, Harvard University Press.

Lyons, John (1963). *Structural Semantics*, Publication of the Philosophical Society XX.

Maha Boowa, Phra Acharn (1976). *The Venerable Phra Acharn Mun Bhuridatta Thera, Meditation Master*, translated by Siri Buddhasukh, Mahamakut Press, Bangkok.

Malinowski, Bronislaw (1935). *Coral Gardens and Their Magic*, vol. 2, London.

McLuhan, Marshall (1964). *Understanding Media: The Extensions of Man*, McGraw-Hill.

Miller, George A. (1951). *Language and Communication*, McGraw-Hill.

Moore, Sally Falk, and Myerhoff, Barbara G. (eds.) (1977). *Secular Ritual*, Van Gorcum, Assen, The Netherlands.

Munn, Nancy I. (1973). *Walbiri Iconography*, Cornell University Press.

——— (n.d.). 'The Symbolism of Perceptual Qualities: A Study of Trobriand Ritual Aesthetics'.

Needham, Rodney (1967). 'Percussion and Transition' in *Man* (NS), vol. 2, no. 4, pp. 606–14.

Peacock, James L. (1968). *Rites of Modernization*, University of Chicago Press.

Radcliffe-Brown, A. R. (1964). *The Andaman Islanders*, Free Press Paperback Edition (first published in 1922).

Rappaport, Roy A. (1971). 'Ritual Sanctity and Cybernetics', *American Anthropologist* 73 (1), pp. 59–76.

——— (1974). 'Obvious Aspects of Ritual', *Cambridge Anthropology* vol. 2, no. 1.

Richards, A. I. (1956). *Chisungu*, London.

Rosaldo, Michelle Zimbalist (1975). 'It's All Uphill: The Creative Metaphors of Ilongot Magical Spells' in *Sociocultural Dimensions of Language Use*, ed. Mary Sanches and B. G. Blount, Academic Press.

Sacks, H., Schegloff, E., and Jefferson, G. (1974). 'A Simplest Systematics for the Organization of Turn-Taking for Conversation' in *Language*, vol. 50, no. 4, pp. 696–735.

Sapir, J. David, and Crocker, J. C. (1977). *The Social Use of Metaphor, Essays in the Anthropology of Rhetoric*, University of Pennsylvania Press, Philadelphia.

Schegloff, Emanuel A. (1972). 'Sequencing in Conversational Openings' in *Directions in Sociolinguistics, the Ethnography of Communication*, eds. John J. Gumperz and Dell Hymes: Holt, Rinehart & Winston, Inc.

Searle, John R. (1969). *Speech Acts, An Essay in the Philosophy of Language*, Cambridge University Press.

Singer, Milton (1972). *When a Great Tradition Modernizes: An Anthropological Approach to Indian Civilization*, Pall Mall Press, London.

Skorupski, John (1976). *Symbol and Theory, A Philosophical Study of Theories of Religion in Social Anthropology*, Cambridge University Press.

Staal, Frits (1975). *Exploring Mysticism, A Methodological Essay*, University of California Press.

Strathern, Andrew and Marilyn (1968), 'Marsupials and Magic: A Study of Spell Symbolism Among the Mbowamb' in *Dialectic in Practical Religion* (ed. E. R. Leach), Cambridge Papers in Social Anthropology No. 5, Cambridge University Press.

Suzuki, D. T. (1970). *Essays in Zen Buddhism*, Rider & Co., London.

Tambiah, S. J. (1968). 'The Magical Power of Words' in *Man* (NS), vol. 3, no. 2.

———— (1970). *Buddhism and the Spirit Cults in Northeast Thailand*, Cambridge University Press.

———— (1973). 'Form and Meaning of Magical Acts' in *Modes of Thought*, eds. Robin Horton and Ruth Finnegan, Faber & Faber, London.

———— (1977). 'The Cosmological and Performative Significance of a Thai Cult of Healing Through Meditation' in *Culture, Medicine and Psychiatry* 1, pp. 97–132.

Turner, Terence (n.d.). 'Narrative Structure and Mythopoesis: A Critique and Reformulation of Structuralist Concepts of Myth, Narrative, and Poetics.'

Wallace, Anthony F. C. (1966). *Religion: An Anthropological View*, Random House, New York.

Yalman, Nur (1966). 'Dual Organization in Central Ceylon' in *Anthropological Studies in Theravada Buddhism*, Manning Nash *et al.*, Cultural Report Series No. 13, South-east Asia Studies, Yale University.

Liminality and Communitas

VICTOR W. TURNER

Facts of publication: *Turner, Victor W. 1969. "Liminality and Communitas," The Ritual Process: Structure and Anti-Structure, 94–97, 106–113, 125–129. Chicago: Aldine. Copyright © 1969 by Victor W. Turner. Excerpted with the permission of Aldine de Gruyter, a Division of Walter de Gruyter, Inc., 200 Saw Mill River Road, Hawthorne, NY 10532.*

Liminality and communitas have become two of the most widely used concepts in ritual studies. Arnold van Gennep was the first to use the image of a threshold (limen) *as a metaphor for being "betwixt and between" social states. Liminality refers to the transition, or middle, phase of a rite of passage. Later, Turner introduced the notion of the liminoid, by which he meant this same threshold state as manifested in industrial cultures outside the bounds of formal ritual.*

Communitas refers to the kind of social relationship that typifies liminal moments. For Turner communitas is the dialectical opposite of social structure, or what he sometimes calls "the status system." In a situation characterized by communitas participants are not hierarchically related but dwell in a communion of equality that Martin Buber, the Jewish philosopher, called I-Thou relation.

Other works by Turner containing important statements on ritual are Dramas, Fields, and Metaphors: Symbolic Action in Human Society *(Ithaca, NY: Cornell University Press, 1974) and* From Ritual to Theatre *(New York: Performing Arts Journal, 1982).*

About the author: Dates: *1920–83, Glasgow, Scotland.* **Education:** *B.A., University College, London; Ph.D., Victoria University of Manchester.* **Field(s):** *symbolic anthropology; African studies.* **Career:** *Lecturer,* *then Senior Lecturer, 1954–63, Victoria University of Manchester; Professor of Anthropology, 1963–68, Cornell University; Professor of Anthropology and Social Thought, 1968–77, University of Chicago; William R. Kenan Professor of Anthropology, 1977–83, University of Virginia.* **Publications:** Schism and Continuity in African Society *(Manchester University, 1957);* Ndembu Divination: Its Symbolism and Techniques *(Manchester University, 1961);* Chihamba the White Spirit *(Manchester University, 1962);* Essays in the Ritual of Social Relations *(Manchester University, 1963);* Lunda Medicines and the Treatment of Disease *(Rhodes Livingston Museum, 1964);* The Drums of Affliction *(Oxford University, 1968);* The Forest of Symbols: Essays in African Religion *(Cornell University, 1967); editor, with others,* Political Anthropology *(Aldine, 1966);* The Ritual Process *(Aldine, 1969);* Dramas, Fields, and Metaphors *(Cornell University, 1974);* Revelation and Divination in Ndembu Ritual *(Cornell University, 1975); with Edith Turner,* Image and Pilgrimage in Christian Culture: Anthropological Perspectives *(Columbia University, 1978);* Process, Performance, and Pilgrimage *(Concept, 1979);* From Ritual to Theatre *(Performing Arts Journal, 1982);* On the Edge of the Bush: Anthropology as Experience*, ed. Edith L.B. Turner (University of Arizona, 1985).* **Additional:** *Fellow, Institute for Advanced Study, Princeton, NJ; Fellow, Center for Advanced Study in the Behavioral Sciences, Stanford, CA; Editor: Symbol, Myth, and Ritual Series (18 volumes, Cornell University); Guest Curator, Smithsonian Institution's exhibit, "Celebration: A World of Art and Ritual"; Rivers Memorial Medal, Royal Anthropological Institute.*

FORM AND ATTRIBUTES OF RITES OF PASSAGE

In this [reading] I take up a theme I have discussed briefly elsewhere (Turner, 1967, pp. 93–111), note some of its variations, and consider some of its further implications for the study of culture and society. This theme is in the first place represented by the nature and characteristics of what Arnold van Gennep (1960) has called the "liminal phase" of *rites de passage.* Van Gennep himself defined *rites de passage* as "rites which accompany every change of place, state, social position and age." To point up the contrast between "state" and "transition," I employ "state" to include all his other terms. It is a more inclusive concept than "status" or "office," and refers to any type of stable or recurrent condition that is culturally recognized. Van Gennep has shown that all rites of passage or "transition" are marked by three phases: separation, margin (or *limen,* signifying "threshold" in Latin), and aggregation. The first phase (of separation) comprises symbolic behavior signifying the detachment of the individual or group either from an earlier fixed point in the social structure, from a set of cultural conditions (a "state"), or from both. During the intervening "liminal" period, the characteristics of the ritual subject (the "passenger") are ambiguous; he passes through a cultural realm that has few or none

of the attributes of the past or coming state. In the third phase (reaggregation or reincorporation), the passage is consummated. The ritual subject, individual or corporate, is in a relatively stable state once more and, by virtue of this, has rights and obligations vis-à-vis others of a clearly defined and "structural" type; he is expected to behave in accordance with certain customary norms and ethical standards binding on incumbents of social position in a system of such positions.

Liminality

The attributes of liminality or of liminal *personae* ("threshold people") are necessarily ambiguous, since this condition and these persons elude or slip through the network of classifications that normally locate states and positions in cultural space. Liminal entities are neither here nor there; they are betwixt and between the positions assigned and arrayed by law, custom, convention, and ceremonial. As such, their ambiguous and indeterminate attributes are expressed by a rich variety of symbols in the many societies that ritualize social and cultural transitions. Thus, liminality is frequently likened to death, to being in the womb, to invisibility, to darkness, to bisexuality, to the wilderness, and to an eclipse of the sun or moon.

Liminal entities, such as neophytes in initiation or puberty rites, may be represented as possessing nothing. They may be disguised as monsters, wear only a strip of clothing, or even go naked, to demonstrate that as liminal beings they have no status, property, insignia, secular clothing indicating rank or role, position in a kinship system—in short, nothing that may distinguish them from their fellow neophytes or initiands. Their behavior is normally passive or humble; they must obey their instructors implicitly, and accept arbitrary punishment without complaint. It is as though they are being reduced or ground down to a uniform condition to be fashioned anew and endowed with additional powers to enable them to cope with their new station in life. Among themselves, neophytes tend to develop an intense comradeship and egalitarianism. Secular distinctions of rank and status disappear or are homogenized. The condition of the patient and her husband in *Isoma* had some of these attributes—passivity, humility, near-nakedness—in a symbolic milieu that represented both a grave and a womb. In initiations with a long period of seclusion, such as the circumcision rites of many tribal societies or induction into secret societies, there is often a rich proliferation of liminal symbols.

Communitas

What is interesting about liminal phenomena for our present purposes is the blend they offer of lowliness and sacredness, of homogeneity and comradeship. We are presented, in such rites, with a "moment in and out of time," and in and out of secular social structure, which reveals, however fleetingly, some recognition (in symbol if not always in language) of a generalized social bond that has ceased to be and has simultaneously yet to be fragmented into a multiplicity of structural ties. These are the ties organized in terms either of caste, class, or rank hierarchies or of segmentary oppositions in the stateless societies beloved of political anthropologists. It is as though there are here two major "models" for human interrelatedness, juxtaposed and alternating. The first is of society as a structured, differentiated, and often hierarchical system of politico-legal-economic positions with many types of evaluation, separating men in terms of "more" or "less." The second, which emerges recognizably in the liminal period, is of society as an unstructured or rudimentarily structured and relatively undifferentiated

comitatus, community, or even communion of equal individuals who submit together, to the general authority of the ritual elders.

I prefer the Latin term "communitas" to "community," to distinguish this modality of social relationship from an "area of common living." The distinction between structure and communitas is not simply the familiar one between "secular" and "sacred," or that, for example, between politics and religion. Certain fixed offices in tribal societies have *many* sacred attributes; indeed, every social position has *some* sacred characteristics. But this "sacred" component is acquired by the incumbents of positions during the *rites de passage*, through which they changed positions. Something of the sacredness of that transient humility and modelessness goes over, and tempers the pride of the incumbent of a higher position or office. This is not simply, as Fortes (1962, p. 86) has cogently argued, a matter of giving a general stamp of legitimacy to a society's structural positions. It is rather a matter of giving recognition to an essential and generic human bond, without which there could be *no* society. Liminality implies that the high could not be high unless the low existed, and he who is high must experience what it is like to be low. No doubt something of this thinking, . . . years ago, lay behind Prince Philip's decision to send his son, the heir apparent to the British throne, to a bush school in Australia for a time, where he could learn how "to rough it."

Dialectic of the Developmental Cycle

From all this I infer that, for individuals and groups, social life is a type of dialectical process that involves successive experience of high and low, communitas and structure, homogeneity and differentiation, equality and inequality. The passage from lower to higher status is through a limbo of statuslessness. In such a process, the opposites, as it were, constitute one another and are mutually indispensable. Furthermore, since any concrete tribal society is made up of multiple personae, groups, and categories, each of which has its own developmental cycle, at a given moment many incumbencies of fixed positions coexist with many passages between positions. In other words, each individual's life experience contains alternating exposure to structure and communitas, and to states and transitions. . . .

LIMINALITY CONTRASTED WITH STATUS SYSTEM

Let us now, rather in the fashion of Lévi-Strauss, express the difference between the properties of liminality and those of the status system in terms of a series of binary oppositions or discriminations. They can be ordered as follows:

Transition/state

Totality/partiality

Homogeneity/heterogeneity

Communitas/structure

Equality/inequality

Anonymity/systems of nomenclature

Absence of property/property

Absence of status/status

Nakedness or uniform clothing/distinctions of clothing

Sexual continence/sexuality

Minimization of sex distinctions/maximization of sex distinctions

Absence of rank/distinctions of rank

Humility/just pride of position

Disregard for personal appearance/care for personal appearance

No distinctions of wealth/distinctions of wealth

Unselfishness/selfishness

Total obedience/obedience only to superior rank

Sacredness/secularity

Sacred instruction/technical knowledge

Silence/speech

Suspension of kinship rights and obligations/kinship rights and obligations

Continuous reference to mystical powers/intermittent reference to mystical powers

Foolishness/sagacity

Simplicity/complexity

Acceptance of pain and suffering/avoidance of pain and suffering

Heteronomy/degrees of autonomy

This list could be considerably lengthened if we were to widen the span of liminal situations considered. Moreover, the symbols in which these properties are manifested and embodied are manifold and various, and often relate to the physiological processes of death and birth, anabolism and catabolism. The reader will have noticed immediately that many of these properties constitute what we think of as characteristics of the religious life in the Christian tradition. Undoubtedly, Muslims, Buddhists, Hindus, and Jews would number many of them among their religious characteristics, too. What appears to have happened is that with the increasing specialization of society and culture, with progressive complexity in the social division of labor, what was in tribal society principally a set of transitional qualities "betwixt and between" defined states of culture, and society has become itself an institutionalized state. But traces of the *passage* quality of the religious life remain in such formulations as: "The Christian is a stranger to the world, a pilgrim, a traveler, with no place to rest his head." Transition has here become a permanent condition. Nowhere has this institutionalization of liminality been more clearly marked and defined than in the monastic and mendicant states in the great world religions.

For example, the Western Christian Rule of St. Benedict "provides for the life of men who wish to live in *community* and devote themselves entirely to God's service by *self-discipline*, prayer, and *work*. They are to be essentially *families*, in the care and under the *absolute control* of a father (the abbot); individually they are bound to personal *poverty, abstention from marriage*, and *obedience to their superiors*, and by the vows of stability and conversion of manners [originally a synonym for "*common life*," "monasticity" as distinguished from secular life]; a moderate degree of austerity is imposed by the night office, fasting, abstinence from fleshmeat, and *restraint in conversation*" (Attwater, 1962, p. 51—my emphases). I have stressed features that bear a remarkable similarity to the condition of the chief-elect during his transition to the public installation rites, when he enters his kingdom. The Ndembu circumcision rites (*Mukanda*) present further parallels between the neophytes and the monks of St. Benedict. Erving Goffman (*Asylums*, 1962) discusses what he calls the "characteristics of total institutions." Among these he includes monasteries, and devotes a good deal of attention to "the stripping and leveling processes which . . . directly cut across the various social distinctions with which the recruits enter." He then quotes from St. Benedict's advice to the abbot: "Let him make no distinction of persons in the monastery. Let not one be loved more than another, unless he be found to excel in good works or in obedience. Let not one of noble birth be raised above him who was formerly a slave, unless some other reasonable cause intervene" (p. 119).

Here parallels with *Mukanda* are striking. The novices are "stripped" of their secular clothing when they are passed beneath a symbolic gateway; they are "leveled" in that their former names are discarded and all are assigned the common designation *mwadyi*, or "novice," and treated alike. One of the songs sung by circumcisers to the mothers of the novices on the night before circumcision contains the following line: "Even if your child is a chief's son, tomorrow he will be like a slave"—just as a chief-elect is treated like a slave before *his* installation. Moreover, the senior instructor in the seclusion lodge is chosen partly because he is father of several boys undergoing the rites and becomes a father for the whole group, a sort of "abbot," though his title *Mfumwa tubwiku*, means literally "husband of the novices," to emphasize their passive role.

MYSTICAL DANGER AND THE POWERS OF THE WEAK

One may well ask why it is that liminal situations and roles are almost everywhere attributed with magico-religious properties, or why these should so often be regarded as dangerous, inauspicious, or polluting to persons, objects, events, and relationships that have not been ritually incorporated into the liminal context. My view is briefly that from the perspectival viewpoint of those concerned with the maintenance of "structure," all sustained manifestations of communitas must appear as dangerous and anarchical, and have to be hedged around with pre-

scriptions, prohibitions, and conditions. And, as Mary Douglas (1966) has . . . argued, that which cannot be clearly classified in terms of traditional criteria of classification, or falls between classificatory boundaries, is almost everywhere regarded as "polluting" and "dangerous" (passim).

To repeat what I said earlier, liminality is not the only cultural manifestation of communitas. In most societies, there are other areas of manifestation to be readily recognized by the symbols that cluster around them and the beliefs that attach to them, such as "the powers of the weak," or, in other words, the permanently or transiently sacred attributes of low status or position. Within stable structural systems, there are many dimensions of organization. . . . Mystical and moral powers are wielded by subjugated autochthones over the total welfare of societies whose political frame is constituted by the lineage or territorial organization of incoming conquerors. In other societies—the Ndembu and Lamba of Zambia, for example—we can point to the cult associations whose members have gained entry through common misfortune and debilitating circumstances to therapeutic powers with regard to such common goods of mankind as health, fertility, and climate. These associations transect such important components of the secular political system as lineages, villages, subchiefdoms, and chiefdoms. We could also mention the role of structurally small and politically insignificant nations within systems of nations as upholders of religious and moral values, such as the Hebrews in the ancient Near East, the Irish in early medieval Christendom, and the Swiss in modern Europe.

Many writers have drawn attention to the role of the court jester. Max Gluckman (1965), for example, writes: "The court jester operated as a privileged arbiter of morals, given license to gibe at king and courtiers, or lord of the manor." Jesters were "usually men of low class—sometimes on the Continent of Europe they were priests—who clearly moved out of their usual estate. . . . In a system where it was difficult for others to rebuke the head of a political unit, we might have here an institutionalized joker, operating at the highest point of the unit . . . a joker able to express feelings of outraged morality." He further mentions how jesters attached to many African monarchs were "frequently dwarfs and other oddities." Similar in function to these were the drummers in the Barotse royal barge in which the king and his court moved from a capital in the Zambezi Flood Plain to one of its margins during the annual floods. They were privileged to throw into the water any of the great nobles "who had offended them and their sense of justice during the past year" (pp. 102–104). These figures, representing the poor and the deformed, appear to symbolize the moral values of communitas as against the coercive power of supreme political rulers.

Folk literature abounds in symbolic figures, such as "holy beggars," "third sons," "little tailors," and "simpletons," who strip off the pretensions of holders of high rank and office and reduce them to the level of common humanity and mortality. Again, in the traditional "Western," we have all read of the homeless and mysterious "stranger" without wealth or name who restores ethical and legal equilibrium to a local set of political power relations by eliminating the unjust secular "bosses" who are oppressing the smallholders. Members of despised or outlawed ethnic and cultural groups play major roles in myths and popular tales as representatives or expressions of universal-human values. Famous among these are the good Samaritan, the Jewish fiddler Rothschild in Chekhov's tale "Rothschild's Fiddle," Mark Twain's fugitive Negro slave Jim in *Huckleberry Finn*, and Dostoevsky's Sonya, the prostitute who redeems the would-be Nietzschean "superman" Raskolnikov, in *Crime and Punishment.*

All these mythic types are structurally inferior or "marginal," yet represent what Henri Bergson would have called "open" as against "closed morality," the latter being essentially the normative system of bounded, structured, particularistic groups. Bergson speaks of how an in-group preserves its identity against members of out-groups, protects itself against threats to its way of life, and renews the will to maintain the norms on which the routine behavior necessary for its social life depends. In closed or structured societies, it is the marginal or "inferior" person or the "outsider" who often comes to symbolize what David Hume has called "the sentiment for humanity," which in its turn relates to the model we have termed "communitas."

MILLENARIAN MOVEMENTS

Among the more striking manifestations of communitas are to be found the so-called millenarian religious movements, which arise among what Norman Cohn (1961) has called "uprooted and desperate masses in town and countryside . . . living on the margin of society" (pp. 31–32) (i.e., structured society), or where formerly tribal societies are brought under the alien overlordship of complex, industrial societies. The attributes of such movements will be well known to most of my readers. Here I would merely recall some of the properties of liminality in tribal rituals that I mentioned earlier. Many of these correspond pretty closely with those of millenarian movements: homogeneity, equality, anonymity, absence of property (many movements actually enjoin on their members the destruction of what property they possess to bring nearer the coming of the perfect state of unison and communion they desire, for property rights are linked with structural distinctions both vertical and horizontal), reduction of all to the same status level, the wearing of uniform apparel (sometimes for both sexes), sexual continence (or its antithesis, sexual community, both continence and sexual community liquidate marriage and the family, which legitimate structural status), minimization of sex distinctions (all are "equal in the sight of God" or the ancestors), abolition of rank, humility, disregard for personal appearance, unselfishness, total obedience to the prophet or leader, sacred instruction, the maximization of religious, as opposed to secular, attitudes and behavior, suspension of kinship rights and obligations (all are siblings or comrades of one another regardless of previous secular ties), simplicity of speech and manners, sacred folly, acceptance of pain and suffering (even to the point of undergoing martyrdom), and so forth.

It is noteworthy that many of these movements cut right across tribal and national divisions during their initial momentum. Communitas, or the "open society," differs in this from structure, or the "closed society," in that it is potentially or ideally extensible to the limits of humanity. In practice, of course, the impetus soon becomes exhausted, and the "movement" becomes itself an institution among other institutions—often one more fanatical and militant than the rest, for the reason that it feels itself to be the unique bearer of universal-human truths. Mostly, such movements occur during phases of history that are in many respects "homologous" to the liminal periods of important rituals in stable and repetitive societies, when major groups or social categories in those societies are passing from one cultural state to another. They are essentially phenomena of transition. This is perhaps why in so many of these movements much of their mythology and symbolism is borrowed from those of traditional *rites de passage*, either in the cultures in which they originate or in the cultures with which they are in dramatic contact.

. . . .

LIMINALITY, LOW STATUS, AND COMMUNITAS

The time has now come to make a careful review of a hypothesis that seeks to account for the attributes of such seemingly diverse phenomena as neophytes in the liminal phase of ritual, subjugated autochthones, small nations, court jesters, holy mendicants, good Samaritans, millenarian movements, "dharma bums," . . . and monastic orders. Surely an ill-assorted bunch of social phenomena! Yet all have this common characteristic: they are persons or principles that (1) fall in the interstices of social structure, (2) are on its margins, or (3) occupy its lowest rungs. This leads us back to the problem of the definition of social structure. One authoritative source of definitions is *A Dictionary of the Social Sciences* (Gould and Kolb, 1964), in which A. W. Eister reviews some major formulations of this conception. . . . Many modern sociologists regard social structure as "a more or less distinctive arrangement (of which there may be more than one type) of specialized and mutually dependent *institutions* [Eister's emphasis] and the institutional organizations of positions and/or of actors which they imply, all evolved in the natural course of events, as groups of human beings, with given needs and capacities, have interacted with each other (in various types or modes of interaction) and sought to cope with their

environment" (pp. 668–669). Raymond Firth's (1951) more analytical conception runs as follows: "In the types of societies ordinarily studied by anthropologists, the social structure may include critical or basic relationships arising similarly from a class system based on relations with the soil. Other aspects of social structure arise through membership in other kinds of persistent groups, such as clans, castes, age-sets, or secret societies. Other basic relations again are due to position in a kinship system" (p. 32).

Most definitions contain the notion of an arrangement of positions or statuses. Most involve the institutionalization and perdurance of groups and relationships. Classical mechanics, the morphology and physiology of animals and plants, and, more recently, with Lévi-Strauss, structural linguistics have been ransacked for concepts, models, and homologous forms by social scientists. All share in common the notion of a superorganic arrangement of parts or positions that continues, with modifications more or less gradual, through time. The concept of "conflict" has come to be connected with the concept of "social structure," since the differentiation of parts becomes opposition between parts, and scarce status becomes the object of struggles between persons and groups who lay claim to it.

The other dimension of "society" with which I have been concerned is less easy to define. G. A. Hillery (1955) reviewed 94 definitions of the term "community" and reached the conclusion that "beyond the concept that people are involved in community, there is no complete agreement as to the nature of community" (p. 119). The field would, therefore, seem to be still open for new attempts! I have tried to eschew the notion that communitas has a specific territorial locus, often limited in character, which pervades many definitions. For me, communitas emerges where social structure is not. Perhaps the best way of putting this difficult concept into words is Martin Buber's—though I feel that perhaps he should be regarded as a gifted native informant rather than as a social scientist! Buber (1961) uses the term "community" for "communitas"; "Community is the being no longer side by side (and, one might add, above and below) but *with* one another of a multitude of persons. And this multitude, though it moves towards one goal, yet experiences everywhere a turning to, a dynamic facing of, the others, a flowing from *I* to *Thou*. Community is where community happens" (p. 51).

Buber lays his finger on the spontaneous, immediate, concrete nature of communitas, as opposed to the norm-governed, institutionalized, abstract nature of social structure. Yet, communitas is made evident or accessible, so to speak, only through its juxtaposition to, or hybridization with, aspects of social structure. Just as in *Gestalt* psychology, figure and ground are mutually determinative, or, as some rare elements are never found in nature in their purity but only as components of chemical compounds, so communitas can be grasped only in some relation to structure. Just because the communitas component is elusive, hard to pin down, it is not unimportant. Here the story of Lao-tse's chariot wheel may be apposite. The spokes of the wheel and the nave (i.e., the central block of the wheel holding the axle and spokes) to which they are attached would be useless, he said, but for the hole, the gap, the emptiness at the center. Communitas, with its unstructured character, representing the "quick" of human interrelatedness, what Buber has called *das Zwischenmenschliche*, might well be represented by the "emptiness at the center," which is nevertheless indispensable to the functioning of the structure of the wheel.

It is neither by chance nor by lack of scientific precision that, along with others who have considered the conception of communitas, I find myself forced to have recourse to metaphor and analogy. For communitas has an existential quality; it involves the whole man in his relation to other whole men. Structure, on the other hand, has cognitive quality; as Lévi-Strauss has perceived, it is essentially a set of classifications, a model for thinking about culture and nature and ordering one's public life. Communitas has also an aspect of potentiality; it is often in the subjunctive mood. Relations between total beings are generative of symbols and metaphors and comparisons; art and religion are their products rather than legal and political structures. Bergson saw in the words and writings of prophets and great artists the creation of an "open morality," which was itself an expression of what he called the *élan vital* or evolutionary "life-force." Prophets and artists tend to be liminal and marginal people, "edgemen," who strive with a passionate sincerity to rid themselves of the clichés associated with status incumbency and role-playing and to enter into vital relations with other men in fact or imagination. In their productions we may catch glimpses of that unused evolutionary potential in mankind which has not yet been externalized and fixed in structure.

Communitas breaks in through the interstices of structure, in liminality; at the edges of structure, in marginality; and from beneath structure, in inferiority. It is almost everywhere held to be sacred or "holy," possibly because it transgresses or dissolves the norms that govern structured and institutionalized relationships and is accompanied by experiences of unprecedented potency. The processes of "leveling" and "stripping," to which Goffman has drawn our attention, often appear to flood their subjects with affect. Instinctual energies are surely liberated by these processes, but I am now inclined to think that communitas is not solely the product of biologically inherited drives released from cultural constraints. Rather is it the product of peculiarly human faculties, which include rationality, volition, and memory, and which develop with experience of life in society—just as among the Tallensi it is only mature men who undergo the experiences that induce them to receive *bakologo* shrines.

The notion that there is a generic bond between men, and its related sentiment of "humankindness," are not epiphenomena of some kind of herd instinct but are products of "men in their wholeness wholly attending." Liminality, marginality, and structural inferiority are conditions in which are frequently generated myths, symbols, rituals, philosophical systems, and works of art. These cultural forms provide men with a set of templates or models which are, at one level, periodical reclassifications of reality and man's relationship to society, nature, and culture. But they are more than classifications, since they incite men to action as well as to thought. Each of these productions has a multivocal character, having many meanings, and each is capable of moving people at many psychobiological levels simultaneously.

There is a dialectic here, for the immediacy of communitas gives way to the mediacy of structure, while, in *rites de passage*, men are released from structure into communitas only to return to structure revitalized by their experience of communitas. What is certain is that no society can function adequately without this dialectic. Exaggeration of structure may well lead to pathological manifestations of communitas outside or against "the law." Exaggeration of communitas, in certain religious or political movements of the leveling type, may be speedily followed by despotism, overbureaucratization, or other modes of structural rigidification. For, like the neophytes in the African circumcision lodge, or the Benedictine monks, or the members of a millenarian movement, those living in community seem to require, sooner or later, an absolute authority, whether this be a religious commandment, a divinely inspired leader, or a dictator. Communitas cannot stand alone if the material and organizational needs of human beings are to be adequately met. Maximization of communitas provokes maximization of structure, which in its turn produces revolutionary strivings for renewed communitas. The history of any great society provides evidence at the political level for this oscillation.

I mentioned earlier the close connection that exists between structure and property, whether this be privately or corporately owned, inherited, and managed. Thus, most millenarian movements try to abolish property or to hold all things in common. Usually this is possible only for a short time—until the date set for the coming of the millennium or the ancestral cargoes. When prophecy fails, property and structure return and the movement becomes institutionalized, or the movement disintegrates and its members merge into the environing structured order. . . .

BIBLIOGRAPHY

Attwater, Donald (Ed.). 1962. *A Catholic encyclopedia.* New York: Macmillan.

Buber, Martin. 1961. *Between man and man.* (Trans. by R. G. Smith). London and Glasgow: Fontana Library.

Cohn, Norman. 1961. *The pursuit of the millennium.* New York: Harper Torch Books.

Douglas, Mary. 1966. *Purity and danger.* London: Routledge and Kegan Paul.

Firth, Raymond. 1951. *Elements of social organization.* London: Watts.

Fortes, Meyer. 1962. Ritual and office. In Max Gluckman (Ed.), *Essays on the ritual of social relations.* Manchester: Manchester University Press.

Gennep, Arnold van. 1960. *The rites of passage.* (Trans. by Monika B. Vizedom and Gabrielle L. Caffee.) London: Routledge and Kegan Paul.

Gluckman, Max. 1965. *Politics, law and ritual in tribal society.* Chicago: Aldine Publishing Company.

Goffman, Erving. 1962. *Asylums.* Chicago: Aldine Publishing Company.

Gould, J., and W. L. Kolb (Eds.). 1964. *A Dictionary of the social sciences.* London: Tavistock.

Hillery, G. A. 1955. Definitions of community: areas of agreement. *Rural Sociology,* vol. 20.

Richards, Audrey I. 1956. *Chisungu.* London: Faber and Faber.

Turner, Victor W. 1967. *The forest of symbols.* Ithaca, N.Y.: Cornell University Press.

Symbols in Ndembu Ritual

VICTOR W. TURNER

Facts of publication: *Turner, Victor W. 1967. "Symbols in Ndembu Ritual," The Forest of Symbols: Aspects of Nbembu Ritual, 28–32, 35–39, 45–47, 50–55, 58. Ithaca, NY: Cornell University Press. Copyright © 1967 by Cornell University. Reprinted with the permission of Cornell University Press.*

In a section of The Forest of Symbols *prior to the one presented here, Victor Turner treats symbols as the building blocks of rites. Symbols, he argues, ought to be interpreted in relation to social events occurring in time and in view of what the users of those symbols say about them, as well as what they do in relation to them. Symbols, he says, do not merely mean, they also produce action, and dominant (as opposed to instrumental) symbols become the focus of interaction.*

In the selection presented here Turner specifies the characteristics of symbols, explains how they work, and identifies the problems with interpreting them, especially when one is studying ritual as a participant-observer.

See also Nancy D. Munn, "Symbolism in a Ritual Context: Aspects of Symbolic Action," Handbook of Social and Cultural Anthropology, *579–612. Ed. John J. Honigmann. (Chicago: RandMcNally, 1973). For background on Turner's view of symbols see Charles Morris,* Foundation of a Theory of Signs *(Chicago: University of Chicago Press, 1938). For a critical view of current scholarship on Turner see Don Handelman, "Is Victor Turner Receiving His Intellectual Due?"* Journal of Ritual Studies 7.2 (1993): 117–124.

About the author: *See biography for previous selection.*

The simplest property [of a dominant ritual symbol] is that of *condensation.* Many things and actions are represented in a single formation. Secondly, a dominant symbol is a *unification of disparate significata.* The disparate *significata* are interconnected by virtue of their common possession of analogous qualities or by association in fact or thought. Such qualities or links of association may in themselves be quite trivial or random or widely distributed over a range of phenomena. Their very generality enables them to bracket together the most diverse ideas and phenomena. Thus [for the Ndembu of Zambia], the milk tree stands for, *inter alia,* women's breasts, motherhood, a novice at *Nkang'a* [the girls' puberty ritual], the principle of matriliny, a specific matrilineage, learning, and the unity and persistence of Ndembu society. The themes of nourishment and dependence run through all these diverse *significata.*

The third important property of dominant ritual symbols is *polarization of meaning.* Not only the milk tree but all other dominant Ndembu symbols possess two clearly distinguishable poles of meaning. At one pole is found a cluster of *significata* that refer to components of the moral and social orders of Ndembu society, to principles of social organization, to kinds of corporate grouping, and to the norms and values inherent in structural relationships. At the other pole, the *significata* are usually natural and physiological phenomena and processes. Let us call the first of these the "ideological pole," and the second the "sensory pole." At the sensory pole, the meaning content is closely related to the outward form of the symbol. Thus one meaning of the milk tree—breast milk—is closely related to the exudation of milky latex from the tree. One sensory meaning of another dominant symbol, the *mukula* tree, is blood; this tree secretes a dusky red gum.

At the sensory pole are concentrated those *significata* that may be expected to arouse desires and feelings; at the ideological pole one finds an arrangement of norms and values that guide and control persons as members of social groups and categories. The sensory, emotional *significata* tend to be "gross" in a double sense. In the first place, they are gross in a general way, taking no account of detail or the precise qualities of emotion. It cannot be sufficiently stressed that such symbols are social facts, "collective representations," even though their appeal is to the lowest common denominator of human feeling. The second sense of "gross" is "frankly, even flagrantly, physiological." Thus, the milk tree has the gross meanings of breast milk, breasts, and the process of breast feeding. These are also gross in the sense that they represent items of universal Ndembu experience. Other Ndembu symbols, at their sensory poles of meaning, represent such themes as blood, male and female genitalia, semen, urine, and feces. The same symbols, at their ideological poles of meaning, represent the unity and continuity of social groups, primary and associational, domestic, and political.

REFERENCE AND CONDENSATION

It has long been recognized in anthropological literature that ritual symbols are stimuli of emotion. Perhaps the most striking statement of this position is that made by Edward Sapir in the *Encyclopaedia of the Social Sciences* (XIV, 492–493). Sapir distinguishes, in a way which recalls Jung's distinction, between two principal classes of symbols. The first he calls "referential" symbols. These include such forms as oral speech, writing, national flags, flag signaling, and other organizations of symbols which are agreed upon as economical devices for purposes of reference. Like Jung's "sign," the referential symbol is predominantly cognitive and refers to known facts. The second class, which includes most ritual symbols, consist of "condensation" symbols, which Sapir defines as "highly condensed forms of substitutive behavior for direct expression, allowing for the ready release of emotional tension in conscious or unconscious form." The condensation symbol is "saturated with emotional quality." The chief difference in development between these types of symbolism, in Sapir's view, is that "while referential symbolism grows with formal elaboration in the conscious, condensation symbolism strikes deeper and deeper roots in the unconscious, and diffuses its emotional quality to types of behavior and situations apparently far removed from the original meaning of the symbol."

Sapir's formulation is most illuminating. He lays explicit stress on four main attributes of ritual symbols: (1) the condensation of many meanings in a single form; (2) economy of reference; (3) predominance of emotional or orectic quality; (4) associational linkages with regions of the unconscious. Nevertheless, he tends to underestimate the importance of what I have called the ideological (or, I would add, normative) pole of meaning. Ritual symbols are at one and the same time referential and condensation symbols, though each symbol is multireferential rather than unireferential. Their essential quality consists in their juxtaposition of the grossly physical and the structurally normative, of the organic and the social. Such symbols are coincidences of opposite qualities, unions of "high" and "low." We do not need a detailed acquaintance with any of the current depth psychologies to suspect that this juxtaposition, and even interpenetration, of opposites in the symbol is connected with its social function. Durkheim was fascinated by the problem of why many social norms and imperatives were felt to be at the same time "obligatory" and "desirable." Ritual, scholars are coming to see, is precisely a mechanism that periodically converts the obligatory into the desirable. The basic unit of ritual, the dominant symbol, encapsulates the major properties of the total ritual process which brings about this transmutation. Within its framework of meanings, the dominant symbol brings the ethical and jural norms of society into close contact with strong emotional stimuli. In the action situation of ritual, with its social excitement and directly physiological stimuli, such as music, singing, dancing, alcohol, incense, and bizarre modes of dress, the ritual symbol, we may perhaps say, effects an interchange of qualities between its poles of meaning. Norms and values, on the one hand, become saturated with emotion, while the gross and basic emotions become ennobled through contact with social values. The irksomeness of moral constraint is transformed into the "love of virtue."

Before proceeding any further with our analysis, it might be as well to restate the major empirical properties of dominant symbols derived from our classification of the relevant descriptive data: (1) condensation; (2) unification of disparate meanings in a single symbolic formation; (3) polarization of meaning.

DOMINANT AND INSTRUMENTAL SYMBOLS

Certain ritual symbols . . . are regarded by Ndembu as dominant. In rituals performed to propitiate ancestor spirits who are believed to have afflicted their living kin with reproductive disorders, illness, or bad luck at hunting, there are two main classes of dominant symbols. The first class is represented by the first tree or plant in a series of trees or plants from which portions of leaves, bark, or roots are collected by practitioners or adepts in the curative cult. The subjects of ritual are marked with these portions mixed with water, or given them, mixed in a potion, to drink. The first tree so treated is called the "place of greeting" (*ishikenu*), or the "elder" (*mukulumpi*). The adepts encircle it several times to sacralize it. Then the senior practitioner prays at its base, which he sprinkles with powdered white clay. Prayer is made either to the named spirit, believed to be afflicting the principal subject of ritual, or to the tree itself, which is in some way identified with the afflicting spirit. Each *ishikenu* can be allotted several meanings by adepts. The second class of dominant symbols in curative rituals consists of shrines where the subjects of such rituals sit while the practitioners wash them with vegetable substances mixed with water and perform actions on their behalf of a symbolic or ritualistic nature. Such shrines are often composite, consisting of several objects in configuration. Both classes of dominant symbols are closely associated with nonempirical beings. Some are regarded as their repositories; others, as being identified with them; others again, as representing them. In life-crisis rituals, on the other hand, dominant symbols seem to represent not beings but nonempirical powers or kinds of efficacy. For example, in the boys' circumcision ritual, the dominant symbol for the whole ritual is a

"medicine" (*yitumbu*), called "*nfunda*," which is compounded from many ingredients, e.g., the ash of the burnt lodge which means "death," and the urine of an apprentice circumciser which means "virility." Each of these and other ingredients have many other meanings. The dominant symbol at the camp where the novices' parents assemble and prepare food for the boys is the *chikoli* tree, which represents, among other things, an erect phallus, adult masculinity, strength, hunting prowess, and health continuing into old age. The dominant symbol during the process of circumcision is the milk tree, beneath which novices are circumcised. The dominant symbol in the immediate post-circumcision phase is the red *mukula* tree, on which the novices sit until their wounds stop bleeding. Other symbols are dominant at various phases of seclusion. Each of these symbols is described as "*mukulumpi*" (elder, senior). Dominant symbols appear in many different ritual contexts, sometimes presiding over the whole procedure, sometimes over particular phases. The meaning-content of certain dominant symbols possesses a high degree of constancy and consistency throughout the total symbolic system, exemplifying Radcliffe-Brown's proposition that a symbol recurring in a cycle of rituals is likely to have the same significance in each. Such symbols also possess considerable autonomy with regard to the aims of the rituals in which they appear. Precisely because of these properties, dominant symbols are readily analyzable in a cultural framework of reference. They may be regarded for this purpose as what Whitehead would have called "eternal objects."[1] They are the relatively fixed points in both the social and cultural structures, and indeed constitute points of junction between these two kinds of structure. They may be regarded irrespective of their order of appearance in a given ritual as ends in themselves, as representative of the axiomatic values of the widest Ndembu society. This does not mean that they cannot also be studied, as we have indeed studied them, as factors of social action, in an action frame of reference, but their social properties make them more appropriate objects of morphological study than the class of symbols we will now consider.

These symbols may be termed "instrumental symbols." An instrumental symbol must be seen in terms of its wider context, i.e., in terms of the total system of symbols which makes up a given kind of ritual. Each kind of ritual has its specific mode of interrelating symbols. This mode is often dependent upon the ostensible purposes of that kind of ritual. In other words, each ritual has its own teleology. It has its explicitly expressed goals, and instrumental symbols may be regarded as means of attaining those goals. For example, in rituals performed for the overt purpose of making women fruitful, among the instrumental symbols used are portions of fruit-bearing trees or of trees that possess innumerable rootlets. These fruits and rootlets are said by Ndembu to represent children. They are also thought of as having efficacy to make the woman fruitful. They are means to the main end of the ritual. Perhaps such symbols could be regarded as mere signs or referential symbols, were it not for the fact that the meanings of each are associated with powerful conscious and unconscious emotions and wishes. At the psychological level of analysis, I suspect that these symbols too would approximate to the condition of condensation symbols, but here we touch upon the present limits of competence of anthropological explanation. . . .

PROVINCES OF EXPLANATION

I consider that if we conceptualize a dominant symbol as having two poles of meaning, we can more exactly demarcate the limits within which anthropological analysis may be fruitfully applied. Psychoanalysts, in treating most indigenous interpretations of symbols as irrelevant, are guilty of a naïve and one-sided approach. For those interpretations that show how a dominant symbol expresses important components of the social and moral orders are by no means equivalent to the "rationalizations," and the "secondary elaborations" of material deriving from endopsychic conflicts. They refer to social facts that have an empirical reality exterior to the psyches of individuals. On the other hand, those anthropologists who regard only indigenous interpretations as relevant, are being equally one-sided. This is because they tend to examine symbols within two analytical frameworks only, the cultural and the structural. This approach is essentially a static one, and it

does not deal with processes involving temporal changes in social relations.

Nevertheless, the crucial properties of a ritual symbol involve these dynamic developments. Symbols instigate social action. In a field context they may even be described as "forces," in that they are determinable influences inclining persons and groups to action. It is in a field context, moreover, that the properties we have described, namely, polarization of meanings, transference of affectual quality, discrepancy between meanings, and condensations of meanings, become most significant. The symbol as a unit of action, possessing these properties, becomes an object of study both for anthropology and for psychology. Both disciplines, in so far as they are concerned with human actions must conceptualize the ritual symbol in the same way.

The techniques and concepts of the anthropologist enable him to analyze competently the interrelations between the data associated with the ideological pole of meaning. They also enable him to analyze the social behavior directed upon the total dominant symbol. He cannot, however, with his present skills, discriminate between the precise sources of unconscious feeling and wishing, which shape much of the outward form of the symbol; select some natural objects rather than others to serve as symbols; and account for certain aspects of the behavior associated with symbols. For him, it is enough that the symbol should evoke motion. He is interested in the fact that emotion is evoked and not in the specific qualities of its constituents. He may indeed find it situationally relevant for his analysis to distinguish whether the emotion evoked by a specific symbol possesses the gross character, say, of aggression, fear, friendliness, anxiety, or sexual pleasure, but he need go no further than this. For him the ritual symbol is primarily a factor in group dynamics, and, as such, its references to the groups, relationships, values, norms, and beliefs of a society are his principal items of study. In other words, the anthropologist treats the sensory pole of meaning as a constant, and the social and ideological aspects as variables whose interdependencies he seeks to explain.

The psychoanalyst, on the other hand, must, I think, attach greater significance than he now does to social factors in the analysis of ritual symbolism. He must cease to regard interpretations, beliefs, and dogmas as mere rationalizations when, often enough, these refer to social and natural realities. For, as Durkheim wrote (1954, 2–3), "primitive religions hold to reality and express it. One must learn to go underneath the symbol to the reality which it represents and which gives it its meaning. No religions are false, all answer, though in different ways, to the given conditions of human existence." Among those given conditions, the arrangement of society into structured groupings, discrepancies between the principles that organize these groupings, economic collaboration and competition, schism within groups and opposition between groups—in short, all those things with which the social aspect of ritual symbolism is concerned—are surely of at least equal importance with biopsychical drives and early conditioning in the elementary family. After all, the ritual symbol has, in common with the dream symbol, the characteristic, discovered by Freud, of being a compromise formation between two main opposing tendencies. It is a compromise between the need for social control, and certain innate and universal human drives whose complete gratification would result in a breakdown of that control. Ritual symbols refer to what is normative, general, and characteristic of unique individuals. Thus, Ndembu symbols refer among other things, to the basic needs of social existence (hunting, agriculture, female fertility, favourable climatic conditions, and so forth), and to shared values on which communal life depends (generosity, comradeship, respect for elders, the importance of kinship, hospitality, and the like). In distinguishing between ritual symbols and individual psychic symbols, we may perhaps say that while ritual symbols are gross means of handling social and natural reality, psychic symbols are dominantly fashioned under the influence of inner drives. In analyzing the former, attention must mainly be paid to relations between data external to the psyche; in analyzing the latter, to endopsychic data.

For this reason, the study of ritual symbolism falls more within the province of the social anthropologist than that of the psychologist or psychoanalyst, although the latter can assist the anthropologist by examining the nature and interconnections of the data clustered at the sensory pole of ritual symbolism. He can also, I believe, illuminate certain aspects of the stereotyped behavior associated with symbols in field contexts, which the actors themselves are unable to explain. For . . . much of this behavior is suggestive of attitudes that differ radically from those deemed appropriate in terms of traditional exegesis. Indeed, certain conflicts would appear to be so basic that they totally block exegesis.

THE INTERPRETATION OF OBSERVED EMOTIONS

Can we really say that behavior portraying conflict between persons and groups, who are represented by the symbols themselves as being in harmony, is in the full Freudian sense unconscious behavior? The Ndembu themselves in many situations outside *Nkang'a*, both secular and ritual, are perfectly aware of and ready to speak about hostility in the relationships between particular mothers and daughters, between particular sublineages, and between particular young girls and the adult women in their villages. It is rather as though there existed in certain precisely defined public situations, usually of a ritual or ceremonial type, a norm obstructing the verbal statement of conflicts in any way connected with the principle and rules celebrated or dramatized in those situations. Evidences of human passion and frailty are just not spoken about when the occasion is given up to the public commemoration and reanimation of norms and values in their abstract purity.

Yet, as we have seen, recurrent kinds of conflict may be acted out in the ritual or ceremonial form. On great ritual occasions, common practice, as well as highest principle, receives its symbolic or stereotyped expression, but practice, which is dominantly under the sway of what all societies consider man's "lower nature," is rife with expressions of conflict. Selfish and factional interests, oath breaking, disloyalty, sins of omission as well as sins of commission, pollute and disfigure those ideal prototypes of behavior which in precept, prayer, formula, and symbol are held up before the ritual assembly for its exclusive attention. In the orthodox interpretation of ritual it is pretended that common practice has no efficacy and that men and women really are as they ideally should be. Yet, as I have argued above, the "energy" required to reanimate the values and norms enshrined in dominant symbols and expressed in various kinds of verbal behavior is "borrowed," to speak metaphorically in lieu at the moment of a more rigorous language, from the miming of well-known and normally mentionable conflicts. The raw energies of conflict are domesticated into the service of social order.

I should say here that I believe it possible, and indeed necessary, to analyze symbols in a context of observed emotions. If the investigator is well acquainted with the common idiom in which a society expresses such emotions as friendship, love, hate, joy, sorrow, contentment, and fear, he cannot fail to observe that these are experienced in ritual situations. Thus, in *Nkang'a* when the women laugh and jeer at the men, tease the novice and her mother, fight one another for the "porridge of *chipwamp-wilu*," and so on, the observer can hardly doubt that emotions are really aroused in the actors as well as formally represented by ritual custom. ("What's Hecuba to him or he to Hecuba, that he should weep for her?")

These emotions are portrayed and evoked in close relation to the dominant symbols of tribal cohesion and continuity, often by the performance of instrumentally symbolic behavior. However, since they are often associated with the mimesis of interpersonal and intergroup conflict, such emotions and acts of behavior obtain no place among the official, verbal meanings attributed to such dominant symbols. . . .

THE ANALYSIS OF SYMBOLS IN SOCIAL PROCESSES

Let me outline briefly the way in which I think ritual symbols may fruitfully be analyzed. Performances of ritual are phases in broad social processes, the span and complexity of which are roughly proportional to the size and degree of differentiation of the groups in which they occur. One class of ritual is situated near the apex of a whole hierarchy of redressive and regulative institutions that correct deflections and deviations from customarily prescribed behavior. Another class anticipates deviations and conflicts. This class includes periodic

rituals and life-crisis rituals. Each kind of ritual is a patterned process in time, the units of which are symbolic objects and serialized items of symbolic behavior.

The symbolic constituents may themselves be classed into structural elements, or "dominant symbols," which tend to be ends in themselves, and variable elements, or "instrumental symbols," which serve as means to the explicit or implicit goals of the given ritual. In order to give an adequate explanation of the meaning of a particular symbol, it is necessary first to examine the widest action-field context, that, namely, in which the ritual itself is simply a phase. Here one must consider what kinds of circumstances give rise to a performance of ritual, whether these are concerned with natural phenomena, economic and technological processes, human life-crises, or with the breach of crucial social relationships. The circumstances will probably determine what sort of ritual is performed. The goals of the ritual will have overt and implicit reference to the antecedent circumstances and will in turn help to determine the meaning of the symbols. Symbols must now be examined within the context of the specific ritual. It is here that we enlist the aid of indigenous informants. It is here also that we may be able to speak legitimately of "levels" of interpretation, for laymen will give the investigator simple and exoteric meanings, while specialists will give him esoteric explanations and more elaborate texts. Next, behavior directed towards each symbol should be noted, for such behavior is an important component of its total meaning.

We are now in a position to exhibit the ritual as a system of meanings, but this system acquires additional richness and depth if it is regarded as itself constituting a sector of the Ndembu ritual system, as interpreted by informants and as observed in action. It is in comparison with other sectors of the total system, and by reference to the dominant articulating principles of the total system, that we often become aware that the overt and ostensible aims and purposes of a given ritual conceal unavowed, and even "unconscious," wishes and goals. We also become aware that a complex relationship exists between the overt and the submerged, and the manifest and latent patterns of meaning. As social anthropologists we are potentially capable of analyzing the social aspect of this relationship. We can examine, for example, the relations of dependence and independence between the total society and its parts, and the relations between different kinds of parts, and between different parts of the same kind. We can see how the same dominant symbol, which in one kind of ritual stands for one kind of social group or for one principle of organization, in another kind of ritual stands for another kind of group or principle, and in its aggregate of meanings stands for unity and continuity of the widest Ndembu society, embracing its contradictions.

THE LIMITS OF CONTEMPORARY ANTHROPOLOGICAL COMPETENCE

Our analysis must needs be incomplete when we consider the relationship between the normative elements in social life and the individual. For this relationship, too, finds its way into the meaning of ritual symbols. Here we come to the confines of our present anthropological competence, for we are now dealing with the structure and properties of psyches, a scientific field traditionally studied by other disciplines than ours. At one end of the symbol's spectrum of meanings we encounter the individual psychologist and the social psychologist, and even beyond them (if one may make a friendly tilt at an envied friend), brandishing his Medusa's head, the psychoanalyst, ready to turn to stone the foolhardy interloper into his caverns of terminology.

We shudder back thankfully into the light of social day. Here the significant elements of a symbol's meaning are related to what it does and what is done to it by and for whom. These aspects can only be understood if one takes into account from the beginning, and represents by appropriate theoretical constructs, the total field situation in which the symbol occurs. This situation would include the structure of the group that performs the ritual we observe, its basic organizing principles and perdurable relationships, and, in addition, its extant division into transient alliances and factions on the basis of immediate interest and ambitions, for both abiding structure and recurrent forms of conflict and selfish interest are stereotyped in ritual symbol-

ism. Once we have collected informants' interpretations of a given symbol, our work of analysis has indeed just begun. We must gradually approximate to the action-meaning of our symbol by way of what Lewin calls (1949, 149) "a stepwise increasing specificity" from widest to narrowest significant action context. Informants' "meanings" only become meaningful as objects of scientific study in the course of this analytical process. . . .

LEVELS OF SYMBOLIC MEANING

When we talk about the "meaning" of a symbol, we must be careful to distinguish between at least three levels or fields of meaning. These I propose to call: (1) the level of indigenous interpretation (or, briefly, the exegetical meaning); (2) the operational meaning; and (3) the positional meaning. The exegetical meaning is obtained from questioning indigenous informants about observed ritual behavior. Here again one must distinguish between information given by ritual specialists and information given by laymen, that is, between esoteric and exoteric interpretations. One must also be careful to ascertain whether a given explanation is truly representative of either of these categories or whether it is a uniquely personal view.

On the other hand, much light may be shed on the role of the ritual symbol by equating its meaning with its use, by observing what the Ndembu do with it, and not only what they say about it. This is what I call the operational meaning, and this level has the most bearing on problems of social dynamics. For the observer must consider not only the symbol but the structure and composition of the group that handles it or performs mimetic acts with direct reference to it. He must further note the affective qualities of these acts, whether they are aggressive, sad, penitent, joyful, derisive, and so on. He must also inquire why certain persons and groups are absent on given occasions, and if absent, whether and why they have been ritually excluded from the presence of the symbol.

The positional meaning of a symbol derives from its relationship to other symbols in a totality, a *Gestalt*, whose elements acquire their significance from the system as a whole. This level of meaning is directly related to the important property of ritual symbols . . ., their polysemy. Such symbols possess many senses, but contextually it may be necessary to stress one or a few of them only. Thus the *mukula* tree viewed in abstraction from any given ritual context may stand for "matriliny," "huntsmanship," "menstrual blood," "the meat of wild animals," and many other concepts and things. The associational link between its various senses is provided by the red gum it secretes, which Ndembu liken to blood. Now in the boys' circumcision ritual (*Mukanda*) the meaning of *mukula* is determined by its symbolic context. A log of this wood is placed near the site where the boys are circumcised. They are circumcised under a *mudyi* tree, which, as we shall see, stands *inter alia* for motherhood and the mother-child relationship. Then they are lifted over a cutting of the *muyombu* tree, which is customarily planted quickset as a shrine to the village ancestor spirits, and placed still bleeding on the *mukula* log. Here the *mukula* log stands mainly for two things. It represents the wish of the elders that the circumcision wounds will heal quickly (from the fact that *mukula* gum quickly coagulates like a scab). It also represents, I was told, masculinity (*wuyala*) and the life of an adult male, who as hunter and warrior has to shed blood. The rite represents (1) the removal of the boy from dependence on his mother (the passage from the *mudyi* tree); (2) his ritual death and subsequent association with the ancestors (the passage over the *muyombu* tree); and (3) his incorporation into the male moral community of tribesmen (the collective setting on the *mukula* tree where the boys are ceremonially fed as though they were infants by the circumcisers and by their fathers. Each boy is given a ball of cassava mush to be eaten directly from the circumciser's knife). In this rite the position of the *mukula* symbol with reference to other symbolic objects and acts is the crucial semantic factor.

The same symbol may be reckoned to have different senses at different phases in a ritual performance, or rather, different senses become paramount at different times. Which sense shall become paramount is determined by the ostensible purpose of the phase of the ritual in which it appears. For a ritual, like a space rocket, is phased, and each phase is directed towards a limited end which itself be-comes a means to the ultimate end of the total performance. Thus the act of circumcision is the aim and culmination of a symbol-loaded phase of the *Mukanda* ritual, but itself becomes a means to the final end of turning a boy into a tribesman. There is a consistent relationship between the end or aim of each phase in a ritual, the kind of symbolic configuration employed in that phase, and the senses that become paramount in multivocal symbols in that configuration.

I should now like to consider the exegetical meaning of one of the principal Ndembu ritual symbols, the *mudyi* tree. This symbol is found in more than half a dozen different kinds of ritual, but its *locus classicus* is in the girls' puberty ritual (*Nkang'a*). The novice is laid, wrapped in a blanket, at the foot of a slender young *mudyi* sapling. Ndembu say that its pliancy stands for the youth of the girl. The sapling has been previously consecrated by the novice's ritual instructress (*nkong'u*) and her mother. They have trampled down the grass in a circle around the tree, thus making it sacred—"set apart" (*chakumbadyi*) or "forbidden" (*chakujila*). The site, like that of circumcision for the boys, is called *ifwilu* or "the place of dying." Both sites are also known as *ihung'u*, "the place of suffering" or "ordeal." *Ihung'u* is also applied to a hut where a woman is in labor. It is a "place of suffering" because the novice must not move her limbs until nearly nightfall on penalty of being pinched all over by the older women; nor may she eat or speak all day. The association of the *mudyi* tree with suffering and dying should be borne in mind as an aspect of its positional meaning.

Ndembu begin the exposition of *mudyi*'s meaning by pointing out that if its bark is scratched, beads of milky latex are promptly secreted. For this reason they say that *mudyi* or "milk tree" is a symbol (*chinjikijilu*) for "breasts" and "breast milk"—both called in Chindembu *mayeli*. They go on from there to say that *mudyi* means "a mother and her child," a social relationship. They further extend this sense to signify a matrilineage (*ivumu*, literally "a womb or stomach"). A text which I collected well expresses this view:

Mudyi diku kwakaminiyi nkakulula hakumutembwisha ni ankukulula

The milk tree is the place where slept the (founding) ancestress, where they initiated her and another ancestress

mukwawu nimukwawu ni kudi nkaka ni kudi mama ninetu anyana;

and (then) another down to the grandmother and the mother and ourselves the children;

diku kumuchidi wetu kutwatachikili ni amayala nawa chochu hamu.

It is the place where our tribe (or tribal custom—literally "kind") began, also the men in just the same way.

My informant then added the following comments: "The milk tree is the place of all mothers; it is the ancestress of men and women. *Kutembwisha,* "to initiate a girl," means to dance round and round the milk tree where the novice lies. The milk tree is the place where our ancestors slept, to be initiated there means to become ritually pure or white. An uninitiated girl, a menstruating woman, or an uncircumcised boy is called "one who lacks whiteness (*wunabulakutooka*)."

Contextually, a particular novice's milk tree may be termed "her matrilineage." At one phase of the ritual, the leaves of this tree are said to represent "the novice's children"—a sense that is concerned with a future wished-for state of affairs rather than with the past or present.

In other phases of the *Nkang'a* ritual the milk tree is said to stand for "the women" and for "womanhood." It also has the situational sense of "married womanhood."

Finally, the milk tree stands for the process of learning (*kudiza*), especially for learning "women's sense" or "wisdom" (*mana yawambanda*). An informant said that "*mudyi*" is like going to school; "the girl drinks sense as a baby drinks milk."

The semantic structure of *mudyi* may itself be likened to a tree. At the root is the primary sense of "breast milk" and from this proceeds by logical steps series of further senses. The general direction is from the concrete to the increasingly abstract, but there are several different branches along which abstraction proceeds. One line develops as follows: breast, mother-child relationship, matriliny, the Ndembu tribe or tribal custom of which matriliny is the most representative principle. Another line runs: development of the breasts, womanhood, married woman-

hood, childbearing. Yet another goes from suckling to learning the tasks, rights, and duties of womanhood. As with many other Ndembu symbols, derivative senses themselves become symbols pointing to ideas and phenomena beyond themselves. Thus "matriliny," a derivative sense from "the mother-child" relationship, and "breast-milk," by the principle of *pars pro toto*, itself becomes a symbol for Ndembu culture in its totality.

However, despite this multiplicity of senses, Ndembu speak and think about the milk tree as a unity, almost as a unitary power. They can break down the concept "milk tree" cognitively into many attributes, but in ritual practice they view it as a single entity. For them it is something like Goethe's "eternal womanly," a female or maternal principle pervading society and nature. It must not be forgotten that ritual symbols are not merely signs representing known things; they are felt to possess ritual efficacy, to be charged with power from unknown sources, and to be capable of acting on persons and groups coming in contact with them in such a way as to change them for the better or in a desired direction. Symbols, in short, have an orectic as well as a cognitive function. They elicit emotion and express and mobilize desire.

Indeed, it is possible further to conceptualize the exegetic meaning of dominant symbols in polar terms. At one pole cluster a set of referents of a grossly physiological character, relating to general human experience of an emotional kind. At the other pole cluster a set of referents to moral norms and principles governing the social structure. If we call these semantic poles respectively the "orectic" and the "normative" pole, and consider Ndembu ritual symbols in terms of this model, we find that the milk tree stands at one and the same time for the physiological aspect of breast feeding with its associated affectual patterns, and for the normative order governed by matriliny. In brief, a single symbol represents both the obligatory and the desirable. Here we have an intimate union of the moral and the material. An exchange of qualities may take place in the psyches of the participants under the stimulating circumstances of the ritual performance, between orectic and normative poles; the former, through its association with the latter, becomes purged of its infantile and regressive character, while the normative pole becomes charged with the pleasurable effect associated with the breast-feeding situation. In one aspect, the tie of milk, under matriliny, develops into the primary structural tie, but in another aspect, and

here the polar model is apposite, the former stands opposed to and resists the formation of the latter.

BIBLIOGRAPHY

Durkheim, E. 1954. *Elementary Forms of the Religious Life*. London: Allen & Unwin.

Jung, Carl G. 1949. *Psychological Types*. London: Routledge & Kegan Paul.

Lewin, K. 1949. *Field Theory in Social Science*. London: Tavistock Publications.

Sapir, E. "Symbols," *Encyclopedia of the Social Sciences*, XIV. New York: Macmillan.

NOTE

1. I.e., objects not of indefinite duration but to which the category of time is not applicable.

Territorial Passage and the Classification of Rites

ARNOLD VAN GENNEP

Facts of publication: *van Gennep, Arnold. 1960 (1909). The Rites of Passage, 10–13, 15–25. Edited by Monika B. Vizedom and Gabrielle Caffee. Chicago: University of Chicago Press. Copyright © 1960 and renewed 1988 by Monika B. Vizedom. Reprinted with the permission of The University of Chicago Press.*

In this brief excerpt from Arnold van Gennep's classic work The Rites of Passage *we are introduced to his threefold enumeration of ritual phases: separation (preliminal), transition (liminal), incorporation (postliminal). Van Gennep makes clear that by "rites" of passage he does not mean whole rituals but rather phases, gestures, or other parts of some greater whole. Here he also articulates the basic metaphor that is the basis of his theory, namely, territorial passage across an international frontier or physical passage through a doorway (in Latin, a* limen*). On the basis of this one kind of ritualized action, van Gennep then treats societies as if they were rooms separated by doorways, portals, or passageways. Transition from one social status (or "room") to the next requires means of negotiating them, namely rites of passage.*

For an application of van Gennep's views see Thomas Leemon, The Rites of Passage in a Student Culture *(New York: Teacher's College, 1972).*

About the author: Dates: *1873–1957, French, born in Ludwigsburg, Germany.* **Education:** *École Pratique des Hautes Études (France); École des Langues Orientales (France).* **Field(s)**: *anthropology; ethnography; folklore.* **Career:** *Ministry of Agriculture, Paris; Professor of Ethnology, University of Neuchâtel (Switzerland), 1912–1915.* **Publications:** Mythes et legendes d'Australie *(E. Guilmoto, 1906);* Religions, mœurs et legendes *(Société du Mercure de France, 1908–14);* Le Folklore *(Stock, 1924);* Essai sur le culte populaire des saints fransciscains en Savoie *(J. Vrin, 1927);* Manuel de folklore français contemporain *(A. Picard, 1937–1958);* The Rites of Passage, *(University of Chicago, 1960 [1909]);* The Semi-Scholars *(Routledge, 1967);* Culte populaire des sainte en Savoie *(G.-P. Maisonneuve & Larose, 1973). See also* Bibliographie des oeuvres d'Arnold van Gennep *(Paris, 1964).*

I have tried to assemble here all the ceremonial patterns which accompany a passage from one situation to another or from one cosmic or social world to another. Because of the importance of these transitions, I think it legitimate to single out *rites of passage* as a special category, which under further analysis may be subdivided into *rites of separation, transition rites*, and *rites of incorporation*. These three sub categories are not developed to the same extent by all peoples or in every ceremonial pattern. Rites of separation are prominent in funeral ceremonies, rites of incorporation at marriages. Transition rites may play an important part, for instance, in pregnancy, betrothal, and initiation; or they may be reduced to a minimum in adoption, in the delivery of a second child, in remarriage, or in the passage from the second to the third age group. Thus, although a complete scheme of rites of passage theoretically includes preliminal rites (rites of separation), liminal rites (rites of transition), and postliminal rites (rites of incorporation), in specific instances these three types are not always equally important or equally elaborated.

Furthermore, in certain ceremonial patterns where the transitional period is sufficiently elaborated to constitute an independent state, the arrangement is reduplicated. A betrothal forms a liminal period between adolescence and marriage, but the passage from adolescence to betrothal itself involves a special series of rites of separation, a transition, and an incorporation into the betrothed condition; and the passage from the transitional period, which is betrothal, to marriage itself, is made through a series of rites of separation from the former, followed by rites consisting of transition, and rites of incorporation into marriage. The pattern of ceremonies comprising rites of pregnancy, delivery, and birth is equally involved. I am trying to group all these rites as clearly as possible, but since I am dealing with activities I do not expect to achieve as rigid a classification as the botanists have, for example.

It is by no means my contention that all rites of birth, initiation, marriage, and the like, are only rites of passage. For, in addition to their over-all goal—to insure a change of condition or a passage from one magico-religious or secular group to another—all these ceremonies have their individual purposes. Marriage ceremonies include fertility rites; birth ceremonies include protection and divination rites; funerals, defensive rites; initiations, propitiatory rites; ordinations, rites of attachment to the deity. All these rites, which have specific effective aims, occur in juxtaposition and combination with rites of passage—and are sometimes so intimately intertwined with them that it is impossible to distinguish whether a particular ritual is, for example, one of protection or of separation. This problem arises in relation to various forms of so-called purification ceremonies, which may simply lift a taboo and therefore remove the contaminating quality, or which may be clearly active rites, imparting the quality of purity.

In connection with this problem, I should like to consider briefly the pivoting of the sacred.[1] Characteristically, the presence of the sacred (and the performance of appropriate rites) is variable. Sacredness as an attribute is not absolute; it is brought into play by the nature of particular situations. A man at home, in his tribe, lives in the secular realm; he moves into the realm of the sacred when he goes on a journey and finds himself a foreigner near a camp of strangers. A Brahman belongs to the sacred world by birth; but within that world there is a hierarchy of Brahman families some of whom are sacred in relation to others. Every woman, though congenitally impure, is sacred to all adult men; if she is pregnant, she also becomes sacred to all other women of the tribe except her close relatives; and these other women constitute in relation to her a profane world, which at that moment includes all children and adult men. Upon performing so-called purification rites, a woman who has just given birth re-enters society, but she takes her place only in appropriate segments of it—such as her sex and her family—and she remains sacred in relation to the initiated men and to the magico-religious ceremonies. Thus the "magic circles" pivot, shifting as a person moves from one place in society to another. The categories and concepts which embody them operate in such a way that whoever passes through the various positions of a lifetime one day sees the sacred where before he has seen the profane, or vice versa. Such changes of condition do not occur without disturbing the life of society and the individual, and it is the function of rites of passage to reduce their harmful effects. That such changes are regarded as real and important is demonstrated by the recurrence of rites, in important ceremonies among widely differing peoples, enacting death in one condition and resurrection in another. These rites are rites of passage in their most dramatic form.

The Territorial Passage

Territorial passages can provide a framework for the discussion of rites of passage. Except in the few countries where a passport is still in use, a person in these days may pass freely from one civilized region to another.[2] The frontier, an imaginary line connecting milestones or stakes, is visible—in an exaggerated fashion—only on maps. But not so long ago the passage from one country to another, from one province to another within each country, and, still earlier, even from one manorial domain to another was accompanied by various formalities. These were largely political, legal, and economic, but some were of a magico-religious nature. For instance, Christians, Moslems, and Buddhists were forbidden to enter and stay in portions of the globe which did not adhere to their respective faiths.

It is this magico-religious aspect of crossing frontiers that interests us. To see it operating fully, we must seek out types of civilization in which the magico-religious encompassed what today is within the secular domain.

The territory occupied by a semicivilized tribe is usually defined only by natural features, but its inhabitants and their neighbors know quite well within what territorial limits their rights and prerogatives extend. The natural boundary might be a sacred rock, tree, river, or lake which cannot be crossed or passed without the risk of supernatural sanctions. Such natural boundaries are relatively rare, however. More often the boundary is marked by an object—a stake, portal, or upright rock (milestone or landmark)—whose installation at that particular spot has been accompanied by rites of consecration. Enforcement of the interdiction may be immediate, or it may be mediated by frontier divinities (such as Hermes, Priapus,[3] or the deities represented on the Babylonian *kudurru*). When milestones or boundary signs (e.g., a plow, an animal hide cut in thongs, a ditch) are ceremonially placed by a defined group on a delimited piece of earth, the group takes possession of it in such a way that a stranger who sets foot on it commits a sacrilege analogous to a profane person's entrance into a sacred forest or temple.

The idea of the sanctity of a territory so delimited has sometimes been confused with the belief in the sanctity of the entire earth as the Earth Mother.[4] In China, according to the most ancient documents, the deity was not the earth as such, but each plot of ground was sacred for its inhabitants and owners.[5] It seems to me that the ease of Loango,[6] the territory of Greek cities, and that of Rome,[7] are all analogous.

The prohibition against entering a given territory is therefore intrinsically magico-religious. It has been expressed with the help of milestones, walls, and statues in the classical world, and through more simple means among the semicivilized. Naturally, these signs are not placed along the entire boundary line. Like our boundary posts, they are set only at points of passage, on paths and at crossroads. A bundle of herbs, a piece of wood, or a stake adorned with a sheaf of straw may be placed in the middle of the path or across it.[8] The erection of a portal,[9] sometimes together with natural objects or crudely made statues,[10] is a more complicated means of indicating the boundary. The details of these various procedures need not concern us here.[11]

Today, in our part of the world, one country touches another; but the situation was quite different in the times when Christian lands comprised only a part of Europe. Each country was surrounded by a strip of neutral ground which in practice was divided into sections or marches. These have gradually disappeared, although the term "letter of marque"[12] retains the meaning of a permit to pass from one territory to another through a neutral zone. Zones of this kind were important in classical antiquity, especially in Greece, where they were used for market places or battle-fields.[13]

The same system of zones is to be found among the semicivilized, although here boundaries are less precise because the claimed territories are few in number and sparsely settled. The neutral zones are ordinarily deserts, marshes, and most frequently virgin forests where everyone has full rights to travel and hunt. Because of the pivoting of sacredness, the territories on either side of the neutral zone are sacred in relation to whoever is in the zone, but the zone, in turn, is sacred for the inhabitants of the adjacent territories. Whoever passes from one to the other finds himself physically and magico-religiously in a special situation for a certain length of time: he wavers between two worlds. It is this situation which I have designated a transition, and one of [my] purposes . . . is to demonstrate that this symbolic and spatial area of transition may be found in more or less pronounced form in all the ceremonies which accompany the passage from one social and magico-religious position to another.

* * *

With this introduction we now turn to some descriptions of territorial passages. When a king of Sparta went to war, he sacrificed to Zeus; if the prognostication was favorable, a torchbearer took fire from the altar and carried it in front of the army to the frontier. There the king sacrificed again, and if the fates again decreed in his favor he crossed the frontier with the torchbearer still preceding the army.[14] The rite of separation from one's own land at the moment of entering neutral territory was clearly acted out in this procedure. Several rites of frontier crossing have been studied by Trumbull,[15] who cites the following example: when General Grant came to Asyut, a frontier point in Upper Egypt, a bull was sacrificed as he disembarked. The head was placed on one side of the gangplank and the body on the other, so that Grant had to pass between them as he stepped over the spilled blood.[16] The rite of passing between the parts of an object that has been halved, or between two branches, or under something, is one which must, in a certain number of cases, be interpreted as a direct rite of passage by means of which a person leaves one world behind . . . and enters a new one.[17]

The procedures discussed apply not only in reference to a country or territory but also in relation to a village, a town, a section of a town, a temple, or a house. The neutral zone shrinks progressively till it ceases to exist except as a simple stone, a beam, or a threshold (except for the pronaos, the narthex, the vestibule, etc.).[18] The portal which symbolizes a taboo against entering becomes the postern of the ramparts, the gate in the walls of the city quarter, the door of the house. The quality of sacredness is not localized in the threshold only; it encompasses the lintels and architrave as well.[19]

The rituals pertaining to the door form a unit, and differences among particular ceremonies lie in technicalities: the threshold is sprinkled with blood or with purifying water; doorposts are bathed with blood or with perfumes; sacred objects are hung or nailed onto them, as on the architrave. Trumbull, in the monograph which he devoted to "the threshold covenant," bypassed the natural interpretation, although he wrote that the bronze threshold of Greece "is an archaic synonym for the enduring border, or outer limit, of spiritual domain."[20] Precisely: the door is the boundary between the foreign and domestic worlds in the case of an ordinary dwelling, between the profane and sacred worlds in the case of a temple. Therefore to cross the threshold is to unite oneself with a new world. It is thus an important act in marriage, adoption, ordination, and funeral ceremonies.

Rites of passing through the door need be stressed no further at this point. . . . It will be noted that the rites carried out on the threshold itself are transition rites. "Purifications" (washing, cleansing, etc.) constitute rites of separation from previous surroundings; there follow rites of incorporation (presentation of salt, a shared meal, etc.). The rites of the threshold are therefore not "union" ceremonies, properly speaking, but rites of preparation for union, themselves preceded by rites of preparation for the transitional stage.

Consequently, I propose to call the rites of separation from a previous world, *preliminal rites*, those executed during the transitional stage *liminal (or threshold) rites*, and the ceremonies of incorporation into the new world *postliminal rites*.

The rudimentary portal of Africa is very probably the original form of the isolated portals which were so highly developed in the Far East,[21] where they not only became independent monuments of architectural value (for example, porticoes of deities, of emperors, of widows) but also, at least in Shintoism and Taoism, are used as ceremonial instruments.[22] This evolution from the magic portal to the monument seems also to have occurred in the case of the Roman arch of triumph. The victor was first required to separate himself from the enemy world through a series of rites, in order to be able to return to the Roman world by passing through the arch. The rite of incorporation in this case was a sacrifice to Jupiter Capitoline and to the deities protecting the city.[23]

In the instances cited thus far the efficacy of the ritual portal has been direct. But the portal may also be the seat of a particular deity. When "guardians of the threshold" take on monumental proportions, as in Egypt, in Assyro-Babylonia (winged dragons, the sphinx, and all sorts of monsters),[24] and in China (in the form of statues), they push the door and the threshold into the background; prayers and sacrifices are addressed to the guardians alone. A rite of spatial passage has become a rite of spiritual passage. The act of passing no longer accomplishes the passage; a personified power insures it through spiritual means.[25]

The two forms of portal rituals mentioned above seldom occur in isolation; in the great majority of cases they are combined. In the various ceremonies one may see the direct rite combined with the indirect, the dynamistic rite with the animistic, either to remove possible obstacles to the passage or to carry out the passage itself.

Among the ceremonies of territorial passage those pertaining to the crossing of mountain passes should also be cited. These include the depositing of various objects (stones, bits of cloth, hair, etc.), offerings, invocations of the spirit of the place, and so forth. They are to be found, for instance, in Morocco (*kerkour*), Mongolia, Tibet (*obo*), Assam, the Andes, and the Alps (in the form of chapels). The crossing of a river is often accompanied by ceremonies,[26] and a corresponding negative rite is found where a king or a priest is prohibited from crossing a certain river or any flowing water. Likewise, the acts of embarking and disembarking, of entering a vehicle or a litter, and of mounting a horse to take a trip are often accompanied by rites of separation at the time of departure and by rites of incorporation upon return.

Finally, in some cases the sacrifices associated with laying the foundation for a house and constructing a house fall into the category of rites of passage. It is curious that they have been studied in isolation, since they are part of a homogeneous ceremonial whole, the ceremony of changing residence.[27] Every new house is *taboo* until, by appropriate rites, it is made *noa* (secular or profane).[28] In form and dynamics, the lifting of this taboo resembles those pertaining to a sacred territory or woman: there is washing or lustration or a communal meal. Other practices are intended to insure that the

house remains intact, does not crumble, and so forth. Scholars have been wrong in interpreting some of these practices as survivals and distortions of an ancient custom of human sacrifice. Ceremonies to lift a taboo, to determine who will be the protecting spirit, to transfer the first death, to insure all sorts of future security, are followed by rites of incorporation: libations, ceremonial visiting, consecration of the various parts of the house, the sharing of bread and salt or a beverage, the sharing of a meal. (In France, a housewarming is given, called literally, "hanging the pothook.") These ceremonies are essentially rites identifying the future inhabitants with their new residence. When the inhabitants—for instance, a betrothed man or a young husband and his family or his wife—build the house themselves, the ceremonies begin at the very start of construction.

Rites of entering a house, a temple, and so forth, have their counterpart in rites of exit, which are either identical or the reverse. At the time of Mohammed, the Arabs stroked the household god when entering and when leaving,[29] so that the same gesture was a rite of incorporation or a rite of separation, depending on the case. In the same way, whenever an Orthodox Jew passes through the main door of a house, a finger of his right hand touches the mezuzah, a casket attached to the doorpost which contains a piece of paper or a ribbon upon which is written or embroidered the sacred name of God (Shaddai). He then kisses the finger and says, "The Lord shall preserve thy going out and thy coming in from this time forth evermore."[30] The verbal rite is here joined to the manual one.

It will be noted that only the main door is the site of entrance and exit rites, perhaps because it is consecrated by a special rite or because it faces in a favorable direction. The other openings do not have the same quality of a point of transition between the familial world and the external world. Therefore thieves (in civilizations other than our own) prefer to enter otherwise than through the door; corpses are removed by the back door or the window; a pregnant or menstruating woman is allowed to enter and leave through a secondary door only; the cadaver of a sacred animal is brought in only through a window or a hole; and so forth. These practices are intended to prevent the pollution of a passage which must remain uncontaminated once it has been purified by special ceremonies. Spitting or stepping on it, for instance, [is] forbidden. But sometimes the sacred value of the threshold is present in all the thresholds of the house. In Russia I saw houses in which little horseshoes, used to protect the heels of boots, were nailed on the threshold of every room. In addition, every room in these houses had its own icon.

In order to understand rites pertaining to the threshold, one should always remember that the threshold is only a part of the door and that most of these rites should be understood as direct and physical rites of entrance, of waiting, and of departure—that is, as rites of passage.

NOTES

1. This pivoting was already well understood by Smith (see *The Religion of the Semites*, pp. 427–28 and discussion of "taboo," pp. 152–53, 451–54, etc.). Compare the passage from sacred to profane, and vice versa, among the Tarahumara and the Huichol of Mexico as described by Karl Sofus Lumholtz, *Unknown Mexico: A Record of Five Years' Exploration among the Tribes of Western Sierra Madre* (London: C. Scribner's Sons, 1903), *passim*.

2. [It should be remembered that van Gennep wrote in the first decade of the twentieth century.] (Vizedom & Caffee note)

3. Here is my interpretation (as yet to be fully demonstrated) of the almost universal association between landmarks and the phallus: (1) There is an association of the stake or the upright rock with the penis in erection; (2) the idea of union associated with the sexual act has a certain magical significance; (3) pointed objects (horns, fingers, etc.) are believed to protect through their power to "pierce" the evil influences, the wicked jinn, etc.; (4) *very seldom* is there the idea of the fecundity of the territory and its inhabitants. The phallic symbolism of landmarks has almost no truly sexual significance.

4. Several interpretations by Dieterich (in *Mutter Erde*), which I believe to be incorrect, will be discussed with reference to birth and childhood.

5. "In the ancient Chinese religion there was a god of the soil for each district (no doubt for twenty-five families); the king had a god of the soil for his people and one for his own personal use; the same was true for each feudal lord, each group of families, each imperial dynasty. Those gods presided over war, which was created us a punishment; they were fashioned from a piece of wood and associated with gods of the harvest. It seems to me that the earth goddess came later as a result of several syncretisms" (Eduard Chavannes, "Le dieu du sol dans l'ancienne religion chinoise," *Revue de l'histoire des religions*, XLIII [1901], 124–27, 140–44).

6. Cf. E. Dennett, *At the Back of the Black Man's Mind: Or Notes on the Kingly Office in West Africa* (London: Macmillan, 1906), and Eduard Pechüel-Loesche, *Volkskunde von Loango* (Stuttgart: Strecher & Schroeder, 1907).

7. Cf. W. Warde Fowler's interesting discussion titled "Lustratio" in *Anthropology and the Classics*, ed. Robert R. Marett (Oxford, 1908), pp. 173–78. My readers will, I hope, accept the view that *lustratio* is nothing more than a rite of territorial separation, cosmic or human (e.g., return from war).

8. To the references given by H. Grierson in *The Silent Trade* (Edinburgh, 1903), pp. 12–14, n. 4 (where, unfortunately, the rites of appropriation and the taboos of passage have been confused), add: Dennett, *At the Back of the Black Man's Mind*,

pp. 90, 153, n. 192; Pechüel-Loesche, *Volkskunde von Loango*, pp. 223–24, 456, 472, etc.; J. Büttikofer, *Reisebilder aus Liberia* (Leiden, 1890), II, 304; van Gennep, *Tabou et totémismo à Madagascar*, pp. 183–86 (taboos of passage); J. M. M. Van der Burght, *Dictionnaire français Kirundi: Avec l'indication succincte de la signification swahili et allemande augmente d'une introduction et de 196 articles ethnologiques sur les Urundi et les Warundi* (Bar-le-Duc: Société d'Illustration Catholique, 1904), s.v. "Iviheko," etc. The custom of planting a stake surmounted with a sheaf of straw to prohibit the entrance into a path or field is very widespread in Europe.

9. Paul B. du Chaillu (in *L'Afrique sauvage: Nouvelles excursions au pays des Ashongos* [Paris: Michel Levy Frères, 1868], p. 38, from the English; *Journey to Ashango Land* [New York, D. Appleton Co, 1867]), mentions a portal with sacred plants, chimpanzee skulls, etc. (in the Congo). Portals formed by two stakes driven into the ground with a pole running between them, on which hang skulls, eggs, etc., are often found on the Ivory Coast as taboos of passage and protection against the spirits (oral report by Maurice Delafosse); Pechüel-Loesche, *Volkskunde von Loango*, figures on p. 224, 472, etc.

10. See among others for Surinam, K. Martin. "Bericht uber eine Reise ins Gebiet des oberen Surinam," *Bijdragen tot de Taai-Land on Volkekunde von Nederlands* Indie (The Hague). XXXV (1886), 28–29. Figure 2 shows a statue with two faces which I compared to *Janus bifrons* in an article of the same title in *Revue des traditions populaires*, XXII (1907), No. 4, 97–98. It confirms Frazer's theory in *Lectures on the Early History of the Kingship*, p. 289.

11. Occasionally in Loango a palisade is erected across the road (Du Chaillu, *L'Afrique sauvage*, p. 133) to prevent diseases from entering the territory of the villages; Büttikofer (*Reisebilder aus Liberia*, p. 304) mentions a barricade of straw matting used to prevent access to sacred forests where initiation rites take place; perhaps the barriers made from branches and from straw matting found in Australia and in New Guinea serve this purpose, rather than simply that of hiding from the profane what is going on there, as is usually thought.

12. Letters of marque originally constituted a license from a sovereign authorizing a subject to seek reprisals against subjects of a hostile state for injuries inflicted by that state. In later times these letters enabled privateers to commit acts against a hostile nation which otherwise would have been considered piracy. In Europe, letters of marque were abolished by the Congress of Paris in 1856. (See *Oxford English Dictionary*.)]

13. On the subject of sacred zones and bands of neutral territory, see Grierson, *The Silent Trade*, pp. 29, 56–59; and on frontiers and signs of sacred frontiers in Palestine and Assyro-Babylonia, see H. Gressmann, "Mythische Reste in der Paradieserzählung," *Archiv für Religionswissenschaft*, X (1907), 361–63 n. On the feast of the Terminalia in Rome, see W. Warde Fowler, *The Roman Festivals of the Period of the Republic* (London: Macmillan, 1899), pp. 325–27. It seems likely that the Capitoline Hill was originally one of those neutral zones of which I speak (Fowler, p. 317), as well as a frontier between the city of the Palatine and that of the Quirinal: see also *Roscher's Lexikon*, s.v. "Jupiter," col. 668, and W. Warde Fowler in *Anthropology and the Classics* pp. 18] ff. on the subject of the pomerium.
14. See Frazer, *The Golden Bough*, I, 305.
15. H. Clay Trumbull, *The Threshold Covenant: Or the Beginning of Religious Rites* (New York: Charles Scribner's Sons, 1896), pp. 184–96. I wish to thank Mr. Salomon Reinach for lending me this book, which is difficult to find.
16. *Ibid.*, p. 186. Trumbull's thesis is that the blood which was shed is a symbol, if not an agent of union.
17. A collection of these rites has been published in *Mélusine: Recueil de mythologie, littérature populaire, tradition, et usages* (Paris: Gaidoz & Rolland, 1878–1912). A few imply the transfer of a disease, but what are commonly called rites of purification suggest the idea of a transition from the impure to the pure. All these ideas, and the rites to which they correspond, often form a single ceremonial grouping.
18. For details on the rites of passage pertaining to the threshold, I refer you to Trumbull's *The Threshold Covenant*. Some prostrate themselves before the threshold, some kiss it, some touch it with their hands, some walk upon it or remove their shoes before doing so, some step over it, some are carried over it, etc. See also William Crooke, "The Lifting of the Bride," *Folk-lore*, XIII (1902), 238–42. All these rites vary from people to people and become more complicated if the threshold is the seat of the spirit of the house, the family, or the threshold god.
19. For a detailed list of Chinese practices with reference to doors, see Justus Doolittle, *Social Life of the Chinese with Some Account of the Religious, Governmental, Educational, and Business Customs and Opinions with Special but Not Exclusive Reference to Fuhchau* (New York: Harper, 1865), I, 121–22; II, 310–12; Wilhelm Grube, *Zur pekinger Volkskunde* (Berlin, 1902), pp. 93–97. On magical ornamentation pertaining to the door, see Trumbull, *The Threshold Covenant*, pp. 69–74, 323.
20. I cannot share Trumbull's view that the threshold is a primitive altar and the altar a transplanted threshold, nor can I attribute a greater importance to the presence of blood in rites pertaining to the threshold than to the use of water or simple contact. All these are rites of incorporation or union.
21. [This statement appears to be primarily speculative.]
22. For China, see Gisbert Combaz, *Sépultures impériales de la Chine* (Brussels: Vromant & Co., 1908), pp. 27–33; Doolittle, *Social Life of the Chinese*, II, 299–300. For Japan, see W. E. Griffis, in Trumbull, *The Threshold Covenant*, Appendix, pp. 320–24; B. H. Chamberlain, *Things Japanese: Notes on Various Subjects Connected with Japan for the Use of Travellers*

and Others (London: Paul, 1891, p. 356, s.v. "torii"); N. Gordon Munro, "Primitive Culture in Japan," *Transactions of the Asiatic Society of Japan*, XXXIV (1906), 144.
23. For the order of rites of triumph, see Le Père Bernard de Montfaucon, O.S.B., *Antiquités expliquées et représentées en figures* (Paris: F. Delaulne, 1719), 2d ed.; IV, 152–61.
24. Regarding these divinities and the rites pertaining to them, see Eugène Lefebure, *Rites égyptiens: Construction et protection des édifices* (Paris: E. Leroux, 1890); for the Assyrian winged bulls, see p. 62.
25. Regarding the divinities of the threshold, see (in addition to Trumbull, *The Threshold Covenant*, pp. 94 ff.): L. R. Farnell, "The Place of the Sonder-götter in Greek Polytheism," in *Anthropological Essays Presented to E. B. Tylor*, p. 82; and Frazer, *The Golden Bough*. In China they are ordinarily Shen-Shu and Jü-Lü (see Jan M. de Groot and Eduard Chavannes, *Les fêtes annuellement célébrées à Emouy* [Paris, 1886], pp. 597 ff.) but in Peking also Ch'in-Ch'iung and Yü-chih-Kung (see Grube, *Zur pekinger Volkskunde*). For Japan see Isabella L. Bird, *Unbeaten Tracks in Japan: Travels in the Interior, Including Visits to the Aborigines of Yozzo and the Shrine of Nikko* (London: J. Murray, 1905), I, 117, 273; Revon, "Le shinntoisme," pp. 389, 390; Munro, "Primitive Culture in Japan," p. 144, etc.
26. See among others H. Gaidoz, *Étude de la mythologie gauloise*, Vol. I: *Le dieu gaulois du soleil et le symbolisme de la roue* (Paris: E. Leroux, 1886), p. 65; I recall the ceremonies of construction and of the opening of bridges (cf. "pontifex"). As for rites of passing between or under something, they have been collected in *Mélusine* and by almost all folklore students. They should all be discussed again, but it will be impossible to do so at this time. Therefore I will cite only the following, taken from Stepan Petrovitch Krašeninnikov, *Histoire et description du Kamtchatka*, trans. from the Russian by M. de Saint Pré (Amsterdam: M. M. Rey, 1760), I, 130–31; and see p. 136: "Soon afterward, they brought birch branches into the yurt, according to the number of families represented. Each Kamchadal took one of these branches for his family, and after bending it into a circle he made his wife and children pass through it twice; as they emerged from this hoop, they began to spin around. Among them this is called being purified of one's faults."

It is apparent from the detailed descriptions by Krašeninnikov that the birch is a sacred tree for the Kamchadals and that it is used ritually in most of their ceremonies. Two interpretations are possible: direct sanctification may occur under the influence of the birch, which is considered *pure*, or a transference of impurity from the people to the birch may take place. The latter seems to be in keeping with the rest of the ceremony: "When all had been purified, the Kamchadals came out of the yurt with these small branches through the *župan*, or the lower opening, and they were followed by their relatives of both sexes. As soon as they were out of the yurt, they passed through the birch circle for the second time and then stuck the little branches in the snow, bending the end towards the east. After throwing all their *tonšič* on this spot and shaking their clothing, the Kamchadals re-entered the yurt by the ordinary opening and not by the *župan*." In other words, they rid themselves of the sacred material impurities which had accumulated in their clothes, and of their most important ritual object, the *tonšič* (which together with "sweet grass," etc., comprises their category of sacra). The branches, which had been endowed with the sacred, are thrown away.

The passage through the sacred arcs automatically removes from the celebrants the sacred characteristics which they acquired by performing the complicated ceremonies that this rite terminates. These circles form the portal which separates the sacred world from the profane world, so that, once they have entered the profane, the performers of the ceremony are again able to use the big door of the hut.

27. Regarding construction sacrifices, see Paul Satori ("Über das Bauopfer," *Zeitschrift für Ethnologie*, XXX [1898], 1–54), who did not see that a few of them are rites of appropriation. For French rites, see Paul Sébillot, *Le folk-lore de la France* (Paris: E. Guilmoto, 1907), IV, 96–98; and for various theories, see Trumbull, *The Threshold Covenant*, pp. 45–57, and Edvard Alexander Westermarck, *The Origin and Development of Moral Ideas* (London: Macmillan, 1906–8), I, 461. Those rites fall into a wider category which I call the "rites of the first time." The charm 43, 3–15, of the Kausika-

sutra (W. Calland, *Altindisches Zauberrei: Darstellung der altindischen Wunschopfer* [Amsterdam: J. Muller, 1900], pp. 147–48) not only is connected with construction and with entering but also is mentioned in people's and animals' changing of dwellings.

28. For a typical ceremony, see W. L. Hildburgh, "Notes on Sinhalese Magic," *Journal of the Royal Anthropological Institute*, XXXVIII (1908), 190.

29. Smith, *The Religion of the Semites*, pp. 461–62.

30. Trumbull, *The Threshold Covenant*, pp. 69–70, with reference to Syria. [Van Gennep evidently relied on Trumbull for this information. According to *The Jewish Encyclopedia*, ed. Isidore Singer (New York and London: Funk & Wagnalls, 1916), the prayer at the door is translated as "may God keep my going out and my coming in from now on and evermore." The inside of the mezuzah contains the words of Deuteronomy 6 : 4–9 and 11 : 13–21, both of which exhort the Jews to love and obey God, and which command them to write God's name on their doors and gateposts. "Shaddai" is written on the outside of the mezuzah, which is touched and kissed in passing through the door.]

Consumption Rituals of Thanksgiving Day

MELANIE WALLENDORF
ERIC J. ARNOULD*

Facts of publication: *Wallendorf, Melanie, and Eric J. Arnould. 1991. " 'We Gather Together': Consumption Rituals of Thanksgiving Day," Journal of Consumer Research 18: 13–14, 17–31. Copyright © 1991 by The Journal of Consumer Research, Inc. Reprinted with the permission of the author and The University of Chicago Press.*

Thanksgiving Day is perhaps the most widely practiced rite in the United States. Because of its commercial and secular character, it is rarely considered a ritual occasion and has been overlooked by students of ritual. Not only do consumer researchers Wallendorf and Arnould show how ritually complex Thanksgiving is, they also argue that the activities of this holiday constitute a discourse among consumers about cultural categories and principles. They assert that ritualized consumption activities construct, as well as reflect, culture.

Further readings on ritual and consumption can be found in Russell Belk, Melanie Wallendorf, and John F. Sherry Jr., "The Sacred and Profane in Consumer Behavior: Theodicy on the Odyssey," Journal of Consumer Research 16 (1989):1–38.

*The authors thank Helen Anderson, Ann Carl, Bob Kafes, Jane Courtland, Deb Heisley, Sheldon Fishman, Marjorie Lyles, Grant McCracken, Heather McManus, Gayathri Mani, Bob Netting, Lisa Penaloza, Dennis Rook, John Sherry, David Snow, and Jerry Zaltman for their generous insights and helpful comments on earlier portions and presentations of this work. The authors would most especially like to thank their 100 junior collaborators, who were students in Professor Wallendorf's marketing research classes in the fall term of 1988. Their openness, eagerness to learn, and hard work made it possible to study Thanksgiving Day celebrations in situ.

About the author: *Melanie R. Wallendorf* **Dates:** *1952– , Jefferson City, MO, U.S.A.* **Education:** *B.B.A., Southern Methodist University; M.A., University of Pittsburgh; Ph.D., University of Pittsburgh.* **Field(s):** *consumer behavior; sociology of consumption, marketing.* **Career:** *Professor of Marketing and of Comparative Culture and Literary Studies, University of Arizona.* **Publications:** *with Russell Belk, "The Sacred Meaning of Money,"* Journal of Economics and Psychology *11 (1990): 35–67; with Russell Belk and John F. Sherry Jr. "The Sacred and the Profane in Consumer Behavior: Theodicy on the Odyssey,"* Journal of Consumer Research *16 (1989): 1–38; with Russell Belk and John F. Sherry Jr., "A Naturalistic Inquiry into Buyer and Seller Behavior at a Swap Meet,"* Journal of Consumer Research *14 (1988): 449–470; with Daniel Nelson, "An Archaeological Examination of Ethnic Differences in Body Care Rituals,"* Psychology and Marketing, *3 (1987): 273–289; with Michael Reilly, "A Comparison of Group Differences in Food Consumption Using Household Refuse,"* Journal of Consumer Research, *14 (1987), 289–294; with Michael Reily, "Ethnic Migration, Assimilation, and Consumption,"* Journal of Consumer Research, *10 (1983): 292–302.*

About the author: *Eric Arnould:* **Dates:** *1951– , Chicago, IL, U.S.A.* **Education:** *B.A., Bard College; M.A., University of Arizona; Ph.D., University of Arizona.* **Field(s):** *consumer behavior; services marketing; development anthropology; anthropology of markets and marketing.* **Career:** *Associate Professor of Marketing, 1994–present, University of South Florida; Associate Professor of Marketing, 1991–1994, California State University, Long Beach; Assistant Professor of Anthropology, 1990–1991, University of Colorado at Denver; Research Associate, 1986–1990, Office of Arid Lands Studies, University of Arizona.* **Publications:** *editor, with Robert Netting and Richard R. Wilk,* Households: Changing Form and Function *(University of California, 1984); with Richard R. Wilk, "Why Do the Natives Wear Adidas? Anthropological Approaches to Consumer Research,"* Advances in Consumer Research *12 (1984): 748–758. "Toward a Broadened Theory of Preference Formation and the Diffusion of Innovations: Cases from Zinder Province, Niger Republic,"* Journal of Consumer Research *16 (1989): 239–267; "Changing the Terms of Rural Development: Collaborative Research in Cultural Ecology in the Sahel,"* Human Organization *49.4 (1990). 339–354, with Linda L. Price, "River Magic: Hedonic Consumption and the Extended Service Encounter,"* Journal of Consumer Research *20 (1993): 24–45; with Melanie Wallendorf, "Market-Oriented Ethnography: Interpretation Building and Marketing Strategy,"* Journal of Marketing Research *(forthcoming);* **Additional:** *"The long-term themes of my research fall into the following categories: consumption ritual, diffusion of innovations, household organization and decision making, services marketing, West African market organization, and economic development. My current research includes study of the relationship between channel structure and consumer outcomes in West Africa, the affective and ritual dimensions of commercial service encounters, and U.S. holiday consumption behaviors. Underlying each of these topical interests is an overall curiosity about the relationship between marketing and culture and culture and consumer behavior."*

Thanksgiving Day is a national holiday celebrated in the United States on the fourth Thursday in November. The day is set aside by decree of the national government so its citizens can give thanks for what they have. Thanksgiving commonly is celebrated by eating what participants regard as a traditional feast featuring a whole stuffed turkey as the main meat dish. Prototypical consumption of the meal occurs within nuclear- and extended-family units in private households. Televised morning parades and afternoon football games bracket the repast taken in early or mid-afternoon. Many regard the day as opening the holiday season (Myers 1972), which extends to Christmas one month later and then to New Year's celebrations the following week.

Thanksgiving Day is a collective ritual that celebrates material abundance enacted through feasting. We interpret the consumption rituals of Thanksgiving Day as a discourse among consumers about cultural categories and principles. We read the holiday as a discussion and negotiation carried on symbolically through consumption. Like other holidays (Caplow and Williamson 1980), the cultural discourse of Thanksgiving Day negotiates larger meanings that are difficult, if not impossible, for many participants to acknowledge, articulate, and negotiate verbally. Unlike the personal rituals described by Rook (1985), more universal themes of American culture are emphasized. Unlike the annual rituals of conflict described by Dirks (1988), Thanksgiving Day celebrations both mark and prove to participants their ability to meet basic needs amply through consumption. So certain is material plenty for most U.S. citizens that its annual celebration is taken for granted, unlike the harvest celebrations of some groups (Cohen and Coffin 1987; Mennell 1985). Not just a moment of bounty, but a culture of enduring prosperity is celebrated.

Systematic study of Thanksgiving Day celebrations can aid our understanding of contemporary U.S. consumer behavior in at least four ways. First, it provides a vehicle to explore the ways consumption actively constructs culture. Consumption is not treated here as a passive response to exogenous cultural factors, as the relationship between culture and consumption is depicted in most consumer-behavior textbooks (for an alternative treatment, see McCracken 1986). Instead, consumption is viewed as an active force in the construction of culture. Second, study of the Thanksgiving Day celebration opens the possibility of developing an understanding of the linkages and ellipses between self-conscious consumer ideology[1] on the one hand and observed consumer praxis[2] on the other. Third, studying the celebration of Thanksgiving Day adds to our understanding of the meanings attached to material abundance and satisfaction through consumption. Finally, the study of Thanksgiving Day challenges us to unravel the complexity of the notion of tradition and the role of manufactured products vis-à-vis homemade ones. Despite being a major holiday, Thanksgiving Day, for the most part, has been ignored by social scientists (for an exception, see Linton and Linton 1949) and consumer researchers alike. . . .

THE MEANINGS OF THANKSGIVING DAY

Five conceptual themes are used to organize our interpretation of the meanings of Thanksgiving Day:

(1) negotiation of abundance; (2) extensiveness of inclusion; (3) resolution of universalism and particularism: (4) negotiation of values, such as cleanliness, not wasting, and hard work; and (5) negotiation of the role of produce and branded food products vis-à-vis tradition and homemade foods. In this discussion, we organize data materials around these five conceptual themes rather than chronologically as they might appear throughout the day.

Thanksgiving Day Consumption as Negotiated Abundance

Thanksgiving Day ritual is guided by no written liturgy; the details of its celebration, like the past and future, are actively negotiated among participants, and not always harmoniously. Emic[3] understandings revealed in depth interviews gloss Thanksgiving Day enactments as stable over time. Yet active negotiation of change and variation over the life cycle as well as across historical epochs (Appelbaum 1984) in making "the plans" and celebrating the holiday are apparent in participant-observation notes. Meanings and emotions, beliefs and values are the emergent artifacts of this ritual process, not all of which are recognized by informants.

In particular, Thanksgiving Day ritual negotiates the presence and meaning of abundance to the household and more broadly to the culture. In this section we discuss the way elements of the ritual are employed in negotiating abundance.

Abundance Embodied. Since Thanksgiving Day is a celebration of material plenty, participants deliberate to insure that everyone agrees there is abundance. In conformity with Puritan tradition (Farb and Armelagos 1980; Mennell 1985), the primary focus is the quantity of food rather than its quality. It tends to be wholesome but plain and simple rather than complex. The amount of food, rather than elaboration and delicacy, is foremost in people's minds (Mennell 1985). More dishes are served at the observed feasts than at everyday dinners. Jokes, a telling cultural form (Freud [1905] 1960), are made. Someone facetiously asks whether 14 potatoes will make enough mashed potatoes for six people, yet preparations in the kitchen continue.

The abundance celebrated on Thanksgiving Day

resonates (McQuarry 1989) across many components of the menu. "Stuffing" and "loading" are redundant at the meal. The turkey is stuffed. Mashed potatoes are loaded with butter and then topped with gravy. The relish tray contains stuffed green olives and pitted black olives that children stuff with their fingers, despite parental disapproval. Pie crusts are filled with fruit or flavored custards and topped with whipped cream, ice cream, or meringue. The themes of stuffing and loading in food are echoed in other elements of the feast. The table or buffet is loaded with serving dishes. The house is filled with people who crowd around the table to eat. Sometimes there is a cornucopia centerpiece filled with the harvest's abundance. Even variations resonate with the theme; a hostess of Italian descent delivered the correct metonymic[4] message by choosing cannoli a pastry filled with cream, for dessert.

Thanksgiving Day abundance is also represented on the plates of participants. Photographs show plates so loaded with food that they are difficult to balance while walking from buffet to table. Unlike the typical service of one main course and two side dishes at everyday dinners (Douglas 1972), Thanksgiving plates are filled with so many different foods that they run together.

To insure that the feast represents abundance to everyone, an almost universal topic of after-dinner conversation is that everyone has overeaten and is painfully full. Men's postures are noticeably different from that before the meal. Stuffed bellies feel more comfortable outstretched, with hips forward on the chair seat and arms sometimes resting overhead on the back of the chair. This contrasts with the more upright before-dinner posture.

So important is it that the group come to consensus about the experience of surfeit that when—but not if—to serve dessert takes a particular form . . . . When the hostess first offers dessert, participants decide to wait because they are "too full." Instead of feeling rejected, the hostess feels successful in feeding them well. The time-lapse between dinner and dessert varies from a few minutes to clear the dishes to several hours.

Unlike everyday dinners, Thanksgiving Day celebrants verbally negotiate consensus about the experience of material abundance. Physical pain is commonly evoked, but people are proud and pleased to have "eaten too much." Semiotically, they embody[5] (Merleau-Ponty [1945] 1962, [1942] 1963) the material surplus and ability to meet basic needs that will be taken for granted the rest of the year. To preclude later questioning of whether surfeit abides, they prove decisively and even painfully its universality. Not even one participant should voice continued hunger. Diners meet urgings to eat just one more small serving of a preferred dish with the insistence that they are stuffed. During the meal, some may say that they want to "save room for pie," but later confess to having no more room. It would feel good to wait a while before proceeding. Their personal storehouses, like the granaries of the agriculturally based consumer culture they each metonymically echo, are charged with the basics. Food at this moment reflects more than personal preferences; it unconsciously mirrors social relations and processes. Fullness will endure (Barthes 1975; Mennell 1985). By negotiating consensus about a desire to delay having dessert, participants agree on their fullness. Lest there be any doubt, they then stuff themselves once again with dessert and later with leftovers, proving that threats of future material scarcity are quickly and easily held at bay.

Abundance is also embodied by pregnant women who guarantee familial continuity. . . . Some families making special mention of welcoming a new family member at the meal-opening prayer or toast. Pregnancy assures a sufficient quantity of family members and in this way is connected to the Thanksgiving Day celebration of abundance. The pregnant woman is a living cornucopia, a metaphor of continued abundance, the ritual message of Thanksgiving Day.

Forgetting as a Consequence of Abundance.
The Thanksgiving Day celebration is so complex and semiotically dense in number of foods and people that very often not everything goes according to the host and hostess's plans. Since there is no written liturgy to insure exact replication each year, sometimes things are forgotten. Participants regard forgetting as unusual in their emic perspective. However, an etic[6] perspective based in reading many sets of fieldnotes indicates that forgetting something and resolving this minor disruption through forgiveness is a common part of the event.

Reading the fieldnotes, we learn that this family forgot to say the prayer and that hostess forgot to prepare the rolls. In the emic perspective, forgetting is an understandable consequence of the abundance of the feast; there is "just so much" to do, eat, and remember that something was forgotten. From an etic perspective, resolving this incident negotiates the importance of abundance and defines what is really important. Resolution is guided but not dictated by the emic ideology of Thanksgiving Day as a celebration of family togetherness, a theme that was revealed in depth interviews. . . .

Reassurance by other participants that all is well in spite of something being forgotten is important. The lesson made visible is that, even when striving to achieve abundance, omissions and human failings are ordinary and acceptable. . . . Abundance is important, but omissions are accepted.

When functioning properly, the ritual, like the family it represents, is robust and tolerant of variation. When functioning improperly, forgetfulness may construct or resurrect intolerance and lack of acceptance. Thus forgetfulness, when accompanied by acceptance and forgiveness, reinforces the core familial values associated with the ritual. The emic perspective that forgetting is unusual and tangential differs from but contributes to the emergent etic perspective. Because forgetting is emically regarded as unusual, it is actively discussed and resolved. This leads to the etic interpretation that forgetfulness is a widespread and ordered part of the negotiated ritual message that celebrates and enacts abundance and family togetherness through consumption.

Mealtime Hush as a Consequence of Abundance.

As we also found in our own fieldwork, fieldnotes written by some junior collaborators mention that conversation during the meal dropped to little besides occasional requests to pass condiments or a serving plate or compliments on a particular dish. . . . There is just so much food that people focus on incorporating its abundance rather than on talking during this period of time. . . . As each person chooses to concentrate on consuming without self-restraint, there is no talk (Mennell 1985).

Taking a Walk as a Consequence of Abundance.

In a number of instances, after the meal is finished and sometimes before dessert is served, par-

ticipants decide to take a stroll. When this action is suggested, almost everyone agrees that it would feel good because they are so full. Some may claim to be too full to do anything but take a nap on the sofa. When a walk is taken, there is usually no destination in mind, and length and pace are determined by local weather. Because it takes place after the integrative meal, the walk may include a mixed-gender group as well as a mixed-age group. It is an activity that draws a boundary around the group rather than within it. Subgroups may form for conversation during the walk, depending on the size of the group walking. . . . In deciding to take a walk, as in the decisions to delay dessert or take a nap, participants affirm their agreement about experiencing abundance (satiety). Through these actions, they prove abundance to themselves.

Type of Abundance Celebrated.

The kind of surfeit proved at Thanksgiving Day is not an abundance of fun and frivolity or elaborate luxury. Instead, foods served are plain, not highly spiced. They are simple unities (green beans) rather than complex blends (green bean soufflé with ginger). . . . Like baby food, the food at Thanksgiving is served baked, boiled, and mashed. Its soft texture and plain flavor is safe for young and old alike. Foods such as sweet and white potatoes remain close to their agricultural form and are not transformed into elaborate gourmet cuisine. Yet this plain food is served on the best china: Jell-O on Royal Doulton china eaten using Reed and Barton silver. It is not the food that would be served on the same china to dinner-party guests. On this day, the best china (form) celebrates (contains) plainness and a surplus of the basics (contents).

Because it is a celebration of abundance of the basics, in most households Thanksgiving Day is not associated with heavy alcohol consumption. . . . The theme of serving items that retain closeness to their agricultural form (rather than a distilled form) is echoed.

The Role of Fasting.

In order to prove decisively the ability of the group to provide a profusion of life-sustaining basics, Thanksgiving Day requires that participants come together in a state of hunger. This is partially accomplished by consuming the meal in early to midafternoon, sufficiently later than the customary midday meal, so as to make inquiries about the turkey's progress and expected time of completion routine. Not uncommonly, people said they fasted for a period of time prior to the meal, so they could save their appetite for the feast. In one household, no appetizers are served so everyone will save their hunger for the meal. In other households, women diet for a period of time, perhaps a week prior to the holiday. And in several households, fathers and college-age daughters made a pact to eat nothing on Thanksgiving Day prior to the dinner. Few males mentioned dieting or fasting, although many skipped lunch while waiting for a midafternoon meal. Fasting, then bingeing, enables even those participating in the ideology of thinness (Nichter and Moore 1990) to be included in negotiating the importance of abundance, if only at one meal.

Abundance of Basics Echoed in Clothing. Clothing also reflects the theme of plainness and modest origins. Enticing sequins and lamé are reserved for New Year's Eve; Thanksgiving Day clothing is unadorned and ordinary. Two prototypical styles of dress are [common]. The first more refined style of dress is reminiscent of Norman Rockwell's art. This style recalls the bygone practice of attending church before the Thanksgiving Day meal; women in boiled-wool jackets and plaid skirts with plain stockings and low-heel pumps accompanied by men in grey suits and white shirts can easily move from Episcopalian church services to the meal. Children are dressed to resemble small adults. This pattern of dress, retained in some upper-class families, appears to be diminishing in prevalence. . . .

For most people, dress is more casual, including jeans and sweaters, fleece sweat suits, and running shoes. Adults dress like large children. Soft fabric (fleece linings or velour finishes) and elastic gathered waistbands are . . . more comfortable; they recall the contemporary one-piece, all-purpose infant garment, sometimes known as "Dr. Dentons." This is clothing that can move from mealtime to playtime to naptime without a change.

Abundance of Plainness as Infantilism. The related metaphors of abundance and simplicity reinforce our notion that Thanksgiving is not a holiday like Christmas that reifies childhood delights (Caplow et al. 1982); instead, Thanksgiving Day satisfactions are more closely linked to infancy. Despite its deeper historical roots, Thanksgiving Day is mythically connected to the infancy of the nation. For Americans as individuals, oral gratification at Thanksgiving allows each participant to return to the contentment and security of an infant wearing comfortable soft clothing who falls asleep after being fed well. Sitting in relative silence, each participant is fed plain soft foods by a nurturing woman and then is taken outside for a walk. Some participants even mash their food together. . . . By "smooshing" their food together, participants enact an infantile pattern and use their food to mirror the family togetherness celebrated on this holiday. In so doing, they also reduce their food to a substance resembling the food fed to infants.

Thanksgiving Day is the cultural equivalent in the ritual calendar of Freud's oral stage of development in an individual's life. Epigenetically, Thanksgiving Day as oral stage must precede rituals that occur later in the American ritual calendar. Greed and retentiveness are culturally negotiated at Christmas, as is hedonic sexual fulfillment on New Year's Eve. In this way, the ritual calendar annually takes the culture through oral, anal, and genital stages of development before completing the holiday season and returning the culture to the everyday world of adult instrumentality.

Extensiveness of Inclusion

Depth interviews reveal that informants think of Thanksgiving Day as a day of family togetherness. Yet, who is to be included in the family circle, how inclusion is enacted, and the roles of each participant are actively negotiated through consumption. These negotiations and inclusion actions are discussed in the following sections.

Negotiating Life-Cycle Changes. Change and variation over the life cycle are negotiated year by year in making and carrying out "the plans." Decisions about whether grandmother is getting too old to handle having the festivities at her house involve deliberations about the degree of productivity expected of the elderly in American culture and the relative productivity of the middle generation. The holiday is an occasion that demands discourse and a decision that negotiates the relative roles (care givers/care receivers) of family members in the domestic cycle.

. . . The issue of what to do with boyfriends and girlfriends [of the unmarried members of the household], especially ones who may later become spouses and thereby extended family members, becomes a focus of negotiation. When girlfriends and boyfriends are from the same town, it is often resolved by including them in a part of the dinner. It is safe to have them come by for dessert, the peripheral course of the meal, after they eat the main course (and sometimes also dessert) with their own families. Boyfriends and girlfriends who have families in different towns may elect to go together to the family of one or the other. This situation is more difficult if it involves incorporating the nonfamily member into the family for more than a few hours or a day. . . . The overnight guests of their boyfriend's or girlfriend's family reported anxiety and nervousness, while typically adding that the host family is nice. The situation and the task of inclusion seem to account for their feelings more than their relationships with the particular people involved. Ideally, this is a time when differences between two families are made visible to the young couple and the possibility of resolution affirmed.

For a growing number of families, divorce forces the negotiation of new family roles and struggles over new ways of enacting the Thanksgiving Day ideology of family togetherness. This challenge is met creatively by many families. It is often resolved by requiring the offspring of divorced couples to consume two feasts in sequence. From an etic perspective . . ., through the children, divorced couples are connected tangentially on this ritual occasion.

Inclusion in Adult World through Advice. The domestic cycle stage characteristic of the households [with college] student[s] sets the scene for discussions regarding progress in college and possible graduate schools or jobs. Males who are fictive (e.g., godfathers, honorary uncles) or distant (e.g., uncles) kin initiate discussions with some college-age students about job plans. Some even suggested that the student should call on them to set up interviews when the time came. Thanksgiving Day events have as one of their foci the incorporation of college-age

students into the corporate world of grown-ups. Helpfulness on the part of the parental generation reconnects the migrant college student to family and friends who are likely to be geographically close to the parents. Such help may increase the chances that the college student will move "back to Michigan" or "back to Chicago."

Enacting Togetherness by Viewing Photographs. Strategies chosen by intact families for enacting family togetherness are patterned. Many families spend part of the day looking at old family pictures, constructing togetherness by reviewing and rehearsing their understanding of a shared past. Especially at feasts that include new or potential family members (such as girlfriends or boyfriends), re-viewing a family photo album includes the newcomer in stories and myths that charter inclusion in the group. Participants do not think of photoviewing as a compulsory part of the ritual in the way that serving turkey is, nor is it linked ideologically to a feast held by Pilgrims and Native Americans (Appelbaum 1984; Greninger 1979). Nonetheless, viewing old family pictures together is a fairly common activity for families. Emically, it is regarded as an individual and unique choice. Etically, it is interpreted as an activity that holds the cultural contents of the ritual. It defines the scope and legitimacy of the group by anchoring it in the past.

Constructing Togetherness through Storytelling. Topics of conversation during the day are somewhat consistent across households, although these patterns are not emically recognized. Stories are often repeated and, like photographs, are regarded as unique to the family. Frequently the stories are told while the whole group is assembled at the table after eating has finished. They could be termed stories of bad times. . . . Some stories about unique, unpleasant events are told to encourage laughter at the past crisis. . . . When successfully told, the point of the story is that, in telling of the disagreeable experience, listeners and storyteller alike (usually who were both present for the original event) are connected in laughing it off. . . . Unpleasant incidents are co-opted to support the value of a strong family. This is culture constructed.

However, such stories are not always successfully told. Intrafamily hostilities and long-term feuds can be rekindled. When stories are told and subsequent collective laughter is discouraged or the punch line about the power of love is omitted, such stories recall prior feelings of alienation and disappointment. This element of family ritual then fails.

Stories about prior holiday consumption experiences are a part of household or family charter, joining listeners in membership and its meanings (Levy 1981). Stories might be about bad Thanksgivings, such as the year the turkey did not defrost in time or the year the pit-roasted turkeys were spoiled by one bad one. Other bad stories told on this day are about other times, such as the time little brother lied to his parents about wrecking the car. In some stories, the oldest generation tells how hard life was many years ago, as with one grandmother who immigrated from Hungary in 1911. By recounting stories of family origins or painful events, such as the recent death of a family member, the family proves to itself that it withstands such shocks (Levy 1981). Participants do not regard storytelling as a prescribed part of the celebration, yet etically we see it as a common event that delivers an important ritual message about endurance and togetherness.

Inclusion of Pets and Those with "Nowhere Else to Go." Another activity that is fairly common, although regarded emically as unique, is the inclusion of pets by serving them part of the festive food. Unlike aspects of the holiday that may be systematically avoided in photographs, this is one that commands a photograph, along with remarks about how "cute" it is. This act expresses values of inclusion and generosity. The whole family participates in the holiday, even animals who, by consuming the same foods, are designated honorary family members.

The inclusion of pets echoes the frequent inclusion of unrelated singles or others described as having "nowhere else to go." This action resolves the culturally problematic position of persons whose families cannot accomplish the togetherness required on this day. It also allows other families to demonstrate generosity and abundance by constructing fictive kin for the day.

There are limits to inclusion, however. Pets are not served at the family table. Like children who eat their feast at a separate table, the pet is fed its share of turkey separately.

In summary, Thanksgivings arrange the re-collected past through stories and photographs, solidify the present through a collective hush while eating and then through a collective walk, and arrange the future through advice and other rituals of inclusion. From an etic perspective all of these events can be regarded as part of the common modern praxis of Thanksgiving Day, although emic ideology would see them as unique.

Resolution of Universalism and Particularism

Thanksgiving Day celebrations are regarded by many participants as being the same for everyone; to them Thanksgiving Day represents cultural universals. That which is universalistic is the same for all; it does not express individualism (Parsons 1951).

Emic understanding of this holiday assumes universality of participation for all Americans. Not only does this ideology assume that all do the same thing on this day ("turkey and all the rest"), but also that the meal has remained unchanged over the years. People go about the preparations as if the Pilgrims and Indians ate (Butterball) turkeys with (Pepperidge Farm) stuffing and (Ocean Spray) jellied cranberry sauce. They understand the celebration as universalistic and unchanging, although evident in the data are many features that are historically and socially particularistic.

Emic understanding of Thanksgiving as universal led many informants to express surprise about the focus of the research project. Some declared that other holidays, such as Christmas, are more interesting and more exciting. When asked what is served at their holiday table, the surprisingly common response is that theirs is the same as everyone's. However, when pushed for further details, evidence of behavioral particularism embedded in a universalistic ideology accumulates in an etic perspective. Particularism, the opposing pattern variable to universalism (Parsons 1951), is expressive of special individual position or ties. In examining the praxis of Thanksgiving Day, we see that behavioral elements regarded as universal are augmented with little traditions that are particular to a family, time period, geographic area of residence or origin, class, gender, or age group. After discussing universalistic elements, we discuss each of these six forms of particularism in the sections that follow.

Universalism in Cuisine and Service. There are some (almost) universal elements of these celebrations. Survey data reflect nearly universal participation [in celebrating] the holiday. Turkey is featured in all of the feasts recorded in the participant-observation data, including the [college students] who prepared frozen TV dinners for themselves while studying. . . . In this regard, "all" are the same.

Particularism Reflected in Little Traditions. Beyond certain focal points, the details of the meals reflect differences regarded as traditions by particular families. What is conceptually important about these little traditions is the way they are embedded in universalistic ideology. . . . "Traditional" inclusions mentioned were the sweet-potato pie, the Jell-O salad, the sweet potatoes with marshmallows and pecans, the blackberry salad, Grandma's homemade noodles, and the fruit salad with whipped cream. The definite article linguistically marks the definitive ritual article. When planning their celebration, one woman explained to her brother-in-law. . . . that this year they would not have a "real" Thanksgiving. When further queried, she said, "We won't be having the broccoli casserole.". . .

In [the selection and preparation of] foods, tradition and continuity are celebrated, but in ways that are particular to certain families. Through the consumption of foods regarded as traditional, participants partake of their collective past (Cohen and Coffin 1987).

Ideology of Stability and Historically Particular Praxis. Celebrants also make assumptions about the timeless character of larger national traditions and the little traditions of families. In the United States, universalism at Thanksgiving is connected to a timeless sense of patriotic nationalism and unification (Caplow and Williamson 1980). Contemporary Americans tend to believe that the holiday was invented by the Pilgrims in 1621 without any historical precedent in their native lands of Holland or England. This nationalistic myth persists despite alternative historical sources for Thanksgiving Day in

ancient holidays such as the Hebrew celebration of Sukkoth, the Feast of the Tabernacles; Greek festivals honoring Demeter, the goddess of harvests and grain; the Roman festival of Cerealia held in honor of Ceres, the goddess of grain; the midautumn and harvest festivals in the Orient; and even Native American tribes' harvest festivals, such as the Vikita ceremony of the Tohono O'Odham (Hayden [1937] 1987). The American meaning of Thanksgiving Day is thought to be so universal that, during World War II, a celebration for U.S. troops was held in Westminster Abbey (Hatch 1978).

The timelessness of traditions extends to emic understandings of family little traditions. Fieldnotes from participant observation and depth interviews frequently refer to things that a family "always" did or does. While pointing out emically meaningful patterns, this material likely also indicates some mythic distortion of memory over time as well as a counterpoint to the fascination with change and newness in contemporary consumer culture (Campbell 1987). Reference to "always" looks no further back than the grandparent's generation. This explains how Thanksgiving Day praxis may change relatively rapidly through time, a kind of moving average of central themes and differentially shared (class, regional) elaborations, while being protected by an ideology that glosses the celebration as stable. This ideology of stability deflects questioning about actual changes in Thanksgiving Day consumption.

Yet, several changes have occurred in American Thanksgiving Day celebrations in their more than 350-year history. Few households now serve mince pie, a onetime tradition. The focus on hunting and wild game is reduced (Ramsey 1979); the emphasis on the bounty of agriculture has increased. Churchgoing is now rare. Prayer persists for some but is combined or replaced with a more secular meal-opening toast for many. The home-centered, active family games that were once prevalent (Applebaum 1984) are often replaced by the passive spectacle of professional sports and nationally broadcast parades hosted by department stores and filled with commercial floats. Hosting by the grandparent's household is giving way to hosting by the middle generation. And, most directly important for an understanding of contemporary consumer culture, a profusion of branded products rather than foods produced by the household are consumed. Through taken-for-granted acceptance of changes, participants perceive universalism in their celebrations when in fact the praxis of their feasting is particular to contemporary times and household groups.

Particularism Reflected in Regional Differences. Other particularistic elements reflect regional differences, especially in the stuffing. One family with eastern roots always has oyster stuffing, while a southern family has cornbread stuffing, evoking the New World crop adopted from Native American agriculture (Tannahill 1988). A Western family with a Greek heritage includes pine nuts in their stuffing. A Korean-American family substitutes rice. Metonymically the turkey represents a universalistic shell filled with ethnic and regional differences in contents. All are Americans on the surface; participants nonetheless differ in their core heritages and regional loyalties. If decreasingly evident, they are still present. Such regionalism is rooted in the history of the holiday, more firmly anchored in New England than in the South (Greninger 1979).

Particularism Reflected in Class Differences. Also represented in the praxis of Thanksgiving Day are American class divisions. These are vividly illustrated in participant-observation fieldnotes and photographs alongside comments that "we do what everyone does." Upper-middle- and upper-class feasts are more formal in etiquette as shown in the table setting and food service. Greater attention to sets of matching objects such as china and silver eating utensils establishes a form of universalism across participants at the feast. However, there is simultaneously greater individualism as opposed to collectivism in the food service. Color and pattern coordination of dishes, beverage containers, napkins, tablecloths, and floral centerpieces is evident. Sometimes there are placecards. Upper-class feasts feature food products more carefully separated from their branded packaging; butter is molded into shapes and served individually on china bread plates with silver butter knives.

In lower-middle-class families, we find less formal table settings and food service, with fewer utensils per person and increasing informality of beverage service. The aesthetic becomes more cluttered, with mixtures of sets of dishes and glassware providing a less universalistic visual portrait. Some beverages are served in cans. Paper napkins appear on colorful tablecloths. Increasing collectivism is evident in the bowls of Jell-O salad rather than individual molds on individual matching china salad plates found in higher class families. As we move even further down the social class hierarchy, foods are more likely to be served buffet style from their cooking pots, rather than transferred to serving platters placed on a sideboard. In some cases, celebrants do not all sit down together but rotate places at a table that is too small to accommodate all simultaneously.

Butter or margarine service is one of the most consistent class markers. At one pole are decoratively molded individual pats of butter served on individual matched china bread-and-butter plates. At an intermediate point, we see butter passed on a central china plate, then carved and transferred by individuals to their own bread and butter plates. Further down the hierarchy, a stick of butter or margarine on a decoratively laid out buffet is transferred by individuals to the edges of their china dinner plates. At the opposite pole, there is a plastic tub of margarine, a collective knife laid across its perimeter. From the tub, individuals transfer the margarine onto the foods on their plates. Thus, although all are together, feasts held by members of different classes reflect different levels of collectivism and individualism, a form of particularism, in the service and selection of foods.

Particularism Reflected in Age Segregation. Another form of particularism enacted within the household on this day is age segregation. Both before and after the meal, age-segregated groups of participants form on the basis of work obligations or play interests of each age group. Groups of children may play together, while teenagers help or participate in Ping-Pong tournaments in blended families. The meal, however, brings age groups together. It temporarily homogenizes gender and age distinctions that have organized the day's interactions up to this point. Participants usually eat at the same table. . . . In other cases, all may eat at the same time; but children, or those so regarded for the day (as with some unmarried teenage and young adults) may sit separately. . . .

Particularism Reflected in Gender Segregation. The most widespread and vivid segregation during this universal feast of togetherness is based on gender. Although regarded as a day of rest by men, in most households Thanksgiving Day is a day of both ritual and physical labor for women. Frequently, food shopping and meal preparation begin several days prior to the feast, culminating on Thanksgiving Day with women attending to last-minute details. On the feast day women are bound closely to the kitchen by basting and other chores. . . .

When the meal is finally served, the fact that the mom will not sit down but instead continues working to insure that all are served is testimony to the day not being a workfree holiday for everyone. . . . The fact that the hostess is frequently the last to sit down enacts her conventional role as family caretaker and caterer. . . .

Men's role at most feasts is to be served or, in some households, to "help" but not assume primary responsibility for planning, preparing, and presenting the feast. In many households, men's help is in the form of symbolic labor, such as lifting the cooked turkey from the oven or carving it. Enacting a stereotyped hunter-gatherer gender distinction unsupported by the ethnographic record (Leibowitz 1986), in typical Thanksgiving feasts the man presents the "hunted" bird (actually purchased in a supermarket after being raised in a feed pen), while the woman presents the gathered berries (from a can) and cultivated vegetables (also purchased in the supermarket). Seldom [do] men [prepare] side dishes or [work] on dishes other than the focal point of the meal, namely turkey and stuffing. Their symbolic labor, especially the carving, is a public event that is often watched by an audience and recorded in ordinary snapshots. Unlike the days of hidden labor that women put into ironing tablecloths, polishing silver, and molding gelatin salads, men's symbolic labor is public, focal, and worthy of historical documentation in photographs, a finding that parallels those concerning men's typical involvement in childcare (Hochcheil 1989). Differences between men's and women's labor in producing the feast event highlight gender distinctions that operate the rest of the year. However, on this one day, women's domestic labor, taken for granted most of the time, is celebrated.

Thanksgiving Day gender segregation occurs in households organized around sharp gender lines as well as in those that are typically more creative about the division of labor. Cleaning up after the feast is usually either women's work . . . or, like other postmeal activities, performed by a mixed-gender group. . . .

Both gender and age segregation diminish after the incorporating ritual meal, because, when successful, the meal homogenizes such distinctions in a moment of universal connection or *communitas* (Turner 1969). After the meal women are freer to watch a televised football game with men despite its usual association with males (Arens 1981). Women may also nap on the sofa, play games that underscore group cohesion (even highly competitive games of Monopoly), take a walk with others, or join any conversation. Similarly, men are freer to assist in cleanup than in preparation. Thus, the Thanksgiving Day feast both enacts and resolves gender distinctions.

In summary, Thanksgiving Day ideology affirms universalism while praxis reflects, maintains, and constructs pervasive social differences. From an etic perspective, Thanksgiving Day celebrates both the universalistic ideology of American society, as well as its particularistic divisions by time period, family, region, class, gender, and age. Thanksgiving Day celebrations use consumption to replicate relatively enduring elements of social structure by constructing several varieties of behavioral particularism within a prevailing ideology of universality. Encapsulation of the celebration in family groups deflects questions about the paradoxical coexistence of universalistic consciousness and particularistic praxis.

Negotiating the Values of Cleanliness, Not Wasting, and Hard Work

In preparing, consuming, and cleaning up from the Thanksgiving dinner, several important cultural values traceable to Puritan, if not Pilgrim, ancestors are made visible. Thanksgiving Day enacts values placed on cleanliness, frugality, and hard work.

Cleanliness is enacted through washing and polishing the serving utensils and dishes employed during the meal. . . . Rather than simplify the burden by using paper plates, servers . . . [use] a great many dishes in the preparation, service, and consumption of the meal. Even the gold-rimmed china and the delicate crystal that "must be" washed by hand are used in quantity. In some households, seldom-used dishes and silver are washed and polished in the days before the holiday. Linens may be washed and specially ironed. Discussions of when and how much cleaning to do negotiate the importance of this value in the household.

Similarly, the feast and its surrounding events enact a belief in the value of hard work. . . . Through the ritual labor of preparing the meal at home, the beliefs that hard work pays off and cleanliness is next to godliness are enacted (Tannahill 1988). It is the unpaid domestic cooking and cleaning usually associated with women rather than professional cooking at restaurants associated with men (Mennell 1985) that is honored.

After working hard to prepare so much food, women puzzle over how and where to store the leftovers. Unlike potlatch harvest rituals among Native Americans of the Northwest Coast in which material surplus is ritually destroyed (Codere 1950), the Thanksgiving Day surplus is encased in plastic wrap, foil, or Tupperware containers to be used later. . . . In many households, even the turkey carcass is saved for soup. Through the careful wrapping of the leftover food, the early-American belief in frugality is dramatized. It is curious that the encasing of leftovers in plastic is done near a waste can filled with packaging from the purchased food products. Packaging waste is tolerated, while wasting food is not. What is saved are the remnants of the sacred "labor of love" and what is thrown away (cans, bottles, etc.) represents waste from profane commercial concerns (Belk, Wallendorf, and Sherry 1989).

Negotiating the Role of Produce and Branded Food Products

Emic descriptions of Thanksgiving Day frequently refer to food dishes that are "made from scratch" or "homemade." This is an interesting etymological[7] reference to scratching the soil to plant a seed to grow food that is then transformed into edible dishes at home. This linguistic expression in fieldnotes is accompanied by photographs showing women basting Butterball turkeys, adding diced celery to Pepperidge Farm bread cubes to make stuff-

ing, stirring cans of Swanson chicken broth into Butterball turkey drippings to make gravy, gently removing Ocean Spray cranberry sauce from the can, stirring ice cubes with Jell-O powder to dissolve it and then adding Dole canned pineapple chunks, and filling Pet-Ritz frozen pie crusts with Libby canned pumpkin that will later be topped with Cool Whip dessert topping. These practices raise a dilemma posed by contemporary consumer culture: How do mass-produced, commercially process and delivered food products come to serve a ritual purpose? How is it that women are perceived to be doing all of the cooking when in fact they are collaborating with a predominantly male-managed manufacturing process in this endeavor? Our final theme then, concerns the processes through which a celebration of material plenty and agrarian cultural roots is created using produce and branded food products purchased in urban supermarkets.

Quintessential Foods. One solution to the problem of sacralizing commercial products is the use of quintessential holiday foods (Belk, Wallendorf, and Sherry 1989) that are so connected with the holiday that they come to represent it. Turkey, stuffing, cranberry sauce, and pie are such essential ingredients and universal symbols of the tradition of Thanksgiving (Appelbaum 1984) that some refer to the holiday as "turkey day." However, mincemeat pie is no longer commonly served, evidence that even quintessential elements of tradition are negotiated over time.

Temporal Separation. Temporal separation marks ritual foods by distinguishing them from everyday ones. . . . For most households, roast turkey, stuffing, cranberry sauce, and perhaps butter are rarely consumed at times other than Thanksgiving or Christmas. Turkey is made particular to the holiday in part by temporal anomaly. Interestingly, turkey was less frequently incorporated into the Thanksgiving Days of previous times when foods used were actually homegrown or hunted. . . . As reliance on purchased food products has increased, turkey produced on industrial farms (Sherpell 1986) has become more "traditional," not because of its historical lineage, which also includes both deer and chicken pie (Appelbaum 1984; Hechtlinger 1977), but because of its temporal separation.

Packaging. The transformation involved in cooking and serving branded products purchased in supermarkets is key to the creation of a ritual with unique meaning for participants. Decommodification and singularization (Kopytoff 1986) or sacralization (Belk, Wallendorf and Sherry 1989) of commodities is required for them to serve expressive ritual purposes (Cheal 1989). The transformation process begins by discarding packaging materials and price tags. The price tag, but not the label showing quaint vineyard scenes, is scraped off wine bottles. Turkeys, unlike shirts or jeans, are not permitted to bear external brand marks (Sherry 1986). Hence, turkey wrappers are disposed of and cranberry sauce is removed from the can. Pie boxes may be kept backstage or put in the garbage. Relish trays are constructed from the contents of an array of bottles and cans, none of which are displayed on the table in middle-class homes. For some products, the transformation process ends here.

Special Ingredients. For other products, the transformation process continues. Recipes combine special ingredients to transform and decommodify purchased products. Through recipes, tubers, turkeys, and grains become "homemade" in the emic sense, although they are not literally produced by scratching the soil to plant a seed. Special ingredients (purchased in a supermarket) are added to further particularize branded products (also purchased). Turkeys are basted with canned pineapple juice, frozen orange juice, or canned chicken broth. Regional markers are added to stuffing mix, such as oysters or chestnuts, as are other ingredients such as mushrooms or wine. In fact, stuffing, as well as particular kinds of basting juice and procedures, is the most common method of decommodifying the main course. The additions sacralize the purchased commodity and transform it into a little family tradition. As is also true of the pies, particularized contents are used to fill a universal container. This transmutation brings commercialization under control by the firm hand of tradition exercised by the female guardians of family values (Greer 1970).

Jell-O-brand gelatin is appropriate to the Thanksgiving feast because of its ability to deliver several messages. Oddly, it is not disguised but is referred to by its brand name. It supplants the homemade puddings typically prepared for early-American Thanksgiving Days (Appelbaum 1984; Hechtlinger 1977). Jell-O is loaded with particularizing additions: black-cherry Jell-O with Bing cherries in one family, lime Jell-O with pineapple and miniature marshmallows in another. Then it is molded into a special form and, like the turkey and the pies, is offered as a whole from which each person may partake. Ordinarily, Jell-O is regarded as proper for children or for those with gastrointestinal illness but not for adult dinner parties. At Thanksgiving, the congealed mass represents both the transmutation of a mass-produced consumer product into an element of tradition and the congealing of family differences into a bounded, molded whole.

Root vegetables such as tubers that are inexpensive unbranded bulk staples provide a conventional message about the common agrarian roots of America. They celebrate humble origins and reflect working-class eating patterns (Mennell 1985; Salaman 1949). They are less commodified at the point of purchase than are branded food products but are nonetheless singularized with special ingredients. These modifications usually use other staple ingredients such as butter, eggs, milk, and sugar that load the food product with meaning as well as additional calories. Miniature marshmallows load yams in a way that is equivalent to whipped cream on pumpkin pie. The omnipresent addition of milk and egg products echoes the message of this as a celebration of (mother) earth's bounty (Myers 1972).

Butter or margarine is a special ingredient added to almost every dish. Noteworthy is the frequent use of butter rather than the margarine used in everyday dinners. Butter increases the richness (both in dollar value and cholesterol) of the Thanksgiving Day meal. Instead of resulting from the more recent health concerns about cholesterol, margarine's everyday popularity over butter can be traced to branding, advertising, and the distribution management skills of margarine manufacturers. Butter, traditionally produced at local dairies, remains a product category with only one national brand (*Consumer Reports* 1989). Butter is "natural," unlike margarine, and recalls the country's agrarian roots. Frequent use of butter on this day delivers a message about the triumph of nature over commerce. Using butter also proves the family's power over the commodification and homogeneity represented by branding, at least within the ritual context.

The addition of special ingredients to branded food products implies that a cultural process besides sacralization is occurring. As part of the ritual, the preparation of foods brings some aspect of life firmly under control. Nationally branded food products have the capacity to deliver the same uniform product to all, protecting consumers from seasonal fluctuations in availability (Mennell 1985). But they also have the capacity to obliterate individual difference and familial uniqueness. By co-opting mass-produced branded products in creating a ritual meal, the food preparer proves familial values can triumph over the powerful homogenizing influences of consumer culture.

The meanings associated with noncommodified domestic culture (Kopytoff 1986; McCracken 1988) rather than commercialized mass culture prevail on this day. Having negotiated and proven values that are invisible most of the time, Thanksgiving ritual then permits the service of dessert to be bound by fewer strictures than the earlier service of the relish tray and main course. By the time dessert is served, familial values have been proven and solidified such that the appearance of Cool Whip or Redi-Whip in its branded packaging is not a threat to the ritual message.

Service. Serving the meal on special dishes is another solution used to convert processed food products into ritual foods. So served, the food products partake of the meanings congealed in the serving dishes and flatware inherited from family ancestors (McCracken 1988). This traditionalizes foods, even those purchased in the supermarket. For example, most people rarely consume cranberry sauce, which lacks a referent in the natural everyday world of most participants. (who knows what a cranberry bog is, where they are, and the type of plant on which cranberries grow?) Because of this, jellied cranberry sauce can be served with can ridges intact, as if it were naturally made that way. Served on silver or crystal dishes rather than directly from the can, it is reclaimed from the world of manufacturers

and particularized. Served whole and intact, jellied cranberry sauce resonates with the whole bird, whole pies, and molded gelatin from which all partake and metonymically rejoices in the ideal, intact family.

Reappropriation. Why do people both use manufacturers and work so hard to disguise them? The answer lies in the way food preparation enables the household to symbolically reclaim the production process taken over by manufacturers in the historical separation of production from consumption (Aries 1962; Dholakia 1987; Durkheim [1893] 1933; Ewen and Ewen 1982; Forty 1986). . . .

Through elaborate preparations using manufactured food products, families make a claim about the immanent productive potential of the household, a claim often frustrated in an economy where the product of wage labor is usually only indirectly relevant to household needs. The more food dishes prepared, the more tableware to be washed, and the more manufactured products transformed, the more evocative and powerful this message.

CONCLUSIONS

Ethnographic study of Thanksgiving Day celebrations informs our understanding of U.S. consumer behavior in several ways. First, it illustrates how Americans use ritual consumption to construct culture. We have shown how informants vigorously recollect past meanings, negotiate future meanings, and assemble present meanings of family, regionalism, material abundance, gender, and age through Thanksgiving Day consumption rituals to construct a model of social life.

Second, this study explores the linkages and cleavages between consumer ideology on the one hand and consumer practice on the other. Our etic reframing of the varied experiences of universal and particular practices brings into focus the contradictions between emic representations of action and behavior itself. We unpack notions of "always" and "from scratch.". . . We assimilate the emic particularism of "forgetting," bad stories, delaying dessert, and not talking much while eating, to the universal.

Third, our study of Thanksgiving Day celebrations contributes to our comprehension of the meanings consumers attach to material surplus and satisfaction. Many consumers associate the satisfaction of basic wants with an ideal of household form, both of which reference ideas of the pooling and redistribution behaviors of agrarian, even preindustrial, households. There is a further association of satisfaction and abundance with an infantile stage of development. The epigenetic center of later holidays celebrating other aspects of materialism, such as the Christmas dialectic of generosity versus retentiveness, and the New Year's dialectic of adult hedonism versus moral restraint, lies in the Thanksgiving Day celebration of basic abundance.

Finally, people actively reappropriate a sense of satisfaction from manufactures through decommodifying actions. Rather than reconstruct the agrarian traditions celebrated, ritual preparers co-opt manufactured products to deliver the message of familial solidarity and productive potentiality. Most important for consumer research, the study of Thanksgiving Day assists us in unraveling the notion of "tradition" and the role of manufactured products vis-à-vis homemade ones from both emic and etic perspectives. We show how branded food products are reclaimed from the world of commodities and reassembled into little traditions through varying household actions. But these processes are not limited to Thanksgiving Day. Through such transformation processes, households define their immanent productive power, their ability to produce abundance for their members. Through the consumption rituals of Thanksgiving Day, households make visible their values and deliver a cultural message about the meaning of abundance.

NOTES

1. Consumer ideology: Consumers' beliefs and doctrine about how a consumption event should be.
2. Praxis: Habitual or established practice or custom.
3. Emic: That which reflects the consciously available perspective of individual informants.
4. Metonym: A figure of speech in which a word is used to reference or evoke a related idea or bundle of meaning.
5. Embody: To make tangible or represent through the body and bodily sensations.
6. Etic: That which reflects the interpretation of the researcher.
7. Etymological: Historical derivation or origin of a word.

REFERENCES

Appelbaum, Diana Karter (1984), *Thanksgiving: An American Holiday, an American History*, New York: Facts on File.

Arens, W. (1981), "Professional Football: An American Symbol and Ritual," in *The American Dimension: Cultural Myths and Social Realities*, ed. Susan P. Montague and W. Arens, Palo Alto, CA: Mayfield, 1–9.

Aries, Philippe (1962), *Centuries of Childhood: A Social History of Family Life*. trans. Robert Baldick, New York: Vintage.

Barthes, Roland (1975), "Toward a Psychosociology of Contemporary Food Consumption," in *European Diet from Pre-industrial to Modern Times*, ed. Elborg Foster and Robert Forster, New York: Harper & Row.

Belk, Russell W., Melanie Wallendorf, and John F. Sherry, Jr. (1989), "The Sacred and the Profane in Consumer Behavior: Theodicy on the Odyssey," *Journal of Consumer Research*, 16 (June), 1–38.

Campbell, Colin (1987), *The Romantic Ethic and the Spirit of Modern Consumerism*, Oxford: Basil Blackwell.

Caplow, Theodore, H. Bahr, B. Chadwick, R. Hill, and Margaret Holmes Williamson (1982), *Middletown Families*, Minneapolis: University of Minnesota Press.

———— and Margaret Holmes Williamson (1980), "Decoding Middletown's Easter Bunny: A Study in American Iconography," *Semiotica*, 32 (3/4), 221–232.

Cheal, David (1989), "The Postmodern Origin of Ritual," *Journal for the Theory of Social Behavior*, 18 (3), 269–290.

Codere, Helen (1950), *Fighting with Property*, American Ethnological Society Monograph no. 18, Washington, DC: American Ethnological Society.

Cohen, Hennig and Tristram Potter Coffin (1987), *The Folklore of American Holidays*, Detroit: Gale Research.

Consumer Reports, (1987), "Butter vs. Margarine," 54 (September), 551–556.

Dholakia, Ruby Roy (1987), "Feminism and the New Home Economics: What Do They Mean for Marketing?" in *Philosophical and Radical Thought in Marketing*, ed. Fuat Firal et al., Lexington, MA: Lexington, 341–357.

Dirks, Robert (1988), "Annual Rituals of Conflict," *American Anthropologist*, 90 (December), 856–870.

Douglas, Mary (1972), "Deciphering the Meal," *Daedalus*, 101, 61–81.

Durkheim, Émile ([1893] 1933), *The Division of Labor in Society*, trans. George Simpson, New York: Free Press.

Ewen, Stuart and Elizabeth Ewen (1982), *Channels of Desire: Mass Images and the Shaping of American Consciousness*, New York: McGraw-Hill.

Farb, Peter and George Armelagos (1980), *Consuming Passions: The Anthropology of Eating*, New York: Washington Square.

Forty, Adrian (1986), *Objects of Desire: Design and Society from Wedgewood to IBM*, New York: Pantheon.

Freud, Sigmund ([1905] 1960), *Jokes and Their Relation to the Unconscious*, trans. James Strachey, New York: Norton.

Greer, Germaine (1970), *The Female Eunuch*, London: MacGibbon & Kee.

Greninger, Edwin (1979), "Thanksgiving: An American Holiday," *Social Science*, 54 (Winter), 3–15.

Hatch, Jane M. (1978), *The American Book of Days*, New York: Wilson.

Hayden, Julian D. ([1937] 1987), "The Vikita Ceremony of the Papago," *Journal of the Southwest*, 29 (Autumn), 273–324.

Hechtlinger, Adelaide (1977), *The Seasonal Hearth: The Woman at Home in Early America*, Woodstock, NY: Overlook.

Hochchiel, Arlie (1989), *The Second Shift*, New York: Viking.

Kopytoff, Igor (1986), "The Cultural Biography of Things: Commoditization as Cultural Process," in *The Social Life of Things*, ed. Arjun Appadurai, Cambridge: Cambridge University Press, 64–94.

Leibowitz, Lila (1986), "In the Beginning . . .: The Origins of the Sexual Division of Labour and the Development of the First Human Societies," in *Women's Work, Men's Property: The Origins of Gender and Class*, ed. Stephanie Coontz and Peta Henderson, London: Verso, 43–77.

Levy, Sidney J. (1981), "Interpreting Consumer Mythology: A Structural Approach to Consumer Behavior," *Journal of Marketing*, 45 (Summer), 49–61.

Linton, Ralph and Adelin Linton (1949), *We Gather Together: The Story of Thanksgiving*, New York: Schuman.

McCracken, Grant (1986), "Culture and Consumption: A Theoretical Account of the Structure and Movement of the Cultural Meaning of Consumer Goods," *Journal of Consumer Research*, 13 (June), 71–84.

———— (1988), *Culture and Consumption*, Bloomington: Indiana University Press.

McQuarry, Edward F. (1989), "Advertising Resonance: A Semiological Perspective," in *Interpretive Consumer Research*, ed. Elizabeth C. Hirschman, Provo, UT: Association for Consumer Research, 97–114.

Mennell, Stephen (1985), *All Manners of Food: Eating and Taste in England and France from the Middle Ages to the Present*, Oxford: Basil Blackwell.

Merleau-Ponty, Maurice ([1945] 1962), *The Phenomenology of Perception*, trans. Colin Smith, London: Routledge & Kegan Paul.

———— ([1942] 1963), *The Structure of Behavior*, trans. Alden L. Fisher, Boston: Beacon.

Myers, Robert J. (1972), *Celebrations: The Complete Book of American Holidays*, Garden City, NY: Doubleday.

Nichter, Mimi and Nancy Moore (1991), "Fat Talk: Body Image among Adolescent Girls," *Mirrors of the Body: Anthropological Perspectives*, ed. Nicole Sault, Philadelphia: University of Pennsylvania Press. . . . .

Parsons, Talcott (1951), *The Social System*, New York: Free Press.

Ramsey, Patricia (1979), "Beyond 'Ten Little Indians' and Turkeys: Alternative Approaches to Thanksgiving," *Young Children*, (September), 28–52.

Rook, Dennis (1985), "The Ritual Dimension of Consumer Behavior," *Journal of Consumer Research*, 12 (December), 251–264.

Salaman, Redcliffe N. (1949), *The History and Social Influence of the Potato*, Cambridge: Cambridge University Press.

Sherpell, James (1986), *In the Company of Animals: A Study of Human-Animal Relationships*, New York: Blackwell.

Sherry, John F., Jr. (1986), "Cereal Monogamy: Brand Loyalty as Secular Ritual in Consumer Culture," paper presented at the Association for Consumer Research Annual Conference, Toronto.

Tannahill, Reay (1988), *Food in History*, New York: Crown.

Turner, Victor W. (1969), *The Ritual Process: Structure and Antistructure*, Ithaca, NY: Cornell University Press.

Legal Ritual

PETER A. WINN*

Facts of publication: *Winn, Peter A. 1991. "Legal Ritual," Law and Critique 2(2): 207–232. Reprinted with the permission of Law and Critique, Deborah Charles Publications, Liverpool, UK.*

Peter Winn not only thinks ritual pervades the law, he believes it ought to. Ritual is not merely an archaic remnant in need of purging from contemporary practice. Rather it is essential to humane governance, since it makes uniform structures possible with a minimum of force. Winn argues his claim on the basis of anthropological theory and then illustrates it with a case study, that of the Miranda decision, which set in motion the American litany of arrest: "You are under arrest. You have a right to remain silent. . . ." Drawing on J. L. Austin's theory of performative utterance, Winn argues that such a rite is constitutive. It does not merely describe or illustrate the act of arresting. Rather it brings that state into being; it is an actual part of making an arrest.

About the author: Dates: *1957–   , Rochester, NY, U.S.A.* **Education:** *B.A., Williams College; M.Phil., University of London; J.D., Harvard Law School.* **Field(s):** *jurisprudence, trial practice.* **Career:** *Special Assistant United States Attorney, Northern District of Texas at Dallas; Special Assistant Attorney General, Texas Attorney General's Office, Austin, Texas.* **Publications:** *"Legal Ritual," Law and Critique 2.2 (1991); "Standing on Ceremonies: Legal Rituals, Regulative Rules and the Metaphysics of Jurisprudence," in P. Kevelson, ed., Semiotics and the Human Sciences, vol. 3 (Peter Lang, 1992).* **Additional:** *"Although my conclusions comport with the experience of most practicing lawyers (who rarely view my work as controversial), legal academics rarely address, and never acknowledge as legitimate, the obvious presence of ritual in the modern legal system. The resistance of legal academics to the study of ritual stems, I believe, from an unwillingness to modify the prevailing jurisprudential model, in which it is assumed a priori that ritual cannot exist as a legitimate element."*

INTRODUCTION

Ritual and ceremony pervade the law. This should not be an embarrassment. Ritual characterizes nearly all human social institutions, especially legal institutions charged with resolving social conflict. But the concept of ritual is rarely used in legal analysis; even more rarely is it the subject of formal academic studies. When mentioned at all, ritual is discussed in the context of legal apologetics.[1] More often, it is treated as some defect in a legal system.[2] Although rarely used to understand modern indus-

trial legal systems, the concept of ritual is frequently used to address the legal systems of non-industrial societies[3] and those of ancient historical societies.[4] The following passage from a book about Roman law by Barry Nicholas provides an illustration:

> Primitive systems are given to the use of forms. Legal consequences do not follow from a mere agreement or from a simple expression of intention. If rights are to be created or transferred, some particular act must be performed or some particular words must be uttered. The act or the words (or both) are the form, and it is the form which produces the legal consequences.[5]

Nicholas implicitly contrasts the "primitive" Roman legal system with "modern" ones, but the phenomenon Nicholas describes certainly exists in

*The opinions expressed herein are those of the author and not necessarily those of the Texas Attorney General. Special thanks to Todd D. Rakoff, David Kertzer, David Park and Jane Kaufman Winn for their comments on earlier drafts of this article.

"modern" legal systems as well. No system of law is either wholly ritualistic or wholly based on the intentions of individuals. All legal systems contain elements of ritual as well as elements of positive law.

Recently, the distinction between "primitive" and "modern" systems, because of its implicit ethnocentrism, has been subject to criticism.[6] There has been an increased willingness to reinterpret "primitive" legal systems to show that they, too, are "rational"—that is, underlying their rituals and ceremonies are intelligible structures which form the basis of legitimate social institutions.[7] However, the converse project of understanding the "primitive" or ritualistic elements within our own "rational" legal system has been largely neglected.[8] The enduring rituals in our system of law are either rationalized as serving some intelligible "function" or dismissed as archaic residuals which enlightened lawyers, judges and legislators should work to purge. It is one thing to assert that "primitive" people are really like us. It is another thing to admit that we are really like them.

AN ANTHROPOLOGICAL THEORY OF RITUAL

Before analyzing the role of ritual in a legal system, something needs to be said about the concept of ritual in general. Ritual has been used to describe an extremely wide variety of behaviour. A person's standard morning routine of bathing, dressing and drinking a cup of coffee is spoken of as [a] morning ritual, ethnologists speak of the stereotyping and fixity of form of ritualized animal signals[9] and psychologists speak of the ritualistic repetitive behaviour of neurotics.[10] However, in this paper, I will be focusing on ritual in the anthropological sense—that is, in the sense of traditional or customary rituals accompanying birth, marriage and death.

From an anthropological point of view, ritual is characterized by standardized, repetitive interpersonal symbolic actions, patterned according to social customs, which involve constant form over time, and which influence or orient human affairs. Ritual subsumes contradictions and creates the possibility of determinate social action. The impact of rituals depends not on the intentions of the partici-

pants, but on the definition of the ritual action itself. The power of ritual in general depends on its ability to create, order and structure human social institutions.[11]

Ritual is often thought of as linked to religious worship or to belief in the supernatural.[12] This is partly because ritual usually has been studied in societies where everything has religious or magical significance.[13] However, as societies become more secular they do not lose the need for "sacred" rituals to create and highlight those events which are imbued with meaning beyond the ordinary.[14] Ritual is not synonymous with "magic" in the sense of the supernatural. Rather, much of what is denigrated as belief in magic and superstition itself reflects a much more complex set of social relations than those words connote. Mary Douglas gives an illustration:

> Once when a band of !Kung Bushmen had performed their rain rituals, a small cloud appeared on the horizon, grew and darkened. Then rain fell. But the anthropologists who asked if the Bushmen reckoned the rite had produced the rain, were laughed out of court.[15]

The Bushmen knew that their rain dance did not literally "cause" the rain, but was part of a cultural system for categorizing their world, a world in which society and nature are not rigorously demarcated from each other.

Industrial societies have more clearly demarcated the natural from the social world and are more likely to understand the natural world through scientific concepts and technology. However, ritual remains important in industrial societies in the creation and maintenance of social institutions, and to orient and relate people to one another in the context of these institutions. Among these institutions, of course, are law and religion.

Legal rituals have important structural similarities to religious rituals, and like religious ritual, cannot be understood solely in terms of belief structures. In the late nineteenth century, it was common for theologians to study a religion's mythological beliefs in order to understand the nature of the religion. As a secondary enterprise, it was thought that one could easily explain the religion's rites as derivative from the beliefs of the religion's adherents. As a people's religious beliefs changed over time, so too, it was thought, would their religious rituals. Robertson Smith's study of ancient Judaism revealed that just the opposite took place—that although a people's religious beliefs might change over time, their concrete ritual practices did not. The rites remained constant while the explanations for these rites in terms of their religious beliefs varied widely.[16] It is now widely recognized that rites are prior and beliefs secondary in the understanding of religion—that is, some religious beliefs are often best understood as rationalizations of the continuing practice of the religious rites.[17] As Clifford Geertz writes, "it is primarily—out of the context of concrete acts of religious observance that religious conviction emerges on the human plane."[18]

It is one of the theses of this article that the relationship of legal rituals to the justifications given for their use is structurally similar to the relationship of religious rituals to the mythological justifications given for them—that is, Robertson Smith's insight about religious ritual applies to legal ritual as well. Just as in the understanding of religious institutions, rite can be structurally more central than religious belief, so too, in the understanding of legal institutions, the concrete legal rituals themselves can be structurally more important than the justifications given for them. The link between magico-religious practices and legal institutions is not new. Marcel Mauss noted the close relationship between certain magical practices and the creation of jural relations,[19] and Bronislaw Malinowski described the function sorcery can play in the administration of a system of justice.[20] Mauss and Malinowski limited themselves, however, to descriptions of archaic and primitive societies. They invariably refused to turn their critical eyes upon their own society.[21] Thus, they failed to recognize how their work on ritual could contribute to the understanding of modern social institutions.

Early anthropologists failed to recognize the presence of ritual within modern society in part because they viewed language as an essentially neutral conveyer of thoughts, beliefs and intentions. Anthropologists, presented with cases where words were perceived to have an effect independent of the thoughts and intentions of the utterer, were therefore inclined to attribute this effect to a superstitious belief in the magical power of certain words, not to any independent power of language. Language, according to this thinking, remained neutral.

Contemporary *analytic philosophy* has revealed that we sometimes use words not simply to communicate thoughts and intentions but directly to create social events and social institutions. In this use of language, words, rather than merely serving as messengers of thought, are themselves critical transforming acts. One of the first to analyze such utterances was J. L. Austin. In a series of lectures and articles he called such utterances "performatives."[22] He noted that these utterances were not statements about some state of affairs. Instead, they were the very execution of the act itself.

For example, the statement, "I give and bequeath my watch to my brother," accompanied by the handing over of the watch, is not a report of an act of mine; it is the very act of giving. In a marriage ceremony, the "I do" is not a report of some inner act of acceptance; it is the act which creates the marriage. It takes no stretch of the imagination to see that what Austin called a "performative" is simply what anthropologists have called a "ritual."[23]

Moreover, determinate ritual action can occur whether or not a specific thought or propositional content is attached to it by the ritual participant. To have undergone a marriage ceremony makes one married. One is married whatever one's thoughts or intentions were during the occasion. The fact that one may have been in an emotional state of panic and one's mind utterly blank does not alter the legal relation which was created by virtue of the execution of the ritual. Even if one of the parties was not sincere at the moment of his or her declarations of the vows, this will not void the legal relation created by them.[24]

Likewise, a promise, in exchange for valid consideration, creates a binding legal obligation of the person making the promise. The intentions of the promisor are largely irrelevant to the creation of this obligation. If the promise was in fact made in exchange for consideration, but the promisor had no intention to bind himself, evidence of his lack of intention will not constitute a defense in an action to enforce the contract. The promise of a liar may be enforced against him even if the person to whom the promise was made may have known or reasonably believed that the liar had no intention of performing the contract.[25] In this example, the ritual of the contract, not the intentions of the parties, creates the obligation.[26]

Although a ritual has a determinate consequence—by means of the marriage ceremony, for instance, one becomes married—ritual often lacks a determinate content. A particular marriage ceremony may mean different things to different people, even different things to the same person. The symbolism of the marriage ceremony has multifaceted resonances, but it is empty of any specific propositional content—that is, the meaning attached to the marriage ceremony cannot be determined to be either true or false.[27] The sentence "the cat is on the mat" is meaningful if there are in the world such entities as cats and mats which stand in a certain relationship to each other. But the ceremony of a marriage has no specific meaning outside of the ritual context itself. If one assumes that all meaning can be characterized by propositional expressions, rituals have no meaning whatsoever.[28] However, when one sees that ritual is a type of social action, not merely a type of verbal expression, one can uncover in ritual a rich network of symbolic meaning.

Because ritual is formalized social action, not expression, different meanings can be attributed to a single ritual action. There can often be more than one—sometimes mutually inconsistent—interpretations of the ritual's meaning. This ambiguity can be understood as essential to the working of ritual; it is not a weakness but a strength of ritual in that it permits group solidarity and action in the absence of actual consensus or agreement.[29] To a certain extent, rituals, especially ceremonial rituals, can contain and defuse the contradictions of a society. In the essential ambiguity of the ritual, a course of action can be selected in which all the conflicting principles and ideologies of the society are both expressed and subsumed.[30] Needless to say that, to the extent that critical, analytic thought, instead of ritual action, is applied to the conflict situations, the contradictions underlying the conflict are more likely to appear and the conflicts will become more difficult to resolve.[31]

Within the sacred space of ritual ceremony, our perception of legitimate social ends and activities is framed and ordered, even if these social ends and activities are internally contradictory. The greater the sense of these contradictions, the greater the sense of the reality of the ritual activity in which the contradictions can all coexist. Thus ritual takes contradiction, and transforms it to shape our understanding of the social order in which we live.

A THEORY OF LEGAL RITUAL

At the outset, it is important to define a few central terms. The concepts of rule, form and ritual are often confused in discussions about the value of "bright line" rules versus discretionary standards,[32] or the value of formal reasoning versus substantive reasoning.[33] Legal rituals are not rules of law. A rule of law is a general maxim which applies to more than one person on more than one occasion. Although rules of law can often be expressed with the same logical form as laws of physical science,[34] rules of law are created by acts of will, apply within a human community and have normative force only within that community.[35] Rules of law regulate human social behaviour. A rule may regulate that behaviour by specific or vague prescriptions; it might require drivers to stay on the right side of the road, or require them to drive with a reasonable standard of care. One has a duty to learn the rule and regulate one's behaviour accordingly. If one's behaviour is challenged, the rule is applied to the behaviour to determine whether or not the behaviour is within the scope of the rule. But the behaviour exists apart from the rule regulating it, and, if necessary, the behaviour can be described without reference to the regulative rule.

A legal ritual on the other hand is a legal *event*. It is something that is *done*. A rule of law can be expressed abstractly, but a legal ritual exists only in the concrete actions of a particular group of human beings. The execution of a will, the conveyance of real property, the execution of a bank's collateral note or agreement, the making of a formal plea in court, are rituals which may or may not express intentions, but if the proper forms are observed, the legal transaction is completed. Technically speaking, legal consequences do not "follow" from the proper execution of the legal ritual. The proper execution of the legal ritual *constitutes* the legally significant event.

A legal form is a fixed pattern of legally significant words which is consistently used to execute specific legal rituals. Legal forms are rarely drafted from "scratch." They are nearly always prepared in advance by attorneys, even if attorneys are not present when the forms are executed by business persons. Attorneys themselves usually model their forms on other forms from previous transactions or on models found in form books. Sometimes, "fill in the blank" standardized forms are used.[36] Different names and factual information are inserted into the form, while the form recites the legally operative language characteristic of the specific legal transaction.

Legal forms are not legal rituals but are *used* in legal rituals. For instance, the execution of a collateral note, the conveyance of real property, the execution of a writ, the signing of a will, the making of a residential lease, all may involve the use of standard or customary forms. But the form for the collateral note does not create a negotiable instrument by itself, the quitclaim form does not itself convey real property, the writ of execution form alone does not enforce a judgment, a form will alone is not a will, a standard realtor's lease form does not create a tenancy. Not until a form is used in the proper circumstances by the proper parties does the legal event which is the ritual come into existence. Until then, the form remains an inert set of marks on paper or in the files of a computer.

Legal forms and legal rituals are not products of regulative rules of law. The specifications of the proper form and the proper circumstances necessary for the completion of a legal ritual can be expressed so that they may appear to be regulative rules of law; but these specifications are in reality what the philosopher John Searle has called *constitutive* rules.[37] Constitutive rules do not merely regulate, they create or define new forms of behaviour.[38] They are less like the rules of the road and more like the rules of a game. Searle gives the example of a constitutive rule of chess, "a checkmate is made when the king is attacked in such a way that no move will leave it unattacked."[39] A constitutive legal rule might be, "a will is a written declaration of a person over the age of eighteen disposing of property at his death signed at its end by that person and by two attesting witnesses." The rules of chess do not regulate an independently existing activity of playing chess; without such rules there would be no such game. Likewise, without the rules governing the execution of wills the legal event known as making a will would not exist. The activity of driving exists independent of the rule requiring one to do so on the right side of the street; but the activities of playing chess or making wills do not exist independent of their constitutive rules.[40]

Constitutive rules are created as a matter of convention or definition, not by virtue of their containing imperative force or information about the world.[41] A regulative rule is likely to have the form "Do X" or "If Y do X," and is expressed in the imperative case: for instance, "drive on the right side of the street" or "if you drive, stay on the right side of the street." A constitutive rule, on the other hand, is more likely to have the form "X counts as Y" and/or "X counts as Y in context C." In other words, the rules of "checkmating" or "will making," simply provide part of the definition of "checkmate" or "will."[42]

Systems of constitutive rules create the possibility of new forms of behaviour which could not exist independent of those rules. Searle calls these new forms of behaviour "institutional facts," as opposed to "brute facts." Brute facts are statements about physical or mental events. They are statements such as "This stone is next to that stone," "Bodies attract with a force inversely proportional to the square of the distance between them and directly proportional to the product of their mass," and "I have a pain."[43] Institutional facts are statements about actions within social institutions, statements such as "Mr. Smith married Miss Jones," "Dodgers beat the Giants three to two in eleven innings," "Green was convicted of larceny," and "Congress passed the Appropriations Bill."[44] Statements about institutional facts cannot be reduced to physical or psychological events.[45] The physical or psychological events only count as part of an institutional fact if they occur in the context of a system of constitutive rules.

Legal rituals, then, are institutional facts which exist in the context of systems of constitutive rules. As such, legal rituals are concrete, visible sets of symbolic acts which give life to social institutions. For instance, the creation and maintenance of the legal entity known as a corporation is almost entirely a creation of legal rituals. The corporation is created when one chooses a suitable name, files certain documents with and obtains a certificate of incorporation. Formal meetings of the shareholders are held to elect a board of directors and resolutions of the board of directors are required to elect and authorise the officers of the corporation. In addition, the board must meet regularly, enact by-laws, vote on board resolutions and ratify the actions of its officers.[46] Apart from the enactment of these legal rituals nothing has changed in the physical world. The business may continue to employ the same people and sell to the world the same goods. But the shareholders of the corporation now have liability only to the extent of their interest in the corporation, and the corporation can continue to do business after the death of its founders, and local managers wearing a corporate logo identify themselves not with individual mangers or directors but with the institution known as Ford, IBM or the Southern Pacific Railroad. Through such rituals, the corporation takes on a life of its own.

RITUAL AND POLICY: EVALUATION OF LEGAL RITUAL

The study of law is often confined to the process of making rules, interpreting them, applying them to specific cases and sanctioning violations—that is, law is studied as a system of regulative rules.[47] A regulative rule is understood in terms of its purposes, the policies or the principles it serves.[48] For instance, the income tax deduction for mortgage interest payments which is permitted homeowners serves the governmental policy of encouraging individual home ownership. The rule, "no vehicles in the park," serves the purpose of keeping the park free for pedestrians. There is obviously an intimate relationship between the expression of the regulative rule, the rule's purpose or policy and the rule's actual impact on human behaviour.[49]

Even among non-governmental entities a clearly understood policy can be just as effective a means for controlling individual behaviour, and exercising the purposes of the controlling group, as a regulation enacted by a government.[50] Policy, in some cases, has a tendency to blur into regulative rules. For example, a government agency may refuse to accept bids by a private contractor when the contractor has failed to comply with civil rights "guidelines." Thus, regulative rules are evaluated in terms of their effectiveness in promoting the policies they are designed to promote and achieving the purposes they are designed to achieve. On the other hand, it is not proper to analyze constitutive rules in terms of purposes and policies. No one, for instance, would seek to find a policy for the rule of checkmate in chess.[51] The rule is a matter of definition or convention. To attempt to find a policy underlying the rule of checkmate confuses a constitutive rule with a regulative rule, a category mistake.[52] Constitutive rules in the law are no different from constitutive rules in chess; it makes no sense to try to understand them in terms of their policies or purposes. For example, Lon Fuller, in an attempt to find a purpose underlying the requirement of a seal in the execution of certain types of debt instruments, suggests that the seal performed a cautionary function:

> A formality may also perform a cautionary or deterrent function by acting as a check against inconsiderate action. The seal in its original form performed this function remarkably well. The affixing and impressing of a wax wafer—symbol in the popular mind of legalism and weightiness—was an excellent device for introducing the circumspective frame of mind appropriate in one pledging his future.[53]

Fuller's reasoning does not bear close scrutiny. One could equally argue that the purpose of the rule of checkmate is to make chess players cautious about permitting their king to be exposed to danger. Fuller confuses a constitutive rule with a regulative one, then seeks to find a purpose underlying the constitutive rule, as if, like a regulative rule, it was intended to serve a determinate purpose or policy. Just as one must understand the rules of chess to understand the rule of checkmate, to understand the legal ritual of a debt instrument under seal one must place it in the context of the English civil pleading system, the legal game, so to speak, in which the constitutive rule of the seal played a role. In the old English pleading system, against an action, or lawsuit, brought on a sealed instrument the defendant could not plead *non debet*, he could not deny he owed the money.[54] The only plea available to the defendant was *non est factum suum*, it is not my deed or seal.[55] If a defendant made the plea of *non est factum suum* and a jury found that the sealed instrument was indeed the defendant's, the defendant was sent to prison for making the plea.[56] Fuller cites no historical or scientific study to support his assertion that the seal caused people using it to be "cautious." Whatever such a study might show we would still feel that people using sealed instruments *should* be cautious. However, this is because we feel they should know the rules of the game, not because the ritual of a seal magically produces in them some independent psychological state of mind.[57] In general, people tend to be cautious with legal rituals not because of any magical quality rituals possess but because there is an understanding of the institutional structure in which the rituals play a role.[58]

Another purpose often posited for legal rituals is that of serving as evidence of a transaction. For instance, the requirement that a gift be "handed over" to be valid is sometimes explained by saying that the "handing over" ritual serves an evidentiary function. According to this argument, the delivery of the donor and acceptance by the donee serves to prove the intention of the donor to give the gift and the intention of the donee to accept it.[59] The problem with this type of argument is that what is presented as "evidence" of an intention to make a gift and to receive it is none other than the legally significant event itself. The ritual of "handing over" involved in gift giving is simply part of the legal and conventional meaning of a "gift."[60] The reference to "evidence of an intention" is unnecessary to the explanation. It is needed only to keep the analysis of the ritual convention consistent with a legal metaphysics where law is thought to be a rational system based on intentions—a place where no ritual, no matter how benign, is welcome.

The same mistake is made by P. S. Atiyah when he discusses the legal necessity of a promise to repay borrowed money in contract law. Atiyah argues that the ritual of the promise serves as evidence that the transaction was not a gift, evidence that the borrower had in fact received the money, evidence of the amount owed, evidence of which party or par-

ties had the legal duty to repay the debt, and so forth.[61] These things listed by Atiyah as "good evidence," however, are simply the formal attributes of the legal relationship created by the promise itself. A necessary attribute of a promise to repay just *is* that it is not a gift, *is* for a sum certain, *is* made by a definite party, and so forth. It is as if Atiyah had argued that a marriage ceremony was "good evidence" of there being certain obligations between a certain man and a certain woman and then proceeded to list a husband's duties to his wife and a wife's duties to her husband. Of course, neither the promise to repay nor the marriage ceremony is "evidence" of legal duties—they are the ritual conventions used to *create* them.

Atiyah's concept of "evidence" is not the familiar one used by practicing attorneys. To Atiyah's example of a promise as "evidence," a trial lawyer would respond by asking what *evidence* there was of the promise, whether it was in a writing or an oral statement, whether witnesses were present, and so forth. The point of evidence is to prove that the promise, the constitutive ritual itself, occurred. That proven, the promise is not in turn evidence of something else, such as the intention of the promisor to bind himself to the terms of the promise. The promise is itself the thing to be proven, the legally significant event itself which, in part, *creates* the obligation to repay the money.[62]

In each case discussed above there is only a tangential relationship between the purpose posited for a legal ritual and the actual ritual practice. The "purpose" seems to be more rationalization than reason. While such "purposes" may sometimes be accomplished by the ritual, they always seem inadequate to explain it, especially when these "purposes" change over time. In this respect, legal ritual bears a startling resemblance to the religious rituals analyzed by Robertson Smith. In law as in religion, ritual has an internal dynamic which is structurally prior to the purposes given for the practice.[63] Just as it sometimes is a mistake to analyze religious rituals in theological terms, it is a mistake to analyze constitutive rules and legal rituals as expressing intentions, policies and purposes.

This does not mean that legal rituals are neutral in terms of their influence on society or that they cannot be changed, but the legal frameworks upon which contracts are formed, wills are executed and trials tried, are sometimes more resistant to change than discrete regulative rules. To understand a constitutive rule, one must examine how the rule works within the entire legal system, not only the limited areas where the rule manifests itself. It also tends to be more difficult to predict the effect of a change of such rules on the overall legal system. Accordingly, if one wishes to change or reform a constitutive rule, one must understand that the entire legal "game" may also be transformed.

For example, in the late fifteenth century the rules of chess were changed so that a pawn which reached the eighth rank could be promoted as part of the same move to a queen, rook, bishop or knight of the same colour. When this change took place, some argued that the acceptance of a plurality of Queens was tantamount to condoning adultery; others argued that it violated logic for a player to have the possibility of having more power than his initial forces.[64] What actually happened no one anticipated. Chess became infinitely more dynamic, nearly all the endgame knowledge garnered during the previous eight or nine centuries was rendered obsolete, and middle game play was radically transformed.[65] Likewise, in the late 18th and early 19th century when the constitutive rules of contract formation were simplified and clarified, permitting a wide variety of actions on contract, dramatic and unexpected changes took place throughout the legal system. These changes interacted with the changes taking place in the underlying economy to move contract law from a legal backwater into the very centre of the legal stage.[66]

One should think of legal rituals as providing the framework or context in which regulative rules operate. An issue involving the interpretation of a regulative rule and its application to the facts will be presented to a court and debated in the context of pleading, motions and, if a trial is required, the presentation of testimony. Within that context it may be possible to analyze a specific regulative rule in terms of a specific purpose. But any ritual component of that context can be understood only in the wider context of an interrelated system of constitutive rules.

LEGAL RITUAL AND THE GOVERNANCE OF SOCIETY

The Confucian philosophers were among the first to explore the legitimate role of ritual in the governance of society. Confucius argued strenuously that people's behaviour is not a simple product of rational deliberation based on rules and sanctions.[67] He pointed out that human action takes shape through the rituals in which people in the society participate.[68] Confucius understood that social institutions are not "free standing," but are constructed out of an intricate matrix of ceremonies and rituals.[69]

For Confucius, *li*, or ritual, meant those objective prescriptions of human behaviour, whether involving rite, ceremony, manners or general deportment, that bind human beings together in networks of interacting roles within the family as well as in political society.[70] Confucius recognized that ritual could modify behaviour in ways more powerful than regulative rules. Direct commands, he noted, bring to the subject's mind the possibility of doing the opposite, and can lead to instability. Rituals, as social action, not verbal expression, have no contraries and can produce harmony of wills and actions without provoking recalcitrance.[71] [Persons finding themselves] playing [their] appointed part[s] in *li* [are] already in harmony with others. It no more occurs to [such] person[s] to act otherwise than it occurs to a dancer to move to a different rhythm than that being played by the orchestra.[72]

No society has a uniform or consistent set of moral ideals; and legal ritual permits social action in the face of ideological contradiction.[73] Society cannot be governed only by legislation enforced by the physical power of the state.[74] Legal ritual makes uniform structure and order possible with minimum exercise of force.

As we have seen, gifts, deeds, wills, motions and trials do not have independent reality apart from the rituals attendant upon their creation. These rituals are events which mark, define and alter the rights and duties of people within a community—*create* these very institutional facts. In legal ritual, the social facts against which one judges the legitimacy of the ritual are themselves constituted by the ritual. In the words of an anthropologist, Maurice Bloch, "what is being said is the right thing because by the acceptance of the formalization of language it has become the only thing."[75] Through legal ritual, as through religious ritual, the world as lived and the world as imagined are fused through the agency of a single set of symbolic forms.[76]

Ritual is not a politically neutral process; it has an intimate relationship with society's ideology. Not only does ritual limit awareness of the scope of conflict and contradiction, it can transform conflict into a reaffirmation of certain social structures and values.[77] If this aspect of ritual has been praised as a conservative force in society,[78] it has also been criticized, especially by Marxists, for the same reason. Douglas Hay has articulated the view that legal ritual necessarily supports the existing ideology; that like religion, legal ritual is a social opiate, subsuming contradictions and unjust inequalities, permitting unjust social orders to survive. In his discussion of 18th century English criminal law Hay addresses how minor technical errors in an indictment, or written charge, could doom a prosecution otherwise founded on excellent evidence:

> If a name or date was incorrect, or if the accused was described as a "farmer" rather than the approved term "yeoman," the prosecution could fail. The courts held that such defects were conclusive . . . These formalisms in the criminal law seemed ridiculous to contemporary critics [who] argued that the criminal law, to be effective, must be known and determinate, instead of capricious and obscure . . . But it seems likely that the mass of Englishmen drew other conclusions from the practice. The punctilious attention to forms, the dispassionate and legalistic exchanges between counsel and the judge, argued that those administering and using the laws submitted to its rules. The law thereby became something more than the creature of a ruling class—it became a power with its own claims, higher than those of prosecutor, lawyers, and even the great scarlet-robed assize judge himself. To them, too, of course, the law was The Law. The fact that they reified it, that they shut their eyes to its daily enactment in Parliament by men of their own class, heightened the illusion. When the ruling class acquited men on technicalities they helped instil a belief in the disembodied justice of the law in the minds of all who

watch. In short, its very inefficiency, its absurd formalism, was part of its strength as ideology.[79]

Hay's analysis of the ideological role of ritual is shared by other Marxist anthropologists.[80] But the analysis of ritual as irrational and illusory raises the question: how does ritual manage to create such an illusion? Whence comes the respect accorded to legal ritual and ceremony? Is the mere fact that courts and lawyers adhere to ritual enough to ensure that the lower classes will be impressed by this fact too? Why is a court's adherence to legal ritual—as opposed to genuine impartiality—a particularly useful way to earn the respect of the public? Hay is right that ritual works to strengthen the respect accorded to the legal system, but his analysis fails to account for how complex the ritual process can be. The rituals of the search warrant, criminal indictment by grand jury, and, perhaps the most dramatic example of all, a death warrant for the execution of a defendant convicted of a capital crime, all humanize what otherwise would seem starkly brutal acts of aggression.

Of course, ritual has been used to support extremely repressive societies, and can be instrumental not only in covering up social contradictions, but also in crushing opponents of the regime and contradictory points of view.[81] But it is a mistake to assume that ritual strengthens any particular ideology, or is necessarily conservative. Sometimes a ritual may be instrumental in challenging or overthrowing a prevailing ideology.[82] Even more important, at times, rituals can be instrumental in transforming and humanizing social conflicts. In this latter role, ritual has a wider purpose—to establish a meaningful relationship between the values a people hold and the general order of existence within which it finds itself. In this latter role, ritual is a means by which human beings construe and construct their world—thus, a form of meaning itself.[83]

EVALUATION OF LEGAL RITUAL

If ritual exists necessarily as a part of all societies, if it can be oppressive as well as humanizing and if it resists evaluation in terms of its purposes or policies, how does one evaluate ritual—how does one distinguish good ritual from bad? First, one clearly does not evaluate legal rituals in terms of the principles or policies supposedly served by those rituals. As we have seen, these principles and policies are more often than not rationalizations of a given ritual practice. Second, a legal ritual must be understood in terms of the entire game in which it plays a role, not simply in terms of discrete "effects" attributed to the legal ritual. Beyond these conclusions, there is no general set of valuative criteria which can be applied in the abstract to "judge" the legitimacy of legal rituals. Each ritual must be evaluated on a case by case basis, in the overall context of the "game" in which it plays a role.

In the remainder of this article, I use ritual theory to evaluate a familiar ritual practice in the legal system. I briefly evaluate the Miranda rule in criminal procedure to show how ritual theory can help us understand the true value of a legal practice which makes little sense from the point of view of policy. The case study is in the nature of a sketch, and does not purport to be an exhaustive treatment of the subject. However, I try to indicate the limitations of policy-based valuative tools and to point out how ritual theory can help us better understand and evaluate legal practices.

CASE STUDY: MIRANDA

In the late 60's and early 70's, American society suffered from severe fissures in the social fabric. These were occasioned by a war that was very unpopular, particularly among the young who were asked to fight it, by a civil rights movement which brought to public attention discrimination against people of colour, and by a demographic surge of young people holding values quite different from older members of the population in positions of authority. The police quickly became associated with the conservative forces hostile to the forces of change.

In this context, a series of Supreme Court decisions came down strictly applying to the field of criminal procedure the Constitutional requirements of search warrants, showings of probable cause for arrest, neutral and detached magistrates, and the right to independent counsel. Perhaps the most controversial change in this "procedural revolution" was the ritual of the "Miranda" warning.[84]

The *Miranda* decision set out a prescribed litany that a police officer was required to recite to a person immediately upon taking him into custody: (1) that he is under arrest, (2) that he has a right to remain silent, (3) if he gives up the right to remain silent, any statement he does make may be used as evidence against him, (4) that he has the right to the presence of an attorney and (5) that if he cannot afford an attorney, one will be appointed for him. Unless and until these warnings [are] given, no evidence obtained in the interrogation may be used against the accused.[85]

The express purpose given for the imposition of *Miranda* was to eliminate a perceived danger of the police obtaining "coerced" confessions from criminal suspects. Of course, actual practice showed that even when *Miranda* warnings were given the number of confessions made by suspects in custody remained about the same.[86] Even if *Miranda* had the intended effect, it could be argued that throwing out a conviction based on evidence seized or a confession obtained without first giving a "Miranda" warning, is undesirable. The failure to comply with this ritual has arguably little or no effect on the fundamental question of the accused's guilt or innocence of the crime with which he was charged. *Miranda*, accordingly, has been criticized as judicial legislation which made little or no sense from a point of view of policy.[87] The actual decision was hardly popular and probably decreased public respect for the judiciary.

However, as a legal ritual, *Miranda* does more than create a mindless hoop for law enforcement officers to jump through. First, *Miranda* ties into a rich vein of ideological symbolism. Ritual can be used as it is here, to relate local participants to higher levels of social organization and wider networks of legal symbolism. In the case of *Miranda*, the ritual tied and subordinated local police . . . and local state courts to the federal judiciary, to the Supreme Court and to the Constitution.

Furthermore, as legal ritual, the administration of *Miranda* warnings has been highly successful in disrupting prior patterns of behaviour and attitudes between the police and the public. Before *Miranda*, one could be dragged off to jail without ceremony, in a behaviour pattern therapists might have called "underritualized."[88] The administration of *Miranda* rites imposed a kind of therapeutic distancing process on the parties, defusing the tension otherwise engendered by the arrest, and humanizing the parties involved, especially the policeman administering the ceremony. Miranda is as effective as it is because in part it involves such dramatic role-reversal. It goes against the grain for a policeman, interested in investigating the facts, to tell a suspect that he need not talk to him. *Miranda* provides a salient marker to symbolize the rite of passage of an accused from freedom into police custody. *Miranda*, illogical as it may seem from a strict policy analysis, makes for compelling legal theatre.

Miranda has been so dramatic and effective a ritual that it has quickly become associated in the public mind with the very nature of being arrested, appearing repeatedly in television and film accounts of police work. The public perception of *Miranda* is not mistaken. The giving of *Miranda* warnings now have become a *constitutive* part of the making of a valid arrest—part of the very meaning of being arrested.

Miranda, leading occasionally to unmeritorious acquittals, hardly has increased respect for judges, but it may well have increased the public respect for police. . . .[89] It also may have contributed to a much more professional self-image of the police . . . themselves. By providing a structure for the imposition of force by police . . . on citizens, the rituals of the criminal procedural revolution—and *Miranda* in particular—have helped to humanize the American criminal process.

NOTES

1. Lon Fuller, "Consideration and Form", *Columbia Law Review* 45 (1945), 799, 800.
2. T. Arnold, *Symbols of Government* (New Haven: Yale University Press, 1935), 22. "When they do recognize a taboo, they condemn it, instead of realizing that such is the stuff which binds society together and makes it orderly and comfortable in its spirit."
3. B. Malinowski, *Crime and Custom in Savage Society* (Totowa, N.J.: Littlefield, Adams & Co., 1926, 1982 ed.); M. Gluckman, *Politics, Law and Ritual in Tribal Society* (Chicago: Aldine, 1965), and *The Judicial Process Among the Barotse of Northern Rhodesia* (Manchester: Manchester University Press, 1955, rev. ed. 1967).
4. See, e.g., R. Pound, *Introduction to the Philosophy of Law* (New Haven: Yale University Press, 1922, 1954 ed.). Also see E. Durkheim, "The Nature and Evolution of Contract", in *Durkheim and the Law*, ed. S. Lukes and A. Scull (New York: St. Martins Press, 1983), 199–200.
5. B. Nicholas, *An Introduction to Roman Law* (Oxford: Clarendon Press, 1965), 61.
6. See, e.g., Mary Douglas, *Purity and Danger: an Analysis of the Concepts of Pollution and Taboo* (London: Routledge & Kegan Paul, 1966, 1984 ed.), 61. Also see generally E. W. Said, *Orientalism* (New York: Vintage, 1979).
7. E. A. Hoebel, *The Law of Primitive Man* (New York: Atheneum, 1974); Victor Turner, *The Ritual Process* (Chicago: Aldine, 1969), 8: ". . . certain regularities that emerged from the analysis of numerical data, such as village genealogies and censuses and records of succession to office and inheritance of property, became fully intelligible only in the light of values embodied and expressed in symbols at ritual performances." Also see Sally F. Moore, "Legal Liability and Evolutionary Interpretation", in *Law as Process* (London: Routledge & Kegan Paul, 1978), 83–134; L. Rosen, "Equity and Discretion in a Modern Islamic Legal System", *Law and Society Review* 15 (1980–1981), 217–45.
8. But see Moore, "Introduction", *Law as Process, supra* n.7, at 1–31. Also see C. Geertz, "Fact and Law in Comparative Perspective", in *Local Knowledge: Further Essays in Interpretive Anthropology* (New York: Basic Books, 1983), 167–234.
9. J. M. Cullen, "Some Principles of Animal Communication", in *Non-Verbal Communication*, ed. R. A. Hinde (Cambridge: Cambridge University Press, 1972), 116.
10. M. D. Mather. "The Treatment of an Obsessive-Compulsive Patient by Discrimination Learning and Reinforcement of Decision-Making", *Behaviour Research and Therapy* 8 (1970), 315–18.
11. See e.g., V. Turner, *The Forest of Symbols: Aspects of Ndembu Ritual* (Ithaca, N.Y.: Cornell University Press, 1967), 19; D. I. Kertzer, *Ritual Politics and Power* (New Haven: Yale University Press, 1988), 8; R. Firth, *Elements of Social Organization* (London: Watts, 1951), 222; E. M. Ahern, *Chinese Ritual and Politics* (Cambridge: Cambridge University Press, 1981), 1.
12. Turner, *supra* n.11, at 10; Firth, *supra* n.11, at 222.
13. "Introduction", in *Secular Ritual*, eds. S. F. Moore and B. G. Myerhoff (Assen, The Netherlands: Van Gorcum, 1977), 3.
14. *Ibid.*
15. Douglas, *supra* n.6, at 58.
16. W. Robertson Smith, *Lectures on the Religion of the Semites* (London: S. A. Cook, 1927), 3rd ed., esp. lectures vi–xi.
17. R. Benedict, "Ritual", *Encyclopedia of the Social Sciences* 13 (1937), 396–397. "The rite is similarly more stable and more fundamental than the rationalizations that universally accompany it. As soon as it receives traditional form the ritual itself becomes a standard of reference; 'from it proceed the random whys, and to it return the indeterminate therefores.' "
18. C. Geertz, "Religion As a Cultural System", in *The Interpretation of Cultures* (New York: Basic Books, 1973), 112; T. Jennings, "On Ritual Knowledge", *Journal of Religion* 62

(1982), 116: "Ritual Knowledge is gained not by detached observation or contemplation but through action. . . ."

19. M. Mauss, *A General Theory of Magic* (New York: W. W. Norton & Company, 1902–03, Brain Trans. 1972, 1975 Reprint), 19. "Magic has been linked with a system of jural obligations, since in many places there are words and gestures which are binding sanctions."

20. Malinowski, *supra* n.3, at 93–94.

21. Mauss, *supra* n. 19, at 19. "It is true that legal actions may often acquire a ritual character and that contracts, oaths and trials by ordeal are to a certain extent sacramental. Nevertheless, the fact remains that although they contain ritual elements they are not magical rites in themselves. If they assume a special kind of efficacy or if they do more than merely establish contractual relations between persons, they cease to be legal actions and do become magical or religious rites. Ritual acts, on the contrary, are essentially thought to be able to produce much more than a contract: rites are eminently effective; they are creative; they *do* things." (Emphasis in original).

   In light of the later work of J. L. Austin, see *infra*, at note 22, it is difficult to understand the distinction Mauss is trying to draw between rites which "do things" and "merely establishing contractual relations between persons" as if this were not *doing* something too.

22. J. L. Austin, "Performative Utterances", *Philosophical Papers*, eds. J. O. Urmson and G. J. Warnock (Oxford: Oxford University Press, 1961, 1970 ed.), 233; *How To Do Things With Words* (New York: Oxford University Press, 1962, 1965 ed.).

23. S. J. Tambiah, "A Performative Approach to Ritual", in *Culture, Thought and Social Action: An Anthropological Perspective* (Cambridge, Massachusetts: Harvard University Press, 1985), 123–166.

24. Of course, if there was no intention whatsoever to become married by virtue of the ceremony, one can sometimes undo the marriage, but only by virtue of executing another ritual, that of annulment.

25. See David Hume, *A Treatise of Human Nature*, bk. III, pt. ii, sec. 5 (Oxford: Clarendon Press, 1739, 1896 ed.), 524. "Nay, even this we must not carry so far as to imagine that one, whom, by our quickness of understanding, we conjecture, from certain signs, to have an intention of deceiving us, is not bound by his expression or verbal promise, if we accept of it."

26. *Ibid.* "All these contradictions are easily accounted for, if the obligation of promises be merely a human invention for the convenience of society; but will never be explain'd, if it be something real and natural, arising from any action of the mind or body."

27. For discussion of characteristics of propositional meaning, see G. Frege, "Thoughts", in *Logical Investigations*, ed. P. T. Geach, trans. P. T. Geach and R. H. Stoothoff (Oxford: Basil Blackwell, 1977).

28. See F. Stahl, "The Meaninglessness of Ritual", *Numen* 26 (1979), 2.

29. Kertzer, *supra* n.11, at 69: "It is the very ambiguity of the symbols employed in ritual action that makes ritual useful in fostering solidarity without consensus"; J. Fernandez, "Symbolic Consensus in a Fang Reformative Cult", *American Anthropologist* 67 (1965), 902.

30. Turner, *The Ritual Process, supra* n. 7, at 10–13. See also Arnold, *supra* n.2, at 44. "Legal institutions must constantly reconcile ideological conflicts, just as individuals reconcile them by shoving inconsistencies back into a sort of institutional subconscious mind."

31. Barbara G. Myerhoff, "We don't wrap herring in a printed page: Fusion, fiction and continuity in secular ritual", *Secular Ritual, supra* n. 13, at 199–200. "The fiction underlying ritual is twofold: first, that rituals are not made-up productions, and second, that the contradictions embraced by their symbols have been erased."

32. D. Kennedy, "Form and Substance in Private Law Adjudication", *Harvard Law Review* 89 (1976), 1685, 1693.

33. P. S. Atiyah, "Form and Substance in Contract Law", in *idem, Essays on Contract* (Oxford: Clarendon Press, 1986), 93–94; P. S. Atiyah and R. S. Summers, *Form and Substance in Anglo-American Law: A Comparative Study of Legal Reasoning, Legal Theory, and Legal Institutions* (Oxford: Clarendon Press, 1987).

34. C. G. Hempel, *Philosophy of Natural Science* (Englewood Cliffs, N.J.: Prentice-Hall, 1966), ch. 5.

35. The nature of the "normative force" of law is largely irrelevant to the themes of this paper. Legal positivists hold that the "normative force" of law depends on the expectation of sanction or punishment upon its violation. H. L. A. Hart, *The Concept of Law* (Oxford: Clarendon Press, 1961), 6–7. Alternative theories maintain that laws express certain norms of behaviour which are obeyed not out of fear of the sanction attendant upon their transgression, but because of certain shared beliefs about a proper code of behaviour. Lon Fuller, "Positivism and Fidelity to Law", *Harvard Law Review* 71 (1958), 630.

36. Standard lease and contract forms for transactions involving real estate are available from realtors' associations, standard promissory notes from banking associations, standard construction contracts are available from the American Institute of Architects, and so forth. There also are thousands of other commercially produced forms, for different legal transactions. For example, the Blumberg company of New York has a sales catalogue which lists 30 different forms for affidavits, 26 different forms for deeds, 42 forms for mortgages, 31 different types of contracts, several kinds of forms for bills of sale, special forms for the enforcement of judgments and releases and sells a form kit for the incorporation of a business. Blumberg also sells pleading forms for City Court, New York Supreme Court, U.S. District Court, and various courts of appeals. These forms are now available on computer software.

37. J. R. Searle, *Speech Acts: An Essay in the Philosophy of Language* (Cambridge: Cambridge University Press, 1969), 33–42.

38. *Ibid.*, at 33.

39. *Ibid.*, at 34.

40. *Ibid.*, at 33–34.

41. But see K. Olivecrona, *Law as Fact* (London: Stevens & Sons, 2nd ed., 1971), 221–222. Olivecrona rejects the view that performatives have effects independent of intentions.

42. Searle, *supra* n. 37.

43. *Ibid.*, 50–53.

44. *Ibid.*, 51.

45. *Ibid.*

46. Forms for all of these actions are conveniently provided by manufacturers of legal forms. The sale of such corporate "form kits" as Blumberg's "Black Beauty" first manufactured in the 1870's and still used today, may have played an important role in the growth of the corporate form of business. See generally R. E. Seavoy, *The Origins of the American Business Corporation, 1784–1855* (Westport, Conn.: Greenwood Press, 1982); A. D. Chandler, Jr., *The Visible Hand: The Managerial Revolution in American Business* (Cambridge, Mass.: Belknap Press, 1977).

47. See, e.g., E. A. Hoebel, *The Law of Primitive Man* (New York: Atheneum, 1974), 28; O. W. Holmes, "The Path of the Law", *Harvard Law Review*, 10 (1897), 457; S. Macaulay, *Private Government* (Madison: Disputes Processing Research Program of University of Wisconsin Law School, 1986), 1.

48. See, e.g., O. W. Holmes, *The Common Law*, ed. DeWolfe (Boston: Little, Brown & Company, 1881, 1963 ed.), 8; Pound, *supra* n. 4, at 77.

49. See generally R. von Ihering, *Law as a Means to an End*, trans. I. Husik (Boston: Boston Book Company, 1913); H. L. A. Hart, *supra* n.35, esp. chapters 1–3. The link of regulative rules to purposes and policies must include the *caveat* that, "neither politicians nor scientists can fully, nor, often, even satisfactorily predict the consequences of legislation." Moore, *Law as Process, supra* n.7, at 7. Moore makes a profound critique of the conventional self-image of law in the American legal profession as an intentionally constructed framework of social order.

50. See, e.g., Macaulay, *Private Government, supra* n.47.

51. The constitutive rule of checkmate should be distinguished from regulative rules of tournament play, such as the "touch move" rule and rules setting time limitations on play.

52. For discussion of the term category mistake, see G. Ryle, *The Concept of Mind* (New York: Barnes and Noble, 1949), 1–20.

53. Lon Fuller, "Consideration and Form", *Columbia Law Review* 45 (1945), 799, 801.

54. S. F. C. Milsom, *Historical Foundations of the Common Law* (Toronto: Butterworths, 1981, 2nd ed.), 250.

55. *Ibid.*

56. *Ibid.*

57. The modern day legal ritual of sworn affidavits is properly understood in the context of motion practice, and in the wider context of the practice of Courts ruling "on the record." Less important (although not irrelevant) to the understanding of affidavits is the possible criminal prosecution for a false statement and the possible religious damnation associated with the swearing of a false oath.

58. For instance, in Taiwan, the "chop" (or personal seal) is used instead of manual signatures to execute checks, promissory notes and other financial instruments and continues to play much the same role that the seal recently did in the West. Interestingly, business people typically keep their "chops" in safety deposit vaults, and the use of checks is not widespread

among consumers. See Jane K. Winn, "Taiwan Ends Criminal Penalties for Bad Checks in Move to Reform its Financial System", *East Asian Executive Reports* 8:8 (August 15, 1988), 9.

59. See e.g., *Danby v. Tucker*, 31 W.R. 578 (1883).

60. This was recognized by Lord Esher in *Cochrane v. Moore*, (1890) 25 Q.B.D. 57: "I have come to the conclusion that in ordinary English language, and in legal effect, there cannot be a 'gift' without a giving and a taking. The giving and taking are the two contemporaneous reciprocal acts which constitute a 'gift.' They are a necessary part of the proposition that there has been a 'gift.' They are not evidence to prove that there has been a gift, but fact to be proved to constitute the proposition that there has been a gift."

61. P. S. Atiyah, *The Rise and Fall of Freedom of Contract* (Oxford: Clarendon Press, 1979), 144–145.

62. The Statute of Frauds, which requires that written documents accompany certain types of transactions, is often given as an example of "the evidentiary function" of legal rituals. This is a mistake. The Statute of Frauds is a regulative rule, not a constitutive one. It provides a defense to action on an oral promise (the legal ritual) which is deemed waived if not affirmatively pleaded by the defendant: Atiyah, *ibid.*, at 205–208.

63. Robertson Smith, *supra* n.16, at lectures vi–xi.

64. D. Hooper and K. Whyld, *The Oxford Companion to Chess* (Oxford: Oxford University Press, 1984), 267.

65. *Ibid.*, at 145.

66. L. M. Friedman, *History of American Law* (New York: Touchstone, 2nd ed. 1985), 275–279; M. J. Horwitz, *The Transformation of American Law, 1780–1860* (Cambridge, Massachusetts: Harvard University Press, 1977), ch.6; Atiyah, *supra* n.61.

67. *Confucian Analects*, Bk. II; Ch. 3, transl. Legge (Taipei: Southern Materials Center, Inc., 1983 ed.). "If the People be led by laws, and uniformity sought to be given them by punishments, they will try to avoid the punishment, but have no sense of shame. If they be led by ritual, they will have the sense of shame, and moreover will become good." See also H. Fingarette, *Confucius—The Secular as Sacred* (New York: Harper & Row, 1972), 28.

68. J. G. A. Pocock, "Ritual, Language, Power: An essay on the apparent meanings of ancient Chinese philosophy", *Political Science* 16 (1964), 6.

69. B. I. Schwartz, *The World of Thought in Ancient China* (Cambridge, Mass.: Belknap Press, 1985). 67–75. See also Douglas, *supra* n.6, at 62 ("As a social animal, man is a ritual animal. If ritual is suppressed in one form it crops up in others, more strongly the more intense the social interaction. Without the letters of condolence, telegrams of congratulations and even occasional postcards, the friendship of a separated friend is not a social reality. It has no existence without the rites of friendship. Social rituals create a reality which would be nothing without them.")

70. Schwartz, *supra* n. 69, at 67.

71. *Confucian Analects*, Bk. II, Ch. 3, *supra* n. 67.

72. Pocock, *supra* n.68, at 6.

73. See Arnold, *supra* n.2, at 10–17.

74. In modern times, the police, the telephone and the automo-

bile have revolutionized the ability of state bureaucracies to exercise power quickly and efficiently, but it is a mistake to conclude that such technological advances permit a society to be governed in the absence of ritual.

75. M. Bloch, "Introduction", in *Political Language and Oratory in Traditional Society*, ed. Maurice Bloch (London: Academic Press, 1975), 22.

76. Geertz, *supra* n.18, at 112.

77. See works cited *supra* n.30.

78. Malinowski, *supra* n.3 at 13.

79. D. Hay, "Property, Authority and the Criminal Law", in *Albion's Fatal Tree: Crime and Society in Eighteenth-Century England* (New York: Pantheon Books, 1975), 32–33. One problem with Hay's analysis is that it confuses the constitutive rules of criminal procedure with the enactment of regulatory rules by Parliament.

80. See e.g. M. Bloch, "Symbols, Song, Dance and Features of Articulation: Is Religion an Extreme Form of Traditional Authority?", *European Journal of Sociology* 15 (1974), 55–81; Bloch, *supra* n.75, at 1–28.

81. See B. Bettleheim, *The Informed Heart* (Glencoe: Free Press, 1960), 290–291 (Analysis of the Nazi ritual salute and its powerful political and psychological effectiveness in undermining dissent). Also see R. Bartlett, *Trial by Fire and Water: The Mediaeval Judicial Ordeal* (Oxford: Clarendon Press, 1986). (Analysis of the use of the ritual of the ordeal to consolidate the power of Charlemagne.)

82. Kertzer, *supra* n.11, at 151–173. (Many examples of use of ritual by opposition political groups); Eva Hunt, "Ceremonies of Confrontation and Submission: The Symbolic Dimension of Indian-Mexican Political Interaction", in *Secular Ritual, supra* n. 13, at 124–47 (use of ritual by peasants to develop points of view opposed to ruling class).

83. T. Jennings, "On Ritual Knowledge", *Journal of Religion* 62 (1982), 116.

84. *Miranda* v. *Arizona*, 384 U.S. 436 (1966).

85. *Ibid.*, at 444, 478–479.

86. See G. M. Caplan, "Questioning Miranda", *Vanderbilt Law Review* 38 (1985).

87. W. Gangi, "Confessions: Historical Perspective and a Proposal", *Houston Law Review* 10 (1973), 1087, 1103 ". . . [I]n an effort to eliminate swearing contests and protect the accused from police misconduct, Miranda constructed 'prophylactic and deterrent rules that result in the release of the factually guilty even in cases in which blotting out the illegality would still leave an adjudicative factfinder convinced of the accused's guilt.' "

88. Janine Roberts, "Definition, Functions, and Typology of Rituals", in *Rituals in Families and Family Therapy*, ed. Imber-Black, Roberts and Whiting (New York: W.W. Norton & Company, 1988), 26–33.

89. For a brief, though provocative, essay arguing for a reappraisal of the Warren Court, see M. J. Horwitz, "The Warren Court", *University of Chicago Law Review* 55 (1988), 450, 456.

Appendix:
Classification of the Selections

Here each of the selections from *Readings in Ritual Studies* is classified in several ways, allowing teachers to select their own range of subtopics. I have attempted to code each selection under six headings: ritual component, ritual type, religious tradition, geographical location, historical period, and academic discipline. Some articles could not be coded in all six ways; others appear in more than six subcategories.

Instructors who wish to organize a course so as to survey ritual theory across the disciplines or according to ritual type can easily do so. Use of *Readings* in this manner will likely be successful. Use of it to compare rites across religious traditions, cultural areas, historical periods, or geographical locations is possible but will probably be less successful. As is always the case with anthologies, compromises had to be made, so I have noted which categories have no illustrative selections so readers can see the gaps in this text's selections. Works that may seem obvious candidates for inclusion are sometimes missing. Perhaps their theoretical importance was overshadowed by the need to represent a discipline newly interested in ritual or by a selection that concentrates on an understudied ritual component. I compiled a list of obvious names important to the study of ritual. In effect, it was a seventh criterion, along with the main six. However, I sometimes opted for lesser-known names in order to represent disciplines whose voices would not be heard if I had attended only to those with long histories of studying ritual. Since the aim is to represent contemporary interdisciplinary research, older, classical selections (for example, those by Freud, Durkheim, Eliade, van Gennep) are kept to a minimum and usually made shorter than the main selections.

This classification system is a modified version of one that I first published in a bibliographical work called *Research in Ritual Studies* (Metuchen, NJ: Scarecrow Press, 1972). Originally, its purpose was to facilitate the cataloging of an archive of articles on ritual. Later, it was modified and used to classify articles submitted to the *Journal of Ritual Studies*, of which I was a founding editor.

The primary purpose of the codes is less to facilitate the analysis of rites than to organize bibliography. The scheme is subject to ongoing revision. For instance, the depth of subdivision in the rites of passage section has come about because of my own growing interest in that area; what was originally a cluster of topics became a set of subdivisions (2.1.1 through 2.1.5). Other means of classification could be developed that would reflect other priorities and other views of ritual.

The scheme could be read for its theoretical implications, but that would be troublesome if one were to assume that ritual rather than research on ritual is the object of classification. For example, the outline would seem to imply that rites have component parts and that there are distinct types of ritual. Both assumptions, however, are problematic. Any definition of types is likely to be culture-specific, and the notion of parts works better when considering objects than when studying actions and social processes. Nevertheless, I retain the division into components and types because research on ritual is conducted and written as if components and types were realities.

To take a second example, books on ritual may confine themselves to a single religious tradition, but rites themselves can appear in nonreligious traditions or in more than one religious tradition. Similarly, articles on ritual may focus on a single geographical area or historical period, even though rites themselves sometimes migrate across geographical or religious boundaries and survive through multiple eras.

So users of the outline do well to remember its

bibliographical purpose and to take care in drawing general conclusions about ritual from it.

1: RITUAL COMPONENTS

1.1: Ritual Action

Babcock, Barbara A. Arrange me into disorder: fragments and reflections on ritual clowning

Bell, Catherine. Constructing ritual

Driver, Tom F. Transformation: the magic of ritual

Erikson, Erik H. The development of ritualization

Freud, Sigmund. Obsessive actions and religious practices

Geertz, Clifford. Deep play: notes on the Balinese cockfight

Gill, Sam D. Disenchantment: a religious abduction

Goffman, Erving. Interaction ritual: deference and demeanor

Grimes, Ronald L. Ritual criticism and infelicitous performances

Handelman, Don, and Lea Shamgar-Handelman. Holiday celebrations in Israeli kindergartens

MacAloon, John J. Olympic games and the theory of spectacle in modern societies

Peña, Manuel H. Ritual structure in a Chicano dance

Schechner, Richard. Restoration of behavior

Smith, Bardwell. Buddhism and abortion in contemporary Japan: *mizuko kuyō* and the confrontation with death

Tambiah, Stanley J. A performative approach to ritual

Turner, Victor W. Liminality and communitas

1.2: Ritual Space

Babcock, Barbara A. Arrange me into disorder: fragments and reflections on ritual clowning

Bell, Diane. Women's business is hard work: central Australian aboriginal women's love rituals

Combs-Schilling, M. Elaine. Etching patriarchal rule: ritual dye, erotic potency, and the Moroccan monarchy

Eliade, Mircea. Ritual and myth

Peña, Manuel H. Ritual structure in a Chicano dance

Smith, Jonathan Z. The bare facts of ritual

van Gennep, Arnold. Territorial passage and the classification of rites

1.3: Ritual Time

Bell, Diane. Women's business is hard work: central Australian aboriginal women's love rituals

Burkert, Walter. The function and transformation of ritual killing

Combs-Schilling, M. Elaine. Etching patriarchal rule: ritual dye, erotic potency, and the Moroccan monarchy

Eliade, Mircea. Ritual and myth

Handelman, Don, and Lea Shamgar-Handelman. Holiday celebrations in Israeli kindergartens

MacAloon, John J. Olympic games and the theory of spectacle in modern societies

Myerhoff, Barbara. A death in due time: construction of self and culture in ritual drama

Peña, Manuel H. Ritual structure in a Chicano dance

Turner, Victor W. Liminality and communitas

Wallendorf, Melanie, and Eric J. Arnould. Consumption rituals of Thanksgiving Day

1.4: Ritual Objects

Bell, Diane. Women's business is hard work: central Australian aboriginal women's love rituals

Burkert, Walter. The function and transformation of ritual killing

Combs-Schilling, M. Elaine. Etching patriarchal rule: ritual dye, erotic potency, and the Moroccan monarchy

Geertz, Clifford. Deep play: notes on the Balinese cockfight

Goethals, Gregor T. Ritual: Ceremony and Super-Sunday

Handelman, Don, and Lea Shamgar-Handelman.

Holiday celebrations in Israeli kindergartens

Wallendorf, Melanie, and Eric J. Arnould. Consumption rituals of Thanksgiving Day

1.5: Ritual, Symbol, and Metaphor

Bell, Diane. Women's business is hard work: central Australian aboriginal women's love rituals

Bergesen, Albert. Political witch-hunt rituals

Bynum, Caroline Walker. Women's stories, women's symbols: a critique of Victor Turner's theory of liminality

Campany, Robert F. Xunzi and Durkheim as theorists of ritual practice

d'Aquili, Eugene G., and Charles D. Laughlin Jr. The neurobiology of myth and ritual

Douglas, Mary. Dirt: purity and danger

Handelman, Don, and Lea Shamgar-Handelman. Holiday celebrations in Israeli kindergartens

Hardin, Richard F. "Ritual" in recent literary criticism: the elusive sense of community

Kertzer, David I. Ritual, politics, and power

Lévi-Strauss, Claude. The effectiveness of symbols

MacAloon, John J. Olympic games and the theory of spectacle in modern societies

Myerhoff, Barbara G. A death in due time: construction of self and culture in ritual drama

Rappaport, Roy A. The obvious aspects of ritual

Turner, Victor W. Liminality and communitas

Turner, Victor W. Symbols in Ndembu ritual

1.6: Ritual, Society, and Group

Bell, Diane. Women's business is hard work: central Australian aboriginal women's love rituals

Bergesen, Albert. Political witch-hunt rituals

Combs-Schilling, M. Elaine. Etching patriarchal rule: ritual dye, erotic potency, and the Moroccan monarchy

Durkheim, Emile. Ritual, magic, and the sacred

Erikson, Erik H. The development of ritualization

Geertz, Clifford. Deep play: notes on the Balinese cockfight

Girard, René. Violence and the sacred: sacrifice

Goffman, Erving. Interaction ritual: deference and demeanor

Kertzer, David I. Ritual, politics, and power

Myerhoff, Barbara G. A death in due time: construction of self and culture in ritual drama

Peña, Manuel H. Ritual structure in a Chicano dance

Turner, Victor W. Liminality and communitas

Wallendorf, Melanie, and Eric J. Arnould. Consumption rituals of Thanksgiving Day

Winn, Peter A. Legal ritual

1.6.1: Women in Ritual

Bell, Diane. Women's business is hard work: central Australian aboriginal women's love rituals

Bynum, Caroline Walker. Women's stories, women's symbols: a critique of Victor Turner's theory of liminality

Combs-Schilling, M. Elaine. Etching patriarchal rule: ritual dye, erotic potency, and the Moroccan monarchy

Davis-Floyd, Robbie E. Ritual in the hospital: giving birth the American way

Laird, Joan. Women and ritual in family therapy

Smith, Bardwell. Buddhism and abortion in contemporary Japan: *mizuko kuyō* and the confrontation with death

1.6.2: Men in Ritual

Combs-Schilling, M. Elaine. Etching patriarchal rule: ritual dye, erotic potency, and the Moroccan monarchy

Crapanzano, Vincent. Rite of return: circumcision in Morocco

Geertz, Clifford. Deep play: notes on the Balinese cockfight

1.6.3: Children in Ritual

Crapanzano, Vincent. Rite of return: circumcision in Morocco

Davis-Floyd, Robbie E. Ritual in the hospital: giving birth the American way

Handelman, Don, and Lea Shamgar-Handelman. Holiday celebrations in Israeli kindergartens

Gill, Sam D. Disenchantment: a religious abduction

1.7: Ritual and The Self

d'Aquili, Eugene G., and Charles D. Laughlin Jr. The neurobiology of myth and ritual

Douglas, Mary. Dirt: purity and danger

Erikson, Erik H. The development of ritualization

Gill, Sam D. Disenchantment: a religious abduction

Girard, René. Violence and the sacred: sacrifice

Jennings, Theodore W., Jr. On ritual knowledge

Lévi-Strauss, Claude. The effectiveness of symbols

Myerhoff, Barbara G. A death in due time: construction of self and culture in ritual drama

Smith, Bardwell. Buddhism and abortion in contemporary Japan: *mizuko kuyō* and the confrontation with death

1.8: Ritual and Divine Beings

Durkheim, Emile. Ritual, magic, and the sacred

Gill, Sam D. Disenchantment: a religious abduction

Smith, Bardwell. Buddhism and abortion in contemporary Japan: *mizuko kuyō* and the confrontation with death

1.9: Ritual Language

Bell, Diane. Women's business is hard work: central Australian aboriginal women's love rituals

Bynum, Caroline Walker. Women's stories, women's symbols: a critique of Victor Turner's theory of liminality

d'Aquili, Eugene G., and Charles D. Laughlin Jr. The neurobiology of myth and ritual

Grimes, Ronald L. Ritual criticism and infelicitous performances

Hardin, Richard F. "Ritual" in recent literary criticism: the elusive sense of community

Lévi-Strauss, Claude. The effectiveness of symbols

Staal, Frits. The meaninglessness of ritual

Tambiah, Stanley J. A performative approach to ritual

1.10: Ritual Qualities and Quantities

Bell, Diane. Women's business is hard work: central Australian aboriginal women's love rituals

Turner, Victor W. Symbols in Ndembu ritual

1.11: Ritual and Cosmology

Bell, Diane. Women's business is hard work: central Australian aboriginal women's love rituals

Douglas, Mary. Dirt: purity and danger

Eliade, Mircea. Ritual and myth

1.12: Ritual Sound

Bell, Diane. Women's business is hard work: central Australian aboriginal women's love rituals

2: RITUAL TYPES

2.1: Rites of Passage

2.1.1: GENERAL WORKS

Peña, Manuel H. Ritual structure in a Chicano dance

Turner, Victor W. Liminality and communitas

van Gennep, Arnold. Territorial passage and the classification of rites

2.1.2: BIRTH AND CHILDHOOD

Davis-Floyd, Robbie E. Ritual in the hospital: giving birth the American way

Handelman, Don, and Lea Shamgar-Handelman. Holiday celebrations in Israeli kindergartens

Lévi-Strauss, Claude. The effectiveness of symbols

Schechner, Richard. Restoration of behavior

2.8: Worship, Liturgy

Jennings, Theodore W., Jr. On ritual knowledge

Rappaport, Roy A. The obvious aspects of ritual

2.9: Ritual Magic

Bell, Diane. Women's business is hard work: central Australian aboriginal women's love rituals

Douglas, Mary. Dirt: purity and danger

Driver, Tom F. Transformation: the magic of ritual

Smith, Jonathan Z. The bare facts of ritual

Tambiah, Stanley J. A performative approach to ritual

2.10: Ritual Healing

Driver, Tom F. Transformation: the magic of ritual

Laird, Joan. Women and ritual in family therapy

Lévi-Strauss, Claude. The effectiveness of symbols

2.11: Interaction Ritual

Erikson, Erik H. The development of ritualization

Freud, Sigmund. Obsessive actions and religious practices

Geertz, Clifford. Deep play: notes on the Balinese cockfight

Goffman, Erving. Interaction ritual: deference and demeanor

Peña, Manuel H. Ritual structure in a Chicano dance

2.12: Ritual and Altered States of Consciousness

d'Aquili, Eugene G., and Charles D. Laughlin Jr. The neurobiology of myth and ritual

2.13: Ritual Inversion

Babcock, Barbara A. Arrange me into disorder: fragments and reflections on ritual clowning

Turner, Victor W. Liminality and communitas

2.14: Ritual Drama

Babcock, Barbara A. Arrange me into disorder: fragments and reflections on ritual clowning

Geertz, Clifford. Deep play: notes on the Balinese cockfight

Gill, Sam D. Disenchantment: a religious abduction

Goethals, Gregor T. Ritual: Ceremony and Super-Sunday

Hardin, Richard F. "Ritual" in recent literary criticism: the elusive sense of community

Kertzer, David I. Ritual, politics, and power

MacAloon, John J. Olympic games and the theory of spectacle in modern societies

Schechner, Richard. Restoration of behavior

2.15: Experimental Ritual

Schechner, Richard. Restoration of behavior

Smith, Bardwell. Buddhism and abortion in contemporary Japan: *mizuko kuyō* and the confrontation with death

2.16: Commemorative Ritual

Handelman, Don, and Lea Shamgar-Handelman. Holiday celebrations in Israeli kindergartens

Kertzer, David I. Ritual, politics, and power

Myerhoff, Barbara G. A death in due time: construction of self and culture in ritual drama

Smith, Bardwell. Buddhism and abortion in contemporary Japan: *mizuko kuyō* and the confrontation with death

Wallendorf, Melanie, and Eric J. Arnould. Consumption rituals of Thanksgiving Day

3. RITES BY LOCATION

3.1: Comparative or Cross-Cultural Studies of Ritual

Campany, Robert F. Xunzi and Durkheim as theorists of ritual practice

Lévi-Strauss, Claude. The effectiveness of symbols [the Cuna of Panama]

Smith, Jonathan Z. The bare facts of ritual [the Ainu of Japan, circumpolar peoples]

Turner, Victor W. The forest of symbols [the Ndembu of Zambia]

3.3: Rites Located by Geographical Area

3.3.1: RITUAL IN NORTH AMERICA

Babcock, Barbara A. Arrange me into disorder: fragments and reflections on ritual clowning

Davis-Floyd, Robbie E. Ritual in the hospital: giving birth the American way

Driver, Tom F. Transformation: the magic of ritual

Gill, Sam D. Disenchantment: a religious abduction

Goethals, Gregor T. Ritual: Ceremony and Super-Sunday

Goffman, Erving. Interaction ritual: deference and demeanor

Jennings, Theodore W., Jr. On ritual knowledge

Kertzer, David I. Ritual, politics, and power

Laird, Joan. Women and ritual in family therapy

Peña, Manuel H. Ritual structure in a Chicano dance

Wallendorf, Melanie, and Eric J. Arnould. Consumption rituals of Thanksgiving day

Winn, Peter A. Legal ritual

3.3.2: RITUAL IN LATIN AMERICA

Lévi-Strauss, Claude. The effectiveness of symbols

Peña, Manuel H. Ritual structure in a Chicano dance [Hispanic North America]

3.3.3: RITUAL IN AFRICA

Combs-Schilling, M. Elaine. Etching patriarchal rule: ritual dye, erotic potency, and the Moroccan monarchy

Crapanzano, Vincent. Rite of return: circumcision in Morocco

Douglas, Mary. Dirt: purity and danger

Turner, Victor W. Symbols in Ndembu ritual

3.3.4: RITUAL IN EUROPE

Babcock, Barbara A. Arrange me into disorder: fragments and reflections on ritual clowning

Burkert, Walter. The function and transformation of ritual killing

Bynum, Caroline Walker. Women's stories, women's symbols: a critique of Victor Turner's theory of liminality

Girard, René. Violence and the sacred: sacrifice

3.3.5: RITUAL IN THE MIDDLE EAST, NEAR EAST, OR WEST ASIA

Grimes, Ronald L. Ritual criticism and infelicitous performances

Handelman, Don, and Lea Shamgar-Handelman. Holiday celebrations in Israeli kindergartens

3.3.6: RITUAL IN EAST ASIA

Bergesen, Albert. Political witch-hunt rituals

Campany, Robert F. Xunzi and Durkheim as theorists of ritual practice

Smith, Bardwell. Buddhism and abortion in contemporary Japan: *mizuko kuyō* and the confrontation with death

Staal, Frits. The meaninglessness of ritual

3.3.7: RITUAL IN AUSTRALIA AND OCEANIA

Bell, Diane. Women's business is hard work: central Australian aboriginal women's love rituals

Geertz, Clifford. Deep play: notes on the Balinese cockfight

3.3.8: RITUAL IN CIRCUMPOLAR REGIONS

Smith, Jonathan Z. The bare facts of ritual

3.3.9: RITUAL IN THE CARIBBEAN

No selections

3.4: Rites Located by Historical Period

3.4.1: PREHISTORIC RITUAL

Burkert, Walter. The function and transformation of ritual killing

3.4.2: RITUAL FROM THE SECOND MILLENIUM B.C.E. THROUGH THE THIRD CENTURY C.E.

Burkert, Walter. The function and transformation of ritual killing

Campany, Robert F. Xunzi and Durkheim as theorists of ritual practice

Girard, René. Violence and the sacred: sacrifice

Grimes, Ronald L. Ritual criticism and infelicitous performances

3.4.3: RITUAL FROM THE FOURTH CENTURY C.E. THROUGH THE EIGHT CENTURY C.E.

Bynum, Caroline Walker. Women's stories, women's symbols: a critique of Victor Turner's theory of liminality

3.4.4. RITUAL FROM THE NINTH CENTURY C.E. THROUGH THE SIXTEENTH CENTURY C.E.

Bynum, Caroline Walker. Women's stories, women's symbols: a critique of Victor Turner's theory of liminality

3.4.5 RITUAL FROM THE SEVENTEENTH CENTURY C.E. THROUGH THE NINETEENTH CENTURY C.E.

Babcock, Barbara A. Arrange me into disorder: fragments and reflections on ritual clowning

Campany, Robert F. Xunzi and Durkheim as theorists of ritual practice

Combs-Schilling, M. Elaine. Etching patriarchal rule: ritual dye, erotic potency, and the Moroccan monarchy

Smith, Jonathan Z. The bare facts of ritual

3.4.6 RITUAL IN THE TWENTIETH CENTURY

Babcock, Barbara A. Arrange me into disorder: fragments and reflections on ritual clowning

Bell, Catherine. Constructing ritual

Campany, Robert F. Xunzi and Durkheim as theorists of ritual practice

Combs-Schilling, M. Elaine. Etching patriarchal rule: ritual dye, erotic potency, and the Moroccan monarchy

Crapanzano, Vincent. Rite of return: circumcision in Morocco

Davis-Floyd, Robbie E. Ritual in the hospital: giving birth the American way

Douglas, Mary. Dirt: purity and danger

Driver, Tom F. Transformation: the magic of ritual

Durkheim, Emile. Ritual, magic, and the sacred

Erikson, Erik H. The development of ritualization

Freud, Sigmund. Obsessive actions and religious practices

Geertz, Clifford. Deep play: notes on the Balinese cockfight

Gill, Sam D. Disenchantment: a religious abduction

Girard, René. Violence and the sacred: sacrifice

Goethals, Gregor T. Ritual: Ceremony and Super-Sunday

Goffman, Erving. Interaction ritual: deference and demeanor

Grimes, Ronald L. Ritual criticism and infelicitous performances

Handelman, Don, and Lea Shamgar-Handelman. Holiday celebrations in Israeli kindergartens

Hardin, Richard F. "Ritual" in recent literary criticism: the elusive sense of community

Jennings, Theodore W., Jr. On ritual knowledge

Kertzer, David I. Ritual, politics, and power

Laird, Joan. Women and ritual in family therapy

Lévi-Strauss, Claude. The effectiveness of symbols

MacAloon, John J. Olympic games and the theory of spectacle in modern societies

Peña, Manuel H. Ritual structure in a Chicano dance

Rappaport, Roy A. The obvious aspects of ritual

Schechner, Richard. Restoration of behavior

Smith, Bardwell. Buddhism and abortion in contemporary Japan: *mizuko kuyō* and the confrontation with death

Smith, Jonathan Z. The bare facts of ritual

Tambiah, Stanley J. A performative approach to ritual

Turner, Victor W. Liminality and communitas

Turner, Victor W. Symbols in Ndembu ritual

van Gennep, Arnold. Territorial passage and the classification of rites

Wallendorf, Melanie, and Eric J. Arnould. Consumption rituals of Thanksgiving Day

Winn, Peter A. Legal ritual

4: DISCIPLINES USED TO STUDY RITUAL

4.1: Ritual in Religious Studies

Bell, Catherine. Constructing ritual

Campany, Robert F. Xunzi and Durkheim as theorists of ritual practice

Eliade, Mircea. Ritual and myth

Gill, Sam D. Disenchantment: a religious abduction

Grimes, Ronald L. Ritual criticism and infelicitous performances

Smith, Bardwell. Buddhism and abortion in contemporary Japan: *mizuko kuyō* and the confrontation with death

Smith, Jonathan Z. The bare facts of ritual

4.1.1 RITUAL IN THEOLOGY

Driver, Tom F. Transformation: the magic of ritual

Jennings, Theodore W., Jr. On ritual knowledge

4.2 Ritual in Anthropology

Babcock, Barbara A. Arrange me into disorder: fragments and reflections on ritual clowning

Bell, Catherine. Constructing ritual

Bell, Diane. Women's business is hard work: central Australian aboriginal women's love rituals

Burkert, Walter. The function and transformation of ritual killing

Combs-Schilling, M. Elaine. Etching patriarchal rule: ritual dye, erotic potency, and the Moroccan monarchy

Crapanzano, Vincent. Rite of return: circumcision in Morocco

Davis-Floyd, Robbie E. Ritual in the hospital: giving birth the American way

Douglas, Mary. Dirt: purity and danger

Geertz, Clifford. Deep play: notes on the Balinese cockfight

Handelman, Don, and Lea Shamgar-Handelman. Holiday celebrations in Israeli kindergartens

Kertzer, David I. Ritual, politics, and power

Lévi-Strauss, Claude. The effectiveness of symbols

MacAloon, John J. Olympic games and the theory of spectacle in modern societies

Myerhoff, Barbara G. A death in due time: construction of self and culture in ritual drama

Peña, Manuel H. Ritual structure in a Chicano dance

Rappaport, Roy A. The obvious aspects of ritual

Tambiah, Stanley J. A performative approach to ritual

Turner, Victor W. Liminality and communitas

Turner, Victor W. Symbols in Ndembu ritual

van Gennep, Arnold. Territorial passage and the classification of rites

4.3: Ritual in Sociology

Bergesen, Albert. Political witch-hunt rituals

Campany, Robert F. Xunzi and Durkheim as theorists of ritual practice

Durkheim, Emile. Ritual, magic, and the sacred

Girard, René. Violence and the sacred: sacrifice

Goffman, Erving. Interaction ritual: deference and demeanor

4.4: Ritual in Literature

Babcock, Barbara A. Arrange me into disorder: fragments and reflections on ritual clowning

Hardin, Richard F. "Ritual" in recent literary criticism: the elusive sense of community

4.5: Ritual in Philosophy

Babcock, Barbara A. Arrange me into disorder: fragments and reflections on ritual clowning

Grimes, Ronald L. Ritual criticism and infelicitous performances

Staal, Frits. The meaninglessness of ritual

4.6: Ritual in History, Classics, and Archaeology

Burkert, Walter. The function and transformation of ritual killing

Bynum, Caroline Walker. Women's stories, women's symbols: a critique of Victor Turner's theory of liminality

4.7: Ritual in Communications, Journalism, and Media Studies

Goethals, Gregor T. Ritual: Ceremony and Super-Sunday

4.8: Ritual in Psychology

Erikson, Erik H. The development of ritualization

Freud, Sigmund. Obsessive actions and religious practices

Laird, Joan. Women and ritual in family therapy

Lévi-Strauss, Claude. The effectiveness of symbols

Smith, Bardwell. Buddhism and abortion in contemporary Japan: *mizuko kuyō* and the confrontation with death

4.9: Ritual in Education

Handelman, Don, and Lea Shamgar-Handelman. Holiday celebrations in Israeli kindergartens

4.10: Ritual in Performance Studies and Theater

Goethals, Gregor T. TV ritual

MacAloon, John J. Olympic games and the theory of spectacle in modern societies

Schechner, Richard. Restoration of behavior

4.11: Ritual in Music

Peña, Manuel H. Ritual structure in a Chicano dance

4.12: Ritual in Dance

Peña, Manuel H. Ritual structure in a Chicano dance

4.13: Ritual in Kinesics, Kinesiology, and Sports

MacAloon, John J. Olympic games and the theory of spectacle in modern societies

4.14: Ritual in Architecture

No selections

4.15: Ritual in Political Science and Economics

Bergesen, Albert. Political witch-hunt rituals

Kertzer, David I. Ritual, politics, and power

4.16: Ritual in Business and Advertising

Wallendorf, Melanie, and Eric J. Arnould. Consumption rituals of Thanksgiving day

4.17: Ritual in Law

Girard, René. Violence and the sacred: sacrifice

Winn, Peter A. Legal ritual

4.18: Ritual in Medicine, Genetics, Biology, and Ethology

d'Aquili, Eugene G., and Charles D. Laughlin Jr. The neurobiology of myth and ritual

Davis-Floyd, Robbie E. Ritual in the hospital: giving birth the American way